Lecture Notes in Computer Science 9335

Commenced Publication in 1973
Founding and Former Series Editors:
Gerhard Goos, Juris Hartmanis, and Jan van Leeuwen

More information about this series at http://www.springer.com/series/7407

Francesco Corman · Stefan Voß
Rudy R. Negenborn (Eds.)

Computational Logistics

6th International Conference, ICCL 2015
Delft, The Netherlands, September 23–25, 2015
Proceedings

 Springer

Editors
Francesco Corman
Delft University of Technology
Delft
The Netherlands

Rudy R. Negenborn
Delft University of Technology
Delft
The Netherlands

Stefan Voß
University of Hamburg
Hamburg
Germany

ISSN 0302-9743   ISSN 1611-3349   (electronic)
Lecture Notes in Computer Science
ISBN 978-3-319-24263-7   ISBN 978-3-319-24264-4   (eBook)
DOI 10.1007/978-3-319-24264-4

Library of Congress Control Number: 2015948712

LNCS Sublibrary: SL1 – Theoretical Computer Science and General Issues

Springer Cham Heidelberg New York Dordrecht London

Printed on acid-free paper

Springer International Publishing AG Switzerland is part of Springer Science+Business Media
(www.springer.com)

Preface

Computational logistics comprises the planning and implementation of large, complex logistics tasks using computations and advanced decision support and control. It is applied in various areas, such as for finding the most efficient scheduling/plan for the transport of passengers or goods. Optimization models and solution algorithms are integrated with advanced computer technology for getting satisfactory results in appropriate time and providing interactivity, visualization, etc., for a better understanding and problem solution. Computational logistics also involves the use of information systems and modern communication and information technology for the design, planning, and control of large-scale logistics networks as well as the complex tasks within them.

The International Conference on Computational Logistics (ICCL) provides an opportunity for researchers and practitioners in the field of computational logistics to present their latest results and findings in a fruitful and open-minded environment. This volume of the Lecture Notes in Computer Science series consists of selected papers presented at the 6th International Conference on Computational Logistics, held and organized by Delft University of Technology (TU Delft), Department of Maritime & Transport Technology, in Delft, The Netherlands, September 23–25, 2015.

The Department of Maritime & Transport Technology proposes new tools for design, control, simulation, and optimization that are based on fundamental innovations and new insights gained into the physics of continuous transport phenomena, as well as the development of agile logistic control systems for transport systems using distributed intelligence. This research is carried out in close cooperation with several other research groups within TU Delft. TU Delft aims to make a significant contribution towards a sustainable society for the twenty-first century by conducting ground breaking scientific and technological research and by helping to translate theoretical knowledge into technological innovations and activity of economic and social value. Logistics is an important pillar in this – especially for the business ecosystem of The Netherlands. The Netherlands holds a top position at international level as far as logistics, handling of good flows, and chains of (inter)national logistics operations are concerned. With only 0.25 % of the world's population and 1 % of world production, The Netherlands still provides 3.7 % of world trade. It is the Dutch government's ambition to strengthen this international position: The Netherlands aims to reach in 2020 the European number 1 position in the World Logistics Performance Index. The Port of Rotterdam, a stone's throw from Delft and one of the largest ports worldwide, is a crucial interconnecting factor in reaching and maintaining such a top position. The port strives to become the most efficient, safe, and sustainable port in the world–automation, advanced decision support, control, and information (community) systems are the core technologies constantly being developed further for facilitating this.

The special theme of ICCL 2015 is Coordination for Real-Time Logistics. This refers to the scientific and practical interest of approaches that are able to control and coordinate in real time multiple components involved in transport and logistics processes. A general trend especially in computational logistics is to strengthen its theoretical and modeling basis. To achieve system performance, the distributed nature of logistical transport processes (in space, stakeholders, and time dimensions) needs to be taken into account explicitly; inclusion of coordination in control schemes specifically tailored for logistical processes is therefore crucial. This would allow day-to-day, hour-to- hour, minute-to-minute, real-time control of operations. For instance, transport flows over multiple modes (including rail, water, intermodality, and/or synchromodality), need to be controlled, while dealing with real-time dynamics. In general, uncertainty phenomena require that action plans are not merely determined, but also updated in real time by some form of closed loop depending on actual circumstances.

After a thorough review process, a grand total of 66 contributions were accepted, prepared by researchers from over 30 countries. Compared with previous ICCL conferences, this marks a great increase in academic output, making this year's ICCL a cornerstone in the visibility and participation in this emerging field. Following the focus of the papers accepted, the contributions were grouped into the following themes:

- Part I: Transport over Ground
- Part II: Transport over Water
- Part III: Internal Coordination within a System
- Part IV: External Coordination among Systems

While we believe that these proceedings provide insights into the state-of-the-art of the field, we also expect that the development of these themes will continue to grow. To support this, a few critical areas have been recognized as the frontier where a better match between practical needs, policy requirements, and innovative academic contributions is sought. These include further integration of mono-approaches; fostering usage of large-scale computational techniques to tackle the complexity of coordination; the application of innovative models that are already used for specific modes, such as vehicular traffic, to more complex multimodal or synchromodal situations; and inclusion of autonomy in the vehicles.

Organizing a conference and publishing the proceedings takes significant effort, for which we are endowed to the support of a large group of people. The greatest thanks go to the authors, who kept the scientific debate open and at a high qualitative standard. In addition, we greatly appreciate the valuable cooperation with the members of the International Organizing Committee and Program Committee, who worked hard at organizing and evaluating the papers to achieve a high scientific standard. A special thanks goes to the enthusiastic local organizers in Delft, in particular Céline Dohmen and Wouter Beelaerts-van Blokland. We moreover thank conference partners Dinalog, Transport Institute TU Delft, Science Centre Delft, and TransportNET.

ICCL 2015 in Delft was the sixth of its kind, after Shanghai (2010, 2012), Hamburg (2011), Copenhagen (2013), and Valparaíso (2014). The contributions presented at ICCL 2015, and the papers in these proceedings, show that computational logistics is getting ready to be put to work. We look forward to the next steps!

September 2015

Rudy R. Negenborn
Francesco Corman
Stefan Voß

Organization

Organizing Committee

General Chair

Rudy R. Negenborn   Delft University of Technology, The Netherlands

Program Chair

Francesco Corman   Delft University of Technology, The Netherlands

Special Sessions Chair

João Nabais   Instituto Politécnico de Setúbal, Portugal
Rafael Carmona   Universidad Anahuac Mexico Norte, Mexico

Tutorial Chair

José Maestre   Universidad de Sevilla, Spain

Publications Chair

Stefan Voß   University of Hamburg, Germany

International Program Committee

Panagiotis Angeloudis	Imperial College London, UK
Behzad Behdani	Wageningen University, Wageningen, The Netherlands
Khalid Bichou	Imperial College, London, UK
Miguel Ayala Botto	Instituto Superior Técnico, Lisbon, Portugal
Jürgen W. Böse	TU Hamburg-Harburg, Hamburg, Germany
Buyang Cao	Tongji University, Shanghai, China and ESRI, Redlands, USA
José Ceroni	Pontificia Universidad Católica de Valparaíso, Valparaíso, Chile
Loon Ching Tang	National University of Singapore, Singapore
Marielle Christiansen	Norwegian University of Science and Technology, Trondheim, Norway
Francesco Corman	Delft University of Technology, Delft, The Netherlands
Joachim Daduna	University of Economics and Law Berlin, Berlin, Germany
Rommert Dekker	Erasmus University, Rotterdam, The Netherlands
Karl F. Doerner	Johannes Kepler University, Linz, Austria
Wolfgang Domschke	TU Darmstadt, Darmstadt, Germany

Roberto Domínguez Cañizares	Universidad de Sevilla, Sevilla, Spain
Mark Duinkerken	Delft University of Technology, Delft, The Netherlands
Kjetil Fagerholt	Norwegian University of Science and Technology, Trondheim, Norway
Enzo Frazzon	Universidade Federal de Santa Catarina, Florianópolis, Brazil
Monica Gentili	University of Salerno, Salerno, Italy
Rinze Geertsma	Delft University of Technology, Delft, The Netherlands
Rosa González	Pontificia Universidad Católica de Valparaíso, Valparaíso, Chile
Peter Greistorfer	Karl-Franzens-Universität Graz, Austria
Hans-Otto Günther	Seoul National University, South Korea and TU Berlin, Germany
Richard Hartl	University of Vienna, Vienna, Austria
Geir Hasle	Sintef, Oslo, Norway
Leonard Heilig	University of Hamburg, Hamburg, Germany
Sin Ho	Aarhus University, Aarhus, Denmark
Patrick Jaillet	Massachusetts Institute of Technology (MIT), Cambridge, MA, USA
Rune Moller Jensen	IT University, Copenhagen, Denmark
Herbert Kopfer	University of Bremen, Bremen, Germany
René de Koster	Rotterdam School of Management, Rotterdam, The Netherlands
Ioannis Lagoudis	Malaysia Institute for Supply Chain Innovation, Malaysia
Jasmine Siu Lee Lam	Nanyang Technological University, Singapore
Gilbert Laporte	Cirrelt, Montreal, Canada
Janny Leung	Chinese University, Hong Kong, China
Le Li	Delft University of Technology, Delft, The Netherlands
Shijie Li	Delft University of Technology, Delft, The Netherlands
Xiao Lin	Delft University of Technology, Delft, The Netherlands
André Ludwig	University of Leipzig, Leipzig, Germany
Vittorio Maniezzo	University of Bologna, Cesena, Italy
Rudy R. Negenborn	Delft University of Technology, Delft, The Netherlands
Gerardo de la O	Friends University, Wichita, USA
Carlos Oscampo-Martinez	Technical University of Catalonia, Barcelona, Spain
Dario Pacino	DTU, Lyngby, Denmark
Ana Paias	Cidade Universitaria, Lisbon, Portugal
Guenther Raidl	Vienna University of Technology, Vienna, Austria
Jana Ries	Portsmouth University, Portsmouth, UK
Bart van Riessen	Delft University of Technology, Delft, The Netherlands
Simona Sacone	University of Genoa, Italy
Juan Jose Salazar	University of La Laguna, Tenerife, Spain
Frederik Schulte	University of Hamburg, Hamburg, Germany

Xiaoning Shi	University of Hamburg, Germany and Jiaotong University, Shanghai, China
L. Douglas Smith	University of Missouri, St. Louis, USA
Matthijs Spaan	Delft University of Technology, Delft, The Netherlands
Lori Tavasszy	Delft University of Technology, Delft, The Netherlands
Kevin Tierney	Paderborn University, Paderborn, Germany
Stefan Voß	University of Hamburg, Hamburg, Germany
Jaap Vleugel	Delft University of Technology, Delft, The Netherlands
Bart Wiegmans	Delft University of Technology, Delft, The Netherlands
David Woodruff	UC Davis, Davis, USA
Jianbin Xin	Delft University of Technology, Delft, The Netherlands
Tsz Leung Yip	Hong Kong Polytechnic University, Hong Kong, China
Huaron Zheng	Delft University of Technology, Delft, The Netherlands
Shiyuan Zheng	Shanghai Maritime University, Shanghai, China

Contents

Internal Coordination within a System

External Coordination among Systems

Transport Over Ground

Ant Metaheuristic with Adapted Personalities for the Vehicle Routing Problem

Nicolas Zufferey[1], Jaime Farres[2]([✉]), and Rémy Glardon[3]

[1] Geneva School of Economics and Management, GSEM - University of Geneva,
Blvd du Pont-d'Arve 40, 1211 Geneva 4, Switzerland
n.zufferey@unige.ch
[2] ETSEIB, Universitat Politècnica de Catalunya, Barcelona, Spain
jaimefarres@gmail.com
[3] LGPP, École Polytechnique Fédérale Lausanne, Lausanne, Switzerland
remy.glardon@epfl.ch

Abstract. At each generation of an ant algorithm, each ant builds a solution step by step by adding an element to it. Each choice is based on the *greedy force* (short term profit or heuristic information) and the *trail* system (central memory which collects information during the search process). Usually, all the ants of the population have the same characteristics and behaviors. In contrast in this paper, a new type of ant metaheuristic is proposed. It relies on the use of ants with different personalities. Such a method has been adapted to the well-known vehicle routing problem, and even if it does not match the best known results, its performance is encouraging (on one benchmark instance, new best results have however been found), which opens the door to a new ant algorithm paradigm.

Keywords: Evolutionary metaheuristics · Ant algorithms · Vehicle routing problem · Combinatorial optimization

1 Introduction

As exposed in [33], modern methods for solving complex optimization problems are often divided into *exact* methods and *metaheuristic* methods. An exact method guarantees that an optimal solution is obtained in a finite amount of time. However, for a large number of applications and most real-life optimization problems, which are typically NP-hard, such methods need a prohibitive amount of time to find an optimal solution. For these difficult problems, it is preferable to quickly find a satisfying solution. If solution quality is not a dominant concern, then a simple *heuristic* can be employed, but if quality plays a critical role, then a more advanced *metaheuristic* procedure is recommended. There are mainly two classes of metaheuristics: *local search* and *population based* methods. The former type of algorithm works on a single solution (e.g., descent local search, tabu search, variable neighborhood search), whereas the latter makes a population of (pieces of) solutions evolve (e.g., genetic algorithms, ant colonies, adaptive

© Springer International Publishing Switzerland 2015
F. Corman et al. (Eds.): ICCL 2015, LNCS 9335, pp. 3–15, 2015.
DOI: 10.1007/978-3-319-24264-4_1

memory algorithms). The reader interested in a recent book on metaheuristics is referred to [16].

As presented in [21,34], in most ant algorithms, the role of each ant is to build a solution step by step. At each step, an ant adds an element to the current partial solution. Each *decision* or *move* m is based on two ingredients: the *greedy force* $GF(m)$ (short-term profit) and the *trail* $Tr(m)$ (information obtained from other ants). The probability $p_i(m)$ that ant i chooses decision m is given by Equation (1), where α and β are parameters, and M_i is the set of admissible decisions that ant i can make.

$$p_i(m) = \frac{GF(m)^\alpha \cdot Tr(m)^\beta}{\sum\limits_{m' \in M_i} GF(m')^\alpha \cdot Tr(m')^\beta} \tag{1}$$

Let M be the set of all possible decisions. When each ant of the population has built a solution, the trails are generally updated as follows: $Tr(m) = \rho \cdot Tr(m) + \Delta Tr(m)$, $\forall m \in M$, where $0 < \rho < 1$ is a parameter representing the evaporation of the trails, which is usually close or equal to 0.9, and $\Delta Tr(m)$ is a term which reinforces the trails left on decision m by the ant population. That quantity is usually proportional to the number of times the ants have made decision m, and to the quality of the obtained solutions when decision m was made. More precisely, let N be the number of ants, then: $\Delta Tr(m) = \sum_{i=1}^{N} \Delta Tr_i(m)$, where $\Delta Tr_i(m)$ is proportional to the quality of the solution provided by ant i if it has made decision m. The pseudo-code of a classical ant method is given in Algorithm 1. A *generation* consists in performing steps (1) to (4). A stopping condition can be a maximum number of generations or a maximum time limit.

It is important to mention that the goal of this paper is not to propose a new state-of-the-art method for the vehicle routing problem (*VRP*), but its main contribution consists in designing a new type of ant metaheuristics. The paper is organized as follows. In Section 2, the most well-known extensions and variants of the classical ant algorithm are discussed. The *VRP* is presented in Section 3, where state-of-the-art metaheuristics are briefly reviewed. In Section 4, five new algorithms are proposed for the *VRP*, and the results are presented in Section 5. A conclusion is given in Section 6, where the main contributions of this paper are highlighted.

Algorithm 1. Classical ant metaheuristic

While no stopping condition is met, **do:**

1. for $i = 1$ to N, do: ant i builds a solution s_i step by step based on Equation (1);
2. *intensification* (optional): apply a local search to some solutions of $\{s_1, \ldots, s_N\}$;
3. update s^* (best encountered solution during the search);
4. update the trails by the use of a subset of $\{s_1, \ldots, s_N\}$;

Output: solution s^*.

---

2 Ant Algorithms

As presented in [11], ant algorithms have been developed for many problems of different types. Several variants or extensions of the above Algorithm 1 can be found in the literature. Some of them are briefly discussed below.

Elitist Ants Trails. It is one of the first improvement of the classical ant algorithms. It biases the trail updating rule to converge faster to the most promising area of the search space. For example, at the end of each generation, only the best ants of the generation can update the trail system [3].

Pseudo-random Proportional Selection. For each ant, this rule is used at each iteration of the constructing process. It selects with probability q_0 the element that maximizes $GF(m)^\alpha \cdot Tr(m)^\beta$, and uses Equation (1) with probability $(1 - q_0)$. This selection rule is one of the most used and has proved to be a very easy way to regulate the balance between intensification and diversification through the parameter q_0. It was first presented in [12].

Bounded Trails. This variant was first presented in the MAX-MIN ant system in [29]. It consists in having upper and lower bounds for the trail values. The lower bound avoids the algorithm to discard some solutions and ensures the asymptotic convergence, as every solution has always a probability above 0 of being generated. The upper bound avoids the algorithm to focus all its attention to a region of the search space. This mechanism has a strong diversification ability.

Candidate Lists. It consists in reducing the number of possible choices to decrease the computational effort at each iteration of the constructing process. For example, only the e (parameter) elements with the best greedy forces can be chosen for a move. For instance in [13], only the e closest clients can be chosen in the construction of a solution of the traveling salesman problem.

Hyper-cube Framework. Presented for the first time in [2], this technique uses weighting parameters w_s (each w_s is proportional to the quality of solution s) in the trail updating rule. It limits the trail values to interval $[0, 1]$ and it has been theoretically proved to continuously increase the expectation of the average solution quality over time.

Multiple Ant Colony System ($MACS$). It consists in several groups of ants that have their own trail system. In most $MACS$, there exists some kind of interaction or exchange of information between the different groups. A $MACS$ can optimize different objective functions. In this case, each colony focuses on optimizing its own objective function and interacts with the other ones to create a global best solution. This is the case for the VRP with time windows, for which a $MACS$ was first proposed in [14]. Having more than one trail system provides the algorithm with a very important diversification potential.

Other Ant Paradigms. In most ant algorithms, the role of each ant is to build a solution in a constructive way, basing each decision on the greedy force and the trails. However, different roles are possible for each individual ant, ranging from a negligible help in the decision process to a refined local search such a tabu search (e.g., [25,32,34,35]).

3   Presentation of the *VRP* and Literature Review

The *VRP* is one of the most popular problems in combinatorial optimization because of its obvious applications in transportation. It consists in designing the route of each of the k identical vehicles with the aim of minimizing the total traveled distance f (or the total cost or the total travel time). All vehicles are initially in a depot, where each route starts and ends. Each client v (with demand $D(v)$) has to be visited once by the collection of routes. The problem is defined in an undirected graph $G = (V, E)$, where $V = \{v_0, v_1, \ldots, v_n\}$ is the vertex set and $E = \{(v_i, v_j) \mid v_i, v_j \in V, i < j\}$ is the edge set. Note that v_0 is the depot and the other vertices are clients. The following lexicographical approach is generally used: minimize k, then the total distance f. The two most well-known constraints associated with the VRP are: (1) *capacity*: each vehicle has a limited capacity Q, thus the demand of each route cannot exceed Q; (2) *autonomy*: each vehicle has a limited autonomy A, thus the total duration of each route cannot exceed A. Several extensions of the *VRP* can be found in the literature. In this paper, only the capacity constraint is considered, which is the most studied version of the *VRP*.

A few ant algorithms have been proposed in the literature for the *VRP* (see [27]), but none belongs to the best *VRP* metaheuristics. The first ant algorithm for the *VRP* was presented in [4]. In the most basic version, each ant constructs a solution by choosing the next client (among the non visited ones plus the depot) to visit according to Equation (1). When the selection of a client leads to an infeasible solution, the route is closed and another route is started. The greedy force of an edge is the inverse of its length. The trail updating rule is based on an elitist technique. Some variations of this algorithm have been tested in the literature. The most successful variations are described below. The distance between two clients is not the only relevant heuristic information. In [3], a new probability rule is described and includes the *savings* s_{ij} (advantage of combining two cities i and j as consecutive elements in a tour) and the *capacity utilization* (portion of the vehicle capacity used if the next considered client is chosen). In [26], local search procedures (e.g. the well-known *2-opt* heuristic based on the *cross exchange*, the move *swap* or *reinsert*) have improved the performance of the discussed ant algorithms. A mutation operator which belongs to the genetic algorithm paradigm is introduced in [1]. With a certain probability (which is dynamically managed during the search), the algorithm selects two tours from parent solutions and exchanges two nodes (unfeasible solution are penalized but not forbidden). The resulting solution is improved with the *2-opt* heuristic. When updating the trail of an edge (i, j) with a solution s, two components are considered: the value of s and the contribution of the length of (i, j) to the tour it belongs to.

For survey papers on the *VRP*, the reader is referred to [7–9,15,17,19]. Many algorithms have been developed for the *VRP*. Among them, there are some successful classical heuristics such as Clarke & Wright, Two-matching, Sweep, 1-Petal and 2-Petal, as tested in [8]. However, the best performance is achieved by metaheuristics (e.g. [10,22,23,28,30,31]). Such competitive metaheuristics are all discussed below.

Adaptive Memory (*AM*). *AM* [28] has been proved to be a good algorithm for the *VRP* and introduces a very innovative approach. At each generation of *AM*, an offspring solution s is built route by route from a central memory M (which contains routes), then s is improved with a local search, and the resulting solution is used to update M (i.e. routes of M are replaced with routes of s).

Unified Tabu Search (*UTS*). *UTS* [10] has been proved to be a very flexible algorithm (easily adapted to variations of the *VRP*) with competitive quality and speed. *UTS* relies on a tabu search using an objective function which dynamically penalizes the constraint violations (the penalty component is likely to be increased if the last iterations violate the constraints).

Granular Tabu Search (*GTS*). *GTS* [30] has been proved to be a very balanced algorithm in terms of speed and quality. It uses a tabu search framework and relies on the use of *granular* neighborhoods to discard the edges that rarely would belong to a competitive solution. *GTS* uses a granularity threshold which is dynamically adjusted.

Active Guided Evolution Strategies (*AGES*). *AGES* [22] has been proved to be very efficient (it is one of the best *VRP* method), with a reasonable speed. *AGES* is a combination of several procedures (including local search techniques), but an important drawback is its significant number of parameters.

Edge Assembly-Based Memetic Algorithm (*EAMA*). *EAMA* [23] combines an edge-assembly crossover with well-known local search procedures. It allows infeasible solutions with respect to capacity and route duration constraints after invoking the crossover.

Unified Solution Framework for Multi-Attribute *VRP* (*USFMA*). *USFMA* [31] is to be able to tackle a wide range of *VRP* variants. Using a diversity management process, the proposed method is a hybrid genetic algorithm relying on problem-independent local search and genetic operators.

4   New Algorithms for the *VRP*

4.1   *GR*: A Greedy Constructive Algorithm with Restarts

There are many constructing algorithms for the *VRP*, such as the *savings* algorithm [6]. Most of them are deterministic and as a consequence generate always the same solution. We propose a greedy constructing procedure *GR* with randomness, able to generate different solutions if restarted, which is the core procedure of the proposed ant metaheuristics. It works with a given number k of vehicles and it is restarted as long as a given time limit is not reached. At the end, the best generated solution is returned to the user.

GR consists in sequentially constructing each of the k routes. The procedure starts a new route R by choosing randomly an unserved client $v \in \{v_1, \dots, v_n\}$, and creates a tour $v_0 - v - v_0$. Let $C(R)$ be the capacity of route R (defined as the vehicle capacity, minus the demands $D(R)$ of all the clients belonging to R). Then, for all the unserved clients v such that $D(v) \le C(R)$ (called the R-available clients), a move $m = (v, p, R)$ can be performed, which consists in inserting client v at position p (between two clients v_i and v_j, or between the depot v_0 and one client v_i) in route R. To do it, the greedy force $GF(v, p, R)$ is first computed for each R-available client v, for each position p of the considered route R. $GF(v, p, R)$ is defined by dividing the distance $d(v, v_0)$ between v and the depot v_0 by the augmentation $\Delta f_R(v, p)$ of the length of R if it is extended by inserting client v at position p. This greedy force is new and in contrast with the existing greedy forces proposed in the literature, it favors the insertion of clients located far away from the depot, which is likely to reduce the number of *isolated* clients (i.e. an unserved client v with a large $d(v, v_0)$ value). If too many isolated clients are left for the next routes, such routes are likely to be long. However, the consideration of $\Delta f_R(v, p)$ avoids the insertion of isolated clients located far away from the route R under construction. When the greedy force of each R-available move has been computed, all the possible choices have been identified and evaluated for the considered route R. At this moment, the *greedy force threshold* $GFT(R)$ is computed as $q_A \cdot \max_{v,p} GF(v, p, R)$. It is the largest available greedy force, multiplied by parameter q_A (tuned to 0.9) which regulates the amount of possible moves and corresponds to a candidate list technique. At the end of each iteration, the selected move m is randomly chosen among the ones whose greedy forces are above the threshold.

At each iteration of GR, these three mains steps are performed for the considered route R (i.e., compute the $GF(m)$'s, then $GFT(R)$, and finally select a move m) until there is no more R-available client v. When this occurs, a new route is started by choosing randomly an unserved client. The process stops when all the clients have been served (feasible solution), or when it is not anymore possible to serve a client with one of the k vehicles (unfeasible solution).

4.2 ANT: An Ant Algorithm with Two Phases

In ANT, the role of each ant is to build a solution with a 2-phase algorithm denoted $2PH$, where a trail value is associated with each edge. In the first phase (P1), the routes are sequentially built and extended as in GR, whereas in the second phase (P2), the unserved clients are sequentially considered to fill any of the existing routes. In other words, (P1) works tour by tour, whereas (P2) works client by client (by order of decreasing demands, which improves the likelihood of the solution to be feasible). The transition between the two phases is one of the challenging issues. The key idea is to stop the construction of a route R in (P1) when only poor R-available insertions are possible (i.e. do not fill route R

just to fill it, because these R-available clients might be much more efficiently served by other routes).

Based on Algorithm 1, each generation of ANT consists in the following steps: (1) construct a solution with each of the N (parameter tuned to 12) ants, using $2PH$; (2) is skipped; (3) update $s^\star$; (4) update the trails and compute a *trail threshold* TT, which is used to decide when to move from (P1) to (P2) in $2PH$ (in the next generation). More precisely, the role of TT is to detect when the potential of (P1) becomes poor, in the sense that even if a client v is inserted at the best position in the considered route R (as it can be done in (P1)), it could be much better to assign v to another vehicle (as it can be done in (P2)). TT is computed as $\min(t_B \cdot T_B, t_S \cdot T_S)$, where t_B and t_S are parameters respectively tuned to 0.2 and 3, T_B is the average trail value in the best encountered solution $s^\star$ during the search, and T_S is the average trail value in the whole trail system.

The trails are updated as follows. First, for each edge (i,j), the evaporation coefficient ρ is used to set $Tr(i,j) = \rho \cdot Tr(i,j)$. Then, the N_b (parameter tuned to 4) best solutions (i.e. the *elite* solutions) of the last generation are used to reinforce the trails of the edges that appear in the elite solutions. More precisely, for each elite solution s, $Tr(i,j)$ is augmented by $(1 - \rho) \cdot w \cdot [f(s)/f^\star]$, where $f^\star$ is the value of $s^\star$, and w is a weighting parameter tuned to 0.1. One can remark that parameter ρ (tuned to 0.975) can regulate the balance between the evaporation and the reinforcement of the trails.

(P1) is derived from GR with the two following differences: (1) the probability of a move is proportional to its associated trail value; (2) (P1) stops when the trail of the selected move is below TT (i.e. (P1) does not only stop because of non sufficient capacity). More precisely, let $p(v, p, R)$ be the probability to insert client v at position $p = (v_i, v_j)$ in route R. Such a probability depends on the trail $Tr(v, p, R) = \max[Tr(v_i, v), Tr(v, v_j)]$. Consequently, a sequence of clients that appears to be good in the previous generations is more likely to be created. The "maximum" is used (instead of the "summation") because at that stage, many edges are going to be broken by the insertion of the next clients.

(P2) starts by calculating the greedy force $GF(v, p, R)$ of the considered client v for each position $p = (v_i, v_j)$ of each existing route R that has a sufficient remaining capacity to serve v. In contrast with (P1), the trail is computed as $Tr(v, p, R) = Tr(v_i, v) + Tr(v, v_j)$. The summation is performed because unlike in (P1), the added edges are likely to stay in the final solution. As in (P1), the probability of a move (among the ones above GFT) is proportional to its trail value. If a client v cannot be placed in any route R because $D(v) > C(R)$, the solution is unfeasible.

Because of the sequential use of the greedy forces and the trails, there is no need to use parameters α and β of Equation (1), which results in a significant reduction of the computational effort and a better overall performance, as discussed in [35]. We have now all the ingredients to summarize $2PH$ in Algorithm 2.

Algorithm 2. *2PH*: The two-phases algorithm associated with each ant

---

(P1) While there is a free vehicle, do:

1. select a free vehicle;
2. select randomly an unserved client v and build the route $R = v_0 - v - v_0$;
3. while there is at least a R-available client v, do:
   (a) compute $GF(v, p, R)$ for each R-available client v;
   (b) compute $GFT(R)$;
   (c) select a move $m = (v, p, R)$ (based on their trail values) among the moves such that $GF(v, p, R) \geq GFT(R)$;
   (d) if $Tr(m) < TT$, STOP (select another free vehicle, if any);

(P2) For each unserved client v (ordered by decreasing demand), do:

1. if there is no route R such that $D(v) \leq C(R) - D(R)$, STOP (unfeasible solution);
2. for each route R such that $D(v) \leq C(R) - D(R)$, compute $GF(v, p, R)$ and $Tr(v, p, R)$;
3. compute GFT (over all the possible moves and routes at that step);
4. select a move $m = (v, p, R)$ (based on their trail values) among the moves such that $GF(v, p, R) \geq GFT(R)$;

Output: feasible/unfeasible *VRP* solution.

4.3   *AL*: *ANT* Enhanced with Local Search Techniques

Often, in order to get competitive results, it is unavoidable to apply a local search method (e.g., a descent method, tabu search) to the solutions provided by the classical constructive ants [35]. Widely used neighborhood structures for the *VRP* are: (1) the forward and backward *Or-exchange* [24], where the neighborhood structure consists in moving a client from a route to another; (2) the *2-opt* [20], where a move consists in removing two edges of a route and rebuilding the solution by creating a different pair of edges. *2-opt* appears to be very efficient while combined with the forward and backward *Or-exchange* (in one configuration of the algorithm proposed in [22], these are the only three local search procedures used). Moreover, the *2-opt* local search is the most used in literature for the *VRP* because of its simplicity, its speed and its capacity to improve the solutions by making intra-route improvements.

At the end of each generation, before updating the trail system (i.e. at step (2) of Algorithm 1), the following local search techniques are sequentially applied to the elite solutions: the *2-opt*, the forward *Or-exchange*, the backward *Or-exchange*. This sequence of three local search procedures is restarted until no more improvement is encountered by any of the procedure.

4.4   *ALM*: *AL* Enhanced with a Central Memory

ALM is derived from *AL* by adding an intensification component at the beginning of *2PH*, before (P1). This component (P0) consists in copying some of the routes of $s^\star$ when generating a solution s with the considered ant. More precisely, each route R of $s^\star$ has a probability $p(R)$ to be copied in s, which depends on two elements: the *saturation* $Sat(R)$ of R and the mutual *attractiveness* $Att(R)$ of the clients belonging to R. The probabilities $p(R)$ are updated at each generation, after $s^\star$ has been updated (i.e. at the end of step (3) of Algorithm 1).

On the one hand, the saturation $Sat(R)$ of a route R is defined as $D(R)/C(R)$. The larger it is, the better R is filled (which favors the likelihood of a solution to be feasible). On the other hand, let M be a central memory containing the elite solutions of the M_b (parameter tuned to 10) previous generations. For a given client v, we define $f_M(v)$ as the average length of the routes in M which serve v. In addition, $f_R(s^\star)$ is the length of R in $s^\star$. The attractiveness $Att(R)$ of the clients belonging to route R of $s^\star$ can now be defined as $\prod_{v \in R} f_R(s^\star)/f_M(v)$. The larger it is, the better are likely to be the solutions which group together the clients of R. Finally, probability $p(R)$ is computed as in Equation (2), where q_M is a parameter (tuned to 0.4) which can regulate the influence of $s^\star$ on the solution s generated by the involved ant. Note that if $p(R)$ exceeds 1, we simply set $p(R) = 1$.

$$p(R) = q_M \cdot Sat(R) \cdot Att(R) = q_M \cdot \frac{D(R)}{C(R)} \cdot \prod_{v \in R} \frac{f_R(s^\star)}{f_M(v)} \tag{2}$$

4.5   *ALMP*: **ALM with Different Ant Personalities**

The idea of *ALMP* is to assign a specific personality to each of the N ants of the population. The personality intervenes anytime the ant makes a decision, which consists in selecting a move among the ones above *GFT*. Four ant personalities are proposed: *Normal Ants (NA)*, *Follower Ants (FA)*, *Moody Ants (MA)* and *Innovative Ants (IA)*. These characteristics are likely to belong to any group of individuals working together to reach a common goal. In order to work with a well-balanced ant society, we propose to use $N/4$ ants of each personality (remind that N was tuned to 12).

NA corresponds to the average ant personality as presented in Subsection 4.2. *NA* selects a move proportionally to its trail value.

FA corresponds to the personality that strictly follows what others have done previously. *FA* always selects the move with the largest trail value. This behavior aims at intensifying the search.

MA corresponds to *NA* with probability $(1 - p_{MA})$, but with a probability p_{MA} (parameter tuned to 0.4), it changes its mood and starts behaving apparently against the goal. *MA* selects a move proportionally to the trail values with probability $(1 - p_{MA})$, and inverse-proportionally to the trail values with probability p_{MA}. This behavior aims at strongly diversifying the search.

IA corresponds to the personality that tends to behave in an unusual way, but with the intention to reach the goal. *IA* corresponds to *FA* with probability $(1 - p_{IA})$ (intensification role), but with a probability p_{IA} (parameter tuned to 0.2), it changes its mood and make a random decision (diversification role). *IA* selects the move with the largest trail values with probability $(1 - p_{IA})$, and randomly with probability p_{IA}. For this personality, the value of parameter q_A which appears in $GFT = q_A \cdot \max_{v,p} GF(v, p, R)$ is lower than usual (it is tuned to 0.8 instead of 0.9), which means that the number of possible choices is larger than for the other personalities, which favors the exploration of new solutions.

5   Results

The algorithms have been coded in C++ and compiled by Microsoft Visual Studio 2013. The tests have been run in a Windows 7 PC with an Intel Core2 Quad Q9400 of 2.66GHz and 4MB of RAM in 32-bit but only using one of the 4 processors of the PC. To make the results comparable to other results obtained with other computers, a GFlops test has been performed with the software LinX 0.6.5. The obtained result is 9.1 GFlops. For each proposed algorithm, the stopping condition is $5 \cdot n$ seconds, where n is the number of clients of the considered instance. The results are averaged over 9 runs. The considered instances are all the benchmark instances from [5, 17] which do not have the autonomy constraint. More precisely, the instances are 1 to 5, 11 and 12 from [5], and 9 to 20 from [17]. For each instance, the smallest number k of vehicles and the best-known solution value f^* are taken from [22]. As already presented above, the parameters are tuned to the following values: $q_A \in \{0.8, 0.9\}$, $N = 12$, $t_B = 0.2$, $t_S = 3$, $N_b = 4$, $w = 1$, $\rho = 0.975$, $M_b = 10$, $q_M = 0.4$, $p_{MA} = 0.4$, and $p_{IA} = 0.2$.

The results are provided in Table 1. The five first columns indicate respectively: the instance name (starting with a "C" if from [5], and with a "G" if from [17]), the number n of clients, the number k of vehicles, the instance saturation Sat computed as the total demand divided by the total capacity of the vehicles, the time t^* (in seconds) to get the best known value f^* (obtained from [22]). Column 6 indicates on the one hand the average percentage gap between GR and f^*, and on the other hand the average computing time (in brackets) needed to get the best results of GR. Columns 7 to 10 provide the same information, but for ANT, AL, ALM and $ALMP$, respectively. The times (indicated in seconds) are all re-scaled according to the above mentioned computer (based on the corresponding GFlops performance), so that they can be fairly compared. Average results are given in the last line. Remind that for the VRP, minimizing k is more important than minimizing the total traveled distance f. In this respect G14 is of particular interest, as the newly proposed algorithms are able to generate solutions with $k = 29$ vehicles instead of $k = 30$ (as it is the case in the existing literature). This indicates that the proposed algorithm $2PH$ has a strong ability to find feasible solutions with large values of Sat. For this reason, C14 is not considered to compute the average results in the last line of Table 1.

From Table 1, it can be concluded that every ingredient (i.e., a trail system, local search procedures, a central memory, and various personalities) successively added to GR to derive $ALMP$ is useful, as the average percentage gap is reduced step by step from 12.5% to 11% to 7.5% to 3.7% to 3.3%. Other experiments, which are not detailed here, confirm this statement: it was observed that each ingredient improves significantly the solution values even if other time limits are used (ranging from n to $5 \cdot n$ seconds). In addition, it was also observed that *ALMP* with the proposed mix of personalities is better than if only one personality is used (i.e. there is no personality which outperforms the proposed mix of personalities).

Table 1. Results on well-known benchmark instances

Inst.	n	k	Sat	t^*	GR	ANT	AL	ALM	ALMP
C01	50	5	97.1%	1	2.4% [82s]	1.4% [130s]	0.3% [88s]	0.9% [25s]	1.3% [46s]
C02	75	10	97.4%	22	11.3% [187s]	8.7% [177s]	3.9% [121s]	1.8% [98s]	1.4% [124s]
C03	100	8	91.1%	4	13.9% [280s]	9.0% [299s]	1.6% [251s]	0.4% [176s]	0.5% [211s]
C04	150	12	93.1%	41	19.9% [338s]	15.1% [229s]	4.4% [491s]	2.0% [364s]	1.7% [630s]
C05	199	16	99.6%	8640	20.0% [289s]	20.2% [575s]	13.0% [446s]	6.2% [721s]	5.5% [746s]
C11	120	7	98.2%	4	12.0% [233s]	6.3% [232s]	4.3% [287s]	4.0% [155s]	0.9% [309s]
C12	100	10	90.5%	1	10.6% [322s]	7.6% [227s]	1.2% [223s]	0.0% [92s]	0.0% [58s]
G09	255	14	95.9%	1441	11.7% [671s]	9.8% [736s]	8.1% [757s]	2.9% [562s]	3.1% [1006s]
G10	323	16	95.0%	300	13.2% [716s]	11.9% [848s]	8.8% [1081s]	4.2% [1353s]	4.1% [1492s]
G11	399	18	94.3%	1763	14.6% [1009s]	13.2% [1249s]	9.7% [1270s]	5.3% [1716s]	5.1% [1833s]
G12	483	19	98.4%	2591	12.6% [1573s]	12.4% [1496s]	11.8% [793s]	5.9% [2161s]	4.8% [2324s]
G13	252	26	96.7%	1600	10.4% [539s]	9.9% [607s]	8.4% [472s]	3.0% [1061s]	3.2% [886s]
G14	*320*	*29*	*98.9%*	*N/A*	*1255 [791s]*	*1261 [867s]*	*1245 [775s]*	*1170 [1510s]*	*1173 [1516s]*
G15	396	33	97.7%	110	12.0% [985s]	11.9% [1075s]	10.2% [849s]	5.8% [1743s]	5.3% [1899s]
G16	480	37	96.7%	3200	14.1% [1429s]	13.3% [1168s]	11.1% [1419s]	7.3% [1957s]	6.2% [2136s]
G17	240	22	98.2%	121	10.0% [638s]	9.7% [495s]	6.6% [271s]	1.7% [994s]	1.7% [1064s]
G18	300	27	100.0%	600	10.0% [663s]	10.5% [648s]	9.0% [904s]	3.6% [1256s]	3.6% [1312s]
G19	360	33	98.2%	93	12.9% [979s]	12.9% [916s]	10.1% [640s]	5.0% [1619s]	5.2% [1747s]
G20	420	38	99.5%	920	12.9% [1620s]	13.4% [988s]	11.7% [1312s]	6.0% [2026s]	5.8% [1964s]
Avg.					**12.50%**	**11.00%**	**7.50%**	**3.70%**	**3.30%**

6   Conclusion

In this paper, the ant algorithm paradigm is extended. As in classical ant metaheuristics, each ant makes decisions based on two ingredients: the greedy force on the one hand, and the trail system on the other hand. The main contribution of this paper is to assign a specific personality to each ant. The resulting method is applied to the famous vehicle routing problem (*VRP*), and it can be adapted to any combinatorial optimization problem. In the *VRP* context, a new type of greedy force is proposed, which, in contrast with the existing ant methods for the *VRP*, favors clients located far away from the depot (this augments the likelihood of a solution to be feasible).

The performance of the best proposed metaheuristic with ant personalities is encouraging, even if it does not match the state-of-the-art results. On one instance, new best results has however been found. Note that the proposed ant algorithm can be used even if the number k of vehicles is not known in advance, by solving a series of k-*VRP* instances (i.e., with a fixed value of k), starting with an upper bound on k and decreasing it step by step as long as a feasible solution is found.

Future works include the adaptation of the ant algorithm with personalities to other problems (especially the ones for which classical ant algorithms have shown a high potential). Another avenue of research could consist in managing a variable fleet of vehicles (see for instance [18]) to generate VRP solutions over a planning horizon.

References

1. Bin, Y., Zhong-Zhen, Y., Baozhen, Y.: An improved ant colony optimization for vehicle routing problem. European Journal of Operational Research **196**, 171–176 (2009)
2. Blum, C., Dorigo, M.: The hyper-cube framework for ant colony optimization. IEEE Trans Syst Man Cybernet Part B **34**(2), 1161–1172 (2004)
3. Bullnheimer, B., Hartl, R.F., Strauss, C.: A new rank-based version of the Ant System: A computational study. Central European Journal for Operations Research and Economics **7**(1), 25–38 (1999)
4. Bullnheimer, B., Hartl, R.F., Strauss, C.: An improved Ant System algorithm for the Vehicle Routing Problem. Annals of Operations Research **89**, 319–328 (1997)
5. Christofides, N., Mingozzi, A., Toth, P.: The vehicle routing problem. In: Combinatorial Optimization, pp. 315–338 (1979)
6. Clarke, G., Wright, J.R.: Scheduling of vehicles from a central depot to a number of delivery points. Operations Research **12**(4), 568–581 (1964)
7. Cordeau, J.-F., Gendreau, M., Hertz, A., Laporte, G., Sormany, J.-S.: New heuristics for the vehicle routing problem. In: Logistics Systems: Design and Optimization, pp. 270–297. Springer (2005)
8. Cordeau, J.-F., Gendreau, M., Laporte, G., Potvin, J.-Y., Semet, F.: A Guide to Vehicle Routing Heuristics. Journal of the Operational Research Society **53**(5), 512–522 (2002)
9. Cordeau, J.-F., Laporte, G.: Tabu search heuristics for the vehicle routing problem. In: Metaheuristic Optimization via Memory and Evolution: Tabu Search and Scatter Search, pp. 145–163. Kluwer, Boston (2004)
10. Cordeau, J.-F., Laporte, G., Mercier, A.: A Unified Tabu Search Heuristic for Vehicle Routing Problems with Time Windows. Journal of the Operational Research Society **52**, 928–936 (2001)
11. Dorigo, M., Birattari, M., Stuetzle, T.: Ant colony optimization - artificial ants as a computational intelligence technique. IEEE Computational Intelligence Magazine **1**(4), 28–39 (2006)
12. Dorigo, M., Gambardella, L.M.: Ant colony system: a cooperative learning approach to the traveling salesman problem. IEEE Transactions on Evolutionary Computation **1**(1), 53–66 (1997)
13. Dorigo, M., Stuetzle. T.: The ant colony optimization metaheuristic: algorithms, applications, and advances. In: Glover, F., Kochenberger, G. (eds.) Handbook of Metaheuristics, vol. 57, pp. 251–285 (2003)
14. Gambardella, L.M., Taillard, E., Agazzi, G.: MACS-VRPTW: a multiple ant colony system for vehicle routing problems with time windows. In: New Ideas in Optimization, pp. 63–76. McGraw-Hill, London (1999)
15. Gendreau, M., Laporte, G., Potvin, J.-Y.: Metaheuristics for the VRP. In: The Vehicle Routing Problem, pp. 129–154. SIAM Monographs on Discrete Mathematics and Applications, Philadelphia (2002)

16. Gendreau, M., Potvin, J.-Y.: Handbook of Metaheuristics. International Series in Operations Research & Management Science, vol. 146. Springer (2010)
17. Golden, B.L., Wasil E.A., Kelly, J.P., Chao, I.-M.: Metaheuristics in vehicle routing. In: Fleet Management and Logistics, pp. 33–56. Kluwer, Boston (1998)
18. Hertz, A., Schindl, D., Zufferey, N.: A solution method for a car fleet management problem with maintenance constraints. Journal of Heuristics 15(5), 425–450 (2009)
19. Laporte, G., Semet, F.: Classical heuristics for the capacitated VRP. In: The Vehicle Routing Problem, pp. 109–128. SIAM Monographs on Discrete Mathematics and Applications, Philadelphia (2002)
20. Lin, S.: Computer solutions of the traveling salesman problem. Bell System Technical Journal 44, 2245–2269 (1965)
21. Luyet, L., Varone, S., Zufferey, N.: An ant algorithm for the steiner tree problem in graphs. In: Giacobini, M. (ed.) EvoWorkshops 2007. LNCS, vol. 4448, pp. 42–51. Springer, Heidelberg (2007)
22. Mester, D., Braysy, O.: Active-guided evolution strategies for large-scale capacitated vehicle routing problems. Computers & Operations Research 34(10), 2964–2975 (2007)
23. Nagata, Y., Braysy, O.: Edge assembly-based memetic algorithm for the capacitated vehicle routing problem. Networks 54(4), 205–215 (2009)
24. Or, I.: Traveling salesman-type combinatorial problems and their relation to the logistics of regional blood banking. PhD thesis, Nortwester University, USA (1976)
25. Plumettaz, M., Schindl, D., Zufferey, N.: Ant local search and its efficient adaptation to graph colouring. Journal of the Operational Research Society 61, 819–826 (2010)
26. Reimann, M., Doerner, K.F., Hartl, R.F.: Analyzing a unified ant system for the VRP and some of its variants. In: Cagnoni, S. (ed.) EvoIASP 2003, EvoWorkshops 2003, EvoSTIM 2003, EvoROB/EvoRobot 2003, EvoCOP 2003, EvoBIO 2003, and EvoMUSART 2003. LNCS, vol. 2611, pp. 300–310. Springer, Heidelberg (2003)
27. Reimann, M., Doerner, K., Hartl, R.F.: D-Ants: Savings Based Ants Divide and Conquer the Vehicle Routing Problem. Computers & Operations Research 31(4), 563–591 (2004)
28. Rochat, Y., Taillard, E.: Probabilistic diversification and intensification in local search for vehicle routing. Journal of Heuristics 1, 147–167 (1995)
29. Stuetzle, T., Hoos, H.: MAX-MIN Ant System. Future Generation Computer Systems 16(9), 889–914 (2000)
30. Toth, P., Vigo, D.: The Granular Tabu Search and Its Application to the Vehicle-Routing Problem. INFORMS Journal on Computing 15(4), 333–346 (2003)
31. Vidal, T., Crainic, T.G., Gendreau, M., Prins, C.: A unified solution framework for multi-attribute vehicle routing problems. European Journal of Operational Research 234, 658–673 (2014)
32. Zufferey, N.: Heuristiques pour les Problèmes de la Coloration des Sommets d'un Graphe et d'Affectation de Fréquences avec Polarités. PhD thesis, École Polytechnique Fédérale de Lausanne (EPFL), Switzerland (2002)
33. Zufferey, N.: Metaheuristics: some Principles for an Efficient Design. Computer Technology and Applications 3(6), 446–462 (2012)
34. Zufferey, N.: Optimization by ant algorithms: Possible roles for an individual ant. Optimization Letters 6(5), 963–973 (2012)
35. Zufferey, N.: Design and classification of ant metaheuristics. In: Proceedings of the 22nd Euromicro International Conference on Parallel, Distributed, and Network-Based Processing, pp. 339–343 (2014)

The Round-Trip Ridesharing Problem with Relay Stations

Kamel Aissat[1,2]($\boxtimes$) and Ammar Oulamara[1,2]

[1] University of Lorraine - LORIA, Nancy, France
{kamel.aissat,ammar.oulamara}@loria.fr
[2] University of Lorraine, Ile de Saulcy, Metz, France

Abstract. In this work, we investigate the potential benefits of introducing relay stations in the round-trip ridesharing problem. In the classical round-trip ridesharing system, the pick-up and drop-off locations for the rider don't differ from his origin and destination, respectively, for both outgoing and return trips. This system is straightforward but inflexible and unbalanced as it puts the whole detour effort on the driver's shoulders. In this paper, we propose to consider a meeting location as flexible and to determine its optimal position minimizing total travel cost for the round-trip. The meeting locations correspond to relay stations in which riders find ridesharing vehicles. The introduction of relay stations in the round-trip ridesharing problem creates dependency between the outgoing and return trips, in the sense that the relay stations must be chosen in such a way as to minimize the combined travel cost of the outgoing and return trips. In this setting, the rider is supposed to drive to the relay station with his private car and to park it there, so the return trip has to drop him there to get his car back. We present efficient algorithms to solve this problem and, finally, we perform a comparative evaluation using a real road network and real dataset provided by a local company. Our numerical results show the effectiveness of our system, which improves participants' cost-savings and matching rate compared to the classical round-trip ridesharing system.

1 Introduction

The growth of the nation combined with the need to meet mobility, environmental, and energy objectives require other alternative transportation systems. In fact, public transportation systems are insufficient to address the needs of commuters in terms of flexibility and availability. One potential solution to meet these requirements without expanding service area or increasing service frequency of public transportation, is to use ridesharing services. Ridesharing service is based on better use of vehicle by connecting drivers and riders so they can share all or part of their commute, cutting transportation costs for the participants while reducing traffic congestion and pollution. Both drivers and riders benefit from this service; the drivers save money by sharing the trips' cost, and the riders obtain their travels with attractive costs. The effective use of new

© Springer International Publishing Switzerland 2015
F. Corman et al. (Eds.): ICCL 2015, LNCS 9335, pp. 16–30, 2015.
DOI: 10.1007/978-3-319-24264-4_2

communication capabilities, including mobile technology and global position-ing system (GPS), enabled the emergence of dynamic or real-time ridesharing systems. It consists in automatically and instantly matching riders and drivers through a network service by using a smartphone both as a geolocation and a communication device. Several research has been reported recently in the fields of ridesharing, as in [1] and [6]. The authors in [3] consider the one-way ridesharing problem with intermediate meeting locations. Their system is defined as follows: given a set of drivers' offers already in the system, and a new rider's request, they determine a best driver, a best pick-up and drop-off locations, and a sharing cost rate between rider and driver for their common path. In [9], an approach that allows a dynamic scheduling of ridesharing requests (offers and demands), in a context which also involves standard public transportation modes is proposed. This approach is based upon dynamic labelling of the nodes of some transit network together with a filtered search for existing potential riders and drivers.

Although ridesharing provides many advantages, some users are reluctant to participate as rider in such a service. This concerns especially users who are not ready to drop their private cars for a ride with others drivers if their return trips are not ensured by the ridesharing service.

Very few researches are focused on the round-trip ridesharing problem. In [2], the authors study the round-trip ridesharing problem in which given a set of potential users, each user can be either a driver or a rider, and the objective is to minimize the vehicle-kilometers. The decision consists in assigning a role to each user and finding the optimal matching of drivers with riders. When a user is assigned as a rider, their system ensures another matching for the return trip. In [8], the authors propose an approach that synchronizes an outgoing path and a return path in a location, while minimizing the global cost of the two paths. This problem which is defined as the 2-Way Multi Modal Shortest Path problem doesn't take into consideration ridesharing as a mode of transport. Furthermore, in existing round-trip ridesharing systems, a rider's origin can't differ from his pick-up location. However, in some situations, the rider accepts to travel with his private car to a relay station which can be considered as a new pick-up location, more or less close to his initial starting location, where he will be picked up by the driver and dropped off at his ending location. In this case the ridesharing system should guarantee the existence of a new matching for the rider's return trip passing though the relay station, i.e, a matching with another driver that accepts to share his car with the rider and drop him off where his car was left.

In this study, we pursue a two-fold goal.

(i) The primary purpose is to increase the opportunity to obtain a matching between drivers and riders. Indeed, if the rider accepts to travel on his own car to a relay station close to driver's origin, the driver will make less detour to pick-up the rider. Additionally, this allows to reduce the total travel cost.

(ii) The second goal is to ensure for the rider the return trip via the relay station where he left his private car. In fact, the rider will not accept to leave his car in a relay station to participate in a ridesharing service, if the return trip passing through this relay station is not ensured by the system.

To the best of our knowledge, our work is the first to consider the round-trip ridesharing problem with relay stations. This problem consists in minimizing the total cost of the round-trip. In this study, we consider a practical setting by exploiting a real road network of the French Lorraine region with a validation of the proposed solutions on real data.

The remainder of the paper is structured as follows. Section 2 describes our model of ridesharing. Section 3 explains the algorithmic details. Section 4 presents detailed experimental analysis of our algorithms. Finally, concluding remarks and future research are included in Section 5.

2   Problem Description and Notation

The road network is represented by a weighted graph $G = (V, E)$, where V is the set of nodes and E the set of edges. Nodes model intersections and edges depict street segments. In our model, for an edge $(i, j) \in E$ we associate two weights $c(i, j)$ and $\tau(i, j)$, where $c(i, j)$ represents the traveling cost and $\tau(i, j)$ the traveling time between i and j, respectively. A path in a graph G is represented by a vector $\mu = (u, \dots, v)$ of nodes in which two successive nodes are connected by an edge of E. The cost $c(\mu)$ of path μ is the sum of costs of all edges in μ. A shortest-path between a source node u and a target node v is the path with minimal cost among all paths from u to v. In the following a shortest-path between node u and node v will be represented by $u \to v$.

An offer i of ridesharing is represented by $o_i = (s_i, e_i, [t_i^{\min}, t_i^{\max}], \Delta_i)$ where s_i is the starting location, e_i the ending location, $[t_i^{\min}, t_i^{\max}]$ the departure time window and Δ_i is the detour time. A detour time is the maximal time that the driver accepts as overtime of his shortest-path from s_i to e_i. When a driver travels in round-trip, we generate two offers separately, one for outgoing trip and another for return trip.

A demand of ridesharing is represented by $d = (s', e', [t_{\min}^{out}, t_{\max}^{out}], [t_{\min}^{ret}, t_{\max}^{ret}], \Delta_d^{out}, \Delta_d^{ret})$ where s' is the starting location, e' is the ending location, $[t_{\min}^{out}, t_{\max}^{out}]$ and $[t_{\min}^{ret}, t_{\max}^{ret}]$ are the outgoing departure time window and return departure time window, respectively, and Δ_d^{out} and Δ_d^{ret} are the detour time of the outgoing and return trips, respectively.

In our road graph G, traveling costs of drivers and riders are distinguished, more precisely, an edge (i, j) has a nonnegative traveling cost $c_k(i, j)$ depending on the fact that the edge is used by driver, i.e., $k = o$, or by rider, i.e., $k = d$.

In [2], authors consider a constraint on saved cost of traveling $cs(o_i, d)$ as a necessary condition of a feasible matching between a rider's request and a driver's offer. The saved cost of traveling is defined as the difference between the travel cost of the driver including serving the rider and the travel costs of the driver and the rider if each of them travels alone, i.e

$$cs(o_i, d) = c_o(s_i \to e_i) + c_d(s' \to e')$$
$$- \left(c_o(s_i \to s') + c_o(s' \to e') + c_o(e' \to e_i) \right) \qquad (1)$$

Thus, a feasible matching is accepted only if the cost of a *Joint trip* is less than the cost of the separate trips, i.e., $cs(o_i, d) > 0$. If the cost of *Joint trip* is more expensive than the cumulated cost of the individual trips of the driver and the rider, then the matching will not be not considered (see Figure 1).

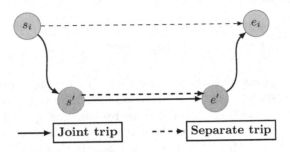

Fig. 1. Example of single rider, single driver ride-share matching.

In order to increase the opportunity of matching, the rider may accept to be picked-up in relay station v. More precisely, the rider travels with his private car from his starting location s' to relay station v. He parks his car at relay station v, and he shares a ride with driver i, from relay station v till his end location e'. Whereas, a driver i travels from his starting location s_i to relay station v, he picks up the rider traveling together till end location e', where the rider is dropped off, and finally the driver continues to his ending location e_i. The system should guarantee to the rider the existence of a second feasible matching with another driver j to reach the relay station v from e' in the return trip. The travel paths of the rider d, the driver i and the driver j are depicted in Figure 2.

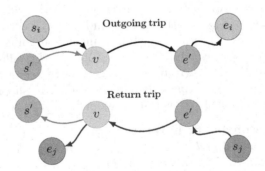

Fig. 2. Round-trip ridesharing with v as a relay station.

2.1   Matching Constraints

In ridesharing systems a matching between drivers and riders can be established only when constraints of matching are satisfied. In our approach, we consider two constraints of matching, namely, the timing constraint, and the travel cost constraint.

Definition 1. (time synchronization)
We say that a demand d and an offer o_i form a time synchronization at relay station v in outgoing trip if and only if there exists $\beta \geq 0$, where,

$$\beta = \min \begin{cases} t_{o_i}^{\max} + \tau_{o_i}(s_i \to v) - (t_{\min}^{out} + \tau_d(s' \to v)) & \text{(2a)} \\ t_{\max}^{out} + \tau_d(s' \to v) - (t_{o_i}^{\min} + \tau_{o_i}(s_i \to v)) & \text{(2b)} \end{cases}$$

Equation (2a) means that when a rider leaves his starting location s' at $t_{\min}^{out}$ to reach the relay station v, he must arrive no later than the latest arrival time of the driver at the relay station v. The same reasoning is applied for the driver in equation (2b). Thus, when $\beta \geq 0$, the arrival time window for the driver and the rider at the relay station v will coincide. So, they can meet each other in this station at time $\max \left\{ t_{\min}^{out} + \tau_d(s' \to v), t_{o_i}^{\min} + \tau_{o_i}(s_i \to v) \right\}$.

Definition 2. (reasonable fit in outgoing trip)
We say that a demand d and an offer o_i form a reasonable fit in outgoing trip with v as a relay station if and only if d and o_i form a time synchronization at relay station v in outgoing trip, and

$$c_o(s_i \to e_i) + c_d(s' \to e') - (c_o(s_i \to v) + \\ c_d(s' \to v) + c_o(v \to e') + c_o(e' \to e_i)) \geq 0 \qquad (3)$$

$$\tau_o(s_i \to v) + \tau_o(v \to e') + \tau_o(e' \to e_i) \leq (\tau_o(s_i \to e_i) + \Delta_i) \qquad (4)$$

$$\tau_d(s' \to v) + \tau_o(v \to e') \leq (\tau_d(s' \to e') + \Delta_d^{out}) \qquad (5)$$

The constraint (3) ensures that the incurred cost in the ridesharing is more attractive than the cost when the driver and the rider travel alone. The constraints (4) and (5) concern the detour time in outgoing trip. The term $\tau_o(s_i \to e_i) + \Delta_i$ in (4) (resp. $\tau_d(s' \to e') + \Delta_d^{out}$ in (5)) allows to limit the amount of time that the driver (resp. rider) passes in traveling in outgoing trip. We consider that the service times to pick-up and drop-off of riders are not significant and can be considered as instantly done.

Definition 3. (reasonable fit in return trip)
We say that a demand d and an offer o_j form a reasonable fit in return trip with v as a relay station if and only if d and o_j form a time synchronization at location e' in return trip, such that :

$$c_o(s_j \to e_j) + c_d(e' \to s') - (c_o(s_j \to e') + \\ c_o(e' \to v) + c_d(v \to s') + c_o(v \to e_j)) \geq 0 \qquad (6)$$

$$\tau_o(s_j \to e') + \tau_o(e' \to v) + \tau_o(v \to e_j) \leq (\tau_o(s_j \to e_j) + \Delta_j) \qquad (7)$$

$$\tau_o(e' \to v) + \tau_d(v \to s') \leq (\tau_d(e' \to s') + \Delta_d^{ret}) \qquad (8)$$

The constraint (6) considers the travel cost-savings by both rider d and driver j in return trip. Whereas, the constraints (7) and (8) consider the detour time for the driver and the rider, respectively.

Lemma 1. *A demand d and two offers o_i and o_j form a reasonable fit in round-trip, if and only if, there exists a relay station v, where d and o_i form a reasonable fit in outgoing trip with v as a relay station in outgoing trip, and, d and o_j form a reasonable fit in return trip with v as a relay station.*

2.2 Objective of Ridesharing System

In the following we use the term *round-trip-path* $\langle d, i, j, v \rangle$ to describe the round-trip of rider's demand d with the driver i in outgoing trip and the driver j in return trip, passing through the relay station v.

A shortest *round-trip-path* $\langle d, i, j, v \rangle$ is the *round-trip-path* with minimal cost, denoted by $c(\langle d, i, j, v \rangle)$, such that

$$c(\langle d, i, j, v \rangle) = c(\langle d, i, v \rangle)_{out} + c(\langle d, j, v \rangle)_{ret} \qquad (9)$$

where

$$c(\langle d, i, v \rangle)_{out} = c_o(s_i \to v) + c_d(s' \to v) + c_o(v \to e') + c_o(e' \to e_i) \qquad (10)$$

and

$$c(\langle d, j, v \rangle)_{ret} = c_o(s_j \to e') + c_o(e' \to v) + c_o(v \to e_j) + c_d(v \to s') \qquad (11)$$

In a nutshell, for a demand d, our objective is to determine, an offer o_i in the outgoing trip, a relay station v, and an offer o_j in return trip such that the cost of *round-trip-path* is minimized, and the demand d form a reasonable fit in round-trip with the offer o_i and the offer o_j having v as a relay station.

3 Algorithmic Details

In this section, we explain the algorithmic details of our solving approaches. Note that the system is launched when a rider request enters the system, but when a driver proposes an ridesharing offer, some informations are stored.

3.1 Adding Offer

Each new offer entering into the system generates new ridesharing opportunities. For this purpose, when an offer o_i is added to the system, we store all possible relay stations for this offer, then we determine the costs $c_o(s_i \to v)$ and $c_o(v \to t_i)$. More precisely, we denote by $N^\uparrow(s_i)$, $N^\downarrow(t_i)$ the *forward search space* from a source s_i and the *backward search space* from target t_i, respectively. A forward search space $N^\uparrow(s_i)$ is a set of triplets: node, cost and time $(v, d^\uparrow_{s_i}, \tau^\uparrow_{s_i})$ such that there is a path from s_i to v with cost $d^\uparrow_{s_i}$ and travel time $\tau^\uparrow_{s_i}$ to reach node v. A backward search space $N^\downarrow(t_i)$ is a set of triplet: node, cost, and time $(v, d^\downarrow_{t_i}, \tau^\downarrow_{t_i})$

such that there is a path from v to t_i with cost $d_{t_i}^{\downarrow}$ and travel time $\tau_{t_i}^{\downarrow}$ to reach t_i from v.

Based on the constraints of *detour time*, we can limit the search spaces when we compute these costs without considering any demand. In our proposed approach, we started by computing the set $N^{\downarrow}(t_i)$ using reverse Dijkstra Algorithm, and for each settled node v, we check the constraint $\tau_o(v \rightarrow t_i) \leq (\tau_o(s_i \rightarrow t_i) + \Delta_i)$. The search procedure is stopped at the first settled node v which violates this constraint. In the second step, we compute the forward search space $N^{\uparrow}(s_i)$, using Dijkstra Algorithm [4]. The search procedure is stopped when the first node v that violates the time constraint $\tau_o(s_i \rightarrow v) \leq (\tau_o(s_i \rightarrow t_i) + \Delta_i)$ is settled. Finally, we keep a node v in $N^{\uparrow}(s_i)$ only if $(\tau_o(s_i \rightarrow v) + \tau_o(v \rightarrow t_i)) \leq (\tau_o(s_i \rightarrow t_i) + \Delta_i)$.

At each iteration, when a node v which corresponds to relay station is selected in the set $N^{\uparrow}(s_i)$, we add the entries in the *bucket* $B(v)$, i.e.,

$$B(v) := B(v) \cup \{(i, d_{s_i}^{\uparrow}, \tau_{s_i}^{\uparrow})\}. \tag{12}$$

The bucket serves to store for a relay station v, all trips which can pass via this location without violating the lower bound on constraint of *detour time*.

To take into consideration the drivers having already begun their trips, we must update their locations at each time unit. For simplicity, we consider only drivers who have not yet started their trips when the rider enters the system.

3.2   Adding a Demand

For given demand d, the objective of the matching procedure is to select the *best fit in round-trip* by scanning the potential buckets in round-trip. More precisely, we determine a class $\mathcal{C}$ of potential relay stations, where the *detour time* constraint of the demand d is respected simultaneously in the *outgoing* and *return trips*. Algorithm 1 allows to recover the class $\mathcal{C}$ of potential relay stations.

Algorithm 1. Potential relay stations in round-trip

Require: Graph $G(V, E)$, demand d.

Ensure: Class of potential relay stations in round-trip $\mathcal{C}$.

1: Set $\mathcal{C}_{out} = \emptyset$ and $\mathcal{C}_{ret} = \emptyset$.
2: Compute $N^{\uparrow}(s')$, using a forward one-to-all Dijkstra algorithm from s' with rider cost bounded by $(\tau_d(s' \rightarrow t') + \Delta_d^{out})$.
3: Compute $N^{\downarrow}(t')$, using a backward one-to-all Dijkstra algorithm from t' with driver cost bounded by $(\tau_d(s' \rightarrow t') + \Delta_d^{out})$, for each settled relay station v that satisfied the equation (5), $\mathcal{C}_{out} = \mathcal{C}_{out} \cup \{v\}$.
4: Compute $N^{\downarrow}(s')$, using a backward one-to-all Dijkstra algorithm from s' with rider cost bounded by $(\tau_d(t' \rightarrow s') + \Delta_d^{ret})$.
5: Compute $N^{\uparrow}(t')$, using a forward one-to-all Dijkstra algorithm from t' with driver cost bounded by $(\tau_d(t' \rightarrow s') + \Delta_d^{out})$, for each settled relay station v that satisfied the equation (8), $\mathcal{C}_{ret} = \mathcal{C}_{ret} \cup \{v\}$.
6: $\mathcal{C} = \mathcal{C}_{out} \cap \mathcal{C}_{ret}$.

Steps 4 and 5 allow to store all nodes v that satisfy the constraint of detour time for the rider in outgoing trip (5). The same reasoning is applied in steps 6 and 7 on the constraint of detour time in the return trip (8). Finally in the step 8, we keep in a class $\mathcal{C}$ only nodes that satisfy both constraints (5) and (8).

Once the class of potential relay stations $\mathcal{C}$ is determined, it remains to scan each bucket of this class and select the relay station v with the minimum cost of the *round-trip-path*. The scanning method of buckets is described in the Algorithm 2.

Thus, the *best fit in round-trip* for a given demand d is computed by Algorithm 3.

Complexity. The runtime of Dijkstra's Algorithm using Fibonacci Heaps is bounded by $O(|V|\log|V| + |E|)$. Hence, the worst-case complexity of the Algorithm 3 is $O(4(|V|\log|V| + |E|) + \sum_{v \in \mathcal{C}} |B(v)|)$ where $|B(v)|$ is the number of offers in the bucket v.

Algorithm 2. Scan bucket $B(v)$

Require: $B(v)$, demand d.
Ensure: *round-trip-path* $c(d, i^\star, j^\star, v)$.
1: Initialization: Cost_out $\leftarrow \infty$, Cost_ret $\leftarrow \infty$, $i^\star \leftarrow -1$, $j^\star \leftarrow -1$.
2: **for all** i in $B(v)$ **do**
3:     **if** o_i and d form a reasonable fit in outgoing trip with v as a relay station **then**
4:         Compute $c(\langle d, i, v \rangle)_{out}$ as described in (10)
5:         **if** $c(\langle d, i, v \rangle)_{out} <$ Cost_out **then**
6:             Cost_out $\leftarrow c(\langle d, i, v \rangle)_{out}$
7:             $i^\star \leftarrow i$
8:         **end if**
9:     **end if**
10:     **if** o_i and d form a reasonable fit in return trip with v as a relay station **then**
11:         Compute $c(\langle d, i, v \rangle)_{ret}$ as described in (11)
12:         **if** $c(\langle d, i, v \rangle)_{ret} <$ Cost_ret **then**
13:             Cost_ret $\leftarrow c(\langle d, i, v \rangle)_{ret}$
14:             $j^\star \leftarrow i$
15:         **end if**
16:     **end if**
17: **end for**
18: $c(\langle d, i^\star, j^\star, v \rangle) \leftarrow$ Cost_out + Cost_ret

---

Algorithm 3. Adding a demand

Require: Graph $G(V, E)$, demand d.
Ensure: driver $i^\star$, driver $j^\star$, best relay station $v^\star$ and $c(\langle d, i^\star, j^\star, v^\star \rangle)$.
1: Compute $\mathcal{C}$ using Algorithm 1
2: **for all** v in $\mathcal{C}$ **do**
3:     Scan a Bucket $B(v)$ using Algorithm 2
4:     Store the minimum cost $c(\langle d, i^\star, j^\star, v^\star \rangle)$
5: **end for**

3.3   Total Gain in Round-trip

The *Matching procedure* described above, ensures for the rider a gain simultaneously in the *outgoing* and *return* trips (i.e, constraints (3) and (6)). In this way, the sharing of the *cost-savings* between the ride-share partners in the *outgoing* trip is independent of ride-share partners in the *return* trip. But in practice, the gain must be ensured in *round-trip*, not necessarily in both *outgoing* trip and *return* trip. For example, we can have a negative *cost-savings* in outgoing trip equal to -3   between the rider d and the driver i. In the return trip, the rider d can be matched with the driver j with *cost-savings* equal to 8   . Thus, the rider can recover the cost that he lost in outgoing trip (i.e, -3   ). The main difficulty here lies in the way of sharing the saved cost, which depends both on the rider-share partners in outgoing and return trips. Note that the sharing procedure of saved cost in not considered in this study.

To take into account the total gain in round-trip instead of separate gain in outgoing and return trips, we just need to modify the lines 5, 12 and 20 in Algorithm 2. More precisely, in the lines 5 and 12, we only check the constraints of *detour time* in outgoing and return trips, respectively. Finally, in line 20, we must ensure the constraint of the *cost-savings* between the rider d, the driver $i^\star$ and the driver $j^\star$, defined as follows:

$$c_d(s' \to t') + c_o(s_{i\star} \to e_{i\star}) + c_d(t' \to s')$$
$$+ c_o(s_{j\star} \to e_{j\star}) - c(\langle d, i^\star, j^\star, v \rangle) \geq 0 \qquad (13)$$

In some cases, either the driver or the rider may ask for a minimum rate of the saved cost in his trip. For instance, the driver requires at least 10% of the saved cost relative to his initial travel cost. In that case, we extend model to take into account that requirement. More precisely, an offer and a demand of ridesharing will be represented by $o_i = (s_i, e_i, [t_i^{\min}, t_i^{\max}], \Delta_i, \sigma_{o_i})$ and $d = (s', e', [t_{\min}^{out}, t_{\max}^{out}], [t_{\min}^{ret}, t_{\max}^{ret}], \Delta_d^{out}, \Delta_d^{ret}, \sigma_d)$, respectively, where σ_{o_i} (σ_d) is the minimum percentage of cost-saving fixed by the driver (rider) relative to his shortest path. In such case, the constraint of the *cost-savings* between the rider d, the driver $i^\star$ and the driver $j^\star$, defined as follows:

$$c_d(s' \to t') + c_o(s_{i\star} \to e_{i\star}) + c_d(t' \to s') + c_o(s_{j\star} \to e_{j\star}) - c(\langle d, i^\star, j^\star, v \rangle)$$
$$\geq \sigma_{o_i} \cdot c_o(s_{i\star} \to t_{i\star}) + \sigma_{o_j} \cdot c_o(s_{j\star} \to t_{j\star}) + \sigma_d \cdot c_d(s' \to t') \quad (14)$$

3.4   Removing Offers

To remove an offer o_i, we need to remove its entries from the buckets. In order to accelerate the time calculation of the system, we classify buckets according to calendar date. Furthermore, for each calendar date, we have not defined an order in which the entries of a bucket are stored. This makes adding operation of an offer very fast, but removing it, requires scanning the buckets. Thus, scanning all buckets is prohibitive as there are too many entries. Instead, it is faster to compute $N^\uparrow(s_i)$ and $N^\downarrow(t_i)$ in order to obtain the set of buckets which contains an entry of this offer o_i. Then, we only need to scan those buckets and remove the entries of offer o_i.

4   Experiments

Computational experiments have been conducted to compare the performance of the proposed algorithms. In this section, the classical approach of round-trip ridesharing was denoted by CRT, the round-trip ridesharing with relay stations while ensuring for the rider a gain in the *outgoing* and *return trips* was denoted by RTR, and the round-trip ridesharing with relay stations while ensuring for the rider a total gain in round-trip was denoted by RTRG. The results of experiments were evaluated in terms of quality, number of matchings and running-time.

Environment.   The algorithms were coded in C# and run using an Intel(R) Core(TM) I7-3520M CPU 2.90 Ghz, with 8 GB RAM memory. A binary heap was used as the priority queue data structure.

Offers-demands Data.   In our experiments, we use a real data provided by Covivo company[1]. These data concern employees of Lorraine region traveling between their homes and their work places. The real data instance is composed of 756 offers and 757 demands in *round-trip*. In our experiments, for each offer in round-trip, we generate two offers separately, one for outgoing trip and another for return trip. Thus, the number of generated offers reach 1512. Concerning the demands, each rider owns a private car that he might use during a part of his trip. The set of offers and demands are filtered in the way that we can never find an offer and a demand which have both the same starting and ending locations. The time window for each trip is fixed as follows. For the outgoing trip from home to work, the early departure time and the latest departure time are fixed at 7:30 a.m. and at 8:00 a.m, respectively. For the return trip, the early departure time and the latest departure time are fixed at 18:00 p.m. and at 18:15 p.m, respectively. The detour time of the driver (rider) is fixed to at most 20% of his initial trip duration.

Road Networks.   Our road network of the French region Lorraine was derived from the publicly available data of OpenStreetMap[2] (OSM) and was provided by GeoFabrik[3]. It consists of 7 978 30 nodes and 2 394 002 directed edges. Each node in the road network can be a relay station in which the driver and the rider can meet each other. OSM is used in several projects and it facilitates the map integration or exploitation. For instance, OsmSharp is an open-source mapping tool designed to work with OpenStreetMap-data. In our experiments, we use OsmSharp's routing and OSM data processing library to test our shortest paths computations on real data sets.

Computational Results.   To facilitate our analysis, we divide the set of offers and demands into six main classes, and each class represents a geographical city (see Table 1). For each class, we compute the following parameters that allow us to compare the efficiency of different solution approaches.

---

[1] http://www.covivo.fr
[2] http://www.openstreetmap.org/
[3] http://www.geofabrik.de/

- Average success rate of matching ($\mathcal{M}$): the number of matched demands divided by the total number of demands within each class.
- Average cost-savings rate in round-trip ($\mathcal{C}$) : the sum of cost-savings rate in round-trip generated by the matched demands divided by the total number of matched demands within each class.

Table 1. Performance of three approaches

Classes (Cities)	# demands	CRT	RTR		RTRG	
		$\mathcal{M}$ (%)	$\mathcal{M}$ (%)	$\mathcal{C}$ (%)	$\mathcal{M}$ (%)	$\mathcal{C}$ (%)
Nancy	311	94.2	97.1	35.2	97.1	35.2
V.L.N	199	96.4	98.4	32.7	98.4	32.7
Metz	38	68.4	94.7	22.7	97.3	21.8
Luneville	107	95.3	99	25.7	99	25.7
Toul	74	91.8	97.2	27.8	97.2	27.8
Epinal	28	60.7	82.1	21.2	89.2	20.2

Results of Table 1 show that RTR and RTRG outperform CRT in terms of successful matching ($\mathcal{M}$) over the all six classes.

The gap between CRT and RTR (RTRG) of successful matching decreases with the offers' density in the concerned classes. For instance, the gap between CRT and RTR (RTRG) reaches 26.3% (28.9%) in Metz class and 21.4% (28.5%) in Epinal class. In fact, when the density of offers is low and the offers are distant from demands, this implies that drivers must make long detours to pick-up the riders, however, the detour time and the detour cost limit the successful matching. Nevertheless, when the rider accepts to travel with his own car to a relay station (RTR and RTRG approaches), this allows to reduce the detour of the drivers, therefore more successful matchings are found. Note also that in RTR and RTRG, the rate of successful matching are the same in all classes, except in Metz and Epinal classes where RTRG outperforms RTR with a slight ratio that does not exceed the 7.1%.

Regarding results in Epinal and Metz classes, RTRG is less efficient than RTR in terms of cost-savings ($\mathcal{C}$). This is due to the fact that the average cost-savings ($\mathcal{C}$) is calculated over instances where successful matching is found, and RTRG detects more matchings than RTR. In order to have a better idea on the performance of CRT, RTR and RTRG in terms of cost-savings, we evaluate the additional cost-savings that our approaches provide compared to the classical ridesharing CRT on instances in which successful matching is found by three approaches (CRT, RTR and RTRG), hereafter denoted by $\mathcal{I}$. Then, we compare the approaches RTR and RTRG on instances where a matching is found only by both RTR and RTRG, hereafter denoted by $\mathcal{H}$. The results are reported in Table 2. In column $\mathcal{C_I}$, the average cost-savings in round-trip on set of instances $\mathcal{I}$ are shown. In column $\mathcal{C_H}$, the average cost-savings in round-trip on set of instances $\mathcal{H}$ are shown.

Table 2. Additional cost-savings

Classes (Cities)	$\mathcal{C}_\mathcal{I}$			$\mathcal{C}_\mathcal{H}$	
	CRT (%)	RTR (%)	RTRG (%)	RTR (%)	RTRG (%)
Nancy	31	36.2	36.2	35.2	35.2
V.L.N	29.7	33.3	33.3	32.7	32.7
Metz	25	32.3	32.3	22.7	22.7
Luneville	25.9	26.8	26.8	25.7	25.7
Toul	26.4	29.4	29.4	27.8	27.8
Epinal	25	28.7	28.7	21.2	21.2

From the Table 2, we can see that the generated cost-saving is significant in both approaches RTR and RTRG compared to CRT for all classes. Indeed, the average cost-savings per round-trip reaches 36.2% with our approaches. Furthermore, the two approaches RTR and RTRG have the same cost-savings for the detected matchings. In the case where a matching is detected only by RTRG, the cost-savings of round-trip can never exceed 25%. Indeed, in outgoing trip (resp. return trip), we can never save more than 25% of the round-trip. Since RTR approach does not detect a matching, then either outgoing trip or return trip generates a negative cost-savings. So the cost-savings that RTRG saves in case RTR found no matching does not exceed 25%. Thus, the major advantage of the RTRG approach compared to RTR was in increasing the matching rate while conserving attractive cost-savings.

To illustrate the effectiveness of the whole system, we evaluate the time to add/remove a demand and an offer depending on the existing numbers of offers and buckets in the system. Tables 3 and 4 summarize the time needed to add/remove a demand and an offer depending on the numbers of offers and buckets. Each entry in the Table 3 is an average value over instances in each class.

From Table 3, the average time of adding a demand increases linearly with the number of buckets and the number of offers in buckets. In CRT, we only need to scan two buckets corresponding to vertices of the starting and ending locations of the demand. However, in RTR and RTRG, we need to scan all

Table 3. Adding demand

Classes (Cities)	# buckets		# offers in buckets $[\cdot 10^3]$			Runtime [s]		
	CRT	RTR	CRT	RTR	RTRG	CRT	RTR	RTRG
Nancy	2	285	0.064	48	48	0.19	0.44	0.44
V.L.N	2	374	0.090	47	47	0.24	0.55	0.56
Metz	2	2442	0.010	39	39	2.77	3.39	3.52
Luneville	2	1700	0.043	44	44	0.55	1.73	2.03
Toul	2	832	0.041	48	48	0.49	1.45	1.51
Epinal	2	3740	0.006	31	31	3.5	5.29	5.45

buckets in *the set of potential relay stations* C. The slight difference in running-time between RTR and RTRG (< 0.2 sec) is due to the way in which we scan a bucket. Contrary to RTR approach, in RTRG, we check the *constraint of cost-savings* only after having verified all offers contained in the bucket that satisfy *the constraint of detour time*. Thus, the number of filtered offers in bucket is less important compared to the RTR approach.

In order to evaluate the time needed to add and to remove an offer, we have fixed three offers o_1, o_2 and o_3 composed of 99, 239 and 549 buckets, respectively. These offers are added/removed from the system according to the number of offers already contained in these buckets.

From Table 4, we observe that the time to add an offer o_i is independent of the number of offers already in the system. The main time is spent in computing $N^{\uparrow}(s_i)$ and $N^{\downarrow}(t_i)$. However, removing the offer requires scanning these buckets. Thus, the run-time to add and remove offers remains at microseconds scale.

Figure 3 gets a better visualization of the running time of adding and removing offer.

Table 4. Adding and removing offer

Offer	# buckets	# offers in buckets	Add [s]	Remove [s]
o_1	99	100	0.03	0.032
		250	0.03	0.041
		550	0.03	0.053
o_2	239	100	0.05	0.052
		250	0.05	0.062
		550	0.05	0.074
o_3	549	100	0.08	0.083
		250	0.08	0.093
		550	0.08	0.1

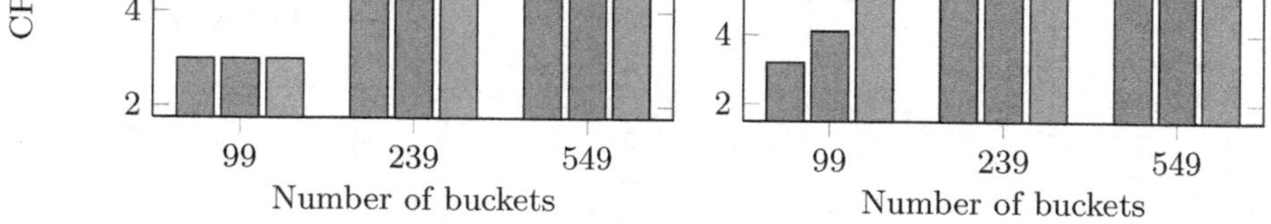

Fig. 3. Adding and removing offers depending on the number of buckets and offers in the system.

Summarizing these results, the two approaches RTI and RTIG provide efficient results in terms of successful matching, cost-savings and running-time. They can also solve the problem of ridesharing with a high number of offers and relay stations within a few seconds of computation time.

5   Conclusion

This paper sets out methods for round-trip ridesharing that allow the rider to use his private car in order to reach a relay station, more or less close to his initial starting location. The decision making process on the choice of the relay station relates to the density of offers passing via this location. This approach was validated by experiments based on real data of ridesharing in the French Lorraine region. The main advantages of this approach are increasing the opportunity of matching between riders and drivers and then a significant reduction of the total travel cost compared to the classical approach of round-trip ridesharing. As perspectives, several extensions can be considered. For example, the case where some ride-share participants announce trips in which they are flexible to serve as drivers or riders. Ride-share matching optimization in this case must not only determine the best relay station, but also assign a role to each of the participants. For future work, it may be interesting to consider the approach described in [5] by allowing riders to switch between several drivers while guaranteeing their return trips. Secondly, some procedures for sharing saved costs between the outgoing and return trip of one round-trip will be investigated. Finally, a natural avenue for future research is accelerating our approach using Contraction Hierarchies [7].

References

1. Agatz, N., Erera, A., Savelsbergh, M., Wang, X.: Optimization for dynamic ride-sharing: A review. European Journal of Operational Research **223**, 295–303 (2012)
2. Agatz, N., Erera, A., Savelsbergh, M., Wang, X.: Dynamic ride-sharing: a simulation study in metro atlanta. Transportation Research Part B, Methodological **45**, 1450–1464 (2011)
3. Aissat, K., Oulamara, A.: A posteriori approach of real-time ride-sharing problem with intermediate locations. In: Proceedings of the 4rd International Conference on Operations Research and Enterprise Systems, ICORES 2015, Lisbon, Portugal, January 10–12, 2015 (2015)
4. Dijkstra, E.: A note on two problems in connexion with graphs. Numerische Mathematik **1**, 269–271 (1959)
5. Drews, F., Luxen, D.: Multi-hop ride sharing. In: Proceedings of the Sixth Annual Symposium on Combinatorial Search, pp. 71–79 (2013)
6. Furuhata, M., Dessouky, M., Brunet, F.O.M., Wang, X., Koenig, S.: Ridesharing: The state-of-the-art and future directions. Transportation Research Part B: Methodological **57**, 28–46 (2013)
7. Geisberger, R., Sanders, P., Schultes, D., Vetter, C.: Exact routing in large road networks using contraction hierarchies. Transportation Science **46**, 388–404 (2012)

8. Huguet, M.J., Kirchler, D., Parent, P., Calvo, R.W.: Efficient algorithms for the 2-way multi modal shortest path problem. Electronic Notes in Discrete Mathematics **41**, 431–437 (2013)
9. Varone, S., Aissat, K.: Muti-modal transportation with public transport and ride-sharing mutli-modal transportation using a path-based method. In: Proceedings of the 17th International Conference on Enterprise Information Systems, ICEIS 2015, vol. 1, Barcelona, Spain, April 27–30, 2015 (2015)

A Hierarchical Model for the Cash Transfer System Design Problem

Engin Topaloglu[1], Abdullah Dasci[2]([✉]), and M. Hasan Eken[3]

[1] Turkiye Is Bankasi, 34330 Besiktas, Istanbul, Turkey
[2] Sabanci University, 34956 Tuzla, Istanbul, Turkey
dasci@sabanciuniv.edu
[3] Istanbul Commerce University, 34134 Beyoglu, Istanbul, Turkey

Abstract. This paper presents a hierarchical model that incorporates strategic, tactical, and operational decisions of cash transfer management system of a bank. The aim of the model is to decide on the location of cash management centers, the number and routes of vehicles, and the cash inventory management policies to minimize the cost of owning and operating a cash transfer system while maintaining a pre-defined service level. Owing to the difficulty of finding optimal decisions in such integrated models, an iterative solution approach is proposed in which strategic, tactical, and operational problems are solved separately via a feedback mechanism. Numerical results show that such an approach is quite effective in reaching at greatly improved solutions with just a few iterations, making it a very promising approach for similar models.

Keywords: Location · Vehicle routing · VRP · Cash transfer · Inventory management

1 Introduction

A major function of a bank is to act as an intermediary between its clients by collecting deposits from some while dispensing cash to the others. Typically, banks perform these operations via their branches and automated banking machines located across a geographical market. Since such transactions are naturally uncertain, cash positions at branches change randomly throughout the day.

Effective management of cash positions at branches is critical. Banks do not prefer to carry extra cash due to opportunity cost is associated with it. Any extra cash can be deposited to central banks or loaned to other banks for overnight interest. Furthermore, extra cash makes banks susceptible to theft, fraud, and so on. Falling short of necessary cash, however, is also undesirable and perhaps, even more harmful. Client requests for withdrawal should be met immediately or with very little delay as failure to do so may have severe negative consequences such as loss of goodwill or even loss of confidence.

Therefore, banks need to transfer cash in and out of branches to manage these inventories in a rational way. A cash transfer system has two main sets of cost

© Springer International Publishing Switzerland 2015
F. Corman et al. (Eds.): ICCL 2015, LNCS 9335, pp. 31–45, 2015.
DOI: 10.1007/978-3-319-24264-4_3

items. The first set includes operational costs of managing a system such as fixed and variable costs related to the cash management centers (CMCs) and armored vehicles (AVs) while the second set includes opportunity and shortage costs of having too much or too little cash at the branches. An effective management of a cash transfer system should trade-off these costs when making design and operational decisions in the system.

In this paper we present a hierarchical model and an iterative solution approach for a cash transfer management system design problem. Our model falls into the general class of integrated location-routing-inventory models. The literature on integrated models for any pair of these decisions is relatively well developed. A comprehensive review on integrated location-routing, location-inventory, and inventory-routing problems is provided by Shen (2007). Other papers, such as Melo, Nickel, and Saldanha-da-Gama (2009) as well as Klibi, Martel, and Guitouni (2010) give a review of supply chain design models that include integrated facility location models. In cash logistics context, recently there are few papers for inventory-routing problems (Wagner 2010 and van Anholt et al. 2013). However, the literature that consider all three levels of decisions is scant and those that present such integrated models report a very limited results.

In one of the earlier works Ambrosino and Scutella (2005) study a detailed location-routing model in a four-layer distribution network. A more concise model that considers inventories in a similar manner is presented in Hiassat and Diabat (2011). However, neither papers gave any numerical experimentation of a reasonable detail but rather solved only a very small instance. Shen and Qi (2007) is perhaps the first study that explicitly considers cycle and safety inventory costs and routing in a location problem. However, they do not consider detailed routing decisions; instead they develop an approximation for the routing cost and incorporate it in a nonlinear program.

The model closest to ours is given in Javid and Azad (2010), in which authors study a capacitated facility location problem that explicitly considers routing and inventory decisions. They first formulate the problem as a mixed-integer convex problem, which is solved by LINDO for small sized problems. The largest problem that was solved to optimality within 12 hours by LINDO had three potential DCs, two vehicles, and nine customers. For larger size problems they utilize a hybrid Tabu Search and Simulated Annealing heuristic method. They solved problems as large as 50 potential DCs, 65 vehicles, and 400 customers.

Our paper introduces a novel addition to this growing literature. First, the very few models that explicitly include routing and inventory decisions along with location decisions consider a "traditional" inventory management setting. We on the other hand deal with a cash inventory setting, which is perhaps the first considered in a network design problem here. Even though cash inventory management is an area that has not received enough attention in logistics literature, with the continuing general economic climate of low-interest borrowing, logistics and other operational costs have become more important determinants of the profitability of financial institutions. Our work offers a step towards addressing this research gap in the literature.

Secondly, we propose an iterative solution method for the problem, instead of dealing with approximate integrated models or meta-heuristics as most past works do. We obtain promising results on the performance of an iterative approach that solves a series of simpler problems with updated parameters. Finally, we generate problem instances based mostly on the real-life data we obtained from a commercial bank. Some of this data can be used in future studies.

In the rest of this paper we first present the model and the iterative approach. Section 3 contains the description of parameter estimation and instance generation followed by reporting of the set of numerical experiments. We conclude the paper with few remarks and avenues for future research in Section 4.

2   The Model

Our approach consists of a series of well-known problems for strategic, tactical, and operational decisions and an iterative solution method to reach an optimal or near-optimal solution. We consider a location problem at the strategic level, a vehicle routing problem at the tactical level, and a cash management problem at the operational level. The fourth problem, termed as a vehicle number determination problem, is a peculiar tactical problem that ties these three problems in the iterative solution approach we developed. Each of the following subsections is devoted to the exposition of one problem and its relationship to the other problems as well as to the overall iterative procedure.

2.1   Strategic Problem: An Uncapacitated Facility Location Problem (UFLP)

The strategic problem is an extension of the standard UFLP that determines the CMC locations and CMC-branch assignments so as to minimize the total cost. In addition to the location and assignment variables, we defined a third set of decision variables for the number of vehicles to take transportation capacity and cost of the AVs into account, albeit approximately. These extensions add a bit more realism to the fixed and variable cost structures and are expected to lead to better location decisions.

We consider an uncapacitated case, as it is usually easy to increase capacity at these centers by acquiring additional machinery or hiring new personnel. The vehicles also have annual fixed costs such as tax, insurance, as well as personnel costs. Transportation costs are incorporated approximately through CMC-branch assignment as typical in facility location problems.

Let the index $i \in I = \{1, 2, \ldots, m\}$ represent the alternative CMC locations and the index $j \in J = \{1, 2, \ldots, n\}$ represent the branches. The decision variables used in our version of UFLP are:

$$y_i = \begin{cases} 1, & \text{if CMC at location } i \text{ opened,} \\ 0, & \text{otherwise,} \end{cases}$$

$z_i =$ The number of AVs assigned to CMC at location i.

$$x_{ij} = \begin{cases} 1, \text{ if the branch } j \text{ is assigned to CMC at location } i, \\ 0, \text{ otherwise.} \end{cases}$$

The parameters are given as:

f_i : Fixed cost of opening a CMC at location i,

g_i : Fixed cost of an AV assigned to CMC at location i,

a_{ij} : Direct trip cost between locations i and j,

s_{ij} : Direct travel time between the CMC at location i and the branch at j,

S : Maximum total time an AV can be used in a year.

Our iterative approach requires some of these parameters to be revised at each iteration. To facilitate it, we also define the following iteration parameters:

α^{t-1} : System-wide ratio of total route length to total direct travel (including backhaul),

k_j^{t-1} : The number of cash transfer requests made by branch j.

These parameters are revised at each iteration of the algorithm and the superscript $(t-1)$ refers to the values obtained in the previous iteration. Although the impact of α and k are combined in the formulation, we chose to separately represent them since they are obtained from different problems. Given all the variables and parameters, the strategic problem can be formulated as follows:

$$\text{Minimize} \quad \sum_{i \in I} f_i y_i + \sum_{i \in I} g_i z_i + \sum_{i \in I} \sum_{j \in J} \alpha^{t-1} k_j^{t-1} a_{ij} x_{ij} \tag{1}$$

$$\text{subject to} \quad \sum_{i \in I} x_{ij} = 1, \text{ for all } j \in J, \tag{2}$$

$$x_{ij} \leq y_i, \text{ for all } i \in I, j \in J, \tag{3}$$

$$\sum_{i \in J} \alpha^{t-1} k_j^{t-1} s_{ij} x_{ij} \leq S z_i, \text{ for all } i \in I, \tag{4}$$

$$y_i \text{ and } x_{ij} \in \{0,1\}, \text{ for all } i \in I \text{ and } j \in J, \tag{5}$$

$$z_i \in \{0,1,\ldots\} \text{ for all } i \in I. \tag{6}$$

Objective function (1) includes the fixed costs of CMCs and AVs and the direct transportation cost, which is adjusted with a routing factor and the approximate number of trips to a particular branch. Constraints (2) and (3) are the standard constraints in UFLP which ensure that each branch is assigned to one open CMC. Constraints (4) ensure that there are enough vehicles that cover the anticipated total travel time at each CMC. This constraint provides a rough-cut estimate of the minimum number of vehicles without considering the detailed routing issues. Finally, (5) and (6) define the binary and general integer variables.

2.2   Tactical Problem: A Vehicle Routing Problem (VRP)

Our tactical model is a version of VRP, in which the location of CMCs and CMC-branch assignments from the UFLP are given as input. A VRP is solved for each CMC to determine the number of vehicles and their routes that minimize the total vehicle and traveling costs. Let n_i denote the number of branches assigned to CMC i and the set $J_i = \{1, \ldots, n_i\}$ denote those branches. Indices $j = 0$ and $j = n_i + 1$ are used to indicate the start and the end of the tours, i.e., the CMC location. For notational conciseness we also define new sets as $\underline{J}_i = J_i \cup \{0\}$ and $\overline{J}_i = J_i \cup \{n_i + 1\}$. Furthermore, let

$$u_{jk} = \begin{cases} 1, & \text{if the branch } k \text{ is visited immediately after branch } j, \\ 0, & \text{otherwise, and} \end{cases}$$

$t_j = $ The time branch j starts receiving the service.

The problem parameters are defined as:
s_{jk} : Trip time from branch j to branch k,
h : Average service time at a branch,
B : The length of a shift,
M : A large number.
We also define an iterative parameter β^{t-1} as the average aggregate trip frequency of routes. Our VRP can be modeled as:

$$\text{Minimize} \quad g_i \sum_{j \in J_i} u_{0j} + \beta^{t-1} \sum_{j \in J_i} \sum_{k \in \overline{J}_i} a_{jk} u_{jk} \tag{7}$$

$$\text{subject to} \quad \sum_{j \in \underline{J}_i, j \neq k} u_{jk} = 1, \text{ for all } k \in J_i, \tag{8}$$

$$\sum_{k \in \overline{J}_i, k \neq j} u_{jk} = 1, \text{ for all } j \in J_i, \tag{9}$$

$$t_j \geq s_{0j} - M(1 - u_{0j}), \text{ for all } j \in J_i, \tag{10}$$

$$t_k \geq t_j + s_{jk} + h - M(1 - u_{jk}), \text{ for all } j \in J_i \text{ and } k \in \overline{J}_i, \tag{11}$$

$$t_{n_i+1} \leq B, \tag{12}$$

$$u_{jk} \in \{0,1\}, \text{ and } t_j \geq 0 \text{ for all } j \in J_i \text{ and } k \in \overline{J}_i. \tag{13}$$

The objective function consists of the fixed vehicle costs and the total trip costs. Constraints (8-11) are standard constraints in VRPs. Constraints (8) ensure that each branch is visited by a vehicle and (9) ensure that each vehicle also leaves a branch it has visited. Constraints (10) and (11) ensure that vehicles are given sufficient time for service and travel between visiting branches. Finally, the condition on the shift length is given in (12) and the non-negativity and binary restrictions are given in (13).

While CMC locations and assignments to branches are given as input from the strategic model, here the number of vehicles for each CMC is found by re-optimizing a more detailed representation of the vehicle and trip costs.

2.3 Operational Problem: A Cash Management Problem Under Uncertainty (CMPU)

At the operational level, we solve a cash management problem at each branch where cash transactions are uncertain. In CMPU, the cash positions of the branches are continuously reviewed and at any period one has to decide if any action of cash transfer to or from the branch should take place and if so, what should be the transfer amounts. In general, each of these actions incur fixed and variable costs, which are defined in our context as:

K_1 : Fixed cost of transferring money from a branch to a vehicle,

K_2 : Fixed cost of transferring money from a vehicle to a branch,

k_1 : Unit variable cost of transferring money from a branch to a vehicle,

k_2 : Unit variable cost of transferring money from a vehicle to a branch.

Hence, when the cash position of a branch changes from x to y, the transfer cost can be written as:

$$A(x, y) = \begin{cases} K_1 + k_1(x - y), & \text{if } y < x, \\ 0 & \text{if } y = x, \\ K_2 + k_2(y - x), & \text{if } y > x. \end{cases}$$

Under a variety of conditions, several authors, such as Girgis (1968), Porteus (1972), Porteus and Neave (1972), and Constantinides and Richard (1978), show that a "two-sided" generalization of (s, S) policy from inventory management, i.e., (u, U, D, d), is an optimal policy for the cash management problem. The four parameters defining this policy suggest that if the cash position falls to or below u, enough cash is obtained to raise the cash position up to U and if the cash position rises to or above d, enough cash is removed from the branch to bring the cash position down to D.

While the form of the optimal policy is known, it is rather challenging to compute the optimal policy parameters. The problem, however, can be somewhat simplified for our setting. First, it would not be a very strong assumption to take the fixed costs of cash transfers between the branch and the vehicle as equal, i.e., $K_1 = K_2$, since in both cases, the vehicles take similar routes and similar actions are taken at the time of transfer such as counting money, approvals, and so on. Second, the variable portion of the cash transfer can be assumed negligible as compared to the fixed costs, i.e., $k_1 = k_2 = 0$, because much of the personnel cost is already sunk in our setting. Under these conditions, Milbourne (1983) has shown that a (u, z, d) policy would be optimal. This policy is a special case of the two-sided policy described above, with $z = U = D$.

Despite these simplifications, however, computation of policy parameters remains a challenge under general net transaction distributions. Furthermore, while it is relatively easy to estimate the cost of holding excess cash (such as the overnight interest rate), estimating the cost of cash shortage is not straightforward. Shortage cost includes the cost of borrowing at the interbank interest rate, but sometimes it might not be feasible or desirable to borrow from another institution. Moreover, one also needs to account for the cost of lost goodwill. Therefore, rather than finding all three policy parameters with an estimated cost of shortage, we assume that the management sets a "service-level" that restricts the probability of cash shortage when a cash transfer to the branch is awaited. This service level helps us to set the lower threshold u independent of other parameters and then compute the remaining two parameters, z and d. Our treatment is analogous to approximating (s, S) policy parameters with an

Economic Order Quantity - ReOrder Point (EOQ-ROP) approach in inventory management.

The model we have chosen towards this end is that of Miller and Orr (1966). Their results are based on two key assumptions: cash transfers are immediate and cash movements at a branch have zero mean, i.e., deposits and withdrawals cancel each other, on average. Under these conditions Miller and Orr has calculated the optimal decisions as

$$z^* = \sqrt{\frac{3Kn_t\mu_t^2}{4r}} \text{ and } d^* = 3z^*,$$

where
  μ_t : Mean cash transaction size,
  K : Fixed cost of transferring money to or from a branch,
  n_t : Mean number of cash transactions on a day, and
  r : Daily interest rate.

While in our case most branches have nonzero net transaction average, we nonetheless use Miller and Orr's model as an approximation. We find the (z^*, d^*) as described above and then add u^* to these values to obtain the triple policy parameters $(u^*, z^* + u^*, d^* + u^*)$, where u^* is computed by using the service level and the next transaction distribution. After calculation of these parameters we find the average cash levels and the average number of transactions via a simulation.

2.4   Integrating Problem: The Vehicle Number Determination Problem (VNDP)

The last problem acts as an integrating problem among UFLP, VRP, and CMPU and it resulted from the practice of the bank from which this study derives. While both UFLP and VRP take the number of vehicles into account, their treatments are based on simplifying assumptions: UFLP determines the minimum number of vehicles based on "adjusted" direct distance and VRP, on the other hand assumes that each branch will be visited every day. VNDP offers a correction via a probabilistic analysis of branches' transfer requests. It uses VRP and CMPU results from the previous iteration while modifying the parameters to be used in UFLP and VRP in the next iteration.

Now suppose that VRP produces k_i routes for CMC i. Let there be n_{ik} branches represented by the set $J_{ik} = \{1, 2, \ldots, n_{ik}\}$ on each route $k \in K_i = \{1, 2, \ldots, k_i\}$. Also, let p_j^{ik} denote the probability that a branch $j \in J_{ik}$ requests a cash transfer on a given day. These probabilities are assumed to be independent across branches. The probability that at least one branch on route $k \in K_i$ requests a transfer can be expressed as:

$$P_{ik} = 1 - \prod_{j \in J_{ik}} (1 - p_j^{ik}),$$

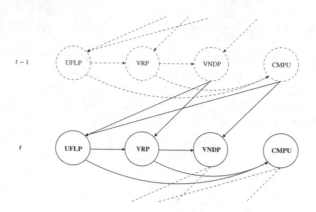

Fig. 1. The structure of the iterative algorithm

where probabilities (p_j^{ik}) are calculated via simulation of the CMPU. Then, the probability distribution of the number of routes used on a day would be a multinomial distribution for each CMC i with probabilities, $P_{i1}, P_{i2}, \ldots, P_{ik_i}$. Hence, for CMC i, the probability that all routes need to be served on a particular day is given as $q_{ik_i} = \prod_{k=1}^{k_i} P_{ik}$. Similarly, the probability that $(k_i - 1)$ routes to be used is given as $q_{i(k_i-1)} = \sum_{k'=1}^{k_i}(1 - P_{ik'}) \prod_{k \neq k'} P_{ik}$, and so on. The expected number of vehicles is then found by enumerating all probabilities q_{ik} for $1, 2, \ldots, k_i$ routes and then taking the expectation, i.e.

$$NoV[\text{VNDP}] = \sum_{k=0}^{k_i} k q_{ik}. \tag{14}$$

This calculation is based on the fact that whether a single branch or all the branches in a route requests a service, one vehicle is used. Also, note that this particular setup is based on the practice of the bank where routes are determined and fixed before any daily operations take place (more on this later). Total distance however, would depend on how many branches (an which branches) are visisted on a particular day. This is taken into account in finding the expected total distance, which is given as:

$$Dist[\text{VNDP}] = \sum_{i=1}^{m} P_{ik} U_{ik}, \tag{15}$$

where U_{ik} be the distance of the kth route of CMC i. This quantity is used to revise the distance correction factor used in UFLP as well as to compute the total transportation cost.

In our solution method, these four problems are solved iteratively with some parameters updated at each iteration. Figures 1 and 2 depict the structure of the algorithm at different levels of detail. In nutshell, UFLP uses CMPU results

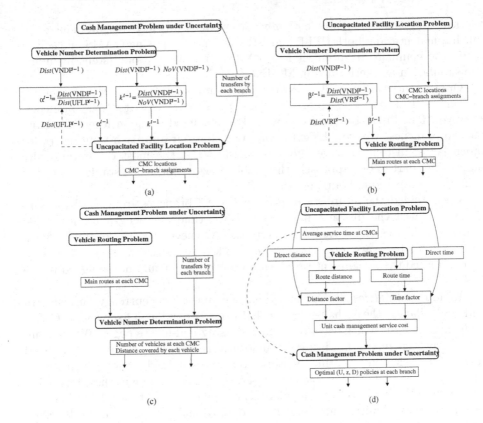

Fig. 2. The components of the iterative algorithm: (a) Uncapacitated Facility Location Problem, (b) Vehicle Routing Problem, (c) Vehicle Number Determination Problem, and (d) Cash Management Problem under Uncertainty

to determine the expected cash transfer requests at each branch, while using the VNDP's results to adjust the transportation cost and time parameters. VRP uses UFLP results on the CMC locations and CMC-branch assignments and VNDP's results to adjust the distance parameter. VNDP uses VRP results to obtain the routes and CMPU's results to obtain the number of transfers, which are used to calculate the branches' transfer request probabilities. Finally, CMPU uses the results of UFLP and VRP to find the transfer request fixed costs at each branch and hence the policy parameters, which in turn determine the service request frequencies on of the branches.

3   A Numerical Study

The main purpose of this study is to investigate the convergence properties of our approach. We are also interested in how much an iterative approach would likely to improve the system over a piece-meal approach, i.e., solving strategic, tactical, and operational problems only once without any feedback mechanism. In our implementation, both UFLP and VRP are modeled using GAMS and solved using the commercial optimizer LINDO. Other computational steps including the simulation are performed in MS Excel.

Our instances are partially based on data obtained from a bank that operates in Turkey. It is the largest private bank in Turkey with its 1,300 branches. However, for illustrative purposes, we only considered a region where the bank had 86 branches. We would like to point out that our approach would work for much larger instances as well because in the VRP, the most computationally demanding part of our approach, the problem sizes tend to be stable due to the constraint on working hours in a day.

We obtained the addresses of each of the 86 branches from the bank and then generated the distance matrices in both time and length using Google Maps, which uses the actual road network. Whenever the travel time from a CMC candidate location to a branch and back exceeds the nine-hour work day, we eliminated the assignment variables, so the branch would not assigned to the CMC.

Table 1 summarizes all the cost estimations in the local currency Turkish Lira and US Dollars at the exchange rate at that time. A portion of fixed cost of CMCs is the leasing cost, which we have estimated using real-estate pages. We came up with an average figure that is used at all locations. For other components of fixed costs such as cleaning, heating, lighting, etc. we just added a fixed percentage of the leasing cost. The second cost is that of the AVs. According to the information provided by the bank, AVs are regular commercial vehicles that are modified for certain security requirements. AVs can be operational for an average of 10 years. The straight-line depreciation of the price of an AV and an verage maintenance cost is used as the AV annual cost. The variable AV cost is essentially the mileage cost due to gas.

Above estimates do not include labor cost. Under the current operations all labor costs are fixed. There are four types of personnel employed in the cash transfer system: drivers, security guards, clerks, and supervisors. To calculate the cost of these personnel we used the minimum wage as a basis. First we have estimated how much a minimum wage personnel cost to a company including health and pension benefits, vacation pay, and so on. Roughly, drivers and security guards cost twice as much as a minimum wage personnel. The clerks and supervisors cost three and four times that amount, respectively.

In the current operations, each AV is assigned four personnel; one of each. This number might seem excessive, but in the current mode of operation, drivers are required to be in the vehicle at all times and not to perform any other task. According to Turkish regulations, security personnel is also barred from performing any other function. A clerk is needed to perform all the transactions and exchanges and a supervisor is to oversee all the operations. A CMC is typically staffed with three personnel; also one of each, except a driver. These personnel costs are added to costs of CMCs and AVs to obtain the fixed costs.

Table 1. Cost estimations

Cost type	TL	USD
CMC annual cost	77,581	43,100
AV annual cost	5,104	2,835
AV variable cost (per km)	0.68	0.38
Minimum wage	11,088	6,160
Driver or guard cost	22,176	12,320
Clerk cost	33,264	18,480
Supervisor cost	44,352	26,640
Total CMC annual fixed cost	177,373	98,540
Total AV annual fixed cost	127,071	90,595

We now turn to the estimation of the cash transaction parameters at the branches, which include the nature of cash movements at each branch, fixed cost of cash transfers, and the daily interest rate. The last one is perhaps the easiest one to estimate (we have simply divided the interbank borrowing rate, which was 8% at the time, by 365 days). We are also aware that this is particularly high; in most developed economies this rate is extremely low.

While in most cash management literature fixed cost is usually readily available (as transferring money from one investment option to another entails some fees) in our case, it includes the fixed effort of transferring the cash from a vehicle to a branch (or, vice versa) as well as the transportation cost portion that can be allocated to the branch. For the first portion, we have estimated the average times the branch and vehicle personnel spend in the money exchange and multiply it with hourly wage rates to estimate a fixed labor cost. The transportation cost portion is rather more crude; we have identified the total route transportation cost and divided it among the branches based on a weight computed from the direct distances to CMC. Hence, farther branches received a larger share of the transportation cost while closer branches received a smaller share.

We now move on with the description of demand parameters. We need to introduce some notation to facilitate the exposition. Let,

$\mu_w, \sigma_{\mu w}^2$: Mean and variance of the size of withdrawals,

n_w, σ_{nw}^2 : Mean and variance of the number of daily withdrawals,

$\mu_d, \sigma_{\mu d}^2$: Mean and variance of the size of deposits,

n_d, σ_{nd}^2 : Mean and variance of the number of daily deposits,

The number of transactions at a branch is then $n_t = n_w + n_d$ and the weighted average cash movement size is $\mu_t = (n_w \mu_w + n_d \mu_d)/n_t$. Although Miller and Orr (1966) model assume roughly equal sized withdrawals and deposits, in our cases we have observed that on average there are roughly three to four times more withdrawals than deposits, while the average deposit size is roughly three to four times that of withdrawals.

To compute the lower threshold u^* of the triple policy we need to estimate the lead-time and lead-time cash withdrawal (or deposit) demand. The mean of daily cash demand is simply $\mu = n_w \mu_w - n_d \mu_d$ and its variance is

$\sigma^2 = n_w\sigma_{\mu w}^2 + \mu_w^2\sigma_{nw}^2 + n_d\sigma_{\mu d}^2 + \mu_d^2\sigma_{nd}^2$. In our numerical experiments, we have also observed that normal distribution is a fairly good approximation for the net daily transactions, although the actual distribution have fatter tails. Finally we have set the lead time as the one fourth of the route travel time between a branch and its CMC and assumed that it is same for all branches at a route. The rationale is that the most a particular branch is away from the CMC is about half the route and we used the half of that time (the average) as the approximation of the lead-time. Finally, we set the risk of running out of cash during cash transfer lead-time as 1% (i.e., 99% service level).

We have tested our approach on 12 problem instances, each of which has the same parameters except the demand parameters. The instances are only differentiated with respect to the cash demand parameters. To estimate the means and variances of the sizes and numbers of deposits and withdrawals, we used monthly data for a 12-month period, each month corresponding to an instance. We refer to these instances as "January", "February", etc.

To initialize the procedure, we start with solving a CMPU for each branch assuming that each branch is also a CMC. In this case the fixed cost of transferring money consists only of the labor portion. We expected branches put a substantially high number of transfer requests since the cost of doing so is rather low at the beginning. Based on those results we generate average transfer requests at each branch and start "Iteration 1" by solving a UFLP considering only the CMC costs and the direct transportation cost. Subsequently, we solve VRPs and VNDPs for each CMC and then CMPU at each branch to end the first iteration. We then move to the second iteration and continue until all three iteration parameters (α, β, and k_j) converge.

Tables 2 and 3 report our results at varying in details. We choose to give only the January's results in detail (Table 2) as other instances were similar. As expected, there are substantially high number of cash transfer requests and low cash levels at the initialization stage (Iteration 0). However, the solution quickly moves to a converging pattern and by the fourth iteration it converges to a solution. One of the decisions, the number of vehicles, shows a noteworthy pattern. This decision is found in UFLP, VRP, and VNDP. Although UFLP is not able to capture the impact of this variable sufficiently, it does not present an obstacle for the convergence of the algorithm. We also observed that the impact of VNDP on revising the number of vehicles is basically negligible (refer to Equation (14)). However its impact on the distance correction is important (see Equation (15)).

In Table 3 we only reported those of the summary results (marked with "*" in Table 2). The results are somewhat similar to those of January instance. Eight of the other instances took four iterations; one took five, and two took three iterations. Each instance's iterative pattern is also similar where the problems quickly converge to a lower number of CMC locations and AVs and mostly settle there. From this table we also observe that the iterative solution approach improves greatly upon a piece-meal approach. For example, in January, the total cost at the end of Iteration 1 (would be the result of a piece-meal approach)

Table 2. Detailed results of the January instance

Problem	Iteration (t)	0	1	2	3	4
UFLP	Number of CMCs*	86	14	10	10	10
UFLP	Number of vehicles		11.8	6.9	8.3	10.0
UFLP	Total distance		1,622,953	1,141,654	942,083	942,083
VRP	Number of vehicles		18	17	17	17
VRP	Total route length		3,803	4,190	4,190	4,190
VRP	Total distance		959,679	1,057,302	1,057,302	1,057,302
VNDP	Number of vehicles*		18	17	17	17
VNDP	Total distance*		957,457	947,365	946,300	946,300
CMPU	Total number of requests	28,428	17,724	16,704	16,704	16,704
CMPU	Total average cash level*	9,618,084	24,898,274	27,535,662	27,535,662	27,535,662
Iteration parameters						
UFLP	Distance correction (α^t)	0.67	0.59	0.83	1.00	1.00
VRP	Distance correction (β^t)	0.67	1.00	0.90	0.90	0.90
Costs						
UFLP	CMC fixed costs	15,262,196	2,484,544	1,774,674	1,774,674	1,774,674
VNDP	AV fixed costs		2,655,043	2,507,541	2,507,541	2,507,541
VNDP	Travel cost		652,961	646,079	645,353	645,353
CMPU	Cash holding cost	769,447	1,991,862	2,202,853	2,202,853	2,202,853
	Total cost*	16,031,643	7,784,410	7,131,147	7,130,421	7,130,421

is 7,784,410. It is reduced to 7,130,421 as a result of the iterative approach, which corresponds to about 8.4% improvement. The average improvement over 12 instances is 7.8%, which indicates that a substantial improvement in total cost can be obtained by an iterative approach.

In summary, both the convergence and the improvement results indicate that an iterative approach such as ours presents a great promise as a viable solution approach in the improvement of such design and operational decisions. One final noteworthy result is that most of the improvement in these instances came at the end of Iteration 2, while the algorithm uses the remaining steps to ensure convergence of the algorithm. Knowing that such great improvements can be obtained in a few iterations is a further credit to an iterative approach.

4   Concluding Remarks

This paper presents a novel addition to the scant but growing literature of cash logistics operations. The overall problem is potentially very difficult to solve and even to model in an integrated fashion. Therefore, an iterative approach such as ours that solves a series of location, routing, and cash inventory problems is an attractive one.

Our approach and the model are open to several improvements and extensions. Some of our modeling choices came from the particular practices we observed at the bank, which might not be valid or desirable in other cases. Firstly, the cash management problem that we model here is based on a number of assumptions that might not hold in other banking environments. For example, in general, some branches have net withdrawals while the others have net deposits. Hence, the cash management policy parameters must be found

Table 3. Summary results on 12 instances

Instance	Iteration (t)	0	1	2	3	4	5
Jan	Number of CMCs	86	14	10	10	10	
	Number of vehicles		18	17	17	17	
	Total distance		957,457	947,365	946,300	946,300	
	Total average cash level	9,618,084	24,898,274	27,535,662	27,535,662	27,535,662	
	Total cost	16,031,643	7,784,410	7,131,147	7,130,421	7,130,421	
Feb	Number of CMCs	86	13	10	10	10	
	Number of vehicles		18	17	17	17	
	Total distance		966,150	902,489	904,540	904,540	
	Total average cash level	7,954,135	22,532,743	24,567,775	24,567,775	24,567,775	
	Total cost	15,898,527	7,423,629	6,863,111	6,864,511	6,864,511	
Mar	Number of CMCs	86	14	10	10	10	10
	Number of vehicles		20	17	17	17	17
	Total distance		994,626	1,005,494	997,635	1,001,523	1,001,523
	Total average cash level	11,903,928	28,726,610	33,080,877	33,080,877	33,080,877	33,080,877
	Total cost	16,214,510	8,411,030	7,614,407	7,609,047	7,611,699	7,611,699
Apr	Number of CMCs	86	14	9	9	9	
	Number of vehicles		19	19	19	19	
	Total distance		960,376	977,459	972,778	972,778	
	Total average cash level	8,340,658	23,916,725	27,049,245	27,049,245	27,049,245	
	Total cost	15,929,449	7,855,380	7,230,294	7,227,102	7,227,102	
May	Number of CMCs	86	14	11	11	11	
	Number of vehicles		19	18	18	18	
	Total distance		977,670	856,824	854,915	854,915	
	Total average cash level	9,548,230	25,731,865	30,164,435	30,164,435	30,164,435	
	Total cost	16,026,055	8,012,385	7,604,672	7,603,370	7,603,370	
Jun	Number of CMCs	86	14	11	11		
	Number of vehicles		19	19	19		
	Total distance		973,696	928,029	928,029		
	Total average cash level	9,548,230	24,757,850	27,745,785	27,745,785		
	Total cost	16,026,055	7,931,754	7,607,242	7,607,242		
Jul	Number of CMCs	86	14	10	10		
	Number of vehicles		19	17	17		
	Total distance		977,670	955,171	955,171		
	Total average cash level	8,828,137	24,122,858	27,498,010	27,498,010		
	Total cost	15,968,447	7,883,664	7,133,459	7,133,459		
Aug	Number of CMCs	86	13	10	10	10	
	Number of vehicles		19	17	16	16	
	Total distance		971,967	1,021,075	1,020,822	1,020,822	
	Total average cash level	9,691,987	27,062,211	30,421,063	30,421,063	30,421,063	
	Total cost	16,037,555	7,937,456	7,412,247	7,264,573	7,264,573	
Sep	Number of CMCs	86	15	12	12	12	
	Number of vehicles		19	18	18	18	
	Total distance		960,033	902,765	901,199	901,199	
	Total average cash level	9,008,141	26,093,475	28,959,204	28,959,204	28,959,204	
	Total cost	15,982,847	8,206,753	7,717,051	7,715,984	7,715,984	
Oct	Number of CMCs	86	14	10	10	10	
	Number of vehicles		19	17	17	17	
	Total distance		977,645	958,301	957,318	957,318	
	Total average cash level	8,673,301	28,051,644	32,771,237	32,771,237	32,771,237	
	Total cost	15,956,060	8,197,950	7,557,451	7,556,781	7,556,781	
Nov	Number of CMCs	86	14	10	10	10	
	Number of vehicles		19	17	16	16	
	Total distance		967,954	919,875	923,733	923,733	
	Total average cash level	8,996,093	25,429,554	29,259,249	29,165,969	29,165,969	
	Total cost	15,981,884	7,981,574	7,250,286	7,097,953	7,097,953	
Dec	Number of CMCs	86	14	10	10	10	
	Number of vehicles		19	17	17	17	
	Total distance		977,670	996,579	995,629	995,629	
	Total average cash level	9,560,877	27,679,537	31,601,283	31,601,283	31,601,283	
	Total cost	16,027,066	8,168,198	7,489,960	7,489,312	7,489,312	

by observing these differences among the branches and the corresponding vehicle routing problem could also be revised to take advantage of such differences among the branches. Secondly, the vehicle routing part can also be made more dynamic. However, that would necessitate a different and potentially a much more difficult version of the vehicle routing problem. Thirdly, an integrated approach could also be developed albeit possibly with more simplifying assumptions. Finally, a real-time control and decision support system can be developed for some of the tactical and operational decisions.

References

1. Ambrosino, D., Scutella, M.G.: Distribution network design: New problems and related models. European Journal of Operational Research **165**(3), 610–624 (2005)
2. Bloomberg.com. Highest and cheapest gas prices by country (2013)
3. Constantinides, G.M., Richard, S.F.: Existence of optimal simple policies for discounted-cost inventory and cash management in continuous time. Operations Research **26**(4), 620–636 (1978)
4. Girgis, N.M.: Optimal cash balance levels. Management Science **191**(3), 650–660 (1968)
5. Hiassat, A.H., Diabat, A.: A location-inventory-routing problem with perishable products. In: Proceedings of the 41st International Conference on Computers and Industrial Engineering (2011)
6. Javid, A.A., Azad, N.: Incorporating location, routing and inventory decisions in supply chain network design. Transportation Research Part E: Logistics and Transportation Review **46**(5), 582–597 (2010)
7. Klibi, W., Martel, A., Guitouni, A.: The design of robust value-creating supply chain networks: A critical review. European Journal of Operational Research **203**(2), 283–293 (2010)
8. Milbourne, R.: Optimal money holding under uncertainty. International Economic Review **31**(1), 685–698 (1983)
9. Miller, M.H., Orr, D.: The demand for money by firms. The Quarterly Journal of Economics **80**(3), 413–435 (1966)
10. Saldanha-da-Gama, F., Melo, M.T., Nickel, S.: Facility location and supply chain management a review. European Journal of Operational Research **196**(2), 401–412 (2009)
11. Porteus, E.: Equivalent formulations of the stochastic cash balance problem. Management Science **19**(3), 250–253 (1972)
12. Porteus, E.L., Neave, E.H.: The stochastic cash balance problem with levied against the balance. Management Science **18**(11), 600–602 (1972)
13. Shen, Z.-J.: Integrated supply chain design models: A survey and future research directions. Journal of Industrial and Management Optimization **3**(1), 1–27 (2001)
14. Shen, Z.-J., Qi, L.: Incorporating inventory and routing costs in strategic location models. European Journal of Operational Research **179**, 372–389 (2007)
15. Van Anholt, R.G., Coelho, L.C., Laporte, G., Vis, I.F.A.: An Inventory-Routing Problem with Pickups and Deliveries Arising in the Replenishment of Automated Teller Machines. Working Paper no. CIRRELT-2013-71, Montreal, Canada (2013)
16. Wagner, M.: Analyzing Cost Structures of Inventory-Routing: Application to Cash Supply Chains. Lecture Notes in Management Science **2**, 110–122 (2010)

A Decision Support Model for Routing and Scheduling a Fleet of Fuel Supply Vessels

Marielle Christiansen[1], Kjetil Fagerholt[1(✉)], Nikolaos P. Rachaniotis[2],
Ingeborg Tveit[1], and Marte Viktoria Øverdal[1]

[1] Department of Industrial Economics and Technology Management,
Norwegian University of Science and Technology, Trondheim, Norway
kjetil.fagerholt@iot.ntnu.no
[2] Department of Economics, Democritus University of Thrace, Xanthi, Greece

Abstract. We consider a real fuel supply vessel routing and scheduling problem faced by a Hellenic oil company with a given fleet of fuel supply vessels used to supply customer ships outside Piraeus Port. The supply vessels are loading fuel at refineries in the port area before delivering it to a given set of customer ships within specified time windows. A customer ship may place orders of more than one fuel type, and all orders placed by a customer ship do not have to be serviced by the same vessel, meaning customer splitting is possible. Fuel transported to the customer ships is allocated to compartments on board the supply vessels, and fuels of different types cannot be mixed in the same compartment. The objective is to design routes and schedules for the supply vessels while maximizing the company's profit. We propose a mixed-integer programming (MIP) model for the problem and provide a computational study based on real instances.

Keywords: Maritime transport · Routing · Scheduling · Split loads

1 Introduction

Maritime transportation planning problems have attracted considerable attention in the literature in the last decades; see the surveys by Christiansen et al. (2013). However, even though fuel refilling is an important task for ships entering ports, the planning problem considered in this paper, where incoming customer ships are supplied with fuel by a given fleet of specialized fuel supply vessels, has, to the authors' knowledge, not been studied previously in the Operations Research literature. As a case study, we consider a Hellenic oil company operating in the broader area of Pireaus Port illustrated in Figure 1. The figure also shows where incoming customer ships anchor, waiting to be supplied by the company's fuel supply vessels within given agreed time windows. The supply vessels load at refineries in the inner part of the port before supplying the customer ships. The refineries offer different types of fuel, and a customer ship can order quantities of several fuel types to be delivered within the same time window. Fuel transported to the customer ships is allocated to compartments on board the supply vessels, and fuels of different types cannot be mixed in

© Springer International Publishing Switzerland 2015
F. Corman et al. (Eds.): ICCL 2015, LNCS 9335, pp. 46–60, 2015.
DOI: 10.1007/978-3-319-24264-4_4

the same compartment. Some customer ships are mandatory to service, while other customer ships are optional and can be supplied if the company has the available capacity. The planning problem consists of determining routes and schedules for the fleet of supply vessels such that the profit is maximized and all mandatory customer ships are serviced within their time windows. The vessels can perform more than one voyage during the planning horizon. The problem also includes determining which optional customers to service, as well as allocating the different types of fuel to separate compartments within the supply vessels, which add substantial complexity to the problem. The problem can be considered as a version of the multi-trip vehicle routing problem with time windows, see for example Nguyen et al. (2013) and Cattaruzza et al. (2014). In addition, we have a multi-compartment routing problem, see for instance Mendoza et al. (2010).

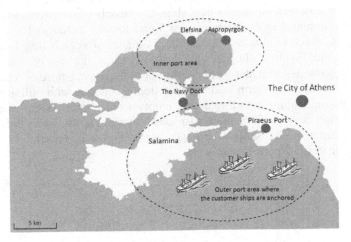

Fig. 1. Map of Piraeus port area

The fuel supply business in Piraeus Port has long traditions, and the business is to a large extent characterized by manual efforts in determining routes and schedules for the fuel supply vessels. However, many complicating factors and the large amount of money involved indicate that some decision support could be of good use.

The objective of this paper is to introduce this planning problem to the research community, and to propose a mixed-integer-programming (MIP) model for the problem that can support decision-making.

The outline of the remaining of the paper is as follows: Section 2 presents the planning problem in more detail followed by a MIP model in Section 3. Computational results are reported and discussed in Section 4, while concluding remarks are provided in Section 5.

2   Problem Description

A given heterogeneous fleet of supply vessels is used to supply customer ships anchored in a port area. The customer ships place orders of different fuel types. The supply vessels load all fuel types at refineries. Since the distances within the refineries are almost negligible for this particular case study, we assume that the refineries can be modeled as a single depot. In the start of a planning horizon, some vessels may not be available for loading until some specified time. After finishing loading at the depot, the supply vessels start sailing to the customer ships. The sailing time between the depot and the customer ships is dependent on the hour of the day because sailing is not allowed in the area of the navy dock at night time, and vessels that would like to sail between the inner and outer port area in this period must sail around Salamina Island (Figure 1). The sailing times between different customer ships are assumed independent of time and which customer ships the vessels sail between. Loading time at the depot is assumed independent of vessel and loading quantity. The depot has a berth capacity, which implies that a maximum number of vessels may load simultaneously at a time. Figure 2 illustrates the customer ships, the supply vessels and the depot. The vessels may wait at a customer ship or at the depot before operation starts.

A vessel's voyage starts with loading at the depot, continue with sailing to and servicing the customer ships before returning empty to the depot. Within the planning horizon, a vessel may perform more than one voyage. Hence, every time a vessel loads at the depot, it also starts a new voyage. In Figure 2, vessel 1 executes two voyages, while vessel 2 performs only one.

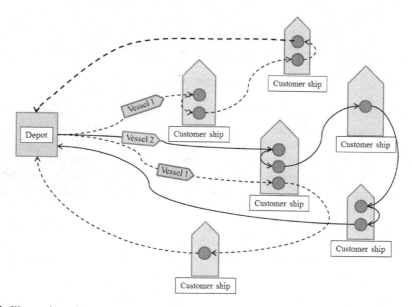

Fig. 2. Illustration of the customer ships, vessels and the depot. The customer ships' demands range from one to three different orders. One of the customer ships is serviced by both vessels, while the other customer ships are operated by only one vessel. Vessel 1 sails two voyages, while vessel 2 only sails one voyage.

A customer ship may place orders of different fuel types to be delivered at the same time. Each customer ship states a time window in which all its orders must be serviced. All orders at a customer ship do not need to be serviced by the same supply vessel, but if they are, the operation of the orders must happen continuously. If several vessels are servicing different orders at the same customer ship, there is an upper time limit between starting the first and the last order operations. In addition, only one vessel may service a customer ship at a time. The supply vessels are obliged to service contract customers, while spot customers can be serviced if the supply vessels have sufficient capacity. There are given quantities for the contract orders, while the spot orders' quantities are flexible within given upper and lower limits specified by the customers. The company must operate either all or none of a given spot customer's orders.

The supply vessels have a different number of compartments with given capacities where the fuels are loaded. A compartment may carry several fuel types, but it may only contain one fuel type at a time. The same fuel type may be carried in several compartments at the same supply vessel, and large orders may be split between compartments. Moreover, if different customer ships order the same fuel type, the orders may be allocated to the same compartment.

The planning problem consists of determining routes and schedules for the fleet of supply vessels such that the profit is maximized and all mandatory customer ships are serviced within their time windows. The profit equals the revenue through operation of contract and spot customers subtracted fixed daily costs and variable sailing costs. The problem also includes determining which optional customers to service, as well as allocating the different types of fuel to separate compartments within the supply vessels.

3   Mathematical Model

In this section, we propose a MIP model for the problem. Section 3.1 introduces some modelling choices and definitions that are used in the mathematical model. Section 3.2 describes the notation used, while the objective function and the constraints of the mathematical model are presented in Section 3.3.

3.1   Modeling Approach

We have chosen to develop a discrete time model due to the time dependent sailing time between the inner and outer port area. With discrete time representation, the planning horizon is divided into time periods of equal lengths.

Nodes are introduced to describe the orders placed by the customer ships. A node, a customer node and an order represent the same, and the terms may be used interchangeably. In addition to the nodes representing the orders, we include a depot node and a dummy end node. The depot node represent both refineries, while the dummy end node represent a fictive node where the vessels end up after operating all scheduled nodes in the planning horizon.

The vessel may execute multiple voyages during the planning horizon. In the mathematical model the numbering of voyages is related to each supply vessel.

The time window of a customer ship is defined by two parameters. One parameter represents the start of the time window and is the first time period a vessel may start servicing one of the customer ship's nodes. The other parameter represents the end of the time window, meaning that this is the last possible time period for servicing the customer ship. Notice that the end of the time window here is defined as the time period where operations must be finished, while in most relevant literature the time windows are defined as time periods which service may start.

3.2 Notation

Indices

v	supply vessel
i, j	Node
0	the depot node
d	the dummy end node
u	customer ship
f	fuel type
c	Compartment
m	Voyage
t	time period

Sets

$\mathcal{V}$	supply vessels
$\mathcal{N}$	customer nodes
$\mathcal{N}^T$	Nodes (total), $\mathcal{N} \cup \{0\} \cup \{d\}$
$\mathcal{U}$	customer ships
$\mathcal{U}^C \subseteq \mathcal{U}$	contract customer ships
$\mathcal{U}^O \subseteq \mathcal{U}$	spot customer ships
$\mathcal{N}_u \subseteq \mathcal{N}$	nodes that belong to customer ship u
$\mathcal{F}$	fuel types
$\mathcal{F}_c \subseteq \mathcal{F}$	fuel types allowed on compartment c
$\mathcal{C}_v$	compartments on supply vessel v
$\mathcal{M}_v$	voyages for vessel v
$\mathcal{T}$	time periods
$\mathcal{T}^{DAY} \subseteq \mathcal{T}$	time periods that represent a day's first time period. For example, when the planning horizon starts with time period 0 and one time period represent one hour, time periods 0, 24, 48 etc. are time periods in the set.
$\mathcal{S}^x$	possible combinations of (v, i, j, m, t) for variable x_{vijmt}
$\mathcal{S}^y$	possible combinations of (v, i, m, t) for variable y_{vimt}
$\mathcal{S}^w$	possible combinations of (v, i, m, t) for variable w_{vimt}

Parameters

T_{vijt}^{SA}	sailing time when vessel v sails directly between nodes i and j when arriving at node j in time period t
T_{vijt}^{SD}	sailing time when vessel v sails directly between node i and j when departing node j in time period t
T_{vi}^{O}	vessel $v's$ operating time at node i
$\underline{T_u}$	start of time window of customer ship u
$\overline{T}_u$	end of time window of customer ship u
T_u^D	maximum time difference between start of operation of the first and last node at customer ship u
T_v^M	the minimum time a vessel may use on any voyage
T_v^E	the earliest time vessel v is available for operation
H	number of time periods within 24 hours
B	berth capacity of the depot
D_{if}	demanded quantity of fuel type f for contract node i
$\underline{D_{if}}$	minimum accepted quantity of fuel type f for spot node i
$\overline{D}_{if}$	maximum accepted quantity of fuel type f for spot node i
Q_{cv}	load capacity of compartment c on vessel v
C_v^F	fixed daily cost of using vessel v
C_v^S	sailing cost per time period with vessel v
R_f	revenue per quantity delivered of fuel type f

Variables

x_{vijmt}	1, if vessel v starts sailing in time period t from node i directly to node j on voyage m/ 0, otherwise
y_{vimt}	1, if vessel v starts operating node i in time period t on voyage m / 0, otherwise
w_{vimt}	1, if vessel v is waiting in time period t at node i on voyage m/ 0, otherwise
γ_{vum}	1, if vessel v operates all nodes at customer ship u on voyage m/ 0, otherwise
z_u	1, if spot customer ship u is operated/ 0, otherwise
δ_{vt}	1, if vessel v is utilized the day that start with time period t/ 0, otherwise
k_{vfcm}	1, if compartment c on vessel v is allocated to fuel type f on voyage m/ 0, otherwise
l_{vijfcm}	quantity of fuel type f in compartment c of vessel v when sailing directly from node i to j on voyage m
q_{vifm}	delivered quantity of fuel type f to spot node i by vessel v on voyage m

3.3   Model

Objective Function

The objective function (1) represents the company's profit. It comprises the revenue from operating spot orders, variable sailing costs and daily fixed costs of using the vessels. The revenue from the contract orders is not included in the objective function since they can be considered as fixed. By including daily fixed costs in this way, the model will strive towards solutions where the vessels are busy some days, and are doing nothing other days. This is assumed to be practical in the real case problem, as long breaks in the utilization of a vessel allow for necessary repairs and time off.

$$
max\ \Pi = \sum_{m\in\mathcal{M}_v}\sum_{f\in\mathcal{F}}\sum_{i\in\mathcal{N}}\sum_{v\in\mathcal{V}}R_f q_{vifm}
$$
$$
-\sum_{t\in\mathcal{T}}\sum_{v\in\mathcal{V}}C_v^F\delta_{vt}
$$
$$
-\sum_{t\in\mathcal{T}}\sum_{m\in\mathcal{M}_v}\sum_{j\in\mathcal{N}^T}\sum_{i\in\mathcal{N}^T}\sum_{v\in\mathcal{V}}C_v^S T_{vijt}^{SD}x_{vijmt} \tag{1}
$$

Flow constraints

The flow or routing constraints are given as follows:

$$
\sum_{t=\underline{T}_u}^{\bar{T}_u-T_{vi}^O}\sum_{m\in\mathcal{M}_v}\sum_{v\in\mathcal{V}}y_{vimt}=1 \qquad\qquad \forall i\in\mathcal{N}_u, u\in\mathcal{U}^C \tag{2}
$$

$$
\sum_{t=\underline{T}_u}^{\bar{T}_u-T_{vi}^O}\sum_{m\in\mathcal{M}_v}\sum_{v\in\mathcal{V}}y_{vimt}-z_u=0 \qquad\qquad \forall i\in\mathcal{N}_u, u\in\mathcal{U}^O \tag{3}
$$

$$
\sum_{t\in\mathcal{T}}y_{v0mt}\le 1 \qquad\qquad \forall v\in\mathcal{V}, m\in\mathcal{M}_v \tag{4}
$$

$$
\sum_{\tau=0}^{t-T_v^M}y_{v0(m-1)\tau}-y_{v0mt}\ge 0 \qquad\qquad \forall v\in\mathcal{V}, m\in\mathcal{M}_v, t\in\mathcal{T} \tag{5}
$$

$$
y_{vim(t-T_{vi}^O)}=\sum_{j\in\mathcal{N}^T}x_{vijmt} \qquad\qquad \begin{aligned}&\forall v\in\mathcal{V}, i\in\mathcal{N}\cup\{0\},\\ &m\in\mathcal{M}_v, t\in\mathcal{T}\end{aligned} \tag{6}
$$

$$\sum_{j \in \mathcal{N} \cup \{0\}} x_{vjim(t-T^{SA}_{vjit})} + w_{vim(t-1)}$$
$$= y_{vimt} + w_{vimt}$$
$$\forall v \in \mathcal{V}, i \in \mathcal{N}, \quad m \in \mathcal{M}_v, t \in \mathcal{T} \qquad (7)$$

$$\sum_{j \in \mathcal{N}} x_{vj0m(t-T^{SA}_{vj0t})} + w_{v0m(t-1)}$$
$$= y_{v0(m+1)t} + w_{v0mt}$$
$$\forall v \in \mathcal{V}, m \in \mathcal{M}_v, t \in \mathcal{T} \qquad (8)$$

$$\sum_{t \in \mathcal{T}} y_{v01t} - \sum_{t \in \mathcal{T}} \sum_{m \in \mathcal{M}_v} \sum_{j \in \mathcal{N}} x_{vjdmt}$$
$$= 0$$
$$\forall v \in \mathcal{V} \qquad (9)$$

$$\sum_{\tau=t}^{t+(H-1)} \sum_{m \in \mathcal{M}_v} \sum_{i \in \mathcal{N} \cup \{0\}} (y_{vim\tau}$$
$$+ \sum_{j \in \mathcal{N} \cup \{0\}} x_{vijm\tau})$$
$$- H\delta_{vt} \le 0$$
$$\forall v \in \mathcal{V}, t \in \mathcal{T}^{DAY} \qquad (10)$$

$$x_{vijmt} \in \{1,0\} \qquad \qquad \forall (v,i,j,m,t) \in \mathcal{S}^x \qquad (11)$$

$$y_{vimt} \in \{1,0\} \qquad \qquad \forall (v,i,m,t) \in \mathcal{S}^y \qquad (12)$$

$$w_{vimt} \in \{1,0\} \qquad \qquad \forall (v,i,m,t) \in \mathcal{S}^w \qquad (13)$$

$$z_u \in \{1,0\} \qquad \qquad \forall u \in \mathcal{U}^o \qquad (14)$$

$$\delta_{vt} \in \{1,0\} \qquad \qquad \forall v \in \mathcal{V}, t \in \mathcal{T}^{DAY} \qquad (15)$$

Constraints (2) ensure that every contract node is serviced only once, by one vessel on one voyage. The constraints also control that the customer nodes are serviced within their time windows. Constraints (3) hold for the nodes at the spot customer ships. If these nodes are serviced, each node can only be serviced by one vessel on one voyage within its time window. They also ensure that either all or none of the nodes for a given spot customer ship are serviced. Furthermore, constraints (4) make sure that the vessels operate at the depot at most once on each voyage. Constraints (5) control that a vessel cannot start a new voyage if it has not ended the previous voyage. The constraints also ensure that the previous voyage takes at least time T^M_v, which is the minimum time any vessel may use on a voyage. In constraints (6), it is described that when a vessel has finished servicing a node, it must start sailing to a customer node, the depot node or the dummy end node. Even when the same supply vessel is servicing two different nodes belonging to the same customer ship, it must start sailing after operating the first node. The sailing times between the nodes will in that case be zero. Since the sailing time between nodes at the same customer ship is zero, sailing variables and operating variables may equal 1 in the same time periods. Constraints (7) make sure that a vessel either starts waiting or operating at a customer node when the vessel arrives at the node. Moreover, if a vessel waits at a node in a time period, it is restricted to either operate or wait at the node in the following time period. Constraints (8) are equivalent to the previous constraints, but concern the depot node. They make sure that when a vessel arrives at the depot, it must either start loading at the depot for a new voyage or wait at the depot on the current voyage. If a vessel waits at the depot in a time period, it may start operating on a new voyage or keep waiting on the current voyage in the next time period. Constraints (9) control that every vessel, if it is used at all, executes the fictive sailing to the dummy end node once during the planning horizon. Constraints (10) ensure that the variable δ_{vt} equals 1 if a given vessel is utilized the day which starts with time period t. Waiting is not included, since it is possible to wait at the depot which in practice corresponds to not utilizing the vessel. Finally, the binary restrictions for the variables are given in (11)-(15).

Time Constraints

The time or schedule constraints are as follows:

$$\gamma_{vum} - \frac{\sum_{t \in \mathcal{T}} \sum_{i \in \mathcal{N}_u} y_{vimt}}{|\mathcal{N}_u|} \leq 0 \qquad \forall v \in \mathcal{V}, u \in \mathcal{U}, m \in \mathcal{M}_v \quad (16)$$

$$\gamma_{vum} - \frac{\sum_{t \in \mathcal{T}} \sum_{i \in \mathcal{N}_u} y_{vimt}}{|\mathcal{N}_u|} \geq \frac{1 - |\mathcal{N}_u|}{|\mathcal{N}_u|} \qquad \forall v \in \mathcal{V}, u \in \mathcal{U}, m \in \mathcal{M}_v \quad (17)$$

$$\left(y_{vimt} - y_{v(i+1)m\left(t+T_{vi}^O\right)} \right) + \gamma_{vum} \leq 1 \qquad \begin{array}{c} \forall v \in \mathcal{V}, i \in \mathcal{N}_u, u \in \mathcal{U}, \\ m \in \mathcal{M}_v, t \in \mathcal{T} \end{array} \quad (18)$$

$$y_{vimt} + y_{v'jn\left(\tau+T_u^D\right)} \leq 1 \qquad \begin{array}{c} \forall v, v' \in \mathcal{V}, i, j \in \mathcal{N}_u | i \neq j, u \in \mathcal{U}, \\ m \in \mathcal{M}_v, n \in \mathcal{M}_{v'}, t, \tau \in \mathcal{T} | \tau > t \end{array} \quad (19)$$

$$\sum_{\tau=\max\{0, t-T_{v0}^O+1\}}^{t} \sum_{m \in \mathcal{M}_v} \sum_{v \in \mathcal{V}} y_{v0m\tau} \leq B \qquad \forall t \in \mathcal{T} \quad (20)$$

$$\sum_{\tau=\max\{0, t-T_{vi}^O+1\}}^{t} \sum_{m \in \mathcal{M}_v} \sum_{i \in \mathcal{N}_u} \sum_{v \in \mathcal{V}} y_{vim\tau} \leq 1 \qquad \forall u \in \mathcal{U}, t \in \mathcal{T} \quad (21)$$

$$\gamma_{vum} \in \{1, 0\} \qquad \forall v \in \mathcal{V}, u \in \mathcal{U}, m \in \mathcal{M}_v \quad (22)$$

Constraints (16) and (17) force the γ_{vum} variables to 1 if all nodes at the same customer ship are serviced by the same vessel. Constraints (18) further control that the nodes at such customer ships are operated continuously. Note that the constraints assume that the nodes are serviced in a specific order, which reduces symmetry. When a vessel services all nodes at a customer ship, this must happen on the same voyage, since continuous operation by the same vessel will never happen on two different voyages. If a customer ship is serviced by more than one vessel, constraints (19) narrow the time span where the nodes at the customer ship can be operated. It is desirable that the nodes of a customer ship are operated continuously without any waiting in between. Since the operating times vary with vessel and the fact that the operating sequence of the nodes are not known a priori, these constraints give some possibilities for waiting in between. All operation of nodes at a given customer ship must start within an interval, T_u^D, calculated from the vessels' operating times at the customer ship. Constraints (20) ensure that in any time period, the company cannot have more than B vessels loading at the depot. In addition, a customer ship can only be operated by one vessel at the time. Constraints (21) take care of this. Finally, the binary requirements for the γ_{vum} variables are given in (22).

Load Constraints

The load management on board the ships is taken into account by the following constraints:

$$\sum_{c \in C_v} \sum_{j \in \mathcal{N} \cup \{0\}} l_{vjifcm} - \sum_{t \in \mathcal{T}} D_{if} y_{vimt}$$
$$- \sum_{c \in C_v} \sum_{j \in \mathcal{N}^T} l_{vijfcm} = 0 \qquad\qquad \begin{array}{l} \forall v \in V, i \in \mathcal{N}_u, \\ u \in \mathcal{U}^C, \quad (23) \\ f \in \mathcal{F}, m \in \mathcal{M}_v \end{array}$$

$$\sum_{c \in C_v} \sum_{j \in \mathcal{N} \cup \{0\}} l_{vjifcm} - q_{vifm} - \sum_{c \in C_v} \sum_{j \in \mathcal{N}^T} l_{vijfcm} = 0 \qquad \begin{array}{l} \forall v \in V, i \in \mathcal{N}_u, \quad (24) \\ u \in \mathcal{U}^O, \\ f \in \mathcal{F}, m \in \mathcal{M}_v \end{array}$$

$$\sum_{t \in \mathcal{T}} \underline{D}_{if} y_{vimt} \le q_{vifm} \le \sum_{t \in \mathcal{T}} \overline{D}_{if} y_{vimt} \qquad\qquad \begin{array}{l} \forall v \in V, i \in \mathcal{N}_u, \quad (25) \\ u \in \mathcal{U}^O, \\ f \in \mathcal{F}, m \in \mathcal{M}_v \end{array}$$

$$\sum_{c \in C_v} \sum_{f \in \mathcal{F}_c} l_{vijfcm} - \sum_{t \in \mathcal{T}} \sum_{c \in C_v} Q_{vc} x_{vijmt} \le 0 \qquad\qquad \begin{array}{l} \forall v \in V, i \in \{0\}, \quad (26) \\ j \in \mathcal{N}, m \in \mathcal{M}_v \end{array}$$

$$\sum_{c \in C_v} \sum_{f \in \mathcal{F}_c} l_{vijfcm} - \sum_{t \in \mathcal{T}} (\sum_{c \in C_v} Q_{cv} - \sum_{f \in \mathcal{F}_c} D_{if}) x_{vijmt}$$
$$\le 0 \qquad\qquad \begin{array}{l} v \in V, u \in \mathcal{U}^C, \quad (27) \\ i \in \mathcal{N}_u, \\ j \in \mathcal{N}^T, m \in \mathcal{M}_v \end{array}$$

$$\sum_{c \in \mathcal{C}_v} \sum_{f \in \mathcal{F}_c} l_{vijfcm} - \sum_{t \in \mathcal{T}} (\sum_{c \in \mathcal{C}_v} Q_{cv} - \sum_{f \in \mathcal{F}_c} \underline{D}_{if}) x_{vijmt}$$
$$\leq 0$$
$$\qquad \begin{aligned} &v \in \mathcal{V}, u \in \mathcal{U}^o, \\ &i \in \mathcal{N}_u, \\ &j \in \mathcal{N}^T, m \in \mathcal{M}_v \end{aligned} \quad (28)$$

$$\sum_{f \in \mathcal{F}_c} k_{vfcm} \leq 1 \qquad \begin{aligned} &v \in \mathcal{V}, c \in \mathcal{C}_v, \\ &m \in \mathcal{M}_v \end{aligned} \quad (29)$$

$$l_{vijfcm} - \min \{ Q_{vc}, \sum_{k \in \mathcal{N}_u | u \in \mathcal{U}^C} D_{kf}$$
$$+ \sum_{k \in \mathcal{N}_u | u \in \mathcal{U}^O} \overline{D}_{kf} \} k_{vfcm} \leq 0 \qquad \begin{aligned} &\forall v \in \mathcal{V}, \\ &i,j \in \mathcal{N} \cup \{0\}, \\ &f \in \mathcal{F}_c, c \in \mathcal{C}_v, \\ &m \in \mathcal{M}_v \end{aligned} \quad (30)$$

$$\sum_{c \in \mathcal{C}_v} \sum_{f \in \mathcal{F}_c} \sum_{j \in \mathcal{N}} l_{vjifcm} = 0 \qquad \begin{aligned} &\forall i \in \{0\} \cup \{d\}, \\ &v \in \mathcal{V}, m \in \mathcal{M}_v \end{aligned} \quad (31)$$

$$k_{vfcm} \in \{1,0\} \qquad \begin{aligned} &\forall v \in \mathcal{V}, f \in \mathcal{F}_c, \\ &c \in \mathcal{C}_v, m \in \mathcal{M}_v \end{aligned} \quad (32)$$

$$l_{vijfcm} \geq 0 \qquad \begin{aligned} &\forall v \in \mathcal{V}, \\ &i \in \mathcal{N} \cup \{0\}, \\ &j \in \mathcal{N} \cup \{0\}, \\ &f \in \mathcal{F}_c, c \in \mathcal{C}_v, \\ &m \in \mathcal{M}_v \end{aligned} \quad (33)$$

$$q_{vifm} \geq 0 \qquad \begin{aligned} &\forall v \in \mathcal{V}, i \in \mathcal{N}, \\ &m \in \mathcal{M}_v, f \in \mathcal{F} \end{aligned} \quad (34)$$

The difference in load within a supply vessel's compartments before and after operating a customer node equals the demanded fuel quantity of the node. This is ensured by constraints (23) and (24) for contract and spot nodes, respectively. Constraints (25) ensure that the quantity delivered to the spot nodes are within the upper and lower limits. The load variables, l_{vijfcm}, can be denoted as arc-load flow variables. Agra et al. (2013) describe the advantages of having arc-load flow variables instead of more common load variables, where the latter do not include a destination node j. They state that using the arc-flow load variables strengthen the model. Constraints (26)-(28) control that the l_{vijfcm} variables are assigned non-zero values only if the given vessel, v, sails directly between nodes i and j, and that the compartments' capacity limits are not exceeded. Constraints (29) ensure that only one fuel type is allocated to a compartment on each voyage. The constraints also make sure that a compartment is only loaded with a fuel type that it is allowed to carry. Constraints (30) control that the arc-flow load variables only take values for combinations of fuel type and compartment if the fuel type is actually allocated to that compartment. To facilitate the reading, we introduce constraints (31) to ensure that the vessels do not carry any load when returning to the depot or the dummy end node. Finally, the binary and non-negativity requirements for the variables related to loading are given in (32)-(34).

We have tested several types of valid inequalities to strengthen the linear relaxation of the model. Neither clique nor cover inequalities improved the solution process, so they are not included. Instead we include the promising valid inequalities (35) ensuring that a spot node i cannot be operated by a vessel v if the vessel is not utilized the day the node has its time window.

$$q_{vifm} - D_{if}\delta_{vt} \leq 0 \qquad \forall v \in \mathcal{V}, i \in \mathcal{N}_u, u \in \mathcal{U}^O, f \in \mathcal{F}, m \in \mathcal{M}_v, \qquad (35)$$
$$t \in \mathcal{T}^{DAY} | t \leq \underline{T}_u < (t + H)$$

4   Computational Study

This section presents a computational study performed on a number of test instances generated from real data from the company. The model described in the previous section has been implemented in Mosel and solved using the commercial optimization software Xpress v7.3 64-bit on an HP DL 165 G6 computer with two AMD Opteron 24312 4.0 GHz processors, 24 GB of RAM and running on a Linux operating system. Section 4.1 describes the test instances, while computational results are presented and discussed in Section 4.2.

4.1   Test Instances

The test cases are generated based on data regarding customer ships and their fuel orders provided by the company. The shipping company's vessel fleet consisted of three vessels. Information regarding the vessels' compartments, load capacities, costs and pumping rates was also given. The vessels have between 5 and 7 compartments and the total load capacities are in the range of approximately 1300 to 3000 m³. The pumping rates vary between 180 to 320 m³/h.

Since the sailing times for this problem are small compared to the operating times at the customer ships and the depot (3 to 12 hours), we have approximated the sailing times between customer ships and between the depot and the customer ships to one hour. Exceptions are the sailing time between the depot and the customer ships during night time, which is four hours because of the navy dock closure, and the time to the dummy end node, which is set to 0. Taking these sailing times into account, we have chosen to use a time discretization of 1 hour.

The customer ships had between one and three different orders each. Most customer ships had a wide time window specifying service within a given day (i.e. during a period of 24 time periods). However, some of the ships had requested morning deliveries where the deliveries had to be made between 7 am in the morning and 2 pm on the given day.

The number of time periods to include in the planning horizon was set to the end time of the latest time window of the customer ships: $|\mathcal{T}| = \max_{(i \in \mathcal{N})} \bar{T}_u$. This varied between 48 and 96 hours (i.e. two to four days). The start of the planning horizon was set to $t = 0$. Since the vessels were already engaged in fuel deliveries (from the previous planning period), they were given different times for when they became available. Vessel 1 became available for loading at the depot from time period $t = 17$, meaning $T_1^E = 17$, while vessels 2 and 3 were available from $t = 7$ and $t = 0$, respectively.

Table 1. Test cases with varying number of customer ships that have placed orders on different days

Test Case	# Ships day 1	# Ships day 2	# Ships day 3	# Total ships	# Time periods
4_4_0	4	4	0	8	72
3_3_2	3	3	2	8	96
10_0_0	10	0	0	10	48
5_5_0	5	5	0	10	72
6_6_0	6	6	0	12	72
4_4_4	4	4	4	12	96

Table 1 shows the different test cases used in the computational study. Since we did not have any data whether the customer orders were mandatory or optional, we assumed all were the latter in our tests.

4.2   Computational Experiments and Results

Table 2 shows the best obtained solutions within a time limit of 10,000 seconds running time. The table shows the results from running the model without and with the valid inequalities (35).

Table 2. Test results from testing the basic mathematical model on test cases with spot nodes. The numbers in front of the '/' show the results obtained without the valid inequalities (35), while the numbers after the '/' are with.

Test Case	After 10,000 seconds		
	Objective Function Values	Best Bounds	Gaps (%)
4_4_0	2492/2492	2513/2514	0.8/0.9
3_3_2	2483/2490	2498/2505	0.6/0.6
10_0_0	2659/2950	2989/2990	11.0/1.3
5_5_0	2329/777	2990/2987	22.1/74.0
6_6_0	1011/1032	2490/3488	59.4/70.4
4_4_4	2148/3257	3476/3476	38.2/6.3

As shown in the table, we were not able to find proven optimal solutions within the given time limit. This gives a good indication of the problem's complexity. However, for four of the six test cases, we are able to find solutions with reasonably small gaps of 6.3 % and less. We may also note that the model with the valid inequalities yields a better solution to four of the test cases, while the one without provides a better solution only on test case 5_5_0. The model without the valid inequalities is however best at finding better upper bounds on four of the six test cases.

Since we experienced large difficulties in solving the problem, we also tested two simplified versions of the model. In the first version, denoted *NoCS*, we remove the possibility of customer splitting. The motivation behind this is that there are only very few cases where the company actually performs a customer splitting (which is something that our results also showed). Furthermore, reducing this possibility will reduce the model's complexity, and one might actually obtain better solutions within the given time limit despite that the feasible space is reduced.

In the second simplified version of the model, denoted *ES50_NoCS*, we additionally eliminated the complicating stowage of orders to separate compartments in the vessels. This means that we assume in the model that all orders can be mixed in a single compartment only considering the total capacity. Because of this we risk that the solutions obtained are not feasible with respect to the real stowage problem. Therefore, we have tested this with running the simplified model with reduced ship capacities, which makes it easier to find feasible stowage plans for the solutions obtained. Actually, tests showed that we had to reduce the capacity of the ship to as little as 50 % of the original capacity to achieve solutions that always where feasible with respect to the real allocation requirements. This feasibility check was done by solving a stowage model for the given route of each ship, which becomes a much simpler problem to solve.

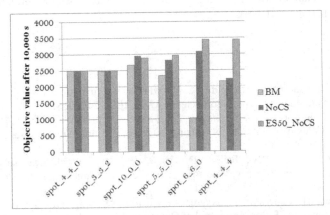

Fig. 3. Comparing the objective values after 10,000 seconds for the basic model (BM), without customer splitting (NoCS), and without stowage and customer splitting (ES50_NoCS)

Figure 3 compares the objective values for the two simplified model versions with the original one (without the valid inequalities). We can see that for the two smallest test cases, the three model versions gave similar results. However, for the four other test cases both simplified models gave better results. The model without both customer splitting and stowage (ES50_NoCS) gave best results for all test cases except for 10_0_0. If we compare the best results obtained with the simplified model version with the best upper bound provided in Table 2, it can be shown that these solutions are in fact very close to the optimal solutions. This indicates that these simplification strategies can be a good way to provide good decision support to a decision maker in a real planning situation when limited time is available. To respond to spot order inquiries, there is typically need for a solution within approximately 10 minutes. The ES50_NoCS model with neither stowage nor customer splitting provided solutions within this time limit. In addition, the model can be solved during the night to produce a schedule for the next days. The other two models can be useful for this purpose.

5   Concluding Remarks

We have proposed a mixed integer programming model for a combined fuel supply vessel scheduling and fuel allocation problem. Three versions of the model have been evaluated using data for a real-life problem; a basic model which comprises all relevant aspects as shown in Section 3, a simplified version of the model without customer splitting, and another simplified version without stowage and customer splitting.

Test results showed that the two simplified models provided significantly better solutions within a time limit of 10,000 seconds compared to the basic model.

The fuel supply vessel routing and scheduling problem is important for the shipping industry and includes several challenges for the research community. In order to solve even larger instances of the problem in limited time, interesting future research could be to integrate some heuristic elements to the solution method presented, develop advanced metaheuristics for the problem or methods based on branch-and-price (see e.g. Barnhart et al., 1998).

References

1. Agra, A., Christiansen, M., Delgado, A.: Mixed integer formulations for a short sea fuel oil distribution problem. Transportation Science 47(1), 108–124 (2013)
2. Barnhart, C., Johnson, E.L., Nemhauser, G.L., Savelsbergh, M.W.P., Vance, P.H.: Branch-and-price: Column generation for solving huge integer programs. Operations Research 46(3), 316–329 (1998)
3. Cattaruzza, D., Absi, N., Feillet, D., Vigo, D.: An iterated local search for the multi-commodity multi-trip vehicle routing problem with time windows. Computers and Operations Research 51, 257–267 (2014)
4. Christiansen, M., Fagerholt, K., Nygreen, B., Ronen, D.: Ship routing and scheduling in the new millennium. European Journal of Operational Research 228(3), 467–483 (2013)
5. Mendoza, J.E., Castanier, B., Guéret, C., Medaglia, A.L., Velasco, N.: A memetic algorithm for the multi-compartment vehicle routing problem with stochastic demands. Computers and Operations Research 37(11), 1886–1898 (2010)
6. Nguyen, P.K., Crainic, T.G., Tolouse, M.: A tabu search for time-dependent multi-zone multi-trip vehicle routing problem with time windows. European Journal of Operational Research 231(1), 43–56 (2013)

An Approximate Dynamic Programming Approach to Urban Freight Distribution with Batch Arrivals

Wouter van Heeswijk[✉], Martijn Mes, and Marco Schutten

Department of Industrial Engineering and Business Information Systems, University of Twente, P.O. Box 217, 7500 AE Enschede, The Netherlands
{w.j.a.vanheeswijk,m.r.k.mes,m.schutten}@utwente.nl

Abstract. We study an extension of the delivery dispatching problem (DDP) with time windows, applied on LTL orders arriving at an urban consolidation center. Order properties (e.g., destination, size, dispatch window) may be highly varying, and directly distributing an incoming order batch may yield high costs. Instead, the hub operator may wait to consolidate with future arrivals. A consolidation policy is required to decide which orders to ship and which orders to hold. We model the dispatching problem as a Markov decision problem. Dynamic Programming (DP) is applied to solve toy-sized instances to optimality. For larger instances, we propose an Approximate Dynamic Programming (ADP) approach. Through numerical experiments, we show that ADP closely approximates the optimal values for small instances, and outperforms two myopic benchmark policies for larger instances. We contribute to literature by (i) formulating a DDP with dispatch windows and (ii) proposing an approach to solve this DDP.

Keywords: Urban distribution · Transportation planning · Consolidation · Approximate dynamic programming

1 Introduction

In the field of urban freight logistics, the need for consolidation centers at the edge of urban areas is becoming increasingly important [11]. Due to the external costs of freight transport – such as congestion, air pollution, and noise hindrance – more efficient goods transport within the city center is necessary. Governments seek to reduce the negative influence of large trucks in urban areas. Imminent regulations are, e.g., restricted access areas, and road pricing for heavy vehicles. Such developments spur the need for transshipments at the edge of urban areas. Transshipments allow both for bundling goods – such that vehicle capacity can be used more efficiently – and dispatching environment-friendly vehicles such as electric vans on the last mile. However, the introduction of an additional transshipment in the supply chain also poses new challenges. The challenge we study is inspired by a project on urban freight logistics, in which various logistics partners participate.

© Springer International Publishing Switzerland 2015
F. Corman et al. (Eds.): ICCL 2015, LNCS 9335, pp. 61–75, 2015.
DOI: 10.1007/978-3-319-24264-4_5

We adopt the perspective of the party in charge of the consolidation center, to which we refer as the 'hub operator'. We focus on the timing of dispatching orders for delivery, in an environment where the batch arrivals of goods at the hub are not fully controlled by the hub operator. Hub operators are generally small parties that deploy rules-of-thumb for dispatching orders. They have a certain degree of knowledge of order arrivals over a relatively short horizon; order arrivals are usually announced at most 24 hours in advance. The operators also have expectations regarding future order arrivals – e.g., based on historical data – which can be modeled as stochastic arrivals.

We consider an extension of the Delivery Dispatching Problem (DDP) that includes dispatch windows as an order characteristic. This extension is particularly relevant in an urban distribution context, where deliveries within specified time windows are the norm. As opposed to traditional DDPs, we consider a finite planning horizon, allowing to capture time-dependent arrival processes (e.g., holiday weeks). Commonly studied shipment consolidation policies fall short to aid decision-making in this context. It does not suffice to determine when to dispatch the orders in inventory, one also needs to determine which subset of orders to dispatch. In our DDP, order batches are dynamically revealed to the hub operator. Some orders may arrive at the consolidation center without advance notice, others orders may be scheduled to arrive at a future point in time. After orders have physically arrived at the consolidation center, they can be dispatched to the customers in the city. An arriving batch may contain orders with dispersed destinations, various dispatch windows, distinct load sizes, etc. Directly distributing an arriving batch may therefore render poor solutions. Instead, waiting for future batches to arrive could yield order clusters for which better solutions are available. This entails waiting for known batches, but also the inclusion of future orders that may have uncertain properties. Based on both the available knowledge regarding current orders and anticipation of new orders, the operator is able to make informed waiting decisions.

Due to the dynamic and stochastic nature of our DDP – combined with the large amount of states – we must deal with various computational challenges. We consider our study to be part of a two-phase solution approach. In the first phase – which is the scope of this paper – the hub operator decides which orders to dispatch at the current decision moment. The dispatch decision is based on known information and probabilistic arrivals; estimates for the direct costs and downstream costs are used. In the second phase, the operator solves a detailed VRP for the selected set of orders. With this paper, we aim to contribute to existing literature with (i) the formulation of a Markov model for DDPs with dispatch windows, and (ii) an approach to provide high-quality solutions for larger-sized DDPs.

2   Literature Review

In this section, we analyze the existing literature on the DDP and related topics. We refer to recent literature studies for overviews of these problems, and highlight several studies that address problems comparable to ours. We address various solution approaches, and discuss their suitability for our problem type. Finally, we point out the literature gap that we aim to address.

Optimization problems that are both stochastic and dynamic are notoriously hard to solve [10]. The use of stochastic information in transportation problems is recognized as an important aspect of optimization, yet its incorporation in solution methods is still an ongoing development [10,14]. Mathematical programming and (meta)heuristics have traditionally been applied to handle high-dimensional problems in transportation. However, these methods generally do not cope well with stochastic information being revealed over time [10]. Suitable solution approaches tend to be either based on stochastic modeling or scenario sampling [5,8]; the latter is generally applied to fit heuristics and mathematical programs towards stochastic problems. Incorrect sampling may misrepresent the stochastic process [5]. Stochastic models represent all possible outcomes, and therefore in general require more computational effort. As a result, they are better fit for preprocessed decisions than for online decision-making.

We classify our problem as a DDP. In a DDP, orders arrive according to a stochastic process and are dispatched in batches [6]. Solving the DDP yields a shipment consolidation policy, indicating when to dispatch orders held in inventory. We briefly described the DDP in the introduction. For a more elaborate definition we refer to Minkoff [6], who states that all eligible routes are pre-defined input for DDPs. The performance of shipment consolidation policies is generally evaluated based on efficiency (vehicle capacity utilization) and/or timeliness (time between order arrival and dispatch). Policies are either recurrent (i.e., dependent on the state of the problem) or non-recurrent [9]; we study a DDP with a recurrent policy. The stochastic and dynamic nature of such DDPs gives rise to Markov decision problems [6]. Although a Markov decision model is a useful framework to describe decision problems with dynamic and stochastic elements, practical implementations generally suffer from intractably large state spaces and expected values that cannot be calculated exactly [6,8,9]. Relatively little work has been done on optimizing consolidation policies; the majority of DDP literature focuses on testing the performance of existing policies [1,7]. Most DDP literature only considers weight and arrival time as order properties, while results are valid for a limited set of distributions. A more generic approach based on a batch Markovian arrival process is presented by Bookbinder et al. [1]; allowing for arrival properties that follow any distribution. Although able to cope with a variety of arrival processes, enumeration of the transition matrix is still required. Even when applying techniques to simplify this procedure, complete enumeration is computationally challenging to describe batch arrivals consisting of order types with multiple stochastic properties such as dispatch windows.

Although the Vehicle Routing Problem (VRP) addresses routing decisions rather than dispatching, some characteristics are shared. Unlike the DDP, the inclusion of time windows is a common property of VRPs. Ritzinger et al. [12] provide an overview of dynamic and stochastic VRP literature, which generally considers re-optimization during the execution of routes. A particularly relevant class they describe considers dynamic order requests combined with stochastic customer information. For this class, they distinguish between preprocessed decision support (the sub-class we study) and online decision making. For preprocessed decision support, a number of stochastic modeling approaches is mentioned. Solutions for online decision problems tend to focus more on sampling.

Another subject related to the DDP is the Inventory Routing Problem (IRP) [6]. The IRP is concerned with repeated stock replenishment from a facility to a fixed set of delivery locations, the decision when to visit a location, and the quantity of product to be delivered are the decision of the facility. Each location consumes the product at a given – possibly stochastic – rate. As such, the IRP also considers a dispatching decision. However, deliveries in an IRP are not order-based; goods can be dispatched to any customer at any decision moment. Furthermore, one or several types of goods have to be distributed along multiple customers. Coelho et al. [3] provides a recent overview of IRP literature. They state that for the solution of stochastic IRPs, generally either Markov models are solved in a heuristic manner, or mathematical programming is applied. For IRPs with both dynamic and stochastic properties they mention only few works. Coelho et al. [2] solve a problem in this IRP class heuristically, forecasting a single scenario based on exponential smoothing of historical data.

Finally, we refer to several Service Network Design (SND) studies mentioned in SteadiSeifi et al. [14]. SND is concerned with the selection and timing of transportation services. Known solution approaches make use of mathematical programming, (meta)heuristics, and graph theory. Most SND studies focus on deterministic instances. Lium et al. [5] propose a stochastic extension to their mathematical program, adding scenarios to reflect uncertain future demand. The authors state that generating a compact yet representative scenario tree is one of the key challenges in this approach.

We did not encounter existing DDP literature that mathematically formulates a dispatch problem for orders with time windows. We aim to contribute to literature by formulating our DDP as a Markov decision process that captures both the stochastic and dynamic nature of the order arrival process. Dynamic programming (DP) can be used to solve such models to optimality, but instance sizes quickly grow too large for exact solutions. Topaloglu and Powell [15] present a stochastic modeling framework for solving dynamic resource-allocation problems, proposing the application of approximate dynamic programming (ADP). Various successful ADP applications can be found in transportation literature [8,14]. Following frameworks such as [9,10,15], we develop an ADP approach to solve our DDP with dispatch windows.

3   Problem Formulation

This section introduces the planning problem. We describe the problem in a generic way, making it applicable to a variety of instances. We assume that the characteristics of arriving orders are stochastic and have a known associated probability distribution. Our problem formulation allows to include both deterministic and stochastic future orders. We consider a finite planning horizon, during which batches of orders can arrive at the consolidation center. Dispatching decisions are made at fixed decision moments within the planning horizon, with constant time intervals separating the decision moments. We model the arrival rates of order batches, the number of orders in a batch, order sizes, order destinations, and dispatch times as stochastic variables. When a batch of orders arrives at the center, the exact properties of the orders are revealed.

The decision problem that we address is the choice of which orders to dispatch at the current decision moment. To make an informed decision, we require insight in the effects of postponing the dispatch of orders. Postponed orders may be combined with future orders against lower costs than when dispatched at the current decision moment. We therefore consider optimization over a planning horizon; orders not known at the current decision moment are probabilistic. We assess all possible realizations of stochastic order arrivals, and plan these arrivals as if they were actual orders. For both the deterministic and stochastic orders belonging to a given realization, we compute the costs of dispatching. The costs of dispatching stochastic orders are required to quantify the expected costs. By incorporating stochastic order arrivals, we can compute the expected costs of the various dispatch decisions for the currently known orders.

Consider an urban area with a fixed set of potential order destinations, which are delivered via a consolidation center at the edge of the area. Our representation of the urban distribution network is as follows. Let $\mathcal{G} = \{\mathcal{V}, \mathcal{A}\}$ be a directed and complete graph with $\mathcal{V}$ being the set of vertices and $\mathcal{A}$ being the set of arcs. $\{0\} \in \mathcal{V}$ represents the consolidation center in the network. The remaining vertices signify the subset of order destinations $\mathcal{V}' = \{1, 2, \ldots, |\mathcal{V}'|\}$, with $\mathcal{V}' = \mathcal{V} \setminus \{0\}$. The distances between any pair of vertices in the graph are known.

We consider a planning horizon that contains decision moments with fixed intermediate time intervals. Let $\mathcal{T} = \{0, 1, \ldots, T\}$ be the set containing all decision moments, and $t \in \mathcal{T}$ describe any decision moment within the planning horizon. We consider a homogeneous fleet (i.e., a set of identical vehicles), although our method is able to cope with heterogeneous fleets as well. We distinguish between sets of primary vehicles $\mathcal{Q}^{pr}$ and secondary vehicles $\mathcal{Q}^{se}$. We assume that the secondary fleet has an infinite size, and is either an actual transport alternative (e.g., renting an additional vehicle in case of shortage) or a dummy fleet with infinite costs. A dummy fleet serves as bound on capacity, without having to explicitly calculate the capacity constraints for each decision. We only assign vehicles in $\mathcal{Q}^{se}$ if no more vehicles in $\mathcal{Q}^{pr}$ are available. We assume that dispatching a secondary vehicle is always more expensive than dispatching a primary vehicle. To ease the presentation, we assume that every dispatched vehicle has a fixed route duration of $\tau_{route} \geq 1$ (this assumption can be easily relaxed). When dispatching at t, the vehicle will be available again at $t + \tau_{route}$. For decision-making purposes, we keep track of the availability of primary vehicles now and in the future. Let $r \in [0, \tau_{route} - 1]$ be the number of time intervals before a dispatched vehicle returns. Because all vehicles are available again at $t + \tau_{route}$, we only keep track of availability up to $t + \tau_{route} - 1$. Let $q_{t,r}$ denote the number of primary vehicles available for dispatch at $t + r$. It follows that $q_{t,0}$ vehicles are available for dispatch at t. We record primary fleet availability in the vector $Q_t = (q_{t,0}, q_{t,1}, \ldots, q_{t,t+\tau_{route}-1})$.

Every order is characterized by four properties: destination, load size, earliest dispatch time, and latest dispatch time. The order destination (i.e., the customer location) is represented by a vertex $v \in \mathcal{V}'$. Let $\mathcal{L} = \{\frac{1}{k}, \frac{2}{k}, \ldots, 1\}$ be the discretized set of viable load sizes, with integer $k \geq 1$, and 1 representing a full load for an urban vehicle. The size of an order is given by $l \in \mathcal{L}$. The hard dispatch window of an order is given by earliest dispatch time $e \in \mathcal{E}$ and latest dispatch time $d \in \mathcal{D}$. Both indices are relative to the decision moment t; at the decision moment $t + 1$ all indices of orders in inventory are reduced by 1. Only orders with $e = 0$ can be dispatched. Order types with $e > 0$ describe pre-announced future orders, that will be delivered to the hub at time $t + e$. We define a maximum length of the dispatch window τ_{window}, such that $d \in [e, e + \tau_{window}]$. Every unique combination of the four properties represents an order type. Let $I_{t,v,l,e,d} \in \mathbb{Z}_+$ be the number of a given order type in inventory at t. We denote the information regarding all known orders at t as $I_t = (I_{t,v,l,e,d})_{v \in \mathcal{V}', l \in \mathcal{L}, e \in \mathcal{E}, d \in \mathcal{D}}$. The state of the system at t, $S_t \in \mathcal{S}$, combines primary fleet availability with available orders, and is represented by

$$S_t = (Q_t, I_t)_{\forall v \in \mathcal{V}', l \in \mathcal{L}, e \in \mathcal{E}, d \in \mathcal{D}} \ , \forall t \in \mathcal{T}. \tag{1}$$

For $t \geq 1$, let $\mathcal{O}_t = \{0, 1, \ldots, o_t^{max}\}$ be the set containing the number of possible order arrivals between decision moments $t - 1$ and t. Let $o_t \in \mathcal{O}_t$ be a realization of the number of orders arriving between $t - 1$ and t. Furthermore, we set $l^{max} \in \mathbb{Z}_+$ as the maximum number of orders that can be held in inventory, i.e., the maximum inventory remaining after a decision.

For every decision moment t in the planning horizon, we decide which orders in inventory to dispatch. Orders that are not dispatched remain in inventory, and are available at the next decision moment. Let the integer variable $x_{t,v,l,e,d}$ describe the number of a specific order type to be dispatched at t. A feasible action at decision moment t is given by

$$x_t(S_t) = (x_{t,v,l,e,d})_{\forall v \in \mathcal{V}', l \in \mathcal{L}, e \in \mathcal{E}, d \in \mathcal{D}}, \tag{2}$$

where

$$\sum_{v \in \mathcal{V}', l \in \mathcal{L}, e \in \mathcal{E}, d \in \mathcal{D}} (I_{t,v,l,e,d} - x_{t,v,l,e,d}) \leq l^{max}, \tag{3}$$

$$x_{t,v,l,e,d} \leq I_{t,v,l,e,d} \ , \forall v \in \mathcal{V}', \forall l \in \mathcal{L}, \forall e \in \mathcal{E}, \forall d \in \mathcal{D} \ , \tag{4}$$

$$x_{t,v,l,e,0} = I_{t,v,l,e,0} \ , \forall v \in \mathcal{V}', \forall l \in \mathcal{L}, \forall e \in \mathcal{E} \ , \tag{5}$$

$$x_{t,v,l,e,d} = 0 \ , e > 0 \ , \forall v \in \mathcal{V}', \forall l \in \mathcal{L}, \forall d \in \mathcal{D} \ , \tag{6}$$

$$x_{t,v,l,e,d} \in \mathbb{Z}_+ \ , \forall v \in \mathcal{V}', \forall l \in \mathcal{L}, \forall e \in \mathcal{E}, \forall d \in \mathcal{D} \ . \tag{7}$$

Constraint (3) ensures that after dispatching, no more than the maximum inventory remains at the consolidation center. According to Constraint (4), it is not possible to dispatch more orders of a certain type than available at the decision moment t. Constraint (5) states that all orders that have reached their latest dispatch time must be dispatched. Constraint (6) prevents orders with an earliest dispatch time in the future from being dispatched. Constraint (7) states that only nonnegative integer amounts of orders can be dispatched. The set of feasible actions in a given state is described by $\mathcal{X}_t(S_t)$.

4 Markov Model

We model the operator's decision problem as a Markov model. This model considers all possible realizations of orders arrivals during the planning horizon. With this knowledge, we can make the optimal dispatch decision for the current decision moment. In realistic instances, the state space, action space, and outcome space for such a model will be intractably large. Exactly solving the Markov model is therefore not possible within a reasonable time. In Section 6, we solve some toy-sized instances of the Markov model using DP. The ADP approach as outlined in Section 5 is applied to larger instances.

Every action $x_t(S_t)$ has associated direct costs $C(S_t, x_t)$. The direct costs are the sum of fixed dispatching costs per vehicle, variable transportation costs, and handling costs. As the focus of this paper is on the consolidation policy, we do not explicitly consider routing. Instead, we use the classic approximation of Daganzo [4] to estimate the transportation costs for a dispatched set of orders. This approximation is known to provide good estimates of total route distances [13], given constraints on vehicle capacity, number of destinations, and shape of the service area. These constraints are likely to be fulfilled in an urban distribution setting. The approximation is based on the average distances between the depot and the customers, the number of customer locations visited, the size of the service area, and the capacity of the vehicles. We consider fixed handling costs per visited customer; note that this provides an incentive to simultaneously deliver multiple orders to a customer.

To model the uncertainties with respect to the properties of arriving orders, we introduce six stochastic variables. These are (i) the number of orders arriving O_t, (ii) the destination V, (iii) the order size L, (iv) the earliest dispatch time E, (v) the length of the dispatch window D_{window}, and (vi) the latest dispatch time $D = E + D_{window}$. The corresponding probability distributions are discrete and finite. To capture all probability distributions into a single variable, we define the exogenous information variable $\tilde{I}_{t,v,l,e,d} \in \mathbb{Z}_+, t \geq 1$, which indicates the number of arrivals of a specific order type. Furthermore, we introduce a generic variable W_t that describes all exogenous information, i.e., all orders arriving between $t-1$ and t:

$$W_t = [\tilde{I}_{t,v,l,e,d}]_{\forall v \in \mathcal{V}', \forall l \in \mathcal{L}, \forall e \in \mathcal{E}, \forall d \in \mathcal{D}} \ , t \geq 1. \tag{8}$$

There exists a finite number of realizations of W_t. Let Ω_t be the set of possible batch arrivals between $t-1$ and t, and $\omega_t \in \Omega_t$ be a realization of the random variables occurring with $P(W_t = \omega_t)$.

We proceed to describe the transition from a state S_t to the next state S_{t+1}. The transition is affected by the action x_t and the new arrivals W_{t+1}. We first describe the effects of x_t. Orders not dispatched at t remain in inventory, hence must be included in S_{t+1}. As indices e and d are adjusted over time, we introduce two new variables to properly process the conversion. Let $e' = \max\{0, e-1\}$ and $d' = d-1$. Since $e < 0$ does not affect our decision making, capping e' at 0 reduces the number of possible order types. Let $\bar{q}_t \in \{0, \ldots, |\mathcal{Q}^{pr}|\}$ be the number of primary vehicles dispatched at t; combined with Q_t this information suffices to compute Q_{t+1}. We represent new arrivals with the information variable W_{t+1}. This gives us the transition function

$$S_{t+1} = S^M(S_t, x_t, W_{t+1}), \tag{9}$$

where

$$I_{t+1,v,l,e',d'} = I_{t,v,l,e,d} - x_{t,v,l,e,d} + \tilde{I}_{t+1,v,l,e',d'}, \tag{10}$$
$$\forall t \in \mathcal{T}, \forall v \in \mathcal{V}', \forall l \in \mathcal{L}, \forall e \in \mathcal{E}, \forall d \in \mathcal{D},$$

$$q_{t+1,r} = \begin{cases} q_{t,r+1} - \bar{q}_t & \text{if } r < \tau_{route} - 1 \\ |\mathcal{Q}^{pr}| & \text{if } r = \tau_{route} - 1 \end{cases}, \forall r \in [0, \tau_{route} - 1]. \tag{11}$$

Constraint (10) states that for every order type, we have the amount of the order type in state S_t, minus the amount of the order type that was dispatched, plus the amount of the order type that arrived between t and $t+1$. Constraint (11) ensures that Q_{t+1} is consistently updated. Having described the transition function, we now introduce the optimality equation that must be solved:

$$V_t(S_t) = \min_{x_t \in \mathcal{X}_t(S_t)} \left(C(S_t, x_t) + \sum_{\omega_{t+1} \in \Omega_{t+1}} P(W_{t+1} = \omega_{t+1}) V_{t+1}(S_{t+1} | S_t, x_t, \omega_{t+1}) \right). \tag{12}$$

We proceed to describe the state space. Between every two consecutive decision moments $t-1$ and t, we can have $o_t \in \{0, \ldots, |\mathcal{O}_t| - 1\}$ new orders arriving. Every arriving order can have any of the unique order types, given the constraints on the dispatch window. Before the new arrivals occur, we can have up to l^{max} orders in inventory. Hence, we can have at most $l^{max} + |\mathcal{O}_t| - 1$ orders at a given decision moment. A state can be any feasible combination of order types available at t, combined with any vector Q_t.

Next, we describe the action space. At every decision moment, we decide which orders to dispatch. Every combination of orders to dispatch represents a unique action. Orders that are not dispatched remain in inventory, and may be dispatched at the next decision moment. As we do not consider routing options, a unique selection of orders to dispatch equals exactly one action.

The transition from one state to another is determined by the current state, the used action, and the realization of the random variables. The remaining inventory before new orders arrive is deterministic. The probability of o_t orders arriving is given by $P(O_t = o_t)$. The probability of an arriving order being of a certain order type is given by the multivariate distribution $P(V, L, E, D)$. V, L and E are independent random variables, while D is the sum of the realizations of E and D_{window}.

The outcome space is dependent on the state S_t, the action x_t, and the realization of new arrivals ω_{t+1}. Orders not shipped at decision moment t are with certainty included in S_{t+1}. As route duration is deterministic, so is the change in fleet availability. Therefore, only the order arrivals account for stochasticity. To account for the multiple permutations corresponding to o_t order arrivals, we multiply the probability of o_t orders arriving with a multinomial coefficient. We obtain the following probability function for new arrivals:

$$P(W_t = \omega_t) = P(O_t = o_t)\frac{o_t!}{\prod\limits_{\tilde{I}_{t,v,l,e,d} \in \omega_t} \tilde{I}_{t,v,l,e,d}!}$$

$$\prod\limits_{v \in \mathcal{V}', l \in \mathcal{L}, e \in \mathcal{E}, d \in \mathcal{D}} P(V = v, L = l, E = e, D = d)^{\tilde{I}_{t,v,l,e,d}} \quad, t \geq 1.$$

(13)

5   Solution Approach

Realistic-sized problems are intractably large for DP. We resolve computational problems with the state- and outcome space with our ADP approach, while partially addressing the dimensionality of the action space in this paper. We retain the full level of detail in the state description, without enumerating the full state space. By means of Monte Carlo simulation, we approximate the exact values of the DP method [9]. In our ADP implementation, we use the concept of the post-decision state [9]. The post-decision state S_t^x is the state immediately after action x_t, but before the arrival of new information ω_{t+1}. Given our action x_t, we have a deterministic transition from S_t to the so-called post-decision state S_t^x. We express this transition in the function

$$S_t^x = S^{M,x}(S_t),$$

(14)

where

$$I_{t,v,l,e,d} = I_{t,v,l,e,d} - x_{t,v,l,e,d},$$

(15)

$$\forall t \in \mathcal{T}, \forall v \in \mathcal{V}', \forall l \in \mathcal{L}, \forall e \in \mathcal{E}, \forall d \in \mathcal{D},$$

$$q_{t,r} = q_{t,r} - \bar{q}_t \quad, \forall r \in [0, \tau_{route} - 1].$$

(16)

The post-decision state has a corresponding value function

$$V_t(S_t^x) = \mathbb{E}\{V_{t+1}(S_{t+1})|S_t^x\}.$$

(17)

Adopting the concept of the post-decision state allows us to represent our problem as a deterministic minimization problem. Although this reduces the computational effort, Equation (17) still requires to evaluate all states in the outcome space. We therefore replace this value function with a single value function approximation $\bar{V}_t^{n-1}(S_t^x)$. n is an iteration counter, representing that we use an estimate from iteration $n-1$ at iteration n. At every decision moment, we take the best action given our value function approximation. Incoming arrivals are generated according to Equation (13). Utilizing the post-decision state and value function approximation for future costs, we solve Equation (18) to minimize the value $\hat{v}_t^n$:

$$\hat{v}_t^n = \min_{x_t \in \mathcal{X}_t(S_t)} (C_t(S_t, x_t) + \bar{V}_t^{n-1}(S_t^x)). \tag{18}$$

Once we obtain our estimate $\hat{v}_t^n$, we can update $\bar{V}_{t-1}^{n-1}(S_{t-1}^x)$. For this, we use the following function:

$$\bar{V}_{t-1}^n(S_{t-1}^x) \leftarrow U^V(\bar{V}_{t-1}^{n-1}(S_{t-1}^x), S_{t-1}^x, \hat{v}_t^n). \tag{19}$$

Table 1 provides an outline of our ADP algorithm.

Table 1. ADP algorithm with post-decision states

Step 0 Initialize		
	Step 0a:	Initialize $\bar{V}_t^0(S_t)$, $\forall t \in \mathcal{T}$, $\forall S_t \in \mathcal{S}$
	Step 0b:	Set iteration counter to $n = 1$, and set the maximum number of iterations to N.
	Step 0c:	Select an initial state S_0.
Step 1 For $t = 0$ to T do:		
	Step 1a:	Find the best action $\tilde{x}_t^n$ by solving Equation (18).
	Step 1b:	If $t > 0$, then update $\bar{V}_t^{n-1}(S_t)$ using Equation (19).
	Step 1c:	Obtain the post-decision state S_t^x via Equation (14).
	Step 1d:	Obtain a sample realization W_{t+1}, calculate S_{t+1} with Equation (9)
Step 2 Set $n := n + 1$.		
	If $n \leq N$, then go to Step 1.	
Step 3 Return $\bar{V}_t^N(S_t^x), \forall t \in \mathcal{T}$.		

We briefly discuss two options for the function U^V to update $\bar{V}_t^n(S_{t-1}^x)$: lookup and value function approximation (VFA). With the lookup approach, we store an estimate $\bar{V}_t^n(S_t^x)$ for every post-decision state, which is updated based on our observation at the next decision moment. We can speed up this procedure by first completing a full iteration, and then update all post-decision values at once (a procedure known as double pass, see [9]). Although the lookup ADP resolves several computational challenges of dynamic programming, we still need to visit a state to learn about its value. Instead, we want to learn about the value of many states with a single observation. To achieve this, we make use of VFA with the so-called basis function approach, see [9]. Let $\mathcal{F}$ be a set of features, with $f \in \mathcal{F}$ being some variable that partially explains the costs of being in a state. Relevant features for our dispatch problem are, e.g., the total volume of orders in inventory, the number of orders with $d = 0$, and the number of distinct destinations. Let $\phi_f(S_t^x)$ be a basis function of feature f – for example, a cross-product or a polynomial of f – that returns a certain value given S_t^x. Let θ_f^n be a weight corresponding to feature f. Our value function approximation becomes

$$\bar{V}_t^n(S_t^x) = \sum_{f \in \mathcal{F}} \theta_f^n \phi_f(S_t^x), \forall t \in \mathcal{T}. \tag{20}$$

Following [9], the weights θ_f^n are updated using recursive least squares for nonstationary data. Using this procedure, we are able to learn about the value of many states by sampling just a single state. Using VFA, it is therefore not necessary to visit all states in the state space to learn about their value, allowing to handle large state spaces. The key difficulty with VFA is to define basis functions that closely approximate the exact values of states. Good insight in the structure of the problem is required to select features that allow to accurately approximate the true values.

After learning the appropriate weights by completing the procedure in Table 1, VFA can be applied for practical decision making. By calculating the values for the post-decision states corresponding to our initial state, we are able to obtain the best action given the estimate. Only the features of the states, the basis functions, and the corresponding weights are necessary for decision making.

6   Numerical Experiments

First, we solve a toy-sized instance with dynamic programming. We show how both the lookup approach and the VFA approach approximate the exact DP values. Next, we consider larger problems. As these instances are too large to solve exactly, we cannot show convergence results for these. For all instances, we compare the ADP-based simulation results to the results of two myopic benchmark policies, showing how the inclusion of future information impacts decision quality. The first benchmark policy ('Postpone') we deploy in this paper is given in Table 2. It aims to postpone as many orders as possible, until a suitable consolidation opportunity arises or the latest dispatch time is reached. The second benchmark policy ('DirectShipment') always ships orders as soon as possible, as long as primary vehicle capacity is available. 'DirectShipment' sorts and assigns orders just as 'Postpone' describes, and also dispatches secondary vehicles only when necessary. We found that in practice, consolidation policies of comparable complexity are applied by hub operators, followed by manual fine-tuning.

We first describe the properties of our toy problem. We consider a fleet of two primary vehicles; secondary vehicles are twice as expensive as primary vehicles. We consider three distinct customer locations, a random order size from $\{0.2, 0.4, 0.6, 0.8, 1\}$, a maximum inventory of two orders, and a maximum of two arrivals per decision moment. We fix the tour length at $\tau_{route} = 1$. We set $e = 0$ for all orders, and select d from $\{0, 1\}$. All probability distributions are

Table 2. Benchmark policy – Postpone

Step 0 Sort orders.	
Step 0a:	Sort available orders based on lowest d.
Step 0b:	Sort available orders with same d based on smallest size.
Step 1 While orders with $d = 0$ are unassigned do:	Assign order with $d = 0$ to vehicle.
Step 2 While remaining inventory exceeds l^{max} do:	Assign first order on list to vehicle.
Step 3 While capacity from already dispatched vehicles remains do:	Assign first order on list to vehicle.

uniform. We define a planning horizon with five decision moments. Although an extremely small problem, the state space already contains about 140,000 states.

The features we use for our VFA are (i) a constant, (ii) the number of vehicles available at the decision moment, (iii) the number of distinct order destinations, (iv) the total volume of orders in inventory, and (v) the square of the volume of orders in inventory. In Figure 1 and Figure 2, we show for two initial states (one without initial inventory, the other with four orders at the decision moment) how both the lookup approach and the VFA approach converge to the optimal values found with DP. In the first number of iterations, the estimates fluctuate due to the inability to accurately compute expected costs. However, by learning the values of visited states, ADP starts recognizing good actions.

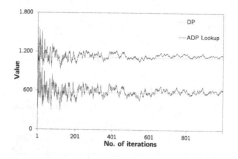

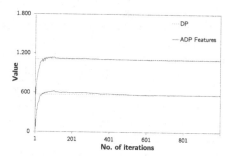

Fig. 1. Approximation of exact value with Lookup

Fig. 2. Approximation of exact value with VFA

From here on, we focus only on ADP with VFA using basis functions. By completing the algorithm in Table 1, we obtain a set of weights for every decision moment. When in a given state, with these weights we estimate the values of all reachable post-decision states. Hence, ADP results in a policy, which we use to solve a deterministic decision problem. We apply the learned policy in a Monte Carlo simulation on a variety of initial states, comparing its performance

Table 3. Comparison between ADP and benchmark policies for small instances

	Average costs	Standard deviation	Average deviation from optimal	Lowest deviation from optimal	Highest deviation from optimal
DP	876	–	–	–	–
ADP	881	0.00145	0.60%	0.45%	0.99%
Postpone	908	0.03205	3.76%	1.98%	9.41%
DirectShipment	1033	0.02040	12.23%	8.52%	18.66%

Table 4. Comparison between ADP and benchmark policies for larger instances

Primary vehicles	Max. arrivals per time unit	Max. inventory	Earliest dispatch	Costs ADP (normalized)	Costs DirectShipment	Costs Postpone
2	10	20	$\{0\}$	100	109.2	109.7
8	10	20	$\{0\}$	100	112.3	113.6
3	15	15	$\{0\}$	100	111.6	112.1
5	15	30	$\{0\}$	100	111.9	113.0
5	15	30	$\{0,1\}$	100	113.5	113.9
5	15	30	$\{0,1,2\}$	100	114.9	115.8

to both DP and the benchmark policies. For all simulations, we use the same realizations of order arrivals, and perform 10,000 simulation replications over the planning horizon. We do this for ten initial states, selected to represent a variety of properties. Table 3 shows the comparison between DP, ADP, and the two benchmark policies. The percentages indicate the average difference in costs between the optimal solution and the simulation results. By applying our ADP policy, we incur costs that are on average 0.60% higher than the optimal solution, as such outperforming both benchmark policies. Also, the standard deviation in solution quality is much lower than for the benchmark policies. With ADP, we postpone 24% less orders than 'Postpone' does. For the initial states where 'DirectShipment' actually postpones orders – for some initial states it never will – ADP postpones 203% more.

Finally, we perform tests on six larger instances, with 10 customers, 10 order sizes, a maximum dispatch window length of 2, and a time horizon of 10. Tunable parameters are mentioned in Table 4. The size of the state space follows from the multinomial coefficients for all possible combinations of order arrivals, and is $\gg 10^{30}$ for all these instances. Clearly, an exact benchmark for such instances cannot be provided.

Table 4 shows the results of our experiments on the six larger instances. When the size of the action space exceeds a predefined threshold, we only partially enumerate the action space based on customer locations. We subsequently apply the same priority rules as the heuristic to assign orders to a given action. On average, ADP outperforms the policy 'DirectShipment' by 12.23% and the policy 'Postpone' by 13.02%. The results show how incorporating future information (both deterministic and stochastic) improves dispatching decisions. In the case of pre-announced orders, the outperformance is stronger due the myopic nature of the benchmark policies.

7   Conclusions

In this paper, we proposed an ADP approach to make dispatch decisions at urban consolidation centers. We optimized decisions for a finite planning horizon, taking into account stochastic order arrivals during this horizon. We have shown that ADP is able to closely approximate the optimal values obtained by DP for toy-sized instances of our problem. For larger instances, ADP clearly and consistently outperforms both myopic benchmark policies, indicating the added value of considering future information.

The ADP approach as described in this paper resolves the intractability of the state space and outcome space. However, we have not thoroughly addressed the size of the action space, which in the worst case increases exponentially with the number of orders in the system. A possible approach to tackle this problem – without affecting the quality of decision-making – is to express the single-period, single-state decision problem as an integer linear program, that can be solved to optimality with less computational effort. This requires the basis functions in the VFA to be defined in such a way that they are linear with the decision problem. Additionally, heuristic approaches to reduce the action space – as touched upon in this paper – are considered for future research.

Our numerical experiments have shown that even for small instances, simple consolidation policies that ignore future information are inadequate to capture the complexity of waiting decisions. Further research will focus on the evaluation of realistically-sized instances and comparison with more sophisticated benchmark policies. The basis functions as proposed in this paper may not work well on every instance. Insights in appropriate VFAs for a variety of problem structures will yield a valuable contribution to existing literature. Both the ADP approach and its benchmarks need to be refined in order to provide an in-depth analysis of the applicability of ADP on realistic-sized dispatch problems.

References

1. Bookbinder, J.H., Cai, Q., He, Q.M.: Shipment consolidation by private carrier: the discrete time and discrete quantity case. Stochastic Models **27**(4), 664–686 (2011)
2. Coelho, L.C., Laporte, G., Cordeau, J.F.: Dynamic and stochastic inventory-routing. Technical Report CIRRELT 2012–37, CIRRELT (2012)
3. Coelho, L.C., Cordeau, J.F., Laporte, G.: Thirty years of inventory routing. Transportation Science **48**(1), 1–19 (2014)
4. Daganzo, C.F.: The distance traveled to visit n points with a maximum of c stops per vehicle: An analytic model and an application. Transportation Science **18**(4), 331–350 (1984)
5. Lium, A.G., Crainic, T.G., Wallace, S.W.: A study of demand stochasticity in service network design. Transportation Science **43**(2), 144–157 (2009)

6. Minkoff, A.S.: A markov decision model and decomposition heuristic for dynamic vehicle dispatching. Operations Research **41**(1), 77–90 (1993)
7. Mutlu, F., Çetinkaya, S., Bookbinder, J.: An analytical model for computing the optimal time-and-quantity-based policy for consolidated shipments. IIE Transactions **42**(5), 367–377 (2010)
8. Pillac, V., Gendreau, M., Guéret, C., Medaglia, A.L.: A review of dynamic vehicle routing problems. European Journal of Operational Research **225**(1), 1–11 (2013)
9. Powell, W.B.: Approximate Dynamic Programming: Solving the Curses of Dimensionality, vol. 842. John Wiley & Sons (2011)
10. Powell, W.B., Topaloglu, H.: Stochastic programming in transportation and logistics. Handbooks in Operations Research and Management Science **10**, 555–635 (2003)
11. Quak, H.: Sustainability of urban freight transport: Retail distribution and local regulations in cities. No. EPS-2008-124-LIS. Erasmus Research Institute of Management (ERIM) (2008)
12. Ritzinger, U., Puchinger, J., Hartl, R.F.: A survey on dynamic and stochastic vehicle routing problems. International Journal of Production Research, 1–17 (2015). (ahead-of-print)
13. Robusté, F., Estrada, M., López-Pita, A.: Formulas for estimating average distance traveled in vehicle routing problems in elliptic zones. Transportation Research Record: Journal of the Transportation Research Board **1873**(1), 64–69 (2004)
14. SteadieSeifi, M., Dellaert, N., Nuijten, W., Van Woensel, T., Raoufi, R.: Multimodal freight transportation planning: A literature review. European Journal of Operational Research **233**(1), 1–15 (2014)
15. Topaloglu, H., Powell, W.B.: Dynamic-programming approximations for stochastic time-staged integer multicommodity-flow problems. INFORMS Journal on Computing **18**(1), 31–42 (2006)

Emission Vehicle Routing Problem with Split Delivery and a Heterogeneous Vehicle Fleet

Benedikt Vornhusen[✉] and Herbert Kopfer

Chair of Logistics, University of Bremen, Bremen, Germany
{bvornhusen,kopfer}@uni-bremen.de
http://www.logistik.uni-bremen.de

Abstract. In order to reduce the greenhouse effect caused by road haulage, new methods for transportation planning need to be developed. The amount of combusted diesel on a route segment of a tour depends to a large extend on the travel distance, the curb weight and the actual payload of the vehicle traversing that segment. Both, using an adequate mixed fleet and allowing split deliveries, open up options for reducing greenhouse gas (GHG) emissions caused by transportation. A MIP-model for a GHG based vehicle routing problem with a mixed fleet and split deliveries is presented. To demonstrate the achieved potential for emission reduction, we analyze results of applying our model to instances generated for homogeneous and mixed fleets.

Keywords: Greenhouse gases · Emission vehicle routing · Split delivery · Heterogeneous fleet

1 Introduction

In Germany, 3.5 billion tons of freight were transported in 2013 and thereof 83% on road. The transportation sector is still growing and an increase of about 1.9% in 2014 is expected [1]. Additionally, road transportation is the most increasing transportation mode. Thus a high ratio of the total emissions resulting from freight transportation is induced by road haulage. The impact of road freight transportation to environment has become crucial in the last years. Hence, many researchers deal with this issue, and recently at least 59 papers were published on this topic [3]. Most of these papers have been published in the last four years. This shows that the consideration of the environmental impact of freight transport accrued recently.

There exist few studies focusing on the possibility of reducing air pollutants by employing a heterogeneous vehicle fleet instead of a homogeneous fleet. Kopfer and Kopfer [8] introduce the emission vehicle routing problem with vehicle classes (EVRP-VC). The EVRP-VC is an extension of the classical vehicle routing problem (VRP) by introducing a heterogeneous vehicle fleet and an objective function which minimizes the total CO_2 emissions caused by differently sized vehicles. In contrast to most heterogeneous vehicle routing problems

© Springer International Publishing Switzerland 2015
F. Corman et al. (Eds.): ICCL 2015, LNCS 9335, pp. 76–90, 2015.
DOI: 10.1007/978-3-319-24264-4_6

in literature, the model introduced in [8] does not only consider heterogeneity of vehicles related to restrictions, e.g. capacity. The heterogeneity of vehicles is also relevant with respect to the objective function since the fuel consumption of vehicles out of different vehicle classes is calculated in the objective function in dependence of the size of the used vehicles. In [8], the EVRP-VC is compared with the VRP. It has been shown that through the utilization of a mixed fleet with vehicles of different size instead of a homogeneous fleet significant reductions in emissions are possible.

Our study extends the EVRP-VC to the EVRPTWSD-VC by increasing the number of vehicle classes from 4 to 6, by introducing time windows, and by allowing split deliveries. The VRP with split deliveries (VRPSD) is originally introduced by [4]. Introducing split deliveries allows serving a customer more than one time by different vehicles. Thereby, the demand of a customer can be satisfied by several vehicles with each vehicle delivering only a part of the entire customer demand. Since the solution space of the VRPSD is larger than that of the VRP, allowing split deliveries may enable the reduction of the total travel distance of optimal solutions of the VRP. The EVRPTWSD-VC can also be considered as a VRPSD enriched (modified) by including time windows, by introducing an objective function which minimizes the total emissions instead of the total driven distances and by introducing a heterogeneous vehicle fleet with six vehicle classes.

This article analyzes the effects on emission reductions which are realizable due to the existence of different vehicle classes available for vehicle routing and the effects of allowing split deliveries. The article is structured as follows. In Section 2, relevant methods for the calculation of greenhouse gas (GHG) emissions and approaches for vehicle routing with the specific goal of minimizing GHG emissions of a mixed vehicle fleet are discussed. In Section 3, parameters of vehicle specific functions for emission calculation are derived. A mathematical model for the EVRPTWSD-VC is proposed in Section 4. Validations of the proposed model as well as experiments on the potential for emission-savings are conducted in Section 5. The last Section concludes the paper.

2   Ecological Approaches for Mixed Vehicle Routing

The calculation of GHGs emitted through road haulage is very complex since there are many factors with a more or less strong influence on emissions. An overview of factors which affect fuel consumption and emissions is given in [3]. These factors are divided into five categories: vehicle, environment, traffic, driver and operations related factors. In Demir et al. [2] further relevant factors with impact on fuel consumption and emissions are considered, e.g. engine type and vehicle design. Due to the wide spectrum of possible factors, numerous emission models are available. Several of these models are analyzed and compared by [2]. They differ in their modeling structures, modeling approaches and data requirements. Demir et al. [3] categorize these models into factor models, macroscopic and microscopic models.

Hereafter, macroscopic models which are able to differentiate between diverse types of vehicles are mentioned. Some of these models calculate the energy or fuel consumption, while some other models refer to GHG emissions.

The online tool EcoTransIT World (short: EcoTransIT) designed by Knörr et al. [6] offers the possibility to consider seven types of vehicles with specific characteristics. It introduces vehicle types of different size and enables the calculation of emitted GHGs in dependence of the size and other vehicle specific factors.

The model provided in the norm DIN EN 16258 [12] is similar to the approach proposed by EcoTransIT. Like EcoTransIT, the DIN model enables to determine the consumption data without any on-road measured values. Only information concerning the payload, vehicle type and travel distance must be available. But the DIN norm provides the calculation of emissions for only four vehicle types. It calculates the amount of consumed diesel instead of emissions. In order to compare values calculated for diesel consumption with emission-oriented values computed by other approaches, conversion from energy consumption to GHG emissions is made.

MEET (Methodology for calculating Emissions and Energy of Transport) is a further method for the approximation of the quantity of emissions caused by transportation [5]. Meet calculates in dependence of several vehicle specific coefficients the emissions for an unloaded vehicle at speed v. Four vehicle types are considered. For including the additional emissions caused by vehicle load, MEET applies a load correction function which is dependent on the vehicle category, too.

An analysis about the influence of road gradient and payload is conducted by Scott et al. [13] within a CO_2 minimizing vehicle routing approach. Four vehicle categories are considered and thereby the effect of gradient and payload on a singe vehicle is discussed. The used traveling salesman problem instances are based on real life examples.

There are few approaches for vehicle routing with the specific goal of minimizing GHG emissions of a mixed vehicle fleet. Kwon et al. [10] consider a heterogeneous vehicle fleet with the objective of minimizing carbon emissions. By their mathematical model a cost-benefit assessment of the value for purchasing or selling carbon emission rights can be made. They develop and apply tabu search algorithms for their experiments and demonstrate that the amount of carbon emissions can be decreased by carbon trading without increasing the costs for transportation.

Koç et al. [7] investigate the fleet size and mix pollution-routing problem to quantify the benefits of using a flexible fleet with respect to fuel consumption, emissions and costs. Speed optimization is an important part in this work. Nevertheless, their tests demonstrate that using a heterogeneous fleet without speed optimization allows for higher benefits than using a homogeneous vehicle fleet with speed optimization.

Kopfer et al. [9] investigate the EVRP-VC introduced in [8]. Four vehicle types with a total weight of 3.5to, 7.5to, 12to and 40to are included in their study. They demonstrate that through the utilization of a heterogeneous vehicle fleet significant reductions (up to 20%) in emissions are possible especially if the customer requests are small. In particular, they demonstrate that replacing a tour for a single big vehicle by several tours for vehicles of different size can result in a considerable reduction of emissions. However, compared to a homogeneous fleet with only big vehicles, using a mixed fleet implies increased totally driven distances and additional routes to be performed by the vehicles. Additionally, if the demand of some of the customers exceeds the capacity of some vehicles types, it is not possible to serve any customer by any vehicle of the mixed fleet. This limitation of the solution space of the heterogeneous problem could possibly be compensated by having additional vehicle classes and by allowing that customers with a high demand are served by more than one vehicle.

3   Calculation of Emissions

Vehicle routing with the specific goal of minimizing GHG emissions requires the anticipation of the amount of emissions which will be induced by the realization of planned transportation processes. Exact, detailed and complete information on these processes is not available at planning time. That is why, as far as planning activities are concerned, the amount of emissions associated with transportation has to be predicted; i.e. the emissions must be estimated in advance, in dependence on vehicle routing and scheduling decisions. Since we focus with respect to vehicle routing on decisions which can exclusively and independently be made by the transportation planner through fixing a transportation plan, we restrict the calculation of the estimated amount of emissions to be based on the following factors: travel distances, type of used vehicles, payload over the course of tour fulfillment.

Calculating the estimated amount of GHG emissions on the basis of the above factors is possible by using one of the models presented in [5], [6], [12] and [13]. The models from [5] and [12] do not consider light goods vehicles, i.e. it is not possible to calculate the emission values for small $3.5to$ vehicles. Since EcoTransIT [6] is fitting nearly perfectly to the vehicle classes that we decided to consider within our research, we use [6] for calculating fuel consumption and emissions.

EcoTransIT is a tool which can be used online. It provides the well-to-wheel (WTW) calculation for energy consumption in kWh, the greenhouse effect in $kgCO_2e$ and the emissions itemized in all GHGs. WTW calculations include the entire emissions resulting from the transport and all effects which arise out of the production and distribution of the consumed fuel [11]. EcoTransIT is available in a standard and an extended mode. In the extended mode it is possible to include vehicle specific information. First, the weight of cargo must be specified. Second, the vehicle class with respect to size has to be specified. Note that the maximum weight which can be transported is equal to the load capacity of the chosen vehicle type. EcoTransIT considers seven vehicle classes with a total weight up to 60 tons. The consideration in this paper is restricted to the first six vehicle classes of EcoTransIT. The heaviest vehicle considered has a total weight of 40 tons which corresponds to the weight of the heaviest regularly allowed trucks on most European roads. A further input parameter is the specific weight of cargo, i.e. the ratio of weight and volume of transported goods. It can be chosen between heavy, average and light cargo. In dependence of the specific weight, the capacity with respect to weight is restricted to 30%, 60% and 100% of the original capacity if light, average or heavy cargo is specified, respectively. In this study, the transportation of heavy cargo is assumed. EcoTransIT uses country specific values for road gradients. Here, the gradient for Germany is used. With the previously specified parameter values, EcoTransIT is applied for calculating the emissions and energy consumption of vehicles from the six considered vehicle classes for varying values of payload q. Since EcoTransIT cannot calculate the values for an empty (i.e. unloaded) vehicle, the series of calculations is started with the payload $q = 0.5to$ and is increased by $0.5to$ steps up to the maximal vehicle capacity. Based on the results of the application of EcoTransIT, discrete values for the emissions (measured in $kgCO_2e/100km$) respectively the energy consumption (measured in $kWh/100km$) are determined in dependence of the payload q. Figure 1 shows the values for the greenhouse effect respectively energy consumption in dependence on the payload q for all six vehicle classes. The values

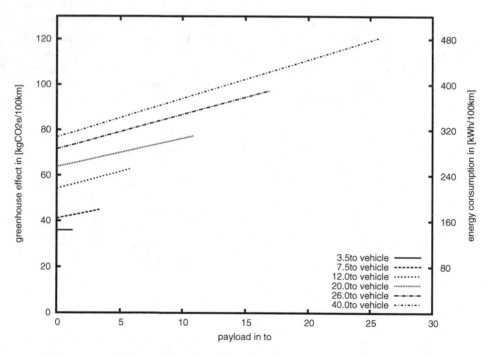

Fig. 1. Energy consumption and greenhouse effect in dependence of payload according to EcoTransIT.org

in Figure 1 show that the greenhouse effect is linearly dependent on the payload q. That is why the function $E_v(q)$ for the GHG emissions of a vehicle of class v can be described as:

$$E_v(q) = a_v + b_v \cdot q \tag{1}$$

with a_v being the parameter for the emission of an empty vehicle of type v ($v = 1, .., 6$) and b_v representing the parameter for the emissions caused by the payload q. Table 1 shows the values for the parameters a_v and b_v, which can be derived from the results generated by EcoTransIT. Table 1 additionally shows the load capacity Q_v and the emission function $E_v(q)$ for all vehicle classes v. It

Table 1. Six vehicle categories - EcoTransIT

Vehicle category	Vehicle type	Load capacity Q_v (to)	a_v	b_v	$E_v(q)$ ($\frac{kgCO_2e}{100km}$)
V_{40}	6 $(26 - 40to)$	26	76.82	1.70	$76.82 + \frac{1.70}{to}q$
V_{26}	5 $(20 - 26to)$	17	71.57	1.52	$71.57 + \frac{1.52}{to}q$
V_{20}	4 $(12 - 20to)$	11	63.76	1.25	$63.76 + \frac{1.25}{to}q$
V_{12}	3 $(7.5 - 12to)$	6	54.18	1.49	$54.18 + \frac{1.49}{to}q$
$V_{7.5}$	2 $(3.5 - 7.5to)$	3.5	41.07	1.14	$41.07 + \frac{1.14}{to}q$
$V_{3.5}$	1 $(\leq 3.5to)$	1.5	35.89	0.00	$35.89 + \frac{0.00}{to}q$

is obvious that, without any load, big vehicles have higher fuel consumption than small vehicles (values of a_v in Table 1). According to Table 1, the proportional factor for the additional energy required for carrying payload (values of b_v in Table 1) increases for increasing vehicle size, except for the V_{12} vehicle class. That is not directly plausible. Additionally, it is amazing that the smallest vehicle produces a constant amount of emissions, no matter whether it is loaded or unloaded. This is in contrast to the values used for fuel consumption in [8] where the values assumed for the parameter b_v invariably increase for decreasing vehicle size. Applying [12] for calculating the emissions for V_{40} vehicles yields that such a vehicle emits $73.55kgCO_2e/100km$ in case that it is unloaded, and further emits $1.79kgCO_2e/100km$ for every ton payload. This is roughly conforming to the values of Table 1. According to [13], the payload does not have a significant impact on the air pollutants emitted by light goods vehicles. This is conforming to the results derived for Table 1, too.

Intensive comparisons of diverse emission models demonstrate that the results obtained by various models differ substantially in terms of fuel consumption and emissions ascribed to the fulfillment of a transportation task on a given route [2]. Moreover, it is shown that the results generated by applying the models differ from those results which can be obtained by on-road experiments. Some models provide estimations which are closer to on-road measured values for heavy vehicles while the results of other models are closer to on-road values for light vehicles. This proves that there is an urgent need for more research on models which can be used for predicting reliable values for the expected amount of emissions based on some key factors and specific parameters of transportation processes. Nevertheless, all current research on GHG emission based vehicle routing has to rely on the actual state of the art for emission calculation. As far as the research presented in this paper is concerned, it is important to mention that all values used for the calculation of emissions in the following sections have been derived by using EcoTransIT.

4   A Mathematical Model

The EVRPTWSD-VC can be defined on a graph $G = (N, A)$, where N is the set of nodes and $A = N \times N$ is the set of arcs. There are n customers and one depot which are represented by nodes $i \in N$, $N = \{0, ..., n\}$. The node $i = 0$ depicts the depot. All customers i have a request of π_i which has to be transported from the depot to the customer node. Each arc $(i, j) \in A$ is associated with a travel distance d_{ij}. It is assumed that the travel time t_{ij} which is needed to drive along an arc $(i, j) \in A$ is proportional to d_{ij}, i.e. $t_{ij} = const \cdot d_{ij}$ with const being the constant average speed of the vehicles. All customers have to be visited within a predefined time window $[t_i^a, t_i^b]$ and they are associated with a service time t_i^s. The service at the customer nodes must be started within the given time windows. A vehicle fleet $K = \{1, ..., m\}$ with a sufficiently high number of vehicles for each vehicle class is available for the fulfillment of the customer requests. All vehicles $k \in K$ are stationed at the depot and exhibit a specific capacity of Q_k according to the vehicle class v they belong to (see Table 1).

A specific vehicle can visit every node only once. But split delivery allows visiting a customer more than one time by different vehicles.

The following decision variables are necessary to develop the MIP model for the EVRPTWSD-VC. Binary variable x_{ijk} will be equal to one if the vehicle $k \in K$ travels along the arc $(i, j) \in A$ and zero otherwise. Binary variable y_{ik} will be one if vehicle $k \in K$ visits the customer $i \in N$. The decision variable q_{ijk} indicates the load which is carried by vehicle $k \in K$ on arc $(i, j) \in A$. To denote the portion of the request of customer $i \in N$ which is transported by vehicle $k \in K$, the variable z_{ik} is necessary. The operation at customer $i \in N$ starts at time w_{ik}. Finally, u_{ik} is introduced to integrate the Miller-Tucker-Zemlin constraint.

$$\min \sum_{i=0}^{n} \sum_{j=0}^{n} \sum_{k=1}^{m} d_{ij} \cdot (a_k \cdot x_{ijk} + b_k \cdot q_{ijk}) \tag{2}$$

$$\text{s.t.} \sum_{i=0}^{n} x_{ijk} = \sum_{i=0}^{n} x_{jik} \qquad \forall j \in N, \forall k \in K \tag{3}$$

$$\sum_{i=0}^{n} x_{ijk} = y_{jk} \qquad\qquad \forall j \in N, \forall k \in K \qquad (4)$$

$$\sum_{j=1}^{n} x_{0jk} \leq 1 \qquad\qquad \forall k \in K \qquad (5)$$

$$u_{ik} - u_{jk} + n \cdot x_{ijk} \leq n - 1 \qquad \forall i \in N, \forall j \in N \setminus \{0\}, \forall k \in K \quad (6)$$

$$\sum_{i=1}^{n} z_{ik} \leq Q_k \qquad\qquad \forall k \in K \qquad (7)$$

$$\sum_{k=1}^{m} z_{ik} = \pi_i \qquad\qquad \forall i \in N \setminus \{0\} \qquad (8)$$

$$z_{ik} \leq \pi_i \cdot y_{ik} \qquad\qquad \forall i \in N \setminus \{0\}, \forall k \in K \qquad (9)$$

$$\sum_{i=0}^{n} q_{ijk} - \sum_{i=0}^{n} q_{jik} = z_{jk} \qquad \forall j \in N \setminus \{0\}, \forall k \in K \qquad (10)$$

$$q_{ijk} \leq Q_k \cdot x_{ijk} \qquad\qquad \forall i, j \in N, \forall k \in K \qquad (11)$$

$$t_i^a \leq w_{ik} \leq t_i^b \qquad\qquad \forall i \in N, \forall k \in K \qquad (12)$$

$$w_{ik} + t_{ij} + t_i^s - M \cdot (1 - x_{ijk}) \leq w_{jk} \quad \forall i \in N \setminus \{0\}, \forall j \in N, \forall k \in K \quad (13)$$

$$q_{ijk} \geq 0 \qquad\qquad \forall i, j \in N, \forall k \in K \qquad (14)$$

$$u_{ik} \geq 0 \qquad\qquad \forall i \in N, \forall k \in K \qquad (15)$$

$$z_{ik} \geq 0 \qquad\qquad \forall i \in N, \forall k \in K \qquad (16)$$

$$x_{ijk} \in \{0, 1\} \qquad\qquad \forall i, j \in N, \forall k \in K \qquad (17)$$

$$y_{ik} \in \{0, 1\} \qquad\qquad \forall i \in N, \forall k \in K \qquad (18)$$

The EVRPTWSD-VC is described by the mathematical model (2) to (18). The objective function (2) minimizes the total amount of emitted CO_2e units in dependence of the total weight of the vehicles on each arc. Constraints (3) and (4) enforce that each node will be visited only once by the same vehicle. All vehicles can leave the depot at most once (constraint (5)). Restriction (6) forbids self-cycles due to the Miller-Tucker-Zemlin formulation. The constraints (7) to (12) are used to enable split delivery. Equation (7) ensures that the vehicle specific capacity limitations are met. Each customer must receive the total demand by one or more vehicles (constraint (8)). Vehicles must not load any goods which are destined for customers they do not visit (constraint (9)). The actual load carried on an arc is computed in equation (10) and this load has to comply with the vehicles capacities (constraint (11)). Restrictions (12) and (13) are guaranteeing that a customer will be served within its time window. Constraints (14) to (16) ensure that the decision variables are always positive.

$$\sum_{k=1}^{m} y_{ik} = 1 \qquad\qquad \forall i \in N \setminus \{0\} \qquad (19)$$

To demonstrate the impact of split deliveries, two different scenarios are opposed by analyzing problems with and without allowing customer demands to be split. Thus, we consider a second optimization problem (EVRPTW-VC) without split deliveries. The EVRPTW-VC is identical to the EVRPTWSD-VC, except that split deliveries are prohibited. Equation (19) ensures that every request is delivered by exactly one vehicle. Thus, adding (19) to the above model (2) to (18) yields a model for the EVRPTW-VC. If in the model for the EVRPTWSD-VC respectively EVRPTW-VC the values of all parameters a_k and b_k are identical for all $k \in K$, then these models reduce to describe the corresponding homogeneous problems EVRPTWSD and EVRPTW.

5   Computational Study

In this section, a computational study is conducted to evaluate the possible reduction of the amount of CO_2e by allowing split deliveries and by utilizing heterogeneous instead of homogeneous vehicle fleets. Additionally, the effects on the totally traveled distance and the number of used vehicles are analyzed. All test instances are solved on an Intel(R) Core(TM) i5-4200M at 2.50GHz with 8GB memory using IBM ILOG CPLEX 12.5.1.

5.1   Generation of Instances

Since the model for the EVRPTWSD-VC presented in Section 4 is hard to solve for a commercial solver, only small instances consisting of 10 customers are tested. The test instances are generated similar to the well-known VRP instances from Solomon [14]. In our paper, only the generation of randomly spread customer nodes is considered. Thus, all nodes are scattered in a square of 300×300. For each instance, the depot is placed in the middle of the square at $[150, 150]$ while the coordinates of all customer nodes are determined randomly. A large time window for the depot is set to $[0, 800]$. The width of this time window has no influence on the results of our experiments. To reduce the bias possibly caused by the characteristics of the customer time windows, they are chosen as follows. The beginning of the time window t_i^a at customer i is set to t_{0i} which is a lower bound for the earliest possible arriving time. The end of each time window t_i^b is determined randomly. Under consideration of the service time t_i^s of about 20 time units it is randomly chosen within the interval $[t_{0i} + t_i^s, t_0^b - t_{i0} - t_i^s]$. Thus the size of all customer time windows varies. In case of a heterogeneous fleet (EVRPTWSD-VC), the vehicle fleet consists of ten vehicles for every vehicle class, and in case of a homogeneous fleet (EVRPTWSD) it consists of ten vehicles of one predefined type. Consequently, there is no lack of vehicles; i.e. the number of available vehicles has no restricting effect on the solution space.

Two different types of test sets have been generated: test set R with randomly generated coordinates of the customer nodes and test set RM with no customers in the interval $[100, 200]$ on the y-axis; i.e., for all instances out of RM there are no nodes in the middle of the square near the depot. For every test set, ten configurations of customer locations have been generated. The customer demands are additionally diversified for each customer configuration. For each single customer configuration, demands from the interval $]0, 6] \subset \mathbb{R}$ are randomly generated and assigned to the customers. This is repeated five times resulting in five test instances with different customer demands for any specification of customer locations. To sum up, $2 \cdot 10 \cdot 5 = 100$ instances were generated and tested.

5.2   Computational Results

The models EVRPTW and EVRPTWSD (i.e. the models restricting to one single vehicle type) presented in Section 4 have been solved for all hundred test instances. The instances are solved for the three homogeneous fleets with the vehicle classes: V_{12}, V_{20} and V_{26}, respectively. Further, EVRPTW-VC and EVRPTWSD-VC have been solved for the heterogeneous fleet composed of sufficient vehicles out of all six vehicle classes. For all experiments the values for a_v and b_v are taken from Table 1. The computation time for solving a single test instance was limited to one hour.

Table 2. Test set R with homogeneous fleets

	EM	EM(SD)	D	D(SD)	#V	#V(SD)	#SD
	1012.77	993.89	1752.88	1719.58	6.8	6.6	1.2
	849.17	846.06	1471.73	1463.32	6.8	6.6	1.0
	1093.13	1071.59	1897.75	1850.86	7.0	6.4	1.4
	1269.94	1228.16	2209.38	2124.04	7.2	6.4	1.2
V_{12}	1172.93	1154.59	2024.97	1993.82	6.8	6.4	1.0
	1130.88	1092.00	1956.84	1885.70	6.8	6.6	0.8
	1128.98	1103.66	1963.97	1914.17	7.2	6.8	2.0
	1014.85	978.62	1759.20	1690.60	7.0	6.6	0.6
	984.62	977.08	1703.97	1688.19	6.8	6.6	0.6
	859.98	844.70	1489.68	1460.62	7.0	6.4	2.0
	895.70	895.70	1312.14	1312.14	4.4	4.4	0.0
	720.73	710.51	1052.26	1034.12	4.0	4.0	0.6
	915.14	910.18	1334.17	1325.74	4.0	4.0	0.4
	1103.31	1094.82	1614.82	1602.08	4.0	4.0	0.2
V_{20}	1012.66	1005.49	1469.68	1459.18	4.0	4.0	0.2
	959.66	929.82	1401.20	1356.97	4.4	4.4	0.6
	937.76	928.10	1382.56	1355.53	4.4	4.0	0.6
	859.34	857.98	1257.11	1255.90	4.4	4.4	0.2
	825.30	824.14	1203.80	1201.57	4.2	4.0	0.2
	765.43	765.43	1128.37	1128.37	4.2	4.2	0.2
$\varnothing V_{26}$	906.89	906.89	1151.88	1151.88	3.28	3.28	0

The solutions for test set R (test instances with randomly distributed customer locations) are presented in Table 2. Each row in Table 2 refers to the result of one customer configuration averaged over the five random generations and assignments of customer demands. The columns EM respectively EM(SD) render the emitted emissions in $kgCO_2e$ for routing a homogeneous fleet without allowing splits respectively routing the fleet including the possibility of split deliveries. The columns D respectively D(SD) contain the averaged values for the totally driven distances in case of non-split respectively in case of possible split deliveries. The average number of used vehicles without respectively with splits is shown in the columns #V respectively #V(SD). The average number of customers which were served by more than one vehicle is shown in column #SD. Table 3 presents the results for the test set RM in analogy to Table 2.

All test instances without allowing split deliveries have been solved to optimality within a few minutes or faster. In contrast, the EVRPTWSD is hard to solve, especially for instances with small vehicle types. For this model, solutions for instances with V_{12} vehicles come up with an average optimality gap of 2.02% for set R (rows of V_{12} in Table 2) and 2.15% for set RM (rows of V_{12} in Table 3). Solving homogeneous instances with smaller vehicles yields even bigger gaps. That is why we did not perform extensive experiments for homogeneous fleets with vehicles smaller than 12 tons gross weight in our study. Even four of the

Table 3. Test set RM with homogeneous fleets

	EM	EM(SD)	D	D(SD)	#V	#V(SD)	#SD
	1011.18	990.67	1770.70	1727.19	6.2	5.6	1.0
	1081.59	1049.74	1880.65	1823.13	5.8	5.6	1.0
	883.54	870.66	1537.84	1514.27	6.0	5.8	1.0
	1040.10	999.28	1814.62	1735.04	6.4	5.6	1.4
V_{12}	1025.47	1020.34	1782.94	1775.39	6.0	5.6	0.6
	1156.03	1139.09	2000.58	1975.52	5.8	5.8	0.6
	1066.98	1051.04	1858.12	1826.67	5.8	5.4	1.6
	1130.12	1120.39	1975.16	1954.42	6.2	5.8	0.6
	1176.95	1144.04	2047.29	1985.61	6.0	5.8	0.8
	1214.04	1137.71	2120.55	1974.35	6.4	5.4	1.6
	920.67	915.12	1367.17	1358.68	3.8	3.6	0.4
	887.59	877.61	1292.69	1276.19	3.4	3.2	0.8
	752.57	752.57	1106.97	1106.97	3.6	3.6	0.0
	823.20	822.70	1201.66	1201.66	3.4	3.4	0.4
V_{20}	906.10	895.76	1321.23	1294.98	3.4	3.2	0.4
	1097.75	1097.75	1594.57	1594.57	3.6	3.6	0.0
	983.83	983.83	1455.26	1455.26	3.6	3.6	0.0
	1052.54	1052.54	1571.30	1571.30	4.0	4.0	0.0
	1012.50	1009.17	1470.86	1463.14	3.4	3.2	0.2
	1024.94	1017.71	1505.80	1491.31	3.4	3.2	0.4
$\varnothing V_{26}$	989.09	988.63	1270.96	1269.92	3.08	3.06	0.04

solutions of instances of the set RM with V_{20} vehicles exhibit a small optimality gap with an average value of 0.34% in case of split delivery. All other test instances have been solved to optimality.

In case of using a homogeneous fleet with V_{12} vehicles, nearly every solution consists of one or more split deliveries. The experiments on both, the R and RM test sets, demonstrate that there are fewer splits made if the vehicles constituting the homogeneous fleet are becoming bigger. In case of a homogeneous fleet with V_{26} vehicles there are no splits at all for the test set R and only two test cases with splits for all fifty instances of RM. Further tests on a homogeneous fleet with V_{40} vehicles yield that there are no splits made for all 100 test cases.

The comparisons of the values of columns EM and EM(SD) demonstrate the reduction of CO_2e emissions achieved by split deliveries in case of homogeneous fleets. Deploying V_{12} vehicles, CO_2e emissions could be reduced by 2.08% on average for test set R and by 2.38% for set RM. The at most reachable reduction is even higher since it corresponds to the above values augmented by the optimality gap. Over all instances of R respectively RM, a maximal reduction of 3.57% respectively 6.29% has been reached. In addition to the reduction of GHGs, travel distance can be reduced by allowing splits. On average 2.33% and 2.58% less distance is achieved for the V_{12} instances of the test set R and RM, respectively. Moreover, 5.76% fewer vehicles have been used due to split delivery for instances in R and 6.93% for instances in RM.

Increasing the size of the vehicles of a homogeneous fleet leads to decreasing effects of split deliveries with respect to savings in emissions, travel distance and number of realized splits. Allowing splits for V_{20} vehicles yields an average reduction of about 0.79% and 0.40% in emissions and 0.93% and 0.54% in travel distances by solving the R and RM instances, respectively. For homogeneous fleets with V_{26} vehicles there are no appreciable effects of allowing splits.

There are some other interesting findings from Tables 2 and 3. As expected, the amount of used vehicles decreases with increasing capacity of the vehicles of the homogeneous fleets. Allowing split delivery has a significantly stronger effect on the reduction of travel distance than on the reduction of emissions. Further, instances of the test set RM generally require fewer tours to be fulfilled than instances of the set R; e.g., V_{12} instances with split delivery averagely consist of 6.54 tours for R and 5.64 for RM. But with respect to the magnitude of the effects of introducing split deliveries there are no remarkable differences between the sets R and RM.

Comparing V_{20} and V_{26} fleets with respect to the values of columns EM and D in Table 2 and 3, yields that using V_{26} fleets results in less travel distance but more GHG emissions. The V_{20} fleet averagely emits 2.65% less GHG than the V_{26} fleet in case of EVRPTW, and 3.21% in case of EVRPTWSD. It had to be expected that V_{26} fleets lead to less travel distance than V_{20} fleets since bigger vehicles allow for larger tours with more efficient bundling effects. But the fact that V_{20} fleets produce less emission is remarkable. It demonstrates that, from ecological point of view (i.e. minimizing greenhouse emissions) and for homogeneous fleets, V_{20} vehicles are superior to all other vehicle types considered for fulfilling the transportation requests of the test sets R and RM. In other words the V_{20} fleet is the one which is fitting best to the test cases used in our experiments for emission reduction. These results expose that adapting the size of the vehicles of a homogeneous fleet is a challenging but worthwhile optimization task which cannot be analyzed in more detail in this paper.

Table 4. Test set R with heterogeneous fleet

EM(-VC)	EM (SD-VC)	D(-VC)	D(SD-VC)	#V (-VC)	#V (SD-VC)	#SD
825.46	824.57	1354.37	1402.06	4.8	5.0	0.2
645.27	645.14	908.88	924.47	3.4	3.6	0.2
824.31	824.31	1152.38	1152.38	3.0	3.0	0.0
950.57	950.57	1482.95	1482.95	4.2	4.2	0.0
935.18	935.18	1412.62	1412.62	4.4	4.4	0.0
833.91	833.91	1242.54	1242.54	4.6	4.6	0.0
821.87	821.86	1156.08	1156.25	3.0	3.0	0.2
698.05	698.05	945.75	945.75	3.2	3.2	0.0
775.79	775.07	1225.37	1225.51	4.6	4.6	0.4
711.63	711.45	1124.64	1124.77	4.4	4.4	0.4

In Tables 4 and 5, the results of solving the models of the heterogeneous problems presented in Section 4 are shown for the test sets R and RM with and without allowing split deliveries. All test instances of Tables 4 and 5 could have been solved to optimality within the given time limit of one hour.

Table 5. Test set RM with heterogeneous fleet

EM(-VC)	EM (SD-VC)	D(-VC)	D(SD-VC)	#V (-VC)	#V (SD-VC)	#SD
767.21	765.48	1324.17	1345.36	4.0	4.0	0.2
728.48	728.48	1092.81	1092.81	3.4	3.4	0.0
664.05	664.05	980.11	980.11	3.0	3.0	0.0
770.63	768.02	1091.65	1082.33	3.0	2.8	0.2
790.20	784.10	1234.46	1237.56	3.4	3.4	0.2
987.95	985.70	1655.68	1661.17	4.2	4.2	0.4
883.64	876.44	1506.70	1551.19	4.2	4.4	0.4
974.80	971.11	1634.74	1651.02	4.4	4.4	0.4
914.25	911.54	1353.52	1364.41	3.4	3.4	0.2
906.45	906.16	1431.79	1439.03	3.8	3.8	0.2

Comparing the GHG emissions EM(-VC) of the heterogeneous fleet (Table 4) in case that no split deliveries are allowed with the emissions EM and EM(SD) of the best homogeneous fleet (V_{20} vehicles in Table 2) demonstrates that a tremendous reduction of the greenhouse effect can be achieved by using a heterogeneous fleet. In case that no split deliveries are allowed for the V_{20} fleet, the reduction amounts to 10.82%, and to 10.11% if split deliveries are allowed for the V_{20} fleet. For the test set RM the results are similar: 11.35% without split deliveries and 11.28% with split deliveries for the V_{20} fleet.

Allowing split deliveries for the heterogeneous fleet too (columns EM(SD-VC)), yields only a slight further reduction by 0.02% for R and 0.32% for the set RM. The results of the experiments show that, in case of a mixed fleet, improvements achieved by split deliveries are small since the capacities of the differently sized vehicle are mostly utilized to a high degree. Summarized over all 50 test cases with 500 customer services for R respectively RM, there have occurred only 7 respectively 11 split deliveries performed by the heterogeneous fleet. These results show that replacing a homogeneous fleet by a heterogeneous fleet has a great benefit with respect to GHG emissions while additionally allowing split deliveries for the heterogeneous fleet only results a negligible additional benefit.

6   Conclusion

This study analyzes the effects of introducing a heterogeneous fleet and allowing split deliveries on vehicle routing problems whose objective function is minimizing the amount of emitted GHG. It is difficult to get reliable and reasonable values for predicting the amount of GHG emissions that will be caused by the vehicle routes of a transportation plan. Since most of the factors which have an effect on the amount of emitted GHG are not known in advance (i.e. before the tour is started) or cannot be influenced by the transportation planner, we restrict to calculate the estimated amount of emissions based on three factors: length of tours, type of used vehicles and load of the vehicles over the course of their tours. In our study, we decided to use EcoTransIT for deriving concrete parameter values for the factors that we use for calculating the expected amount of GHG emissions of a transportation plan.

The computational experiments of Section 5 show that allowing split deliveries for homogeneous fleets has the positive effect of reducing the GHG emissions by 1.03% (averaged over all test cases) while the travel distances and the number of used vehicles averagely decrease by 1.30% and 3.69%, respectively. Replacing a homogeneous fleet with a gross weight of 12, 20 or 26 tons by a heterogeneous fleet with 6 different vehicle classes with gross weights from 3.5 to 40 tons has the effect of reducing the GHG emissions by 16.16% (also averaged over all test cases) while the travel distances and the number of used vehicles averagely decrease by 14.00% and 15.49%, respectively. Consequently, introducing a heterogeneous fleet has a much stronger positive effect on GHG emissions than allowing split deliveries. Doing both, does not provide the benefits which could have been hoped for, since the effect of allowing a heterogeneous fleet to serve customers by split deliveries, has only minor effects which sometimes even might be negative with respect to travel distance. But the results of the experiments clearly demonstrate the substantial ecological benefits of using heterogeneous fleets.

References

1. Bundesamt für Güterverkehr: Marktbeobachtung Güterverkehr: Jahresbericht 2013 (2014)
2. Demir, E., Bektaş, T., Laporte, G.: A comparative analysis of several vehicle emission models for road freight transportation. Transportation Research Part D: Transport and Environment **16**(5), 347–357 (2011)
3. Demir, E., Bektaş, T., Laporte, G.: A review of recent research on green road freight transportation. European Journal of Operational Research **237**(3), 775–793 (2014)
4. Dror, M., Trudeau, P.: Savings by split delivery routing. Transportation Science, 141–145 (1989)
5. Hickman, J., Hassel, D., Joumard, R., Samaras, Z., Sorenson, S.: Methodology for calculating transport emissions and energy consumption (1999)
6. Knörr, W., Seum, S., Schied, M., Kutzner, F., Anthes, R.: Ecological Transport Information Tool for Worldwide Transports. Technical report (2011). http://www.ecotransit.org/download/ecotransit_background_report.pdf (accessed September 28, 2014)
7. Koç, Ç., Bektaş, T., Jabali, O., Laporte, G.: The fleet size and mix pollution-routing problem. Transportation Research Part B: Methodological **70**, 239–254 (2014)
8. Kopfer, H.W., Kopfer, H.: Emissions minimization vehicle routing problem in dependence of different vehicle classes. In: Kreowski, H.-J., Scholz-Reiter, B., Thoben, K.-D. (eds.) Dynamics in Logistics. Lecture Notes in Logistics, pp. 48–58. Springer (2013)
9. Kopfer, H.W., Schönberger, J., Kopfer, H.: Reducing greenhouse gas emissions of a heterogeneous vehicle fleet. Flexible Services and Manufacturing Journal **26**(1–2), 221–248 (2014)
10. Kwon, Y.-J., Choi, Y.-J., Lee, D.-H.: Heterogeneous fixed fleet vehicle routing considering carbon emission. Transportation Research Part D: Transport and Environment **23**, 81–89 (2013)
11. McKinnon, A., Piecyk, M.: Measuring and managing CO2 emission (2011). http://cefic-staging.amaze.com/Documents/IndustrySupport/Transport-and-Logistics/Sustainable%20Logistics/McKinnon%20Report%20Transport%20GHG%20emissions%2024.01.11.pdf (accessed November 06, 2014)
12. Schmied, M., Knörr, W.: Berechnung von Treibhausgasemissionen in Spedition und Logistik gemäß DIN EN 16258: Begriffe, Methoden, Beispiele 2. aktualisierte Auflage. Edited by Deutscher Speditions-und Logistikverband eV Öko-Institut eV (2013)
13. Scott, C., Urquhart, N., Hart, E.: Influence of topology and payload on CO2 optimised vehicle routing. In: Applications of Evolutionary Computation, pp. 141–150 (2010)
14. Solomon, M.M.: Algorithms for the vehicle routing and scheduling problems with time window constraints. Operations Research **35**(2), 254–265 (1987)

A Combined Liquefied Natural Gas Routing and Deteriorating Inventory Management Problem

Yousef Ghiami[1,2](✉), Tom Van Woensel[1,2], Marielle Christiansen[3], and Gilbert Laporte[4]

[1] School of Industrial Engineering and Innovation Sciences, OPAC and Eindhoven University of Technology, 5600 MB Eindhoven, The Netherlands
{y.ghiami,t.v.woensel}@tue.nl

[2] Dinalog, the Dutch Institute for Advanced Logistics, 4813 DA Breda, The Netherlands

[3] Department of Industrial Economics and Technology Management, Norwegian University of Science and Technology, 7491 Trondheim, Norway
marielle.christiansen@iot.ntnu.no

[4] CIRRELT and HEC Montréal, 3000 Chemin de la Côte-Sainte-Catherine, Montréal H3T 2A7, Canada
gilbert.laporte@cirrelt.ca

Abstract. Liquefied Natural Gas (LNG) is becoming a more crucial source of energy due to its increased price competitiveness and environmental friendliness. We consider an inventory routing problem for inland distribution of LNG from storage facilities to filling stations. Here, an actor is responsible for the inventory management at the storage facilities and filling stations, as well as the routing and scheduling of a heterogeneous fleet of vehicles. A characteristic of the problem is that a constant rate of LNG evaporates each day at the storage facilities and filling stations. This is in contrast to maritime LNG inventory routing problems where the evaporation is considered at the ships only. The combined LNG routing and deteriorating inventory management problem is modelled with both an arc-flow and a path-flow formulation. Both models are tested and compared on instances motivated from a real-world problem.

Keywords: Inventory routing problem · Deteriorating inventory · Liquefied natural gas · Arc-flow model · Path-flow model

1 Introduction

Inventory-routing problems (IRPs) are receiving more and more attention from the research community due to the increasing demand for new applications. IRPs integrate routing and inventory decisions by taking into account the trade-off between holding costs and routing costs. For an overview of the literature of IRPs see [4].

© Springer International Publishing Switzerland 2015
F. Corman et al. (Eds.): ICCL 2015, LNCS 9335, pp. 91–104, 2015.
DOI: 10.1007/978-3-319-24264-4_7

A subset of the IRP literature is dedicated to maritime transportation applications that address liquefied natural gas (LNG) distribution networks due to its fast growing market. In these networks, the natural gas is cooled down to a temperature of approximately ($-162°C$) where the gas reaches its liquid state and turns into LNG. This also reduces the volume of the gas by a factor of 610, which makes transportation and storage more efficient. The LNG is kept at a boiling state in the LNG distribution networks, so some of the LNG evaporates, and this gas, called boil-off, is used by some ships as fuel. A constant rate of the cargo capacity of the ship cargo tanks is boiling off each day during a voyage at sea, so some LNG is lost during transportation. As a general rule, about 0.15 % of storage content is lost every day. However, the boil-off rate depends on the vessel and the type of voyage [5]. This evaporation property is another main characteristic of LNG that makes it an interesting research topic. LNG is transported by ships from distant origins to ports close to a market from which inland distribution starts. Examples of maritime IRP applications for LNG can be found in [1], [8], [9], [10], [11], [13], [14], [15], and [16].

The existing literature of IRP for LNG distribution networks only addresses ship routing and scheduling and not inland distribution of LNG (see [3], and [4]). In addition, no evaporation of LNG in the storages at the ports are considered. In inland distribution, evaporation persists in storage facilities and filling stations. Current research on inland distribution operations shows that the evaporation of LNG in storage facilities and filling stations can be higher than experienced in LNG ships, and should be considered. However, the loss of LNG while it is transported between storage facilities and filling stations is almost zero due to short travelling time, and can therefore be disregarded.

In the literature, products like LNG are categorised as deteriorating inventory, an item of which a percentage of on-hand inventory is constantly lost due to, for instance, decay, evaporation, or spoilage. Reviews of deteriorating inventory are conducted by [2], [7], and [12]. According to the deteriorating inventory literature, deterioration rate varies and it can take relatively large values depending on the case (see [6]).

To our knowledge, no existing IRP model has considered deterioration in the storages. From a modelling point of view, incorporating deterioration at the storage facilities and filling stations into IRP does not add to the complexity of the problem. However, it introduces new trade-offs in the model that may have a large influence on the solution depending on the application.

The focus of this paper is the design of an LNG distribution network within the Netherlands. Such a system distributes LNG from storage facilities, usually located close to ports such as the Gate Terminal in Rotterdam, to a group of filling stations that are geographically scattered all over the country (or a larger area).

The remainder of this paper is organised as follows. Section 2 introduces the IRP application studied in this paper. The IRP is modelled with both arc-flow and path-flow formulations in Sections 3 and 4, respectively. In Section 5 some computational analyses are conducted to highlight the differences between the arc-flow and path-flow formulations for this specific application and also to show the effects of deterioration on the total cost function. This is followed by concluding remarks in Section 6.

2 Problem Description

LNG is transported by tankers from its origins to storage facilities located close to its market. The scope of the inland distribution network studied in this paper includes these storage facilities and the downstream customers (filling stations).

Storage facilities receive LNG in large quantities from tankers and hold the commodity to meet the filling stations' demand. These replenishments induce large fixed costs to the distribution system due to the high fixed cost of operating tankers and also costly loading and unloading operations. In order to keep LNG in its liquid state, the temperature of storage facilities and filling stations should be held at a very low level which results in a variable holding cost. LNG is subject to constant evaporation while kept in tank (storage facility or filling station). Filling stations place orders to storage facilities for LNG quantities and incur a fixed ordering cost.

The infrastructure of LNG distribution network in the Netherlands is at its early stage and currently there are only a few operating filling stations. There are, however, industrial customers who use LNG as the main fuel for their business. From a modelling point of view these customers are the same as filling stations with a demand rate that should be met by the same distribution network.

In this distribution network two modes of transportation are used, namely road, and sea that can deliver LNG from storage facilities to filling stations. Accessibility and flexibility make road by far the dominating mode for transportation in this distribution network. Apart road, a large network of water canals all over the country makes sea (short-sea shipping) an efficient mode for transportation in this network. Due to limited accessibility, rail has not yet been part of this distribution system. In order to benefit from the low transportation cost that rail can offer, there is an ongoing research on *containerised* LNG. Only after the establishment of this concept, intermodal transportation will be an option for this distribution network where containers of LNG could be transferred from one mode to another.

We consider a group of vehicles that belong to road or sea. The distance between each pair of nodes in this network can be traversed with different costs since the two vertices may be connected by more than one vehicle. Due to accessibility limits, not all vehicles can operate between each pair of vertices in this network. In this case, the travel cost between the two nodes is considered to be suitably large. Each time that a filling station or storage facility is visited by a vehicle, a fixed cost is incurred due to loading and unloading operations. No boil-off gas is assumed when LNG is being transported by a vehicle between storage facilities and filling stations. Figure 1 depicts an example of an LNG inland distribution network in the Netherlands.

The goal of this LNG inland distribution problem is to maximise the total profit of the system by setting the inventory and routing policies for pick-up

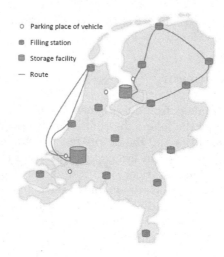

Fig. 1. LNG inland distribution network in the Netherlands

(storage facilities) and delivery (filling stations) points using the fleet of hetero-geneous vehicles. The revenues of the network are earned by the filling stations that meet the demand of the final customers. The cost function of the system includes fixed purchasing cost at the filling stations and at the storage facilities, variable purchasing cost at the storage facilities, holding cost at all nodes, routing cost, and vehicle fixed visiting cost.

It should be noted that the variable purchasing cost paid by the filling stations is a revenue for the storage facilities, hence in the total profit function of the integrated system they cancel out. It is assumed that the demand at the filling stations is known and shortages are not allowed. This means that the revenue function of the system (earned at the filling stations) is independent of the decision variables. It then seems logical to discard the revenue functions and replace the profit maximisation objective with a cost minimisation objective.

3   Arc-Flow Model

In this section we use an arc-flow formulation to model the problem described in Section 2. LNG is delivered from a set of storage facilities (pick-up points), $\mathcal{N}^P = \{1, ..., m\}$ to a set of filling stations (delivery points), $\mathcal{N}^D = \{m+1, ..., m+n\}$, using a set of vehicles, $\mathcal{V} = \{1, ..., k\}$. It is assumed that these vehicles belong to a set of vertices defined as $\mathcal{N}^V = \{m+n+1, ..., m+n+k\}$. Depending on the mode used for transporting LNG, the distance between two vertices may vary. The set of all storage facilities and filling stations in the network is given by $\mathcal{N}' = \mathcal{N}^P \cup \mathcal{N}^D$. A percentage (θ_i) of LNG constantly evaporates while being kept in node i $(i \in \mathcal{N}')$. It is assumed that there is no evaporation while LNG is being transported by vehicles.

In order to model this IRP with an arc-flow formulation we consider a graph $\mathcal{G} = (\mathcal{N}, \mathcal{A}_v)$, where $\mathcal{N} = \mathcal{N}^P \cup \mathcal{N}^D \cup \mathcal{N}^V$ is the set of all vertices in the distribution network and $\mathcal{A}_v = \{(i, j) : i, j \in \mathcal{N}, i \neq j, v \in \mathcal{V}\}$ is the arc set using a specific vehicle. The set of periods in the planning horizon is given by $\mathcal{T} = \{1, ..., H\}$.

In each period we define a route as follows. A vehicle starts its trip from its parking place towards a storage facility. After loading LNG, it visits a series of filling stations on the route to unload some quantities of LNG and eventually returns to its parking place. Each vehicle can visit a maximum of one storage facility on a route, whereas one storage facility can be visited by multiple vehicles during one period. We define binary variables w_{ivt} equal to one if and only if vehicle v visits vertex i ($i \in \mathcal{N}'$) during period t to load (or unload) LNG. In its visit to vertex i during period t, vehicle v loads (unloads) a quantity of q_{ivt}. To construct a route we define binary variables x_{ijvt} ($(i, j) \in \mathcal{A}_v$) equal to one if and only if vehicle v visits vertex j immediately after vertex i in period t.

The storage facilities and filling stations have an inventory capacity of $\bar{S}_i$ and a minimum allowed inventory level $\underline{S}_i$ ($i \in \mathcal{N}'$). The inventory level at storage facility or filling station i at the end of period t is given by the variable s_{it}. The initial inventory level at the beginning of the planning horizon at storage facility or filling station i is given by S_{i0}. At the beginning of period t, storage facility $i \in \mathcal{N}^P$ places an order quantity of y_{it} to its upstream supplier and instantly receives the replenishment. We define binary variable z_{it} equal to one if and only if storage facility i replenishes its inventory at time period t. Storage facility i dispatches a total quantity of $\sum_{v \in \mathcal{V}} q_{ivt}$ to filling stations at the beginning of period t. Having dealt with upstream suppliers and filling stations at the start of period t, storage facility i is left with the remaining inventory that gets depleted with rate θ_i due to deterioration throughout period t before ending with an inventory level of s_{it}.

At the start of period t, filling station $i \in \mathcal{N}^D$ receives a total amount of $\sum_{v \in \mathcal{V}} q_{ivt}$ after which the inventory level decreases throughout the period due to the demand rate D_{it} and deterioration rate θ_i.

Vehicle $v \in \mathcal{V}$ has a capacity of $\bar{V}_v$ and costs C_{ijv}^T to operate between vertices i and j ($(i, j) \in \mathcal{A}_v$). A suitably large value is assigned to C_{ijv}^T whenever vehicle v cannot travel on arc (i, j). A fixed cost of C_v^{FV} is incurred when vehicle v visits a vertex. In each trip, due to practical limitations, vehicle v can visit a maximum number of $\bar{N}_v^D$ filling stations.

3.1 Inventory Level at Vertices

The inventory level at filling station $i \in \mathcal{N}^D$ at the beginning of period t is the sum of the inventory level at the end of the previous period and the quantities delivered by the vehicles at the start of the period:

$$s_{it}^D(t' = 0) = s_{i(t-1)} + \sum_{v \in \mathcal{V}} q_{ivt}. \tag{1}$$

This inventory level is depleted throughout the period due to demand and evaporation. The evaporation results in a continuous loss of θ_i percent of on-hand inventory. The following differential equation represents the changes in the inventory level during period t:

$$\frac{ds_{it}^D(t')}{dt'} = -\theta_i s_{it}^D(t') - D_{it}. \tag{2}$$

Solving this differential equation leads to the following inventory level at the filling station i in period t. Note that t is the unit of time of which we analyse the inventory level and t' is the time parameter of which the value changes from $t' = 0$ (the start of the period) to $t' = 1$ (the end of the period):

$$s_{it}^D(t') = -\frac{D_{it}}{\theta_i} + K\,e^{-\theta_i t'}, \tag{3}$$

where K is a positive constant. Considering the initial inventory of filling station i at period t presented in (1) as the boundary condition, the inventory level of this station throughout period t is obtained as

$$s_{it}^D(t') = -\frac{D_{it}}{\theta_i} + \left[s_{i(t-1)} + \sum_{v \in \mathcal{V}} q_{ivt} + \frac{D_{it}}{\theta_i} \right] e^{-\theta_i t'}. \tag{4}$$

Equation (4) gives the exact inventory level of the filling station at any moment during period t. The inventory level at the end of period t ($t' = 1$) is hence given by

$$s_{it} = \left[s_{i(t-1)} + \sum_{v \in \mathcal{V}} q_{ivt} \right] e^{-\theta_i} - \frac{D_{it}}{\theta_i} \left(1 - e^{-\theta_i} \right), \qquad \forall i \in \mathcal{N}^D,\, t \in \mathcal{T}. \tag{5}$$

In storage facility $i \in \mathcal{N}^P$ the inventory level changes according to a different pattern since the demand is realised in batches at the beginning of each period. Since all inventory transactions are performed at the start of each period, the inventory level decreases over the period due to evaporation only. The inventory level at storage facility i at the beginning of period t after the above-mentioned transactions is given by

$$s_{it}^P(t' = 0) = s_{i(t-1)} + y_{it} - \sum_{v \in \mathcal{V}} q_{ivt}. \tag{6}$$

The changes of inventory level at this storage facility over period t is shown by the following differential equation:

$$\frac{ds_{it}^P(t')}{dt'} = -\theta_i s_{it}^P(t'). \tag{7}$$

Considering the boundary condition shown in (6), solving differential equation (7) results in the following inventory level for storage facility i over time period t:

$$s_{it}^P(t') = \left[s_{i(t-1)} + y_{it} - \sum_{v \in \mathcal{V}} q_{ivt} \right] e^{-\theta_i t'}. \tag{8}$$

The inventory level at the end of this time period is hence given by

$$
s_{it} = \left[s_{i(t-1)} + y_{it} - \sum_{v \in \mathcal{V}} q_{ivt} \right] e^{-\theta_i}, \qquad \forall i \in \mathcal{N}^P,\ t \in \mathcal{T}. \tag{9}
$$

In the following section, we derive the objective function and the constrains using inventory levels of storage facilities and filling stations.

3.2 Objective Function and Constraints

Replenishment at filling station i in period t incurs a fixed purchasing cost of C_i^F. The sum of all these costs over the planning horizon is given by

$$
FC^D = \sum_{i \in \mathcal{N}^D} \sum_{v \in \mathcal{V}} \sum_{t \in \mathcal{T}} C_i^F w_{ivt}. \tag{10}
$$

At the start of period t, storage facility i receives a quantity y_{it} for which it pays a unit price of C_{it}^P. This replenishment also results in a fixed cost of C_i^F for the storage facility. The total (fixed and variable) purchasing cost incurred by all the storage facilities over the planning horizon is as follows:

$$
FC^P = \sum_{i \in \mathcal{N}^P} \sum_{t \in \mathcal{T}} (C_i^F z_{it} + C_{it}^P y_{it}). \tag{11}
$$

The cost of routing includes fixed and variable costs. The total value of all fixed costs of vehicle v in period t is $\sum_{i \in \mathcal{N}'} C_v^{FV} w_{ivt}$. The variable cost of a route is obtained by summing up the transportation cost between each two nodes on the route: $\sum_{i \in \mathcal{N}} \sum_{j \in \mathcal{N}, (i,j) \in \mathcal{A}_v} C_{ijv}^T x_{ijvt}$. The total routing cost is hence given by

$$
\begin{aligned}
RC^A = &\sum_{v \in \mathcal{V}} \sum_{t \in \mathcal{T}} \sum_{i \in \mathcal{N}} \sum_{j \in \mathcal{N}, (i,j) \in \mathcal{A}_v} C_{ijv}^T x_{ijvt} \\
&+ \sum_{v \in \mathcal{V}} \sum_{t \in \mathcal{T}} \sum_{i \in \mathcal{N}'} C_v^{FV} w_{ivt}.
\end{aligned} \tag{12}
$$

In order to obtain the total holding cost at filling station $i \in \mathcal{N}^D$ over the planning horizon, the holding cost of each period is first calculated using the inventory level presented in (4). It is assumed that a unit holding cost of C_i^H is incurred per unit of time when keeping LNG at vertex $i \in \mathcal{N}^P$:

$$
\begin{aligned}
HC_{it}^D &= \int_0^1 C_i^H s_{it}^D(t')dt' \\
&= \frac{C_i^H \left[1 - e^{-\theta_i} \right]}{\theta_i} \left[s_{i(t-1)} + \sum_{v \in \mathcal{V}} q_{ivt} + \frac{D_{it}}{\theta_i} \right] - \frac{C_i^H D_{it}}{\theta_i}.
\end{aligned} \tag{13}
$$

The total holding cost of all filling stations is hence given by

$$
HC^D = \sum_{i \in \mathcal{N}^D} \sum_{t \in \mathcal{T}} HC_{it}^D. \tag{14}
$$

The inventory holding cost at the storage facilities is obtained in a similar way to filling stations. Using the inventory level at storage facility $i \in \mathcal{N}^P$ presented in (8), the inventory holding cost over period t at the storage facility is

$$
\begin{aligned}
HC_{it}^P &= \int_0^1 C_i^H s_{it}^P(t') dt' \\
&= \frac{C_i^H \left[1 - e^{-\theta_i}\right]}{\theta_i} \left[s_{i(t-1)} + y_{it} - \sum_{v \in \mathcal{V}} q_{ivt} \right].
\end{aligned}
\tag{15}
$$

The total holding cost incurred at all the storage facilities is then

$$
HC^P = \sum_{i \in \mathcal{N}^P} \sum_{t \in \mathcal{T}} HC_{it}^P.
\tag{16}
$$

Considering all the costs obtained in this section, the objective function of the model is

$$
\text{Minimise } TC^{ARC} = FC^D + FC^P + RC^A + HC^D + HC^P.
\tag{17}
$$

The constraints on the inventory levels at the filling stations and the storage facilities are presented in (5) and (9), respectively. The remaining constraints are as follows:

$$
s_{i(t-1)} + \sum_{v \in \mathcal{V}} q_{ivt} \leq \bar{S}_i, \qquad \forall i \in \mathcal{N}^D, t \in \mathcal{T},
\tag{18}
$$

$$
s_{i(t-1)} + y_{it} - \sum_{v \in \mathcal{V}} q_{ivt} \leq \bar{S}_i, \qquad \forall i \in \mathcal{N}^P, t \in \mathcal{T},
\tag{19}
$$

$$
s_{it} \geq \underline{S}_i, \qquad \forall i \in \mathcal{N}', t \in \mathcal{T},
\tag{20}
$$

$$
\sum_{i \in \mathcal{N}^P} w_{ivt} \leq 1, \qquad \forall v \in \mathcal{V}, t \in \mathcal{T},
\tag{21}
$$

$$
\sum_{i \in \mathcal{N}^D} w_{ivt} \leq \bar{N}_v^D, \qquad \forall v \in \mathcal{V}, t \in \mathcal{T},
\tag{22}
$$

$$
y_{it} \leq (\bar{S}_i - \underline{S}_i) z_{it}, \qquad \forall i \in \mathcal{N}^P, t \in \mathcal{T},
\tag{23}
$$

$$
\sum_{i \in \mathcal{N}^P} q_{ivt} = \sum_{j \in \mathcal{N}^D} q_{jvt}, \qquad \forall v \in \mathcal{V}, t \in \mathcal{T},
\tag{24}
$$

$$
q_{ivt} \leq \min\{\bar{S}_i - \underline{S}_i, \bar{V}_v\} w_{ivt}, \qquad \forall i \in \mathcal{N}', v \in \mathcal{V}, t \in \mathcal{T},
\tag{25}
$$

$$
\sum_{j \in \mathcal{V}, j \neq v} w_{(m+n+j)vt} = 0, \qquad \forall v \in \mathcal{V}, t \in \mathcal{T},
\tag{26}
$$

$$
x_{(m+n+v)ivt} = w_{ivt}, \qquad \forall i \in \mathcal{N}^P, v \in \mathcal{V}, t \in \mathcal{T},
\tag{27}
$$

$$
\sum_{i \in \mathcal{N}^P} w_{ivt} = \sum_{j \in \mathcal{N}^D} x_{j(m+n+v)vt}, \qquad \forall v \in \mathcal{V}, t \in \mathcal{T},
\tag{28}
$$

$$\sum_{j\in\mathcal{N},(j,i)\in\mathcal{A}_v} x_{jivt} + \sum_{j\in\mathcal{N},(i,j)\in\mathcal{A}_v} x_{ijvt} = 2w_{ivt}, \qquad \forall i \in \mathcal{N},\ v \in \mathcal{V},\ t \in \mathcal{T}, \quad (29)$$

$$\sum_{i\in\mathcal{M}}\sum_{j\in\mathcal{M},i\neq j} x_{ijvt} \leq \sum_{i\in\mathcal{M}} w_{ivt} - w_{kvt}, \qquad \forall \mathcal{M} \subseteq \mathcal{N}^D,\ k \in \mathcal{M},\ v \in \mathcal{V},\ t \in \mathcal{T},$$

$$(30)$$

$$q_{ivt} \geq 0, \qquad \forall i \in \mathcal{N}',\ v \in \mathcal{V},\ t \in \mathcal{T}, \qquad (31)$$

$$y_{it} \geq 0, \qquad \forall i \in \mathcal{N}^P,\ t \in \mathcal{T}, \qquad (32)$$

$$z_{it} \in \{0,1\}, \qquad \forall i \in \mathcal{N}^P,\ t \in \mathcal{T}, \qquad (33)$$

$$w_{ivt} \in \{0,1\}, \qquad \forall i \in \mathcal{N}',\ v \in \mathcal{V},\ t \in \mathcal{T}, \qquad (34)$$

$$x_{ijvt} \in \{0,1\}, \qquad \forall (i,j) \in \mathcal{A}_v,\ v \in \mathcal{V},\ t \in \mathcal{T}. \qquad (35)$$

Constraints (18) and (19) keep the inventory level at vertex i at the start of period t less than or equal to the available capacity, while constraints (20) impose the minimum acceptable inventory level at vertex i during period t. Constraints (21) and (22) limit the number of storage facilities and filling stations visited by vehicle v in period t to one and $\bar{N}_v^D$, respectively. Constraints (23) guarantee that order quantities received by storage facilities stay within the allowed limits. Constraints (24) control that the sum of the amounts delivered to filling stations by a vehicle equals the amount picked up by the vehicle from assigned storage facility. Constraints (25) link the routing variables to the quantities delivered to the filling stations. Each vehicle has a designated parking place, which is imposed by constraints (26). Constraints (27) and (28) ensure that a vehicle (if assigned) starts its route from its parking place and at the end of the route traverses an arc from one of the filling stations to it parking place. Constraints (29) and (30) represent degree constraints and subtour eliminations constraints, respectively. Constraints (31)–(35) impose non-negativity and integrality conditions to the relevant decision variables.

4   Path-Flow Model

In order to model this distribution system with a path-flow formulation, we consider all sets defined in Section 3 except for arc set $\mathcal{A}_v$ which is replaced with path set $\mathcal{R}_v$. Here a path is defined as the shortest route that consecutively connects a parking place of a particular vehicle, a storage facility, a group of filling stations and finally the same parking place.

In this formulation all the feasible paths are generated a priori. In order to generate a feasible path for a specific vehicle in the path-flow model, it should visit one storage facility, and a maximum number of filling stations, and eventually its parking place from which it starts the trip. To do so we generate all the subsets of $\mathcal{N}^D$ that include a maximum of $\bar{N}_v^D$ filling stations. We then complete each generated path by adding different combinations of "vehicle-storage facility". In order to guarantee the shortest path, we optimise the order of the filling stations on the path.

Binary parameter A_{ivr} equals to one if and only if vehicle $v \in \mathcal{V}$ visits vertex $i \in \mathcal{N}'$ on path $r \in \mathcal{R}_v$. We define binary variable λ_{vtr} equal to one if and only if vehicle v traverses path r in period t. Parameter C_{vr}^T includes the transportation cost (C_{ijv}^T) and a fixed visiting cost (C_v^{FV}) incurred when vehicle v follows path r. This parameter also includes the set-up cost that each filling station should pay when visited by a vehicle (C_i^F, $i \in \mathcal{N}^D$).

In the path-flow model the inventory level calculations of storage facilities and filling stations stay the same as presented in Section 3.1.

4.1   Objective Function and Constraints

In this section, we include the same costs in the objective function as in Section 3.2, however due to changes in the decision variables the cost formulations are modified accordingly.

The sum of all fixed and variable transportation costs and set-up costs at the filling stations is obtained as follows:

$$RC^P = \sum_{v \in \mathcal{V}} \sum_{t \in \mathcal{T}} \sum_{r \in \mathcal{R}_v} C_{vr}^T \lambda_{vtr}. \tag{36}$$

This cost function is equivalent to the sum of costs presented in (10) and (12). The cost functions (11), (14), and (16) remain unchanged. The objective function of the path-flow formulation is hence given by

$$\text{Minimise } TC^{PATH} = FC^P + RC^P + HC^D + HC^P. \tag{37}$$

The constraints of the path-flow formulation are as follows. The inventory levels at the filling stations and storage facilities are as presented in (5) and (9), respectively. Constraints (18) and (19) define upper bounds on the inventory levels at vertices while constraints (20) set lower bounds. Constraints (23) are to limit the batch sizes that are received by storage facilities while constraints (24) guarantee the sum of delivered quantities in a trip is equal to the amount picked up from the storage facility. The following constraints link the routing and quantity variables:

$$q_{ivt} \le \sum_{r \in \mathcal{R}_v} \min\{\bar{S}_i - \underline{S}_i, \bar{V}_v\} A_{ivr} \lambda_{vtr}, \qquad \forall i \in \mathcal{N}', \, v \in \mathcal{V}, \, t \in \mathcal{T}. \tag{38}$$

We define the following constraints to ensure that in time period t, vehicle v can travel on at most one path:

$$\sum_{r \in \mathcal{R}_v} \lambda_{vtr} \le 1, \qquad v \in \mathcal{V}, \, t \in \mathcal{T}. \tag{39}$$

Finally, non-negativity and integrality conditions are imposed by constraints (31)–(33) together with the following:

$$\lambda_{vtr} \in \{0,1\}, \qquad \forall r \in \mathcal{R}_v, \, v \in \mathcal{V}, \, t \in \mathcal{T}. \tag{40}$$

Having all the paths determined a priori, there is no need for the routing constraints (21)–(22) and (26)–(30).

In the next section we analyse two numerical examples to compare the two formulations when the size of an instance changes and also to study the effect of deterioration on the objective function.

5   Computational Results

In this section we present two numerical examples. In the first one we conduct a comparison between the two formulations introduced in this paper to see how they perform when the size of the network increases. In the second example we show how deterioration rate can influence the optimal solution.

5.1   Example 1

The two formulations described in Sections 3 and 4 were implemented in Java using CPLEX. The code was run on a personal computer with Intel V 2.00GHz processor and 8.00 GB RAM. In the computational analysis, one storage facility is assumed to serve a group of filling stations using a fleet of four vehicles over a two-day period.

In order to construct all feasible paths in the path-flow model, we first generate all the subsets of $\mathcal{N}^D$. In the next step we assign one vehicle and one storage facility to the subsets. Since all the nodes of the path are determined, we have a travelling salesman problem. We solve this problem using the tabu search algorithm, coding in Java, to minimise the travelling cost of the path.

Having all the paths generated, we run the two models for different instances. The result of this analysis is reported in Table 1. It should be noted that for the path-flow formulation, the runtime does not include the time used for path generation.

The initial results show that the path-flow formulation solves the same problem much faster than the arc-flow formulation. Enumerating paths can take a relatively long time, however, it is a one-off task to perform. This means for

Table 1. Computational results when the number of filling stations varies

n m k H	Arc-flow				Path-flow			
	Runtime	Number of			Runtime	Number of		
		Variables	Constraints	Nodes		Variables	Constraints	Nodes
5 1 4 2	0.4	865	822	176	0.3	313	78	487
7 1 4 2	2.0	1237	3802	414	1.0	1101	98	1263
9 1 4 2	109.2	1673	18686	2719	5.5	4193	118	2705
10 1 4 2	1025.1	1915	41232	8546	94.0	8299	128	37739
11 1 4 2	18111.2	2173	90402	21958	716.9	16501	138	215330
12 1 4 2	100418.3	2447	196916	23269	9751.0	32895	148	1384076

a given number of filling stations we need to generate the paths once and the path-flow model could be solved very frequently (i.e. on a daily basis) using these generated paths. This can continue until a new filling station is added to the network which necessitates generating the new set of all paths. This however is not applicable to the arc-flow model as we should include all the subtour elimination constraints each time that we run the model.

5.2   Example 2

The deterioration rate for LNG in deep-sea shipping is around 0.15%. LNG inland distribution networks are evolving. Therefore, it is hard to give a specific rate for the boil-off. However, based on the current practices, we can say that the rate is higher than what is the case in sea shipping operations. Here we run the IRP developed in this paper for deterioration rate changing from 0 to 2%.

In order to illustrate the effect of the evaporation we analyse two different networks and obtain the change in the objective function when the deterioration is taken into account. The results of this analysis are illustrated in Table 2.

Table 2. The effects of the deterioration on the total cost function

					Deterioration rate (%)				
				0.0	0.5	1.0	1.5	2.0
				Total	Increase in			
n	m	k	H	cost	total cost* (%)			
4	1	3	6	9239	1.03	1.67	2.27	2.91
6	1	3	6	14063	2.99	3.88	4.54	5.23

*Compared with the case with no deterioration

Table 2 shows that a network of four filling stations, one storage facility, and three vehicles over a six-day planning horizon incurs a total cost of 9239 when no deterioration is taken into account. This experiment shows that if for instance the real deterioration rate is as high as 2%, the accurate total cost is 2.91% more than the case when the deterioration is not modelled.

We examine the same network with an increase in the number of the filling stations while the number of vehicles remains unchanged. The initial results show that in cases where the transportation resources are tight the model tends to keep more inventory in filling stations which results in more deterioration. The analysis of this network shows that for example the total cost of the system increases by 5.23% when there is a deterioration rate of 2%.

6   Conclusion

We have analysed an IRP for LNG inland distribution network taking into account the evaporation property of the item. We have modelled the distribution network with both arc-flow and path-flow formulations. The basic variant of each formulation has been derived and solved by CPLEX.

The results of the computational analysis conducted in this paper show that the path-flow formulation can solve the problem faster compared with the arc-flow model. Moreover, the analysis indicates that disregarding the deterioration rate even in a small instance of this model could result in a relatively large underestimation in the total cost. These initial results suggest that the deterioration property should be incorporated into the model as the underestimation may be significant depending on the instance. The computational analysis also shows that including deterioration in the model does not add to the complexity of the problem.

References

1. Andersson, H., Christiansen, M., Desaulniers, G.: A new decomposition algorithm for a liquefied natural gas inventory routing problem. International Journal of Production Research (2015). doi:10.1080/00207543.2015.1037024
2. Bakker, M., Riezebos, J., Teunter, R.H.: Review of inventory systems with deterioration since 2001. European Journal of Operational Research **221**(2), 275–284 (2012)
3. Christiansen, M., Fagerholt, K., Nygreen, B., Ronen, D.: Ship routing and scheduling in the new millennium. European Journal of Operational Research **228**(3), 467–483 (2013)
4. Coelho, L., Cordeau, J.-F., Laporte, G.: Thirty years of inventory routing. Transportation Science **48**(1), 1–19 (2014)
5. Fodstad, M., Uggen, K.T., Rømo, F., Lium, A.-G., Stremersch, G., Hecq, S.: LNGScheduler: A rich model for coordinating vessel routing, inventories and trade in the liquefied natural gas supply chain. Journal of Energy **3**(4), 31–64 (2010)
6. Ghiami, Y.: Models for production and inventory systems for deteriorating items with a supply-chain perspective. Doctoral Thesis, Southampton Business School, University of Southampton (2014)
7. Goyal, S.K., Giri, B.C.: Recent trends in modeling of deteriorating inventory. European Journal of Operational Research **134**(1), 1–16 (2001)
8. Grønhaug, R., Christiansen, M., Desaulniers, G., Desrosiers, J.: A branch-and-price method for a liquefied natural gas inventory routing problem. Transportation Science **44**(3), 400–415 (2010)
9. Halvorsen-Weare, E.E., Fagerholt, K.: Routing and scheduling in a liquefied natural gas shipping problem with inventory and berth constraints. Annals of Operations Research **203**(1), 167–186 (2013)
10. Halvorsen-Weare, E.E., Fagerholt, K., Rönnqvist, M.: Vessel routing and scheduling under uncertainty in the liquefied natural gas business. Computers & Industrial Engineering **64**(1), 290–301 (2013)
11. Papageorgiou, D.J., Nemhauser, G.L., Sokol, J., Cheon, M.S., Keha, A.B.: MIRPLib - A library of maritime inventory routing problem instances: Survey, core model, and benchmark results. European Journal of Operational Research **235**(2), 350–366 (2014)
12. Raafat, F.: Survey of literature on continuously deteriorating inventory models. Journal of the Operational Research Society **42**(1), 27–37 (1991)

13. Rakke, J.G., Andersson, H., Christiansen, M., Desaulniers, G.: A new formulation based on customer delivery patterns for a maritime inventory routing problem. Transportation Science **49**(2), 384–401 (2015)
14. Rakke, J.G., Stålhane, M., Moe, C.R., Andersson, H., Christiansen, M., Fagerholt, K., Norstad, I.: A rolling horizon heuristic for creating a liquefied natural gas annual delivery program. Transportation Research Part C **19**(5), 896–911 (2011)
15. Shao, Y., Furman, K.C., Goel, V., Hoda, S.: A hybrid heuristic strategy for liquefied natural gas inventory routing. Transportation Research Part C **53**, 151–171 (2015)
16. Stålhane, M., Rakke, J.G., Moe, C.R., Andersson, H., Christiansen, M., Fagerholt, K.: A constructive and improvement heuristic for a liquefied natural gas inventory routing problem. Computers & Industrial Engineering **62**(1), 245–255 (2012)

An Ant Colony-Based Matheuristic Approach for Solving a Class of Vehicle Routing Problems

Umman Mahir Yıldırım[1,2(✉)] and Bülent Çatay[2]

[1] School of Industrial Engineering, Eindhoven University of Technology,
5600 MB, Eindhoven, The Netherlands
U.M.Yildirim@tue.nl, mahiryldrm@sabanciuniv.edu
[2] Faculty of Engineering and Natural Sciences, Sabanci University, 34956, Istanbul, Turkey
catay@sabanciuniv.edu

Abstract. We propose a matheuristic approach to solve several types of vehicle routing problems (VRP). In the VRP, a fleet of capacitated vehicles visits a set of customers exactly once to satisfy their demands while obeying problem specific characteristics and constraints such as homogeneous or heterogeneous fleet, customer service time windows, single or multiple depots. The proposed matheuristic is based on an ant colony optimization (ACO) algorithm which constructs good feasible solutions. The routes obtained in the ACO procedure are accumulated in a pool as columns which are then fed to an integer programming (IP) optimizer that solves the set-partitioning (-covering) formulation of the particular VRP. The (near-)optimal solution found by the solver is used to reinforce the pheromone trails in ACO. This feedback mechanism between the ACO and IP procedures helps the matheuristic better converge to high quality solutions. We test the performance of the proposed matheuristic on different VRP variants using well-known benchmark instances from the literature. Our computational experiments reveal competitive results: we report six new best solutions and meet the best-known solution in 120 instances out of 193.

Keywords: Vehicle routing problem · Matheuristic · Ant colony optimization

1   Introduction

There is an increasing trend towards matheuristics in the recent literature as they incorporate relatively fast and effective solutions while preserving the solution quality. Matheuristics can do so by combining heuristics/metaheuristics with exact solution approaches. According to Boschetti et al. (2009), the interoperation of metaheuristics and mathematical programming techniques yields the matheuristics. The metaheuristic further exploits the features derived by the mathematical model of the problem. Bertazzi and Speranza (2011) simply define a matheuristic as any heuristic that uses mathematical programming in one of its solution steps such as solving sub-problems, solving parts of an instance, restricting the search space and exploring neighborhoods.

© Springer International Publishing Switzerland 2015
F. Corman et al. (Eds.): ICCL 2015, LNCS 9335, pp. 105–119, 2015.
DOI: 10.1007/978-3-319-24264-4_8

Matheuristics have been widely used to solve various VRPs. Doerner and Schmid (2010) define three matheuristic categories based on set-partitioning/set-covering formulations, local branching and decomposition within the VRP context. They further label the first category as integrative approaches where the set-partitioning/set-covering component is responsible for the selection of the routes based on a given subset of feasible routes. The feasible routes are iteratively accumulated in this pool by means of a heuristic/metaheuristic. Different VRP variants have been solved adopting this approach.

Groër et al. (2010) and Kelly and Xu (1999) solve the CVRP using a set-partitioning based approach whereas Groër et al. (2011) combine a local search heuristic with integer programming (IP). Alvarenga et al. (2007) hybridize a genetic algorithm with set-partitioning formulation of the VRPTW. For the same problem, Yıldırım and Çatay (2014) implement a matheuristic using parallel ant colony optimization (ACO). Using an IP-based heuristic, Gulczynski et al. (2011) solve the periodic VRP. Pirkwieser and Raidl (2009) solve the periodic variant with time windows using a multiple variable neighborhood search. For the split delivery VRP, Archetti et al (2008) implemented a Tabu Search (TS) approach. They identified the promising parts of the solution space with the TS and further explored them using IP. Recently, Subramanian et al. (2012) and Subramanian et al. (2013) have coupled iterated local search (ILS) with mixed IP (MIP) in a matheuristic framework. The most recent study belongs to Boschetti and Maniezzo (2015) who apply a set-covering based matheuristic to a real-world city logistics problem tailored for mid-sized cities. The set-partitioning/set-covering based matheuristic approach is also adopted in a stochastic environment by Mendoza and Villegas (2012) to solve the stochastic VRP.

A survey on matheuristics can be found in Maniezzo et al. (2010). For a detailed survey on matheuristics for Rich VRP and for routing problems, we refer the reader to Doerner and Schmid (2010) and Archetti and Speranza (2014), respectively.

This brief review shows that matheuristics have been applied to many VRPs. Yet, most were developed for a particular variant of the problem. In this study, we propose a general solution approach that is applied to a class of VRPs. The contributions of the paper are as follows: First, we propose a matheuristic framework capable of solving different variants of the VRP. Second, we compare the performance of using set-covering formulation to that of using set-partitioning formulation within the IP procedure. Although the gain was questioned in the literature (Russell and Chiang, 2006), to the best of our knowledge these two formulations have never been compared extensively in a matheuristic context. Furthermore, we investigate a novel implementation of ACO tailored for solving the heterogeneous VRP (HVRP) and multi-depot VRP (MDVRP). Finally, we report improved solutions on six problem instances.

The remainder of this paper is structured as follows. Section 2 presents the proposed matheuristic and its implementation to different VRP variants. Computational experiments and results are given in Section 3. Section 4 concludes the paper.

2   The Proposed Matheuristic

2.1   Description

The proposed matheuristic (namely MathAS) is based on two main components: an ant system (AS) that generates feasible routes and an IP optimizer. The generated routes are fed into the set-covering (SC) or set-partitioning (SP) formulation of the VRP where they are regarded as columns of the model. The chance of obtaining (near-)optimal solutions increases with the increasing number of distinct columns in the IP model.

A major advantage of using an ant-based approach is its ease of parallel implementation. In our matheuristic, we implement an agent-level based parallelization where ants in the colony construct their solutions in parallel. At the end of each iteration these solutions are collected within a solution pool and are used to update the pheromone trails, a structure that mimics the implicit communication mechanism of the real ants.

We use the elitist version of the rank-based AS of Bullnheimer et al. (1999) which has two main components. The first component is pheromone trail intensity (τ_{ij}), which is the cumulative pheromone amount between customers i and j. The second component, namely visibility (η_{ij}), corresponds to the desirability of visiting customer j after customer i. Note that τ_{ij} is updated after each iteration whereas η_{ij} is a static information. For an ant k currently located at customer i, the selection of the next customer is based on these two components and given with the following random proportional rule:

$$p_{ij}^k = \frac{[\tau_{ij}]^\alpha [\eta_{ij}]^\beta}{\sum_{l \in N_i^k} [\tau_{il}]^\alpha [\eta_{il}]^\beta} \tag{1}$$

where N_i^k refers to the set of customers that can be visited after customer i and are unvisited by the kth ant. The relative weight of the pheromone trail intensity τ_{ij} and the visibility η_{ij} are controlled by the non-negative parameters α and β respectively.

The pheromone trails are initialized by setting them equal to the inverse of the total distance found in an initial solution. The initial solution is obtained by using the nearest neighbor heuristic. In the pheromone update procedure, the pheromone trails are first evaporated and then reinforced using a subset of best performing ants. The amount of pheromone deposited on each arc of the pheromone network depends on the rank of the solution quality found by the ants. The pheromone update procedure is performed as follows:

$$\tau_{ij} \leftarrow (1-\rho)\tau_{ij} + \sum_{k=1}^{w-1} \Delta\tau_{ij}^k, \forall (i,j) \tag{2}$$

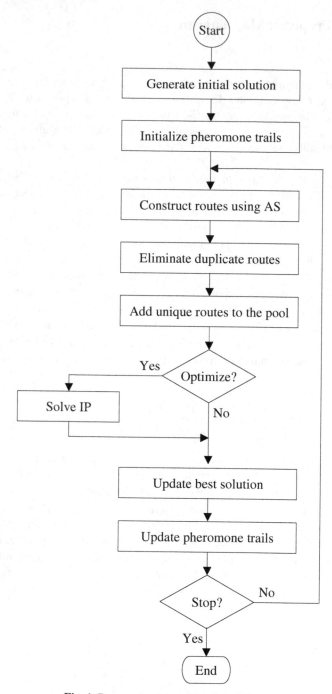

Fig. 1. Proposed ant-based matheuristic

where ρ $(0 < \rho \leq 1)$ is a parameter to control the evaporation rate. (i,j) and $\Delta\tau_{ij}^{k}$ refer to the arc between customers i and j and the amount of pheromone on that arc deposited by ant k respectively. The pheromone deposited is inversely proportional to the rank of the ant in the colony in terms of solution quality. In other words, among the best w-1 ants and the ant that has found the best solution so far (the best-so-far ant, bs), the pheromone amounts deposited by the kth ant ($\Delta\tau_{ij}^{k}$) and bs ($\Delta\tau_{ij}^{bs}$) are $(w-k)/L_k$ and w/L_{bs} respectively. Here, L_k and L_{bs} denote the length (cost) of the complete solution built by k^{th} ant and bs.

At the end of each iteration, all the routes are collected in a solution pool. This step includes a check procedure to eliminate duplicate routes (Yıldırım and Çatay, 2014). After a predetermined number of iterations, the IP model is solved in an attempt to find a better solution. This solution is used to further enhance the pheromone trails.

When the SC formulation is used in the IP procedure, the solution might be infeasible in terms of the number of visits made to a customer; i.e. a customer may be serviced by multiple vehicles. To overcome this problem, the algorithm includes a post-processing step which keeps the cheapest visit and removes the other(s). The general framework of MathAS is given in Fig. 1.

2.2   Implementation to VRP Variants

In this section we give the definitions and the implementation details of the VRP variants considered in this study. Note that the proposed method is generic in the sense that it is capable of solving different VRP variants. That is, the main framework of the algorithm is common for all of the variants. Nevertheless, we also utilize variant dependent implementations for the Heterogeneous VRP and the Multi-depot VRP.

Capacitated VRP
The capacitated VRP (CVRP) aims to serve a set of geographically dispersed customers with known demands by using a homogeneous fleet of capacitated vehicles located at a central depot. The objective is to determine the best set of routes that minimizes either the total distance travelled or the number of routes while complying with the following constraints: (i) every route starts and ends at the central depot; (ii) each customer is assigned to a single route; and (iii) the vehicle capacity is not exceeded. We apply MathAS to CVRP in its basic form as described above.

Open VRP
Open VRP (OVRP) differs from CVRP in the sense that the vehicles do not have to return to the depot after the last visited customer. The implementation of MathAS is the same as in the CVRP; however, the ants are not allowed to return to the depot.

Heterogeneous VRP
VRP with heterogeneous fleet (HVRP) extends the CVRP by introducing a fleet with a limited number of vehicles with different capacities. In addition, a fixed and a variable cost are also introduced for each vehicle. The problem is referred to as fleet size mix problem (FSM) when the fleet size is not limited.

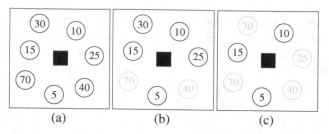

Fig. 2. Solving the HVRP problem for each vehicle type separately

In the case of HVRP, MathAS uses multiple ant colonies, each solving a CVRP using a homogenous fleet of a different vehicle type. Fig. 2 shows an example which includes seven customers (circles) and a depot (square). The numbers in the circles represent the demands for the corresponding customer. Suppose the fleet consists of three vehicle types with capacities of 80, 30 and 20. Since the first vehicle type is large enough, all customers can be serviced (Fig. 2.a). On the other hand, the second vehicle type cannot accommodate the demand sizes 70 and 40. So, the problem is reduced as shown in Fig 2.b by eliminating these customers and solved by AS using the second vehicle type only. A similar reduction approach is applied for the third vehicle type as shown in Fig. 2.c. At the end of this procedure three ant colonies provide a collection of solutions to three different homogeneous VRP problems. Then, MathAS combines this pool of routes into to the set of columns and solves the IP formulation of HVRP using an optimizer.

Multi-Depot VRP
In the Multi-Depot VRP (MDVRP) multiple depots are available to serve the customers and there is no restriction on the number of customers that each depot can serve. In this case, we implement MathAS in a similar fashion as in HVRP: each ant colony solves a sub-problem which consists of the CVRP using a different depot. After collecting all the routes found in the sub-problems into a single set of columns, the IP model of the original MDVRP is solved using an optimizer.

VRP with Time Windows (VRPTW)
VRPTW extends the CVRP by introducing the earliest and latest visiting times for each customer, namely time windows. Although the implementation is similar to that of CVRP, time window violation is checked each time a new customer is visited. Here, we use the Time-based AS (TbAS) approach proposed in Yildirim and Çatay (2012) which utilizes the time-window restriction in the visibility mechanism of AS. Basically, TbAS divides the planning horizon into several time intervals and considers the timing of the visit to a node as implicit heuristic information in the route construction phase. So, it creates a separate pheromone network for each time interval and allows the ants to deposit pheromones on the relevant arcs of the pheromone network corresponding to the time interval within which the node is visited.

The pheromone mechanism of TbAS is illustrated in Fig. 3. The planning horizon is divided into three time intervals and a pheromone network is associated with each interval as shown in Fig. 3.a. In the bottom network, the arcs emanating from the depot to the customers have more pheromone trails since this network belongs to the first time interval (e.g. morning). On the other hand, the pheromone levels on the arcs directed from the customers to the depot are higher on the top network as it corresponds to the last time interval (e.g. evening). The middle network shows the pheromones accumulated on the arcs which are traversed in the second time interval (e.g. noon). In Fig. 3.b we observe that the vehicle routes overlap with the pheromone trails on the three networks. The details of TbAS can be found in Yildirim and Çatay (2012).

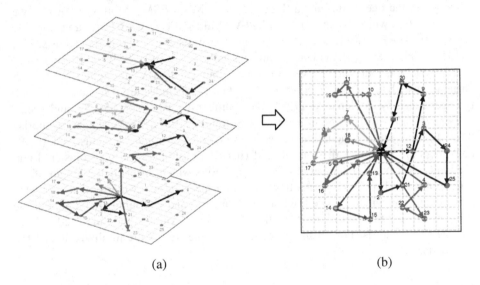

(a)   (b)

Fig. 3. The pheromone mechanism of TbAS: (a) pheromone trails on three separate networks; (b) vehicles routes (Yildirim and Çatay, 2012)

3   Computational Study

In this section, we investigate the performance of the proposed method on VRP variants summarized in the previous section. We report the results obtained by both SP and SC formulations of the corresponding VRP variant.

We coded our algorithm in C# and performed 10 runs for each instance on an Intel Core i7 4770 3.40 GHz computer with 16 GB RAM and 64-bit Windows 7 operating system. The IP-solver is IBM ILOG CPLEX version 12.6. We used a time limit of 300 seconds in each call. For all the problems, the parameter values were set as in Yıldırım and Çatay (2014).

3.1 Benchmark Instances

The tests for CVRP are conducted on 14 instances of Christofides et al. (1979), CMT1-CMT14. Half of the instances have a time limit within which all of the customers must be served. In addition, the customers are clustered in the last four instances whereas they are randomly dispersed in the others. The number of customers ranges between 50 and 199. The OVRP data set includes the same problems.

We use instances of Cordeau et al. (1997) for testing the performance of MathAS on the MDVRP. The number of depots varies between two and five while the number of customers ranges between 50 and 100.

For HVRP, we consider the cases where the fleet is limited (HVRP) as well as the cases where the fleet is unlimited (Fleet Size and Mix – FSM). More specifically, we tackle the following variants: (i) HVRPFV: limited fleet, with fixed and variable costs, (ii) HVRPV: limited fleet, with variable costs but without fixed costs, (iii) FSMFV: unlimited fleet, with fixed and variable costs, (iv) FSMF: unlimited fleet, with fixed costs but without variable costs, and (v) FSMV: unlimited fleet, with variable costs but without fixed costs. The data set includes eight instances of each type generated by Golden et al. (1984). The number of customers is 50, 75, and 100.

For VRPTW, we use 56 instances of Solomon (1987). The instances comprise three different sets, all including 100 customers: (i) C: customers are clustered, (ii) R: customers are randomly distributed, and (iii) RC: customers are both clustered and randomly distributed. Each set also has two subsets which differ by the length of the time windows. Type-1 problems have narrow time windows while type-2 problems have wider time windows. We use both the truncated and real-numbered data. For the former, the optimal solutions for all instances are known and are used in our comparative analysis. For all the problems, our objective is the minimization of the total distance.

3.2 Results

The computational results for all the VRP variants are summarized in Table 1. In this table, "BKS" refers to the average of the best-known solutions reported in the literature for the corresponding VRP set. For the CVRP and MDVRP data sets, we use the best results reported in Subramanian et al. (2013) as benchmarks. For OVRP, HVRP and VRPTW with real-numbered data, we compare our results with those provided in Reinholz and Schneider (2013), Subramanian et al. (2012) and Yıldırım and Çatay (2014), respectively. For all VRPTW instances with truncated distances except R208, the optimal solutions are available in Roberti (2012). The optimal distance for R208 is obtained from Röpke (2014). Note that BKS refers to the optimal solutions for this data set. "MathAS–SC" and "MathAS–SP" indicate the proposed method which utilizes set-covering and set-partitioning formulations, respectively. The "Best" and "Average" columns report the average of the best and the average of the average solutions for each problem class in 10 runs. The computational times are given under the column "CT" in seconds.

Table 1. Computational results

| VRP Set | BKS | MathAS-SC | | | MathAS-SP | | |
		Best	Average	CT	Best	Average	CT
CVRP	976.03	981.74	987.72	444.08	981.31	995.31	399.78
With time limits	909.63	919.37	925.96	497.06	916.31	937.41	451.24
Without time limits	1042.42	1044.12	1049.49	391.10	1046.32	1053.22	348.32
OVRP	646.77	647.29	650.78	1330.45	648.92	655.68	1197.97
With time limits	632.94	634.15	636.88	1489.18	633.94	642.05	1352.37
Without Time limits	660.60	660.43	664.68	1171.73	663.89	669.32	1043.58
HVRP	3166.63	3190.18	3205.17	329.92	3197.21	3217.82	306.70
HVRPFV	5081.59	5130.66	5146.05	328.68	5147.59	5170.24	308.96
HVRPV	1227.85	1248.10	1250.60	318.19	1251.84	1254.85	292.74
FSMFV	4344.43	4370.38	4400.97	288.45	4367.32	4418.14	271.15
FSMF	4103.44	4117.53	4134.00	355.88	4136.06	4150.95	330.97
FSMV	1071.06	1083.91	1091.50	355.80	1084.24	1092.81	327.34
MDVRP	743.01	758.33	777.40	351.97	763.19	809.07	332.92
VRPTW^R	966.94	967.47	969.51	274.66	967.56	969.38	217.99
Type 1	1114.14	1114.24	1115.35	147.10	1114.40	1115.40	104.43
Type 2	829.89	830.83	833.72	393.43	830.85	833.43	323.72
VRPTW^T	963.09	963.77	966.41	366.52	963.85	966.30	243.01
Type 1	1110.33	1110.36	1111.12	194.85	1110.49	1111.30	126.40
Type 2	826.01	827.29	831.68	526.36	827.32	831.30	351.58

^{R}: with real-numbered data

^{T}: with truncated data

In CVRP instances, the average gap is 0.50% for SC and 0.44% for SP where eight best-known solutions out of 14 problems are met. The average gap for problems with 199 customers is 1.43%. For the remaining 12 problems with a maximum number of 150 customers, the average gap decreases to 0.06%.

In OVRP instances, the average gap is 0.10% and 0.34% where the highest gap is 0.88% and 1.06% (observed in the smallest instance in size) for SC and SP formulations, respectively. Five of the best-so-far solutions are met and the best known solutions for three instances are improved (by 0.12% on the average).

The average gap in seven MDVRP instances is 2.07% and 2.72% for SC and SP, respectively. These results show that the approach of solving the MDVRP as multiple single depot VRPs in the AS phase is not very efficient in obtaining high quality solutions.

Table 2. Summary of the performance of proposed method on different VRP variants

Problem class	# of Problems	%Gap MathAS-SC	%Gap MathAS-SP	BKS Met	BKS Improved
CVRP	14	0.50	0.44	8	-
OVRP	14	0.10	0.34	5	3
MDVRP	7	2.07	2.71	-	-
HVRPFV	8	0.97	1.30	-	-
HVRPV	8	1.65	1.95	3	-
FSMFV	10	0.60	0.53	6	-
FSMF	10	0.34	0.79	4	-
FSMV	10	1.20	1.23	3	-
VRPTW^R	56	0.06	0.06	45	3
VRPTW^T	56	0.07	0.08	46	-

^{R}: with real-numbered data
^{T}: with truncated data

For the HVRPFV, HVRPV, FSMFV, FSMF and FSMV, the average performance is mediocre although not as good as in the other VRP variants. The average gap values are below 1.30% except HVRPV where the average gap is 1.65% and 1.95% for SC and SP formulations, respectively. Overall, the algorithm performs better in instances where the fleet size is not limited.

In VRPTW instances using real data, MathAS performs better on type-1 problems where the average gap is 0.01% for SC formulation. This gap slightly increases to 0.02% when implementing MathAS-SP. We reached all of the best-known values for type-1 problems, except R102 where the gap is only 0.01%. We also obtained a new best value for the instance R107. For type-2 problems the performance of the method is relatively worse. Nevertheless, we obtained new best distance also for R210 and RC208 problems.

The same pattern in problems with real-numbered distances is also observed for the problems with truncated distances. Using MathAS-SC, the average gaps for type-1 and type-2 problems are 0.00% and 0.15%, respectively whereas the average gaps for MathAS-SP are 0.01% and 0.16% for type-1 and type-2 problems, respectively. We found the optimal solutions for all type-1 problems, except RC106. For type-2 problems, we succeeded to find 17 optimal solutions in 27 instances.

The summary of the performance of MathAS on different VRP class is given in Table 2. The table includes the average % deviations from the best-known solutions published the literature and the number of instances in which the best-known solutions are matched/improved. The detailed new best solutions are provided in the Appendix.

Comparison of SP and SC Formulations
Concerning the use of the SC or SP formulation in the IP phase, we did not observe any superiority of one formulation over the other considering all problem types solved. However, we can conclude that using the SC formulation yields slightly better results on the average whereas implementing the SP formulation decreases the computational effort.

For the CVRP and OVRP instances with route duration restriction, the performance of SC is inferior to that of SP in terms of best solutions. Taking into account the average performance, SP performs slightly better in VRPTW type-2 instances for both real-numbered and truncated data. In all other cases, the average performance of SC is slightly better.

This increase in performance comes with an extra burden on the computational effort. When the SC formulation is used, the computational time is 11% more for the CVRP and the OVRP compared to using the SP formulation. For the VRPTW, this gap reaches up to 26% and 51% for real-numbered and truncated data, respectively.

4   Conclusion and Future Research

In this study, we proposed a matheuristic for solving different variants of the VRP. We show that the proposed method performs well on a range of routing problems. Best known results are obtained in 62% of all instances. We improved three best-known solutions in the VRPTW real-numbered data and three best-known solutions in the OVRP data. We observe relatively poor performance on HVRP and MDVRP variants. This shows that decomposing the problem into single-vehicle (in HDVRP) and single-depot (in MDVRP) problems in the AS may not be an effective approach in achieving high quality solutions.

We also tested the claim of Russell and Chiang (2006) and compared the implementation of SC and SP formulations in the IP solver phase. Our results did not reveal any significant difference. Moreover, we utilized parallelism to reduce the computational time. However, a parallel implementation by devising multiple ant colonies evolving on different processors may lead to improved performance with respect to the solution quality as well as processor load balance. The introduced structure for HVRP and MDVRP can further be utilized for an efficient parallelization. In this case, each entity (either a vehicle or a depot) will be assigned to a separate ant colony.

Acknowledgment. This research was partially supported by The Scientific and Technical Research Council of Turkey 2214 scholarship to the first author.

Appendix

Table 3. New best solutions for OVRP

Problem	Route		Distance
cmt08			**641.553**
	1	0-28-76-77-3-79-78-34-35-71-66-65	76.914
	2	0-26-12-80-68-29-24-54-4-55-25-39-67	92.894
	3	0-89-18-83-60-5-99-59-92-98-37-100-91-16-86	65.099
	4	0-6-96-93-85-61-84-17-45-8-46-36-49-64	98.449
	5	0-52-31-88-7-82-48-47-19-11-63-90-32	82.246
	6	0-53-58-40-21-73-72-74-22-41-75-56-23	57.123
	7	0-27-69-1-50-33-81-9-51-20-30-70-10-62	80.560
	8	0-13-94-95-97-87-2-57-15-43-42-14-44-38	88.268
cmt10			**869.800**
	1	0-105-26-149-195-179-54-130-165-55-25-170-67	56.202
	2	0-132-69-162-101-70-30-32-131-160-128-20-188-66	60.569
	3	0-94-95-97-87-172-42-142-14-192-119-44-140-38	59.145
	4	0-111-50-102-157-33-185-78-34-164-135-35-136-65	62.935
	5	0-28-184-76-196-116-77-158-3-79-129-169-121-29	43.132
	6	0-166-83-199-114-8-174-46-124-168-47-36-143-49	68.318
	7	0-13-117-151-92-37-98-100-193-91-191-141-16-86	45.456
	8	0-112-183-6-96-99-104-59-93-85-61	31.261
	9	0-180-198-110-4-155-139-187-39-56-186-23	50.974
	10	0-53-40-21-73-171-74-72-197-75-133-22-41-145	50.509
	11	0-27-176-1-122-51-81-120-9-103-161-71	57.898
	12	0-89-18-82-48-123-19-107-175-11-64	60.559
	13	0-167-127-190-31-10-189-108-90-126-63-181	46.939
	14	0-146-52-153-106-194-7-182-88-148-62-159	39.253
	15	0-138-154-12-109-177-80-150-68-134-163-24	39.199
	16	0-156-147-60-118-5-84-173-113-17-45-125	51.228
	17	0-152-58-137-2-115-178-144-57-15-43	46.222
cmt13			**835.956**
	1	0-40-43-45-59-65-61-62-64-60-63-66	135.273
	2	0-104-103-68-79-80-56-58-55-53-52-54-57	111.563
	3	0-37-38-39-42-41-44-46-49-47-48-50-51	110.481
	4	0-119-81	14.142
	5	0-109-21-20-23-26-28-31-34-36-35-32-29	106.217
	6	0-87-92-89-91-90-114-18-118-108	24.314
	7	0-95-96-93-94-97-115-110-98	30.261
	8	0-107-67-69-70-71-74-75-72-78-77-76-73	76.693
	9	0-105-106-102-101-99-100-116	20.850
	10	0-2-1-3-4-5-6-9-10-11-15-14-13	73.188
	11	0-88-82-111-86-85-112-84-117-113-83	22.763
	12	0-7-8-12-17-16-19-25-22-24-27-30-33	103.140
	13	0-120	7.071

Table 4. New best solutions for VRPTW (real-numbered data)

Problem	Route		Distance
R107			**1072.118**
	1	0-28-76-79-78-29-24-68-80-12-0	82.100
	2	0-26-39-23-67-55-4-25-54-0	127.042
	3	0-52-7-62-11-63-90-32-66-20-51-50-0	114.944
	4	0-2-57-43-15-41-22-75-56-74-72-73-21-0	103.079
	5	0-53-40-58-0	24.359
	6	0-48-47-36-64-49-19-82-18-89-0	126.000
	7	0-60-83-45-46-8-84-5-17-61-85-93-0	113.470
	8	0-94-96-92-59-99-6-87-13-0	62.747
	9	0-95-97-42-14-44-38-86-16-91-100-37-98-0	105.742
	10	0-27-69-30-88-31-10-70-1-0	86.165
	11	0-33-81-65-71-9-35-34-3-77-0	126.471
R210			**906.187**
	1	0-95-92-42-15-23-67-39-75-72-73-21-40-53-0	125.795
	2	0-6-94-96-99-59-87-97-13-58-0	57.818
	3	0-18-83-45-61-16-86-44-38-14-43-57-2-41-22-74-56-4-55-25-54-26-0	198.200
	4	0-28-12-76-3-79-29-78-81-9-20-66-32-90-63-10-70-31-0	150.767
	5	0-52-7-82-48-47-36-19-88-62-11-64-49-46-8-84-17-85-98-37-100-91-93-5-60-89-0	219.950
	6	0-27-69-1-30-51-33-71-65-35-34-24-80-68-77-50-0	153.657
RC208			**778.926**
	1	0-94-92-95-67-62-50-34-31-29-27-26-28-30-32-33-76-89-63-85-51-84-56-91-80-0	198.990
	2	0-61-42-44-39-38-36-35-37-40-43-41-72-71-93-96-54-81-0	133.001
	3	0-69-98-88-2-6-7-79-73-78-12-14-47-17-16-15-13-9-11-10-53-60-8-46-4-45-5-3-1-70-100-55-68-0	227.168
	4	0-90-65-82-99-52-83-64-49-19-18-48-21-23-25-77-58-75-97-59-87-74-86-57-24-22-20-66-0	219.767

References

1. Alvarenga, G.B., Mateus, G.R., de Tomi, G.: A genetic and set partitioning two-phase approach for the vehicle routing problem with time windows. Computers and Operations Research **34**(6), 1561–1584 (2007)
2. Archetti, C., Speranza, M.: A survey on matheuristics for routing problems. EURO Journal on Computational Optimization **2**, 223–246 (2014)
3. Archetti, C., Speranza, M., Savelsbergh, M.: An optimization-based heuristic for the split delivery vehicle routing problem. Transportation Science **42**, 22–31 (2008)

4. Bertazzi, L., Speranza, M.G.: Matheuristics for inventory routing problems. In: Montoya-Torres, J.R., Juan, A.A., Huatuco, L.H., Faulin, J., Rodriguez-Verjan, G.L. (eds.) Hybrid Algorithms for Service, Computing and Manufacturing Systems: Routing and Scheduling Solutions. IGI Global, Hershey (2011)

5. Boschetti, M.A., Maniezzo, V., Roffilli, M., Bolufé Röhler, A.: Matheuristics: optimization, simulation and control. In: Blesa, M.J., Blum, C., Di Gaspero, L., Roli, A., Sampels, M., Schaerf, A. (eds.) HM 2009. LNCS, vol. 5818, pp. 171–177. Springer, Heidelberg (2009)

6. Boschetti, M., Maniezzo, V.: A set covering based matheuristic for a real-world city logistics problem. International Transactions in Operational Research 22, 169–196 (2015)

7. Bullnheimer, B., Hartl, R.F., Strauss, C.: A new rank-based version of the ant system: A computational study. Central European Journal of Operations Research 7, 25–38 (1999)

8. Christofides, N., Mingozzi, A., Toth, P.: The vehicle routing problem. In: Chrisofides, N., Mingozzi, A., Toth, P., Sandi, C. (eds.) Combinatorial Optimization, pp. 315–338. Wiley, Chichester (1979)

9. Cordeau, J.-F., Gendreau, M., Laporte, G.: A tabu search heuristic for periodic and multi-depot vehicle routing problems. Networks 30(2), 105–119 (1997)

10. Doerner, K.F., Schmid, V.: Survey: matheuristics for rich vehicle routing problems. In: Blesa, M.J., Blum, C., Raidl, G., Roli, A., Sampels, M. (eds.) HM 2010. LNCS, vol. 6373, pp. 206–221. Springer, Heidelberg (2010)

11. Golden, B.L., Assad, A.A., Levy, L., Gheysens, F.G.: The fleet size and mix vehicle routing problem. Computers and Operations Research 11, 49–66 (1984)

12. Groër, C., Golden, B., Wasil, E.: A library of local search heuristics for the vehicle routing problem. Mathematical Programming Computation 2, 79–101 (2010)

13. Groër, C., Golden, B., Wasil, E.: A parallel algorithm for the vehicle routing problem. Informs Journal on Computing 23, 315–330 (2011)

14. Gulczynski, D., Golden, B., Wasil, E.: The period vehicle routing problem: new heuristics and real-world variants. Transportation Research Part E-Logistics 47, 648–668 (2011)

15. Kelly, J.P., Xu, J.: A set-partitioning-based heuristic for the vehicle routing problem. Informs Journal on Computing 11, 161–172 (1999)

16. Maniezzo, V., Stützle, T., Voß, S.: Matheuristics: Hybridizing Metaheuristics and Mathematical Programming. Springer, New-York (2010)

17. Mendoza, J.E., Villegas, J.G.: A multi-space sampling heuristic for the vehicle routing problem with stochastic demands. Optimization Letters 7, 1503–1506 (2013)

18. Pirkwieser, S., Raidl, G.R.: Multiple variable neighborhood search enriched with ILP techniques for the periodic vehicle routing problem with time windows. In: Blesa, M.J., Blum, C., Di Gaspero, L., Roli, A., Sampels, M., Schaerf, A. (eds.) HM 2009. LNCS, vol. 5818, pp. 45–59. Springer, Heidelberg (2009)

19. Russell, R.A., Chiang, W.-C.: Scatter search for the vehicle routing problem with time windows. European Journal of Operational Research 169(2), 606–622 (2006)

20. Reinholz, A., Schneider, H.: A Hybrid (1+1)-Evolutionary Strategy for the Open Vehicle Routing Problem. Advances in Metaheuristics, Operations Research/Computer Science Interfaces Series 53, 127–141 (2013)

21. Roberti, R.: Exact Algorithms for Different Classes of Vehicle Routing Problems. Dissertation in Control System Engineering and Operational Research. University of Bologna, Italy (2012)

22. Röpke, S.: Personal communication (2014)
23. Solomon, M.M.: Algorithms for the vehicle routing and scheduling problems with time window constraints. Operations Research **35**(2), 254–265 (1987)
24. Subramanian, A., Penna, P.H.V., Uchoa, E., Ochi, L.S.: A hybrid algorithm for the heterogeneous fleet vehicle routing problem. European Journal of Operational Research **221**(2), 285–295 (2012)
25. Subramanian, A., Uchoa, E., Ochi, L.S.: A hybrid algorithm for a class of vehicle routing problems. Computers and Operations Research **40**, 2519–2531 (2013)
26. Yildirim, U.M., Çatay, B.: A time-based pheromone approach for the ant system. Optimization Letters **6**(6), 1081–1099 (2012)
27. Yıldırım, U.M., Çatay, B.: A parallel matheuristic for solving the vehicle routing problems. In: de Sousa, J.F., Rossi, R. (eds.) Computer-based Modelling and Optimization in Transportation. AISC, vol. 262, pp. 477–489. Springer International Publishing, Heidelberg (2014)

Transport Over Water

A Hybrid Reactive Tabu Search for Liner Shipping Fleet Repositioning

Mark Becker and Kevin Tierney[✉]

Decision Support and Operations Research Lab, University of Paderborn,
Paderborn, Germany
bmark@mail.upb.de, kevin.tierney@upb.de

Abstract. We solve the liner shipping fleet repositioning problem
(LSFRP), a key problem in the liner shipping industry, using a hybrid
reactive tabu search and simulated annealing algorithm in combination
with novel local search neighborhoods. Liner carriers reposition vessels
between services in order to add, remove or modify services in their network. Repositioning vessels costs between hundreds of thousands and
millions of dollars, meaning finding cost efficient repositioning plans is
an important goal for liner carriers. We introduce a reactive tabu search
approach and hybridize it with simulated annealing, allowing us to find a
combined \$147,000 in additional profit over the state-of-the-art approach
across 44 public LSFRP instances.

1 Introduction

Liner shipping networks transported over 1.5 billion tons of containerized cargo on
more than 5,000 seagoing container vessels in 2013 [20], making liner shipping a key
component of the world economy. Vessels are regularly *repositioned* between services in liner shipping networks to align networks with seasonal cargo fluctuations
and shifting macroeconomic conditions. Repositioning vessels involves creating a
plan for a set of vessels that moves (i.e., repositions) the vessels from one route to
another route in the network. Since repositioning a single vessel can cost hundreds
of thousands of US dollars, optimizing the repositioning activities of vessels is an
important problem for the liner shipping industry.

The Liner Shipping Fleet Repositioning Problem (LSFRP), first introduced
in [18], and more recently considered in [16,9,19], involves finding sequences of
activities that move vessels between services (routes) in a liner shipping network while considering cargo flows. The LSFRP maximizes the profit earned on
the subset of the network affected by the repositioning, balancing sailing costs
and port fees against cargo revenues, while respecting important liner shipping
specific constraints dictating the creation of services and movement of cargo.

Exact approaches for solving the LSFRP have recently made significant
advances [15], however heuristics are still critical for solving the LSFRP in practice. Repositioning coordinators require quick feedback when creating repositioning plans in order to experiment with different "what if" scenarios, and to
address minor issues in generated plans (for example, dealing with ship draft

F. Corman et al. (Eds.): ICCL 2015, LNCS 9335, pp. 123–138, 2015.
DOI: 10.1007/978-3-319-24264-4_9

restrictions or tides). Furthermore, on large instances exact approaches sometimes fail to even find a single feasible solution, meaning fast heuristics are absolutely essential for any LSFRP decision support system.

This work presents the following novel contributions:*i*) two novel LSFRP local search neighborhoods, *ii*) a reactive tabu search (RTS) approach for the LSFRP, and *iii*) a hybrid simulated annealing (SA) and RTS algorithm (RTS-SA) for the LSFRP. One of the neighborhoods analyzes undelivered containers on the path of vessels and attempts to modify the path to be able to deliver the containers. The other neighborhood uses an ejection chain style neighborhood for swapping visits between multiple vessels in a single search iteration. Our RTS approach presents an alternative solution approach for solving LSFRP problems and finds optimal solutions for several instances that the state-of-the-art algorithm cannot find. Finally, our RTS-SA approach outperforms all previous heuristic LSFRP approaches, closing the gap to optimality on several instances and significantly increasing the profit earned by solving the LSFRP instances.

We provide a brief overview of the LSFRP in Section 2, followed by a description of our heuristic solution approach in Section 4, including a discussion of the state-of-the-art. Finally, computational results are presented in Section 5.

2   Liner Shipping Fleet Repositioning

We now provide a brief LSFRP description from [19], and refer readers to [16] for a more detailed description and a mathematical model. Liner shipping networks consist of cyclical routes, called services, that visit ports on a regular (usually weekly or biweekly) schedule. Liner carriers regularly adjust their network (many small changes, and several large changes per year) to account for seasonal changes in cargo demands, as well as to adapt to economic growth and decline. Whenever a new service is created, or a service is expanded, vessels must be repositioned from their current service to the service being added or expanded.

Vessel repositioning is expensive due to the cost of fuel and the revenue lost due to cargo flow disruptions. Given that liner shippers around the world reposition hundreds of vessels per year, optimizing vessel movements can significantly increase the efficiency of carriers while reducing the environmental burden of containerized shipping. Furthermore, it allows carriers to better utilize repositioning vessels to transport cargo. The aim of the LSFRP is to maximize the profit earned when repositioning a number of vessels from their initial services to a service being added or expanded, called the goal service.

Liner shipping services are composed of multiple *slots*, each of which represents a cycle that is assigned to a particular vessel. Each slot is composed of a number of *visits* (port calls), i.e., a specific time when a vessel is scheduled to arrive at a port. A vessel that is assigned to a particular slot sequentially sails to each visit in the slot. Vessel sailing speeds can be adjusted throughout repositioning to balance cost savings with punctuality (using slow-steaming, see [13]). The bunker fuel consumption of vessels increases approximately cubically with the speed of the vessel, which we linearize.

Phase-out & Phase-in. The repositioning period for each vessel starts at a specific time when the vessel may cease normal operations. This means the vessel may stop sailing to its regularly scheduled port calls and go somewhere else. Each vessel is assigned a time when it may begin its repositioning, called its *phase-out* time. After this time, the vessel may undertake a number of different activities to reach the goal service. In order to complete the repositioning, each vessel must join a slot on the goal service before a time set by the repositioning coordinator, called the *phase in* time. After this time, normal operations on the goal service begin, and all scheduled visits on the service are to be undertaken.

Cargo and Equipment. Revenue is earned through delivering *cargo* and *equipment* (empty containers). We use a detailed view of cargo flows in which cargo is represented as a set of port to port demands with a cargo type, a latest delivery time, an amount of TEU[1] available, and a revenue per TEU delivered. We subtract the cost of loading and unloading each TEU from the revenue earned to determine the profit per TEU of each cargo demand. Unlike cargo, equipment can be sent from any port where it is in surplus to any port where it is in demand. Cargo and equipment may be either *dry* (standard) or *reefer* (refrigerated) cargo. Vessels have a limited capacity, and are therefore assigned a maximum number of reefer containers and a maximum number of all containers.

Sail-on-Service (SoS) Opportunities. While repositioning, vessels may use user specified services to cheaply sail between two parts of the network. These are called *SoS opportunities*. The two vessels involved in SoS opportunities are referred to as the *repositioning vessel*, which is the vessel under the control of a repositioning coordinator, and the *on-service vessel*, which is the vessel assigned to a slot on the service being offered as an SoS opportunity. Repositioning vessels can use SoS opportunities by replacing the on-service vessel and sailing in its place for a portion of the service. The on-service vessel is either laid up (taken out of service), or chartered out (leased to another party). SoS opportunities save significant amounts of fuel costs, since one vessel is sailing where there would have otherwise been two. SoS opportunities are subject to a number of constraints, which are described in full in [16].

Flexible Visits. Most visits have fixed berthing times, such as those on the phase-out, the phase-in and on SoS opportunities. However, some ports do not have strict berthing windows. If a vessel travels to such a port, the berthing time must be determined. LSFRP instances with flexible visits are difficult to solve because sailing times to and from flexible visits cannot be precomputed.

Asia-CA3 Case Study. Figure 1 shows a subset of a real repositioning scenario in which a vessel must be repositioned from its initial service (the phase-out service), the Chennai-Express, to the goal service (the phase-in service), the Intra-WCSA. The Asia-CA3 service is offered as an SoS opportunity to the vessel

---

[1] A TEU is a *twenty-foot equivalent unit* and represents a single twenty-foot container.

Fig. 1. A subset of a case study of the LSFRP, from [17].

repositioning from Chennai Express to Intra-WCSA. One possible repositioning could involve a vessel leaving the Chennai Express at TPP, and sailing to HKG where it can pick up the Asia-CA3, thus replacing the on-service vessel. The repositioning vessel would then sail along the Asia-CA3 until it gets to BLB, where it can join the Intra-WCSA. No vessel sails on the backhaul of the Asia-CA3, which saves fuel and crew costs, as little cargo is transported on this leg.

3   Literature Review

The LSFRP is not mentioned in the main literature reviews of maritime transportation [6,5]. Although there has been significant work on problems such as the Network Design Problem (NDP) (e.g. [3]), these problems deal with strategic decisions related to building the network and assigning vessels to services excluding the problem of getting vessels to their new services. The vessel schedule recovery problem (VSRP) [4] differs from the LSFRP as it lacks the breadth of activities of the LSFRP due to its short time window.

Although tramp shipping problems (see, e.g., [11]) maximize cargo profit while accounting for sailing costs and port fees as in the LSFRP, they lack liner shipping specific constraints, such as sail-on-service opportunities, phase-in requirements and strict visit times. Airline disruption management (see [10]) differs from the LSFRP in that airline disruption management requires an exact cover of all flight legs over a planning horizon. The LSFRP has no such requirement over visits or sailing legs.

The primary previous work on the LSFRP in the literature is found in [17], [18], [16], [19] and [9] by the authors. The first work on the LSFRP, [17], solved an abstraction of the LSFRP without cargo/equipment flows and SoS parallel sailings using a hybrid of automated planning and linear programming called Linear Temporal Optimization Planning (LTOP). However, LTOP and other automated planning methods are unable to model cargo flows and are thus inapplicable to the version of the LSFRP we solve in this work. A mathematical model of the LSFRP with cargo and equipment flows is introduced in [18] with an extension for a special case in [19]. In both cases, CPLEX is used to solve the model. In [16], the current state-of-the-art simulated annealing algorithm is presented and used to find solutions for instances that CPLEX was unable to solve, both due to running out of memory and exceeding a timeout of one hour. Additionally, the technique is shown to be faster than CPLEX at finding good solutions.

4 A Hybrid Reactive Tabu Search Approach

We first provide an overview of the SA approach in [16] that forms the basis for this work. We then describe our tabu search (TS) approach for the LSFRP, which we then extend to be a reactive TS (RTS) [1]. TS is well-suited to solve the LSFRP given its success in solving routing and transportation problems. The existing local search neighborhoods are rather susceptible to cycles, making TS a natural advancement in LSFRP research. Finally, inspired by [21], we iterate between RTS and SA, using SA to move to a more promising area when RTS gets stuck. We refer to this method as RTS-SA.

We use the same solution representation as in the original SA approach. We store a path through the graph for each vessel, which we briefly describe in the following subsection, starting at the vessel's earliest phase-out port and ending at the graph sink. We then describe the existing local search neighborhoods from the SA, followed by two new neighborhoods for the LSFRP. Then we discuss the RTS based approach along with its hybridization with SA.

4.1 Graph Overview

All previous work on the LSFRP uses a graph as the basis to solve the problem. The vessels follow node disjoint paths through the graph, with each vessel's path starting at a node representing the vessel's earliest phase-out port call. The paths end at a common graph sink, which has an incoming arc from the last visit in each slot of the phase-in service. Due to the disjointness of the paths (excluding the graph sink), the phase-in structure ensures that each slot of the phase-in service is assigned exactly one vessel as is required in a valid service.

The graph also contains special structures to ensure the correct modeling of SoS opportunities, flexible visits, and cabotage restrictions. As the details of these components are not necessary for understanding our new local search neighborhoods and metaheuristic approaches, we omit them and refer interested readers to [16] for a detailed (and formal) description.

4.2 Existing SA Approach

The SA approach in [16] uses a standard SA algorithm with the metropolis acceptance criteria together with a neighborhood chosen uniformly at random in each iteration to generate a new candidate solution. A reheating procedure is used if the search converges before the time limit has expired. We now describe the neighborhoods used in the SA and refer to [16] for more details.

Add/Remove/Swap. The add, remove and swap neighborhoods are "basic" neighborhoods that make a small change to a randomly selected vessel or pair of vessels. The add neighborhood selects a random vessel and a random arc on that vessel's path. The arc is then removed and a random visit is chosen that can be feasibly inserted into the path at the position of the arc. The remove neigh- borhood chooses a random vessel and removes a random visit on the vessel's path. Finally, the swap neighborhood selects two vessels at random and chooses a random visit on the path of one of the vessels. A compatible node is chosen from the path of the other vessel and the visits are swapped between the paths.

These neighborhoods allow the SA to reach any possible solution, meaning the optimal solution will be found given enough time (although we do not prove this). However, in practice these neighborhoods make changes that are too small to quickly find high quality solutions.

Random Path Completion (RPC). A ship is selected uniformly at random along with a visit on its path. All visits subsequent to the chosen visit are removed from the path and replaced with a random path to the graph sink. The visits chosen at random must be feasible, that is none may already be on the path.

Demand Destination Completion (DDC). A ship, is selected uniformly at random along with a visit on its path where demand originates. A demand is chosen that could be loaded at the visit, but cannot be delivered because none of its delivery visits are on the path of the vessel. The neighborhood attempts to connect the current path to one of the destinations of the cargo using a breadth first search. Then, another breadth first search is started from the destination back to any subsequent visit on the path. If no such path exists, or such paths can only be created by introducing a duplicated node into the vessel's path, then the solution is left unchanged.

4.3   Demand Source Completion Neighborhood

A natural extension of the demand destination completion (DDC) neighborhood is the *demand source completion* (DSC) neighborhood. The DSC neighborhood changes the path of a vessel so that it picks up a demand that could be delivered at a port along the path of the vessel, but cannot be delivered because the source port of the demand is not on the vessel path.

The DSC neighborhood first chooses a vessel path uniformly at random to change. Then, a visit t is chosen that contains a demand that could be delivered if the source, s, of some demand was on the path of the vessel. A breadth first search finds a path from any visit before t to s. If a path is found, another breadth first search finds a path from s back to a visit on the vessel's path before t. The vessel's path is then updated with the new paths. If no path is possible either to or from s, then the solution is left unchanged.

Figure 2 shows the difference between the DSC and DDC neighborhoods. A vessel path traveling between a, b, c, d, and e is shown with a thin line. Two demands are present: one from f to c (demand 1) and one from c to g (demand 2). The DSC neighborhood looks at visit c and identifies demand 1 as being deliverable if visit f is part of the path. The DSC neighborhood therefore finds a path to f (from a) and then reconnects f to the path at c. In this process, visit b is removed from the path since it cannot be visited at the same time as f. Likewise, for the DDC neighborhood the original path visits c, so the neighborhood adds port g in order to deliver demand 2.

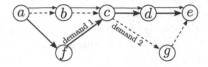

Fig. 2. A vessel path (thin line) changed by the DSC (bold) and DDC (dashed) neighborhoods.

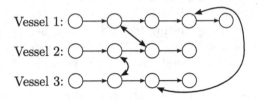

Fig. 3. A sample ejection chain swap sequence for three vessels.

4.4   Ejection Chain Neighborhood

Ejection chains (ECs) were introduced in [8] as a way of overcoming the local optima that occur when using neighborhoods making small changes. An EC consists of a sequence of changes to a solution that are connected to each other. For example, in the traveling salesman problem a node is *ejected* from its location in a solution and placed in a new location, whereby another node is ejected and moved elsewhere in the solution. This process is repeated until the "hole" left by the first ejected node is filled.

In the case of the LSFRP, we use a chain of node swaps between vessel paths as depicted in Figure 3. We make several small departures from the standard EC paradigm so that EC can be used in the LSFRP. First, swaps do not have to be connected, i.e., they need not share any visit. Second, if a swap is not possible between a vessel and any other vessel, no swap is performed. Extending this notion, ECs do not have to be complete. That is, we do not include vessel paths in the chain when no swap is possible. For example, if a vessel is sailing directly from its phase-out port to a phase-in port, there may not be any feasible swap available between that vessel and another.

We justify our modifications of the standard EC paradigm because finding a complete chain in the LSFRP is in most cases impossible. Vessels can be separated by thousands of nautical miles during transit and only "interact" in how they phase-in to a goal service. In such situations no feasible swaps of visits between vessels are possible.

4.5   Reactive Tabu Search

Tabu search (TS) (see, e.g., [7]) is a memory based local search method that prevents cycles during search by storing a list of previously seen solutions (or partial solutions) called a *tabu restriction*. A single iteration of TS explores a neighborhood around a solution and replaces it with the best solution in the neighborhood does not violate the tabu restriction. Designing a TS approach raises three questions: i) How should solutions be represented? ii) How should the tabu list be managed? iii) What neighborhoods should be used?

We answer the first question by maintaining the solution representation of the SA, namely a path for each vessel through the graph. For the second question, we use a reactive approach [1] (RTS) that actively adjusts the length of the *prohibition period* of the tabu list based on the progress of the search. The prohibition period determines how long a solution remains tabu. Finally, we answer the third question by testing two TS approaches for the LSFRP: one that samples the existing and new LSFRP neighborhoods (TS-S) and one that uses modified neighborhood operators to more systematically search the area round each solution (TS-T).

Creating two approaches allows us to more effectively compare TS on the LSFRP to the SA approach. By using the same neighborhoods, we can determine which metaheuristic performs better. Since TS usually benefits from having neighborhoods that perform a strong search around a solution, we also modify all of the neighborhoods used by the SA. We use the information gained in the TS approaches in our RTS approach, which uses the sampling approach of TS-S.

Move-based Prohibitions. Our tabu list uses move-based prohibitions instead of storing complete or partial solutions (see, e.g., [7]). This means that given a new current solution, s, and a previous solution, s^P, the tabu list stores the change $\Delta(s^P, s)$ and prohibits changes that would undo $\Delta(s^P, s)$.

We store tabu prohibitions for three types of changes, which are neighborhood specific. *Swap* moves are created through the swap and EC neighborhoods. Swap moves store two tuples, each containing a vessel and a visit, and are used directly in the swap neighborhood. Note that the position of the visit on the vessel path is not stored. The EC neighborhood stores each swap performed in the chain. Should any of these swaps be encountered in a particular EC move, the entire chain of swaps is considered to be tabu. *Add-Remove* moves involve the addition or removal of a visit from the path of a vessel, as well as the DSC neighborhood. Again, the position of the removal is not stored, rather just the visit and the vessel in a tuple. Combining these neighborhoods into a single operator more effectively removes cycles, as these neighborhoods easily reverse each other. In the DSC neighborhood, the visit that fulfills the selected demand is added to the tabu list. *RPC-DDC* moves store the position in the path of a vessel where a change was started. In the case of RPC, it is the last position before a random path begins. For DDC, it is the position before a path to complete a demand is inserted. Starting the RPC/DDC neighborhoods from the same position is then banned in future iterations of the search.

TS-T Neighborhoods. Due to space restrictions, we do not describe our TS-T approach in detail. The idea behind TS-T is to perform systematic searches of neighborhoods, when possible, in order to find better solutions than a random

---

Algorithm 1. A reactive tabu search algorithm for the LSFRP.

1: **function** RTS-LSFRP($f, V, inc, dec, R, n^{ST}, \ell$)
2:      $s \leftarrow$ INITIALSOLUTION(); $s^* \leftarrow s$; $T \leftarrow \emptyset$; $noImprovementItrs \leftarrow 0$
3:      **while** $noImprovementItrs < \bar{r}^{ltrs}$ and $\neg terminate$ **do**
4:          $N \leftarrow$ REMOVETABU($T, f(s^*),$ NEIGHBORS(s, n^{ST}))
5:          **if** $N \neq \emptyset$ **then**
6:             $s^P \leftarrow s$; $s \leftarrow \operatorname{argmax}_{s' \in N}\{f(s')\}$
7:             **if** $f(s) > f(s^*)$ and FEASIBLE(s) **then**
8:                 $s^* \leftarrow s$; $noImprovementItrs \leftarrow 0$
9:             **else**
10:                 $noImprovementItrs \leftarrow noImprovementItrs + 1$
11:             **if** $R = true$ **then**
12:                 $\alpha \leftarrow$ REACTIVEUPDATE($T, V, \Delta(s^P, s), inc, dec, \alpha, itr$)
13:                 $T \leftarrow$ REACTIVETABUUPDATE($T, \Delta(s^P, s), \alpha$)
14:             **else**
15:                 $T \leftarrow$ TABUUPDATE($T, \Delta(s^P, s), \ell$)
16:          **else**
17:             $noImprovementItrs \leftarrow noImprovementItrs + 1$
18:          $itr \leftarrow itr + 1$
19: **return** s^*

---

sampling provides. This comes, of course, at the expense of increased CPU time. We create such neighborhoods for the add, remove, and swap neighborhoods, as a systematic search is possible. In the case of DSC, DDC and RPC, a complete search of the neighborhood would take exponential time in the size of the problem. We therefore continue using a sampling approach for these neighborhoods.

RTS Algorithm for the LSFRP. Algorithm 1 encompasses the RTS, TS-S and TS-T approaches. The RTS-LSFRP function accepts the following parameters. The parameter f is the objective function to maximize, V is the set of graph nodes, inc and dec describe the amount to increase and decrease the prohibition period of the reactive tabu list, respectively, R indicates whether or not the tabu list should be managed reactively, n^{ST} determines the type of neighborhood to use (stochastic sampling or systematic neighborhoods) and ℓ is the fixed prohibition period for non-reactive TS.

The tabu search first generates an initial solution and initializes the incumbent solution s^* and the tabu list, T. The tabu search continues until either a maximum number of non-improving iterations occurs or a user-specified termination criteria is met, such as a CPU time limit. The set N is given the non-tabu neighborhood around the current solution s on line 4. When n^{ST} is set to S, the TS-S algorithm is carried out. In TS-S, a neighborhood is selected from the SA neighborhoods union the DSC and EC neighborhoods uniformly at random and a solution is sampled. This process is repeated $n^{mult}|V|$ times to form a set of solutions. For TS-S, we take into account an aspiration criteria that accepts tabu solutions into the neighborhood if they improve on the incumbent. When n^{ST} is set to T, the TS-T algorithm is used, and all of the TS neighborhoods are queried for neighbors.

The best solution in the neighborhood replaces the current solution on line 6, and the incumbent is updated if the solution is feasible and the best seen so far. A counter, *noImprovementItrs*, is incremented whenever a new incumbent solution is not found or the neighborhood is empty. When this counter reaches the value $\bar{r}^{Itrs}$ the search terminates.

On line 11, if R is set to true, the reactive tabu list update is carried out on lines 12 and 13. We describe the function REACTIVEUPDATE in Algorithm 2, which updates the prohibition period α that is then used in REACTIVETABUUP-DATE. REACTIVETABUUPDATE removes any entry in the tabu list that exceeds the prohibition period and adds the change from the previous solution to the current solution to the tabu list. In the case of TS-T and TS-S, the prohibition period is set to a fixed length specified by the user.

The REACTIVEUPDATE function in Algorithm 2 shows how the prohibition period is updated reactively in response to the progress of the search. This function is based on the memory_based_reaction function in [2] The parameters V, *inc* and *dec* are as in Algorithm 1. Parameter T is the tabu list, Δ is the change being performed to the solution in the search, α is the current period of prohibition and *itr* is the current search iteration. The global variables *repInterval*^{avg} and α_t represent the average amount of time it takes to see a change a second time and the time of the last increase of the prohibition period, respectively. The parameter *repInterval*^{avg} is initialized to 1 and α_t to 0.

When a change is encountered that has already been seen (line 3) the time since that change was last seen is computed. If the time it took to encounter this change a second time is less than twice the size of the problem (number of nodes), then the prohibition period is increased and the average repetition interval is updated. We use a repetition interval of twice the number of nodes in the graph. Since most neighborhoods operate on a small portion of the problem, seeing a particular change multiple times within twice the size of a problem likely indicates a cycle. This is, of course, a parameter that could be tuned.

When the last time the prohibition period was updated becomes greater than the average time between seeing the same change, the prohibition period is decreased. Intuitively, when a change is not seen for a long period of time, the prohibition period can be decreased since the risk of encountering a cycle is low.

4.6 Hybrid RTS-SA Approach

When RTS encounters a solution with an empty neighborhood due to tabus, it must discontinue its search. The question becomes how to continue searching if a time/iteration budget has not yet expired. One option is using random changes to the incumbent solution as in [1], or a perturbation strategy as in iterated local search [12]. Another option is the use an SA algorithm starting from the incumbent solution. Hybridizing RTS and SA is shown in [21] to be effective

---

Algorithm 2. Reactive update of the prohibition period.

1: **function** REACTIVEUPDATE($T, V, \Delta, inc, dec, \alpha, itr$)
2:    **global** $repInterval^{avg}$, α_t
3:    **if** $\Delta \in T$ **then**
4:        $repInterval \leftarrow itr - \text{TIMELASTSEEN}(T, \Delta)$
5:        **if** $repInterval < 2|V|$ **then**
6:            $repInterval^{avg} \leftarrow (0.1)\,repInterval + (0.9)\,repInterval^{avg}$
7:            $\alpha \leftarrow \alpha * inc$; $\alpha_t \leftarrow itr$
8:    **if** $itr - \alpha_t > repInterval^{avg}$ **then**
9:        $\alpha \leftarrow \max\{1, \alpha * dec\}$; $\alpha_t \leftarrow itr$
10: **return** α

---

for several combinatorial graph problems. This has the advantage over random changes that the search process is guided. Furthermore, no problem specific perturbation routine is required as in ILS. Finally, we choose an online hybridization approach over an offline algorithm selection procedure as in, e.g., [14], due to the low number of instances currently available.

The hybridized approach works by first performing an iteration of the SA algorithm from [16] including the DSC and EC neighborhoods. Then, we alternate between RTS and SA, waiting until each approach converges before switching to the next approach. The current best solution found is passed from each solution procedure to the next. When no improving solution is found in an iteration of SA and RTS a counter is incremented. The RTS-SA algorithm stops when this counter reaches a number provided by the user or another termination criteria is reached (CPU time, iterations).

5   Computational Evaluation

We evaluate the following claims: i) the DSC neighborhood results in better performance than not using it; ii) the EC neighborhood provides better performance than not using it; iii) using neighborhood sampling in TS (TS-S) provides better performance than using the systematic neighborhoods (TS-T); and iv) the RTS-SA approach provides better performance than the current state-of-the-art approach with and without the DSC and EC neighborhoods.

We define the *performance* of a single execution of an approach as the objective function value of the best solution found after 10 minutes of CPU time. We evaluate each solution approach over 25 independent executions on each of the 44 instances in the public LSFRP dataset from [16]. The instances range in size from 3 to 11 vessels and contain up to 379 nodes and 11972 arcs in the graph. The number of container demands in the multi-commodity flow varies between just 20 demands to as many as 1423. All experiments in this section are performed on Intel Xeon E5-2670 2.6GHz processors with 4 GB of RAM.

5.1 Neighborhood Effectiveness

We first investigate the performance of the DSC and the EC neighborhoods. In order to test neighborhoods individually, we disable the non-basic neighborhoods (RPC and DDC). For both the DSC and EC neighborhoods, we investigate their performance for both RTS and RTS-SA.

Demand Source Completion (DSC) Neighborhood. A performance overview of the DSC neighborhood can be seen in Figure 4. For both the RTS and RTS-SA algorithms, a number of instances gain in performance thanks to the neighborhood, with only several instances showing worse performance.

In terms of the best performance found over 25 runs on each instance, using the DSC neighborhood is always better (or equal) to not using the neighborhood for RTS. The neighborhood shows its strongest performance on instances with at least 1000 demands, which is not so surprising, given that without this neighborhood the search will only carry profitable demands by chance. In terms of average performance over the 25 runs, 11 instances have better performance without the DSC neighborhood, but 16 have better performance with it.

On the RTS-SA algorithm, performance is more mixed, with the DSC neighborhood improving the best performance on 8 instances, but degrading performance on 7. We see a similar picture in the average case. We hypothesize that the stronger metaheuristic guidance allows it to occasionally overcome the shortcomings of basic neighborhoods. Although Figure 4b shows a number of points where the DSC neighborhood improves performance, these are mainly due to multiple runs of the same instances. We believe the clear performance gains on some instances make the neighborhood nonetheless worthwhile for RTS-SA.

Ejection Chain (EC) Neighborhood. The EC neighborhood's effectiveness is shown in Figure 5. Although gains can be clearly seen when combining the neighborhood with RTS, the neighborhood has little effect with the RTS-SA hybrid. Ejection chain neighborhoods are not traditionally combined with SA

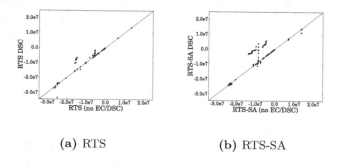

(a) RTS   (b) RTS-SA

Fig. 4. DSC neighborhood objective function values. Points above the line indicate better performance using the neighborhood.

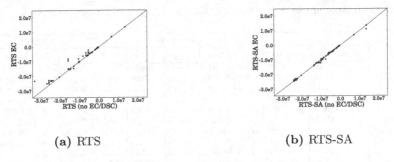

(a) RTS   (b) RTS-SA

Fig. 5. EC neighborhood objective function values.

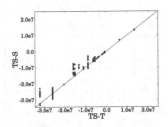

Fig. 6. Objective function of TS-S against TS-T.

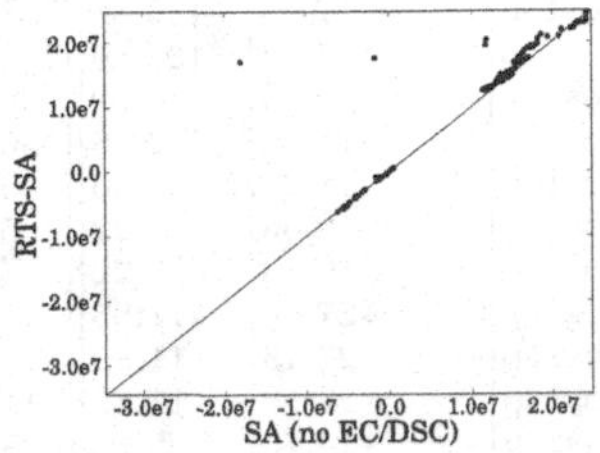

Fig. 7. Objective function of RTS-SA against the state-of-the-art SA.

approaches in the literature, although in principle they should work together. Using the EC neighborhood only in combination with RTS within the RTS-SA hybrid might provide better performance.

The ejection chain neighborhood is most effective on two groups of instances: repos11p through repos14p and repos33p through repos41p, which represent 4 different groups of instances. The instances are concentrated geographically around Africa and south-east Asia, although this seems unlikely to be the reason for better performance of the EC neighborhood.

5.2 TS-S vs. TS-T

Figure 6 shows that the TS-S variant outperforms TS-T on most instances. The computational cost of fully exploring the add, remove and swap neighborhoods is clearly too high to outweigh the benefit of having the best solution in the neighborhood. This is likely due to the simplicity of the neighborhoods, which do not make large changes in the objective function in a single step.

5.3 RTS-SA

We now compare the performance of RTS-SA to the state-of-the-art approach. Figure 7 provides an overview of the performance of RTS-SA to the current state-of-the-art. RTS-SA has better performance than the state-of-the-art SA

Table 1. Best objective (in tens of thousands) over 25 runs per instance.

ID	SA Baseline	Optimal	SA [16] Obj.	Score	SA (DSC/EC) Obj.	Score	RTS Obj.	Score	RTS-SA Obj.	Score
repos1p	-52.30	-39.83	-39.83	0.000	-39.83	0.000	-39.83	0.000	-39.83	0.000
repos2p	-52.30	-39.83	-39.83	0.000	-39.83	0.000	-39.83	0.000	-39.83	0.000
repos3p	-72.11	-61.77	-61.77	0.000	-61.77	0.000	-61.77	0.000	-61.77	0.000
repos4p	-55.44	-46.62	-46.62	0.000	-46.62	0.000	-46.62	0.000	-46.62	0.000
repos5p	-15.76	-8.21	-8.21	0.000	-8.21	0.000	-8.21	0.000	-8.21	0.000
repos6p	-15.76	-8.21	-8.21	0.000	-8.21	0.000	-8.21	0.000	-8.21	0.000
repos7p	-12.08	-11.49	-11.49	0.000	-11.49	0.000	-11.49	0.000	-11.49	0.000
repos8p	-15.76	-8.21	-11.54	0.405	-12.44	0.514	-8.21	0.000	-8.21	0.000
repos9p	-15.76	-8.21	-11.54	0.405	-12.44	0.514	-8.21	0.000	-8.21	0.000
repos10p	7.83	137.61	137.61	0.000	137.61	0.000	137.61	0.000	137.61	0.000
repos11p	7.83	137.61	137.61	0.000	137.61	0.000	137.61	0.000	137.61	0.000
repos12p	7.83	138.55	138.55	0.000	138.55	0.000	138.55	0.000	138.55	0.000
repos13p	7.83	138.86	138.86	0.000	138.86	0.000	138.86	0.000	138.86	0.000
repos14p	7.83	138.86	138.86	0.000	138.86	0.000	138.86	0.000	138.86	0.000
repos15p	-119.14	-36.59	-36.59	0.000	-36.59	0.000	-36.59	0.000	-36.59	0.000
repos16p	-228.99	-36.59	-36.59	0.000	-36.59	0.000	-36.59	0.000	-36.59	0.000
repos17p	-18.74	-9.36	-9.36	0.000	-9.36	0.000	-9.36	0.000	-9.36	0.000
repos18p	-12.33	5.22	5.22	0.000	5.22	0.000	5.22	0.000	5.22	0.000
repos19p	-12.33	5.22	5.22	0.000	5.22	0.000	5.22	0.000	5.22	0.000
repos20p	-27.13	-11.85	-11.85	0.000	-11.85	0.000	-11.85	0.000	-11.85	0.000
repos21p	-27.13	-11.85	-11.85	0.000	-11.85	0.000	-11.85	0.000	-11.85	0.000
repos22p	-27.13	-11.85	-11.85	0.000	-11.85	0.000	-11.85	0.000	-11.85	0.000
repos23p	-14.13	5.22	5.22	0.000	5.22	0.000	5.22	0.000	5.22	0.000
repos24p	-62.96	-53.89	-53.89	0.000	-53.89	0.000	-53.89	0.000	-53.89	0.000
repos25p	-66.33	-53.13	-53.13	0.000	-53.13	0.000	-53.13	0.000	-53.13	0.000
repos26p	-66.33	-53.13	-53.13	0.000	-53.13	0.000	-53.13	0.000	-53.13	0.000
repos27p	-51.10	-28.20	-28.20	0.000	-28.20	0.000	-28.20	0.000	-28.20	0.000
repos28p	-50.37	-32.13	-32.13	0.000	-32.13	0.000	-32.13	0.000	-32.13	0.000
repos29p	-48.91	-32.13	-32.13	0.000	-32.13	0.000	-32.13	0.000	-32.13	0.000
repos30p	-29.66	5.72	5.35	0.064	5.35	0.064	3.21	0.439	4.86	0.150
repos31p	-41.60	-12.08	-12.08	0.000	-12.08	0.000	-12.08	0.000	-12.08	0.000
repos32p	-37.90	-10.92	-10.92	0.000	-10.92	0.000	-10.92	0.000	-10.92	0.000
repos33p	-40.85	-10.92	-11.53	0.056	-11.41	0.044	-10.92	0.000	-11.41	0.044
repos34p	-352.99	-2.01	-2.22	0.106	-2.01	0.002	-3.26	0.620	-2.01	0.002
repos35p	-1245.56	-	130.35	-	132.16	-	131.34	-	134.69	-
repos36p	-695.71	160.02	151.15	0.055	153.65	0.040	157.51	0.016	149.30	0.067
repos37p	-810.86	139.31	126.54	0.092	129.32	0.072	134.01	0.038	131.28	0.058
repos38p	-695.71	-	149.03	-	151.99	-	154.96	-	154.86	-
repos39p	-512.87	161.53	148.64	0.080	150.21	0.070	146.75	0.091	148.09	0.083
repos40p	-512.87	161.53	148.64	0.080	149.23	0.076	150.36	0.069	151.24	0.064
repos41p	-227.27	-39.60	-49.43	0.248	-49.50	0.250	-52.31	0.321	-50.98	0.287
repos42p	-202.30	253.60	243.06	0.042	243.65	0.039	221.20	0.128	248.49	0.020
repos43p	-159.66	223.98	177.13	0.209	188.92	0.157	163.60	0.270	191.58	0.145
repos44p	-239.09	254.06	186.67	0.265	207.35	0.184	182.91	0.280	211.28	0.168
⊘	-156.96	-	33.59	0.050	34.58	0.048	33.19	0.054	35.05	0.026

on many instances, as can be seen on the top right of the figure. Moreover, RTS-SA is able to obtain roughly $147,000 in additional profit summed across all 44 instances, and narrows the gap to optimality on 9 instances. Table 1 shows the best objective found for each public instance on the various methods and a score showing the gap each approach closes between an initial solution and the optimal solution. A score of 0 indicates an optimal solution is found. A full description of the properties of the instances is given in [16]. The instances are sorted from small to large.

The RTS-SA approach finds two additional optimal solutions over the state-of-the-art SA (repos8p and repos9p). Using the DSC and EC neighborhoods with the original SA is not enough to find optimal solutions on these instances, however RTS and RTS-SA do find the optimal solutions. Inspecting these solutions reveals that vessels do not carry any of the 50 cargo demands available. Instead, RTS is able to find low cost paths for the vessels. The allure of profits likely tricks SA, while RTS is able to avoid this trap because of tabu restrictions. Another interesting result is that RTS itself actually does not outperform even the original SA. RTS achieves an average performance over all instances of 33.19, slightly worse than the original SA. This further confirms the importance of using algorithm selection and hybridization approaches for solving problems.

6   Conclusion

We presented a hybrid reactive tabu search and simulated annealing algorithm for the LSFRP. We introduced two novel neighborhoods for use in both simulated annealing and reactive tabu search. One of these neighborhoods exploits the demand structure of the problem in order to find good solutions, the other attempts to make a chain of changes in order to modify multiple vessel paths in a single step. The addition of these neighborhoods within the hybrid search approach is able to find roughly \$147,000 in additional profit on the public set of LSFRP instances. For future work, a larger dataset of instances is necessary to create a more systematic comparison of approaches. Another question is whether neighborhoods performing a deeper analysis of multiple port visits can be developed to lower the optimality gap on large instances.

References

1. Battiti, R., Tecchiolli, G.: The reactive tabu search. ORSA journal on computing **6**(2), 126–140 (1994)
2. Battiti, R., Tecchiolli, G.: Training neural nets with the reactive tabu search. IEEE Transactions on Neural Networks **6**(5), 1185–1200 (1995)
3. Brouer, B.D., Alvarez, J.F., Plum, C.E.M., Pisinger, D., Sigurd, M.M.: A base integer programming model and benchmark suite for liner-shipping network design. Transportation Science **48**(2), 281–312 (2014)
4. Brouer, B.D., Dirksen, J., Pisinger, D., Plum, C.E.M., Vaaben, B.: The Vessel Schedule Recovery Problem (VSRP) - A MIP model for handling disruptions in liner shipping. European Journal of Operational Research **224**(2), 362–374 (2013)
5. Christiansen, M., Fagerholt, K., Nygreen, B., Ronen, D.: Maritime transportation. Handbooks in operations research and management science **14**, 189–284 (2007)
6. Christiansen, M., Fagerholt, K., Nygreen, B., Ronen, D.: Ship routing and scheduling in the new millennium. European Journal of Operational Research **228**(3), 467–483 (2013)
7. Gendreau, M., Potvin, J.-Y.: Tabu search. In: Gendreau, M., Potvin, J.-Y. (eds.) Handbook of Metaheuristics. International Series in Operations Research and Management Science, vol. 146, pp. 41–59. Springer, US (2010)
8. Glover, F.: Multilevel tabu search and embedded search neighborhoods for the traveling salesman problem. Univ. of Colorado, Graduate School of Business (1991)

9. Kelareva, E., Tierney, K., Kilby, P.: CP methods for scheduling and routing with time-dependent task costs. EURO Journal on Computational Optimization **2**(3), 147–194 (2014)

10. Kohl, N., Larsen, A., Larsen, J., Ross, A., Tiourine, S.: Airline disruption management-perspectives, experiences and outlook. Journal of Air Transport Management **13**(3), 149–162 (2007)

11. Korsvik, J.E., Fagerholt, K., Laporte, G.: A large neighbourhood search heuristic for ship routing and scheduling with split loads. Computers and Operations Research **38**(2), 474–483 (2011)

12. Loureņo, H.R., Martin, O.C., Stützle, T.: Iterated local search. In : Glover, F., Kochenberger, G.A. (eds.) Handbook of Metaheuristics. International Series in OR & MS, vol. 57, pp. 320–353. Springer (2003)

13. Meyer, J., Stahlbock, R., Voß, S.: Slow steaming in container shipping. In: HICSS-45, pp. 1306–1314. IEEE (2012)

14. Smith-Miles, K., Baatar, D., Wreford, B., Lewis, R.: Towards objective measures of algorithm performance across instance space. Computers and Operations Research **45**, 12–24 (2014)

15. Tierney, K.: Optimizing Liner Shipping Fleet Repositioning Plans. Operations Research/Computer Science Interfaces Series, vol. 57. Springer (2015)

16. Tierney, K., Áskelsdóttir, B., Jensen, R.M., Pisinger, D.: Solving the liner shipping fleet repositioning problem with cargo flows. Transportation Science (2014)

17. Tierney, K., Coles, A.J., Coles, A.I., Kroer, C., Britt, A.M., Jensen, R.M.: Automated planning for liner shipping fleet repositioning. In: McCluskey, L., Williams, B., Silva, J.R., Bonet, B. (eds.) Proceedings of ICAPS-2012, pp. 279–287 (2012)

18. Tierney, K., Jensen, R.M.: The liner shipping fleet repositioning problem with cargo flows. In: Hu, H., Shi, X., Stahlbock, R., Voß, S. (eds.) ICCL 2012. LNCS, vol. 7555, pp. 1–16. Springer, Heidelberg (2012)

19. Tierney, K., Jensen, R.M.: A node flow model for the inflexible visitation liner shipping fleet repositioning problem with cargo flows. In: Pacino, D., Voß, S., Jensen, R.M. (eds.) ICCL 2013. LNCS, vol. 8197, pp. 18–34. Springer, Heidelberg (2013)

20. United Nations Conference on Trade and Development (UNCTAD). Review of maritime transport (2013)

21. Voß, S., Fink, A.: Hybridizing reactive tabu search with simulated annealing. In: Hamadi, Y., Schoenauer, M. (eds.) LION 2012. LNCS, vol. 7219, pp. 509–512. Springer, Heidelberg (2012)

Risk Analysis and Quantification of Vulnerability in Maritime Transportation Network Using AIS Data

Kiyotaka Ide[1(✉)], Loganathan Ponnambalam[2], Akira Namatame[1],
Fu Xiuju[2], and Rick Siow Mong Goh[2]

[1] Department of Computer Science, National Defense Academy of Japan, Yokosuka, Japan
ed13001@nda.ac.jp
[2] Computing Science, Institute of High Performance Computing, A*STAR, Singapore, Singapore

Abstract. The risk analysis and vulnerability quantification in the global maritime transportation networks are important to maintain the healthy economy in today's world. In this paper, we analyze the auto identification system (AIS) data that provides us with the real-time location of vessels. The AIS data of a Japanese company was used to compute the throughputs of the ports for the vessel it operates and the topology of the global maritime transportation network during a certain time period. Firstly, we computed the conventional un-weighted node-level characteristics and compared it with the port throughput. This comparison shows the statistically significant correlations, especially, with the in-degree and the Page-Rank. Secondly, we modeled and simulate to quantify the vulnerability and importance of each port identified from the AIS data. The simulation results indicate that Singapore is the most robust and influential port when disrupted. In addition, we introduce a method to compute the vulnerability and importance analytically. Subsequent research will be required to extend the proposed analysis to the complete data sets for all cargo-ships and utilize the high performance computing technologies to accelerate the computation.

Keywords: Automatic identification system · AIS · Complex network analysis · Open data analysis · Risk assessment · Maritime transportation network

1   Introduction

Increase in globalization, outsourcing and inter-dependencies have increased the complexity in the structures of global maritime transportation networks (GMTN). These increasing complexity render the global maritime transportation system face "systemic risks". The systemic risks represented the risks that are caused or enlarged the inter-dependencies in the systems. Since the complexity and inter-dependencies of the GMTN has become increasingly complicated, we believe that the risk assessment and vulnerability quantification focusing on the network structures in the GMTN are meaningful. In addition, it is reported that 90% of the global trade of goods are via the global cargo-ship network, which consists of about 60,000 cargo-ships and more than 5,000 ports [1,2]. The recent tragic disasters such as the earthquake in

© Springer International Publishing Switzerland 2015
F. Corman et al. (Eds.): ICCL 2015, LNCS 9335, pp. 139–151, 2015.
DOI: 10.1007/978-3-319-24264-4_10

and the flood in Thailand in 2011 highlight the importance of risk in transportation networks and hence, remind companies' executives the importance of the of the GMTN. However, quantification of the disruption risks in GMTNs is a challenging issue due to the fact that high inter-dependencies render the origin of the risks unclear and difficult to be identified. There are a number of the antecedents that conduct complex network analysis of the GMTNs. For instance, based on a database of vessel movements, Ducruet et al. [3-5] applied the conventional techniques of analysis, such as centrality measures, to the global liner shipping network in 1996 to 2006. Montes et al. [6] also applied the techniques of the complex network analysis to analyze the database of containership and general cargo vessel positions between 2008 and 2011. The relevance of the time intervals for this analysis, in terms of length and immediacy, will lead us to an accurate and dynamic diagnostic for the evolution during the crisis years in the transport patterns of the two traffics considered. Woolley-Meza et al. [1] investigate the two types of transportation networks: world air-transportation network and global cargo ship network. This study utilized the technique based on effective distances, shortest paths and shortest path trees for strongly weighted symmetric networks, which results in the most significant features both networks can be better reflected to a shortest path tree representation. Also, their investigation results indicate that the effective shortest path distance highly correlates with node centrality measures, and they derive and discuss a functional relationship between node characteristics and resilience a network disruption from their network analysis results. Kaluza et al. [2] investigate AIS data of the GMTN which shows characteristic of the GMTN on three different types of carriers, namely bulk dry carriers, container ships and oil tankers. They compare the empirical data with theoretically estimated traffic flows by the gravity model, which highlights that analysis on the real network are more practical for international policy makings.

The objective of this paper is to develop quantification methodologies to identify vulnerable port(s) and important port(s) based on the real-time observation of the GMTNs. The existing studies introduced above are mainly focused on the analysis of the historical data on a single-year basis or multi-year basis. In addition, studies in the literature mainly analyze the stochastic characteristics of GMTNs from the complex analysis point of view. Such analysis is able to only provide good academic insights however difficult to be utilized by practitioners for actual operations. Therefore, in work, we conduct the series of analysis of the automatic identification system (AIS) data which are available online in real time. In this paper, we analyze the open AIS for the cargo-ships belonging to a specific company on a single-month or several-months basis. In addition, we also suggest a method for modeling and simulation risk identification of port in the GMTNs. To model and simulate the maritime transportation in the GMTNs, lack of information is one of the big difficulties that we encounter. For instance, the information of the contents inside the cargo-ships cannot be easily known. Therefore, analyzing the risks with the deterministic manners resignificant efforts on collecting information and computations varying day by day. Therefore, using the probabilistic approach is one of the possible approaches to address this limitation. We develop a methodology based on the probabilistic diffusion dynamics model, namely Susceptible-Infected- Susceptible (SIS) model [7-12], to analyze the vulnerability and importance of the ports in the GMTNs extracted from the collected AIS data. Probabilistic diffusion dynamics model on complex network has been widely applied into various fields, such as epidemics, computer virus spread, and information diffusion on SNS [7-9]. In this work, we applied the SIS model into the risk assessment in the GMTNs. In the SIS model, each node is probable to take one of the two states, susceptible and infected. Then, the susceptible state can propagate to the neighbor infected state nodes at the infection probability, β, and an infected node can return to the susceptible state at the recovery probability, δ. One of the noteworthy insights in the SIS model is that an epidemic outbreak appears when the effective infection rate, which is the ratio between β and δ, increases above a certain threshold. Recent works in complex network study reveal that the epidemic threshold can be approximated by the inverse of the maximum eigenvalue of the adjacency matrix [13, 14]. In our application to the risk assessment of the GMTNs, nodes with the infected state represent the ports which are suffered by the out of services of the cargo-ships. The susceptible state represents the normally operative ports, however are possible to be suffered by the out of services of the cargo-ships.

This paper consists of six sections; in the following third section, the AIS data set used in this study and their sources are introduced. The fourth section reports the analysis of the AIS data that we collected; in this section, we compute the port and link throughputs and constructed the weighted topology then analyzed the node-level characteristics from the network analysis point of view. The fifth section introduces our methods of modeling and simulation for the risk assessments of the ports in the GMTNs. We propose the indices to quantify the risks of the ports in the GMTN, both the simulation-based and the analytical indices. Also, the sixth section concludes this paper.

2   Data Collection

In this paper, we try to estimate the GMTNs utilizing the auto identification system (AIS) data. The AIS is an automatic vessel tracking system to identify and locate vessels by electronic data exchange with other nearby ships, AIS base station, and satellites. In the AIS data set, the information of call sign of each vessel, time, and location are included. There are several resources to acquire the AIS data set. One of the reliable strategies to collect the AIS data set is to purchase the commercial data set or a license to use the commercial databases. For example, One of the most famous commercial data sources is the database of Lloyd's List (http://www.lloydslistintelligence.com/llint/ais.htm).

Another strategy that can be utilized is to use the open data sources. There are some services that provide with free licenses to use their AIS databases when the users share their collected local AIS data (http://www.marinetraffic.com and http://www.vesseltracker.com). In addition, there are some web services that provides the free trial licenses or free data search functions (http://www.marinetraffic.com and http://sailwx.info/). However, the reliability and completeness of the open data sources may need to be improved because these data sources rely on the data sets shared by the volunteers. Therefore, we combined the data acquired from several sources and tried to improve the accuracies of the data as much as possible.

The dataset that we collected includes the AIS data for about 430 cargo ships belonging to a Japanese company. Approximately 180,000 records had been collected for 3 months since December 1st 2014 to February 28th 2015. A record in the dataset includes the information of the vessel name, call sign, build year, class, time, location (Latitude and Longitude), flag, home port, and the operator. For most of the vessels, datasets had been collected one-hour basis; However, because the data collection based on the voluntary activities, there are some vessels whose time span for the data collection is shorter than the a hour, such as half an hour.

3   Data Analysis

3.1   Throughput Calculations

Using the AIS data that we acquired, firstly, we computed throughputs for the primary 835 ports [15] in the GMTN and the links (routes) connecting the ports. In this paper, the port or link throughput is simply defined by the counts of the AIS records that represent a vessel's stays on the port or the link (i.e. route). Because of the AIS records are basically recorded every fixed time, we can extent to the throughput time for a port or a link. For the port throughput calculations, we searched the two continuous records from the timeline of the AIS data set between which the distance are within 100m for a specific ship. As the second step, we search the port within a circle of 10 km-radius from the location of the records, which were found in the previous step. Then, for the third step, a count of the port throughput is added for the port identified in the second step. Since this calculation counts the two sequenced data of timeline, the significance of the port throughput directly relates to length of time that ships are calling at the ports. For the link throughput calculation, in the case that a new port is selected in the second step of the port throughput calculation, we connect the two ports as a route of the cargo ship transportation. In the case that the existing routes are selected in the previous step, a count is added to the link throughput for the route. Figure 1 visualizes the collected AIS data and the calculated port throughput from December 1st 2014 to February 28th 2015 by utilizing GoogleMaps API. Figure 2 shows the time evolution of the accumulated number of the port throughput for the 17 ports that were identified in the port throughput calculations. As can be seen in this figure, Singapore shows the largest accumulated number constantly and Hong-Kong and Oakland are the second and third largest ports.

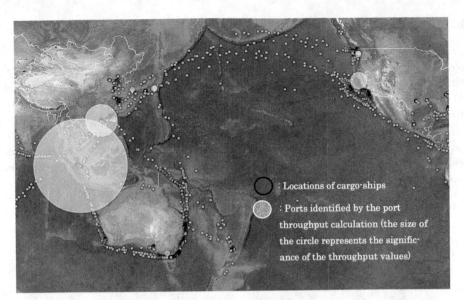

Fig. 1. Visualization of the collected AIS data and the calculated port throughput from December 1st 2014 to February 28th 2015 by utilizing GoogleMaps API. The red dots in the map indicates the locations of the ships within the time window, and the yellow circles shows the location of the ports identified in the port throughput calculation and the size of the yellow circles represent the significances of the throughput

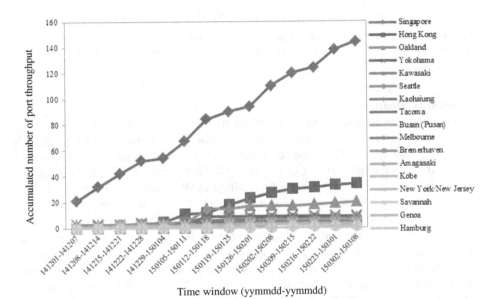

Fig. 2. Time evolution of the port throughput

3.2   Network Analysis

Force-Directed Graph

We then constructed and visualize the network topology utilizing the collected AIS data sets. Figure 3 shows the force-directed graph drawn by Data-Driven Document.js (D3.js) for an arbitrary time window ((a) from Dec. 1st 2015 to Jan. 31st 2015 and (b) from Jan. 1st 2015 to Feb. 28th 2015). D3.js is a JavaScript library for manipulating documents that based on data. In the algorithm to draw the force-directed graph, the nodes which have closer port throughput in closer proximity, while the nodes which have different port throughput are farther apart. The thickness of the links is proportional to the amounts of the link throughput.

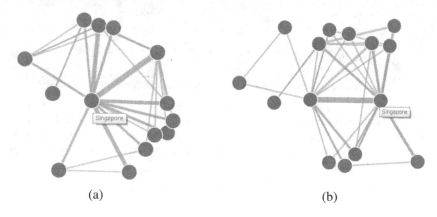

(a)   (b)

Fig. 3. Force-directed graph drawn by Data-Driven Document.js (D3.js) utilizing the collected AIS data sets for time window (a) from Dec. 1st 2015 to Jan. 31st 2015 and (b) from Jan. 1st 2015 to Feb. 28th 2015

Centrality Measures

The centrality is an index to evaluate the relative importance of a node in a network. In this work, we measured the seven conventional centrality measures, namely In-degree, Out-degree, Closeness centrality [16, 17], Betweenness centrality [18], Information centrality [19], Load centrality [20], and PageRank [21] in the non-weighted network for arbitrary time windows. We then investigated as to how only the topological features without the weights of throughputs relates to the port throughputs computed from the actual AIS data. If we found any correlations between the centrality measures and the data-driven throughput, we can predict the future throughput only based on the network topology, which will be important information when we design and reconstruct the cargo-ship transportation networks. We examined the correlation between the centrality measures and the port throughputs, and then drew three types of fitting curves, namely the liner fitting curves, log fitting curves, and exponential fitting curves. We then examined the coefficient of determination to quantify the degree of the correlation between port throughput and the each centrality measure.

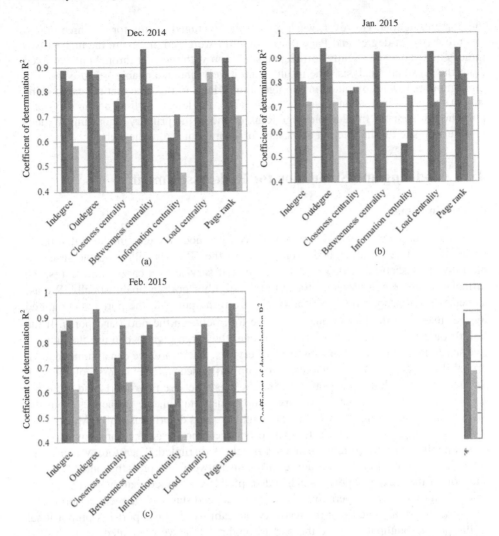

Fig. 4. The comparison results between the centrality measures in un-weighted networks and the port throughputs extracted from the data analysis. Each bar chart represents the coefficients of determination for the three types of fitting curves, namely the liner fitting curve, log fitting curve, and exponential fitting curve for the time spans of (a) Dec. 2014, (b) Jan. 2015, (c) Feb. 2015, and (d) the average of the three months

Figure 4 shows the comparison results of the networks for (a) December 2014, (b) January 2015, (c) February 2015, and (d) the average of the three months. As can be seen in these figures, the conventional centrality measures except the information centrality constantly shows fairy good positive correlation for the both of the liner fitting and the log fitting. However, since the data we collected are still not sufficient and the degree of correlation has been evolving time by time, we cannot explicitly conclude that which centrality measure in the unweight network is the best to estimate the port throughput. However, when we see the averaged results for the three month (Figure 4-(d)) In-degree and Page Rank of the un-weighted graph are the highest two indices that show statistically sufficient correlation with the port throughput extracted from the AIS data analysis. The result is intuitively understandable because the port throughput that was computed in our algorithm relates to the time that the cargo ships stay at the ports, and when the in-degree is large, the length of time a ship stays at a port should increase. In addition, Page Rank is one of the primary algorithms to identify the web site for the Internet users stay for a long time from the web.

4   Modeling and Simulation for Risk Assessment

4.1   Modeling

To assess and quantify the risks in the GMTNs, we modeled and simulated that influences of a failure on a cargo-ship propagate in the GMTNs following the susceptible-infected-susceptible (SIS) model. If an out of service of a cargo-ship occurs, the influences can be considered to travel to the neighbor ports probabilistically. We assumed that the propagation probability β_{ij} from the port i to the port j is computed by the inverse of the link throughput of the link between the port i and port j. If the link throughput between two ports is over one, the cargo owners can use the alternative sea freights and maintain their normal services. Therefore, we can assume that the probability that the out-of-service cargo-ship influences is the inverse of the link throughput of the link (i.e. if only sea freight exists between two ports and there are no alternative way to operate the cargo-ship transportation, the influences from the disruption of the sea freight travel to the neighbor ports deterministically. Meanwhile, if two sea freights are planned to operate between the ports, the cargo owners can commute the other sea freight when a sea freight is disrupted. Therefore, we can consider that the probability of influence diffusion between the ports becomes half). In addition, if there exists a port i which is disrupted, we assumed that the port i is probable to return to normal operations (i.e. non-influenced state) at the recovery probability δ_i. And, we assumed that the recovery probability δ_i on a port i is proportional to the port throughput because the port throughput that we computed relates to the length of time which a cargo-ship stays at the port. In addition, if the length of time that a cargo-ship calls at the port is long, the probability of the mitigation from the influences at the port should be high, and hence, the assumption.

4.2   Quantification Method of the Risks

To quantify the risk in the GMTN, we defined two indices, Vulnerability index (VI) and Amplification index (AI). The VI is defined as the average fraction of the influenced ports from the initial shock on each node as changing the nodes of the initial shock. Therefore the VI is an index that quantifies how easy the ports in the GMTN are influenced by the failures of the cargo-ships in the GMTN. The AI is defined as the average fraction of the influenced ports that an initial shock at a target port caused as changing the initially shocked node. The AI is an index that quantifies how significant a port influences and defuses the influences when the failures occur on the port.

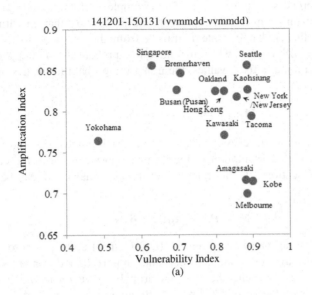

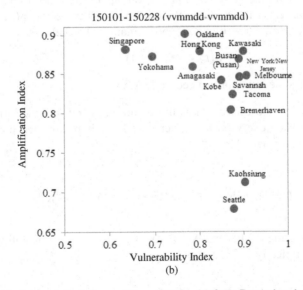

Fig. 5. The comparison results between VI and AI for (a) from December 1st 2014 to January 31st 2015 and (b) from January 1st 2015 to February 28th 2015

4.3   Analytical Approach

In this sub-section, we propose the numerical frameworks to compute VI and AI analytically utilizing the transition probability matrix $\mathbf{M}$. The (i, j) element of the transition probability matrix $\mathbf{M}$ represents the transition probability from state i to the state j in the stochastic processes. In the SIS model in complex network, the (i, j) element of the transition probability matrix $\mathbf{M}$ represents the probability that an entity, such as infected state in the epidemic context, travels from the ith node to the jth node. Therefore, in the SIS model, when the infection probability β and the recovery probability δ for a node is fixed values, the transition probability matrix $\mathbf{M}_{fixed}$ can be obtained as,

$$\mathbf{M}_{fixed} = \beta\mathbf{A} + (1 - \delta)\mathbf{I}, \tag{1}$$

where $\mathbf{A}$ represents the adjacency matrix of the underlying networks, and $\mathbf{I}$ represents the unit matrix. For the assumption of the influence propagation in the GMTNs described in the sub-section 5.1, the transition probability matrix $\mathbf{M}$ can be computed as follows,

$$\mathbf{M} = \mathbf{B} + diag(\mathbf{e} - \boldsymbol{\delta}). \tag{2}$$

Here, $\mathbf{B}$ represents the matrix in which the (i, j) element corresponds to the inverse value of the link throughput between ith port and jth port. In addition, $\mathbf{e}$ is an all-one column vector and $\boldsymbol{\delta}$ represents the recovery probability vector in which the ith elements correspond with the normalized port throughput of ith port. In the probabilistic diffusion dynamics on network, the influenced probability vector, $\mathbf{p}(t)$, at time t can be computed utilizing the transition probability matrix $\mathbf{M}$ as below,

$$\mathbf{p}(t) = \mathbf{M}^{t-1}\mathbf{p}(0), \tag{3}$$

where $\mathbf{p}(0)$ denotes the initial influenced probability.

Then, because AI can be considered as the accumulated ratio of the influenced ports for infinite time when every port is selected as the initial damaged port, AI can be analytically calculated as follows,

$$\text{AI} = (\mathbf{I} + \mathbf{M} + \mathbf{M}^2 + \mathbf{M}^3 + \cdots + \mathbf{M}^t + \cdots)\mathbf{e}. \tag{4}$$

In addition, utilizing the transposed matrix of the transition probability matrix, $^{\mathrm{T}}\mathbf{M}$, the VI can be analytically calculated as follows,

$$\text{VI} = \left(\mathbf{I} + {}^{\mathrm{T}}\mathbf{M} + {}^{\mathrm{T}}\mathbf{M}^2 + \cdots + {}^{\mathrm{T}}\mathbf{M}^t + \cdots\right)\mathbf{e}. \tag{5}$$

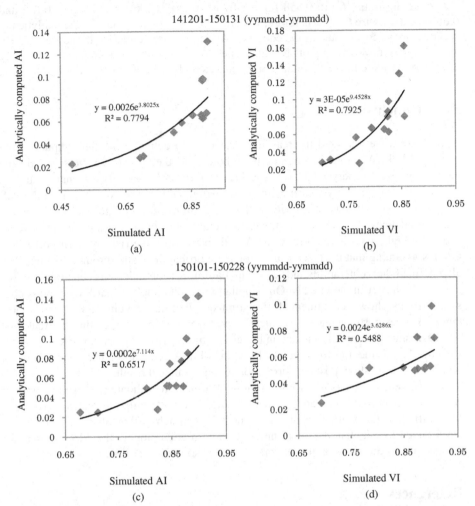

Fig. 6. Comparison results between the simulated indices (AI and VI) in the horizontal axis and the analytically calculated indices in the vertical axis. (a) Comparison results between the simulated AI and the analytically calculated AI for the data sets from Dec. 1st 2014 to Jan. 31st 2015, (b) comparison results between the simulated VI and the analytically calculated VI for the data sets from Dec. 1st 2014 to Jan. 31st 2015, (c) comparison results between the simulated AI and the analytically calculated AI for the data sets from Jan. 1st 2015 to Feb. 28th 2015, and (c) comparison results between the simulated VI and the analytically calculated VI for the data sets from Jan. 1st 2015 to Feb. 28th 2015

Figure 6 shows the comparison results between the simulated indices (AI and VI) in the horizontal axis and the analytically calculated indices (AI and VI) in the vertical axis for the data sets from December 1st 2014 to January 31st 2015 ((a) and (b)) and from January 1st 2015 to February 28th 2015 ((c) and (d)). As can be seen in this figure, the analytically computed indices by equations (4) and (5) show positive exponential correlation to the simulated indices. Also, Spearman's rank correlation are

0.787 for the figure 6-(a), 0.858 for the figure 6-(b), 0.706 for the figure 6-(c), and 0.883 for the figure 6-(d). Therefore, we can conclude the methods for the analytically computations , formulated as the equation (4) and (5) are validated. In the figure 6-(b) and 6-(d), we remove the plots for the highest two largest ports (Singapore and Hong Kong) to calculate the exponential fitting curves and the coefficients of determination.

5   Conclusion

In this work, we analyzed the real-time AIS data to compute the throughputs of the ports and links. We then constructed the topology of the GMTN for the selected time period. Firstly, we analyzed the GMTNs based on the complex network analysis theory to compute the centrality measures in the un-weighted GMTN extracted from the AIS data. From our analysis, it is evident that centralities, except information centrality, show good linear and log correlations. Especially, the in-degree and the Page-Rank show the highest positive correlations. We then assessed the risks of each port in the GMTN assuming that the risks would propagate probabilistically through the links. We also defined the vulnerability index (VI) and amplification index (AI) that quantify the risks of each port in the GMTN. Our simulation results implied that Singapore is constantly robust, however influential, if disrupted. The relative vulnerability and importance of other ports changes dynamically over time, which implies that the real-time risk assessment is crucial to maintain the global maritime transportation systems. Also, we introduce a method to compute the vulnerability and importance analytically, of which the results show positive correlation to the simulated results.

The current work has its own limitations. We need to validate the results from our risk assessment and vulnerability quantification methods utilizing realistic risk data. In addition to the validation of the proposed approach with realistic risk data, we would need to establish the environment to obtain and compute the AIS data sets for all the vessels and analyze the network characteristics for real-time risks.

References

1. Woolley-Meza, O., et al.: Complexity in human transportation networks: a comparative analysis of worldwide air transportation and global cargo-ship movements. Eur. Phys. J. B **84**, 589–600 (2011)
2. Kaluza, P., Kolzsch, A., Gastner, M.T., Blasius, B.: The complex network of global cargo ship movements. J. R. Soc. Interface **7**, 1093 (2010)
3. Ducruet, C., et al.: Centrality and vulnerability in liner shipping networks: revisiting the Northeast Asian Port hierarchy. Maritime Policy and Management **37**(1), 17–36 (2010)
4. Ducruet, C., et al.: Structure and dynamics of liner shipping networks. In: 2010 Annual Conference of the International Association of Maritime Economics, Lisbon, pp. 7–9 (2010)
5. Ducruet, C., et al.: Structure and dynamics of transportation networks: models, methods and applications. In: Rodrigue, J.P., Notteboom, T.E., Shaw, J. (eds.) The SAGE Handbook of Transport Studies, SAGE, pp. 347–364 (2013)

6. Montes, C.P., Seoane, M.J.F., Laxe, F.G.: General cargo and containership emergent routes: A complex networks descriotion. Transport Policy **2**, 4126–4140 (2012)
7. Albert, R., Barabasi, A.L.: Statistical mechanics of complex networks. Reviews of Modern Physics **74**, 47–94 (2002)
8. Dorogovtsev, S.N., Mendes, J.F.F.: Evolution of networks. Advances in Physics **51**, 1079–1187 (2002)
9. Newman, M.E.J.: The structure and function of complex networks. SIAM Review **45**, 167–256 (2003)
10. Dorogovtsev, S.N., Goltsev, A.V., Mendes, J.F.F.: Critical phenomena in complex networks. Reviews of Modern Physics **80**, 1275 (2008)
11. Pastor-Satorras, R., Vespignani, A.: Epidemic dynamics and endemic states in complex networks. Physical Reviews E **63**, 066117 (2001)
12. Boguña, M., Pastor-Satorras, R., Vespignani, A.: Absence of Epidemic Threshold in Scale-Free Networks with Degree Correlations **90**, 028701 (2003)
13. Wang, Y., Chakrabarti, D., Wang, C., Faloutsos, C.: Epidemic spreading in real networks: an eigenvalue viewpoint. In: Proceedings of SRDS, pp. 25–34 (2003)
14. Van Mieghem, P., Omic, J.S., Kooij, R.E.: Virus spread in networks. IEEE/ACM Trans. Net. **17**(1), 1–14 (2009)
15. Hinkelman, E.G.: Dictionary Of International Trade, 8th edn. World Trade Press, Brno (2008)
16. Bavelas, A.: Communication patterns in task-oriented groups. J. Acoust. Soc. Am. **22**(6), 725–730 (1950)
17. Sabidussi, G.: The centrality index of a graph. Psychometrika **31**, 581–603 (1966)
18. Freeman, L.: A set of measures of centrality based upon betweenness. Sociometry **40**, 35–41 (1977)
19. Stephenson, K., Zelen, M.: Rethinking centrality: methods and examples. Soc. Netw. **11**, 1–37 (1989)
20. Newman, M.E.J.: Scientific collaboration networks: II. Shortest paths, weighted networks, and centrality, Phys. Rev. E **64**, 016132 (2001)
21. Brin, S., Page, L.: The anatomy of a large-scale hypertextual Web search engine. Computer Networks and ISDN Systems **30**, 107–117 (1998)

A Branch-and-Price Method for a Ship Routing and Scheduling Problem with Stowage Constraints

Magnus Stålhane[(✉)]

Department of Industrial Economics and Technology Management,
Norwegian University of Science and Technology, Trondheim, Norway
magnus.stalhane@iot.ntnu.no

Abstract. In this paper we study a maritime pickup and delivery problem with time windows and stowage constraints. The problem is inspired by a real life ship routing and scheduling problem from a sub-segment of shipping known as *project shipping*. What is unique about this sub-segment is that they transport unique and specialized cargoes, that make stowage onboard the ships complex, and thus must be considered when creating routes and schedules for the ships. To solve this problem we propose a branch-and-price method, including a novel way of solving the subproblems using a labeling algorithm. To speed up the solution process we relax some of the restrictions in the subproblem, giving us a simpler subproblem that may produce infeasible paths. The computational results show the branch-and-price method provides optimal solutions to many instances previously unsolved by the literature, and that it is competitive with the tabu search heuristic for many instances.

Keywords: Maritime transportation · Branch-and-price · Vehicle routing · Stowage

1 Introduction

In this paper we study a ship routing and scheduling problem with stowage constraints. The problem stems from a sub-segment of tramp shipping, called project shipping, which specializes in transporting unique and oddly shaped cargoes. These cargoes may for instance be parts of an oil platform, train cars, reactors, yachts, or wind turbines. Due to the special shape of each cargo, stowage onboard the ship is more of an issue in this segment of shipping, than in wet or dry-bulk shipping where cargoes are poured into tanks or cargo holds. Often an engineering team is used to assess how to store and secure the cargo onboard the ship so that it is not damaged during transportation, and to ensure the stability of the ship during the voyage. The cargo can be stored either on the deck, or in the cargo hold below deck. The engineering team estimates the area above deck, and the volume below deck that is needed to store the cargo. Some cargoes can be stored both above and below deck, while others can only be stored in one of the two.

© Springer International Publishing Switzerland 2015
F. Corman et al. (Eds.): ICCL 2015, LNCS 9335, pp. 152–165, 2015.
DOI: 10.1007/978-3-319-24264-4_11

In addition to the stowage considerations, project shipping also has some other unique characteristics. One is that contracts are often offered to transport a set of cargoes. Thus, the shipping company must commit itself to service all cargoes in the set, or none of them. Such cargoes are referred to in this paper as *coupled cargoes*. Another unique aspect is that some contracts require that the cargoes are transported directly from the pickup port to the discharge port, and that no other cargoes may be onboard the ship concurrently. In this paper we refer to these cargoes as cargoes that require a *dedicated ship*.

Apart from the aspects mentioned above, the ship routing and scheduling problem of a project shipping company is the same as that of a tramp shipping company, and may be defined as a maritime version of the pickup and delivery problem with time windows (PDPTW)([4]). The problem consists of transporting a set of cargoes using a fixed fleet of ships. Each cargo has a given size/quantity and must be picked up and delivered at specified ports within pre-determined time windows. In maritime transportation the cargoes are usually divided into contracted (or mandatory) cargoes that must be serviced, and optional (or spot) cargoes that may be serviced if it is profitable and the fleet has sufficient capacity. The fleet of ships is heterogeneous and may have different draft, cargo capacity, speed, cost structure, and initial position. The objective of the problem is to find one route and schedule for each ship, so that the total profit of the shipping company is maximized.

The problem studied in this paper was first presented by [7]. They present an arc-flow model of the problem, as well as a tabu search heuristic to obtain good primal solution to larger instances. A similar problem from project shipping has also been studied by [1] and [12]. What separates their problem from the one studied in this paper is that they consider temporal synchronization of the deliveries of the coupled cargoes, but do not consider stowage onboard the ships, nor cargoes that require direct sailing. In [1] three path-flow formulations are presented and solved using a priori path generation, while [12] presented a branch-and-price method. Numerical experiments show that the branch-and-price method is superior to a priori path generation.

Branch-and-price (B&P) has been one of the most successful methods for solving different variants of the maritime PDPTW, e.g. [3], [11], [14], [6]. A ship routing and scheduling problem with flexible cargo quantities is studied in [3], while [11] presents a variant where each cargo can be split among several ships. In [14] a problem that combines ship routing and scheduling with bunkering decisions for the ships is described, and [6] studies a problem that combines routing and scheduling decisions with inventory management in the ports.

There are several other types stowage problems that have been discussed in the literature, including those presented by [13], [9], and [5]. In [13] and [5] the stowage of containers onboard ships is considered with respect to both stability of the ships and efficient loading and unloading of the containers, while [9] considers a stowage problem in RoRo shipping where cars are stowed on decks onboard specialized ships.

The purpose of this paper is to present a new exact solution method to the ship routing and scheduling problem with stowage constraints. The method is based on branch-and-price, where the master problem is solved as a linear program, while the supbroblem is solved as an elementary shortest path problem using a labeling algorithm. Section 2 gives a formal description of the problem and a mathematical model. In Section 3 the details of the branch-and-price solution method is given, before a computational study is given in Section 4. Finally, some concluding remarks are made in Section 5.

2 Problem Description and Mathematical Model

We define the problem of transporting n cargoes on a graph $G = (\mathcal{N}, \mathcal{A})$, where $\mathcal{N} = \{1, \ldots, 2n\}$ is the set of nodes, and $\mathcal{A}$ is the set of arcs connecting pairs of nodes in the graph. The set $\mathcal{N}$ can be divided into the set of pickup nodes, $\mathcal{N}^P = \{1, \ldots, n\}$, and the set of delivery nodes, $\mathcal{N}^D = \{n+1, \ldots, 2n\}$. The set $\mathcal{N}^P$ can further be divided into the set of pickup nodes associated with contracted cargoes, $\mathcal{N}^C$, that have to be transported, and the set of pickup nodes associated with optional (or spot) cargoes, $\mathcal{N}^O$.

Associated with each cargo $i \in \{1, \ldots, n\}$ is a unique pickup node $i \in \mathcal{N}^P$, a delivery node $(n+i) \in \mathcal{N}^D$, and a revenue R_i for transporting the cargo. Each node $i \in \mathcal{N}$ has a time window $[\underline{T}_i, \overline{T}_i]$ which gives an earliest and a latest time for start of service at the node.

Further, let $\mathcal{N}^{DS} \subseteq \mathcal{N}^P$ be the set of pickup nodes where the corresponding cargo requires a dedicated ship, i.e. no other cargoes can be onboard the ship concurrently. This also implies that a ship servicing this cargo will travel directly from the pickup node to the corresponding delivery node. Thus, the set $\mathcal{A}$ is constructed so that for each node $i \in \mathcal{N}^{DS}$ the only arc extending from node i is the arc $(i, n+i)$. In addition, we have a set $\mathcal{K}$ of sets of optional coupled cargoes $\mathcal{N}^K_k$ where $k = 1, \ldots, |\mathcal{K}|$. For these sets either all cargoes in the set have to be transported, or none of them.

The available fleet is heterogeneous and considered fixed during the planning horizon. The set of ships $\mathcal{V}$ is indexed by v, and each ship v has two storage areas onboard, one below deck with capacity K^V_v and one above deck with capacity K^A_v. The below deck capacity is limited by the volume of the cargo hold, while the above deck capacity is limited by the deck area. Each cargo i has a given area Q^A_i and a given volume Q^V_i that the engineering team has estimated is sufficient to securely store the cargo above/below deck. If a cargo cannot be placed above/below deck the corresponding value is set to infinity. The cargo may not be moved during a voyage, thus once a cargo is placed either above or below deck it must remain there until it is unloaded.

Each ship v has a starting position $o(v)$, an artificial ending position $d(v)$, and a graph $G_v = (\mathcal{N}_v, \mathcal{A}_v)$ associated with it. The set of vertices $\mathcal{N}_v \subseteq \mathcal{N} \cup \{o(v), d(v)\}$, and the set of arcs $\mathcal{A}_v \subset \mathcal{N}_v \times \mathcal{N}_v$ define the feasible movements for ship v. For each arc $(i, j) \in \mathcal{A}_v$ there is a corresponding non-negative cost C_{ijv}, and a time T_{ijv} for traversing that arc. Included in the traversal time is both the service time at node i and the sailing time from node i to node j. We assume that the triangle inequality holds for both travel times and travel costs.

Note that not all ships are allowed to pick up all cargoes due to the shape/size of the cargoes themselves, or draft/width limitations at the origin or destination ports.

A route r for a ship v corresponds to a feasible path from $o(v)$ to $d(v)$ in G_v. The path is feasible if for each pickup node i visited, the corresponding delivery node $n + i$ is visited afterwards, the deck and cargo hold capacities of the ship is never violated, and the time windows are respected at every node. The total profit of route r, P_{vr}, is the sum of the revenue of the cargoes transported, minus the sum of the arc costs of traversing the corresponding path. The objective is to find the set of routes, one for each ship, that maximizes the total profit of the fleet over the planning horizon.

To present the mathematical formulation of the problem, we need to introduce some additional notation. Let $\mathcal{R}_v$ be the set of all feasible routes for ship v, and let coefficient A_{ivr} be equal to 1 if ship v transports cargo i when sailing route r, and 0 otherwise. Finally, let variables λ_{vr} be equal to one if route r is sailed by ship v, and 0 otherwise, while z_k are the variables representing whether the cargoes in coupled cargo set k are transported or not. The path-flow formulation of the problem is defined as follows:

$$(MP) \max \sum_{v \in \mathcal{V}} \sum_{r \in \mathcal{R}_v} P_{vr} \lambda_{vr}, \tag{1}$$

subject to:

$$\sum_{v \in \mathcal{V}} \sum_{r \in \mathcal{R}_v} A_{ivr} \lambda_{vr} = 1, \qquad \forall i \in \mathcal{N}^C, \tag{2}$$

$$\sum_{v \in \mathcal{V}} \sum_{r \in \mathcal{R}_v} A_{ivr} \lambda_{vr} \leq 1, \qquad \forall i \in \mathcal{N}^O, \tag{3}$$

$$\sum_{v \in \mathcal{V}} \sum_{r \in \mathcal{R}_v} A_{ivr} \lambda_{vr} = z_k, \qquad k = 1, \ldots, |\mathcal{K}|, \forall i \in \mathcal{N}_k^{\mathcal{K}}, \tag{4}$$

$$\sum_{r \in \mathcal{R}_v} \lambda_{vr} = 1, \qquad \forall v \in \mathcal{V}, \tag{5}$$

$$\lambda_{vr} \in \{0, 1\}, \qquad \forall v \in \mathcal{V}, r \in \mathcal{R}_v, \tag{6}$$

$$z_k \in \{0, 1\}, \qquad k = 1, \ldots, |\mathcal{K}|. \tag{7}$$

The objective function (1) maximizes the total profit of the shipping operations. Constraints (2) state that all mandatory cargoes must be transported, while constraints (3) ensure that all optional cargoes are serviced at most once. Constraints (4) state that either all or none of the cargoes in a coupled set must be lifted, while constraints (5) limit each ship to sail exactly one route. Finally, constraints (6) and (7) put binary restrictions on the variables.

3   Solution Method

The path-flow model presented above assumes that all routes for all ships are known. As the number of feasible routes through the network increase exponentially as a function of the number of cargoes, generating all of them is impractical, or even impossible, for most realistic instances of the problem. To circumvent this problem, we introduce a solution method based on branch-and-price ([2]), where only a small number of routes are explicitly generated, while the remaining routes are considered implicitly.

Branch-and-price combines a branch-and-bound (B&B) tree-search to obtain integral solutions, with a column generation procedure ([8]) to obtain bounds in each node of the B&B-tree. Let RMP represent the MP-model with constraints (6) and (7) relaxed, and the sets R_v replaced with $\hat{R}_v$ containing only a small subset of all routes. In each node of the B&B-tree the method iterates between solving the RMP and a set of subproblems that finds new routes with a positive reduced cost. These new routes are then added to $\hat{R}_v$, and a new iteration is started by re-solving the RMP. Once no more routes with a positive reduced cost can be found, we have proved that the solution is optimal, and thus a valid upper bound of the current B&B-node. If the solution of the node satisfies the integral requirement of constraints (6) and (7), a new feasible solution to the original problem has been found, otherwise we either prune the node, or branch on some property of the problem to create two new nodes, depending on the objective value.

In the following we present the details of our branch-and-price method. In Section 3.1 we formulate the subproblem that gives the maximum reduced cost route for a given ship, before we present the details of the labeling algorithm used to solve the subproblem in Section 3.2. In Section 3.3 we explain how the computational effort of the labeling algorithm may be improved by an acceleration strategy, before presenting how the branching is performed in the B&B-tree to obtain integral solutions in Section 3.4.

3.1   Subproblem

In order to formulate the subproblem for ship v, $SP(v)$, we need to define some additional notation. Let α_i^*, γ_{ik}^*, and β_v^* be the optimal values of the dual variables of constraints (2) and (3), (4), and (5), respectively, for a given solution of the RMP. To make the formulation more readable we assume that γ_{ik}^* exists, but with a value of zero if cargo i is not part of coupled cargo set k. Further, let x_{ijv} be equal to one if arc (i,j) is used by ship v, and zero otherwise. Variable y_i is equal to 1 if the cargo picked up at node i is stored above deck, and 0 if it is stored below deck. Finally, let l_{iv}^A and l_{iv}^V be the capacity used above and below deck on ship v after leaving node i, and t_{iv} be the start of service at node i. The subproblem for ship v may then be formulated in the following way:

$$(SP(v)) \max -\beta_v^* + \sum_{i \in \mathcal{N}^P} \sum_{j \in \mathcal{N}_v} \left(R_i - \alpha_i^* - \sum_{k=1}^{k=|\mathcal{K}|} \gamma_{ik}^* \right) x_{ijv} - \sum_{(i,j) \in \mathcal{A}_v} C_{ijv} x_{ijv}, \quad (8)$$

subject to:

$$\sum_{j \in \mathcal{N}_v} x_{o(v)jv} = 1, \quad (9)$$

$$\sum_{j \in \mathcal{N}_v} x_{jiv} - \sum_{j \in \mathcal{N}_v} x_{ijv} = 0, \qquad i \in \mathcal{N}_v \setminus \{o(v), d(v)\}, \qquad (10)$$

$$\sum_{i \in \mathcal{N}_v} x_{id(v)v} = 1, \qquad\qquad\qquad\qquad\qquad (11)$$

$$l_{iv}^A \le y_i Q_i^A, \qquad\qquad \forall v \in \mathcal{V}, i \in \mathcal{N}^{DS}, \qquad (12)$$

$$l_{iv}^V \le (1 - y_i) Q_i^V, \qquad\qquad \forall v \in \mathcal{V}, i \in \mathcal{N}^{DS}, \qquad (13)$$

$$(l_{iv}^A + Q_j^A y_j - l_{jv}^A) x_{ijv} \le 0, \qquad \forall j \in \mathcal{N}^P, (i,j) \in \mathcal{A}_v, \qquad (14)$$

$$(l_{iv}^A - Q_j^A y_j - l_{(n+j)v}^A) x_{i(n+j)v} \le 0, \qquad \forall j \in \mathcal{N}^P, (i, (n+j)) \in \mathcal{A}_v, \qquad (15)$$

$$(l_{iv}^V + Q_j^V (1 - y_j) - l_{jv}^V) x_{ijv} \le 0, \qquad \forall j \in \mathcal{N}^P, (i,j) \in \mathcal{A}_v, \qquad (16)$$

$$(l_{iv}^V - Q_j^V (1 - y_j) - l_{(n+j)v}^V) x_{i(n+j)v} \le 0, \quad \forall j \in \mathcal{N}^P, (i, (n+j)) \in \mathcal{A}_v, \qquad (17)$$

$$l_{iv}^A \le K_v^A \sum_{j \in \mathcal{N}_v} x_{ijv}, \qquad\qquad \forall i \in \mathcal{N}^P, \qquad (18)$$

$$l_{iv}^V \le K_v^V \sum_{j \in \mathcal{N}_v} x_{ijv}, \qquad\qquad \forall i \in \mathcal{N}^P, \qquad (19)$$

$$l_{(n+i)v}^A + Q_i^A y_i \le K_v^A \sum_{j \in \mathcal{N}_v} x_{ijv}, \qquad \forall i \in \mathcal{N}^P, \qquad (20)$$

$$l_{(n+i)v}^V + Q_i^V (1 - y_i) \le K_v^V \sum_{j \in \mathcal{N}_v} x_{ijv}, \qquad \forall i \in \mathcal{N}^P, \qquad (21)$$

$$(t_{iv} + T_{ijv} - t_{jv}) x_{ijv} \le 0, \qquad \forall (i,j) \in \mathcal{A}_v, \qquad (22)$$

$$\sum_{j \in \mathcal{N}_v} x_{ijv} - \sum_{j \in \mathcal{N}_v} x_{(i+n)jv} = 0, \qquad \forall i \in \mathcal{N}^P, \qquad (23)$$

$$t_{iv} + T_{i(n+i)v} - t_{(n+i)v} \le 0, \qquad \forall i \in \mathcal{N}^P, \qquad (24)$$

$$\underline{T}_i \le t_{iv} \le \overline{T}_i, \qquad\qquad \forall i \in \mathcal{N}_v, \qquad (25)$$

$$l_{iv}^A \ge 0, \qquad\qquad \forall i \in \mathcal{N}_v, \qquad (26)$$

$$l_{iv}^V \ge 0, \qquad\qquad \forall i \in \mathcal{N}_v, \qquad (27)$$

$$x_{ijv} \in \{0,1\}, \qquad\qquad \forall (i,j) \in \mathcal{A}_v, \qquad (28)$$

$$y_i \in \{0,1\}, \qquad\qquad \forall i \in \mathcal{N}^P. \qquad (29)$$

The objective of the subproblem is to find the path through the network with the highest reduced cost. Constraints (9) – (11) conserve the flow through the network from the origin to the artificial destination of the ship. Further, constraints (12) and (13) ensure that there are no other cargoes on-board the ship when leaving the pickup node of a cargo demanding a dedicated ship, while constraints (14) – (21) keep track of the load on-board the ship, both above and below deck. Constraints (22) make sure that the start of service at two consecutive nodes are at least separated by the sailing time between them. Pairing and precedence between a pickup node and the corresponding delivery node is handled by constraints (23) and (24), and constraints (25) ensure that the start of service at each node is within the time window if the node is serviced. Finally constraints (26) and (27) ensure that the loaded quantities above and below deck are non-negative, while constraints (28) and (29) put binary restrictions on the arc-flow and stowage decision variables, respectively.

3.2   A Labeling Algorithm for the Subproblems

The subproblems presented above are variants of the elementary shortest path problem with resource constraints (ESPPRC). In [10] an efficient labeling algorithm to solve the ESPPRC for the PDPTW is presented. We use a modified version of the algorithm proposed in their paper to solve $SP(v)$.

The subproblems are solved as shown in Algorithm 1. U is the set of unprocessed labels, initially only containing the label L_0 representing a path that consists of only the ship's origin node, $o(v)$. While there are labels left in U, the $removefirst(U)$ function removes one label from U according to some criteria. This label, representing a path ending at node i, is extended along all arcs $(i, j) \in \mathcal{A}_v$, creating new labels, L'. If the new extended label ending at node j is resource feasible, it is checked for dominance, and if it is not dominated by any other label, it is added to U and the set $\mathcal{L}_j$ containing all non-dominated labels at node j. Any labels in $\mathcal{L}_j$ that are dominated by L' are removed from both $\mathcal{L}_j$ and U. Once there are no more unprocessed labels left in U we filter out the paths represented by the labels in $\mathcal{L}_{d(v)}$ with positive reduced cost, and add them to the set $\mathcal{P}$, which is then returned by the algorithm.

In the following we describe which resources are stored in a label, what the resource extension functions look like, what constitutes a feasible extension, and how labels are compared for dominance.

Labels. Each label contain the following resources:

1. η - the node of the label
2. ϕ - the predecessor label
3. t - the earliest time service can start at the node
4. c - the accumulated reduced cost
5. $\mathcal{V}$ - the set of cargoes picked up (and possibly delivered)
6. $\mathcal{O}^A$ - the set of cargoes currently onboard and placed above deck
7. $\mathcal{O}^V$ - the set of cargoes currently onboard and placed below deck

The notation $t(L)$ is used to refer to the arrival time at the node of label L and similar notation is used for the rest of the data (i.e., $\eta(L)$, $\phi(L)$, $c(L)$, $\mathcal{V}(L)$, $\mathcal{O}^A(L)$, and $\mathcal{O}^V(L)$).

Algorithm 1. Pseudo-code of labeling algorithm for ship v

Input: graph $G_v = (\mathcal{N}_v, \mathcal{A}_v)$
$U = \{L_0\}$
while $U \neq \emptyset$ **do**
  $L = removefirst(U)$
  let i be the last node of the path represented by label L
  for each node $j : (i,j) \in \mathcal{A}_v$ **do**
    create new label L' extending L to node j
    if L' is resource feasible **then**
      if no label in $\mathcal{L}_j$ dominates L' **then**
        remove all labels in $\mathcal{L}_j$ and U that are dominated by L'
        $\mathcal{L}_i = \mathcal{L}_j \cup \{L'\}$
        $U = U \cup \{L'\}$
      end if
    end if
  end for
end while
for $L \in \mathcal{L}_{d(v)}$ **do**
  if reduced cost of $L > 0$ **then**
    add the path represented by L to $\mathcal{P}$
  end if
end for
return $\mathcal{P}$

Label Extension. When extending a label L along an arc $(\eta(L), j)$, we create up to two new labels L' at node j. If j is a pickup node we create one label where $y_i = 1$, and one label where $y_i = 0$. If it is not a pickup node, only one label is created. The resources of the new label L' are updated according to the following resource extension functions:

$$\eta(L') = j \tag{30}$$

$$\phi(L') = L \tag{31}$$

$$t(L') = \max\{\underline{T}_j, t(L) + T_{\eta(L)jv}\} \tag{32}$$

$$c(L') = c(L) - C_{\eta(L)jv} + \begin{cases} R_j - \alpha_j^* - \sum_{k=1}^{k=|\mathcal{K}|} \gamma_{jk}^* & \text{if } j \in \mathcal{N}^P \\ -\beta_v & \text{if } j = d(v) \\ 0 & \text{otherwise} \end{cases} \tag{33}$$

$$\mathcal{V}(L') = \begin{cases} \mathcal{V}(L) \cup \{j\} & \text{if } j \in \mathcal{N}^P \\ \mathcal{V}(L) & \text{otherwise} \end{cases} \tag{34}$$

$$\mathcal{O}^A(L') = \begin{cases} \mathcal{O}^A(L) \cup \{j\} & \text{if } j \in \mathcal{N}^P \wedge y_i = 1 \\ \mathcal{O}^A(L) \setminus \{j - n\} & \text{if } j \in \mathcal{N}^D \\ \mathcal{O}^A(L) & \text{otherwise} \end{cases} \tag{35}$$

$$\mathcal{O}^V(L') = \begin{cases} \mathcal{O}^V(L) \cup \{j\} & \text{if } j \in \mathcal{N}^P \wedge y_i = 0 \\ \mathcal{O}^V(L) \setminus \{j - n\} & \text{if } j \in \mathcal{N}^D \\ \mathcal{O}^V(L) & \text{otherwise} \end{cases} \tag{36}$$

Equations (30) – (33) update the current node, the predecessor label, the time spent, and the accumulated reduced cost of the label, respectively. Equation (34) updates the set of cargoes serviced on the path represented by the label , while equation (35) and (36) updates the cargoes above and below deck by adding (removing) a cargo from the set when visiting a pickup (delivery) node.

An extension of an arc is feasible if:

$$t(L') \leq \overline{T}_j, \tag{37}$$

$$\sum_{i \in \mathcal{O}^A(L')} Q_i^A \leq K_v^A, \tag{38}$$

$$\sum_{i \in \mathcal{O}^V(L')} Q_i^V \leq K_v^V, \tag{39}$$

$$\mathcal{O}^A(L') \cup \mathcal{O}^V(L') = \{j\} \vee j \notin \mathcal{N}^{DS}, \tag{40}$$

and one of the following hold:

$$0 < j \leq n \wedge j \notin \mathcal{V}(L) \tag{41}$$

$$n < j \leq 2n \wedge j - n \in \mathcal{O}^A(L) \cup \mathcal{O}^V(L) \tag{42}$$

$$j = d(v) \wedge \mathcal{O}^A(L) = \mathcal{O}^V(L) = \emptyset \tag{43}$$

Dominance Criterion

Proposition 1. *A label L_1 dominates L_2 if:*

1. $\eta(L_1) = \eta(L_2)$
2. $t(L_1) \leq t(L_2)$
3. $c(L_1) \geq c(L_2)$
4. $\mathcal{V}(L_1) \subseteq \mathcal{V}(L_2)$
5. $\mathcal{O}^A(L_1) \subseteq \mathcal{O}^A(L_2)$
6. $\mathcal{O}^V(L_1) \subseteq \mathcal{O}^V(L_2)$

This dominance criterion is the same as the one presented by [10] with the exception of 5. and 6. which are new to this problem. The correctness of this dominance criterion may be proved similarly to the proof presented by [10].

3.3   Acceleration Strategy

One problem with the method presented above, is that there are potentially many feasible ways to store a given set of cargoes. This may lead to generating many labels that represent the same path through the network, and since the stowage only affects feasibility, all these labels will have the same reduced cost when reaching the end node, $d(v)$.

One way to circumvent this problem, and get an easier subproblem, is to relax the constraint that the cargo cannot move between storages during a voyage. This may be handled in the labeling algorithm by simply storing the cargoes onboard the ship at any given time, $\mathcal{O}(L) = \mathcal{O}^A(L) \bigcup \mathcal{O}^V(L)$, instead of storing information regarding whether the cargo is stored above or below deck. An advantage of this is that we only generate one new label whenever extending a label to a new pickup node, instead of two.

To ensure feasibility of the new label, we replace equations (38) and (39) with the following mathematical program for a given label L:

$$\min w^A + w^V, \tag{44}$$

$$\text{subject to:} \tag{45}$$

$$\sum_{i \in \mathcal{O}(L)} Q_i^A y_j - w^A \le K_v^A, \tag{46}$$

$$\sum_{i \in \mathcal{O}(L)} Q_i^V (1 - y_j) - w^V \le K_v^V, \tag{47}$$

$$y_i \in \{0, 1\}, \forall i \in \mathcal{O}(L), \tag{48}$$

$$w^A, w^V \ge 0. \tag{49}$$

If there exist a feasible solution with a value of zero, then there exists a feasible stowage plan for the cargoes currently onboard. We solve this mathematical problem with a simple depth-first dynamic program which terminates if a feasible solution with value zero is found. With this modification we have the same labels as [10], and may use the same dominance criterion, i.e. $1 - 4$ from proposition 1, and $\mathcal{O}(L_1) \subseteq \mathcal{O}(L_2)$.

The optimal path produced by the modified algorithm may then be checked to see if it is stowage feasible using a simple dynamic programing algorithm. By doing this we get three possible outcomes.

1. The optimal path has a non-positive reduced cost
2. The optimal path has a positive reduced cost and is stowage feasible
3. The optimal path has a positive reduced cost, but it not stowage feasible

In the first case we have proved that no positive reduced cost path exists for the given ship, and in the second case the path may be added to the RMP which may then be re-solved. Only in the third case do we need to solve the exact pricing problem, since in this case it is possible that a stowage feasible solution with a positive reduced cost has been excluded by the dominance test.

3.4   Branching

To perform branching in the B&B tree, we consider the following four branching strategies that are used in a hierarchical fashion.

1. branch on the value of the z_k variables in the master problem
2. branch on whether an optional cargo is tranported or not
3. branch on whether a given ship transports a given cargo or not
4. branch on whther a given ship traverses a given arc or not

The first two branchsing strategies can be handled just by making changes to the master problem, either by fixing the corresponding z_k variable, or by by replacing the $\leq$ with an $=$ for the corresponding constraint in (3), and change the coefficient to 0 in the zero branch.

The third branching strategy may be implemented either by removing the nodes representing the given cargo from the subproblem of the ship in the case of the zero-branch, or by removing the same nodes from the subproblems of all other ships in the case of the one-branch. Finally, the fourth branching strategy may be imposed by removing the arc from the subproblem of the given ship in the case of the zero-branch, or by forcing the ship to traverse the given arc in the case of the one-branch. This branch also forces us to change the dominance criteria so that a label can only dominate another label if it has traversed a superset of the one-branch arcs that another label has traversed.

The nodes in the B&B tree are processed in a best first order, depending on the upper bound of their parent.

4   Computational Study

The solution method presented in this paper has been implemented in Java 6.0 and uses the XpressMP 1.19.0 LP-solver through its BCL interface. The computational experiments have been run on an HP DL 160 G5 computer with an Intel Xeon QuadCore E5472 3.0 GHz processor, 16 GB of RAM and running on a Linux operating system. The Java-code is run as a single thread, thus not taking advantage of the multi-core processor.

4.1   Test Results

Table 1 shows the test instances used by [7] to test their tabu search heuristic. We have tested our branch-and-price method on the same set of instances. A comparison of the computing times may be seen in Table 2. We see that the branch-and-price method is able to solve all but the largest test instance within the two hour limit, and thus has proved optimality of seven previously unsolved instances. Further, we see that the computing time used by the branch-and-price method is competitive with running the tabu search for 10 000 iterations.

It is also interesting to note that the full pricing problem is never solved for any of the instances, because the maximum positive reduced cost path produced by the accelerated version of the pricing problem are always stowage feasible. This indicates that the simplified stowage constraints considered in the accelerated version of the subproblem are sufficient to get feasible paths through the network for realistic instances of the problem.

An added contribution is that we are able to present improved optimality gaps for the tabu search heuristics presented in [7]. As their arc-flow model could only solve the six smallest instances, we give the optimality gap of the solutions provided by the tabu search heuristic for all instances in Table 3. The table shows that the average optimality gap is less than 2.02 % for all instances when running the tabu search for 1000 iterations, while it is less than 0.7 % when running the tabu search for 10 000 iterations. Thus we have shown that the tabu search heuristic performs even better than what was shown in the original paper.

Table 1. Overview of the instances used by [7]. We present the number of ships ($| \mathcal{V} |$), the number of cargoes (n), tne number of cargo sets ($| \mathcal{K} |$), and the number of cargoes that demand direct sailing ($| \mathcal{N}^{DS} |$). Each cargo set contains exactly two cargoes.

Instance	1	2	3	4	5	6	7	8	9	10	11	12	13	14
Ships	3	2	3	3	3	4	3	4	4	5	5	6	6	8
Cargoes	6	8	8	10	10	10	12	12	14	18	20	30	40	63
Cargo sets	4	5	5	4	6	6	8	8	8	11	13	19	26	38
Direct sailing	1	1	1	0	0	0	1	1	1	1	1	2	2	2

Table 2. Comparison of the solution times obtained by branch-and-price to the computing times presented by [7]. All computational times are given in seconds.

Instance	Arc-flow model	Tabu search Heuristic		Branch-and-price
		1000 Iterations	10 000 iterations	
1	7	7	69	1
2	5 759	10	94	1
3	514	9	94	1
4	129	11	112	1
5	128	11	108	1
6	630	11	103	1
7	>7200	14	139	10
8	>7200	15	146	9
9	>7200	17	163	3
10	>7200	19	185	11
11	>7200	22	221	41
12	>7200	28	272	277
13	>7200	71	697	1343
14	>7200	151	1597	>7200

Table 3. Optimality gap for the tabu search heuristic given as tabu search solution divided by the optimal solution.

	1000 Iterations		10 000 iterations	
Instance	best. Sol	avg. Sol	best. Sol	avg. Sol
1	1.0000	1.0000	1.0000	1.0000
2	1.0000	1.0000	1.0000	1.0000
3	1.0000	1.0000	1.0000	1.0000
4	0.9960	0.9960	0.9960	0.9960
5	1.0000	1.0000	1.0000	1.0000
6	1.0000	1.0000	1.0000	1.0000
7	1.0000	1.0000	1.0000	1.0000
8	1.0000	1.0000	1.0000	1.0000
9	1.0000	1.0000	1.0000	1.0000
10	1.0000	0.9940	1.0000	1.0000
11	0.9961	0.9898	0.9961	0.9961
12	0.9994	0.9818	1.0000	0.9988
13	1.0000	0.9798	1.0000	0.9991
14	0.9913	0.9849	0.9939	0.9931

5   Concluding Remarks

In this paper we have presented an exact solution method, based on branch-and-price, to solve a ship routing and scheduling problem with stowage constraints. The master problem is formulated as a path-flow model and is solved as a linear program, while the subproblems, one for each ship, is solved as an elementary shortest path problem with resource constraints using a labeling algorithm. To speed up the solution process we relax some of the restrictions in the subproblem, giving us a simpler subproblem that may produce infeasible paths. The computational results show the branch-and-price method provides optimal solutions to many instances previously unsolved by the literature, and that it is competitive with the tabu search heuristic for many instances. Further, the tests show that the best known primal solutions from the literature are very close to the optimal solution.

References

1. Andersson, H., Duesund, J., Fagerholt, K.: Ship routing and scheduling with cargo coupling and synchronization constraints. Computers & Industrial Engineering **61**(4), 1107–1164 (2011)
2. Barnhart, C., Johnson, E.L., Nemhauser, G.L., Savelsbergh, M.P.W., Vance, P.H.: Branch-and-price: Column generation for solving huge integer programs. Operations Research **46**(3), 316–329 (1998)
3. Brønmo, G., Nygreen, B., Lysgaard, J.: Column generation approaches to ship scheduling with flexible cargo sizes. European Journal of Operational Research **200**, 139–150 (2010)

4. Christiansen, M., Fagerholt, K., Nygreen, B., Ronen, D.: Ship routing and scheduling in the new millennium. European Journal of Operational Research **228**(3), 467–483 (2013)

5. Dubrovsky, O., Levitin, G., Penn, M.: A genetic algorithm with a compact solution encoding for the container ship stowage problem. Journal of Heuristics **8**(6), 585–599 (2002)

6. Engineer, F., Furman, K., Nemhauser, G., Savelsbergh, M., Song, J.: A branch-price-and-cut algorithm for single-product maritime inventory routing. Operations Research **60**(1), 106–122 (2012)

7. Fagerholt, K., Hvattum, L.M., Johnsen, T.A.V., Korsvik, J.E.: Routing and scheduling in project shipping. Annals of Operations Research **36**(1), 94–118 (2011)

8. Lübbecke, M., Desrosiers, J.: Selected topics in column generation. Operations Research **53**(6), 1007–1023 (2005)

9. Øvstebø, B.O., Hvattum, L.M., Fagerholt, K.: Optimization of stowage plans for roro ships. Computers & Operations Research **38**(10), 1425–1434 (2011)

10. Røpke, S., Cordeau, J.F.: Branch-and-cut-and-price for the pickup and delivery problem with time windows. Transportation Science **43**(3), 267–286 (2009)

11. Stålhane, M., Andersson, H., Christiansen, M., Cordeau, J.F., Desaulniers, G.: A branch-price-and-cut method for a ship routing and scheduling problem with split loads. Computers & Operations Research **39**, 3361–3375 (2012)

12. Stålhane, M., Andersson, H., Christiansen, M.: A branch-and-price method for a ship routing and scheduling problem with cargo coupling and synchronization constraints. EURO Journal on Transportation and Logistics, 1–23 (2014). http://dx.doi.org/10.1007/s13676-014-0061-5

13. Steenken, D., Winter, T., Zimmermann, U.: Stowage and transport optimization in ship planning. In: Grtschel, M., Krumke, S., Rambau, J. (eds.) Online Optimization of Large Scale Systems, pp. 731–745. Springer, Heidelberg (2001)

14. Vilhelmsen, C., Lusby, R., Larsen, J.: Tramp ship routing and scheduling with integrated bunker optimization. EURO Journal on Transportation and Logistics **3**(2), 143–175 (2014)

Trajectory Tracking Control for Underactuated Surface Vessels Based on Nonlinear Model Predictive Control

Chenguang Liu[1,2(✉)], Huarong Zheng[3], Rudy R. Negenborn[3], Xiumin Chu[1], and Le Wang[1,4]

[1] Engineering Research Center for Transportation Safety, Ministry of Education, Wuhan University of Technology, Wuhan, Peoples Republic of China
{liuchenguang,chuxm}@whut.edu.cn, xileyicheng@163.com
[2] School of Energy and Power Engineering, Wuhan University of Technology, Wuhan, Peoples Republic of China
[3] Maritime and Transport Technology, Delft University of Technology, Delft, The Netherlands
{h.zheng-1,R.R.Negenborn}@tudelft.nl
[4] School of Logistics Engineering, Wuhan University of Technology, Wuhan, Peoples Republic of China

Abstract. An autonomous vessel can improve the intelligence, efficiency and economy of shipping logistics. To realize autonomous navigation control of underactuated vessels (USVs), this paper presents a controller that can make USV track a reference trajectory with only 2 inputs, i.e., surge and yaw. A nonlinear state-space model with 2 inputs considering environmental disturbances induced by wind, current and waves for a 3 degree of freedom (DOF) surface vessel is considered. Based on this model, a trajectory tracking controller using Nonlinear Model Predictive Control (NMPC) is designed. System constraints on inputs, input increment and output are incorporated in the NMPC framework. Simulation results show that the controller can track an ellipse trajectory well and that the tracking errors are within acceptable ranges, while system constraints are satisfied.

Keywords: Underactuated surface vessels · Nonlinear model predictive control · Trajectory tracking · Environmental disturbances

1 Introduction

As an important transport mode, shipping plays an increasing role in logistics. An autonomous ship can improve the intelligence and efficiency and decrease the cost at the same time during logistics management. An autonomous ship doesn't require allocating seafarers, servers and related living facilities, so more space can be placed with cargo and the expenditure becomes lower. Meanwhile, in consideration that near 80 % ship accidents can be attributed to human factor, an autonomous ship can avoid this risk largely [1]. Trajectory tracking control is a basic problem that has received general concern for autonomous navigation of underactuated surface vessels (USVs). The challenge of the problem appears relevant because of the fact that the motion of the underactuated surface vessels possesses three degrees of freedom (yaw, sway, and

© Springer International Publishing Switzerland 2015
F. Corman et al. (Eds.): ICCL 2015, LNCS 9335, pp. 166–180, 2015.
DOI: 10.1007/978-3-319-24264-4_12

surge, neglecting the motion in roll, pitch and heave), whereas there are typically only two controls available (surge force and yaw moment) [2].

Model Predictive Control (MPC), Sliding Mode Control (SMC), Line of Sight (LOS), PID and Intelligent Control have been used for trajectory tracking of USVs [3,4,5,6,7,8]. This paper will focus on MPC in USVs motion control [9,10]. In [4], a recurrent neural networks method to solve the optimal value of an MPC quadratic programming problem is proposed, and the MPC real-time computation has been improved. [10] used MPC to realize tracking control of a four degrees of freedom vessel with the consideration of actuator saturation and speed constraints. [11] used NMPC based on linear matrix inequalities (LMIs) to achieve the motion control of USVs with the consideration of input constraints. Therefore, MPC shows potential in solving trajectory tracking control problems of USVs. Compared with linear MPC, NMPC based trajectory tracking controllers can have better performance with higher accuracy.

Tracking controllers should consider system constraints such as input range because a vessel's mechanical capacities are limited. The controller this paper proposes can set different constraints according to different vessels and mechanical conditions of the same vessel. Also, the controller considers output constraints (trajectory range) because a vessel's trajectory should be limited, as it will be prohibited to approach channel boundaries and some obstacles. In addition, environmental disturbances, i.e., wind, current and waves always affect trajectory control of an USV, therefore the controller has considered disturbances in three DOF.

This paper is organized as follows. Firstly, we build the state-space model with the only 2 inputs for a USV in Section 2. Then, a trajectory tracking controller based on NMPC is designed in Section 3. Simulation results are presented in Section 4 to illustrate the tracking performance of our controller. Finally, the conclusion and direction for future work are given in Section 5.

2   Underactuated Surface Vessel Model Considering Disturbances

Fossen [12] has done many valuable studies on kinetics and kinematics models of vessels. The vessel model we use in this paper is also based on the state-space model proposed by Fossen. To simplify modeling, only three forces and moments (surge force, sway force and yaw moment) are considered, neglecting heave, roll and pitch forces and moments. An USV only has two inputs (surge force and yaw moment) powered by propeller and steering engines. The environmental disturbances can also be divided into three DOF [13]. To simplify the disturbances model, we set disturbances in the three DOF with random values in a certain range. Force and moment analyses of USV are shown in Fig. 1.

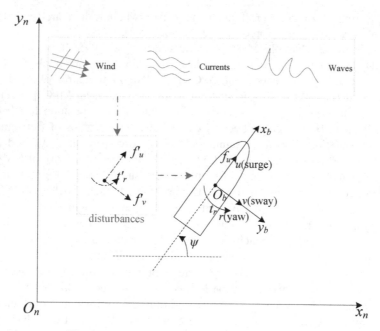

Fig. 1. Force and moment analyses of an USV [13]

In Fig.1, two reference systems need to be considered for modeling ship maneuvering dynamics. One is the body fixed coordinate system denoted by $\{b\}=(x_b,y_b,z_b)$; the other is the inertial reference system denoted by $\{n\}=(x_n,y_n,z_n)$. Suppose ship material is uniform and x-z plane is symmetric, then[14]

$$I_{xy} = I_{yz} = 0,\qquad(1)$$

where, I_{xy} and I_{yz} are respectively inertia moments of the x-y plane and the y-z plane. Kinematic and kinetic models of USVs are shown in (2):

$$\begin{aligned}
&\dot{\boldsymbol{\eta}}(t) = \mathrm{T}(\boldsymbol{\eta}(t))\boldsymbol{v}(t)\\
&\mathbf{M}\dot{\boldsymbol{v}}(t) + \mathbf{C}(\boldsymbol{v}(t))\boldsymbol{v}(t) + \mathbf{D}\boldsymbol{v}(t) = \boldsymbol{\tau}(t) + \boldsymbol{\tau}_{\text{wind}}(t) + \boldsymbol{\tau}_{\text{wave}}(t) + \boldsymbol{\tau}_{\text{current}}(t),
\end{aligned}\qquad(2)$$

where, $\boldsymbol{\eta}(t)$ is the position and course in $\{n\}=(x_n,y_n,z_n)$, and $\boldsymbol{v}(t)$ is the velocity in $\{b\}=(x_b,y_b,z_b)$, and $\tau(t)$ is control vector. $\tau_{\text{wind}}(t)$, $\tau_{\text{wave}}(t)$ and $\tau_{\text{curent}}(t)$ are the disturbances forces due to wind, waves and current respectively. These vectors are further defined as:

$$\boldsymbol{\eta}(t)=\begin{bmatrix}x(t)\\y(t)\\\psi(t)\end{bmatrix},\ \boldsymbol{v}(t)=\begin{bmatrix}u(t)\\v(t)\\r(t)\end{bmatrix},\ \boldsymbol{\tau}(t)=\begin{bmatrix}f_{\mathrm{u}}(t)\\f_{\mathrm{v}}(t)\\t_{\mathrm{r}}(t)\end{bmatrix}\qquad(3)$$

$$\boldsymbol{\tau}_{\text{wind}}(t) = \begin{bmatrix} f_{\text{u1rand}}(t) \\ f_{\text{v1rand}}(t) \\ t_{\text{r1rand}}(t) \end{bmatrix}, \boldsymbol{\tau}_{\text{current}}(t) = \begin{bmatrix} f_{\text{u2rand}}(t) \\ f_{\text{v2rand}}(t) \\ t_{\text{r2rand}}(t) \end{bmatrix}, \boldsymbol{\tau}_{\text{wave}}(t) = \begin{bmatrix} f_{\text{u3rand}}(t) \\ f_{\text{v3rand}}(t) \\ t_{\text{r3rand}}(t) \end{bmatrix} \tag{4}$$

$$\boldsymbol{\tau}_{\text{d}}(t) = \boldsymbol{\tau}_{\text{wind}}(t) + \boldsymbol{\tau}_{\text{wave}}(t) + \boldsymbol{\tau}_{\text{current}}(t) := \begin{bmatrix} \alpha \cdot (rand(\cdot)\text{-}0.5) \\ \alpha \cdot (rand(\cdot)\text{-}0.5) \\ \alpha \cdot (rand(\cdot)\text{-}0.5) \end{bmatrix}, \alpha \geq 0, rand(\cdot) \in [0,1] \tag{5}$$

In (5), $x(t)$ and $y(t)$ stand for the position along x_n and y_n axis in $\{n\}$, $\psi(t)$ stands for ship course (heading angle) in $\{n\}$. $u(t)$, $v(t)$ and $r(t)$ respectively stand for the speed of surge, sway direction and rate of yaw in $\{b\}$ respectively. Respectively, $f_u(t)$, $f_v(t)$, $t_r(t)$ stand for the forces of surge and sway, moment of yaw. For an underactuated vessel, there is no force of sway powered by lateral thruster. Environmental disturbance forces could be divided into three directions which are surge, sway and yaw in $\{b\}$, it is shown as (5) [15]. In (5), α is disturbances weight. System matrices $\mathbf{M}$, $\mathbf{C}(v(t))$ and $\mathbf{D}$ stand for inertia, centrifugal force and damping matrix respectively, which are defined as[14]

$$\mathbf{M} := \begin{bmatrix} m_{11} & 0 & 0 \\ 0 & m_{22} & m_{23} \\ 0 & m_{32} & m_{33} \end{bmatrix}, \mathbf{D} := \begin{bmatrix} d_{11} & 0 & 0 \\ 0 & d_{22} & d_{23} \\ 0 & d_{32} & d_{33} \end{bmatrix}, \mathbf{C} := \begin{bmatrix} 0 & 0 & -c_{31} \\ 0 & 0 & c_{23} \\ c_{31} & -c_{23} & 0 \end{bmatrix}, \tag{6}$$

where $c_{23} = m_{11}u(t)$ and $c_{31} = m_{22}v(t) + \frac{1}{2}(m_{23} + m_{32})r(t)$. The Jacobian matrix $\mathbf{T}(\boldsymbol{\eta}(t))$ transforms the body-fixed velocities $v(t)$ into the inertial velocities $\dot{\boldsymbol{\eta}}(t)$, which is given by:

$$\mathbf{T}(\boldsymbol{\eta}(t)) = \begin{bmatrix} \cos(\psi(t)) & -\sin(\psi(t)) & 0 \\ \sin(\psi(t)) & \cos(\psi(t)) & 0 \\ 0 & 0 & 1 \end{bmatrix} \tag{7}$$

3   Nonlinear Predictive Model Control

The trajectory tracking principle of USVs based on MPC is illustrated in Fig. 2. The first control input of the optimal input array in every loop is adopted by the USV's trajectory tracking controller. In real circumstance, the measure procedure is realized by state measure sensors. For NMPC, at first continuous state space should be discretized; then objective function should designed considering multi-objective; at last system constraints should be considered in the NMPC model.

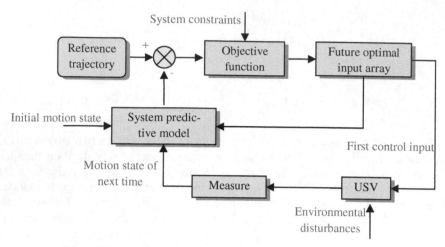

Fig. 2. The trajectory tracking principle of USVs based on MPC

3.1   Model Discretization

From (2), we can easily see that the state-space model of USVs is nonlinear. In order to better study control problem, (2) can be transformed into:

$$\dot{x}(t) = f\left(x(t), u(t), \tau_d(t)\right)$$
$$y(t) = g\left(x(t)\right), \tag{8}$$

where, $x(t) = \left[x(t), y(t), \psi(t), u(t), v(t), r(t)\right]^T$ stands   for   system   state; $u(t) = [f_u(t), f_r(t)]^T$ stands for surge and sway control input; $\tau_d(t) = [f_{du}(t), f_{dv}(t), f_{dr}(t)]$ stands for environmental disturbance forces, which is defined in (5). Function f and g $(\mathbb{R}^6 \times \mathbb{R}^3 \rightarrow \mathbb{R}^6)$ is defined as:

$$f\left(x(t), u(t), \tau_d(t)\right) = \begin{bmatrix} T(p_1 x(t))(p_2 x(t)) \\ M^{-1}\left(-C(p_2 x(t))(p_2 x(t)) - D(p_2 x(t)) + p_3 u(t) + \tau_d(t)\right) \end{bmatrix}$$
$$g\left(x(t)\right) = \begin{bmatrix} 1 & 0 & 0 & 0 & 0 & 0 \\ 0 & 1 & 0 & 0 & 0 & 0 \end{bmatrix} x(t), \tag{9}$$

where $p_1 = [0\ \ 0\ \ 1\ \ 0\ \ 0\ \ 0]$, $p_2 = \begin{bmatrix} 0 & 0 & 0 & 1 & 0 & 0 \\ 0 & 0 & 0 & 0 & 1 & 0 \\ 0 & 0 & 0 & 0 & 0 & 1 \end{bmatrix}$, $p_3 = \begin{bmatrix} 1 & 0 \\ 0 & 0 \\ 0 & 1 \end{bmatrix}$.

Differential equations in (9) are hard to solve analytically. They are therefore usually solved using numerical solutions. Euler Method and 4-step Runge-Kutta are widely adopted in solving arithmetic solutions. Form of Euler Method is simple, but precision is relatively low. The 4-step Runge-Kutta is used in high precision applications occasion. This paper uses 4-step Runge-Kutta to discrete (10). The $n+1$ moment iterative equation relative to n moment is as follows:

$$x(n+1)=f\left(x(n),u(n),\tau_{\mathrm{d}}(n)\right)+\frac{T}{6}\left(k_1+2k_2+2k_3+k_4\right) \tag{10}$$

In (10), T stands for the time interval between two control steps, and k_1, k_2, k_3, k_4 are defined as:

$$k_1 = f\left(x(n),u(n),\tau_{\mathrm{d}}(n)\right)$$

$$k_2 = f\left(x(n)+\frac{T}{2}k_1,u\left(n+\frac{T}{2}\right),\tau_{\mathrm{d}}\left(n+\frac{T}{2}\right)\right)$$

$$k_3 = f\left(x(n)+\frac{T}{2}k_2,u\left(n+\frac{T}{2}\right),\tau_{\mathrm{d}}\left(n+\frac{T}{2}\right)\right)$$

$$k_4 = f\left(x(n)+Tk_2,u(n+T),\tau_{\mathrm{d}}(n+T)\right).$$

To simplify the calculation process, we assume that input and disturbances remains unchanged during T. Therefore,

$$u\left(n+\frac{T}{2}\right)=u(n),\tau_{\mathrm{d}}\left(n+\frac{T}{2}\right)=\tau_{\mathrm{d}}(n)$$

Equation (10) can be also denoted as

$$x(n+1)= f_{\mathrm{d}}\left(x(n),u(n),\tau_{\mathrm{d}}(n)\right) \tag{11}$$

In order to realize increment range constraints, it is necessary to transform (11) into (13) where $\Delta u(n)$ is independent variable. The transforming process is as follows.

Define $\xi(n)=\begin{bmatrix} x(n) \\ u(n-1) \end{bmatrix}$ and $\Delta u(n)=u(n)-u(n-1)$. Transformed (12) is shown as below.

$$\xi(n+1)=f_{\mathrm{d}}\left(\mathbf{p}_4\xi(n),\mathbf{p}_5\xi(n)+\Delta u(n),\tau_{\mathrm{d}}(n)\right)= f_{\mathrm{d}}'\left(\xi(n),\Delta u(n),\tau_{\mathrm{d}}(n)\right) \tag{12}$$

where

$$\mathbf{p}_4=\begin{bmatrix} 1 & 0 & 0 & 0 & 0 & 0 & 0 & 0 \\ 0 & 1 & 0 & 0 & 0 & 0 & 0 & 0 \\ 0 & 0 & 1 & 0 & 0 & 0 & 0 & 0 \\ 0 & 0 & 0 & 1 & 0 & 0 & 0 & 0 \\ 0 & 0 & 0 & 0 & 1 & 0 & 0 & 0 \\ 0 & 0 & 0 & 0 & 0 & 1 & 0 & 0 \end{bmatrix},\quad \mathbf{p}_5=\begin{bmatrix} 0 & 0 & 0 & 0 & 0 & 0 & 1 & 0 \\ 0 & 0 & 0 & 0 & 0 & 0 & 0 & 1 \end{bmatrix}$$

3.2   Objective Function Design

The objective function should consider output errors, control input values and incremental inputs if it needs to guarantee the controller to track the trajectory effectively and steadily. The objective function is defined as (13) [16].

$$J(k) = \sum_{i=1}^{N_p} \left\| \boldsymbol{\eta}(k+i) - \boldsymbol{\eta}_{\mathrm{ref}}(k+i) \right\|_Q^2 + \sum_{i=1}^{N_c-1} \left\| \Delta \boldsymbol{u}(k+i) \right\|_R^2, \tag{13}$$

where, Q and R are weight matrices; N_p is the prediction horizon; N_c is the control horizon; $\boldsymbol{\eta}(k+i)$ and $\boldsymbol{\eta}_{\mathrm{ref}}(k+i)$ stands for the real and reference trajectory in the next $k+i$ step from moment k, respectively.

3.3   System Constraints

For USVs, motion trajectory range and movement speed of the propeller driven by motor and steering engine are limited because of their mechanical properties, so the input range and input increment range should be considered in the optimization as constraints. Meanwhile, to guarantee safety, trajectory position should be limited into a certain range to avoid collisions and stranding. Input range, input increment range and output range can be denoted by as follows:

$$\Delta \mathbf{u}_{\min}(t+k) \le \Delta \boldsymbol{u}(t+k) \le \Delta \mathbf{u}_{\max}(t+k), k = 0,1,2,\cdots,N_c-1 \tag{14}$$

$$\mathbf{u}_{\min}(t+k) \le \boldsymbol{u}(t+k) \le \mathbf{u}_{\max}(t+k), k = 0,1,2,\cdots,N_c-1 \tag{15}$$

$$\boldsymbol{\eta}_{\min}(t+k) \le \boldsymbol{\eta}(t+k) \le \boldsymbol{\eta}_{\max}(t+k), k = 0,1,2,\cdots,N_p-1 \tag{16}$$

From (13), we know $\Delta \boldsymbol{u}(t)$ is an independent variable, so the constraints of $\boldsymbol{u}(t)$ and $\boldsymbol{\eta}(t)$ should be transformed into function of $\Delta \boldsymbol{u}(t)$. The transforming process is shown as follow.

Define

$$U_t = \mathbf{1}_{N_c} \otimes \boldsymbol{u}(t-1) \tag{17}$$

$$A = \begin{bmatrix} 1 & 0 & \cdots & \cdots & 0 \\ 1 & 1 & 0 & \cdots & 0 \\ 1 & 1 & 1 & \ddots & 0 \\ \vdots & \vdots & \ddots & \ddots & 0 \\ 1 & 1 & \cdots & 1 & 1 \end{bmatrix}_{N_c \times N_c} \otimes I_{N_u} \tag{18}$$

In (17) and (18), $\mathbf{1}_{N_c}$ is the column vector whose row number is N_c; I_{N_u} is the identity matrix whose dimension is N_u ($N_u=2$ in this paper); $\otimes$ is the Kronecker product symbol which stands for an operation on two matrices of arbitrary size resulting in a block matrix.

Define

$$\Delta U_t = \begin{bmatrix} \Delta u(t) \\ \Delta u(t+1) \\ \cdots \\ \Delta u(t+N_c-1) \end{bmatrix} \tag{19}$$

According to (17) – (19), (15) can be transformed into:

$$U_{min} \le A\Delta U_t + U_t \le U_{max} \tag{20}$$

In (20), U_{min} and U_{max} stand for the minimum and maximum set in control time domain.

$$U_{min} = 1_{N_c} \otimes u_{min}, \; U_{max} = 1_{N_c} \otimes u_{max} \tag{21}$$

Equation (16) can be transformed as follows.

$$Y_{min} \le \begin{bmatrix} \eta(k) \\ \eta(k+1) \\ \vdots \\ \eta(k+N_p-1) \end{bmatrix} \le Y_{max} \tag{22}$$

$$\begin{bmatrix} \eta(k) \\ \eta(k+1) \\ \vdots \\ \eta(k+N_p-1) \end{bmatrix}^T = \begin{bmatrix} 1 & 0 & 0 & 0 & 0 & 0 & 0 & 0 \\ 0 & 1 & 0 & 0 & 0 & 0 & 0 & 0 \end{bmatrix} \begin{bmatrix} \xi(k) \\ \xi(k+1) \\ \vdots \\ \xi(k+N_p-1) \end{bmatrix}^T \tag{23}$$

$$Y_{min} = 1_{N_c} \otimes \eta_{min}, \; Y_{max} = 1_{N_c} \otimes \eta_{max} \tag{24}$$

4   Simulation Experiment

To illustrate the performance of the trajectory tracking controller for USVs, this paper analyzes the tracking errors and performances based on the model of CyberShip II [17].

4.1   Model Parameters

For own case, system matrices **M** and **D** are assigned as follows.

$$M = \begin{bmatrix} 25.8 & 0 & 0 \\ 0 & 33.8 & 1 \\ 0 & 1 & 2.8 \end{bmatrix}, D = \begin{bmatrix} 0.72 & 0 & 0 \\ 0 & 0.89 & 0.03 \\ 0 & 0.03 & 1.9 \end{bmatrix}$$

The power parameters of CyberShip II are:

- The maximum force of surge f_u is 2 N which corresponds to 686 kN of the corresponding full scale vessel.
- The maximum moment of yaw t_r is 1.5 Nm which corresponds to 36015 kNm of the corresponding full scale vessel.
- The maximum nominal speed is 0.2 m/s which corresponds to 1.7 m/s of the corresponding full scale vessel.

4.2   Simulation Parameters

The simulation experiments of trajectory tracking controller this paper proposes are implemented in MATLAB 2010a. During the simulation experiment, (x_{ref}, y_{ref}) is the reference trajectory and (x,y) is the real trajectory. The tracking errors are defined as follows:

$$d_{error} = \sqrt{(x_{ref} - x)^2 + (y_{ref} - y)^2} \tag{25}$$

Simulations are first run under the settings of $N_p=3$, $N_c=3$, $T=2$ with an initial position at $(x_0, y_0, \psi_0, u_0, v_0, r_0) = (-0.5, 0, \pi/3, 0, 0, 0)$.

For all simulations, the ellipse reference trajectory (x_{ref}, y_{ref}) is used:

$$\begin{aligned} x_{ref} &= 4 \cdot \sin\left(0.02 \cdot N_{ref} \cdot t_{sample}\right) \\ y_{ref} &= 2 \cdot \left(1 - \cos\left(0.02 \cdot N_{ref} \cdot t_{sample}\right)\right) \end{aligned} \tag{26}$$

In (26), $N_{ref}=158$ is the number of reference positions. $t_{sample}=2$s is sample time. In (13), $Q=\begin{bmatrix} 100 & 0 \\ 0 & 100 \end{bmatrix}$, $R=\begin{bmatrix} 1 & 0 \\ 0 & 1 \end{bmatrix}$.

The parameters above of the controller are verified with the comprehensive consideration of the real-time and tracking accuracy.

In MATLAB, calculation of the next step state value array $\xi(n+1)$, $\xi(n+2)$, ... , $\xi(n+k)$ in (11) with the 4-step Runge-Kutta relative the present state $\xi(n)$ can be realized by the use of the ODE 45 function by setting T, $\Delta u(n+1), \Delta u(n+2), ..., \Delta u(n+k)$, $\Delta \tau(n+1), \Delta \tau(n+2), ..., \Delta \tau(n+k)$ and $\xi(n)$.

The optimal solutions in this paper are calculated with *fmincon* function which attempts to find a constrained minimum of a scalar function ($J(k)$ in this paper) of several variables starting at an initial estimate in MATLAB.

4.3   Results

Results are shown with environmental disturbances, input constraints, input increment constraints and output constraints. The simulation time tracking the complete trajectory is about 1800 seconds.

1. Environmental Disturbances

This part does some experiments to illustrate the performances of the controller under the different environmental disturbances, and relevant results are analyzed.

(a)   No Environmental Disturbances

The environmental disturbance and constraint parameters are set as Table 1. The tracking result is shown in Fig. 1. The experiment results show that the trajectory errors with no environmental disturbances are within 0.2 m.

Table 1. Parameters setting

Environmental disturbances	$\alpha=0$
Input constraints	$\begin{bmatrix} -2 \\ -1.5 \end{bmatrix} \leq u \leq \begin{bmatrix} 2 \\ 1.5 \end{bmatrix}$
Input increment constraints	$\begin{bmatrix} -3 \\ -3 \end{bmatrix} \leq \Delta u \leq \begin{bmatrix} 3 \\ 3 \end{bmatrix}$
Output constraints	$\begin{bmatrix} -5 \\ -10 \end{bmatrix} \leq \eta \leq \begin{bmatrix} 5 \\ 10 \end{bmatrix}$

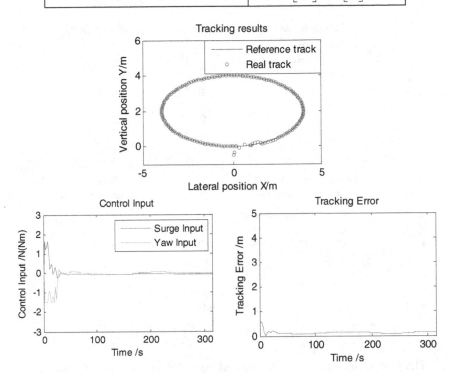

Fig. 3. Simulation results of trajectory tracking without environmental disturbances

(b) Environmental Disturbances

Compared to Table 1, the environment disturbances are set as Table 2. The tracking result are shown in Fig. 4. From Fig. 4, the inputs fluctuate more seriously because of environment disturbances. There are different performances with different environmental disturbance values, and the tracking errors have the same trend with the environmental disturbance values.

Table 2. Parameters setting

Environmental disturbances	$\alpha=0.4$
Input constraints	$\begin{bmatrix} -2 \\ -1.5 \end{bmatrix} \leq u \leq \begin{bmatrix} 2 \\ 1.5 \end{bmatrix}$
Input increment constraints	$\begin{bmatrix} -3 \\ -3 \end{bmatrix} \leq \Delta u \leq \begin{bmatrix} 3 \\ 3 \end{bmatrix}$
Output constraints	$\begin{bmatrix} -5 \\ -10 \end{bmatrix} \leq \eta \leq \begin{bmatrix} 5 \\ 10 \end{bmatrix}$

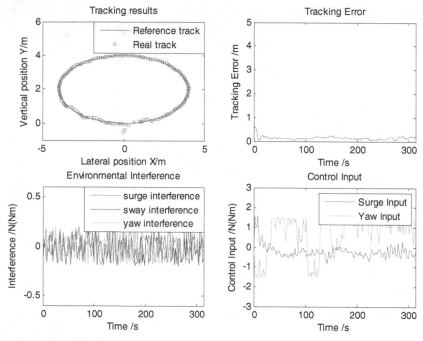

Fig. 4. Simulation results of trajectory tracking with environmental disturbances

2. Input Constraints

For comparison, we set tighter inputs as shown in Table. Results with parameters of Table 3 are shown in Fig. 5. The tracking errors have the inverse trend with input constraints within limits.

Table 3. Parameters setting

Environmental disturbances	$\alpha=0.4$
Input constraints	$\begin{bmatrix} -1 \\ -1 \end{bmatrix} \leq u \leq \begin{bmatrix} 1 \\ 1 \end{bmatrix}$
Input increment constraints	$\begin{bmatrix} -3 \\ -3 \end{bmatrix} \leq \Delta u \leq \begin{bmatrix} 3 \\ 3 \end{bmatrix}$
Output constraints	$\begin{bmatrix} -5 \\ -10 \end{bmatrix} \leq \eta \leq \begin{bmatrix} 5 \\ 10 \end{bmatrix}$

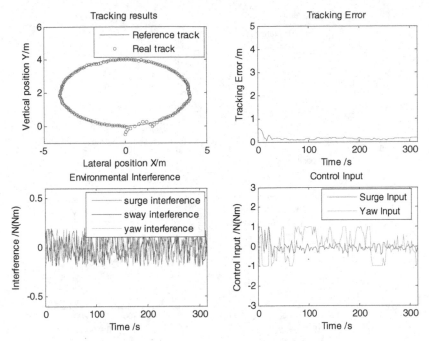

Fig. 5. Simulation results of trajectory tracking

3. Input Increment Constraints

Input increment constraints of Table 4 are smaller than that in Table 3. Results of experiments with parameters of Table 4 are shown in Fig. 6. Compared to Fig. 5, we can find easily that Δu could make sense in Fig. 6. When the Δu is set to be too small, the controller cannot track the trajectory well. The tracking errors have the inverse trend with input increment constraints within limits.

Table 4. Parameters setting

Environmental disturbances	$\alpha=0.4$
Input constraints	$\begin{bmatrix} -1 \\ -1 \end{bmatrix} \leq u \leq \begin{bmatrix} 1 \\ 1 \end{bmatrix}$
Input increment constraints	$\begin{bmatrix} -0.2 \\ -0.2 \end{bmatrix} \leq \Delta u \leq \begin{bmatrix} 0.2 \\ 0.2 \end{bmatrix}$
Output constraints	$\begin{bmatrix} -5 \\ -10 \end{bmatrix} \leq \eta \leq \begin{bmatrix} 5 \\ 10 \end{bmatrix}$

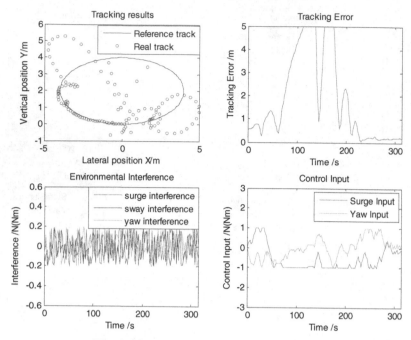

Fig. 6. Simulation results of trajectory tracking

4. Output Constraints

The output constraints are used to limit the trajectory range. In real channel environment, the navigation route of the vessel should be limited because of channel scale and obstacles. To set the output constraints is to make a vessel navigate more safely.

Output constraints of Table 5 are smaller than that in Table 1. The experimental with parameters of Table 5 is shown in Fig. 7. Compared to Fig. 3, we can find easily that the output constraints make sense because the tracking trajectory does not extend the range of η set in advance. The tracking errors have the inverse trend with output constraints.

Table 5. Parameters setting

Environmental disturbances	$\alpha=0$
Input constraints	$\begin{bmatrix} -2 \\ -1.5 \end{bmatrix} \leq u \leq \begin{bmatrix} 2 \\ 1.5 \end{bmatrix}$
Input increment constraints	$\begin{bmatrix} -3 \\ -3 \end{bmatrix} \leq \Delta u \leq \begin{bmatrix} 3 \\ 3 \end{bmatrix}$
Output constraints	$\begin{bmatrix} -3.8 \\ -0.5 \end{bmatrix} \leq \eta \leq \begin{bmatrix} 3.8 \\ 3.8 \end{bmatrix}$

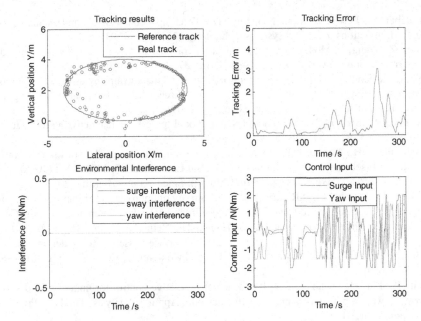

Fig. 7. Simulation results of trajectory tracking

5   Conclusion and Future Work

Aiming at the trajectory tracking of USVs, a trajectory tracking controller based on NMPC with the consideration of environmental disturbances and kinds of consideration is proposed. The experimental results under different conditions show that it is necessary to set such constraints, and constraints make the controller closer to the reality.

The proposed controller can be also applied to unmanned aerial vehicle (UAV) and underwater vehicle. However, the parameter instability of the system is lack of consideration, the stabilities of the controller is also lack of certification, and the real-time of NMPC calculation should be improved in real applications. In the future, the environmental disturbances should be considered with the real features of wind, current and waves, and the performances of the controller will be tested with a real vessel or model ship.

References

1. Duan, A.Y., Zhao, Y.: Brief Discussion on the Problems of Safety Management of Carrying Cargo on Deck (in Chinese). Ship and Ocean Engineering **35**, 124–126 (2006)
2. Serrano, M.E., Scaglia, G.J.E., Godoy, S.A., et al.: Trajectory Tracking of Underactuated Surface Vessels: A Linear Algebra Approach. IEEE Transactions on Control Systems Technology **22**, 1103–1111 (2014)

3. Lefeber, E., Pettersen, K.Y., Nijmeijer, H.: Tracking control of an underactuated ship. IEEE transactions on control systems technology **11**, 52–61 (2003)
4. Yan, Z., Wang, J.: Model predictive control for tracking of underactuated vessels based on recurrent neural networks. Oceanic Engineering **37**, 717–726 (2012)
5. Wang, X: Study on path following control for underactuated ships by using analytic model predictive control (in Chinese). School of Naval Architecture, Ocean and Civil Engineering, Shanghai Jiao Tong University, Shanghai (2009)
6. Moreira, L., Soares, C.G.: Autonomous ship model to perform manoeuvring tests. Journal of Maritime Research **8**, 29–46 (2011)
7. Ashrafiuon, H., Muske, K.R., McNinch, L.C., et al.: Sliding-mode Tracking Control of Surface Vessels. IEEE Transactions on Industrial Electronics **55**, 4004–4012 (2008)
8. Chen, H.: Model Predictive Control (in Chinese). Science Press, Beijing (2013)
9. Zheng, H., Negenborn, R.R., Lodewijks, G.: Survey of approaches for improving the intelligence of marine surface vehicles. In: Proceedings of the 16th International IEEE Conference on Intelligent Transportation, The Hague, The Netherlands, pp. 1217–1223 (2013)
10. Li, Z., Sun, J., Oh, S.: Path following for marine surface vessels with rudder and roll constraints: an MPC approach. In: American Control Conference, ACC 2009, pp. 3611–3616. IEEE (2009)
11. Liu, L., Liu, Z., Zhang, J.: LMI-based model predictive control for underactuated surface vessels with input constraints. In: Abstract and Applied Analysis. Hindawi Publishing Corporation (2014)
12. Perez, T., Fossen, T.I.: Kinematic Models for Manoeuvring and Seakeeping of Marine Vessels. Modeling, Identification and Control **28**, 19–30 (2007)
13. Fossen, T.I.: Handbook of Marine Craft Hydrodynamics and Motion Control. John Wiley & Sons, New Jersey (2011)
14. Zheng, H., Negenborn, R.R., Lodewijks, G.: Trajectory tracking of autonomous vessels using model predictive control. In: Proceedings of the 19th IFAC World Congress, Cape Town, South Africa, pp. 8812–8818 (2014)
15. Do, K.D., Jiang, Z.P., Pan, J.: Universal controllers for stabilization and tracking of underactuated ships. Systems and Control Letters. **47**, 299–317 (2002)
16. Gong, J.W., Jiang, Y., Xu, W.: Model Predictive Control of Unmanned Vehicle (in Chinese). Beijing Institute of Technology Press, Beijing (2014)
17. Skjetne, R., Smogeli, Ø.N., Fossen, T.I.: A Nonlinear Ship Manoeuvering Model: Identification and adaptive control with experiments for a model ship. Modeling, Identification and Control **25**, 3–27 (2004)

Cooperative Distributed Collision Avoidance Based on ADMM for Waterborne AGVs

Huarong Zheng[✉], Rudy R. Negenborn, and Gabriel Lodewijks

Department of Maritime & Transport Technology,
Delft University of Technology, Delft, The Netherlands
{h.zheng-1,R.R.Negenborn,G.Lodewijks}@tudelft.nl

Abstract. This paper investigates cooperative waterborne AGVs which are appealing for intelligent transport in port areas. The systems are with independent dynamics and objectives but coupling constraints due to collision avoidance requirements. The goal is to develop an algorithm that locally solves subproblems while minimizing an overall objective in a cooperative distributed way. The proposed approach is based on the decomposition-coordination iterations of the alternating direction method of multipliers (ADMM). In particular, we separate the variables into two sets: one concerned with collision avoidance constraints, and the other concerned with local problems; and add consensus constraints for these two. Local subproblems can be solved fully in parallel. Furthermore, optimization problems are formulated and solved in a receding horizon way. Successive linearizations of nonlinear vessel dynamics as well as the non-convex collision avoidance constraints about a shifted optimal trajectory from a previous step are implemented to maintain a trade-off between computational complexity and optimality. Simulation results are presented to illustrate the effectiveness of the proposed algorithm for cooperative distributed collision avoidance.

Keywords: Distributed model predictive control · Alternating direction method of multipliers · Collision avoidance · Waterborne AGVs

1 Introduction

The Port of Rotterdam is expecting more than 30 million Twenty-foot Equivalent Unit (TEU) per year towards 2035 [1] and the port authority is seeking innovative and efficient ways to handle the expected large throughput of containers in the port area. Automated Guided Vehicles (AGVs) have been put into practice (e.g., at ECT Delta Terminal and APM Terminal in the Port of Rotterdam) and proved to be able to improve efficiency and save energy in Automated Container Terminals. Correspondingly, we have proposed the concept of waterborne Automated Guided Vessels (waterborne AGVs) [2] for transport of containers among various terminals known as Inter Terminal Transport (ITT). Nonetheless, when multiple waterborne AGVs (also referenced to as subsystems, vessels or agents

© Springer International Publishing Switzerland 2015
F. Corman et al. (Eds.): ICCL 2015, LNCS 9335, pp. 181–194, 2015.
DOI: 10.1007/978-3-319-24264-4_13

hereafter) encounter each other, autonomous collision avoidance still remains an issue.

One straightforward approach for this problem is using one centralized controller being responsible for all subsystems. In contrast, multiple controllers can also be distributed throughout the system, each taking care of a local subproblem or a part of the centralized problem. Communication and coordination is required when interactions exist between subsystems to resolve conflicts between local performances and system-wide constraints or performances. In general, distributed approaches are preferable over centralized ones [3]. However, decomposing the non-convex coupling due to collision avoidance of waterborne AGVs minimizing overall performances is challenging for distributed control design.

Collision avoidance problems in the literature are generally dealt with by priority [4], potential field [5], optimization [6], velocity obstacles [7] and artificial intelligence [8] based methods. It comes naturally that conflicts will disappear if vessels are prescribed relative priorities according to certain rules (e.g., COLREGs) as has been done in [4], but system flexibility and optimality could be degraded with fixed rules. Potential fields model conflicts as repulsive forces which drive the vessel away to avoid collisions. However, traditional potential functions are struggling with local minima [5]; multi-criteria design and system constraints are usually difficult to be incorporated in such potential functions as well. The method of velocity obstacles [7], slightly different, works on agents' velocity space and calculates a set of velocities which might lead to collisions in the future; however, such a method assumes constant current velocity which might not hold in complex situations. We settle the distributed collision avoidance problem using an optimization based control strategy – model predictive control (MPC) [9] because of its capability of handling system constraints explicitly and flexibility in controller design. Separations of vessels from collisions are guaranteed by Euclidian distance based hard constraints which bring about online non-convex optimizations for MPC. A more detailed literature review on applications of MPC in vessel motion control problems can be found in [2].

However, non-convex optimization problems are generally hard to solve and decompose if not impossible. A widely applied approach for non-convex collision avoidance constraints is to approximate them by mixed-integer programming (MIP) problems [10]. Much of the current research on distributed collision avoidance based on MIP formulations assumes constant trajectories from other subsystems and sequentially solve local subproblems [6]. This approach fails, however, when the assumption of small changes of other subsystems' trajectories does not hold. Global problems are reproduced and solved by each subsystem knowing all subsystems' dynamics and measured states in [11] and thus can discard the former assumption. However, computational and privacy issues arise. In [12], global optimizations are avoided by parameterizing other subsystems' decision variables in a reduced order decision space achieving a distributed scheme by sequential computations. But still, knowledge about system-wide dynamics is required. Most of the above approaches are solving either local or global problems sequentially which means other subsystems need to be idle; moreover, the involvement of integer variables leads to exponential computational complexity with the increase of prediction horizon and number of vessels involved.

In this paper, we propose to take advantage of the shifted optimal trajectory from a previous step MPC optimization problem and linearize the collision avoidance constraints about it to obtain convex but time-varying incremental collision avoidance constraints. This method suits well with our successive linearization framework for nonlinear vessel dynamics. Furthermore, system decompositions are achieved by a technique recently gaining increasing attentions for solving large scale optimization problems – alternating direction method of multipliers (ADMM) [13]. ADMM enjoys both the good robustness of the method of multipliers and separability of dual decomposition and has been applied for collision avoidance problems of road vehicles with linear dynamics [14]. More specifically for our problem, vessels are able to solve local problems without taking into account the coupling collision avoidance constraints explicitly first. A coordinator will then take care of the collision avoidance constraints with collected relative vessel position information. Extra consensus constraints on position states between the coordinator and vessels are introduced. Iterative communication and computation proceed until the consensus constraints are met, indicating overall safety and optimality are cooperatively attained. Moreover, since in each iteration, local problems are solved in a fully parallel way, all vessels are treated equally and no vessel needs to be idle waiting for other vessels' computation.

The remainder of this paper is organized as follows. Firstly, in Section 2, we introduce the 3 degree-of-freedom (DOF) surface vessel dynamic models for both experimental simulation and MPC controller design. Then in Section 3, the cooperative collision avoidance problem and a centralized formulation based on a network model and convexified collision avoidance constraints are presented. Distributed cooperative collision avoidance based on ADMM in a receding horizon way is formulated in Section 4. In Section 5, simulation experiments, results and analysis are presented, followed by concluding remarks and future research directions in Section 6.

2   Vessel Models for Simulation and Prediction

We briefly introduce in this section two vessel models which are required for the cooperative distributed collision avoidance controller design in the following sections. One is the continuous nonlinear vessel dynamic model for system simulation and the other for receding horizon system trajectory predictions.

2.1   A Marine Surface Vessel Model

Following the vectorial setting in [15], behavior of a 3 DOF surface vessel p considering a constant current (fixed speed and angle in the inertial frame) and neglecting other environmental disturbances are mathematically modeled as the following two ordinary differential equations[1]:

$$\dot{\boldsymbol{\eta}}_p = \boldsymbol{R}(\psi_p)\boldsymbol{\nu}_p,$$

$$\dot{\boldsymbol{\nu}}_p = (\boldsymbol{M}_{\mathrm{RB}} + \boldsymbol{M}_{\mathrm{A}})^{-1}$$

$$\left(\boldsymbol{\tau}_p - (\boldsymbol{D}_l + \boldsymbol{D}_{\mathrm{nl}}(\boldsymbol{\nu}_{\mathrm{r},p}) + \boldsymbol{C}_{\mathrm{A}}(\boldsymbol{\nu}_{\mathrm{r},p}))\,\boldsymbol{\nu}_{\mathrm{r},p} - \boldsymbol{C}_{\mathrm{RB}}(\boldsymbol{\nu}_p)\boldsymbol{\nu}_p + \boldsymbol{M}_{\mathrm{A}}r_p\boldsymbol{S}^{\mathrm{T}}\boldsymbol{\nu}_{\mathrm{c}}\right),$$

(1)

with subscripts $\cdot_p$ indicating vessel p, $\left[\boldsymbol{\eta}_p{}^{\mathrm{T}}\ \boldsymbol{\nu}_p{}^{\mathrm{T}}\right]^{\mathrm{T}}$ as the system states and $\boldsymbol{\tau}_p$ as system inputs, and

$$\boldsymbol{\eta}_p = \begin{bmatrix} x_p \\ y_p \\ \psi_p \end{bmatrix}, \quad \boldsymbol{\nu}_p = \begin{bmatrix} u_p \\ v_p \\ r_p \end{bmatrix}, \quad \boldsymbol{\tau}_p = \begin{bmatrix} \tau_{u,p} \\ \tau_{v,p} \\ \tau_{r,p} \end{bmatrix},$$

(2)

where x_p, y_p and ψ_p are displacements and heading angle in inertial frame, respectively. Linear velocities in surge and sway are expressed in body-fixed frame as u_p and v_p, respectively and r_p is angular velocity of heading angle. Control input vector is constituted of surge, sway forces and yaw moment represented by $\tau_{u,p}$, $\tau_{v,p}$ and $\tau_{r,p}$, respectively. States in inertial and body-fixed frames are related by the rotation matrix:

$$\boldsymbol{R}(\psi_p) = \begin{bmatrix} \cos(\psi_p) & -\sin(\psi_p) & 0 \\ \sin(\psi_p) & \cos(\psi_p) & 0 \\ 0 & 0 & 1 \end{bmatrix}.$$

In (1), $\boldsymbol{\nu}_{\mathrm{r},p} = \boldsymbol{\nu}_p - \boldsymbol{\nu}_{\mathrm{c}} = \left[u_{\mathrm{r},p}\ v_{\mathrm{r},p}\ r_{\mathrm{r},p}\right]^{\mathrm{T}}$ is the relative velocity in the body-fixed frame between ship hull and the fluid. Other terms in (1) as $\boldsymbol{M}_{\mathrm{RB}}$, $\boldsymbol{M}_{\mathrm{A}}$, $\boldsymbol{C}_{\mathrm{A}}(\boldsymbol{\nu}_{\mathrm{r},p})$, $\boldsymbol{C}_{\mathrm{RB}}(\boldsymbol{\nu}_p)$, $\boldsymbol{D}_l$ and $\boldsymbol{D}_{\mathrm{NL}}(\boldsymbol{\nu}_{\mathrm{r},p})$ are all 3×3 matrices describing effects caused by rigid body and hydrodynamics. Specific expressions are omitted here due to length limits and interested readers are referred to [2] for details.

2.2 Successively Linearized Prediction Models for MPC

Conventionally, MPC calculates a sequence of optimal control inputs in a receding horizon way but only implements the first element of the sequence and disregard the rest. To maintain a trade-off between computational complexity and optimality, we take advantage of the whole calculated sequence of control inputs and successively linearize the nonlinear model (1) about a shifted optimal trajectory from a previous step.

For simplicity, the nonlinear dynamics of (1) for vessel p are generalized as:

$$\dot{\boldsymbol{x}}_p(t) = \boldsymbol{f}(\boldsymbol{x}_p(t), \boldsymbol{u}_p(t)),$$

(3)

where $\boldsymbol{f} : \mathbb{R}^6 \times \mathbb{R}^3 \to \mathbb{R}^6$ is a continuous nonlinear smooth function with system states $\boldsymbol{x}_p = \left[\boldsymbol{\eta}_p{}^{\mathrm{T}}\ \boldsymbol{\nu}_p{}^{\mathrm{T}}\right]^{\mathrm{T}}$ and control inputs $\boldsymbol{u}_p = \boldsymbol{\tau}_p$.

---

[1] Time indices for system states and control inputs are left out in this section for notational simplicity; and system state-independent matrices (e.g., $\boldsymbol{M}_{\mathrm{RB}}$, $\boldsymbol{M}_{\mathrm{A}}$ etc.) are the same for all homogenous waterborne AGVs.

For numerical simulations, continuous time model (3) is usually discretized with zero-order-hold assumption as:

$$x_p(k+1) = x_p(k) + \int_{kT_s}^{(k+1)T_s} f(x_p(k), u_p(k))\mathrm{d}t, \tag{4}$$

where T_s is the sampling time and k is a discrete time step standing for time instant kT_s. Consider at time step $k-1$ ($k > 1$) in MPC, the calculated optimal control input sequence is $u_p(k-1+i|k-1)$ for $i = 0, 1, ..., N_p - 1$, where N_p is the prediction horizon. Conventionally, the first element $u_p(k-1|k-1)$ is applied to the system and the rest are disregarded. For linearizations at step k, however, we make extensive use of this 'tail' to build a seed trajectory $\left(x_p^0(k+i|k), u_p^0(k+i|k)\right)$ for $i = 0, 1, ..., N_p - 1$, where

$$u_p^0(k+i|k) = u_p(k+i|k-1) \tag{5}$$

for $i = 0, 1, ..., N_p - 2$ and

$$u_p^0(k+N_p-1|k) = u_p(k+N_p-2|k-1). \tag{6}$$

Then, with an initial state $x_p^0(k|k) = x_p(k)$, solutions for (3) at time steps $k+i$, i.e., $x_p^0(k+i|k)$ for $i = 1, 2, ..., N_p$ can be calculated according to (4)[2]. Hereby, $k+i|k$ stands for the ith element of the predicted trajectories at step k and the superscript $\cdot^0$ denotes a seed trajectory. Small perturbations around the seed trajectory are denoted as $(\Delta x_p(k+i|k), \Delta u_p(k+i|k))$ for $i = 0, 1, ..., N_p - 1$ and satisfy

$$\begin{aligned} x_p(k+i|k) &= x_p^0(k+i|k) + \Delta x_p(k+i|k), \text{ for } i = 0, 1, ..., N_p \\ u_p(k+i|k) &= u_p^0(k+i|k) + \Delta u_p(k+i|k), \text{ for } i = 0, 1, ..., N_p - 1. \end{aligned} \tag{7}$$

Substituting (7) into (4), the term in the integrator, by applying Taylor's series and neglecting the higher order terms than the first order, can be written as:

$$\begin{aligned} &f(x_p^0(k+i|k) + \Delta x_p(k+i|k), u_p^0(k+i|k) + \Delta u_p(k+i|k)) \\ &= f(x_p^0(k+i|k), u_p^0(k+i|k)) + A_{c,p}(k+i|k)\Delta x_p(k+i|k) \\ &+ B_{c,p}(k+i|k)\Delta u_p(k+i|k), \end{aligned} \tag{8}$$

where

$$A_{c,p}(k+i|k) = \left.\frac{\partial f}{\partial x_p}\right|_{\left(x_p^0(k+i|k), u_p^0(k+i|k)\right)}, B_{c,p}(k+i|k) = \left.\frac{\partial f}{\partial u_p}\right|_{\left(x_p^0(k+i|k), u_p^0(k+i|k)\right)}$$

are continuous Jacobian state and input matrices, respectively and can also be discretized with zero-order-hold assumption to get corresponding $A_{d,p}$ and $B_{d,p}$ and we reach the discrete linearized incremental model

[2] Ordinary differential equation solvers (e.g., ode45 in MATLAB [16]) are able to provide higher precision ODE solutions with specified tolerance.

$$\Delta \boldsymbol{x}_p(k+i+1|k) = \boldsymbol{A}_{\mathrm{d},p}(k+i|k)\Delta \boldsymbol{x}_p(k+i|k) + \boldsymbol{B}_{\mathrm{d},p}(k+i|k)\Delta \boldsymbol{u}_p(k+i|k), \quad (9)$$

with an initial state $\Delta \boldsymbol{x}_p(k|k) = 0$ since $\boldsymbol{x}_p{}^0(k|k) = \boldsymbol{x}_p(k)$. To this end, we are able to predict future system behavior in a linear way for nonlinear system (1) by (7) and (9).

3   Centralized Predictive Collision Avoidance

When a waterborne AGV is in the proximity of other waterborne AGVs where potential collision avoidance might happen, pair-wise couplings arise since certain distance needs to be maintained in order to guarantee safety. Solving local problems independently will not necessarily satisfy these coupling constraints and amount to overall optimality any more. Non-convex Euclidean distance based collision avoidance constraints are first convexified based on which a centralized formulation over the network model is presented to tackle the cooperative collision avoidance problem in this section.

3.1   A Network Model

We consider a network with N_v waterborne AGVs each equipped on board with a processing unit, measurement and communication devices. An undirected graph topology $\mathcal{G}(k)$ is utilized to denote couplings among subsystems at time step k:

$$\mathcal{G}(k) = (\mathcal{V}, \mathcal{E}(k)), \quad (10)$$

where $\mathcal{V} = \{1, 2, ..., N_v\}$ is a time invariant set of waterborne AGVs under consideration attached to the vertices of the graph and $\mathcal{E}(k) \subseteq \mathcal{V} \times \mathcal{V}$ the set of time-varying edges. Behaviors of each vessel $p \in \mathcal{V}$ are described by independent dynamic models detailed in Section 2.1. Pair-wise couplings between vessels are described by edges $e_{p,q} = \{(p, q) | p \in \mathcal{V}, q \in \mathcal{V}\} \in \mathcal{E}(k)$ which are updated each time new measurements are available considering the maximum possible plan length as:

$$e_{p,q} = (p, q) \begin{cases} \in \mathcal{E}(k), & \text{for } d_{p,q}(k) \leqslant 2u_{\max}T_s N_{\mathrm{p}} + l \\ \notin \mathcal{E}(k), & \text{otherwise}, \end{cases} \quad (11)$$

where

$$d_{p,q}(k) = h\left(\boldsymbol{r}_p(k), \boldsymbol{r}_q(k)\right) = \|\boldsymbol{r}_p(k) - \boldsymbol{r}_q(k)\|_2, \quad (12)$$

as the Euclidean distance between vessels p and q at time step k and $\boldsymbol{r}_\star(k) = \begin{bmatrix} x_\star & y_\star \end{bmatrix}^{\mathrm{T}} = \begin{bmatrix} 1 & 1 & 0 & 0 & 0 & 0 \end{bmatrix}\boldsymbol{x}_\star(k)$ for $\star \in \{p, q\}$ as current measured vessel positions; l being the vessel length. The above logic implies that the collision avoidance coupling constraint emerges when there is a possibility of collision over the next receding horizon if two vessels are sailing at their maximum speeds. This is a relatively conservative logic but guarantees safety.

3.2   Convexified Collision Avoidance Constraints

Without loss of generality, $\mathcal{G}(k)$ is considered to be connected and for each pair of two vessels $(p, q) \in \mathcal{E}(k)$, we enforce a collision avoidance coupling constraint as

$$d_{p,q}(k + i|k) \geqslant d_s \tag{13}$$

for $i = 1, 2, ..., N_{\mathrm{p}}$ where d_s is a safe separation distance. Integration of inequalities (13) results in non-convex optimization problems which are generally hard to solve. Following the idea of successive linearization and again, taking advantage of the "seed trajectory" as introduced in Section 2.2, we successively approximate non-convex constraints (13) as time-varying convex constraints. According to (7),

$$\boldsymbol{r}(k + i|k) = \boldsymbol{r}^0(k + i|k) + \Delta \boldsymbol{r}(k + i|k), \text{ for } i = 0, 1, ..., N_{\mathrm{p}}. \tag{14}$$

Then the distance between vessel p and vessel q can be approximated according to Taylor Theory as:

$$
\begin{aligned}
d_{p,q}(k + i|k) = {}& d_{p,q}^0(k + i|k) + \boldsymbol{C}(k + i|k)\Delta \boldsymbol{r}_p(k + i|k) + \\
& \boldsymbol{D}(k + i|k)\Delta \boldsymbol{r}_q(k + i|k) \geqslant d_s,
\end{aligned}
\tag{15}
$$

where

$$\boldsymbol{C}(k + i|k) = \left.\frac{\partial h}{\partial \boldsymbol{r}_p}\right|_{\left(\boldsymbol{r}_p^0(k+i|k),\boldsymbol{r}_q^0(k+i|k)\right)}, \boldsymbol{D}(k + i|k) = \left.\frac{\partial h}{\partial \boldsymbol{r}_q}\right|_{\left(\boldsymbol{r}_p^0(k+i|k),\boldsymbol{r}_q^0(k+i|k)\right)}.$$

This convexifying framework is expected to work well since linearizations are conducted at every prediction step and thus are expected to only result in negligible linearization errors. Moreover, states in (13) become incremental states in (15) which are consistent with the ones as introduced in Section 2.2.

3.3   Centralized Formulation

We can now formulate the centralized problem based on individual waterborne AGVs problem as formulated in [2] for the defined connected graph $\mathcal{G}(k)$ in Section 3.1 with convexified collision avoidance constraints in Section 3.2 as

$$\min_{\Delta \boldsymbol{u}_1(k)...\Delta \boldsymbol{u}_{N_v}(k)} \sum_{p=1}^{N_v} J_p(k), \tag{16}$$

subject to, for $i = 0, 1, ..., N_{\mathrm{p}} - 1$,

$$(\Delta \boldsymbol{x}_p(k + i|k), \Delta \boldsymbol{u}_p(k + i|k)) \in \mathcal{C}_p, \tag{17a}$$

and for $p, q \in \mathcal{V}(k)$ and $(p, q) \in \mathcal{E}(k)$

$$(14), (15) \tag{17b}$$

where $J_p(k)$ is individual vessel cost and readers are referred to [2] which deals with single waterborne AGV control problem for more details.

There are two types of constraints in the centralized problem: N_v sets of independent constraints (17a) for each vessel $p \in \mathcal{V}$ and $|\mathcal{E}(k)|$ (cardinality of $\mathcal{E}(k)$) sets of coupling collision avoidance constraints (17b) for each pair of $p, q \in \mathcal{V}$ and $(p, q) \in \mathcal{E}(k)$. Solving centralized problem (16) - (17) provides globally optimal solutions that generate cooperative and safe vessel behavior. However, centralized approaches suffer drawbacks compared with distributed approaches which are to be presented in the next section.

4   Cooperative Distributed Collision Avoidance

Waterborne AGVs with separate transportation tasks are distributed by nature while system wide goals such as safety and minimal total energy consumption are also prerequisites. This section proposes a cooperative distributed collision avoidance algorithm based on the decomposition-coordination procedure of ADMM [13].

4.1   ADMM Based Decomposition for Waterborne AGVs

For notational simplicity, let capitalized letters denote state/input sequences over the prediction horizon N_p in this paper, e.g., $\boldsymbol{X}(k) = [\boldsymbol{x}(k+1|k)...$ $\boldsymbol{x}(k+N_p|k)]^{\mathrm{T}}$. Observing the centralized problem (16) formulated in Section 3.3, the barriers for a distributed approach lie only in the coupling collision avoidance constraints (17b) for which we introduce an indicator function $\boldsymbol{g}\left(\tilde{\boldsymbol{R}}(k)\right)$ as

$$\boldsymbol{g}\left(\tilde{\boldsymbol{R}}(k)\right) = \begin{cases} 0, & \text{for } \tilde{\boldsymbol{R}}(k) \in \mathcal{C}_{\mathrm{ca}} \\ \infty, & \text{otherwise,} \end{cases} \tag{18}$$

where $\tilde{\boldsymbol{R}}(k) \in \mathcal{R}^{2 \times N_v \times N_p}$ is a copy of the position variables $\boldsymbol{R}(k)$ of all coupling vessels over the prediction horizon at step k and $\mathcal{C}_{\mathrm{CA}}$ the convex sets of the $|\mathcal{E}(k)|$ coupling collision avoidance constraints (17b) w.r.t. $\tilde{\boldsymbol{R}}(k)$.

Adding extra consensus constraints for $\tilde{\boldsymbol{R}}(k)$ and $\boldsymbol{R}(k)$ as

$$\boldsymbol{R}(k) = \tilde{\boldsymbol{R}}(k). \tag{19}$$

To this end, the centralized problem (16) can be rewritten as

$$\min_{\Delta \boldsymbol{U}_1(k)...\Delta \boldsymbol{U}_{N_v}(k)} \sum_{p=1}^{N_v} J_p(k) + \boldsymbol{g}\left(\tilde{\boldsymbol{R}}(k)\right), \tag{20}$$

subject to, for $p = 1, 2, ..., N_v$ and $i = 0, 1, ..., N_p - 1$, (17a) and (19).

The above formulation now suits well the format of ADMM. An augmented Lagrangian for the formulation [13] is

$$
\mathcal{L}_\rho\left(\boldsymbol{X}(k), \tilde{\boldsymbol{R}}(k), \boldsymbol{\lambda}(k)\right) = \min_{\Delta U_1(k)...\Delta U_{N_v}(k)} \sum_{p=1}^{N_v} J_p(k) +
$$
$$
g\left(\tilde{\boldsymbol{R}}(k)\right) + \boldsymbol{\lambda}(k)^{\mathrm{T}}\left(\boldsymbol{R}(k) - \tilde{\boldsymbol{R}}(k)\right) + (\rho/2)\left\|\boldsymbol{R}(k) - \tilde{\boldsymbol{R}}(k)\right\|_2^2, \tag{21}
$$

subject to (17a) with $\boldsymbol{\lambda}(k) \in \mathcal{R}^{2 \times N_v \times N_p}$ being the dual variable of (19) and ρ a positive step size. The first term in (21) as well as (17a) are separable with respect to each subsystem. Then the ADMM decomposition-coordination procedure at each iteration consists of the following steps:

– Step 1:

$$
\left(\boldsymbol{X}_p^{j+1}(k), \Delta \boldsymbol{U}_p^{j+1}(k)\right) := \underset{\boldsymbol{X}_p(k), \Delta U_p(k)}{\arg\min}
$$
$$
\left(J_p(k) + \boldsymbol{\lambda}(k)^{j\mathrm{T}}\left(\boldsymbol{R}_p(k) - \tilde{\boldsymbol{R}}_p^j(k)\right) + (\rho/2)\left\|\boldsymbol{R}_p(k) - \tilde{\boldsymbol{R}}_p^j(k)\right\|_2^2\right) \tag{22}
$$

subject to (17a) for $p = 1, 2, ..., N_v$;
– Step 2:

$$
\tilde{\boldsymbol{R}}^{j+1}(k) := \underset{\tilde{\boldsymbol{R}}(k)}{\arg\min}
$$
$$
\left(g\left(\tilde{\boldsymbol{R}}(k)\right) + \boldsymbol{\lambda}(k)^{j\mathrm{T}}\left(\boldsymbol{R}^{j+1}(k) - \tilde{\boldsymbol{R}}(k)\right) + (\rho/2)\left\|\boldsymbol{R}^{j+1}(k) - \tilde{\boldsymbol{R}}(k)\right\|_2^2\right) \tag{23}
$$

– Step 3:
$$
\boldsymbol{\lambda}^{j+1}(k)^{\mathrm{T}} := \boldsymbol{\lambda}^j(k)^{\mathrm{T}} + \rho\left(\boldsymbol{R}^{j+1}(k) - \tilde{\boldsymbol{R}}^{j+1}(k)\right), \tag{24}
$$

where the superscript j denotes iteration j.

Computations of Step 1 are done parallelly on board of all vessels involved in $\mathcal{G}(k)$. Having collected updated states (only position states $\boldsymbol{R}^{j+1}(k)$ are required) of all vessels from Step 1, Step 2 is carried out by a coordinator (e.g., the port authority) which is implemented as Euclidean projections onto $\mathcal{C}_{\mathrm{ca}}(k)$ as

$$
\tilde{\boldsymbol{R}}_p^{j+1}(k) := \prod_{\mathcal{C}_{\mathrm{ca}}(k)}\left(\boldsymbol{R}^{j+1}(k) + \boldsymbol{\lambda}^j(k)/\rho\right), \tag{25}
$$

and can be expressed as the following optimization problem

$$
\tilde{\boldsymbol{R}}_p^{j+1}(k) := \underset{\tilde{\boldsymbol{R}}(k)}{\arg\min}\left\|\tilde{\boldsymbol{R}}(k) - \left(\boldsymbol{R}^{j+1}(k) + \boldsymbol{\lambda}^j(k)/\rho\right)\right\|_2^2 \tag{26}
$$

subject to

$$
\tilde{\boldsymbol{R}}(k) \in \mathcal{C}_{\mathrm{CA}}(k). \tag{27}
$$

Step 3 updates dual variables based on $\boldsymbol{R}^{j+1}(k)$ and $\tilde{\boldsymbol{R}}^{j+1}(k)$ from the former two steps.

4.2   Stopping Criteria

A convergence proof of ADMM has been provided in [13] and references therein under two mild assumptions. However, convergence to a high accuracy can be very slow while to a modest accuracy usually are within tens of iterations, which is practically acceptable for our control purposes. Primal and dual residuals for (20) with respect to (19) are defined as

$$r^j(k) = \boldsymbol{R}^j(k) - \tilde{\boldsymbol{R}}^j(k), \; s^j(k) = \rho \left(\tilde{\boldsymbol{R}}^j(k) - \tilde{\boldsymbol{R}}^{j-1}(k) \right). \tag{28}$$

A reasonable termination criterion to reach a small objective sub-optimality [13] is then

$$\left\| r^j(k) \right\|_2 \leqslant \varepsilon^{\mathrm{pri}}, \; \left\| s^j(k) \right\|_2 \leqslant \varepsilon^{\mathrm{dual}}, \tag{29}$$

where $\varepsilon^{\mathrm{pri}} > 0$ and $\varepsilon^{\mathrm{dual}} > 0$ are primal and dual feasibility tolerances, respectively. These tolerances can be further specified using an absolute and relative criterion as [13]

$$\varepsilon^{\mathrm{pri}} = \sqrt{2N_v N_p} \varepsilon^{\mathrm{abs}} + \varepsilon^{\mathrm{rel}} \max \left\{ \left\| \boldsymbol{R}^j(k) \right\|_2, \left\| \tilde{\boldsymbol{R}}^j(k) \right\|_2 \right\}, \tag{30}$$

$$\varepsilon^{\mathrm{dual}} = \sqrt{2N_v N_p} \varepsilon^{\mathrm{abs}} + \varepsilon^{\mathrm{rel}} \left\| \boldsymbol{\lambda}^j(k) \right\|_2. \tag{31}$$

Values of $\varepsilon^{\mathrm{rel}}$ might be 10^{-3} or 10^{-4} while $\varepsilon^{\mathrm{abs}}$ is problem specific depending on the scale of the variable values of the application.

5   Simulation Experiments

5.1   Controller and Scenario Setups

Control parameters of both controllers are set as the same with a prediction horizon $N_{\mathrm{p}} = 30$. Weight parameters are given as:

$$\boldsymbol{w}_1 = \begin{bmatrix} 10 & 0 & 0 \\ 0 & 10 & 0 \\ 0 & 0 & 5 \end{bmatrix}, \; \boldsymbol{w}_2 = I_{3 \times 3}, \boldsymbol{w}_3 = I_{3 \times 3}, \, w_4 = 5.$$

System sampling time $T_{\mathrm{s}} = 1\mathrm{s}$. System constraints are based on the actual limitations of the vessel model we use [17]:

$$\begin{bmatrix} 0 \\ -0.1 \\ -15\pi/180 \end{bmatrix} \leqslant v \leqslant \begin{bmatrix} 0.3 \\ 0.1 \\ 15\pi/180 \end{bmatrix}, \text{ and } |\boldsymbol{\tau}_{\mathrm{max}}| = \begin{bmatrix} 2 & 2 & 1.5 \end{bmatrix}^{\mathrm{T}}.$$

Maximum iterations j_{max} is set to 100; absolute tolerance $\varepsilon^{\mathrm{abs}} = 10^{-3}$ and relative tolerance $\varepsilon^{\mathrm{rel}} = 10^{-3}$. Algorithms in this article are implemented using

YALMIP (version 20131002) [18] in MATLAB 2011b [16]. Optimization problems are solved by Cplex (version 12.5.1) [19]. All the simulations are run on a platform with Intel (R) Core (TM) i5-3470 CPU @3.20 GHz.

We carry out simulations on two vessels encountering each other as a case study to illustrate the effectiveness of the proposed cooperative distributed collision avoidance algorithm and compare its performance with the centralized baseline. For both cases, as shown in Figure 1, there are two waterborne AGVs in a cross scenario: vessel 1 starts from A and is expected to follow the path A → B with an arrival time of 130 s; vessel 2 starts from C and is expected to follow the path C → D also with an arrival time of 130 s. That means if no collision avoidance actions are taken, the two vessels will collide at the center of the square. We will show that, however, both our centralized and distributed controllers will succeed in avoiding collisions while still achieve transportation tasks, i.e., track shortest path smoothly and arrive at destinations on time in an energy efficient way.

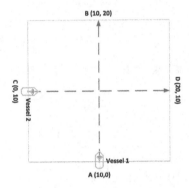

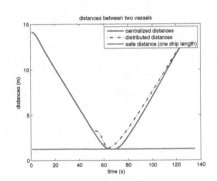

Fig. 1. Cross scenario for two waterborne AGVs

Fig. 2. Distances of two waterborne AGVs

5.2 Simulation Results and Discussions

Figure 2 shows the Euclidean distances between two vessels which are above the safe distance all the time in both simulations. Figure 3a and Figure 3b further show the trajectories from the centralized controller (simulation 1) and the distributed controller (simulation 2), respectively. It can be seen that in both simulations, vessel 1 and vessel 2 are able to track the reference path well. Both vessels arrive at the their own destinations on time at 130 s and 134 s, respectively, in two simulations, despite the possibly time consuming behavior for collision avoidance in the conflicting area. Blue dots in Figure 3a and Figure 3b are the position of vessel 1 at $t = 69s$; red squares are the positions of vessel 2 at the same time. This illustrates that although the trajectories of two vessels cross each other spatially, they do not cross each other temporally at the same time. However, observing relative positions of the two vessels in Figure 3

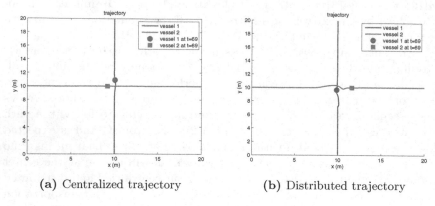

(a) Centralized trajectory   **(b)** Distributed trajectory

Fig. 3. Trajectories of two vessels

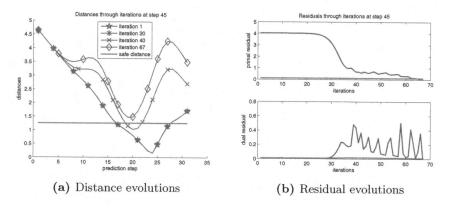

(a) Distance evolutions   **(b)** Residual evolutions

Fig. 4. Convergence behavior of distances and residuals over N_p at $k = 45$

and 4, it can be seen that centralized controller resolves the conflict by having vessel 2 slow down first to give way to vessel 1 while, conversely, the problem by distributed controller is solved by making vessel 1 wait for vessel 2's passing first. Collisions are successfully avoided in both cases.

Comparing with the centralized baseline, the distributed approach attains the cooperative behavior by decentralized computation and coordination which is in line with the decentralized nature of waterborne AGV systems. The convergence behavior of the decomposition - coordination scheme is shown in Figure 4a and Figure 4b taking the 67 iterations at time step 45 for example. Figure 4a shows the distance evolutions between two vessels as iterations proceeds. During the first iterations, distances at several steps of the prediction horizon are below the safe distance; but by iterative communication and coordination, both vessels adjust their initial calculated trajectories to guarantee a certain distance from each other. At the end of iterations when stopping criterion are met, distances between 2 vessels have been driven above the safe distance line. In Figure 4b, the difference between two sets of position variables: one from parallel local solutions for each vessel and the other from collision avoidance constraints, i.e. primal residuals converge to the primal tolerance as iteration proceeds, which means local vessel's solutions finally also satisfy collision avoidance constraints. Also, dual residuals which are the difference between current iteration solution and the previous step solution converge to the dual tolerance.

6   Conclusions and Future Research

Scenarios with multiple waterborne AGVs are considered in this paper which proposes a cooperative distributed collision avoidance controller based on alternating direction method of multipliers (ADMM) in the framework of model predictive control (MPC). A network model is defined based on graph theory for vessels which are coupled by non-convex minimum distance separation constraints. Shifted optimal trajectories are taken advantage of to convexify the coupling constraints. Iterative decomposition-coordination is achieved via ADMM. In particular, we introduce indicator functions which are updated using Euclidean projections over the convexified sets due to collision avoidance constraints. The remaining problem is readily further splitted and solved by each vessel since they have separable objectives and local constraints. Fully parallelized computations are possible in this setting which fits well for the physically distributed nature of waterborne AGVs. Extra consensus constraints converge through reasonable iterations which also generate feasibility and optimality convergence to a practical accuracy. Results from numerical simulations illustrated the effectiveness of the proposed algorithm.

Future research will be dedicated to improving the convergence behavior of the algorithm possibly by exploring the specific structure of our problem. Furthermore, hydrodynamic interactions for vessels in close proximity might also amount to couplings in system dynamics; and more case studies are to be done for ITT scenarios in the port area to demonstrate waterborne AGVs' potential in logistics.

Acknowledgments. This research is supported by the China Scholarship Council under Grant 201206 950021 and the Maritime Project "ShipDrive: A Novel Methodology for Integrated Modeling, Control, and Optimization of Hybrid Ship Systems" (project 13276) of the Dutch Technology Foundation STW.

References

1. Port of Rotterdam Authority. Port Vision 2030 (December 2011). http://www.portofrotterdam.com/en/Port/port-in-general/port-vision-2030/Pages/default.aspx (accessed: November 13, 2014)

2. Zheng, H., Negenborn, R.R., Lodewijks, G.: Predictive path following with arrival time awareness for waterborne AGVs. Transportation Research Part C: Emerging Technologies (Submitted to 2015)
3. Negenborn, R.R., Maestre, J.M.: On 35 approaches for distributed MPC made easy. In: Distributed Model Predictive Control Made Easy, pp. 1–37. Springer (2014)
4. Naeem, W., Irwin, G.W., Yang, A.: COLREGs-based collision avoidance strategies for unmanned surface vehicles. Mechatronics **22**(6), 669–678 (2012)
5. Mezouar, Y., Chaumette, F.: Path planning for robust image-based control. IEEE Transactions On Robotics and Automation **18**(4), 534–549 (2002)
6. Richards, A., How, J.P.: Robust distributed model predictive control. International Journal of Control **80**(9), 1517–1531 (2007)
7. Kuwata, Y., Wolf, M.T., Zarzhitsky, D., Huntsberger, T.L.: Safe maritime autonomous navigation with colregs, using velocity obstacles. IEEE Journal of Ocean Engineering **39**(1), 110–119 (2014)
8. Statheros, T., Howells, G., Maier, K.M.: Autonomous ship collision avoidance navigation concepts, technologies and techniques. Journal of Navigation **61**(01), 129–142 (2008)
9. Camacho, E.F., Bordons, C.: Model predictive control. Springer, Heidelberg (2013)
10. Schouwenaars, T., De Moor, B., Feron, E., How, J.: Mixed integer programming for multi-vehicle path planning. In: Proceedings of European control conference, pp. 2603–2608. Seminário de Vilar, Porto (2001)
11. Keviczky, T., Borrelli, F., Fregene, K., Godbole, D., Balas, G.J.: Decentralized receding horizon control and coordination of autonomous vehicle formations. IEEE Transactions on Control Systems Technology **16**(1), 19–33 (2008)
12. Kuwata, Y., How, J.P.: Cooperative distributed robust trajectory optimization using receding horizon MILP. IEEE Transactions on Control Systems Technology **19**(2), 423–431 (2011)
13. Boyd, Stephen, Parikh, Neal, Chu, Eric, Peleato, Borja, Eckstein, Jonathan: Distributed optimization and statistical learning via the alternating direction method of multipliers. Foundations and Trends in Machine Learning **3**(1), 1–122 (2011)
14. Ong, H.Y., Gerdes, J.C.: Cooperative collision avoidance via proximal message passing. In: Proceedings of 2015 American Control Conference, Chicago, USA (2015) (to appear)
15. Fossen, T.I.: Handbook of marine craft hydrodynamics and motion control. John Wiley and Sons Ltd., West Sussex (2011)
16. MATLAB: Version 7.13 (R2011b). The MathWorks Inc., Natick (2011)
17. Skjetne, R.: The maneuvering problem. Ph.D. thesis, Norwegian University of Science and Technology, Trondheim (2005)
18. Lofberg, J.: YALMIP: a toolbox for modeling and optimization in matlab. In: Proccedings of 2004 IEEE International Symposium on Computer Aided Control Systems Design, Taipei, Taiwan, pp. 284–289 (2004)
19. ILOG: IBM ILOG CPLEX Optimizer (2010). http://www-01.ibm.com/software/integration/optimization/cplex-optimizer/

A Matheuristic for the Liner Shipping Network Design Problem with Transit Time Restrictions

Berit Dangaard Brouer[1], Guy Desaulniers[2], Christian Vad Karsten[1]([⊠]),
and David Pisinger[1]

[1] DTU Management Engineering, Technical University of Denmark,
Produktionstorvet, Building 426, 2800 Kgs. Lyngby, Denmark
{blof,chrkr,dapi}@dtu.dk
[2] Department of Mathematics and Industrial Engineering,
Polytechnique Montréal and GERAD, C.P. 6079, Succ. Centre-Ville,
Montréal, QC H3C 3A7, Canada
guy.desaulniers@gerad.ca

Abstract. We present a mathematical model for the liner shipping network design problem with transit time restrictions on the cargo flow. We extend an existing matheuristic for the liner shipping network design problem to consider transit time restrictions. The matheuristic is an improvement heuristic, where an integer program is solved iteratively as a move operator in a large-scale neighborhood search. To assess the effects of insertions/removals of port calls, flow and revenue changes are estimated for relevant commodities along with an estimation of the change in the vessel cost. Computational results on the benchmark suite *LINER-LIB* are reported, showing profitable networks for most instances. We provide insights on causes for rejecting demand and the average speed per vessel class in the solutions obtained.

Keywords: Liner shipping · Network design · Transit time

1 Introduction

The *liner shipping network design problem with transit time restrictions*, LSNDP-TT, is a core planning problem facing container carriers. The problem is to design a set of cyclic routes for container vessels to provide transport for commodities in an origin-destination (OD) matrix respecting transit time restrictions of each individual commodity. The objective of the problem is to maximize the profit of the liner shipping company through the revenues gained from container transport taking into account the fixed cost of deploying vessels and the variable cost related to the operation of the routes and the handling cost of cargo transport. As a consequence of maximizing profits the liner shipping network design problem generally allows rejection of some commodities if deemed unprofitable.

Recent literature on liner shipping network design allows arbitrary transit times for all commodities [Agarwal and Ergun, 2008; Brouer et al., 2014a,b;

© Springer International Publishing Switzerland 2015
F. Corman et al. (Eds.): ICCL 2015, LNCS 9335, pp. 195–208, 2015.
DOI: 10.1007/978-3-319-24264-4_14

Gelareh et al., 2010; Liu et al., 2014; Mulder and Dekker, 2014; Plum et al., 2014; Reinhardt and Pisinger, 2012; Wang and Meng, 2014] although it is generally acknowledged that transit times are decisive for the competitiveness of the network design. This means that from the customer perspective liner shipping network design has multiple objectives as the customers prefer minimal transit times along with low freight rates. However, providing low freight rates by minimizing the cost of the network is likely to result in prolonged transit times as exemplified in Karsten et al. [2015]. Likewise designing a network to minimize transit times is likely to result in a very costly network since speed increases. Initial work to construct a multi-criteria objective function is presented in Alvarez [2012] that considers a bi-linear expression for the inventory cost of the cargo on board vessels, but the level of service calculations are not computationally tractable in the already very complex liner shipping network design models. However, the inventory cost of commodities on board vessels is only indirectly a concern to the carrier, when excessive transit times result in the customers switching to a different carrier. Hence, the carriers concern is to ensure a maximal transit time corresponding to the market level of service. Wang and Meng [2014] introduce deadlines on commodities in a non-linear, non-convex mixed-integer programming (MIP) formulation of liner shipping network design with transit time restrictions. As a consequence the model does not allow transshipment of cargo, which is another common trait of the liner shipping network design problem.

In this paper we present a capacitated multicommodity network design formulation for the liner shipping network design problem allowing for an arbitrary number of transshipments and enabling restrictions on transit time of individual commodities. We also propose an adaptation of the matheuristic of Brouer et al. [2014b] that considers transshipment times to show that it is tractable to incorporate the transit time restrictions in a heuristic context.

The paper is organized as follows: Section 2 reviews related work to the Liner Shipping Network Design Problem, LSNDP, and related areas in maritime and public transportation. Section 3 introduces our mathematical model. Section 4 expands the IP used as a move operator in Brouer et al. [2014b] to consider transit times and the column generation algorithm used to evaluate the cargo flow considering transit times. Section 5 reports computational results for the benchmark suite *LINER-LIB*. We end the paper by drawing conclusions and discussing extensions in Section 6.

2   Literature Review

Meng et al. [2014] and Christiansen et al. [2013] provide broader reviews of recent research on routing and scheduling problems within liner shipping. Here we review selected works on the LSNDP and the inclusion of transit time considerations.

Brouer et al. [2014a] present a thorough problem description of the LSNDP along with a mathematical model and a benchmark suite of data instances. Incorporating transit times into LSNDP is highlighted as an important area for future research. To accommodate future research needs the benchmark instances contain maximum transit time for all OD pairs and these instances are used for the computational results of this paper. Brouer et al. [2014b] develop a matheuristic for the LSNDP. The matheuristic is an *improvement* heuristic according to the categorization in the survey on matheuristics by Archetti and Speranza [2014] meaning that an integer program is used as a move operator. The present paper extends the method of Brouer et al. [2014b] to include transit times.

Alvarez [2012] presents mathematical expressions for the inventory cost of containers during transport. No computational results are reported as the mathematical expressions are not easily incorporated into existing models of the LSNDP. In Wang et al. [2013] an integer program for deciding minimum cost container paths for a single OD pair respecting transit time and cabotage restrictions is considered. Karsten et al. [2015] present a column generation algorithm for a time constrained multicommodity flow (MCF) problem applied to a liner shipping network. A resource constrained shortest path problem is solved for each origin using a specialized label setting algorithm. Different topologies of graphs for liner shipping networks are presented. Computational results for solving the MCF problem with and without transit times on global-sized liner shipping networks are reported. The solution times for the time constrained MCF problem is comparable to solving the MCF problem without transit time restrictions. The algorithm of Karsten et al. [2015] is used in the matheuristic presented in this paper for evaluating a given network during the search. A liner shipping network design problem considering transit time restrictions is presented in Wang and Meng [2014]. The model excludes transshipments between services. The problem is proven to be NP-hard and is formulated as a non-linear, non-convex mixed integer program. A column generation based heuristic is developed and a case study is presented for a network of 12 main ports on the Asia-Europe trade lane with three different vessel classes. The model is suggested as an aid to planners in a liner shipping company and the case study provides high quality network suggestions and important insights to assist the planners. The authors suggest incorporation of transshipments along with transit time restrictions as an area of future research.

In this paper we present a mathematical model considering cargo transit time restrictions and transshipments allowed between services. We develop a heuristic solution method incorporating ideas and methods of several of the works mentioned in this section.

3   Mathematical Model for the LSNDP-TT

In the following we introduce the notation used to formulate the LSNDP-TT mathematically. An instance of the LSNDP-TT consists of the following sets:

- P: Set of ports with an associated port call cost c_p^e, (un)load cost c_U^p, c_L^p, transshipment cost c_T^p and berthing time b_p spent on a port call.
- K: Set of demands, where each demand has an origin $O_k \in P$, a destination $D_k \in P$, a quantity, q_k, a revenue per unit, z_k, a reject penalty per unit $\tilde{z}_k$ and a maximal transit time, t_k.

- E: Set of vessel classes with specifications for the weekly charter rate, f_e, capacity U_e, minimum (v_{min}^e) and maximum (v_{max}^e) speed limits in knots per hour, bunker consumption as a function of the speed, g_v^e and bunker consumption per hour, when the vessel is idle at ports h^e. There are N_e vessels available of class $e \in E$. The price for one metric ton of bunker is denoted c_B.
- D: Matrix of the direct distances d_{ij}^e between all pairs of ports $i,j \in P$ and for all vessel classes $e \in E$. The distance may depend on the vessel class draft as the panama canal is draft restricted. Along with d_{ij}^e follows an indication of the cost l_{ij}^e associated with a possible traversal of a canal.

A solution to the LSNDP is a subset of the set of feasible services S. A service consists of a set of ports $P' \subseteq P$, a number of vessels, and an average sailing speed. A service is cyclic but may be non-simple, that is, ports can be visited more than once. In this model we allow a single port to be visited twice, yielding a so-called *butterfly* route. The service time T_s is the time needed to complete the cyclic route. A weekly frequency of port calls is obtained by deploying multiple vessels to a service. Let $e(s) \in E$ be the vessel class assigned to a service s and $n_{e(s)}$ the number of vessels of class $e(s)$ required to maintain a weekly frequency. A round trip may last several weeks but due to the weekly frequency exactly one round trip is performed every week. Let v_s be the service speed in nautical miles per hour.

The mathematical model of the LSNPD-TT relies on a set of service variables and a path flow formulation of the underlying time constrained MCF problem. To describe the service network of the LSNDP-TT, we define F^s to be the port sequence $p_1^s, p_2^s, \ldots, p_m^s$ for the service $s \in S$. Let $|s|$ denote the number of unique ports in a service $s \in S$ and $|F^s| = m$ the number of port calls in s.

Furthermore we define a directed graph, $G(V, A)$, with vertices V and arcs A. $V = V_P \cup V_R$ is the set of vertices, where V_P is the subset of vertices representing the unique ports $p \in P$, and V_R is the subset of service vertices representing all port calls by all services. $V_R = \bigcup_{s \in S} V_{F^s}$ and V_{F^s} is the subset of vertices representing the port calls $p_1^s, p_2^s, \ldots, p_m^s$ of service F^s, $s \in S$. $p(v)$ is a function mapping a vertex $v \in V_R$ (i.e., a port call) to its actual port $p \in P$. The set of arcs in the graph can be divided into (un)load arcs, transshipment arcs, sailing arcs, and forfeited arcs, i.e. $A = A_L \cup A_U \cup A_T \cup A_S \cup A_K$. These sets are formally defined below and we associate with each arc $a \in A$ a cost c_a, traversal time t_a, and capacity C_a.

- $A_L = \{(p, v) \,|\, p \in V_P, v \in V_{F^s}\}$ and $A_U = \{(v, p) \,|\, v \in V_{F^s}, p \in V_P\}$ are respectively the sets of loading/unloading arcs representing a departure/arrival at port p visited in F^s, $c_a = c_L^p$, and $c_a = c_U^p$ is the (un)loading cost for a container at the associated port $p \in V_P$, $t_a = 0$, and C_a is unlimited.
- $A_T = \{(v, u) \,|\, v \in V_{F^s}, u \in V_{F^{s'}}\}$ is the set of transshipment arcs representing a transshipment between services F^s and $F^{s'}$ defined for every pair (v, u) where $p(v) = p(u)$, $c_a = c_T^p$ is the transshipment cost for a container at the associated port $p \in V_P$, t_a is the transshipment time, and C_a is unlimited.

- $A_S = \{(v, u) \mid s \in S, v, u \in V_{F^s}, v = p_h^s, u = p_{((h+1) \bmod m)}^s\}$ is the set of sailing arcs representing a sailing between two consecutive port calls v and u in F^s, $c_a = 0$ as sailing costs are directly incurred by the vessels, $t_a = d_{ij}/v_s + b_j$ meaning the time in hours to traverse the edge plus the berthing time at the arriving port for each sailing, and $C_a = U_{e(s)}$.
- $A_K = \{(v, u) \mid v, u \in V_P, \exists k \in K : O_k = v \land D_k = u\}$ is the set of forfeiting arcs representing a rejection of transporting the cargo k between v and u in P, $c_a = \tilde{z}_k + z_k$ is the penalty associated with rejecting the cargo k, $t_a = t_k$ is the maximum transit time for k, and $C_a = q_k$.

We use the path flow formulation of the time constrained MCF problem as described in Karsten et al. [2015]. Let Ω_k be the set of all feasible paths for commodity k including forfeiting the cargo. Let $\Omega(a)$ be the set of all paths using arc $a \in A$. The cost of a path ρ is denoted as c_ρ and it includes the revenue obtained by transporting one unit of commodity k sent along path $\rho \in \Omega_k$. The real variable x_ρ denotes the amount of commodity k sent along the path. Let the weekly cost of a service be $c_s = n_{e(s)}f_{e(s)} + \sum_{(i,j) \in A_S} \left(c_B(h^{e(s)}b_p + g_{v(s)}^{e(s)}d_{ij}^{e(s)}) + c_j^{e(s)} + l_{ij}^{e(s)} \right)$ accounting for fixed cost of deploying the vessel and the variable cost in terms of the fuel and port call cost of one round trip. Define binary service variables y_s indicating the inclusion of service $s \in S$ in the solution.

Then the mathematical model of the LSNDP-TT can be formulated as follows.

$$\min \quad \sum_{s \in S} c_s y_s + \sum_{k \in K} \sum_{\rho \in \Omega_k} c_\rho x_\rho \tag{1}$$

$$\text{s.t.} \quad \sum_{\rho \in \Omega_k} x_\rho = q_k \qquad\qquad k \in K \tag{2}$$

$$\sum_{\rho \in \Omega(a)} x_\rho - U_{e(s)} y_s \leq 0 \qquad\qquad s \in S, a \in A_S \tag{3}$$

$$\sum_{s \in S : e(s) = e} n_{e(s)} y_s \leq N_e \qquad\qquad e \in E \tag{4}$$

$$x_\rho \in \mathbb{R}^+ \qquad\qquad \rho \in \Omega_k,\ k \in K \tag{5}$$

$$y_s \in \{0, 1\} \qquad\qquad s \in S \tag{6}$$

The objective (1) minimizes cumulative service and cargo transportation cost. As the cargo transportation cost includes the revenue of transporting the cargo this is equivalent to maximizing profit. *The cargo flow constraints* (2) along with non-negativity constraints (5) ensure that all cargo is either transported or forfeited. *The capacity constraints* (3) link the cargo paths with the service capacity installed in the transportation network. *The fleet availability constraints* (4) ensure that the selected services can be operated by the available fleet. Finally, constraints (6) define the service variables as binary.

The mathematical model extends the problem description of the LSNDP presented in Brouer et al. [2014a] to handle transit times. The model enforces a weekly frequency resulting in a weekly planning horizon. The path flow formulation of the MCF problem considers transit time restrictions in the definition of a feasible path for a given commodity. Column generation is applied for solving the path flow formulation of the MCF problem, where reduced cost columns are generated by solving a shortest path problem. Introducing transit time restrictions changes the subproblem to a resource constrained shortest path problem and thus the complexity of the subproblem becomes NP-hard. The label setting algorithm from Karsten et al. [2015] is used to solve the cargo routing problem with transit time restrictions during the execution of our algorithm.

In the LSNDP-TT the sailing speed is decisive for the cost of a given service as well as the feasible solution space of the multicommodity flow problem. The majority of all commodities are subject to transshipments and transit time may depend on the choice of speed on multiple services. As a consequence lowering the speed to reduce the cost of a service may make existing cargo routings infeasible due to an increase in transit times. Likewise, increasing speed may result in increased flow in the network as the set of feasible paths increase, but at the same time it will increase the cost of service through the additional fuel burn. The service variables of (1)-(6) are defined for an average speed on all sailings on a round trip and assume a fixed weekly frequency and the resulting speed and cost change from in- or de-creasing by one vessel may be quite significant. However, the proposed algorithm is not optimizing speeds of the individual sailings. The feasible deployment of vessels to maintain weekly frequency will be limited by the minimum and maximum speed.

4   Algorithm

The algorithm presented in this paper is an extension of the matheuristic for the LSNDP presented in Brouer et al. [2014b]. The algorithm proposed in Brouer et al. [2014b] uses a greedy knapsack based construction heuristic to create an initial set of services, S. Then the core of the matheuristic is executed iteratively to try to improve these using a MIP for each service. The algorithm terminates either when no profitable moves can be found or when a computational time limit is reached. We use the same overall framework in the following and a detailed description and flow chart of the algorithm can be found in Brouer et al. [2014b]. The central component in the latter matheuristic is an improvement heuristic, where an integer program is solved as a move operator in a large-scale neighborhood search. The integer program is iteratively solved for a single service using estimation functions for changes in the flow due to insertions and removals of port calls in the service investigated. The solution of the integer program provides a set of moves in the composition of port calls and fleet deployment. Flow changes and the resulting change in the revenue are estimated by solving a series of resource constrained shortest path problems on the residual graph of the current network. This is done for relevant commodities to the insertion/removal of a port call along with an estimation of the change in the vessel related cost with the current fleet deployment.

Given a total estimated change in revenue of rev_i and port call cost of $c_i^{e(s)}$ Figure 1(a) illustrates estimation functions for the change in revenue (Θ_i^s) and duration increase (Δ_i^s) for inserting port i into service s controlled by the binary variable γ_i. The duration controls the number of vessels needed to maintain a weekly frequency of service. Figure 1(b) illustrates the estimation functions for the change in revenue (Υ_i^s) and decrease in duration (Γ_i^s) for removing port i from service s controlled by the binary variable λ_i. Insertions/removals will affect the duration of the service in question and hence the needed fleet deployment modeled by the integer variable ω_s representing the change in the number of vessels deployed.

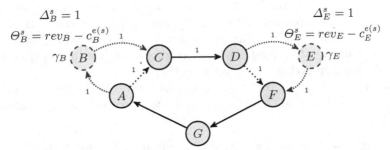

(a) Blue nodes are evaluated for insertion corresponding to variables γ_i for the set of ports in the neighborhood N^s of service s.

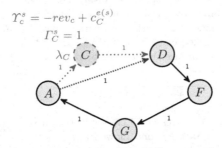

(b) Red nodes are evaluated for removal corresponding to variables λ_i for the set of current port calls F^s on service s.

Fig. 1. Illustration of the estimation functions for insertion and removal of port calls

4.1 Estimated Revenue Loss ζ_x Due to Transit Time Changes

For considering the transit time in the IP, it is necessary to estimate how insertions and removals of port calls will affect the duration of the existing flow on the service. This means that existing flow must be estimated to have sufficient

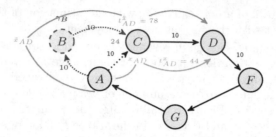

Fig. 2. Insertions/removals affect transit time of the flow. Commodity k_{AD} has a maximum transit time of 48 hours and the insertion of γ_B will make path variable x_{AD} infeasible

slack in transit time for the insertions performed or alternatively, existing flow will result in a loss of revenue if it cannot be rerouted within the available transit time on a different path. Figure 2 illustrates a case of a path variable in the current basis of the MCF model, which becomes infeasible due to transit time restrictions when inserting port B on its path.

In order to account for the transit time restrictions of the current flow, constraints (14) are added to the IP and a penalty, ζ_x corresponding to losing the

Table 1. Overview of sets, constants, and variables used in the IP

Sets

N^s	Set of neighbors (potential port call insertions) of s.
X^s	Set of path variables on service s in current flow solution with positive flow.
$N^x \subseteq N^s$	Subset of neighbors with insertion on current path of variable $x \in X^s$.
$F^x \subseteq F^s$	Subset of port calls on current path of variable $x \in X^s$.
L_i	Lock set for port call insertion $i \in N^s$ or port call removal $i \in F^s$.

Constants

Y_s	Distance of the route associated with s.
K_s	Estimated average speed of the service s.
M_e	Number of undeployed vessels of class e in the current solution.
I_s	Maximum number of insertions allowed in s.
R_s	Maximum number of removals allowed in s.
Δ_i^s	Estimated distance increase if port call $i \in N^s$ is inserted in s.
Γ_i^s	Estimated distance decrease if port call $i \in F^s$ is removed from s.
Θ_i	Estimated profit increase of inserting port call $i \in N^s$ in s.
Υ_i	Estimated profit increase of removing port call $i \in F^s$ from s.
ζ_x	Estimated penalty for cargo lost due to transit time.
s_x	Slack time of path variable x.

Variables

λ_i	1 if port call $i \in F^s$ is removed from s, 0 otherwise.
γ_i	1 if port call $i \in N^s$ is inserted in s, 0 otherwise.
$\omega_s \in \mathbb{Z}$	Number of vessels added (removed if negative) to s.
α_x	1 if transit time of path variable $x \in X^s$ is violated, 0 otherwise.

cargo, is added to the objective if the transit time slack for an existing path variable becomes negative. This is handled through the variable α_x, where x refers to a path variable with positive flow in the current solution and s_x refers to the current slack time according to the transit time restrictions of the variable. For ease of reading, Table 1 gives an overview of additional sets, constants, and variables used in the IP.

Given this notation, the IP is:

$$\max \quad \sum_{i \in N^s} \Theta_i \gamma_i + \sum_{i \in F^s} \Upsilon_i \lambda_i - f_{e(s)} \omega_s - \zeta_x \alpha_x \tag{7}$$

$$\text{s.t.} \quad \frac{Y_s}{K_s} + \sum_{i \in F^s} b_{p(i)} + \sum_{i \in N^s} (\frac{\Delta_i^s}{K_s} + b_{p(i)}) \gamma_i - \sum_{i \in F^s} (\frac{\Gamma_i^s}{K_s} + b_{p(i)}) \lambda_i \leq 24 \cdot 7 \cdot (n_{e(s)} + \omega_s) \tag{8}$$

$$\omega_s \leq M_e \tag{9}$$

$$\sum_{i \in N^s} \gamma_i \leq I_s \tag{10}$$

$$\sum_{i \in F^s} \lambda_i \leq R_s \tag{11}$$

$$\sum_{j \in L_i} \lambda_j \leq |L_i|(1 - \gamma_i) \qquad\qquad i \in N^s \tag{12}$$

$$\sum_{j \in L_i} \lambda_j \leq |L_i|(1 - \lambda_i) \qquad\qquad i \in F^s \tag{13}$$

$$\sum_{i \in N^x} (\frac{\Delta_i^s}{K_s} + b_{p(i)}) \gamma_i - \sum_{i \in F^x} (\frac{\Gamma_i^s}{K_s} + b_{p(i)}) \lambda_i - UB\alpha_x \leq s_x \qquad x \in X^s \tag{14}$$

$$\lambda_i \in \{0,1\}, \ i \in F^s \quad \gamma_i \in \{0,1\}, \ i \in N^s \quad \alpha_x \in \{0,1\}, \ x \in X^s$$

$$\omega_s \in \mathbb{Z}, \ s \in S$$

The objective function (7) maximizes the estimated profit increase obtained from removing and inserting port calls, accounting for the estimated change of revenue, transshipment cost, port call cost and fleet cost. As opposed to the IP proposed in Brouer et al. [2014b] the change in revenue may be related to not transporting cargo for which the path duration is estimated to exceed the transit time of the commodity. The number of vessels needed on the service (assuming a weekly frequency) after insertions/removals is estimated in constraint (8) accounting for the change in the service time given the current speed K_s. Constraint (9) ensures that the solution does not exceed the available fleet of vessels. Note that ω_s does not need to be bounded from below by $-n_{e(s)}$ because it is not allowed to remove all port calls. Constraints (10) and (11) limit the number of port call insertions and removals to minimize the error in the computed estimates. The set of port calls affected by an insertion or a removal is fixed by the lock set constraints (12) and (13), respectively. Finally, constraint (14) activates the estimated penalty for lost cargo due to an estimated violation of the transit time for the commodity on this particular path.

Table 2. The instances of the benchmark suite with indication of the number of ports ($|P|$), the number of origin-destination pairs ($|K|$), the number of vessel classes ($|E|$), the minimum (min v) and maximum number of vessels (max v), and the solution time limit in seconds (t.l.). The instances can be found at http://www.linerlib.org

Category	Instance and description	$|P|$	$|K|$	$|E|$	min v	max v	t.l.
Single-hub	**Baltic** Baltic sea, Bremerhaven as hub	12	22	2	5	7	300
	WAF West Africa, Algeciras as hub	19	38	2	33	51	900
Multi-hub	**Mediterranean** Mediterranean, Algeciras, Tangier, and Gioia Tauro as hubs	39	369	3	15	25	1200
Trade-lane	**Pacific** (Asia-US West)	45	722	4	81	119	3600
	AsiaEurope Europe, Middle East and Far east regions	111	4000	6	140	212	14400
World	**Small** 47 Main ports worldwide identified by Maersk Line	47	1764	6	209	317	10800

5 Computational Results

The matheuristic was tested on the benchmark suite *LINER-LIB 2012* described in Brouer et al. [2014a]. Table 2 gives an overview of the instances. We have revised the transit time restrictions for a small number of the origin-destination pairs in order to meet critical transit times as our model operates with average sailing speeds. The pairs where the transit times have been revised are those that cannot be satisfied by a direct sailing at 14 knots. The number of revised pairs is 6, 15, 106, and 32 for WAF, Pacific, WorldSmall, and EuropeAsia respectively. They have been revised according to the most recent published liner shipping transit times.

The matheuristic has been coded in C++ and run on a linux system with an *Intel(R) Xeon(R) X5550* CPU at *2.67GHz* and *24 GB* RAM. The algorithm is set to terminate after the time limits imposed in Brouer et al. [2014a] if the stopping criterion of the embedded simulated annealing procedure is not fulfilled at the time limit.

We fix the berthing time, b_p, to 24 hours for all ports as in Brouer et al. [2014a] and the transshipment time, t_a, is fixed to 48 hours for every connection as the schedule is not considered.

5.1 Computational Results for *LINER-LIB 2012*

Table 3 shows that the algorithm can find profitable solutions (negative objective values) for Baltic, WAF, WorldSmall and AsiaEurope. Pacific is unprofitable although both fleet deployment and transport percentage is high. In most instances except the Mediterranean around 85% to 95% of the available cargo is transported on average. At the same time as little as 80% of the fleet in terms of volume is utilized suggesting that further improvements may be achievable as the larger instances all terminate due to the imposed computational time limits.

Table 3. Best and Average of 10 runs on an *Intel(R) Xeon(R) X5550* CPU at *2.67GHz* with *24 GB* RAM. Weekly objective value (**Z(7)**); percentage of fleet deployed: as a percentage of the total volume **D(v)**, and as a percentage of the number of ships **D(|E|)**. **T(v)** is the percentage of total cargo volume transported and (**S**) is the execution time in CPU seconds; time means the solution time limit has been reached

Instance	Z(7)	D(v) (%)	D(|E|) (%)	T(v) (%)	(S)
Best - Baltic 1	**-14050**	**100.0**	**100.0**	**87.4**	**101**
Average Baltic	74480	100.0	100.0	86.7	108
Best - WAF 10	$-5.59 \cdot 10^6$	**83.3**	**85.7**	**97.0**	**255**
Average WAF	$-4.87 \cdot 10^6$	83.3	85.2	94.3	354
Best -Med 5	$2.42 \cdot 10^6$	**91.9**	**95.0**	**86.9**	**710**
Average Med	$2.70 \cdot 10^6$	90.5	94.0	78.9	737
Best - Pacific 2	$3.05 \cdot 10^6$	**95.0**	**91.0**	**93.3**	**time**
Average Pacific	$3.65 \cdot 10^6$	94.0	91.9	94.0	time
Best - WorldSmall 5	$-3.54 \cdot 10^7$	**82.0**	**85.2**	**91.1**	**time**
Average WorldSmall	$-3.15 \cdot 10^7$	82.3	85.4	90.9	time
Best - AsiaEurope 9	$-1.67 \cdot 10^7$	**84.6**	**90.9**	**88.8**	**time**
Average AsiaEurope	$-1.45 \cdot 10^7$	83.9	91.9	88.5	time

Table 4 shows that most services operate relatively close to their design speed for the smaller classes, apart from the WorldSmall instances where average service speed is higher than design speed. The large vessel classes generally have high average speeds. For the WorldSmall and AsiaEurope, we can see in Table 3 that we have excess fleet and by comparing **D(v)** and **D(|E|)** it can be seen that it is mainly the large vessel classes that are undeployed. This is somewhat surprising as this contradicts the economy of scale of larger vessels. However, Table 4 also shows that the WorldSmall and AsiaEurope operate at very high

Table 4. Average speed per vessel class over ten runs. Last two rows indicate the design speed and max speed of the corresponding vessel classes. F is Feeder, P is Panamax

Instance	F450	F800	P1200	P2400	Post P	Super P
Baltic	10.8	13.7				
WAF	11.5	13.2				
Med	11.9	13.7	13.9			
Pacific	12.0	14.2	15.9	18.2		
WorldSmall	12.7	15.5	17.5	19.4	19.4	18.2
AsiaEurope	11.7	13.7	16.5	18.0	19.7	17.6
Design Speed	**12.0**	**14.0**	**18.0**	**16.0**	**16.5**	**17.0**
Max speed	**14.0**	**17.0**	**19.0**	**22.0**	**23.0**	**22.0**

speeds for the large vessel classes. An explanation could be the fact that we cannot swap vessel classes very well in the algorithm and we are perhaps not able to fill the larger vessels because we have very good utilization on the small services. This needs further investigation.

Table 5 gives statistics on the rejected demand in the solutions. The primary causes are that existing paths do not meet transit time restrictions, that there is no residual capacity or that the OD pair is not connected in the graph. For the smaller instances (Baltic,WAF and Mediterranean) rejection of demand is primarily because the OD pairs are not connected, indicating that it is unprofitable to call these ports. For the larger instances (Pacific, WorldSmall, and AsiaEurope) the demand is primarily rejected due to the transit times that cannot be met (with some variation), and in WorldSmall a significant amount of cargo is also rejected due to lack of capacity. In general comparing the percentage not connected in number of demands (k) compared to the volume (v) not connected indicates that it is the demands with low volume that are not connected. Often these demands are from small feeder ports not visited by the solution because the total volume is very low and it is deemed unprofitable by the algorithm.

Table 5. Statistics on the rejected demand reporting average (μ) and standard deviation (σ) over ten runs. $|R|$ is the number of rejected OD pairs; **tt(k)** is the percentage of OD pairs rejected due only to transit time; **C(k)** is the percentage of OD pairs rejected due only to lack of capacity; **tt,C(k)** is the percentage of OD pairs rejected due to both transit time and lack of capacity; **L(k)** is the percentage of OD pairs not connected; **FFE** is the volume of the rejected demand; **tt(v)** is the percentage of the volume rejected due only to transit time; **C(v)** is the percentage of the volume rejected due only to lack of capacity; **tt,C(v)** is the percentage of volume rejected due to both transit time and lack of capacity; **L(v)** is the percentage of volume rejected because O and D are not connected

Instance		$|R|$	tt(k) (%)	C(k) (%)	tt,C(k) (%)	L(k) (%)	FFE	tt(v) (%)	C(v) (%)	tt,C(v) (%)	L(v) (%)
Baltic	μ	10	0.0	20.8	0.0	79.2	653	0.0	66.4	0.0	33.6
	σ	1	0.0	6.7	0.0	6.7	57	0.0	6.8	0.0	6.8
WAF	μ	7	3.4	16.2	0.0	80.4	489	2.8	28.1	0.0	69.1
	σ	2	7.4	12.5	0.0	9.3	230	6.9	28.4	0.0	26.1
Med	μ	113	32.9	0.7	5.1	61.2	1590	41.9	0.7	7.4	50.0
	σ	25	11.1	0.9	3.1	12.2	521	13.0	1.2	5.1	14.6
Pacific	μ	190	53.4	2.7	15.9	28.0	2629	51.5	10.1	27.6	10.8
	σ	21	11.8	2.3	8.3	5.7	708	17.0	9.5	14.2	4.9
WorldSmall	μ	238	38.3	27.8	23.4	10.5	11635	42.7	24.3	25.9	7.2
	σ	22	11.8	4.9	9.6	13.6	1008	13.5	6.5	10.5	9.5
AsiaEurope	μ	810	37.2	11.7	26.4	24.8	8836	41.6	15.4	31.2	11.9
	σ	66	5.6	5.4	4.0	4.4	871	10.3	6.7	8.9	2.9

6   Conclusions

We have presented a model for the LSNDP-TT introducing transit time restrictions on each individual commodity while maintaining the ability to transship between services. We have extended the matheuristic of Brouer et al. [2014b] to handle transit time restrictions. The core component of the matheuristic is an integer program considering a set of removals and insertions to a service. We extend the integer program to consider how removals and insertions influence the transit time of the existing cargo flow on the service. Each iteration of the matheuristic provides a set of moves for the current set of services and fleet deployment, which lead to a potential improvement in the overall revenue. The evaluation of the cargo flow for a set of moves requires solving a time constrained multi-commodity flow problem using column generation.

The introduction of transit time constraints changes the estimation functions for the improvement heuristic and the pricing problem of the column generation algorithm from an ordinary shortest path problem to a resource constrained shortest path problem. We apply the specialized label setting algorithm of Karsten et al. [2015] to achieve satisfactory performance.

Extensive computational tests show that it is possible to generate profitable networks for the majority of the instances in *LINER-LIB* and especially for the larger instances the approach generates networks of good quality. However some demand is not served and the fleet is not utilized completely, especially for the larger vessel classes, suggesting that further algorithmic improvements may lead to even better solutions. We expect that especially speed optimization on individual legs as well as more flexibility in terms of possible vessel class swaps could improve the algorithmic performance in terms of profitability for the generated networks as well as the amount of met demand.

Acknowledgments. This project was supported by the Danish Maritime Fund project, "competitive liner shipping network design".

References

Agarwal, R., Ergun, O.: Ship scheduling and network design for cargo routing in liner shipping. Transportation Science **42**(2), 175–196 (2008)

Alvarez, J.F.: Mathematical expressions for level of service optimization in liner shipping. Journal of the Operational Research Society **63**(6), 709–714 (2012)

Archetti, C., Speranza, M.G.: A survey on matheuristics for routing problems. EURO Journal on Computational Optimization **2**, 223–246 (2014)

Brouer, B., Alvarez, J., Plum, C., Pisinger, D., Sigurd, M.: A base integer programming model and benchmark suite for liner shipping network design. Transportation Science **48**(2), 281–312 (2014a)

Brouer, B., Desaulniers, G., Pisinger, D.: A matheuristic for the liner shipping network design problem. Transportation Research Part E: Logistics and Transportation Review **72**, 42–59 (2014b)

Christiansen, M., Fagerholt, K., Nygreen, B., Ronen, D.: Ship routing and scheduling in the new millennium. European Journal of Operational Research **228**(3), 467–483 (2013)

Gelareh, S., Nickel, S., Pisinger, D.: Liner shipping hub network design in a competitive environment. Transportation Research Part E: Logistics and Transportation Review **46**(6), 991–1004 (2010)

Karsten, C.V., Pisinger, D., Ropke, S., Brouer, B.D.: The time constrained multi-commodity network flow problem and its application to liner shipping network design. Transportation Research Part E: Logistics and Transportation Review **76**, 122–138 (2015)

Liu, Z., Meng, Q., Wang, S., Sun, Z.: Global intermodal liner shipping network design. Transportation Research Part E: Logistics and Transportation Review **61**, 28–39 (2014)

Meng, Q., Wang, S., Andersson, H., Thun, K.: Containership routing and scheduling in liner shipping: Overview and future research directions. Transportation Science **48**(2), 265–280 (2014)

Mulder, J., Dekker, R.: Methods for strategic liner shipping network design. European Journal of Operational Research **235**(2), 367–377 (2014)

Plum, C., Pisinger, D., Sigurd, M.M.: A service flow model for the liner shipping network design problem. European Journal of Operational Research **235**(2), 378–386 (2014)

Reinhardt, L.B., Pisinger, D.: A branch and cut algorithm for the container shipping network design problem. Flexible Services and Manufacturing Journal **24**(3), 349–374 (2012)

Wang, S., Meng, Q.: Liner shipping network design with deadlines. Computers and Operations Research **41**(1), 140–149 (2014)

Wang, S., Meng, Q., Sun, Z.: Container routing in liner shipping. Transportation Research Part E: Logistics and Transportation Review **49**(1), 1–7 (2013)

A Positioning System Based on Monocular Vision for Model Ship

Shuo Xie[1,2], Chenguang Liu[1,2(✉)], Xiumin Chu[1], and Xue Ouyang[1,3]

[1] Engineering Research Center for Transportation Safety, Ministry of Education,
Wuhan University of Technology, Wuhan, People's Republic of China
{760137081,670489920}@qq.com, {liuchenguang,chuxm}@whut.edu.cn
[2] School of Energy and Power Engineering, Wuhan University of Technology,
Wuhan, People's Republic of China
[3] School of Logistics Engineering, Wuhan University of Technology, Wuhan,
People's Republic of China

Abstract. High precision positioning for a ship is important during logistics automation on water. This paper has proposed a positioning system of model ship based on monocular vision. Firstly an image of the experiment pool can be obtained by the camera on shore before the image is filtered and corrected in the preprocessing. Then the system uses binarization area and color threshold to identify a ship target. Finally ship real-time information which includes position, navigation speed and course can be obtained by transforming the image coordinate into the inertial coordinate, and the ship track will be displayed on the positioning software at the same time. Experimental results show that real-time and positioning precision of this system can meet automatic navigation demand for model ship.

Keywords: Monocular vision · Color threshold · Coordinate transforming · Positioning system

1 Introduction

With the development of logistics automation on water, a real-time positioning system for a ship is needed. It can provide navigation information such as position, speed and course for the ship navigation in automatic logistics.

1.1 The Research Background

At present, GPS, inertial navigation, radar and computer vision equipment are widely used in ship positioning system [1].

GPS has the advantage of wide scope of coverage, but the positioning accuracy is not high enough. Zheng L. F. puts forward a mobile ship positioning technology based on GPSOne. On the basis of the fusion of CDMA network, this technology can solve the positioning error of A-GPS. But the precision can only reach meter-scale, does not meet the demand of the real-time ship positioning [2].

© Springer International Publishing Switzerland 2015
F. Corman et al. (Eds.): ICCL 2015, LNCS 9335, pp. 209–221, 2015.
DOI: 10.1007/978-3-319-24264-4_15

Optical gyro inertial system, which is also currently used, has been applied on land vehicles. But the cost of inertial system is very high, and it has accumulative error after working for a few hours. Xu X. F. uses the navigation information of GPS to correct the error of inertial system. But the result is also not stable enough after working in a period of time [3].

Radar is more accurate. With the development of High-Frequency (HF) radars, the precision can reach centimeter according to the research of HF radar measurements accuracy by Essen H. H [4]. But high precision radar equipment is very expensive for ship positioning system.

Visual positioning system acquires continuous image sequence of moving target by a video camera. Then the designed algorithm in image sequence is used to detect, track and positioning the target. After that, the trajectory is reconstructed and three-dimensional coordinates of the target are outputted [5,6,7]. Li X. F. designed a ship tracking and positioning system based on binocular vision, which is divided into four modules: camera calibration, target tracking, stereo matching and parallax position. This system can achieve real-time tracking and provide precise location of ship [8].

1.2   The Research Significance

The positioning system for an autonomous navigation ship should have a certain precision for automatic collision avoidance and route planning. Accuracy of visual poisoning system is higher than GPS and inertial system and it costs lower than radar. With comprehensive consideration, visual positioning is chosen for research. But there are also some issues in ship visual positioning system nowadays.

In the aspect of recognition, grey image binarization is mostly adopted in the ship visual positioning system. Jin X. D. uses Histogram-based threshold to detect the object and background in the gray image of a ship [9] Xie D. L. used computer vision to match the shape feature of container ship's grey image [10]. But the color characteristics of the target are not reserved completely in those methods and will be affected by other noise colors. A stable ship recognition method has not been given for real-time identification yet.

In the aspect of positioning, the localization algorithm used for ship location is always complex. Wang J. provide a relatively simple method of locating ship by measuring the distance based on monocular camera by using projective geometry and camera intrinsic parameters. But the parameters of this method are not easy to be measured in real time applications [11]. A simple localization algorithm which input can be easily measured should be given for real-time positioning.

1.3   Work of this Paper

This paper puts forward a monocular vision positioning system based on an color threshold of each channel in RGB model. Because the color of ship background image is simple (the water color), this method has a good applicability for the experiment of ship recognition. And in order to get high precision and real-time performance, a simple localization algorithm based on pin-hole imaging is given.

In this paper, the positioning system is expounded in two parts. The first part is the ship target recognition. An identification method is explained in detail in this part. Then in the second part, a coordinate transformation is given. It is used to get the navigation motion state of the ship. Finally the experimental method is introduced and the results are analyzed to verify the accuracy of the system.

2   Ship Target Recognition

2.1   Color Feature Recognition

To identify a ship from an image, the positioning system needs to segment image which contained objective vessels. Wang J. T. studied several kinds of color image segmentation algorithms. He said that among all the segmentation methods, the image segmentation based on color is used widely, and threshold segmentation is one of the most common methods in color segmentation because that method is simple, needs small amount of calculation and performs stable [12]. Through setting a certain threshold the method can divide an image into the interesting color area (such as the color of the model ship) and the others (such as water, distractions, etc.).

In order to get better ship image segmentation in the experiment, the ship is covered with the marked color (red) before doing experiment. In this paper， *RGB* color space is used and the steps of color threshold segmentation are shown as follows:

$$r = \frac{R}{R+G+B}$$

$$g = \frac{G}{R+G+B} \tag{1}$$

$$b = \frac{B}{R+G+B}$$

r, g, b are called the chromaticity coordinates, and $r + g + b = 1$. Then threshold of each channel is set.

$$THA(r_{min}) \leq r \leq THA(r_{max})$$

$$THA(g_{min}) \leq g \leq THA(g_{max}) \tag{2}$$

$$THA(b_{min}) \leq b \leq THA(b_{max})$$

In the recognition of ship, some photos of the red ship are taken and the range of the *RGB* value in each pixel in these photos is obtained. Then experience threshold value is set:

$$THA(r_{\min}) = 0.6 \quad THA(r_{\max}) = 1$$

$$THA(g_{\min}) = 0 \quad THA(g_{\max}) = 0.2 \tag{3}$$

$$THA(b_{\min}) = 0 \quad THA(b_{\max}) = 0.2$$

The normalization method can reduce influence caused by the change of brightness. But only the relative luminance component of r, g and b are wiped off. The influence by the color saturation is not separated from normalized RGB model. However, after experimental comparison, it is found that the difference of the three channels (r, g and b) is in a certain range. Namely, the difference is little affected by the light. This paper proposed an improved threshold processing method, which can better identified the ship under different illumination by joining the criterion in the second step of experience threshold processing. And the criterion is as follow:

If the pixel meets: $r-g>THA(r-g)\&\&r-b>THA(r-b)$, then it is the red pixel.

THA () represents the threshold of the current identification mode. Parameters that are in brackets represent the color difference. Such as *THA (r - g)* is the value difference between red and green.

In the experiment, through constantly adjusting color threshold, the system can recognize the ship under different light conditions accurately.

2.2   Binarization and Contour Detection

In this paper model ship is selected as the research object, which size is 1/32 of a certain torpedo by narrowing. The model ship's length is 958 mm and width is 243mm.When the ship sails on the water, the area of the hull part is within limits in the captured image. Therefore, the following target detection process is put forward:

1. In the previous step of color recognition, another single channel image is built to obtain the point which meets the color threshold in the original image. And the system sets that point's grey value as 255 (white) and other point's grey value as 0 (black).
2. With OpenCV library function, contour sequences of the binarization image are extracted and the outlines are drawn on the original image.
3. For each contour sequence, the threshold value (Smin and Smax) is set to limit the contour area and the sequence which can satisfy the threshold condition is saved.
4. The contour which appears nearby the one in previous frame in reasonable sports area is selected as recognized contour. The area is a fan which determined by the largest ship heading course and speed change. Reasonable radius is decided by constraint conditions, such as real ship speed, course angle.
5. If the final contour is not uniqueness, this frame will be excluded and the process will be done in the next frame.

3   Ship Motion State Computing

After recognizing by the image threshold, a feature point is needed to represent the center of ship. In this paper the center of circumscribed circle of the ship contour is

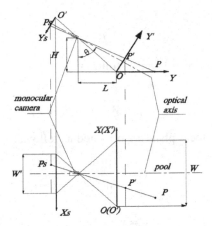

Fig. 1. Transformation of the ship coordinate

selected. By the conversion of ship's coordinates in imaging plane, the ship's coordinates in real water scene can be obtained. It is as shown in Fig. 1.

The meanings of physical quantities are as follows:

H: height from horizontal plane to the camera (in cm);
L: horizontal distance from the shore to the camera (in cm);
Θ: angle between focal plane $X\,'O'\,Y\,'$ and the horizontal plane (in degree);
W: width of observed water shore (in cm);
W': image horizontal width (in pixel);

Point P in the Fig. 1 represents the location of ship in the pool and Ps represents the location of ship in the camera image. So the XOY plane represents the water level and the $X_sO_sY_s$ plane represents the image plane. The monocular camera is overlooking the water at a certain point of view with the angle Θ and the height H. Create a focal plane $X\,'O'\,Y\,'$ though the coastline, then the corresponding point $P\,'$ can be obtained. The coordinate transformation between P and Ps can be divided into two steps by camera geometry: Ship in camera coordinate system $X_sO_sY_s$ transforms into focal plane coordinate system $X\,'O'\,Y\,'$. And then it transforms further into the inertial coordinate system XOY.

3.1   Camera Coordinates to Focal Plane Coordinate

A single pixel on the image taken by an industrial imaging lens in the experiment is a square. Assuming that the distance from focus plane to the camera is Z, the product of physics lens' focal length and each unit size of the image is f. These formulas can be given by the principle of camera imaging:

$$x' = x_s \frac{z}{f}$$

$$y' = y_s \frac{z}{f} \tag{4}$$

Then the proportional relation is given as follow:

$$\frac{z}{f} = \frac{W}{W'} \tag{5}$$

So the coordinates of the focus plane are obtained as follows:

$$x' = x_s \frac{W}{W'}$$

$$y' = y_s \frac{W}{W'} \tag{6}$$

3.2　Focal Plane Coordinate to Inertial Coordinate

The geometric relationship between focal plane coordinate and inertial coordinate has been shown in the Fig. 1.The coordinate transformation formula is shown as follows, which is used to transform the point $P'(x',y')$ in focal plane to the point $P\ (x,y)$ in water surface in two-dimensional coordinates.

$$x = \frac{H \cdot \left(\tan\theta - \dfrac{L}{H} \right) \cdot \sin(2\theta) \cdot x'}{2H - \left(\tan\theta - \dfrac{L}{H} \right) \cdot \sin(2\theta) \cdot y' \cdot \sin\theta}$$

$$y = \frac{1}{2} \left(\sin\theta - \frac{L \cdot \cos\theta}{H} \right) \cdot \sin(2\theta) \cdot y' \tag{7}$$

$$+ \frac{\left(2L + \left(\sin\theta - \dfrac{L \cdot \cos\theta}{H} \right) \cdot \sin(2\theta) \cdot y' \right) \cdot \left(\tan\theta - \dfrac{L}{H} \right) \cdot \sin(2\theta) \cdot y' \cdot \sin\theta}{2 \left(2H - \left(\tan\theta - \dfrac{L}{H} \right) \cdot \sin(2\theta) \cdot y' \cdot \sin\theta \right)}$$

　　The formula above is calculated based on the geometric relation as shown in Fig. 1. Physical quantities in the formula above have been given, and can be obtained by actual measurement. But there is a deviation between point P in image coordinate and the ship center point in practical 3d scene, as shown in Fig. 2.

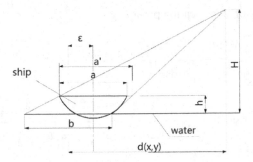

Fig. 2. Position deviation

In cross section, b is the equivalent length of ship in the image obtained by camera. The horizontal distance from the center to the camera is $d(x,y)$, which changes with position parameter. As shown in Figure 2, the longest horizontal line of ship's projection in each axis direction is on the top surface and the height from ship surface to the water is h.

First of all, along the x axis, $d(x,y) = y$. so there is a geometric relationship in this picture:

$$\left(y+\frac{b}{2}\right)\left(\frac{H-h}{H}\right)-\left(y-\frac{b}{2}\right)\left(\frac{H-h}{H}\right)=a' \tag{8}$$

$$\text{Get:} b=\frac{a\times H}{H-h} \tag{9}$$

Actual distance of the ship center to camera horizontal is as follow:

$$D=\left(y+\frac{b}{2}\right)\left(\frac{H-h}{H}\right)-\frac{a}{2}=y\frac{H-h}{H}+\left(\frac{a'}{2}-\frac{a}{2}\right) \tag{10}$$

So the deviation in y axis is:

$$\varepsilon_y=D-y=y\frac{h}{H}-\left(\frac{a'}{2}-\frac{a}{2}\right) \tag{11}$$

Because $\left(\dfrac{a'}{2}-\dfrac{a}{2}\right)\approx 0$, so the deviation is as follow:

$$\varepsilon_y=y\frac{h}{H} \tag{12}$$

In the same way in x axis:

$$\varepsilon_x=x\frac{h}{II} \tag{13}$$

The final coordinates of ship location point is:

$$x = \frac{H \cdot \left(\tan\theta - \dfrac{L}{H}\right) \cdot \sin(2\theta) \cdot x_s \cdot \dfrac{W}{W'}}{2H - \left(\tan\theta - \dfrac{L}{H}\right) \cdot \sin(2\theta) \cdot y_s \cdot \dfrac{W}{W'} \cdot \sin\theta} \left(1 - \frac{h}{H}\right)$$

$$y = \begin{bmatrix} \dfrac{1}{2}\left(\sin\theta - \dfrac{L \cdot \cos\theta}{H}\right) \cdot \sin(2\theta) \cdot y_s \dfrac{W}{W'} + \dfrac{\left(2L + \left(\sin\theta - \dfrac{L \cdot \cos\theta}{H}\right) \cdot \sin(2\theta) \cdot y_s \dfrac{W}{W'}\right)}{2\left(2H - \left(\tan\theta - \dfrac{L}{H}\right) \cdot \sin(2\theta) \cdot y_s \dfrac{W}{W'} \cdot \sin\theta\right)} \left(1 - \dfrac{h}{H}\right) \\ \cdot \left(\tan\theta - \dfrac{L}{H}\right) \cdot \sin(2\theta) \cdot y_s \dfrac{W}{W'} \cdot \sin\theta \end{bmatrix} \tag{14}$$

3.3   Motion State Computing

Ship Speed Computing

The raw data after image processing are just static coordinates of ship in images. In order to get dynamic speed information, considering the image sampling period T is very short, the real motion of ship during this time can be seen as a uniform motion. So assuming that ship position in adjacent frames are $P1(x1, y1)$ and $P2 (x2, y2)$, in the time interval T between two frames, the average speed can be taken as the current speed of ship

$$v = \frac{\sqrt{(x_2 - x_1)^2 + (y_2 - y_1)^2}}{T} \tag{15}$$

In actual calculation, $T(s)$ is obtained by gathering the numerical difference in the timer, and can ensure the accuracy of speed.

Ship Course Computing

Because T is small, relationships between course angle ψ and ship coordinates in adjacent frames are as follows:

$$\psi = \begin{cases} \arcsin\left(\dfrac{x_2 - x_1}{\sqrt{(x_2 - x_1)^2 + (y_2 - y_1)^2}}\right) & if : x_2 - x_1 > 0, y_2 - y_1 > 0 \\[3mm] \pi - \arcsin\left(\dfrac{x_2 - x_1}{\sqrt{(x_2 - x_1)^2 + (y_2 - y_1)^2}}\right) & if : x_2 - x_1 > 0, y_2 - y_1 < 0 \\[3mm] 2\pi - \arcsin\left(\dfrac{x_2 - x_1}{\sqrt{(x_2 - x_1)^2 + (y_2 - y_1)^2}}\right) & if : x_2 - x_1 < 0, y_2 - y_1 < 0 \\[3mm] \pi + \arcsin\left(\dfrac{x_2 - x_1}{\sqrt{(x_2 - x_1)^2 + (y_2 - y_1)^2}}\right) & if : x_2 - x_1 < 0, y_2 - y_1 > 0 \end{cases} \tag{16}$$

4   Experimental Analysis

4.1   Experimental Platform

Experimental equipments are as follows: industrial camera and a proper length of cable, the battery, power inverter and an computer. Before the start of the experiment, the camera must be fixed in the experimental pool at a certain height to ensure the pool is in the scope of the camera view. Then the 12v battery power supplies the industrial camera and computer. Camera is connected to the computer through the front-end ports. Besides, experiment ship is labeled with red stickers for camera recognition. As follows:

Fig. 3. Experimental platform

In this paper, software of ship positioning system is based on C++ platform, combining with OpenCV open-source library vision. It can be a good experimental real-time positioning system. The software interface is shown in Fig. 4(the blue color was added in the experiment).

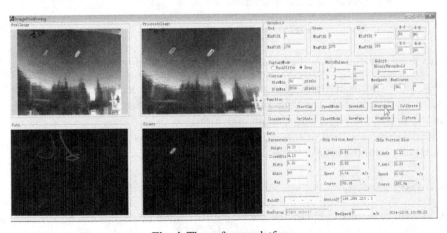

Fig. 4. The software platform

4.2   Experimental Method

1. Firstly, after the program is running, the angle of the camera must be adjust at the same time. Then the pool coastline is paralleled with the image horizontal line to make sure that the camera is installed correctly.
2. Then, the calibration can be started. The pool coastline in the image must be overlap with lower edge of the image for convenience. The top left corner in the image will be corresponded to the right bottom of coastline. Then the origin of the coordinate system was automatic calibrated by the software.
3. After the calibration is completed, fixed parameters of positioning system are measured:
   (a) Height distance of the camera to experimental water (H);
   (b) Horizontal distance of the camera to experimental water coastline (L);
   (c) Width of the coastline captured by camera (W);
   (d) Angle of the camera optical axis between the vertical (θ);
   (e) Height from the ship surface to the water surface (h).
4. Then the ship can be put into the pool, color threshold and binarization area are adjusted to make sure that the outline of the ship can be detected accurately. Ideally, after the binarization threshold segmentation, only ship area can be trapped. Gaussian filtering is applied to make the binarization image smooth:

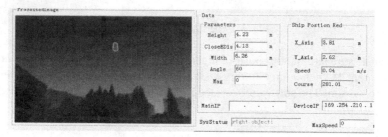

Fig. 5. Identify complete interface

At this point, the corresponding location information is displayed in the window.

5. When the ship is navigating in different position, ship location outputted by the software is recorded. The rangefinder measurement is used to get the true location of the ship in the vessel's pool at the same time.
6. The database is started to store the recorded data in order to guarantee the system's reliability until the measurement sample is reached.

4.3   Data Analysis

This system is mainly to obtain the position information of ship. It can be verified by real location measured with distance measuring equipment (such as laser range finder and so on). But the speed and course information provided by navigation equipment have a cumulative error, so their accuracies are hard to verify in experiment. The following analysis is in view of the location accuracy.

According to the introduction above, automatic ship positioning system should have a centimeter level accuracy. In order to validate the precision of this positioning system, the actual real-time location measured by laser range finder is used to compared with the one measured by software as shown in the left of Fig. 6. The x, y axis represent the coordinates of experiment pool, red point represent the location of point measured by software and blue point represent the actual location of point measured by range finder:

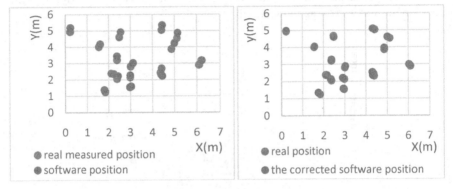

Fig. 6. Positioning contrast

Then the error percentages of x axis and y axis in each point can be calculated. It can be seen that the valid points are evenly distributed cover the pool, and the x, y axis error percentages of experimental measured data are on the high side. Then the first 4 sets of data are selected to correct the error percentage, that is to say, the average error percentage of the former four points is taken as a system error and used to correct the ones of the follow points. Then the revised comparison result between the corrected software position and the real position can be obtained as shown in the right of Fig. 6. Original distance of the contrasted points is decreased after correcting as shown in the Fig. 7.

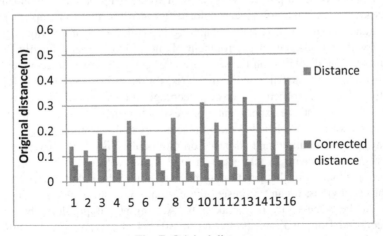

Fig. 7. Original distance

Among the external parameters which mostly affect the positioning accuracy are the width of the observed water coastline and the distance of the nearest coast to the camera in x axis and y axis respectively through the formula derived above. Difficulties in the accurate measurement of these two physical parameters are different which related to the installation method of the monocular camera. After calibration of the origin, the width of coastline can be directly measured, but the horizontal distance L from the camera center to the coastline is obtained by quadratic measurement because that the camera is installed in a certain height. As results, the y axis error is a little higher than the x axis error as shown in Fig. 8.

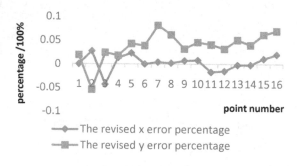

Fig. 8. Error percentage contrast

In a word, the original distance error can fall below 10 cm after corrected as shown in Fig. 7. Considering the influences of the external parameters in experiment, the location accuracy of this positioning system can meet the requirement of centimeter level.

5   Conclusion

This paper puts forward a positioning system of model ship based on monocular vision. This system uses the normalized color difference threshold in ship image segmentation, and the ship motion state computing is given by transformation algorithm combining with the installation environment of monocular camera. Finally the real-time information is displayed on the software. To test and verify the accuracy of the system positioning, the actual location measured by the laser rangefinder is for reference. In the related experiment, the error percentage of each coordinate has been calculated respectively and the experimental process has been analyzed. The positioning accuracy of the system is verified to meet the experimental requirements.

Anyway, this positioning method based on monocular vision is just verified in the experimental environment. In this paper, a model ship with red color is chosen for identification. Problem of this positioning method is that the color feature of experimental ship is obvious. It can't represent the normal color of a real ship, and the recognition will be affected by the weak light. Aiming at this problem, this research can be deepened from two aspects. On the one hand, the adaptive color difference threshold can be applied in the positioning system in order to position a ship with ordinary color in different illumination. On the other hand, infrared camera can be used to instead of ordinary monocular camera, and infrared light source can be placed on the ship. Then this positioning system can overcome the influence of light, and be applied on real ship automatic positioning system.

The application of this positioning system is very extensive, it can offer shore side real-time monitoring platform for automatic water transportation. For example, it can provide the accurate positioning information for unmanned ship automatic collision avoidance system. With the development of image processing technology, the system can be researched more deeply.

References

1. Hofmann W.B., Lichtenegger H., Collins J.: Global Positioning System: Theory and Practice. Springer Science & Business Media (2013)
2. Zheng, L.F.: Mobile Location Services Based on GPSone Technology Application in VTS. Marine Technology 46–47 (2009)
3. Xu, X.F.: Research on Error Emendation of Strap-down Inertial Navigation System Based on GPS. Computer Measurement & Control 2518–2521 (2013)
4. Essen, H.H., Gurgel, K.W., Schlick, T.: On the Accuracy of Current Measurements by Means of HF Radar. Oceanic Engineering 472–480 (2002)
5. Zhou, T.: 3D Reconstruction Based on Monocular Vision. Xidian University (2014)
6. Li, R.M., Lu, L.L., Jin, G.D.: Research Overview of Location Method for Monocular Vision. Modern Computer 9–12 (2011)
7. Zhou, N.: Research on Camera Location based on monocular vision. Nanjing University of Aeronautics and Astronautics 30–33 (2007)
8. Li, X.F., Song, Y.N., Xu, R.H., Chen, J.: Tracking and Positioning of Ship Based on Binocular Vision. Journal of Nanjing University of Information Science & Technology (Natural Science Edition) 46–52 (2015)
9. Jin X. D.: Real time Detection and Classification of Ship by Computer Vision. Shanghai Maritime University (2007)
10. Xie, D.L.: Study on Container Position System Based on Computer Vision. Tianjin University of Science and Technology (2006)
11. Wang, J.: Study of Ship Locating Principle by Measuring Distance Based on the Monocular Camera Machine Vision. Navigation of China 8–11 (2005)
12. Wang, J.T.: A Survey on Color Image Segmentation Techniques. Information Security and Technology 76–80 (2015)

Improvement of Navigation Conditions Using Model Predictive Control - The Cuinchy-Fontinettes Case Study

Klaudia Horváth[1,2,3]($\boxtimes$), Eric Duviella[1,2,3], Lala Rajaoarisoa[1,2,3], Rudy R. Negenborn[1,2,3], and Karine Chuquet[1,2,3]

[1] Mines Douai, IA, Douai, France
hklau85@gmail.com,
{eric.duviella,lala.rajaoarisoa}@mines-douai.fr,
R.R.Negenborn@tudelft.nl, karine.chuquet@vnf.fr
[2] Department of Maritime and Transport Technology,
TU Delft, Delft, The Netherlands
[3] VNF, DT Nord-Pas de Calais, SEME, PARME Hydro, Lille, France

Abstract. A considerable shift from road transport to inland navigation and railway is expected in the following years in France. By focusing on inland navigation, this expected increase of transport will require an efficient management of the infrastructure and water. Inland navigation requires water levels kept within the navigation rectangle. Hence it is necessary to design efficient control algorithms for water levels. Model Predictive Control (MPC) is proposed to regulate the water level of canals with locks. This controller maintains the level close to the navigation objective by rejecting disturbances mainly caused by lock operations. In this paper, MPC is designed by considering realistic constraints on the dynamics of the gates and the available supplied discharges. It allows taking into account several operating conditions that correspond to normal, drought and flood situations. MPC strategy is tested on a numerical simulation of the Cuinchy-Fontinettes reach that is located in the north of France.

Keywords: Navigation canal · Control · Waves · Resonance

1 Introduction

Inland navigation presents economical and ecological conditions that motivate governments of several European countries to promote it [8,10]. A considerable shift from road transport to inland navigation and railway is expected in the following years in France [13]. Responding to the expected increase of inland waterway transport requires the improvement of the inland navigation network management by the proposal of advanced control strategies. Indeed, the navigation can be accommodated only in a safe manner if the water level of each canal

This work is a contribution to the GEPET'Eau project which is granted by the French ministery MEDDE - GICC, the French institution ORNERC and the DGITM.

© Springer International Publishing Switzerland 2015
F. Corman et al. (Eds.): ICCL 2015, LNCS 9335, pp. 222–237, 2015.
DOI: 10.1007/978-3-319-24264-4_16

is close to the Normal Navigation Level (NNL) and inside a defined navigation rectangular, *i.e.* an interval around the NNL. This implies minimum canal width and depth for the boats to pass and maximum water depth to avoid bridges.

There are different algorithms to control canals, an overview of the different algorithms is given by [6,9]. One of the control techniques applied to water systems is Model Predictive Control (MPC). It can be applied to different kind of water systems [17]. MPC is used for flow control; controlling the ecological flow rate of a dam river system [12] or maintaining the desired flow in irrigation canals [14]. There are several water level control applications using MPC, for example for irrigation canals [20] or drainage canals [19]. MPC was also implemented on laboratory canals [1,4] and tested on a real irrigation canal [18]. MPC can be used for different water systems to achieve different management objectives. It can be used to control water quality [21], for risk mitigation [22]. The control of water systems used for navigation is dealt with [11]. In this work we focus on the objective of water level control of a navigation canal. Similar approach is used as in the above mentioned works of controlling irrigation canals [18].

The level of the navigation canals is mainly disturbed by the operation of the lock. When an upstream lock is operated, it is filled from the upstream reach if a boat is going to the upstream direction or water is released downstream if the boat is going downstream. These water intakes and releases can initiate waves that disturb the water level. The disturbance depends on the size of the lock chamber. MPC aims at keeping the level of the canals inside the navigation rectangle by operating the gates. However, the constraints imposed by the working conditions of the gates was not taken into account. Moreover, only one operating point that corresponds to the management of the canals in normal situation is considered. In real case, navigation canals can be impacted by drought and flood periods which enforce the operators to modify the operating points. That is the reason why the designed control approach has to be robust to several operating points.

In this work, [3] is improved in two aspects. First, the constraints imposed by the hydraulic structures are taken into account. Secondly, several operating points are considered. The management of the navigation reach in drought and flood situation is addressed, implying different setpoints for the controller. The controller is tested on the Cuinchy-Fontinettes navigation reach located in the north of France (Figure 1).

This paper is organized as follows. The proposed models are presented in section 2. Section 3 is dedicated to the design of the MPC strategy. The Cuinchy-Fontinettes reach case study is described in section 4. Finally, the performance of the proposed approach is illustrated in Section 5 using simulation studies. Section 6 concludes this paper and provides direction for future research.

2   Modeling

Different models are used for simulation of open channels and for control purposes: simple linear models for control design, and more complex, distributed,

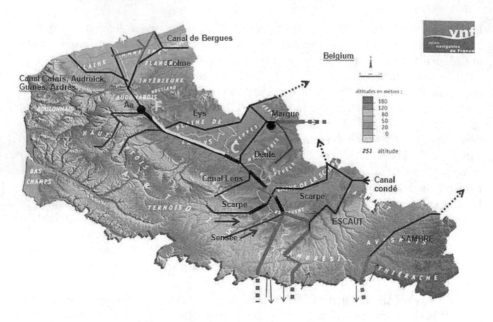

Fig. 1. The Cuinchy-Fontinettes reach

non-linear models to test the developed controllers. This section introduces the different models of the control structures and the constraints they impose.

2.1 Nonlinear Model for Simulation Purposes

In order to evaluate the proposed controller, a non-linear model is used. The Saint-Venant equations representing the open channel flow are solved numerically using the Preissmann-scheme by the software SIC [7]. The model has been validated using real data before the test of the controllers.

2.2 Linear Model for Control Purposes

The Integrator Delay Zero (IDZ) model is used to model the open water channel for control purposes [5]. Similarly to the frequently used Integrator Delay (ID) model [15], the model captures the two most important phenomena: integrator and delay. The IDZ model is an extension of the ID model in order to account for the high frequency behaviour: it takes into account the first increase in water level in a step response. This first fast response is clearly seen in such system, therefore the choice was the IDZ model. Further work can be to test different models for the same system. On low frequencies the canal pool can be modelled as an integrator, that is the water level increases with the integral value of the discharge, like a tank. The value of this integrator is the reciprocal of the surface of the canal reach, i.e. the backwater area, A_s. The backwater area can be approximated by the product of the width and the length of the canal:

$$A_s = BL, \tag{1}$$

where B is the width and L is the length of the canal reach.

The delay is the time it takes for a wave to travel from one end to the other end of the canal. It is slightly different in the upstream (τ_u) and in the downstream direction (τ_d), due to the direction of the waves, and it can be obtained as:

$$\tau_u = \frac{L}{C - V} \qquad (2)$$

and

$$\tau_d = \frac{L}{C + V} \qquad (3)$$

where V is the velocity and C is the celerity, given by:

$$C = \sqrt{gH} \qquad (4)$$

where g is the acceleration of gravity and H is the water level.

The IDZ model contains a zero, that accounts for the first fast increase in water level after a disturbance occurs. The calculation of the zero is not detailed here, *see* [5]. The general form of the transfer functions can be written as:

$$\frac{h(s)}{q(s)} = \frac{p_1 s + 1}{A_s s} e^{-\tau s}, \qquad (5)$$

where h is the water level and q is the discharge, the parameter p_1 accounts for the zero and τ can be τ_s or τ_d depending of the direction of the disturbance.

2.3   Modelling Hydraulic Structures

The modelling of the two main gate types used in navigation canals are discussed below.

Undershot Gate. An undershot gate is a bottom opening in a wall (Figure 2). The basic condition to have any flow, is that the upstream level (H_1) is higher than the downstream (H_2). An undershot gate can be operated under free flow or submerged conditions. The condition of submergence in terms of the gate opening and the water depths [16]:

$$L_{sub} = 0.7463 \frac{H_2^{2.389}}{H_1^{1.389}} \qquad (6)$$

where L_{sub} is the maximum gate opening resulting in submerged flow.
Thus the flow conditions depend on the opening and the corresponding maximum submerged opening such that:

$$\begin{array}{ll} \text{free} & \text{if } L \geq L_{sub} \\ \text{submerged} & \text{if } L < L_{sub}. \end{array} \qquad (7)$$

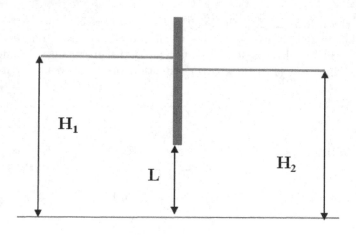

Fig. 2. Undershot gate

Then this should be combined with the physical constraints on the gate opening:

$$L \in [L_{\min}, L_{\max}] \tag{8}$$

Combining the expression for the flow regimes (7) and the physical constraints on gate opening (8), the free and submerged gate opening limits can be obtained. Then the free flow discharge for an undershot gate Q_{gf} is calculated as:

$$Q_{gf} = L B_a C_{gf} \sqrt{2gH_1} \tag{9}$$

where B_a is the width of the gate, C_{gf} is the gate discharge coefficient for free flow and

$$L \in [L_{\text{minfree}}, L_{\text{maxfree}}], \tag{10}$$

where

$$L_{\text{maxfree}} = L_{\max} \tag{11}$$

$$L_{\text{minfree}} = max(L_{\min}, L_{\text{sub}}). \tag{12}$$

The discharge for submerged conditions (Q_{gs}) is obtained as:

$$Q_{gs} = L B_a \sqrt{2g} C_{gs} \sqrt{H_1 - H_2} \tag{13}$$

where C_{gs} is the gate discharge coefficient for submerged case and

$$L \in [L_{\text{minsub}}, L_{\text{maxsub}}], \tag{14}$$

where

$$L_{\text{maxsub}} = min(L_{\max}, L_{\text{sub}}) \tag{15}$$

$$L_{\text{minsub}} = L_{\min}. \tag{16}$$

2.4 Overshot Gate

For an overshot gate (or sharp crested weir) the flow goes over the crest. Hence the upstream water level should be higher than the crest and higher than the downstream water level.

Therefore the conditions to be flow present in the downstream direction is $H_1 > W$ and $H_1 > H_2$ where W is the height of the gate (crest of the weir), see Figure 3.

The physical constraints on W are:

$$W \in [W_{\min}, W_{\max}]. \tag{17}$$

The free flow operation condition is for an overflow gate with gate height W [7]:

$$\begin{matrix} \text{free} & \text{if } W \geq W_{sub} \\ \text{submerged} & \text{if } W < W_{sub} \end{matrix} \tag{18}$$

where [7]:

$$W_{sub} = 3H_2 - 2H_1. \tag{19}$$

The free flow discharge Q_{Wf} of an overshot gate then can be obtained as:

$$Q_{Wf} = 2/3 C_w B_w \sqrt{2g}(H_1 - W)^{1.5} \tag{20}$$

where B_w is the width of the gate and C_w is the weir discharge coefficient and

$$W \in [W_{\text{minfree}}, W_{\text{maxfree}}] \tag{21}$$

where

$$W_{\text{minfree}} = max(W_{\min}, W_{sub}) \tag{22}$$

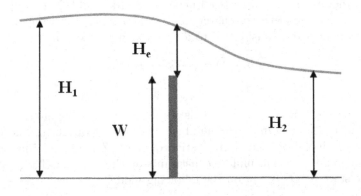

Fig. 3. Overshot gate

$$W_{\text{maxfree}} = W_{\text{max}}. \tag{23}$$

The flow over a submerged overshot gate can be obtained as [2]:

$$Q_{Ws} = \frac{3\sqrt{3}}{2} 2/3 C_w B_w \sqrt{2g} \sqrt{H_1 - H_2}(H_1 - W) \tag{24}$$

where Q_{Ws} is the discharge of a submerged overflow gate and

$$W \in [W_{\text{minsub}}, W_{\text{maxsub}}] \tag{25}$$

where

$$W_{\text{minsub}} = W_{\text{min}} \tag{26}$$

$$W_{\text{maxsub}} = min(W_{\text{max}}, W_{\text{sub}}). \tag{27}$$

2.5   Lock Operations

The locks are modelled as input/offtake of constant discharge. During the time of the lock operation constant discharge is assumed in order to fill the lock chambers. The time of the lock operations, and the daily number of lock operations is approximated using real data. As they are not controlled, they are considered as unknown disturbances for the controller, hence they are not modelled for the controller.

3   Control Development

The objective is to keep the water level close enough to the NNL while the inputs do not exceed the constraints imposed by the hydraulic structures. MPC strategy is chosen due to its ability to handle constraints.

The controller development is described in detail in [3], here a brief summary is given. Using the IDZ model, all the canal pools are modelled in continuous time, then the models are discretized using zero order hold. The input of these models is the change of the discharge, and the output is the water level error. Then these models are transformed to a minimal state-space model:

$$\begin{aligned} x(k+1) &= Ax(k) + Bu(k) \\ y(k) &= Cx(k) \end{aligned} \tag{28}$$

where A is an $n \times n$, B is $n \times m$, and C is $p \times n$ matrix, n is the number of states, m the number of inputs and p the number of measured variables. The matrices A, B, C are derived from the discretization of the IDZ model in (5).

In order to be able to formulate constraints on the input discharge $Q^d(k)$ we extend the state by Q^d to obtain the following model

$$\begin{aligned} z(k+1) &= \tilde{A}z(k) + \tilde{B}u(k) \\ e(k) &= \tilde{C}z(k) \end{aligned} \tag{29}$$

where $z(k) = \left[x^T(k), Q^d(k)\right]^T$ and

$$\tilde{A} = \begin{bmatrix} A & 0 \\ 0 & I_m \end{bmatrix} \quad \tilde{B} = \begin{bmatrix} B \\ I_m \end{bmatrix},$$
$$\tilde{C} = \begin{bmatrix} C & 0 \end{bmatrix}$$

where I_m denotes the $m \times m$ identity matrix.
Then, the following objective function is minimized:

$$\min_{u = (u(k|k), u(k+1|k), \ldots, u(k+\lambda-1|k)) \in \mathbb{R}^{m\lambda}} J(z, u)$$

$$J(z, u) = \sum_{j=1}^{\lambda} z\left(k + j\,|k\right)^T Pz\left(k + j\,|k\right) + \sum_{j=0}^{\lambda-1} u\left(k + j\,|k\right)^T Ru\left(k + j\,|k\right),$$

subject to the following constraints:

$$z(k \mid k) = z$$

(30)

$$\forall j = 1, \ldots, \lambda:$$
$$z(k + j + 1 \mid k) = \hat{A}z(k + j \mid k) + \hat{B}u(k + j \mid k)$$
$$e(k + j \mid k) = \hat{C}z(k + j \mid k)$$
$$z_{min} \leq z(k + j \mid k) \leq z_{max}$$

where P and R are weighing matrices. This optimization problem is a quadratic programming problem.

4   The Cuinchy Fontinettes Reach - Case Study

The Cuinchy-Fontinettes reach (CFR) is the main studied part of the inland navigation network of the north of France, because this reach has a strategic location for navigation and water resource management. Indeed, it allows navigation from the French ports to Belgian and Dutch ports. It is 42 km long, 50 m wide, with an average water depth of about 3.8 m and an average discharge of 0.6 m^3/s. The normal navigation level to be maintained is 19.52 m.

CFR is principally used for navigation. The locks that are located upstream at Cuinchy and downstream at Fontinettes correspond to volume of 3700 m^3 and 25000 m^3, respectively. The lock operations lead to strong disturbances that cause long lasting waves along the CFR. When a boat is going to the downstream direction, first the lock of Cuinchy releases 3700 m^3 water, then when the boat arrives downstream, the lock of Fontinettes is filled with 25000 m^3 water within about 20 minutes. The operation of the lock of Fontinettes causes an about 15 cm drop in the water level downstream. The objective is to keep to water level between the range of navigation: 15 cm around the NNL.

It is a completely artificial channel that is perpendicular to the direction of the runoff (overland flow due to excess stormwater). The CFR can be supplied from different sources (Figure 4). First, by the navigation discharge of

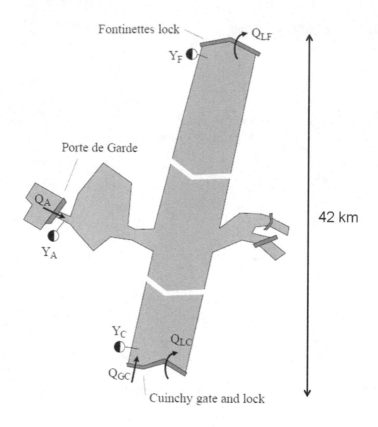

Fig. 4. Scheme of the Cuinchy-Fontinettes reach with the locks, gates and limnimeters

the Cuinchy lock upstream (Q_{LC}). Secondly, it can be supplied by a overshot gate located close to the Cuinchy lock, i.e. the Cuinchy gate (Q_{GC}). Finally, in the central part of the CFR, the gate 'Porte de Garde' is also controlled (Q_A), located at Aire-sur-la-Lys. This undershot gate can supply or empty the CFR depending of the levels of the CFR and of the river upstream the gate. The operation of the downstream lock withdraws water from the CFR (Q_F).

The CFR is equipped with three limnimeters (sensitive water level gages), located in the upstream part, at Cuinchy (Y_C), in the central part at Aire-sur-la-Lys, next to the overshot gate (Y_A) and in Fontinettes, downstream (Y_F). The water level is measured using a sampling period of 1 minute.

For all these reasons, the control of the CFR is a stake for the inland navigation network manager. Especially when drought and flood occurs. During these periods, the navigation setpoint is modified. In case of drought the NNL is reduced as higher priority is given for e.g. drinking water supply than to navigation. In case of flood, the NNL is raised in order to be able to store more water volume in the canal. The goal is to design an MPC that is robust under all these situations.

The gates of Cuinchy and of Aire-sur-la-Lys are controlled. Their characteristics are given below:

Gate of Cuinchy. The gate of Cuinchy is an overshot gate working under free flow conditions, with possible gate positions of 20.78-22.5 m. The upstream base NNL is 21.48 m. The width of the gate is 6m. The gate is modelled using the free flow overflow gate equation.

Gate of Aire-sur-la-Lys. The gate of Aire-sur-la-Lys is an undershot gate and should always work under submerged conditions. The minimum gate opening is 0, the gate can be closed. The position of the gate can be between 19.17m and 20.16m.

5 Results and Discussion

This section presents simulation experiments for three different situations: normal operation conditions, drought and flood situation. The controller is used with the same tuning while the different situations require different setpoints and operation conditions, summarized in Table 1.

Table 1. Summary of the conditions of the different scenarios

Scenario	Setpoint	Allowed difference from setpoint	Water level of confluences
Normal	NNL	± 15cm	NNL
Drought	NNL-10cm	± 15cm	NNL-10cm
Flood	NNL+30cm	± 25cm	NNL+30cm

Normal operation. First, the normal operation of the system is shown. The control objective is to keep the water level in a 15 cm range around the NNL. As in all situations, the locks of Cuinchy and Fontinettes are operating during the whole day. The locks are opened and closed in different periods - when boats are crossing. An example of a typical daily lock operation that is used during these tests is shown in Figure 5. The lock operations upstream, at Cuinchy (dashed line) cause an increase in discharge, while the operations of Fontinettes cause discharge valleys. Note that the discharge change is much bigger for Fontinettes.

The controlled water levels for this situation are shown in Figure 6. The valleys caused by the operations of Fontinettes are clearly seen. All three water levels are kept within the range of navigation, while the controller was acting respecting the constraints.

In order to keep the water levels within the navigation limits, the gate of Aire-sur-la-Lys is always at the maximum opening (Figure 7, the light gray line is the maximum, the dark gray line would be the opening of Aire-sur-la-Lys, but it is covered). The opening of the gate of Cuinchy reaches the maximum only at certain points (e.g. the peaks at 1h, 3h and 5h).

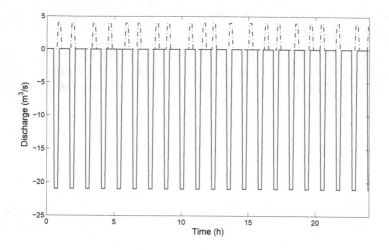

Fig. 5. Lock operations, with negative sign the water taken out of the canal

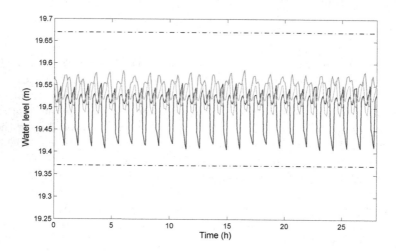

Fig. 6. Water levels in normal situation, black: Fontinettes, dark gray: Cuinchy, light gray: Aire-sur-la-Lys, dashed line: NNL

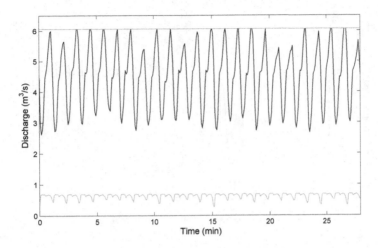

Fig. 7. Discharges in normal situation, black: Cuinchy, dark gray: Aire-sur-la-Lys (coincides with the maximum), maximum Aire-sur-la-Lys and Cuinchy: light gray

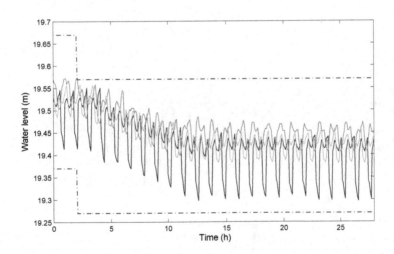

Fig. 8. Water levels in drought situation, black: Fontinettes, dark gray: Cuinchy, light gray: Aire-sur-la-Lys, dashed line: NNL

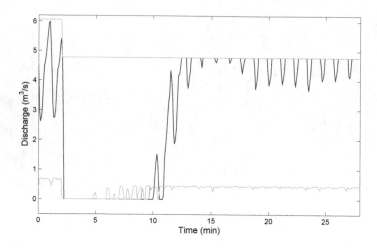

Fig. 9. Discharge in drought situation, black: Cuinchy, dark gray: Aire-sur-la-Lys, light gray: maximum allowed discharges

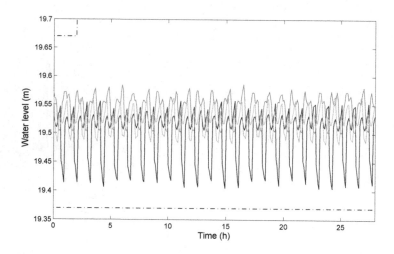

Fig. 10. Water levels in flood situation, black: Fontinettes, dark gray: Cuinchy, light gray: Aire-sur-la-Lys, dashed line: NNL

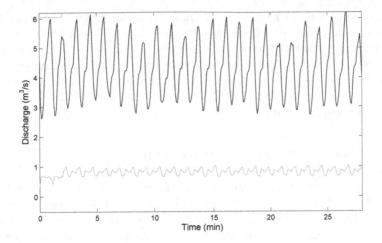

Fig. 11. Discharge in flood situation, black: Cuinchy, dark gray: Aire-sur-la-Lys, light gray: maximum allowed discharges

Drought situation. For a drought period all NNLs are decreased by 10 cm due to the lack of water. In this case the setpoint of the CFR is 19.42 m. The water levels are also decreased on the upstream side of the gates. Thus, the controller has to bring the system to a different operation point. The new scenario is introduced after two hours, and the controller has to bring all the water levels between the new limits, while respecting all the constraints. It can be seen in Figure 8 that during the full operation all levels are kept within the navigation limits.

The control actions are shown in Figure 9. In the first two hours the discharge of Cuinchy (black line) is not reaching the maximum, but the discharge at Aire-sur-la-Lys does. After the change the discharge of Cuinchy drops to the minimum (zero) for several hours, in order to reach the new NNL. The discharge at Aire-sur-la-Lys also drops to zero, until about 14 hours. Then in order to keep the situation the discharge at Cuinchy increases again to maximum, while the discharge at Aire-sur-la-Lys (dark gray) is kept under its maximum (light gray). Note that the maximum of Cuinchy is a constant, while the maximum of Aire-sur-la-Lys changes over time. The reason is that the maximum possible discharge at Cuinchy is determined only by the upstream water level, since the structure there is an overshot gate. On the other hand, at Aire-sur-la-Lys, the fixed maximum gate opening corresponds to different discharges, depending both on the upstream and downstream water levels.

Flood situation. In case of flood, the water level of the confluences is supposed to increase by 30 cm. Also the maximum of the normal navigation range is 15 cm more than the usual. The water levels increase at 2 h. Figure 10 shows that all water levels are kept, even within the original range of navigation. The response of the controller can be seen in Figure 11. Note that the maximum possible discharge for Cuinchy has increased as the upstream water level increased. Also for

Aire-sur-la-Lys a slight in increase in the maximum discharge - and hence in the implemented one - can be noticed. It is interesting to note that the discharges are very similar to that of the normal situation. In this case as the water level upstream of the structure at Aire-sur-la-Lys is increased, the maximum possible discharge is bigger. Therefore Aire-sur-la-Lys is able to provide more water to counterbalance the operation of lock Fontinettes, and there is less fluctuation in the discharge from upstream.

6 Conclusions and Future Research

Model predictive control has been applied for the management of a navigation reach in normal, drought and flood period. The constraints on the control input were expressed using the properties of the hydraulic structures and are changing at every optimization step. The controller was able to handle the constraints imposed by the hydraulic structures and keep the water level within the range of navigation allowing the transport over water. In the same time it was able to handle different scenarios where other objectives (like the transport or storage of water) enjoyed priority.

Future research consists of extending the proposed controller for more navigation reaches, in the future a centralized controller is planned to control the system taking into account the interactions between different reaches. The application can be extended to include also the main rivers of Belgium and the Netherlands.

References

1. Begovich, O., Ruiz, V.M., Besançon, G., Aldana, C., Georges, D.: Predictive control with constraints of a multi-pool irrigation canal prototype. Latin American applied research **37**(3), 177–185 (2007)
2. Bos, M.: Discharge measurement structures, Recon Technical Report. Technical report, NASA STI, May 1976
3. Horváth, K., Petreczky, M., Rajaoarisoa, L., Duviella, E., Chuquet, K.: Model predictive control of water level in a navigation canal - the cuinchy-fontinettes case study. In: Proceedings of the European Control Conference, p. 1337, June 24–27, 2014
4. Lemos, J.M., Machado, F., Nogueira, N., Rato, L.M., Rijo, M.: Adaptive and non-adaptive model predictive control of an irrigation channel. Networks and Heterogeneous Media **4**(2), 303–324 (2009)
5. Litrico, X., Fromion, V.: Simplified modeling of irrigation canals for controller design. Journal of Irrigation and Drainage Engineering **130**(5), 373–383 (2004)
6. Malaterre, P.-O.: Classification of canal control algorithms. Journal of Irrigation and Drainage Engineering **124**(1), 3–10 (1998)
7. Malaterre, P.-O., Baume, J.P.: Sic 3.0, a simulation model for canal automation design. In: Proceecings of the International Workshop on Regulation of Irrigation Canals: State of Art of Research and Applications, vol. I, pp. 68–75. L.A.A.A.-C.N.R.S., April 1997

8. Mallidis, I., Dekker, R., Vlachos, D.: The impact of greening on supply chain design and cost: a case for a developing region. Journal of Transport Geography **22**, 118–128 (2012)
9. Mareels, I., Weyer, E., Ooi, S., Cantoni, M., Li, Y., Nair, G.: Systems engineering for irrigation systems: Successes and challenges. Annual Reviews in Control **29**(2), 191–204 (2005)
10. Mihic, S., Golusin, M., Mihajlovic, M.: Policy and promotion of sustainable inland waterway transport in Europe Danube river. Renewable and Sustainable Energy Reviews **15**(4), 1801–1809 (2011)
11. Ocampo-Martinez, C., Negenborn, R. (eds.): Transport of Water versus Transport over Water. Springer International Publishing (2015)
12. Puig, V., Romera, J., Quevedo, J., Cardona, C.M., Salterain, A., Ayesa, E., Irizar, I., Castro, A., Lujan, M., Charbonnaud, P., Chiron, P., Trouvat, J.-L.: Optimal predictive control of water transport systems: Arret-Darre/Arros case study. Water Science and Technology **60**(8), 2125–2133 (2009)
13. RÉGION NORD-PAS DE CALAIS. L'essentiel de la strategie regionale climat (2014)
14. Rodellar, J., Gómez, M., Martín, J.P.: Vide. Stable predictive control of open-channel flow. Journal of Irrigation and Drainage Engineering **115**(4), 701–713 (1989)
15. Schuurmans, J.: Open-channel flow model approximation for controller design. Applied Mathematical Modelling **19**(9), 525–530 (1995)
16. Swamee, P.K.: Sluice gate discharge equations. Journal of Irrigation and Drainage Engineering **118**(1), 56–60 (1992)
17. van Overloop, P.-J.: Model predictive control on open water systems. PhD thesis, Delft University of Technology, Delft, The Netherlands (2006)
18. van Overloop, P.-J., Clemmens, A., Strand, R., Wagemaker, R., Bautista, E.: Real-time implementation of model predictive control on Maricopa-Stanfield irrigation and drainage district's WM canal. Journal of Irrigation and Drainage Engineering **136**(11), 747–756 (2010)
19. van Overloop, P.-J., Weijs, S., Dijkstra, S.: Multiple model predictive control on a drainage canal system. Control Engineering Practice **16**(5), 531–540 (2008)
20. Wahlin, B.T.: Performance of model predictive control on asce test canal 1. Journal of Irrigation and Drainage Engineering **130**(3), 227–238 (2004)
21. Xu, M., Negenborn, R.R., van Overloop, P.-J., van de Giesen, N.: De Saint-Venant equations-based model assessment in model predictive control of open channel flow. Advances in Water Resources **49**, 37–45 (12/2012)
22. Zafra-Cabeza, A., Maestre, J.M., Ridao, M.A., Camacho, E.F., Sánchez, L.: Hierarchical distributed model predictive control for risk mitigation: an irrigation canal case study. In: American Control Conference (ACC), July, 29, 2011, pp. 3172–3177 (2011)

A Survey on the Ship Loading Problem

Cagatay Iris[✉] and Dario Pacino

Department of Transport, Technical University of Denmark,
Kgs. Lyngby, Denmark
{cagai,darpa}@transport.dtu.dk

Abstract. Recent statistics show that large container terminals can process more than 30 million containers a year, and are constantly in search for the better ways to optimize processing time, deliver high quality and profitable services. Some of the terminal decisions are, however, dependent on externalities. One of those is the ship loading process. Based on the stowage plan received by liner shippers, terminal operators plan the execution of load and discharge operations. In this paper we present a literature review for the Ship Loading Problem, where stowage and loading sequencing and scheduling are integrated to improve the efficiency of the ship handling operations. We present a survey of the state-of-the-art methods and of the available benchmarking data.

1 Introduction

The World economy has always relied on the ability of transporting goods. With the introduction of containerized shipping, global supply chains have flourished and are now demanding more cost efficient and reliable transport. Liner shippers have responded by increasing the capacity of their fleet, deploying vessels of over 18.000 Twenty Equivalent Units (TEUs). Capacity is, however, not enough. A reliable service requires the goods to arrive on time, and it is here that container terminals play a major role. Recent statistics show that container terminal throughput, totaling worldwide 651.1 million TEUs in 2013 [38], is estimated to increase by 5.6%.

As it can be seen from recent literature surveys [6,7,21,36], there is an increased interest on the use of optimization techniques for the planning of terminal operations. Moreover, there is a growing trend on integration approaches trying to increase the flexibility of the currently rigid hierarchical planning practices.

With this paper, we aim at bringing the readers' attention to the Ship Loading Problem (SLP), where integration efforts go beyond terminal operations and try to reach the liner shipper as well. Traditionally, the liner shipper is responsible for generating stowage plans suitable for the current and future ports. Stowage coordinators spend great effort in generating plans that are both feasible in terms of vessel stability and efficient in terms of load and discharge operations. Terminals then plan the container sequencing accordingly. The position of a container in the vessel can, however, have a large impact on the needed transportation

© Springer International Publishing Switzerland 2015
F. Corman et al. (Eds.): ICCL 2015, LNCS 9335, pp. 238–251, 2015.
DOI: 10.1007/978-3-319-24264-4_17

time of the container to and from the yard. More control over stowage planning would enhance the terminal's ability to efficiently plan ship handling operations. Common ground for both liner shippers and terminal operators, is the class based stowage plan. Class based stowage plans assign classes of containers to positions in the vessel rather than specific containers. Since the assignment of specific containers to each class has no impact for the objective of the liner shipper [34], this then leaves terminal operators with two planning decisions: 1) generating an operative stowage plan (a detailed stowage plan assigning containers to classes [32]) 2) sequencing of container load operations. Container sequencing is governed by precedences dictated by the physical position of the containers on the vessel e.g. the load sequence between two containers in the same stack (or row) cannot be changed, while it can if the containers belong to two different stacks. The integration between these two planning decisions allows a degree of freedom that, according to existing literature (e.g. [32,37]), has a large impact on terminal costs and handling time.

In this paper we present a literature study of the SLP and its variants. We wish to illustrate the current state-of-the-art methods and identify interesting research opportunities. Also, we survey the currently used benchmarks and point out missing features in the conclusion. This paper is the pioneering literature review on SLP. We believe that structuring such a problem definition will contribute to better position future research papers in the field.

This paper is organized as follows: First, the SLP is introduced in Section 2. The literature and benchmark review are presented in Section 3, including a comprehensive comparison table. Finally, Section 4 draws conclusion and presents future research directions.

2   The Ship Loading Problem

When a container vessel arrives at port, handling equipment is immediately mobilized to service the ship. The management of loading operations, planning of the equipments to use and their scheduling is what we define as the SLP. In this sense, equipment scheduling heavily relies on the stowage plan of the vessel and on the sequence in which the containers are to be loaded. As depicted in Figure 1, we define the SLP as the integration of four terminal planning problems: operational stowage planning, load sequencing, equipment assignment and equipment scheduling.

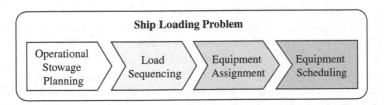

Fig. 1. Ship Loading Problem composition

Let us then define the SLP by describing each of those problems and their interaction. The term *operational stowage plan* was first introduced in [32] to distinguish between the stowage planning problem (solved by the liner shipper) and the operational refinement of it done by the terminal. Briefly, during stowage planning, an assignment of containers to vessel positions is performed. The assignment must fulfill stability requirement for its entire journey (not only the current port), while minimizing overstowage (re-handling of containers) and handling time. A class based stowage plan, is a plan where container types are assigned to vessel positions rather than actual containers, thus leaving the final match between containers and container classes to the terminal. We refer to this last container assignment as the *operational stowage planning problem*. The advantage of letting the terminal perform this operation can be easily described. Since the liner shipper has no knowledge of the yard arrangement, a detailed stowage plan might be costly in terms of transportation time. In Figure 2, it is shown how transportation time can be reduced by switching the assignment of two containers (c_1, c_2) that belong to the same class (t_1). Container classes are defined by their weight, length , height , etc. We refer the reader to [34] for a more in-depth description.

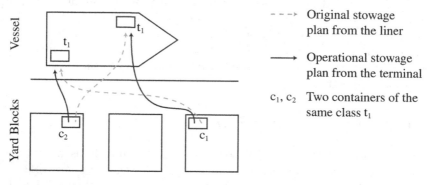

Fig. 2. Operational stowage planning

Independently on whether the terminal receives a detailed or class based stowage plan, there is still a degree of flexibility, the optimization of the loading sequence. The *Load Sequencing* problem aims at better utilizing the yard equipment during vessel handling. The sequence in which containers must be loaded is governed by physical rules, e.g. the sequence between two containers destined to the same row cannot be changed. It is, however, up to the terminal to decide the sequence of containers on different rows or bays. Some terminal use predefined loading policies, such as "sea to land" where containers are loaded row or tier wise for the sea to the land side. This decision can also be seen as an optimization problem. Figure 3 shows an example where an optimized load sequence can greatly improve the total handling time (the value in parenthesis). Once a loading sequence if finalized, further handling time improvements can be

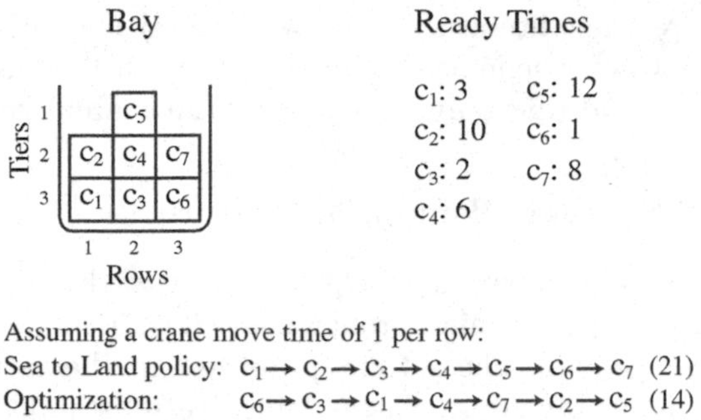

Bay   Ready Times

c_1: 3 c_5: 12
c_2: 10 c_6: 1
c_3: 2 c_7: 8
c_4: 6

Assuming a crane move time of 1 per row:
Sea to Land policy: $c_1 \rightarrow c_2 \rightarrow c_3 \rightarrow c_4 \rightarrow c_5 \rightarrow c_6 \rightarrow c_7$ (21)
Optimization: $c_6 \rightarrow c_3 \rightarrow c_1 \rightarrow c_4 \rightarrow c_7 \rightarrow c_2 \rightarrow c_5$ (14)

Fig. 3. Load sequencing example

achieved by allowing the pre-marshaling ([11]) of yard blocks. This is, however, outside the scope of the SLP.

Load sequencing, can only be done given the ready times of each container. By ready time we mean the time a container is ready to be loaded on the vessel, that being by a quay crane (QC) or reach stacker. The ready times depend on the equipment assigned to the vessel (QCs, straddle carriers, reach stackers, trucks etc.). At the same time the load sequence influences the scheduling of the equipment, thus making the integration of load sequencing and *equipment assignment and scheduling* an obvious choice.

Each of the previously mentioned planning problems defines the SLP, no matter whether they are solved hierarchically or as an integrated problem. The main objective of the SLP is the minimization of the total handling time. This can be interpreted as a minimization of re-handles in the yard and of the transportation times. Secondary objectives can be the minimization of costs associated to the used equipment. Hard constraints are mainly related to the stability requirements of the vessels and to the capacity of the terminal equipment.

3 Literature Review

The SLP is not well studied in the literature. The variety of settings, assumptions, and objectives considered in previous studies highlights the lack of a commonly accepted view of the problem. As mentioned in the previous section, we define the SLP as a combination of the operational stowage planning problem, the load sequencing problem and the equipment assignment and scheduling problem. Most of the works present in the literature can be classified as belonging to one of those sub problems, yet some authors present some integration efforts. The information needed to classify a problem has been inferred from the context, if not explicitly provided by the authors.

During our literature review we compare contributions based on three main aspects: problem structure, objective function and solution approach. The problem structure identifies the output of the planning problem, the constraints and assumption wrt. yard equipment, use of loading policies etc. Table 1 presents a comparison of the relevant literature. It is worth noticing that the number of scientific works is not overwhelming. From now on, we will assume the terminal as the decision maker and that only loading operations are taken into account.

3.1   Operational Stowage Planning Literature

To the best of the authors' knowledge, [32] is the only work that focuses entirely on the operational stowage planning problem. In [32], the input of the problem is a class-based stowage plan. The authors propose a mathematical formulation for the assignment of containers to classes. Since vessel stability contraints are already fulfilled in the class-based stowage plan, only stack weight capacity and weight sorting requirements are modelled. The model aims at minimizing the total travel distance and the number of re-handles in the yard. It assumed that the terminal is operated by straddle carriers, and that there are no restrictions on the number of available vehicles. Since the mathematical formulation does not scale to realistic instance, a two-phase Tabu Search algorithm is proposed. A comparison with container terminal data, reveals that the model underestimates the yard re-handles, which the authors attribute to the stochastic nature of the problem.

Stowage Planning with Terminal Considerations. In our definition of the SLP, we assume that stowage planning is the responsibility of the liner shipper. A number of works in the literature, however, do not share the same idea (e.g. [3,35,40]). In these works, it is assumed that the terminal has full control over the positioning of containers in the vessel. The optimization problem that needs to be solved is then the *stowage planning problem*. Since it is not the scope of this survey to review stowage planning literature, we limit ourselves to the description of those works that include aspects of terminal optimization. It is also debatable (at least for liner shipping), whether the terminal should be responsible for the stowage plan.

The work presented in [14] is one of the first stowage planning model that considers the minimization of yard-rehandles. The model formulates the stability of vessel only in terms of GM (the distance between the center of gravity and the metacenter). No distiction is made between the different container types or their destinations. An estimate of the number of re-handles is calculated and included in the objective function as well. The estimate is shown to be a fair estimation of the real re-handles. In a later paper [15], the authors include trim and healing (longitudinal and transversal listing of the vessel) to the model. The stability constraints are still handled as an objective rather than a constraint. Also, the improved model includes the modeling of a yard with multiple rows. Due to the model complexity, the authors propose a solution approach based on genetic algorithms. As in [32], there are no restrictions in terms of handling equipment.

In [3], a stowage planning model is used to analyze the impact of two different load policies: pre-marshaling ([11]), and the sort and store policy. The model distinguished between container length, weight, discharge port and power requirements. Vessel stability is heuristically handled by balancing the front-back and right-left side of the vessel (an in-depth description of the model can be found in [4]). The generated stowage plan is then evaluated in terms of yard re-handles using the two policies. The stowage planning model was also used for the implementation of the sort and store procedure, which resembles just-in-time planning where the stowage plan is repetitively computed for the current subset of available containers. The authors argue that equipment costs must be taken into consideration before a clear conclusion can be drawn.

Another terminal efficiency analysis, that uses a stowage planning model, is presented in [35]. Here the same stowage planning problem as in [4] is considered. The problem is solved using a 3D-Bin Packing approach that, included into a hierarchical heuristic procedure, models the assignment of containers to QC. In a first phase the set of containers is heuristically distributed among the cranes. The containers are then assigned to the vessel by the stowage planning procedure. Mind that here, as an extra requirement, a stowage planner has identified subsections of the vessels to be used for containers with specific discharge ports. The generated plan is then evaluated in terms of quay crane productivity. A simplified version of this problem is studied in [40] where the authors wish to minimize the concentration of containers coming from the same yard block and thus focus on decreasing the interference in the yard. A mathematical model is presented, but no comments are given to the effectiveness of the approach in terms of terminal operations.

3.2   Load Sequencing Problem Literature

Literature on the Load Sequencing Problem is scarse. To the best of the authors' knowledge, only five works focus on this problem, yet the approach to the problem is very different. Differently than all the works surveyed until now, [31] approaches the minimization of containers reshuffles directly within the vessel. The authors argue that the best loading sequence can be obtained by allowing changes to the stowage plan of each bay. The problem deals with finding a sequence of container moves that converts a given arrival configuration of a bay into a detailed stowage plan configuration within minimum service time. The objective is defined as the total processing time of container moves and empty crane movement. This definition of the problem enables the exploitation of quay crane double cycling (i.e., alternating loading and unloading operations), and minimizes internal reshuffles within bays. The approach assumes that a departure configuration is given for the vessel, then no considerations are made to the impact of the stowage changes on the next port of calls. The proposed model is solved using a Greedy Randomized Adaptive Search Procedure (GRASP).

The following works move the focus on yard operations. In [26] the aim is the generation of balanced Quay Crane (QC) loading plans with respect to Transfer Crane (TC) assignment. The objective is the minimization of the total travel distance between all TCs and their setup cost when moved to pick up containers in a different yard block. The authors propose the following approach to cope with the complexity of the problem. Given a detailed stowage plan, containers are grouped into classes (by size and destination, effectively generating a class-based stowage plan). Then, in a hierarchical manner, the load sequencing is performed. Since containers of the same class are distributed among different yard bays, the method first performs an overall sequencing deciding how many containers should be moved from which yard-bay to which vessel bay. In a second stage, the detailed sequencing of each container within the container groups is calculated. The second stage problem is solved using the beam search heuristic proposed in [18], while for the first stage, the authors propose an ant colony optimization, a tabu search and a hybrid of these methods.

In [5], the decision is to determine the loading sequence of containers with the aim of minimizing the number of re-handles. It is assumed that a detailed stowage plan is given, that only one QC is available, and that the relocation of containers within a yard bay is allowed. The authors have proposed a two-stage algorithm. In the first stage, a heuristic is developed to load the containers which do not need any rehandling. In the second phase, a dynamic programming algorithm with heuristic rules is presented to solve the load sequencing problem for all of the remaining containers. The results are compared with an alternative re-handling strategy, where load containers are chosen from stacks with the smallest number of blocked containers. Re-handles are then reassigned to random stacks. The number of relocations is shown to be reduced by 46.5% compared to the alternative strategy.

Another work on the load sequencing problem is presented in [16]. Differently than [5], the authors consider multiple QCs for loading a ship, and evaluate three different container relocation strategies: nearest-stack, lowest-stack, and an optimization strategy. These strategies determine where the blocking containers will be moved. Firstly, a mathematical model of the problem is formulated. A genetic algorithm is then presented and tested for two versions. One version assumes that a certain loading sequence is given, while the other also determines the loading sequence along with the relocation strategy within a yard bay. The results show that the number of re-handles is reduced up to 30% compared to state-of-the art solutions which assumes a given load sequencing strategy.

A different approach is taken in [27], where the focus is on the calculation of the exact number of rehandles for a given load sequencing policy. They do this by simulating the picking strategies with a discrete-event based simulation model. The simulation model considers the availability of straddle carriers, the number of reshuffles to reach a stacked container, and the availability of buffer space under the crane. Tests on the impact of multiple QCs on the operational efficiency of the loading plan are performed. The authors argue that the turnaround time of vessel loading is significantly reduced when assigning more straddle carriers and note that the number of rehandles does not change (see also [28] for a simulation-based optimization approach for both loading and unloading operations).

3.3   Equipment Assignment and Scheduling Literature

Many works in the literature touch on different aspects of equipment management. Some examples are the determination of the number of the yard equipment to use [39], the assignment of equipment to QCs and/or containers during the loading operations [8, 12, 17, 20, 25, 33], and sequencing and scheduling of these yard equipment [8–10, 17, 20, 22–24, 29].

Each of these problems has been studied extensively in the literature. For this survey, we decided to concentrate on two of the most popular works that incorporate the all above mentioned equipment management problems, and that are concentrated around container loading.

The focus in [19] is the optimal routing of one TC in a container yard during loading operations. They decide the number of containers that a TC picks up at each yard-bay and they also determine the sequence of yard-bays that a TC visits during the loading of the vessel. It is assumed that QC work schedule is given, which defines how many containers of a specific type (size and destination) should be loaded in which vessel-bay at what time interval. The objective of the presented mathematical model minimizes the total container handling time, which consists of the setup time at each yard-bay and the travel time between yard-bays.

The work presented in [8] looks at the vehicle dispatching problem, which also assumes a given QC work schedule. The authors assume that a fixed number of vehicles has been assigned to serve each QC. The problem aims at minimizing the ship berthing time. They propose a greedy heuristic to solve the problem. For the single-crane case, they prove that the greedy algorithm is optimal. This does not hold for the multiple crane case. For multiple QC case, they provide a modification of the greedy algorithm which, compared to the results obtained with a mathematical model, finds better solutions than the original algorithm.

QCs are also considered as quay-side equipment which are attributed to the ship loading. In the most of the SLP studies, a QC working plan is given as input to the problem [17, 18, 20]. This plan holds the QC split which points out which specific QC will work on each bay. Once a QC working plan is given, the QC scheduling for bay areas (see [30]) can be generated. The QC scheduling problem is, however, outside the scope of the SLP.

3.4   Integration Efforts

The literature on integration efforts for the SLP is also rather limited. To the best of the authors' knowledge, only one of the surveyed works actively models and optimizes the container sequencing. The other integration efforts focus on the combination of operational stowage planning and equipment planning, where a loading policy is assumed (e.g. sea-land, fill each stack first. etc.), leaving no space for the sequence optimization.

The pioneering paper on SLP is [37], which focuses on the generation of operative stowage plans and the allocation/schedule of straddle carriers. They assume that a given fixed number of straddle carriers is available for each QC.

The problem described in [37] relies on the assumption that only one QC operates and disregards the equilibrium constraints of the vessel in the detailed stowage plan. A just-in-time scheduling model is solved when a group of container is ready to be retrieved from the yard. This model assigns each container to a specific slot and a straddle carrier. Later, in the same paper, the authors extend the approach to include multiple QCs. This is done by first solving the crane split problem and then applying the single crane heuristic to each QC. Authors assume two loading strategies: column-wise, where each stack is filled in sequence, or layer-by-layer. The objective is the minimization of lateness of the QC moves and the transportation time between the yard and the quay area. To solve the problem, the authors present a mathematical model and a best-fit heuristic which can be applied for all QCs in parallel.

Another integration approach is [18]. Given the QCs schedule, this work combines operational stowage planning, load sequencing and TC scheduling, making this, to the best of the authors knowledge, the most complete integration effort. With respect to operational stowage planning, the presented non-linear mathematical model incorporates vessel stability considerations by imposing weight and height limit constraints on the stacks of the vessel. The sequencing is part of the model decisions, however, a column-wise policy is encoded into the objective. Only the travel time costs of the TCs can force the sequence away from this policy. The actual schedule for the loading of the containers is also modelled, aiming at minimizing reshuffles, TCs travel times and interferences. A two stage approach is used to solve the problem. The first stage sequences yard-clusters (like the first stage of [26]), while the second sequences individual containers. Both stages are solved using beam search. In a later paper [17], the authors propose a genetic algorithm and a simulated annealing heuristic for solving the first stage problem. Although this problem is similar to [26], we include it in this section since the scheduling of Yard Cranes (YCs) is also included. Here the objective is the minimization of the makespan for the YCs.

In [1], we find an integration approach that combines detailed yard equipment planning and scheduling, with operative stowage planning. A terminal operated by reach-stackers is considered. This work is particullary interesting for its presentation of a full mathematical model that includes all the aspects regarding reach-stackers routing and operations at the yard for each container. It is assumed that a selection is made between column-wise or layer-by-layer loading policy. Moreover it assumes that containers are expected to be loaded sea-to-land. As in previous approaches, the use of loading policies leaves no space for sequencing optimization. The model minimizes the number of rehandling, the movement of reach-stacker (i.e. distance traveled on the ground by the transport vehicles) and vessel instability. A solution of the model establishes which sections of the yard provide the containers of the needed type (with given numbers of containers) and generates a feasible tour of the yard to pick them up. A Tabu Search algorithm is described for solving the problem. A lagrangian relaxation approach is proposed by the same author in a later work [2].

Table 1. Ship loading problem literature abstract

Year	Authors	A1	A2	A3	A4	B1	B2	C1	C2	D1	D2	D3	E1	E2	E3	F1	F2	F3	G1	G2	G3	H1	H2	Type	T_w	T	T_{y-q}	S_v	E_q	Q_k	X1	Y1	Y2	Y3	Z1	Z2	Z3	Z4	Z5	Z6	Z7
2014	Monaco et. al. [32]	*				*	*	*		*					*				*			*		Min			*			*	*										
2003	Ambrosino et. al. [3]	*				*	*	*		*			*						*			*		Min	*						*										
2006	Imai et.al. [15]	*				*	*	*		*			*				*		*			*		Min				*		*	*										
2007	Sciomachen et. al. [35]	*				*		*		*						*			*			*		Min	*					*											
2013	Zhao et. al. [40]	*				*		*		*			*							*		*		Min				*						*							*	
2005	Lee et. al. [26]		*			*	*	*		*			*				*			*		*		Min		*							*	*								
2015	Bian et. al. [5]	*				*	*	*		*			*	*			*			*		*		Min				*		*	*		*							*	
2015	Ji et. al. [16]	*				*	*	*		*			*	*			*			*		*		Min			*	*		*	*		*							*	
2010	Meisel et. al. [31]		*			*	*	*			*		*	*		*				*		*	*	Min		*															*	
2012	Legato and Maza [27]	*				*	*	*	*			*	*			*	*			*		*	*	Min	*					*					*						*	
2001	Steenken et. al. [37]	*				*	*	*	*			*	*			*				*		*		Min	*	*						*	*						*			
2004	Kim et. al. [18]	*				*	*	*			*		*			*				*		*		Min	*			*		*	*									*		
2006	Alvarez [1]	*			*	*	*	*			*		*	*		*				*		*		Min		*											*				*	
2006	Jung and Kim [17]	*				*	*	*			*		*	*		*				*	*	*		Min		*		*		*										*	*	
2008	Alvarez [2]	*			*	*	*	*		*			*	*		*			*	*		*		Min		*		*			*						*				*	
2012	Hu et. al. [13]	*	*	*	*	*	*	*	*	*			*	*		*			*	*		*	*	Min		*		*		*	*											*

†Problem Structure = {A: Solution Outcome: (1: Detailed Stowage Plan, 2: Class-based Stowage Plan, 3: Load sequencing plan, 4: Yard Equipment Planning), B: Terminal Aspect: (1: QC Operations, 2: Yard Operations), C: Number of QCs: (1: One, 2: Multiple), D: Equilibrium and Stability constraints: (1: Explicitly, 2: Implicitly, 3: Is not considered), E: Rehandles at yard or bay: (1: Approximation, 2: Exact number, 3: Is not considered), F: Type of yard equipment (1: Stradle carriers, 2: RTGs, RMGSs or Yard cranes, 3: Reach stakers), G: Loading Policy: (1: Sea-to-land, 2: Other policy, 3: Optimal policy), H: Formulation type: (1: Integrated, 2: Hierarchical)}

‡Objective Function = {T_w: Total weighted loading time (handling, waiting, transhipment etc.) or makespan, T: Tardiness of operations, T_{y-q}: Yard-to-quay transport time, S_v: Number of container rehandles/reshuffles on/for vessel, E_q: Violation of equilibrium constraints, Q_k: Quay cranes related objective}

§Solution Approaches = {X: Exact Solutions: (1: Novel mathematical models), Y: Decomposition and Exact Algorithms, Z: Heuristic, Simulation, AI approaches: (1: Beam search, 2: Tabu search, 3: Ant colony optimization, 3: Tabu search, 4: Greedy/GRASP heuristics, 5: Local search, 6: Genetic Algorithms, 7: Simulation}

A summary of the surveyed literature can be found in Table 1. The reader can compare the different manuscripts in terms of problem structure, objective function and solution approach.

4   Conclusions and Future Research Directions

This paper has presented a description of the SLP as a combination of operational stowage planning, load sequencing and equipment management. The relevant literature has been surveyed and a comparison table has been provided. The study shows that, aside from yard equipment scheduling, little work has been done on the optimization of loading operations.

It is worth noticing that the lack of literature, does not only apply to the integrated SLP but also to the planning problems composing it. Many works have appeared in the past two decades on stowage planning, yet very few focus on the interface with the terminal, and those that do, often look at the problem only from the terminal side.

An explanation for the scarce amount of research in this field, could be explained by the general lack of benchmark data. Each paper presents indications of the nature of the data, but no detailed information. It would be beneficial to have a public benchmark for the SLP, which could then also be used for its subproblems.

Of notice, it is also the use of load policies for the container sequencing. Since most of the surveyed papers have industrial collaborations, this tendency could be explained as a lack of interest from the terminals.

We see the integration of yard equipment into the SLP models as the nearest research challenge. In almost none of the papers we surveyed (with exception of [39] which focuses on routing), yard equipment such as straddle carriers are considered as a limited resource for the complete SLP. Optimized resource utilization can have a large impact, especially on short-sea terminals, since the available resources can be utilized to service other operations (e.g. hinterland operations). Another major challenge is the integration of operational stowage planning with optimal load sequencing.

The larger number of containers handling (with ship capacities over 15.000 TEUs) puts more pressure on terminal resources. In this respect, other main resources, namely manpower and QCs, can be further detailed in the SLP formulations. For example, the effects of QC double cycling (which is a method to increase the efficiency of QC operations) on the SLP can be analyzed.

With respect to solution techniques, the literature focuses mainly to heuristic methods. However, exact decomposition algorithms might efficiently solve some reasonable sized problems to optimality.

References

1. Alvarez, J.F.: A heuristic for vessel planning in a reach stacker terminal. Journal of Maritime Research **3**(1), 3–16 (2006)
2. Alvarez, J.F.: Optimization Algorithms for Maritime Terminal and Fleet Management. Ph.D. thesis, Universitat Pompeu Fabra (2008)
3. Ambrosino, D., Sciomachen, A.: Impact of yard organisation on the master bay planning problem. Maritime Economics & Logistics **5**(3), 285–300 (2003)
4. Ambrosino, D., Sciomachen, A., Tanfani, E.: Stowing a containership: the master bay plan problem. Transportation Research Part A: Policy and Practice **38**(2), 81–99 (2004)
5. Bian, Z., Shao, Q., Jin, Z.: Optimization on the container loading sequence based on hybrid dynamic programming. Transport (ahead-of-print) 1–10 (2015)
6. Bierwirth, C., Meisel, F.: A survey of berth allocation and quay crane scheduling problems in container terminals. European Journal of Operational Research **202**(3), 615–627 (2010)
7. Bierwirth, C., Meisel, F.: A follow-up survey of berth allocation and quay crane scheduling problems in container terminals. European Journal of Operational Research **244**(3), 675–689 (2015)
8. Bish, E., Chen, F., Leong, Y., Nelson, B., Ng, J., Simchi-Levi, D.: Dispatching vehicles in a mega container terminal. OR Spectrum **27**(4), 491–506 (2005)
9. Bose, J., Reiners, T., Steenken, D., Voß, S.: Vehicle dispatching at seaport container terminals using evolutionary algorithms. In: Proceedings of the 33rd Annual Hawaii International Conference on System Sciences, vol. 2, p. 10, January 2000
10. Cao, J.X., Lee, D.H., Chen, J.H., Shi, Q.: The integrated yard truck and yard crane scheduling problem: Benders decomposition-based methods. Transportation Research Part E: Logistics and Transportation Review **46**(3), 344–353 (2010)
11. Caserta, M., Voß, S.: A corridor method-based algorithm for the pre-marshalling problem. In: Giacobini, M., Brabazon, A., Cagnoni, S., Di Caro, G.A., Ekárt, A., Esparcia-Alcázar, A.I., Farooq, M., Fink, A., Machado, P. (eds.) EvoWorkshops 2009. LNCS, vol. 5484, pp. 788–797. Springer, Heidelberg (2009)
12. Grunow, M., Guenther, H.O., Lehmann, M.: Strategies for dispatching AGVs at automated seaport container terminals. OR Spectrum **28**(4), 587–610 (2006)
13. Hu, W., Hu, Z., Shi, L., Luo, P., Song, W.: Combinatorial optimization and strategy for ship stowage and loading schedule of container terminal. Journal of Computers **7**(8), 2078–2092 (2012)
14. Imai, A., Nishimura, E., Papadimitriou, S., Sasaki, K.: The containership loading problem. International Journal of Maritime Economics **4**(2), 126–148 (2002)
15. Imai, A., Sasaki, K., Nishimura, E., Papadimitriou, S.: Multi-objective simultaneous stowage and load planning for a container ship with container rehandle in yard stacks. European Journal of Operational Research **171**(2), 373–389 (2006)
16. Ji, M., Guo, W., Zhu, H., Yang, Y.: Optimization of loading sequence and rehandling strategy for multi-quay crane operations in container terminals. Transportation Research Part E: Logistics and Transportation Review **80**, 1–19 (2015)
17. Jung, S., Kim, K.: Load scheduling for multiple quay cranes in port container terminals. Journal of Intelligent Manufacturing **17**(4), 479–492 (2006)
18. Kim, K.H., Kang, J.S., Ryu, K.R.: A beam search algorithm for the load sequencing of outbound containers in port container terminals. OR Spectrum **26**(1), 93–116 (2004)

19. Kim, K.H., Kim, K.Y.: An optimal routing algorithm for a transfer crane in port container terminals. Transportation Science **33**(1), 17–33 (1999)
20. Kim, K.H., Kim, K.Y.: Routing straddle carriers for the loading operation of containers using a beam search algorithm. Computers and Industrial Engineering **36**(1), 109–136 (1999)
21. Kim, K.H., Lee, H.: Container terminal operation: current trends and future challenges. In: Lee, C.Y., Meng, Q. (eds.) Handbook of Ocean Container Transport Logistics. International Series in Operations Research and Management Science, vol. 220, pp. 43–73. Springer International Publishing (2015)
22. Kim, K.Y., Kim, K.H.: Heuristic algorithms for routing yard-side equipment for minimizing loading times in container terminals. Naval Research Logistics (NRL) **50**(5), 498–514 (2003)
23. Lau, H., Zhao, Y.: Integrated scheduling of handling equipment at automated container terminals. Annals of Operations Research **159**(1), 373–394 (2008)
24. Lee, D.H., Cao, Z., Meng, Q.: Scheduling of two-transtainer systems for loading outbound containers in port container terminals with simulated annealing algorithm. International Journal of Production Economics **107**(1), 115–124 (2007). special Section on Building Core-Competence through Operational Excellence
25. Lee, L., Chew, E., Tan, K., Wang, Y.: Vehicle dispatching algorithms for container transshipment hubs. OR Spectrum **32**(3), 663–685 (2010)
26. Lee, Y.H., Kang, J., Ryu, K.R., Kim, K.H.: Optimization of container load sequencing by a hybrid of ant colony optimization and tabu search. In: Wang, L., Chen, K., S. Ong, Y. (eds.) ICNC 2005. LNCS, vol. 3611, pp. 1259–1268. Springer, Heidelberg (2005)
27. Legato, P., Mazza, R.M.: Managing container reshuffling in vessel loading by simulation. In: Proceedings of the 2013 Winter Simulation Conference: Simulation: Making Decisions in a Complex World, pp. 3450–3461. IEEE Press (2013)
28. Legato, P., Mazza, R., Trunfio, R.: Simulation-based optimization for discharge/loading operations at a maritime container terminal. OR Spectrum **32**(3), 543–567 (2010)
29. Li, C.L., Vairaktarakis, G.L.: Loading and unloading operations in container terminals. IIE Transactions **36**(4), 287–297 (2004)
30. Meisel, F., Bierwirth, C.: A unified approach for the evaluation of quay crane scheduling models and algorithms. Computers and Operations Research **38**(3), 683–693 (2011)
31. Meisel, F., Wichmann, M.: Container sequencing for quay cranes with internal reshuffles. OR spectrum **32**(3), 569–591 (2010)
32. Monaco, M.F., Sammarra, M., Sorrentino, G.: The terminal-oriented ship stowage planning problem. European Journal of Operational Research **239**(1), 256–265 (2014)
33. Nishimura, E., Imai, A., Papadimitriou, S.: Yard trailer routing at a maritime container terminal. Transportation Research Part E: Logistics and Transportation Review **41**(1), 53–76 (2005)
34. Pacino, D., Delgado, A., Jensen, R.M., Bebbington, T.: Fast generation of near-optimal plans for eco-efficient stowage of large container vessels. In: Böse, J.W., Hu, H., Jahn, C., Shi, X., Stahlbock, R., Voß, S. (eds.) ICCL 2011. LNCS, vol. 6971, pp. 286–301. Springer, Heidelberg (2011)
35. Sciomachen, A., Tanfani, E.: A 3d-bpp approach for optimising stowage plans and terminal productivity. European Journal of Operational Research **183**(3), 1433–1446 (2007)

36. Steenken, D., Voß, S., Stahlbock, R.: Container terminal operation and operations research-a classification and literature review. OR Spectrum **26**(1), 3–49 (2004)
37. Steenken, D., Winter, T., Zimmermann, U.T.: Stowage and transport optimization in ship planning. In: Groetschel, M., Krumke, S.O., Rambau, J. (ed.) Online Optimization of Large Scale Systems, pp. 731–745. Springer (2001)
38. UNCTAD: Review of maritime transport. Tech. rep. (2014)
39. Vis, I.F.A., de Koster, R.M.B.M., Savelsbergh, M.W.P.: Minimum vehicle fleet size under time-window constraints at a container terminal. Transportation Science **39**(2), 249–260 (2005)
40. Zhao, N., Mi, W., Mi, C., Chai, J.: Study on vessel slot planning problem in stowage process of outbound containers. Journal of Applied Sciences **13**, 4278–4285 (2013)

Characterization of the Portuguese SSS into the Europe: A Contribution

Teresa Pereira[1,2](✉), José Rocha[1], José Telhada[2], and Maria Sameiro Carvalho[2]

[1] IPP/ESEIG, Escola Superior de Estudos Industriais e de Gestão, Instituto Politécnico do Porto, CIEFGEI, Rua D. Sancho I, 981 4480-876, Vila do Conde, Portugal
teresapereira@eseig.ipp.pt, josesrocha@gmail.com
[2] Centro Algoritmi, Escola de Engenharia, Universidade do Minho,
Campus de Azurém 4800-058, Guimarães, Portugal
{maria.pereira,jose.telhada,maria.carvalho}@algoritmi.uminho.pt

Abstract. Nowadays, Short Sea Shipping (SSS) is an essential part in European multi-modal transport system, representing approximately thirty-seven per cent of intra-Community transactions in tonnes per kilometre (tkm). Since 2001, the European Shortsea Network (ESN) in partnership with the short-sea Promotion Centres (SPC) of each Member State of the European Union (EU) have managed to make significant progress in the promotion and development of this mode of transport.

This paper aims to assess and analyse the SSS of containerised goods in Portugal and its articulation with other EU routes and also other transport modes. The current SSS infrastructure, how the sector is organized, as well as the future perspectives for the sector are also analysed for the case of Portugal.

The analyses are based on a survey that was carried out on the logistics operators, navigation agents, freight forwarders, and the leading imports and exports manufacturers in Portugal.

Keywords: Sort Sea Shipping (SSS) · Intermodal transport · Containerized freight · Survey

1 Introduction

Freight transport is a vital component in any economy. It is an economic indicator on the contribution to the economic growth of each country or region. Transport networks facilitate good and people movement, being considered essential to the competitiveness and growth of the economies. As such, efficient transport networks generate savings for businesses, making the production and distribution more efficient and generating economies of scale. The recent trends at the global level, combined with the efficiency of transport networks, enabled the decentralization of production methods and leaded to a significant growth of freight transport flows, both at domestic and international levels. However, this growth raised several problems, mainly due to road mode increase, such as air pollution, road accidents, road congestion and the

© Springer International Publishing Switzerland 2015
F. Corman et al. (Eds.): ICCL 2015, LNCS 9335, pp. 252–266, 2015.
DOI: 10.1007/978-3-319-24264-4_18

corresponding energy consumption, and social problems [3]. Also the concept of mobility drives the world economy. The mobility of people and goods allowed the massification of the transport sector. Distances became shorter than ever, new forms of business transactions and business strategies were developed changing the way companies are managed, and new services based on the transport sector were developed, thus creating numerous opportunities and challenges, leading to globalisation. In this way, the issues of mobility and, more specifically, sustainable mobility, became the main focus of the concerns relating to the fulfilment of the goals of the strategy Europe 2020 programme launched by the European Commission [1]:

- Reduction in at least 20% of the emissions of greenhouse gases;
- Increase in the use of 20% energy from renewable sources;
- Increase in energy efficiency 20%.

The concept of Short Sea Shipping (SSS) aroused in the beginning of last decade of last century, and its definition is not consensual among the various authors [4]. For Denisis [3] and Lombardo [15], the definition given by the U.S. Maritime Administration (MARAD) is considered the most consensual: the SSS is a means of transport of goods by waterway that does not exceed the limits of the ocean where navigates and uses the shorelines and channels for the carriage of goods. Yonge and Henesey [21] define the SSS as freight for distances considered short or to nearby coastal ports. Paixão et al. [23] define the SSS as containing certain criteria such as the type of ship, the markets in question, the logistical needs and the services offered. According to English et al. [6], SSS is based on commercial transportation of goods or passengers by national and international shipping, being a subsector of shipping which operates in coastal and inland waterways and that does not cross any ocean, competing often with road and rail networks. Musso et al. [21] proposed four criteria to define SSS:

- Geographic criteria, based on the size of the route;
- Supply criteria, based on the type and size of vessels or belonging to a longer path;
- Commercial criteria, in which it competes with land transport, distinguishing between feeder traffic, intraregional traffic and the nature of the load to be carried;
- Legal criteria.

In European Union (EU), SSS means the movement of goods and passengers by sea between ports situated in EU Member States (EU-28), or between these and non-European ports at the coast lines in the seas surrounding Europe: cases of the Baltic, Black Sea and the Mediterranean. It includes both shipping national and international transport feeder services and transport between islands, rivers and lakes [1].

The SSS sector is responsible for about 5% of European GDP, contributing to employ approximately 10 million people. The existence of efficient transport systems is essential for European companies to compete in the global economy. Many European companies operating in the transport sector are world leaders in traffic management systems, logistics, infrastructure and manufacture of transport equipment [5].

The SSS has become one of the priorities of EU transport policy, with the objective of reducing the use of road transport. The SSS has been seen as the only mode of transport able to compete with road transport, minimizing the problems referred to, since it offers sustainable and value-added services (e.g. door-to-door) at competitive cost when compared with road transport. Since 2001, the European Commission (EC) has been trying to increase the use of the SSS through its use-friendly policies and funding programs to expansion of the SSS, in order to provide the desired services. Several EU countries have been transposing and implementing EU legislation and directives, aiming to exploiting the economic benefits offered by the SSS. United Kingdom, Italy and Netherlands are the best examples of countries that offer SSS services able to compete with road transport. These countries have in common the direct access to the sea, and long coastlines (except Netherlands). It is relevant that a country like Netherlands, with a coastline quite smaller when compared to most other European countries with coastline, is the country that uses sea transport that includes Deep Sea Shipping-DSS. The Netherlands is in fact a candidate to SSS leadership in Europe. In 2013, it ranked third in SSS cargo transportation, reaching 15% of all cargo via SSS in EU-28, following the United Kingdom (17.6% of the total cargo) and Italy (15.6%). Portugal represented only 2% of SSS [7].

The success of the SSS in one country cannot be merely measured by the coastline length and direct access to the sea. In order to conclude that there is a well-organised sea transport service in any country, other criteria/aspects have to be factored in. The SSS concept is much more complicated and its success depends on various other factors and variables that will be discussed throughout this paper.

SSS is an essential part in EU multi-modal transport system representing approximately 37% of intra-community transactions in tonnes per kilometre (tkm). Since 2001, the European Shortsea Network (ESN) in partnership with the short-sea Promotion Centres (SPC) of each Member State of the European Union (EU) have managed to make significant progress in the promotion and development of this mode of transport.

In Portugal, more than one-third of the primary energy is absorbed by the transport sector. It is argued that sustainable mobility is the way to reduce its energy intensity in order to promote competitiveness, as well as reduce the costs associated with moving from domestic to external markets of consumption. Once the transport and logistics sector represent high costs for companies, it becomes clear that the focus should be on using more efficient transport modes and integrated intelligent transport networks, as a means to enhance the competitiveness of these companies, capturing the attention of economic agents and investment.

This paper is organized as follows. Section 2 describes the SSS evolution and characterization. Section 3 describes the survey methodology used in this research. Section 4 reports and discusses the results of the survey. Finally, Section 5 summarizes the main conclusions and some suggestions for further work.

2   SSS Evolution and Characterization: A Literature Review

The SSS challenge is to be a low-cost component in the handling of cargo in intermodal and integrated transportation system. Medda and Trujillo [20] intended to assess what are the determining factors for the success of the SSS and its development.

The authors found that the use of alternative transport modes to road transport would only be significant if there was a clear benefit for the carrier in terms of cost, time, or both. In this way, these authors stated that the SSS would only be an alternative if the advantages for its use were familiar and since the SSS was able to adapt to the needs of demand of transport services, offering the same services door-to-door road transport offers, whereas only in this way the SSS would be a real and competitive alternative to road transport [20]. This concept attracted much attention in the EU over the last decade. Unfortunately, not all intentions and promises have yet to be met and the desired modal transfer, road-sea, is not held, despite the strong will and financial programmes implemented by the EU.

According to Perakis and Denisis [25] and López-Navarro et al. [16], the main motivation of the EU for the SSS promotion and its expansion was due to other environmental benefits that the SSS could offer when compared with the other modes of freight transport, mainly road transport. Due to high external costs of this mode of transport, the EU has supported firmly the SSS through various funding programmes that lead to modal shift from road transport to shipping. López-Navarro et al. [16] consider that, although it is desirable that the SSS constitutes an alternative to road transport, both modes of transport can be complementary, as long as EU policies to achieve sustainable mobility align accordingly.

Denisis [3] states that the road freight can and should be a partner and complementary mode to the SSS. Road mode would be a long distance partner, rather than competitor, leading thus to a higher growth of SSS operations. The SSS for long distances is more competitive due to efficiency in terms of fuel utilization and economy of scale. Port authorities, taking advantage of the SSS, began rerouting container cargo to smaller ports and satellites and increased their storage capacity, aiming to improve the efficiency of their terminals [3].

Perakis and Denisis [25] conclude that the trends in the logistics sector, in particular the decentralization of production and logistics services procurement logistics operators, would benefit even more the SSS. In fact, modern logistics has become an integral part of the production process, due to the needs of industry in adopting just-in-time production and fast transportation services, resulting in reduced inventory costs. These needs could be met only by door-to-door services for transport goods [3]. In general, industrial companies are not enabled to own and operate these transportation services with effectiveness and/or efficiently. For being effective and efficient, reliable and secure, these transportation services requires a combination of road transport with the SSS. For the intermodal transfer be done successfully, ports must offer efficient services in order to facilitate the transfer and the coordination of the goods by the various modes of transport. There are needs in terms of communication and exchange of information between the modes, since the routes and timetables must be synchronized between the parties. A quick and efficient transfer of goods from one mode to the other is crucial to the success of the SSS, as well as for the sustainability of freight transport [25].

López-Navarro et al. [16] refer that the SSS has success if it is developed and geared towards inter-modality, by encouraging cooperation between the shipping agents and freight transport companies. However, these authors believe that these companies have the difficult choice of deciding which mode of transport to be used, since the use of SSS, for road haulage transport companies, implies a radical adjustment to their traditional way of operating. Good performances and corresponding success of SSS is only possible by means of long-term partnerships and cooperation. The two modes should not compete among themselves, as it is the case in most cases, but rather cooperate to multimodal transport chains [16].

Paixão at al. [23] explore the reasons why SSS operators continue to concentrate on the problems detected by various EU documentation concerning transport and SSS, proving not to be the solution required for the transfer of road traffic to the SSS. The authors conclude that, despite the huge effort of EU for the desired transfer of freight transport from road to sea mode, SSS is still short of the expectations generated by the EU and continues with plenty of delay with regard to the use of road transport. One of the reasons cited for this, according to the authors, is the fact that maritime operators of SSS have been specializing in port-to-port services, instead of door-to-door services, as do operators of road transportation. Another reason cited by the authors is the lousy marketing management, giving rise to a bad image about SSS service. This is seen as a disadvantage when compared with road transport. All these reasons eventually result in low investment in the promotion of SSS who perceive these short-term results to be due to the uncertainty of this market [23]. The empirical research conducted by the authors identified eight factors in which the SSS service could create a robust strategy and, what are the necessary attributes to integrate the SSS within a more competitive multimodal logistics chains. According to Paixão et al. [23] these factors are: cost, reliability and quality of service; guarantee of service; corporate image; investment policy; involvement in the industry; logistics network design and speed; post-market; and existence of policies for managing operational and commercial relations with freight agents.

García-Menéndez and Feo-Valero [9] found out that the determining factors for modal choice (truck with full charge or a freight container ship) used in Spain, when the goal was to carry cargo (motor vehicles, agricultural and ceramic products, and appliances) to the rest of Europe. Their findings reveal that variables such as the accessibility of ports, the distance travelled by land, the INCOTERM used, the value of the load, the amount of cargo transported and the type of company are important in the choice of transport mode. These as well as cost and time variables, are the main factors [20]. In contrast, Koi Yu Ng [14] found out that the competitiveness of the SSS was not affected by other factors but monetary and time related costs.

In order to achieve greater equality in modal shifts, the SSS is currently an important mode of transport in the European transport planning. However, despite all the attention and promotion given by the EU to the SSS, some issues have been raised regarding the real capacity of the SSS to compete with road transport, because it is necessary to overcome considerable obstacles, be satisfactorily efficient and cohesive across the multimodal chain [14].

In order to compete with road transport, the maritime highways began to be promoted by the EU latter in the last century. However, according to Gouvernal et al. [10], other factors represented a decisive role in the success or failure of maritime highways. Their success depends on the maritime distance to be travelled, the road transport costs, the costs necessary for the promotion of SSS and competition with road transport, transported volumes, the places where are held between transfer modes, as well as regulatory issues relating to the rest of the truck drivers represent an important role for sustainable maritime highways viability [10]. Despite having the potential to be an alternative way to the road mode, the SSS mode has challenges that prevent a greater use, since most ports do not have the necessary capacity for inter-modal SSS operations. A greater integration of the SSS in the supply chain requires some important progress in the logistics sector [20].

As described, the development of conventional SSS still faces a set of problems, limiting this mode of transport to be an efficient alternative to road transport in terms of delivery cost and time.

The SSS presents benefits and constrains. Denisis [3] refers the benefits of SSS:

- Improving energy efficiency in the countries;
- Reduction of air pollution;
- Reduction of congestion on the roads;
- Reduction of road accidents;
- Reduction of noise caused by road traffic of trucks;
- Infrastructure costs lower than construction and maintenance of roads;
- Increase the capacity of the transport networks;
- Increased productivity of ports;
- Possibility for companies to be socially responsible.

Medda and Trujillo [20] identified the following constrains:

- Unfavourable image, in the sense that it is considered an antiquated mode of transport;
- Low frequency;
- Low reliability, due to non-fulfilment of departure and arrival;
- Quality and safety, since there is an increased risk of damage to the goods transported;
- Complicated transport logistics, being required their integration into door-to-door service;
- Documentary and administrative complex procedures;
- Need for efficient ports, port services and connections to the hinterland.

3   Survey Methodology

The methodology used in this research includes a literature review on the characteristics of the SSS transport sector, primary data collected from a survey (enquiry), and secondary information gathered from official statistics of EU-28 and Portugal (in particular).

The survey has been focussed on the Portuguese SSS characterization. The enquiry comprised the following main questions:

- (Q1) – What are the most important factors influencing modal choice for freight?
- (Q2) – In particular, what are the most important factors to choose SSS mode, and what are the main factors/attributes of a sea port that guarantee the success of SSS?
- (Q3) – What are the most important factors to promote a better integration between SSS and other modes?

The questionnaire is divided into three sessions: (1) enterprise and respondent characterization, logistics and sea partners; (2) Portuguese SSS characterization (used ports for import/entrances, for exports and for transhipment of Portuguese trade), transport mode selection, type of cargo traded, cargo unit used, transport modes used, main factors considered important to each mode, mode service assessment, used ports; and (3) reasons to use SSS and intermodal modes, and factors that are important to promote a better integration of SSS and intermodal mode.

The Q1 main question is based on the criteria extracted from the work of Pereira et al. [27], which factors are cost, lead time, transit time, service level, frequency, reliability, flexibility and environmental impact.

Main questions Q2 and Q3 were built on previous works [e.g., 19, 20, 23, 24, 27].

The answers to qualitative nature questions of the survey used a 1-5 Likert scale (1-less important to 5- extremely important).

Data Collection and Sample

The analysis of the survey population and the definition of the survey data collection strategy were based on the 2013-2014 Ports and Shipping Directory [29] and other online sites [e.g., 26], and the SABI database [30]. The survey was developed in *Google Docs* and an email list was built from [26, 29, 30], composed by all 50 listed sea shipping operators (SSO), all the 55 logistics operators (LO), all 171 forwarders, all 267 transporters and other related companies operating in Portugal. The email list was completed, from [30], by adding 494 major exports/imports manufacturing companies (preferred contact: logistics head responsible of each company). The population was composed by around a thousand (987) companies operating in Portugal. Due the population is stratified, the sample size should be slightly above 100 in order to achieve 95% confidence level and a margin of error not higher than 9%.

The survey was both distributed at the participants of the "ShortSea14- European Conference" realized in 12-13 of May in Lisbon and send by e-mail, at the same period. The e-mail was resubmitted twice to non-respondents at begin of June and middle of September. At the end, 106 valid responses had been obtained (147 emails were returned with an error or changed address alert; 71 companies have referred not used the SSS mode; 32 companies have informed that do not respond due reasons of security or confidentiality of business data; the remaining do not reply at all).

Statistical analyses were performed by the SPPS software tool pack, version 21. Descriptive statistical analyses were used for quantitative nature data. For the qualitative data, main questions Q2 and Q3, with eight and twelve variables respectively, it was used the Components Analysis (CA) and Factors Analysis (FA). MacCallum et al. [18] recommend a minimum sample size of 100 responses and Guadagnoli and Velicer [12] refer a minimum of 100 to 200 observations, which is also recommended by several authors [e.g., 12]. MacCallum et al. [17] define that, as a rule, for the sample size a ratio of valid responses per existing variables should be greater than 5 (in this case, it was greater than 8).

CA and FA are exploratory multivariate analysis techniques that turns a set of correlated variables into a smaller set of independent variables, linear combinations of the original variables, known as components and factors. After performing the Varimax matrix rotation, the CA becomes FA. Both of these techniques are usually seen as a data reduction methods but, beyond this goal, one of the main advantages of each one is that they allow to reduce the information of multiple correlated variables into one or more independent linear combinations (components or factors), representing most of the information present in the original variables [19, 28].

4   Survey Results and Discussion

4.1   EU and Portuguese Context

Portugal has 7 freight sea ports: Sines, Setúbal, Lisbon, Figueira da Foz, Aveiro, Leixões and Viana. The ports of Sines, Leixões and Lisbon are, by this order, the main container ports, followed by Setúbal port. The port of Viana has a very small expression in the Portuguese sea freight, except for bulk cargo. According to the Portuguese Office of Mobility and Transports (IMTT) [31], regarding the type of cargo, container cargo concerned 76.7% and the fractional cargo 22.3% of total freight, reflecting the high level of containerisation that Portuguese ports move. The movement of containers by the Portuguese ports, in 2013, was approximately 2.2 million TEUs, corresponding to an increase in its drive to 25.8%. Concerning container cargo, in 2013, Sines port represented 42.5 %, Lisbon port represented 24%, and Leixões port represented 28.6%. These ports accounted for 96% of the total TEUs handled by Portuguese ports, in 2013.

According to Eurostat [7], EU-28 SSS represented, in 2013, 1.75 billion tonnes, represented around 60% of all sea transported cargo [7]. Considering the EU-28 SSS total amount in that year, United Kingdom accounted for 17.6%, Italy 15.6%, Netherlands 15%, Spain 10.8%, as the countries that accounted for more than 10% of the total amount; Portugal represented 2.25% only [7]. The main European users of the SSS are Netherlands, United Kingdom, Spain, Italy, Turkey and Germany. The main European SSS ports are Rotterdam, Antwerp and Hamburg. The main cargo transported corresponds to solid bulk cargo.

The SSS in Portuguese ports reached a total of 78.8 million in 2013 and, of these, 66 million tonnes moved into international transactions [32]. The ports reached 26.8 million tons that had international destination. The represented a growth of 29% for 2012, continuing the recovery observed since 2010 (15.2% in 2010, 14.4% in 2011 and 13.3% in 2012). The most significant growth was recorded in the port of Sines, growing 27.8%, followed by the port of Aveiro, Figueira da Foz and Setúbal, with growth rates of 20.2%, and 15.7% 19.7%, respectively. In the ports of Lisbon and Leixões, the growth was below the double digits, with 8.6% and 3.4%, respectively. Only the port of Viana do Castelo has a loss, when compared with the same period of the previous year, registering -1.3% [31, 32].

4.2   Survey Results

The sample is composed by 106 valid responses to the enquire (10.1% of the population): 27% are manufacturing companies, 25% are SSO, 16% are transport operators, 15% are forwarders and 14% are logistic operators (others: 3%); adjusted to the strata of the population in percentage, being the SSO 20% higher.

Respondents are administrators or CEOs (22.6%), logistics head chiefs (18.9%), 9.4% owners (9.4%), logistics department collaborators (9.4%), operation management head chiefs (8.5%), sales head chiefs (7.5%), marketing head chiefs (3.8%).

About 65% of the respondents has a business volume higher than 5 million euros per year, about 13% between 2.5 and 5 million euros, 5% between 1 and 2.5 million, and the remaining has less than a million. Concerning the number of employees, 18.5% referred less than 25, 19.8% between 26 and 50, and 62.3% more than 50. Concerning the companies' location, 34% of the companies are located in great Lisbon, 32.2% in great Porto, 7.5% in the north and 24.5% in the centre of Portugal. More than 70% of the companies are located in the hinterland of the ports in the north region of Portugal (e.g. Leixões) and in the centre-south (e.g. Sines specialized in petroleum products and container cargo; Lisbon and Setúbal ports, both specialized in container cargo). About 25% of respondent companies are located in the hinterland of the ports of Aveiro, specialized bulk cargo, near Porto at 75 km, and Leixões, specialized in container cargo, Ro-Ro and bulk cargo. The Leixões and Lisbon ports are the most used (for about 70% of the companies).

Concerning the freight responsibility, 31% of the companies enquired uses third part logistics for the cargo transport. Approximately 31% companies appealed, in 2013, the services of transport undertakings for the carriage of their goods, 23.6% used its own fleet for freight, 7.5% used a logistics operator, 3.8% used navigation agents and 8.5% referring that the question is not applicable.

Concerning the type of cargo transported in 2013, 33% of the companies referred that operates machines and vehicles while, 30% operates metallurgical products, 30% operate as payload type, textiles and garment, foodstuffs and fodder, 5.7% operates auto parts.

The main Portuguese SSS partners of enquired companies are Spain, Netherlands, United Kingdom and France, in accordance with governmental statistics. The main types of cargo are the liquid and solid bulk and container cargo of 20, 40 and 45-feet.

Question 1 – What are the most important factors influencing modal choice for freight?

Concerning Q1 – transport mode used: 23.6% of enquired companies use the road mode in more than 80% of the cases, 20.8% between 50%-80% of the cases, 20.8% between 20%-50% of the cases, 18.9% less than 20% of the cases and 13.2% do not use the road mode. Concerning rail mode, 66% of enquired companies do not use this mode, 23.6% referred the rail mode usage in less than 20% of the cases, only 1.9% has referred to use rail mode in more than 80% of the cases. Considering SSS, 10.4% of enquired companies use the SSS mode in more than 80% of the cases, 6.6% between 50%-80% of the cases, 18.9% between 20%-50% of the cases, 28.3% in less than 20% of the cases and 25.5% do not use this mode. The companies that reported having used the SSS during the year of 2013 for the carriage of goods, at least 84% of these companies, used the road mode as complementary transport. It should be noted that about 7% of the companies that used the SSS, used another mode.

Around 70% of the enquired companies uses the Leixões, Lisbon, Setúbal, Sines ports. The main ports used by undertakings, for incoming and outgoing goods by order of importance, are: Leixões, Lisbon, Setúbal, Sines, Aveiro, and the Spanish Vigo, Algeciras and Barcelona ports. The port of Leixões is the main port used for the movement of goods to be used by about 85% of the Portuguese companies, followed by Lisbon (about 50% of the companies surveyed) and Sines is the third most used port to be referenced by 36% companies. Refer that two Spanish ports are used for the entry and exit of goods: Algeciras by 14% companies and Barcelona by 10%. The main ports used by undertakings, for the transhipping entrance of goods, are in this order of importance, Rotterdam (61%), Algeciras (42%), Antwerp (28%), Barcelona (26%) and Hamburg (18%), confirming the statistical characterization performed the main ports of the SSS, with the presence of 3 European ports identified in the Top-20 of the European ports in the year 2013 (except Barcelona). For incoming and outgoing goods, Germany, Benelux, Spain, France, United Kingdom, are European countries with whom Portugal has the largest commercial transactions, confirming, statistics pertaining to 2013 year. According to the results and, as expect, the road transport is the most widely used mode of transport, in year 2013, with 84% companies surveyed have referred to this mode for goods receipt and 74% for goods exited. In contrast, the transport mode less used is rail transport (approximately 20% companies). SSS is the second most widely used mode for freight by enquired Portuguese companies. At least 70% companies uses this mode for sending goods, while for the goods receipt, its use down to 55%. Access to the inland port is mainly outland, effected by road transport. Intermodal mode of transport presents a low use by Portuguese companies in the cargo movement. About 40% uses this mode for goods exit and 21% uses for the goods receipt. Concerning intermodal transport, the most commonly used modes are the combination of road transport with rail and road with the SSS.

Concerning the SSS mode choice, relatively to other transport mode, by the enquired companies, 38.7% have referred that they choose SSS mode for the environmental impact, 35.8% by the cost, 22.6% by the service level, 17.9% by the intermodal integration, 17.9% by reliability, 17% by the frequency, 13.2% by the transit time and 13.2% by the service availability. Despite Road mode 60% by the frequency, 58.5% by the service availability, 50% referred the by transit time, 42.5% by the service level, 41.5% by reliability, 37.7% by the cost, 31.1% by the intermodal integration, and 6.6% for the environmental impact. Intermodal and rail mode as very low values, less than 5.7% and 15.1%, the higher values, both in the intermodal and rail modes by the environmental impact, the other are less than 2.8%.

Question Q2 – In particular, what are the most important factors to choose SSS mode, and what are the main factors/attributes of a sea port that guarantee the success of SSS?

The main factors referred were:

— Road/train mode accessibility
— Inter-modal infrastructures
— Port operations availability
— Effectiveness of the pier
— Consortia with ship-owners
— Lower port costs.

The three main factors referred as the most important in a sea port to guarantee the SSS success were: 76.6% referred the port operation available (76.6%), the road/train mode accessibility (75.5%), intermodal infrastructures (50.0%), 36.8% has referred the effectiveness of the Pier, 14.2% the consortia with ship-owners and the others with less than 6%.

Concerning the Q2 second part - the important factors to use SSS as freight transport, we used CA to extract them because, as referred in the session 4, the sample size is considered statistically acceptable. As explained in Session 3, the 8 variables presented in this question, were extracted from previews work from [27], reduced to the eight referred variables as important: environmental impact, Cost, Service level, Intermodal integration, Reliability, Frequency, Transit time and Service availability, we use the FA of CA. Normality Kolmogorov-Smirnov and Shapiro-Wilk tests has been used with a significance level of 5%, considered as normal distributions all eight variables, not requiring any issued any transformation on data obtained. The Bartlett's sphericity test provided a result very significant ($\chi2 \approx 588.421$; df28), featuring a p-value less than 0.001, value by which we reject null hypothesis, concluding that all the variables are significantly correlated. The results obtained have granted legitimacy to the use of the CA method, showed that the matrix contains a significant correlations between the eight variables. We have a 0.86 Kaiser-Meyer-Olkin measure (KMO) that is considered good between 0.8-0.9 values [28]. Factors with eigenvalue greater than 1 were retained, as well as one factor that cumulatively explained a 64.399% variance in the original data. The rotation was not possible due the variance values. The correlation between Reliability, Flexibility, transit time and frequency are the ones that have correlation with the largest single factor retained with a value exceeding 0.8. Thus the main factor in the choice of the SSS as mode of transport is its reliability.

Question Q3 – What are the most important factors to promote a better integration between SSS and other modes?

These 1-5 Likert questions were composed by twelve factors:
— Ports and terminals with logistical services privatized;
— Appropriate land access;
— Reduction of tariffs applied to SSS;
— Creation of new infrastructures; Ro-Ro services;
— Frequency of service;
— Cargo track and tracing;

— Providing door-to-door delivery services;
— Entry into new markets;
— Provision of new services;
— Logistics strategic inventory management (just in time, quick response, lean);
— Less bureaucracy.

As Q3 are qualitative nature, we also use FA of CA to analyse the. Normality Kolmogorov-Smirnov and Shapiro-Wilk tests has been used with a significance level of 5%, considered as normal distributions all twelve variables, not requiring any issued any transformation on data obtained. The Bartlett's sphericity test provided a result very significant ($\chi 2 \approx 596.256$; df66), featuring a p-value less than 0.001, value by which we reject null hypothesis, concluding that all the variables are significantly correlated. The results obtained have granted legitimacy to the use of the CA method, showed that the matrix contains a significant correlations between the twelve variables. We have a 0.849 KMO value, which, as referred is considered good. The measures of Adequacy of sample (MAS) in the anti-image matrix are between 0.8-0.9, showed that all variables should be considered in the AC. The commonalities analysis showed that all variables have a strong correlation with the extracted factors, since the percentage of common variance of variables extracted factors is greater than 50% for all variables, explaining at least 54.4% of the total variance. Factors with eigenvalue greater than 1 are detained, were detained three factors that cumulatively explain variance 67.175% of the original data. While the total variance explained by three factors (67.175%) does not vary with the rotation, the same happens with the variance explained for each factor. The first factor, Provision of new services, explains the variance 44.828%, the second factor, Ports and terminals with logistical services privatized, explains 13.587% and the third, reduction of the tariffs applied to SSS, explains 8.760%. Cumulatively, those explain the 67.175% variability of the twelve original variables.

5   Conclusions

The survey suggest that the success of the SSS may be possible if it is integrated into the intermodal transport and logistics chain. The SSS offers plenty of advantages, however, also presents drawbacks. SSS offers many benefits as it allows withdraw trucks from the roads, thus reducing congestion on the roads, causing fewer traffic accidents and contributing to improving air quality. The SSS allows lower infrastructure costs than the construction and maintenance of highways, increasing the productivity of the seaports, mainly the secondary ports, offering also the possibility for companies to become socially responsible. The disadvantages of the SSS are: it offers low frequency of the services and low completion of hourly windows (unlike road transport). The complexity of service integration into the logistics chain, the bureaucracy and the need for the existence of efficient ports with connections to the hinterland are other disadvantages.

Despite having the potential to be an alternative way to road mode, SSS has challenges that prevent its greater usage, since most maritime networks do not have the necessary intermodal capacity for this, except in specialized ports in this kind of services. To combat this problem, the maritime highways and investment in modern and efficient port platforms play a preponderant role to the EU panorama of SSS. The perspectives of the SSS service are thus quite promising, in that the many advantages outweigh the obstacles to their growth, offering enough benefits for the transport sector to national economies, society and environment.

Most companies surveyed are located in the hinterland of these ports the main Portuguese ports: Leixões, Lisbon, Sines and Setúbal, reflecting the general geographical location of the entire population (of companies).

The survey has leaded to conclude that road freight transport is selected because it offers fast services, low cost for short and medium distances, high frequency, high capacity for various types of cargo, door-to-door services, high flexibility and mobility, as well fast cargo loading and unloading, despite its high polluting rate per ton-km. SSS and rail are basically selected by the most socially responsible companies.

The three main factors referred as the most important in a sea port to guarantee the SSS success are the port operation available, the road/train mode accessibility and the intermodal infrastructures.

A better integration of SSS with other transport modes will require the development of new services, the privatization of ports and logistics terminals services, as well as the reduction of SSS rates.

Future research may extend the analyses herein presented to other EU countries, contributing to the findings for EU policy-making concerning the promotion of SSS. Optimization and simulation techniques can be used in order to confirm that the success of SSS can be achieved with an appropriated integration of intermodal transport into leader companies' logistics chains. This may be accomplished by optimizing or simulating intermodal supply chains with different scenarios and under competition with different transportation modes.

Acknowledgments. This research was funding by BInt-ICD/IPP-BST/CIEFGEI/02/2014 under Santander Totta funding.

References

1. CE: The Development of Short Sea Shipping in Europe: A Dynamic Alternative in a Sustainable Transport Chain, COM (1999). 317 final: European Commission
2. Corres, A., Tselentis, B., Tzannatos, E.: An inland waterway option for sustainable freight transport in southeastern Europe. In: 6th International Conference on Maritime Transport, Barcelona, June 25–27, 2014
3. Denisis, A.: An Economic Feasibility Study of Short Sea Shipping Including the Estimation of Externalities with Fuzzy Logic. The University of Michigan, Naval Architecture and Marine Engineering (2009)
4. Douet, M., Cappuccilli, J.F.: A review of Short Sea Shipping policy in the European Union. Journal of Transport Geography **19**, 968–976 (2011)

5. ENEI, G.d.T.: Estratégia de Investigação e Inovação para uma Especialização Inteligente 2014–2020 (2014). http://www.fc.ul.pt/sites/default/files/fcul/investigacao/ENEI%20V% 20F%20%20Maio%202014_SE%5B1%5D.pdf (accessed October 15, 2014)
6. English, G., Hackston, D.C., Frost, J.: Define, Defend and Promote - The Need to Differentiate Short Sea Shipping from International Shipping in the Application and Development of IMO Conventions and National Regulations and Policies. Research and Traffic Group, s.l. (2013)
7. Eurostat: Eurostat (2014). http://ec.europa.eu/eurostat/data/database (accessed December 27, 2014)
8. Fafaliou, I., Lekakou, M., Theotokas, I.: Is the European shipping industry aware of corporate socialresponsibility? The case of the Greek-owned short sea shipping companiea. Marine Policy **30**, 412–419 (2006)
9. García-Menéndez, L., Feo-Valero, M.: European Common Transport Policy and Short-Sea Shipping: Empirical Evidence Based on Modal Choice Models. Transport Reviews: A Transnational Transdisciplinary Journal **29**(2), 239–259 (2009)
10. Gouvernal, E., Slack, B., Franc, P.: Short sea and deep sea shipping markets in France. Journal of Transport Geography **18**, 97–103 (2009)
11. Grosso, M., Lynce, A.R., Silla, A., Vaggelas, G.K.: Short Sea Shipping, intermodality and parameters influencing pricing policies: the Mediterranean case. NETNOMICS: Economic Research and Electronic Networking **33**(1), 47–67 (2010)
12. Guadagnoli, E., Velicer, W.E.: Relation of Sample Size to the Stability of Component Patterns. Psychological Bulletin **103**(2), 265–275 (1988)
13. Henstra, D., Ruijgrok, C., Tavasszy, L.: Globalized trade, logistics and intermodality: european perspectives. In: Leinbach, T.R., Capineri, C. (eds.) Globalized Freight Transport: Intermodality, E-Comerce, Logistics and Sustainability, pp. 135–163. Edward Elgar Publishing Limited, UK (2007)
14. Koi, Yu., Ng, A.: Competitiveness of short sea shipping and the role of port: the case of North Europe. Maritime Policy & Management: The flagship journal of international shipping and port research **36**(4), 337–352 (2009)
15. Lombardo, G.A.: Short Sea Shipping: Practices, Opportunities and Challenges. Transport-Gistics, Inc., White Papers Series (2004)
16. López-Navarro, M.Á., Moliner, M.Á., Rodríguez, R.M., Sánchez, J.: Accompanied versus Unaccompanied Transport in Short Sea Shipping between Spain and Italy: An Analysis from Transport Road Firms Perspective. Transport Reviews **31**(4), 425–444 (2011)
17. MacCallum, R.C., Widaman, K.F., Preacher, K.J., Hong, S.: Sample Size in Factor Analysis: The Role of Model Error. Multivariate Behavioral Research **36**(4), 611–637 (2001)
18. MacCallum, R.C., Widaman, K.F., Zhang, S., Hong, S.: Sample Size in Factor Analysis. Psychological Bulletin **4**(1), 84–99 (1999)
19. Maroco, J.: Análise Estatística com utilização do SPSS, 2ª Edição ed. Edições Sílabo, Portugal (2003)
20. Medda, F., Trujillo, L.: Short-sea shipping: an analysis of its determinants. Maritime Policy & Management: The flagship journal of international shipping and port research **37**(3), 285–303 (2010)
21. Musso, E., Paixão Casaca, A.C., Lynce, A.R.: Economics of Short Sea Shipping. In: Costas Th., G. (ed.) The Handbook of Maritime Economics and Business, 2nd edn, pp. 391–430. Lloyd's List, s.l. (2010)
22. Yonge, M., Henesey, L.: A Decision Tool for Identifying the Prospects and Opportunities for Short Sea Shipping. In: EUA, 85th Annual Meeting of the Transportation Research (2005)

23. Paixão Casaca, A.C., Marlow, P.B.: The competitiveness of short sea shipping in multi-modal logistics supply chains: service attributes. Maritime Policy & Management: The flagship journal of international shipping and port research **32**(4), 363–382 (2005)
24. Paixão Casaca, A.C., Marlow, P.B.: Logistics strategies for short sea shipping operating as part of multimodal transport chains. Maritime Policy & Management: The Flagship Journal of International Shipping and Port Research **36**(1), 1–19 (2009)
25. Perakis, A.N., Denisis, A.: A survey of short sea shipping and its prospects in the USA. Maritime Policy & Management **35**(6), 591–614 (2008)
26. MOPTC, M.d.O.P.T.e.C.: Portugal Logístico - Rede Nacional de Plataformas Logísticas-Apresentação (2008). http://www.imtt.pt/sites/imtt/portugues/plataformaslogisticas/paginas/plataformaslogisticas.aspx (accessed in October 16, 2014)
27. Pereira, M., Adelaide, M., Resgate, L., Telhada, J.: Multicriteria Methodology to Mode of Transport Choosing – The Portuguese Case. XI Congreso Galego de Estatística e Investi-gación de Operacións, A Coruña (2013)
28. Pestana, M.H., Gageiro, J.N.: Análise de dados para ciências sociais - A complementari-dade do SPSS. 5ª Edição ed. Edições Sílabo, Portugal (2008)
29. Carmo, A.T.d.: Directório Portos & Transportes 2013–2014, 10ª Edição ed. Albano T. Do Carmo, Portugal (2013)
30. SABI, S.d.A.d.B.I.: Sistema de Análise de Balanços Ibéricos - SABI (2014). http://www.bvdinfo.com/en-gb/our-products/company-information/national-products/sabi (accessed in June 17, 2014)
31. Instituto da Mobilidade e dos Transportes, I.: Instituto da Mobilidade e dos Transportes (2014). http://www.imtt.pt/ (accessed in January 03, 2015)
32. Instituto Nacional de Estatística: Instituto Nacional de Estatística (2014). www.ine.pt (accessed in January 03, 2015)

Yard Crane Dispatching to Minimize Total Weighted Vessel Turnaround Times in Container Terminals

Shell Ying Huang[✉] and Ya Li

School of Computer Engineering, Nanyang Technological University,
Singapore 639798, Singapore
{assyhuang,LIYA}@ntu.edu.sg

Abstract. In traditional approaches, the objective of yard crane (YC) dispatching is usually to minimize makespan of YC operations or to minimize vehicle waiting time. However, one of the most important objectives of terminal operation management is to minimize total weighted vessel turnaround time. We prove that minimizing the maximum tardiness of vehicle jobs from one vessel will minimize the vessel's turnaround time. Therefore minimizing the total weighted maximum tardiness of all YCs' jobs will minimize the total weighted vessel turnaround time. We propose algorithm MTWMT to minimize total weighted maximum job tardiness. We compare the performance of our algorithm with the optimal algorithms RBA* and MMS-RBA* from earlier studies. RBA* minimizes total vehicle waiting time while MMS-RBA* minimizes makespan. Experimental results confirm that MTWMT is most effective in reducing total weighted vessel turnaround time.

Keywords: Yard crane scheduling and dispatching · Optimization · Container terminal

1 Introduction

One of the most important objectives in terminal operations is to reduce vessel turnaround time (Steenken *et al.* 2004). Quite often a terminal operator may treat the vessels from different shipping lines with different priorities, because some shipping lines are more 'favoured' customers than others, or because it is more important to shorten the turnaround time for big ocean crossing vessels than for small regional feeders. Therefore the objective is to minimize the total weighted turnaround time for vessels.

In a container terminal, the storage yard is organized in a number of yard blocks. In a yard block, containers are arranged in a number of rows and slots as shown in Figure 1. In traditional container terminals, vehicles travel along lanes to load/unload containers at the side of a yard block. YCs need to move among different slot locations to serve vehicle jobs. When a YC is busy serving other vehicle(s), a vehicle needs to wait. A vehicle may also need to wait for the YC to move to its job location. Therefore the sequence in which a YC serves the vehicles has great impact on the vehicle delays in the storage yard. Previous studies have pointed out that YC

© Springer International Publishing Switzerland 2015
F. Corman et al. (Eds.): ICCL 2015, LNCS 9335, pp. 267–280, 2015.
DOI: 10.1007/978-3-319-24264-4_19

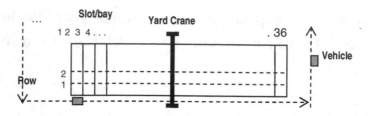

Fig. 1. A yard block with slots (yard bays) & rows

operations are of great importance and likely to be a potential bottleneck to the overall terminal performance (Li *et al.* 2009). Deciding the job sequence for a YC which we refer to as the YC dispatching problem is investigated in this paper.

In many works presented in the past, the objective is to minimize the total (average) vehicle waiting time (Ng and Mak, 2005a and 2005b; Kumar and Omkar, 2008; Guo *et al.*, 2011); or to minimize the makespan (Jung and Kim, 2006; Lee *et al.*, 2007), that is, the total time taken to finish a set of jobs by the YC. Minimizing vehicle waiting times helps vehicles to return to the QCs as soon as possible after they arrive at the yard blocks. However, minimization of QC waiting time for vehicles is not guaranteed. The YC service order is to minimize total vehicle waiting time. Thus it may result in some vehicles returning to the quayside earlier than they are needed while others are late for the QCs. Minimizing makespan for a YC enables the YC to finish a set of jobs as soon as possible. This optimizes the YC productivity. Optimal productivity of a YC is often achieved with minimum gantry movements to reduce the YC unproductive times. This does not necessarily minimize vehicle delays in reaching the QCs.

To help minimize the total weighted vessel turnaround time the algorithm should help minimize the total weighted operational delay in loading and unloading of various vessels. We introduce the concept of vehicle job tardiness at a yard block. The vehicle job tardiness is the lateness in completing a job with respect to the deadline of the vehicle job.

For a loading job, based on *the time a QC needs the vehicle at the quayside*, the time this vehicle should leave the yard block with the container to travel to the quayside is the deadline of this vehicle job. It is the time the QC needs the vehicle minus the expected travel time from the yard block to the QC (assuming no traffic congestions). Once a vehicle is assigned to this loading job, *the vehicle's arrival time at the yard block* can be derived or predicted based on the expected travel time of the vehicle and when the vehicle is expected to move towards the container block.

Even though an unloading job is less critical to the QCs, longer times needed to store a container in the storage yard also directly lead to interruptions of QCs' unloading process (Kemme, 2010). A deadline set for the vehicle will help the YC finish the job so that it can return to the QC to be part of a continuous supply of vehicles to the QC. The deadline of an unloading job can be set as a certain amount of time after its arrival at a yard block such that the total time for a vehicle to be served at a QC, travel to a YC, be served by a YC and travel back to a QC in within a reasonable cycle time.

For external vehicles carrying export or import containers, a deadline for a storing or retrieving job at the yard block will allow the terminal operator to guarantee a quality of service to the external truck companies. For example, the terminal operator may guarantee that 15 minutes after an external truck's arrival, its retrieval or delivery of a container will complete and it is able to leave. This will help the truck company to plan their transport operations.

Each loading or unloading job is associated with a vessel. Each vessel has a weight representing the priority the terminal operator assigns to the vessel. To allow the YC dispatching algorithm to help minimizing the total weighted vessel delays, the weight of the vessel is assigned to the weight of all its loading or unloading jobs. For jobs associated with external vehicles, we can assign a suitable weight as if it is for a (virtual) vessel.

Given the weights, the deadlines of the vehicle jobs and their predicted arrival times at the yard block, the YC dispatching algorithm computes its serving sequence with the ultimate objective of minimizing the total weighted delay to vessels. We prove that minimizing maximum tardiness for jobs of a vessel will minimize the delay to this vessel. When multiple vessels are loading and unloading at the same time, minimizing total weighted maximum tardiness for all jobs will minimize the total weighted vessel turnaround time. We propose a dispatching algorithm that will plan all jobs for all YCs for continuous planning windows with the objective of minimizing total weighted maximum tardiness. In the performance evaluation of the algorithms, we compare our approach with the optimal algorithm to minimize total vehicle waiting time (Guo *et al.*, 2011) and the optimal algorithm to minimize YC makespan (Huang *et al.*, 2014). The computational costs of the algorithms are also examined. We show that our approach produces much better results in reducing the total weighted vessel delay.

The rest of the paper is structured as follows. Firstly, we review the related studies in Section 2. A formal description of the YC dispatching problem and a discussion on the objective function for YC dispatching are presented in Section 3. Then the algorithm is proposed in Section 4. The experimental evaluations are presented in Section 5. Conclusion is drawn in the last section.

2   Related Work

The YC dispatching problem was studied by Kim and Kim (1999) where they considered the loading operations only for a single YC with a given load plan and a given bay plan. A Mixed Integer Programming (MIP) model is proposed to minimize the total gantry time of the YC. The solutions focus on the sequence of bay visits and the number of containers to be picked up at each bay while the individual container pickup sequence within a specific bay is left to the crane operator. Later, Kim and Kim (2003) and Kim et al. (2004) extended the study of this problem by comparing exact optimization, a beam search heuristic and a Genetic Algorithm (GA).

Ng and Mak (2005a, 2005b) developed branch-and-bound heuristics to schedule the single YC for a given set of loading and unloading jobs with different ready times.

Their objective is to minimize the total job waiting time. Kumar and Omkar (2008) used particle swarm optimization with genetic algorithm operators to handle YC jobs with different ready times to minimize total job waiting time. It is known that for large problems, the MIP model has limited applicability due to the excessive computational times. On the other hand, heuristics cannot guarantee optimal solutions. Guo et al. (2011) applied A* search to compute optimal single YC dispatching sequence based on vehicle arrival times to minimize vehicle waiting times.

Petering et al. (2009) performed simulation analysis of real-time yard crane control systems and concluded that the main goal of a YC dispatching system should be to minimize the waiting times both in yard and at the quay. In other words, considering the vehicle waiting time in yard blocks alone is not the best for the overall terminal performance.

Huang et al. (2014) presented an algorithm MMT-RBA* for YC dispatching to minimize the maximum job tardiness of a vessel in order to minimize the vessel's turnaround time. They also presented an algorithm MMS-RBA* to minimize YC makespan to compare with MMT-RBA*. This paper extends the MMT-RBA* approach to minimize total weighted maximum tardiness across multiple yard blocks and multiple planning windows.

3   The Formulation of the YC Dispatching Problem

3.1   General Description

Container terminals normally operate continuously 24 hours a day. Operation planning is done through planning windows which tries to optimize a set of operations in near future with an objective. For yard crane dispatching, if there is one YC working in each yard block, the operation of a YC is independent from the other YCs in the sense that they do not interfere with each other. A dispatching algorithm is used to plan the operations of one YC in a time window which may be a fixed length in time (periodic planning) or a fixed number of future jobs.

In our formulation, the following notations are used:

$J_y = \{1, 2, \ldots, n_y\}$,   the set of job IDs in the block of a YC y for a planning window
a_{yi} the arrival time of job i at the yard block of YC y.
p_{yi} the process time of job i by YC y.
d_{yi} the deadline of job i at YC y.
v_i the weight of vessel i/the weight of job i
m_{yij} the time for YC y to move from the position of job i to that of job j.
S_{yi} the time YC y starts processing job i.
C_{yi} the time YC y completes processing job i.

J_y is the set of jobs to be sequenced for the YC y for a planning window. When discussing the solution of the general YC dispatching problem for one YC, we drop the subscript y in the notation. m_{0j} is the YC gantry time from its position at the start of the time window to the position of job j. C_0 is the time the YC is available to start to move to the position of its first job in the YC dispatching sequence.

The completion time for job i is equal to its start time plus process time, that is, $C_i = S_i + p_i$. When vehicle arrivals can be predicted and the next job is decided, a YC is able to start moving towards the next job location before the actual vehicle arrival. This is referred to as the pre-gantry ability. Job starting time with pre-gantry ability is shown in Equation (1). The advantage of the pre-gantry ability is the possibility of utilizing YC idle time between jobs to transfer between different job locations.

$$ S_j = \max \left(C_i + m_{ij} \cdot a_j \right) \tag{1} $$

Job process time p_i is the YC service time for the job. It is a sequence dependent variable which cannot be pre-determined and can be modelled by embedded simulation to compute p_i dynamically during the planning of the YC dispatching sequence.

3.2   The Objective Function

Our objective is to minimize total weighted vessel turnaround time. The turnaround time of a vessel is determined by the longest crane serving the vessel, that is, the crane that completes its loading/unloading operations last. Under the assumption that the workload of the QCs serving a vessel is evenly distributed (achieved by a good stowage planning algorithm for a vessel), a QC that experiences the longest delay in its operations will lengthen the vessel's turnaround time. Consider this example: there are 10 jobs coming to a yard block. Minimizing the total waiting time of the vehicles may result in zero tardiness for 9 jobs but a large tardiness in one job. This large tardiness will cause a long delay in the QC's loading operation of this container. Once this loading operation is delayed, the whole sequence of this QC's operations will be delayed since the loading sequence has to be observed. If this delay is the longest among the delays to the QCs serving the same vessel, it directly results in a lengthened stay for this vessel.

Theorem 1: Consider a sequence of l containers to be loaded by one QC. Each vehicle carrying one of these containers has a scheduled time to reach its QC in order to keep the QC continuously working. Let $\{d_1, d_2, ..., d_l\}$ be the tardiness of the vehicles in reaching the QC (some tardiness may be zero when a vehicle is not late). The delay to the QC in completing this sequence of jobs is $\max(d_1, d_2, ..., d_l)$.

Proof: If there is only one job ($l = 1$), the delay to the QC in completing the sequence is d_1. Assume that the delay to the QC in completing a sequence of k jobs is $\max(d_1, d_2, ..., d_k)$ and the next job has a delay of d_{k+1}. If $d_{k+1} \leq \max(d_1, d_2, ..., d_k)$, the vehicle arrives at the QC before (or at the time) the QC completes the kth loading operation. There is no delay in the $(k+1)^{th}$ job. So the delay of this QC after the $(k+1)^{th}$ loading operation is $\max(d_1, d_2, ..., d_k)$ which is $\max(d_1, d_2, ..., d_{k+1})$. If $d_{k+1} > \max(d_1, d_2, ..., d_k)$, the QC will need to wait for the vehicle for a time period of $d_{k+1} - \max(d_1, d_2, ..., d_k)$. The delay of this QC after the $(k+1)^{th}$ loading operation is d_{k+1}. So the delay of this QC after the $(k+1)^{th}$ loading operation is also $\max(d_1, d_2, ..., d_{k+1})$. Therefore the delay to the QC in completing a sequence of l jobs is $\max(d_1, d_2, ..., d_l)$.

Corollary 1: If there are m QCs serving the same vessel, the delay to each QC k with l jobs will be $max(d_{1k}, d_{2k}, ..., d_{lk})$, $k = 1, 2, ..., m$. The delay to the vessel will be from the QC which suffers the longest delay, that is $max_{k \in set\ of\ QCs}\left(max_{j \in set\ of\ jobs\ for\ QC\ k}(d_{jk})\right) = max(d_{jk})$. In other words, the delay to a vessel is the maximum job tardiness of all the jobs of the vessel.

The l x m jobs from one vessel usually spread over multiple yard blocks and multiple planning windows. For example, there are 10 jobs from a vessel which go to 2 blocks and spread over 3 planning windows. For each planning window, we may do integrated planning for the two blocks to minimize the maximum tardiness of the jobs. But to achieve global optimum, we should do global planning of the two blocks over the 3 windows since the completion time in a block from one window will affect the tardiness of jobs in the next window. Furthermore, these two blocks may also have jobs from other vessels and these vessels may have jobs going to other blocks in the same time period. It is not feasible to plan for all blocks and all planning windows together. So planning will be done by a dispatching algorithm for each block and for each planning window.

Corollary 2: The jobs of a vessel h generally spread over a number of planning windows and a number of yard blocks. Let p be the number of planning windows and y be the number of blocks. The jobs in this vessel will be involved in p x y planning by the dispatching algorithm. Let $i \in$ set of jobs in one such planning. The delay to the vessel h at the end of the jth planning $(j = 1, 2, ..., py)$ will be $max(D_{hj-1}, max_{i,k}(d_{ik}))$. $k \in$ set of QCs serving vessel h. D_{hj-1} is the delay to vessel h at the end of the previous planning.

Therefore translating the terminal operator's objective of minimizing total weighted vessel turnaround time to the YC dispatching objective in one planning, we get

$$min_{job\ sequences}\left(\Sigma_{h \in set\ of\ vessels}\ v_h\ max\left(D_{hj-1}, max_{i \in set\ of\ jobs\ for\ vessel\ h}(T_i)\right)\right)$$
with $D_{h0} = 0$, $h \in$ set of vessels.   (2)

j for different vessel is different because of the different arrival times of vessels. When the first operation from a vessel comes to the storage yard $j = 0$ for that vessel.

4   MTWMT- Dispatching to Minimize Total Weighted Maximum Tardiness

As proposed in the last section, YC dispatching will be performed block by block and planning window by planning window. In each planning window, our algorithm plans in increasing order of the earliest deadline of the blocks. Optimal algorithm MTWMT computes dispatching decisions for one block each time.

Given a YC dispatching problem of n jobs, there are $n!$ possible dispatching solutions in total. The dispatching problem can be transformed into a tree-search problem as shown in Figure 2. The root of the tree is the start node before the first job is selected. Each path from the start node to a leaf node in the tree represents a complete dispatching sequence of height n.

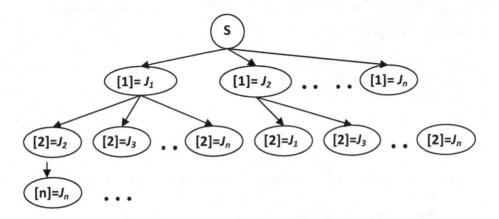

Fig. 2. Search Space of the Problem

The dispatching problem is strongly NP-hard (Narasimhan and Palekar 2002). Exhaustive search that guarantees optimality would be time-consuming to perform. We propose to use the Recursive Backtracking (RB) approach with an A*-like heuristic to prune the search tree by an evaluation function $f(x)= max(D_{hj-1}, g(x) + h(x))$. A* search is a method to reduce search time while ensuring optimality. $g(x)$ is the cost from the start node to x and $h(x)$ is the estimated lowest cost from x to a goal node. If $h(x)$ never overestimates the true cost h*(x), i.e. $h(x) \leq h^*(x)$, the heuristic $h(x)$ is admissible. When coupled with an admissible heuristic $h(x)$, pure A* search is optimally effective (if $f(x)= g(x) + h(x)$). The efficiency of the search depends very much on a good heuristic to effectively prune the search space. RB will quickly find the first solution by a depth first search of n nodes in a problem of size n. It would then backtrack to examine other solutions. If a better solution is encountered during the backtracking process, the knowledge of current best solution will be updated accordingly. Therefore, RB is an anytime algorithm such that a current best solution may be provided if a real time constraint demands it. RB greatly reduces memory usage by keeping only the nodes on current path while the pure A* search (the best f(x) first) may run out of memory a long time before a best solution is obtained.

Note that since $f(x)= max(D_{hj-1}, g(x) + h(x))$, the solution obtained may not be optimal with respect to the jobs involved in the current planning. This does not prevent the algorithm to optimize on D_{hyp}. The algorithm, MTWMT is presented in Figure 3.

To accelerate the search process, instead of choosing the next job randomly, we proposed a technique called prioritized search order which is more likely to discover a good dispatching sequence early in the planning process. The prioritized search order is in jobs' increasing deadlines (line 2 of **YCDispatching**() in Figure 3).

The algorithm takes as input the predicted job arrival time, its deadline and which vessel this job is associated with (and the vessel weight) for each job coming to the YC's block in the planning window. It also takes in the time the YC is available to start the first job in the planning window and its initial location. This will be the time and position of the YC when this YC finishes its last job in the previous planning window. The third argument in MTWMT(), D, is D_{hj-1} in Equation (2).

```
J = {J₁, J₂, ... , Jₙ}
YCDispatching (J)
{
1    newJ = φ;  optimalJ = φ;  CurSmallest = ∞;
2    sort J into increasing order of job deadlines;
3    MTWMT(J, newJ, D);    // D is D_{hj-1}
}


MTWMT(J, newJ, D)
{
1    FOR each job J_i ∈ J    // Select J_i as the job to serve after jobs in newJ;
2          Remove J_i from J and append J_i to newJ;
3          Simulation to get the value of g(J_i) from start to this job J_i;
4          Estimate lower bound cost h(J_i) from this job ;
5          IF f( J_i ) based on g(J_i), h(J_i) and D is smaller than CurSmallest
6                IF J is not empty
7                      MTWMT(J, newJ, D);
8                ELSE  // f( J_i ) is the real cost and is smaller than CurSmallest
9                      Update CurSmallest as  f( J_i ) ;
10                     Update optimalJ = newJ;  //Store Optimal List
}
```

Fig. 3. Pseudocode of MTWMT().

The objective of our tree search is to find a path from the start node to a leaf node (a dispatching sequence of n jobs) with minimum $f(x)$ where $f(x)$ is the total weighted maximum tardiness. The edge weight from node i to node j in the tree is the tardiness of job j if the YC is to do job j immediately after finishing job i. It is computed by

$$T_j = W_{ij} = \max (0, \max (C_i + m_{ij}, a_j) + p_j - d_j) \tag{3}$$

The evaluation function $f(x)$ in line 5 of **MTWMT()** in Figure 3 will be

$$f(x) = combine(g(x), h(x), D) \tag{4}$$

$g(x)$ is the list of maximum tardiness for vessels resulted from the jobs already planned in the partial sequence from start node to node x (line 3 of **MTWMT()** in Figure 3). For each vessel k, the maximum tardiness is

$$MT(k) = \max(W_{i,i+1}), i = 0, 1, ..., x-1 \tag{5}$$

where $(i, i+1)$ is an edge in the path from start node to node x and job $i+1$ is associated with vessel k. $g(x)$ is therefore

$$g(x) = \{ MT(k) \mid k \in set\ of\ vessels\} \tag{6}$$

The total weighted maximum tardiness for vessels from the partial sequence is simply the sum of the weighted $MT(k)$, that is, $\sum_{k \in set\ of\ vessels} v_k MT(k)$. However, this is not computed because we will combine $g(x)$ with $h(x)$ to obtain $f(x)$ as discussed later. Therefore line 3 of **MTWMT()** in Figure 3 will just compute Equation (6).

Similarly, $h(x)$ will be the list of estimated lower bound of the maximum tardiness for vessels from the jobs not planned yet. For these jobs, the lower bound tardiness will be the job tardiness if the job is done at the earliest possible time after the current job x. So the lower bound of job tardiness will be computed by

$$LBW_j = max(0, max\ (C_x + m_{xj}, a_j) + p_i - d_j)\quad J_j \in set\ of\ jobs\ not\ planned\ yet \qquad (7)$$

For each vessel k, the lower bound maximum tardiness from the unplanned jobs is

$$MT'(k) = max(LBW_j)\quad J_j \in set\ of\ jobs\ associated\ with\ vessel\ k\ and\ not\ planned$$
yet $\qquad (8)$

$h(x)$ is therefore

$$h(x) = \{\ MT'(k) \mid k \in set\ of\ vessels\}$$

To compute the value of $f(x)$ by combining $h(x)$, $g(x)$ and D (Equation (2)), we compute

$$f(x) = \sum_{k \in set\ of\ vessels} v_k max\big(MT(k), MT'(k), D_{k,j-1}\big)$$

$$(9)$$

Preposition 1: $h(x)$ is admissible
Proof: The tardiness LBW_j as expressed by Equation (7) is the minimum for each job that is not planned yet. It is the job tardiness if it were served immediately after job x or after the job has arrived, whichever is later and the minimum job processing time by the YC is incurred. It follows that $MT'(k)$ as computed by Equation (8) is the lower bound of the maximum tardiness for vessel k among the jobs not planned yet.

Thus $h(x)$ can never overestimate the maximum tardiness for each vessel from node x to the leaf node and is hence admissible.

Since $MT(k)$ is the longest delay to vessel k from the jobs already planned in the partial job sequence, and $MT'(k)$ is the lower bound of the maximum tardiness among the jobs not planned yet, $max(MT(k), MT'(k))$ returns the lower bound of the vessel $k's$ tardiness for all job sequences where the planned partial sequence is the prefix. $f(x)$ computed by Equation (9) is the minimum increase in the total weighted maximum tardiness for all vessels for all job sequences where the planned partial sequence is the prefix. This will direct the search to find a job sequence that tries to minimize the total weighted maximum tardiness of vessels among all sequences of the n jobs. Being a greedy approach, this does not guarantee the optimal total weighted vessel turnaround time.

5   Performance Evaluation

5.1   Design of Experiments

To evaluate the performance of the proposed YC dispatching algorithms, simulation experiments were carried out. The YC dispatching models are programmed in C++ language under Microsoft Visual Studio 2010 using Dell Precision T3500, Windows 7 64-bit OS, Intel(R) Xeon(R) CPU with 3.2GHz and 6GB RAM.

We consider the yard crane operations in a terminal with high volumes for transhipment containers. Since the import containers are usually delivered to a yard block designated specifically to import containers, the majority of the vehicles coming to a non-import block are serving vessel loading/unloading operations. We will consider such vehicle jobs only. We simulate scenarios where q QCs are loading/unloading containers from/to b yard blocks. Within a planning window, each QC will load/unload from a small number of yard blocks (YCs) when serving a vessel. We decide the job deadlines for a sequence of jobs from a QC based on a QC rate of 20-35 containers per hour, with a small amount of randomness. This is not the peak rate that a QC can work but it is a realistic rate. Each yard block has one YC to serve the vehicles. Parameter settings in the experiments were obtained from real world terminal models as in past projects (Guo *et al.* 2007). A yard block has a size of 36 slots. The linear gantry speed of an YC is 7.8km/hour. The jobs that come to a yard block will have a randomly generated slot and row number. Other recent studies using randomized container locations include, for example, Zeng and Yang (2009). Time for one container move by a YC ranges from 95 seconds to 120 seconds. The different YC operation speed is used to help achieve a certain job arrival rate to YC service rate ratio (average YC utilization in Table 1).

Table 1. Setting of experiment.

Serving vessel	QC	Working with yard blocks	Serving vessel	QC	Working with yard blocks
1 (vessel weight = 1)	QC1	1, 2, 3	2 (vessel weight = 2)	QC5	1, 3, 5
	QC2	4, 5, 6		QC6	2, 4, 6
	QC3	7, 8, 9		QC7	7, 9, 11
	QC4	10, 11, 12		QC8	8, 10, 12
Job due time	The due time of the first job from each QC is a random value drawn from $480 + U(0, 120)$ seconds after the beginning of the planning window, other job's due time is a random variable drawn from $U(102, 132)$ seconds after the due time of its previous job.				
Job arrival time	The job arrival time is $U(102, 360)$ seconds before the job's due time.				
Planning window	20 planning windows. Each QC has 15 job requests. 15x8 job requests distributed to 12 yard blocks evenly. Each yard block (YC) has 10 jobs.				
Average YC utilization	85%				

Experiment Set (Table 1) simulates a continuous time period of 20 planning windows of typical operating environment of YC operations. Each YC works continuously from one planning window to the next. Just before the beginning of each planning window, the YC dispatching algorithm works out the job sequence for a YC. Therefore, after finishing the last job in the planned job sequence of a window, the YC moves to serve the first job of the planned job sequence of the next window. In each planning window, each of the 8 QCs will have 15 job requests. A total of 120 job requests are distributed evenly to the 12 yard blocks. 20 windows will make a total of 120x20 jobs from the 8 QCs serving 2 vessels. Therefore a total of 1200 loading and unloading jobs are simulated for each vessel. This simulates the entire loading and unloading service of a vessel.

We compare the following algorithms:

- MTWMT: the algorithm minimizes total weighted maximum job tardiness (Section 4)
- RBA*: the algorithm (Guo *et al.*, 2011) minimizes total job waiting time
- MMS-RBA*: the algorithm minimizes makespan of jobs (Huang *et al.*, 2014)

QCs generate jobs according to the setup in the respective tables for a planning window. The generated jobs are distributed into the job list for each yard block (YC). In each yard block, the YC dispatching algorithm plans the job sequence for the job list of the planning window. We report the maximum tardiness for each vessel at the end of the planning window for each algorithm. This is the maximum tardiness of the most delayed QC for the vessel. We also report the total weighted maximum tardiness for vessels at the end of the planning window for each algorithm. For each experimental setting, 50 independent runs are conducted and the average results are reported.

5.2   Results and Discussions

The performance of the YC dispatching algorithm is measured by the average of the total weighted maximum tardiness for vessels from the 50 independent runs. The maximum tardiness for a vessel is computed from the tardiness of the QCs serving this vessel. The tardiness of a vessel v in simulation run r is

$$VT_{r,v} = max_{q \in set\ of\ QCs\ serving\ v} \left(max_{i \in set\ of\ jobs\ for\ QC\ q}(d_i) \right) \qquad (10)$$

The total weighted tardiness of vessels in simulation run r is

$$TWVT_r = \sum_{j \in set\ of\ vessels} v_j VT_{r,j} \qquad (11)$$

The average of the tardiness of vessel v over the 50 independent runs is

$$VT_{mean,v} = \frac{1}{50} \sum_{r=1}^{50} VT_{r,v} \qquad (12)$$

The average of the total weighted tardiness of vessels over the 50 independent runs is

$$TWVT_{mean} = \frac{1}{50}\sum_{r=1}^{50} TWVT_r \qquad (13)$$

The total weighted tardiness ratio of another algorithm x against MTWMT is defined as

$$TWVTR_{x,MTWMT} = \frac{TWVT_{mean}\ under\ x - TWVT_{mean}\ under\ MTWMT}{TWVT_{mean}\ under\ MTWMT} \qquad (14)$$

where $TWVT_{mean}$ is computed by Equation (13).

Table 2 shows the individual vessel tardiness and the total weight vessel tardiness from the 50 runs of the experiments. Column 4 of the table confirms that MTWMT algorithm is the most effective in reducing total weight vessel turnaround time. It is better than minimizing total vehicle waiting time by 20% and better than minimizing makespan by 76%. This proves that minimizing total weighted maximum tardiness in YC dispatching is able to serve better the objective of minimizing total weighted vessel turnaround time than the other two objectives. Column 2 and 3 show that MTWMT is also able to produce better individual vessel turnaround time. When vessel 2 gets more favourable treatment than vessel 1 because of its higher weightage in MTWMT, vessel 1 is not unduly penalized.

Table 2. The vessel tardiness and the total weighted tardiness of vessels, $TWVT_{mean}$ (seconds) and the total weighted tardiness ratio of algorithm RBA* against MTWMT, $TWVTR_{RBA*,MTWMT}$.

	$VT_{mean,vessel1}$	$VT_{mean,vessel2}$	$TWVT_{mean}$ ($TWVTR_{x,MTWMT}$)
MTWMT	139.49	67.56	274.61(0.0%)
RBA*	331.52	331.65	331.61(20.76%)
MMS-RBA*	349.24	550.50	483.41(76.04%)

Table 3. The average computational time (seconds).

	MTWMT	MMS-RBA*	RBA*
20	37.26	203.34	26.19

Table 3 shows the average CPU time of the various algorithms. MTWMT takes a longer time than RBA*. This may not seem intuitive because if the current maximum vessel delay is already big, the algorithm may not need to spend time to optimize the job sequence of the current block as long as it does not make it worse. However, this is not true because a near-optimal sequence is needed such that the YC will finish the current set of jobs efficiently in order not to incur large tardiness in future planning windows. This is why MTWMT takes more time than RBA*. As said in Huang et al.(2014), the A* heuristic in MMS-RBA* presented in that paper may not be very effective in pruning the search space. However, it serves to show that minimizing makespan is not a good way to minimize total weighted vessel turnaround time.

6   Conclusions

We propose to minimize the total weighted maximum tardiness among the vehicle jobs for solving the YC dispatching problem. We prove that this objective will minimize total weighted delay to vessels thus minimize total weighted vessel turnaround time. We present optimal algorithm MTWMT-RBA* to minimize total weighted maximum job tardiness. Optimal algorithm MTWT-RBA* to minimize total weighted job tardiness and optimal algorithm MMS-RBA* to minimize makespan are also proposed for comparison with MTWMT-RBA*.

In real operations, containers involved in a YC job may not be on top of the stack. To handle such jobs, some containers have to be moved first. Such scenarios are very often ignored in some other studies. In order to consider such jobs in the planning of YC dispatching sequence, simulation is embedded in our optimization algorithms to help provide accurate YC service times. This results in a more accurate evaluation of job tardiness.

Simulation experiments are conducted to evaluate all algorithms proposed, together with the optimal algorithm RBA* to minimize total job waiting time and the Earliest Due Date First heuristic. The performance of the dispatching algorithms in managing one planning window are evaluated under 2 distributions of QC rates, 3 distributions of job slackness, 3 YC utilization rates and 3 planning window sizes. Evaluation is also conducted simulating the entire vessel loading and unloading process for vessel visits with 240 and 1200 total container moves per visit respectively. Our results show that MTWMT-RBA* is the best algorithm to minimize total weighted vessel turnaround time among all tested algorithms under the tested scenarios.

Future work includes investigations into dynamic optimization algorithms that are effective under uncertainty: when predicted vehicle arrival times have noise.

References

1. Cao, Z., Lee, D.H., Meng, Q.: Deployment strategies of double-rail-mounted gantry crane systems for loading outbound containers in container terminals. International Journal of Production Economics **115**, 221–228 (2008)
2. Carlo, H.J., Vis, I.F.A., Roodbergen, K.J.: Storage yard operations in container terminals: Literature overview, trends, and research directions. European Journal of Operational Research **235**(2), 412–430 (2014)
3. Guo, X., Huang, S.Y., Hsu, W.J., Low, M.Y.H., Chan, T.H., Liu, J.H.: Vehicle Dispatching with real time location information in container terminals. In: Proceedings of the European Modeling and Simulation Symposium (2007)
4. Guo, X., Huang, S.Y., Hsu, W.J., Low, M.Y.H.: Dynamic Yard Crane Dispatching in Container Terminals with Predicted Vehicle Arrival Information. Advanced Engineering Informatics **25**(3), 472–484 (2011)
5. Guo, X., Huang, S.Y.: Dynamic Space and Time Partitioning for Yard Crane Workload Management in Container Terminals. Transportation Science **46**(1), 134–148 (2012)
6. Huang, S.Y., Tay, Z.C.: A Framework for Automated Real Time Management of Container Handling Equipment. In: The 2013 International Conference on Logistics and Maritime Systems (2013)

7. Jung, S.H., Kim, K.H.: Load scheduling for multiple quay cranes in port container terminals. Journal of Intelligent Manufacturing **17**, 479–492 (2006)
8. Kemme, N.: RMG crane scheduling and stacking. In: Bose, J.W. (eds) Handbook of Terminal Planning. Springer (2010)
9. Kim, K.H., Kang, J.S., Ryu, K.R.: A beam search algorithm for the load sequencing of outbound containers in port container terminals. OR Spectrum **26**, 93–116 (2004)
10. Kim, K.M., Kim, K.Y.: An optimal routing algorithm for a transfer crane in port container terminals. Transportation Science **33**(1), 17–33 (1999)
11. Kim, K.Y., Kim, K.H.: Heuristic algorithms for routing yard-side equipment for minimizing loading times in container terminals. Naval Research Logistics **50**, 498–514 (2003)
12. Kumar, M.M., Omkar, S.N.: Optimization of yard crane scheduling using particle swarm optimizartion with genetic algorithm operators (PSOGAO). Journal of Scientific & Industrial Research **67**, 335–339 (2008)
13. Lee, D.H., Cao, Z., Meng, Q.: Scheduling of two-transtainer systems for loading outbound containers in port container terminals with simulated annealing algorithm. International Journal of Production Economics **107**, 115–124 (2007)
14. Li, W., Wu, Y., Petering, M., Goh, M., d. Souza, R.: Discrete time model and algorithms for container yard crane scheduling. European Journal of Operational Research **198**, 165–172 (2009)
15. Narasimhan, A., Palekar, U.S.: Analysis and Algorithm for the Transtainer Routing Problem in Container Port Operation. Transportation Science **36**(1), 63–78 (2002)
16. Ng, W.C.: Crane scheduling in container yards with intercrane interference. European Journal of Operational Research **164**, 64–78 (2005)
17. Ng, W.C., Mak, K.L.: An effective heuristic for scheduling a yard crane to handle jobs with different ready times. Engineering Optimization **37**(8), 867–877 (2005a)
18. Ng, W.C., Mak, K.L.: Yard crane scheduling in port container terminals. Applied Mathematical Modelling **29**(3), 263–276 (2005b)
19. Park, T., Choe, R., Ok, S.M., Ryu, K.R.: Real-time scheduling for twin RMGs in an automated container yard. OR Spectrum **32**, 593–615 (2010)
20. Petering, M.E.H., Wu, Y., Li, W., Goh, M., d. Souza, R.: Development and simulation analysis of real-time yard crane control systems for seaport container transhipment terminals. OR Spectrum **31**, 801–835 (2009)
21. Stahlbock, R., Voss, S.: Efficiency consideration for sequencing and scheduling of double-rail-mounted gantry cranes at maritime container terminals. International Journal of Shipping and Transport Logistics **2**(1), 95–123 (2010)
22. Steenken, D., Voß, S., Stahlbock, R.: Container terminal operation and operations research – a classification and literature review. OR Spectrum **26**, 3–49 (2004)
23. Zeng, Q., Yang, Z.: Integrating simulation and optimization to schedule loading operations in container terminals. Computers & Operations Research **36**(6), 1935–1944 (2009)

A Two Phase Approach for Inter-Terminal Transport of Inland Vessels Using Preference-Based and Utility-Based Coordination Rules

Shijie Li[✉], Rudy R. Negenborn, and Gabriel Lodewijks

Faculty of Mechanical, Maritime and Materials Engineering,
Delft University of Technology, Mekelweg 2, 2628 CD Delft, The Netherlands
{s.li-2,R.R.Negenborn,G.Lodewijks}@tudelft.nl

Abstract. While inland vessels are becoming more important in container transport between terminals in the port and the hinterland, in a large sea port like port of Rotterdam, only 62% of the inland vessels leave the port on time. Poor alignment of inland vessels leads to significant uncertainty in waiting times of vessels at terminals, low utilization of terminal quay resources, and long sojourn time of vessels in the port. To improve this, it is important to find the sequences in which vessels visit different terminals in an efficient way. This paper presents a novel approach to find the visiting sequence of groups of inland vessels in a large seaport with the objective of better alignment of activities. The approach consists of two phases, namely single vessel optimization and multiple vessel coordination. The single vessel optimization problem is first solved using mixed integer programming, preference-based and utility-based coordination rules are then used to solve the multiple vessel coordination problem. We evaluate the performance of the proposed approach with respect to departure time of the last vessel, total sojourn time and waiting time. Simulation results show improvements with earlier departure time, as well as much shorter sojourn time and waiting time.

1 Introduction

Nowadays, larger ports are being constructed to keep up with the growth of containerized shopping. Large ports usually consist of multiple terminals serving container ships, railways, and other forms of hinterland transportation. Containers are often transferred between terminals, and this movement is called inter-terminal transportation [6]. In large sea ports like Rotterdam and Antwerp, inland container vessels are an important means of transport containers inter-terminals in the port, as well as the hinterland. In the Port of Rotterdam, on a typical day, around 25 inland vessels visit on average 8 different container terminals [5]. The sequence in which the vessels visit different terminals, referred to as rotations [1], decides to a large extent the sojourn times of the vessels

© Springer International Publishing Switzerland 2015
F. Corman et al. (Eds.): ICCL 2015, LNCS 9335, pp. 281–297, 2015.
DOI: 10.1007/978-3-319-24264-4_20

in the port. A vessel rotation is the sequence in which a vessel visits the different terminals in a large port. In this paper, rotation plan includes the sequence, arrival/departure time of visiting different terminals, as well as the number of containers to load and unload at each terminal.

Inter-terminal transport involves the movement of containers between terminals in a pot [6]. The inter-terminal transport of inland vessel is characterized by the short traveling distances, and lack of external traffic interaction, limited internal interaction between operators. There are have been several publications on improving the efficiency of transport of inland vessels between terminals in a large seaport, a review can be found in [4]. All these research are from a perspective of enhancing the alignment of terminals and inland vessels. In this paper, we take a different perspective: by enhancing the cooperation and coordination of inland vessel operators themselves, we aim to improve the efficiency of the inter-terminal transport of inland vessels. Thus, the inland vessels considered in this paper only operate in the port area. The terminals operators are considered as in practice: they serve the vessels first-come-first-served. We focus on reaching agreements among vessel operators.

We propose a two phase approach that integrates mixed-integer programming (MIP) with coordination rules to improve the efficiency of inter-terminal transport of inland vessels, which concerns investigation of generating automatically efficient rotation plans for a given set of vessels, with the aim of reducing sojourn time and waiting time of those vessels in the port area. The problem solving in this approach consists of two phases. The first phase is defined as single vessel optimization problem. In this phase, for each vessel there is a vessel agent that is in charge of its local problem. Hence, multiple unconnected local problems for different vessels are considered. Due to the fact that the generated rotation plans for different vessels may be conflicting with each other, those rotation plans need to be coordinated. The second phase is defined as a multiple vessel coordination problem, in which vessels will coordinate and communicate with each other based on the solutions obtained from the first phase. We design two coordination rules for the multiple vessel coordination problem to coordinate the arrival and departure time of vessels.

This paper is organized as follows. In Section 2, we present the structure of the proposed method. In Section 3, we introduce the formulation of the single vessel optimization approach based on MIP. Two multiple vessel coordination rules based on the solutions from single vessel optimization are introduced in Section 4. Experimental results are presented in Section 5. Conclusions and future work are presented in Section 6.

2   Coordination Framework

The problem considered in this paper concerns finding the best rotation plans for inland vessels in a large seaport. In such ports, there is a certain transport demand for moving containers from one terminal to another. The inland vessel transport considered acts as a feeder service, which means that vessels do not

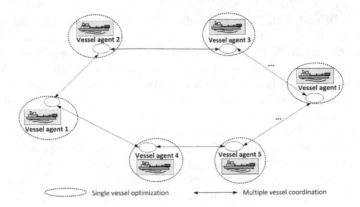

Fig. 1. Structure of proposed methodology

necessarily need to meet all transport demands from different terminals. The reason we consider this is to determine in what sequence an inland vessel can transport a maximum number of containers between terminals.

The structure of the proposed approach is shown in Figure 1. The first phase is defined as single vessel optimization. In this phase, given a set of individual vessels, and the number of containers that need to be transported from one terminal to another, we aim to find the optimal rotation plans, which consist of visiting sequence, arrival and departure time, as well as the number of containers to load and unload at different terminals of these vessels. The objective is to transport as many containers as possible, and minimize sojourn times of these vessels in the port. We formulate the problem based on MIP for individual vessel agents, considering constraints on vessel capacity, required number of containers to be transported, as well as time constraints for arrival and departure. In this phase, each vessel does not take into account other vessels, thus, constraints from other vessel will not be included in the MIP formulation. The solution obtained after solving the single vessel optimization problem for an individual vessel agent is the rotation plan. The optimal solution is the rotation plan with the maximum number of containers transported in minimum time. Aside from the optimal solution, each vessel agent also obtains a set of feasible solutions but not optimal. For example, the solution with maximum number of containers transported in longer time, or the solution with the less number of containers transported in longer time. Those solutions are all possible rotation plans for the vessels, and we refer to all these solutions as solution pool. Those solutions will be used in the next phase.

Real vessel operators would always choose the optimal solutions in those solution pools, since they would like to transport more containers in a shorter time. However, there may be conflicts between these optimal solutions for different vessels. For example, one vessel may arrive at the terminal when another vessel has already arrived at the terminal earlier and has not left yet (overlapping arrival/departure time windows), the vessel then has to wait until the other vessel leaves. In addition, if more vessels arrive at the same terminal at almost the same time, there will be a queue for them to be served due to the limited capacity of the terminal. This will cause waiting for the vessels at the terminal. This waiting might be especially long for the vessel that arrives latest, since the terminals serve vessels first-come-first-served. As a result, the actual sojourn time considering the waiting time will actually be much longer than what is generated in the rotation plan.

If one or more of the vessel agents chooses another solution (rotation plan), with a different sequence and arrival/departure time, the situation could be improved when the overlapping arrival/departure time windows happens and thus reduce waiting time. Even though the solutions they have changed to are not optimal from a purely local individual perspective, considering the reduction on the waiting time, the actual sojourn time may still be much less than the actual sojourn time of the optimal solutions. Therefore, coordination between the vessel agents is needed to decide the best rotation plan with less waiting and sojourn time, by considering the rotation plans of the other vessels.

In the second phase, we define a multiple vessel coordination problem that aims to find the optimal rotation plans after taking the rotation plans of the other vessels into account. The multiple vessel coordination use the solution pool (rotation plans) generated from the single vessel optimization. We design and implement two coordination rules, preference-based and utility-based rules, for the vessel agents to interact with each other. In this phase, given the solution pools of a set of vessels obtained from single vessel optimization, vessel agents exchange the sequence, arriva/departure time at different terminals based on the coordination rules, to estimate their possible waiting time and sojourn time for different solutions, so as to decide the best option of solutions (rotation plans).

3   Single Vessel Optimization

3.1   Problem Description

The problem considered in this paper consists of finding the rotations of inland vessels in a sea port, while transport maximum number of containers in minimum time. In practice, inland vessel operators already have the information of the set of terminals to be visited, number of containers to be transported from one terminal to another, as well as the distance between any two terminals before they enter the port area. In addition, due to the capacity limits of terminal quay resources, limited number of vessels can be served simultaneously at the same terminal. Furthermore, in order to find out how many containers each vessel can load and unload at terminals with different rotations for a single round-trip, the vessels do not need to transport all containers from one terminal to another. Therefore, we make the following assumptions:

- When the inland container vessel arrives in the port area, the vessel operator is assumed to have the following information beforehand: (1) the set of the terminals that has to be visited; (2) the number of containers that need to be transported from one terminal to another; (3) the sailing time between any two terminals.

- Each terminal will be visited exactly once.
- It is not necessary for the vessel to satisfy all the container transport demand from different terminals.
- The vessel will start and end at the same terminal to make a round-trip.
- Each terminal can serve at most 1 vessels, at the same time.

3.2 Mathematical Formulation

The single vessel optimization problem is formulated as a mixed-integer linear program. Table 1 shows the parameters used. Table 2 shows the decision variables considered in formulating the single vessel optimization problem. x_{ij}^m is used to decide the sequence of vessels' visits to terminals. In addition, we consider the rotation plan as a series of segments. For example, if vessel m needs to visit 10 terminals, then there are 10 segments on its rotation plan. $k_{ij}^m = 4$ represents that on the segment 4 of the rotation plan of vessel m, this vessel should travel from terminal i to j. Variables a_i^m and d_i^m are the arrival and departure time at terminal i, respectively. a_i^m and d_i^m together constitute the arrival/departure time window at different terminals. z_{ij}^m is the number of containers transported directly from terminal i to terminal j. Thus, it not only includes the number of containers that need to be transported from i to j but also the number of containers that need to be transported from i to other terminals after visiting terminal j.

Table 1. Parameters

Symbols	Definitions
n^m	the set of terminals that vessel m needs to visit in the port;
τ_{ij}^m	traveling time for vessel m from terminal i to j;
w_i^m	waiting time of vessel m at terminal i;
C^m	number of containers that need to be transported from terminal i to j by vessel m;
r_{ij}^m	Inter-agent utility functions
$t_i^{\text{uft}}/t_i^{\text{lft}}$	average loading/unloading time, per loaded container at terminal i.

The total sojourn time includes the service time, waiting time and the traveling time. To consider the number of containers transported in the objective function, we transform the difference between required and actual number of containers transported into a penalty time. Parameter p_1 and p_2 are the weight assigned to sojourn time and penalty time, by introducing weights we can find the balance of whether to minimize the total round-trip time, or maximize the total number of containers transported.

Table 2. Decision variables

Symbols	Definitions
x_{ij}^m	$x_{ij}^m = 1$ if vessel m will travel from terminal i to j, otherwise $x_{ij}^m = 0$;
k_{ij}^m	the segment during which vessel m is traveling from i to j;
a_i^m / d_i^m	arrival/departure time of vessel m at/from terminal i.;
z_{ij}^m	number of containers directly transported from terminal i to terminal j.

The objective for a single vessel agent is to minimize the total sojourn time in the port, as well as to maximize the number of containers transported. We formulate the objective function for vessel m as follows,

$$\min \quad p_1 \left(\sum_{i=1}^n \sum_{j=1}^n z_{ij}^m (t_i^{\text{uft}} + t_i^{\text{lft}}) + \sum_{i=1}^n w_i^m + \sum_{i=1}^n \sum_{j=1}^n x_{ij}^m \tau_{ij}^m \right)$$

$$+ p_2 \left(\sum_{i=1}^n \sum_{i=1}^n (\mathrm{r}_{ij}^m - z_{ij}^m)(t_i^{\text{uft}} + t_i^{\text{lft}}) \right)$$

For each vessel m, we introduce the following constraints,

$$z_{ij}^m \le r_{ij}^m \sum_{q=1}^n x_{iq}^m \qquad \forall i, j = 1, 2, \ldots, n; \tag{1}$$

$$z_{ji}^m \le r_{ji}^m \sum_{q=1}^n x_{qi}^m \qquad \forall i, j = 1, 2, \ldots, n; \tag{2}$$

$$\sum_{j=1}^n z_{ij}^m \le \sum_{j=1}^n r_{ij}^m \qquad \forall i = 1, 2, \ldots, n; \tag{3}$$

$$\sum_{j=1}^n z_{ji}^m \le \sum_{j=1}^n r_{ji}^m \qquad \forall i = 1, 2, \ldots, n; \tag{4}$$

$$\sum_{i=1, i \ne q}^n x_{iq}^m - \sum_{j=1, j \ne q}^n x_{qj}^m = 0 \qquad \forall q = 1, 2, \ldots, n; \tag{5}$$

$$d_i^m = a_i^m + w_i^m + s_i^m \qquad \forall i = 1, 2, \ldots, n; \tag{6}$$

$$s_i^m = \sum_{q=1}^n z_{iq}^m \cdot t_i^{\text{lft}} + \sum_{p=1}^n z_{pi}^m \cdot t_i^{\text{uft}} \qquad \forall i = 1, 2, \ldots, n; \tag{7}$$

$$x_{ij}^m + x_{ji}^m \le 1 \qquad \forall i, j = 2, \ldots, n; \tag{8}$$

$$k_{1i}^m = 1, \qquad k_{i1}^m = K \qquad \forall i = 2, \ldots, n; \tag{9}$$

$$x_{pi}^m = 1 \wedge x_{iq}^m = 1 \iff k_{pi}^m + 1 = k_{iq}^m \qquad \forall i, p, q = 1, 2, \ldots, n; \qquad (10)$$

$$x_{ij}^m = 1 \iff d_i^m + \tau_{ij} - a_j^m = 0 \qquad \forall i, j = 1, 2, \ldots, n; \qquad (11)$$

$$x_{ij}^m = 1 \iff \sum_{q=1}^{i} \sum_{s=j}^{n} z_{qs}^m \leq C \qquad \forall i, j = 1, 2, \ldots, n; \qquad (12)$$

$$x_{ij}^m = 1 \iff \sum_{q=i}^{n} \sum_{s=1}^{j} z_{qs}^m \leq C \qquad \forall i, j = 1, 2, \ldots, n; \qquad (13)$$

Constraints (1) and (2) ensure that the number of containers transported directly from terminal i to j is less than the sum of all required number of containers transported from i to j. Constraint (3) and (4) ensure that the actual transported containers between terminals is less or equal to the required of the number of containers need to be transported.

Constraint (5) is network constraint that ensures the route are connected. Constraint (6) defines the departure time from terminal i, which consists of arrival time, waiting time and service time. s_i^m is the service time at terminal i, which is defined in constraint (7).

Constraint(8) ensures that there will be no round-trip between two terminals. Constraint (9) ensures that the vessel starts and ends at the same terminal 1. Constraint (10) ensures the consecutiveness of the rotations. If vessel travels from i to j, then the arrival at j will be the sum of departure from j and traveling time τ_{ij}, as defined in constraint (11). Constraints (12) and (13) ensure that the number of containers on board will not exceed the capacity of the inland vessel at any segment of the trip.

3.3 Solution Method

Methods for solving the single vessel optimization problem are commercially available. We can get the optimal solutions, which are the rotation plans for the vessels to transport more containers in shorter time. Aside from that, we also obtain different feasible solutions (rotations with longer time or less containers). Based on these solutions, vessel agents can get different rotation plans, and for each rotation plan, there is a corresponding objective value from which we can get the sojourn time and the number of transported containers between terminals. Those rotation plans and the corresponding sojourn time and transported containers will be used as input for the multiple vessel coordination.

4 Multiple Vessel Coordination

4.1 Problem Description

In practice, there is no coordination for inland vessels, and terminals always serve inland vessels first-come-first-served. This means that vessel agents will choose the optimal solution directly from the solution pool, without communicating with any other vessel agent. The best situation is that there is no conflict between those optimal solutions, in which the vessel agents do not need to spend time waiting at any terminal. Nevertheless, it happens frequently that rotation plans are conflicting with each other at certain terminals. If one vessel takes the priority, then the rest of the vessels have to adjust their rotation plans accordingly. This will cause domino effects that make the total sojourn time and total waiting time of all vessels increase substantially. Therefore, coordination between inland vessels is needed.

To ensure that all vessels can finish the loading/unloading process in the port area as soon as possible, and prevent unnecessary waiting time, and thus reduce the congestion in the port area, coordination between vessel agents is needed. To accomplish this task, we propose two coordination rules, which involve a sequence of information exchange to establish a formal agreement among multiple vessel agents. The information the vessel agents share with each other include arrival/departure time at each terminal.

The coordination rules use solutions obtained from the single vessel optimization, including both optimal and feasible solutions. We use those solutions to build what we define as a solution network. Figure 2 illustrates a solution network. Different blocks in the figure represent the arrival/departure time window vessels at terminals. Different colors represent different terminals. The blocks that are connected with the same line indicate that these blocks formulate a complete rotation plan together. Some of the rotation plans are conflicting with each other (the time windows are overlapping), which means some of the vessels have to wait to be serviced at certain terminals due to limited terminal quay capacity.

Each vessel agent has a group of candidate rotation plans, resulting from the first phase. The coordination is based on the segments of the rotation plans. We formulate the problem as a sequence of coordination steps based on the segments $s1$, $s2$, $s3$, For example, if vessel m needs to visit 10 terminals, then there are 10 segments on its rotation plan. Each coordination step consists of obtaining agreement on one segment. We use coordination rules to handle conflicts. Initially, each vessel agent chooses n candidate plans with the same number of containers transported, but with different sojourn time. The criteria for choosing candidate plans are be set in different ways, depending on the objective. In this paper, we aim to ensure that the vessels can transport as many containers as possible and finish the transportation task efficiently. Therefore, we choose candidate plans with the same largest number of containers transported, but with different sojourn times. Then the agent ranks these candidate plans based on the sojourn time. The shorter the corresponding sojourn time is, the higher the ranking of the candidate plan will be. After that, each agent has a preference profile indicating the priorities of different candidate plans, and their corresponding utility values. The priorities of rotation plans are represented as an order of rankings. For example, if a vessel agent has n possible rotation plans in the solution pool, then the highest ranking, which is the best option for the agent is 1, while the least-preferred solution is n. The utility value is represented

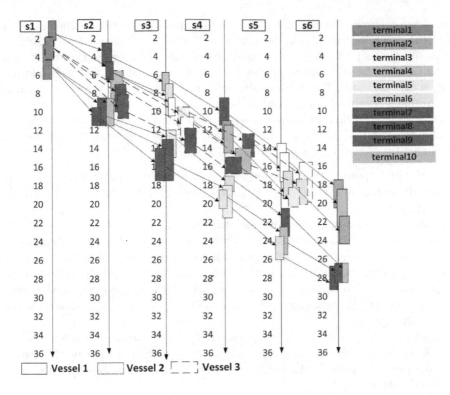

Fig. 2. Sequence-based solution network

by the sojourn time of the rotation plan. Thus,the preference profile of a vessel agent consists of rankings and utility values of several candidate rotation plans.

In each coordination step, vessel agents update the ranking of rotation plans in the preference profile. When the coordination has finished, agents will get the optimal rotation plan that ranks first in the preference profile. Agents only exchange information with respect to the possible time window of arrival/departure and terminal ID (the terminal the vessels will visit) to decide on the rankings of the candidate plans. Other information that will affect the agents decision, such as the utility value and the number of containers transported will not be shared with other agents. This means that the agents can have a better coordination plan without sacrificing to share the important decision-related information such as the number of containers the vessel load/unload per terminal and total time of stay in the port area. All preference profiles are kept private for each vessel agent. The detailed description of the coordination rules is given below.

4.2   Preference-Based Coordination

As we described in the previous section, initially, each vessel agent has a solution pool consisting of optimal and sub-optimal solutions. For each solution, the vessel agent has preferences over different solutions. This information is kept in what we define as preference profile, in which the solutions are ranked according to the vessel agent's preferences. As a result, we define this coordination rule based on the rankings of solutions as preference-based coordination. For each solution there is also corresponding utility value, which is the sojourn time the solution. The problem solving is based on the segments on the vessel's rotation plan, in which each coordination step consists of one segment on the rotation plans. Assume that we have multiple vessels coming into the port area, the preference-based coordination rule is described as follows:

1. In the first coordination step, vessel agents exchange information about the possible terminal ID and possible arrival/departure time in the first segment of their rotation plans.
2. Based on the information from the other vessels, each vessel agent checks if the possible terminal it will visit is the same as the other vessel agents: if it is not the same, the vessel agent will then keep the ranking order of the corresponding rotation plan in the preference profile, and the coordination process moves to the next coordination step.; if it is the same as the other vessel agents, the vessel agent checks if their arrival/departure time windows are overlapping.
3. If there is no overlapping between arrival/departure time windows of the considered vessels, the original ranking of the rotation plan in the preference profile will be kept, and the coordination process moves to the next coordination step.
4. If overlapping of arrival/departure time windows happens, the vessel agents compare the arrival times. Since terminals always serve inland vessels first-come-first-served, the vessels arrives later will also be served later. Therefore, the vessel agent with later arrival time will put the ranking of the corresponding rotation plan one position lower and updates preference profile, while the vessel agent with earlier arrival time will keep the original preference profile.
5. In the next coordination step, based possible terminal ID and possible arrival/departure time in the corresponding segment of the vessels' rotation plans, the above-mentioned process will go through again.

After final coordination step has been finished, the preference profiles of all considered vessel agents have been updated with all segments on the rotation plans. Based these preference profiles, each vessel agent will choose the rotation plan with the highest ranking as the best option. The reason is that this plan has the least conflicting rotation plans with other vessel agents.

4.3 Utility-Based Coordination

Utility-based problem solving is based on the similar procedure as the preference-based coordination. The difference is that this coordination rule updates the utility value of the candidate rotation plans in the coordination process instead of ranking orders in the preference profiles. Therefore, we define this coordination rule as utility-based coordination rule.

1. In the first coordination step, vessel agents exchange information about the possible terminal ID and possible arrival/departure time in the first segment of their rotation plans.
2. Each vessel agent checks the if the terminal it will visit is the same as any other vessel agents: if it is not the same, the vessel agent keep the original utility value in the preference profile; if it is not the same, the vessel agent checks if the arrival/departure time windows are overlapping with other vessel agents.
3. If there is no overlapping between arrival/departure time windows, the preference profiles of vessel agents will not be changed and the coordination process moves to the next coordination step.
4. When overlapping of arrival/departure time window happens for two vessel agents, similar to the preference-based coordination, the vessel agent with later arrival time has to wait until the vessel agent with earlier arrival leaves the terminal. This waiting time is calculated as the difference of the arrival time of the late arrived vessel and the departure time of the early arrived vessel. As a matter of fact, usually there will be more than two vessels with overlapping time windows, therefore we choose the maximum waiting time caused by the other vessels, and define it as maximal possible waiting time. This maximal possible waiting time will be added to the corresponding utility value of the rotation plan in the preference profile.
5. In the next coordination step, based possible terminal ID and possible arrival/departure time in the corresponding segment of the vessels' rotation plans, the above-mentioned process will go through again.

After the final coordination step has been finished, the preference profiles of all considered vessel agents have been updated with all segments on the rotation plans. Based these preference profiles, each vessel agent will choose the rotation plan with the minimum utility value as the best option. This utility value obtained after coordination is the sum of original sojourn time of the corresponding rotation plan, and possible waiting time caused by the conflicts with other vessel agents. Therefore, the plan with minimum utility value has the shortest possible sojourn time, and it is thus considered as the best option.

4.4   No Coordination

In practice, there is currently no coordination between inland vessel operators. In order to compare the performance of the multiple vessel coordination with the existing situation, we use the situation in which there is no vessel coordination as benchmark. In this situation, after the single vessel optimization for individual vessels, the corresponding vessel agents simply choose the solution (rotation plan) with the maximum number of transported containers in shortest sojourn time.

5   Simulation Experiments

In this section, simulation experiments are carried out to assess and analyze the effectiveness of the proposed approaches. We first present the rotation plans generated from the single vessel optimization and then compare the performance of the multiple vessel coordination rules. To evaluate the performance of the rules, we choose 3 performance indicators, including departure time of the last vessel, which is the time when the last vessel leaves the port area, total sojourn time, which is the sum of the sojourn time of all vessels, and the total waiting time, which is the sum of the waiting time of all vessels. In addition, terminals serve vessels first-come-first-served in our tests. Our experiments are performed on an Intel Core i5-2400 CPU with RAM 4GB under Windows 7 system. For the MIP problem we used CPLEX 12.6 MIP solver. The coordination rules are implemented based on Matlab.

5.1   Scenario Description

In our experiments, we use the situation in practice, in which the terminal operators will serve the vessels first-come-first-served. In addition, when an initial rotation plan is chosen, the vessel operators will not change it afterwards but stick to it. When a certain terminal is occupied, the other vessels that arrive at the same time have to wait to be handled instead of going to other terminals. The reason is that in real cases, the vessel operators will not change their plans all of a sudden during the sailing process between terminals.

We set up 4 cases to evaluate the performance of the proposed approaches. Firstly, we use a single vessel instance to show the generated possible rotation plans from single vessel optimization. Secondly, we set up typical example of multiple vessels entering the port area within a 5 hours range, to show the performance after multiple vessel coordination. Besides, according to [3] and [2], the modal share of inland waterway transport needs to be raised in the future. Subsequently, we can foreseen that there will be more inland vessels enter the port area each day. Therefore, we double the number of the vessels in the settings in another case. In addition, we also narrow the range of terminals that vessels visit to show how the approach performs in a more crowded situation in the port area.

We use the following four cases:

- Case 1: 1 vessel, 8 terminals (terminal ID ranging from 1 to 10);
- Case 2: 8 vessel, in which 6 vessels visit 8 terminals (terminal ID ranging from 1 to 10), while 2 vessels visit 6 terminals (terminal ID ranging from 1 to 10) ;
- Case 3: 16 vessels, in which 9 vessels visit 8 terminals (terminal ID ranging from 1 to 10), while 6 of them visit 6 terminals (terminal ID ranging from 1 to 10);
- Case 4: 16 vessels, in which 9 vessels visit 8 terminals (terminal ID ranging from 1 to 8), while 6 vessels visit 6 terminals terminals (terminal ID ranging from 1 to 6);

Case 1 is used to show the possible rotation plans from single vessel optimization, for a typical inland vessel (capacity of 120 TEUs) that will visit 8 terminals in the port. Case 2 is an typical example of current situation in the port of Rotterdam. In Case 3, we doubled the number of vessels in our experimental settings, in which the vessels will visit any of the terminals with the ID from 1 to 10. In addition, to show how the approach performs for even crowded situation in the port area, in Case 4 we narrowed the range of terminals that vessels visit to 1 to 8 for 8 terminals instances, and 1 to 6 for 6 terminals instances.

Our tests parameters are chosen randomly: the number of containers that need to be transported ranges from 150 TEUs to 350 TEUs, and capacity of the inland vessels ranges from 90 TEUs to 150 TEUs. The arrival time of the vessels considered in our cases are within a range of five hour's length. Therefore, we coordinate the inland vessels every five hours. The distances between terminals are represented with different traveling times. For each case, we run 10 experiments with different parameters to show the maximum, minimum, and average performance of the proposed approaches.

5.2 Rotation Plans

Figure 3 shows 5 possible rotation plans for a typical inland vessel generated from the single vessel optimization. Different colors represent different terminals. Each block is an arrival/departure time window at the terminal. The length of a block shows the time the vessel stays at a terminal. The height of a block shows the number of containers loaded and unloaded at a terminal. This could give the vessel operator references about the sequence and time to enter and leave terminals, as well as the number of containers to load and unload. In this figure, we choose 5 rotation plans from the solution pool obtained after the single vessel optimization as an example. These rotation plans have the same maximum number of total transported containers. Among those rotation plans, the plan with ID = 5 gives the shortest sojourn time, which means it is the option in which the transportation tasks are done most efficiently, if no other vessels are present. However, if we consider the other vessels in the port, this option might not be optimal. The other vessels may arrive earlier or at the same time at the same terminal, which will cause waiting and delay in the previously chosen plan. Thus, coordination is needed to coordinate sets of inland vessels. Case 2 to Case 4 show the possible improvements after coordination in the following sections.

5.3 Departure Time of the Last Vessel

Table 3 shows the maximum, minimum, and average ratio[1]of the time when the last vessel leaves the port area, as well as the optimality ratio. We define the optimality ratio as the percentage of experiments in which the departure time

---

[1] $\text{ratio} = \dfrac{\text{departure time of the last vessel generated from coordination rules}}{\text{departure time of the last vessel generated from benchmark}}$

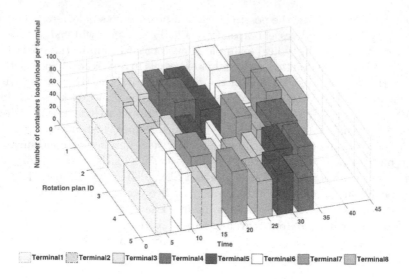

Fig. 3. Possible rotation plans for typical inland vessel (capacity: 120 TEU)

Table 3. Performance comparison with different coordination rules w.r.t departure time of the last vessel

		Max(%)	Min(%)	Avg.(%)	Optimality(%)
	Case 2	114.3	84	95	80
	Case 3	105	91.9	99	60
Preference-based	Case 4	103	90.6	96.6	90
	Case 2	107	85.9	94.6	80
	Case 3	101	87.2	91.7	90
Utility-based	Case 4	99.1	91	93.7	100

of the last vessel of proposed rules is less than the benchmark scenario in all 10 experiments of each case. In 76% and 90% of all cases, the two coordination rules generate earlier departure time comparing with benchmark, respectively, indicating that utility-based coordination outperforms preference-based coordination with respect to optimality. In addition, utility-based coordination outperforms preference-based coordination in 50% of the experiments in Case 2, 100% of the experiments in Case 3, and 90% of the experiments in Case 4 with earlier departure time of the last vessel. Utility-based coordination also outperforms preference-base coordination with respect to maximum and average ratio of departure time of the last vessel. Comparing with the benchmark, although the two rules have a longer departure time, the minimum and average departure time of the last vessel is much shorter.

Table 4. Performance comparison with different coordination rules w.r.t total sojourn time

		Max(%)	Min(%)	Avg.(%)	Optimality(%)
	Case 2	106	91.7	98.1	60
	Case 3	103	98	100	50
Preference-based	Case 4	104	98.2	101	10
	Case 2	105	87.1	97.3	80
	Case 3	104	94.2	98.2	70
Utility-based	Case 4	102	91.9	99.3	50

5.4 Total Sojourn Time

Table 4 shows the maximum, minimum, and average ratio [2] of total sojourn time of all vessels, as well as the optimality ratio. As we can see, the performance improvements of both coordination rules on total sojourn time of all vessels are less significant than departure time of the last vessel, each with optimality ratio of 43% and 66%, respectively. In addition, in all cases, the maximum total sojourn time of the two rules is even longer than the benchmark scenario, and the average total sojourn time only performs slightly better than the benchmark. Among all experiments, utility-based coordination outperforms preference-based coordination in 80% of the experiments in Case 2, 80% of the experiments in Case 3 and 90% of the experiments in Case 4 with shorter total sojourn time.

5.5 Total Waiting Time

Table 5 shows the maximum, minimum, and average ratio [3] of total waiting time of all vessels, as well as the optimality ratio. In all cases, the two coordination rules generate much shorter waiting times compared with the benchmark scenario. In addition, in Case 1, in 30% of the experiments, preference-based coordination rule has better performance than utility-based coordination, while in 70% of the experiments, utility-based coordination outperforms preference-based coordination rule. In Case 2 and Case 3, in all experiments, utility-based coordination outperforms preference-based coordination with much shorter waiting times.

Additionally, comparing with Case 2, Case 3 and Case 4 show less improvements on the waiting time. The reason is that in Case 3 and Case 4, the number of vessels has doubled, while the number of terminals to visit remains the same. Thus, the port area is more crowed, and the actual improvement that can be made is therefore limited. Besides, comparing with Case 3, the vessels in Case 4 have more similar rotation plans (due to the narrower range of terminals), which means the overlapping of arrival/departure time window happens more frequently in Case 4 than in Case 3. Subsequently, the improvement on waiting time in Case 4 is slightly less than in Case 3.

---

[2] $\text{ratio} = \dfrac{\text{total sojourn time generated from coordination rules}}{\text{total sojourntime generated from benchmark}}$

[3] $\text{ratio} = \dfrac{\text{total waiting time generated from coordination rules}}{\text{total waiting time generated from benchmark}}$

Table 5. Performance comparison with different coordination rules w.r.t total waiting time

		Max(%)	Min(%)	Avg.(%)	Optimality(%)
	Case 2	96	53.9	71.9	100
	Case 3	100	75.4	91.7	100
Preference-based	Case 4	96.3	85.5	92.2	100
	Case 2	96.2	57.5	70.4	100
	Case 3	96.2	75.4	82.8	100
Utility-based	Case 4	91.3	68.4	85	100

5.6   Discussion

To conclude, utility-based coordination outperforms preference-based coordination rules with respect to departure time of the last vessel, total sojourn time, and total waiting time at most of the time. Additionally, experimental results show that the proposed rules have substantial improvements in total waiting time with on average 30% reduction for 8 vessels instances, and average 17% reduction for 16 vessels instances.

The above experimental results show that the proposed approach can generate efficient rotation plans for not only individual vessel but also multiple vessels. For single vessel, the proposed approach can generate optimal rotation plans with maximized number of containers transported in shortest amount of time. When there are multiple vessels in the port area, the proposed approach can reduce the departure time of the last vessel, total sojourn time, and total waiting time by applying the coordination rules.

6   Conclusions and Future Research

This paper addresses the optimization of inter-terminal transport of inland vessels using an integrated approach consisting of two phases: single vessel optimization and multiple vessel coordination. In the first phase, individual vessels will gets the optimal and sub-optimal rotation plans for visiting different terminals. However, when there are more vessels entering the port area at the same time, conflicts of arrival/departure time windows at certain terminals may happen, which leads to long waiting times. To solve this problem, in the second phase we implemented two coordination rules to coordinate the arrival/departure time of different vessels. Experimental results show that the proposed approach can improve efficiency of the inter-terminal transport of inland vessels, with reduced departure time of the last vessel, sojourn time and waiting time.

From the application perspective, provided the required container volume transported between terminals, and the number of vessels comes into the port area within a certain time range, the proposed approach can give vessel operators with a higher chance to obtain better rotation plans. The problem formulation and solution method given in this research could be very practical tools for vessel operators as well as terminal operators. They can test different solutions of the problem and decide which are more suitable for their own needs. Therefore, the planning of inland vessels in a large seaport could be improved by applying the proposed approach.

For the future research, this study can be extended in several directions. Firstly, due to the fact that as the number of vessels increases, the complexity of the problem also increases, it takes much longer computation time and puts higher memory requirements for the solver. Therefore is it is important to find out other heuristics that can find optimal solutions in a more efficient way. Secondly, for the multiple vessel coordination, two coordination rules we proposed, although they are efficient they do not guarantee optimality. Therefore, other optimization techniques and solvers, such as constraint programming, distributed constraint optimization, large neighborhood search, A* algorithm, as well as other advanced heuristics can be investigated and applied to better coordinate the inland vessels. It would also be interesting to keep track of how long it takes for all containers from one destination to another. Then coordination between inland vessels can be more enhanced by sharing part of container transport volume. In addition, the geographical scale of the problem can also be extended by taking inland waterway transport into account. Therefore, not only the containers transported inter-terminal but also containers transported from hinterland terminals to sea-port terminals will be considered.

Acknowledgments. This research is supported by the China Scholarship Council under Grant 201206680009 and the Maritime Project "ShipDrive: A Novel Methodology for Integrated Modeling, Control, and Optimization of Hybrid Ship Systems" (project 13276) of the Dutch Technology Foundation STW.

References

1. Douma, A.M.: Aligning the operations of barges and terminals through distributed planning. Ph.D. thesis, University of Twente, Enschede, The Netherlands, December 2008
2. European Commission: Europe 2020: a strategy for smart, sustainable and inclusive growth: communication from the Commission. Publications Office (2010)
3. European Commission: White paper on transport. Roadmap to a single European Transport Area-towards a competitive and resource efficient transport system (2011)
4. Li, S., Negenborn, R.R., Lodewijks, G.: A distributed constraint optimization approach for vessel rotation planning. In: González-Ramírez, R.G., Schulte, F., Voß, S., Ceroni Díaz, J.A. (eds.) ICCL 2014. LNCS, vol. 8760, pp. 61–80. Springer, Heidelberg (2014)
5. Moonen, H., Van de Rakt, B., Miller, I., Van Nunen, J., Van Hillegersberg, J.: Agent technology supports inter-organizational planning in the port. In: Managing Supply Chains: Challenges and Opportunities, pp. 201–225 (2007)
6. Tierney, K., Voß, S., Stahlbock, R.: A mathematical model of inter-terminal transportation. European Journal of Operational Research **235**(2), 448–460 (2014)

Learning Maritime Traffic Rules Using Potential Fields

Ewa Osekowska$^{(\boxtimes)}$ and Bengt Carlsson

Blekinge Tekniska Högskola, 371 79, Karlskrona, Sweden
{ewa.osekowska,bengt.carlsson}@bth.se,
http://www.bth.se/com/ewo.nsf

Abstract. The Automatic Identification System (AIS) is used to identify and locate active maritime vessels. Datasets of AIS messages
recorded over time make it possible to model ship movements and analyze traffic events. Here, the maritime traffic is modeled using a potential
fields method, enabling the extraction of traffic patterns and anomaly
detection. A software tool named STRAND, implementing the modeling method, displays real-world ship behavior patterns, and is shown to
generate traffic rules spontaneously. STRAND aids maritime situational
awareness by displaying patterns of common behaviors and highlight-
ing suspicious events, i.e., abstracting informative content from the raw
AIS data and presenting it to the user. In this it can support decisions
regarding, e.g., itinerary planning, routing, rescue operations, or even
legislative traffic regulation. This study in particular focuses on identification and analysis of traffic rules discovered based on the computed
traffic models. The case study demonstrates and compares results from
three different areas, and corresponding traffic rules identified in course
of the result analysis. The ability to capture distinctive, repetitive traffic
behaviors in a quantitative, automatized manner may enhance detection
and provide additional information about sailing practices.

Keywords: Anomaly detection · Visualization · Potential fields · Automatic identification system · Traffic modeling

1 Introduction

Maritime traffic modeling has the purpose of capturing information and extracting the knowledge of the ways the traffic functions. That way it can provide
insights to non-expert users, without the need for a lengthy hands-on experience
[10, 18]. Similarly, anomaly detection aids the identification of potentially dangerous incidents from the vastness of vessel tracking data, without the cumbersome
manual analysis [13].

The skill set of an experienced navigator involves the knowledge of many non-
written, de-facto traffic rules, commonly followed in seamen's practice. Route
planning and maneuvering often requires semi-intuitive familiarity with the
physics of vessel's movement in various marine circumstances, which is usually

© Springer International Publishing Switzerland 2015
F. Corman et al. (Eds.): ICCL 2015, LNCS 9335, pp. 298–312, 2015.
DOI: 10.1007/978-3-319-24264-4_21

acquired in a non-formal way, over years of practice. Similarly, decisions regarding detection of abnormal behaviors in maritime traffic are still mainly taken on the basis of a human expertise. The operator keeping track of vessel movements must monitor the open sea and harbors in order to identify suspicious behaviors and critical situations, often with assistance of available automated maritime traffic tracking systems.

Much of what occurs in the maritime domain is difficult to observe and assess, as vessel movements cannot reflect navigating activities and intentions in a direct manner [2,3]. Nevertheless, such observations may be enabled and aided by tools automatically extracting information from the traffic data, providing a visual representation of typical traffic behaviors, and warning about out-of-the ordinary movements and events (see traffic model and detection example in figure 1). In this study several such non-written traffic regularities and de facto rules are demonstrated and analyzed, showing that the current state of automatization may enable capturing the knowledge so far only obtainable through human learning.

Fig. 1. STRAND user interface; example of traffic patterns and detections in the open sea area

Automatic Identification System (AIS) transponders are used to identify and locate vessels at the sea, by electronically exchanging data with other nearby AIS transponders on ships, airplanes and fixed receiving stations. The AIS system provides by far the most comprehensive automated description of current traffic state, including vessel position, course, speed, time of day and type of vessel. By inspecting AIS data history it is possible to observe precise ship tracks, and hence, to get an indirect view of the process of piloting.

This approach defines traffic models as a collection of typical traffic behavior patterns, computed using past traffic records. All collected AIS data is analyzed with the use of the potential field concept adapted for data abstraction and representation.

The general idea in applying potential fields for maritime traffic is, for the observed movement of each vessel, to assign charges along its track. A collection of charges distributed over an area generates a potential field, which is locally weaker or stronger depending on the density and strength of surrounding charges. Just like road traffic, the marine traffic tends to concentrate locally in certain areas. The distances between ships tend to be smallest in harbors and river systems and largest on open sea. As a result, in some areas traffic is precisely regulated, while in others it is less restrained.

Given such a model of traffic, a behavior is regarded as normal if it is same as or similar to situations frequently observed in the traffic records, in terms of time, space, speed, course, etc. A detection of anomalous (unusual) behavior is triggered by novel traffic behaviors, not previously observed by the system. In that perspective, the developed method subscribes to another branch of detection domain — namely, the novelty detection.

This method may be regarded as opposite to expert system based solutions, as it reveres definition of what merits a detection. Here, an anomalous behavior is not defined directly, but implicitly — as a deviation from normal behavior automatically learned from a large amount of data.

Contrary to a sea chart, no background data such as waterway obstacles and the sea shore is used for extracting traffic patterns using potential fields. The tool visualizing the potential fields starts with a "blank sheet" filling it with accumulated data from the AIS, i.e., making the obstacles apparent as the local lacks of data instead of a pre-drawn template. This presents a possible double advantage. Firstly, the traffic model is constructed based on the present traffic conditions, e.g., a recently sunken wreck obstructing a waterway would be reflected by the potential fields as a lack of potential in that area. Secondly, the potential fields extract and visually express traffic patterns of, e.g., typical speed or course in an area, and can even spontaneously reflect traffic rules.

Previous studies of potential field based traffic data modeling, as well as the anomaly detection based on it, demonstrated the applicability of the method and investigated its performance [1,5]. Quite surprisingly, this method was also found to result in often characteristically asymmetric traffic patterns, which indicated underlying regularities in the traffic, some of which were, in reality, not formalized or even counterintuitive. Namely, in some areas ships deviating from their course to the left are considered to be more anomalous than if they deviated to the right. In other areas, traveling with speed higher than the most common local speed is less (or in other cases — more) anomalous, than slowing down to the next slower speed range.

A closer investigation, and cross-examination with the type of area being modeled, it became apparent that the character of the perceived persistent irregularities and asymmetries is deterministic, and it seems to follow either man-made traffic rules or regular practices in sailing, commonly known by sailors, but not formally defined. The modeling and detection system STRAND will be further shown in this publication to deliver results allowing to grasp and clearly define such regularities and rules in the maritime traffic.

The rest of the paper is organized as follows. Section 2 presents the background of self-learning anomaly detection decision systems based on different techniques such as machine learning, AI or statistics. In section 3 a traffic modeling and detection system STRAND is presented. The main results regarding anomaly detection and generating traffic rules are presented in section 4. Finally a discussion and a summary of the major findings conclude the paper.

2   Background and Method

In the maritime domain, the sheer amount of data that has to be processed in order to interpret traffic situations is a major challenge. Advanced, self-learning anomaly detections are typically built on some form of machine learning, i.e., the study of algorithms that learn in some sense [10,17]. The algorithm is presented with a set of training data to extract the model out of, to subsequently classify new input, test data (in the case of anomaly detection typically into the classes: anomalous and normal) and to predict how a modeled system will behave in the future.

The additional challenge in case of the maritime traffic captured by AIS, is that there can be no definite knowledge of all truly anomalous incidents. One may, however, make an indefinite assumption that the vast majority of traffic activities occurs correctly, and actually dangerous or malicious incidents happen scarcely, even though the maritime domain, being a part of a shared logistic chain, functions as an avenue for a multitude of opportunities and threats [4]. Therefore, the approach followed here represents neither fully supervised or unsupervised learning, with the classifier (detector) learning normal behavior from the given example of all past behaviors, but having no well formed idea about unwanted behavior as such.

An often practiced and sensible way to track anomalous behavior given the described conditions is by identifying the deviation from normality, i.e., studying models of maritime traffic, representing normal traffic behaviors. Ristic et al. [14] applied statistics to extract normal behavior patterns from primary data and consequently anomalies as lack of recorded motion relevant to normal trajectories and velocity. Riveiro and Falkman [12] combined user interaction with visualization techniques to obtain rule-based anomaly detection. In another study, Riveiro et al. [15] applied a visual approach (self-organizing maps) with nonparametric statistics (density estimation by Gaussian mixture modeling) and probabilistic theory (Bayes theorem).

Different machine learning techniques have been addressed by Perera and Oliveira [7] (neural networks), Laxhammar and Falkman [9] (Similarity based Nearest Neighbour). Rhodes et al. [16] applied a proprietary solution for normalcy learning.

Potential fields, not previously used for anomaly detection, were developed in the AI community as a navigation and decision making mechanism mainly for the development of game AI [6]. The potential fields applied here to model maritime traffic are analogous to actual physical phenomenon of potential fields, e.g., electrostatic or gravitational [19], and are described in a similar manner. The three main concepts derived from the physical potential fields are: the *charge accumulation*, the *decay* of potential fields, and the *distribution* of potential around a charge.

$$c_{lat_k, lon_k} = \langle c^1_{lat_k, lon_k}, c^2_{lat_k, lon_k}, \ldots, c^n_{lat_k, lon_k} \rangle \tag{1}$$

Each vessel tracked by AIS is characterized by a collection of static parameters (e.g., name, flag, type), as well as the current state of its dynamic behavior (e.g., speed, course, location; equation 1). The total charge at a location is calculated as the sum of all local charges (as in equation 2), i.e., the greater an electric charge is, the stronger the electric potential field that surrounds it. A higher potential field indicates visits by more vessels at a location.

$$C_{lat_k, lon_k} = \sum_{t=0}^{\tau} c_{lat_k, lon_k} \tag{2}$$

A field decay effect enables maritime traffic to evolve over time, i.e., to compare and follow trends of the changeable maritime traffic behaviors over time. It is an alternative to other constructs dealing with the real time continuity, such as a sliding time frame or a data window [11,14]. The field decay is here implemented as an exponential decrease of the charge (expressed by equation 3). The prototype builds a normal model based on a real world AIS data set spanning 20 days.

$$C_{lat_k, lon_k}(t) = \sum_{t=0}^{\tau} d(t) c_{lat_k, lon_k}, \tag{3}$$

where d(t) is a non-increasing decay function with limit at zero, describing the decrease of a local charge over time.

Each local charge gives rise to a local potential, most intensive in the location of the charge and dissipates with increasing radius. A global potential field is instantiated by merging local charges. The intensity of the field varies depending on the strength of the surrounding local charges and the distance to them (described by equation 4).

$$P_{lat_k, lon_k}(t) = \sum_i \frac{1}{2\pi\sigma^2} e^{-\frac{(lat_k - lat_i)^2 + (lon_k - lon_i)^2}{2\sigma^2}} C_{lat_i, lon_i} \tag{4}$$

3   STRAND

A maritime traffic modeling and detection system STRAND (Seafaring TRansport ANomaly Detection) computes and displays distinctive traffic patterns as potential fields, extracted from the maritime surveillance data. In the AIS-based maritime surveillance case, static parameters for the vessels (identification number, call sign and name) as well as current state of its dynamic behavior (course, speed, time of day, location) are collected. STRAND further discretizes course and speed. Course is divided into 8 equal intervals: N, NE, E and so on. Speed ranges are not equal in size, and correspond to the speed classes common in maritime circles, ranging from Static (0–1 knot) Very slow (1–7), Slow (7–14), Medium (14–22), Fast (22–30), Very fast (30–45), Ultra fast (45–60), to exceeding 60 knots. The time of day divides 24 hours into four equal time slots: Morning (6–12), Afternoon (12–18), Evening (18–24), and Night (0–6).

Besides using the aforementioned parameters, the STRAND system requires setting a grid size for the potential field. The grid size in essence defines the resolution of the traffic model, i.e., the map of potentials. It has been shown, that this parameter has a direct impact on the number of detected anomalies, and if set improperly may strongly overfit or underfit the data. The number of generic anomaly detections decreases when the grid size is enlarged, on the other hand bigger grid sizes might lead to excluding detections of real anomalies.

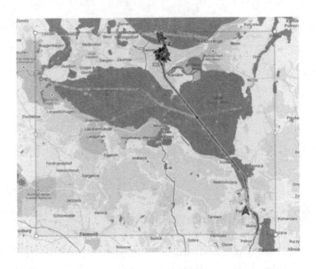

Fig. 2. River area with Szczecin Bay

In figure 1 depicting the STRAND interface, the small black arrows represent vessels conforming to the normal behavior patterns, and all anomalously behaving vessels are marked by larger red arrows. Each red arrow indicates a vessel outside the potential field of at least one type, e.g., navigating in a wrong direction. Also an abnormal speed, vessel type or time of day may indicate an anomalous behavior. Besides the shown open sea area, two other areas are chosen for investigation: the estuary of the Oder River along with the bay of Szczecin representing the river case (figure 2), and the harbor case of the Gdansk bay with ports of Gdansk, Gdynia and others (figure 3). The shown open sea area between Sweden and Poland in the Baltic Sea (figure 1) covers two main routes outside the east coast of Sweden, each represented by a double line. The red color indicates a strong potential field with traffic in two directions, NE and SW. At the bottom of the folded open sea, are the increased potential fields indicating close proximity to the bay of Szczecin, i.e., traffic to and from the harbor of Gdynia and Gdansk.

Fig. 3. Harbor area of Gdansk Bay

4   Anomalies and Discovered Rules

The potential field based method, implemented by the STRAND system, produces different results, based on the specific scenario settings. Each potential field is specific to one AIS metric (i.e., waypoint, speed, course or daytime). The geographic area, in which to aggregate charges and distribute potential, is delimited by two pairs of latitude and longitude bounds. The time selection is necessary for limiting the traffic records, based on which the fields are created, as well as to determine the moment in traffic that should undergo the anomaly detection. Additionally, a classification threshold is set to draw a line between the potential levels determining the distinction between anomalous and normal behavior.

All of the above parameters are constant throughout the experiments in this study. i.e., the time frame, detection moment, and detection threshold remain the same. The three selected areas have unchanged bounds, and for each of them a complete set of all potential fields is built and used for detection.

The focal point is the grid size influencing the resolution of the vessel traffic model. A larger grid size means a lower resolution, and if increased too high, may cause under fitting the underlying traffic patterns, and exceedingly lowering the sensitivity. On the other hand, high-resolution grids may result in over fitting the model and making the detection too sensitive.

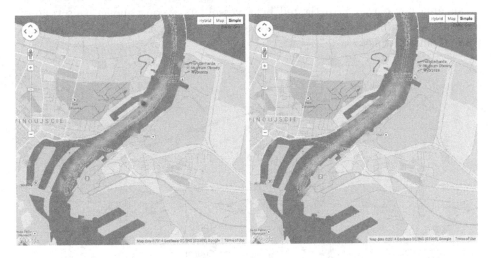

Fig. 4. Traffic patterns for course SW (to the left) and NE (to the right)

Visualization of the potential fields lets a STRAND system user get an overview of the past and present traffic. This is dissimilar from an ordinary visualization of the AIS data plotting. The difference can be seem in the example figure 4 where ships seem to get closer to the opposite riverbank either to dock or to cut the turn. On the other hand, the north-eastern traffic seems to keep to the right bank in the south, but gets somewhat diffused towards the mouth of the river. The distribution of the potential also enables interpretation of the probable reason for that NE traffic diffusion: a point at the western riverbank in the middle of both images appears to be a frequent destination for tracked vessels, some of which seem to show disregard to traffic rules when departing in north-eastern direction. That behavior occurred often enough to build up a relatively strong traffic pattern, and if repeated — it will be concerned normal from a course-specific point of view. If speed, daytime and type of ship are evaluated, new anomalies may occur. In such manner, the potential field based method may act as a way of not only finding typical behavior patterns, anomalies and monitoring normal behavior, but also finding actual traffic rules and local traffic regularities individual to specific areas.

4.1   Anomalies

Figure 5 displays anomaly detection statistics for maritime traffic as a function of grid size. The plot represents the numbers of detections of types: waypoint, course, speed, daytime and total. The total is a sum of all positive detections regardless of type where course, speed and daytime are detections made separately for these parameters. The specific detections may overlap, e.g., a ship may travel with anomalous course and time of day, but at a speed that is normal for its location. The waypoint detection is triggered when a vessel is observed in an area not earlier investigated by a vessel. As a consequence this type of anomaly also indicates anomalous speed, course and daytime, i.e., provide multiple anomaly values.

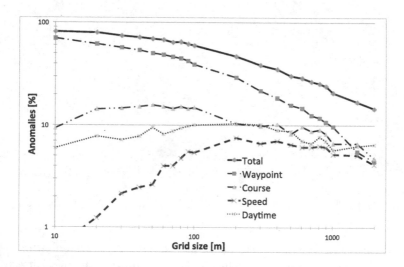

Fig. 5. Percentage of anomalies for different grid sizes

In practice, the STRAND system recognizes the waypoint detections as a deficit of any manner of recorded vessel presence at an examined location. The observed tendency is that for oversensitive detection settings (where the grid is too dense), the proportion between the generic (waypoint) and specific detection (course, speed, daytime) is strongly skewed towards the former type. The reason being that in a small size grid the distances between waypoints recorded in fact relatively close to one another, are so many grid nodes apart, that they cannot create a common potential field (i.e., a traffic pattern).

In figure 6, the waypoint plots (solid lines) show a lot of positive detections for small grid sizes, especially at open sea. The earlier decline in the number of

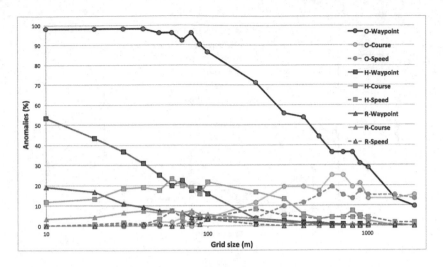

Fig. 6. Anomalies for open sea (O), harbor (H) and river (R) cases

anomalies for the harbor, and especially the river case, suggests that a smaller grid size should be more suitable for these cases.

Both course and speed reaches a peak around the grid size 600–800m for the open water case at the same time as the number of waypoint anomalies get reasonable low in number. For the harbor case there is a similar peak around 60–80m grid size where the peak of the river case is between 30–100m but with fewer anomalies. Both open sea and harbor detects around 25% possible anomalies where the river case holds less than 10% alarms for course deviations. Also for speed deviations there is a higher percentage for the open sea (20%) than for the harbor and river cases (below 10%).

4.2   Traffic Rules at Sea

Besides the already mentioned parameters, added experimental sets are produced by performing detection on data with altered speed and course. For speed, the velocity may increase or decrease relative to the current speed. As seen in figure 7, the grid size is an important metric optimized individually for each area under examination, dependent on the location type (e.g., proximity to the shore), and the conditions imposed by this position (e.g., density of vessels and practically or formally limmited speeds). In the following examples we have chosen a grid size of 30 meters for the harbor and river cases and 800 meters for the open sea case.

As seen in the diagram (figure 7), altered speeds raise the percentage of anomalies for all investigated areas. For two of them: the harbor and river, the amount of anomalies is quite low for the real speed metric value. The experiment for increased speed shows that detection count is multiple times higher, compared to driving with normal or decreased speed.

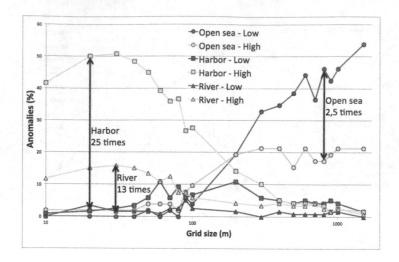

Fig. 7. Altered speed detections for open sea, harbor and river cases

For the open sea, the initial amount of anomalies is about 10 times higher than for the harbor and river case. Unlike to the dense-traffic cases, at the open sea it is a more unexpected behavior to drive slower than usual, rather than to increase the speed.

In all of the cases, the results seem to provide quite intuitive and logical findings. Harbor areas as well as river paths often have speed limits depending on narrow passages and dense traffic. Anomalies normally amount to a few percent for normal and lowered speed, may raise to 50 percent and more of all traffic with increased speed for the harbor case. For the open sea the opposite is true: reducing speed or stopping results in far more anomaly detections, but increasing the speed seems almost as normal as the typical behavior. At the open sea, where most traffic follows straight, lengthy lines it is usual to develop high consistent speed, and any changes to that (i.e., slowing down) may be symptoms of problems with the affected vessel [8].

The comparative detection case study for original and altered vessel courses, was preceded by two additional investigations, which object was the course discretization. The first experiment has to do with granularity: should course be divided into smaller or larger sections? The comparison was performed for course bins of 45, 36 and 22.5 degrees, e.g., sailing NE versus NNE. Finer granularity moderately increased the number of anomalies without changing the overall results, and it did not provide ground for increasing the precision of course binning. The second experiment examined whether the offset of course bins has any influence on anomaly detection (i.e., does it matter if the bins start at 0, 18 or 22.5 degrees?). The observed differences were small and inconsistent over the whole range of grid sizes, indicating that the shift in direction introduces no additional bias, i.e., the STRAND tool seems to be robust against shifting the course binning offset. Therefore the subsequent investigation was performed for course binning of 45 degrees with -22.5 offset (i.e., the bin: North-East indicates course from 22.5 to 67.5 degrees).

For the investigated grid size, the deviations from course are less apparent than for the speed parameter as seen in figure 8. Traffic on rivers is not dissimilar from traffic on land roads, with elongated routes without crossings, where the ships hold a direction determined by the shape of river, its banks and current. The diagram in figure 8 shows that the anomaly results for vessels deviating from their course to the left are at least 67% higher, for a grid size up to 80 meters. The opposite course alteration (to the right) results in barely any increase in anomaly count. These observations make it apparent that turning left from the typical course is much more uncommon than turning right.

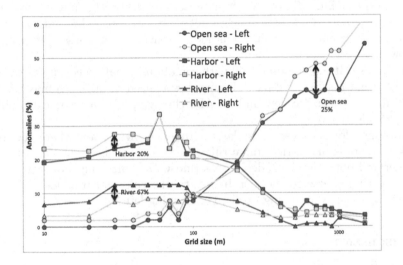

Fig. 8. Altered course detections for open sea, harbor and river cases

In the harbor case there is no such consistent leverage for either altered course, and the local differences between left and right course amount up to 20%. Nevertheless, the overall increase of anomalies for altered courses compared to the original course is quite stable and reaches up to 50%. That observation corresponds to harbor traffic properties, which are characterized by more vessel routes crossing at various angles (unlike land roads), depending on traffic to and from the quays, anchorage areas, etc., and not quite as precisely defined waterways.

The open sea case displays a slightly larger increase of anomaly counts for course deviation towards right (up to 25%) but also a large overall increase of anomalies for altered courses compared to the original (exceeding 100%). In this case the difference between left and right course alteration is more consistent and seems to show that the deviation from course to the left is not as anomalous as deviation to the right. One may interpret it as a highway-like traffic organization, where temporary course alterations to the left may sometimes be acceptable (e.g., while overtaking another vessel), rather than turning to the right and abandoning the "highway" altogether, but are still unusual.

The performed experiment investigated the influence of speed and course alterations on the anomaly detection results. By interpreting just these two metrics, the study resulted in identification of a set of traffic rules apparent in the modeled traffic. The discovered rules include speed regularities (lower and upper de-facto speed limits), and course rules (keeping to the right side on rivers, and following the straight lines at the sea):

- Upper speed limits are significant for both harbor and river situations. This is consistent with the real physical vessel traffic on narrow or closed waterways, where speed limitations are often present and strictly upheld. In harbor and river areas speed is regularly limited by law, obstacles and (or) sailing practice, therefore exceeding it is more dangerous and less common than slowing down or even stopping.
- At open sea it is common to sail with certain minimal speeds, and exceeding them is not disadvantageous. Slowing down speed at open sea may result in disrupting the traffic flow and may be the symptom of technical problems at the affected vessel.
- Traveling along a river is similar to traveling on a road, where the driver follows simple and strict traffic rules, in this case: the right-side rule. The generated potential fields depict this rule with a high increase in anomalies for altering course to the left. In reality the rule and practice is to avoid shifting towards oncoming traffic, i.e., turning left.

5   Discussion

One of the main objectives underlying the design of this traffic modeling method is making its mechanisms, working and logic observable to the user. The anomaly detection was designed in a way that enables observing the basis on which it occurs: the patterns (potential fields) constituting the normal behavior model. That way the method offers background information regarding the circumstances of traffic incidents. According to the experimental findings, this method can also support gaining overall knowledge about the traffic regulations, and even particular traffic rules and practices.

Prof. Edwin Hutchins [18] performed an extended analysis of ship navigation and its actual practice aboard large ships in a naval setting. Cognitive skills observed in the actual practice aboard were shared organically among multiple crew members, constituting the collective traffic awareness. Their actions as vessel navigators determine the way the ship sails, which can in turn be monitored and captured the vessel tracking systems. The developed traffic modeling can be perceived as reverse engineering of this process, where the workings of a system or mechanism are analyzed based on the data it produces. In STRAND, the navigational practices are captured and visualized by the concept of potential fields.

Therefore the distributed cognitive processes of ship navigation may partly be handled by potential fields.

This study's findings regarding speed limits and keep-right rule appear to correspond with real-world sailing practice and common sense, which provide a user with an additional layer of traffic information. In that way the user is better informed and empowered to correctly interpret the anomalies reported by STRAND. The patterns and rules are depicted twofolds: by visual patterns rendered over a map, providing insights instantaneously understood by human users, and quantitative distinction between different behavior types, e.g., as seen in this study.

Same as any anomaly detection method used for maritime traffic, potential fields implemented in STRAND are prone to numerous misdetections. These, if occurring often, affect user's trust in the system, and can undermine its purpose. This is why providing the insight into the detection basis and modeling mechanism is vital. It can facilitate the analysis of detections by providing the necessary background information needed to quickly assess the real severity of the anomalous incident. The gained awareness helps speed up the selection of serious incidents among all the detections, and may mitigate the negative influence of false detections on user's trust.

There are various potential benefits and practical applications of the described traffic modeling method, and its ability to capture traffic rules, depending on the user group. From a ship navigator point of view, the display of patterns of correct or normal behavior, aids the choice of the safest and most optimal path. From traffic safeguarding perspective, the anomaly detection based on potential fields may help quickly and comprehensively inspecting possible traffic incidents. Finally, from authorities' point of view, the clear overview of traffic may help recognize traffic regulation and legislation issues.

6   Conclusion

The STRAND prototype system demonstrates the applicability of the proposed method and its capability to capture traffic patterns and even rules. The three aspects of potential field theory: charge accumulation, potential decay and dissipation; enable the modeling of vessel traffic and rendering the traffic regularities easily comprehensible and observable to the system users, by the means of customizable visualizations and anomaly detection.

An advantage of the method is the ability to create normal traffic models based solely on the traffic history, without the need for expert knowledge, therefore the extracted information is not affected by bias or polluted with outdated or inaccurate data. The additional benefit of the method, demonstrated, analyzed and discussed in this study, is the ability to grasp behaviors common in the sailing practices in a way that can be easily expressed as a traffic rule.

References

1. Osekowska, E., Axelsson, S., Carlsson, B.: Potential fields in modeling transport over water. In: Transport of Water versus Transport over Water, pp. 259–280 (2015)
2. Bichou, K., Szyliowicz, J.S., Zamparini, L.: Maritime Transport Security: Issues, Challenges and National Policies. Comparative Perspectives on Transportation Security Series (2014)
3. Coutroubis, A.D., Kiourktsoglou, G.: Maritime piracy analysis. In: Maritime Transport Security: Issues, Challenges and National Policies, p. 98 (2014)
4. Acciaro, M., Serra, P.: Maritime supply chain security: a critical review. In: IFSPA 2013, Trade Supply Chain Activities and Transport: Contemporary Logistics and Maritime Issues, p. 636 (2013)
5. Osekowska, E., Axelsson, S., Carlsson, B.: Potential fields in maritime anomaly detection. In: Proceedings of the 3rd International Conference on Models and Technologies for Intelligent Transport Systems (2013)
6. Hagelbäck, J.: Multi-agent potential field based architectures for real-time strategy game bots. Blekinge Institute of Technology (2012)
7. Perera, L.P., Oliveira, P.: Maritime Traffic Monitoring Based on Vessel Detection, Tracking, State Estimation, and Trajectory Prediction. IEEE Transactions on Intelligent Transportation Systems **13**(3), 1188–1200 (2012)
8. Cariou, P., Notteboom, T.: Bunker costs in container liner shipping: are slow steaming practices reflected in maritime fuel surcharges? In: Notteboom, T. (ed.) Current Issues in Shipping Ports and Logistics, pp. 69–82 (2011)
9. Laxhammar, R., Falkman, G.: Sequential conformal anomaly detection in trajectories based on Hausdorff distance. In: Proc. of the 14th Int. Conf. on Information Fusion (FUSION) (2011)
10. Witten, I.H., Eibe, F.: Data Mining: Practical Machine Learning Tools and Techniques. Morgan Kaufmann Series in Data Management Systems (2011)
11. Brax, C., Karlsson, A., Andler, S.F., Johansson, R., Niklasson, L.: Evaluating precise and imprecise state-based anomaly detectors for maritime surveillance. In: Proceedings of the 13th Conference on Information Fusion (FUSION) (2010)
12. Riveiro, M., Falkman, G.: Interactive visualization of normal behavioral models and expert rules for maritime anomaly detection. In: Proc. of the Sixth Int. Conf. on Computer Graphics, Imaging and Visualization (2009)
13. Chandola, V., Banerjee, A., Kumar, V.: Anomaly detection: A survey. ACM Computing Surveys **41**(3), 1–58 (2009)
14. Ristic, B., Scala, B.L., Morelande, M., Gordon, N.: Statistical analysis of motion patterns in AIS data: anomaly detection and motion prediction. In: Proc. of the 11th Int. Conf. on Information Fusion (2008)
15. Riveiro, M., Falkman, G., Ziemke T.: Visual analytics for the detection of anomalous maritime behavior. In: Proc. of the 12th Int. Conf. on Information Visualisation (2008)
16. Rhodes, B.J., Bomberger N.A., Seibert, M., Waxman, A.M.: Seecoast: automated port scene understanding facilitated by normalcy learning. In: Proceedings of the Military Communications Conf. (2006)
17. Mitchell, T.M.: Machine Learning. McGraw-Hill (1997)
18. Hutchins, E.: Cognition in the Wild. MIT Press, Cambridge (1995)
19. Jekeli, C.: Alternative methods to smooth the Earth's gravity field. In: Reports of the Department of Geodetic Science and Surveying. Report 327 (1981)

Internal Coordination within a System

Bootstrap Estimation Intervals Using Bias Corrected Accelerated Method to Forecast Air Passenger Demand

Rafael Bernardo Carmona-Benítez[(✉)] and María Rosa Nieto-Delfín

School of Business and Economics, Universidad Anáhuac México Norte, Av. Universidad Anáhuac no. 46, Col. Lomas Anáhuac 52786, Huixquilucan, State of Mexico, Mexico
{rafael.carmona,maria.nieto}@anahuac.mx

Abstract. The aim of this paper is to propose an approach for forecasting passenger (pax) demand between airports based on the median pax demand and distance. The approach is based on three phases. First, the implement of bootstrap procedures to estimate the distribution of the mean pax demand and the median pax demand for each block of routes distance; second, the estimate pax demand by calculating boostrap confidence intervals for the mean pax demand and the median pax demand using bias corrected accelerated method (BCa); and third, by carrying out Monte Carlo experiments to analyse the finite sample performance of the proposed bootstrap procedure. The results indicate that in the air transport industry it is important to estimate the median of the pax demand.

Keywords: Air passenger demand · Bootstrap · Forecast · Monte carlo simulation · Bias corrected accelerated method

1   Introduction

In the commercial aviation industry, air passenger (pax) demand plays an important role. Forecasting and estimating the air pax demand is important for network planning, network management, fleet assignment, manpower planning [15], aircraft routing, flight scheduling, and revenue management. In the case of the airline industry, demand is the number of passengers that are willing to fly between two different airports, cities, regions, and countries or even global [3]. Airlines make decisions with these information such as to open new routes, increase or decrease number of services, and buy aircrafts and equipment to handle the increment of pax demand per route based on their pax forecasting [9]. Airlines makes these decisions to calculate the total number of people that are willing to fly from an origin (O) city/airport to a destination (D) city/airport [3].

The aim of this paper is to propose an approach for forecasting pax demand between airports based on the median pax demand and distance. Normally, what is done is to forecast the mean demand and companies based their analysis and planning on this point estimate. On the other hand, this paper proposes an approach based on bootstrap methodology for estimating pax demand by constructing confidence bands using the bias corrected accelerated method (BC$_a$) [8]. The main contribution of this paper is an approach to forecast the median pax demand and the corresponding confidence bands.

© Springer International Publishing Switzerland 2015
F. Corman et al. (Eds.): ICCL 2015, LNCS 9335, pp. 315–327, 2015.
DOI: 10.1007/978-3-319-24264-4_22

This paper is organized as follows: Section 2 describes previous work on forecasting methods applied to estimate pax demand. Section 3 describes the bootstrap methodology. Section 4 shows the BC_a method by implementing it to estimate confidence bands for the mean pax demand and the median pax demand using the DOT US Consumer Report data [6]. Monte Carlo experiments to analyze the finite sample performance of the proposed approach are presented. Finally, Section 5 concludes the paper.

2   Air Pax Forecasting Demand Methods

This paper studies different methods from time-series because its aim is to forecast the median pax demand by route distance.

[10, 11] develop a model to generate pax demand data, from O to D (OD pair), based on Grey model (GM) theory. [12] use a GM model to calculate Chinese passenger volume from 1990-2007. [18] develop a passenger traffic forecast based on GM theory and the Markov chain. [4] develops a passenger traffic forecast based on GM theory and the Markov chain. [6] develop two gravity models for calculating airline pax volume between routes for a given time interval. [16] develops a gravity model based on the spatial interaction between OD pair. [5] develop a logit model for aggregate air travel itinerary shares at major US airlines. [1] develop a neural model to calculate Brazilian pax per km transport demand (PKTD).

Known distributions functions can be used to forecast airlines pax demand [17]. [2] probe that pax demand behaves as the Poisson distribution function. [17] Show that pax demand does not behave as a single uniform distribution but they behave as a Gamma distribution function. [19] forecast airlines pax demand using three distributions: Normal, Gamma and Weibull. [3] finds that airlines pax demand, between O and D airports, behaves as a log normal distribution function.

On other hand, this paper does not assume well knowns distributions functions. A bootstrap approach for the distribution of the pax demand, the mean pax demand, and the median pax demand is proposed.

3   Bootstrap Estimation Intervals for Pax Demand

3.1   Bootstrap Methodology

The instrument used for describing the pax demand distribution is the kernel distribution, which is a nonparametric technique to estimate the density function of a random variable by smoothing the data using a bandwidth that controls the smoothness.

The bootstrap methodology is applied to analyze the power to capture the behaviour of pax demand in the airline industry and it is compared to the pax demand kernel distribution. The methodology is explained as follows:

The bootstrap, as defined by [7], is a simulation method that can be used for statistical inference purposes, for example, for estimating the mean pax demand or the median pax demand. The method is based on a simulation of the real distribution of the data by randomly sampling, with replacement, the original data.

Suppose that we have independent and identically distributed observations $Pax = (Pax_1, ..., Pax_n)$ with an unknown probability distribution function F.

$$Pax_1, ..., Pax_n \sim F \qquad (1)$$

The empirical distribution function is defined as the cumulative distribution function that mass $(1/n)$ at each data point (Pax_i):

$$\hat{F}(Pax) = \frac{1}{n} \sum_{i=1}^{n} I(Pax_i \leq Pax) \qquad (2)$$

Where:

I	= the indicator function	[-]
n	= sample size	[-]

The bootstrap considers that the real distribution of the pax demand, F, can be approximated by the distribution $\hat{F}$.

The bootstrap methodology, is a computer based method, which depends on the concept of bootstrap sample A bootstrap sample $Pax^* = (Pax_1^*, ..., Pax_n^*)$ is defined as a random sample of size n drawn with replacement from the original data: $Pax = (Pax_1, ..., Pax_n)$.

$$Pax_1^*, ..., Pax_n^* \sim \hat{F} \qquad (3)$$

This processes is repeated B times for creating B bootstrap samples.

The interest is forecasting specific statistics, the mean pax demand, $\mu(F)$, and the median pax demand, $\mu e(F)$. For this purpose, in each bootstrap sample B, an estimation of the mean pax demand and the median pax demand are calculated, named respectively, bootstrap mean pax demand, $\mu^*(\hat{F})$ and bootstrap median pax demand, $\mu e^*(\hat{F})$. Finally, obtaining B values for each measure:

$$\mu^*(\hat{F}) = (\mu_1^*, ..., \mu_B^*) \qquad (4)$$

$$\mu e^*(\hat{F}) = (\mu e_1^*, ..., \mu e_B^*) \qquad (5)$$

With this results, a distribution function for $\mu^*(\hat{F})$, and for $\mu e^*(\hat{F})$ can be constructed.

$$\mu_1^*, ..., \mu_B^* \sim \hat{F}_\mu \qquad (6)$$

$$\mu e_1^*, ..., \mu e_B^* \sim \hat{F}_{\mu e} \qquad (7)$$

3.2   Confidence Bands Methods

The bootstrap replicates of the mean pax demand and the median pax demand simulates its distribution function. The objective is to calculate nonparametric confidence
bands for these measures.

Let us assume that $\hat{F}_\mu(Pax)$ represents the cumulative bootstrap distribution function for the mean pax demand and, $\hat{F}_{\mu e}(Pax)$ represents the cumulative bootstrap
distribution function for the median pax demand.

In this paper, the BC_a method is implemented for calculating bootstrap confidence
bands [8].

3.2.1   The Bias Corrected Accelerated Method (BCa)

[8] Improve the performance of the BC method by using a bias constant z_0 and also
some acceleration constant α. The $1 - 2\alpha$ confidence band is calculated as follows:

$$\mu \in \left(\hat{\mu}^*(\alpha_1), \hat{\mu}^*(\alpha_2)\right) \tag{8}$$

Where:

$$\alpha_1 = \left(\hat{z}_0 + \frac{\hat{z}_0 + z_\alpha}{1 - \hat{\alpha}(\hat{z}_0 + z_\alpha)}\right) \tag{9}$$

$$\alpha_2 = \left(\hat{z}_0 + \frac{\hat{z}_0 + z_{1-\alpha}}{1 - \hat{\alpha}(\hat{z}_0 + z_{1-\alpha})}\right) \tag{10}$$

$$z_0 = \Phi^{-1}\left(\hat{F}_\mu(Pax)\right) \tag{11}$$

$\Phi(x)$ is the distribution function of a Normal random variable x.

An estimation of the acceleration α is given in terms of a resampling technique
named jackknife developed by [13, 14]. Assume that $Pax_{(i)}$ is the original data with
the ith point deleted, let $\mu_{(i)}^*(\hat{F})$ be the bootstrap mean pax demand for these data.

The jackknife estimate of α is given by

$$\hat{\alpha} = \frac{\sum_{i=1}^n \left(\mu_{(.)}^*(\hat{F}) - \mu_{(i)}^*(\hat{F})\right)^3}{6\left(\sum_{i=1}^n \left(\mu_{(.)}^*(\hat{F}) - \mu_{(i)}^*(\hat{F})\right)^2\right)^{3/2}} \tag{12}$$

Where:

$$\mu_{(.)}^*(\hat{F}) = \frac{\sum_{i=1}^n \mu_{(i)}^*(\hat{F})}{n} \tag{13}$$

Similar calculations are used for the bootstrap median pax demand.

4   Empirical Application and Monte Carlo Experiments

4.1   Experimental Data

The Airline Fares Consumer Report has been published annually by the US Department of Transportation Office of Aviation Analysis. The data includes information of approximately 18,000 routes operated by US airlines inside the United States. Only those carriers with a 10% or greater market share are listed. The reports include non-directional market passenger numbers, revenue, nonstop and track mileage broken down by competitors. In this study, only the total number of passenger demand data is used, and it is calculated for each route connecting two cities. The pax demand data is organized by distance block and divided into full service carriers (FSC) and low cost carriers (LCC) because of the purpose of analyzing with an airline business model. As a consequence, data is integrated into eight different distance block. The first distance block goes from 0 to 250km; the second distance block goes from 250 to 500km; the third distance block goes from 500 to 750km; the fourth distance block goes from 750 to 1000km; the fifth distance block goes from 1000 to 1500km; the sixth distance block goes from 1500 to 2000km; the seventh distance block goes from 2000 to 2500km; and the last distance block includes greater than 2500km. This paper uses the data from 2007, and the proposed approach is validated comparing these results with data from 2008.

4.2   Pax Demand Distribution per Distance Block

First, we analyze the distribution of the pax demand to estimate the mean pax demand and the median pax demand. Figure 1 and Figure 2 show the kernel distribution for pax demand per distance block. In both figures, we observe that the distributions are right bias for all distance block. Nevertheless, the right bias is less pronounced in the first, second and third blocks distance, meaning that pax demand is more scattered in comparison with the other distance blocks. For the other blocks, the pax demand is more cumulative to the left side of their distributions, but there exist positive probability to forecast high pax demand values.

Figure 1 and Figure 2 demonstrate the error of forecasting the mean which only forecasts symmetric information. An alternative measure is the median, which divides the distribution exactly in the fifty percent accumulated data. Therefore, this paper proposes to forecast the pax demand based on the median pax demand.

Figure 3 and Figure 4 demonstrate that the distance blocks distribution is properly simulated by the bootstrap estimation method. What more, the bootstrap distribution captures the right bias of the pax demand what proves the ability of this method to simulate the real distribution function.

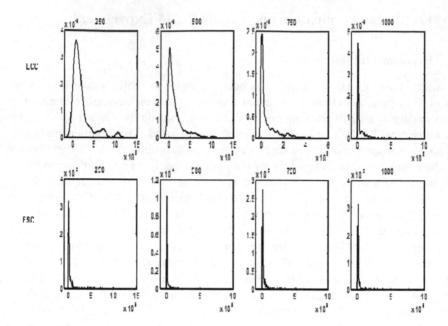

Fig. 1. Kernel distribution for pax demand

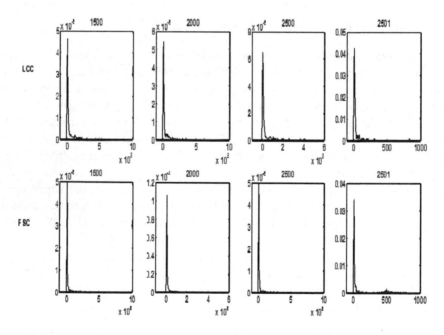

Fig. 2. Kernel distribution for pax demand

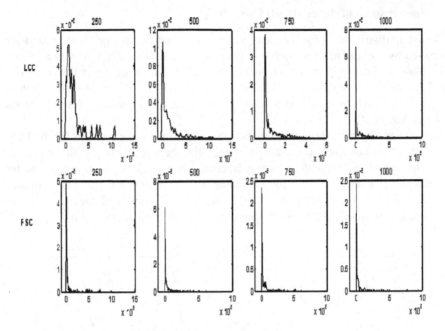

Fig. 3. Bootstrap distribution for pax demand

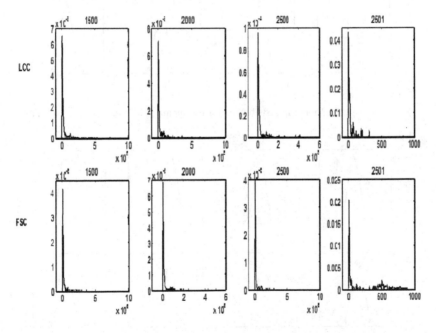

Fig. 4. Bootstrap distribution for pax demand

4.3   Bootstrap Confidence Bands Using BC$_a$

The bootstrap distributions for the mean pax demand and the median pax demand are constructed by simulating B = 1000 bootstrap replicates. For each bootstrap replicate we calculate the bootstrap mean pax demand and bootstrap median pax demand, with these 1000 bootstrap means and medians pax demand the bootstrap distribution is constructed for each measure. This procedure is performed for each distance block and airline business type.

Figure 5 and Figure 6 show the distribution for the mean pax demand for the LCC and FSC airlines. The line represents the normal distribution function with the respective confidence band. The dotted line represents the bootstrap distribution function for the mean pax demand with the corresponding BC$_a$ confidence band. These figures proves that the normal distributions fit the bootstrap distributions function and the confidence bands are equal for all distance block and for both airline business types.

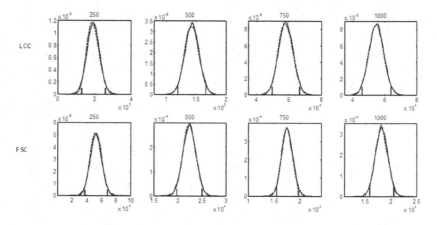

Fig. 5. Bootstrap distribution for the mean pax demand

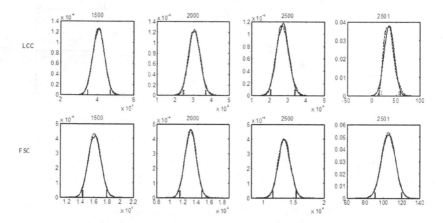

Fig. 6. Bootstrap distribution for the mean pax demand

Figure 7 and Figure 8 show the distribution for the median pax demand for the LCC and FSC airlines. The line represents the normal distribution function with the respective confidence band. The dotted line represents the bootstrap distribution function for the median pax demand with the corresponding BC_a confidence band. LCC airlines bootstrap distribution is leptokurtic as it is shown in the first four bocks distance (Figure 7) what is opposite to the normal distribution function which is flatter. Therefore, higher probability exists for some points with the bootstrap distribution in comparison with the normal distribution. Thus, confidence bands are shorter with the bootstrap distribution than with the normal distribution what allows taking decisions based on confidence bands with short width. Figure 7 shows that for the first four blocks for FSC airlines, the bootstrap distribution function is even more leptokurtic than in the LCC airlines cases. The results prove that the normal distributions do not represent the behavior of the distribution for the median pax demand.

Figure 8 shows the behavior of the last four distance block for both airline business models. The behavior is similar for both airline business models. These results are consistent with the behavior of the airline industry because the unit operation cost is minimized as distance growths, then LCC airlines are less competitive against the FSC airlines because both achieve similar operations cost. It is the reason why low cost long-haul airlines are difficult to operate [3].

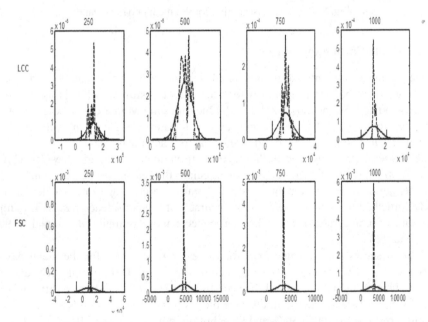

Fig. 7. Bootstrap distribution for the median pax demand

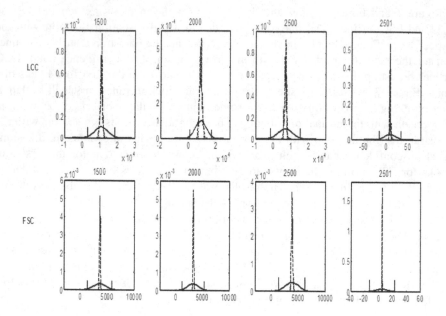

Fig. 8. Bootstrap distribution for the median pax demand

4.4   Monte Carlo Experiments

Monte Carlo experiments are implemented to analyze the finite sample performance of the proposed bootstrap approach for constructing estimation bands for the mean pax demand and the median pax demand. One thousand Monte Carlo experiments are generated for B = 1000 bootstrap replicates which mean one million experiments are evaluated. The result is 1000 confidence bands for each measure.

The experiments presented in this section are validated comparing results with the DOT 2008 data [6], this data is used to calculate the real mean pax demand and the real median pax demand for this particular year. The coverage rate is calculated for the BC_a method to validate the forecast accuracy of the confidence bands. The aim is to obtain coverage rates near to the confidence bands nominal value equal to 90%, 95%, and 99%.

Table 1 shows the coverage rates for the estimation bands for the mean pax demand using the BC_a methods. The BC_a method covers the 100% for the LCC and FSC airline business models in the all distance blocks. The BC_a method slightly overestimate for the coverage rate for all distance blocks (confidence intervals calculated with a confidence level of 90%, 95% and 99% but the coverage rate is 100% in all cases). The confidence bands calculated with the bootstrap approach and using the BC_a method provides an accurate forecast because the real mean pax demand of 2008 is included in the confidence bands for a number B of bootstrap replicates, what means all confidence bands contain the real values of the mean pax demand per distance block for 2008 data [6]. Therefore, the bootstrap approach presented in this paper appears to be an accurate method for forecasting the mean pax demand for the case of the US air transport industry.

Table 1 also presents the bootstrap confidence bands width for the mean pax demand in thousands. The results show that FSC bootstrap confidence bands width are narrower than LCC bootstrap confidence bands width. It is because the LCC mean pax demand is greater than FSC mean pax demand in those routes where both business models operate for all block route distances. It means LCC move in average more paxs than FSC per route. However, the number of FSC routes is greater than the number of LCC routes. Therefore, FSC transport more paxs than LCC in total for the case of the US air transport industry.

Table 1. Monte Carlo experiments for the mean pax demand

Block	90% Estimation intervals coverage rates and width for mean pax demand							
	250	500	750	1000	1500	2000	2500	2501
LCC	100%	100%	100%	100%	100%	100%	100%	100%
LCC width	115.75	39.27	14.37	15.05	10.35	10.75	11.41	18.18
FSC	100%	100%	100%	100%	100%	100%	100%	100%
FSC width	25.73	4.49	3.53	3.95	3.01	2.84	3.26	3.65
Block	95% Estimation intervals coverage rates and width for mean pax demand							
	250	500	750	1000	1500	2000	2500	2501
LCC	100%	100%	100%	100%	100%	100%	100%	100%
LCC width	138.26	46.52	17.06	17.81	12.13	12.50	13.23	20.31
FSC	100%	100%	100%	100%	100%	100%	100%	100%
FSC width	31.05	5.25	4.09	4.69	3.58	3.34	3.82	4.35
Block	99% Estimation intervals coverage rates and width for mean pax demand							
	250	500	750	1000	1500	2000	2500	2501
LCC	100%	100%	100%	100%	100%	100%	100%	100%
LCC width	185.08	61.05	22.68	23.70	16.21	16.90	18.56	30.12
FSC	100%	100%	100%	100%	100%	100%	100%	100%
FSC width	40.84	7.02	5.57	6.32	4.82	4.46	5.15	5.77

Table 2 shows the coverage rates for the estimation bands for the median pax demand using the BC_a method described in Section 3. The BC_a method covers the 100% for the LCC and FSC airline business models for all distance blocks. As it happens for the mean pax demand, in the case of the median pax demand, the BC_a method slightly overestimates for all distance blocks. The confidence bands calculated with the approach proposed in this paper using the BC_a method provides an accurate forecast because 100% of the confidence bands contain the real values of the median pax demand per distance block for 2008 data [6].

Table 2 also presents the bootstrap confidence bands width for the median pax demand. The results show that FSC bootstrap confidence bands width are narrower than LCC bootstrap confidence bands. Hence, FSC transport more paxs than LCC in total and this is consistent with the results shown in Table 1.

The bootstrap confidence bands calculated for the mean pax demand are wider than those for the median pax demand using the three confidence levels meaning that the uncertainty with respect to the real median pax demand is minimized. Therefore, for forecasting the air pax demand it is better to use the bootstrap distribution for the median pax demand and BCa method for constructing bootstrap confidence bands.

Table 2. Monte Carlo experiments for the median pax demand

Block	90% Estimation intervals coverage rates and width for median pax demand							
	250	**500**	**750**	**1000**	**1500**	**2000**	**2500**	**2501**
LCC	100%	100%	100%	100%	100%	100%	100%	100%
LCC width	84.72	34.86	8.52	4.09	2.26	3.61	1.74	4.18
FSC	100%	100%	100%	100%	100%	100%	100%	100%
FSC width	3.49	0.61	0.30	0.31	0.30	0.26	0.42	0.45
Block	95% Estimation intervals coverage rates and width for median pax demand							
	250	**500**	**750**	**1000**	**1500**	**2000**	**2500**	**2501**
LCC	100%	100%	100%	100%	100%	100%	100%	100%
LCC width	95.22	36.81	9.88	5.00	2.95	4.13	2.21	4.98
FSC	100%	100%	100%	100%	100%	100%	100%	100%
FSC width	3.73	0.72	0.35	0.39	0.34	0.31	0.50	5.05
Block	99% Estimation intervals coverage rates and width for median pax demand							
	250	**500**	**750**	**1000**	**1500**	**2000**	**2500**	**2501**
LCC	100%	100%	100%	100%	100%	100%	100%	100%
LCC width	111.35	54.53	14.32	8.06	3.70	5.06	2.97	7.65
FSC	100%	100%	100%	100%	100%	100%	100%	100%
FSC width	5.24	0.95	0.44	0.51	0.45	0.41	0.65	0.60

5   Conclusions

The pax demand real distribution is right bias according with the kernel distribution function from the [6] data. Therefore, this paper results demonstrates the importance of estimating the median pax demand instead of the mean pax demand. The implementation of bootstrap procedures to estimate the distribution of the mean pax demand and the median pax demand allows making statistical inference of these parameters. The main contribution of this paper is using the BC_a method to calculate bootstrap confidence bands for the mean pax demand and the median pax demand for the first time. Finally, this paper demonstrates, by carrying out Monte Carlo experiments, the forecast accuracy of the bootstrap confidence bands using the BC_a method. Even when the coverage rates for the estimation bands for the mean and the median pax demand using the BC_a method are 100% accurate, bootstrap confidence bands are shorter for the median pax demand than for the mean pax demand, which is an advantage when forecasting because it is better to take decisions based on bootstrap confidence bands with narrow width, and the uncertainty with respect to the real median pax demand is minimized

References

1. Alekseev, K.P.G., Seixas, J.M.: Forecasting the air transport demand for passengers with Neural Modelling. In: The VII Brazilian Symposium on Neural Networks IEEE Computer Society Washington, Recife, Brazil, pp. 86–91 (2002)
2. Beckmann, M.J., Bobkoski, F.: Airline demand: An analysis of some frequency distributions. Naval research logistics quarterly **5**(1), 43–51 (1958)

3. Carmona-Benitez, R.B.: The design of a large scale airline network (PhD Dissertation). Delft University of Technology, The Netherlands: TRAIL Research School, pp. 81–106 (2012)
4. Carmona-Benitez, R.B., Carmona-Paredes, R.B., Lodewijks, G., Nabais, J.L.: Damp trend Grey Model forecasting method for airline industry. Expert System with Applications **40**(12), 4915–4921 (2013)
5. Coldren, G.M., Koppelman, F.S., Kasturirangan, K., Mukherjee, A.: Modelling aggregate air travel itinerary shares: logit model development at a major US airline. Journal of Air Transport Management **9**(6), 841–851 (2003)
6. DOT US Department of Transportation: Domestic Airline Fare Consumer Report (2005–2008). http://ostpxweb.dot.gov/aviation/X-50%20Role_files/airportcompdefinition.htm (cited 26/02/2011)
7. Efron, B.: Bootstrap methods: another look at the jackknife. Annals of Statistics **7**, 1–26 (1979)
8. Efron, B.: Better bootstrap with dense intervals (with discussion). Journal of the American Statistical Association **82**, 171–200 (1987)
9. Grosche, T., Rothlauf, F., Heinzl, A.: Gravity models for airline passenger volume estimation. Journal of Air Transport Management **13**, 175–183 (2007)
10. Hsu, C.I., Wen, Y.H.: Application of Grey theory and multi objective programming towards airline network design. European journal of operation research **127**(1), 44–68 (2000)
11. Hsu, C.I., Wen, Y.H.: Reliability evolution for airline network design in response to fluctuation in passenger demand. Omega – The International Journal of Management Science **30**(3), 197–213 (2002)
12. IATA: Successful Vision 2050 Meeting Concludes – Building a Sustainable Future (2011b). http://www.iata.org/pressroom/pr/pages/2011-02-14-01.aspx (cited 22/08/2011)
13. Quenouille, M.H.: Problems in Plane Sampling. The Annals of Mathematical Statistics **20**(3), 355–375 (1949)
14. Quenouille, M.H.: Notes on Bias in Estimation. Biometrika **43**(3–4), 353–360 (1956)
15. Shaw, R.: Forecasting air traffic: are there limits to growth? Futures **11**(3), 185–194 (1979)
16. Shen, G.: Reverse-fitting the gravity model to inter-city airline passenger flows by an algebraic simplification. Journal of Transport Geography **16**(4), 213–217 (2004)
17. Swan, M.: A System Analysis of Schedule Air Transportation Networks. Report FTL-R79-5. MIT, Cambridge (1979)
18. Wei, Z., Jinfu, Z.: Passenger traffic forecast based on the Grey-Markov method. In: IEEE International Conference on Grey Systems, pp. 630–633 (2009)
19. Zeni, R.H.: Improved forecast accuracy in revenue management by unconstraining demand estimates from censored data, in: Dissertation.com, PhD in management program, New Jersey, United States of America (2001)

On a Pooling Problem with Fixed Network Size

Dag Haugland[1]([✉]) and Eligius M.T. Hendrix[2]

[1] Department of Informatics, University of Bergen, Bergen, Norway
dag.haugland@ii.uib.no
[2] Computer Architecture, Universidad de Málaga, Málaga, Spain
Eligius@uma.es

Abstract. The computational challenge offered by most traditional network flow models is modest, and large scale instances can be solved fast. The challenge becomes more serious if the composition of the flow has to be taken into account. This is in particular true for the pooling problem, where the relative content of certain flow components is restricted. Flow entering the network at the source nodes has a given composition, whereas the composition in other nodes is determined by the composition of entering flows. At the network terminals, the flow composition is subject to restrictions. The pooling problem is strongly NP-hard. It was recently shown that at least weak NP-hardness persists in an instance class with only two sources and terminals, and one flow component subject to restrictions. Such instances were also shown to be solvable in pseudo-polynomial time if a particular fixed-size instance class, called atomic instances, can be solved in terms of a constant number of arithmetic operations. This work proves existence of such a closed-form solution to atomic instances.

Keywords: Pooling problem · Complexity · Global optimization · Network flow

1 Introduction

In many industrial and logistics applications of network flow models, including petroleum refining and pipeline transportation of natural gas, the composition of the flow is not homogeneous across the network. Crude oils supplied to a refinery have contamination levels depending on their sources of origin. Major components of natural gas are methane, ethane, butane and propane, but the proportions in which they occur are not equal for all gas wells. For environmental or technical reasons, constraints on the final composition are often imposed at the terminal nodes of the flow network. It is therefore essential for network flow models to recognize not only the product flow, but also how the flow composition

The work of the second author has been funded by grants from the Spanish Ministry of Science and Innovation (TIN2008-01117,TIN2012-37483), and Junta de Andalucía (P11-TIC-7176), in part financed by the European Regional Development Fund (ERDF).

© Springer International Publishing Switzerland 2015
F. Corman et al. (Eds.): ICCL 2015, LNCS 9335, pp. 328–342, 2015.
DOI: 10.1007/978-3-319-24264-4_23

evolves from network sources to terminals. In particular, the models must reflect updates of the composition at nodes where differently composed flows are pooled. This implies a computationally challenging problem referred to as the *pooling problem*.

The pooling problem exhibits strong resemblance with well-studied logistics models like the minimum cost flow problem. Another classical related problem is Stigler's diet problem [7,17], which asks for the minimum cost diet requiring a certain amount of specified nutrients. The problem is easy to extend to a multi-diet version where groups of people have each their own requirements. Nutritional contents differ between sources, that is, the various foods of which diets can be composed, and the optimal mix must be found for each terminal (group of people). Conceptually, the multi-diet version coincides with the pooling problem in bipartite networks. Thanks to this simple network structure, with exclusively direct links between sources and terminals, diet problems are nothing but linear programs (LPs). However, when extending the problem to more general network structures, this is no longer the case.

Standard pooling problems are defined for networks with three layers of nodes. Between source and terminal nodes, there is a layer of nodes referred to as *pools*. Even for networks with only one pool, the problem is strongly NP-hard [2]. The computational complexity is more favorable if there are more limitations on the number of nodes. Polynomial time algorithms have been developed for the case of a unique pool and an additional bound on either the number of terminals [12] or the number of sources [13]. Because of the intractability of the general problem, mainly heuristic approaches [5,9,14] have been applied to large instances. Most of them are based on linearization, which appears natural as the problem is an LP if the flow composition is known in every node.

Floudas and Visweswaran [10] reported the first exact solution algorithm for the pooling problem. Later, algorithms based on branch-and-bound [4,11, 16,18,19], Lagrangian relaxation [1,3,6] and integer programming [8] have been studied. The pooling problem survey by Misener and Floudas [15] has a comprehensive list of references to work in this area.

The pooling problem remains NP-hard for networks with only two sources and two terminals, and only one flow component subject to constraints [12]. A recent study [13] analyses a dynamic programming (DP) algorithm for such instances. It concludes that the algorithm runs in pseudo-polynomial time if a special class of fixed-size instances, referred to as atomic instances, can be solved in terms of a constant number of comparisons and arithmetic operations on rational numbers. Pseudo-polynomiality means that the running time is bounded by a polynomial in the numerical values of the input data, but it might be exponential in the instance size. This is a weaker condition than polynomiality, which requires running time bounded by a polynomial in the number of binary digits needed to represent the input. The contribution from the current work is a proof of the desired tractability of atomic instances, concluding pseudo-polynomial running time of the DP-algorithm. In the next section, we introduce notation used, and present a mathematical formulation of the pooling problem.

In Section 3, the DP-algorithm is briefly reviewed, and a closed-form solution to atomic instances is derived in Section 4.

2   Mathematical Formulation of the Pooling Problem

In this section, we describe the pooling problem in graph notation, where costs and returns are on the nodes of the graph. We restrict the attention to cases where only one flow component is subject to constraints. The relative content of this component is referred to as the *quality* of the flow. Let $D = (S, P, T, \mathcal{A})$ be a digraph, where the disjoint node sets S, P, and T consist of *sources*, *pools* and *terminals*, respectively, and the arc set $\mathcal{A} \subseteq (S \times P) \cup (P \times T)$ links sources with pools and pools with terminals. Let $S_p = \{s \in S : (s, p) \in \mathcal{A}\}$ denote the set of neighbor source nodes of pool $p \in P$, and define analogously $T_p = \{t \in T : (p, t) \in \mathcal{A}\}$, $P_s = \{p \in P : (s, p) \in \mathcal{A}\}$ for $s \in S$, and $P_t = \{p \in P : (p, t) \in \mathcal{A}\}$ for $t \in T$.

The following data are associated with the network: Let $c_i \in \mathbb{Q}$ be the unit cost of in/out flow of node $i \in S \cup T$, $b_i \in \mathbb{Q}$ the capacity at node $i \in S \cup P \cup T$, $q_s \in \mathbb{Q}$ the quality at source $s \in S$, and let $u_t \in \mathbb{Q}$ be the upper quality bound at terminal $t \in T$. We assume that not all qualities q_s are equal.

To formulate the problem as a bilinear program, we define the continuous variables x_{ij} as the flow along arc $(i, j) \in \mathcal{A}$, and w_p as the quality in pool $p \in P$. This yields the model:

$$\zeta(D) = \min_{x, w} \sum_{s \in S} c_s \sum_{p \in P_s} x_{sp} + \sum_{t \in T} c_t \sum_{p \in P_t} x_{pt}, \tag{1}$$

$$\text{s.t.} \qquad \sum_{p \in P_s} x_{sp} \leq b_s \qquad\qquad s \in S, \tag{2}$$

$$\sum_{p \in P_t} x_{pt} \leq b_t \qquad\qquad t \in T, \tag{3}$$

$$\sum_{s \in S_p} x_{sp} = \sum_{t \in T_p} x_{pt} \leq b_p \qquad p \in P, \tag{4}$$

$$\sum_{s \in S_p} q_s x_{sp} - w_p \sum_{t \in T_p} x_{pt} = 0 \qquad p \in P, \tag{5}$$

$$\sum_{p \in P_t} w_p x_{pt} - u_t \sum_{p \in P_t} x_{pt} \leq 0 \qquad t \in T, \tag{6}$$

$$x_{ij} \geq 0 \qquad\qquad (i, j) \in \mathcal{A}, \tag{7}$$

where (2)–(3) are capacity constraints at sources and terminals, respectively, (4) are capacity and flow conservation constraints at pools, (5) ensure that w_p equals the quality of the blend in pool p, and (6) are quality constraints at terminals.

In the more general multi-quality version of the problem, each of the vectors q and u are defined for a set of quality parameters (flow components). The quality variables are indexed over the same set, and so are constraints (5)–(6).

3   A DP-Algorithm for Instances with Two Sources and Terminals

Recent studies [12,13] of the complexity of the pooling problem analyze the instance class with $|S| = |T| = 2$. While a reduction from a bin packing problem shows that the pooling problem remains at least weakly NP-hard when

$|S| = |T| = 2$ [12], instances with either $|S| = 1$ or $|T| = 1$ can be solved in poly-nomial time by linear programming. With respect to $|S| + |T|$, networks in the class under study are thus probably at minimum for NP-hard instance classes.

Henceforth, we associate network nodes with integers. We let $S = \{0, 1\}$, and for reasons to become clear later, we let $T = \{7, 8\}$. For any flow in D, we let $(J_2, \ldots, J_6)$ be a partition of P such that all $p \in J_2$ (all $p \in J_6$) receive zero flow from source 1 (source 0), and such that all $p \in J_3$ (all $p \in J_5$) send zero flow to terminal 8 (terminal 7). Ties are broken arbitrarily. Pools in J_4 receive positive flow from both sources and send positive flow to both terminals. The following propositions (see [13] for proofs) lead to a DP-algorithm:

Proposition 1. *If $|S| = |T| = 2$, (1)–(7) has an optimal flow for which $|J_4| \leq 1$.*

Proposition 2. *Let $|S| = |T| = 2$, and let the pool partition $(J_2, \ldots, J_6)$ cor-respond to an optimal flow and satisfy $|J_4| \leq 1$. Then $\zeta(D) = \zeta(\bar{D})$, where $\bar{D} = (S, \bar{P}, T, \bar{A})$ is the digraph with S, T, c, q and u defined as in the origi-nal problem, $\bar{P} = \{2, \ldots, 6\}$, node capacities $\bar{b}_k = \sum_{p \in J_k} b_p$ ($k = 2, \ldots, 6$) and $\bar{b}_i = b_i$ ($i \in S \cup T$), and arcs $\bar{A}$ defined such that nodes 0, 1, 7, and 8 have neighbor pools $\bar{P}_0 = \bar{P} \setminus \{6\}$, $\bar{P}_1 = \bar{P} \setminus \{2\}$, $\bar{P}_7 = \bar{P} \setminus \{5\}$, and $\bar{P}_8 = \bar{P} \setminus \{3\}$, respectively.*

The instance with fixed-size network $\bar{D}$ (see Fig. 1) is henceforth referred to as an *atomic* instance. According to its definition, it consists of the same sources and terminals as the original network, whereas all pools in J_k ($k = 2, \ldots, 6$) are aggregated into a joint pool with capacity equal to the total pool capacity in J_k. Consistently with the definition of J_k ($k \neq 4$), exactly one node in $S \cup T$ is a non-neighbor of the corresponding atomic pool. Propositions 1–2 show that in instances with $|S| = |T| = 2$, $\zeta(D) = \min_{J_2,\ldots,J_5} \zeta(\bar{D})$, where minimization is defined over all partitions of P where $|J_4| \leq 1$.

A DP-algorithm is suitable for optimizing the partition. Denote the original pools by $P = \{p_1, \ldots, p_m\}$, where $m = |P|$. At stage $n = 1, \ldots, m, m + 1$ of the DP, each pool $p_1, \ldots, p_{n-1}$ has been assigned to some set J_k, whereas

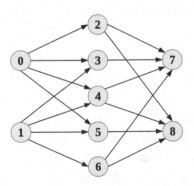

Fig. 1. Atomic instance

pools $p_n, \ldots, p_m$ are left to be assigned. The state variable is the capacity vector $\bar{b} \in \mathbb{Q}^5$, where $\bar{b}_k$ is the total capacity currently assigned to J_k.

The cost function $z_n(\bar{b})$ represents the minimum obtainable cost given state $\bar{b}$ at stage n. At stage $m+1$, all pools are allocated, and $z_{m+1}(\bar{b}) = \zeta(\bar{D})$ with pool capacities $\bar{b}$ in $\bar{D}$. The assignment of p_n made at stage $n \le m$, is represented by a unit vector in the feasible set

$$E(\bar{b}) = \left\{ e = (e_2, \ldots, e_6) \in \{0,1\}^5, \sum_{k=2}^{6} e_k = 1, e_4 = 0 \text{ if } \bar{b}_4 > 0 \right\}.$$

With $z_1(0)$ equal to the minimum cost in (1)–(7), optimizing the assignment yields the backward recursion formula ($n = 1, \ldots, m$):

$$z_n(\bar{b}) = \min_{\bar{b} \in E(\bar{b})} z_{n+1}(\bar{b} + b_{p_n} e). \tag{8}$$

It is straightforward to derive a DP-algorithm from (8). A running time analysis [13] shows that such an algorithm computes $z_1(0)$ in $\mathcal{O}\left((\tau + |P|) \left(\sum_{p \in P} b_p \right)^4 \right)$ time, where τ is the time required to solve an atomic instance. Dependency on $\sum_{p \in P} b_p$ shows that the running time is not polynomial. If $\zeta(\bar{D})$ can be computed in terms of a *constant number of elementary operations* on rationals, then τ increases linearly with the number of binary digits needed to code the input data $(\bar{D}, c, q, u, \bar{b})$. This is because the running time of each arithmetic operation is proportional to the lengths of the bit strings of the operands. It then follows that τ is bounded by a logarithmic function of the numerical values of the input data, and, consequently, that the DP-algorithm runs in pseudo-polynomial time.

In the remainder of the text, we prove that atomic instances are tractable in the above sense if some mild assumptions on the costs are satisfied. The above discussion then implies that the class of instances where $|S| = |T| = 2$, $|P|$ is arbitrary, and the cost assumptions hold, is solvable in pseudo-polynomial time.

4   Solving Atomic Instances by a Constant Number of Operations

Without loss of generality [12], let $q_0 = 0$ and $q_1 = 1$. From the definition of atomic instances, the following formulation is then derived: $\zeta(\bar{D}) =$

$$\min_{x,w} \quad c_0 x_{04} + c_1 x_{14} + c_7 x_{47} + c_8 x_{48} + (c_0 + c_7)(x_{03} + x_{27}) +$$
$$(c_0 + c_8)(x_{05} + x_{28}) + (c_1 + c_7)(x_{13} + x_{67}) + (c_1 + c_8)(x_{15} + x_{68}), \tag{9}$$
$$x_{03} + x_{04} + x_{05} + x_{27} + x_{28} \le \bar{b}_0, \quad x_{13} + x_{14} + x_{15} + x_{67} + x_{68} \le \bar{b}_1, \tag{10}$$
$$x_{27} + x_{28} \le \bar{b}_2, x_{03} + x_{13} \le \bar{b}_3, x_{04} + x_{14} \le \bar{b}_4, x_{05} + x_{15} \le \bar{b}_5, x_{67} + x_{68} \le \bar{b}_6, \tag{11}$$
$$x_{03} + x_{13} + x_{27} + x_{47} + x_{67} \le \bar{b}_7, \quad x_{05} + x_{15} + x_{28} + x_{48} + x_{68} \le \bar{b}_8, \tag{12}$$
$$x_{13} + x_{67} + w_4 x_{47} - u_7(x_{03} + x_{13} + x_{27} + x_{47} + x_{67}) \le 0, \tag{13}$$
$$x_{15} + x_{68} + w_4 x_{48} - u_8(x_{05} + x_{15} + x_{28} + x_{48} + x_{68}) \le 0, \tag{14}$$

$$x_{04} + x_{14} - x_{47} - x_{48} = 0, \tag{15}$$
$$x_{14} - (x_{47} + x_{48})w_4 = 0, \tag{16}$$
$$x_{03}, x_{04}, x_{05}, x_{13}, x_{14}, x_{15}, x_{27}, x_{28}, x_{47}, x_{48}, x_{67}, x_{68} \geq 0. \tag{17}$$

In this section, we demonstrate how (9)–(17) is solved in terms of a constant number of comparisons and arithmetic operations. To this end, it is crucial to avoid computations of roots of higher order (quintic) algebraic equations, since no general closed-form solution exists.

4.1   Assumptions

A pooling problem instance with $\min\{|S_p|, |T_p|\} = 1$ for all $p \in P$ can be formulated as an LP [12]. This means that if $J_4 = \emptyset$, the corresponding atomic instance is an LP with constant size, and is obviously solvable in terms of a constant number of operations. We exclude such simple instances from further consideration, and assume that all partitions $(J_2, \ldots, J_6)$ corresponding to optimal flows in D satisfy $|J_4| = 1$. Consequently, it is henceforth assumed that all optimal flows in $\bar{D}$ satisfy $x_{04}, x_{14}, x_{47}, x_{48} > 0$.

Let the quality bounds u_7 and u_8 fulfill $0 \leq u_7 \leq u_8 \leq 1$. Flow quality can be thought of as a contamination level, meaning that sources 0 and 1 are perfectly clean ($q_0 = 0$) and fully contaminated ($q_1 = 1$), respectively. The following cost assumptions are made: The market value of the flow is increasing with decreasing contamination. Purchasing is therefore more expensive at source 0 than at source 1, implying $c_0 > c_1$, and sales prices at terminal 7 are higher than at terminal 8, i.e. $c_7 < c_8$. Further, the purchase cost c_0 at source 0 is larger than the sales price $-c_8$ at terminal 8 ($c_0 + c_8 > 0$), which means that it is not profitable to produce the poor quality product at 8 exclusively from the good quality supply at 0. Finally, both terminals are *profitable*, i.e. $(1 - u_t)c_0 + u_t c_1 + c_t < 0, t = 7, 8$, meaning that flow satisfying the quality specifications with zero slack gives positive profit. A non-profitable terminal can be excluded from consideration, and the problem reduces to an LP.

4.2   Augmenting Paths and Cycles

In the following, we consider paths and cycles in $\bar{D}$ where traversal of arcs in their reverse direction is allowed. The underpinning idea is that in any optimal solution, there exists no path of forward and backward arcs along which flow can be augmented, such that feasibility is retained while costs are reduced. With respect to a current feasible flow, x, assigned to $\bar{D}$, we say that such a path or cycle is *flow augmenting* if it is feasible to increase the flow along it by some positive amount. Increasing the flow along a reverse arc (j, i) on a path is equivalent to reducing x_{ij} ($(i, j) \in \bar{A}$). Obviously, x is positive on all reverse arcs of a flow augmenting path. If (i, j) and (j, k) are consecutive forward arcs on a flow augmenting path or cycle, then $\sum_{\ell:(j,\ell) \subset \bar{A}} x_{j\ell} < \bar{b}_j$. If (i, j) is the last arc on the path, and $(i,j) \in \bar{A}$ ((i,j) is a forward arc), then $\sum_{\ell:(\ell,j)\in\bar{A}} x_{\ell j} < \bar{b}_j$. If (i,j) is the first arc on the path, and $(i,j) \in \bar{A}$, then $\sum_{\ell:(i,\ell)\in\bar{A}} x_{i\ell} < \bar{b}_i$.

Meeting the above requirements is not sufficient to qualify as a flow augmenting path or cycle. It also has to be verified that all quality constraints are satisfied after flow augmentation. For such verification, the following observations turn out to be useful:

Observation 1: Increasing flow from pools with better quality, while decreasing flow by the same amount from pools of poorer quality, improves the quality at a terminal.

Observation 2: Consider a path or cycle that does not intersect terminal $t \in T$. If a flow augmentation does not improve (deteriorate) the quality at any of the pools $p \in \bar{P}$ for which $x_{pt} > 0$, but deteriorates (improves) the quality at at least one such pool, then also the quality at t is deteriorated (improved).

Observation 3: A cyclic flow augmentation deteriorates the quality at terminal $t \in T$ if and only if it improves the quality at the other terminal $t' \neq t$.

It is straightforward to see that augmenting flow on a cycle leaves the total costs unchanged. The same does not hold for paths in general, and absence of flow augmenting paths with negative total cost is therefore a necessary optimality condition. More generally, if x is an optimal flow, then there cannot exist flow augmenting cycles that generate another (also optimal) flow, for which a flow augmenting path with negative cost exists. These observations are used extensively in the following derivations of stronger necessary optimality conditions.

4.3 Optimality Conditions on Flow in the Atomic Network

In the analysis to follow, we make frequent references to the qualities in nodes 4, 7, and 8, defined respectively as $w_4 = \frac{x_{14}}{x_{04}+x_{14}}$,

$$w_7 = \frac{x_{13} + w_4 x_{47} + x_{67}}{x_{27} + x_{03} + x_{13} + x_{47} + x_{67}}, \quad w_8 = \frac{x_{15} + w_4 x_{48} + x_{68}}{x_{28} + x_{48} + x_{05} + x_{15} + x_{68}}. \quad (18)$$

Lemma 1. *If $\bar{D}$ is assigned optimal flow, then $w_7 = u_7$.*

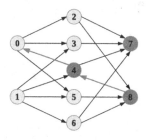

Fig. 2. Proving non-optimality of $w_7 < u_7$ and $w_8 < u_8$ (Lemma 1)

Proof. Assume first $w_7 < u_7$ and $w_8 < u_8$. Then $(8, 4, 0)$ (see Fig. 2) is a flow augmenting path with total cost $-c_0 - c_8 < 0$, contradicting optimality of the assigned flow.

Assume next that x is an optimal flow with $w_7 < u_7$ and $w_8 = u_8$. Because $w_7 < w_8$, there exists a pool $p \neq 4$ such that x is positive on either of the paths $(0, p, 7)$ and $(1, p, 8)$. Consequently, $\max\{x_{68}, x_{15}, x_{27}, x_{03}\} > 0$, implying that at least one of the cycles $(8, 6, 7, 4, 8)$, $(7, 2, 8, 4, 7)$, $(5, 1, 4, 0, 5)$, and $(3, 0, 4, 1, 3)$ (see Fig. 3) is flow augmenting. Continued fulfillment of the quality bound at terminal 8 follows from Observation 1 in the cases of $(8, 6, 7, 4, 8)$ and $(7, 2, 8, 4, 7)$, from Observation 2 with $t = 8$ in the case of $(3, 0, 4, 1, 3)$, and from Observation 2 ($t = 7$) combined with Observation 3 in the case of $(5, 1, 4, 0, 5)$.

Since the flow augmentation reduces w_8, there exists some optimal flow satisfying both quality bounds with strict inequality, contradicting the first part of the proof. $\square$

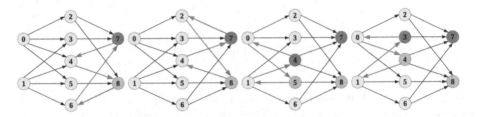

Fig. 3. Flow augmenting cycles (Lemma 1)

Lemma 2. *If x is an optimal flow in $\bar{D}$ such that $w_8 < u_8$, then $x_{02} = x_{27} = \bar{b}_2$, $x_{03} = x_{37} = \bar{b}_3$, $x_{15} = x_{58} = \bar{b}_5$, and $x_{16} = x_{68} = \bar{b}_6$.*

Proof. If $\max\{x_{05}, x_{28}, x_{13}, x_{67}\} > 0$, then the reverse of one of the cycles studied in the proof of Lemma 1 is flow augmenting. Because an augmentation along any of these cycles generates a quality $w_7 < u_7$, this is a contradiction of Lemma 1. Hence, $x_{05} = x_{28} = x_{13} = x_{67} = 0$, yielding $x_{02} = x_{27}$, $x_{03} = x_{37}$, $x_{15} = x_{58}$, and $x_{16} = x_{68}$.

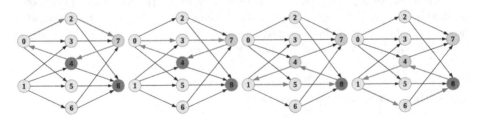

Fig. 4. Proof of Lemma 2

Assume $x_{27} < \bar{b}_2$. Then $(7, 4, 0, 2, 7)$ (see Fig. 4) is a flow augmenting cycle (see Observation 2 with $t = 8$ and Observation 3 with $t' = 7$) generating $w_7 < u_7$, contradicting Lemma 1. Consequently, $x_{02} = x_{27} = \bar{b}_2$.

By choosing the augmenting cycles (Fig. 4) $(7,4,0,3,7)$, $(8,4,1,5,8)$, and $(8,4,1,6,8)$, respectively, the remaining parts are proved analogously. □

Lemma 3. *There exists an optimal flow x in $\bar{D}$ such that either $x_{04} + x_{14} = \bar{b}_4$ or $x_{05} = x_{28} = x_{13} = x_{67} = 0$.*

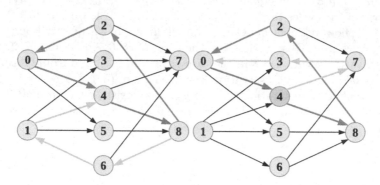

Fig. 5. Proof of Lemma 3

Proof. Assume x is an optimal flow such that $x_{04} + x_{14} < \bar{b}_4$ and $x_{28} > 0$. By Lemmata 1–2, $w_8 = u_8 \geq u_7 = w_7$. Thus, there exists a path $H = (s, p, t)$, along which x is positive, where either $(s, t) = (0, 7)$ or $(s, t) = (1, 8)$, and $p \neq 4$. Neither $C_1 = (8, 2, 0, 4, 8)$ nor $C_2 = (t, p, s, 4, t)$ is a flow augmenting cycle (see Fig. 5 for illustrations in the cases of $H = (1, 6, 8)$ and $H = (0, 3, 7)$). This is because flow augmentation along C_1 implies $w_7 < u_7$ and $w_8 > u_8$, while augmentation along C_2 implies $w_7 > u_7$ and $w_8 < u_8$. By choosing $\varepsilon > 0$ sufficiently small, and $\delta = \frac{x_{14}\varepsilon}{x_{04}}$ if $H = (1, p, 8)$ (left part of Fig. 5), and $\delta = \frac{x_{47}\varepsilon}{x_{48}}$ if $H = (0, p, 7)$ (right part of Fig. 5), qualities w_7 and w_8 remain unchanged upon augmentations ε and δ along C_1 and C_2, respectively. Hence, there exists a feasible flow, corresponding to ε and δ chosen in the suggested proportions, such that the flow through $p = 4$ equals $\bar{b}_4$, or such that at least one of the arcs $(2, 8)$, (s, p), and (p, t) receives zero flow, while the other two arcs have non-negative flow. In the former event, or if the flow at arc $(2, 8)$ is zero, the proof in the case of x_{28} is complete. Otherwise, the above arguments can be repeated for some other path H, until either the flow through 4 equals $\bar{b}_4$ or the flow along $(2, 8)$ is zero.

To prove $x_{05} = 0$, $x_{13} = 0$, and $x_{67} = 0$, analogous arguments can be used. Because none of the arcs $(2, 8)$, $(0, 5)$, $(1, 3)$, or $(6, 7)$ are part of any of the augmenting cycles, the proof is complete. □

Lemma 4. *There exists an optimal flow x in $\bar{D}$ satisfying at least one of the conditions*

(i) $x_{04} + x_{14} = \bar{b}_4$,
(ii) $x_{02} = x_{27} = x_{03} = x_{37} = 0$,
(iii) $x_{15} = x_{58} = \bar{b}_5$ and $x_{16} = x_{68} = \bar{b}_6$.

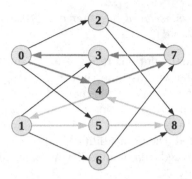

Fig. 6. Proof of Lemma 4

Proof. Let x be optimal, and assume $x_{04} + x_{14} < \bar{b}_4$. By Lemma 3 we have $x_{02} = x_{27}$, $x_{03} = x_{37}$, $x_{15} = x_{58}$ and $x_{16} = x_{68}$. Assume further that $x_{0i} = x_{i7} > 0$ and $x_{1j} = x_{j8} < \bar{b}_j$ for some $i \in \{2, 3\}$ and $j \in \{5, 6\}$. Then, both cycles $C_1 = (7, i, 0, 4, 7)$ and $C_2 = (8, 4, 1, j, 8)$ (see Fig. 6 in the case of $i = 3$ and $j = 5$) have slack capacity. Augmentations $\delta > 0$ and $\varepsilon > 0$ along C_1 and C_2, respectively, leave w_7 and w_8 unchanged if $\varepsilon = \dfrac{x_{14} x_{48} \delta}{x_{04} x_{47} + (x_{04} + x_{14}) \delta}$. The proof is complete by observing that for an appropriate choice of δ, the augmented flow x' is non-negative, and satisfies either $x'_{04} + x'_{14} = \bar{b}_4$, $x'_{0i} = x'_{i7} = 0$, or $x'_{1j} = x'_{j8} = \bar{b}_j$. □

Lemma 5. *There exists an optimal flow x in $\bar{D}$ satisfying at least one of the conditions*

 (i) $x_{04} + x_{14} = \bar{b}_4$,
 (ii) $w_8 = u_8$,
 (iii) $x_{02} + x_{03} + x_{04} + x_{05} = \bar{b}_0$,
 (iv) $x_{13} + x_{14} + x_{15} + x_{16} = \bar{b}_1$,
 (v) $x_{28} + x_{48} + x_{58} + x_{68} = \bar{b}_8$.

Proof. Let x be optimal, and assume that none of the conditions are satisfied. Because $w_8 < u_8$, we have $c_0 x_{04} + c_1 x_{14} + c_8 x_{48} \leq 0$, since otherwise a cost reduction would be obtained by reducing the flow along $(0, 4)$, $(1, 4)$ and $(4, 8)$. Sufficiently small flow adjustments on these arcs are feasible if the quality w_4, and thereby the quality w_7, are unchanged, which is achieved by retaining the ratio between x_{04} and x_{14}. It follows that the flow along the three said arcs can be increased without increasing costs, until either of the capacities $\bar{b}_0$, $\bar{b}_1$, $\bar{b}_4$, or $\bar{b}_8$ is reached. □

Lemma 6. *All optimal flows in $\bar{D}$ satisfy both the conditions:*

 (i) *Full capacity flow is assigned to either one of the nodes 0, 1, 4, and 7, or to both of the pools 2 and 3.*

(ii) Full capacity flow is assigned to either one of the nodes 0, 1, 4, and 8, or to both of the pools 5 and 6.

Proof. Let x be an optimal solution. If $x_{04} + x_{14} = \bar{b}_4$, the proof is complete. By Lemma 3, we can otherwise assume that $x_{05} = x_{28} = x_{13} = x_{67} = 0$. If x violates (i), the flow to $t = 7$ can be augmented along paths $(0, 4, 7)$, $(1, 4, 7)$, and $(0, 2, 7)$ or $(0, 3, 7)$, without alteration of qualities w_4, w_7, or w_8. Thus $t = 7$ receives flow from the sources $s = 0$ and $s = 1$ in the same proportions as before. Since the flow is augmented, the profitability condition $c_0(1 - u_7) + c_1 u_7 + c_7 < 0$ implies that the costs are reduced, contradicting optimality of x. The proof of condition (ii) is analogous.   □

It is easily observed that Lemmata 3–5 are compatible in the sense that there exist optimal solutions satisfying the conditions mentioned in each lemma.

We now go on to analyze the case where the capacity of pool 4 is fully utilized, and show that $x_{04} + x_{14} = \bar{b}_4$ leads to a bilinear program with a unique bilinear term. This particular problem is considered in the next section. In Section 4.6, we use Lemmata 3–6 to analyze the case where $x_{04} + x_{14} < \bar{b}_4$.

4.4   A Bilinear Program with a Single Bilinear Term

In this section, we first take a side step that will turn out to be useful in the sequel. We analyze a bilinear extension of the LP $\min\{c^T x : Ax \le b, x \ge 0\}$, where A is an $m \times n$ rational matrix, and b and c are rational vectors of length m and n, respectively. To the objective function, we add a linear term in a new scalar variable, $y \ge 0$, and a bilinear term in the new variable and one of the original variables, x_1, yielding the new objective function $\min_{x,y}(\gamma_1 y + \gamma_2 y x_1 + \sum_{j=1}^{n} c_j x_j)$, for rational constants γ_1 and γ_2. All constraints $i = 1, \ldots, m$ are extended analogously, such that constraint i reads $d_i y + a_{i0} y x_1 + \sum_{j=1}^{n} a_{ij} x_j \le b_i$ for rational constants a_{i0} and d_i.

The bilinear program is equivalent to minimizing the univariate function $f(y)$, defined by

$$f(y) = \gamma_1 y + \min_x (\gamma_2 y x_1 + \textstyle\sum_{j=1}^{n} c_j x_j), \tag{19}$$

$$\text{s.t.}\quad a_{i0} y x_1 + \textstyle\sum_{j=1}^{n} a_{ij} x_j \le b_i - d_i y \quad i = 1, \ldots, m, \tag{20}$$

$$x_1, \ldots, x_n \ge 0 \quad\quad j = 1, \ldots, n. \tag{21}$$

Assume that for any fixed non-negative value of y, the LP (19)–(21) is feasible and bounded. The minimum value of $f(y)$ can be found by expressing all basic solutions to (19)–(21) as functions of y, evaluating the objective function (19) value of the solutions, and minimize with respect to y. The only constraints that apply are non-negativity of all basic variables.

We focus on expressing the basic solutions. Because only one column of the coefficient matrix in (20) depends on y, the determinant of any basis matrix is a function of the form $\alpha_0 + \alpha_1 y$, for some constants α_0 and α_1. Likewise, replacing any of the columns $j = 2, \ldots, n$ by the right hand side, which also depends on

y, gives a determinant of the form $\beta_{j0} + \beta_{j1}y + \beta_{j2}y^2$, for constants β_{j0}, β_{j1} and β_{j2}. Cramer's rule hence shows that any basic solution can be written

$$x_1(y) = \frac{\beta_{10} + \beta_{11}y}{\alpha_0 + \alpha_1 y}, \quad x_j(y) = \frac{\beta_{j0} + \beta_{j1}y + \beta_{j2}y^2}{\alpha_0 + \alpha_1 y} \quad (j = 2, \ldots, n).$$

The problem $\min_y \left\{ \gamma_1 y + \gamma_2 y x_1(y) + \sum_{j=1}^{n} c_j x_j(y) : y, x_1(y), \ldots, x_n(y) \geq 0 \right\}$ has an optimal solution where either the derivative of the objective function vanishes or $x_j(y) = 0$ for some $j = 1, \ldots, n$. All such solutions are found by taking roots of polynomials of degree at most 2. For the LP-basis, B, in question, the best value of y thus becomes $y^B = r_0^B \pm \sqrt{r_1^B}$, where r_0^B and r_1^B are rational numbers depending on the LP-basis. It follows that the best achievable value for the given choice of LP-basis is of the form $z_0^B + z_1^B \sqrt{r_1^B}$, where also z_0^B and z_1^B are rational. Consequently, an optimal value of y is found by minimizing $z_0^B + z_1^B \sqrt{r_1^B}$ over all LP-bases B.

We next show that if m and n are fixed, $\min_{y \geq 0} f(y)$ is computed in terms of a constant number of comparisons and arithmetic operations on rational numbers. For a fixed number of pairs (B_1, B_2) of LP-bases, we must check whether $z_0^{B_1} + z_1^{B_1} \sqrt{r_1^{B_1}} \leq z_0^{B_2} + z_1^{B_2} \sqrt{r_1^{B_2}}$. Because both numbers are irrational, there is no upper bound on the number of bit operations required to compare them directly. To accomplished the comparison, we utilize the fact that if $a_1, r_1, a_2, r_2 \in \mathbb{Q}$, $a_1 > a_2$, $r_1 < r_2$, and $(a_1 - a_2)^2 \leq r_1 + r_2$, then $a_1 + \sqrt{r_1} \leq a_2 + \sqrt{r_2}$ if and only if $4 r_1 r_2 \leq \left(r_1 + r_2 - (a_1 - a_2)^2 \right)^2$. The comparison hence runs in time proportional to the total bit lengths of the rational numbers involved. In conclusion, a constant number of rational number operations, each of which runs in time proportional to the bit lengths of the operands, suffice for computing $\min_{y \geq 0} f(y)$.

Observe that if more than one column in (21) depend on y, then $x_1(y), \ldots, x_n(y)$ are given as roots of polynomials of degree higher than 2. In such an extended version of the problem, computing the optimal y in a finite number of operations is not straightforward. To conclude that (19)–(21) can be solved fast, the assumption that y occurs in only one column is therefore essential.

4.5 Full Capacity Utilization at the Center Pool

Consider the case where the flow through the center pool 4 is at full capacity, i.e. $x_{04} + x_{14} = x_{47} + x_{48} = \bar{b}_4$. By (16), we thus get $w_4 = x_{14}/\bar{b}_4$, which substitutes w_4 in (13)–(14). Further, we substitute x_{04} by $\bar{b}_4 - x_{14}$, and x_{47} by $\bar{b}_4 - x_{48}$. Consequently, the atomic pooling problem (9)–(17) now amounts to minimizing a linear objective subject to the bilinear quality constraints

$$\tfrac{x_{14}}{\bar{b}_4} \left(\bar{b}_4 - x_{48} \right) + (1 - u_7)(x_{13} + x_{67}) - u_7(x_{03} + x_{27} - x_{48}) \leq u_7 \bar{b}_4, \quad (22)$$

$$\tfrac{x_{14}}{\bar{b}_4} x_{48} + (1 - u_8)(x_{15} + x_{68}) - u_8(x_{05} + x_{28} + x_{48}) \leq 0, \quad (23)$$

and a set of linear constraints.

With x_{14} and x_{48} in the roles of y and x_1, respectively, the problem is translated into the form (19)–(21). Because the numbers of constraints and variables are constant in atomic instances, the conclusion of Section 4.4 proves the following:

Lemma 7. *When full capacity utilization at pool 4 is imposed, $\zeta(\bar{D})$ is computed in terms of a constant number of comparisons and arithmetic operations on rationals.*

4.6   Convergence in a Constant Number of Arithmetic Operations

Proposition 3. *Atomic instances fulfilling the cost assumptions of Section 4.1 are solved in terms of a constant number of operations on rational numbers.*

Proof. An optimal solution, x, satisfies one of the following conditions:

(i) $x_{04} + x_{14} = \bar{b}_4$,
(ii) $x_{04} + x_{14} < \bar{b}_4$ and $w_8 = u_8$,
(iii) $x_{04} + x_{14} < \bar{b}_4$ and $w_8 < u_8$.

By imposing condition (i), Lemma 7 shows that the problem is solved by a constant number of comparisons and arithmetic operations. Otherwise, Lemma 3 shows that we can fix $x_{05} = x_{28} = x_{13} = x_{67} = 0$. Further, combining $w_4 = \frac{x_{14}}{x_{04}+x_{14}}$, (18), and Lemma 1, yields

$$x_{14}x_{47} - u_7\,(x_{47} + x_{27} + x_{03})\,(x_{04} + x_{14}) = 0. \tag{24}$$

Assume that condition (ii) is imposed. Then, Lemma 4 shows that either $x_{02} = x_{27} = x_{03} = x_{37} = 0$ applies, or $x_{15} = x_{58} = \bar{b}_5$ and $x_{16} = x_{68} = \bar{b}_6$ apply. In the former case, terminal 7 receives flow exclusively from the center pool 4, implying $w_4 = w_7 = u_7$. Thus, the problem becomes an LP with a constant number of variables and constraints, which obviously is solved in terms of a constant number of operations. In the latter case, we are left with a problem in variables x_{04}, x_{14}, x_{47}, x_{48}, and $x_{27} + x_{03}$, subject to (24) and conservation of flow at pool 4 (15). Besides, $w_8 = u_8$ implies

$$u_8\,(x_{48} + \bar{b}_5 + \bar{b}_6) = x_{14} + \bar{b}_5 + \bar{b}_6 - u_7\,(x_{47} + x_{27} + x_{03}), \tag{25}$$

and by Lemma 6, at least one of the equations $x_{27}+x_{03}+x_{04} = \bar{b}_0$, $x_{14}+\bar{b}_5+\bar{b}_6 = \bar{b}_1$, $x_{27} + x_{03} = \bar{b}_2 + \bar{b}_3$, and $x_{27} + x_{03} + x_{47} = \bar{b}_7$ applies. It is easily verified that in either case, it is possible to select one variable Y_1, and express the remaining variables as a univariate rational function of the form:

$$Y_j = \frac{f_j(Y_1)}{d(Y_1)}, \qquad j = 2, \ldots, 5, \tag{26}$$

where $\{Y_1, \ldots, Y_5\} = \{x_{27} + x_{03}, x_{04}, x_{14}, x_{47}, x_{48}\}$, f_j $(j = 2, \ldots, 5)$ are second order polynomials, and d is an affine function. Consequently, we are left with a univariate optimization problem of the form

$$\min_{Y_1} \quad \xi_1 Y_1 + \sum_{j=2}^{5} \xi_j \frac{f_j(Y_1)}{d(Y_1)}, \tag{27}$$

$$\text{s.t. } \alpha_{i1} Y_1 + \sum_{j=2}^{5} \alpha_{ij} \frac{f_j(Y_1)}{d(Y_1)} \leq \beta_i, \ i = 1, \dots, k. \tag{28}$$

for rational constants k, ξ_j, α_{ij}, and β_i ($i = 1, \dots, k$, $j = 1 \dots, 5$). It follows that the points satisfying (28) with equality are the zeroes of a second order polynomial. Putting the derivative of the objective function (27) to zero yields

$$\xi_1 d^2(Y_1) + \sum_{j=2}^{5} \xi_j \left(f_j'(Y_1) d(Y_1) - f_j(Y_1) d'(Y_1) \right) = 0.$$

All boundary points, and all interior points where the derivative of the objective function vanishes, are thus found by solving second order algebraic equations. An optimal solution of the form $r_0 \pm \sqrt{r_1}$ is found by enumerating all such points.

If condition (iii) is imposed, Lemma 2 shows that we are left with a problem in variables x_{04}, x_{14}, x_{47}, and x_{48}. By assuming full capacity flow at either $\bar{b}_0$, $\bar{b}_1$, or $\bar{b}_8$ (Lemma 5), also one of the flows x_{04}, x_{14} and x_{48} can be fixed. Elimination by means of (24) and (15) shows that all variables can be expressed as rational functions of x_{47} of the form (26). Following the analysis of condition (ii), an optimal solution is found in terms of a constant number of operations.

The proof is complete by observing that the best solution satisfying either of conditions (i)–(iii) is found by comparing a fixed number of real values of the form $r_0 \pm \sqrt{r_1}$, which is accomplished in a constant number of operations on rationals. □

5   Conclusions and Further Research

The research question investigated in this paper is whether a specific type of pooling problems can be solved in a constant number of operations on rationals. Using an augmenting path approach, we have answered the question in the affirmative. The interest in this contribution is that it provides the argument that has been missing to answer a more general question in computational logistics. By virtue of the main proposition proved, it is concluded that the pooling problem can be solved in pseudo-polynomial time if only one quality parameter is defined, and the network contains only two sources and only two terminals.

Several related research topics deserve further investigation. The tractability of the class of problem instances in question might be exploitable for more general networks, where the numbers of sources, terminals and quality parameters are arbitrary. The challenge will be to combine solutions to instances induced by subnetworks with only two sources and terminals, to form feasible solutions to the original problem instance. Further, the augmenting path operations, used merely for proving theorems in the current work, might have wider applicability for algorithm construction. How to make efficient use of flow augmentation in local improvement methods for general pooling problems, is a research topic that deserves attention.

References

1. Adhya, N., Tawarmalani, M., Sahinidis, N.V.: A Lagrangian approach to the pooling problem. Ind. Eng. Chem. Res. **38**(5), 1965–1972 (1999)
2. Alfaki, M., Haugland, D.: Strong formulations for the pooling problem. J. Global Optim. **56**(3), 897–916 (2013)
3. Almutairi, H., Elhedhli, S.: A new Lagrangian approach to the pooling problem. J. Global Optim. **45**(2), 237–257 (2009)
4. Audet, C., Brimberg, J., Hansen, P., Le Digabel, S., Mladenović, N.: Pooling problem: alternate formulations and solution methods. Manage. Sci. **50**(6), 761–776 (2004)
5. Baker, T.E., Lasdon, L.S.: Successive linear programming at Exxon. Manage. Sci. **31**(3), 264–274 (1985)
6. Ben-Tal, A., Eiger, G., Gershovitz, V.: Global minimization by reducing the duality gap. Math. Program. **63**(1–3), 193–212 (1994)
7. Dantzig, G.B.: The diet problem. Interfaces **20**(4), 43–47 (1990)
8. Dey, S., Gupte, A.: Analysis of MILP techniques for the pooling problem. Oper. Res. **63**(2), 412–427 (2015)
9. DeWitt, C.W., Lasdon, L.S., Waren, A.D., Brenner, D.A., Melham, S.: OMEGA: An improved gasoline blending system for Texaco. Interfaces **19**(1), 85–101 (1989)
10. Floudas, C.A., Visweswaran, V.: A global optimization algorithm (GOP) for certain classes of nonconvex NLPs: I. Theory. Comput. Chem. Eng. **14**(12), 1397–1417 (1990)
11. Foulds, L.R., Haugland, D., Jörnsten, K.: A bilinear approach to the pooling problem. Optimization **24**, 165–180 (1992)
12. Haugland, D.: The computational complexity of the pooling problem. Accepted for publication in J. Global Optim., DOI:10.1007/s10898-015-0335-y (2015)
13. Haugland, D., Hendrix, E.M.T.: Pooling problems with polynomial solution algorithms, submitted to J. Optimiz. Theory App. (2015)
14. Haverly, C.A.: Studies of the behavior of recursion for the pooling problem. ACM SIGMAP Bulletin **25**, 19–28 (1978)
15. Misener, R., Floudas, C.A.: Advances for the pooling problem: modeling, global optimization, and computational studies. Appl. Comput. Math. **8**, 3–22 (2009)
16. Misener, R., Thompson, J.P., Floudas, C.A.: APOGEE: Global optimization of standard, generalized, and extended pooling problems via linear and logarithmic partitioning schemes. Comput. Chem. Eng. **35**, 876–892 (2011)
17. Stigler, G.J.: The cost of subsistence. J. Farm Econ. **27**(2), 303–314 (1945)
18. Sahinidis, N.V., Tawarmalani, M.: Accelerating branch-and-bound through a modeling language construct for relaxation-specific constraints. J. Global Optim. **32**(2), 259–280 (2005)
19. Visweswaran, V., Floudas, C.A.: Computational results for an efficient implementation of the GOP algorithm and its variants. In: Grossmann, I.E. (ed.) Global Optimization in Chemical Engineering, pp. 111–153. Kluwer Academic Publishers (1996)

Optimizing Constraint Test Ordering
for Efficient Automated Stowage Planning

Zhuo Qi Lee[✉], Rui Fan, and Wen-Jing Hsu

School of Computer Engineering, Nanyang Technological University,
Singapore, Singapore
{zqlee,fanrui,hsu}@ntu.edu.sg

Abstract. Containers stowage optimization is a long-standing problem
in the maritime industry. Since the problem was shown to be NP-hard,
it is computationally challenging to obtain an optimal solution. We first
review an efficient 2-phase block stowage scheme which can generate a
feasible initial solution in just a few minutes. Since the algorithm relies
heavily on checking whether any constraints will be violated by stowing
a container at a specific location, we investigate the impact of changing
the order in which the constraints are checked on the execution time
of the algorithm. We evaluate seven different strategies for ordering the
sequence in which the constraints are tested. Experiments based on real
stowage instances show that, by strategically reordering the constraints
test sequence, we can achieve 2 times speedup on the stowage planning
algorithm on average, and up to 33 times speedup in certain instances.

Keywords: Maritime logistics · Stowage plans · Optimization ·
Heuristics

1 Introduction

Containerization of goods is one of the most important technologies which has
enabled efficient and high volume transportation of goods. With the increase in
the volume of international trade, large scale containerships are built to meet
the demand of the market. The task of stowage planning is to assign containers
stowage locations on the containership such that the number of containers that
can be transported between ports is maximized without violating the safety and
stability constraints while minimizing the operational cost. In addition, a good
stowage plan also balances the workload of the quay cranes when loading or
unloading the containers at the ports.

The container stowage plans are conventionally devised by human planners
who have to go through years of training. The quality of the stowage plan is
highly dependent on the planner's experience. With the trend to transit from relatively smaller containerships (capacity of a few thousand Twenty-foot Equivalent
Units or TEUs) to large scale containerships (more than 15000 TEUs capacity),
the stowage planning process has become extremely taxing. It may take experienced human planners several hours of effort to devise a feasible stowage plan.

© Springer International Publishing Switzerland 2015
F. Corman et al. (Eds.): ICCL 2015, LNCS 9335, pp. 343–357, 2015.
DOI: 10.1007/978-3-319-24264-4_24

Hence, shipping lines face an increasingly daunting challenge to hire and retain sufficiently qualified and experienced planners.

In view of the challenges above, automated stowage plan generation has become a trend. Since the containers stowage optimization problem was shown to be NP-hard [4], obtaining the optimal stowage plan is computationally infeasible. Various heuristics are employed to generate feasible solution within reasonable amount of time. In this paper, we present an improvement, in terms of plan generation efficiency, over an existing stowage algorithm whose performance, including both the quality of solution and execution time, has been investigated empirically and reported in [11–15]. For the sake of completeness, we briefly describe the overall approach of the algorithm.

The rest of the paper is organized as follows. In Section 2 we provide an overview on the container stowage optimization problem. In Section 3, we present the overall approach of the two-phase stowage heuristics. In Section 4, we show how to further improve the execution efficiency of the stowage algorithm. Empirical results on the improvement of stowage planning time is reported in Section 5. We conclude the paper in Section 6.

2   Preliminary

In this section, we briefly introduce the types of containers and typical structure of a containership, some of the main considerations in generating a stowage plan, and a review of the literature on the container stowage optimization problem.

2.1   Types of Containers and Ship Structure

The containers can be categorized into four main types, i.e., normal containers, out-of-gauge containers (OOG), refrigerated containers (reefer), and dangerous goods

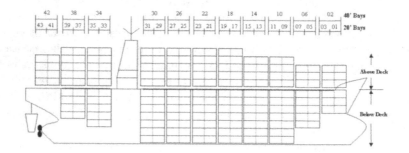

Fig. 1. Cross section view of a containership. The space on the ship is divided into discrete locations where the x-axis direction in the figure corresponds to the bays and the y-axis direction corresponds to the tiers. Bays for stacking 40 ft containers are indexed with even numbers while bays for stacking 20 ft containers are indexed with odd numbers. Two consecutive 20 ft bays form a single 40 ft bay

(DG). The typical length of a container is 20 ft, 40 ft, 45 ft, 48 ft, or 53 ft while the width and height are 8 ft and 8.5 ft respectively. When at least one of the dimension is greater than the typical range, the container is categorized as OOG. High cube (HC) container is a special case of OOG where both the width and length of a HC container are of a typical size but the height is greater than a typical container by one ft. Reefer containers need to be located near electricity plug to keep its content refrigerated. DGs need to be handled with care and are usually placed away from each other as well as heat sources and living quarters. An empty container weighs between 2.2 to 4.8 tons depending on the size, while a loaded container may weigh up to 30 tons.

Figure 1 shows the cross section view of a containership. The space on the ship is divided into discrete locations where the x-axis direction in Figure 1 corresponds to the bays and the y-axis direction corresponds to the tiers. Bays for stacking 40 ft containers are indexed with even numbers while bays for stacking 20 ft containers are indexed with odd numbers. Two consecutive 20 ft bays form a single 40 ft bay. The locations are divided into above-deck and below-deck locations by hatch covers. Figure 2 shows a slice of a 40 ft bay. The x-axis direction in Figure 2 corresponds to rows which are indexed starting from the middle. The y-axis direction corresponds to the tiers.

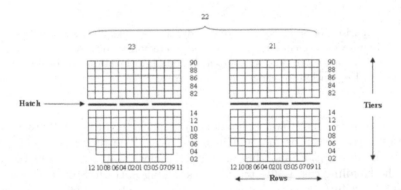

Fig. 2. A slice of 40 ft bay (two consecutive 20 ft bays) from the containership. The x-axis direction in the figure corresponds to rows which are indexed starting from the middle. The y-axis direction corresponds to the tiers. Hatch covers divide the locations into above- and below- deck

2.2   Stowage Constraints and Considerations

A feasible stowage plan is an assignment of locations to the containers such that the containership can transport the goods safely between the ports. The safety requirements can be categorized into three main types: (i) DG constraints; (ii) stacking constraints; (iii) balance and weight distribution constraints [13, 16, 17].

As mentioned previously, certain DG containers which contain flammable objects must not be placed close to the heat sources. In addition, some DGs may emit hazardous gas and must not be placed near to the living quarters or close to other DG which may react to the emitted gas. The stacking constraints specify whether different types of containers can be stacked on one another. In addition, the total weight and height of a stack cannot exceed a specified limit. In the balance and weight distribution constraints, the forces applied onto the ship structure (such as the buoyancy of the vessel and weights of the containers) are considered. The containers have to be distributed such that the ship can maintain balance during the voyage while ensuring that the differences in weight distribution exert minimal damage on the ship structure (such as shear force and bending moments). In the case where the balance and weight distribution cannot be satisfied by swapping the locations of containers, the ballast tanks are filled with water to achieve balance.

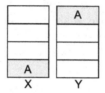

Fig. 3. Comparison of handling costs of two different stacks. Stack X requires 3 operations to remove containers on top of A, one operation to retrieve container A, and additional 3 operations to put the containers back into location. Meanwhile, stack Y only requires 1 operation to retrieve container A

However, a feasible stowage plan does not guarantee profit as there are other operational costs such as fuel and handling cost. The fuel cost is affected by the weight distribution and the amount of ballast water used. On the other hand, the handling cost is affected by the stacking pattern. Stowing a container destined for a further port on top of another container which is destined for a nearer port is said to be an *overstow*. Overstows induce additional handling cost as the containers can only be accessed when all the containers that are stacked on top are removed. Figure 3 shows an example of overstow and compares the handling cost incurred in removing a container. The containerships are also charged port dues for the duration of stay at a port. Part of the contributing factor to the port stay duration is the workload distribution between the bays [15]. The cost incurred for staying at a port for an extended period of time is especially significant for mega-vessels [1,15].

2.3 Related Works

The container stowage optimization problem, which is also known as the Master Bay Plan Problem, was shown to be NP-hard in [6]. Since it is computationally challenging to obtain an optimal solution, many studies are conducted to devise near optimal solution, rather than the optimal, to the problem. The existing approaches for solving the problem can mainly be divided into the following three categories: (i)linear programming (LP) based, e.g., [4,5,8]; (ii) meta-heuristics based, e.g., [2,3,11], and (iii)heuristics based, e.g., [2,9,15].

In the linear programming based approaches, the optimization problem is formulated with the LP framework, i.e., expressing the objective function and constraints as a collection of linear functions. Then, the problem can be solved by using a LP solver.

Meta-heuristics frameworks, such as Genetic Algorithm (GA), Ant Colony Optimization, and Tabu Search usually starts with a randomly generated stowage plan. The initial stowage plan is then incrementally altered using the framework's operations repeatedly. When a certain criterion is met, such as the execution time exceeded the time limit or an adequate solution has been obtained, the algorithm will return with the best solution found throughout the whole process.

While most of the algorithms above provide good solution to the Master Bay Plan Problem, some may not be applicable to real world usage due to either the implicit simplifying assumptions made [13], or the long period of time required to generate a good feasible solution [3].

Heuristics based algorithm are devised by observing the patterns and rule-of-thumbs utilised by the human planners. Although these approaches usually do not offer theoretical guarantee on the quality of the solution, they can generate multiple feasible solutions quickly and the pattern of solution generated can be easily modified by the human planners [14].

3   Two-Phase Stowage Planning Approach

In the following, we briefly describe an efficient two-phase stowage heuristics whose performance, including both the quality of solution returned and execution time, has been investigated empirically and reported in [11–15].

The algorithm applies a divide-and-conquer approach. The container stowage problem is divided into two phases. In the first phase, the focus is on maximizing the number of containers that can be allocated onto the containership without causing any overstow issue. In the second phase, the safety and balance of the ship is enhanced by swapping the locations of containers and adjusting the ballast tanks. Since the main concern of the paper is about optimizing the efficiency of the allocation phase, we do not cover the adjustment phase. Interested reader may refer to [13,16,17].

3.1   Allocation Phase

To reduce the solution search space for allocating the containers, the locations on the containership are divided into blocks [15]. Firstly, the locations are grouped according to the hatch covers and also their position, i.e. above deck or below deck, on a bay-by-bay basis. Then, the pair of groups symmetric around the central location are combined into a block. This heuristic is introduced so that the weight distribution around the center of the ship is relatively balanced.

The allocation starts from the group of containers with the furthest POD. Based on this group of containers, available blocks which would not have the over-stow issue by accepting the containers with the current POD are included into the candidate list. Subsequently, the list of candidate blocks is sorted according to the block's workload and its compatibility to the current POD being considered. The order of the set of blocks with the same priority is randomized by means of a randomization seed.

When allocating containers, a block of the highest priority is selected. A cell is retrieved from this block. Then, the containers are tested against a collection of constraints for the eligibility to be allocated in the currently selected cell based on the types and weights. The first container in the group that satisfies all of the constraints is allocated to the current cell and is removed from the list of containers to be allocated. In the case where all eligible cells in the current block are tested, another block is retrieved from the list of candidate blocks and the process continues until either all cells from the candidate blocks have been considered or the group of containers are fully allocated. The containers that remain after exhausting the list of candidate blocks are added to the rejection list. This process is repeated for the group of containers with a closer POD and ends after the group of containers with the closest POD have been processed. The containers in the rejection list have to be allocated manually by the human planner.

4   Reordering of Constraint Tests

As described in the previous section, the allocation phase relies heavily on the result of constraints checks. Figure 4 shows examples of constraint test sequence. Checking a constraint ϕ_i would incur certain cost c_i. While some constraints are easy to check, such as the constraint on the type match between the container and the cell, some other constraints may be costly to check, such as the DG segregation constraints. All of the constraints have to be checked to ensure that a container can be allocated to a certain cell. However, when one of the constraints is violated, the remaining sequence of constraints need not be checked. Thus, the efficiency of the checking process can be improved if majority of the constraint checks can be skipped by strategically ordering the sequence in which the constraints are checked.

Intuitively, one may order the constraints in ascending order of cost. However, a constraint with a low test cost may not be violated frequently and thus is contributing to the constraint test overhead most of the time. On the other hand, one may also order the constraints in terms of the likelihood p_i in which a constraint is violated. Unfortunately, a constraint which is likely to be violated may also be very costly to test. A good strategy is to order the sequence of constraint tests in terms of the cost effectiveness of the tests. The cost effectiveness

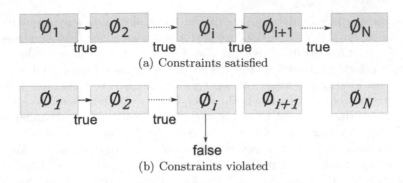

(a) Constraints satisfied

(b) Constraints violated

Fig. 4. Examples of constraint test sequence. (a) the scenario where a container satisfies all of the constraints. The total cost for this set of tests is the sum of the individual costs, $C = \sum_{k=1}^{N} c_k$. (b) the scenario where the i-th constraint test result is false. The total cost for this set of tests is the sum of the cost of the first i tests, $C = \sum_{k=1}^{i} c_k$

of a constraint test ϕ_i is given by $\sigma_i = \frac{p_i}{c_i}$. In fact, it was shown in [7,10] that, such an ordering is optimal, i.e., the expected cost of getting the constraint test results is the lowest. For the sake of completeness, we state the following theorem from [7,10].

Theorem 1. *Given a sequence of tests $\Phi = \{\phi_1, \phi_2, \phi_3, ..., \phi_N\}$ that are both statistically independent and have no precedence requirements, the costs of the tests are given by $c_1, c_2, c_3, ..., c_N$ respectively, and each test terminates the whole test sequence with probability $p_1, p_2, p_3, ..., p_N$ respectively. The cost of a sequence of tests is given by $C = \sum_{k=1}^{i} c_k$, where i is the index of the first test with sufficient termination condition. If the tests are ordered in non-increasing order of cost effectiveness, $\sigma_k = \frac{p_k}{c_k}$, then the expected time of the sequence of tests by using this order is the lowest among all possible permutations of the test sequence.*

However, the trouble of applying Theorem 1 is that, the tests are assumed to be statistically independent and both costs and probabilities of the tests are known. For the container allocation phase, both costs and probabilities of violation may vary between different instances of the problem. In addition, the constraint test results may exhibit certain periodicity with respect to the locations of the cells being considered. For instance, the twenty-foot containers can only be allocated to the lowest tiers below deck, and the type-matching constraint for twenty-foot containers will be violated periodically. Hence, we also consider reordering the constraint test sequence dynamically by placing the most recently violated constraint item to the first of the sequence. Moreover, this strategy will not incur large amount of preprocessing time required for using Theorem 1.

While the Recent-First (RC) strategy may partially adapt to the periodicity of the constraint test result, moving a constraint test directly to the top of the test abruptly may destroy the initial order of the test very quickly. While the violation probability distribution of the constraint tests may vary across the instances, the cost distribution of the constraint tests stays roughly the same. Based on this observation, we introduce a strategy that emulates the Cost-Effective-First strategy dynamically. Figure 5 shows the normalized cost distribution for the constraint tests. The test sequence is initialized with the Lowest-Cost-First order. Since the top two most expensive constraint tests are of a different order from the rest of the tests, they are not reordered dynamically. For the rest of the constraint tests, they are dynamically reordered similar to the RC strategy. However, instead of moving the recently violated constraint to the top of the test sequence, it is moved half the distance to the top. For instance, when the constraint test at position #10 of the test sequence is violated at the current step, it will be moved to position #5 in the next step. Thus, a constraint test will only be moved to the front of the test sequence if it is violated frequently, or it will be replaced by other constraint tests that are more frequently violated. Since the cost of the constraint tests are very similar, this strategy emulates the Cost-Effective-First strategy dynamically.

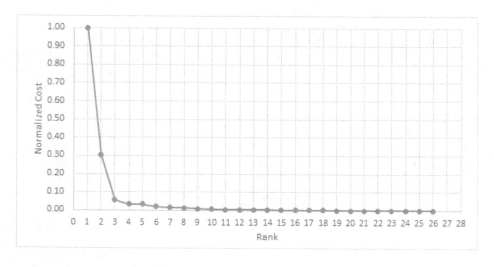

Fig. 5. Cost distribution of the constraint tests

In the next section, we present experimental results which compare the differences in overall time spent in checking constraints by using the sequence of constraint tests based on the different approaches, namely,

- **Rnd**: Random Arbitrary Order
- **Heu**: A heuristic order devised by the programmer manually
- **LCost**: Lowest-Cost-First
- **HProb**: Highest-Probability-First
- **CostEff**: Cost-Effective-First
- **RC**: Recently-Violated-First
- **RCR**: Recently-Violated-First with Restriction

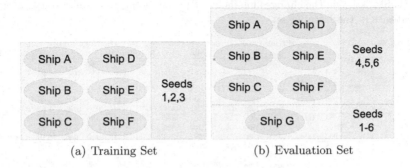

(a) Training Set   (b) Evaluation Set

Fig. 6. Partition of instances into training set and evaluation set

5   Experiments

We conducted experiments on the allocation phase based on real stowage planning instances which include 7 different containerships and stowage demands from several ports. Since the allocation phase makes use of randomization to determine the order in which blocks of equivalent priority are considered for allocation, we use 6 different seeds and treat them as different instances. Then we partition the set of instances into training set and evaluation set. Figure 6 shows how the instances are partitioned. We obtain an estimation of the cost and probability for each constraint based on the training set. Using the estimated values, we order the sequence in which the constraints are checked using the strategies as mentioned in the previous section. Except for the RC and RCR strategy, the other strategies follow the same sequences of constraints tests as dictated by the respective strategies.

The detailed timings are tabulated in Table 1 and Table 3 for the training set and evaluation set respectively. The timings in both tables are given in milliseconds. The column labelled "Overhead" denotes the amount of overhead time spent in the main program logic. The columns labelled "Rnd", "Heu", "LCost", "HProb", "CostEff", "RC", and "RCR" denote the total time spent in checking constraints by using the strategies respectively. The columns under "Overall Timing Ratio" are the ratio between the total time spent in the allocation phase by the respective strategy and the Rnd order (i.e., overhead is included). The last 3 rows compare the total time spent across all instances in the table.

From the "Total" row of Table 1, the time spent in the allocation phase by the CostEff strategy is 0.38 of that by the Rnd ordering (or 62% reduction). On the other hand, the RC and RCR strategies reduce the fraction of time spent by 62% and 64% respectively. In certain cases, the overall time spent in the allocation phase can be reduced by a very significant amount. For instance, the instance from the training set with Vessel E, port 51, seedID 3, the total time spent in the allocation phase is cut down to 0.03 of the base case timing, i.e. achieving a speedup of 33 times.

Table 1. Statistics on the changes in efficiency by using different constraint test ordering strategies in the training set

Vessel	POL	Seed ID	Overhead	Rnd	Heu	Lcost	Hprob	CostEff	RC	RCR	Heuristic	Lcost	Hprob	CostEff	RC	RCR
						Timings (milliseconds)					Overall ratio (based on Rnd)					
A	11	1	424	26	21	21	21	22	28	22	0.99	0.99	0.99	0.99	1.00	0.99
		2	293	17	16	16	16	17	15	18	1.00	1.00	1.00	1.00	0.99	1.00
		3	290	13	13	13	15	15	13	13	1.00	1.00	1.01	1.01	1.00	1.00
	12	1	1016	26157	3820	2319	13843	2264	2641	1818	0.18	0.12	0.55	0.12	0.13	0.10
		2	570	23422	2242	1362	10268	1300	2013	1071	0.12	0.08	0.45	0.08	0.11	0.07
		3	531	23502	2265	1326	10401	1242	1621	951	0.12	0.08	0.45	0.07	0.09	0.06
	13	1	1482	19871	8692	4075	5281	4001	3486	3732	0.48	0.26	0.32	0.26	0.23	0.24
		2	1131	17030	6662	3104	3816	3164	2986	2983	0.43	0.23	0.27	0.24	0.23	0.23
		3	950	18500	6489	2956	3159	2771	2540	2694	0.38	0.20	0.21	0.19	0.18	0.19
B	21	1	1778	28325	10447	7667	7721	7080	5520	5999	0.41	0.31	0.32	0.29	0.24	0.26
		2	1067	12223	3943	2113	2820	1996	1873	1975	0.38	0.24	0.29	0.23	0.22	0.23
		3	1155	38110	23685	22268	22644	21962	21020	22664	0.63	0.60	0.61	0.59	0.56	0.61
	22	1	564	603	368	230	178	193	123	197	0.80	0.68	0.64	0.65	0.59	0.65
		2	542	727	392	171	134	139	101	136	0.74	0.56	0.53	0.54	0.51	0.53
		3	424	740	246	130	131	118	92	101	0.58	0.48	0.48	0.47	0.44	0.45
	23	1	1501	34890	15614	13303	11090	11920	9727	10098	0.47	0.41	0.35	0.37	0.31	0.32
		2	1315	29146	7536	6631	6182	5792	5880	5562	0.29	0.26	0.25	0.23	0.24	0.23
		3	1191	31700	6724	4994	4359	4313	4062	3785	0.24	0.19	0.17	0.17	0.16	0.15
	24	1	1866	35149	11626	12522	10242	11482	10619	9594	0.36	0.39	0.33	0.36	0.34	0.31
		2	1386	24721	3797	4213	4445	3615	4837	3515	0.20	0.21	0.22	0.19	0.24	0.19
		3	1081	5439	1166	723	734	587	569	497	0.34	0.28	0.28	0.26	0.25	0.24
C	31	1	546	4370	2187	1604	2329	1684	1641	1465	0.56	0.44	0.58	0.45	0.44	0.41
		2	231	3816	359	282	966	193	157	150	0.15	0.13	0.30	0.10	0.10	0.09
		3	366	3822	1793	1457	1888	1445	1402	1401	0.52	0.44	0.54	0.43	0.42	0.42
	32	1	295	1969	803	374	574	255	232	228	0.48	0.30	0.38	0.24	0.23	0.23
		2	249	995	426	247	397	309	319	322	0.54	0.40	0.52	0.45	0.46	0.46
		3	149	831	202	106	158	106	113	95	0.36	0.26	0.31	0.26	0.27	0.25
D	41	1	1034	1926	1236	768	632	676	569	561	0.77	0.61	0.56	0.58	0.54	0.54
		2	597	2060	549	336	356	343	330	302	0.43	0.35	0.36	0.35	0.35	0.34
		3	751	4873	3165	2974	2964	2802	3019	2829	0.70	0.66	0.66	0.63	0.69	0.64
	42	1	778	7403	6319	6284	7021	6638	6967	6349	0.87	0.86	0.95	0.91	0.95	0.87
		2	479	648	176	151	179	164	145	143	0.58	0.56	0.58	0.57	0.55	0.55
		3	521	4953	4459	4289	4405	4385	4464	4185	0.91	0.88	0.90	0.90	0.95	0.86
	43	1	2083	37876	12521	12236	12158	11786	10828	9457	0.37	0.36	0.36	0.35	0.32	0.29
		2	1405	49909	34727	30481	31618	30306	30960	29280	0.70	0.62	0.64	0.62	0.63	0.60
		3	1291	88077	68590	63896	64881	65595	70733	63920	0.78	0.73	0.74	0.75	0.81	0.73
	44	1	1264	24150	19341	10596	10926	10033	11070	9672	0.81	0.47	0.48	0.44	0.49	0.43
		2	1013	14279	10443	2031	2384	2145	2192	1825	0.75	0.20	0.22	0.21	0.21	0.19
		3	877	12069	7910	349	861	300	243	249	0.68	0.09	0.13	0.09	0.09	0.09
	45	1	2264	37441	14836	12541	13826	12426	11977	9887	0.43	0.37	0.41	0.37	0.36	0.31
		2	1584	29340	6551	3505	4016	3069	3354	2339	0.26	0.16	0.18	0.15	0.16	0.13
		3	1674	30703	4820	3301	3646	3030	4144	2515	0.20	0.15	0.16	0.15	0.18	0.13
	46	1	1462	34224	30606	27986	28905	27512	31109	27217	0.90	0.83	0.85	0.81	0.91	0.80
		2	1481	5582	1324	638	992	542	651	485	0.40	0.30	0.35	0.29	0.30	0.28
		3	1029	6991	1512	778	1464	618	581	534	0.32	0.23	0.31	0.21	0.20	0.19
	47	1	1146	12647	1233	948	866	834	1901	722	0.17	0.15	0.15	0.14	0.22	0.14
		2	810	13753	535	367	365	275	1293	239	0.09	0.08	0.08	0.07	0.14	0.07
		3	756	13262	479	276	299	253	653	218	0.09	0.07	0.08	0.07	0.10	0.07
E	51	1	484	11179	393	974	286	301	267	259	0.08	0.13	0.07	0.07	0.06	0.06
		2	256	12845	427	737	267	280	207	186	0.05	0.08	0.04	0.04	0.04	0.03
		3	202	10339	241	553	149	158	118	124	0.04	0.07	0.03	0.03	0.03	0.03
	52	1	385	3013	2356	563	1340	566	531	461	0.81	0.28	0.51	0.28	0.27	0.25
		2	168	2232	1363	311	1170	326	400	276	0.64	0.20	0.56	0.21	0.24	0.18
		3	157	2037	1336	364	647	328	457	375	0.68	0.24	0.37	0.22	0.28	0.24
	53	1	583	5741	2991	3015	2951	2892	2711	2688	0.57	0.57	0.56	0.55	0.52	0.52
		2	308	2630	881	856	735	698	690	698	0.40	0.40	0.36	0.34	0.34	0.34
		3	246	3382	1827	1889	1729	1644	1699	1669	0.57	0.59	0.54	0.52	0.54	0.53
	54	1	1680	36309	29020	27801	27830	27153	24966	25879	0.81	0.78	0.78	0.76	0.70	0.73
		2	914	54797	47128	46585	46266	45649	44927	46831	0.86	0.85	0.85	0.84	0.82	0.86
		3	949	38342	32465	33334	32751	31852	30443	31802	0.85	0.87	0.86	0.83	0.80	0.83
F	61	1	795	38781	5412	5233	3083	3260	2463	2356	0.16	0.15	0.10	0.10	0.08	0.08
		2	456	34419	3165	2967	1818	1687	1836	1426	0.10	0.10	0.07	0.06	0.07	0.05
		3	426	32729	3288	2852	1611	1681	1835	1358	0.11	0.10	0.06	0.06	0.07	0.05
	62	1	402	8213	396	974	499	343	253	254	0.09	0.16	0.10	0.09	0.08	0.08
		2	217	7538	251	533	287	221	169	127	0.06	0.10	0.06	0.06	0.05	0.04
		3	207	8082	249	500	326	191	115	113	0.06	0.09	0.06	0.05	0.04	0.04
	63	1	659	4470	2042	1529	1568	1498	1498	1407	0.53	0.43	0.43	0.42	0.42	0.40
		2	423	3730	1277	1003	924	863	854	771	0.41	0.34	0.32	0.31	0.31	0.29
		3	386	3479	1120	801	701	641	665	569	0.39	0.31	0.28	0.27	0.27	0.25
Total			56990	1142567	490494	412332	443514	393949	398217	373643	0.46	0.39	0.42	0.38	0.38	0.36
										Min	0.04	0.07	0.03	0.03	0.03	0.03
										Max	0.91	0.88	0.95	0.91	0.95	0.87

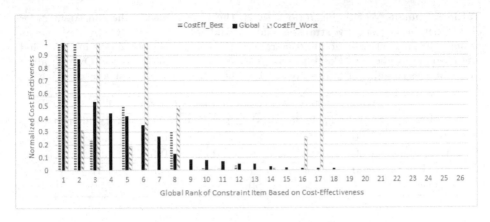

Fig. 7. Comparison of the Cost-Effectiveness distribution between the best and worst cases of CostEff strategy against the global distribution. Both the best case and worst case are taken from the training set. The best case corresponds to Vessel E, port 51, seedID 3; the worst case corresponds to Vessel D, port 42, seedID 1. The cost-effectiveness distribution of the best case matches the global distribution better as compared to the worst case. For example, the constraintID 17 is very cost-effective for the worst case instance, but is among the least cost-effective globally

The final row of the table shows the worst case among the instances for each of the strategies (excluding the instances from Vessel A with POL 11 as these values are too small). The "RCR" strategy has the best worst-case performance which is 0.87 of the overall time spent by the Rnd order. However, the "HProb" and "RC" strategies has the worst performance, which is 0.95 of the overall time spent by the Rnd order. The results for the evaluation set can be interpreted similarly.

Figure 7 compares the cost-effectiveness distributions of the best and worst cases for the CostEff strategy to the global distribution. As shown in the figure, in the worst case instance, the instance's distribution is very different from the global distribution. For example, the constraintID 17 is very cost-effective for the particular instance, but is among the least cost-effective globally. We summarize the statistics on the changes in the total execution time in Table 2.

Table 2 shows a surprising result. Both "RC" and "RCR" strategies have matching or even lower overall time as compared to the "CostEff" strategy. We believe that this is due to the "periodicity" of the violation probability for the constraint tests. As mentioned previously, the probability that an individual constraint is violated may be subject to the pair of container and cell being considered. Thus, the probability of violation for certain constraints may be higher (or lower) at specific stages of the allocation. Although Theorem 1 gives an optimal ordering of constraint tests when the probability of violation is considered globally, local fluctuation in the violation probability may change the optimal order of constraint tests locally. Thus, by dynamically reordering the recently violated constraint, the "RC" strategy is emulating the "HProb" ordering dynamically

Table 2. Summary of timing ratio between the time taken by the constraint order obtained from the respective strategies and the Rnd order. The "RCR" strategy appears to have the greatest reduction in constraint check timing for both the training set and evaluation set while the "CostEff" strategy has a similar performance. Overall, all of the strategies examined successfully reduced the time spent in constraint checking

	Rnd	Heu	Lcost	Hprob	CostEff	RC	RCR
Total Timing	3099313	1742635	1568152	1647536	1534348	1568135	1507896
Training Set	1.00	0.46	0.39	0.42	0.38	0.38	0.36
Evaluation Set	1.00	0.63	0.58	0.60	0.57	0.59	0.57
Overall (Rnd)	1.00	0.56	0.51	0.53	0.50	0.51	0.49
Overall (Heu)	1.78	1.00	0.90	0.95	0.88	0.90	0.87

while the "RCR" strategy is emulating the "CostEff" strategy dynamically. We note that, when the costs of individual constraint tests are the same, the strategy by Theorem 1 is equivalent to the "HProb" strategy.

6   Discussions and Conclusions

We summarise the findings in the following:

- Reordering the sequence in which the constraints are tested improves the efficiency of the stowage algorithm.
- The time spent in checking constraints can be reduced significantly for certain instances (up to 97% reduction).
- CostEff, RC, and RCR have the best overall improvement of about 50% reduction in time spent on checking constraints.
- RC and RCR can match the performance of CostEff by adapting to the 'periodicity' in the constraint violation pattern dynamically.
- Both CostEff and RCR use historical data in ordering. However, RCR does not require the probability distribution, which may vary between different instances.

While the Cost-Effective-First strategy [7, 10] has a good overall improvement on the efficiency, it assumes independence between the individual constraint tests and requires training data. In addition, the strategy may overlook the periodicity in which the individual constraint tests are violated. On the other hand, both RC and RCR have matching or better performance in reducing the total time spent in checking constraints. We believe that this is due to the dynamic reordering nature of the strategy which may better match the 'periodic' nature of the constraint tests. While this may suggest that a better dynamically reordering approach is feasible, the overhead induced in changing the constraint test sequences dynamically may offset the benefit brought about when implementing such a strategy. We plan to incorporate the dependencies between the constraints in the next phase of efficiency optimization.

Table 3. Statistics on the changes in efficiency by using different constraint test ordering strategies in the evaluation set

Vessel	POL	Seed ID	Timings (milliseconds)								Overall ratio (based on Rnd)					
			Overhead	Rnd	Heuristic	Lcost	Hprob	CostEff	RC	RCR	Heu	Lcost	Hprob	CostEff	RC	RCR
A	11	4	293	15	19	12	12	18	12	12	1.01	0.99	0.99	1.01	0.99	0.99
		5	289	13	12	20	13	13	13	13	1.00	1.02	1.00	1.00	1.00	1.00
		6	298	13	12	12	12	14	12	12	1.00	1.00	1.00	1.00	1.00	1.00
	12	4	538	22622	2399	1321	10300	1283	1678	1012	0.13	0.08	0.47	0.08	0.10	0.07
		5	558	22271	2188	1323	10293	1219	2259	1019	0.12	0.08	0.48	0.08	0.12	0.07
		6	541	22723	2330	1337	10373	1245	2231	955	0.12	0.08	0.47	0.08	0.12	0.06
	13	4	1074	17300	6970	3632	3921	3632	3494	3620	0.44	0.26	0.27	0.26	0.25	0.26
		5	1146	18540	7482	4070	4394	4018	3666	3897	0.44	0.26	0.28	0.26	0.24	0.26
		6	1017	15969	6204	3048	3556	3172	2934	2874	0.43	0.24	0.27	0.25	0.23	0.23
B	21	4	1263	214570	193436	194366	194824	194758	190903	196866	0.90	0.91	0.91	0.91	0.89	0.92
		5	1425	202448	186124	186891	188557	184821	179762	187816	0.92	0.92	0.93	0.91	0.89	0.93
		6	1342	173058	157720	158861	162090	158381	154285	162179	0.91	0.92	0.94	0.92	0.89	0.94
	22	4	415	236	121	70	71	70	58	66	0.82	0.74	0.75	0.74	0.73	0.74
		5	376	502	214	98	103	99	82	167	0.67	0.54	0.55	0.54	0.52	0.62
		6	386	370	199	104	107	107	86	99	0.77	0.65	0.65	0.65	0.62	0.64
	23	4	1126	46091	20329	19485	19003	18673	17929	18486	0.45	0.44	0.43	0.42	0.40	0.42
		5	1063	28201	6768	4583	6035	4191	3374	2999	0.27	0.19	0.24	0.18	0.15	0.14
		6	1288	45081	21596	20026	19468	18841	18648	18793	0.49	0.46	0.45	0.43	0.43	0.43
	24	4	1396	36726	8961	9556	8697	8631	9043	8461	0.27	0.29	0.26	0.26	0.27	0.26
		5	1042	23100	4110	4055	3422	3591	3645	3390	0.21	0.21	0.18	0.19	0.19	0.18
		6	1141	25170	5000	5507	4828	5086	5421	4863	0.23	0.25	0.23	0.24	0.25	0.23
C	31	4	205	2091	336	254	679	217	134	166	0.24	0.20	0.39	0.18	0.15	0.16
		5	327	4315	1193	1027	1685	980	964	892	0.33	0.29	0.43	0.28	0.28	0.26
		6	344	3724	1780	1362	1793	1430	1351	1269	0.52	0.42	0.53	0.44	0.42	0.40
	32	4	163	2034	439	154	381	140	387	129	0.27	0.14	0.25	0.14	0.25	0.13
		5	169	813	177	82	135	73	76	79	0.35	0.26	0.31	0.25	0.25	0.25
		6	189	1710	593	168	329	124	215	115	0.41	0.19	0.27	0.16	0.21	0.16
D	41	4	630	1682	844	371	393	322	347	293	0.64	0.43	0.44	0.41	0.42	0.40
		5	734	1286	567	261	240	246	276	227	0.64	0.49	0.48	0.49	0.50	0.48
		6	598	1253	817	190	182	157	173	145	0.76	0.43	0.42	0.41	0.42	0.40
	42	4	540	583	170	197	156	158	145	135	0.63	0.66	0.62	0.62	0.61	0.60
		5	519	855	224	211	224	187	195	171	0.54	0.53	0.54	0.51	0.52	0.50
		6	453	20071	17242	17410	17483	18037	19986	17653	0.86	0.87	0.87	0.90	1.00	0.88
	43	4	1661	89924	69238	65836	66200	70404	76326	65288	0.77	0.74	0.74	0.79	0.85	0.73
		5	1441	30124	9658	6402	6681	5809	7069	5228	0.35	0.25	0.26	0.23	0.27	0.21
		6	1168	48948	31038	28756	29937	28817	33782	28454	0.64	0.60	0.62	0.60	0.70	0.59
	44	4	909	18826	14576	6831	7472	7071	7977	6604	0.78	0.39	0.42	0.40	0.45	0.38
		5	1041	36436	29083	21252	21451	20944	24574	20764	0.80	0.59	0.60	0.59	0.68	0.58
		6	874	12742	8100	365	794	290	227	241	0.66	0.09	0.12	0.09	0.08	0.08
	45	4	1723	29927	8612	6829	7040	6568	8572	6038	0.33	0.27	0.28	0.26	0.33	0.25
		5	1482	22536	4241	2284	2880	2102	2337	1898	0.24	0.16	0.18	0.15	0.16	0.14
		6	1663	24435	5359	3183	3863	2757	3756	1869	0.27	0.19	0.21	0.17	0.21	0.14
	46	4	1190	34240	31635	28377	28491	28116	34782	27589	0.93	0.83	0.84	0.83	1.01	0.81
		5	1416	51442	50023	46605	47622	46484	54856	45446	0.97	0.91	0.93	0.91	1.06	0.89
		6	1383	44875	41604	38759	39784	38990	46044	38427	0.93	0.87	0.89	0.87	1.03	0.86
	47	4	718	10214	526	206	235	167	307	177	0.11	0.08	0.09	0.08	0.09	0.08
		5	787	13004	588	320	339	261	1091	240	0.10	0.08	0.08	0.08	0.14	0.07
		6	711	7673	518	255	261	203	1066	177	0.15	0.12	0.12	0.11	0.21	0.11
E	51	4	207	10652	263	579	183	168	150	176	0.04	0.07	0.04	0.03	0.03	0.04
		5	220	12419	302	697	219	196	150	153	0.05	0.07	0.04	0.03	0.03	0.03
		6	212	10185	281	565	176	155	142	162	0.05	0.07	0.04	0.04	0.03	0.04
	52	4	164	2860	1790	395	1125	339	369	348	0.65	0.18	0.43	0.17	0.18	0.17
		5	163	1881	1260	296	771	287	408	286	0.70	0.22	0.46	0.22	0.28	0.22
		6	156	2089	1377	319	793	307	358	319	0.68	0.21	0.42	0.21	0.23	0.21
	53	4	304	3434	1746	1826	1723	1621	1711	1657	0.55	0.57	0.54	0.51	0.54	0.52
		5	288	5503	3265	3308	3154	3135	3121	3059	0.61	0.62	0.59	0.59	0.59	0.58
		6	277	2335	506	455	355	336	286	256	0.30	0.28	0.24	0.23	0.22	0.20
	54	4	863	19781	14357	13736	14192	13113	12533	13085	0.74	0.71	0.73	0.68	0.65	0.68
		5	865	39021	32265	32128	31698	30924	30333	32175	0.83	0.83	0.82	0.80	0.78	0.83
		6	1052	38351	32254	32373	31749	31246	30050	32264	0.85	0.85	0.83	0.82	0.79	0.85
F	61	4	432	32797	3371	2924	1576	1665	1915	1403	0.11	0.10	0.06	0.06	0.07	0.06
		5	416	32850	3133	3059	1660	1575	1580	1343	0.11	0.10	0.06	0.06	0.06	0.05
		6	416	34916	3370	3151	1767	1669	1893	1361	0.11	0.10	0.06	0.06	0.07	0.05
	62	4	196	7690	254	527	284	154	133	132	0.06	0.09	0.06	0.04	0.04	0.04
		5	188	7737	253	501	278	167	120	123	0.06	0.09	0.06	0.04	0.04	0.04
		6	180	7770	235	482	289	147	125	110	0.05	0.08	0.06	0.04	0.04	0.04
	63	4	407	3574	1546	1054	961	866	971	829	0.49	0.37	0.34	0.32	0.35	0.31
		5	401	3462	1143	829	746	639	688	668	0.40	0.32	0.30	0.27	0.28	0.28
		6	350	3367	899	694	571	502	545	474	0.34	0.28	0.25	0.23	0.24	0.22

Table 3. (Continued)

Vessel G	POL	Seed ID	Timings (milliseconds)							Overall ratio (based on Rnd)
71		1	928	7218	2157	1560	2004	1511	1269	1371	0.38 0.31 0.36 0.30 0.27 0.28
		2	636	6675	1149	756	827	693	698	688	0.24 0.19 0.20 0.18 0.18 0.18
		3	614	13181	8642	6595	8099	6735	6272	6168	0.67 0.52 0.63 0.53 0.50 0.49
		4	424	9577	4336	3257	4116	3385	3008	3229	0.48 0.37 0.45 0.38 0.34 0.37
		5	505	6691	1031	638	639	538	565	549	0.21 0.16 0.16 0.14 0.15 0.15
		6	414	6097	936	657	618	549	496	507	0.21 0.16 0.16 0.15 0.14 0.14
	72	1	791	3094	2417	404	607	296	245	238	0.83 0.31 0.36 0.28 0.27 0.26
		2	470	12797	10628	7579	9345	7312	7053	7237	0.84 0.61 0.74 0.59 0.57 0.58
		3	609	2875	1980	150	754	132	106	137	0.74 0.22 0.39 0.21 0.21 0.21
		4	488	5002	4542	2338	3096	2263	2147	2259	0.92 0.51 0.65 0.50 0.48 0.50
		5	680	2468	1799	161	695	127	107	113	0.79 0.27 0.44 0.26 0.25 0.25
		6	622	5755	4926	2908	3488	2744	2611	2667	0.87 0.55 0.64 0.53 0.51 0.52
	73	1	910	3351	1552	1244	1795	1140	790	567	0.58 0.51 0.63 0.48 0.40 0.35
		2	648	2917	1084	579	863	547	488	539	0.49 0.34 0.42 0.34 0.32 0.33
		3	576	1968	694	352	1641	344	307	325	0.50 0.36 0.87 0.36 0.35 0.35
		4	663	1748	698	404	523	368	350	387	0.56 0.44 0.49 0.43 0.42 0.44
		5	604	1513	628	381	560	368	338	338	0.58 0.47 0.55 0.46 0.44 0.44
		6	643	2387	822	618	908	578	488	494	0.48 0.42 0.51 0.40 0.37 0.38
	74	1	658	1501	881	291	328	223	190	201	0.71 0.44 0.46 0.41 0.39 0.40
		2	512	1064	545	149	248	164	210	128	0.67 0.42 0.48 0.43 0.46 0.41
		3	370	4796	4316	2855	3916	2708	2597	2951	0.91 0.62 0.83 0.60 0.57 0.64
		4	384	1427	787	289	431	272	263	257	0.65 0.37 0.45 0.36 0.36 0.35
		5	374	1226	633	114	201	99	98	90	0.63 0.31 0.36 0.30 0.30 0.29
		6	405	1159	612	111	175	98	98	85	0.65 0.33 0.37 0.32 0.32 0.31
	75	1	954	3313	1455	705	1165	667	579	581	0.56 0.39 0.50 0.38 0.36 0.36
		2	613	1989	878	192	549	187	181	183	0.57 0.31 0.45 0.31 0.31 0.31
		3	586	2264	879	235	399	200	208	198	0.51 0.29 0.35 0.28 0.28 0.28
		4	511	1664	697	158	397	144	148	160	0.56 0.31 0.42 0.30 0.30 0.31
		5	589	2000	800	170	335	147	160	179	0.54 0.29 0.36 0.28 0.29 0.30
		6	557	2017	856	212	685	196	179	195	0.55 0.30 0.48 0.29 0.29 0.29
Total			66546	1833210	1128605	1032284	1080486	1016863	1046382	1010717	0.63 0.58 0.60 0.57 0.59 0.57
									Min		0.04 0.07 0.03 0.03 0.03 0.03
									Max		1.01 1.02 1.00 1.01 1.06 1.00

Acknowledgments. The study is supported by grants from the NOL Fellowship programme and the co-funding from SMI. The authors would like to thank Mr. Si Thu Myint for his assistance in proof-reading the manuscript.

References

1. Singapore port marine notice, April 2013. http://www.mpa.gov.sg/sites/circulars_and_notices/pdfs/port_marine_notices/pn13-47.pdf (accessed March 25, 2015)
2. Ambrosino, D., Anghinolfi, D., Paolucci, M., Sciomachen, A.: A new three-step heuristic for the master bay plan problem. Maritime Economics and Logistics 11(1), 98–120 (2009)
3. Ambrosino, D., Anghinolfi, D., Paolucci, M., Sciomachen, A.: An experimental comparison of different heuristics for the master bay plan problem. In: Festa, P. (ed.) SEA 2010. LNCS, vol. 6049, pp. 314–325. Springer, Heidelberg (2010)
4. Ambrosino, D., Sciomachen, A., Tanfani, E.: Stowing a containership: the master bay plan problem. Transportation Research Part A: Policy and Practice 38(2), 81–99 (2004)
5. Ambrosino, D., Sciomachen, A., Tanfani, E.: A decomposition heuristics for the container ship stowage problem. Journal of Heuristics 12(3), 211–233 (2006)
6. Avriel, M., Penn, M., Shpirer, N.: Container ship stowage problem: complexity and connection to the coloring of circle graphs. Discrete Applied Mathematics 103(13), 271–279 (2000)

7. Berend, D., Brafman, R., Cohen, S., Shimony, S., Zucker, S.: Optimal ordering of independent tests with precedence constraints. Discrete Applied Mathematics **162**, 115–127 (2014)
8. Chen, C., Lee, S., Shen, Q.: An analytical model for the container loading problem. European Journal of Operational Research **80**(1), 68–76 (1995)
9. Cruz-Reyes, L., H., P.H., Melin, P., H., H.J.F., O., J.M.: Constructive algorithm for a benchmark in ship stowage planning. In: Castillo, O., Melin, P., Kacprzyk, J. (eds.) Recent Advances on Hybrid Intelligent Systems. SCI, vol. 451, pp. 393–408. Springer, Heidelberg (2013)
10. Garey, M.: Optimal task sequencing with precedence constraints. Discrete Mathematics **4**(1), 37–56 (1973)
11. Liu, F., Low, M.Y.H., Hsu, W.J., Huang, S.Y., Zeng, M., Win, C.A.: Randomized algorithm with tabu search for multi-objective optimization of large containership stowage plans. In: Böse, J.W., Hu, H., Jahn, C., Shi, X., Stahlbock, R., Voß, S. (eds.) ICCL 2011. LNCS, vol. 6971, pp. 256–272. Springer, Heidelberg (2011)
12. Liu, F., Low, M.Y.H., Huang, S.Y., Hsu, W.-J., Zeng, M., Win, C.A.: Stowage planning of large containership with tradeoff between crane workload balance and ship stability. In: Proceedings of the International MultiConference of Engineers and Computer Scientists 2010 (IMECS 2010), vol. III (2010)
13. Low, M., Zeng, M., Hsu, W., Huang, S.Y., Liu, F., Win, C.A.: Improving safety and stability of large containerships in automated stowage planning. IEEE Systems Journal **5**(1), 50–60 (2011)
14. Win, C.A., Low, M.Y.H., Huang, S.Y., Hsu, W.-J., Liu, F., Zeng, M.: An efficient block-based heuristic method for stowage planning of large containerships with crane split consideration. In: Proceedings of the International MultiConference of Engineers and Computer Scientists 2010 (IMECS 2010), vol. II (2010)
15. Xiao, X., Low, M.Y.H., Liu, F., Huang, S.Y., Hsu, W.J., Li, Z.: An efficient block-based heuristic method for stowage planning of large containerships with crane split consideration. In: The International Conference on Harbour, Maritime and Multimodel Logistics Modelling and Simulation (2009)
16. Zeng, M., Low, M., Hsu, W., Huang, S.Y., Liu, F., Win, C.A.: Automated stowage planning for large containerships with improved safety and stability. In: Proceedings of the 2010 Winter Simulation Conference (WSC), pp. 1976–1989, December 2010
17. Zeng, M., Low, M., Hsu, W.J., Huang, S.Y., Liu, F., Win, C.A.: Proceedings of the International MultiConference of Engineers and Computer Scientists 2010 (IMECS 2010), vol. III, March 2010

Probabilistic Analysis of Online Stacking Algorithms

Martin Olsen[✉] and Allan Gross

Department of Business Development and Technology,
Aarhus University, Aarhus, Denmark
{martino,agr}@auhe.au.dk

Abstract. Consider the situation where some items arrive to a storage location where they are temporarily stored in bounded capacity LIFO stacks until their departure. We consider the problem of deciding where to put an arriving item with the objective of using as few stacks as possible. The decision has to be made as soon as an item arrives and we assume that we only have information on the departure times for the arriving item and the items currently at the storage area. We are only allowed to put an item on top of another item if the item below departs at a later time. We assume that the numbers defining the storage time intervals are picked independently and uniformly at random from the interval $[0,1]$. We present a simple polynomial time online algorithm for the problem and prove the following: For any positive real numbers $\epsilon_1, \epsilon_2 > 0$ there exists an $N > 0$ such that the algorithm uses no more than $(1 + \epsilon_1)OPT$ stacks with probability at least $1 - \epsilon_2$ if the number of items is at least N where OPT denotes the optimal number of stacks. The result even holds if the stack capacity is $o(\sqrt{n})$ where n is the number of items.

1 Introduction

In this paper, we consider the situation where some items arrive to a storage location where the items are temporarily stored in LIFO stacks until their departure. When an item arrives we are faced with the problem of deciding where to store the item. We will refer to this problem as the stacking problem. The stacking problem has many applications within real world logistics. As an example, the items could be containers and the storage location could be a container terminal or a container ship [3]. The items could also be steel bars [11], trains [5] or the storage location could simply be a warehouse storing anything that could be stacked on top of each other.

We focus on the variant of the stacking problem given by the following assumptions: 1) We have to make a decision on where to store an item as soon as it arrives. When an item i arrives at time x_i we are informed on the departure time y_i of the item but we have no information on future items. In other words, we look at an *online* version of the problem and we look for online algorithms solving the problem. 2) The numbers x_i and y_i could be any real numbers. This

© Springer International Publishing Switzerland 2015
F. Corman et al. (Eds.): ICCL 2015, LNCS 9335, pp. 358–369, 2015.
DOI: 10.1007/978-3-319-24264-4_25

means that we restrict our attention to what we will refer to as the *continuous* case as opposed to the *discrete* case where we only have a few possibilities for x_i and y_i. 3) We are only allowed to put an item i on top of an item j if $y_i \leq y_j$. Another way of saying this is that we do not allow *rehandling* or *relocations* of items. 4) The objective is to use as few stacks as possible given a bound b on the stack height. There are several real world applications for algorithms solving this variant for the stacking problem. Two examples for applications are track assignment for trains at train depots [5] and stacking of containers in container terminals.

The basis for our analysis is a stochastic model for generating instances for the stacking problem. The numbers defining the storage time intervals are simply picked independently and uniformly at random from the interval $[0, 1]$. The main contribution of our paper is a proof of the existence of a simple polynomial time online algorithm for the stacking problem that we consider such that the following holds: For any positive real numbers $\epsilon_1, \epsilon_2 > 0$ there exists an $N > 0$ such that the algorithm uses no more than $(1 + \epsilon_1)OPT$ stacks with probability at least $1 - \epsilon_2$ if the number of items is at least N where OPT denotes the optimal number of stacks. In other words, we show that the competitive ratio of the online algorithm – the number of stacks used divided by OPT – converges to 1 in probability using terminology from probability theory. Our results do *not* require the stack capacity b to be a fixed constant but $b = o(\sqrt{n})$ is sufficient where n is the number of items. We believe that similar results hold for many other stochastic models as discussed in the final part of the paper.

The paper also contributes methodologically because we demonstrate an alternative or supplementary way of evaluating online stacking rules: Assuming a natural probability distribution on problem instances, we analyze a simple online stacking algorithm using probability theory and prove that the algorithm performs well. It is important to note that algorithms almost identical to our algorithm have been presented previously in the literature [3,14]. Consequently, the main contributions of our paper are the results on the performance of the algorithm and the demonstration of the use of probabilistic analysis for obtaining the results.

1.1 Related Work

The offline variant of the stacking problem where all information is provided before any decisions are made is NP-hard for any fixed bound $b \geq 6$ on the stacking height [4] as can be seen from reduction from the coloring problem for permutation graphs [6]. This variant of the problem is also NP-hard in the unbounded case as shown by Avriel et al. [2]. Tierney et al. [13] show that the problem of deciding if it possible to accommodate all the items in a *fixed* number of bounded capacity stacks without relocations can be solved in polynomial time but the running time of their offline algorithm is huge even for a small (fixed) number of stacks.

Cornelsen and Di Stefano [4] and Demange et al. [5] consider the problem in the context of assigning tracks to trains arriving at a train station/depot.

Cornelsen and Di Stefano consider unbounded capacity stacks (train tracks) but Demange et al. consider "our" problem with bounded capacity stacks. Demange et al. present lower and upper bounds around 2 for online algorithms for the problem restricted to the situation where all trains are at the train depot at some point in time – this condition is known as *the midnight condition*. Demange et al. also present lower and upper bounds for the unbounded stack capacity case.

Wang et al. [14] also consider the stacking problem but in the context of stowage of container ships and present a Mixed Integer Linear Program for solving it. Wang et al. present algorithms almost identical to the one we present and analyze. Wang et al. look at the discrete case assuming that the number of ports is relatively low compared to the number of containers and show that their algorithms use no more than $OPT + P$ stacks where P is the number of ports where containers are loaded. It should be noted that this is an upper bound that also can be achieved if containers loaded at the same port simply are stacked on top of each other (sorted according to the length of their voyage). Borgman et al. [3] also present an online algorithm similar to the one we present and compare it with other rules for online stacking using discrete-event simulation.

Finally, we mention the work of Rei and Pedroso [11] and König et al. [8] on related problems within the steel industry and the PhD Thesis of Pacino [9] on container ship stowage.

1.2 Outline of the Paper

In Section 2 we look at the link between stacking problems and the coloring problems for overlap graphs and interval graphs and introduce some terminology used in the paper. We also consider some results from the field of probability theory that form the basis for the probabilistic analysis of our online algorithm. Our algorithm is introduced in an offline and an online version in Section 3. Finally, we present the analysis of the algorithm and our main result in Section 4.

2   Preliminaries

In this section we present most of the terminology used in this paper and some results from probability theory that we will use later.

2.1   Connections to Graph Coloring

For each item i we have an interval $I_i = [x_i, y_i]$ specifying the time interval that the item has to be temporarily stored. We assume that items cannot arrive and depart at exactly the same time to make it easier to formulate the constraint on the stacking height.

It is well known that the problem that we consider can be formulated as a graph coloring problem and we will use graph coloring terminology in the remaining part of the paper in order to make the presentation generic. We say that two intervals $I_1 = [x_1, y_1]$ and $I_2 = [x_2, y_2]$ *overlap* if and only if $x_1 < x_2 <$

$y_1 < y_2$ or $x_2 < x_1 < y_2 < y_1$. We can put an item on top of another item if and only if their corresponding intervals do not overlap so our problem can now be formally defined as follows where b is the maximum allowed stack height:

Definition 1. *The b-OVERLAP-COLORING problem:*

- *Instance: A set of n intervals $\mathcal{I} = \{I_1, I_2, \ldots, I_n\}$ where all the end points of the intervals are distinct.*
- *Solution: A coloring of the intervals using a minimum number of colors such that the following two conditions hold:*
  1. *Any two overlapping intervals have different colors.*
  2. *For any real number x and any color d there will be no more than b intervals with color d that contain x.*

It should be stressed that we look for online algorithms for the problem processing the intervals in the order of increasing starting points of the intervals.

The problem can be viewed as a graph coloring problem for the graph with a vertex for each interval and an edge between any two vertices where the corresponding intervals overlap. Such a graph is known as an *overlap graph*. We let χ_b denote the minimum number of colors for a solution.

An *interval graph* is a graph where each vertex corresponds to an interval and with an edge between two vertices if and only if the corresponding intervals *intersect*. It is well known that we can obtain a minimum coloring of an interval graph if we use the following simple online algorithm processing the intervals in increasing order of their starting points: If we can reuse a color we do it – otherwise we pick a new color that we have not used earlier on. The clique number of a graph is the size of a maximum clique. Interval graphs are members of the family of *perfect* graphs implying that all interval graphs can be colored with a number of colors corresponding to their clique number.

2.2   Increasing Subsequences and Patience Sorting

The algorithm we present in Section 3 and the probabilistic analysis performed in Section 4 is based on some results from the theory on increasing subsequences and the method of Patience Sorting that we now will introduce. Patience Sorting [1] is a method originally invented for sorting a deck of cards. Now imagine that we have a small deck of cards as follows where the top of the deck is the leftmost card (the underlined cards will be explained later):

$$9, \underline{2}, \underline{4}, 8, 1, 7, \underline{6}, 3, 5, \underline{10}$$

We now take the top card 9 and start a new pile. We now remove the other cards from the initial deck one by one from the top of the deck. Each time we remove a card we try to put it in another pile with a top card with a higher value than the removed card. If it is possible, we choose such a pile where the top card has the smallest value. If not, we start a new pile. The card 2 goes on top of the card 9 but we have to start two new piles with the cards 4 and 8 respectively.

The card 1 can be put on top of the card 2, etc. Finally, we face the following four piles:

$$1, 2, 9 \qquad 3, 4 \qquad 5, 6, 7, 8 \qquad 10$$

It is now easy to sort the cards by repeatedly picking the smallest top card. This is the Patience Sorting method and we refer the reader to the work by Aldous [1] for more details.

Let L_n be the random variable representing the resulting number of piles for the Patience Sorting method on a deck with n cards. It is worth noting that L_n is identical to the length of the longest increasing subsequence for the sequence of cards defined by the deck. To illustrate this there are several increasing subsequences that have length 4 for the sequence shown above (for example the subsequence 2, 4, 6, 10 that is underlined) but no increasing subsequence with length 5 or more – and the number of piles needed is 4. Each pile represents a decreasing subsequence and L_n is the minimum number of decreasing subsequences into which the sequence can be partitioned. Let μ and σ denote the expected value and the standard deviation of L_n respectively under the assumption that the permutation corresponding to the deck of cards is picked uniformly at random. The asymptotic behavior of L_n is described as follows where σ_∞ is a positive constant [1, 10]:

$$\mu \leq 2\sqrt{n} \tag{1}$$

$$\sigma = \sigma_\infty n^{\frac{1}{6}} + o(n^{\frac{1}{6}}) \tag{2}$$

These facts are crucial for the analysis of the online algorithm we present later in this paper.

3   The Algorithm

Before we present our stacking strategy we need to introduce a little more terminology. A *chain* of intervals is a sequence of intervals $I_1 \supseteq I_2 \supseteq I_3 \supseteq \ldots \supseteq I_m$. The intervals in a chain represent items that may be stacked on top of each other. We refer to the intervals I_1 and I_m as the *bottom* and the *top* of the chain respectively. For a given number b, we can split a chain into chains of cardinality b or less in a natural way: The intervals I_1 to I_b form the first chain, the next b intervals I_{b+1} to I_{2b} form the next chain, etc. A partition of $\mathcal{I}$ into chains is a set of chains such that each interval is a member of exactly one chain.

We present two versions of our algorithm named A and B that produce the same coloring for any instance of the b-OVERLAP-COLORING problem. Algorithm A is an offline version and algorithm B is an online version. Algorithm A is presented in order to make it easier for the reader to understand the coloring strategy used.

We are now ready to describe algorithm A that consists of 4 steps listed in Fig. 1. In the first step, we partition $\mathcal{I}$ into a minimum number of chains as illustrated in Fig. 2. In the second step, we split the chains into chains of cardinality b or less as described above. The interval graph of the bottoms of the chains is colored in the third step using the simple algorithm described in Section 2.1. Finally, in the fourth step, all the remaining intervals are colored with the color at the bottom of their chain. The steps 2, 3 and 4 are illustrated in Fig. 3 for the case $b = 2$. It is not hard to see that the coloring produced satisfies the conditions from Definition 1: All the chains produced in Step 2 have cardinality at most b and chain bottoms with the same color do not intersect.

Algorithm A($\mathcal{I}$, b):
    Step 1: Partition $\mathcal{I}$ into a minimum number c of chains.
    Step 2: Split the chains into chains of cardinality b or less.
    Step 3: Color the interval graph formed by the bottoms of the chains with χ_b' colors.
    Step 4: Color any interval not at the bottom of a chain with the color of the bottom of its chain.

Fig. 1. The offline version of our algorithm

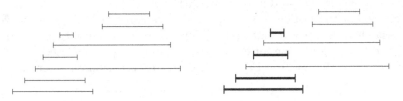

Fig. 2. The initial phase of algorithm A is illustrated here. To the left we see the intervals forming the instance. The two chains created in step 1 are shown to the right.

We now prove that it is possible to transform algorithm A into an online version, algorithm B, that is listed in Fig. 4.

Lemma 1. *There is an online algorithm for the b-OVERLAP-COLORING problem processing the intervals in increasing order of the starting points that produces a coloring identical to the coloring produced by Algorithm A. The time for processing one interval is $O(\log n)$ for the algorithm.*

Proof. Let π be a permutation of the integers from 1 to n such that $x_{\pi(i)} < x_{\pi(j)}$ for $i < j$. Now we consider the sequence where the i'th number is $y_{\pi(i)}$. There is a simple one-to-one correspondence between a decreasing subsequence of this sequence and a chain of intervals from the set $\mathcal{I}$: If we start at the bottom of a chain and move upward then the x-values increase and the y-values decrease. This means that we obtain a partition of $\mathcal{I}$ into a minimum number of chains if we apply the Patience Sorting method described in Section 2.2 and partition the sequence into a minimum number of decreasing subsequences.

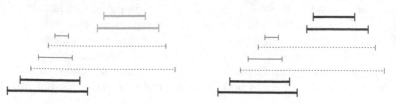

Fig. 3. This figure illustrates the final phase of algorithm A for the case $b = 2$. The four chains produced in step 2 are shown to the left and the coloring produced in the steps 3 and 4 is shown to the right. The algorithm generates a coloring using $\chi'_b = 3$ colors.

The intervals are processed in increasing order of their starting points when the Patience Sorting method is used and decisions on an interval are made without considering intervals with bigger starting points. The same goes for the splitting into smaller chains and the coloring of the chain bottoms and the other intervals. This means that we can construct an online algorithm processing the intervals in increasing order of the starting points that produces the same coloring as the coloring produced by algorithm A.

Each step of the Patience Sorting method requires $O(\log n)$ time if we use binary search to locate the right pile. Keeping track of unused colors can also be handled in $O(\log n)$ time for each step if a priority queue is used (A priority queue is used for the set $\mathcal{D}$ in Fig. 4 that stores information on when the colors expire). $\qquad\square$

4   Probabilistic Analysis

Let ω' be the clique number of the interval graph formed by the set of intervals $\mathcal{I}$. We remind the reader that c is the minimum number of chains formed in Step 1 of algorithm A.

Lemma 2. *The coloring produced by algorithms A and B uses χ'_b colors satisfying*

$$\chi'_b \leq \frac{\omega'}{b} + c \ . \tag{3}$$

Proof. For any real number x we let g_x denote the number of intervals in $\mathcal{I}$ that contain x and g^b_x denote the number of chain bottoms produced in step 2 containing x. As mentioned in Section 2.1, any interval graph can be colored with a number of colors corresponding to the size of the largest clique of the graph:

$$\chi'_b = \max_x g^b_x \ . \tag{4}$$

Now consider an interval that is a bottom of a chain produced in step 2 of algorithm A but not a bottom of one of the chains produced in step 1. If such

Algorithm B($\mathcal{I}$, b):
   Assumption on $\mathcal{I} = \{[x_1, y_1], [x_2, y_2], \ldots, [x_n, y_n]\}$: $i < j \Rightarrow x_i < x_j$

  1: $\mathcal{C} \leftarrow \emptyset$
  2: $\mathcal{D} \leftarrow \emptyset$
  3: $\chi \leftarrow 0$
  4: **for** $i \in \{1, 2, \ldots, n\}$ **do**
  5:     *bottom* $\leftarrow$ false
  6:     Let $\mathcal{H}$ be the set of chains in $\mathcal{C}$ where
       the top of the chain contains I_i.
  7:     **if** $\mathcal{H} = \emptyset$ **then**
  8:         Add a new chain to $\mathcal{C}$ consisting of I_i.
  9:         *bottom* $\leftarrow$ true
10:     **else**
11:         Let c_J be the chain in $\mathcal{H}$ with a top interval
           $J[x_J, y_J]$ with the smallest value of y_J.
12:         Put I_i on top of c_J.
13:         Let d be the color assigned to J.
14:         **if** there are less than b intervals in c_J with color d **then**
15:            Assign color d to I_i.
16:         **else**
17:            *bottom* $\leftarrow$ true
18:         **end if**
19:     **end if**
20:
21:     **if** *bottom* = true **then**
22:         Let $\mathcal{G} = \{(d, y) \in \mathcal{D} : y < x_i\}$
23:         **if** $\mathcal{G} = \emptyset$ **then**
24:            $\chi \leftarrow \chi + 1$
25:            Assign color χ to I_i.
26:            $\mathcal{D} \leftarrow \mathcal{D} \cup \{(\chi, y_i)\}$
27:         **else**
28:            Pick any $(d, y) \in \mathcal{G}$.
29:            Assign color d to I_i.
30:            $\mathcal{D} \leftarrow (\mathcal{D} \setminus \{(d, y)\}) \cup \{(d, y_i)\}$
31:         **end if**
32:     **end if**
33: **end for**

Fig. 4. The online version of our algorithm. Please note that we assume the intervals in $\mathcal{I}$ to appear in increasing order of their starting points.

an interval contains a number x then the $b - 1$ intervals directly below it in the chain will also contain x. There are at least $g_x^b - c$ such intervals that contain x so we obtain the following inequality:

$$(g_x^b - c)b \leq g_x \ . \tag{5}$$

We now rearrange this inequality:

$$\max_x g_x^b \le \frac{\max_x g_x}{b} + c \ . \tag{6}$$

We now use (4) and $\omega' = \max_x g_x$. $\square$

As mentioned in Section 1.1, Wang et al. [14] prove a weaker result than stated in the lemma using similar arguments for the discrete case where we consider the continuous case (If P is the number of ports where containers are loaded then we obviously have $c \le P$).

We will use the following random process for generating stacking problem instances that was also used by Scheinerman [12] in a study of random interval graphs: Let $A_1, B_1, A_2, B_2, \ldots, A_n, B_n$ be independent random variables that are uniformly distributed on $[0, 1]$. Let $I_i = [X_i, Y_i]$ where $X_i = \min(A_i, B_i)$ and $Y_i = \max(A_i, B_i)$ The instance generated by the procedure is $\mathcal{I} = \{I_1, I_2, \ldots, I_n\}$. It should be noted, that the end points of the intervals in $\mathcal{I}$ are distinct with probability 1 according to [12].

As mentioned earlier, we let χ_b denote the minimum number of colors for a solution to the b-OVERLAP-COLORING problem. Our aim is to show that the competitive ratio $\frac{\chi_b'}{\chi_b}$ of algorithm B is close to 1 with high probability. Formally, we say that an event E_n occurs *with high probability*, abbreviated whp, if $P(E_n) \to 1$ as $n \to +\infty$ where we assume that the underlying probability distribution corresponds to the random process for generating instances. There is a number α contained in ω' intervals implying $\chi_b \ge \frac{\omega'}{b}$. Using Lemma 2, we now conclude that the competitive ratio is not bigger than $1 + c/\left(\frac{\omega'}{b}\right)$. We will now show that the competitive ratio is $1 + O(bn^{-\frac{1}{2}})$ whp. The strategy of our proof is to show that $c = O(\sqrt{n})$ whp and combine this with the fact $\omega' = \Omega(n)$ whp shown by Scheinerman [12]. We start by showing $c = O(\sqrt{n})$ whp:

Lemma 3. *The set of intervals $\mathcal{I}$ is partitioned into less than $5\sqrt{n}$ chains whp in Step 1 of Algorithm A.*

Proof. Consider the random variables A_i and B_i, $i \in \{1, 2, \ldots, n\}$. Let a_i and b_i denote the values observed for A_i and B_i respectively. We introduce another partition π' on the integers from 1 to n defined by $a_{\pi'(i)} < a_{\pi'(j)}$ for $i < j$. We now look at the sequence of b-values with $b_{\pi'(i)}$ as the i'th number in the sequence. We use the Patience Sorting method from Section 2.2 on the b-sequence and obtain c' decreasing subsequences. We split each subsequence into two decreasing subsequences if there is a point where the b-values become smaller than their corresponding a-values. It is not hard to see that we can form a chain of intervals for each of the up to $2c'$ subsequences we obtain by the splitting procedure – see Fig. 5. Since $c \le 2c'$ we have the following:

$$P(c \ge 5\sqrt{n}) \le P\left(c' \ge \frac{5}{2}\sqrt{n}\right) \ . \tag{7}$$

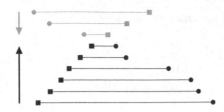

Fig. 5. The figure shows a decreasing subsequence for the sequence of b-values. The squares and circles correspond to a-values and b-values respectively. The decreasing subsequence can be split into a grey chain and a black chain of intervals.

The B-variables are independent and drawn from the same probability distribution so c' and L_n have the same distribution where L_n is the length of the longest increasing subsequence for a permutation of n numbers chosen uniformly at random (see Section 2.2):

$$P\left(c' \geq \frac{5}{2}\sqrt{n}\right) = P\left(L_n \geq \frac{5}{2}\sqrt{n}\right) . \tag{8}$$

Using (1) we get the following:

$$P\left(L_n \geq \frac{5}{2}\sqrt{n}\right) \leq P\left(|L_n - \mu| \geq \frac{1}{2}\sqrt{n}\right) . \tag{9}$$

From (2) we observe that $\sigma \leq \frac{3}{2}\sigma_\infty n^{\frac{1}{6}}$ for n sufficiently big. By using Chebyshevs inequality [7] we now get the following for n sufficiently big:

$$P\left(|L_n - \mu| \geq \frac{1}{2}\sqrt{n}\right) \leq \frac{\sigma^2}{(\frac{1}{4}n)} \leq \frac{\frac{9}{4}\sigma_\infty^2 n^{\frac{1}{3}}}{(\frac{1}{4}n)} = 9\sigma_\infty^2 n^{-\frac{2}{3}} . \tag{10}$$

From (7), (8), (9) and (10) we now get the following for n sufficiently big:

$$P(c < 5\sqrt{n}) \geq 1 - 9\sigma_\infty^2 n^{-\frac{2}{3}} . \tag{11}$$

From (11) we conclude that $c < 5\sqrt{n}$ whp.   □

We now present the main theorem of the paper:

Theorem 1. *There is an online algorithm for the b-OVERLAP-COLORING problem processing the intervals in increasing order of their starting points such that*

$$\frac{\chi'_b}{\chi_b} \leq 1 + O(bn^{-\frac{1}{2}}) \ whp \tag{12}$$

The time for processing one interval is $O(\log n)$.

Proof. Algorithm B is an online algorithm computing the same coloring as algorithm A according to Lemma 1. From Lemma 2 and Lemma 3 we conclude that

$\chi'_b \leq \frac{\omega'}{b} + 5\sqrt{n}$ whp. The minimum number of colors χ_b satisfies $\chi_b \geq \frac{\omega'}{b}$ so we now have the following:

$$\frac{\chi'_b}{\chi_b} \leq 1 + \frac{5b\sqrt{n}}{\omega'} \text{ whp} \tag{13}$$

Finally, we use that ω' is $\frac{n}{2} + o(n)$ whp [12]. □

A corollary of Theorem 1 is that $\frac{\chi'_b}{\chi_b}$ converges to 1 in probability if $b = o(\sqrt{n})$. Another thing to note is that the underlying constant for the big O notation is not that big (around 10).

Future Directions

We believe that Theorem 1 – or a similar result – holds for many other stochastic models for generating stacking problem instances. To be more specific, we believe that there are other relevant random processes for generating instances having the following properties: 1) $c = o(n)$ whp, and 2) $b\chi_b = \Omega(n)$ whp. Intuitively, we would expect the average chain size $\frac{n}{c}$ to tend to infinity as n tends to infinity implying $c = o(n)$ unless all the intervals have the same length. As noted in the proof of Lemma 3, then we only use the independence of the B-variables and the fact that these variables are drawn from the same distribution to prove $c = o(n)$ whp so property 1) holds for other models as well. Property 2) seems easier to handle. Property 2) can be shown to hold for any random process where intervals with end points in $[0,1]$ are drawn independently from the same distribution. Analyzing the behavior of c for other stochastic models in an attempt to extend the scope for our results thus seems to be an interesting challenge.

As a final note, we also believe that similar results hold for stacking algorithms similar to the one we have presented. If this is the case it would be interesting to compare the rates of convergence.

Acknowledgments. This work has been supported by the Danish Council for Strategic Research project EcoSense (11-115331).

References

1. Aldous, D., Diaconis, P.: Longest increasing subsequences: From patience sorting to the baik-deift-johansson theorem. Bull. Amer. Math. Soc. **36**, 413–432 (1999)
2. Avriel, M., Penn, M., Shpirer, N.: Container ship stowage problem: complexity and connection to the coloring of circle graphs. Discrete Applied Mathematics **103**(1–3), 271–279 (2000)
3. Borgman, B., van Asperen, E., Dekker, R.: Online rules for container stacking. OR Spectrum **32**(3), 687–716 (2010)
4. Cornelsen, S., Di Stefano, G.: Track assignment. Journal of Discrete Algorithms **5**(2), 250–261 (2007)
5. Demange, M., Di Stefano, G., Leroy-Beaulieu, B.: On the online track assignment problem. Discrete Applied Mathematics **160**(7–8), 1072–1093 (2012)

6. Jansen, K.: The mutual exclusion scheduling problem for permutation and comparability graphs. Information and Computation **180**(2), 71–81 (2003)
7. Kobayashi, H., Mark, B.L., Turin, W.: Probability, Random Processes, and Statistical Analysis: Applications to Communications, Signal Processing, Queueing Theory and Mathematical Finance. Cambridge University Press (2012)
8. König, F.G., Lübbecke, M., Möhring, R.H., Schäfer, G., Spenke, I.: Solutions to real-world instances of PSPACE-complete stacking. In: Arge, L., Hoffmann, M., Welzl, E. (eds.) ESA 2007. LNCS, vol. 4698, pp. 729–740. Springer, Heidelberg (2007)
9. Pacino, D., Jensen, R.M.: Fast Generation of Container Vessel Stowage Plans: using mixed integer programming for optimal master planning and constraint based local search for slot planning. PhD thesis, IT University of Copenhagen (2012)
10. Pilpel, S.: Descending subsequences of random permutations. Journal of Combinatorial Theory, Series A **53**(1), 96–116 (1990)
11. Rei, R.J., Pedroso, J.P.: Tree search for the stacking problem. Annals OR **203**(1), 371–388 (2013)
12. Scheinerman, E.R.: Random interval graphs. Combinatorica **8**(4), 357–371 (1988)
13. Tierney, K., Pacino, D., Jensen, R.M.: On the complexity of container stowage planning problems. Discrete Applied Mathematics **169**, 225–230 (2014)
14. Wang, N., Zhang, Z., Lim, A.: The stowage stack minimization problem with zero rehandle constraint. In: Ali, M., Pan, J.-S., Chen, S.-M., Horng, M.-F. (eds.) IEA/AIE 2014, Part II. LNCS, vol. 8482, pp. 456–465. Springer, Heidelberg (2014)

Dynamic Multi-period Freight Consolidation

Arturo Pérez Rivera[✉] and Martijn Mes

Department of Industrial Engineering and Business Information Systems,
University of Twente, P.O. Box 217, 7500 AE Enschede, The Netherlands
{a.e.perezrivera,m.r.k.mes}@utwente.nl

Abstract. Logistic Service Providers (LSPs) offering hinterland transportation face the trade-off between efficiently using the capacity of long-haul vehicles and minimizing the first and last-mile costs. To achieve the optimal trade-off, freights have to be consolidated considering the variation in the arrival of freight and their characteristics, the applicable transportation restrictions, and the interdependence of decisions over time. We propose the use of a Markov model and an Approximate Dynamic Programming (ADP) algorithm to consolidate the right freights in such transportation settings. Our model incorporates probabilistic knowledge of the arrival of freights and their characteristics, as well as generic definitions of transportation restrictions and costs. Using small test instances, we show that our ADP solution provides accurate approximations to the optimal solution of the Markov model. Using larger problem instances, we show that our modeling approach has significant benefits when compared to common-practice heuristic approaches.

Keywords: Intermodal transportation · Transportation planning · Consolidation · Time horizon · Approximate dynamic programming

1 Introduction

Over the last decade, the hinterland transportation industry has experienced a change towards network oriented services. Many Logistic Service Providers (LSPs) now offer services such as pick-up, intermediate storage, long-haul, and last-mile delivery of freight. With this change, new challenges arise for LSPs who organize their processes (and possibly carriers) seeking the highest efficiency of their entire transportation network. We investigate one of such challenges faced by a LSP in The Netherlands. On a daily basis, this Dutch LSP transports containers from the East of the country to different terminals in the port of Rotterdam using reserved capacity on a barge. The costs of the long-haul are fixed, but the last-mile costs come from the time required for sailing, waiting, and handling of containers at around 12 container terminals spread over a distance of 40km in Rotterdam, and the use of trucks for urgent containers. The challenge is then to consolidate containers in such a way that only a few close-by terminals are visited each day and the reserved barge capacity is used efficiently over time.

© Springer International Publishing Switzerland 2015
F. Corman et al. (Eds.): ICCL 2015, LNCS 9335, pp. 370–385, 2015.
DOI: 10.1007/978-3-319-24264-4_26

In operations research terms, we study the planning problem that arises when a company transports freights from a single origin to different destinations, periodically. The destinations of these freights are far away and closer among themselves than to the origin. For this reason, the long-haul is the same in every trip, independent of which freights were consolidated at the origin. However, the last-mile route varies according to the destinations of the freights that were consolidated at the beginning of the long-haul. In addition, there is an alternative mode that can be used to transport freights directly from their origin to their destination. The objective of the company is to reduce its total costs over time and to use the vehicle's capacity efficiently.

In companies with the aforementioned characteristics, costs savings are only possible in the last-mile and in the use of the alternative transportation mode. The first source of costs is influenced by factors such as unloading time, waiting time, service reliability, etc. As a result, combinations of destinations might have different last-mile costs even when the distance between them is the same. The second source of costs depends on the use of the alternative mode. Properly balancing the consolidation and postponement of freights is therefore a challenge for the company but also a necessity for its efficient operation.

For several reasons, minimizing costs over time through freight consolidation is not straightforward. First, the number of freights that arrive, and their characteristics, vary from day to day. This uncertainty makes it difficult to know which freights to postpone for future trips. Second, each freight has a time-window for transportation. Furthermore, not all freights which arrive on the same day have the same destination or time-window. Third, the objective of carrying as many freights as possible in the long-haul vehicle each day can be conflicting with the objective of reducing last-mile costs in the long run. To handle these planning challenges and to reduce costs over time, we propose the use of a Markov model and a solution algorithm based in Approximate Dynamic Programming (ADP).

The remaining of this paper is organized as follows. In Section 2, we briefly introduce the relevant scientific literature on dynamic multi-period freight consolidation and outline our contribution to it. In Section 3, we present the mathematical notation of the problem characteristics and the formulation of the Markov model. Also in this section, we present our ADP approach. In Section 4, we carry out a series of numerical experiments, as well as a discussion of our results and approach. We close with conclusions and future research directions in Section 5.

2   Literature Review

In this section, we briefly study the literature on freight consolidation in intermodal transportation networks. In particular, we look at papers about dynamically choosing transportation modes for different types of freights. We shortly examine advantages, limitations, and extension opportunities, of both models and solution methods proposed in these papers. For a comprehensive literature study on tactical and operational planning problems in intermodal transportation networks we refer to the reviews [12] and [5].

The problem in this paper falls into the category of Dynamic Service Network Design (DSND). Most DSND models assume deterministic demand [12]. In addition, most models consider the context of a single carrier and cyclically scheduled services where there are hardly any time-dependencies, even when there are multi-period horizons [5]. Although there are exceptions to these shortcomings, models seem to focus on one exception at a time and leave out the rest. For example, models which include *multiple modes* of transportation, such as [9], usually do not incorporate time issues. On the other hand, the few models which include *time dependencies*, such as [3], are developed for a single mode. The few models that include *uncertainty* in the demand, such as [6], are usually developed for the road transportation mode.

Most DSND solution approaches are based on graph theory, mathematical programming techniques, and heuristics [12,14]. Solutions based on graph theory cannot deal with time-dependencies for large instances and assume deterministic demand most of the time. To avoid these shortcomings and handle the complexities of large size problems, mathematical programming techniques such as cycle-based variables [2], branch-and-price [1], or column generation [9] have been proposed. With a similar goal, metaheuristic extensions such as Tabu Search [4,13] have been vastly proposed [12]. A disadvantage of most of these heuristics and mathematical programming techniques is that they are less suitable for stochastic settings. Further design such as stochastic scenarios [6] or probabilistic constraints is required to incorporate stochastic elements. Nevertheless, the need and the benefits of introducing stochastic elements into DSND formulations have been widely recognized in practice [8].

As mentioned by Wieberneit [14], realistic instances of DSND problems are difficult to solve with the exact approaches presented in the literature. Although these exact approaches have been studied for some years now [7], research about the use of approximations and decompositions, especially for stochastic multi-period problems, has been scarce [8,12,14]. Considering these challenges and opportunities, we believe our contribution to the scientific literature of DSND problems and intermodal transportation planning is two-fold. First, we develop a Markov model that handles complex time dependencies, incorporates stochastic demand (and its characteristics), for a multi-period horizon, and has a generic definition of costs. Second, we develop a solution algorithm, based on Approximate Dynamic Programming (ADP), that makes the aforementioned model computationally applicable to realistic-size problems.

3   Problem Description and Formulation

We consider a dynamic multi-period long-haul freight consolidation problem in which decisions are made on consecutive periods t over a finite horizon $\mathcal{T} = \{0, 1, 2, ..., T^{max} - 1\}$. For simplicity, in the remaining of the paper we refer to a period as a day. The main decision at each day is which of the known and released-for-transport freights to transport using the long-haul vehicle. Each freight must be delivered to a given destination d from a group of destinations

$\mathcal{D}$ within a given time-window. The time-window of a freight begins at a release-day $r \in \mathcal{R} = \{0, 1, 2, ..., R^{max}\}$ and ends at a due-day $r + k$, where $k \in \mathcal{K} = \{0, 1, 2, ..., K^{max}\}$ defines the length of the time-window. The arrival-day t of a freight is the moment when all its information is known to the planner. Note that r influences how long the freights are known before they can be transported, and thus influences the degree of uncertainty in the decisions.

New freights become available as time progresses. These freights and their characteristics are unknown before they arrive, but the planner has some probabilistic knowledge about them as follows. F is the discrete and finite random variable describing the variation in the total number of freights arriving per day. D is the random variable describing the variation in the destination of each freight, with domain $D \in \mathcal{D}$. R and K are two random variables with domains $R \in \mathcal{R}$ and $K \in \mathcal{K}$, respectively, which describe the variation of the time-window of each freight. Between two consecutive days, a number of freights f arrive with probability p_f^F, independent of the arrival day. Each freight has destination d with probability p_d^D, release-day r with probability p_r^R, and time-window length k with probability p_k^K, independent of the day and of other freights.

Each day, there is only one long-haul vehicle which transports at most Q freights. Its cost is $C_{\mathcal{D}'}$, where $\mathcal{D}' \subseteq \mathcal{D}$ denotes the subset of destinations visited. There is also an alternative transport mode for each destination d which has unlimited transport capacity, but can only be used for freights whose due-day is immediate (i.e., $r = k = 0$). Its cost is B_d per freight to destination d.

3.1   Markov Model

In this section, we model the characteristics described before into stages, states, decision variables, transitions, and optimality equations of a Markov model. The *stages* correspond to the days of the planning horizon denoted by t. At each stage t, there are known freights with different characteristics. We define $F_{t,d,r,k}$ as the number of known freights at stage t whose destination is d, whose release-day is r stages after t, and whose time-window length is k (i.e., its due-day is $r + k$ stages after t). The *state* of the system at stage t is denoted by S_t and is defined as the vector of all freight variables $F_{t,d,r,k}$, as seen in (1).

$$S_t = [F_{t,d,r,k}]_{\forall d \in \mathcal{D}, r \in \mathcal{R}, k \in \mathcal{K}}, \ \forall t \in \mathcal{T} \tag{1}$$

The main *decision* made at each stage is which released freights (i.e., freights with $r = 0$) to consolidate in the long-haul vehicle. Note that the capacity of the long-haul vehicle is Q freights. We use the integer variable $x_{t,d,k}$ as the number of freights that are consolidated in the long-haul vehicle at stage t, which have destination d and are due k stages after t. We denote the vector of decision variables at stage t as x_t. Due to the time-window of freights, the possible values of these decision variables are state dependent. Thus, the feasible space of decision vector x_t, given a state S_t, is as follows:

$$x_t = [x_{t,d,k}]_{\forall d \in \mathcal{D}, k \in \mathcal{K}}, \ \forall t \in \mathcal{T} \tag{2a}$$

s.t.

$$\sum_{d \in \mathcal{D}} \sum_{k \in \mathcal{K}} x_{t,d,k} \leq Q, \tag{2b}$$

$$0 \leq x_{t,d,k} \leq F_{t,d,0,k}, \ |F_{t,d,0,k} \in S_t, \ \forall d \in \mathcal{D}, k \in \mathcal{K} \tag{2c}$$

As mentioned earlier, four discrete and independent random variables describe the arrival of freights, and their characteristics, over time: $\{F, D, R, K\}$. We combine them into a single arrival information variable $\widetilde{F}_{t,d,r,k}$ which represents the freights that arrived from outside the system between stages $t - 1$ and t with destination d, release-day r, and time-window length k. We denote the vector of all arrival information variables at stage t as $\boldsymbol{W}_t$, as seen in (3).

$$\boldsymbol{W}_t = \left[\widetilde{F}_{t,d,r,k} \right]_{\forall d \in \mathcal{D}, r \in \mathcal{R}, k \in \mathcal{K}}, \ \forall t \in \mathcal{T} \tag{3}$$

The consolidation decision $\boldsymbol{x}_t$ and arrival information $\boldsymbol{W}_t$ have an influence on the *transition* of the system between stages $t - 1$ and t. In addition, the relative time-windows have an influence on the transition between related freight variables. To represent all of these relations, we introduce the transition function S^M, as seen in (4a). In this function, we define freight variables $F_{t,d,r,k}$ at stage t with destination d as follows. First, freights which have been released at stage t (i.e., $r = 0$) and have a time-window length of k are the result of: (i) freights from the previous stage $t - 1$ which were already released, had time-window length $k + 1$, and were not transported (i.e., $F_{t-1,d,0,k+1} - x_{t-1,d,k+1}$), (ii) freights from the previous stage $t - 1$ with next-stage release-day (i.e., $r = 1$) and time-window length k (i.e., $F_{t-1,d,1,k}$), and (iii) the new (random) arriving freights with the same characteristics (i.e., $\widetilde{F}_{t,d,0,k}$) as seen in (4b). Second, freights which have not been released at stage t (i.e., $r \geq 1$) are the result of: (i) freights from the previous stage $t - 1$ with a release-day $r + 1$ and that have the same time-window length k, and (ii) the new freights with the same characteristics (i.e., $\widetilde{F}_{t,d,r,k}$), as seen in (4c). Third, freights which have the maximum release-day (i.e., $r = R^{max}$) are the result only of the new freights with the same characteristics (i.e., $\widetilde{F}_{t,d,R^{max},k}$), as seen in (4d).

$$S_t = S^M \left(S_{t-1}, \boldsymbol{x}_{t-1}, \boldsymbol{W}_t \right), \ \forall t \in \mathcal{T} | t > 0 \tag{4a}$$

s.t.

$$F_{t,d,0,k} = F_{t-1,d,0,k+1} - x_{t-1,d,k+1} + F_{t-1,d,1,k} + \widetilde{F}_{t,d,0,k}, \ |k < K^{max} \tag{4b}$$

$$F_{t,d,r,k} = F_{t-1,d,r+1,k} + \widetilde{F}_{t,d,r,k}, \ |r \geq 1 \tag{4c}$$

$$F_{t,d,R^{max},k} = \widetilde{F}_{t,d,R^{max},k}, \tag{4d}$$

$$\forall d \in \mathcal{D}, \ r \in \mathcal{R}, \ r + 1 \in \mathcal{R}, \ k \in \mathcal{K}, \ k + 1 \in \mathcal{K}$$

The cost of a decision $\boldsymbol{x}_t$ at a state $\boldsymbol{S}_t$ depends on the destinations visited and the use of the alternative mode. Note that last-mile costs $C_{\mathcal{D}'}$ depend on the subset of destinations $\mathcal{D}' \subseteq \mathcal{D}$ from the freights consolidated in the long-haul vehicle. Note also that there is an alternative transportation cost B_d per urgent freight (i.e., $r = k = 0$) to destination d that is not consolidated in the long-haul vehicle. To determine the total costs, we introduce two auxiliary variables:

(i) $y_{t,d} \in \{0,1\}$, which gets a value of 1 if any freight with destination d is consolidated in the long-haul vehicle at stage t and 0 otherwise, as seen in (5b), and (ii) $z_{t,d} \in \mathbb{Z}$ which counts how many urgent freights to destination d were not transported in the long-haul vehicle, as seen in (5c). Thus, the costs at stage t are defined as seen in (5a).

$$C(S_t, x_t) = \sum_{\mathcal{D}' \subseteq \mathcal{D}} \left(C_{\mathcal{D}'} \cdot \prod_{d' \in \mathcal{D}'} y_{t,d'} \cdot \prod_{d'' \in \mathcal{D} \setminus \mathcal{D}'} (1 - y_{t,d''}) \right) + \sum_{d \in \mathcal{D}} (B_d \cdot z_{t,d}) \tag{5a}$$

s.t.

$$y_{t,d} = \begin{cases} 1, & \text{if } \sum_{k \in \mathcal{K}} x_{t,d,k} > 0 \\ 0, & \text{otherwise} \end{cases}, \forall d \in \mathcal{D} \tag{5b}$$

$$z_{t,d} = F_{t,d,0,0} - x_{t,d,0}, \forall d \in \mathcal{D} \tag{5c}$$

The objective of the model is to minimize the costs in (5a), under the uncertainty in the arrival of freights and their characteristics, over a finite horizon. Therefore, we need the optimal decision for each of the possible states, for each stage in the horizon. We define a policy π as a function that maps each possible state S_t to a decision vector x_t^π. Thus, the formal objective of the Markov model is to find the policy $\pi \in \Pi$ which minimizes the expected costs over the planning horizon, given an initial state S_0, as seen in (6):

$$\min_{\pi \in \Pi} \mathbb{E} \left\{ \sum_{t \in \mathcal{T}} C(S_t, x_t^\pi) | S_0 \right\} \tag{6}$$

Following Bellman's principle of optimality, the best policy π for the planning horizon can be found solving a set of stochastic recursive equations which consider current-stage and expected next-stage costs, as seen in (7). The recursion between stages t and $t + 1$ uses the arrival information vector W_{t+1} and the transition function S^M. Remind that W_{t+1} is the result of the discrete and finite random variables describing the arrival process of freights, and thus has also a discrete and finite number of realizations. We denote the set of all possible realizations of the arrival information vector with Ω, i.e., $W_t \in \Omega, \forall t \in \mathcal{T}$. For each realization $\omega \in \Omega$, there is an associated probability p_ω^Ω.

$$\begin{aligned} V_t(S_t) &= \min_{x_t} (C(S_t, x_t) + \mathbb{E}\{V_{t+1}(S_{t+1})\}), \forall t \in \mathcal{T} \\ &= \min_{x_t} \left(C(S_t, x_t) + \mathbb{E}\left\{ V_{t+1}\left(S^M(S_t, x_t, W_{t+1})\right)\right\}\right) \\ &= \min_{x_t} \left(C(S_t, x_t) + \sum_{\omega \in \Omega} \left(p_\omega^\Omega \cdot V_{t+1}\left(S^M(S_t, x_t, \omega)\right)\right)\right) \end{aligned} \tag{7}$$

A realization ω is the vector of all freight variables $\widetilde{F}_{d,r,k}^\omega$ which capture the random arrival process. Its probability p_ω^Ω depends in three aspects of the realization, as seen in (8a). First, it depends in the total number of freights arriving f and its probability p_f^F, , as seen in (8b). Second, in the the probability that $\widetilde{F}_{d,r,k}^\omega$ freights will have destination d, release-day r and time-window length k

(i.e., $\left[p_d^D \cdot p_r^R \cdot p_k^K\right]^{\widetilde{F}_{d,r,r+k}^\omega}$). Third, in a multinomial coefficient β since the order in which freights arrive does not matter, but "repetition" in freight characteristics is allowed. From a combinatorial perspective [11], β counts the number ways of assigning the total number of arriving freights f to each freight variable $\widetilde{F}_{d,r,k}^\omega$, as seen in (8c).

$$p_\omega^\Omega = \beta \cdot p_f^F \cdot \prod_{d \in \mathcal{D}, r \in \mathcal{R}, k \in \mathcal{K}} \left(\left[p_d^D \cdot p_r^R \cdot p_k^K\right]^{\widetilde{F}_{d,r,k}^\omega}\right) \tag{8a}$$

s.t.

$$f = \sum_{d \in \mathcal{D}, r \in \mathcal{R}, k \in \mathcal{K}} \widetilde{F}_{d,r,k}^\omega \tag{8b}$$

$$\beta = \frac{f!}{\prod_{d \in \mathcal{D}, r \in \mathcal{R}, k \in \mathcal{K}} \left(\widetilde{F}_{d,r,k}^\omega!\right)} \tag{8c}$$

Solving the recursion in (7) with dynamic programming will yield the optimal solution to the aforementioned model. However, as with most Markov models, ours suffers from the dimensionality issues mentioned by Powell [10], which make it computationally intractable (see Section 4.3). Nevertheless, it is the foundation for solving larger problems as will be explained in the following section.

3.2   Approximate Dynamic Programming Solution Algorithm

Approximate Dynamic Programming (ADP) is a modeling framework, based on a Markov model, that offers several strategies for tackling the curses of dimensionality in large, multi-period, stochastic optimization problems [10]. The output of ADP is the same as in the Markov model, i.e., a policy or function π that maps each possible state $\boldsymbol{S}_t$ to a decision vector $\boldsymbol{x}_t^\pi$, for each stage t in the planning horizon. This policy is derived from an approximation of the optimal values of the Bellman's equations. To do this approximation, a series of constructs and algorithmic manipulations of the base Markov model are needed, as seen in Algorithm 1. The ADP solution can be applied to realistic-size instances because two of the dimensionality issues are completely avoided. The first dimensionality issue corresponds to the set Ω containing all possible realizations ω of the arrival information. This issue is avoided through the construct of a post-decision state $\boldsymbol{S}_t^{n,x}$ and an approximated next-stage cost $\bar{V}_t^n(\boldsymbol{S}_t^{n,x})$, which we explain in the next paragraphs. The second dimensionality issue corresponds to the state space which contains all possible permutations of accumulated freights for each possible realization of the arrival information. This issue is avoided through the so-called "forward dynamic programming" algorithmic strategy, which solves the Bellman's equations by stepping forward in time, and repeats this process for N iterations. We elaborate on this strategy later in this section.

Algorithm 1. ADP Based Solution Algorithm

Require: $F, D, R, K, \mathcal{D}, T^{max}, R^{max}, K^{max}, [C_{\mathcal{D'}}]_{\forall \mathcal{D'} \subseteq \mathcal{D}}, B_d, Q, S_0, N$
Ensure: Sets $\mathcal{T}, \mathcal{R}, \mathcal{K}, \Omega$ are defined
1: Initialize $\bar{V}_t^0, \ \forall t \in \mathcal{T}$
2: $n \leftarrow 1$
3: **while** $n \leq N$ **do**
4:      $S_0^n \leftarrow S_0$
5:      **for** $t = 0$ to $T^{max} - 1$ **do**
6:          $\hat{v}_t^n \leftarrow \min_{x_t^n} \left(C\left(S_t^n, x_t^n \right) + \bar{V}_t^{n-1} \left(S^{M,x}\left(S_t^n, x_t^n \right) \right) \right)$
7:          **if** $t > 0$ **then**
8:              $\bar{V}_{t-1}^n(S_{t-1}^{n,x*}) \leftarrow U^V(\bar{V}_{t-1}^{n-1}(S_{t-1}^{n,x*}), S_{t-1}^{n,x*}, \hat{v}_t^n)$
9:          **end if**
10:         $x_t^{n*} \leftarrow \arg\min_{x_t^n} \left(C\left(S_t^n, x_t^n \right) + \bar{V}_t^{n-1} \left(S^{M,x}\left(S_t^n, x_t^n \right) \right) \right)$
11:         $S_t^{n,x*} \leftarrow S^{M,x}\left(S_t^n, x_t^{n*} \right)$
12:         $W_t^n \leftarrow \text{RandomFrom}\left(\Omega \right)$
13:         $S_{t+1}^n \leftarrow S^M\left(S_t^n, x_t^{n*}, W_t^n \right)$
14:     **end for**
15: **end while**
16: **return** $\left[\bar{V}_t^N \right]_{\forall t \in \mathcal{T}}$

A post-decision state $S_t^{n,x}$ is the state directly after decision x_t^n given state S_t^n but before the arrival information W_t^n is known. In our model, the post-decision state contains all post-decision freight variables $F_{t,d,r,k}^{n,x}$, as seen in (9). To define the values of the post-decision state vector, we use the transition function $S^{M,x}$, as seen in (10a). This function works in the same way of the DP transition function defined in (4a), with the difference that the new arrival information W_t^n is not included.

$$S_t^{n,x} = \left[F_{t,d,r,k}^{n,x} \right]_{\forall d \in \mathcal{D}, r \in \mathcal{R}, k \in \mathcal{K}}, \ \forall t \in \mathcal{T} \tag{9}$$

$$S_t^{n,x} = S^{M,x}\left(S_t^n, x_t^n \right), \ \forall t \in \mathcal{T} \tag{10a}$$

s.t.

$$F_{t+1,d,0,k}^{n,x} = F_{t,d,0,k+1}^n - x_{t,d,k+1}^n + F_{t,d,1,k}^n, \tag{10b}$$

$$F_{t+1,d,r,k}^{n,x} = F_{t,d,r+1,k}^n \mid r \geq 1, \tag{10c}$$

$$\forall d \in \mathcal{D}, \ r \in \mathcal{R}, \ r + 1 \in \mathcal{R}, \ k \in \mathcal{K}, \ k + 1 \in \mathcal{K} \tag{10d}$$

In the forward dynamic programming algorithmic strategy, the Bellman's equations are solved only for one state at each stage. Just as in the Markov model, the feasible decisions x_t^n for state S_t^n in these equations are defined by (2a). However, some modifications are necessary to apply this algorithmic strategy. Besides the construct of the post-decision state, the construct of an approximated next-stage cost $\bar{V}_t^n(S_t^{n,x})$ is necessary. This construct replaces the standard expectation in Bellman's equations, as seen in (11).

$$\bar{V}_t^n(S_t^{n,x}) = \mathbb{E}\left\{ V_{t+1}\left(S_{t+1} \right) \mid S_t^x \right\} \tag{11}$$

Using the post-decision state and the approximated next-stage cost, the original Bellman's equations from (7) are converted to the ADP forward optimality equations, as seen in (12). Note that for each feasible decision x_t^n, there is an associated post-decision state $S_t^{n,x}$ obtained using (10a). The ADP forward optimality equations are solved first at stage $t = 0$ and S_0, and then for subsequent stages and states until the end of the horizon. To advance "forward" in time, from stage t to $t+1$, a Monte Carlo simulation of the random information Ω is done. In this simulation, a sample W_t^n from Ω is obtained. With this information, transition in the algorithm is done using the same DP transition function defined in (4a), as seen in Algorithm 1 lines 12 and 13.

$$\hat{v}_t^n = \min_{x_t^n} \left(C\left(S_t^n, x_t^n\right) + \bar{V}_t^{n-1}\left(S^{M,x}\left(S_t^n, x_t^n\right)\right)\right) \tag{12}$$

Immediately after the forward optimality equations are solved, the approximated next-stage cost $\bar{V}_t^n(S_t^{n,x})$ is updated retrospectively, as seen in (13). The rationale behind this update is that, at stage t, the algorithm has seen new arrival information (via the Monte Carlo simulation) and has taken a decision in the new state S_t^n which incurs a cost. This means that the approximated next-stage cost that was calculated at the previous stage $t-1$, i.e., $\bar{V}_{t-1}^{n-1}(S_{t-1}^{n,x})$, has now been observed at stage t. To take advantage of this observation and improve the approximation, the algorithm updates this approximated next-stage cost using the old approximation, i.e., $\bar{V}_{t-1}^{n-1}(S_{t-1}^{n,x})$, the new approximation, i.e., the value $\hat{v}_t^n$ corresponding to the optimal decision that solves (12), and the decision x_t^n that resulted in the value $\hat{v}_t^n$. We use U^V to denote the process that takes all of the aforementioned parameters and "tunes" the approximating function, as seen in (13). Note that in Algorithm 1 line 8, the parameters used for the update have the superscript * indicating the optimal decision made at stage $t-1$ and its corresponding post-decision state.

$$\bar{V}_{t-1}^n(S_{t-1}^{n,x}) \leftarrow U^V(\bar{V}_{t-1}^{n-1}(S_{t-1}^{n,x}), S_{t-1}^{n,x}, \hat{v}_t^n), \ \forall t \in \mathcal{T} \tag{13}$$

Two of the largest challenges of ADP are: (i) to find an accurate approximation function $\bar{V}_t^n(S_t^{n,x})$ of the value of a post-decision state $S_t^{n,x}$, and (ii) to define an appropriate updating process U^V for this function. For our problem, we use the concept of post-decision state "features". A feature of a post-decision state is a quantitative characteristic that explains, to some extent, what the value of that post-decision state is. In our problem, features such as the number of urgent freights, the number of released freights that are not urgent, and the number of freights which have not been released for transport, can explain part of the value of a post-decision state. We define a set of features $\mathcal{A}$ for which the value of each feature $a \in \mathcal{A}$ is obtained using a function $\phi_a(S_t^{n,x})$. We assume the approximated next-stage value of a post-decision state can be expressed by a weighted linear combination of the features, using the weights θ_a for each feature $a \in \mathcal{A}$, as seen in (14).

$$\bar{V}_t^n(S_t^{n,x}) = \sum_{a \in \mathcal{A}} \left(\phi_a(S_t^{n,x}) \cdot \theta_a\right) \tag{14}$$

The use of features and weights for approximating the value function $\bar{V}_t^n(S_t^{n,x})$ is comparable to the use of regression models for fitting data to a (linear) function. In that sense, the independent variables of the regression would be the post-decision features and the dependent variable would be the post-decision value. However, in contrast to regression models, the data in our ADP is generated iteratively inside an algorithm and not all at once. Therefore, the updating process U^V for the approximating function in (14) cannot be based on solving systems of equations as in traditional regression models. Instead, we use a recursive least squares method for non-stationary data, in a double-pass procedure, to "fine-tune" the weight θ_a for each feature $a \in \mathcal{A}$. This method is based in regression models, and explained in detail in [10].

4 Numerical Experiments

In this section, we carry out two types of numerical experiments to test our model and approach. In the first experiment, we test the accuracy of our ADP algorithm. This experiment shows how good the chosen basis functions approximate the true value of a state in the Markov model. In the second experiment, we compare the policy performance from our ADP algorithm. This experiment shows the value of incorporating stochastic (i.e., future) information in the daily decisions compared to using a today-only heuristic. For both experiments we use a planning horizon of $T^{max} = 5$ and consider that there are no next-stage costs at the end of the horizon, i.e., $V_{T^{max}}(\boldsymbol{S}_{T^{max}}) = 0$. We use two small and two large instances as seen in Table 1. The instances differ among themselves in the long-haul vehicle capacity: (i) the small ones have $Q = \{2, 5\}$ and (ii) the large ones $Q = \{4, 10\}$.

Table 1. Random variables in the numerical experiments

Input Parameter	Small Instances	Large Instances
1. Freights arriving per day (F)	$\{1, 2\}$	$\{1, 2, 3, 4\}$
$\rightarrow$Probability (p_f^F)	$\{0.8, 0.2\}$	$\{0.25, 0.25, 0.25, 0.25\}$
2. Destinations (D)	$\{1, 2, 3\}$	$\{1, 2, 3, 4, 5, 6, 7\}$
$\rightarrow$Probability (p_d^D)	$\{0.1, 0.8, 0.1\}$	$\{0.1, 0.2, 0.1, 0.1, 0.3, 0.1, 0.1\}$
3. Release-days (R)	$\{0\}$	$\{0, 1, 2\}$
$\rightarrow$Probability (p_r^R)	$\{1\}$	$\{0.3, 0.3, 0.4\}$
4. Time-window lengths (K)	$\{0, 1, 2\}$	$\{0, 1, 2\}$
$\rightarrow$Probability (p_k^K)	$\{0.2, 0.3, 0.5\}$	$\{0.2, 0.3, 0.5\}$
5. Long-haul vehicle Cost $(C_{D'})$	$[250, 1000]$	$[250, 2050]$
6. Alternative mode Cost (B_d)	$[500, 1000]$	$[300, 800]$

The parameters of the ADP algorithm are set as follows. The number of iterations is $N = 2000$. The features $\mathcal{A}$ are related to three characteristics of a post-decision state: (i) the number of freights with each combination of freight characteristics, (ii) the total number of urgent freights (i.e., $r = k = 0$), and (iii) the total number of released and non-urgent freights (i.e., $r = 0$ and $k > 0$). The features related to these characteristics include also counting the number of destinations that fulfill such characteristics (e.g., destinations having urgent freights). We also include a constant feature a' such that $\phi_{a'}(\boldsymbol{S}_t^{n,x}) = 1$ for all post-decision states and stages. Feature weights are initialized with 1, i.e., $\theta_a = 1$ for all features and all stages at iteration $n = 1$. The updating process U^V (i.e., the recursive least squares method for non-stationary data with double-pass procedure) requires a discount factor λ which is defined as $\lambda = 1 - \frac{0.5}{n}$.

4.1 Accuracy Experiment

In this experiment, we compare the optimal value of 20 random initial states $\boldsymbol{S}_0$ obtained with the Markov model against the value obtained with our ADP algorithm. We looked at the solution value range of the Markov model and divided it into 20 segments from which a random state was chosen. This resulted in a sample of states containing freights with the three time-window lengths. Using these time-windows, we name the states from A to T in increasing number of urgent freights ($k = 0$), i.e., State A has no urgent freights and State T has only urgent freights. The results of this comparison can be seen in Figure 1 and Figure 2 for the small instances with $Q = 2$ and $Q = 5$, respectively.

In the left part of the aforementioned figures, we observe the convergence of our ADP algorithm (solid lines) to the optimal value of our Markov model

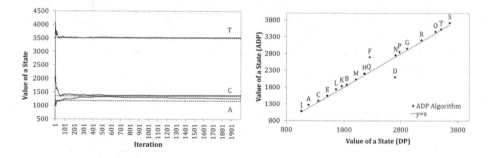

Fig. 1. Accuracy experiment for the small instance with $Q = 2$

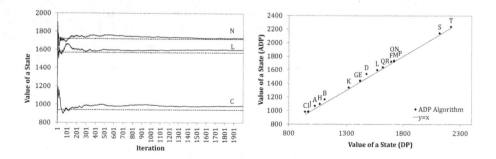

Fig. 2. Accuracy experiment for the small instance with $Q = 5$

(dotted lines). For both figures we only show the states with best, intermediate, and worst convergence. In Figure 1, States T, C, and A converge to 0.6%, 3.0%, and 7.4% of the optimal value. In Figure 2, States N, L, and C converge to 0.5%, 1.9%, and 4.5% of the optimal value. We observe that ADP values fluctuate for some states more than others, and that the number of iterations for convergence varies from state to state and between the instances. In the right part of the figures above, we see that the difference between the optimal values (solid line) and the estimates produced by our ADP algorithm (points) is small. In Figure 1, the average accuracy of all states, excluding the outliers F and D, is of 2.5%. Including the outliers results in an average accuracy of 2.2%, which is lower due to the large underestimation of State D. We further discuss these outliers in Section 4.3. In Figure 2, the average accuracy is of 2.1%. Note that all estimates in this case are above the optimal value, which can be expected in minimization problems [10]. These experiments show how accurate the optimal value can be estimated using ADP. However, these values are just an intermediate result since they are used to define the policy for making consolidation decisions. Thus, to properly compare performance, we test this policy in the following section.

4.2 Policy Performance Experiment

In the second experiment, we compare the output policy of our ADP algorithm with the optimal policy of the Markov model and a heuristic commonly used in practice. We simulate all policies in 2000 runs, using common random numbers for the comparison of arriving freights in the planning horizon. The heuristic consolidates urgent freights that yield the lowest direct costs (i.e., no future costs considered), and then if there is capacity left, fills the long-haul vehicle with released freights that do not add extra costs (i.e., same destinations). The average performance of the different decision policies is shown in Table 2 and 3.

Table 2. Policy performance for the small instances

	$Q = 2$					$Q = 5$				
State	Markov	M. Heuristic	Diff.	ADP	Diff.	Markov	M. Heuristic	Diff.	ADP	Diff.
Small A	1182.3	1343.4	13.6%	1330.0	12.5%	1025.2	1052.5	2.7%	1143.2	11.5%
Small B	1845.0	2887.8	56.5%	1920.1	4.1%	1110.5	1127.7	1.5%	1224.1	10.2%
Small C	1351.9	2414.7	78.6%	1465.6	8.4%	940.3	960.9	2.2%	1019.7	8.4%
Small D	2697.8	2773.6	2.8%	3050.9	13.1%	1475.2	1502.5	1.9%	1593.2	8.0%
Small E	1508.0	1602.0	6.2%	1597.3	5.9%	1418.6	1433.1	1.0%	1523.6	7.4%
Small F	2250.3	2990.0	32.9%	3065.6	36.2%	1692.1	1701.0	0.5%	1791.1	5.9%
Small G	2908.0	3002.0	3.2%	2997.3	3.1%	1418.6	1433.1	1.0%	1523.6	7.4%
Small H	2158.0	2252.0	4.4%	2247.3	4.1%	1068.6	1083.1	1.3%	1173.6	9.8%
Small I	1058.0	1152.0	8.9%	1147.3	8.4%	968.6	983.1	1.5%	1073.6	10.8%
Small J	1058.0	1152.0	8.9%	1147.3	8.4%	968.6	983.1	1.5%	1073.6	10.8%
Small K	1758.0	2202.0	25.3%	1847.3	5.1%	1318.6	1333.1	1.1%	1423.6	8.0%
Small L	1658.0	1802.0	8.7%	1747.3	5.4%	1568.6	1633.1	4.1%	1673.6	6.7%
Small M	2008.0	2502.0	24.6%	2097.3	4.4%	1718.6	1733.1	0.8%	1823.6	6.1%
Small N	2708.0	3202.0	18.2%	2797.3	3.3%	1718.6	1733.1	0.8%	1823.6	6.1%
Small O	3408.0	3902.0	14.5%	3497.3	2.6%	1718.6	1733.1	0.8%	1823.6	6.1%
Small P	2775.7	3122.7	12.5%	2857.7	3.0%	1718.6	1733.1	0.8%	1823.6	6.1%
Small Q	2158.0	3152.0	46.1%	2247.3	4.1%	1618.6	1633.1	0.9%	1723.6	6.5%
Small R	3158.0	4152.0	31.5%	3247.3	2.8%	1618.6	1633.1	0.9%	1723.6	6.5%
Small S	3658.0	4652.0	27.2%	3747.3	2.4%	2118.6	2633.1	24.3%	2223.6	5.0%
Small T	3508.0	3852.0	9.8%	3597.3	2.5%	2218.6	2333.1	5.2%	2323.6	4.7%

Table 3. Policy performance for the large instances

State	Q = 4			Q = 10		
	Heuristic	ADP	Difference	Heuristic	ADP	Difference
Large A	2962.9	2579.4	-12.9%	1723.1	1743.0	1.2%
Large B	9687.9	8729.4	-9.9%	6448.1	5568.0	-13.6%
Large C	5937.9	5579.4	-6.0%	3223.1	2918.0	-9.5%
Large D	1737.9	1754.4	1.0%	1523.1	1543.0	1.3%
Large E	2162.9	1804.4	-16.6%	1523.1	1543.0	1.3%
Large F	1362.9	1254.4	-8.0%	848.1	868.0	2.3%
Large G	1362.9	1254.4	-8.0%	848.1	868.0	2.3%
Large H	2187.9	2079.4	-5.0%	1298.1	1318.0	1.5%
Large I	3585.5	3550.0	-1.0%	1766.3	1782.2	0.9%
Large J	2537.9	2179.4	-14.1%	1523.1	1543.0	1.3%
Large K	3462.9	2979.4	-14.0%	1123.1	1143.0	1.8%
Large L	1778.1	1677.1	-5.7%	1082.4	1101.2	1.7%

In the experiment of Table 2, we observe that the performance of our ADP's policy is, on average, 7.0% away from optimal for the small instance with $Q = 2$ and 7.6% for the one with $Q = 5$. However, the performance of the heuristic is 21.7% and 2.7% for the same instances, respectively. Furthermore, we observe a contrast in the performance between ADP and the heuristic. In the instance with $Q = 2$, ADP outperforms the heuristic in 18 out of the 20 states. In the other one, the exact opposite happens. We elaborate more on this contrast in Section 4.3.

In the experiment of Table 3, the large instances become computationally intractable for the Markov model. Thus, we compare the performance of our ADP's policy against the heuristic. We test 12 random states fulfilling similar considerations as explained in the previous section. We observe that the performance of our ADP's policy is, on average, 8.3% better than the heuristic for the instance with $Q = 4$ and 0.6% better for the one with $Q = 10$. However, in the instance with $Q = 10$, ADP outperforms the heuristic only in 2 out of the 12 states, while with $Q = 4$, ADP outperforms the heuristic in all states. We elaborate more on this contrast in Section 4.3.

Even though the Tables above show performance differences among random, but carefully selected states, it is likely that in real-life problems, states and settings for which a look-ahead policy matters are more common than those for which it does not make a difference. For example, we saw that ADP brings an advantage in states with urgent freights and settings with restrictive capacities, which are common for LSPs. We discuss this, and other critical aspects, in the following section.

4.3   Discussion

In the accuracy experiments, we observe that our ADP approach is able to estimate the optimal value of the Markov model consistently for all states in the two test cases. However, in the $Q = 5$ case, the ADP algorithm approximates the optimal value better (2.1% overestimated) than in the $Q = 2$ case (2.5% overestimated). In this last case, we further observe that in States F and D, ADP significantly overestimates and underestimates the optimal value, respectively. When looking closer at these states, they only have freights with the latest due-day, which in this instance is halfway through the horizon. In finite horizon problems, the beginning and end states of the horizon (i.e., starting or ending conditions) can influence the estimates of the ADP algorithm, if there is not an appropriate balance between exploring and exploiting new knowledge [10]. These issues, however, are less likely to occur in larger and more realistic instances.

In the performance experiments, we observed that ADP performed better than the heuristic in *normal capacity* cases (i.e., where Q equals the maximum number of arriving freights each day). However, in the *large capacity* cases (i.e., Q is 2.5 times the normal capacity), the heuristic seems to outperform the ADP. The reason for this is that, when there is too much capacity, postponing freights for future consolidation does not add any value. Freights "fit" at any decision moment, therefore it is reasonable that consolidating all freights that fit at the cheapest cost (i.e., what the heuristic does) is, in this case, a near-optimal policy. Specifically in this small instance, the heuristic coincides with the optimal policy. When there is no effect of future costs in decisions, such as in the large capacity cases of our problem, look-ahead policies from ADP are simply not near-optimal [10]. Nevertheless, we observe that the value added by ADP with respect to the heuristic is substantial: on average, 10.3% better in the small instance with $Q = 2$ and 8.3% better in the large instance with $Q = 4$.

With respect to computational costs, the Markov model becomes intractable with an increasing problem dimension. Both the set of possible arrival realizations and the state space rapidly expand as the number of freights, destinations, release-days, or time-windows increase. In our experiments, we have 54 and 766479 possible arrival realizations, and 2884 and approximately $8.18 \cdot 10^{18}$ possible states, for the small and large instances, respectively. The ADP algorithm does not suffer from these two dimensions. In this respect, its computational costs are only related to the number of iterations and the size of the action space. The action space, however might rapidly expand as the number of freights and the capacity increases. This is a computational challenge for both the Markov model and the ADP algorithm.

5   Conclusions

We developed a Markov model and an Approximate Dynamic Programming (ADP) solution for the dynamic multi-period freight consolidation problem. The approach is designed to achieve the optimal balance between freights that are consolidated in a long-haul vehicle and freights that are postponed for future trips or alternative transportation modes. The optimal balance is achieved taking into account the probabilistic knowledge in the arrival of freights and their characteristics, the applicable transportation restrictions, and the interdependence of decisions over time.

Through a limited number of numerical experiments, the accuracy of the ADP method and the benefits of the Markov model were shown. These experiments showed that there are some cases where it pays off to have a look-ahead policy (e.g., more restrictive capacities), and some others where a common heuristic is sufficient to achieve the optimal balance between direct shipment and postponement for future consolidation. Furthermore, within the cases where it pays off to have a look-ahead policy, our ADP policy underperforms at some states. This leads to the idea that further research is needed (i) to fine-tune the ADP approximation for different state characteristics, and (ii) to identify in which problem settings (both instance and state characteristics) look-ahead policies (i.e., using the ADP approach) yield the largest benefits. Specifically, more experiments on large problem instances and different benchmark policies are crucial to analyze the value of our approach.

References

1. Andersen, J., Christiansen, M., Crainic, T.G., Gronhaug, R.: Branch and price for service network design with asset management constraints. Transportation Science **45**(1), 33–49 (2011)
2. Andersen, J., Crainic, T.G., Christiansen, M.: Service network design with asset management: Formulations and comparative analyses. Transportation Research Part C: Emerging Technologies **17**(2), 197–207 (2009). selected papers from the Sixth Triennial Symposium on Transportation Analysis (TRISTAN VI)
3. Andersen, J., Crainic, T.G., Christiansen, M.: Service network design with management and coordination of multiple fleets. European Journal of Operational Research **193**(2), 377–389 (2009)
4. Crainic, T.G., Gendreau, M., Farvolden, J.M.: A simplex-based tabu search method for capacitated network design. INFORMS Journal on Computing **12**(3), 223–236 (2000)
5. Crainic, T.G., Kim, K.H.: Intermodal transportation. In: Barnhart, C., Laporte, G. (eds.) Transportation, Handbooks in Operations Research and Management Science, vol. 14, Chapter 8, pp. 467–537. Elsevier (2007)
6. Hoff, A., Lium, A.G., Lokketangen, A., Crainic, T.: A metaheuristic for stochastic service network design. Journal of Heuristics **16**(5), 653–679 (2010)
7. Kim, D., Barnhart, C.: Transportation service network design: models and algorithms. Springer (1999)
8. Lium, A.G., Crainic, T.G., Wallace, S.W.: A study of demand stochasticity in service network design. Transportation Science **43**(2), 144–157 (2009)
9. Moccia, L., Cordeau, J.F., Laporte, G., Ropke, S., Valentini, M.P.: Modeling and solving a multimodal transportation problem with flexible-time and scheduled services. Networks **57**(1), 53–68 (2011)
10. Powell, W.B.: Approximate Dynamic Programming: Solving the Curses of Dimensionality, vol. 1. John Wiley & Sons (2007)
11. Riordan, J.: Introduction to combinatorial analysis. Courier Dover Publications (2002)
12. SteadieSeifi, M., Dellaert, N., Nuijten, W., Woensel, T.V., Raoufi, R.: Multimodal freight transportation planning: A literature review. European Journal of Operational Research **233**(1), 1–15 (2014)

13. Verma, M., Verter, V., Zufferey, N.: A bi-objective model for planning and managing rail-truck intermodal transportation of hazardous materials. Transportation Research Part E: Logistics and Transportation Review **48**(1), 132–149 (2012). select Papers from the 19th International Symposium on Transportation and Traffic Theory
14. Wieberneit, N.: Service network design for freight transportation: a review. OR Spectrum **30**(1), 77–112 (2008)

Synchromodal Container Transportation: An Overview of Current Topics and Research Opportunities

Bart van Riessen[1,2(✉)], Rudy R. Negenborn[2], and Rommert Dekker[1]

[1] Econometric Institute, Erasmus University Rotterdam, Rotterdam, The Netherlands
{vanriessen,rdekker}@ese.eur.nl
[2] Department of Maritime and Transport Technology,
Delft University of Technology, Delft, The Netherlands
r.r.negenborn@tudelft.nl

Abstract. Renewed attention has emerged for the topic of intermodal transportation. Since a couple of years, research has focused on the concept of *synchromodality*. Synchromodality refers to creating the most efficient and sustainable transportation plan for all orders in an entire network of different modes and routes, by using the available flexibility. In this paper we provide an overview of relevant research around three topics related to the case of European Gateway Services, the network orchestrator of container transportation network in the Rotterdam hinterland. For each topic we describe studies with practical relevance and recent results. Finally, we conclude by describing topics for further research with relevance for future practical developments.

Keywords: Synchromodal transportation · Container transportation · Hinterland network · Research overview

1 Introduction

In recent years intermodal networks have received renewed attention for two reasons: focus on shifting containers from truck transportation towards barge or rail transportation and an increased competition on hinterland transportation between players in maritime transportation. Port authorities have put focus on modal shift towards more environmental friendly transportation modes. E.g. the ports of Rotterdam, Antwerp and Hamburg have stated modal split requirements for the hinterland transportation of containers (Van den Berg and De Langen, 2014). In *Port Vision 2030* the Port of Rotterdam Authority (2010) aims for a modal shift in the hinterland transportation of containers. Currently, 55% of the containers are transported by truck between the terminals in the Port of Rotterdam and inland destinations in North-West Europe. In 2035 this must be reduced to 35%. Efficient planning methods for transportation are essential to achieve this, while meeting customer requirements for synchronizing the container supply chain and a further reduction of delivery time, costs and emissions. These trends motivate the use of inland container transportation networks, with multiple possible transport modes. The use of these *intermodal networks* requires new methods to guarantee efficient operation, in terms of cost, reliability and emissions.

© Springer International Publishing Switzerland 2015
F. Corman et al. (Eds.): ICCL 2015, LNCS 9335, pp. 386–397, 2015.
DOI: 10.1007/978-3-319-24264-4_27

Several researchers have stressed the complexity of achieving the required modal shift, i.e. in Veenstra *et al.* (2012) the need for an integrated network approach is emphasised, and Van der Horst and De Langen (2010) mention the mind shift that is required for achieving more integrated inland transportation.

In this paper we describe the developments on the topic of *synchromodal transportation* for the case of the hinterland network of European Gateway Services (EGS), a subsidiary of the Rotterdam container terminal operator ECT. With this paper, we do not aim to provide a complete overview of all developments on synchromodal transportation, but merely an overview of the ongoing research for this Rotterdam case from practice. Synchromodal transportation refers to a concept of optimising all network transportation in an integrally operated network, making of all transportation options in the most flexible way. A more general description follows in the next section. EGS´s developments around implementing this concept are structured around 3 topics: optimisation of integral network planning, methods for real-time decision making for planning and the creation of flexibility in the network planning problem. This paper highlights recent developments and introduces new research opportunities.

1.1   Synchromodal Transportation

The main challenge for a transportation network operator is the continuous construction of an efficient transportation plan. That is, the allocation of containers to available inland services (train, barge or truck). Recently, some studies refer to the concept of synchromodal transportation (Lucassen *et al.*, 2012, SteadiSeafi *et al.*, 2014, Behdani *et al.*, 2014). These studies mention the flexible deployment of modes, the possibility of last minute changes to the transportation plan (*switching*) and a central network orchestrator that offers integrated transport. However, no uniform definition exists yet in literature. The Platform Synchromodality, of which ECT is a partner, defined synchromodality as follows: "Synchromodality is the optimally flexible and sustainable deployment of different modes of transport in a network under the direction of a logistics service provider, so that the customer (shipper or forwarder) is offered an integrated solution for his (inland) transport." (Platform Synchromodality, n.d.). For container transportation, synchromodality focuses on inland barge, rail and/or truck transportation. Creating the transportation plan for the network of inland services is refered to as *planning* in this paper, i.e. allocation all orders to available services in the network. Creating more planning flexibility should help to raise the utilization rate of inland barge and rail capacity and thus decreasing costs and emissions. Also, the planning flexibility can be used to deal with uncertainties and disturbances, and thus increasing the on-time performance and reliability of the transportation.

Since 2007, ECT developed the extended gate concept with the subsidiary EGS. The goal is to provide network-wide synchromodal transportation with this network. The first step was the introduction of regular train services on the corridor between Rotterdam and the inland terminal TCT Venlo. Currently, the concept is extended to around 20 hinterland terminals (European Gateway Services, 2014), with over a hundred barge and rail services between the deep sea ports of Rotterdam and Antwerp and the inland destinations.

1.2   Problem Statement

Although EGS started with the first developments into synchromodal inland container transportation, the inland transportation in this network and for other networks in North-West Europe is still considered per corridor and not for the network as a whole. This is the case for mainly three reasons: Firstly, no suitable methods for creating an integrated network plan exist yet. Secondly, adapting the plan in real-time responding to delays and other changes occurs manually, by planning operators that focus on specific corridors and inland connections. Thirdly, because of the customer's restrictions with its transportation orders, the network orchestrator misses the flexibility to switch between modes and routes and thus cannot achieve the benefits of synchromodal planning.

The goals of this paper is to describe three steps required to **enable synchromodal planning in inland container networks**, specifically for the case of EGS. For achieving this objective, three topics of research are introduced:

1. Integrated network planning: Methods for creating an integrated transportation plan for intermodal transportation networks that are operated by a network orchestrator.
2. Methods for real-time network planning: Methods for creating the transportation plan in real-time and updating it continuously as new information arrives.
3. Creating planning flexibility: Methods for persuading clients to allow flexible transportation planning.

This paper described the research plan for enabling synchromodal transportation and is structured as follows. In Section 2, the general scientific state of the art is described. Section 3 focuses on the recent research specifically for the EGS case and provides preliminary results of the tree topics mentioned above. In Section 4 the expected impact of the research is elaborated on.

2   Scientific State of the Art Related to EGS Topics

2.1   Integrated Network Planning

The global throughput in container transportation continues to grow and constitutes a growing portion of the global transportation (Drewry Shipping Consultants, 2007). Meanwhile, supply chains get increasingly interconnected and shippers demand higher levels of service, such as short delivery times and reliability (Crainic and Laporte, 1997; Crainic, 2000; Veenstra et al., 2012). The logistic expression for integrated transportation is intermodality. The International Transport Forum defined intermodal transportation as: *Multimodal transport of goods, in one and the same intermodal transport unit by successive modes of transport without handling of the goods themselves when changing modes* (UNECE, 2009). The planning of intermodal transportation requires a network-wide approach (Crainic 2000; Jansen et al. 2004; Crainic and Kim 2006). Consolidation of flows between hubs in intermodal networks is cost efficient as it benefits of the economies of scale (Ishfaq and Sox, 2012). Transportation used to be optimized based purely on costs. However, Crainic and Laporte (1997) signal that carriers and transporters cannot only optimize the transportation on cost efficiency anymore. Apart from low tariffs, customers demand for a higher quality of service. According to Crainic and Laporte, quality of service consists of three parts: on-time delivery (time window), delivery speed (service time) and consistency of these aspects. Veenstra et al. (2012) mention reliability as an important quality of service. Ishfaq and Sox (2010) mention six performance targets for intermodal logistic networks: cost, service frequency, service time, delivery reliability, flexibility and safety. They propose methods to optimize the costs of intermodal logistic networks, while meeting service time requirements. The other performance targets are neglected in their work.

Some of the existing tactical service network formulations use strict constraints on delivery time (Ziliaskopoulos and Wardell, 2000) or no due time restrictions (e.g. Crainic, 2000). Strict constraints do not accurately model the flexibility that transportation planners have in consultation with customers. No time restrictions at all neglect the existing time pressure in the container transportation. Several models use formulations that model the economies of scale that occur when cargo is consolidated on an arc (e.g. Ishfaq and Sox, 2012). These abstract formulations of economies of scale cannot directly represent the current situation. The current practice in intermodal container networks is that multiple service and terminal operators cooperate and in this perspective, economies of scale are exploited by selecting services operated by the network operator (self-operated services) or use subcontracted transport. The difference in cost structure between these two cannot be modelled in the existing formulations for the economies of scale. See Van Riessen et al. (2014-c) for a more detailed review of integrated network planning.

2.2   Real-Time Network Planning

For efficient synchromodal transport plans it is essential to allow real-time switching, i.e. real-time planning updates. This was recognized by all studies that referred to synchromodal transportation (Lucassen et al., 2012, SteadiSeafi et al., 2014, Behdani et al., 2014), but not many real-time planning methods that provide a network-wide plan exist yet. The previous section mentioned various planning models that are aimed for solving the network transportation problem offline (Crainic and Laporte, 1997; Crainic, 2000; Crainic and Kim, 2006; Ishfaq and Sox, 2010, 2012, Van Riessen et al. 2014-c). Ziliaskopoulos and Wardell (2000) and Janssen et al. (2004) proposed an online method, but focused on the planning of single corridors. Nabais et al (2013) proposed a more advance method for solving the online problem. This method uses model predictive control to achieve a required modal split, but the approach requires real-time automated data processing and is less insightful to human planning operators. Li (2013) used a sequential linear programming method.

2.3   Creating Planning Flexibility

As Van der Horst and De Langen (2008) stated, the container inland transportation chain lacks information integration and stakeholders do not fully trust each other, making integrated solutions difficult. This is also the experience of EGS. Nonetheless, creating more planning flexibility is vital to enable synchromodal planning. Therefore, the network operator has an incentive to introduce a range of transportation services with varying levels of flexibility. Such new product ranges have been studied recently by Lin (2014) and Wanders (2014). These propositions consider different tariff classes for varying levels of service and the level of decision flexibility that the network operator receives from the customer. In other areas of transportation, incentives of stakeholders are studied with stated preference surveys, e.g. for the valuation of time for travellers (Wee et al., 2013): "travellers are confronted with hypothetical choice situations between a fast, expensive alternative and a cheap one". To our knowledge, no stated preference studies exist that looked specifically into customer incentives for container transportation.

In aviation, the development of revenue management (RM) enabled these industries to increase utilizations (Carmona-Benítez, 2012), e.g. by "selling the right seats to the right customer at the right time" (Zeni, 2001) and by creating customer incentives for using flexible services (Petrick, 2012). The concept of different service propositions in transportation is very similar to the concept of different fare classes for the same flight in aviation. Barnhart et al (2003) give an overview of operations research in airline revenue management. The primary objective of airline revenue management models is to determine the optimal fare mix: how much seats of each booking class should be available, provided the demand forecasts and the limited total number of seats? Some studies on revenue management in freight transportation focused on the online policy: whether to accept or reject an incoming order. Pak and Dekker (2004) proposed a method for judging sequentially arriving cargo bookings based on expected revenues. If the direct revenue of a booking exceeds the decrease in expected future revenue, the order is accepted. Bilegan et al (2013) apply a similar approach on rail freight application. In their approach the decision of accepting or rejecting an arriving transport order is based on the difference in expected revenue with and without that order. In this study we aim to translate fare mix models from airline revenue management towards the setting of intermodal hinterland transportation of containers. The setting of container transportation introduces a new issue to the fare mix problem, as the operator has the opportunity to select from various transport modes, routes and time for some of the containers.

3   Research Topics and Recent Results

We describe the ongoing research on three topics related to the studied case from practice: methods for integrated network plans, methods for real-time planning and methods for creating planning flexibility. All these three aspects contribute to develop synchromodal transportation to such a level that it can be implemented in practice. Finally, all topics combined must lead to a synchromodal network than can be operated and monitored in real-time.

3.1 Integrated Network Planning

The first aspect that is studied considers the development of planning in integrated networks. Two studies are carried out: a new *service network design* method is developed and the *impact of disturbances* is assessed. The initial research for these topics was carried out by the author for his Master's thesis (Van Riessen, 2013). Container transportation is currently organized with A-B connections. However, a network operator carries out services to several closely located inland terminals in the hinterland. A service network between all network locations provides more alternative routes using intermediate transfers. This allows consolidation of flows and an increase of overall capacity. Existing service network design methods are not applied in practice for several reasons: models with more flexible time restrictions are required and self-operated and subcontracted services must be combined. In this research an exact method is developed to determine the optimal number of services on all corridors in the network. The service network design must incorporate combinations of self-operated and subcontracted transport and allow for overdue delivery (at a penalty cost) to model current container transportation networks. For this purpose, a new model must be developed. This part of the research has been carried out and the new *Linear Container Allocation model with Time-restrictions* (LCAT) is described in detail in Van Riessen (2014-c).

Besides, the online planning of the network transportation is important, dealing with continuous disturbances in the network. In case of disturbances, the manual planners have to switch disturbed containers to other routes. This is time-consuming and the network potential for alternatives is not fully used yet. Last-minute switching is often difficult, resulting in delays. For this, an assessment of the impact of disturbances is made. With this assessment, the network operator can find the most important network aspects to improve for increasing reliability and robustness of the transportation and decrease the cost impact of disturbances. In a simulation case study of the EGS network, the quality of online updates of an automated optimal method and a method that mimics the manual updates are compared for various disturbances. This provides insight in the gravity of disturbances and the benefit of automating online planning updates. This study is described in Van Riessen (2014-a).

We recognise two directions for further research in integral network planning for synchromodal networks. Network development in a cooperative synchromodal transportation setting is more complex than the intermodal network design problem. Each addition of a new node or connection may influence the loads on existing ones. However, the sub-contractors of individual connections will aim for stable flows for economic operation. How can the network be expanded in a stable way, without jeopardising the operations of individual sub-contractors? To our knowledge, the problem of stable development of synchromodal network over time has not been studied, yet. Secondly, considering the operational network level, the operational planning of fleet deployment may improve the overall network performance. With a synchromodal transportation plan, the flexibility in transportation routes may be used in conjunction with the operational fleet deployment problem. This creates new and more complex optimisation challenges

3.2   Towards Real-Time Network Planning

A second line of research aims for enabling real-time network planning, to allow syn-chromodal transportation in practice. As mentioned in Section 2, several studies have proposed optimisation methods for determining the optimal allocation of containers to all available inland transportation services, considering capacity, costs, lead times and emissions. The proposed methods are suitable for solving the *offline* planning prob-lem, in which an optimal network plan is created for a batch of transportation orders collectively. Our study of EGS showed that the implementation of a centralised offline approach in intermodal networks is difficult for various reasons:

- The nature of the inland transport logistics requires a real-time approach, and does not allow for integral planning models that are applied in intervals.
- Proposed centralised optimisation methods depend strongly on automation, both for terminals, as for other parts of the supply chain. Such an automation level is of-ten not easy to implement. On top of that, information from direct communication between manual operators is often essential (Douma, 2008).
- Finally, the supply chain of container logistics lacks information integration (van der Horst and de Langen, 2008). In the case of intermodal networks, manual plan-ning operators often do not have real-time capacity information about the inland services.

We proposed a general method for obtaining a real-time DSS that addresses all three aforementioned issues. The model is based on an intrinsic analysis of the offline LCAT model, and translates the offline model's optimal solutions to a decision tree for online decision support. A decision tree is a white box method that is comprehen-sible for manual planners and allows manual changes if necessary. It will therefore more easily be accepted for use in daily practice. The first study of this method has shown the capabilities of providing accurate and easy decision support (Van Riessen, 2014-b). The proposed model is distinguished from existing methods by three aspects. Firstly, the proposed method allows allocating incoming transport orders directly to available inland services, resulting in a stable solution and instant feedback to the customer without the necessity of continuous planning updates. Secondly, the model can be used as a centralised method, but does not require extensive automation. Our method provides an automated system for obtaining the decision support model in advance, the decision tree can then be applied in daily practice, without an automated decision system. Thirdly, the proposed method uses optimal solutions of representa-tive historic transport problems as a baseline for suitable transport allocations. The human planner responsible for a central network planning can check available capac-ity on a proposed service manually. Hence, real-time up-to-date information is not critical for the methods performance. The proposed method can be improved by fu-ture research on two aspects. On the one hand, additional studies may improve the proposed method by iteratively improving the decision tree using online updating or introducing a guided decision tree learning process. On the other hand, new applica-tions of the proposed method must be studied. The decision tree method may be of value in many environments that require real-time decision making. The method is especially promising in situations that lack automated and standardised information exchange, such as planning in a hospital environment or for rail applications.

The balance between optimal real-time network planning and network flexibility is vital. More flexibility increases the problem complexity, but potentially allows better solutions. Also, not all transportation customers are willing to transfer flexibility of the transportation towards the network orchestrator. This balance is not yet studied in detail, but recently a *synchromodal planning game* was developed by several partners, among which EGS, for the purpose of demonstrating the balance between real-time planning complexity and the benefit of flexibility (Buiel *et al*, 2015).

Currently, the effect of real-time decision support in case of disturbances or disruptions is not yet studied. Note that the method described above aims to support decision of incoming transportation orders. In case of a disruption during the operational phase, a different type of real-time decisions must be made in order to solve the disruption and fulfil all transportation requests. Implementing synchromodal transportation means that the right mode and route for a container can be selected at every point in time. As the operational planning is restricted by the amount of planning flexibility allowed by the clients, it is expected that increasing the planning flexibility will allow for more cost-efficient transportation plans. However, finding the optimal plan will become more difficult if flexibility increases, especially in a real-time operational setting. In order to achieve the most cost-efficient and reliable transportation over the entire network, the network operator wants to make the best use of the network planning flexibility that is available. However, it is unclear to what type and amount of flexibility is required, to optimise the achievable cost reduction and reliability increase in the operational phase. E.g., what types of flexibility must be supported by planning methods? Should heuristics consider all possible routes for transportation orders, or can the search space be restricted? New research is required to determine value of planning flexibility for the performance of the real-time planning methods for synchromodal network transportation.

3.3   Creating Planning Flexibility

The research topics on integral and real-time network planning as described in previous sections provide insights into efficient network planning, from an offline and an online perspective, respectively. Also, the potential gain in network performance of several types of planning flexibility is assessed. In the current set-up of the transportation product, customers are hesitant to transfer planning flexibility to the (network) operator. This is for several reasons, i.e. company policy, habituation, but also the pricing mechanism. Achieving planning flexibility requires persuading clients to allow flexible planning of their transportation orders. For that reason, studies into creating planning flexibility are required. As suggested by Lin (2014) and Wanders (2014), the market for inland container transportation can be segmented in groups of customers with different characteristics. These groups are sensitive to different *incentives* that may persuade customers to allow flexibility synchromodal transportation. In order to target those groups, a *revenue management (RM) model for container logistics* is required to balance the customer demand and network transportation options (Barnhart *et al*, 2003).

A revenue management strategy for inland container transportation does not exist yet and must be developed. An integrated study of revenue management and operational planning methods will provide a large contribution to achieving synchromodal transportation. One issue with developing a RM model in practice is the high number of stakeholders involved in a container transport. The decision on service level and price is expected often has to be made between several stakeholders with conflicting incentives, such as the cargo owner, the container owner (shipping line) and the logistic service provider (Van der Horst and De Langen, 2008).

We see opportunity for research on at least four aspects, regarding this topic: market research, product design, development of a pricing strategy and integral analysis of revenue and operations management. First of all, market research is necessary to gain insights in the incentives of different segments of transportation customers. Currently, only qualitative studies into customer preferences have been carried out for container transportation in North-West Europe, e.g. Lucassen *et al.* (2010), Palmer, *et al.* (2012) and Veenstra and Zuidwijk (2012).

Secondly, using the information from such market research, a method must be created for designing transportation products that encourage flexibility and thus synchromodal transportation. By designing transportation products properties according to customer preferences, customers can be targeted with different types of service level (delivery time, reliability), availability and other aspects. This allows addressing service needs more specifically, and enables pricing mechanisms that maximise revenue, by differential pricing (Barnhart *et al*, 2003).

Thirdly, a pricing strategy must be developed. Currently, transportation is priced per service, based on the mode (barge, rail) and the distance. This is typically *cost-plus pricing*. If the network operator will get flexibility to allocate containers to different modes or routes, this pricing mechanism is not suitable: a customer is not willing to pay a high price if his container is planned on an expensive route for the benefit of the entire network plan. The new pricing strategy must balance the need for flexibility in the order pool with maximising revenue. For instance, orders that allow flexible routing with flexible modes may incur a discount on the price. Using a model for product pricing, based on revenue management techniques, allows support for accepting or rejecting customers that are willing to pay a certain price for a transportation product with a certain amount of flexibility. Based on the value of synchromodal planning flexibility for the network performance, this pricing strategy can be set up.

Finally, such a new revenue management strategy is different from other applications as the network operator can use the flexibility in some products to attain a more efficient transportation plan. In this case the pricing strategy is strongly linked to the operations management: promoting planning flexibility is beneficial for the network if the flexibility can be used to achieve a more cost-efficient transportation plan. This is depicted in Figure 1. While the operations management aims to assign transportation slots to a provided set of demand for minimum cost, the revenue management strategy aims to attain demand for a provided set of slots with maximum revenue. In our case, these two approaches are connected by the balance between flexibility and network utilisation. To optimise total profit, these two approaches must be optimised integrally.

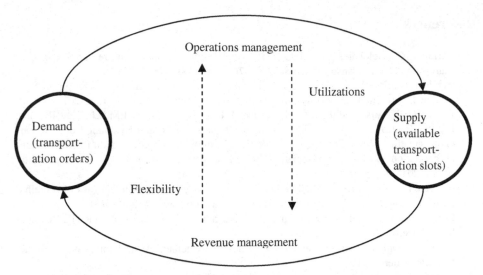

Fig. 1. Revenue management and operations management

4   Conclusion and Outlook

In this paper we have provided an overview of recent and current developments on the topic of operational implementation of synchromodal transportation for the case of European Gateway Services (EGS). The inland transportation network of EGS has focused on separate inland corridors, but is moving towards an integrated network approach of transportation planning: this is referred to as the concept of synchromodal transportation. This transformation is currently in progress. For that, we have highlighted the ongoing research and possibilities for future research regarding three topics:

- Models for integrated network planning
- Methods for real-time decision making for network transportation planning
- Methods for creating flexibility in the transportation planning problem

In this paper we have described the reason for considering these three topics, and summarised recent results for the case of EGS. These results are expected to have practical relevance, as many case studies used in the research are based on the case of EGS and the Rotterdam hinterland. Currently, the most important developments of synchromodal transportation occur in The Netherlands and focus on the Rotterdam hinterland. For wider application of the development of synchromodal transportation, it is important that the general implications of these works will be assessed by comparing the Rotterdam case to other hinterland transportation regions with intermodal networks around the world. In conclusion, although many studies have already been performed on the topic of synchromodal transportation recently, a wide array of extensions and new topics for further research arise. Because of the close connection with developments in practice, we expect that the attention for research on the concept of synchromodal transportation will most likely grow further in the near future.

References

1. Barnhart, C., Belobaba, P., Odoni, A.R.: Applications of operations research in the air transport industry. Transportation Science **37**(4), 368–391 (2003)
2. Behdani, B., Fan, Y., Wiegmans, B., Zuidwijk, R.: Multimodal Schedule Design for Synchromodal Freight Transport Systems. Manuscript submitted for publication (2014)
3. Buiel, E.F.T., Visschedijk, G.C., Lebesque, L.H.E.M., Lucassen, I.M.P.J., Van Riessen, B., Van Rijn, A., Te Brake, G.M.: Syncho Mania – Design and Evaluation of a Serious Game creating a Mind Shift in Transportation Planning. In: Proceedings of the International Simulation and Gaming Association's 46th International Conference, Kyoto, Japan, July 17–21, 2015 (to appear)
4. Bilegan, I.C., Brotcorne, L., Feillet, D., Hayel, Y.: Revenue management for rail container transportation. EURO Journal on Transportation and Logistics, 1–23 (2013)
5. Carmona-Benítez, R.B.: The Design of a Large Scale Airline Network. TRAIL Research School, Delft (2012)
6. Cole, S.: Applied transport economics: policy, management & decision making. Kogan Page Publishers (2005)
7. Crainic, T.G., Laporte, G.: Planning models for freight transportation. European Journal of Operational Research **97**(3), 409–438 (1997)
8. Crainic, T.G.: Service network design in freight transportation. European Journal of Operational Research **122**(2), 272–288 (2000)
9. Crainic, T.G., Kim, K.H.: Intermodal transportation. Transportation **14**, 467–537 (2006)
10. Douma, A.M.: Aligning the operations of barges and terminals through distributed planning. University of Twente (2008)
11. Drewry Shipping Consultants: World container trade and port volumes. Annual container market review and forecast – 2007/08. Nigel Gardiner, London (2007)
12. European gateway services: Direct train Euromax Terminal Rotterdam - DeCeTe Duisburg (2014). http://www.europeangatewayservices.nl/node/231 (retrieved March 10, 2014)
13. Ishfaq, R., Sox, C.R.: Intermodal logistics: the interplay of financial, operational and service issues. Transportation Research Part E: Logistics and Transportation Review **46**(6), 926–949 (2010)
14. Ishfaq, R., Sox, C.R.: Hub location–allocation in intermodal logistic networks. European Journal of Operational Research **210**(2), 213–230 (2011)
15. Ishfaq, R., Sox, C.R.: Design of intermodal logistics networks with hub delays. European Journal of Operational Research **220**(3), 629–641 (2012)
16. Jansen, B., Swinkels, P.C., Teeuwen, G.J., de Fluiter, B.V.A., Fleuren, H.A.: Operational planning of a large-scale multi-modal transportation system. European Journal of Operational Research **156**(1), 41–53 (2004)
17. Lucassen, I.M.P.J., Dogger, T.: Synchromodality pilot study. Identification of bottlenecks and possibilities for a network between Rotterdam, Moerdijk and Tilburg. TNO (2012)
18. Macharis, C., Bontekoning, Y.M.: Opportunities for OR in intermodal freight transport research: A review. European Journal of Operational Research **153**(2), 400–416 (2004)
19. Nabais, J.L., Negenborn, R.R., Benitez, R.B.C., Ayala Botto, M.: A constrained MPC heuristic to achieve a desired transport modal split at intermodal hubs. In: 16th International IEEE Conference on Intelligent Transportation Systems (ITSC), pp. 714–719. IEEE, October 2013
20. Palmer, A, Saenz M.J., Van Woensel, T., Ballot, E.: Characteristics of Collaborative Business Models. ([FP7/2007-2013- SST-2011-RTD-1-7.6)] Ediburgh, UK: CO_3 project. Logistics Research Center (2012)

21. Petrick, A., Steinhardt, C., Gönsch, J., Klein, R.: Using flexible products to cope with demand uncertainty in revenue management. OR Spectrum **34**(1), 215–242 (2012)
22. Platform Synchromodality: What is Synchomodality? (n.d.). http://www.synchromodaliteit.nl/en/definition/ (retrieved March 10, 2014)
23. Port of Rotterdam, Port Vision 2030 (2010). http://www.portofrotterdam.com/en/Port/port-in-general/port-vision-2030/Documents/Port-vision-2030/index.html (accessed February 10, 2014)
24. Van den Berg, R., De Langen, P.W.: An exploratory analysis of the effects of modal split obligations in terminal concession contracts. International Journal of Shipping and Transport Logistics **6**(6), 571–592 (2014)
25. Van der Horst, M.R., de Langen, P.W.: Coordination in hinterland transport chains: a major challenge for the seaport community. Maritime Economics & Logistics **10**(1), 108–129 (2008)
26. Van Riessen, B.: Planning of hinterland transportation in the EGS network. (Master's thesis, Delft University of Technology, The Netherlands, and Erasmus University Rotterdam, The Netherlands) (2013). http://hdl.handle.net/2105/13372
27. Van Riessen, B., Negenborn, R.R., Lodewijks, G., Dekker, R.: Impact and relevance of transit disturbances on planning in intermodal container networks using disturbance cost analysis. Maritime Economics & Logistics (2014-a) (to appear)
28. Van Riessen, B., Negenborn, R.R., Dekker, R.: Online Container Transport Planning with Decision Trees based on Offline Obtained Optimal Solutions. In: Proceedings of the International Forum on Shipping, Ports and Airports (IFSPA 2014), Hong Kong (2014-b)
29. Van Riessen, B., Negenborn, R.R., Dekker, R., Lodewijks, G.: Service network design for an intermodal container network with flexible transit times and the possibility of using subcontracted transport. International Journal of Shipping and Transport Logistics **7**(4), 457–478 (2015)
30. Roso, V., Woxenius, J., Lumsden, K.: The dry port concept: connecting container seaports with the hinterland. Journal of Transport Geography **17**(5), 338–345 (2009)
31. SteadieSeifi, M., Dellaert, N.P., Nuijten, W., Van Woensel, T., Raoufi, R.: Multimodal freight transportation planning: A literature review. European Journal of Operational Research **233**(1), 1–15 (2014)
32. UNECE, ITF, Eurostat. Glossary for Transport Logistics (2009)
33. Veenstra, A., Zuidwijk, R., Van Asperen, E.: The extended gate concept for container terminals: Expanding the notion of dry ports. Maritime Economics & Logistics **14**(1), 14–32 (2012)
34. van Wee, B., Annema, J.A., Banister, D. (eds.): The Transport System and Transport Policy: An Introduction. Edward Elgar Publishing Limited, Cheltenham (2013)
35. Ypsilantis, P., Zuidwijk, R.A.: . Joint Design and Pricing of Intermodal Port-Hinterland Network Services: Considering Economies of Scale and Service Time Constraints (No. ERS-2013-011-LIS). ERIM Report Series Research in Management (2013)
36. Zeni, R.H.: Improved forecast accuracy in revenue management by unconstraining demand estimates from censored data (Doctoral dissertation, Rutgers, The State University of New Jersey) (2001)
37. Ziliaskopoulos, A., Wardell, W.: An intermodal optimum path algorithm for multimodal networks with dynamic arc travel times and switching delays. European Journal of Operational Research **125**(3), 486–502 (2000)

Survey on Operational Perishables Quality Control and Logistics

Xiao Lin[✉], Rudy R. Negenborn, and Gabriel Lodewijks

Department of Maritime & Transport Technology,
Delft University of Technology, Delft, The Netherlands
{X.Lin,R.R.Negenborn,G.Lodewijks}@tudelft.nl

Abstract. Roughly one third of the food is lost worldwide yearly. Much of the loss happens during transport. With the emergence of information and communication technology, new intelligent ways of arranging food transport can be developed. By making transport more intelligent and efficient, the loss of food can be reduced. This survey performs a review on three critical aspects of food transportation, for considerations of an intelligent food transport system. Firstly, the indicators that reflect and factors that affect food quality are discussed. Then, shelf life modeling approaches are analyzed. Thirdly the impacts of shelf life and information technology on the transport system are discussed. Although great achievements have been made, there is much room for further research, as this survey points out, in order to establish a quality-oriented transport system for less food loss.

Keywords: Food transport · Food loss · Kinetic modeling · Shelf life · Quality-oriented transport · Information technology

1 Introduction

An increasing amount of perishables, including foods, flowers, medicine and other products, are produced and consumed worldwide. The modernization of production and transportation has boosted the world market of fresh products. However, a considerably large proportion of food and other perishable goods are still wasted. It is reported that an estimated amount of 1.3 billion tones, roughly one third of the food produced for human consumption, are wasted or lost each year throughout the supply chain, from harvest handling, transport, warehousing to home [27]. Therefore, this survey mainly focuses on the aspect of food in perishables logistics.

The consequences of food wastage and loss are not negligible. Large amounts of wasted perishables are responsible for taking up considerable supply chain capacity and therefore a significant contribution of greenhouse gas emission. The resources that are used for producing the food, namely fresh water, cropland and fertilizer, also get wasted with the food wastage [54]. In the year of 2007, it is estimated that 1.6 billion tones of greenhouse gases worldwide were generated

© Springer International Publishing Switzerland 2015
F. Corman et al. (Eds.): ICCL 2015, LNCS 9335, pp. 398–421, 2015.
DOI: 10.1007/978-3-319-24264-4_28

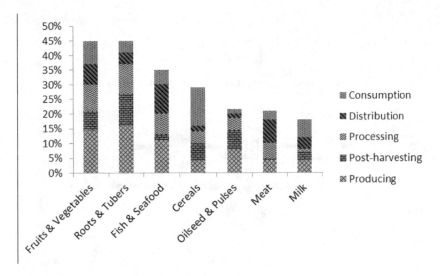

Fig. 1. Yearly food loss categorized by types and stages in supply chain, adapted from [32]

in order to produce and transport the food; one third of it later turned out to have been wasted [27]. In addition, the disposal of wasted food also needs to be handled properly [53].

Food loss happens throughout the supply chains. Figure 1 presents the amount of food loss during different stages of food supply chains, namely production, post-harvesting, processing, distribution and consumption [32]. From the chart we can see that fruits & vegetables, fish & seafood, meat and milk products suffer from great loss during distribution. The goal of establishing greener and more transparent supply chains of perishable goods is undeniably urgent, for if the global food loss and waste can be halved, the saved food can feed more than a million people [32]. Literature highlights issues such as development of demand forecasting [16], better planning of production and distribution [4], better handling in storage and transport [34], improved communication [35], more integrated and effective supply chains [75,82].

Typical Logistic Process of Case Studies. It is not possible to optimize supply chains without knowing how they work. Some literature carries out case studies of perishables logistics. A blueberry logistic process is studied in [24]. The blueberries are picked in Mexico and shipped to the US. During the supply chain, post-harvesting and processing take one day. Distribution, i.e. logistics activities take four to fourteen days, leaving the remaining shelf life of two to seven days for customers to consume. Another case study in literature is banana supply chain from Costa Rica to Germany in [46]. It takes less than a day for bananas from the farm to the port in Central America. After two weeks of sea

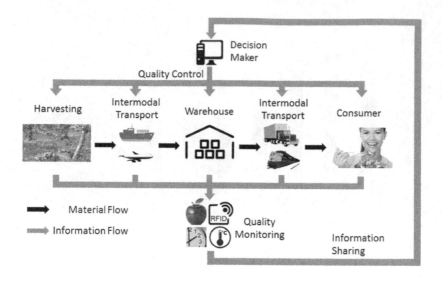

Fig. 2. Intelligent food transport system

transport, it takes three to twelve days to reach chambers for ripening for six days. Then the bananas goes to wholesale trader.

As can be seen above, the travel time of food can be fluctuating largely because of logistic reasons. To reduce the loss during this time, deeper and more comprehensive research is needed in order to establish efficient and organized fresh food supply chains. To solve the problems mentioned above, we propose an intelligent food logistic system. The framework of the intelligent food logistic system we propose is given in Figure 2. In the figure the black arrows are material flows and blue arrows are information flows. Together with the food quality monitoring, shelf life estimation and information technologies used in each stage of the supply chains, a properly organized transport system from production to end users can be established. Information sharing and intermodal transport increases transparency, traceability and flexibility of the transport system. Decision makers cooperate within the frame of the system and perform optimal, quality-oriented transport scheduling. To establish this system, we need to examine how perishable goods lose value throughout the supply chains using proper sensing and modeling technologies and to understand how to predict and control the deterioration process. With this knowledge we may better organize food supply chains to reduce the food loss.

In order to evaluate the possibility of realizing the concept presented in Figure 2 and find gaps between needs and reality, three critical aspects are to be considered. Firstly, an understanding of nature of food, meaning its quality or shelf life and what affect it are of importance. Because the quality affects the price as well as customer satisfaction [72]. Secondly, proper modeling methods

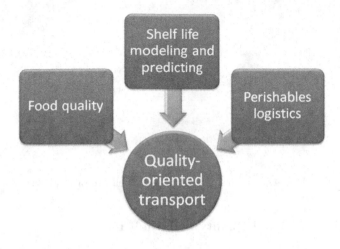

Fig. 3. Overview of the survey

of food quality are needed. The information of food enhances the transparency and is the basis by which logistics process can be scheduled [84]. Thirdly, the information of food quality shall be made full use of [14]. Research as well as investments need to be done on infrastructure, such as refrigerators, sensors or wireless networks for real-time communication and quality control. Therefore, as illustrated in Figure 3, this paper reviews the literature in the following three key aspects:

- food quality and control,
- shelf life modeling, and
- new technologies for food logistics.

The rest of this article is organized as follows. In Section 2, the properties of food quality as well as attributes of food appearance are discussed and the concept of shelf life is defined. Section 3 investigates approaches for shelf life modeling and predicting for food. In Section 4, we discuss approaches for keeping the best quality in cold chain transport. In the final section, we draw conclusions to previous research and discuss open problems that will be encountered when establishing quality-oriented food transport systems.

2   Food Quality and Shelf Life

Food quality, especially of fresh fruit or vegetables, is the determining reason for product acceptance of consumers and affects pricing. It is also the purpose of cold supply chains: to keep foods as fresh as possible during the transport. In order to keep an acceptable quality during the processes of a supply chain, a clear understanding of what quality is and how to quantify it should be obtained firstly. In this section, the definitions of quality and shelf life are given. Then the factors affecting shelf life and food quality quantification are surveyed.

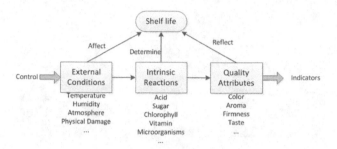

Fig. 4. Features of quality and shelf life of food

2.1 Definition of Food Quality and Shelf Life

The term of "food quality" is a general concept that describes the overall acceptance of food, including attributes such as color, aroma, firmness and taste. Food quality changes as the chemical or biochemical reactions goes on, for example the deterioration and micro-organisms growth. These reactions are affected by various factors, both intrinsic and extrinsic. As Figure 4 illustrates, by controlling external conditions, the rate of internal reactions can be affected. Quality attributes are indicators of these internal reactions, such attributes could be monitored during the transport process. However it is not applicable to plan or schedule transport according to a list of chemical and environmental facts of foods. A simple index of the food quality is needed for higher communication efficiency and faster decision making [56]. Therefore the term "shelf life" is preferred when estimating food quality in supply chains. It can be defined as *"the period that the decreasing quality of perishables remains acceptable for end users"* [85]. It needs to be pointed out that as shelf life counts down, food quality does not always drop, for some fruits and vegetables ripen after harvesting such as bananas and tomatoes.

2.2 Indicators Reflecting and Factors Affecting Food Quality

Attributes that reflect food quality can be used to estimate the shelf life of food. These indicators change along time, because physical, chemical and biochemical reactions are taking place. At the same time, some external conditions can affect the reaction process, resulting in the changes of food quality. Some conditions (e.g., temperature and atmosphere) are the factors that affects food quality as well as the results when foods start respiration and decaying. Table 1 lists indicators, factors and conditions that interacts with food quality and literature addressing them. By understanding these attributes and conditions, we can know how foods decay and how to reduce the loss from it.

Attributes Indicating Food Quality. These attributes, in another word, indicators, reflect food quality. In Table 1 four types of indicators are listed,

Table 1. Types of kinetics models

Item	Role	Reference
Weight loss	Indicator	[40,48]
Color	Indicator	[41,46,81]
Firmness	Indicator	[99]
Chemicals	Indicator	[3,23]
Radiation	Factor	[1]
Physical impact	Factor	[91]
Micro-organisms	Factor	[37]
Humidity	Factor	[11]
Temperature	Interaction	[10,28,30,46,67,92]
Atmosphere	Interaction	[9,26,49,59,69,94]

namely weight loss, color, firmness and chemicals. Weight loss as a function of time is used as an indicator for estimating quality of fresh food in [40,48]. While color change is used as an indicator to examine fresh fruit quality and ripening. A study on tomatoes is conducted, in which color examination was applied for predicting the post-harvest behavior of fresh tomatoes in [41]. Another study monitors banana ripening using peel color change [46]. The degradation of chlorophyll of cucumbers is investigated through the change of green color in [81], in order to predict the remaining time that cucumbers retain their quality within an acceptable range. Firmness is also used for shelf life estimation for nectarine in [99]. Changes in some chemical substance are applied in studies. For instance, shelf life of frozen spinach is modeled using chlorophyll in [23]; and loss of Vitamin C is examined to model quality of fresh melons in [3].

Conditions Affecting Food Quality. Food quality changes along the time. In which chemical and biochemical reactions are the intrinsic reasons. The process of these reactions determines the quality change of food. By controlling some of the external conditions, temperature or humidity for instance, the intrinsic reactions can be accelerated or decelerated, and therefore the shelf life can be shortened or prolonged.

Physical impacts or vibrations can also affect quality of food [91], as well as irradiations [1]. The growth of micro-organisms is not negligible. Bacteria, yeasts and mold may affect the quality and safety of food [37]. Humidity sometimes is also a factor that may affect the quality of food [11].

Temperature and Atmosphere. Temperature and atmosphere are factors as well as indicators relating to food quality. Food is sensitive to temperature and ambient atmosphere because they can affect the rate of reactions taking place inside. And these reactions can in turn affect temperature and atmosphere around because of the heat or gas generated due to respiration [30,44].

Temperature can be a significant factor affecting shelf life [6]. It affects the rate of respiration [30], activity of enzyme [10,67], degradation of nutritious

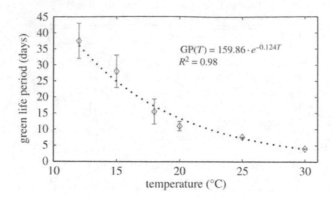

Fig. 5. Time-temperature relationship for bananas [46]

substances [28]. The rate of chemical reactions is closely related to temperature. In addition to chemical aspects, low temperature may do chilling or freezing injury to fresh vegetables or fruits as well [92]. For instance, Figure 5 shows that the higher temperature is, the shorter green life of bananas will be. In other words, the quicker bananas will turn yellow [46]. What is more, when some of bananas ripen, heat is generated due to the chemical reactions happening in these fruits. The heat will then in turn accelerate the ripening process of the rest of fruits nearby.

Atmosphere also plays an essential role in reactions taking place in perishables. Most of the literature considers interactive effects among several factors: it is found that by reducing O_2 and raising CO_2 concentration helps slow down respiration rate and prolongs shelf life of fresh fruit and vegetables [49]; and different concentration of O_2 and CO_2 of atmosphere is found to have an impact on tomato shelf life [94]. Experiments carried out by Duarte and others [26] show that concentration of CO_2 affects firmness of blueberries and thus the shelf life of them. Increased CO_2 concentration enhances the firmness after a storage of 24 days. Similarly, experiments conducted by Ayala-Zavala and others [9] show that strawberries under a higher O_2 concentration remain higher levels of quality attributes after a storage of 14 days at 5°C. In another study, Majidi [69] used modified atmosphere for tomato storage. Results show that with increased CO_2 and reduced O_2, tomatoes' ripen comes later than in normal air and therefore the shelf life is prolonged. Some of the chemicals can affect the ripening process as well as shelf life of some fruit. For instance ethylene is studied and found to be a key factor for ripening of fruits and vegetables [59].

2.3   Discussion

Remaining shelf life should be taken care of during each stage of supply chains. To some extent, the quality of food relates to attributes based on observations. Nevertheless, the changing appearance of food does not completely reflect loss of nutritions as food quality changes [69]. It is pointed out that the criteria for shelf life estimation should be carefully chosen [23]. It is also noted that the loss of nutritious substances should be taken into account, so that shelf life estimation is not only based on appearance. Because nutritions are what consumers get from the food, for instance, Vitamin C in melons [3].

3 Predicting Shelf Life

In Section 2, we have discussed the definition of shelf life and factors affecting shelf life. In order to establish a quality-oriented transport system, it helps to be aware of the goods quality and remaining shelf lives at anytime, anywhere. This requires a thorough understanding of perishing feature of goods, real-time monitoring of the conditions and the ability to predict how goods perish under changing conditions. This section focuses on existing approaches for acquiring quality attributes and models for predicting shelf life.

3.1 Sensing Technology

Sensors are devices that transfer real world attributes into electronic signals. In this survey, the sensors we discuss can be categorized in two groups: destructive sensors and non-destructive sensors. Destructive sensing approaches are methods that take small pieces of tissue from foods for analysis. By which, however, fruits and vegetables can get wounded and may develop further deterioration due to the injury. Therefore, in food transport it is preferred that non-destructive sensors are used, for the measurements can be conducted more often using such sensors without concerning causing too much spoilage.

Destructive Sensors. Penetrometers are effective ways to examine the quality change in food. For instance, firmness of apples, kiwifruits and lemons is measured using penetrometers in [13, 36]. This approach makes the analysis highly accurate, for it directly examines the chemical contents of food. However the pitfall is that it also damages the food, especially to fruits and vegetables. Therefore these approaches are not suitable for consecutive food quality monitoring during supply chains.

Impact analysis and acoustic impulse response are methods for measuring fruit and vegetable quality via striking the surface and detect the response in either time or frequency domain [21, 80]. Although a large variety of food can be tested via this way, whether the striking has further undesirable effect on food remains suspicious.

Non-destructive Sensors. Other approaches are called non-destructive methods in which food is examined without any direct contact. Among all the analysis methods, color is widely used for an indicator of remaining shelf life of food. The change of color can be triggered by the degradation of chlorophyll [23, 46] or the change of carotene [86] or other factors. The sensing of color can be done using cameras and computer vision technology. The technology is used for green and brown detection for the classification of bananas [70] and tomato ripening [65]. The change of temperature and concentration of CO_2, O_2 and ethylene, are indicators as well as triggers of quality changing. The respiration process makes fresh fruit and vegetables consume oxygen and generate carbon-dioxide, heat, and in some cases, ethylene. These reactions, which bring changes to the atmosphere, can in turn affect the rate of the reactions [44]. This brings a better understanding of shelf life estimation and prediction.

3.2   Modeling Methods

The ideal situation of quality monitoring system for food logistics is that every unit is under inspection at anytime. However, this requires large amount of sensors and processing capacity, which can be too expensive for food logistics. One cost-efficient alternative is keeping records of external conditions that affect the quality change and using mathematical models of food shelf life as reference to estimate the status of the quality. These approaches can highly reduce the cost and time for installing sensing, communicating and processing devices. Several models for shelf life estimation and prediction have been proposed in the literature.

Markovian Model. Ledauphin et al. [57] use Markovian model to describe the decaying stages of salmon according to scores given by expert assessors. The stages include "fresh", "decayed" and "very decayed". The transition matrix between different stages is given by the scores from the assessors. The result shows that fresh salmon has a probability of 39% of turning decayed after one week of storage and 2% of turning very decayed. For decayed salmon, it has a probability of 6% of turning very decayed. Nevertheless, the future state of the object only depends on the current state, which may bring inaccuracy to the model. Besides, the external conditions are not considered by Markovian models, meaning that predictions to shelf life cannot be made according to different storage conditions.

Later the model has been extended to a hidden Markov model in [58], using the same dataset and bringing possibility of relating the prediction to external conditions. The paper points out the limitation that the performance of the model strongly depends on data which could be insufficient, and thus leads to inaccuracy. In addition, the scores are given according to the sensory attributes, which makes the evaluation subjective.

Artificial Neural Network. Lin and Block [64] use a 2-stage artificial neural network to predict the remaining shelf life of lettuce under storage in fluctuating temperature and relative humidity. Temperature is selected as the input of the neural network model. The 2-stage neural network is trained using heuristics based on data from experiments. The study indicates that 2-stage neural network has a higher accuracy than 1-stage neural network and regression models. Therefore it has the potential for shelf life prediction.

Another study develops a three-stage artificial neural network to predict shelf life of milk [89]. Experiments are conducted for milk of different quality and volatiles of the milk are detected and used as the input of the neural network. The study also uses a principle component regression model as comparison. The results show that neural network has a higher prediction performance than the principle component regression model.

Other Models. There are other models reported to be utilized in food shelf life or quality evaluation. Chatterjee and others [17] use fuzzy logic analysis to evaluate shelf life of fried potato wedges. Sensory properties of sausages are evaluated using fuzzy logic in [43]. Decision tree is applied in meat quality evaluation in [83].

Although these models can, to some extent, describe the quality decreasing process of food, they are general model and are not explanatory. The accuracy of Markovian models, as mentioned in [58], strongly relies on the size of dataset used for training. A review by Du and Sun [25] points out the limitations of other models mentioned above. Artificial neural networks lack a profound theoretical basis of designing the structure and are black boxes; the performance of fuzzy logic models largely depends on the tunning process; decision trees can be easily understood by human but they are method for approaching discrete value target functions.

Kinetic Modeling. Chemical kinetics is widely applied in modeling food quality and shelf life estimation [90]. The model is based on intrinsic, time dependent features of food. The established kinetic models need to be validated by experiments before they come to actual use. A general kinetic model can be described as follows:

$$r = -\frac{dQ}{dt} = kQ^n, \tag{1}$$

in which r is reaction rate, which can be represented as the decreasing rate of quality overtime $-\frac{dQ}{dt}$. The rate is proportional to the quality Q to the power of n. Variable k is determined by reaction type and external conditions like temperature. When using kinetics for shelf life estimation, shelf life t_{SL} can be calculated from the kinetic model, with a degrading quality indicator at a static external condition:

$$t_{SL} = \frac{f(Q, Q_1)}{k}, \tag{2}$$

where the quality function $f(Q, Q_1)$ represents the actual physiological mechanism, initial quality Q and the lowest acceptable quality Q_1 [42]. The quality function depends on how the concentration of chemical substance affects reaction rate. Variable k can be affected by one or more attributes. In the kinetics

Table 2. Types of kinetics models

Reaction type	Reaction rate	Remaining shelf life
Zero-order	$-\dfrac{dQ}{dt} = k$	$t_{SL} = \dfrac{Q - Q_1}{k}$
First-order	$-\dfrac{dQ}{dt} = kQ$	$t_{SL} = \dfrac{\ln \frac{Q}{Q_1}}{k}$
Second-order	$-\dfrac{dQ}{dt} = kQ^2$	$t_{SL} = \dfrac{\frac{1}{Q_1} - \frac{1}{Q}}{k}$
Logistic	$-\dfrac{dQ}{dt} = kQ(\dfrac{Q}{Q_{\text{inf}}} - 1)$	$t_{SL} = \dfrac{\ln \frac{Q_1 - Q_{\text{inf}}}{Q_1 C_{\text{ba}}}}{k}$
Michaelis-Menten	$-\dfrac{dQ}{dt} = \dfrac{V_{\max}Q}{K_{\text{m}} + Q}$	$-$

model for food quality estimation, it is considered as a variable of reaction rate affected by temperature. This is because of the reason that during food transport, as packaging technology evolves, other attributes can be better controlled than temperature. Therefore temperature is one of the attributes that generates the most uncertainty affecting shelf life of goods [84]. Therefore Arrhenius law [6], which is discussed in Section 3.3, is applied for determining variable k. To identify the type of $f(Q, Q_1)$, experiments are needed for each type of chemicals or food. Labuza [55] categorizes food deterioration in two different orders of kinetics model with different value of k: zero-order and first-order. Chen [18] pointed out that second-order kinetics is suitable for some reactions. Table 2 shows the reaction rate and calculated shelf life of different types of kinetic models.

From literature on modeling food we can see that chemical kinetics is used for various substance in different orders. Zero-order kinetics is frequently used in describing reactions that are not affected by the amount of substance. It is also used for modeling dehydration process in potatoes and onions [50, 71]. Experiments show the degradation of Vitamin C in frozen spinach fits the model of first-order kinetics [23]. First-order kinetic is also proved to be useful in describing peach color change in [8]. Oxidation of extractable color pigments in chili pepper is modeled using second-order kinetics in [18]. In spite of the fact that experiments have shown kinetics models suit many of the reactions, we cannot assume that reactions of a certain substance can fit in one single model.

Other types of kinetic models like logistic models as well as Michaelis-Menten models are reported to be observed by literature [87]. Logistic function is considered as one of the natural processes, and is also reported in shelf life modeling

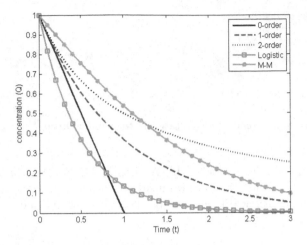

Fig. 6. Reactions having the same initial concentration and rate constant but a varying order n, adapted from [90]

[66]. In Table 2, Q_{inf} is the possible lowest quality and

$$C_{ba} = \frac{Q - Q_{inf}}{Q}.$$

In Michaelis-Menten kinetics, parameter V_{max} the maximum reaction rate. And K_m is the Michaelis constant representing substance concentration when the reaction rate reaches half of the maximum rate. The relationship between concentration of O_2 and respiration rate of stored apples is modeled using Michaelis-Menten kinetics [5]. The table does not list the remaining shelf life calculated by Michaelis-Menten kinetics, because the solution of t_{SL} is not explicit.

Figure 6 illustrates the relationships between time and concentration of substances in different reaction mechanisms. It can be seen that except for zero-order reaction, the reaction rate drops while the concentration is reducing at different rate. In the zero-order model, no difference that concentration makes to reaction rate while in other types the concentration does have impacts on reaction rate.

3.3 Arrhenius Law

As is shown above, chemical kinetics is widely applied in the modeling of food quality. It uses Arrhenius law to determine variable k. Arrhenius law is of significance in describing how temperature affects reaction rate [77]. According to Arrhenius law, the rate constant k of a reaction can be obtained as follows:

$$k = Ae^{-\frac{E_a}{RT}}, \tag{3}$$

in which E_a is the activation energy, while A represents the rate k at which all molecules have sufficient energy to react. R and T are the gas constant and

Fig. 7. Response scale of solid state photochromic OnVu^{TM} TTI [88]

absolute temperature, respectively [90]. Arrhenius law reveals the relationship between temperature and reaction rate inside of perishables. The practical perspective of utilizing chemical kinetics and Arrhenius law is discussed in Section 3.4.

3.4   Time Temperature Integrator

A widely applied technology namely time temperature integrator (TTI, or in some literature, time temperature indicator) was introduced [51]. TTIs are cheap, active labels that shows an easily measurable time-temperature dependent change that reflects the full or partial temperature history of a product to which it is attached. Based on shelf life of products and kinetic response of TTI, the quality of perishables can be monitored and predicted through out the supply chain. The reason for using temperature dependent modeling is that in most food transport, atmosphere and relative humidity is more easily handled than temperature, which means that the change of temperature has a major impact on the uncertainty of deterioration [84]. Figure 7 demonstrates how one type of TTIs work by showing the response scale of them. The dark blue appears after photosensitive compounds are activated to low wavelength light. The color fades at a rate which relates to temperature. Sensitivity to temperature of the TTI can be set at activation using different photochromic compounds and wavelength of UV light exposure.

3.5   Discussion

In conclusion, the advantage of kinetic modeling comparing to other modeling techniques is that, it generates a simple, continuous output via examining the mechanisms of intrinsic reactions of food as well as environmental conditions. This explanatory modeling approach can provide accurate prediction from attributes, and helps establish a smart food transport system.

However, the challenges that we come across cannot be neglected. First of all, due to the complexity of food, there are many reactions happening simultaneously, which differ among types of food. The selection of the criteria is therefore vital for shelf life estimation. Secondly, biological variability often affects the reliability of models. As mentioned in [93], these variations are due to different handling during planting, harvesting and post-harvest activities. Better statistical analysis needs to be applied based on the thorough understanding of the mechanisms. Besides, there is not a general model for all perishables because of the huge differences among different type of food.

4 Impact of Shelf Life on Perishable Supply Chains

As discussed above, shelf life is an important term in perishables supply chains. Technologies for keeping food quality have been developed, which have already had great impact on transport systems. Modern transport technologies, for instance, refrigerated containers [7] and modified atmosphere packaging [61], are widely used for perishables transport. With the temperature and atmosphere controlled, perishables can stay for a longer time during transport. What is more, warehousing strategies are studied in order to manage orders and stocks according to the freshness of perishables to reduce loss. As previous sections have discussed, it is possible to have an estimation of remaining shelf life of perishable goods using proper monitoring and modeling techniques. If this information is made of full use in real-time, the transportation procedure can be scheduled accordingly, reducing the loss of cargo. In addition, the shelf life can also be affected by controlling temperature and other conditions. It will then become possible that shelf life is controllable (as well as ripening process for some fruits and vegetables) during transport by taking initiative to adjust temperature or atmosphere. Then the whole transport system will be brought to a new era.

4.1 Quality Control in Transport

It is common that lower temperatures prolong the shelf life of food. Refrigerated ships for perishables transport started around 1880 [73]. Before 1950, refrigerated ships used one or more chambers to store foods. As the containerization of cargo ships have become the majority of sea transport [37], refrigerated containers, in another word, reefers, emerged afterwards. Carriers can have various types of goods stored in different reefers on the same ship without worrying about the different requirements of goods. Thus these refrigerating containers enabled a more flexible perishables transport using different modalities and enhanced the quality of cool chain logistics [22]. Nowadays more than 90% of the perishables is transported by reefer containers [76]. Figure 8 shows a scheme for reefer containers. Packaging techniques are widely used for keeping the most shelf life of perishables. Modified atmosphere packaging (MAP) creates the initial package atmosphere according to types of products to slow down the process of deterioration [31]. Controlled atmosphere storage (CAS) allows the atmosphere stay static. Figure 9 shows three different storage conditions for tomatoes and the quality index (the quotient of total soluble solids divided by Titratable acid) remains a high level during a longer time for CAS and MAP storage other than cold storage with normal air. Intelligent packaging carried out by Yam [96] are defined as "a packaging system that is capable of carrying out intelligent functions to facilitate decision-making, to extend shelf life, enhance safety, improve

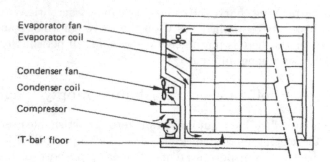

Evaporator fan
Evaporator coil

Condenser fan
Condenser coil

Compressor

'T-bar' floor

Fig. 8. Scheme for reefers [38]

quality, provide information and warn about possible problems". Food quality sensors, indicators and RFID technology have enabled the development of intelligent packaging as well as smart food logistics [39].

The warehousing strategy that was previously used for perishable goods rotation was "first-in-first-out (FIFO)". According to this approach, each distribution center firstly ships the products that arrive first. The approach assumes that all products have the same shelf life. When taking the actual shelf life into account, which requires the monitoring information from the foods, the first-expire-first-out (FEFO, or in some literature, least-shelf-first-out) strategy is able to adjust the rotation sequence and thus can reduce the rejections from consumers due to quality loss. Figure 10 illustrates how FEFO reduces food waste compared with FIFO: the horizontal axis is the quality (or remaining shelf life) at delivery while the vertical axis is the probability, i.e. the proportion of food. The FEFO strategy does not change the average quality of food but reduces the non-acceptable [45].

4.2   The Developing Role of Information Communication Technology

Information communication technology (ICT) can be widely used in different steps of cold supply chains [20], from harvesting[15,29] to warehouse [63], transport [98], etc. With proper use of ICT, perishables supply chains can be better optimized according to real-time information (e.g. demand and remaining shelf life). Ketzenberg et al. [52] measure the importance of information and value of centralized control of a supply chain between one supplier and one retailer. The study shows that the total supply chain profit increases by an average of 5.6% with shared information on shelf life based inventory status and a centralized control scheme. Information sharing helps improve traceability, efficiency, information accuracy and reduce inventory loss [79]. Haass et al. [33] use simulation to show how intelligent containers can reduce the loss of bananas with information sharing and environment controlling. The result indicates that with a proper control 22% of banana spoilage can be reduced. Li and others study a

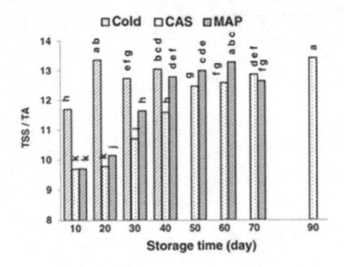

Fig. 9. Ripening and decaying of tomatoes under different atmosphere, adapted from [69]

case of perishables supply chain optimization considering the quality loss due to commodity deterioration. In the simulation scenario it is found that a thorough value loss tracking can help reduce costs by 7% rather than no assessment of value loss [60].

Information Sharing. The sharing of information helps decision makers of transport achieve better operations. Researchers are looking for approaches to integrate this information to fresh supply chains. Lang et al. [56] introduced a cognitive sensor network for transport management, which is installed in a reefer for environment and quality monitoring. Food quality estimation is based on observation and models. The estimation can be applied in decentralized transportation control and management. The approach of quality driven customer order decoupling corridors (qCODC) is introduced for better manage fresh supply chains [68].

RFID Technology. The development of RFID technology enables a fresh supply chain with better traceability and integration [20]. RFID can be one good solution to the integration of information and transport system. Chen et al. [19] propose a food trace system within a smart cold chain system by 2G-RFID-system. Jedermann et al. [47] use RFID temperature data loggers and models for perishable goods to estimate the remaining shelf life which can be used for transport scheduling. However, the utilization and installation of RFID devices requires investments. The use of RFID faces opportunities as well as great challenges [78]. The cost of RFID chips can still be expensive as to be widely applied

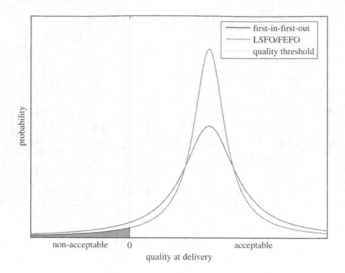

Fig. 10. Comparison of FIFO and FEFO/LSFO [45]

in logistic systems. Yan et al. [97] compare fresh supply chains with and without RFID tags and calculate the total profit. The results show that fresh supply chains with RFID and a reduced cargo loss rate have a higher total profit although costs of devices are taken into account.

Future of ICT in Food Logistics. Although studies on supply chain enhancement using ICT have revealed the opportunities of better utilization of this evolving technology, there are still very few studies in which ICT is implemented in the real cases rather than simulations. Besides, large amount of information can be gained through the monitoring using semi-passive RFID tags in the current studies on smart transport systems [47]. Shelf life prediction can be make using these RFID devices. And a distributed control system is more feasible than a centralized controller in response to quality changes of fresh cargo [74]. By using ICT technology, great changes can be brought to the way of food logistics are organized. All stages of supply chains, such as post-harvest [2], reefer container handling [95], warehousing [42], intermodality [62] can be better organized accordingly. Moreover, with comprehensive, real-time information of quality of food in supply chains, transport providers become able to take initiatives to control the quality change and ripening process, rather than passively react to the deterioration of fresh food [12].

5   Conclusions and Outlook

This survey reviews the literature on features and transportation of foods. We describe the meaning of "quality" and provide a clear definition of shelf life.

Sensing technologies and modeling methods for shelf life estimation and prediction are discussed. Then we perform an analysis about how information of shelf life can impact the transportation of perishable goods. It is shown in literature that great progress has been made in understanding food and has been making good use of the knowledge in all stages of supply chains. The analysis in this research provides background knowledge as a basis of quality-oriented logistic systems.

Nevertheless, problems are becoming more explicit along with the progressing of the research, leaving much room for improvements. It is pointed out that the biological variations among individuals should be better handled, for this is an important source of uncertainties of shelf life. These variations can be caused by planting, post-harvest handling and many other aspects. Besides, because of the complexity of foods, much difference can be seen among different types of food. Therefore, no generic models can describe the quality for all foods. To analyze a certain type of food, careful selection of the criteria for indicators and design of statical analysis of experimental data are significant for modeling and predicting.

Food itself is much more complex than a model. Models with multiple input attributes is not often seen in literature. However, more than one attributes might be considered to develop more accurate models for better predictions. Uncertainties need to be handled using proper techniques (e.g., fuzzy logic). Moreover, this also requires higher capability of devices that monitor shelf life and communicate with transport infrastructures. These challenges call for better modeling approaches with comprehensive evaluation of food deterioration pattern. Apart from fresh food, there are other types of goods being massively transported, medicine and flowers for instance, which also suffer from loss during supply chains. If these commodities are taken into consideration, the intelligent transport systems for perishables can be extended to a much wider range.

The goal of the concept of quality-oriented transport is to solve practical problems. Yet most of the literature is still at theoretical study and is not implemented in real case or operation. Moreover, literature shows that most of studies focus on segments of the supply chain rather than the entire intelligent transport systems, which is likely to be one of the gaps between theory and practice. What is more, The impact of information of food shelf life on transport systems is not negligible. New technologies such as sensors and communication systems can have large amount of data gathered or transmitted that can easily make a centralized controller overloaded. Therefore a distributed control and management system is preferred. Acting as part of the Internet of Things with ICT, the carriers of perishables can negotiate with each other and decide next step of coordination in an agent-based scheme. Information sharing leads to a higher transparency for every stakeholder in perishables supply chains. Intermodal transport can be considered as the cooperative transport system for perishables because its high flexibility.

ICT can bring changes to all stages of supply chains, from producing to end users. In addition, the information of shelf lives makes it possible to arrange for optimal solutions to transport scheduling as well as for temperature or atmosphere controlling. The supply chain will be no longer passively responding to the changes of food quality. Instead, the systems will take the initiative to positively deal with changes that happen within supply chains.

Acknowledgments. This research is supported by the China Scholarship Council under grant 201406950004.

References

1. Akter, H., Khan, S.A.: Effect of gamma irradiation on the quality (colour, firmness and total soluble solid) of tomato (Lycopersicon esculentum mill.) stored at different temperature. Asian Journal of Agricultural Research **6**, 12–20 (2011)
2. Ali, J., Kumar, S.: Information and communication technologies (ICTs) and farmers decision-making across the agricultural supply chain. International Journal of Information Management **31**(2), 149–159 (2011)
3. Amodio, M.L., Derossi, A., Colelli, G.: Modelling sensorial and nutritional changes to better define quality and shelf life of fresh-cut melons. Journal of Agricultural Engineering **44**(1), E6 (2013)
4. Amorim, P., Meyr, H., Almeder, C., Almada-Lobo, B.: Managing perishability in production-distribution planning: a discussion and review. Flexible Services and Manufacturing Journal **25**(3), 389–413 (2013)
5. Andrich, G., Fiorentini, R., Tuci, A., Zinnai, A., Sommovigo, G.: A tentative model to describe the respiration of stored apples. Journal of the American Society for Horticultural Science **116**(3), 478–481 (1991)
6. Aquilanti, V., Mundim, K.C., Elango, M., Kleijn, S., Kasai, T.: Temperature dependence of chemical and biophysical rate processes: Phenomenological approach to deviations from arrhenius law. Chemical Physics Letters **498**(1), 209–213 (2010)
7. Arduino, G., Carrillo Murillo, D., Parola, F.: Refrigerated container versus bulk: evidence from the banana cold chain. Maritime Policy & Management **42**(3), 228–245 (2015)
8. Avila, I.M.L.B., Silva, C.L.M.: Modelling kinetics of thermal degradation of colour in peach puree. Journal of Food Engineering **39**(2), 161–166 (1999)
9. Ayala-Zavala, J.F., Wang, S.Y., Wang, C.Y., González-Aguilar, G.A.: High oxygen treatment increases antioxidant capacity and postharvest life of strawberry fruit. Food Technology and Biotechnology **45**(2), 166–173 (2007)
10. Bahçeci, K.S., Serpen, A., Gökmen, V., Acar, J.: Study of lipoxygenase and peroxidase as indicator enzymes in green beans: change of enzyme activity, ascorbic acid and chlorophylls during frozen storage. Journal of Food Engineering **66**(2), 187–192 (2005)
11. Bhowmik, S.R., Pan, J.C.: Shelf life of mature green tomatoes stored in controlled atmosphere and high humidity. Journal of Food Science **57**(4), 948–953 (1992)
12. Blackburn, J., Scudder, G.: Supply chain strategies for perishable products: the case of fresh produce. Production and Operations Management **18**(2), 129–137 (2009)
13. Botía, P., Navarro, J.M., Cerdá, A., Martínez, V.: Yield and fruit quality of two melon cultivars irrigated with saline water at different stages of development. European Journal of Agronomy **23**(3), 243–253 (2005)

14. Bourlakis, M., Vlachos, I.P., Zeimpekis, V.: Intelligent agrifood chains and networks. John Wiley & Sons Ltd., West Sussex (2011)
15. Caixeta-Filho, J.V.: Orange harvesting scheduling management: a case study. Journal of the Operational Research Society **57**(6), 637–642 (2006)
16. Caixeta-Filho, J.V., van Swaay-Neto, J.M., Wagemaker, A.P.: Optimization of the production planning and trade of lily flowers at Jan de Wit Company. Interfaces **32**(1), 35–46 (2002)
17. Chatterjee, D., Bhattacharjee, P., Bhattacharyya, N.: Development of methodology for assessment of shelf-life of fried potato wedges using electronic noses: Sensor screening by fuzzy logic analysis. Journal of Food Engineering **133**, 23–29 (2014)
18. Chen, S.L., Gutmanis, F.: Auto-oxidation of extractable color pigments in chili pepper with special reference to ethoxyquin treatment. Journal of Food Science **33**(3), 274–280 (1968)
19. Chen, Y., Wang, Y., Jan, J.: A novel deployment of smart cold chain system using 2G-RFID-Sys. Journal of Food Engineering **141**, 113–121 (2014)
20. Chu, H., Wu, G., Chen, J., Fei, F., Mai, J.D., Li, W.J.: Design and simulation of self-powered radio frequency identification (RFID) tags for mobile temperature monitoring. Science China Technological Sciences **56**(1), 1–7 (2013)
21. De Baerdemaeker, J., Lemaitre, L., Meire, R.: Quality detection by frequency-spectrum analysis of the fruit impact force. Transactions of the American Society of Agricultural Engineers **25**(1), 175–178 (1982)
22. Dellacasa, A.: Refrigerated transport by sea. International Journal of Refrigeration **10**(6), 349–352 (1987)
23. Dermesonluoglu, E., Katsaros, G., Tsevdou, M., Giannakourou, M., Taoukis, P.: Kinetic study of quality indices and shelf life modelling of frozen spinach under dynamic conditions of the cold chain. Journal of Food Engineering **148**, 13–23 (2014)
24. do Nascimento Nunes, M.C., Nicometo, M., Emond, J.P., Melis, R.B., Uysal, I.: Improvement in fresh fruit and vegetable logistics quality: berry logistics field studies. Philosophical Transactions of the Royal Society A: Mathematical, Physical and Engineering Sciences **372**(2017), 20130307 (2014)
25. Du, C., Sun, D.: Learning techniques used in computer vision for food quality evaluation: a review. Journal of Food Engineering **72**(1), 39–55 (2006)
26. Duarte, C., Guerra, M., Daniel, P., Camelo, A.L., Yommi, A.: Quality changes of highbush blueberries fruit stored in CA with different CO_2 levels. Journal of Food Science **74**(4), S154–S159 (2009)
27. FAO (2013). Food wastage footprint. http://www.fao.org/docrep/018/i3347e/i3347e.pdf
28. Favell, D.J.: A comparison of the vitamin C content of fresh and frozen vegetables. Food Chemistry **62**(1), 59–64 (1998)
29. Ferrer, J., Mac Cawley, A., Maturana, S., Toloza, S., Vera, J.: An optimization approach for scheduling wine grape harvest operations. International Journal of Production Economics **112**(2), 985–999 (2008)
30. Fonseca, S.C., Oliveira, F.A.R., Brecht, J.K.: Modelling respiration rate of fresh fruits and vegetables for modified atmosphere packages: a review. Journal of Food Engineering **52**(2), 99–119 (2002)
31. Guillard, V., Buche, P., Destercke, S., Tamani, N., Croitoru, M., Menut, L., Guillaume, C., Gontard, N.: A decision support system to design modified atmosphere packaging for fresh produce based on a bipolar flexible querying approach. Computers and Electronics in Agriculture **111**, 131–139 (2015)

32. Gustavsson, J., Cederberg, C., Sonesson, U., van Otterdijk, R., Meybeck, A.: Global food losses and food waste: extent, causes and prevention. FAO (2011)

33. Haass, R., Dittmer, P., Veigt, M., Lütjen, M.: Reducing food losses and carbon emission by using autonomous control-a simulation study of the intelligent container. International Journal of Production Economics (2011)

34. Hailu, M., Workneh, T.S., Belew, D.: Review on postharvest technology of banana fruit. African Journal of Biotechnology **12**(7), 635–647 (2013)

35. Halloran, A., Clement, J., Kornum, N., Bucatariu, C., Magid, J.: Addressing food waste reduction in denmark. Food Policy **49**, 294–301 (2014)

36. Harker, F.R., Maindonald, J.H., Jackson, P.J.: Penetrometer measurement of apple and kiwifruit firmness: operator and instrument differences. Journal of the American Society for Horticultural Science **121**(5), 927–936 (1996)

37. Heap, R., Kierstan, M., Ford, G., Heap, R.D., Ford, G.: Food transportation, 1st edn. Blackie Academic & Professional, London, UK (1998)

38. Heap, R.D.: Design and performance of insulated and refrigerated ISO intermodal containers. International Journal of Refrigeration **12**(3), 137–145 (1989)

39. Heising, J.K., Dekker, M., Bartels, P.V., Van Boekel, M.A.J.S.: Monitoring the quality of perishable foods: opportunities for intelligent packaging. Critical Reviews in Food Science and Nutrition **54**(5), 645–654 (2014)

40. Hertog, M.L.A.T.M.: The impact of biological variation on postharvest population dynamics. Postharvest Biology and Technology **26**(3), 253–263 (2002)

41. Hertog, M.L.A.T.M., Lammertyn, J., Desmet, M., Scheerlinck, N., Nicolaï, B.M.: The impact of biological variation on postharvest behaviour of tomato fruit. Postharvest Biology and Technology **34**(3), 271–284 (2004)

42. Hertog, M.L.A.T.M., Uysal, I., McCarthy, U., Verlinden, B.M., Nicolaï, B.M.: Shelf life modelling for first-expired-first-out warehouse management. Philosophical Transactions of the Royal Society A: Mathematical, Physical and Engineering Sciences **372**, 20130306 (2014)

43. Ioannou, I., Perrot, N., Hossenlopp, J., Mauris, G., Trystram, G.: The fuzzy set theory: a helpful tool for the estimation of sensory properties of crusting sausage appearance by a single expert. Food Quality and Preference **13**(7), 589–595 (2002)

44. Jedermann, R., Lang, W.: Model based estimation of biological heat generation during cold-chain transport and processing. In: Proceedings of 3rd International Institute of Refrigeration International Conference on Sustainability and the Cold Chain, pp. 86–93, London, UK (2014)

45. Jedermann, R., Nicometo, M., Uysal, I., Lang, W.: Reducing food losses by intelligent food logistics. Philosophical Transactions of the Royal Society A: Mathematical, Physical and Engineering Sciences **372**, 20130302 (2014a)

46. Jedermann, R., Praeger, U., Geyer, M., Lang, W.: Remote quality monitoring in the banana chain. Philosophical Transactions of the Royal Society A: Mathematical, Physical and Engineering Sciences **372**, 20130303 (2014b)

47. Jedermann, R., Ruiz-Garcia, L., Lang, W.: Spatial temperature profiling by semi-passive RFID loggers for perishable food transportation. Computers and Electronics in Agriculture **65**(2), 145–154 (2009)

48. Kablan, T., Mathias, K.O., Gilles, D., Robert, W.L., Joseph, A.: Comparative evaluation of the effect of storage temperature fluctuation on modified atmosphere packages of selected fruit and vegetables. Postharvest Biology and Technology **46**(3), 212–221 (2007)

49. Kader, A.A.: Biochemical and physiological basis for effects of controlled and modified atmospheres on fruits and vegetables. Food Technology **40**(5), 99–100 (1986)

50. Kaymak-Ertekin, F., Gedik, A.: Kinetic modelling of quality deterioration in onions during drying and storage. Journal of Food Engineering **68**(4), 443–453 (2005)
51. Kerry, J., Butler, P.: Smart packaging technologies for fast moving consumer goods. Wiley Online Library (2008)
52. Ketzenberg, M., Ferguson, M.E.: Managing slow-moving perishables in the grocery industry. Production and Operations Management **17**(5), 513–521 (2008)
53. Kim, M., Kim, J.: Comparison through a LCA evaluation analysis of food waste disposal options from the perspective of global warming and resource recovery. Science of the Total Environment **408**(19), 3998–4006 (2010)
54. Kummu, M., de Moel, H., Porkka, M., Siebert, S., Varis, O., Ward, P.J.: Lost food, wasted resources: Global food supply chain losses and their impacts on freshwater, cropland, and fertiliser use. Science of the Total Environment **438**, 477–489 (2012)
55. Labuza, T.P.: Application of chemical kinetics to deterioration of foods. Journal of Chemical Education **61**(4), 348 (1984)
56. Lang, W., Jedermann, R., Mrugala, D., Jabbari, A., Krieg-BruIckner, B., Schill, K.: The "Intelligent container" - a cognitive sensor network for transport management. IEEE Sensors Journal **11**(3), 688–698 (2011)
57. Ledauphin, S., Pommeret, D., Qannari, E.M.: A Markovian model to study products shelf-lives. Food Quality and Preference **17**(7), 598–603 (2006)
58. Ledauphin, S., Pommeret, D., Qannari, E.M.: Application of hidden Markov model to products shelf lives. Food Quality and Preference **19**(2), 156–161 (2008)
59. Lelièvre, J., Latche, A., Jones, B., Bouzayen, M., Pech, J.: Ethylene and fruit ripening. Physiologia Plantarum **101**(4), 727–739 (1997)
60. Li, D., Kehoe, D., Drake, P.: Dynamic planning with a wireless product identification technology in food supply chains. The International Journal of Advanced Manufacturing Technology **30**(9–10), 938–944 (2006)
61. Li, J., Song, W., Barth, M.M., Zhuang, H., Zhang, W., Zhang, L., Wang, L., Lu, W., Wang, Z., Han, X., et al.: Effect of modified atmosphere packaging (MAP) on the quality of sea buckthorn berry fruits during postharvest storage. Journal of Food Quality **38**(1), 13–20 (2014a)
62. Li, L., Negenborn, R.R., De Schutter, B.: Receding horizon approach for container flow assignment in intermodal freight transport. Transportation Research Record: Journal of the Transportation Research Board **2410**(1), 132–140 (2014b)
63. Lim, M.K., Bahr, W., Leung, S.C.H.: RFID in the warehouse: A literature analysis (1995–2010) of its applications, benefits, challenges and future trends. International Journal of Production Economics **145**(1), 409–430 (2013)
64. Lin, W., Block, G.S.: Neural network modeling to predict shelf life of greenhouse lettuce. Algorithms **2**(2), 623–637 (2009)
65. López Camelo, A.F., Gómez, P.A.: Comparison of color indexes for tomato ripening. Horticultura Brasileira **22**(3), 534–537 (2004)
66. López-López, A., Beato, V., Sánchez, A., García-García, P., Montaño, A.: Effects of selected amino acids and water-soluble vitamins on acrylamide formation in a ripe olive model system. Journal of Food Engineering **120**, 9–16 (2014)
67. Ludikhuyze, L., Van Loey, A., Indrawati, S.C., Hendrickx, M.: Effects of combined pressure and temperature on enzymes related to quality of fruits and vegetables: from kinetic information to process engineering aspects. Critical Reviews in Food Science and Nutrition **43**(5), 527–586 (2003)
68. Lütjen, M., Dittmer, P., Veigt, M.: Quality driven distribution of intelligent containers in cold chain logistics networks. Production Engineering **7**(2–3), 291–297 (2013)

69. Majidi, H., Minaei, S., Almassi, M., Mostofi, Y.: Tomato quality in controlled atmosphere storage, modified atmosphere packaging and cold storage. Journal of Food Science and Technology 51(9), 2155–2161 (2014)
70. Mendoza, F., Aguilera, J.M.: Application of image analysis for classification of ripening bananas. Journal of Food Science 69(9), E471–E477 (2004)
71. Mishkin, M., Saguy, I., Karel, M.: Dynamic optimization of dehydration processes: Minimizing browning in dehydration of potatoes. Journal of Food Science 48(6), 1617–1621 (1983)
72. Mowat, A., Collins, R.: Consumer behaviour and fruit quality: supply chain management in an emerging industry. Supply Chain Management: An International Journal 5(1), 45–54 (2000)
73. Munton, R., Stott, J.R.: Refrigeration at sea, 2nd edn. Applied Science Publishers, London (1978)
74. Negenborn, R.R., Maestre, J.M.: Distributed model predictive control: an overview and roadmap of future research opportunities. IEEE Control Systems Magazine 34(4), 87–97 (2014)
75. Parfitt, J., Barthel, M., Macnaughton, S.: Food waste within food supply chains: quantification and potential for change to 2050. Philosophical Transactions of the Royal Society B: Biological Sciences 365(1554), 3065–3081 (2010)
76. Port of Rotterdam. Rotterdam, hotspot for cool logistics (2014). http://www.portofrotterdam.com/nl/brochures/rotterdam
77. Ratkowsky, D.A., Olley, J., McMeekin, T.A., Ball, A.: Relationship between temperature and growth rate of bacterial cultures. Journal of Bacteriology 149(1), 1–5 (1982)
78. Ruiz-Garcia, L., Lunadei, L.: The role of RFID in agriculture: applications, limitations and challenges. Computers and Electronics in Agriculture 79(1), 42–50 (2011)
79. Sarac, A., Absi, N., Dauzère-Pérès, S.: A literature review on the impact of rfid technologies on supply chain management. International Journal of Production Economics 128(1), 77–95 (2010)
80. Schotte, S., De Belie, N., De Baerdemaeker, J.: Acoustic impulse-response technique for evaluation and modelling of firmness of tomato fruit. Postharvest Biology and Technology 17(2), 105–115 (1999)
81. Schouten, R.E., Tijskens, L.M.M., van Kooten, O.: Predicting keeping quality of batches of cucumber fruit based on a physiological mechanism. Postharvest Biology and Technology 26(2), 209–220 (2002)
82. Shukla, M., Jharkharia, S.: Agri-fresh produce supply chain management: a state-of-the-art literature review. International Journal of Operations and Production Management 33(2), 114–158 (2013)
83. Song, Y.H., Kim, S.J., Lee, S.K.: Evaluation of ultrasound for prediction of carcass meat yield and meat quality in korean native cattle (hanwoo). Asian Australasian Journal of Animal Sciences 15(4), 591–595 (2002)
84. Taoukis, P.S., Labuza, T.P.: Applicability of time-temperature indicators as shelf life monitors of food products. Journal of Food Science 54(4), 783–788 (1989)
85. Taylor, S., Shewfelt, R.L., Prussia, S.E.: Postharvest handling: a systems approach, 2nd edn. Academic Press, San Diego, U.S (1993)
86. Tijskens, L.M.M., Evelo, R.G.: Modelling colour of tomatoes during postharvest storage. Postharvest Biology and Technology 4(1), 85–98 (1994)
87. Tijskens, L.M.M., Polderdijk, J.J.: A generic model for keeping quality of vegetable produce during storage and distribution. Agricultural Systems 51(4), 431–452 (1996)

88. Tsironi, T., Stamatiou, A., Giannoglou, M., Velliou, E., Taoukis, P.: Predictive modelling and selection of time temperature integrators for monitoring the shelf life of modified atmosphere packed gilthead seabream fillets. LWT-food Science and Technology **44**(4), 1156–1163 (2011)

89. Vallejo-Cordoba, B., Arteaga, G.E., Nakai, S.: Predicting milk shelf-life based on artificial neural networks and headspace gas chromatographic data. Journal of Food Science **60**(5), 885–888 (1995)

90. Van Boekel, M.A.J.S.: Kinetic modeling of food quality: a critical review. Comprehensive Reviews in Food Science and Food Safety **7**(1), 144–158 (2008)

91. Van Zeebroeck, M., Ramon, H., De Baerdemaeker, J., Nicolaï, B.M., Tijskens, E., et al.: Impact damage of apples during transport and handling. Postharvest Biology and Technology **45**(2), 157–167 (2007)

92. Wang, C.: Chilling injury of fruits and vegetables. Food Reviews International **5**(2), 209–236 (1989)

93. Woodward, T.J.: Variation in 'Hayward' kiwifruit quality characteristics. PhD thesis, The University of Waikato, Waikato, New Zealand (2006)

94. Wrzodak, A., Adamicki, F.: Effect of temperature and controlled atmosphere on the storage of fruit from long-life tomatoes. Vegetable Crops Research Bulletin **67**, 177–186 (2007)

95. Xin, J., Negenborn, R.R., Lodewijks, G.: Energy-aware control for automated container terminals using integrated flow shop scheduling and optimal control. Transportation Research Part C: Emerging Technologies **44**, 214–230 (2014)

96. Yam, K.L., Takhistov, P.T., Miltz, J.: Intelligent packaging: concepts and applications. Journal of Food Science **70**(1), R1–R10 (2005)

97. Yan, B., Shi, S., Ye, B., Zhou, X., Shi, P.: Sustainable development of the fresh agricultural products supply chain through the application of RFID technology. Information Technology and Management **16**(1), 67–78 (2014)

98. Zacharewicz, G., Deschamps, J., Francois, J.: Distributed simulation platform to design advanced RFID based freight transportation systems. Computers in Industry **62**(6), 597–612 (2011)

99. Zerbini, P.E., Vanoli, M., Lovati, F., Spinelli, L., Torricelli, A., Rizzolo, A., Lurie, S.: Maturity assessment at harvest and prediction of softening in a late maturing nectarine cultivar after cold storage. Postharvest Biology and Technology **62**(3), 275–281 (2011)

A Rolling Horizon Auction Mechanism and Virtual Pricing of Shipping Capacity for Urban Consolidation Centers

Chen Wang[1]($\boxtimes$), Hoong Chuin Lau[2], and Yun Fong Lim[3]

[1] SAP Innovation Center, Singapore, #14-01, 1 Create Way,
Singapore 138602, Singapore
chen.wang02@sap.com

[2] School of Information Systems, Singapore Management University,
80 Stamford Road, Singapore 178902, Singapore
hclau@smu.edu.sg

[3] Lee Kong Chian School of Business, Singapore Management University,
50 Stamford Road, Singapore 178899, Singapore
yflim@smu.edu.sg

Abstract. A number of cities around the world have adopted urban consolidation centers (UCCs) to address challenges of last-mile deliveries. At the UCC, goods are consolidated based on their destinations prior to their deliveries into city centers. Typically, a UCC owns a fleet of eco-friendly vehicles to carry out such deliveries. Shippers/carriers that make use of the UCC's service hence no longer need to be restricted by time-window and vehicle-type regulations. As a result, they retain the ability to deploy large trucks for the economies of scale from the source to the UCC which is located outside the city center. Furthermore, the resources which would otherwise be spent in the city center can then be utilized for other purposes. With possibly tighter regulation and thinning profit margin in near future, requests for UCC's services will become more and more common, and there is a need for a market mechanism to allocate UCC's resources to provide sustainable services for shippers/carriers in a win-win fashion. An early work of our research team (Handoko et al., 2014) proposed a profit-maximizing auction mechanism for the use of UCC's last-mile delivery service. In this paper, we extend this work with an idea of rolling horizon to give bidders more flexibility in competing for the UCC's resources in advance. In particular, it addresses the needs of many shippers/carriers to be able both plan deliveries weeks ahead and at the same time bid for the UCC's service at the last minute. Under our rolling horizon framework, the capacity of the same truck is up for bid in several successive auctions. To allocate truck capacities among these auctions under future demand uncertainty, we propose a virtual pricing mechanism which makes use of Target-oriented Robust Optimization techniques.

C. Wang—This work was done when the author was a research scientist at Singapore Management University, supported by the A*STAR's Thematic Schematic Research Programme on Collaborative Urban Logistics under grant number 1224200002.

F. Corman et al. (Eds.): ICCL 2015, LNCS 9335, pp. 422–436, 2015.
DOI: 10.1007/978-3-319-24264-4_29

Keywords: Rolling horizon · Virtual pricing · Urban consolidation center

1   Introduction

Last-mile deliveries in urban areas impose serious pressures on environmental, social, and economic well-being of a city. These three aspects are usually referred to as *planet, people*, and *profit* [Quak and Tavasszy, 2011]. On the planet, the impacts are contributed by the use of unsustainable natural resources like the fossil fuel. On the people, the impacts are primarily due to air pollution and noise. On the profit, the impacts include economic losses because of traffic congestion and low utilization of transport vehicles. Addressing these issues, local authorities may introduce time-window or vehicle-type restriction on city delivery operations. The former restriction complicates the scheduling of the last-mile deliveries from the perspective of carriers/shippers, compromising the efficiency of deliveries. The latter, on the other hand, forces carriers/shippers to operate small eco-friendly trucks for deliveries into city centers. These trucks, however, are not efficient for long-distance inter-city transport. Both time-window and the vehicle-type restrictions affect profitability while seeking to address challenges on the planet and people.

Such challenges motivate carriers/shippers to collaborate and consolidate shipments for greater efficiency, which leads to the concept of Urban Consolidation Center (UCC). A UCC is an alliance where orders served by various participating carriers get consolidated. First, the packages are sorted according to their destinations. Then, they are assigned to a sufficient number of vehicles for the actual last-mile deliveries. The cost savings obtained are finally shared among the relevant carriers. As a consequence, higher truck utilization is attained, fewer trucks are required, and lower delivery cost is incurred. This effectively addresses the potential inefficiency due to the time-window restriction.

To-date, there have been a number of UCC establishments with their own transport vehicles that are in compliance with the rules and regulations set by local authorities. These UCCs provide last-mile delivery service at a charge. Occasionally, the UCCs may be governments' initiatives or pilot runs and provide last-mile delivery service free-of-charge. In most cases, carriers/shippers can simply drop their loads off at the UCCs and pay the UCCs accordingly to get the loads delivered into the city center. Examples of these UCCs are La Petite Reine in Paris, France, Westfield Consolidation Center in London, and Binnenstadservice.nl in Nijmegen, the Netherlands. This addresses not only the time-window but also the vehicle-type restrictions. By using a UCC's services, carriers/shippers no longer need to enter city centers. Retaining the use of large trucks for the economies of scale outside city centers thus becomes possible. With these incentives, requests for using a UCC's services would become more common. A UCC could soon receive more demands than what it can serve.

To our knowledge, most—if not all—UCCs operate on some fixed-rate mechanisms and first-come-first-serve basis. We found little literature discussing automated matching of orders to the available fleets of UCCs' transport vehicles for efficient last-mile deliveries. Handoko et al. [2014] recently proposed an auction mechanism for the last-mile delivery via a UCC. Compared to fixed-rate mechanisms, the proposed auction mechanism is distinctively aimed at achieving both operational efficiency and economic viability—both of which are important for the sustainability of the UCC.

The basic auction mechanism proposed by Handoko et al. [2014] is however quite restrictive in the sense that bidders are only allowed to compete for a UCC's resources in a immediate near time period, usually one week. This is somewhat unrealistic as many shippers/carriers plan for their deliveries far in advance. To address this issue, not only the period needs to be lengthened, the auction also needs to be conducted frequently, which leads to a rolling planning horizon. For example, consider a planning horizon of 4 weeks and the UCC starts Auction 1 at the beginning of Week 0 and accept bids for deliveries in Week 1 to Week 4. Prior to the start of Week 1, the UCC selects the winning bids for Auction 1. The UCC then starts Auction 2 at the beginning of Week 1 and accept bids for deliveries in Week 2 to Week 5, and so on. This gives more options for the bidders so that they can choose to bid in advance (four weeks before delivery) or at the very last minute (one week before delivery). Different from the basic auction model, there is an overlap in the planning horizons of two successive auctions. Intuitively, there may be only a few bids for deliveries in Week 4 in Auction 1. Profitable consolidation may thus be impossible when Auction 1 is closed. However, there should be more upcoming bids for deliveries in Week 4 in Auction 2 to Auction 4. Hence, profitable consolidation may in fact be possible. This suggests that the UCC needs to be able to anticipate the potential revenue due to future bids in the upcoming auctions. For deliveries in Week 3 or Auction 1, there may be enough bids to consolidate but some of the bids have low bid prices. Rather than accepting bids with low value to make profitable consolidation, it could be better for the UCC to accept only highly profitable bids in the current auction and reserve some capacity for highly profitable bids in the upcoming auctions. The above observations motivate a virtual pricing approach in this work.

Our contribution in this paper is an auction mechanism that helps to both generate more revenue, as well as provide greater flexibility to bidders. This is achieved by considering a rolling planning horizon in auctions and introducing a virtual pricing approach for capacity reservation. To our knowledge, this is the first auction with rolling horizon in the context of last-mile deliveries via a UCC. Additionally, the proposed pricing approach makes use of Target-oriented Robust Optimization techniques, and can determine a solution that is robust again demand uncertainties. Note that this is not a trivial problem, since the price should not be too conservative nor too optimistic to maximize the profit of a UCC. The value of the proposed mechanism is also verified by computational experiments.

The rest of this paper is then organized as follows. Section 2 briefly reviews some related works on auction in the logistics and transportation. Section 3 elaborates the basic auction mechanism presented in [Handoko et al., 2014] and forms the basis of our extension described in this paper. Section 4 describes the auction mechanism with a rolling horizon and virtual pricing in details. Mathematical formulation of the winner determination problem is also presented therein. Section 5 demonstrates the advantages of the proposed mechanism by numerical experiments. Section 6 describes how the virtual prices can be determined based on the available information. Finally, Section 7 concludes the paper and gives suggestions about future researches.

2 Related Works

Auction has been commonly used in logistics and transportation, for example in the area of collaborative transportation [Agarwal and Ergun, 2010; Özener and Ergun, 2008]. The problem considered in this paper is similar to the one in transportation procurement [Caplice and Sheffi, 2006; Ledyard et al., 2002; Lee et al., 2007; Song and Regan, 2003] in the sense that both allocate delivery jobs to available shipping resources using auction as a selecting tool. But the problems under consideration are also different in several aspects. Transportation procurement select carriers for shippers for large scale (inter-city or state) transportation in a relative long period (one year or two), and therefore what is out for bid are shippers' delivery lanes (or routes). In the context of urban freight, a bipartite bidding scheme involving both carriers and suppliers was proposed in [Duin et al., 2007] where the suppliers get to select the bids submitted by the carriers. The last-mile delivery problem considered in this paper plan the shipping resource allocation for a immediate near future, and what is out for bid is truck capacities. Additionally, last-mile delivery problem deal with package-level jobs while transportation procurement problem considers total volume being shipped in a lane which is usually at truckload or larger levels.

Winner determination problem in logistics auctions can be typically formulated as a Mixed Integer Programming (MIP) problem with an objective of minimizing the cost subject to constraints on delivery time, capacity and other factors. Such an MIP, when optimally solved, guarantees a least-cost solution. However, it is usually computationally expensive even for medium-sized problems. A linear relaxation may be used to come up with a feasible solution in polynomial time [Özener and Ergun, 2008]. Note that despite the numerous literature on logistics auction, we found none pertaining to the use of a UCC. Furthermore, the concept of rolling horizon has been extensively used for decision making[Chand et al., 2002; Mula et al., 2006; Ouelhadj and Petrovic, 2009; Sethi and Sorger, 1991]. However as long as a UCC is concerned, we believe no work has been done regarding an auction of shipping capacities with a rolling planning horizon.

In contrast to traditional auctions where each item for sale is typically one entity and all belongs to one winner once sold, the auction for truck capacities of UCC differs in some ways. First, the capacity of one truck load may be shared by several winning bidders. Second in the case of auction with a rolling planning horizon, bidders in different auctions may compete for the same truck capacity and the truck capacity is gradually assigned in several auctions. Such features make it necessary to develop a method for reserving truck capacity. In this paper, we consider a dynamic virtual pricing approach for this purpose. The literature of dynamic pricing is rich and expanding fast, especially in the area of logistics and inventory control [Bitran and Caldentey, 2003; Elmaghraby and Keskinocak, 2003]. In the context of UCC, the pricing of truck capacity is primarily for the reservation of truck capacity and the "price" is never release to bidders. Therefore, this problem is different from most of the problems considered in the literature and that is why we call it virtual pricing. In this work, we determine the optimal price using robust optimization techniques. Adida and Perakis [2007] proposed a dynamic pricing approach using robust optimization techniques, but it is for a nonlinear continuous time inventory control problem. Our approach is also different in the sense that we propose a target value for the profit of UCC and maximize the uncertainty set that can be accommodated.

3   Problem Description and Auction Mechanism for UCC

An earlier work by Handoko et al. [2014] considered a UCC that operates its own storage resources and delivery trucks. In the value chain of such a UCC, the packages originate from a shipper (for example, a manufacturer). They are transported to the UCC by the shipper or by a carrier (for example, a logistics service provider). The UCC then consolidates them with other packages and then delivers them to a receiver (for example, a retailer, a restaurant, or a hotel in the city center). Since the UCC is not obliged to deliver the packages for all the shippers and carriers, Handoko et al. [2014] proposed an auction mechanism for the UCC to select the packages to deliver. The auction mechanism and the associated winner determination problem will be reviewed in the rest of this section.

It is assumed that there are Z zones in the city center indexed by j. The UCC operates K trucks indexed by k to deliver packages to these zones. Assume there are T periods (for example, each period represents a day) in the planning horizon. Truck k has volume capacity V_k^t in period t. To plan for the last-mile deliveries in its nearest upcoming planning horizon, each shipper or carrier is invited to submit bids for his packages (or bundles of packages) to be delivered to the city center. Each bid i specifies the following information in a tuple: $[v_i, d_i, a_i, \ell_i, p_i]$, where v_i is the volume of the package, $d_i \in [1, Z]$ is the destination of the package, $a_i \in [1, T]$ is the period when the package arrives at the UCC, $l_i \in [1, T]$ is the delivery deadline, and p_i is the bidding price. Let B denote the total number of bids when the auction is closed (after that no more bids are accepted). Based on this information, the UCC selects the packages to serve, and then notifies the bidders about the result arranges the deliveries accordingly.

To determine which bids are to be served such that the profit of the UCC over its planning horizon is maximized, a winner determination problem is to be solved. To model this problem and determine the winning bids, define binary decision variables x_{ik}^t which equals 1 if bid i is delivered by truck k in period t and 0 otherwise. Also define binary decision variables y_{jk}^t which equals 1 if truck k delivers to zone j in period t and 0 otherwise. For notational convenience, define index sets $\mathcal{B} := \{1, 2, \ldots, B\}$, $\mathcal{Z} := \{1, 2, \ldots, Z\}$, $\mathcal{K} := \{1, 2, \ldots, K\}$, and $\mathcal{T} := \{1, 2, \ldots, T\}$. The following constraints are considered in the winner determination problem.

Constraint (i): Each bid is served at most once,

$$\sum_{k \in \mathcal{K}, t \in \mathcal{T}} x_{ik}^t \leq 1, \qquad \forall i \in \mathcal{B}. \tag{1}$$

Constraint (ii): Each truck serves no more than one zone in one period,

$$\sum_{j \in \mathcal{Z}} y_{jk}^t \leq 1, \qquad \forall t \in \mathcal{T}, \forall k \in \mathcal{K}. \tag{2}$$

Constraint (iii): Truck capacity constraint can be expressed as

$$\sum_{i \in \mathcal{B}} v_i x_{ik}^t \leq V_k^t, \qquad \forall t \in \mathcal{T}, \forall k \in \mathcal{K}. \tag{3}$$

Constraint (iv): A truck will visit zone d_i in period t if bid i is served by the truck in period t,

$$x_{ik}^t \leq y_{jk}^t, \qquad \text{for } j = d_i, \forall t \in \mathcal{T}, \forall i \in \mathcal{B}, \forall k \in \mathcal{K}. \tag{4}$$

Constraint (v): Each bid must be served within its delivery time window,

$$x_{ik}^t = 0, \qquad \forall t \notin [a_i, l_i], \forall i \in \mathcal{B}, \forall k \in \mathcal{K}. \tag{5}$$

Constraint (vi): Binary decision variables constraint,

$$x_{ik}^t, y_{jk}^t \in \{0, 1\}, \qquad \forall i \in \mathcal{B}, \forall j \in \mathcal{Z}, \forall k \in \mathcal{K}, \forall t \in \mathcal{T}. \tag{6}$$

Define the following sets of decision variables

$$\mathbf{X} := \left\{ x_{ik}^t, i \in \mathcal{B}, k \in \mathcal{K}, t \in \mathcal{T} \right\}, \tag{7a}$$

$$\mathbf{Y} := \left\{ y_{jk}^t, j \in \mathcal{Z}, k \in \mathcal{K}, t \in \mathcal{T} \right\}. \tag{7b}$$

The set of feasible solutions can be expressed as

$$\mathbb{F} := \left\{ (\mathbf{X}, \mathbf{Y}) | \mathbf{X}, \mathbf{Y} \text{ satisfy (1)-(6)} \right\}. \tag{8}$$

The cost of the UCC consists of two major components: warehousing cost and delivery cost. If a package is stored in the UCC before delivery, it incurs a holding cost, denoted by h per volume per period. For truck k to deliver to zone

j in period t, a delivery cost c_{jk}^t is incurred. Given a solution $(\mathbf{X}, \mathbf{Y})$ and the delivery costs c_{jk}^t, the profit of UCC can be expressed as

$$r(\mathbf{X}, \mathbf{Y}) := \sum_{i \in \mathcal{B}, k \in \mathcal{K}, t \in \mathcal{T}} [p_i - hv_i(t - a_i)] x_{ik}^t - \sum_{j \in \mathcal{Z}, k \in \mathcal{K}, t \in \mathcal{T}} c_{jk}^t y_{jk}^t. \quad (9)$$

The basic Winner Determination Problem (WDP) is to

$$\max r(\mathbf{X}, \mathbf{Y}) \quad (10a)$$
$$s.t. \ (\mathbf{X}, \mathbf{Y}) \in \mathbb{F}. \quad (10b)$$

In the next section, we propose an auction mechanism with a rolling planning horizon based on the above formulation.

4   Proposed UCC Auction with Rolling Horizon

The winner determination problem for the basic UCC auction elaborated in Section 3 assumes that the planning horizons of two consecutive UCC auctions never overlap one another. As mentioned in Section 1, this restricts shippers/carriers as bidders can compete only for the UCC's delivery resources in an immediate near.

In practice, a long planning horizon is often desirable to allow shippers/carriers flexibility to bid for delivery resources not only in the immediate near period but also in the subsequent few periods following the winner determination. Announcement of the results of each auction should remain as frequent so that the losing bidders could have a chance to arrange for some other means of delivery or to alter their bid prices and resubmit their bids in subsequent auctions. The requirement of a long planning horizon and high-frequency updates makes rolling horizon an interesting and significant topic in auction mechanism.

One fact in a UCC's rolling horizon auction mechanism is that the shipping resource in one period is out for bid in a number of successive auctions. For instance if we have a four weeks' planning horizon, the shipping resource in Week 3 is for bid in 3 consecutive auctions. When determining the winners of Auction 1, the auctioneer may intuitively wish to reserve shipping resource for profitable bids yet to come in Auctions 2 and 3. On the other hand when determining the winners of Auction 3, it is intuitive to use as much remaining capacity as possible since capacity left unused will no longer have any potential value.

Motivated by the above observation, we propose a virtual pricing approach for resource reservation. This approach aims to price the unused shipping capacity that still has potential value in upcoming auctions. This is equivalent to introducing virtual bids to the current auction, which could potentially be replaced by real bids of equal or higher values in future auctions. Other than reserving capacity for future auctions, the pricing approach additionally allows selection of highly profitable bids as winners in the current auction although there may not be enough bids to realize profitable consolidation at the current moment.

Precisely, we adjust the profit function as follows. Let q_{jk}^t denote the potential value of one unit of unused truck capacity if truck k delivers to zone z in period t and hereafter we refer to it as *virtual price*. Also Let V_k^t denote the remaining capacity of truck k at day t. If $y_{jk}^t = 1$, the potential value for the remaining capacity of the truck after the auction is $q_{jk}^t(V_k^t - \sum_{i \in \mathcal{B}} v_i x_{ik}^t)$, and 0 otherwise. Additionally if truck k does not deliver to any zone in period t, we assume the potential value is the average potential value of the full truckload $(\sum_{j \in \mathcal{Z}} q_{jk}^t/Z)V_k^t$. Hence, the profit after adjustment can be expressed as

$$\hat{r}(\mathbf{X}, \mathbf{Y}) := r(\mathbf{X}, \mathbf{Y}) + \sum_{j \in \mathcal{Z}, k \in \mathcal{K}, t \in \mathcal{T}} q_{jk}^t \min\{M \cdot y_{jk}^t, \ V_k^t - \sum_i v_i x_{ik}^t\}$$

$$+ \sum_{k \in \mathcal{K}, t \in \mathcal{T}} \left(\left(\sum_{j \in \mathcal{Z}} q_{jk}^t/Z \right) V_k^t \left(1 - \sum_{j \in \mathcal{Z}} y_{jk}^t \right) \right), \quad (11)$$

where M in (11) is a large constant. In the WDP of each auction, we update the value of V_k^t in Constraint (3) and solve the following optimization problem,

$$\max \ \hat{r}(\mathbf{X}, \mathbf{Y}) \tag{12a}$$

$$s.t. \ (\mathbf{X}, \mathbf{Y}) \in \mathbb{F}. \tag{12b}$$

to determine the winning bids. Note that the feasible set $\mathbb{F}$ in Constraint (12b) changes from time to time as the remaining truck capacity changes.

5   Numerical Experiments of the Proposed Mechanism

In this section, we design numerical experiments to, 1) highlight the advantages of an auction with rolling horizon over a single period auction, 2) demonstrate the importance of a proper choice of the virtual price q_{jk}^t.

To make the results clear and easily understandable, we consider a problem with one zone and one truck with capacity 10. The planning horizon is 10 weekdays (2 weeks) and the auction is hold every week. The delivery cost is deterministic and equals 10. For each auction, a total of 30 bids are random generated, and 15 of them bid for the UCC's delivery resources on the first week of the planning horizon and another 15 for resources on the second week. The price-to-volume ratio of the bids is uniformly distributed between 0 and 3.

Rolling Horizon v.s. Single Period. First we compare the auction mechanism with rolling planning horizon with the single period auction mechanism. In a single period auction, the planning horizon is just one week which is the time interval between two successive auctions. We simulate the whole 10 weeks of auctions for 50 times, and compare the average revenues generated by both auction mechanisms. For the auction with rolling planning horizon, we set $q_{11}^t = 0$ for each $t = 1, 2, ..., 5$ and $q_{11}^t = 1$ for each $t = 6, 7, ..., 10$. Our simulation result shows that the average revenue under single period auction is 560, while the average revenue under auction mechanism with a rolling planning horizon

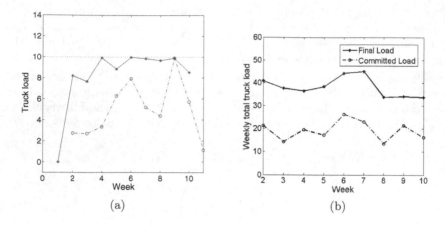

Fig. 1. (a) Truck load of Friday. (b) Weekly total truck load.

is 718 which is a 28.2% improvement. This suggests that the rolling horizon mechanism has the potential to yield more revenue.

Efficacy of an Auction with Rolling Horizon. The auction mechanism with rolling horizon manages to generate more revenue by reserving the truck capacity for more profitable bids. To see this, we first analyze the composition of final truck load. The truck load on Fridays from Week 2 to Week 10 are shown in Figure 1(a). The result of Week 1 is not shown since it is only involved in one auction and no truck load is committed before that auction. In Figure 1(a), the dash-dot line show the truck load committed one week before the delivery date and the solid line show the final truck load. It can be observed that in most of the days, the final truck load contains a portion that is committed one week before the delivery date. For truck load on Monday, Tuesday, Wednesday and Thursday we can also observe the similar pattern, which also lead to a weekly (from Monday to Friday) total truck load as shown in Figure 1(b). From Figure 1(b), we can observe that about half of the weekly truck load are committed one week before and this is shown specifically by the dash line in Figure 2. It can be seen that around 50% of the total load is committed one week before. In Figure 2, the solid line shows the percentage of the total profit that is due to this portion of the final truck load. In most of the ten weeks, the solid line is above the dash line, which means this portion of truck load has a larger value of profit-to-volume ration than the rest part of the truck load. This suggests that by pricing the unused capacity properly (i.e. setting q_{jk}^t appropriately) the winning bids chosen one week before are more profitable.

Effects of Varying Pricing Mechanisms. To further show the importance of the potential value rate, we let q_{11}^t where $t = 6, 7, ..., 10$ change from 0 to 3.4 while keeping $q_{11}^t = 0$ for each $t = 1, 2, ..., 5$ to see how the total revenue (profit) changes with the pricing of the unused capacity. Since the delivery cost remains the same for all cases, we just compare revenue contributed by different types

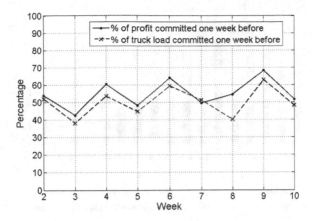

Fig. 2. Percentage of profit and truck load committed in advance (i.e. one week ahead of the actual delivery week).

of bids. The result is shown in Figure 3 where the darker bars at the bottom shows the revenue contributed by the winning bids to be delivered on the second week of the planning horizon and the lighter bars on the top corresponds to the revenue due to the winning bids to be delivered on the first week of the planning horizon. Note that when $q_{11}^t = 0$ for all t, the winning bids are selected exactly according to Problem (10) without any pricing of unused truck capacity, which is the winner determination problem proposed by Handoko et al. [2014]. As q_{11}^t, $t = 6, 7, ..., 10$ increase, the revenue contributed by the winners of the second week's delivery resource first increases and then decreases. The total revenue follows the same trend. Figure 3 also verifies the idea of choosing value of q_{jk}^t described in Section 4. As the expected total volume of the 15 bids is 22.88, the value of q_{jk}^t should be $3 * 10/22.88 = 1.31$ in the ideal case. But due to non-splittable bid volumes and the small number of bids, the best value of q_{jk}^t in the experiment appears around 1 which is smaller than 1.31.

In Figure 3 when $q > 3$, all the shipping capacity is reserved for the very last auction before the delivery date as no bids have the price-to-volume ratio larger than 3. Therefore, there is no winning bids for deliveries on the second week of the planning horizon, and it is equivalent to run a single period auction with one week planning horizon every week without any rolling planning horizon. It can be observed that the auctions with rolling horizon always generates a hight revenue than the single period auctions, which again demonstrates the superiority of a rolling planning horizon.

6   Virtual Price Determination Approaches

Suggested by the last experiment in Section 5, the virtual price q_{jk}^t is a critical parameter in rolling horizon auction mechanism and it has great impact on the

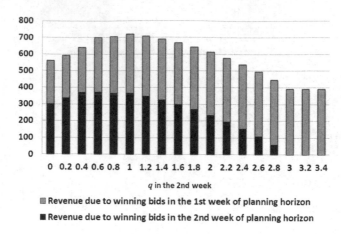

Fig. 3. Revenue v.s. value of q_{11}^t for all $t = 6, 7, ..., 10$.

performance. In this section, we introduce two approaches for the determination of its value, one for the case of known distribution of price-to-volume ratio of all bids and the other one for the case without knowledge of such a distribution.

6.1 The Case with Known Distribution of Price-to-Volume Ratio

For the ideal case, the value of q_{jk}^t can be roughly determined in the way described below. Assume the volume of each bid is relatively small compared with a truck load so that almost all the highly profitable bids can be consolidated in a truck load. We also assume the volume and price of each bid are independent and the distribution of price-to-volume ratio of all bids, denoted by p/v, is available or can be precisely determined from using historical data. Let $F(\cdot)$ denote the cumulative distribution function of the ratio p/v. Then we want to fill the remaining total truck capacity, denoted by V_k, with the bids of the highest price-to-volume ratio. If the total volume of the oncoming bids is V, then the best value of q is $F^{-1}(1 - V_k/V)$. This value is for the optimistic case where all bids of high price-to-volume ratio can be consolidated into the remaining truck load. However, this is almost not possible in reality due to non-splittable volume of a bid and limited number of bids. Therefore, the optimal value of q is usually smaller than $F^{-1}(1 - V_k/V)$ in practice. This is already observed in the results of numerical example in Section 5. In the next section, we will discuss another scenario where the distribution of p/v is unknown and the total volume is also uncertain.

6.2 Pricing Using Robust Optimization

This section consider a scenario that is more realistic. Let n denote the index of future auctions and s_j^n denote the total volume that is to be allocated for zone

j in the future n^{th} auction. Also for a clear presentation, we assume the trucks are homogeneous and q_{jk}^t remains the same for all $k \in \mathcal{K}$. We let q_j^n denote the value of q_{jk}^t that is set for the next N auctions and Z zones. Then typically, s_j^n is a decreasing function of q_j^n in general and may also be subject to uncertainties. In this paper, we assume s_j^n, as a function of q_j^n, takes the following form,

$$s_j^n(q_j^n, \delta_j^n) = (a_j^n - b_j^n q_j^n)(1 + \delta_j^n) \tag{13}$$

where a_j^n and b_j^n are known parameters, δ_j^n is an uncertain factor around 0 and in the range $[\underline{\delta}_j^n, \bar{\delta}_j^n]$. Since q_j^n is the virtual price of remaining capacity, an lower bound of the revenue coming from the winning bids to Zone j in Auction n is

$$\Upsilon(q_j^n, \delta_j^n) := s_j^n q_j^n = q_j^n(a_j^n - b_j^n q_j^n)(1 + \delta_j^n). \tag{14}$$

It has been pointed out [Chen and Sim, 2009] that the primary target of decision makers is to meet certain pre-specified target on profit instead of simply maximizing the profit. This motives us to propose a Target-oriented Robust Optimization (TRO) approach to determine the value of q_j^n. Let V_n denote the total remaining capacity of UCC's truck fleet before auction n and let τ denote the total revenue that is expected from the future N auctions. We aim to determine the vale of q_j^n so that the revenue target is met for an uncertainty set that is as large as possible, so the optimization problem takes the following form.

$$\max_{0 \leq \gamma \leq 1} \gamma \tag{15a}$$

$$s.t. \sum_{j \in \mathcal{Z}} s_j^n(q_j^n, \delta_j^n) \leq V_n, \qquad \forall \delta_j^n \in \left[\gamma \underline{\delta}_j^n, \gamma \bar{\delta}_j^n\right], \ \forall n \in \mathcal{N}; \tag{15b}$$

$$\sum_{n \in \mathcal{N}} \sum_{j \in \mathcal{Z}} \Upsilon(q_j^n, \delta_j^n) \geq \tau, \qquad \forall \delta_j^n \in \left[\gamma \underline{\delta}_j^n, \gamma \bar{\delta}_j^n\right]. \tag{15c}$$

The solution of Problem (15) can be obtained by performing a binary search over γ and solving the following problem a few times.

$$r^*(\gamma) := \max \sum_{t \in \mathcal{N}} \sum_{j \in \mathcal{Z}} q_j^n(a_j^n - b_j^n q_j^n)(1 + \gamma \underline{\delta}_j^n) \tag{16a}$$

$$s.t. \sum_{j \in \mathcal{Z}} (a_j^n - b_j^n q_j^n)(1 + \gamma \bar{\delta}_j^n) \leq V_n, \qquad \forall t \in \mathcal{N}. \tag{16b}$$

6.3   A Numerical Example of Virtual Pricing Using TRO

In this section, we demonstrate the pricing approach proposed in Section 6.2 using an example. The UCC considered in this section is the same as the one in Section 5 with one truck, one zone and a planning horizon of 10 days. We assume the mean of the daily total bid volume increases evenly from 10 on Monday to 30 on Friday, and remains the same for every week. The actual daily total volume is uniformly distributed within $\pm 10\%$ around its mean value. The distribution

Table 1. Parameters in pricing problem

	Monday	Tuesday	Wednesday	Thursday	Friday
a	50	75	100	125	150
b	10	15	20	25	30
$\bar{\delta}$	10%	10%	10%	10%	10%
$\underline{\delta}$	-10%	-10%	-10%	-10%	-10%

of the ratio p/v is the same for all bids, and is uniformly distributed between 3 and 5. Therefore for a pricing problem with a planning horizon of 2 weeks, the parameters is summarized in Table 1.

When we generate detailed bid information, we draw the total daily volume first, and then determine the number of bids so that the average bid volume is 0.5.

Table 2. Optimal virtual prices for weekdays

	Monday	Tuesday	Wednesday	Thursday	Friday
optimal q	4.05	4.37	4.53	4.62	4.68

Virtual Pricing Using Robust Optimization. We choose $\tau = 200$ for Problem (15) which is about 60% of the theoretical maximum mean of revenue in two weeks' time. With this target and the parameters in Table 1, a binary search method determines an optimal $\gamma^* = 0.53$ and Figure 4(a) shows the trajectories of the upper bound and lower bound of γ in the binary search.

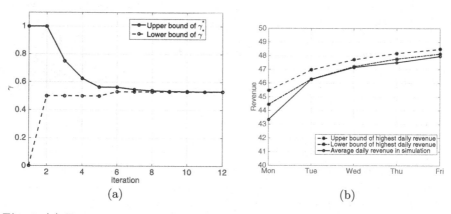

(a)   (b)

Fig. 4. (a) Trajectories of upper and lower bounds of γ in binary search. (b) Average daily revenue of each weekday.

The resultant optimal virtual prices for one unit of shipping capacity on weekdays are given in Table 2.

Daily Revenue. We also conduct simulation to run the UCC for 10 weeks, and therefore 10 auctions are conducted. Assuming that each truck load captures the highest profitable portion of the total bid volume, we can calculate the upper and lower bounds of the theoretically highest revenue of each weekday, and they are shown in Figure 4(b), together with the average revenue of each weekday over the 10 weeks in our simulation. It can be observed that the average daily revenue in our simulation is actually very close to its theoretically highest value. This validate the value of our virtual pricing approach.

7 Conclusion

In this paper, we have presented an auction mechanism for the consolidation of last-mile deliveries into the city centers via a UCC. The proposed mechanism extends existing literature by introducing a rolling planning horizon and a virtual pricing approach. This is essentially equivalent to introducing some virtual bids to the current auction, which may potentially be replaced by the real bids in the upcoming auctions. Simulation results suggest that by setting the virtual price appropriately, more revenue can be made out of the auctions for UCC.

For the determination of an appropriate virtual price, we also proposed approaches for two different scenarios. One is for the ideal case where the distribution of price-to-volume ratio of upcoming bids and the total bid volume are known. In this case, the optimal virtual price can be determined by making use of the distribution function. The other pricing approach is for a more realistic scenario where the distribution of price-to-volume ratio and the total volume are unknown and subject to uncertainties. For this case, we proposed an approach which use Target-oriented Robust Optimization to determine virtual prices that makes the resultant revenue robust against uncertain factors. The validity of the pricing approach is verified by numerical experiments.

The idea of rolling horizon auctions lead to many opportunities for future research. An important one is to construct a heuristics that can determine a good approximation of the solution of winner determination problem. For large problem instances, it is computationally challenging to solve the winner determination problem explicitly. A heuristics that can imitate the pricing mechanism while selecting the winning bids would make the proposed approach application to a large scope of real-life problems. Another future research work is to make the approach more realistic by relaxing some assumptions and/or considering more types of constraints. For example, in the future model we can allow cross-zone delivery, and let the bidder to specify blacklist of bidders that he does not want his packages to be bundle with. A historical data driven pricing mechanism is also of great interest.

References

Adida, E., Perakis, G.: A nonlinear continuous time optimal control model of dynamic pricing and inventory control with no backorders. Naval Research Logistics **54**(7), 767–795 (2007)

Agarwal, R., Ergun, Ö.: Network design and allocation mechanisms for carrier alliances in liner shipping. Operations Research **58**(6), 1726–1742 (2010)

Bitran, G., Caldentey, R.: An overview of pricing models for revenue management. Manufacturing & Service Operations Management **5**(3), 203–229 (2003)

Caplice, C., Sheffi, Y.: Combinatorial auctions for truckload transportation. In: Cramton, P., Shoham, Y., Steinberg, R. (eds.) Combinatorial Auctions, chapter 21, pp. 539–571. MIT Press (2006)

Chand, S., Hsu, V.N., Sethi, S.: Forecast, solution, and rolling horizons in operations management problems: A classified bibliography. Manufacturing & Service Operations Management **4**(1), 25–43 (2002)

Chen, W., Sim, M.: Goad-driven optimization. Operation Research **57**(2), 342–357 (2009)

Elmaghraby, W., Keskinocak, P.: Dynamic pricing in the presence of inventory considerations: Research overview, current practices, and future directions. Management Science **49**(10), 1287–1309 (2003)

Handoko, D., Nguyen, D.T., Lau, H.C.: An auction mechanism for the last-mile deliveries via urban consolidation centre. In: Proceedings of 2014 IEEE International Conference on Automation Science and Engineering, Taipei, Taiwan, pp. 607–612 (2014)

Ledyard, J.O., Olson, M., Porter, D., Swanson, J.A., Torma, D.P.: The first use of a combined-value auction for transportation services. Interfaces **32**(5), 4–12 (2002)

Lee, C.-G., Kwon, R.H., Ma, Z.: A carriers optimal bid generation problem in combinatorial auctions for transportation procurement. Transportation Research Part E: Logistics and Transportation Review **43**(2), 173–191 (2007)

Mula, J., Poler, R., García-Sabater, J.P., Lario, F.C.: Models for production planning under uncertainty: A review. International Journal of Production Economics **103**(1), 271–285 (2006)

Ouelhadj, D., Petrovic, S.: A survey of dynamic scheduling in manufacturing systems. Journal of Scheduling **12**(4), 417–431 (2009)

Özener, O.Ö., Ergun, Ö.: Allocating costs in a collaborative transportation procurement network. Transportation Science **42**(2), 146–165 (2008)

Quak, H., Tavasszy, L.: Customized solutions for sustainable city logistics: the viability of urban freight consolidation centres. In: van Nunen, J.A.E.E., Huijbregts, P., Rietveld, P. (eds.) Transitions Towards Sustainable Mobility, chapter 12, pp. 213–233. Springer, Heidelberg (2011)

Sethi, S., Sorger, G.: A theory of rolling horizon decision making. Annals of Operations Research **29**(1), 387–415 (1991)

Song, J., Regan, A.: Combinatorial auctions for transportation service procurement: The carrier perspective, Technical report, University of California Transportation Center (2003)

van Duin, J.H.R., Tavasszy, L.A., Taniguchi, E.: Real time simulation of auctioning and re-scheduling processes in hybrid freight markets. Transportation Research Part B: Methodological **41**(9), 1050–1066 (2007)

Consolidation of Residual Volumes in a Parcel Service Provider's Long-Haul Transportation Network

Martin N. Baumung[✉] and Halil I. Gündüz

Deutsche Post Chair of Optimization of Distribution Networks,
RWTH Aachen University, 52072 Aachen, Germany
{baumung,guenduez}@dpor.rwth-aachen.de
http://www.dpor.rwth-aachen.de

Abstract. We consider the direct long-haul transportation network of a parcel service provider where transports are carried out using swap bodies. Our focus is on residual volumes, which are not enough to fill a swap body, and investigate how consolidation using hubs can lead to cost reduction through better capacity utilization. We developed a corresponding model minimizing total costs consisting of transportation costs for the swap bodies and costs for the additional sorting required in the hubs.

Keywords: Postal logistics · Parcel industry · Consolidation · Hub location · Long-haul transports · Transportation network

1 Introduction

The courier-express-parcel (CEP) market has been growing consistently in Europe over the last years. According to ATKearney's analysis (see [24]) revenues grew 4 percent per year and volumes rose 6 percent per year from 2009 to 2011 while the overall revenue per shipment declined. Revenues in 2011 were about € 47.2 billion and the volumes were about 5.6 billion shipments. Growth impulses mainly came from lower-margin segments such as business to customer (B2C), e-commerce business, and standard products. Especially in Germany, the standard parcel segment constitutes the largest part of the revenue in 2012 (45%, € 8.17 billion, see [19]), while the express and courier segment represent 34% (€ 6.23 billion) and 21% (€ 3.83 billion), respectively. Standard products that offer broader transit times at less expensive rates have become of major interest for companies trying to optimize their supply chains. CEP companies in many markets responded to this demand with improved service levels for standard products and therefore most domestic and international markets have stronger growth rates in standard products than in express products. Further, the differences in services and transit times blur between express and standard parcel mail delivery in the domestic segment. The increasing market competition,

© Springer International Publishing Switzerland 2015
F. Corman et al. (Eds.): ICCL 2015, LNCS 9335, pp. 437–450, 2015.
DOI: 10.1007/978-3-319-24264-4_30

the service focus of customers and the small margin revenue force CEP logistics service providers to re-evaluate and to continuously improve their networks.

In this work we investigate the domestic standard parcel mail distribution in Germany. A typical structure of a distribution network for standard parcel mail can be described briefly by the following subnetworks (see [25], Fig. 1):

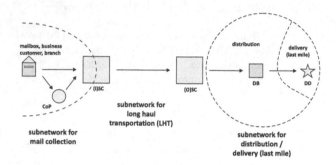

Fig. 1. Subnetworks of a typical distribution network for standard parcel mail.

Mail collection subnetwork: In this network, parcel mail is collected from different mail sources (e.g. mailboxes, business customers, and branches) and transported to sorting centers. Consolidation points (CoP) are used to switch from small vehicles to bigger vehicles, which then transport the mail to the sorting centers.

Long-haul transportation subnetwork (LHT): The subnetwork takes care of the mail exchange between the sorting centers (overnight). A sorting center (SC) is a big automated sorting facility for parcels, which works in two different modes during different time intervals. The input sorting center (ISC) performs sorting with respect to the destination sorting center (SC), while the output sorting center (OSC) performs sorting processes for the distribution and delivery to the final destination. The main idea is to use bigger vehicles for long distances. In Europe the domestic long-haul transportation subnetwork for parcel mail is mostly realized on road transportation mode.

Distribution subnetwork: In this subnetwork, the parcel mail is distributed by transportation from the sorting centers to mini-hubs (called: delivery base (DB)) using vehicle routes. At the mini-hubs a final sorting and the loading of each vehicle in route sequence takes place.

Delivery (last mile) subnetwork: Each driver has an unique allocated delivery district (DD). The driver starts the delivery route at the DB, moves to the DD and visits the households in a predefined sequence and finally returns to the DB.

This brief description of the complex subnetworks in parcel logistics suggests that the problem of optimizing such a network may become complicated.

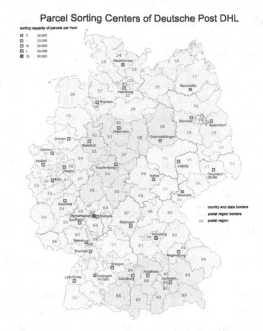

Fig. 2. Parcel sorting center distribution of DPDHL (Source: NordNordWest☺➊◎).

Of course the instances of such networks in different countries differ significantly. For example, the parcel distribution network of Deutsche Post DHL (DPDHL) in Germany in 2011 is characterized by 33 sorting centers (see Fig. 2), 203 delivery bases, 790 million parcels per year, 7,600 vehicles for the parcel mail delivery, and 7,500 delivery districts. All collecting, sorting, long-haul transportation, and delivery processes are important and challenging components of DPDHL's logistics. In particular, the promised service quality of next-day delivery in Germany (for parcels posted before 4 p.m.) for about 85% of the daily standard parcel mail quantity makes the processes more challenging. The focus of this work is on the subnetwork for the long-haul transportation. For motivation and illustration purpose of the residual parcel volume's transportation (RPVT) problem we use the DPDHL network, but not limited thereto, as an example.

The remainder of this article is organized as follows. In Section 2 we introduce the residual volumes hub location problem (RVHLP). Related problems and existing approaches from the literature are surveyed in Section 3. In Section 4 we give an initial mixed integer formulation as a mathematical optimization model and improve the models bounds in Section 5. In Section 6 we survey computational results on well known hub location benchmark and new instances with different residual parcel volumes. Finally, we conclude in Section 7.

2 Residual Volumes Hub Location Problem

Swap bodies are used to carry out the transportation on the considered long-haul transportation network. They are normalized transport carriers, which can be separated from the vehicle and can be swapped between vehicles. Each vehicle can carry one swap body and the capacity of a swap body is limited by the volume and not by the overall weight of the parcels in our case. So far, mostly direct transports between each pair of sorting centers are realized. Direct transports take place overnight between approximately 10 p.m. and 5 a.m. During this time window several fully filled swap bodies (full truck load (FTL)) are shipped between on 33 times 32 sorting center relations (see Fig. 2). At the end of the time window, residual parcel volumes, which are not enough to fill a whole swap body, remain at the sorting centers . Therefore, in general, the last transport on all relations is performed in less than truck load (LTL) mode. Thus, the question arise if substantial cost reduction can be achieved through consolidation of these residual parcel volumes in hubs resulting in a better utilization of swap body capacities.

For each pair of sorting centers a residual parcel volume exists in both directions. In each case we have to decide whether the residual parcel volume is transported directly or through hubs. A splitting of the residual parcel volume is allowed. In the case of a transport via a hub, the parcels have to go through the sorting process again. Therefore, additional sorting costs at the hub per parcel arise. The transportation costs per vehicle consist in general of a distance independent fixed and a distance or time dependent variable component. Transportation costs per vehicle for each relation can be determined in a preprocessing step and correspond to vehicle trip-based costs.

Further, we do not consider fixed location costs as hubs can only be established in existing sorting centers. The transportation time between ISC and a hub may not exceed a maximum duration to guarantee the sorting before the cut-off time of sorting center acting as a hub. Because of the shortage of sorting capacities at the end of the time window, only a restricted number of ISC can be allocated to a hub and a restricted parcel volume can only be transported from a hub to an OSC. In order not to increase the transportation complexity, an ISC can only be allocated to a restricted number of hubs.

The goal of the RPVT problem is to determine the location of hubs and the allocation of sorting centers to the hubs such that the sum of additional sorting and transport costs is minimized.

Note that the requirement of direct transports for full swap bodies is a result of sorting, consignment and co-ordination processes and is not necessarily optimal in term of costs.

Further, note that some hub location decisions for residual volumes are not immediately obvious as for original volumes. The area of the circles in Fig. 3 (a) and (b) corresponds to the original volumes and, respectively, to the residual volumes of 200 real-world postcode districts from the Australian Post (AP) benchmark data set for hub location problems. Depots of postcode districts are the centers of the circles and the values of the residual volumes are calculated by original volumes modulo 1000. As shown in Fig. 3 (a) some circles cover or have an intersection with several other circles and thereby the corresponding depots are predestined to be hubs. In comparison, for the residual volumes this observation is very considerably less marked than for the original volumes (compare Fig. 3 (a) and (b)). Thus, the hub location decision is more difficult for the residual volumes.

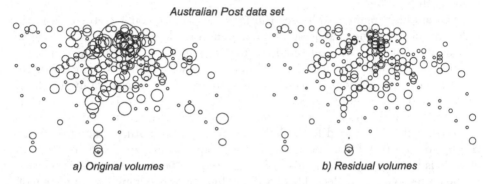

Australian Post data set

a) Original volumes   b) Residual volumes

Fig. 3. Comparison of of original and residual volumes of the Australian Post data set.

3 Literature Review

Network design problems usually consist of two interrelated problems: to determine the number and locations of hubs and to allocate geographic areas/customers (i.e. sorting centers) to them. That kind of decision, i.e. the design of a hub-and-spoke network, is usually made by solving so-called hub location problems, which have been the subject of numerous works. Hub location models are well studied in literature and can be found in [4], [6], [17], or [21]. We refer to [1] and [8] for a comprehensive review and to [8] for an insight to the current status of this research field.

Network design problems have a lot of real world applications, i.e. railroad or airline network design. Applications of network design problems to postal logistics have been studied in several different countries. [2] restructured the logistic system of the Swiss parcel delivery network and decided upon the number, location, capacity, and service areas of different transshipment points. [26] presented a heuristic solution concept for the design and hub transportation network for parcel service providers in Austria and [22] optimized highway transportation at the United States Postal Service. [9] considered a hub and routing problem in postal delivery motivated by observations in the Turkish postal services.

Economies of scale achieved through consolidation of flows is the *raison d'être* for hub-and-spoke networks and is usually modeled by discounting the unit costs of transportation for inter-hub flows with a discount factor $0 < \alpha < 1$ to reflect the consolidation of flows between hub nodes. Let $G = (N, A)$ be a complete graph, where $N = \{1, \ldots, n\}$ denotes the set of sorting centers and potential hub location respectively, then c_{ij} indicates the unit costs of transportation between the nodes i and j for every ordered pair $(i, j) \in N \times N$. Assuming that flows between sorting centers i and j go through paths $i \to k \to l \to j$, where k and l are hub nodes, the total unit costs of transportation can be expressed by $c_{ijkl} = c_{ik} + \alpha c_{kl} + c_{lj}$ with $0 < \alpha < 1$. While this approach is widespread in the literature because of its simplicity, it has been facing substantial criticism (e.g. [7] and [16]).

The criticism mainly addresses the fact that the discount factor α is flow-independent, meaning that it does not depend on the actual hub flow. This is a mismatch between the model and the underlying idea that economies of scale are achieved through consolidation of flows on arcs with high flows, since it often leads to optimal solutions in which some hub arcs carry considerably less flow than most of the non-hub arcs [7]. As a consequence, there is no reason why economies of scale should apply to hub arcs only. Furthermore, it is not clear what value should be used for α. Values used in the literature range from 0.25 [13] up to 0.7-1.0 [11]. Another issue with this approach to modelling economies of scale is the fact that the number of hubs needs to be determined in some way in the corresponding models. This is either done by predefining the number p of hubs to be installed in so-called p−hub Median problems [5] or by assuming that installing a hub in a node k of the network incurs fixed costs F_k in hub location problems [20]. Efficient algorithms for the single allocation p-hub median problem can be found in [13]. Further discussion of the related p-hub center problem were introduced by [15] and [12]. Some authors have tried to avoid the above mentioned criticisms and introduced flow-dependent discount factors, resulting in non-linear objective functions which can be approximated by piecewise linear functions (e.g. [3], [18], and [21]). In a simpler approach, [23] consider flow thresholds for every hub-arc. These must be reached in order for the unit costs of transportation on a particular arc to be discounted. [7] introduced the so-called hub arc location problem, where hub arcs are explicitly selected instead of hub nodes. This usually leads to solutions with hub arcs carrying more flow than in the corresponding hub location problems.

Even if the approaches mentioned above do provide considerable improvements to the way economies of scale are modeled in hub location models, some of the major criticisms mentioned earlier still apply. In all of the works mentioned above, economies of scale still apply to hub arcs only, and the number of hubs still needs to be restricted in some way. To resolve these problems, we have developed a new approach to economies of scale in hub-and-spoke networks, which is trip-based. While in all of the works mentioned above, transportation costs are always incurred by flows between nodes, we chose an approach in which transportation costs are incurred by vehicle trips. This approach has two advantages. If we assume fixed costs $c_f^{fix} = c_f$ for a specific vehicle trip f, then the unit costs of transportation as a function of the vehicles load l_f is given by $\frac{c_f^{fix}}{l_f}$ if $l_f > 0$ and 0 otherwise, which is a very simple but adequate description of economies of scale.

The second advantage of this approach is the fact that it allows easy consideration of different kinds of consolidation. Traditional hub location models only consider the consolidation of items with different origins and destinations on hub arcs, even though, according to [10], there are several ways in which items can be consolidated. The consolidation of items with the same origin and different destinations or with different origins and the same destination, as illustrated in Fig. 4, is of great interest and relevance when optimizing long-haul transports in letter mail networks, since it is a very effective way to reduce transportation costs. In addition to our the trip-based approach we consider sorting costs which are incurred by the additional sorting process required if parcels are not shipped directly but via some hub. Therefore, our objective is not only determined by transportation costs as in most classical hub location models but has to handle the trade-off between transportation cost reduction and additional sorting costs if using a hub for transports.

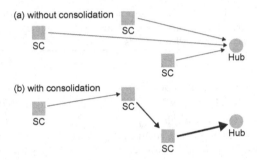

Fig. 4. Consolidation of items with different origins and the same destination according to [10]

4   Model Formulation

In this section we give a formulation for the residual volume hub location problem (RVHLP) as a mixed-integer linear programming problem. An overview of the sets, parameters and decision variables used in the model formulation can be found in Table 1. Consider the complete graph $G = (N, A)$, where $N = \{1, \ldots, n\}$ represents the set of nodes corresponding to origins/destinations as well as potential hub locations and $A \subseteq N \times N$ is the set of arcs representing the direct links between the nodes.

We introduce three types of decision variable to formulate the model. For the number of swap bodies being shipped directly from node i to node j we introduce the decision variable $x_{ij} \in \mathbb{N}_0$ for all $(i, j) \in A$. Other decisions made by the model concern the allocation of non-hub nodes to hubs and the location of hubs. For this we introduce the binary decision variables $z_{ik} \in \{0, 1\}$ for all $(i, k) \in A$, where $z_{ik} = 1$, iff node i is allocated to hub k $(i \neq k)$, and $z_{kk} \in \{0, 1\}$

Table 1. Sets, Parameters and Decision Variables used in the Model Formulation

Symbol	Meaning
N	Set of nodes
A	Set of links
w_{ij}	Parcel volume from node i to node j
d_{ij}	Distance between nodes i and j
t_{ij}	Travel time between nodes i and j
Γ	capacity of a swap body
δ	unit transportation costs
σ	unit sorting costs
p	total number of hubs to be located
s	maximum number of hubs an origin node may be allocated to
r	maximum number of origin nodes that may be allocated to a hub
Λ	maximum parcel volume being shipped from a hub to a destination node
T	maximum travel time allowed between a node and the hub it is allocated to
$x_{ij} \in \mathbb{N}_0$	Decision variable on the number of swap bodies from i to j
y_{ikj}	Decision variable on the fraction of the indirect flow from i to j via hub k
y_{ijj}	Decision variable on the fraction of the direct flow from i to j
$z_{ik} \in \{0,1\}$	Decision variable, $=1$ iff node i is allocated to hub k
$z_{kk} \in \{0,1\}$	Decision variable, $=1$ iff node k is a hub

for all $k \in N$, where $z_{kk} = 1$, iff node k is a hub. Eventually, the model also has to decide upon the parcel flows which can be either indirect or direct. For the indirect flows, the decision variables $y_{ikj} \geq 0$ for all $i, k, j \in N (i \neq j, i \neq k, k \neq j)$ represent the fraction of the parcel volume w_{ij} being shipped from node i to node j via hub k. The direct flows are represented by the decision variables $y_{ijj} \geq 0$ for all $i, j \in N (i \neq j)$, which represent the fraction of the parcel volume w_{ij} being shipped directly from node i to node j.

The overall objective is to determine the cost minimal location of hub nodes, allocation of the remaining nodes to the hub nodes, parcel flows and number of swap bodies on every arc of the network. For this we consider two cost components. The first and more important one is the transportation costs, represented by the total kilometers covered by all of the swap bodies, the second one, the additional sorting costs incurred by the sorting process in the hubs. Let d_{ij} denote the distance between node i and j, then we obtain the following objective function:

$$\min z = \delta \sum_{(i,j) \in A, i \neq j} d_{ij} x_{ij} + \sigma \sum_{i,k,j,k \neq j} w_{ij} y_{ikj}, \tag{1}$$

where δ and σ are user-defined parameters representing the unit transportation costs and the unit sorting costs for parcels being shipped indirectly via some hub respectively. High values of δ lead to solutions with more indirect shipments and high values of σ lead to solutions with more direct shipments.

The objective function is minimized such that the following constraints hold:

$$\sum_k y_{ikj} = 1, \ \forall i, j \in I, i \neq j. \tag{2}$$

These constraints ensure that for every relation between the nodes i and j the total volume w_{ij} is shipped from i to j, either directly from i to j or indirectly via some hub k.

$$\sum_{j,k \neq j} y_{ikj} \leq O_i z_{ik}, \ \forall i, k \in I. \tag{3}$$

Constraints (3) state that indirect flows originating in node i and destined for node j may only be routed via some hub k if the origin node i is allocated to the hub node k. To prevent node i from being allocated to a non-hub node, we can formulate the following constraints:

$$z_{ik} \leq z_{kk}, \ \forall i, k \in I. \tag{4}$$

According to constraints (4), node i may only be allocated to node k if k is a hub node ($z_{kk} = 1$). Since we do not consider fix costs for installing a hub, the total number of hubs to be installed needs to be restricted in some way. Thus we have the constraint:

$$\sum_k z_{kk} = p. \tag{5}$$

This means that a total of p hubs ($1 \leq p \leq n$) is installed in the nodes of the network. We also have the option to restrict the maximum number of hub nodes that a node is allocated to. The corresponding constraints are the following:

$$\sum_{k, i \neq k} z_{ik} \leq s, \ \forall i \in I. \tag{6}$$

This makes sure that node i is allocated to at most s hub nodes. Vice versa it is also possible to restrict the maximum number of non-hub nodes that are allocated to a single hub node. This can be done by formulating the following constraints:

$$\sum_{i, i \neq k} z_{ik} \leq r, \ \forall k \in I. \tag{7}$$

Constraints (7) ensure that at most r nodes are allocated to the hub node k. Besides the location and allocation decisions, the model also has to decide upon the number of swap bodies required on every link of the network. We therefore have the following central constraints:

$$y_{ijj} w_{ij} + \sum_{k, k \neq j} y_{ijk} w_{ik} + \sum_l y_{lij} w_{lj} \leq \Gamma x_{ij}, \ \forall i, j \in I, i \neq j. \tag{8}$$

Constraints (8) guarantee that the total flow on the arc between the nodes i and j does not exceed the overall swap body capacity Γx_{ij} on that arc, where the total flow between the nodes i and j consists from three different types of flows. The direct flow $y_{ijj} w_{ij}$, the indirect flows $y_{ijk} w_{ik}$ from node i via hub j on to some destination nodes k, and the indirect flows $y_{lij} w_{lj}$ from some origin nodes l to node j via hub i.

5   Improving the Bounds Through Valid Inequalities

In this section we describe several valid inequalities that can be added to the model given in Section 4 in order to improve the lower bound obtained from solving the LP-relaxation of the above mentioned problem. First we consider inequalities that take into account the swap body capacity.

$$\left\lceil \sum_{i,j,i\neq j} \frac{w_{ij}}{\Gamma} \right\rceil \leq \sum_{i,j,i\neq j} x_{ij} \tag{9}$$

Restrictions (9) states that the total capacity of all swap bodies used in the network must be greater or equal to the total parcel volume.

$$\left\lceil \sum_{(i,j)\in S\times(I\setminus S)} \frac{w_{ij}}{\Gamma} \right\rceil \leq \sum_{(i,j)\in S\times(I\setminus S)} x_{ij}, \ \forall S \subseteq I \tag{10}$$

In the same way, restrictions (10) must hold for every subset S of the set of nodes I. These restrictions state that the total capacity of all swap bodies heading out of subset S must be greater or equal to the total parcel volume leaving that subset. Since the number of subsets increases exponentially with the total number of nodes, we only consider subsets $S \subseteq I$ with up to four nodes ($|S| \leq 4$).

$$x_{ij} + \sum_{k,k\neq j} y_{ikj} \geq 1, \ \forall i,j \in I, i \neq j \tag{11}$$

As stated in (2), the total parcel volume w_{ij} needs to be shipped from its origin node i to its destination node j for every relation of the network. Either directly from i to j or indirectly via some hub k. Since for a relation the flows may be split, some fraction of the parcel volume may be shipped directly from origin to destination while the remaining fraction may be shipped indirectly via some hub. This is reflected in constraints 11. These state that on every relation from i to j the sum of the number of swap bodies from i to j and the sum over all fractions of indirect flows from i to j via some hubs k needs to be greater or equal to 1. If all of the parcel volume or some fraction of w_{ij} is shipped directly from i to j, then there needs to be at least one swap body from i to j and (2) holds. If the entire parcel volume w_{ij} is shipped indirectly, then $\sum_{k,k\neq j} y_{ikj} = 1$ and (2) holds as well.

6   Results

In this section we describe the results we obtained from numerous computational experiments run in order to evaluate the model proposed in Section 4, the improvements to the lower bound described in section 5. The models have been implemented in the modeling system AIMMS and run on a workstation with an Intel®Core™i7-3770 CPU at 3.40 GHz and 32GB of RAM using Gurobi 6 limited to a single core. The CPU time was limited to four hours.

For our computational experiments we used the well known Australian Post benchmark instances introduced in [14] with sizes $n = 10, 20, 25, 40$, and 50. The capacity Γ of a swap body was set to $\Gamma = 1000$, the unit transportation costs to $\delta = 8$, and the unit sorting costs to $\sigma = 0.1$. Since the total flow remains constant in all of the Australian Post instances, we scaled the values with n^2 in order to have flows of the same order of magnitude on the network's arcs and flows that are in a reasonable proportion the the capacity Γ of a swap body. The values w_{ij} for the parcel flow from node i to node j are then computed as

$$w_{ij} = \overset{o}{w}_{ij} - \left\lfloor \frac{\overset{o}{w}_{ij}}{\Gamma} \right\rfloor \tag{12}$$

where $\overset{o}{w}_{ij}$ is the original flow from the Australian Post instances. For every of the considered sizes $n = 10, 20, 25, 40$, and 50, we solve three different instances with values for p of $p = 2, 4$, and 8. The results we obtained can be found in Table 2.

Table 2. Results with Constraints (2)-(8)

n	p	Solution	LP-bound	CPU time	Gap
10	2	9,101.53	9,101.53	4,403.97	opt.
	4	8,621.74	8,451.77	14,400.00	0.0197
	8	8,474.48	8,175.45	14,400.00	0.0353
20	2	41,643.71	40,863.17	14,400.00	0.0187
	4	41,046.29	38,971.34	14,400.00	0.0506
	8	39,864.15	36,238.97	14,400.00	0.0909
25	2	70,749.55	69,025.27	14,400.00	0.0244
	4	69,781.47	61,457.89	14,400.00	0.1193
	8	68,737.49	60,357.88	14,400.00	0.1219
40	2	189,261.86	160,344.81	14,400.00	0.1528
	4	190,762.20	157,027.54	14,400.00	0.1768
	8	196,096.79	155,971.96	14,400.00	0.2046
50	2	305,857.38	247,793.39	14,400.00	0.1898
	4	301,908.48	244,996.77	14,400.00	0.1885
	8	308,270.31	243,295.70	14,400.00	0.2108

As one can see, only the instance with $n = 10$ and $p = 2$ could be solved to optimality within the time limit of four hours. For the remaining instances, the optimality gap varies from 2 to 21 percent, where the gap typically increases with larger values of n.

Next, we studied the effect of the valid inequalities introduced in Section 5 on the quality of the lower bound provided by the LP relaxation and the quality of the solutions obtained for the above mentioned instances. As one can see from table 3, the LP bound is improved by between 13 and 18% when adding the

Table 3. LP-Bounds with different Constraints

n	LP bound for (2)-(8)	LP bound for (2)-(8)&(10)-(11)
10	6.458,20	7.665,99
20	30.403,37	35.004,64
25	51.317,78	58.533,78
40	135.208,54	153.097,64
50	210.942,98	238.818,53

valid inequalities (10)-(11) to the model's original formulation given in Section 4 consisting of (2)-(8). Unfortunately, this improvement of the LP bound does not translate into a general improvement of the solutions for the instances studied. Table 4 reveals that using a model formulation consisting of constraints (2)-(8) as well as the valid inequalities (10)-(11) does not in general lead to better solutions than using a formulation featuring constraints (2)-(8) only.

We identified different reasons for the large gaps remaining at the end of the solutions process. First, the model given in Section 4 is very difficult to solve, mainly because of the constraints (8). The left-hand side features continuous variables, while the right-hand side is integer, resulting in a poor LP relaxation. Also the peculiarity of considering residual volumes only, adds to the difficulty of the problem. As was previously illustrated in Figure 3, the hub location decision is less obvious when considering residual volumes, since there no longer are nodes prone to become hubs because of their higher volumes compared to other nodes. Furthermore, using artificial data sets seems to add to the difficulty of the problem. For the instances featuring randomly generated volumes but based on the DHL parcel network in Germany (see Figure 2) and realistic cost parameters, we obtained better solutions with gaps in a range of 2 to 4%.

Table 4. Results with Constraints (2)-(8)&(10)-(11)

n	p	Solution	LP-bound	CPU time	Gap
10	2	9,101.53	9,101.53	2,078.21	opt.
	4	8,609.56	8,493.05	14,400	0.0135
	8	8,485.39	8,181.41	14,400	0.0358
20	2	41,758.83	40,850.96	14,400	0.0217
	4	41,007.59	38,885.32	14,400	0.0518
	8	39,753.75	36,182.85	14,400	0.0898
25	2	70,402.97	69,026.97	14,400	0.0195
	4	69,489.33	61,217.68	14,400	0.1190
	8	67,848.46	60,367.35	14,400	0.1103
40	2	191,722.25	161,409.84	14,400	0.1581
	4	191,504.87	158,125.71	14,400	0.1743
	8	201,272.15	157,198.69	14,400	0.2190
50	2	308,219.03	248,544.02	14,400	0.1936
	4	315,750.94	243,917.74	14,400	0.2275
	8	307,656.62	244,033.05	14,400	0.2068

7   Conclusion

In this paper, we address the novel problem of consolidating residual volumes in a parcel service provider's long-haul transportation network. As opposed to most models in literature, we chose a fixed cost based approach to model the transportation costs, in order to take into account the peculiarity of the consolidation of residual volumes. We formulated a mixed integer linear problem to locate the hub nodes, allocate the non-hub nodes to the hubs and determine the number of swap bodies required on every arc of the network.

The proposed model was implemented evaluated by solving artificial test instances. Numerical results indicated that the model is very difficult to solve for realistically sized artificial instances, even though results for real-world instances however are very encouraging. Since the proposed model's LP relaxation proved to be quite weak, we introduced different valid inequalities in order to improve the lower bound. Additional computational results however showed that the achieved improvement of the lower bound does not translate into better solutions.

Since the problem studied in this paper is very difficult to solve, we will consider more efficient model formulations and solution techniques to obtain better solutions. Also, the present model does not consider transportation times and time-related constraints required to give a more accurate picture of the underlying real-world problem. These will be included in future work.

References

1. Alumur, S.A., Kara, B.Y.: Network hub location problems: The state of the art. Eur. J. Oper. Res. **190**(1), 1–21 (2008)
2. Bruns, A., Klose, A., Stähly, P.: Restructuring of swiss parcel delivery services. OR Spectrum **22**, 285–302 (2000)
3. Bryan, D.: Extensions to the hub location problem: Formulations and numerical examples. Geogr. Anal. **30**(4), 315–330 (1998)
4. Campbell, J.F.: Integer programming formulations of discrete hub location problems. Eur. J. Oper. Res. **72**(2), 387–405 (1994)
5. Campbell, J.F.: Hub location and the p-hub median problem. Oper. Res. **44**(6), 923–935 (1996)
6. Campbell, J.F., Ernst, A.T., Krishnamoorthy, M.: Hub location problems. In: Drezner, Z., Hamacher, H.W. (eds.) Facility Location: Applications and Theory, pp. 373–407. Springer, Berlin (2002)
7. Campbell, J.F., Ernst, A.T., Krishnamoorthy, M.: Hub arc location problems: Part i-introduction and results. Manage. Sci. **51**(10), 1540–1555 (2005)
8. Campbell, J.F., O'Kelly, M.E.: Twenty-five years of hub location research. Transport. Sci. **46**(2), 153–169 (2012)
9. Çetiner, S., Sepil, C., Süral, H.: Hubbing and routing in postal delivery systems. Ann. Oper. Res. **181**(1), 109–124 (2007)
10. Crainic, T.G.: Service network design in freight transportation. Eur. J. Oper. Res. **122**(2), 272–288 (2000)
11. Cunha, C.B., Silva, M.R.: A genetic algorithm for the problem of configuring a hub-and-spoke network for a ltl trucking company in brazil. Eur. J. Oper. Res. **179**, 747–758 (2007)

12. Ernst, A.T., Hamacher, H., Jiang, H., Krishnamoorthy, M., Woeginger, G.J.: Uncapacitated single and multiple allocation p-hub center problems. Comput. Oper. Res. **36**(7), 2230–2241 (2009)
13. Ernst, A.T., Krishnamoorthy, M.: Efficient algorithms for the uncapacitated single allocation p-hub median problem. Loc. Sci. **4**, 139–154 (1996)
14. Ernst, A.T., Krishnamoorthy, M.: Solution algorithms for the capacitated single allocation hub location problem. Annals of Operations Research **86**, 141–159 (1999)
15. Kara, B.Y., Tansel, B.Ç.: On the single-assignment p-hub center problem. Eur. J. Oper. Res. **125**(3), 648–655 (2000)
16. Kimms, A.: Economies of scale in hub & spoke network design models: we have it all wrong. In: Morlock, M., Schwindt, C., Trautmann, N., Zimmermann, J. (eds.) Perspectives on Operations Research: Essays in Honor of Klaus Neumann, Gabler Edition Wissenschaft, pp. 293–317. Deutscher Universitäts-Verlag (2006)
17. Klincewicz, J.G.: Hub location in backbone/tributary network design: a review. Loc. Sci. **6**(1–4), 307–335 (1998)
18. Klincewicz, J.G.: Enumeration and search procedures for a hub location problem with economies of scale. Ann. Oper. Res. **110**, 107–122 (2002)
19. Manner-Homberg, H., Symanczyk, W., Miller, J.: Der kep-markt in deutschland - eine kurzstudie im auftrag des bdkep, June 2013
20. O'Kelly, M.E.: Hub facility location with fixed costs. Pap. Reg. Sci. **71**, 293–306 (1992)
21. O'Kelly, M.E., Bryan, D.: Hub location with flow economies of scale. Transport. Res. B-Meth. **32**(8), 605–616 (1998)
22. Pajunas, A., Matto, E.J., Trick, M., Zuluaga, L.F.: Optimizing highway transportation at the united states postal service. Interfaces **37**(6), 515–525 (2007)
23. Podnar, H., Skorin-Kapov, J., Skorin-Kapov, D.: Network cost minimization using threshold-based discounting. Eur. J. Oper. Res. **137**, 371–386 (2002)
24. Salehi, F., Ryssel, L.: Europe's cep market: Growth on new terms, October 2012
25. Sebastian, H.-J.: Optimization approaches in the strategic and tactical planning of networks for letter, parcel and freight mail. In: Dolk, D., Granat, J. (eds.) Decision Support Modeling in Service Networks. LNBIP, vol. 42, pp. 36–61. Springer, Heidelberg (2012)
26. Wasner, M., Zäpfel, G.: An integrated multi-depot hub-location vehicle routing model for network planning of parcel service. Int. J. Prod. Econ. **90**(3), 403–419 (2004)

A Review of Intermodal Rail Freight Bundling Operations

Qu Hu[✉], Francesco Corman, and Gabriel Lodewijks

Department of Marine and Transport Technology,
Delft University of Technology, Delft, The Netherlands
{Q.Hu,F.Corman,G.Lodewijks}@tudelft.nl

Abstract. Bundling freight flows are significant important in intermodal transport, as all stakeholders involved, e.g. infrastructure owners and transport providers have to find the best solution to meet the transport demand with reasonable cost. Therefore, consolidation and spilt of the freight are inevitable during the transport. As a result, extensive operations must be performed to ensure the exchange between freight flows. The aim of this paper is to give an integrated perspective of the railway intermodal bundling operations. Key operations in bundling rail freight are addressed and discussed, literature in relevant area are classified according to the characteristic of operation. Finally, current trends and limitation in these topics are discussed.

Keywords: Intermodal transport · Railway transport · Container terminal · Freight bundling

1 Introduction

Last year, approximately 40 million TEU containers were transported through Shanghai Port. Although the growth rate is slowing down these years, the containerized transport will keep increasing in the near future.

As the container port could never be the origin or destination of any container, ongoing transport is needed in every container port. Thus, larger container port mean larger requirement for hinterland transport capacity. Intermodal transport may be a solution for reducing this pressure, as several transport segments can work collaboratively. The definition of intermodal transport can be found in many relevant literatures, a most widely accepted one is that goods are transported in one and the same transport unit (e.g. a container) by a sequence of at least two different transport modes. Intermodal transport can be seen as a particular type of multimodal transport, while through multimodal transport the transport unit is not necessarily to be the same.

To improve the quality of intermodal transport, various problems in strategic, tactical and operational levels have been addressed and studied. This paper will review the studies concerning rail freight bundling operations. Bundling is a broad conception involves several layers, starting with the consolidation of parcels onto a pallet

© Springer International Publishing Switzerland 2015
F. Corman et al. (Eds.): ICCL 2015, LNCS 9335, pp. 451–463, 2015.
DOI: 10.1007/978-3-319-24264-4_31

and going up to the bundling of a large number of containers onto a trunk line at sea or in the hinterland (Konings, 2008). In (Kreutzberger 2008), bundling is described as the process of transporting goods belonging to different flows in a common vehicle (like truck or train), load unit (like container) and/or shipment unit (like pallet) during part of their journey.

In this paper, we focus on the consolidation of flows. Fig.1 shows some basic types of transport networks. When direct transport between origin and destination is not possible or not economical sufficient, freight flows are concentrated into a new flow or shifted into another transport mode. We consider the bundling related operations as the key actions in intermodal transport because these actions concentrate freight flows from separated transport segments into a better organized and more efficient transport mode.

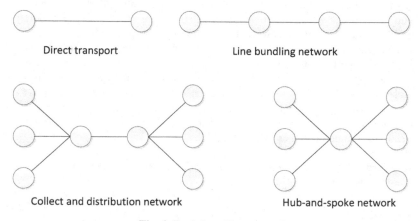

Direct transport   Line bundling network

Collect and distribution network   Hub-and-spoke network

Fig. 1. Basic bundling networks

On strategic level, bundling problems are related to infrastructure construction, which is aimed at providing access between different transport flows. As it is shown in Fig.1, different network can be used to connect the origin and destination and that will impact the transport time and cost. Then, tactical problems concern about how to use the infrastructure, such as when and where to concentrate or split the flows. Transport planners should find optimized routes in the network for their cargos. After these two levels of decisions, a bundling network is formed to process the intermodal transport commodity. To ensure the network working in an efficient way, operational problems are addressed to optimize bundling actions.

However, to keep this paper in a reasonable length, restrictions are proposed follows

- Transport modes considered in this paper include railway, road and water transport;
- Only containerized freight transport is taken into account;
- Only operational problems are reviewed.

The aim of this paper is to give an integrated perspective of the railway intermodal operations. In order to highlight the characteristics of intermodal transport, essential components in separate systems are addressed, and the interface between components is examined throughout the process of rail intermodal transport.

The area of multimodal and intermodal transport has been intensively studied in the last decade. (SteadieSeifi, Dellaert et al. 2014) present a classification of the strategic, tactical, and operational levels of planning in multimodal transport. (Macharis and Bontekoning 2004) review the applications of operational research in intermodal transport. An overview of railway-related intermodal transport can be found in (Caris, Macharis et al. 2008).

This paper is organized as follows. In section 2, background information is given, and the intermodal rail transport network and terminals are introduced. In section 3, we discuss the operational problems in container terminals and railway yards. In section 4, the paper is concluded with a summary and outlook identifying interesting and promising topics for future research.

2   Intermodal Rail Transport Terminals

Literally, bundling means combination of flows, therefore, specialized facilities are needed to perform the freight exchanges. In terms of intermodal transport, bundling operations can be recognized inside and between container terminals. Figure 2 shows a simplified railway network connecting Rotterdam port and inland container terminals. The basic components in a rail-related intermodal network are container terminal, railway shunting yard, rail line and siding. Container terminals can be seen as the connection between railway network and other transport sectors, large amounts of containers are moved on exchange operations carried out inside the terminal. Railway sidings and shunting yards are used to connect different rail lines, and then, bundling the rail cargo inside the railway system.

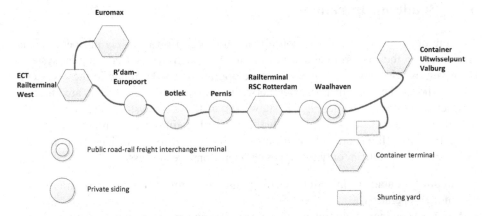

Fig. 2. Schematic chart of railway network

Container terminals are the hubs where containers from deep sea port or road transport section can be transshipped to rail. Review about the container terminal can be found in (Voß, Stahlbock et al. 2004), (Günther and Kim 2006), (Stahlbock and Voß 2007), (Kim and Lee 2015). Usually, a train consists of several **blocks,** and each block is made up of a group of rail wagons or load units with same destination. Shunting (or marshalling, classification) operations are carried out in shunting (or marshalling, classification) yards, aiming at rearranging the rail wagons or load units to form specific trains. Shunting yards differ with each other in terms of layout and facilities. Numerous researches have been carried out on this topic. See (Boysen, Fliedner et al. 2012) for an exhaustive review of related operational problems and challenges. In a traditional way, both in gravity shunting yard or flat shunting yard, trains are split into blocks, and sent to different tracks to form new trains. This problem is NP-hard, so researches usually try to find an approximate optimal solution by heuristics or simulation. (Gatto, Maue et al. 2009) give a review on the traditional shunting process. (Dorda and Teichmann 2013) present a mathematical model and a simulation model of the freight trains shunting process. (Hauser and Maue 2010) develop and evaluate three algorithms for the railway shunting optimization problem.

In this paper, the emphasis is put the emerging shunting yard equipped with cranes, which is a faster alternative to traditional shunting yard (Boysen, Jaehn et al. 2011, Boysen, Fliedner et al. 2013). When compared with the traditional shunting process, this kind of shunting shows higher efficiency due to higher container moving speed, less operations related to split and regrouping the wagons and more parallel operations, etc.

Despite of the difference in layout and facilities applied, a common function is achieved in the container terminals: interconnection. The terminals provide interface to transship freights from different transport segments, which means container terminals ensure the possibility to connect different modes, while shunting yards provide the exchange access between different vehicles or trains.

3   Bundling Operations

As mentioned above, in order to consolidate the cargo flows, variety of operations is carried out in the sea terminal and rail terminals, which makes it a complex system. However, as it is shown in Fig.3, two basic operations can be found in these system. Fig.3.i shows the container transfer between flows/subsystems which are directly connected by cranes, while Fig.3.ii shows when flows/subsystems are not directly linked, an extra transport cycle is needed. It is worth noting that this transport cycle is not a long haul transport, which means it is only performed inside the port area. Therefore, in this article, only two types of operations are addressed:

- Handling container, including loading/unloading to/from vessels or trains and shunting operations;
- Moving container, including quayside transport and inter terminal transport.

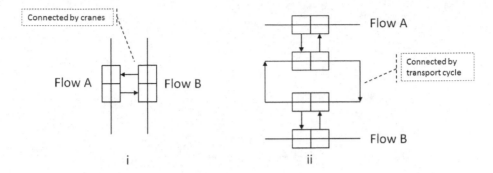

Fig. 3. Basic bundling operations

3.1   Handling Containers

Handling operations are essential in (un)loading, transshipment and sometimes in shunting process. Outbound containers are usually transported to the stack block by extern vehicle. After a certain period of storage, the containers will be sent to train or vessel by intern trucks and then loaded according to the loading plan, vice versa. And shunting usually carried out within storage area or railway shunting yard. Actually, both of the two operations can be seen as the container being moved between two systems using crane. When the connected systems stay static, the handling problem concerns about the movement of cranes. But when one of the connected systems turns out to be dynamic, the synchronization problem should be taken into account. Therefore, the handling can be seen as a crane scheduling problem, the following decisions should be made:

1. Decide on storage positions of containers handled by split moves.
2. Assign each intern truck a parking position.
3. Determine the positions of containers on trains/vessels.
4. Assign container moves to cranes.
5. Determine the sequence of container moves per crane.

The objective of crane scheduling could be minimization of the makespan for serving a given set of vehicles or containers, or maximization the utilization of the cranes, vehicles or ships.

Loading and Unloading

When loading or unloading a set of containers, the maximal number of cranes can be used to serve a vessel of a train is usually given. And each crane can move the container in a certain area, which means the moving area of crane should be determined. As shown in Figure 3, the loading and unloading problem can be seen as scheduling the crane movement to exchange containers between storage area, truck and train/vessel.

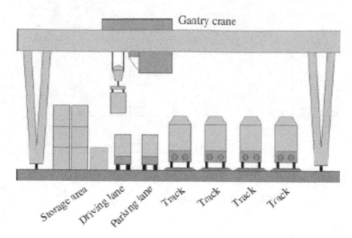

Fig. 4. Schematic representation of a rail–road transshipment yard (Boysen, Fliedner et al. 2013)

Most existing literature use mixed-integer programming (MIP) model to describe the loading and unload process. Each handling operation is split into several tasks, such as lift and drop off, and assigned to crane movements. When making a train loading plan, decision problem 3 is important because the type of wagon will impact the load capacity and load configuration, while it is less of an issue when loading a vessel.

Table 1. Summary of literature on crane scheduling

Reference	Terminal	Decision problem	Model
(Kim and Park 2004)	Sea-Road	4, 5	MIP
(Bierwirth and Meisel 2009)	Sea-Road	4, 5	MIP
(Contu, ebbraro et al. 2011)	Sea-Road	2,4,5	Simulation
(Han, Lu et al. 2010)	Sea-Road	4, 5	MIP
(Corry and Kozan 2006)	Road-Rail	3	MIP
(Corry and Kozan 2007)	Road-Rail	3	MIP
(Kozan 1997)	Road-Rail	4	Simulation
(Bruns and Knust 2010)	Road-Rail	3	MIP
(Froyland, Koch et al. 2007)	Sea-Road-Rail	1, 2, 3	MIP

A trend in crane scheduling is model the crane working combined with berth allocation, vehicle routing or storage planning. (Han, Lu et al. 2010) take berth allocation into account when scheduling the quayside cranes. (Lee, Cao et al. 2009) present an integer programming model in which yard truck scheduling and storage allocation problems are formulated as a whole for heterogeneous import containers. (Chen, Langevin et al. 2013) study the interactions between crane handling and truck transportation in a maritime container terminal by addressing them simultaneously.

Besides, various types of handling equipment other than crane have been studied, (Li and Wang 2008) use a simulation based algorithm to find the optimal deployment of forklifts and container truck when (un)loading container trains. (Anghinolfi, Paolucci et al. 2011) propose a planning procedure for serving freight transportation requests in a railway network with horizontal handling equipment. A 0–1 linear programming is applied to find the optimal assignment of each container to a train sequence and to a specific wagon for each train in the sequence. The authors use a pre-analysis to compute all possible sequences of trains available for serving each order. Based on that, the cost is generated and then used in the objective function. Later, (D.Anghinolf, Caballini et al. 2014) study the same handling system and present a multi-objective problem that maximize the train loading as well as minimize the number of pin changes. Shunting or transship operations faces the problem of in a different way.

Other related research including (Kim and Hong 2006) and (Caserta, Voß et al. 2009) study the blocks relocation problem, a branch-and-bound algorithm is used by the former paper and the later one uses a metaheuristic method.

Shunt Containers with Crane

Shunting containers is another important topic in rail terminal operation. Containers from different origin should be sorted and loaded on the corresponding trains. Although a lot of intermodal containers are transported by direct train, which means the train will reach the destination without be shunted, shunting trains still remain unavoidable in most cases.

When modelling a shunting process with cranes, a new decision problem arises:

6. How to determine the sequence to enter the shunting yards?

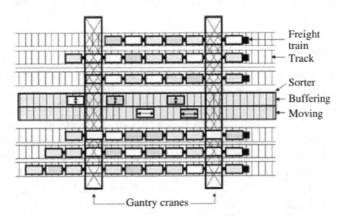

Fig. 5. Schematic representation of a rail–rail transshipment yard (Boysen, Fliedner et al. 2013)

From Figure 4 we can find that a limited number of tracks are crossed by cranes, where trains are dragged in for shunting. Since each container has its target train to be loaded, if the target train is not available, the container will be placed on the storage area, which requires extra movement for the handling resource. Another situation is that when the container is not available for a train, the train may be forced to leave the shunting yard and return after the container is ready.

To solve this problem, (Boysen, Jaehn et al. 2011) propose mathematics model aimed at minimizing the weighted linear combination of extra movement of cranes and train. In that paper, trains processed in parallel track at same time are described as in the same service slot, then, trains are assigned to different service slots. In (Boysen, Jaehn et al. 2010), the author consider an extended problem, another objective concerns the delay of containers is added to the model. (González, Ponce et al. 2008) present a study based on a terminal where containers from Spanish and French trains are exchanged. Because the lack of storage area, the container should be placed on the target wagon, or be placed on a contiguous wagon. Another study about storage constrains can be found in (Bostel and Dejax 1998). The authors present four models with and without explicit storage constraint in loading and shunting operations. The models are 0-1 integer programming and heuristics are developed to solve the problems. In terms of handling equipment and working process, shunting with crane is similar to loading and unloading operation, which means similar methods can be shared in these two problems. (Boysen, Fliedner et al. 2010) use a dynamic programming model in shunting yard with a sorter. A similar model is used in loading planning.

3.2   Moving Containers

This section concerns about the containers' movement inside and between terminals. Since the type of terminals could be different, transport methods used to connect these terminals can be road vehicles, rail vehicles or barges. In this section, two types of transport will be discussed, namely quayside transport and inter terminal transport. See (Voß, Stahlbock et al. 2004) for a detailed review for vehicle routing in container terminal.

Quayside Transport

After being discharged from the vessel, the container should be placed on a vehicle and then transported to storage area. This is the so called quayside transport. As mentioned in previous section, when crane are used as connection between dynamic systems, synchronization problem should be taken into consideration. That is why dispatching quayside vehicle and scheduling crane should be studied integrated. Study like (Chen, Langevin et al. 2013) formulate the problem using a constraint programming model. A similar research can be seen in (Lee, Cao et al. 2009), the authors propose an integer programming model in which yard truck scheduling and storage allocation problems are formulated as a whole for heterogeneous import containers.

Within the topic of vehicle dispatching, parameters such as the set of containers to move, the ready time of each container, the fleet size and configuration are given, the travel time can be calculated through the route, and the objective could be the minimization of delay or the minimization of generalized cost. See (Grunow, Günther et al. 2006) for an exhaustive review, including on-line and off-line dispatching strategies.

(Nguyen and Kim) study the dispatching decision making problem by proposing a heuristic method. In that system, when an automated guided vehicle becoming idle, the dispatching heuristic will be triggered, then a new task will be assigned to the vehicle. Similar research can be found in (Lee, Chew et al. 2010) and (Kim and Bae 2004).

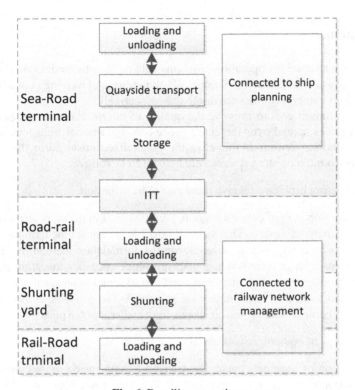

Fig. 6. Bundling operations

Inter Terminal Transport (ITT)

ITT related to the container movement between terminals in a port area. In terms of intermodal transport, ITT ensures the possibility to bundling freight from other trans- port modes, e.g., recall the network in Fig 2, shunting scheme for RSC Rotterdam is party depends on the reliability of ITT connection with upstream terminals like Eu- romax and ECT. Although inter terminal transport is quite common in real word, the amount of research focus on this topic is relatively rare.

(Ottjes, Veeke et al. 2007) develop a simulation model for the Maasvlakte termin- als, and the traffic flow between the terminals tested. (Tierney, Voß et al. 2014) pro- pose the first fully defined mathematical model using a time-space graph, and the objective is to minimize the lateness of container delivery. In the time-space graph, terminals and intersections are represented by nodes, and the connections are represented by weighted arcs. To reflect loading/unloading time in real word, long- term nodes and long-term arcs are introduced. LT (long-term) nodes are copies of the terminal nodes and LT arcs connect a node to its LT counterpart. Based on the graph, the authors present an integer programming model to solve the ITT problem. Then, (Nieuwkoop, Corman et al. 2014) develop the time-space model to find an optimal vehicle configuration with minimized delays. (Schroer, Corman et al. 2014) test 4 different ITT vehicle configurations using a discrete event simulation mode.

4   Conclusion

In this paper, literature on operation problems related to intermodal rail freight bundling are reviewed and classified. Specifically, handling and moving containers inside and between container terminals are discussed respectively.

With the common goal to improve the quality of intermodal rail transport, the reviewed researches spread over the entire process of intermodal transport. Therefore, the aim of bundling actions is minimize the generalized cost and/or the makespan. Some trends from the existing research are addressed as follows.

• Synchronization problems receive more and more attention.

With the development of containerization, facilities used in different terminals are becoming increasingly uniformed. That makes it possible to connect the terminals physically as well as theoretically. For instance, the similar formulation method for crane scheduling can be used in ship (un)loading, stacking block classification, train (un)loading and railway shunting. As a consequence, a trend can be found in terminal operation study is that more and more integrated models are presented. The quayside cranes are usually scheduled with berth allocation, vehicle dispatching and/or storage plan.

• A wider range of equipment is taken into consideration.

The expansion of terminals makes the transport chain inside more complex while more equipment and operations are involved. For both evaluation and planning reason, different configurations of equipment are tested in optimization and simulation models.

Although a considerable number of research have been done in this area, the following problems should be further investigated:

Without doubt, people increasingly attach importance to the synchronization problems, however, this kind of operations can be found inside the terminal. A macroscopic connection can be seen in Figure 5, the sea terminal operations are connected to ship planning process, and the rail terminal operations will impact the railway network management. In terms of railway freight transport, bundling operations should be organized in a network perspective.

ITT is an important research area as it is closely related to the freight bundling, delay in ITT will result in disturbance for downstream systems. More detailed control and evaluate method should be developed, with modern information system, the real-time dispatching for ITT will provide a better connection between terminals. Furthermore, the ITT should be studied combined with loading and storage plan making.

Through an integrated modelling or simulation, the connected terminals can be optimized at the same time.

In terms of algorithm, branch and bound algorithm and local search are the most commonly used method to solve the MIP. Since the complexity increases with the scale of the problem, these algorithms should be developed. On the other hand, other algorithms should be studied and evaluated to find more powerful method.

Robustness of the bundling operation could be a promising research area, which means the operation plan, e.g., loading plan and shunting scheme, should be capable of absorbing, as much as possible, disturbances in upstream systems. The disturbance in bundling operation could be break downs of the facilities as well as unexpected freight flow. The term of unexpected freight flow can be a very large or small flow, which may be a result of peaks in arriving, failure in ITT and etc. Thus, the bundling operation should be resistant against these disturbances.

References

1. Anghinolfi, D., Paolucci, M., Sacone, S., Siri, S.: Freight transportation in railway networks with automated terminals: A mathematical model and MIP heuristic approaches. European Journal of Operational Research 214(3), 588–594 (2011)
2. Bierwirth, C., Meisel, F.: A fast heuristic for quay crane scheduling with interference constraints. Journal of Scheduling 12(4), 345–360 (2009)
3. Bostel, N., Dejax, P.: Models and Algorithms for Container Allocation Problems on Trains in a Rapid Transshipment Shunting Yard. Transportation Science 32(4), 370–379 (1998)
4. Boysen, N., Fliedner, M., Jaehn, F., Pesch, E.: Shunting yard operations: Theoretical aspects and applications. European Journal of Operational Research 220(1), 1–14 (2012)
5. Boysen, N., Fliedner, M., Jaehn, F., Pesch, E.: A Survey on Container Processing in Railway Yards. Transportation Science 47(3), 312–329 (2013)
6. Boysen, N., Fliedner, M., Kellner, M.: Determining fixed crane areas in rail–rail transshipment yards. Transportation Research Part E: Logistics and Transportation Review 46(6), 1005–1016 (2010)
7. Boysen, N., Jaehn, F., Pesch, E.: New bounds and algorithms for the transshipment yard scheduling problem. Journal of Scheduling 15(4), 499–511 (2010)
8. Boysen, N., Jaehn, F., Pesch, E.: Scheduling Freight Trains in Rail-Rail Transshipment Yards. Transportation Science 45(2), 199–211 (2011)
9. Bruns, F., Knust, S.: Optimized load planning of trains in intermodal transportation. OR Spectrum 34(3), 511–533 (2010)
10. Caris, A., Macharis, C., Janssens, G.K.: Planning Problems in Intermodal Freight Transport: Accomplishments and Prospects. Transportation Planning and Technology 31(3), 277–302 (2008)
11. Caserta, M., Voß, S., Sniedovich, M.: Applying the corridor method to a blocks relocation problem. OR Spectrum 33(4), 915–929 (2009)
12. Chen, L., Langevin, A., Lu, Z.: Integrated scheduling of crane handling and truck transportation in a maritime container terminal. European Journal of Operational Research 225(1), 142–152 (2013)
13. Contu, F., Ebbraro, A.D.F., Sacco, N.: A model for performance evaluation and sensitivity analysis of seaport container terminals. In: 18th IFAC World Congress, Milano, Italy (2011)

14. Corry, P., Kozan, E.: An assignment model for dynamic load planning of intermodal trains. Computers & Operations Research **33**(1), 1–17 (2006)
15. Corry, P., Kozan, E.: Optimised loading patterns for intermodal trains. OR Spectrum **30**(4), 721–750 (2007)
16. Anghinolf, D., Caballini, C., Sacone, S.: Optimizing train loading operations in innovative and automated container terminals (2014)
17. Dorda, M., Teichmann, D.: Modelling of Freight Trains Classification Using Queueing System Subject to Breakdowns. Mathematical Problems in Engineering **2013**, 1–11 (2013)
18. Froyland, G., Koch, T., Megow, N., Duane, E., Wren, H.: Optimizing the landside operation of a container terminal. OR Spectrum **30**(1), 53–75 (2007)
19. Gatto, M., Maue, J., Mihalák, M., Widmayer, P.: Shunting for dummies: an introductory algorithmic survey. In: Ahuja, R.K., Möhring, R.H., Zaroliagis, C.D. (eds.) Robust and Online Large-Scale Optimization. LNCS, vol. 5868, pp. 310–337. Springer, Heidelberg (2009)
20. González, J.Á., Ponce, E., Mataix, C., Carrasco, J.: The Automatic Generation of Transhipment Plans for a Train-Train Terminal: Application to the Spanish-French Border. Transportation Planning and Technology **31**(5), 545–567 (2008)
21. Grunow, M., Günther, H.-O., Lehmann, M.: Strategies for dispatching AGVs at automated seaport container terminals. OR Spectrum **28**(4), 587–610 (2006)
22. Günther, H.-O., Kim, K.-H.: Container terminals and terminal operations. OR Spectrum **28**(4), 437–445 (2006)
23. Han, X.-L., Lu, Z.-Q., Xi, L.-F.: A proactive approach for simultaneous berth and quay crane scheduling problem with stochastic arrival and handling time. European Journal of Operational Research **207**(3), 1327–1340 (2010)
24. Hauser, A., Maue, J.: Experimental evaluation of approximation and heuristic algorithms for sorting railway cars. In: Festa, P. (ed.) SEA 2010. LNCS, vol. 6049, pp. 154–165. Springer, Heidelberg (2010)
25. Kim, K.H., Bae, J.W.: A Look-Ahead Dispatching Method for Automated Guided Vehicles in Automated Port Container Terminals. Transportation Science **38**(2), 224–234 (2004)
26. Kim, K.H., Hong, G.-P.: A heuristic rule for relocating blocks. Computers & Operations Research **33**(4), 940–954 (2006)
27. Kim, K.H., Lee, H.: Container Terminal Operation: Current Trends and Future Challenges **220**, 43–73 (2015)
28. Kim, K.H., Park, Y.-M.: A crane scheduling method for port container terminals. European Journal of Operational Research **156**(3), 752–768 (2004)
29. Kozan, E.: Increasing the Operational Efficiency of Container Terminals in Australia. The Journal of the Operational Research Society **48**(2), 151–161 (1997)
30. Kreutzberger, E.: The Innovation of Intermodal Rail Freight Bundling Networks in Europe Concepts, Developments, Performances, TRAIL Research School, Cop., Delft (2008)
31. Lee, D.H., Cao, J.X., Shi, Q.X.: Synchronization of yard truck scheduling and storage allocation in container terminals. Engineering Optimization **41**(7), 659–672 (2009)
32. Lee, L.H., Chew, E.P., Tan, K.C., Wang, Y.: Vehicle dispatching algorithms for container transshipment hubs. OR Spectrum **32**(3), 663–685 (2010)
33. Li, D., Wang, D.: Simulation Based Optimization for the Loading-unloading Strategies of Railway Container Terminal (2008)
34. Macharis, C., Bontekoning, Y.M.: Opportunities for OR in intermodal freight transport research: A review. European Journal of Operational Research **153**(2), 400–416 (2004)

35. Nguyen, V., Kim, K.: Dispatching vehicles considering uncertain handling times at port container terminals. In: Progress in Material Handling Research: Proceedings of the 11th International Material Handling Research Colloquium
36. Nieuwkoop, F., Corman, F., Negenbom, R.R., Duinkerken, M.B., Schuylenburg, M.V., Lodewijks, G.: Decision support for vehicle configuration determination in inter terminal transport system design. In: 2014 IEEE 11th International Conference on Networking, Sensing and Control (ICNSC). Miami, FL, pp. 613–618 (2014)
37. Ottjes, J.A., Veeke, H.P., Duinkerken, M.B., Rijsenbrij, J.C., Lodewijks, G.: Simulation of a multiterminal system for container handling (2007)
38. Schroer, H.J.L., Corman, F., Duinkerken, M.B., Negenborn, R.R., Lodewijks, G.: Evaluation of inter terminal transport configurations at rotterdam maasvlakte using discrete event simulation. In: 2014 Winter Simulation Conference (2014)
39. Stahlbock, R., Voß, S.: Operations research at container terminals: a literature update. OR Spectrum 30(1), 1–52 (2007)
40. SteadieSeifi, M., Dellaert, N.P., Nuijten, W., Van Woensel, T., Raoufi, R.: Multimodal freight transportation planning: A literature review. European Journal of Operational Research 233(1), 1–15 (2014)
41. Tierney, K., Voß, S., Stahlbock, R.: A mathematical model of inter-terminal transportation. European Journal of Operational Research 235(2), 448–460 (2014)
42. Voß, S., Stahlbock, R., Steenken, D.: Container terminal operation and operations research - a classification and literature review. OR Spectrum 26(1), 3–49 (2004)

Cloud-Based Intelligent Transportation Systems Using Model Predictive Control

Leonard Heilig[1]([⊠]), Rudy R. Negenborn[2], and Stefan Voß[1]

[1] Institute of Information Systems (IWI), University of Hamburg,
Hamburg, Germany
{leonard.heilig,stefan.voss}@uni-hamburg.de
[2] Department of Maritime & Transport Technology,
Delft University of Technology, Delft, The Netherlands
r.r.negenborn@tudelft.nl

Abstract. Recent and future technology development make intelligent transport systems a reality in contemporary societies leading to a higher quality, performance, and safety in transportation systems. In a big data era, however, efficient information technology infrastructures are necessary to support real-time applications efficiently. In this paper, we review different control structures based on model predictive control and embed them in cloud infrastructures. We especially focus on conceptual ideas for intelligent road transportation and explain how the proposed cloud-based system can be used for parallel and scalable computing supporting real-time decision making based on large volumes and a variety of data from different sources. As such, the paper provides a novel approach for applying data-driven intelligent transport systems that utilize scalable and cost-efficient cloud infrastructures based on model predictive control structures.

Keywords: Intelligent transport systems · Cloud computing · Big data · Model predictive control

1 Introduction

In the last decade, the development of highly accessible, efficient, and scalable cloud infrastructures has paved the way for processing large quantities of data within tolerable computational time based on available information technology (IT) and techniques such as those from machine learning, signal processing, and data mining. According to Zhang et al. [35], the growing amount of collected data from a variety of sources can potentially lead to a revolution in the development of data-driven intelligent transportation systems (ITS). A data-driven ITS consists of different subcomponents like advanced traffic control systems and public transportation systems, which need to disseminate information processed from large amounts of structured, semi-structured, and unstructured data. This builds the basis for an intelligent transformation of measurements into plausible

© Springer International Publishing Switzerland 2015
F. Corman et al. (Eds.): ICCL 2015, LNCS 9335, pp. 464–477, 2015.
DOI: 10.1007/978-3-319-24264-4_32

actions for individual entities considering the current properties and dynamics of transportation systems in order to improve the overall quality, performance, and safety. In this context, a control structure represents a general concept to describe a system of control agents used to exchange data, make decisions, and choose corresponding actions in a transportation network [31]. Model predictive control (MPC) is a particular useful control methodology for dynamic and complex systems, allowing in principle to use all available information [31]. However, the increased availability of information, possibly required cooperation, and negotiation between control agents may lead to high computational times [31] obstructing the application of real-time decision support. As a result, the transformation from conventional technology-driven ITS into a more multisource and multifunctional data-driven ITS must go hand in hand with the development of appropriate IT infrastructures and learning algorithms that support efficient control structures and control methodologies. That is, modern data-driven ITS aim to combine various data from different sources and apply efficient learning and optimization algorithms for achieving a higher visibility and an enhanced decision support. Especially in the big data era, an efficient collection and processing of large amounts of data will play a key role in ITS [35].

In this paper, we propose a framework to adopt multi-agent single-layer and multi-layer control structures [31] in a cloud environment in order to support large scale data-driven ITS based on MPC algorithms. To the best of our knowledge, the paper presents the first approach of utilizing the scalable nature of cloud environments for implementing high performance data-driven ITS. We see a lot of application potential for data-driven ITS in the domain of maritime shipping and especially in port areas such as with respect to inter-terminal transport (ITT) operations (see, e.g., [12,32,33]), which are highly affected by massive traffic volumes, traffic congestions, and pollution. Therefore, we discuss the contribution of cloud-based data-driven ITS to establish intelligent transport infrastructures and to enable smart traffic management and control. While MPC has been applied in the literature to manage cloud environments, such as with respect to dynamic resource allocation [36], research on cloud-based implementations of MPC structures does not exist so far. In this context, we discuss how computational requirements given by MPC structures can be efficiently satisfied in terms of costs and service quality.

The remainder of this paper is organized as follows. An overview on the purpose and application of ITS is given in Section 2, in particular focusing on port areas. In Section 3, we explain the use of MPC, control structures and cloud computing. The proposed framework and relevant components for MPC multi-agent single-layer and multi-layer control structures are presented in Section 4. Moreover, the section identifies basic requirements and specifies potential benefits of a cloud adoption. This includes a review of existing works aiming to combine ITS and cloud computing. Finally, conclusions and an outlook regarding future research are outlined in Section 5.

2   Intelligent Transportation Systems

Providing accurate traffic information and controlling traffic flows is considered as a major challenge for the involved public institutions and private companies leading to the rapid growth of ITS [13]. An ITS integrates advanced information and communication technologies as well as decision analytics to establish a real-time holistic and accurate transportation management system. The development of ITS varies among countries (see, e.g., [2]), but generally aims to control congestion, increase safety and mobility, and enhance the productivity and effectiveness of the transportation of persons and freight [10]. Obviously, the development of ITS is, to a large extent, linked to the development of advanced information and communication technologies. Underlying technologies are, for instance, global positioning systems (GPS), vehicular ad hoc networks (VANET) [22], wireless sensor networks (WSN), electronic road signs, video vehicle detection, and mobile phone technologies. In this sense, massive amounts of data may need to be integrated to get a holistic view on the current situation, to predict the behaviour of individuals, and to apply control mechanisms in order to achieve a preferable behaviour. This requires advanced methodologies and techniques for collecting, combining, and processing of data to gain information and knowledge for supporting decision making. In this context, El Faouzi et al. [13] provide a survey on data fusion techniques used to combine data from multiple sources in order to reach a better inference such as for advanced driver assistance, automatic incident detection/prevention, and traffic forecasting. Relevant data sources as well as some relevant technologies and processing/learning techniques are depicted in Fig. 1. Several applications can be implemented based on learning and optimization techniques such as real-time traffic control and driver assistant systems that support different actors and actuators in taking the right decisions. While ITS developments were primarily hardware-driven in the early days, today a main driver for the further development of ITS are mathematical models and decision-support systems as well as appropriate IT infrastructures and software components that support those systems [10].

Especially in port areas, the implementation of ITS becomes increasingly important for improving intermodal freight transports. It is increasingly difficult to further extend the transport capacity and improve the transport reliability, in

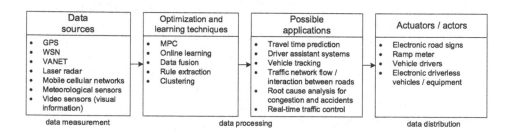

Fig. 1. Multisource and multifunctional data-driven ITS

particular under the constraints, uncertainties, and high degrees of complexity in which ports operate [19]. These conditions are further impacted by increasing trade volumes and larger vessels, changing production patterns, and growing transport volumes in urban areas surrounding the port, leading to traffic congestion, accidents, and environmental pollution [15,19]. An ITS could help to collect data from involved actors (e.g., terminal operators, drayage companies), combine it with external data (e.g., traffic control systems, weather forecasting) and apply decision analytics methods in order to increase the capacity of port transport networks and to improve hinterland connectivity. Thereby, port operators gain important information such as related to traffic patterns and are able to adopt operations and provide context-aware services to involved actors. This may include the prediction of travel times, electronic road tolling, vehicle location and advanced driver assistance to better control the flow of drayage trucks and other transportation means and to provide value-added services such as an online booking of available parking spaces. Moreover, it builds a foundation for fully automated transport with intelligent vehicles [27]. For port operators, cargo-related traffic data is further important to evaluate the performance of truck movements, to identify bottlenecks, and to determine the frequency, costs and environmental burden of recurring events, such as traffic congestion and/or accidents. Consequently, an ITS could not only be used to support operational decisions, but also tactical and strategic decisions such as related to investments in port equipment and infrastructure. In the port area, this is especially important for ITT operations (see, e.g., [12,32,33]), where intermodal freight transport activities carried out by multiple actors have to be coordinated between port facilities given internal data sources (e.g., position of trucks, container arrival) and external data sources (e.g., traffic situation, weather).

3   Model Predictive Control

MPC is an online optimization-based control approach that minimizes an objective function subject to constraints [28]. The idea is to construct models that describe the behaviour of transport networks and make predictions over a certain prediction horizon based on an ongoing measurement of the current state using sensor technology. Given those predictions, an MPC control agent determines at discrete control steps the actions to be chosen in order to obtain the best performance, such as in terms of costs, by solving a respective optimization problem considering desired goals, existing constraints, environmental factors, and existing forecast information [28]. The solution can be implemented by using actuators or based on information exchange among involved actors. However, the on-going data-intensive optimization carried out by multiple MPC control agents results in considerable computational requirements. The complexity is increased by the number of MPC control agents and by considering various sources of structured, semi-structured, and non-structured data (e.g., visual data, etc.) that need to be transformed and processed quickly. Consequently, not only a proper choice of an optimization technique is important for achieving real-time decision support [34], but also an efficient IT infrastructure supporting those computations.

In the recent two decades, several MPC approaches being applied in traffic networks have been proposed in the literature. Hegyi et al. [16] propose an adaptive MPC approach to optimally coordinate variable speed limits and ramp metering in order to reduce congestion. Karimi et al. [21] present an integrated approach for dynamic route guidance and ramp metering control. Negenborn et al. [30] outline a framework for modeling a transportation network into subsystems and apply multi-agent MPC to control the overall network. In [29], the work is extended by proposing a serial scheme to improve the coordination between agents. Simulation experiments show preferable properties of the serial coordination scheme compared to existing parallel schemes. Baskar et al. [4] propose an MPC approach to determine appropriate speed limits and lane allocations for a platoon of intelligent vehicles that communicate with roadside controllers. Zegeye et al. [34] evaluate an MPC control strategy for traffic and emission control. In this context, the authors also point out the extensive computational requirements of MPC optimizations. A related work of Frejo and Camacho [14] compares global and local MPC algorithms in a traffic network managed by ITS signals to control ramp metering and variable speed limits. In summary, recent works show that there are a lot of application potentials and challenges for managing and controlling traffic networks that are dependent on an efficient IT infrastructure.

In particular in large geographically distributed systems, as found in port traffic networks (see, e.g., [28]), consisting of a network of dynamically coupled sub-systems equipped with sensors and actuators, a multi-agent MPC approach becomes attractive whereby a network of control agents (CAs) solves a set of coupled sub-problems [8, 26]. That is, CAs control small subnetworks of the network, measure the state by accessing corresponding sensors and actuators, and aim to improve the behaviour of these subnetworks by considering constraints and costs in their decisions as well as the evolution of the subnetworks connected to their subnetwork with the aim of optimizing the overall network performance [31]. For a detailed overview on MPC the reader is referred to [7, 25].

A control structure defines the communication and interaction between control agents. A single-agent control structure exists when only one CA controls the whole network. Although this may lead to optimal solutions, the computational effort can be significantly high depending on the size and complexity of the overall network. Consequently, the use of multi-agent control structures enables the parallelization of computations by decomposing the overall system into smaller parts that are easier to solve. That being said, the selection of subnetworks and the respective number and computing capacity of CAs, besides the selected solution approach, has a significant impact on the performance of MPC in terms of computational time and solution quality. As more and more objects are equipped with sensors and actuators, such as vehicles and road infrastructure, it becomes increasingly challenging to store and process corresponding large amounts of data and find appropriate traffic strategies efficiently. Further, the amount of data can be characterized by huge fluctuations. Therefore, a static control structure with a fixed number of CAs does not seem appropriate. Instead, a dynamic structure would allow to extend and downsize the network according to the current workload. The latter implies that the size of subnetworks can be dynamically readjusted. During peak times, for instance, the number of CAs that constitute the control structure could be increased to allow a decomposition of the overall network into even smaller parts. Vice versa, the control structure might be reduced down to a single-agent control structure during off-peak times. Note that information exchange constraints may require a minimum number of control agents to be deployed so that it is not always possible to use a single-agent control structure. Further, the computational requirements of CAs might also vary depending on the size of the subnetworks and the current workload, which is usually not equally divided between CAs. A traditional IT infrastructure, which is necessary to host CAs, cannot be efficiently aligned to the actual demand and consequently is under and/or over-provisioned, meaning that it cannot cope with demand peaks or is not fully utilized and costly, respectively. Consequently, the potential performance benefits of dynamic control structures must be supported by flexible IT infrastructures not only for economical reasons, but also to be prepared to meet future big data challenges.

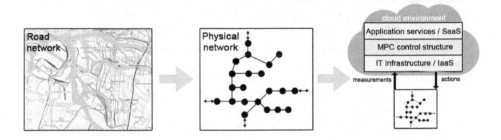

Fig. 2. Cloud-based MPC control structure

A flexible use of computing resources and services is offered by cloud service providers. Cloud computing represents a novel paradigm of providing virtualized computing resources and services through a network [3]. While providers of these resources and services aim to achieve economies of scale and cost reductions by optimizing resource utilization and energy consumption under consideration of guaranteed quality levels, consumers are mostly attracted by on-demand use options, scalability, flexible pricing schemes, and high degree of automation. The relevant service categories are: Infrastructure as a Service (IaaS), Platform as a Service (PaaS), and Software as a Service (SaaS). For a detailed overview on cloud computing the reader is referred to [3,17]. As depicted in Fig. 2, the adoption of a cloud solution shall support an efficient measurement and control of large scale physical networks based on the application of the MPC methodology. That is, cloud resources are provisioned on the IaaS layer in an on-demand fashion by considering the computational requirements of MPC control agents. Based on the implementation of the MPC control structure and other relevant services, such as for collecting traffic information, application services providing tools for collaboration and decision support can be implemented on the SaaS layer. In this regard, cloud consumers can be divided into two main groups: a group of people purchasing and provisioning cloud resources to implement application and decision support services, and a group of decision makers and actors that uses applications and decision support services on the SaaS layer to enhance logistics/traffic operations and collaboration.

4   Cloud-Based Multi-agent MPC Control Structures

Before the implementation of flexible multi-agent single-layer and multi-layer MPC control structures is further explained in Section 4.1 and Section 4.2, respectively, we describe characteristics of the overall cloud solution and provide an overview on related literature aiming to combine ITS and cloud computing. Regarding the above mentioned application scenarios for flexible control structure, we basically identify three essential requirements for IT-enabled MPC infrastructures.

1. *Horizontal and vertical scalability*: The number of computing nodes hosting CAs as well as the computing capacity (e.g., in terms of processor, memory, storage) need to be adjusted to the actual demand of applications in order to maintain performance during peak times and to reduce expenses at off-peak times. In our context, peak times may result from a large number of optimization jobs from multiple control agents at the same time or if the amount of data to be processed is considerably large and complex.
2. *Communication performance*: The communication bandwidth between CAs needs to be sufficient in order to support interactions such as cooperation and negotiation in real-time. Further, a stable network connecting sensors and actuators must be guaranteed.
3. *Costs*: The overall IT infrastructure needs to be cost-efficient while considering computational requirements and the utilization of computing resources.

Cloud IaaS offerings provide the highest autonomy and allow to flexibly configure and deploy computing resources, such as servers and storage systems, for building complete virtual IT infrastructures. Thereby, a dynamic control network can be implemented by hosting involved CAs on a set of interconnected virtual machines (VMs). CA applications may have different requirements, such as with regard to middleware. In [20], we propose an approach to automate and standardize the individual provisioning and deployment of highly scalable applications. Even more importantly, however, are the scaling options and corresponding usage-based pricing schemes of IaaS commercial offerings. Auto-scaling mechanisms, which automatically adopt the underlying cloud infrastructure according to current demand, support both horizontal and vertical scaling. The selection of cloud resources is not only dependent on the physical network to be controlled, but also on individual preferences on computational time and costs. Cloud service providers offer a variety of VM types that have a price per time unit and are characterized by their computing capacities in terms of processor, memory, and bandwidth capacity. In this context, we present a mathematical model and biased random-key genetic algorithm for decision support for selecting those cloud-based computing resources in [18]. Thus, individual requirements of control agents and individual preferences of decision makers in terms of costs and performance can be considered by the selection of appropriate computing resources that are dynamically adopted with regard to the actual demand. Our previous studies build a foundation for the implementation of preference-dependent and flexible cloud infrastructures supporting MPC control structures. A cloud-based infrastructure further builds the basis for PaaS, SaaS and mobile applications. Thus, a standard cloud-based development environment allows a unified implementation of additional means for traffic management that process and integrate the data as well as the allocation and distribution of gained information to certain decision makers and actors being involved in traffic networks. Due to the accessibility of a cloud solution, hardware systems and actors are able to communicate with the cloud environment from everywhere.

The use of cloud computing is also discussed in other works on ITS. Li et al. [24] propose a cloud-based traffic management system. However, the approach describes technologies used in different technology layers rather than explaining the actual distributed processing of data in the proposed traffic management system. In another work, the authors present an explicit approach to process floating car data for urban traffic surveillance with efficient BigTable[1] data management techniques and a MapReduce[2] implementation [23]. Alazawi et al. [1] propose a cloud-based disaster emergency response system based on VANET and mobile technologies. A similar but rather generic approach is presented in [6] facilitating VANET technologies and different communication technologies to combine cloud computing with ITS. It is surprising that the utilization of scalability options is not thematized in recent works nor the implementation of concrete mathematical methods to decompose optimization problems and parallelize computations. To handle large amounts of data and control complex systems in the future, however, it is important to propose novel approaches that consider concrete methods and scalability options. With our approach, we aim to trigger more research in this direction.

In this context, a multi-agent structure builds an essential basis for the parallelization of MPC computations in cloud environments. Each cloud-based CA implements an MPC algorithm to determine its actions in each control cycle. The MPC algorithm firstly measures the current state of the network by using advanced technologies such as GPS, video systems, laser radar, mobile cellular networks, ultrasonic and meterological sensors (see, e.g., [35]). Given this

---

[1] Refers to a high performance distributed storage system for managing structured data [9].

[2] Refers to a programming model that enables fast and simple data processing on large computing clusters [11].

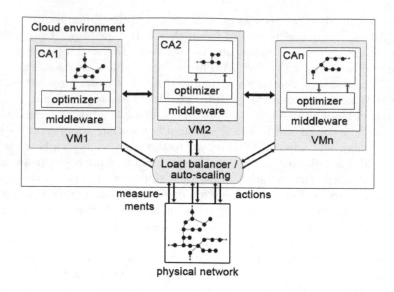

Fig. 3. Cloud-based multi-agent single-layer MPC

data, the actions that optimize the performance over the prediction horizon are determined by considering the dynamics of the whole network over the prediction horizon and constraints, such as in terms of actuator capabilities and initial state at the beginning of the cycle [31]. As indicated, the MPC optimization problem can be parallelized by decomposing the problem (e.g., by decoupling constraints, relaxing some of the state-update equations). That is, individual actions for sub-systems are determined by corresponding CAs that solve a decomposed problem and use a coordination step in each iteration to consider the dynamics of other subnetworks. Consequently, different decomposition techniques shall be available in the proposed framework (see [26]). A temporal Lagrangian decomposition, for instance, is used in [5] to decompose an MPC optimization problem of a power system. The decomposition of transport-related MPC optimization problems need to be further studied. In the following, we discuss how parallelized MPC computations are supported by cloud technologies.

4.1   Multi-agent Single-Layer MPC

In a cloud-based multi-agent single-layer control structure, each CA controls a part of the overall physical network, as depicted in Fig. 3. As the evolution of the subnetwork is influenced by other agents, a communication link between CAs must exist to exchange information on the evolution of the interconnections. Each CA is hosted on a VM equipped with appropriate processing, memory and storage capacities that will be adopted based on its current computational requirements and the size of the subnetwork. Vertical scaling allows a reduction of computational time and thus support real-time decision making scenarios. The

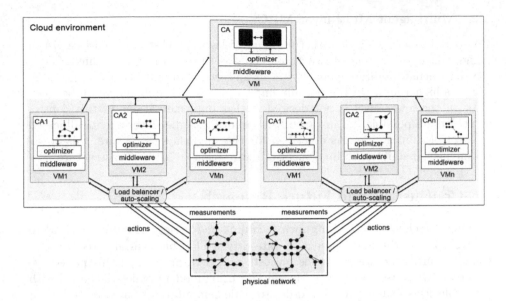

Fig. 4. Cloud-based multi-agent multi-layer MPC

amount of storage capacity corresponds to the amount of collected data and consequently increases over time. A distributed storage system is used for efficiently managing large amounts of data from different sources. Further, deployment processes consider individual middleware requirements, for instance, based on the used sensor and actuator technologies (see [20]).

To find actions that lead to an overall optimal performance, CAs determine actions in several iterations of local problem solving and coordination with neighboring agents. The latter requires an efficient communication link between neighboring agents. To reduce the latency or communication delays between neighboring agents, it would be beneficial to host the VMs in the same location, ideally on the same physical computing resource or in the same server rack, which could be considered during the deployment of CA VMs corresponding to the physical network interconnections.

Horizontal scaling and load balancing is used to distribute computations among a network of VMs. The number of VMs must be determined based on the structure and complexity of the observed physical network as well as on individual preferences of decision makers in terms of cost and performance. A low budget solution, for instance, may use fewer VMs or less equipped VMs leading to a lower computational performance (see [18]). As the amount of data from the subnetworks highly fluctuates, a load balancer and auto-scaling mechanism are used to reorganise the decomposition of the physical network and to automatically assign virtual computing resources.

4.2 Multi-agent Multi-layer MPC

Compared to a single-layer structure, a multi-layer MPC structure uses a CA in a higher layer of the control structure to control the lower layer. The higher layer CA may include additional penalty terms and/or constraints [31]. As depicted in Fig. 4, a higher level CA is especially important when a communication between CAs on the lower level is not desired. Other implementations of this control structure are possible, for instance, with multiple higher layer agents allocated to a set of subnetworks. As described for the single-layer structure, this opens up further possibilities to implement a highly scalable MPC infrastructure.

5 Conclusions and Future Research

Advanced technologies and a growing volume and variety of data may lead to a revolution in the development of data-driven ITS, but will also require efficient IT infrastructures in terms of costs and performance. In this paper, we propose a framework for a cloud-based ITS using model predictive control with a flexible size of subnetworks in order to scale computations based on a decomposition technique. The main purpose of the cloud-based ITS is to control large geographically distributed systems such as traffic networks. Nevertheless, the cloud-based system can be extended by additional functionality on the PaaS and SaaS layer, for instance, to support the allocation and distribution of information among actors being involved in transport operations. We explain the benefits of a cloud solution, especially for multi-agent single-layer and multi-layer MPC control structures, in terms of horizontal and vertical scalability, communication performance, and costs. More importantly, the paper presents incipient stages of utilizing scalability options of cloud infrastructures for parallel computing and storage of large amounts of data supporting real-time decision making in a big data era. So far, this important aspect has not been considered in recent works and consequently requires further research. To further evaluate our approach, we strive to perform simulations with realistic data and a concrete implementation of an MPC optimization problem using a decomposition technique such as Lagrangian decomposition. CloudSim, a framework for simulation of cloud infrastructures, will be used to further evaluate the efficiency of our approach by implementing it in a scalable cloud infrastructure.

References

1. Alazawi, Z., Altowaijri, S., Mehmood, R., Abdljabar, M.B.: Intelligent disaster management system based on cloud-enabled vehicular networks. In: Proceedings of the IEEE 11th International Conference on ITS Telecommunications (ITST 2011), St. Petersburg, Russia, pp. 361–368 (2011)
2. An, S.H., Lee, B.H., Shin, D.R.: A survey of intelligent transportation systems. In: Proceedings of the IEEE 3rd International Conference on Computational Intelligence, Communication Systems and Networks (CICSyN 2011), Bali, Indonesia, pp. 332–337 (2011)

3. Armbrust, M., Fox, A., Griffith, R., Joseph, A.D., Katz, R., Konwinski, A., Lee, G., Patterson, D., Rabkin, A., Stoica, I., et al.: A view of cloud computing. Communications of the ACM **53**(4), 50–58 (2010)

4. Baskar, L.D., De Schutter, B., Hellendoorn, H.: Model-based predictive traffic control for intelligent vehicles: dynamic speed limits and dynamic lane allocation. In: Proceedings of the IEEE Intelligent Vehicles Symposium (IV 2008), pp. 174–179. IEEE, Eindhoven (2008)

5. Beccuti, A.G., Geyer, T., Morari, M.: Temporal lagrangian decomposition of model predictive control for hybrid systems. In: Proceedings of the IEEE 43rd Conference on Decision and Control (CDC 2004), Paradise Island, Bahamas, pp. 2509–2514 (2004)

6. Bitam, S., Mellouk, A.: ITS-cloud: cloud computing for intelligent transportation system. In: Proceedings of the IEEE Communications Software, Services and Multimedia Symposium (Globecom 2012), Anaheim, CA, USA, pp. 2054–2059 (2012)

7. Camacho, E.F., Bordons Alba, C.: Model predictive control, 2nd edn. Springer (2013)

8. Camponogara, E., De Oliveira, L.B.: Distributed optimization for model predictive control of linear-dynamic networks. IEEE Transactions on Systems, Man and Cybernetics, Part A: Systems and Humans **39**(6), 1331–1338 (2009)

9. Chang, F., Dean, J., Ghemawat, S., Hsieh, W.C., Wallach, D.A., Burrows, M., Chandra, T., Fikes, A., Gruber, R.E.: Bigtable: A distributed storage system for structured data. ACM Transactions on Computer Systems **26**(2), 1–26 (2008)

10. Crainic, T.G., Gendreau, M., Potvin, J.Y.: Intelligent freight-transportation systems: Assessment and the contribution of operations research. Transportation Research Part C: Emerging Technologies **17**(6), 541–557 (2009)

11. Dean, J., Ghemawat, S.: MapReduce: simplified data processing on large clusters. Communications of the ACM **51**(1), 107–113 (2008)

12. Duinkerken, M.B., Dekker, R., Kurstjens, S.T.G.L., Ottjes, J.A., Dellaert, N.P.: Comparing transportation systems for inter-terminal transport at the Maasvlakte container terminals. OR Spectrum **28**(4), 469–493 (2006)

13. Faouzi, N.E.E., Leung, H., Kurian, A.: Data fusion in intelligent transportation systems: Progress and challenges – a survey. Information Fusion **12**(1), 4–10 (2011)

14. Frejo, J.R.D., Camacho, E.F.: Global versus local MPC algorithms in freeway traffic control with ramp metering and variable speed limits. IEEE Transactions on Intelligent Transportation Systems **13**(4), 1556–1565 (2012)

15. Giuliano, G., O'Brien, T.: Reducing port-related truck emissions: the terminal gate appointment system at the ports of Los Angeles and Long Beach. Transportation Research Part D: Transport and Environment **12**(7), 460–473 (2007)

16. Hegyi, A., De Schutter, B., Hellendoorn, H., Van Den Boom, T.: Optimal coordination of ramp metering and variable speed control - an MPC approach. In: Proceedings of the American Control Conference (ACC 2002), Anchorage, AK, USA, pp. 3600–3605 (2002)

17. Heilig, L., Voß, S.: A scientometric analysis of cloud computing literature. IEEE Transactions on Cloud Computing **2**(3), 266–278 (2014)

18. Heilig, L., Lalla-Ruiz, E., Voß, S.: A biased random-key genetic algorithm for the cloud resource management problem. In: Ochoa, G., Chicano, F. (eds.) EvoCOP 2015. LNCS, vol. 9026, pp. 1–12. Springer, Heidelberg (2015)

19. Heilig, L., Voß, S.: Information systems in seaports: A categorization and overview. Information Technology and Management (to appear, 2015)

20. Heilig, L., Voß, S., Wulfken, L.: Building clouds: an integrative approach for an automated deployment of elastic cloud services. In: Chang, V., Walters, R., Wills, G. (eds.) Delivery and Adoption of Cloud Computing Services in Contemporary Organizations. IGI Global (to appear, 2015)
21. Karimi, A., Hegyi, A., De Schutter, B., Hellendoorn, J., Middelham, F.: Integrated model predictive control of dynamic route guidance information systems and ramp metering. In: Proceedings of the IEEE 7th International Conference on Intelligent Transportation Systems (ITSC 2004), Washington, DC, USA, pp. 491–496 (2004)
22. Li, F., Wang, Y.: Routing in vehicular ad hoc networks: A survey. IEEE Vehicular Technology Magazine **2**(2), 12–22 (2007)
23. Li, Q., Zhang, T., Yu, Y.: Using cloud computing to process intensive floating car data for urban traffic surveillance. International Journal of Geographical Information Science **25**(8), 1303–1322 (2011)
24. Li, Z., Chen, C., Wang, K.: Cloud computing for agent-based urban transportation systems. IEEE Intelligent Systems **26**(1), 73–79 (2011)
25. Maciejowski, J.M.: Predictive control with constraints. Pearson Education, Essex (2002)
26. Maestre, J.M., Negenborn, R.R. (eds.): Distributed Model Predictive Control Made Easy. Springer, Dordrecht (2014)
27. McGinley, K.: Preparing port container terminals for the future: making the most of intelligent transport systems (ITS). In: Urban Transport XX, vol. 138, pp. 419–427 (2014)
28. Nabais, J.L., Negenborn, R.R., Botto, M.A.: A novel predictive control based framework for optimizing intermodal container terminal operations. In: Hu, H., Shi, X., Stahlbock, R., Voß, S. (eds.) ICCL 2012. LNCS, vol. 7555, pp. 53–71. Springer, Heidelberg (2012)
29. Negenborn, R.R., De Schutter, B., Hellendoorn, J.: Multi-agent model predictive control for transportation networks: Serial versus parallel schemes. Engineering Applications of Artificial Intelligence **21**, 353–366 (2008)
30. Negenborn, R.R., De Schutter, B., Hellendoorn, H.: Multi-agent model predictive control of transportation networks. In: Proceedings of the IEEE International Conference on Networking, Sensing and Control (ICNSC 2006), Fort Lauderdale, FL, USA, pp. 296–301 (2006)
31. Negenborn, R.R., Hellendoorn, H.: Intelligence in transportation infrastructures via model-based predictive control. In: Negenborn, R.R., Lukszo, Z., Hellendoorn, H. (eds.) Intelligent Infrastructures, pp. 3–24. Springer (2010)
32. Nieuwkoop, F., Corman, F., Negenborn, R., Duinkerken, M., van Schuylenburg, M., Lodewijks, G.: Decision support for vehicle configuration determination in inter terminal transport system design. In: Proceedings of the IEEE International Conference on Networking. Sensing and Control (ICNSC 2014), Miami, FL, USA, pp. 613–618 (2014)
33. Tierney, K., Voß, S., Stahlbock, R.: A mathematical model of inter-terminal transportation. European Journal of Operational Research **235**(2), 448–460 (2014)

34. Zegeye, S.K., De Schutter, B., Hellendoorn, H., Breunesse, E.: Reduction of travel times and traffic emissions using model predictive control. In: Proceedings of the American Control Conference (ACC 2009), pp. 5392–5397. IEEE, St. Louis (2009)
35. Zhang, J., Wang, F.Y., Wang, K., Lin, W.H., Xu, X., Chen, C.: Data-driven intelligent transportation systems: A survey. IEEE Transactions on Intelligent Transportation Systems **12**(4), 1624–1639 (2011)
36. Zhang, Q., Zhu, Q., Boutaba, R.: Dynamic resource allocation for spot markets in cloud computing environments. In: Proceedings of the IEEE 4th International Conference Utility and Cloud Computing (UCC 2011), pp. 178–185. IEEE (2011)

Cooperative Relations Among Intermodal Hubs and Transport Providers at Freight Networks Using an MPC Approach

João Lemos Nabais[1,4](✉), Rudy R. Negenborn[2], Rafael Carmona-Benítez[3], and Miguel Ayala Botto[4]

[1] IDMEC/LAETA, School of Business Administration,
Polytechnical Institute of Setúbal, Setúbal, Portugal
joao.nabais@esce.ips.pt
[2] Department of Maritime and Transport Technology,
Delft University of Technology, Delft, The Netherlands
r.r.negenborn@tudelft.nl
[3] School of Business and Economics,
Universidad Anáhuac México Norte, Mexico City, Mexico
rafael.carmona@anahuac.mx
[4] IDMEC/LAETA, Instituto Superior Técnico,
Universidade de Lisboa, Lisbon, Portugal
ayalabotto@tecnico.ulisboa.pt

Abstract. Freight networks are more exposed to unforeseen events leading to delays compromising the delivery of cargo on time. Cooperation among different parties present at freight networks are required to accommodate the occurrence of delays. Cargo assignment to the available transport capacity at the terminal is addressed using a Model Predictive Control approach in this paper, taking into consideration the final destination and the remaining time until due time of cargo. A cooperative framework for transport providers and intermodal hubs is proposed in this paper. The cooperation is based on information exchange regarding the amount of cargo at risk of not reaching the destination on time. The terminal searches for a faster connection at the terminal to allocate the cargo at risk such that the final destination is reached on time. The proposed heuristic is a step towards sustainable and synchromodal transportation networks. Simulation experiments illustrate the validity of these statements.

Keywords: Intermodal container terminals · Freight networks · Model predictive control · Sustainable modal split

1 Introduction

Intermodal hubs are part of freight transportation networks whose main objective is to deliver cargo at the agreed time, and at the agreed location [1,2].

J.L. Nabais—This work was supported by FCT, through IDMEC, under LAETA, project UID/EMS/50022/2013.

© Springer International Publishing Switzerland 2015
F. Corman et al. (Eds.): ICCL 2015, LNCS 9335, pp. 478–494, 2015.
DOI: 10.1007/978-3-319-24264-4_33

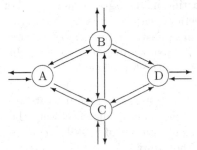

Fig. 1. Intermodal freight network. Circles represent hubs and transport connections are indicated by arrows.

The expected increase in transported container volume will cause the existent infrastructure to reach its limits. In addition, the capacity of deep sea vessels has grown from $1,500$ TEU in 1980 to about $20,000$ TEU at present. This increase in vessel sizes leads to an increase in peak call sizes at terminals. Handling these larger volumes of arriving load takes a significant amount of time and moreover delays other terminal operations. As a consequence, transit times of containers become more delayed. This on its turn affects the connecting transportation means (barge, train and truck), which therefore have to face long waiting times at terminals: in Rotterdam trucks may have to wait up to 6 hours and barges have been reported to wait between 24 and up to 72 hours [3].

When looking into detail at the different economical actors present in freight networks [4], from a control perspective, two main classes of actors appear: 1) the hubs where cargo is stored and can face a transport modality switch towards the final destination and 2) the transport operators which offer transport capacity in different modalities between the existing hubs. Although all actors contribute to the main objective each one has its own objectives and conflicting objectives can be present. A freight network can be represented by a graph $\mathcal{G} = (\mathcal{V}, \mathcal{E})$ [5] where the nodes $\mathcal{V}$ represent intermodal hubs and the links $\mathcal{E}$ represent transport connections made available by transport providers (Fig. 1). Cargo can be transported over freight networks according to the following paradigms: i) merchant haulage in which the shipper or forwarder bears the responsibility; ii) carrier haulage in which the transport provider organizes the transport; and iii) terminal haulage in which the terminal co-determines the transport. Cargo associated to merchant and carrier haulage waits at the terminal for some transport connection to pick it up towards the final destination. The intermodal hub acts for this type of cargo as a warehouse. For cargo in terminal haulage the terminal has the capability to co-assign it to transport connections available at the terminal in accordance to the delivery time and destination.

Cooperation methodologies can be developed at intermodal hubs for the benefit of either the intermodal hub and the transport provider towards the so-called synchromodal transportation [6]. In this work, freight network performance is evaluated taking the client perspective, cargo should be delivered at the right time, on the agreed location in the agreed quantity. For the transport provider, due to delays on connections, cargo can be at risk of not reaching the final destination on time requiring a faster connection to respect due time. Sharing this information with the hub, a suitable connection can be found using a larger set of available connections. For the hub there will be an increase in the throughput and the development of partnerships with transport providers.

A state-space model for cargo evolution over time at intermodal hubs is proposed in this paper. The model follows closely the structural layout of the intermodal hub, in terms of number of possible connections being served at the hub at the same time. The sample time of the model can be chosen accordingly to capture the meaningful arrival and departure pattern of transport connections at the hub, typically measured in hours. For that reason the model is time-invariant and not time varying as in [7]. This makes the model suitable for real-time decisions at the operational level. In particular, the model is used to make predictions regarding over-due cargo. Based on this model, a framework for cooperative relations between intermodal hubs and transport providers is proposed in this paper. Cargo assignment at the hub is addressed using a Model Predictive Control (MPC) approach. MPC has shown successful applications in the process industry [8], and is now gaining increasing attention in fields like supply chains [9], power networks [10], water distribution networks [11], and freight networks [12]. Using mathematical models it is possible to make predictions about the future behavior of cargo at intermodal hubs. In freight networks, costs can be associated to flows and quantities of stored commodities. The MPC controller can determine which actions have to be chosen in order to obtain the best performance. At each time step the controller first obtains the current state of the system it controls. Then, it formulates an optimization problem, using the desired goals, existing constraints, disturbances and prediction information if available.

This paper is organized as follows. Section 2 proposes a state-space model to describe cargo evolution over time at intermodal hubs. Operations management at intermodal hubs in respect to cargo assignment is addressed in Section 3.1. The cooperative framework between intermodal hubs and transport providers is proposed in Section 3.2. The performance of the proposed approach is tested through numerical simulations in Section 4. In Section 5 conclusions are drawn and future research topics are indicated.

2 Intermodal Hub Modeling

Intermodal hubs are part of freight networks and linked through connections offered by transport providers (see Fig. 1). The amount of cargo at an intermodal freight hub changes due to cargo arrivals and cargo departures. A cargo balance at the hub is able to capture this behavior (see Fig. 2). An intermodal freight hub can be a container terminal or a distribution center. In intermodal hubs, decisions regarding cargo assignment to transport connections that will deliver the cargo at a destination hub in a transport network depend on cargo properties. Common cargo properties are: destination, remaining time until due time, weight, volume, dimension, safety hazard and temperature, among others. It is assumed that cargo in intermodal hubs is categorized using three main properties:

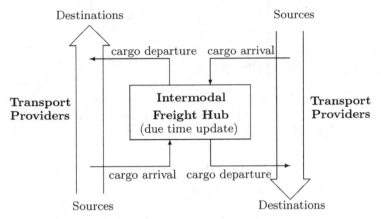

Fig. 2. Cargo balance at an intermodal hub

Cargo Destination: n_{de} is the number of available destinations in the freight network of which the intermodal hub is part. As final destination it is considered the hub location close to the client, such that private information regarding the client is protected. This is a fixed property;

Cargo Type: n_{ct} is the number of different cargo types at the hub, for example, dry and liquid bulk (usually measured in tons), containers (measured in TEU) and general cargo (measured in tons or volume). This is a fixed property;

Remaining Time Until Due Time: n_{dt} is used to include time as a distinguishing factor between cargo that has the same destination. n_{dt} is the number of time steps until due time, Typically measured in hours. This is a time varying property. For the sake of readability, from now on this property will be mentioned as due time.

The number of fixed properties is given by $n_{fp} = n_{ct}n_{de}$. The complete set of commodities is given by n_{fp}, and for each commodity a distinction is made in respect to due time.

The dynamics of an intermodal hub is captured using a state-space representation in this paper. A state-space representation uses a state-space vector to represent the state of the intermodal hub. At each time step k, the state-space vector is updated according to the current state-space vector value, the cargo assigned to transport connections, and the cargo arrivals over a time step. A time step length can be chosen properly for each application, usually measured in hours. With this model representation it is possible to create a prediction of the cargo evolution over time at the hub. For each commodity i ($i = 1, \ldots, n_{fp}$)

a state-space vector $\mathbf{x}_i$ is defined. This vector is used for creating the hub state-space vector $\mathbf{x}$,

$$\mathbf{x}_i(k) = \begin{bmatrix} x^{i1}(k) \\ \vdots \\ x^{ij}(k) \\ \vdots \\ x^{in_{\mathrm{dt}_i}}(k) \end{bmatrix}, \mathbf{x}(k) = \begin{bmatrix} \mathbf{x}_1(k) \\ \mathbf{x}_2(k) \\ \vdots \\ \mathbf{x}_{n_{\mathrm{fp}}}(k) \end{bmatrix}, \tag{1}$$

where $x^{ij}(k)$ represents the amount of cargo of commodity i and due time j at time step k, n_{dt_i} is the number of different due times considered for commodity i. The state-space dimension is given by

$$n_{\mathrm{x}} = \sum_{i=1}^{n_{\mathrm{fp}}} n_{\mathrm{dt}_i}. \tag{2}$$

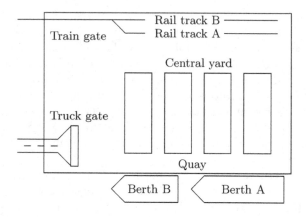

Fig. 3. Structural layout of a generic intermodal container terminal

The control action is the cargo assigned to different transport connections. In contrast with [7], the proposed model follows the structural layout of the hub. This means that the maximum number of transport connections at the terminal is known. In the case of the intermodal terminal represented in Fig. 3, there are a maximum of 5 transport connections available; two on barge modality, two on train modality and one on truck modality. So, for each connection m at the intermodal hub the cargo quantity u^{ij} that is going to be assigned per commodity i and due time j is determined. The control action associated to connection m is denoted by $\mathbf{u}_m$, and all control actions per connection are merged to form the intermodal hub control action vector $\mathbf{u}$,

$$\mathbf{u}_m = \begin{bmatrix} u^{11}(k) \\ \vdots \\ u^{ij}(k) \\ \vdots \\ n^{n_{\mathrm{fp}}n_{\mathrm{dt,fp}}}(k) \end{bmatrix}, \qquad \mathbf{u} = \begin{bmatrix} \mathbf{u}_1(k) \\ \mathbf{u}_2(k) \\ \vdots \\ \mathbf{u}_{n_\mathrm{m}}(k) \end{bmatrix}, \tag{3}$$

where n_m is the number of available transport connections at the intermodal hub, and $n_{\mathrm{dt,fp}} = n_{\mathrm{dt}_{n_\mathrm{fp}}}$ is the number of due times for commodity n_fp. For each available connection there are n_x decision variables. The control action dimension is $n_\mathrm{u} = n_\mathrm{x}n_\mathrm{m}$. It is usual in freight networks to relate a due time to cargo. If cargo is not delivered on-time then contractual penalties will be triggered. Over-due cargo $\mathbf{x}_\mathrm{od}$, defined as the amount of cargo of commodity i that does not reach the final destination on time, can be used as an indicator of client satisfaction and freight network performance. The increment on over-due cargo for commodity i at each time step is the difference between the amount of cargo of commodity i with a due time of one time step at the terminal and the amount of cargo of commodity i with a due time of one time step assigned to the transport connections

$$\Delta\mathbf{x}_\mathrm{od}(k) = \mathbf{A}_\mathrm{dt}\mathbf{x}(k) - \mathbf{B}_\mathrm{dt}\mathbf{u}(k), \tag{4}$$

where the matrix pair $\mathbf{A}_\mathrm{dt}$, $\mathbf{B}_\mathrm{dt}$ is constant. The over-due cargo is

$$\mathbf{x}_\mathrm{od}(k) = \sum_{i=1}^{k} \Delta\mathbf{x}_\mathrm{od}(k). \tag{5}$$

Consider the state-space vector for the over-due cargo over time:

$$\mathbf{x}_\mathrm{od}(k) = \begin{bmatrix} x_{\mathrm{od},1}(k) \\ \vdots \\ x_{\mathrm{od},n_\mathrm{fp}}(k) \end{bmatrix}. \tag{6}$$

The augmented state-space vector for the node is given by $\mathbf{x}_\mathrm{ag}(k) = \left[\mathbf{x}^\mathrm{T}(k)\ \mathbf{x}_\mathrm{od}^\mathrm{T}(k)\right]^\mathrm{T}$. The state-space model is based on cargo volume conservation and on due time update and is given by

$$\mathbf{x}_\mathrm{ag}(k+1) = \mathbf{A}\mathbf{x}_\mathrm{ag}(k) + \mathbf{B}_\mathrm{u}\mathbf{u}(k) + \mathbf{B}_\mathrm{d}\mathbf{d}(k) \tag{7}$$
$$\mathbf{y}(k) = \mathbf{x}_\mathrm{ag}(k) \tag{8}$$
$$\mathbf{x}_\mathrm{ag}(k) \geq \mathbf{0}, \tag{9}$$

where $\mathbf{y}$ is the cargo amount per commodity, matrices $\mathbf{A}$, $\mathbf{B}_\mathrm{u}$, and $\mathbf{B}_\mathrm{d}$ are the state-space matrices.

3   Operations Management at Intermodal Hubs

Operations management at a hub is addressed using a MPC approach. The solution to the optimization problem, formulated by the MPC controller, is an optimal sequence of control actions over the prediction horizon that gives the best predicted performance. The controller implements only the component corresponding to the first time step until the beginning of the next time step, in a receding horizon fashion. At the next time step the MPC controller searches for the solution of a new optimization problem, i.e., by obtaining new information about the current state, available prediction information, and goals.

3.1   MPC Formulation Cargo Assignment at the Hub

The problem to solve is stated from the intermodal hub perspective as follows:

At each time step k, given a known transport capacity per transport modality and destination, how should the existing cargo at the intermodal hub be assigned to the transport capacity available, taking into account that:

1. *cargo should be delivered on time at the agreed location and;*
2. *sustainable transport modalities are preferable options.*

The intermodal hub dynamics are described by model (7)–(9). The cost function of the MPC controller is composed of two components:

Commodity and Due Time: different penalties can be introduced for the combined pair commodity/due time,

$$f_x(\mathbf{x}_{ag}(k), \mathbf{u}(k)) = \mathbf{q}_x^T(k) \left[\mathbf{x}_{ag}(k) - \mathbf{P}_{xu}\mathbf{u}(k) \right], \tag{10}$$

where $\mathbf{q}_x^T(k)$ is a time-varying penalty on the states to allow different priorities over time and $\mathbf{P}_{xu}$ is the projection from the control action space into the state space;

Transport Modality Used: different modalities can be distinguished according to their environmental impact,

$$f_m(\mathbf{u}(k)) = \mathbf{q}_m^T(k)\mathbf{P}_{mu}\mathbf{u}(k), \tag{11}$$

where $\mathbf{q}_m^T(k)$ is a time-varying penalty on the connection to allow different priorities over time and $\mathbf{P}_{mu}$ is the projection matrix from the control action-space into the current connection space with dimension $n_m \times n_u$.

For a prediction horizon N_p the cost function is then defined as,

$$J(\tilde{\mathbf{x}}_{ag,k}, \tilde{\mathbf{u}}_k) = \sum_{l=0}^{N_p-1} f_x(\mathbf{x}_{ag}(k+l), \mathbf{u}(k+l)) + f_m(\mathbf{u}(k+l)) \tag{12}$$

where $\tilde{\mathbf{x}}_{ag,k}$ is the vector composed of the state-space vectors for each time step over the prediction horizon $\left[\mathbf{x}_{ag}^T(k), \ldots, \mathbf{x}_{ag}^T(k+N_p-1) \right]^T$, and $\tilde{\mathbf{u}}_k$ is the vector composed of the control action vectors for each time step over the prediction horizon $\left[\mathbf{u}^{\mathrm{T}}(k), \ldots, \mathbf{u}^{\mathrm{T}}(k + N_{\mathrm{p}} - 1)\right]^{\mathrm{T}}$. The MPC problem for a sustainable transport modal split at the intermodal hub can now be stated as:

$$\min_{\tilde{\mathbf{u}}_k} \ J(\tilde{\mathbf{x}}_{\mathrm{ag},k}, \tilde{\mathbf{u}}_k) \tag{13}$$

$$\text{subject to} \ \ \mathbf{x}_{\mathrm{ag}}(k+1+l) = \mathbf{A}\mathbf{x}_{\mathrm{ag}}(k+l) + \mathbf{B}_{\mathrm{u}}\mathbf{u}(k+l) + \mathbf{B}_{\mathrm{d}}\mathbf{d}(k+l) \tag{14}$$

$$\mathbf{y}(k+l) = \mathbf{x}_{\mathrm{ag}}(k+l), \quad l = 0, \ldots, N_{\mathrm{p}} - 1 \tag{15}$$

$$\mathbf{x}_{\mathrm{ag}}(k+l) \geq \mathbf{0} \tag{16}$$

$$\mathbf{u}(k+l) \geq \mathbf{0} \tag{17}$$

$$\mathbf{P}_{\mathrm{mu}}\mathbf{u}(k+l) \leq \mathbf{u}_{\max}(k+l) \tag{18}$$

$$\mathbf{P}_{\mathrm{xu}}\mathbf{u}(k+l) \leq \mathbf{x}_{\mathrm{ag}}(k+l) \tag{19}$$

$$\mathbf{u}(k+l) \leq \mathbf{u}_{\mathrm{adm}}(k+l) \tag{20}$$

where $\mathbf{u}_{\max}$ is the available transport capacity with dimension n_{m}, $\mathbf{u}_{\mathrm{adm}}$ contains the maximum admissible cargo capacity for each commodity and due time for all transport connections. Constraints (16)–(20) are introduced to represent the assumptions made on the hub behavior: storage quantities are always positive according to constraint (16); constraint (17) imposes that only loading operation is possible; the transport capacity per connection and schedule is bounded through (18); control actions can only assign cargo available at the hub, which is imposed by constraint (19); correct cargo assignment with respect to commodity and due time is imposed using constraint (20).

3.2   Cooperation Between Hubs and Transport Provider

It is assumed that both the hub and transport providers are willing to cooperate: transport providers can reduce the amount of over-due cargo and the hub increases the throughput. The cooperative relation between the hub and transport providers is based on selective information exchange: i) the transport provider p shares the amount of cargo at risk of not being delivered on time $\mathbf{x}_{\mathrm{ri}}^{p}$ (per commodity and due time), after ii) the hub informs the transport provider if a faster connection can be used at the hub to accommodate the transport delay.

The transport provider whenever arriving at the terminal (or prior to the arrival) announces:

- the available transport capacity per commodity according to the future route;
- the unload operation demands;
- the amount of cargo that is in risk of not being delivered on-time to the final destination.

The hub having access to updated information about the available transport capacity and cargo at risk proceeds with the cooperative relation, which is composed of two stages (see Algorithm 1):

Algorithm 1. Cooperative relation between hub and transport provider

---
1: **for** $k = 1 \rightarrow k_{\text{end}}$ **do**
2:     transport connection p announces to the terminal:
                i) available transport capacity
                ii) unload operations demand
                iii) cargo in danger of not being delivered on-time $\mathbf{x}_{\text{ri}}^p$
3:         hub determines $\tilde{\mathbf{u}}_k^0$ for problem (13)–(20) and the over-due cargo $\tilde{\mathbf{x}}_{\text{od}}^0$
4:         hub sets accepted cargo $\mathbf{x}_{\text{ac}}^0$ equal to cargo at risk $\mathbf{x}_{\text{ri}}^p$ from the transport provider
5:         **if** $\mathbf{x}_{\text{ac}}^0 > \delta_{\text{min}}$ **then**
6:             hub sets $l = 1$
7:             hub determines the optimal sequence $\tilde{\mathbf{u}}_k^l$ for problem (13)–(20) using $\mathbf{x}_{\text{ac}}^{l-1}$
8:             hub determines the amount of over-due cargo $\tilde{\mathbf{x}}_{\text{od}}^l$
9:             **while** $(\tilde{\mathbf{x}}_{\text{ac}}^{l-1} > \delta_{\text{min}})$ and $(\tilde{\mathbf{x}}_{\text{od}}^0 < \tilde{\mathbf{x}}_{\text{od}}^l)$ **do**
10:                 hub updates the amount of accepted cargo $\mathbf{x}_{\text{ac}}^l$ using (21)
11:                 hub determines optimal sequence $\tilde{\mathbf{u}}_k^{l+1}$ for problem (13)–(20) using $\mathbf{x}_{\text{ac}}^l$
12:                 hub determines the amount of over-due cargo $\tilde{\mathbf{x}}_{\text{od}}^{l+1}$
13:                 $l = l + 1$
14:             **end while**
15:         **end if**
16:         hub shares the accepted cargo $\mathbf{x}_{\text{ac}}^{l-1}$ with the transport provider
17:         disturbance $\mathbf{d}$ is updated in accordance to accepted cargo $\mathbf{x}_{\text{ac}}^{l-1}$
18:         state of the hub $\tilde{\mathbf{x}}_{\text{ag}}$ is updated using (7)–(9)
19: **end for**

---

first stage: solves the cargo assignment problem (13)–(20) for the cargo located at the hub. From the optimal sequence $\tilde{\mathbf{u}}_k^0$ the hub determines the amount of over-due cargo $\tilde{\mathbf{x}}_{\text{od}}^0$ using model (7)–(9) setting the over-due cargo to zero. The value of $\tilde{\mathbf{x}}_{\text{od}}$ is used as a performance measure. The hub starts by accepting all cargo at risk from the transport provider, $\mathbf{x}_{\text{ac}}^0 = \mathbf{x}_{\text{ri}}^p$, where $\mathbf{x}_{\text{ac}}^0$ is the initial accepted cargo by the hub. Whenever $\mathbf{x}_{\text{ac}}^0$ is positive the hub proceeds to the second stage looking for a connection to allocate the accepted cargo.

second stage: the hub solves the cargo assignment problem (13)–(20) including the accepted cargo $\mathbf{x}_{\text{ac}}^0$ in the disturbance vector $\mathbf{d}$. The solution found $\tilde{\mathbf{u}}_k^l$ is used to determine the over-due cargo $\tilde{\mathbf{x}}_{\text{od}}^l$, where $l = 1, 2, 3, \ldots$ is the iteration index. The amount of over-due cargo $\tilde{\mathbf{x}}_{\text{od}}^l$ is compared with the amount of over-due cargo from the first stage $\tilde{\mathbf{x}}_{\text{od}}^0$: i) if an equal or lower amount of over-due cargo is achieved then the hub unloads from the transport connection the cargo corresponding to the accepted cargo $\mathbf{x}_{\text{ac}}^0$ into the terminal, ii) else in case of a higher amount of over-due cargo, the hub updates the accepted cargo using

$$\mathbf{x}_{\text{ac}}^l = \mathbf{x}_{\text{ac}}^{l-1} \beta, \tag{21}$$

with $0 < \beta < 1$. This stage proceeds until over-due cargo $\tilde{\mathbf{x}}_{\text{od}}^l$ is lower or equal to the initial over-due cargo $\tilde{\mathbf{x}}_{\text{od}}^0$ or the accepted cargo $\mathbf{x}_{\text{ac}}^l$ is smaller than a threshold δ_{min} close to zero.

4   Numerical Experiments

4.1   Setup

Consider the intermodal container terminal A integrated in a transport network composed of 4 intermodal container terminals as illustrated in Fig. 1. The structural layout of the container terminals has been inspired in the case study presented in [13]. The terminal offers three transport modalities: barge, train and truck (see Fig. 3). It is assumed that there are two berth areas for barges, two rail tracks and finally a truck gate.

Without loss of generality, an intermodal terminal with containers as the only type of cargo to be handled is considered, $n_{ct} = 1$. All containers arriving at the terminal are categorized with respect to the final destination, and for each a distinction is made based on the due time. According to the hinterland network $n_{de} = 4$, terminal A is also an available destination. The number of commodities handled at the terminal is $n_{fp} = n_{de} = 4$. A maximum remaining time until due time of 72 hours is considered for all destinations. Using a time step of 3 hours, $n_{dt_i} = n_{dt} = 24$ due times per destination are considered for model (7)–(9). Concerning the cargo destination, it is assumed that cargo is equally distributed over the 4 possible destinations. So, at the beginning of each time step the cargo assignment will be based on the known information at that time: the intermodal terminal state and the cargo arrival forecast or prediction.

In order to respond to the desired hinterland container flows a network of connections and weekly schedules is created [14] (see Tables 1–2). We assume that schedules are a result of agreements between the terminal and transport providers in the freight network, and therefore the terminal has no permission to change it without consent.

The focus is on the interactions between the terminal and transport providers offering transport capacity at the terminal, supporting the outgoing cargo. In this case study four different routes are possible: Route 1, R_1: (A, B, D); Route 2, R_2: (A, B, C, D); Route 3, R_3: (A, C, D) and Route 4, R_4: (A, C, B, D), see Tables 1–2. For truck modality all destinations are available during opening hours, (from 8 a.m. to 24 p.m.). Truck gates are opened for a 16 hours period from Monday to Saturday and the maximum served capacity during the day time is 480 TEU. The reachable time per destination for the pair transport modality

Table 1. Scheduled connections per barge modality

Berth A			Berth B		
Departure	Route	Capacity	Departure	Route	Capacity
06 : 00	R_1	140 TEU	03 : 00	R_1	70 TEU
15 : 00	R_2	140 TEU	12 : 00	R_4	70 TEU
24 : 00	R_3	140 TEU	18 : 00	R_3	70 TEU

Table 2. Scheduled connections per train modality

Rail Track A			Rail Track B		
Departure	Route	Capacity	Departure	Route	Capacity
06 : 00	R_1	40 TEU	03 : 00	R_3	40 TEU
12 : 00	R_2	40 TEU	09 : 00	R_4	40 TEU
18 : 00	R_3	40 TEU	15 : 00	R_1	40 TEU
24 : 00	R_4	40 TEU	21 : 00	R_2	40 TEU

Table 3. Reachable time steps per destination for the pair route – transport modality

Destination	Barge				Train				Truck
	R_1	R_2	R_3	R_4	R_1	R_2	R_3	R_4	
A	–	–	–	–	–	–	–	–	1
B	6	6	–	10	4	4	–	6	2
C	–	10	6	6	–	6	4	4	2
D	12	16	12	16	8	10	8	10	4

and route is shown in Table 3. Destination A is only reachable by truck. The terminal is able to export a maximum of 1430 TEU daily (630 TEU for barge modality, 320 TEU for train modality and 480 TEU for truck modality). The complete model has $n_x = 100$ states and $n_u = 96 \times 5 = 488$ cargo assignments to be determined at each time step.

In respect to due time, it is not equal to have a container with a due time of 4 time steps or a container with a due time of 24 time steps. A container at the terminal with a higher due time gives more freedom for the terminal to assign it towards the final destination. In contrast, a container with a shorter due time creates pressure on the terminal to find an available connection such that due time is respected. This effect can be captured by the *yard pressure* index defined as,

$$x_i^y = \sum_{j=1}^{n_{dt}} x_{n_{dt}(i-1)+j} \cdot \frac{1}{j}, \quad i = 1, \ldots, n_{de}. \tag{22}$$

For testing the framework, it is defined an arrival pattern of cargo for all the connections that pass by the terminal. In order to represent the congestion effect at the end of the week, a peak of cargo arrivals occurs at Friday by a factor of 2. In respect to the cost function, over-due cargo has a strong penalty, while cargo with a due time from 1 to 4 time steps have a smooth penalty to promote the assignment of cargo, other due times have zero penalty. The truck modality has a stronger penalty than the barge and train modality. The simulation runs

Table 4. Over-due cargo and yard pressure for cargo assignment (in bold lowest values per column)

N_p	Over-due cargo [TEU]					Yard pressure				
	A	B	C	D	Total	A	B	C	D	Total
8	597.6	55.8	255.4	1872.5	2781.3	9375.2	7164.4	7885.8	10870.8	35296.2
12	138.8	8.8	61.4	775.9	984.9	6795.4	6025.6	5950.2	6294.4	25065.5
16	**0**	**0**	**0**	**0**	**0**	4282.5	4461.3	4436.6	3395.7	16576.1
24	**0**	**0**	**0**	**0**	**0**	**1370.5**	**2126.0**	1622.3	885.0	6003.7
32	**0**	**0**	**0**	**0**	**0**	1481.9	2386.5	**1459.4**	**597.3**	**5925.1**

for $k = 120$ time steps, which corresponds approximately to 2 weeks. Two case scenarios are considered: i) cargo assignment at the terminal, and ii) cooperation between transport provider and terminal.

4.2 Cargo Assignment at the Terminal

At each time step, the terminal is deciding which cargo to allocate to the available transport capacity at the terminal. With the increase of the prediction horizon, no over-due cargo occurs for a prediction horizon equal or bigger than $N_\mathrm{p} = 16$ (see Table 4). The existence of over-due cargo is related to an increase in yard pressure, and occurs mainly on weekend due to the elimination of truck connections on Sunday (see Fig. 4). The yard pressure decreases with the increase of the prediction horizon (see Table 4), and there is little difference in performance between $N_\mathrm{p} = 24$ and $N_\mathrm{p} = 32$. Recall that the maximum due time at the terminal is 24 time steps. With the increase of the prediction horizon, transport capacity at the terminal is used close to its limit (see Fig. 5–6). Barge modality, which is a slow transport mode, is barely used for low prediction horizons but

Table 5. Transport capacity used and modal split for cargo assignment (in bold the highest values for each column)

N_p	Used capacity [%]				Modal split [%]		
	Barge	Train	Truck	Total	Barge	Train	Truck
8	38.97	90.37	**86.52**	65.53	27.38	**32.46**	**40.16**
12	72.90	93.14	67.04	75.88	44.23	28.89	26.87
16	86.90	93.46	65.37	81.89	48.86	26.86	24.28
24	**99.65**	**96.17**	62.59	**87.56**	**52.40**	25.86	21.74
32	98.29	95.54	61.99	87.31	51.84	26.57	21.60

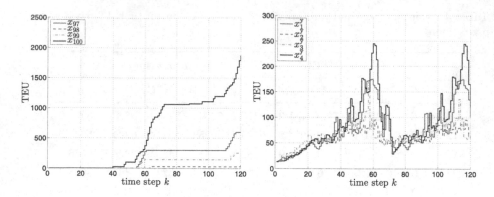

Fig. 4. Lost cargo (left) and yard pressure (right) for $N_p = 8$

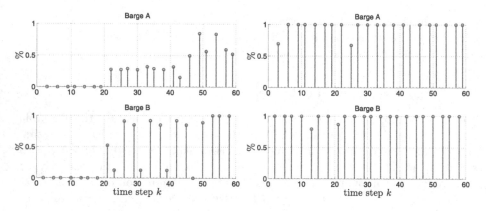

Fig. 5. Used transport capacity of barge modality for cargo assignment for barge modality using $N_p = 8$ (left) and $N_p = 32$ (right)

is used close to full capacity for a prediction horizon of $N_p = 32$ (see Fig. 5). The increase in the use of barge modality is done mainly at the cost of the truck modality (see Fig. 6). For the whole experiment, the used transport capacity at the terminal is around 87% for a prediction horizon of $N_p = 32$, this means that there is some possibility to allow the arrival of more cargo at the terminal (see Table 5). With higher prediction horizons, the modal split favors the barge modality in detriment of the truck modality while the train modality remains approximately constant.

4.3 Cooperation Between Terminal and Transport Provider

In this case scenario, it is assumed that barge connections arriving at berth A are facing a delay (e.g., due to waiting times at seaport). Cargo being transported by barge A with final destination D, arrive at the terminal with a remaining time until due time of 18 hours, that is to say 6 time steps. Barge A can reach

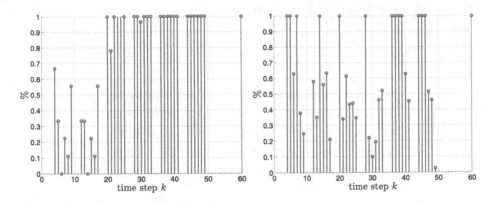

Fig. 6. Used transport capacity of truck modality for cargo assignment for truck modality using $N_p = 8$ (left) and $N_p = 32$ (right).

Table 6. Cooperation details between terminal and transport provider

N_p	Total accepted cargo [TEU]	Max. accepted iteration [TEU]	Min. accepted iteration [TEU]	Increase in used transport [%]	Total iterations	Computation time [s]
8	1091.9	200	0.0	3.60	46	0.31
12	1251.7	200	0.0	6.02	41	0.31
16	1356.3	200	7.0	6.62	36	0.64
24	1373.9	200	7.0	6.64	36	1.27
32	1388.3	200	21.5	6.63	35	2.53

Table 7. Over-due cargo and yard pressure for cooperation between terminal and transport provider (in bold lowest values per column)

N_p	Over-due cargo [TEU]					Yard pressure				
	A	B	C	D	Total	A	B	C	D	Total
8	597.6	55.8	255.4	2236.52	3145.32	9737.3	7184.7	7948.8	12223.5	37094.3
12	168.0	10.8	49.0	792.6	1020.3	7234.1	6035.2	5884.6	7093.5	26247.3
16	**0**	**0**	**0**	**0**	**0**	5090.8	4466.0	4292.6	4057.4	17906.8
24	**0**	**0**	**0**	**0**	**0**	**3404.1**	**2266.2**	1838.2	1491.8	9000.3
32	**0**	**0**	**0**	**0**	**0**	3507.0	2397.3	**1744.9**	**1300.8**	**8950.1**

Table 8. Transport capacity used and modal split for cooperation between terminal and transport provider (in bold highest values per column)

N_p	Used capacity [%]				Modal split [%]		
	Barge	Train	Truck	Total	Barge	Train	Truck
8	39.06	90.10	**98.44**	69.13	27.38	**32.46**	**40.16**
12	72.40	93.19	87.54	81.90	40.70	26.79	32.51
16	88.42	91.01	86.73	88.51	45.99	24.20	29.80
24	**99.55**	95.62	85.02	**94.20**	48.66	23.89	27.45
32	98.19	**97.61**	84.67	93.94	**48.12**	24.46	27.42

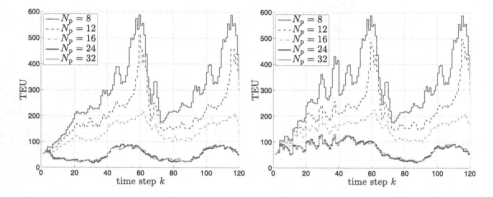

Fig. 7. Yard pressure for cargo assignment (left) and for cooperation between terminal and transport provider (right)

destination D in 12 or 16 time steps depending on the route used. Destination D is reachable on 4 time steps for truck modality (see Table 3). In this case, without cooperation between the transport provider and the terminal the cargo will not be delivered on time. The delays on barge A are assumed to occur for 4 days (from Monday to Thursday in the first week solely), and an amount of 200 TEU is assumed to be delayed for destination D per connection. At berth A 12 connection will be affected, and a total of 2400 TEU are at risk of not being delivered on time. The cooperation between terminal and transport provider allowed the transhipment for the faster transport modality and a reduction of over-due cargo when considering the hub and transport provider together (see Table 6). For a prediction horizon of $N_p = 32$, a total of 1388.3 TEU were accepted for transhipment, with an increase of 2.53 s in computation time using 35 iterations. The transport provider, with the help of the terminal, reduced the amount of cargo at risk in 57.8%. Due to the cooperation among terminal and transport provider, the hub faces an increase of over-due cargo for lower prediction horizon, for $N_p \geq 16$ no over-due cargo occurs (see Table 7). The

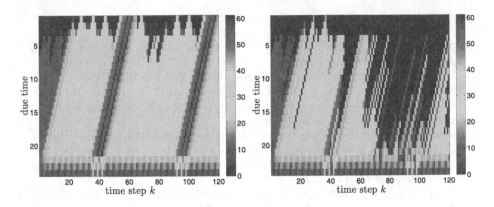

Fig. 8. Yard pressure for destination A for $N_p = 8$ (left) and $N_p = 24$ (right)

yard pressure has increased in comparison to the cargo assignment due to the extra cargo accepted from the delayed connection during the first week (see Fig. 7). The use of a MPC approach allows the cargo assignment in advance giving priority to the lower due time (see Fig. 8). For a prediction horizon of 32 time steps a transport modal split of 48% barges, 25% trains and 27% trucks was achieved (see Table 8).

5   Conclusions and Future Research

The cargo assignment at intermodal hubs according to the terminal haulage is addressed in this paper. A model to monitor the amount of cargo at the terminal over time is proposed. Cargo is categorized in respect to fixed properties, and for each fixed property a distinguish is made in respect to remaining time until due time on destination. The model is suitable for real-time decisions supporting the operational level. In particular, the model can be used to make predictions about the over-due cargo. This is used to guide cooperation between the intermodal hub and the transport provider, using selective information exchange. The extension of this work for a network of intermodal hubs with the presence of different parties is worth to consider, different network topologies and incentives for cooperation can be tested. The development of synchromodal transportation methodologies should be investigated further.

References

1. Stahlbock, R., Voß, S.: Operations research at container terminals: a literature update. Operations Research Spectrum **30**, 1–52 (2008)
2. Carlo, H.J., Vis, I.F.A., Roodbergen, K.J.: Transport operations in container terminals: Literature overview, trends, research directions and classification scheme. European Journal of Operational Research **236**, 1–13 (2014)

3. Contargo, Contargo voert congestietoslag, tech. rep., Nieuwsblad Transport, July 16, 2007
4. Rodrigue, J.-P., Comtois, C., Slack, B.: The Geography of Transport Systems. Taylor and Francis Group (2006)
5. Ahuja, R., Magnanti, T., Orlin, J.: Network Flows. Prentice Hall (1993)
6. SteadieSeifi, M., Dellaert, N., Nuijten, W., van Woensel, T., Raoufi, R.: Multimodal freight transportation planning: A literature review. European Journal of Operations Research **233**, 1–15 (2014)
7. Nabais, J.L., Negenborn, R.R., Botto, M.A.: Model predictive control for a sustainable transport modal split at intermodal container hubs. In: Proceeding of the 10th IEEE International Conference on Networking, Sensing and Control, Paris, pp. 591–596, April 2013
8. Maciejowski, J.: Predictive control with constraints. Prentice Hall, Harlow (2002)
9. Maestre, J., de la Pena, D.M., Camacho, E.: Distributed MPC: a supply chain case. In: 48th IEEE Conference on Decision and Control and 28th Chinese Control Conference, Shanghai, China, pp. 7099–7104, December 2009
10. Geyer, T., Larsson, M., Morari, M.: Hybrid emergency voltage control in power systems. In: Proceedings of the European Control Conference, Cambridge, UK (2003)
11. Negenborn, R.R., Overloop, P., Keviczky, T., De Schutter, B.: Distributed model predictive control of irrigation canals. Networks and Heterogeneous Media **4**, 359–380 (2009)
12. Li, L., Negenborn, R.R., de Schutter, B.: A receding horizon approach for container flow assignment. Journal of the Transportation Research Board **2410**, 132–140 (2014)
13. Alessandri, A., Sacone, S., Siri, S.: Modelling and optimal receding-horizon control of maritime container terminals. Journal of Mathematical Modeling and Algorithms **133**, 6–109 (2007)
14. Nabais, J.L., Negenborn, R.R., Botto, M.A.: A novel predictive control based framework for optimizing intermodal container terminal operations. In: Hu, H., Shi, X., Stahlbock, R., Voß, S. (eds.) ICCL 2012. LNCS, vol. 7555, pp. 53–71. Springer, Heidelberg (2012)

Reducing Port-Related Truck Emissions: Coordinated Truck Appointments to Reduce Empty Truck Trips

Frederik Schulte[1]([✉]), Rosa G. González[2], and Stefan Voß[1]

[1] Institute of Information Systems, University of Hamburg, Hamburg, Germany
{frederik.schulte,stefan.voss}@uni-hamburg.de
[2] Faculty of Engineering and Basic Sciences, Universidad de Los Andes,
Santiago, Chile
rgonzalez@uandes.cl

Abstract. Port-related emissions are a growing problem for urban areas often located directly next to ports highly frequented by trucks and vessels. Empty truck trips are responsible for a significant share of these emissions. Truck appointment systems (TASs) allow scheduling of truck arrivals and enable collaboration among truckers. Though, TASs leveraging the potential to reduce avoidable emissions due to empty trips have hardly been studied. We aim to show how a TAS following this idea may be designed and evaluate the approach. We thus review requirements for a collaborative TAS and develop a discrete-event simulation model to assess coordinated truck appointments in a practical case of drayage. The results indicate that the approach effectively reduces port-related truck emissions, but might create congestion in the port. The considered case refers to drayage processes, but may also be transferred to the hinterland. The developed simulation model assumes a generic truck appointment process and may also serve to analyze diverse cases.

Keywords: Port emissions · Truck appointment system · Empty trips · Empty repositioning · Simulation

1 Introduction

Urban port areas increasingly struggle with port-related emissions—mainly caused by trucks moving full and empty containers between port and hinterland. At many ports the empty container truck trips problem is a major cause for those emissions [6], [14], [13]. This relates to the non-utilization of available slot capacities (i.e., the number of empty or non-empty containers a truck can carry) of trucks in import- and export-related trips [14]. Figure 1 illustrates the occurrence of empty repositioning for different truck routes. Both, not fully utilized slot capacity and empty repositioning trips, increase the number of total trips in a port region and thus cause evitable emissions. There are few studies on TASs at ports like, e.g. [8], but these studies mostly do

© Springer International Publishing Switzerland 2015
F. Corman et al. (Eds.): ICCL 2015, LNCS 9335, pp. 495–509, 2015.
DOI: 10.1007/978-3-319-24264-4_34

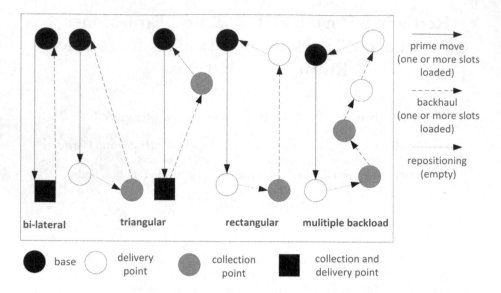

Fig. 1. Basic empty and loaded container truck movements (adapted from [22])

not focus on sharing empty truck capacities. From the perspective of a single carrier, the problem could be modeled mathematically, but this approach would not be as auspicious in cases of collaboration [1]. Simulation models could be a promising alternative, but yet have not been developed for the problem [13]. We aim to introduce and assess collaboration options regarding the number of empty trips, emission savings, capacity utilization, and costs. We develop a discrete-event simulation model and system-based collaborative truck services with real-world data for drayage at the port of San Antonio, Chile. We find that a collaborative TAS may be an effective way to reduce port-related truck emissions, but might have a negative impact on port congestion if not properly integrated in port operations management.

In the following, we present relevant literature, the idea of a collaborative TAS, a discrete-event simulation model with a case study, and conclusions drawn from the study. Section 2 reviews collaboration approaches in transport, TASs, and emission-oriented port logistics. Section 3 introduces requirements for a collaborative TAS and options for its application. Section 4 describes a generic simulation model for the evaluation, complemented by a specific case study in Section 5. Section 6 concludes and gives an outlook on future research ideas.

2   Literature Review

There is few specific literature available on TAS implementations focusing on collaboration or emission reduction. Thus, subsequently we review collaboration approaches in transport (Section 2.1), TAS literature (Section 2.2), and port logistics incorporating emissions (Section 2.3).

2.1 Collaboration in Road Transport

There are various forms of collaboration in road transport applied in industry and discussed in literature. Agarwal et al. [1] have examined different opportunities for collaboration in the business. This includes collaboration set-ups with freight bundling and break-bulk terminals, the formation of alliances to reduce load imbalances, and approaches of carriers to jointly reduce the cost of asset repositioning. From the perspective of a single carrier, the problem could be modeled mathematically and the resulting linear programming model could be solved with reasonable effort. In cases of collaboration, a game theoretic approach has been proposed, but needs to be relaxed significantly for application [26]. Lozano et al. [19] have also proposed a game theoretic approach for a related problem and have conducted numerical experiments, but have also emphasized that further practical requirements need to be incorporated for truly realistic modeling. Besides, few studies [22],[13] have empirically examined challenges and obstacles on the way to consequent collaboration among trucking companies for efficient joint capacity utilization. The study by [13] has analyzed factors enabling and constraining the back-loading of trucks. This work goes back to a large survey to understand the problem of empty running in road transport conducted in Great Britain. Islam and Olsen [13], on the other hand, have provided an exploratory qualitative study by means of interviewing road carriers from the container transport industry. According to them, part of the problem could be addressed with a TAS supporting truck-sharing that yet needs to be evaluated empirically. A successful way to model port-related transport processes with different stakeholders has been introduced by Bielli et al. [5]. The authors make use of discrete-event simulation and an object-oriented modelling approach.

2.2 Truck Appointment Systems

As TASs define when trucks should perform a service (load a container) at ports, these systems naturally have to be considered to plan the point in time when a truck loads its container and, additionally, another container of another trucking company. Zehendner and Feillet [30] have recently demonstrated the multiple benefits a TAS can have on the service quality of trucks, trains, barges and vessels at ports. But generally, there are few studies on TASs, and those existing have hardly considered the impact of a TAS on empty trips at ports and in the hinterland. Among the best described cases in literature are the ports of Los Angeles, Hongkong, and Auckland, as exemplified below.

Giuliano and O'Brian [8] have evaluated a terminal gate appointment system at the ports of Los Angeles and Long Beach. This study has focused on queuing and transaction times without incorporating truck sharing options. The authors have not observed any reduction of these figures, and thus have not found any positive impact on truck emissions. Without explicitly considering a TAS, Englert et al. [6] have examined the impact a potential inland port would have on pollution and congestion caused by empty truck repositioning in the Southern California region of the above ports. The authors have demonstrated that empty truck trips significantly contribute to port area emissions and could be reduced in a collaboratively planned dry port environment. Morais and Lord [23], on the other hand, have provided first evidence on the quantitative impact of truck appointments on greenhouse gas (GHG) emissions, but did not incorporate collaboration. One of the first documented cases of TASs has been studied by Murty et al. [24] in Hongkong. The authors have aimed for the efficient utilization of scarce terminal space and have demonstrated how a TAS, as part of an integrated decision support system, can contribute to achieve this and related objectives. Islam and Olsen [13] have examined empty container truck trips for the case of Auckland. The authors have conducted an interview-based study with road carriers from the container transportation industry and elaborate truck sharing options for reduced emissions of empty container trucks. Based on this study, Islam and Olsen [14] have proposed a re-engineered container truck hauling process and have derived requirements for a TAS incorporating truck sharing options.

Other studies analyzed the impact of truck arrival information on the efficiency of yard and drayage operations [25], [11], [32], [31] or impact of truck announcements on container stacking efficiency [3]. Zhao and Goodchild [32] present a simulation to analyze the impact on container re-handles for different scenarios with partial and perfect information on the truck arrival sequences, observing that partial information is enough to achieve significant benefits with respect to stacking efficiency at the yard. Zhang et al. [31] have developed a model that optimizes the appointment quota of each period optimized subject to the constraints of adjustment quota. The authors have modeled a queuing network of trucks in the terminal and demonstrated that the model can have a positive impact on truck turn times. Van Asperen et al. [3] have focused on the possible effects a TAS could have on stacking operations in the terminal yard.

2.3   Port Logistics Incorporating Emissions

Apart from overall efforts in sustainable port development, there are some dominant issues discussed in the literature of emission-oriented port logistics. Studies with a perspective on logistics operations typically focus on:

- Repositioning of (empty) container trucks [6], [13]

- Hinterland transport [4], [16], [17], [18]

- Terminal operations [12], [20], [28]

- Vessel emissions [10], [27], [29]

While the various kinds of vessel emissions are the topic of many studies, perspectives and approaches differ quite significantly. For instance, [10] focus on governance methods—such as interactive governance for multiple stakeholders involved in causing maritime emissions—to achieve regulatory compliance. On the other hand, there are works emphasizing operational options to effectively reduce the quantitative emission impact of container shipping like [27]. Villalba and Gemechu [29] focus on a single port and derive strategies and policies to reduce emissions in the port area caused by vessels visiting the port.

The repositioning and capacity utilization of (empty) container trucks is an often discussed topic. Studies like the aforementioned ones by Englert et al. [6] and Islam and Olsen [13] have examined the emissions impact of empty logistics resources at ports. Generally, the hinterland transport is a major issue for researchers and practitioners in attempts for more sustainable logistics in port areas. Apart from truck emissions, noise and congestion are in the focus of related studies. Bergqvist and Egels-Zandén [4] have examined approaches to internalize external costs related to green port dues in collaborative transport systems of hinterland logistics and ports. In the same realm, Liao et al. [18] have conducted a quantitative activity-based study to analyze emissions from the port of Taipei. They indicate that there are less emission-intensive transshipment routes possible if planners value the emerging port of Taipei as an alternative to the established ports in the region. In the context of hinterland transport routes, Lättilä et al. [17] have modeled a hypothetical dry port network in Finland. Utilizing an enhanced dry port concept is a promising approach to decrease both emissions and costs. Lam and Gu [16] have reviewed mathematical models for port hinterland intermodal container flows with sustainability aspects and concluded that models should not only focus on costs, but integrate sustainability aspects by means of multi-objective modeling. Regarding sustainable terminal operations, the studies by Henesey et al. [12] and Lun [20] have evaluated sustainable policy-making, while Rijsenbrij and Wieschemann [28] have examined a terminal design for sustainable operations. This work describes how to balance service requirements, costs, and requirements for sustainability using an appropriate terminal design and respective handling systems.

3   A Collaborative Truck Appointment System

TASs basically serve to define time windows in which trucks may arrive at a port or a port area to provide a needed service. Independent from the specific focus of these systems, they offer new opportunities for advanced decision support in and at ports. For the problem of empty truck capacities and resulting emissions a TAS likewise serves as a framework for implementing related planning. There are different options to reduce empty truck capacities, but the most promising are based on the collaboration of trucking companies. Though, the majority of TASs discussed in Section 2.2 do not consider collaboration or capacity sharing among trucking companies. That is, no such system has yet been implemented and evaluated. This section intends to introduce paths for the implementation of TASs incorporating collaboration.

The basic components of advanced truck systems for collaboration are user profiles for trucking companies and exporters as well as a matching procedure for specific services [14]. Truckers are thus able to announce empty capacities, and exporters announce their transport requirements for a specific service. A trucker obviously needs to specify the kind of empty capacity that he can offer and additionally has the opportunity to add preferences on the possible shared services. Similarly, the exporter specifies a certain transport demand and provides information such as container type, points of destination, estimated times of arrival and departure. A basic matching procedure checks origins, destinations, transport constraints, and time windows to propose possible services for collaboration. That is, we assume elementary truck movements that are defined by origin and destination points. Furthermore, special transport vehicles and time windows may be required by the customers. These criteria need to be considered for all planned and demanded container moves. Thus, the matching procedure can validate combination options for container moves based on these criteria. The procedure is basic in a way that it provides feasible solutions that later on need to be evaluated—either by a heuristic or mathematical optimization approach as discussed in Section 4. As a next step, the generated matching options are evaluated based on specific planning models with respect to objectives, such as reduction of emissions and costs. From literature, at least two economically and ecologically relevant problem classes of empty capacities in road transport can be identified: asset repositioning and empty slot transport. The first basically refers to repositioning trucks or empty containers from a prior destination to a new point of demand or a parking position [6]. The latter covers all kinds of problems related to efficient capacity utilization on similar cargo routes such as establishing break-bulk terminals and cycles for collaboration [1]. The proposed TAS can implicitly or explicitly consider these problems. That is, the TAS can either explicitly search a joint optimum for all participating companies and the related problems or implicitly incorporate sub-problems by means of user preferences. In the implicit set-up, the user could thus, e.g., publish his preference for trips that help him solving his asset relocation problem. In the explicit set-up, on the other hand, user preferences are secondary to the overall objectives such as total costs and total emissions. Obviously, the explicit set-up would create better system-wide solutions, but the implicit set-up may be easier to implement in practice. Similarly, one can choose between different approaches to finally create a match between the users. Probably, best results could be created with a multi-objective mixed integer programming formulation considering costs, emissions, and user preferences to define a fixed plan for a specific time window. As this leads to a complex planning approach that might cause resistance among truckers [13], a more flexible iterative approach could be considered, too. For instance, users could iteratively choose from a list of ranked services.

Finally, the system can be implemented in a web-based application enabling users to dynamically interact with their mobile devices. The system then provides all information relevant to its users such as arrival times or navigation data.

4 A Generic Simulation Approach for Collaborative Truck Appointment Systems

Based on requirements elaborated in Section 3, we have designed a discrete-event simulation model for a generic truck appointment process. This section introduces a generic simulation approach that is applied for a specific case in Section 5. The following subsections discuss scope and objectives (Section 4.1), process definition and assumptions (Section 4.2), input and output data (Section 4.3), and an emission-integrated matching procedure (Section 4.4) for the simulation model.

4.1 Scope and Objectives

The potential of an advanced TAS enabling collaboration between trucking companies has not been evaluated to the knowledge of the authors. That is, there are no specific planning models that have been implemented and evaluated scientifically in practice or in simulation models. With this simulation study we thus aim to build the foundation in this direction. We want to demonstrate how planning models could be incorporated in a respective study and discuss appropriate models. Thus, we aim to assess the current transportation impact on sustainability and efficiency objectives. More specific, we aim to evaluate collaboration options with a respective TAS and their impact on emissions, congestion, and costs. This also allows a better understanding of design requirements for collaborative TASs.

For the simulation study, we refer to a conventional set-up of a working day with high utilization. Collaboration based on truck appointments may have a wide impact on port-related logistic processes, but the basic problems of empty capacity sharing and repositioning of empty logistics resources re-occur within the narrow scope of a port and also in a wider scope including the hinterland. We can thus start with a smaller scope and extend in the next step.

4.2 Process Definition and Assumptions

The simulation process depicted in Figure 2 illustrates the basic conditions to be considered for the evaluation of a collaborative TAS at ports. We assume that truck drivers are equipped with mobile devices enabling them to dynamically interact with a TAS and allowing a more flexible truck appointment process. This assumption is made to meet flexibility requirements of truckers. Likewise one could also imagine that the system is operated at a company office and drivers receive orders at transshipment points. The simulated process starts when a truck driver receives a transport order. We assume that this order already contains the truck appointment and potential matches for a collaborative service—both provided by the TAS. That is, as soon as a truck capacity becomes available, a basic matching method (introduced in Section 3) generates feasible solutions for combined trips. This first step already enables a new form of coordinated truck appointments and is likely to improve costs and emissions. In a second step, the generated feasible solutions can now be evaluated for heuristic improvement or mathematical optimization as sketched in Section 4.4. After loading containers at the first demand position, we assume that the trucker could request a new transport and possibly transport additional containers. Finally, the truck needs to be repositioned for a new order or parking. At various steps of this process, the matching method can be called and transport orders updated

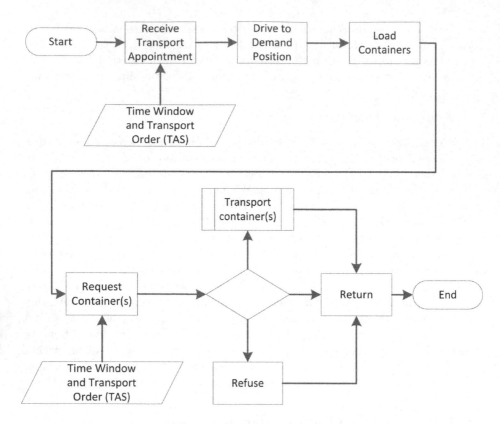

Fig. 2. Simplified Simulated Process

4.3   Input and Output Data

For the sake of realistic modeling of the above process, various types of data sources need to be considered. These sources involve interviews with trucking companies and port operators, observation, and the analysis of existing secondary data. All these sources serve to generate realistic input data for the simulation model such as probability functions for service or demand rates. Interviews might be especially appropriate to gain insights into the questions of how many trucking companies are actually willing to collaborate, what kind of capacity restrictions might exist and would have to be modeled, and how many locations in port and hinterland need to incorporated. Also, interviews are important to understand if there are any current policies to avoid empty trips and to estimate operational costs. Additional operational information might be collected by observations and existing documentation. This applies to transport, waiting, loading, and documentation times as well as to the number of available trucks and the current percentage of empty trips. The analysis of external documentation by port operators or trucking companies in combination with interviews will also serve to gain insight into the distance of truck trips, the number of containers and their destination, operating hours at sea ports and depots as well as the current layout in use at the port. Finally, information gained from trucking companies about truck types in use in combination with external databases will be used for specific calculations of truck emissions at the port and in the hinterland. With this input data the simulation model may provide output data on the percentage of empty trips, emission levels, and time consumption for various sub-processes of the simulated process.

4.4   Emission-integrated Matching Procedure

As discussed in Section 3, port-related empty trips that increase local emissions are caused by the problem classes of asset repositioning and empty slot transport. Respective models that address repositioning [7] and empty slot transport [1] have been reviewed in literature. These models may as well serve as the basis for matching services within a collaborative TAS. Furthermore, synchronization aspects, as reviewed by Mankowska et al. [21], need to be considered. In order to evaluate possible synchronized matches with respect to costs and emissions and independent from a specific problem formulation, these models need to be extended by specific emission objective functions. Considering a basic flow problem, with the set of nodes V and the set of arcs S, a set of order routes O can be introduced to model routes associated with orders during the simulated time period. The set of nodes, V, represents all kinds of locations according to Figure 1. An appropriate bi-criteria formulation has been introduced by Kim et al. [15] and can be adapted for the case of a collaborative TAS. The approach basically applies a cost objective function Z_1 and a second objective function incorporating emissions Z_2. Z_1 thus adds up the total transportation cost:

$$Z_1 = min \sum_{k \in O} \sum_{i,j \in S} C_{ij} x_{ij}^k \tag{1}$$

Z_2 is based on the emissions induced by all considered transport operations:

$$Z_2 = min[\sum_{k \in O} \sum_{i,j \in S} E_{ij} x_{ij}^k + \sum_{k \in O} \sum_{i \in V} E_i y_i^k + \sum_{k \in O} \sum_{j \in V} E_j y_j^k] \tag{2}$$

The functions use the following notation:

V = set of all nodes, i.e., origins i and destinations j in the network;
S = set of all arcs ij connecting origins and destinations in the network;
O = set of all order routes combining sets of arcs in the network;
$x_{ij}^k, ij \in S, k \in O$ = decision variable for transport flow from point i to j;
$y_i^k, i \in V, k \in O$ = decision variable for transshipment at point i;
$C_{ij}, ij \in S$ = cost for transport flow from point i to j;
$E_{ij}, ij \in S$ = emissions for transport flow from i to j; and
$E_i, i \in V$ = emissions during transshipment at point i.

For the proposed bi-objective problem formulation, costs and emissions need to be described in an integrated objective function. Therefore, both terms are typically normalized or scaled. That is, the terms of a multi-objective formulation are divided by a factor that enables their dimensionless representation as sum of single objectives. A common approach for this purpose uses the optimal values of single-objective optimization runs as those scaling factors. That is, in this case, Z_1 and Z_2 as independent objectives first. The resulting objective function can then be implemented in the optimization module of the simulation software for an optimization run based on metaheuristics. Furthermore, additional constraints such as bounds for inventory and vehicle capacities or emission quotas also need to be defined in the optimization module in order to receive near-optimal coordinated order routes. The objective function serves to evaluate potential matching options provided by the basic matching procedure introduced in Section 3. As it evaluates matches with associated order routes, the matching decision implicitly is a routing decision. In the basic set-up with one container type, single-commodity flows are considered. For multi-commodity flows this set-up can easily be extended. x_{ij}^k serves as decision variable, determining whether an empty or full service is performed, without differentiating transport costs of full and empty movements. Emissions are distinguished during transport and transshipment at point i or j. The emission values at different transshipment points may differ because of different infrastructure and loading devices that are used. For instance, fuel based loading devices might be used at some points, while at others electric devices are used. Truck model specific emission data during transport and transshipment is retrieved from the EMFAC2014 and CARB database, respectively [2].

5   Simulation Case Study

As discussed in the previous sections, empty trip problems in a port and in the hinterland have a similar structure. In this section, we model and analyze the the drayage procedures in the port San Antonio, Chile. We first introduce the case (Section 5.1) and then present results of the simulation study (Section 5.2).

5.1   Practical Case

Figure 3 illustrates the basic conditions for the empty container truck trips problem in the case of drayage at the port of San Antonio. There are three major types of transport locations relevant for drayage: depots, custom storage areas (CSAs), and the terminal. In case of San Antonio, five depots, four CSAs, and one terminal are considered in the simulated layout of the port area. Thus, possible truck routes could have all shapes depicted in Figure 1, from bi-lateral to multiple backload. According to these basic route types, a trucker starts at a base (typically the company's location) and returns to this point. In between the truck could serve the terminal, various depots, and custom storage locations.

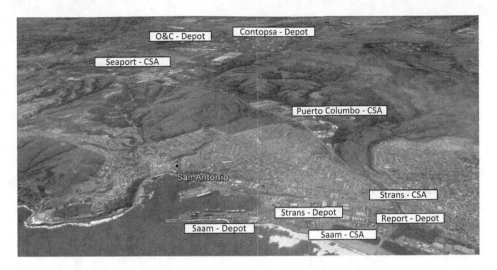

Fig. 3. San Antonio port and hinterland [9]

Depending on each route terminal, CSAs and depots can be understood as delivery, collection, or delivery and collection points. These transport and transshipment processes are usually repeated several times during a day before the trucker returns.

Empty trips thus typically occur when repositioning to the trucker's base point, but are as well likely for movements between delivery and collection points. In the considered case, an empirical analysis has shown that in only 5 % of all drayage transports the potential to combine pick-up and delivery is leveraged in order to reduce empty trips. Coordinated truck appointments require a system that matches empty capacities and demand as introduced in Section 3. Therefore, in the simulation study, we assume a TAS that seeks to leverage this potential by coordinating container pick-ups and deliveries, reducing empty trips and trips with empty slots. For instance, considering a simple case, a truck takes a container from a depot to the terminal and takes another container back to the depot. In comparison to the standard, un-coordinated case, two empty rides are now avoided and respective costs and emissions are saved. In the initial phase, appointments are made directly at the port with a time window of two hours. This set-up follows practical requirements and should reduce acceptance barriers that might exist among truckers if they are urged to accept rigid and inflexible schedules. Also, truckers can decide among options which container to load in a coordinated service and the system does not define a near-optimal plan in the first phase. Since there are no coordinated TASs implemented leveraging any kind of capacity sharing has a significant impact, and more advanced methods should be implemented in the next step after a successful initial phase.

5.2 Results

The case of San Antonio was implemented in a simulation model built with the software Arena. A simulation run assumed one week of high demand in comparison to one of low demand. Depending on the modeled scenario different working hours are assumed. The modeled scenarios can basically be distinguished by their percentage of successfully coordinated pick-ups and deliveries of containers. That is, in Scenario 1, only 5 % of all drayage trips were successfully coordinated, while the rest of the trips involved repositioning of any empty truck to start the next order. The scenarios thus reflect different levels of collaboration which refer to the motivation of truck drivers as well as to operational restrictions. Next to the number of trips, the major cost drivers are waiting and operational times, added up to the total time in the system. Besides that, we analyzed emissions caused during transport and transshipment. Table 1 provides the average results of 50 simulation runs for the defined scenarios.

Table 1. Simulation results averaged over 50 runs

	Coordinated Trips [%]	Time in System [min.]	Total Emissions [tons/day]	Number of Empty Trips [-]
Scenario 1	5	150,2	6,70	504
Scenario 2	15	162,5	6,25	468
Scenario 3	40	195,1	5,70	417
Scenario 4	50	208,0	5,36	393

The values for total time in system and number of empty trucks can be directly obtained from the simulation model. Emissions are calculated according to the formulas introduced in Section 4.4. That is, emissions during transshipment and transport of times of trucks are summed up. The specific emission rates for drayage trucks in the different situations are generated by database query from the EMFAC2014 database [2]. This extensive database is built based on historical data for different kinds of vehicles in different situations. Because most of the trucks used for drayage in San Antonio were already around 15 years old, the emission rates for trucks of that age are considered. These rates furthermore incorporate environmental temperatures and have been derived especially for drayage trucks. Waiting times are derived based on service rates and arrival rates per hour, while emissions for truck transport are derived on rates per kilometer. Service and arrival rates are modeled as Gamma or Weibull distributions based on empirical data. Most reliable data could be obtained for CO_2 emissions. Thus, the presented results only refer to CO_2 emissions, but could easily be extended when respective data becomes available.

The results clearly demonstrate that the approach effectively reduces empty trips and thus port-related emissions. A low number of empty trips itself is no quality criterion for the solutions, but may provide insights about the character of good solutions. For Scenario 4 emissions could be reduced by 20 % in comparison to the current situation. This obviously goes along with a reduction of transportation costs. On the other hand, the average time in system per truck increases significantly when more coordinated trips are made. This is intuitive as coordination of trips means that trucks might have to wait for a second operation. In some cases, this waiting may have a significant impact on congestion in the port areas and thus additionally increases the average time in system for a truck. If, e.g., no operational measures allow a truck to leave the queue or the inner port area during waiting, other trucks waiting can obviously not be served. This effect is especially critical when a truck, due to loading restrictions, cannot load the first available container and thus needs to wait until an appropriate container can be provided.

More generally, these results indicate that operational costs and emissions may be opposing planning objectives and thus need to be modeled separately (as proposed in Section 4.4). That is, trucking companies may not be willing to accept an emissions reducing plan because it goes along with longer truck times in the system, causing lower cost-efficiency. Furthermore, it becomes clear that the implementation of a collaborative TAS can have a significant positive impact on emission and economic metrics, but needs be complemented by congestion management approaches in order to fully leverage the potential of the approach.

6   Conclusion

Prior work, e.g, by Zehendner and Feillet [30], has demonstrated the positive impact of TASs on various operational metrics at ports such as service quality of various transport vehicles. Nevertheless, existing studies on TASs have rarely drawn a connection to the important problem of port-related truck emissions often caused by evitable empty trips. In this study, we propose a collaborative TAS to reduce empty trips and emissions at ports. We evaluate the approach with a simulation model based on a case study with real-world data. We found that a collaborative TAS may be an effective tool to reduce emissions caused by avoidable empty trips, but should be complemented by appropriate congestion management. These findings extend work on a conceptual model for a TAS with collaboration by Islam et al. [14], connecting decision support levels of (truck appointment) systems to mathematical models in empty resource logistics and developing a simulation model to evaluate a basic collaborative TAS in practice. In addition, this study clearly quantifies the emission impact of the evaluated approach. The results also demonstrate that low costs and low emission levels may be opposing planning objectives, providing empirical evidence on the common misconception that operational efficiency improvements naturally go along with a reduction of emissions. Most remarkable, this is the first study to our knowledge to operationally evaluate coordinated truck appointments in a real-world case. The developed simulation model was designed in a generic way for possible application at diverse international ports. Although this practical case considers only drayage, the results encourage the development of similar approaches incorporating port hinterland processes because of the related problem structure. However, it has to be noted that this study only considers drayage and does not apply a sophisticated matching procedure. Future work should, therefore, include the application for an extended regional scope and the development of appropriate matching models.

References

1. Agarwal, R., Ergun, Ö., Houghtalen, L., Ozener, O.Ö.: Collaboration in cargo transportation. In: Optimization and Logistics Challenges in the Enterprise, pp. 373–409. Springer (2009)
2. Air Resources Board: Mobile source emission inventory (2015). http://www.arb.ca.gov/msei/msei.htm
3. van Asperen, E., Borgman, B., Dekker, R.: Evaluating impact of truck announcements on container stacking efficiency. Flexible Services and Manufacturing Journal **25**(4), 543–556 (2011)
4. Bergqvist, R., Egels-Zandén, N.: Green port dues - The case of hinterland transport. Research in Transportation Business & Management **5**, 85–91 (2012)
5. Bielli, M., Boulmakoul, A., Rida, M.: Object oriented model for container terminal distributed simulation. European Journal of Operational Research **175**(3), 1731–1751 (2006)
6. Englert, B., Lam, S., Steinhoff, P.: The impact of truck repositioning on congestion and pollution in the LA Basin. Tech. rep., METRANS (2011)
7. Ergun, Ö., Kuyzu, G., Savelsbergh, M.: Reducing truckload transportation costs through collaboration. Transportation Science **41**(2), 206–221 (2007)
8. Giuliano, G., O'Brien, T.: Reducing port-related truck emissions: The terminal gate appointment system at the Ports of Los Angeles and Long Beach. Transportation Research Part D: Transport and Environment **12**(7), 460–473 (2007)
9. Google Earth: Google Earth (2015). https://earth.google.de
10. Gritsenko, D., Yliskylä-Peuralahti, J.: Governing shipping externalities: Baltic ports in the process of SOx emission reduction. Maritime Studies **12**(10, 21 pages) (2013)
11. Guan, C., Liu, R.: Modeling gate congestion of marine container terminals, truck waiting cost, and optimization. Transportation Research Record: Journal of the Transportation Research Board **2100**, 58–67 (2009)
12. Henesey, L., Notteboom, T., Davidsson, P.: Agent-based simulation of stakeholders relations: an approach to sustainable port and terminal management. In: Proceedings of the IAME Conference, p. 99 (2003)
13. Islam, S., Olsen, T.: Truck-sharing challenges for hinterland trucking companies: A case of the empty container truck trips problem. Business Process Management Journal **20**(2), 290–334 (2014)
14. Islam, S., Olsen, T., Ahmed, M.D.: Reengineering the seaport container truck hauling process: Reducing empty slot trips for transport capacity improvement. Business Process Management Journal **19**(5), 752–782 (2013)
15. Kim, N., Janic, M., van Wee, B.: Trade-off between carbon dioxide emissions and logistics costs based on multiobjective optimization. Transportation Research Record: Journal of the Transportation Research Board **2139**, 107–116 (2009)

16. Lam, J.S.L., Gu, Y.: Port hinterland intermodal container flow optimisation with green concerns: A literature review and research agenda. International Journal of Shipping and Transport Logistics **5**(3), 257–281 (2013)
17. Lättilä, L., Henttu, V., Hilmola, O.P.: Hinterland operations of sea ports do matter: Dry port usage effects on transportation costs and CO2 emissions. Transportation Research Part E: Logistics and Transportation Review **55**, 23–42 (2013)
18. Liao, C.H., Tseng, P.H., Cullinane, K., Lu, C.S.: The impact of an emerging port on the carbon dioxide emissions of inland container transport: An empirical study of Taipei port. Energy Policy **38**(9), 5251–5257 (2010)
19. Lozano, S., Moreno, P., Adenso-Díaz, B., Algaba, E.: Cooperative game theory approach to allocating benefits of horizontal cooperation. European Journal of Operational Research **229**(2), 444–452 (2013)
20. Lun, Y.H.: Green management practices and firm performance: A case of container terminal operations. Resources, Conservation and Recycling **55**(6), 559–566 (2011)
21. Mankowska, D.S., Bierwirth, C., Meisel, F.: Modelling the synchronization of transport means in logistics service operations. In: Böse, J.W., Hu, H., Jahn, C., Shi, X., Stahlbock, R., Voß, S. (eds.) ICCL 2011. LNCS, vol. 6971, pp. 74–85. Springer, Heidelberg (2011)
22. McKinnon, A.C., Ge, Y.: The potential for reducing empty running by trucks: A retrospective analysis. International Journal of Physical Distribution & Logistics Management **36**(5), 391–410 (2006)
23. Morais, P., Lord, E.: Terminal Appointment System Study. Tech. rep.,Transportation Research Board (2006)
24. Murty, K.G., Wan, Y.-W., Liu, J., Tseng, M.M., Leung, E., Lai, K.-K., Chiu, H.W.C.: Hongkong International Terminals gains elastic capacity using a data-intensive decision-support system. Interfaces **35**(1), 61–75 (2005)
25. Namboothiri, R., Erera, A.L.: Planning local container drayage operations given a port access appointment system. Transportation Research Part E: Logistics and Transportation Review **44**(2), 185–202 (2008)
26. Özener, O.Ö., Ergun, Ö.: Allocating costs in a collaborative transportation procurement network. Transportation Science **42**(2), 146–165 (2008)
27. Psaraftis, H.N., Kontovas, C.A.: Ship emissions: logistics and other tradeoffs. In: 10th Int. Marine Design Conference (IMDC 2009), Trondheim, Norway, pp. 26–29 (2009)
28. Rijsenbrij, J.C., Wieschemann, A.: Sustainable container terminals: a design approach. In: Böse, J.W. (ed.) Handbook of Terminal Planning, pp. 61–82. Springer New York (2011)
29. Villalba, G., Gemechu, E.D.: Estimating GHG emissions of marine ports–the case of Barcelona. Energy Policy **39**(3), 1363–1368 (2011)
30. Zehendner, E., Feillet, D.: Benefits of a truck appointment system on the service quality of inland transport modes at a multimodal container terminal. European Journal of Operational Research **235**(2), 461–469 (2014)
31. Zhang, X., Zeng, Q., Chen, W.: Optimization model for truck appointment in container terminals. Procedia - Social and Behavioral Sciences **96**, 1938–1947 (2013)
32. Zhao, W., Goodchild, A.V.: The impact of truck arrival information on container terminal rehandling. Transportation Research Part E: Logistics and Transportation Review **46**(3), 327–343 (2010)

Computational Intelligence to Support Cooperative Seaport Decision-Making in Environmental and Ecological Sustainability

Ana X. Halabi Echeverry[1(✉)], Jairo R. Montoya-Torres[1],
Deborah Richards[2], and Nelson Obregón Neira[3]

[1] Escuela Internacional de Ciencias Económicas y Administrativas, Universidad de La Sabana,
Km 7 Autopista Norte de Bogotá, D.C., Chía (Cundinamarca), Colombia
{ana.halabi,jairo.montoya}@unisabana.edu.co
[2] Computing Department, Macquarie University, Sydney, NSW 2109, Australia
deborah.richards@mq.edu.au
[3] Instituto Geofísico, Universidad Javeriana, Carrera 7 no. 42-27 Piso 7, Bogotá, Colombia
nobregon@javeriana.edu.co

Abstract. The substantial amounts of information that must be gathered, preserved, and used to analyse environmental and ecological impacts on seaports such as the international standards, deserve a direct way to manage and improve those impacts in a seaport through a systematic environmental management system (EMS). We present an artefact called the conceptual intelligent decision-making support module (*i*-DMSS) to enhance cooperative seaport decision-making (COSEADM) in environmental and ecological sustainability. Three interrelated activities of data collection, descriptive and normative modelling, incorporate processes of handling the decision-making side and processes integrating engineering requirements to produce the conceptual *i*-DMSS module. We include two data-driven models to handle the decision-making side of this module and automatically induce domain knowledge. Besides, we deploy and standardise the data-driven models and use the Predictive modelling markup language (PMML) to show advantages of data interoperability. Finally, we offer the rationale of the ontological process to anticipate and provide illustration of how to describe concepts in regard to COSEADM for environmental and ecological sustainability. This module demonstrates how the capture and interoperation of information and decisional structures can be managed.

Keywords: Cooperative decision-making · Seaports · Environmental and ecological sustainability · Intelligent decision support systems

1 Introduction

Factors driving environmental and ecological management worldwide enable connections between incentives and international standards that set the parameters in which a seaport can engage in partnership with other seaports.

© Springer International Publishing Switzerland 2015
F. Corman et al. (Eds.): ICCL 2015, LNCS 9335, pp. 510–525, 2015.
DOI: 10.1007/978-3-319-24264-4_35

Environmental and ecological factors influencing seaport sustainability are suggested in: APPA [1], Kruse [2], Ng & Song [3] and recently in Acciaro et al. [4] and Lam & Notteboom [5]. Figure 1 displays the generic approach to an environmental and ecological scheme proposed in [1] which addresses most of the main challenges mentioned in the literature. However, as stated by Puente-Rodríguez et al. [6a, 6b] key environmental and ecological aspects to be identified largely depend on the social and regulatory context in which the seaports operate. Essentially environmental and ecological factors are influenced by the fact that negative externalities of a seaport mainly reflect on the local level [7]. The cooperative relationship among ports usually incorporates controlling and policing functions within a port jurisdiction[1]. In this line, [2] states that incentives and international standards can help seaports manage continually health, safety and security environments.

Concerning port safety and environmental regulations, the environmental protection management code (IPSEM) is the minimum distinction requirement needed for a port to operate under environmental standards. Regulatory measures recognised and implemented internationally by ports include: the International Ship and Port Facility Security Code (ISPS), the International Maritime Organization (IMO) and the World's Customs Organization (WCO) regulations.

According to the U.S. Environmental Protection Agency EPA, an environmental management system (EMS) can be seen as a systematic approach to manage environmental programs such a as the footprint of a seaport [8]. The substantial amounts of information that must be gathered, preserved, and used to analyse environmental and ecological impacts, and to account on analyses for decision-making has served as the origin of initiatives such as the prototype for the environmental information management system (EIMS) conducted in 2006 by Cambridge Systematics, Inc., with Parsons Brinckerhoff and Venner Consulting, Inc. [9]

Expected benefits of EMS for ports in general are summarised by [2, p. 1] as:

Fig. 1. APPA's approach of an Environmental Awareness Program [4]

- Demonstrate leadership in environmental protection
- Enhance credibility and public image
- Reduce cost and improve efficiency
- Lower environmental liability and improve insurance coverage
- Improve emergency response capability
- Increase staff awareness, competency, involvement and morale
- Establish common management framework to integrate other seaport objectives, such as safety, security, operational efficiency and community relations.

---

[1] Port jurisdiction is an area endorsed and accredited in recent years at the international and local level, including the right of intervention on high seas against vessels having committed violations, such as marine pollution discharges.

Seaports depend on the environment in which they operate to be sustained. Even if ports compete rather than collaborate in many of its functions, the necessity of seaports to collaborate is stronger when the function of the seaport concentrates on operating under the consideration of climate, water, air, soil and use of biodiversity as resources [7,10]. As a result, to integrate EMS functions among seaports such as plans, documents, policy, normativity and performance measurements, is of extremely importance and requires a systematic approach to enhance in future its practice. Following [5,11] and others referenced by the author, we concluded that seaports are able to successfully use EMS to identify and manage environmental and ecological challenges, setting standards and accomplishing international environmental and ecological initiatives, and thus becoming leaders in EMS programmes.

In such a context, the aim of this paper is to present an artifact, called the conceptual intelligent decision-making support module (i-DMSS), devoted to support cooperative seaport decision-making (COSEADM) for the purpose of environmental and ecological sustainability. This module operates on different subsets of data and concentrates on the analysis of influential environmental and ecological factors as well as on a stricter EMS framework based on international schemes, such as The International Organization for Standardization -ISO14001.

To do so, the remainder of this paper is organised as follows: Section 2 presents an overview of the approach followed in this research. Section 3 is devoted to present the conceptual i-DMSS module for cooperative seaport decision-making in environmental and ecological sustainability. A case study on the application of the module is given in Section 4. Finally, some concluding remarks and opportunities for further research are outlined in Section 5.

2   Research Approach

As stated previously, this paper presents an artifact called the conceptual intelligent decision-making support module (called i-DMSS) for cooperative seaport decision-making (COSEADM) for the purpose of environmental and ecological sustainability. Envisaged results of this module will enable decision makers to determine key seaport partners based on EMS aims. This artefact aims at responding the following research question:

How can computational intelligence support cooperative seaport decision-making for environmental and ecological sustainability?

In validating our research question, we first customised a dataset with environmental and ecological factors influencing seaport sustainability as mentioned above. These factors can be grouped in those addressing: 1) reducing air emissions, 2) improving water quality, and 3) minimising impacts of growth, the latest indicating the territorial extension of the seaport and its effects on neighbouring communities. We also documented the dataset with strict EMS frameworks based on international schemes, such as The International Organization for Standardization -ISO14001.

Secondly we related the data collection process with the modelling and interoperation of data structures. Studies in computational intelligence present data-driven mechanisms as the key concept of learning from observations.

Further, we also found the importance of a data-driven approach to develop the promise of our i-DMSS module for COSEADM in environmental and ecological sustainability as being able to:

1. Assist in dealing with complex decision-making, especially if uncertainty of inputs/data for decision-making is present,
2. Provide with a source of quantitative information and periodical results and validation,
3. Allow for handling heterogeneous repositories and merging data with different goals and *foci* and,
4. Allow for acquiring knowledge from the characteristics of the data.

The originality of our i-DMSS module for COSEADM in environmental and ecological sustainability is that it supports analysis of a hierarchy; from raw unstructured data at the lowest level to high level data that has been structured and formalised as one or more ontologies, i.e., use of a common terminology in which modelling and shared knowledge are represented.

Also our approach use two main types of data: 1) historical, factual or declarative knowledge (i.e. what data is used during decision-making, e.g., port performance indicators and regulatory frameworks), and 2) procedural knowledge (i.e. data about how decisions are made, e.g., business intelligence). Both types of data are needed for decisions concerning seaport environmental and ecological sustainability.

We aim to understand and model the effects observed in seaport decision-making for environmental and ecological sustainability, tackling the difficulty of merging information and finding the best possible representations (model) in order to produce an artefact to aid the decision-making process.

3   Overview of the Conceptual i-DMSS Module for Cooperative Seaport Decision-Making in Environmental and Ecological Sustainability

Before describing the structure of the proposed i-DMSS module, a distinction between: Decision support system (DSS), Decision-making support system (DMSS), and Intelligent Decision-making Support System (i-DMSS) is to be made. DSS is a computer-based information system designed for the purpose of improving the process and outcome of decision-making. DMSS is an information system that interactively supports all phases of a user's decision-making process, whilst i-DMSS extends the classical DSS approach by incorporating machine learning to successfully respond to information without human intervention. The developments of DSS so far "have focused on high-level decision-making (strategic decision) but using low levels of representation (data, equation, etc.) because (1) the notion of data representation has not been sufficiently studied and (2) high level decisions are more appealing than small decisions" [12, p. 27].

The classic framework for a decision-oriented DSS development comes from the field of Decision Theory (Stabell, cited in [13]). Stabell's development makes a distinction between "substance (what is used during decision-making) and procedure (how decisions are made)" and relies on three interrelated activities [13, p. 103]:

1. Data collection: including data on current decision-making using various techniques (e.g., historical records);
2. Descriptive modelling: establishing a coherent description of the current decision process;
3. Normative modelling: specifying a norm for how decisions should be made.

We implemented these interrelated activities and incorporated processes of: 1) of handling the decision-making side, and 2) integrating engineering requirements to produce the conceptual *i*-DMSS module for seaport environmental and ecological sustainability. According to IEEE std 1220-2025 [14] processes integrating engineering requirements transform stakeholder' needs and requirements into system products, generating information for decision makers, and providing input for the next level of development.

Next section presents the conceptual design for the decision of COSEADM making for environmental and ecological sustainability considering environmental and ecological factors and strict EMS frameworks based on international schemes.

4   Case Study to Demonstrate the Conceptual *i*-DMSS Module

To demonstrate the conceptual *i*-DMSS module for COSEADM in environmental and ecological sustainability, we identify a potential decision that port authorities may wish to make. In our case study, we consider the situation where we might want to classify subgroups of seaports who are achieving similar environmental management system standards to identify potential cooperation. The assumption is that a port would want to cooperate with other ports who shared their standards. For example, the ports of the United States, Canada, and Australia show similarities in their assessment of policies based on environmental grounds that have led to various consequences for the seaport and their transport systems. In our case study, we show an example of the decision that might be made with the *i*-DMSS module using 44 ports in the coastal zones of the United States. In the next subsections, we first consider the data collection needed to explore COSEADM for environmental and ecological sustainability based on achievement of environmental and ecological standards, followed by discussion of the process needed to make that decision.

4.1   Understanding the Data

The existence of appropriate datasets is essential for a data-driven approach. A feature of the COSEADM for environmental and ecological sustainability is the lack of available datasets that combine data from multiple seaports. It is necessary to handle heterogeneous repositories and merging data with different goals and foci, contributing to the identification of data-levels.

Our dataset is comprised of three data levels: (1) A macro-level that supports a semantic relationship built from computing salient factors pointing to the accomplishment of cross-cutting seaport EMS programs, such as the Global Environmental Program (GEP) that encompasses projects such the Land-Ocean Interactions in the Coastal Zones (LOICZ) as reported by LOICZ Inprint [15]. This level supports inductive representations and complex data associations. (2) Meso-level data supports port performance indicators such as those identified and grouped in section 1, i.e., reduction of air emissions, water quality improvements, and minimisation of port growing impacts. This level provides general associations or flow relationships among micro data. (3) Micro-level of data lowers the analysis to measurements, for example, disposal of oils and chemicals (i.e., nitrogen oxides (NOx), sulphur oxides (SOx), carbon dioxides (CO2) and ozone (O3).

Data collection is possible using accessible data sources such as the following:

- **Bureau of Ocean Energy Management, Regulation and Enforcement** (BOERMRE), http://www.boemre.gov/ld/PDFs/OCSstatusMap8e(3).pdf
- **The Environmental Protection Agency (EPA)** http://water.epa.gov/scitech/datait/databases/cwns/upload/apex-2.pdf
- http://watersgeo.epa.gov/mwm/?layer=LEGACY_WBD&feature=03160205&extra Layers=null
- **The International Maritime Organization (IMO)** https://gisis.imo.org/Public/PRF/Default.aspx
- **US Army Corps of Engineers (USACE)** http://el.erdc.usace.army.mil/odd/SiteQuery.asp
- **United States Department of Agriculture (USDA)**
- http://www.reeis.usda.gov/portal/page?_pageid=193,1&_dad=portal&_schema=P ORTAL
- **United States Geological Survey (USGS)**
- http://gapanalysis.usgs.gov/protected-area-statistics-by-state/
- **US County.org**
- http://uscounty.org/us-counties-descending-by-population.htm

4.2 Descriptive Modelling

In this subsection we show the business process essential to define how the decision of COSEADM for environmental and ecological sustainability is made. Figure 2 depicts what is needed (i.e. the preconditions) and what is to be achieved (i.e. the aims) comprising the module outputs.

The preconditions include: a) the necessary data hierarchy to structure the module (i.e., macro-level, meso-level and micro-level data), b) the context for the decision (i.e., local, US seaports in coastal zones), and c) the dimension (or perspective) for a seaport cooperation, mainly referred to a governance perspective but it can be also seen from logistics operations and transportation perspectives.

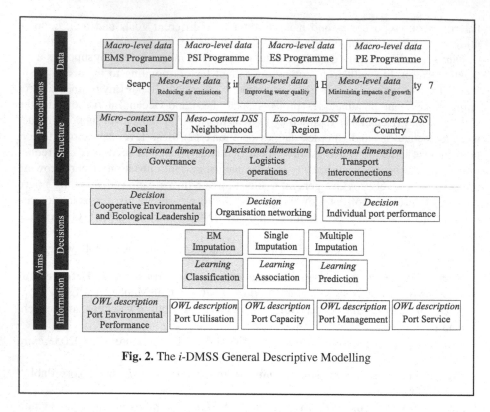

Fig. 2. The *i*-DMSS General Descriptive Modelling

The aims comprise the module outputs: a) specific decisions (referring to case studies implemented such as COSEADM for environmental and ecological sustainability (EMS leadership), b) data-driven models embedded in the module (imputation, computational learning) and knowledge representations dealt with (OWL descriptions). The square boxes in gray underline the main components of the module presented in this paper. Other components correspond to further case studies.

4.3   Normative Modelling

The *i*-DMSS module for COSEADM in environmental and ecological sustainability provides two data-driven models to automatically induce domain knowledge: 1) completion of datasets through the Expectation Maximisation (EM) method of imputation, and 2) construction of a reliable classification process for detecting environmental and ecological benchmarks using Decision Trees (Random Forest) as the classification algorithm. Table 1 lists the two data driven models to induce domain knowledge in the *i*-DMSS module.

Table 1. Data-driven models to induce domain knowledge in this module.

Module's aim	Data-driven models	DM Software
COSEADM for environmental and ecological sustainability	1. EM Method of Imputation and Missing Values	IBM SPSS 19
	2. Supervised classification: Random Forest	Rapid Miner

Metadata has become an essential component of data-driven DSS as a mechanism to capture semantic data (meaning) about raw data. The use of metadata so far has not delved into opportunities, such as supporting users in knowledge discovery and decision support requirements [16]. We collected a selection of important metafeatures to create metadata as presented in Table 2. We use metalearning to take advantage of its main properties. Recently, the literature identifies metalearning as a solution for the automatic prediction of the best classifier [17].

Table 2. Metafeatures module - Case: US west coast, the Gulf and Atlantic coasts.

Metafeatures level	Notation	Value
Number of instances or observations	K	44
Number of variables or attributes	m	27
Number of output values	n	1
Dataset dimensionality	dim_{data}	0.61
Standard deviation of Tbase	$\overline{std_x}$	8,215,818
Coefficient of variation of Tbase	$\overline{varcoeff_x}$	1.241
Skewness of Tbase	$\overline{skew_x}$	1.641
Kurtosis of Tbase	$kurt_x$	5.323
Normalised class entropy	$H(C)_{norm}$	0.239
Normalised attribute entropy	$\overline{H(X)}_{norm}$	0.766
Percentage of missing values	mv.p	0.037
Subset ratio	set.r	0.3

An important issue in knowledge discovery regards to finding the finest classifier. Using the automatic system construction wizard in Rapid Miner 5.0®, the metalearning classification is a straightforward process. This wizard also aids evaluating each classifier and finding the parameterisation for the dataset at hand. We chose Random Forest (RF) as the learning algorithm. Even though RF provides an infinite number of random trees not necessarily optimal, it was useful to test some of them and find the best leaves (rules) during the classification process. Each forest produces a classification for the class StatusEMS. This class introduces the notion of a seaport leader (L), follower (F) and average user (A) of EMS. It has been created numerically using a weighting criterion of 5, 3 or 1 according to the level of compliance with the overviewed environmental and ecological standards reported by the literature, i.e.,

ISO14001, EPA EMS Port Primer, IPSEM, among others, (for detailed information refer to our earlier paper [18]).We identify the characteristics of each of these user types associating to the class 26 factors driving the environmental and ecological management as indicated in section 1.

An interesting classification results are tested in achieving the following parameters:

```
Number of random trees (M) =3; criterion=gain ratio; min-
imal size for split=4; minimal leaf size=2; minimal
gain=0.1; maximal depth=20; confidence level used for the
pessimistic error calculation of pruning= 0.45, and num-
ber of alternative nodes tried when prepruning=3. As ex-
pected, the m variables selected at random from M were
sensitive during the classification
```

The algorithm identifies the most salient variables presented below. We attained an overall accuracy of 70.45% of the RF model, reflecting the largest cohort of average seaport users (A) of EMS, followed by followers and leaders. Although the overall accuracy does not indicate an optimal classification it allows us to identify interesting rules particularly useful for the decision at hand. The topology of RF is presented in Figure 3 to illustrate how the classification can be used to describe the distinct groups of seaports. For example, Rule 5 (R5) identifies 20 out of 28 (A's) and 7 out of 9 (F's). This might indicate that high concentrations of ozone within the area of the seaport followed by none historical encountered problems at receiving ozone sub-stances by the seaport, is an important precedent to classify the seaport among those that should meet additional measures and requirements that otherwise are appropriate for those classified as leaders in EMS programmes. We do not attempt to give a fur-ther explanation of practical implications of the RF classification as it implies the elaboration of a different paper. However, for an understanding of a similar RF classi-fication refers to our earlier paper [18].

O3: *(ordinal)/ O3cont (nominal): fourth-highest daily maximum 8-hour average of ozone concentrations (03 air pollutants) measured ppb (parts per billion) within an area of a state by analysers of CASTNET in 2008 (nominal)*
Inadequacies: *yes/no historical problems encountered at the port reception facility and informed to IMO (International Maritime Organization)*
GAPStatus3: *current GIS acres calculated for a US state under the protection laws for conversion of natural land and water cover for the majority of area, according to the GAP analysis program in the US Geological survey (USGS) and coded 3; and subject to extractive uses of either broad, low intensity type (i.e., logging) or localised intense type (i.e., mining). GAP status3 confers protection to federally listed endan-gered and threatened species throughout the area.*
Type: *Type of port, i.e., deepwater, seaport, river-based*
NMS: *yes/no existence of national marine sanctuaries (NMS) where the port is relatively close located.*
LandFarms: *land in farms given in acres by state and country where the port is located or closely located*

4.4   Data Interoperability

A data-driven model for the *i*-DMSS module automatically determines critical data using packages of statistical software as it has been demonstrated. However, the

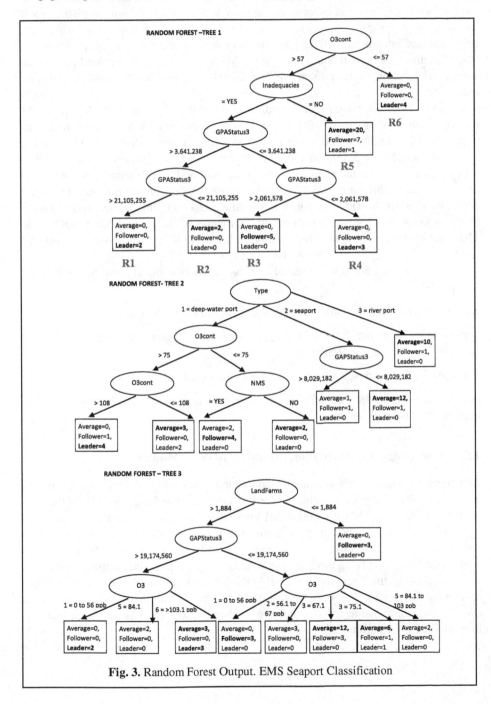

Fig. 3. Random Forest Output. EMS Seaport Classification

necessity to operationally deploy the DM model in a standard language prevails. The PMML technology allows a blend of several independent data mining (DM) solutions resulting in a PMML file containing multiple models. "This is the power of PMML: enabling true interoperability of models and solutions between applications. PMML also allows [shielding] end users from the complexity associated with statistical tools and models [19, p. 5]". The example we provide required the manual identification, collection and integration of data from different sources and the manual application of DM algorithms using different tools. The *i*-DMSS that we envisage should provide an automated solution to time-intensive and error-prone to linked activities inducing knowledge discovery.

Taking into consideration that RapidMiner 5.3® does not support PMML for the RF algorithm as of the time of this paper, it is necessary to export the resulting model object to R by simply invoking the pmml package. Figure 4 shows the process followed in RapidMiner 5.3® and Figure 5 shows the standard procedure used in R to provide *pmml* transformations contained in the RF model. The *pmml* package needs two parameters which are ntree=3 and the transformation object responsible for the continuous normalisation performed on the data, in this case, transform = MinMaxXform [0,1]. Listing 1 shows an extraction of the *pmml* code for RF in R. The generic usage of the *pmml* representation for RF in R 2.13.1 version is as follows [20]:

model refers to a RF object created in R as in the example (Figure 6) provided in [21, p. 250]

model.name refers to the name given to the model in the pmml code.

app.name refers to the name of the application that generated the pmml code. The example shows its use in Rattle.

description refers to descriptive text for the Header element of pmml.

transforms refers to data transformations represented in the package pmml Transformations as explained previously.

4.5   Knowledge Representation within the *i*-DMSS Module

Additionally to handle heterogeneous data sources and types, we propose the use of an ontology-based approach to further look at how the knowledge needed by the conceptual *i*-DMSS module for COSEADM in environmental and ecological sustainability can be represented. We give an illustration using the common knowledge representation known as Ontology Web Language (OWL) of how to describe patterns of port productivity involving environmental and ecological planning, impacts and emissions, relative to the decision of COSEADM for environmental and ecological sustainability. The OWL has been standardised by the World Wide Web Consortium (W3C). Despite its name OWL is not confined to the web but has many applications in modelling information [22].

Ontology also provides a shared conceptualization of common terms between variables (attributes) to make efficient decision support processes. The illustration of the ontological description is provided as a first step to guide future development of a semantic
model towards the COSEADM for environmental and ecological sustainability.

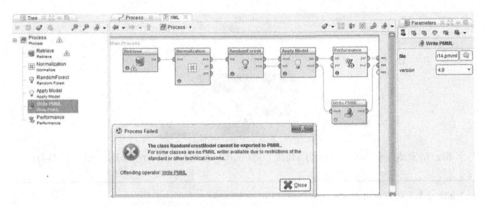

Fig. 4. Computing output RF exported to PMML version 4.0

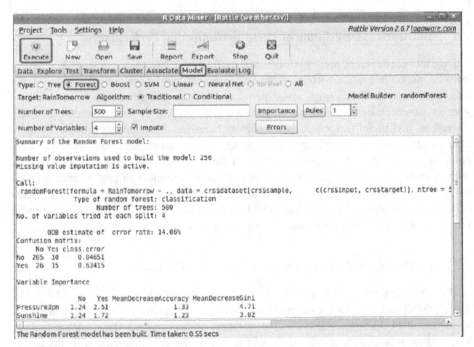

Fig. 5. RF object created in R using Rattle (taken from [Williams (2011, p. 250].

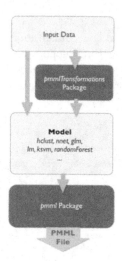

Fig. 6. Standard Procedure of PMML code output for R. Taken from Jena et al. (2013)

Listing 1. Extraction of the *pmml* code

```
> ## S3 method for class 'randomForest'
> pmml(model, model.name="randomForest_Model", app.name="Rattle/PMML",
+ description="Random Forest Tree Model", copyright=NULL, transforms=NULL,
```

4.6   Illustration: Description of Port Environmental Performance

Taking into account that port environmental performance becomes a seaport function of growing public interest, environmental and ecological factors are criteria that will enter into operational choices, capital investments, and cargo routing decisions. The choice of port environmental metrics should be dictated in large part by their intended use [23]. Therefore, traditional factors, such as efficient handling of containers require far more than just quayside space and labour. In these circumstances, seaports that commonly compete for vessel calls (named as "Calls") find themselves compelled to cooperate with other ports to reduce their air emissions through a number of port reception facilities in which final disposal of residues/wastes occur for the sake of environment, safety of workers and population (Facilities) [5]. Listing2 shows the ontological description for port environmental performance combining the criteria above mentioned.

4.7   Challenges in the Development of the *i*-DMSS Module

In defining the *i*-DMSS modular development some considerations need to be made. The *i*-DMSS module provides a guide to describe the decision at hand and challenges simultaneously decision makers and developers to incorporate the decision-making side and engineering requirements. In this sense, we believe this paper fills the gap in the literature presented in [24, 25]. Due to the complexity of the necessities identified, the *i*-DMSS module is required to overcome current concerns about its update and data management as well as the limitations and complications that may rise adopting an easy-to-use platform [24].

OWL:
Class (PortEnvironmentalPerformance) Partial
DataLevels
restriction (*hasA* amongst other things some values From Calls)
restriction (*hasA* amongst other things some values From Facilities)
Paraphrase:
PortEnvironmentalPerformance has *amongst other things*, *both* has *some* values from calls service of vessels of 10,000 DWT or greater (Calls) and *also some* values from port reception facilities in which final disposal of residues/wastes occur for the sake of environment, safety of workers and population (Facilities).

Listing 2. Ontological description of port environmental performance towards the COSEADM for environmental and ecological sustainability.

5   Conclusions and Future Work

The conceptual *i*-DMSS module for COSEADM in environmental and ecological sustainability demonstrates how capturing and interoperate information can be managed. The intelligence has been tackled via data mining for the classification of a seaport leadership in EMS programmes. Using a case study of 44 ports in the coastal zones of the United States, data structures and a hierarchy of data levels exemplify. The fact that Random Forest (RF) was observed to perform well on our dataset indicates that this learning algorithm is appropriate for the decision at hand. Using the rationale of ontologies, we provide illustration of how to describe concepts in regard to this decision. We are required to overcome current concerns about its update and data management as well as the limitations and complications that may rise adopting an easy-to-use platform for the *i*-DMSS module.

References

1. American Association of Port Authorities AAPA. Environmental Management Handbook (1998)
2. Kruse, C.J.: Environmental management systems at ports - a new initiative. In: Proceedings of the 14th Biennial Coastal Zone Conference (2005)
3. Ng, A.K.Y., Song, S.: The environmental impacts of pollutants generated by routine shipping operations on ports. Ocean and Coastal Management **53**, 301–311 (2010)
4. Acciaro, M., Vanelslander, T., Sys, C., Ferrari, C., Roumboutsos, A., Giuliano, G., Kapros, S.: Environmental sustainability in seaports: a framework for successful innovation. Maritime Policy and Management **41**(5), 480–500 (2014). doi:10.1080/03088839.2014.932926
5. Lam, J.S.L., Notteboom, T.: The Greening of Ports: A Comparison of Port Management Tools Used by Leading Ports in Asia and Europe. Transport Reviews **34**(2) (2014)

6. Puente-Rodríguez, D., van Slobbe, E., Al, I.A.C., Lindenbergh, D.E.: Knowledge co-production in practice: Enabling environmental management systems for ports through participatory research in the Dutch Wadden Sea. Environmental Science and Policy (In press, 2015). doi:http://dx.doi.org/10.1016/j.envsci.2015.02.014

7. Puente-Rodríguez, D., Giebels, D., de Jonge, V.N.: Strengthening coastal zone management in the Wadden Sea by applying 'knowledge-practice interfaces'. Ocean and Coastal Management **108**, 27–38 (2015). http://dx.doi.org/10.1016/j.ocecoaman.2014.05.01 7

8. Verhoeven, P.: A review of port authority functions: towards a renaissance? Maritime Policy and Management **37**(3), 247–270 (2010). doi:10.1080/03088831003700645169-189. doi:10.1080/01441647.2014.891162

9. U.S. Environmental Protection Agency (EPA). (n.d). Retrieved from http://water.epa.gov/scitech/datait/databases/cwns/upload/apex-2.pdf

10. National Cooperative Highway Research Program (NCHRP). Prototype software for an environmental information management and decision support system. (2007). Retrieved from http://onlinepubs.trb.org/onlinepubs/nchrp/nchrp_rrd_317.pdf

11. Hall, P., McCalla, R.J., Comtois, C., Slack, B.: Integrating Seaports and Trade Corridors. Ashgate Publishing Ltd. (2011)

12. Verhoeven, P.: European Ports Policy: Meeting Contemporary Governance Challenges. Maritime Policy and Management **36**(1), 79–101 (2009). doi:10.1080/03088830802652320

13. Pomerol, J.C., Adam, F.: Understanding Human decision-making - a fundamental step towards effective intelligent decision support. In: PhillipsWren, G., Ichalkaranje, N., Jain, L.C. (eds.) Intelligent Decision-making: An Ai-Based Approach. SCI, vol. 97, pp. 3–40. Springer-Verlag, Berlin (2008)

14. Gachet, A., Haettenschwiler, P.: Development processes of intelligent decision-making support systems: review and perspective. In: Intelligent Decision-making Support Systems, pp. 97–121. Springer, London (2008)

15. IEEE Standard for Application and Management of the Systems Engineering Process. IEEE Std 1220-2005 (Revision of IEEE Std 1220-1998), 0_1-87. doi:10.1109/IEEESTD.2005.96469

16. INPRINT. INPRINT Newsletter 2010-2014. (2014). Accessed March 15, 2015 (2005)

17. Varga, J., Romero, O., Pedersen, T.B., Thomsen, C.: Towards next generation BI systems: the analytical metadata challenge. In: Bellatreche, L., Mohania, M.K. (eds.) DaWaK 2014. LNCS, vol. 8646, pp. 89–101. Springer, Heidelberg (2014)

18. Abdelmessih, S.D., Shafait, F., Reif, M., Goldstein, M.: Landmarking for Meta-Learning using RapidMiner. German Research Center for Artificial Intelligence, Germany (2010). Retrieved from http://www.mendeley.com/research/landmarking-metalearning-using-rapidminer

19. Halabi Echeverry, A.X., Richards, D., Bilgin, A.: Identifying characteristics of seaports for environmental benchmarks based on meta-learning. In: Richards, D., Kang, B.H. (eds.) PKAW 2012. LNCS, vol. 7457, pp. 350–363. Springer, Heidelberg (2012)

20. Guazzelli, A.: What is PMML? Explore the power of predictive analytics and open standards (2010). Retrieved from http://public.dhe.ibm.com/software/dw/industry/ind-PMML1/ind-PMML1-pdf.pdf

21. Breiman, L., Cutler, A.: Random Forest: Breiman and Cutler's random forests for classification and regression (2009). Retrieved from http://cran.r-project.org/web/packages/randomForest/index.html

22. Williams, G.: Random Forests Data Mining with Rattle and R, pp. 245–268. Springer, New York (2011)

23. Krötzsch, M.: OWL 2 profiles: an introduction to lightweight ontology languages. In: Eiter, T., Krennwallner, T. (eds.) Reasoning Web 2012. LNCS, vol. 7487, pp. 112–183. Springer, Heidelberg (2012)
24. The Tioga Group, I., Moraga, CA. Improving marine container terminal productivity [Report], p. 136 (2010)
25. McIntosh, B.S., Ascough Ii, J.C., Twery, M., Chew, J., Elmahdi, A., Haase, D., Voinov, A.: Environmental decision support systems (EDSS) development – Challenges and best practices. Environmental Modelling and Software 26(12), 1389–1402 (2011). doi:10.1016/j.envsoft.2011.09.009
26. Laniak, G.F., Olchin, G., Goodall, J., Voinov, A., Hill, M., Glynn, P., Hughes, A.: Integrated environmental modeling: A vision and roadmap for the future. Environmental Modelling and Software 39, 3–23 (2013). doi:10.1016/j.envsoft.2012.09.006

A Sample-Based Method for Perishable Good Inventory Control with a Service Level Constraint

Eligius M.T. Hendrix[1]([⊠]), Karin G.J. Pauls-Worm[2], Roberto Rossi[3], Alejandro G. Alcoba[1], and Rene Haijema[2]

[1] Computer Architecture, Universidad de Málaga, Málaga, Spain
{eligius,agutierrez}@uma.es
[2] Operations Research and Logistics, Wageningen University, Wageningen, Netherlands
{karin.pauls,rene.haijema}@wur.nl
[3] Business School, Edinburgh University, Edinburgh, UK
roberto.rossi@ed.ac.uk

Abstract. This paper studies the computation of so-called order-up-to levels for a stochastic programming inventory problem of a perishable product. Finding a solution is a challenge as the problem enhances a perishable product, fixed ordering cost and non-stationary stochastic demand with a service level constraint. An earlier study [7] derived order-up-to values via an MILP approximation. We consider a computational method based on the so-called Smoothed Monte Carlo method using sampled demand to optimize values. The resulting MINLP approach uses enumeration, bounding and iterative nonlinear optimization.

Keywords: Inventory control · Perishable products · MINLP · Chance constraint · Monte carlo

1 Introduction

The basis of our study is a Stochastic programming (SP) model published in [7] for a practical production planning problem over a finite horizon of T periods of a perishable product with a fixed shelf life of J periods. The static dynamic uncertainty YS policy in [7] provides the decision maker with a list of order timings Y and order-up-to levels S. They generate the values for the policy using an approximation based on MILP. The approximation has problems with fulfilling the so-called service level constraints for some of the tested instances. The question in the current paper is how to generate optimal timing and order-up-to values based on Monte Carlo samples of demand; we call this a sample-based approach.

The considered problem has uncertain and non-stationary demand such that one produces to stock. Any unmet demand is backlogged. Mathematically this

© Springer International Publishing Switzerland 2015
F. Corman et al. (Eds.): ICCL 2015, LNCS 9335, pp. 526–540, 2015.
DOI: 10.1007/978-3-319-24264-4_36

means that negative inventory may occur. To keep waste due to out-dating low, one issues the oldest product first, i.e. FIFO issuance. The model assumes a zero lead time. The investigated model aims to guarantee the customer that the probability of not being out-of-stock is higher than a required service level α in every period $t \in \{1, 2, ..., T\}$. I.e. the out of stock probability is less than $1 - \alpha$. The latter implies being mathematically confronted with a chance constraint. This leads to challenging optimization problems, e.g. [2].

Due to dealing with a perishable product, the inventory consists of items of different ages $j = 1, \ldots, J - 1$. Depending on its value at moment t, an order policy should advice the decision maker on the order quantity Q_t. The static dynamic uncertainty YS policy provides a list of order moments $Y \in \{0, 1\}^T$ called an order timing vector, or alternatively it provides at each order the so-called replenishment cycle R_t up to the next order takes place. Given the order timing, we derive theoretical results about the order quantity for the given service level constraints. Besides it provides a list with order-up-to levels S_t. The values generated by the presented MILP model of [7] unfortunately do not exactly fulfil the service level (chance) constraints for all instances. Therefore, our first research question is how to generate values for S_t such that the chance constraints are fulfilled for all instances and expected costs are minimized. Following the concept of Monte Carlo estimation, we present a sample-based model to generate the values S_t. It is known from literature that the corresponding sample-based model called MC-MILP for most instances cannot be solved in reasonable time, e.g. [8]. Therefore, we investigate the possibility to use an equivalent MINLP model based on the Smoothed Monte Carlo method, see [3]. A specific algorithm is designed that uses enumeration and bounding for the integer part Y of the problem leaving us with iteratively solving an NLP problem in the continuous variables S.

We present a more flexible variant of the YS policy that we call YQ(X) policy. It also fixes the best order moments Y but in the order quantity Q_t takes the distribution X of the age of items in stock into account. The second question is how to determine the order quantity. The YQ(X) policy is more difficult to implement for decision support in practice than the YS policy. Our third question is for which cases the YS policy is doing much worse than the YQ(X) policy. We measure how well required service levels are met and estimate the expected cost of all generated policies for the instances provided by [7].

This paper is organised as follows. Section 2 describes the underlying SP model with chance constraints. Section 3 focuses on the properties of the optimal order quantities considering the corresponding basic order-up-to levels and the concept of approximating the chance constraints by samples. Section 4 describes the MC-MILP and MINLP models for generating values for the quantities S_t for the YS policy. Section 5 provides the elaboration of a sample-based algorithm to optimize the YQ(X) policy. In Section 6, we measure numerically for which characteristics of the instances the YS policy provides good enough performance compared to the YQ(X) policy. Section 7 summarizes our findings.

2   Stochastic Programming Model

The stochastic demand implies that the model has random (denoted in bold) inventory variables $\boldsymbol{I}_{jt}$ apart from the initial fixed levels I_{j0}. If the order decision Q_t depends on the inventory levels at the beginning of the period, then Q_t is also a random variable. In the notation, $P(.)$ denotes a probability to express the chance constraints and $E(.)$ is the expected value operator for the expected costs. Moreover, we use $x^+ = max\{x, 0\}$. A formal description of the SP model presented in [7] is given.

Indices
  t period index, $t = 1, \ldots, T$, with T the time horizon
  j age index, $j = 1, \ldots, J$, with J the fixed shelf life
Data
  d_t Normally distributed demand with expectation $\mu_t > 0$ and variance
    $(cv \times \mu_t)^2$ where cv is a given coefficient of variation.
  k fixed ordering cost, $k > 0$
  c unit procurement cost, $c > 0$
  h unit inventory cost, $h > 0$
  w unit disposal cost, is negative when having a salvage value, $w > -c$
  α required service level, $0 < \alpha < 1$

Variables
  $Q_t \geq 0$ ordered and delivered quantity at the beginning of period t
  $\boldsymbol{I}_{jt}$ Inventory of age j at end of period t, initial inventory fixed $I_{j0} = 0$,
    $\boldsymbol{I}_{1t} \in \mathbb{R}$, $\boldsymbol{I}_{jt} \geq 0$ for $j = 2, \ldots, J$.
The total expected costs over the finite horizon is to be minimized.

$$E\left(\sum_{t=1}^{T}\left(g(Q_t) + h\sum_{j=1}^{J-1}\boldsymbol{I}_{jt}^+ + w\boldsymbol{I}_{Jt}\right)\right) = \sum_{t=1}^{T}E\left(g(Q_t) + h\sum_{j=1}^{J-1}\boldsymbol{I}_{jt}^+ + w\boldsymbol{I}_{Jt}\right),$$
$$\tag{1}$$

where procurement cost is given by the function

$$g(x) = k + cx, \quad \text{if } x > 0, \text{ and } g(0) = 0. \tag{2}$$

The chance constraint expressing the required service level is

$$P(\boldsymbol{I}_{1t} \geq 0) \geq \alpha, \ t = 1, \ldots, T. \tag{3}$$

Due to FIFO issuing, if the freshest inventory is negative, no older items are in stock. The inventory dynamics of items of different ages is described by

$$\boldsymbol{I}_{1t} = Q_t - \left(\boldsymbol{d}_t - \sum_{j=1}^{J-1}\boldsymbol{I}_{j,t-1}\right)^+, \ t = 1, \ldots, T \tag{4}$$

for the freshest inventory and

$$I_{jt} = \left(I_{j-1,t-1} - (d_t - \sum_{i=j}^{J-1} I_{i,t-1})^+\right)^+ , \ t = 1, \dots, T, j = 2, \dots, J \quad (5)$$

for older items. These dynamic equations describe the FIFO issuing policy and imply that I_{1t} is a free variable, whereas I_{jt} is nonnegative for the older vintages $j = 2, \dots, J$. Notice that the oldest inventory I_{Jt} perishes and becomes waste. Let

$$X = (I_{1,t-1}, \dots, I_{J-1,t-1}) \quad (6)$$

be the inventory with its age distribution at the beginning of the period. An order policy is a set of rules $Q_t : \mathbb{R}^{J-1} \to \mathbb{R}, t = 1, \dots, T$ which given the inventory state X at the beginning of the period specifies the amount to be ordered by function $Q_t(X)$. [6] show that a straightforward dynamic programming approach to optimize the function $Q_t(X)$ provides not necessarily optimal solutions due to the service level constraint.

For a nonperishable product, a common way to deal with the planning is to define so-called order-up-to levels S_t, e.g. [10]. The decision maker replenishes at order moment t the inventory up to a level S_t. This means a vector S is provided to the decision maker and the order quantity is defined by

$$Q_t(X) = (S_t - \sum_{j=1}^{J-1} X_j)^+, \ t = 1, \dots, T. \quad (7)$$

Considering a fixed timing vector Y combined with order-up-to levels S_t is called an YS policy in [7]. The question is how to generate good values for S_t in case we are dealing with a perishable product and part of the inventory will become waste. We deal with this question in Sections 3 and 4.

Order policies that take the age distribution into account have been studied for stationary demand, see [11]. However, following this concept in a replenishment cycle environment with non-stationary demand requires a time dependent rule $Q_t(X)$. Considering a fixed timing vector Y combined with age dependent order quantities $Q_t(X)$ is called an YQ(X) policy here. The decision maker needs an information system that advices on the order quantity $Q_t(X)$; this is practically more complicated than the YS policy. In Section 5, we investigate how order quantities can be derived using sampled demand. As the YQ(X) policy is wider than the YS policy, it should provide lower expected cost than the case where the age distribution is not taken into account.

First we study the implications of order quantities to fulfil the service level constraint when the order moments are fixed beforehand by vector Y.

3   Replenishment Cycles, Basic Order-Up-To Levels and Estimating the Service Level

In the policies under consideration, the decision maker is provided an order timing vector Y, i.e. $Y_t = 0 \Rightarrow Q_t = 0$. We first focus on the concept of replenishment cycles in Section 3.1 and determine in which cases the so-called basic order-up-to level is the optimal quantity in Section 3.2. For the other order moments, we study the mathematical implications of estimating the service level by a Monte Carlo sampling approach in Section 3.3.

3.1   Replenishment Cycles and Limits on Timing Vector Y

Literature on inventory control e.g. [10] applies the concept of a replenishment cycle, i.e. the length R of the period for which the order of size Q_t is meant. For stationary demand, the replenishment cycle is fixed, but for non-stationary demand the optimal replenishment cycle R_t may depend on order moment t. In our case, replenishment cycle R_t for order moment t is the number of periods such that $Y_t = Y_{t+R_t} = 1$ and no orders take place in between, i.e. $Y_p = 0, p = t+1, .., t+R_t-1$. Notice that for the perishable case with shelf life J, practically the replenishment cycle cannot be larger than the shelf life J; so $R_t \leq J$.

Lemma 1. *Let Y be an order timing vector of the SP model, i.e. $Y_t = 0 \Rightarrow Q_t = 0$. Y provides an infeasible solution of the SP model, if it contains more than $J - 1$ consecutive zeros.*

This means that a feasible order timing vector Y does not contain a consecutive series with more than $J - 1$ zeros.

Let F_T be the set of all feasible order timing vectors Y of length T. The number of elements $|F_T|$ of the set F_T of feasible order timings of T periods and a shelf life of $J + 1 < T$ follows the recursive rule $|F_{T+1}| = 2|F_T| - |F_{T-J}|$ with the initial terms $|F_t| = 2^{t-1}$ for $t < J + 1$ and $|F_{J+1}| = 2^J - 1$ as shown in [1]. F_T is exponential in the horizon T. However, in a practical situation, as explained in [7], one cannot plan far ahead, because the forecasts of demand on which he distribution of d_t is based, is not known. Therefore, we will focus on the provided instances in that paper with $T = 12$.

3.2   Optimal Order Quantities and Basic Order-Up-To Level

A concept that uses the replenishment cycle is that of the basic order-up-to level. In this context, we define the basic order-up-to level $\hat{S}_{R,t}$ as the inventory that should be available at the beginning of period t to cover demand of R periods.

Definition 1. *Let $d_t + .. + d_{t+R-1}$ be the stochastic demand during the replenishment cycle of length R with cumulative distribution function (cdf) $G_{R,t}$. The basic order-up-to level $\hat{S}_{R,t}$ with probability α to fulfil demand is defined by $G(\hat{S}_{R,t}) = \alpha$ such that $\hat{S}_{R,t} = G_{R,t}^{-1}(\alpha)$.*

For the SP problem describing the inventory development of a perishable product, to have $\hat{S}_{R,t}$ in stock at the beginning of period t, i.e. $\sum_j X_t + Q_t \geq \hat{S}_{R,t}$, may not be sufficient, because products in stock may perish during the replenishment cycle. However, for some of the order moments it may be sufficient and also defines the optimum order quantity. First consider an order moment following a replenishment cycle of the length of the shelf life J.

Lemma 2. *Let Y be an order timing vector of the SP model with corresponding cycle R_t and X defined by (6). For an order moment t having $Y_{t-J} = 1, R_{t-J} = J$, the optimal order quantity is $Q_t = \hat{S}_{R_t,t}$.*

Proof. The cost minimisation aims at a value of Q_t as low as possible. Constraints (4) and (5) define that after J periods no (non-perished) inventory is left over from order Q_{t-J}, so $X_{tj} = 0$ for $j = 1, \ldots, J - 1$. To fulfil chance constraint (3), the order quantity should fulfil $Q_t \geq \hat{S}_{R_t,t}$. Minimising its value implies $Q_t = \hat{S}_{R_t,t}$.

$\square$

Second, we may have replenishment cycles of just one period where during the cycle, no products can perish.

Lemma 3. *Let Y be an order timing vector of the SP model and X defined by (6). For an order moment t having $Y_{t+1} = Y_t = 1$ the optimal order quantity is $Q_t = \hat{S}_{1,t} - \sum_j X_j$.*

Proof. For one period demand, chance constraint (3) translates to $P(Q_t + \sum_j X_j \geq d_t) = \alpha \Rightarrow Q_t \geq \hat{S}_{1,t} - \sum_j X_j$. Minimising its value implies $Q_t = \hat{S}_{1,t} - \sum_j X_j$.

$\square$

Independently of the order timing, the best order quantity at a negative stock level always has an order-up-to character.

Lemma 4. *Let Y be an order timing vector of the SP model with corresponding replenishment cycles R_t and X defined by (6). If for $Y_t = 1, X_1 \leq 0$ the optimal order quantity is $Q_t = \hat{S}_{R,t} - X_1$.*

Proof. No old stock is available that can perish during the replenishment cycle. The chance constraint (3) translates to $Q_t + X_1 \geq \hat{S}_{R_t,t}$. Minimising the value of Q_t implies $Q_t = \hat{S}_{R_t,t} - X_1$.

$\square$

Given an order timing vector Y, the theoretical properties give us a hand to determine the optimal order quantities for some of the order moments. The question now is how to deal with the chance constraint and the order quantities for the other order moments. A usual way to deal with that is using samples of the demand series.

3.3   Monte Carlo Estimation of the Service Level

Let for an order period t, d be the stochastic demand vector $(d_t, \ldots, d_{t+R-1})$ during replenishment cycle R, X the starting inventory and Q the order quantity. Let $f(Q, X, d) = I_{1,t+R-1}$ define the end inventory of items with age one period given a realisation d of d following the inventory dynamics with possible perishing according to (4) and (5). Consider the indicator function $\delta : \mathbb{R} \times \mathbb{R}^R \to \{0, 1\}$

$$\delta(Q, d) = \begin{cases} 1 & \text{if } f(Q, X, d) > 0 \\ 0 & \text{otherwise} \end{cases} \tag{8}$$

translating the service level in constraint (3) for period $t + R - 1$ to

$$a(Q) = P(I_{1,t+R-1} \geq 0) = E_d \delta(Q, d). \tag{9}$$

The generic concept of his translations is given in handbooks like [4]. Using sample paths $d_1, \ldots, d_N$ of d to estimate a probability like (9) was called by von Neumann the Monte Carlo method. The idea is that given N sample paths $d_1, \ldots, d_N$ of d, the probability (service level) (9) is estimated by

$$\hat{a}(Q) = \frac{1}{N} \sum_{r=1}^{N} \delta(Q, d_r). \tag{10}$$

As is know from handbooks on statistics (e.g. [5]), considering a set of independent random samples d_r provides the unbiased estimator (10) of $a(Q)$ with standard deviation

$$\sigma(\hat{a}(Q)) = \sqrt{\frac{1}{N}(a(Q) - a(Q)^2)}. \tag{11}$$

The latter is of importance in Monte Carlo approaches to set the number of samples for a desired probabilistic accuracy. Following the usual idea that the binomial distribution is practically normal for a large number of samples, a rule of thumb is to have an accuracy of 2σ. For the particular application aiming at $\alpha = 0.90, 0.95, 0.98$, a sample size of $N = 5000$ gives a rule of thumb accuracy of about 0.005 of the estimator $\hat{a}(Q)$.

The next question is how to use the theoretical findings of Section 3.2 and the estimation method of Section 3.3 in order to find policies where the order timing Y is provided to the decision maker. This means, we should find the best order timing and a way to deal with the order quantity.

4   Fixed Timing Y, Order-Up-To Level S_t

In the YS policy, the decision maker is provided a list of order-up-to levels S_t for each order moment and orders according to (7). Lemmas 2 and 3 are helpful to define the order-up-to level $S_t = \hat{S}_{R,t}$ for specific moments. Sample-based estimation can be used for the service level in each period, for this policy defined as a vector $a(S) = (a_1(S), \ldots, a_T(S))$.

Specifically, for the YS policy, one can write the problem of finding the (discrete) timing Y and (continuous) order-up-to levels S as a Monte Carlo based Mixed Integer Linear Programming (MC-MILP) model. Such a model is given in Section 4.1. When using samples to measure a probability (service level) as function of a continuous variable, the resulting function is piecewise constant in the continuous variable, here S. To be more precise, the implicit equivalent of estimator (10) is a function $\hat{a}_t(S) : \mathbb{R}^T \to \{0, \frac{1}{N}, \frac{2}{N}, \ldots, 1\}$. We will discuss the so-called smoothed Monte Carlo method, such that finding the optimal and feasible S given a timing vector Y becomes a Nonlinear Programming (NLP) problem.

4.1   MC-MILP Optimization of the YS Policy

The sample-based approach for the YS policy can be handled by adding to the SP model a sample index $r = 1, .., N$ to the variables, I_{jtr} and Q_{tr} such that one has replicas of the same variables that describe the actions of the model under each sample r. Furthermore, for the chance constraints one adds a binary variable $\delta_{tr} \in \{0, 1\}$ representing the indicator value that specifies whether demand is fulfilled in period t in sample r

$$- I_{1tr} \leq m_t(1 - \delta_{tr}) \quad r = 1, \ldots, N, \ t = 1, \ldots, T \tag{12}$$

where m_t is an upper bound on the value of the out of stock $-I_{1t}$. This defines a function $\hat{a}_t(S) : \mathbb{R}^n \to \{0, \frac{1}{N}, \frac{2}{N}, \ldots, 1\}$ representing the reached service level under the set of samples. The corresponding chance constraints read

$$\hat{a}_t(S) := \frac{1}{N} \sum_{r=1}^{N} \delta_{tr} \geq \alpha, \ t = 1, \ldots, T. \tag{13}$$

The objective (1) is extended towards

$$\min \frac{1}{N} \sum_{t=1}^{T} \left(kY_t + \sum_{r=1}^{N} (cQ_{tr} + h \sum_{j=1}^{J-1} I_{jtr}^+ + wI_{Jtr}) \right), \tag{14}$$

with order quantity

$$Q_{tr} = (S_t - \sum_{j=1}^{J-1} I_{j,t-1,r})^+, \quad r = 1, \ldots, N, \ t = 1, \ldots, T \tag{15}$$

and the conventional order relation

$$S_t \leq \mathcal{M}Y_t, \quad t = 1, \ldots, T \tag{16}$$

with a big-$\mathcal{M}$ value. The constraints (4) and (5) are extended to each sample

$$I_{1tr} = Q_{tr} - (d_{tr} - \sum_{j=1}^{J-1} I_{j,t-1,r})^+, r = 1, \ldots, N, t = 1, \ldots, T \tag{17}$$

and

$$I_{jtr} = (I_{j-1,t-1,r} - (d_{tr} - \sum_{i=j}^{J-1} I_{i,t-1,r})^+)^+, r = 1, \ldots, N, t = 1, \ldots, T, j = 2, \ldots, J. \tag{18}$$

Notice that the values that we intend to find, i.e. Y_t and S_t are independent of the sample r and the other variables that describe the simulation or evaluation part $Q_{rt}, I_{j,t,r}$ and δ_{tr} depend on the sample.

Solving the MC-MILP model is in most cases practically impossible due to the large number of binary variables δ and many solutions δ that represent the same obtained service levels $a(S)$. The number of samples $N = 5000$ mentioned in Section 3.3, implies defining for each period $N = 5000$ binary variables δ_{rt}. Instead, we will investigate a smoothed Monte Carlo approach as suggested in [3] to estimate the service levels in the MC-MILP model.

4.2   MC Smoothing Approach to the YS Policy

First of all, consider the MC-MILP problem from the point of view of a NLP problem in the continuous variables S when order timing Y is given. The function $\hat{a}_t(S) : \mathbb{R}^n \rightarrow \{0, \frac{1}{N}, \frac{2}{N}, \ldots, 1\}$ in (13) and objective (14) are evaluated by using N sample paths following the dynamics (16), (17) and (18). The difficulty of applying an NLP solver for this problem is that (13) is piecewise constant, i.e. changing the values of S a bit may not change the evaluated value of $\hat{a}_t(S)$.

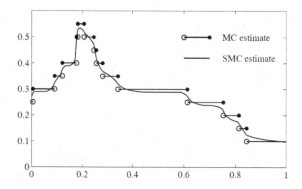

Fig. 1. Illustration of SMC from [3], where the estimated probability on the y-axis depends on varying one parameter on the x-axis

[3] show that one can make the reached service level practically a continuous function by following the MC smoothing approach. Let $z_{rt} = \sum_{j=1}^{J} I_{jtr}$ represent the total amount of product left over at the end of period t in sample r. One can measure, how close $\hat{a}_t(S)$ is to change value by the value of the least nonnegative total inventory $p_t^{[in]}(S) = \min_r\{z_{rt}|z_{rt} \geq 0\}$ and the least negative inventory $p_t^{[out]}(S) = \min_r\{-z_{rt}|z_{rt} < 0\}$. The suggested smoothing function $o_t(S)$ is

$$o_t(S) = \frac{1}{2N}\left(\frac{2p_t^{[in]}(S)}{p_t^{[in]}(S) + p_t^{[out]}(S)} - 1\right). \tag{19}$$

It is proven in [3], that $\hat{a}_t(S) + o_t(S)$ is continuous in the interesting values of S, as illustrated in Figure 1. Moreover, the function $\hat{a}_t(S) + o_t(S)$ deviates at most $\frac{1}{2N}$ from the reached service level $\hat{a}_t(S)$. This deviation is much smaller than the possible estimation error. Using $\hat{a}_t(S) + o_t(S)$ defines the problem $NLPS(Y)$ where constraint (13) in MC-MILP is replaced by

$$\hat{a}_t(S) + o_t(S) \geq \alpha, \ t = 1, \ldots, T \tag{20}$$

as a smooth optimization problem that in principle can be solved by a nonlinear optimization routine. Notice again that only values S_t have to be determined for $Y_t = 1$ and $\exists i = 1, \ldots, J - 1, Y_{t-i} = 1$. For the chance constraints, one only has to focus on the last period of the replenishment cycle $t + R_t - 1$; the demand in between will have a higher probability to be fulfilled. As starting point for the variables S_t in the nonlinear optimization the values $\hat{S}_{R_t,t}$ can be used. Algorithm 1 provides a list of order timing Y^* and order-up-to levels S^* that fulfils the chance constraints arbitrarily close if the number of samples N increases. One can use a lower bound on cost to decide that Y cannot be optimal. A lower bound $LBc(Y)$ on the cost contains the necessary minimum procurement cost $k \sum Y_t + c \sum E(d_t)$. Moreover, the expected inventory at the beginning of a period where no order takes place is at least $\hat{S}_{1,t}$ and the corresponding inventory cost can be added to the lower bound $LBc(Y)$. In an enumeration of Y, if $LBc(Y)$ is greater than the best feasible objective value C^U found so far, Y cannot be the optimal timing.

Algorithm 1. YSsmooth in: samples d_{tr}, cost data, $\alpha, \hat{S}_{R,t}$, out: Y^*, S^*

Set the best function value $C^U := \infty$
Generate a set of feasible order timing Y
for all Y
    if for the lower bound on cost $LBc(Y) < C^U$
        solve $NLPS(Y)$ using $\hat{S}_{R,t}$ values $\rightarrow S$ and cost C
        if $C < C^U$
            save the best found values $C^U := C, S^* := S, Y^* = Y$

---

5 YQ(X): Timing Y, Stock-Age Dependent $Q_t(X)$

The YQ(X) policy fits nearly directly to the results found in Section 3. The decision maker is provided with an order timing vector Y. For each order moment ($Y_t = 1$), the suggested order quantity Q_t depends on the age distribution X of the items in stock. For the order moments fulfilling the conditions of Lemmas 2 and 3, the order quantities are provided by using the pre-calculated basic order-up-to levels $\hat{S}_{R,t}$. For the other order moments, Lemma 4 tells us what to do when confronted with a negative inventory X. For a positive inventory X, the sample-based estimation of Section 3 can be used. At an order moment, i.e. $Y_t = 1$ where the inventory position is positive and $R_t > 1$, the order quantity may be larger than the basic order-up-to level

$$Q_t(X) \geq (\hat{S}_{R_t,t} - \sum_{j=1}^{J-1} X_j)^+ \tag{21}$$

due to the expected out dating of inventory during the replenishment cycle. To compute the optimal order quantity for this case, we have to investigate the total inventory at the end of the replenishment cycle as function of the starting inventory X, the order quantity Q and the demand $d_t, \ldots, d_{t+R-1}$ during the replenishment cycle.

Definition 2. *The function $Z : \mathbb{R} \times \mathbb{R}^J \times \mathbb{R}^R \to \mathbb{R}$ is defined as the transformation $z = Z(Q, X, d)$ giving the total inventory $z = \sum_{j=1}^J I_{j,R-1}$ following the dynamics (4), (5) with starting inventory X, order quantity Q and demand vector $(d_1, \ldots, d_{R-1})$.*

This definition facilitates writing the order quantity we are looking for as the minimum value Q_t for which the chance constraint holds; this is the value of Q_t for which $P(Z(Q_t, X_t, d_t, \ldots, d_{t+R-1}) \geq 0) = \alpha$. The following property of function Z is useful.

Lemma 5. *Let function Z be defined by Definition 2, $R \leq J$, values for Q, X, d given. Let $Z(Q, X, d) = z$, then $\forall q \in \mathbb{R}$, $Z(Q + q, X, d) = z + q$.*

Proof. Due to $R \leq J$ following the equations (4), (5), non of the order quantity Q will be wasted (outdated). An additional amount q will be added to the total end inventory z. □

Theorem 1. *Let function Z be defined by Definition 2, $R \leq J$, starting inventory X given, $z = Z(0, X, d_t, \ldots, d_{t+R-1})$ with cdf Γ. The optimal order quantity in period t is $Q_t = (-\Gamma^{-1}(1 - \alpha))^+$.*

Proof. If $\Gamma^{-1}(1 - \alpha) > 0$, the current stock is enough to fulfil demand with α probability: $P(z \leq 0) < (1 - \alpha) \to P(z \geq 0) > \alpha$. So in that case, $Q_t = 0$ is optimal. For a value $Q_t = -\Gamma^{-1}(1 - \alpha) \geq 0$, we have $P(Z(0, X, d_t, \ldots, d_{t+R-1}) \leq -Q_t) = 1 - \alpha$. This implies $P(Z(0, X, d_t, \ldots, d_{t+R-1}) + Q_t \geq 0) = \alpha$. Using Lemma 5, this translates to $P(Z(Q_t, X, d_t, \ldots, d_{t+R-1}) \geq 0) = \alpha$. So the order quantity Q_t is the minimum value for which the end inventory has a probability of α to be positive. Therefore it is the optimal value.

□

Lemmas 2 and 3 discussed the cases where $Q_t = \hat{S}_{R_t,t} - \sum_{j=1}^{J-1} X_j$ is the optimal solution. A possible deviation from this value in other cases is due to the waste that can occur during the replenishment cycle. Taking this value as benchmark provides a corollary which follows directly from Theorem 1 and Lemma 5.

Corollary 1. *Let function Z be defined by Definition 2, $R \leq J$, starting inventory X given, $z = Z(\hat{S}_{R_t,t} - \sum_{j=1}^{J-1} X_j, X, d_t, \ldots, d_{t+R-1})$ with cdf Γ. The optimal order quantity is $Q_t = \left(\hat{S}_{R_t,t} - \sum_{j=1}^{J-1} X_j - \Gamma^{-1}(1 - \alpha) \right)^+$.*

Algorithm 2. YQ (in: d_{rt},cost data, α, $\hat{S}_{R,t}$), out: Y^*

$C^U := \infty$
Generate a set of feasible order timing Y
for all Y
    if for the lower bound on cost $LBc(Y) < C^U$
        Determine C by simulating N sample paths
        During the simulation
        if $Y_t = 1$
            if starting inventory X not positive or $R_t = 1$ take $Q_t = \hat{S}_{R_t,t} - \sum_{j=1}^{J-1} X_j$
            else simulate the replenishment cycle with N paths from X
            Determine the order quantity Q_t from (23)
    if $C < C^U$
        $C^U := C, Y^* = Y$

In other words, Lemmas 2 and 3 discuss cases where the choice $Q_t = \hat{S}_{R_t,t} - \sum_{j=1}^{J-1} X_j$ gives $\Gamma^{-1}(1 - \alpha) = 0$. Notice, this is also the case if the starting inventory is non-positive, $X_1 \leq 0$, as no waste can be generated. In other cases, waste can be generated and $\Gamma^{-1}(1 - \alpha) < 0$. No analytical form is available to evaluate its value. To estimate the quantile $\Gamma^{-1}(1 - \alpha)$, Monte Carlo simulation can be used as discussed in Section 3.3. Let D be an $N \times T$ matrix with samples $d_{r,t}$. For a starting inventory X, giving the order quantity $Q = \hat{S}_{R_t,t} - \sum_{j=1}^{J-1} X_j$, one can evaluate $z_r = Z(Q, X, d_{r,t}, \ldots, d_{r,t+R-1})$ being the total inventory of sample r at the end of the cycle. The adjusting amount $-\Gamma^{-1}(1-\alpha)$ is estimated by

$$A_t(X) = (-\text{quantile}(\{z_r, r = 1, \ldots, N\}, 1 - \alpha))^+, \tag{22}$$

where $\text{quantile}(\{\}, \alpha)$ is the α sample quantile of set $\{\}$.

The order quantity for any starting inventory according to Corollary 1, can be approximated by

$$Q_t(X) = \hat{S}_{R_t,t} - \sum_{j=1}^{J-1} X_j + A_t(X). \tag{23}$$

This way of approaching the chance constraint is slightly stricter than the original service level constraints. It forces an α probability on positive inventory from any starting inventory X. This is also called a conditional service level constraint, see [9].

The order quantities for the YQ(X) policy are now defined either by the theoretical results, or by the sample-based estimation in (22) and (23). The next question is to generate the best advice for the order timing Y. Algorithm (2) enumerates the possible timing vectors. Here one can make use of Lemma 1 and leave out those with too large periods between two orders. For each vector Y, the average cost is evaluated for a large simulation run that uses different random numbers than the ones in matrix D that are used to determine the order quantities by (22) and (23).

The YQ(X) policy has the advantage that it takes the age distribution into account. However, for the decision maker the required use of tables and possibly interpolation is more hassle than using a simple order-up-to strategy with a list of order-up-to levels of the YS policy. One question is in which cases the policy YQ(X) performs significantly better than the YS policy. The theoretical results already showed that in fact the YQ(X) policy works with basic order-up-to levels $\hat{S}_{R,t}$ for many cases. If costs and demand data are such that we order each period, or alternatively order every J periods, then in fact the YQ(X) policy works with order-up-to levels all the time according to Lemmas 2 and 3.

6 Numerical Study

Not taking the age distribution into account (YS policy) provides an easy to interpret policy. The developed method of Algorithm 1 aims to generate better solutions for the YS policy than the MILP approximation of [7] . Taking the age distribution into account (YQ(X) policy) should even lead to smaller expected costs. We used the experimental design of [7] to investigate the quality of the described policies in terms of how well the required service level is met and what are the expected costs. For which instances does it pay the trouble to take the age distribution into account?

Table 1. Base case with expected demand μ_t. Average cost and reached service level $\hat{\alpha}$ measured by simulating with 5000 runs

t\Cost	demand	MILP [7] 28882		YS Policy 28649		YQ(X) Policy 28205	
	μ_t	S_t	$\hat{\alpha}$	S_t	$\hat{\alpha}$	Y	$\hat{\alpha}$
1	800	1129	94.7%	1129	94.7%	1	1
2	950	1550	99.5%	1550	99.5%	0	98.7%
3	200	0	95.4%	0	95.4%	0	95.2%
4	900	2350	1	2340	1	1	1
5	800	0	98.7%	0	98.5%	0	98.7%
6	150	0	95.3%	0	94.7%	0	95.3%
7	650	1874	1	1874	1	1	1
8	800	0	95.3%.	0	95.3%	0	96.1%
9	900	1271	95.2%	1278	95.2%	1	94.9%
10	300	1333	1	1426	1	1	1
11	150	0	1	0	1	0	1
12	600	0	88.5%	0	95.1%	0	95.1%

We start with the base case with $k = 1500, c = 2, h = .5, w = 0$ $\alpha = 95\%$ from [7] and compare the implications of the reported S_t values by the MILP approach in that paper. The expected demand μ_t given in Table 1 for a time horizon of $T = 12$, and its variance is given by $(cv \times \mu_t)^2$ with variation coefficient $cv = 0.25$. The starting inventory is zero.

Algorithm 1 is used to generate the order-up-to levels S_t of the YS policy. Algorithm 2 generates the timing for the YQ(X) policy. With respect to efficiency, both algorithms required the order of magnitude of 5 minutes in a Matlab implementation. Taking into account the zero starting inventory (the first period we have to order), the number $|F_T|$ of feasible timings Y in this case is 927. Both algorithms also remove more than 200 vectors due to cost bounding.

It is interesting to see that the YS policy (also elaborated in the MILP model) starts by choosing $Q_1 = S_1 = \hat{S}_{1,1}$ and the YQ(X) policy chooses $Q_1 = \hat{S}_{3,1}$, so aiming at covering demand of three periods. Although these numbers are exact, the numerical estimation of the service level via the simulation gives an error within the accuracy as $\hat{\alpha}_1 = 94.7\%$ instead of the used $\alpha = 95\%$. For this specific case, notice that the YS and YQ(X) policies differ in number of orders in the time horizon and both provide a fulfilment of the service level constraints up to the simulation accuracy. This is in contrast to the reported result of the MILP model in [7], where for the last period the α probability was not reached. The YQ(X) policy is 2.4% cheaper than the YS policy for this case.

The illustrative case has been designed such that there is a large difference in cost between the YS and YQ(X) policy. To investigate the question when a large difference occurs, we repeated all 81 experiments of [7] and found the following tendency with respect to the disadvantage of using the more practical YS policy instead of taking the age distribution into account

- No disadvantage if cost structure implies ordering every period, or for a cycle that has the length of the shelf life.
- The disadvantage does not necessarily grow with the forecast error, i.e. larger uncertainty in demand.
- The disadvantage is less when the demand pattern is more stationary.

7 Conclusions

We investigated how order policies can be generated for a specific chance constrained inventory model where the order moments should be fixed in advance for a finite horizon. Focus is on the idea that the chance constraints of the model can be approximated by an approach using Monte Carlo (MC) sampling.

Several theoretical properties have been derived for the optimal order quantities. For those order moments where the analytical results do not apply, sample-based estimation of the service level can be used. For the YQ(X) policy, the order quantity is minimized such that from each starting inventory for a simulated replenishment cycle the chance constraint is just fulfilled. We derived an algorithm to determine the optimal order timing for this order policy.

When investigating the possibility of generating order-up-to levels for a so-called YS policy, one can in principle formulate a MC-MILP problem that is usually unsolvable. We show that such a problem can be approximated arbitrarily near by using the smoothed Monte Carlo method to construct a MINLP problem that is integer in the timing variables Y and continuous in the order-up-to variables S. For each timing vector Y to be evaluated, a continuous $NLPS(Y)$ problem should be solved. A specific algorithm based on enumeration and bounding has been derived to solve the problem.

The YQ(X) policy is more complicated for providing decision support to the decision maker. The derived algorithms and theoretical results have been used to investigate the question for which instances the easier YS policy provides (nearly) the same performance as the more complicated YQ(X) policy. Mainly a wide variation in the demand pattern over the planning horizon provides an advantage for the YQ(X) policy that takes the age distribution into account in the determination of the order quantity.

Acknowledgments. This paper has been supported by The Spanish Ministry (TIN2012-37483-C03-01) and Junta de Andalucía (P11-TIC-7176), in part financed by the European Regional Development Fund (ERDF). The study is co-funded by the TIFN (project RE002).

References

1. Alcoba, A.G., Hendrix, E.M.T., García, I., Ortega, G., Pauls-Worm, K.G.J., Haijema, R.: On computing order quantities for perishable inventory control with non-stationary demand. In: Gervasi, O., Murgante, B., Misra, S., Gavrilova, M.L., Rocha, A.M.A.C., Torre, C., Taniar, D., Apduhan, B.O. (eds.) ICCSA 2015, Part II. LNCS, vol. 9156, pp. 429–444. Springer, Heidelberg (2015)
2. Birge, J.R., Louveaux, F.: Introduction to Stochastic Programming. Springer, New York (1997)
3. Hendrix, E.M.T., Olieman, N.J.: The smoothed Monte Carlo method in robustness optimisation. Optimization Methods and Software **23**, 717–729 (2008)
4. Jacod, J., Protter, P.: Probability Essentials, 2nd edn. Springer, Berlin (2004)
5. Lyman Ott, R., Longnecker, M.T.: An Introduction to Statistical Methods and Data Analysis, 5th edn. Duxbury, Pacific Grove (2001)
6. Pauls-Worm, K.G.J., Hendrix, E.M.T.: SDP in inventory control: non-stationary demand and service level constraints. In: Gervasi, O., Murgante, B., Misra, S., Gavrilova, M.L., Rocha, A.M.A.C., Torre, C., Taniar, D., Apduhan, B.O. (eds.) ICCSA 2015, Part II. LNCS, vol. 9156, pp. 397–412. Springer, Heidelberg (2015)
7. Pauls-Worm, K.G.J., Hendrix, E.M.T., Haijema, R., van der Vorst, J.G.A.J.: An MILP approximation for ordering perishable products with non-stationary demand and service level constraints. International Journal of Production Economics **157**, 133–146 (2014)
8. Rijpkema, W.A., Hendrix, E.M.T., Rossi, R., van der Vorst, J.G.A.J.: Application of stochastic programming to reduce uncertainty in quality-based supply planning of slaughterhouses. Annals of Operations Research (2013) (to appear)
9. Rossi, R., Tarim, S.A., Hnich, B., Prestwich, S.: A global chance-constraint for stochastic inventory systems under service level constraints. Operations Research **13**, 490–517 (2008)
10. Silver, E.A., Pyke, D.F., Peterson, R.: Inventory Management and Production Planning and Scheduling. Wiley (1998)
11. Tekin, E., Gürler, U., Berk, E.: Age-based vs. stock level control policies for perishable inventory systems. European Journal of Operational Research **124**, 309–329 (2001)

Pricing Intermodal Freight Transport Services: A Cost-Plus-Pricing Strategy

Le Li[1]([✉]), Xiao Lin[2], Rudy R. Negenborn[2], and Bart De Schutter[1]

[1] Delft Center for Systems and Control, Delft University of Technology,
Delft, The Netherlands
{l.li-1,b.deschutter}@tudelft.nl
[2] Department of Marine and Transport Technology,
Delft University of Technology, Delft, The Netherlands
{x.lin,r.r.negenborn}@tudelft.nl

Abstract. This paper investigates transport services pricing problems faced by intermodal freight transport operators with fixed transport capacities in an intermodal freight transport network. We first present an optimal intermodal freight transport planning model to minimize the total transport cost. This model captures modality change phenomena, due time requirements, and the possibility to subcontract transport demands. A cost-plus-pricing strategy is proposed to determine the service price as the sum of the operational cost and the targeted profit margins of transport operators under different transport scenarios, i.e., self-transporting, subcontracting, and a combination of them. For the reference transport demand specified by a customer, a list of service packages with different due times, demand sizes, and the determined service prices will be offered to the customer. Based on the urgency of delivering containers and the prices of different service packages, the customer will make the final selection decisions. A case study is given to illustrate the planning model and our proposed pricing strategy.

Keywords: Intermodal freight transport planning · Cost-plus-pricing strategy · Subcontracting · Transport service packages

1 Introduction

Port-hinterland freight transport has been facing challenges from increasing cargo volumes, limited capacities of transport infrastructures, traffic congestion on freeways around the port area, traffic emission issues, etc. The concept of intermodal freight transport provides an innovative solution for realizing efficient and sustainable hinterland transport systems for the deepsea ports, for instance the Port of Rotterdam [1]. Cranic and Kim [2] define intermodal freight transport as "the transportation of a load from its origin to its destination by a sequence of at least two transportation modes, the transfer from one mode to the next being performed at an intermodal terminal." By integrating and coordinating the use of different transport modes available in an intermodal freight

© Springer International Publishing Switzerland 2015
F. Corman et al. (Eds.): ICCL 2015, LNCS 9335, pp. 541–556, 2015.
DOI: 10.1007/978-3-319-24264-4_37

transport network through an efficient ICT system, intermodal freight transport provides the opportunity to obtain an efficient use of the physical infrastructure as well as providing cost and energy efficient transport services. Apart from intermodal freight transport, a number of innovative concepts have been introduced in both the freight transport organization and the supply chain management, such as mode-free booking, extended gateway, synchromodal freight transport, and terminal haulage [1, 3–5].

The topic of intermodal freight transport has been studied intensively in literature [2, 6–11]. Quite a lot of research efforts have been investigating transport planning problem at the strategic, tactical, and operational decision-making levels. However, a successful implementation of intermodal freight transport and also other innovative concepts does not only depend on efficient transport planning, but also on an appropriate pricing strategy for intermodal freight services. Pricing intermodal freight transport services involves determining how much customers should be charged for each service with particular service-related characteristics i.e., origin, destination, the number of containers that have to be transported, and the due time for completing the movement. The pricing strategy will greatly affect the competitiveness of intermodal freight transport, and it also plays an important role in mode choice. Macharis and Bontekoning [6] point out that the pricing for intermodal transport is complicated since several actors are involved relating to different parts of the chain. It requires an accurate cost calculation and insight in the market situation.

The pricing strategies for intermodal freight transport services are often analyzed at two levels, the individual player in the intermodal chain, and the whole door-to-door intermodal freight transport service [11]. At the first, individual player level, pricing strategies for rail haul and drayage operators are evaluated in [12] and [13], respectively. Liu and Yang [14] combines slot allocation and dynamic pricing strategy in container intermodal transport. At the second, whole door-to-door service level, Tsai et al. [15] developed pricing strategies based on minimum logistics cost and logit demand functions for the whole intermodal transport chain. Li and Tayur formulated in [16] a medium-term planning model to jointly consider transport planning and service pricing in intermodal freight transport. Dandotiya et al. [17] developed a joint optimization model for the rail-truck terminal location policy and the pricing strategy for the Delhi-Mumbai freight corridor in India. This study aims to enhance the utilization of the railway infrastructure and shows the interrelation between terminal locations and the price sensitivities of customers while allowing for adequate profit for the railway. A bi-level programming model was proposed by Ypsilantis and Zuidwijk to jointly design the extended gateway services and determine the pricing scheme for profit maximization in [18]. This paper pointed out that for the port-to-door service the corresponding transport service price depends on the best alternative transport service offered by the competition and does not depend on the container transport routing in the network, while for the price of the port-to-port service this is not the case. The best alternative transport service is chosen from the shippers' perspective by evaluating a trade-off among major decision factors, such as transport cost, and transport time. Most of the research work on pricing strategy for intermodal freight transport in the literature is performed at the tactical level [8]. The research presented in the current paper combines the intermodal transport planning operation and the pricing strategy so that the pricing problem is considered in a more detailed level. Moreover, even through there are many cost-related pricing strategies, such as cost-plus pricing, market penetration pricing, discount pricing [12], the current paper will focus on using the basic concept of the cost-plus pricing strategy.

In the current paper we will consider an intermodal freight transport operator that provides port-to-port services in an intermodal freight transport network connecting deep-sea ports and inland terminals. The main contributions of this paper are a new intermodal freight transport network model for minimizing the transport cost of the intermodal freight transport operator and a cost-plus service pricing strategy for facilitating transport operators with given transport capacity in an intermodal freight transport network.This paper considers performing off-line pricing where all transport demands in the planning period are assumed to be known when the transport planning and pricing decisions are being made. It is noteworthy that some transport demands might be rejected by the operator in case that the determined prices of transport services for serving these transport demands are higher than the market prices. The proposed pricing strategy considers the operational cost and the targeted profit margins of intermodal freight transport operators, and also the market price for transporting freight. Therefore, an optimal intermodal freight transport planning model is first developed for representing the characteristic behaviors of the network (e.g., modality changes at intermodal terminals), to guarantee the due time requirements of transport demands, and to capture the possibility of using subcontracted transport services from other transport operators. The introduction of subcontracted transport services in the intermodal container transport network model was first proposed and investigated in [19,20]. The network modeling approach in the current paper is based on the multi-node method that has been proposed and used in [21–23], which works at the tactical container flow level, while extensions are made in this paper to enable the network model to be capable of directly capturing the due time requirements of transport demands and the possibility of doing subcontracting at the operational container transport planning level. After that, the proposed cost-plus-pricing strategy determines intermodal freight transport service prices by adding up the transport operator's operational cost and the targeted profit margins while taking into account different transport scenarios, i.e., self-transporting, subcontracting, and a combination of these two. Moreover, for a reference transport demand a list of transport service packages with different due times, demand sizes, and the determined prices will be provided to the customer. The customer can make the final transport service selection according to his transport urgency and the service prices of different service packages.

The remainder of the paper is organized as follows. Section 2 briefly introduces intermodal freight transport networks and presents an optimal intermodal freight transport planning model. Our proposed cost-plus service pricing strategy

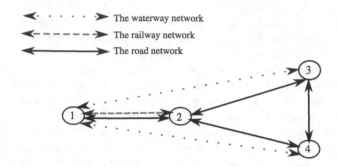

Fig. 1. A graph representation of an intermodal freight transport network. Each doubled-headed arc in the figure represents two directed links with opposite directions.

is explained in detail in Section 3 under different transport scenarios. A simple case study is given in Section 4 to illustrate our proposed pricing approach. Conclusions and directions for future work are given in Section 5.

2   Planning Intermodal Freight Transport

2.1   Intermodal Freight Transport Networks

An intermodal freight transport network is a network of interconnected single-mode transport networks, for instance the road network, the railway network, the inland waterway network. The interconnected network consists of a set of intermodal terminals and a set of transport connections with different modalities among these terminals. Intermodal terminals function as the connecting points for multiple single-mode transport networks, and as the switching points for containers to switch from one modality to another. Unquestionably, certain amounts of transfer time and transfer cost will occur when containers switch among modalities.

By representing intermodal terminals and transport connections as nodes and links, an intermodal freight transport network can be abstracted as a directed graph. Figure 1 shows a graph representation of an intermodal freight transport network with 4 intermodal terminals, 8 freeway connections, 2 railway connections, and 4 inland waterway connections. Adopting the multiple node method used in [24], in [21] an intermodal terminal is modeled as a set of multiple nodes that correspond to each single-mode terminal and the storage yard at this intermodal terminal respectively. The use of multiple nodes enables the analysis of modality change phenomena at intermodal terminals in the same way as the transport connections. This paper will also adopt the multiple node method as used in [21].

Briefly speaking, an intermodal freight transport network can be modeled as a directed graph $\mathcal{G}(\mathcal{V}, \mathcal{E}, \mathcal{M})$. The node set $\mathcal{V}$ is generated using the multiple node method and on the basis of the structure of the physical network and the possibility of changing modalities at intermodal terminals. The node set

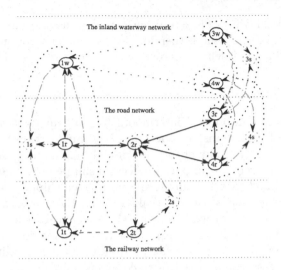

Fig. 2. The intermodal freight transport network model for the network shown in Figure 1. Each doubled-headed arc in the figure represents two directed links with opposite directions.

$\mathscr{V} = \mathscr{V}_{\text{truck}} \cup \mathscr{V}_{\text{train}} \cup \mathscr{V}_{\text{barge}} \cup \mathscr{V}_{\text{store}}$ is a finite nonempty set with the sets $\mathscr{V}_{\text{truck}}$, $\mathscr{V}_{\text{train}}$, $\mathscr{V}_{\text{barge}}$, and $\mathscr{V}_{\text{store}}$ representing truck terminals, train terminals, barge terminals, and storage yards shared by different single-model terminals inside each intermodal terminal of the network, respectively. The modality change set $\mathscr{M}$ is constructed according to the available modalities in this network. This paper formulates the network model for three modalities (i.e., trucks, trains, and barges), but the network model can be extended to include more modalities. The mode change set $\mathscr{M} = \mathscr{M}_1 \cup \mathscr{M}_2$ indicates modalities and modality change types in the network with $\mathscr{M}_1 = \{\text{truck}, \text{train}, \text{barge}, \text{store}\}$ and $\mathscr{M}_2 = \{m_1 \rightarrow m_2 | m_1, m_2 \in \mathscr{M}_1 \text{ and } m_1 \neq m_2\}$. Note that the storage is considered as one type of virtual modality. The link set $\mathscr{E} \subseteq \mathscr{V} \times \mathscr{V} \times \mathscr{M}$ represents all available connections among nodes. The symbol $l_{i,j}^m$ is used to denote link $(i, j, m) \in \mathscr{E}$. All links in the network are categorized as either transport links or transfer links depending on whether a modality change happens on this link or not. Figure 2 gives the intermodal freight transport network model of the network shown in Figure 1. The dotted blue arcs, the solid black arcs, the dashed red arcs, and the dash-dotted green arcs indicate 4 transport links of the inland waterway network, 8 transport links of the road network, 2 transport links of the railway network, and 30 transfer links among nodes with different modalities in the intermodal freight transport network, respectively. The dashed green nodes indicate the storage nodes.

With the above multi-node method based network model, the paper [21] develops a generic intermodal freight transport network model in a discrete-time formulation from an aggregated container flow perspective for optimal container flow assignment. The optimal intermodal freight transport planing model proposed below is also in a discrete-time formulation but considers individual containers in the planning, and is therefore able to directly capture the due time requirements of transport demands ordered in the form of mode-free booking [3].

2.2   Optimal Intermodal Freight Transport Planning Model

This section presents an optimal intermodal freight transport planning model for an intermodal freight transport operator. The transport operator has a fixed transport capacity on each link of the intermodal freight transport network and provides intermodal freight transport services to shippers. Shippers order transport services in a mode-free booking fashion, in which shippers only specify the characteristic information of their containers (i.e., the origin, the destination, the size, and the due time) while leaving the freedom to transport operators to choose appropriate modes of transport for transporting containers under the up-to-date network conditions. In order to guarantee the reliability of transport services, the transport operator strives to complete shippers' orders before their specified due times with the lowest total transport cost possible. Therefore, we choose to consider the due time requirements as hard constraints in the planning. Meanwhile, in practice there are situations that the transport operator does not have enough transport capacity available when some orders from a valued long-term business partners arrive. It is then really important for the transport operator to accept and finish these orders in order to establish a stable cooperation with the business partner. Therefore, we assume that the transport operator can subcontract a part or even the whole order to other transport operators in order to serve the order at the price of making less profit.

An order can be interpreted as a transport demand in the transport planning, and it is defined as a group of containers sharing the origin and destination nodes (e.g., (o, d)) and also a given due time (e.g., $T_{o,d}$). The number of containers corresponding to transport demand $(o, d, T_{o,d})$ (, which belongs to the set of all transport demands $\mathcal{O}_{\mathrm{odt}} \subseteq \mathcal{V} \times \mathcal{V} \times \mathcal{T}$) can be indicated by $d_{o,d,T_{o,d}}$. The due time $T_{o,d}$ is actually the latest time point for finishing transport demand $(o, d, T_{o,d})$, for instance 5:00 pm on April 20, 2015. The proposed optimal intermodal freight transport planning model is a discrete-time model with a time step of T_s (h). The planning horizon of the intermodal freight transport is $N \cdot T_s$ (h) with $N \in \mathbb{N} \backslash \{0\}$. The planning horizon should be large enough to include the due time of all transport demands. The objective, the constraints, and the optimization formulation of the proposed planning model will be explained in detail in the following subsections.

2.2.1   The Objective of the Planning Model

For an intermodal freight transport operator with fixed transport capacities on transport connections in the network, the optimal transport planning consists in determining container routings and making subcontracting decisions by minimizing the total delivery cost while fulfilling the due time requirements of all transport demands in the network. In this optimal intermodal freight transport planning model, the total transport cost J_{total} is the sum of the storage cost, the transport/transfer cost, and subcontracting cost of transport demands in the network and is defined as follows:

$$J_{\text{total}} = \sum_{(o,d,T_{o,d}) \in \mathscr{O}_{\text{odt}}} \left[\sum_{k=1}^{N} \left[\sum_{i \in \mathscr{V}} x_{i,o,d,T_{o,d}}(k) T_{\text{s}} C_{i,\text{store}} + \sum_{(i,j,m) \in \mathscr{E}} x_{i,j,o,d,T_{od}}^{m}(k) T_{\text{s}} C_{i,j,\text{tran}}^{m} \right] \right.$$

$$\left. + d_{i,o,d,T_{o,d}}^{\text{sub}}(1) C_{i,o,d,T_{o,d}}^{\text{sub}} \right], \tag{1}$$

where

- The value of $x_{i,o,d,T_{o,d}}(k)$ (TEU) is the number of containers corresponding to transport demand $d_{o,d,T_{o,d}}$ and staying at node i at time step k. The container storage cost at node $i \in \mathscr{V}$ is given as $C_{i,\text{store}}$ (€/TEU/h).
- The value of $x_{i,j,o,d,T_{od}}^{m}(k)$ (TEU) is the number of containers corresponding to transport demand $d_{o,d,T_{o,d}}$ and traveling on link $l_{i,j}^{m}$ at time step k. The container transport/transfer cost on link $(i,j,m) \in \mathscr{E}$ is given by $C_{i,j,\text{tran}}^{m}$ (€/TEU/h).
- The value of $d_{i,o,d,T_{o,d}}^{\text{sub}}(k)$ (TEU) is the number of containers corresponding to transport demand $d_{o,d,T_{o,d}}$ that have to be subcontracted to other transport operators at time step k. The value of $d_{i,o,d,T_{o,d}}^{\text{sub}}(k)$ corresponds to a planning decision when $i = o$ and $k = 1$, and otherwise it is zero. Here we assume that the subcontracting decision is made about each transport demand only at the time when the demand enters the network. The price that has to be paid for subcontracting one TEU of the transport demand $d_{o,d,T_{o,d}}$ is $C_{i,o,d,T_{o,d}}^{\text{sub}}$ (€/TEU).

2.2.2 The Constraints of the Planning Model

The transport planning has to be performed with respect to multiple constraints on network dynamics, transport capacity, due time requirements, and subcontracting decisions. For each transport demand $d_{o,d,T_{o,d}}$, the network dynamics include node dynamics and link dynamics, and can be formulated as:

$$x_{i,o,d,T_{o,d}}(k+1) = x_{i,o,d,T_{o,d}}(k) + \sum_{(j,m) \in \mathscr{N}_i^{\text{in}}} q_{j,i,o,d,T_{o,d}}^{m,\text{out}}(k)$$

$$- \sum_{(j,m) \in \mathscr{N}_i^{\text{out}}} q_{i,j,o,d,T_{o,d}}^{m,\text{in}}(k) - d_{i,o,d,T_{o,d}}^{\text{out}}(k)$$

$$+ d_{i,o,d,T_{o,d}}^{\text{in}}(k) - d_{i,o,d,T_{o,d}}^{\text{sub}}(k), \tag{2}$$

$$x_{i,o,d,T_{o,d}}(k), d_{i,o,d,T_{o,d}}^{\text{in}}(k), d_{i,o,d,T_{o,d}}^{\text{out}}(k), d_{i,o,d,T_{o,d}}^{\text{sub}}(k) \in \mathbb{N}\backslash\{0\}$$

$$\forall (o,d,T_{o,d}) \in \mathscr{O}_{\text{odt}}, \forall i,j \in \mathscr{V}, \forall m \in \mathscr{M}, \forall k,$$

$$q^{m,\text{out}}_{i,j,o,d,\text{T}_{o,d}}(k) = q^{m,\text{in}}_{i,j,o,d,\text{T}_{o,d}}(k - T^m_{i,j}), \tag{3}$$

$$x^m_{i,j,o,d,\text{T}_{od}}(k+1) = x^m_{i,j,o,d,\text{T}_{od}}(k) + \left(q^{m,\text{in}}_{i,j,o,d,\text{T}_{o,d}}(k) - q^{m,\text{out}}_{i,j,o,d,\text{T}_{o,d}}(k) \right), \tag{4}$$

where

- The value of $q^{m,\text{out}}_{i,j,o,d,\text{T}_{o,d}}(k)$ (TEU) is the number of containers corresponding to transport demand $d_{o,d,\text{T}_{o,d}}$ and leaving link $l^m_{i,j}$ to node j at time step k. The set $\mathcal{N}^{\text{in}}_i$ is defined as

$$\mathcal{N}^{\text{in}}_i = \{(j,m) \mid l^m_{j,i} \text{ is an incoming link for node } i\}.$$

- The value of $q^{m,\text{in}}_{i,j,o,d}(k)$ (TEU) is the number of containers corresponding to transport demand $d_{o,d,\text{T}_{o,d}}$ and entering link $l^m_{i,j}$ from node i at time step k. The set $\mathcal{N}^{\text{out}}_i$ is defined as

$$\mathcal{N}^{\text{out}}_i = \{(j,m) \mid l^m_{i,j} \text{ is an outgoing link for node } i\}.$$

- The transport time on each link $l^m_{i,j}$ is given by $T^m_{i,j}T_{\text{s}}$ (h). Here the transport time on each link is assumed to be constant.
- The value of $d^{\text{in}}_{i,o,d,\text{T}_{o,d}}(k)$ (TEU) is the number of containers corresponding to transport demand $d_{o,d,\text{T}_{o,d}}$ and entering node i from the outside of the network at time step k. The value of $d^{\text{in}}_{i,o,d,\text{T}_{o,d}}(k)$ equals $d_{o,d,\text{T}_{o,d}} - d^{\text{sub}}_{i,o,d,\text{T}_{o,d}}(k)$ when $i = o$ and $k = 1$, and otherwise it is zero.
- The value of $d^{\text{out}}_{i,o,d,\text{T}_{o,d}}(k)$ (TEU) is the number of containers corresponding to transport demand $d_{o,d,\text{T}_{o,d}}$ and arriving at the final destination node i at time step k. The value of $d^{\text{out}}_{i,o,d,\text{T}_{o,d}}(k)$ equals $\sum_{(j,m)\in\mathcal{N}^{\text{in}}_i} q^{m,\text{in}}_{i,j,o,d,\text{T}_{o,d}}(k)$ when $i = d$ (here, we assume that containers coming from each transport demand will immediately leave the network once they arrive at their destinations), and otherwise it is zero.

The transport capacity of an intermodal freight transport operator on each link $l^m_{i,j}$, $C^m_{i,j}$ (TEU), is the maximum number of containers that can traverse within this link. The transfer capacity on each transfer link is basically determined by the equipment capacity and the operation of the intermodal terminal to which this link physically belongs. The transport/transfer capacity constraint on each link $l^m_{i,j}$ applies for the combination of all transport demands $d_{o,d,\text{T}_{o,d}} \in \mathcal{O}_{\text{odt}}$, and can be formulated as follows:

$$\sum_{(o,d,\text{T}_{o,d})\in\mathcal{O}_{\text{odt}}} x^m_{i,j,o,d,\text{T}_{od}}(k) \leq C^m_{i,j}. \tag{5}$$

The due time requirements set the latest times before which the transport demands should be completed. It means that after the set due time of one transport demand its corresponding container flow at the nodes and on the links of the intermodal freight transport network should be zeros. Considering the network dynamics (2)–(4), the due time requirements can be simplified by only requiring the container flow of each transport demand in the network to be zeros at its due time. The due time requirements of all transport demands $d_{o,d,\mathrm{T}_{o,d}} \in \mathscr{O}_{\mathrm{odt}}$ are considered as hard constants in the transport planning, and can be formulated as:

$$x_{i,o,d,\mathrm{T}_{o,d}}(k_{o,d}) = 0, \qquad\qquad \forall i \in \mathscr{V}, \forall (o,d,\mathrm{T}_{o,d}) \in \mathscr{O}_{\mathrm{odt}}, \qquad (6)$$
$$x^m_{i,j,o,d,\mathrm{T}_{o,d}}(k_{o,d}) = 0, \qquad\qquad \forall (i,j,m) \in \mathscr{E}, \forall (o,d,\mathrm{T}_{o,d}) \in \mathscr{O}_{\mathrm{odt}}, \qquad (7)$$

where

- The time step $k_{o,d}$ corresponds to the due time of transport demand $(o,d,\mathrm{T}_{o,d})$ that is assumed to be a multiple of T_{s}. The relation $k_{o,d}T_{\mathrm{s}} = \mathrm{T}_{o,d}$ holds.

This model allows the intermodal freight transport operator to subcontract transport demands to other operators in case of lacking transport capacity or for reducing the total transport cost for serving these transport demands. It is assumed that there is unlimited transport capacity from other operators for serving subcontracted transport demands. However, for each transport demand $(o,d,\mathrm{T}_{o,d}) \in \mathscr{O}_{\mathrm{odt}}$ the number of containers subcontracted to other operators should not be larger than the size of this transport demand. Moreover, recalling the assumption that the subcontracting decision for each transport demand is only made when it enters the intermodal freight transport network at the origin node, the relation is guaranteed by the following constraints:

$$d^{\mathrm{sub}}_{i,o,d,\mathrm{T}_{o,d}}(1) \leq d_{o,d,\mathrm{T}_{o,d}}, \quad \forall (o,d,\mathrm{T}_{o,d}) \in \mathscr{O}_{\mathrm{odt}} \qquad (8)$$

2.2.3 The Optimization Formulation

The optimal intermodal freight transport planning problem can be formulated as the following optimization problem:

$$\min_{\tilde{x}_1,\tilde{x}_2,\tilde{q}^{\mathrm{out}},\tilde{q}^{\mathrm{in}},\tilde{d}^{\mathrm{sub}}} J(\tilde{x}_1,\tilde{x}_2,\tilde{q}^{\mathrm{out}},\tilde{q}^{\mathrm{in}},\tilde{d}^{\mathrm{sub}}) \qquad (9)$$

$$\text{subject to } (2)-(8),$$

where

- $\tilde{x}_1$ contains all $x_{i,o,d,\mathrm{T}_{o,d}}(k)$, for $i \in \mathscr{V}, (o,d,\mathrm{T}_{o,d}) \in \mathscr{O}_{\mathrm{odt}}, k = 1,\cdots,N$.
- $\tilde{x}_2$ contains all $x^m_{i,j,o,d,\mathrm{T}_{od}}(k)$, for $(i,j,m) \in \mathscr{E}, (o,d,\mathrm{T}_{o,d}) \in \mathscr{O}_{\mathrm{odt}}, k = 1,\cdots,N$.
- $\tilde{q}^{\mathrm{out}}$ contains all $q^{m,\mathrm{out}}_{i,j,o,d,\mathrm{T}_{o,d}}(k)$, for $i \in \mathscr{V}, (j,m) \in \mathscr{N}^{\mathrm{out}}_i, (o,d,\mathrm{T}_{o,d}) \in \mathscr{O}_{\mathrm{odt}}, k = 1,\cdots,N$.

- $\tilde{q}^{in}$ contains all $q_{i,j,o,d,\mathrm{T}_{o,d}}^{m,in}(k)$, for $i \in \mathscr{V}, (j,m) \in \mathscr{N}_i^{in}, (o,d,\mathrm{T}_{o,d}) \in \mathscr{O}_{odt}, k = 1, \cdots, N$.
- $\tilde{d}^{sub}$ contains all $d_{i,o,d,\mathrm{T}_{o,d}}^{sub}(1)$, for $(o,d,\mathrm{T}_{o,d}) \in \mathscr{O}_{odt}$.

This problem (9)-10 is a linear integer optimization problem, which can be solved very efficiently using state-of-the-art solvers such as the intlinprog solver in Matlab, and CPLEX.

3   Pricing Intermodal Freight Transport Services

In this paper, we use a cost-plus-pricing strategy to determine the price of intermodal freight transport services. Before introducing the pricing strategy, some important assumptions and issues are listed as follows:

- For an intermodal freight transport service offered by the intermodal freight transport operator, there is always an market price for it and this market price is known to both transport operators and shippers. Therefore, the determined intermodal freight transport service price should not be more expensive than the corresponding market price.
- The intermodal freight transport operator has different targeted profit margins for different types of transport services, M_{self} for the self-operated services and M_{sub} for the subcontracted services. These two profit margins are preset by the transport operator according to its marketing objectives.
- For subcontracted intermodal freight transport services, the targeted profit margin M_{sub} is smaller than M_{self}. Because when the order is carried out by a subcontractor, the main job is done by the subcontractor and the transport operator will have less space to make profit.
- The intermodal freight transport service price is determined and charged at the moment when the order is made by the customer even if the actual execution of the container delivery changes later. For instance, the shipper pays the service price (determined by the operator) of finishing one order when the order is made. This order was planned to be served by trains at the beginning. But some or all containers of this order might be finally moved by trucks instead of the preplanned trains in case of unexpected situations during the container delivery process e.g., train cancellation due to bad weather conditions. In this case the actual operational cost of serving this order will increase since road transport is typically expected to be expensive than railway transport. However, the operator will not be able to charge the shipper any extra costs on this order.
- This paper works for the case of determining off-line pricing. It means that all transport demands in the planning period are known by the operator when he or she plans the freight transport and determines the service price.

With the above mentioned assumptions, our proposed cost-plus-pricing strategy determines the price of intermodal freight transport services as the sum of the operator's operational cost and the targeted profit margins. The operational cost includes the transport cost and the other related cost (e.g., the administration cost). The intermodal freight transport operator provides transport services by using its own transport capacity and subcontracting one part or the full order to other transport operators to serve the order with a predetermined negotiated price when necessary. The corresponding cost calculation and targeted profit margins are different from that of self-operated transport services. Therefore, the proposed pricing strategy should be tailored to take into account different transport scenarios, i.e., self-transporting, subcontracting, and a combination of them.

The optimal intermodal freight transport planning decisions for all transport demands are made by solving problem (9)–(10) in order to minimize the total transport cost. The operational cost and also the corresponding transport service price of each individual transport demand are then calculated and determined according to the transport cost, the other related cost, and the profit margins associated with it. The proposed pricing strategy will be subsequently illustrated for one transport demand in detail. For the sake of notation simplicity, the subscripts $o, d, \mathrm{T}_{o,d}$ for J, $C_{\mathrm{other}}^{\mathrm{self}}$, $C_{\mathrm{other}}^{\mathrm{sub}}$, M_{self}, M_{sub}, P, and P_{market} are omitted in the rest of this paper. For one order or transport demand $(o, d, \mathrm{T}_{o,d})$ with a size of $d_{o,d,\mathrm{T}_{o,d}}$, the operational cost is calculated as

$$C_{\mathrm{cost}}^{\mathrm{self}} = \frac{J}{d_{o,d,\mathrm{T}_{o,d}}} + C_{\mathrm{other}}^{\mathrm{self}}, \quad \text{for the selfoperated case} \tag{10}$$

$$C_{\mathrm{cost}}^{\mathrm{sub}} = C_{i,o,d,\mathrm{T}_{o,d}}^{\mathrm{sub}} + C_{\mathrm{other}}^{\mathrm{sub}}, \quad \text{fort the subcontracted case} \tag{11}$$

where

- The total transport cost J (€) for transport demand $(o, d, \mathrm{T}_{o,d})$ is obtained by solving the planing problem (9)–(10).
- The other cost is assumed to be proportional to the size of the order, but will be different for the self-operated transport service and the subcontracted transport service.

The profit margins for self-conducted transport services and subcontracted transport services are set as M_{self} and M_{sub}, respectively. There are three transport scenarios and the corresponding prices P (€/TEU) are calculated as follows:

- Scenario 1: The order is completely served by the intermodal freight operator itself, i.e., $d_{i,o,d,\mathrm{T}_{o,d}}^{\mathrm{sub}}(1) = 0$. The price is:

$$P = C_{\mathrm{cost}}^{\mathrm{self}} (1 + M_{\mathrm{self}}). \tag{12}$$

- Scenario 2: The order is served by both the intermodal freight operator and subcontractors, i.e., $0 < d_{i,o,d,\mathrm{T}_{o,d}}^{\mathrm{sub}}(1) < d_{o,d,\mathrm{T}_{o,d}}$. The price is:

$$P_{\max} = \rho_{\mathrm{self}} \left(\frac{J - C_{i,o,d,\mathrm{T}_{o,d}}^{\mathrm{sub}} d_{i,o,d,\mathrm{T}_{o,d}}^{\mathrm{sub}}(1)}{d_{o,d,\mathrm{T}_{o,d}} - d_{i,o,d,\mathrm{T}_{o,d}}^{\mathrm{sub}}(1)} + C_{\mathrm{other}}^{\mathrm{self}} \right) (1 + M_{\mathrm{self}}) + \rho_{\mathrm{sub}} C_{\mathrm{cost}}^{\mathrm{sub}} (1 + M_{\mathrm{sub}})$$
$$\tag{13}$$

where ρ_{self} and ρ_{sub} are the percentage of the self-operated containers in the transport demand $(o, d, \text{T}_{o,d})$ and that of the subcontracted containers.

- Scenario 3: The order is served by subcontractors, i.e., $d^{\text{sub}}_{i,o,d,\text{T}_{o,d}}(1) = d_{o,d,\text{T}_{o,d}}$. The price is:

$$P = C^{\text{sub}}_{\text{cost}}\left(1 + M_{\text{sub}}\right). \tag{14}$$

The market price of the transport service to serve the order or transport demand $(o, d, \text{T}_{o,d})$ is P_{market}. In case that the determined price $P > P_{\text{market}}$, the order is not in this transport operator's targeted marketing areas and the transport operator will either recommend another related service packages (e.g., service packages with a longer due time) or decline the order.

Considering the practical booking process, the intermodal freight transport operator will provide several service packages to customers according to their inexplicit reference order information and let the customers select the final service package. The transport service booking procedure is as follows: the customers first specify the reference size of the order in number of containers, the origin and destination pair of the order, and a reference due time. The transport operator will provide the customers with a list of transport service packages with different due times, demand sizes, and determined prices by solving the transport planing problem (9) in multiple times. Generally speaking, a shorter due time or a bigger order size would leads to a higher price. Taking into account the urgency to finish the order and also the price, the customers will determine which transport service package will be selected.

4 Case Study

The case study considers a simple intermodal freight transport network, consisting of three different types of transport networks that are connected at four intermodal terminals. Figure 1 shows the network topology and the four nodes 1, 2, 3, and 4 represent Rotterdam, Tilburg, Nijmegen, and Venlo, respectively. The corresponding network model is given in Figure 2. The network parameters, i.e., transport time, transport cost, transport capacity on links and storage cost and storage capacity at nodes are given in Table 1 and Table 2, respectively. The network is considered to be initially empty. Profit margins for self-operated transport services and subcontracted transport services are $M_{\text{self}} = 5\%$ and $M_{\text{sub}} = 2\%$. The other costs for the self-operated transport service and the subcontracted transport service are $C^{\text{self}}_{\text{other}} = 0.5$ (€/TEU), and $C^{\text{sub}}_{\text{other}} = 0.001$ (€/TEU).

This case study assumes that transport capacity from subcontracting intermodal freight transport services is unlimited. The intermodal freight transport is planned for a period of $N = 24$ hours for different transport demand scenarios by solving the linear integer optimization problem (9). In this paper, we use the dual simplex algorithm in the intlinprog solver in Matlab to solve the optimization problem (9). The simulation experiments are done in a desktop computer with an Intel® Core™ i5-2400 CPU with 3.10 GHz and 4 GB RAM.

Table 1. Network parameters: links. The symbols in the second column, e.g., 1r, correspond to the lables of nodes in the intermodal freight transport network model presented in Figure 2.

Link type	OD pair	Transport time (h)	Transport cost (€/h/TEU)	Transport capacity (TEU)
Road	1r-2r	2	5	20
	2r-3r	1	5	20
	2r-4r	1	5	20
	3r-4r	1	5	20
Rail	1t-2t	2	2	30
Water	1w-3w	6	1	50
	1w-4w	10	1	50
Modality – modality	any	2	2	1000
Modality – storage	any	1	1	1000

Table 2. Network parameters: nodes. The symbols in the first row, e.g., 1s, correspond to the lables of nodes in the intermodel freight transport network model in Figure 2.

	1s	1w	1r	1t	2r	2t	2s	3w	3r	3s	4w	4r	4s
Storage cost (€/h/TEU)	0	0	0	0	0	0	0	0	0	0	0	0	0
Storage capacity	1000	10	10	10	10	10	1000	10	10	1000	10	10	1000

Table 3. Transport demand and subcontracting information. The symbol "/" in the table means either. For instance, the notation "100/200" means that the size of the transport demand could either be 100 TEUs or 200 TEUs.

Origin	Destination	Number (TEU)	Due time (h)	Subcontracting cost (€/TEU)	Subcontracting capacity (TEUs)
1w	4r	100/200	6/12	20/15	unlimited

Table 4. A list of four transport service packages with different operational costs and determined service prices for serving different transport demands (i.e., the number of containers, and the due time)

Demand (TEU)	Due time (h)	Subcontracting cost €/TEU	Demand served (TEU) overall/itself/subcontract	Total transport cost €	Operational cost €/TEU	Price €/TEU
100	6	20	100	1940	–	19.996
			20	340	17.5	
			80	1600	20.001	
	12	15	100	1300	13.5	14.175
			100	1300	13.5	
			0	0	15.001	
200	6	20	200	3940	–	20.198
			20	340	17.5	
			180	3600	20.001	
	12	15	200	2740	–	14.569
			130	1690	13.5	
			70	1050	15.001	

The reference transport demand information (i.e., origin, destination, the number of containers, and due time) and the corresponding subcontracting information (i.e., subcontracting cost, and subcontracting capacity) are presented in Table 3. A list of four transport service packages is provided to the customer in Table 4. This table presents the operational cost of the four different transport service packages and their corresponding intermodal freight transport service price resulted from the proposed pricing strategy in Section 3. It is clear from Table 4 that the demand size and the due time in the transport service packages influence the determined transport service price from the proposed pricing strategy. For transport service packages designed for transport demands with the same size the determined transport service prices decrease significantly as the due times become longer. For instance, for transport service package of 100 TEU the corresponding service price drops 29.1% from 19.996 (€/TEU) for a due time of 6 hours to 14.175 (€/TEU) for a due time of 12 hours. Meanwhile, the enlargement of the size of transport demand may require more expensive transport service packages. This is because the transport operator may encounter a lack of transport capacity and has to do subcontracting, which is typically expensive. For example, for transport service packages tailed to transport demands with a due time of 12 hours the corresponding transport service prices are 14.175 (€/TEU) and 14.569 (€/TEU) for the size of 100 TEU and 200 TEU, respectively. There is a 2.8% rising in the service price. The case study shows that the transport demand with a larger size and/or a shorter due time might require an higher priced service packages.

5   Conclusions

This paper proposes a cost-plus-pricing strategy to determine the price of intermodal freight transport services by adding together the operational cost of the transport operator and also its targeted profit margins under different transport scenarios, i.e., self-transporting, subcontracting, and a combination of them. The transport cost is one important part of the transport operator's operational cost and is minimized by optimizing transport planning based on a discrete-time network model. It assumed that the reference transport demand information such as origin, destination, the number of containers, and due time are given by the customers, and that the transport operator will provide a list of transport service packages with different due times, demand sizes, and also the determined prices to the customer. Based on the urgency of delivering containers and the prices of different service packages, the customer will make the final selection decisions. The simulation results indicate that a shorter due time or a lack of capacity could result in the requirement of transport service with a higher price.

For the future work, we will investigate the application of the proposed pricing strategy for performing on-line dynamic pricing. For the case of dynamic pricing, only transport orders that have already been confirmed earlier are known when the current transport planning and pricing decisions are being made, and other transport orders will arrive later and the transport planning and pricing decisions for the newly arrived orders have to be adjusted accordingly by then. In addition, an integrated approach including joint consideration of intermodal freight transport planning and service pricing will be implemented to investigate the effect of demand response to the transport service price.

Acknowledgments. The authors thank Yashar Araghi from the section of Transport and Logistics, Faculty of Technology, Policy and Management of Delft University of Technology for his valuable discussion and comments. This research is supported by the China Scholarship Council under Grants 2011629027 and 201406950004.

References

1. Port of Rotterdam Authority: Port vision 2030: Port compass, December 2011. http://www.portofrotterdam.com/en/Port/port-in-general/port-vision-2030/ Documents/Port-Vision-2030.pdf
2. Crainic, T., Kim, K.: Intermodal transportation. In: Barnhart, C., Laporte, G. (eds.) Transportation, Ser. Handbooks in Operations Research and Management Science, vol. 14, ch. 8, pp. 467–537. Elsevier (2007)
3. Groen,T., Groen,T., Hofman, W., Janssen, R., Meijeren, J.V., Oonk, M., et al.: Implementatieroadmap Synchromodaliteit. The Netherlands: TNO, Connekt & Dinalog commissioned by the Ministry of Infrastructure and Environment (2011)
4. Veenstra, A., Zuidwijk, R., van Asperen, E.: The extended gate concept for container terminals: Expanding the notion of dry ports. Maritime Economics and Logistics **14**(1), 14–32 (2012)
5. The future of freight transport. Europe Container Terminal, Rotterdam, The Netherlands (2011)
6. Macharis, C., Bontekoning, Y.M.: Opportunities for OR in intermodal freight transport research: a review. European Journal of Operational Research **153**(2), 400–416 (2004)
7. Jarzemskiene, I.: The evolution of intermodal transport research and its development issues. Transport **22**(4), 296–306 (2007)
8. Caris, A., Macharis, C., Janssens, G.: Planning problems in intermodal freight transport: accomplishments and prospects. Transportation Planning and Technology **31**(3), 277–302 (2008)
9. Caris, A., Macharis, C., Janssens, G.: Decision support in intermodal transport: a new research agenda. Computers in Industry **64**(2), 105–112 (2013)
10. SteadieSeifi, M., Dellaert, N., Nuijten, W., Woensel, T.V., Raoufi, R.: Multimodal freight transportation planning: A literature review. European Journal of Operational Research **233**(1), 1–15 (2014)
11. Bontekoning, Y., Macharis, C., Trip, J.: Is a new applied transportation research field emerging? - a review of intermodal rail-truck freight transport literature. Transportation Research Part A: Policy and Practice **38**(1), 1–34 (2004)
12. Yan, S., Bernstein, D., Sheffi, Y.: Intermodal pricing using network flow techniques. Transportation Research Part B **29**(3), 171–180 (1995)
13. Spasovic, L.N., Morlok, E.K.: Using marginal costs to evaluate drayage rates in rail-truck intermodal service. Transportation Research Record, No. 1383 (1993)
14. Liu, D., Yang, H.: Dynamic pricing model of container sea-rail intermodal transport on single OD line. Journal of Transportation Systems Engineering and Information Technology **12**(4), 122–127 (2012)

15. Tsai, J.F., Morlock, E.K., Smith, T.E.: Optimal pricing of rail intermodal freight: models and tests. University of Pennsylvania, Tech. Rep. (1994)
16. Li, L., Tayur, S.: Medium-term pricing and operations planning in intermodal transportation. Transportation Science **39**(1), 73–86 (2005)
17. Dandotiya, R., Nath Banerjee, R., Ghodrati, B., Parida, A.: Optimal pricing and terminal location for a rail-truck intermodal service-a case study. International Journal of Logistics Research and Applications **14**(5), 335–349 (2011)
18. Ypsilantis, P., Zuidwijk, R.A.: Joint design and pricing of intermodal port-hinterland network services: considering economies of scale and service time constraints. ERIM Report Series Research in Management, Tech. Rep. (2013)
19. van Riessen, B., Negenborn, R. R., Lodewijks, G., Dekker, R.: Impact and relevance of transit disturbances on planning in intermodal container networks using disturbance cost analysis. Maritime Economics & Logistics 1–24 (2014)
20. Van Riessen, B., Negenborn, R.R., Dekker, R., Lodewijks, G.: Service network design for an intermodal container network with flexible transit times and the possibility of using subcontracted transport. International Journal of Shipping and Transport Logistics **7**(4), 457–478 (2015)
21. Li, L., Negenborn, R.R., De Schutter, B.: A general framework for modeling intermodal transport networks. In: Proceedings of the 10th IEEE International Conference on Networking, Sensing and Control (ICNSC 2013), Paris, France, pp. 579–585, April 2013
22. Li, L., Negenborn, R.R., De Schutter, B.: A sequential linear programming approach for flow assignment in intermodal freight transport. In: Proceedings of the 16th IEEE International Conference on Intelligent Transport Systems (ITSC 2013), The Hague, The Netherlands, pp. 1124–1230, October 2013
23. Li, L., Negenborn, R.R., De Schutter, B.: Receding horizon approach for container flow assignment in intermodal freight transport. Transportation Research Record **2410**, 132–140 (2014)
24. Boardman, B., Malstrom, E., Butler, D., Cole, M.: Computer assisted routing of intermodal shipments. Computers and Industrial Engineering **33**(1–2), 311–314 (1997)

External Coordination among Systems

Materials Flow Control in Hybrid
Make-to-Stock/Make-to-Order Manufacturing

Filipa Rocha[1], Emanuel Silva[1], Ângela Lopes[1], Luis Dias[1], Guilherme Pereira[1],
Nuno O. Fernandes[2], and S. Carmo-Silva[1(✉)]

[1] Department of Production and Systems, University of Minho,
Campus de Gualtar 4710-057, Braga, Portugal
{lsd,gui,scarmo}@dps.uminho.pt
[2] Instituto Politécnico de Castelo Branco, Av. Empresário 6000-767, Castelo Branco, Portugal
nogf@ipcb.pt

Abstract. Today's company competiveness is favoured by product customisation and fast delivery. A strategy to meet this challenge is to manufacture
standard items to stock for product customisation. This configures a hybrid
environment of make-to-stock and make-to-order. To explore the advantages of
this requires good understanding of production control. Thus, we study production under hybrid MTS-MTO, organising the system in two stages. The 1st
manufactures items to inventory, which are then customised in the 2nd. We analyse how the percentage of tardy orders is affected by the inventory of items required to achieve a given fill rate. The impact of two mechanisms for releasing
orders to both stages is also analysed. Results of a simulation study indicate that
most of the reduction on the percentage of tardy orders is achieved by a moderate increase in the stock level of semi-finished products. Moreover the percentage of tardy orders decreases if suitable controlled release of orders is
exerted.

Keywords: Make-to-Stock/ Make-to-Order (MTO-MTS) · Base-stock ·
CONWIP · DBR, simulation

1 Introduction

For many manufacturing companies, the possibility of having competitive advantage in
relation to their competitors frequently resides in having shorter delivery times and
higher delivery reliability of orders [1]. This requires firmly controlling the internal
throughput times and schedule adherence, while at the same time, devising low inventory
levels and adequate resources' utilisation. This well-known dilemmatic problem can be
solved by the Production Logistics function of a company, which organizes and manages
the entire material flow, from the acquisition of raw materials to the delivery of end
products to customers. Organizing production in a hybrid make-to-stock/make-to-order
(MTS-MTO) manufacturing environment is a strategy that contributes to solve the dilemma. In fact it allows companies to exploit the benefits of delayed differentiation, reducing delivery times and inventory costs in comparison to the pure MTO and MTS

© Springer International Publishing Switzerland 2015
F. Corman et al. (Eds.): ICCL 2015, LNCS 9335, pp. 559–568, 2015.
DOI: 10.1007/978-3-319-24264-4_38

strategies, respectively. It also allows customers to get what and when they want and companies to avoid the costs of shortages and overages. Its application is widely seen as a growing trend in manufacturing [2].

This type of production is common, for example, in the aluminium profiles manufacturing. Companies of this industrial sector instead of making-to-stock, start the production of standard and regular aluminium profiles without confirmed orders, holding a stock of semi-finished products. These are then assigned to customer orders and customized according to specifications. This, for example, can be for a specific surface finishing material or and profiles machining to fit the required application. This customization process is also common in other industries for several different types of products.

In this paper, we focus on the above dilemma in the context of the hybrid MTS-MTO manufacturing environment. The paper specifically deals with a two-stage manufacturing system with unidirectional production flows. In the MTS stage, standard semi-finished products are firstly manufactured and stocked as intermediate inventory. In the MTO stage, semi-finished components are assigned to customer orders for customisation according to specific requirements. The intermediate inventory acts as a buffer or decoupling point between the two stages. High inventory of semi-finished products means high holding costs, whereas low inventory may increase the waiting time of customer orders for semi-finished components, and thus the delivery time. Therefore, in addition to inventory decisions at the MTS stage, order release and dispatching decisions at the MTO stage should determine the company capability to quote short and reliable delivery times to their customers, and thus to remain competitive in the market. In spite of this, most research on inventory location ignores the intricacies of scheduling, typically assuming that orders are processed in the sequence in which they arrive to the production system [3]. Thus, in this paper, we investigate how materials flow's control strategies impacts system performance. The release of orders to the MTS stage is based on inventory replenishment. Two alternative mechanisms have been studied, namely Base-stock [4, 5] and CONstante Work-In-Process (CONWIP) [6]. The release of orders to the MTO stage is based on the capacity availability at the bottleneck workstation. Here Drum-Buffer-Rope (DBR) [7, 8] was applied. The objective is to satisfy the MTO demand within competitive delivery times, while keeping work-in-process (WIP) low at the MTS stage and avoiding stock-outs of semi-finished products at the intermediate buffer. The controlled release of orders to the MTO stage must ensure that orders are not released too early or too late, and maintaining the workload at workstations low and stable. Inventory replenishment at the MTS stage ensures that the semi-finished products' buffer is filled to the required level, without a rigid order release plan.

Research efforts are restricted in the area of materials flow control for the hybrid MTS-MTO manufacturing. Most of the research literature in two-stage production systems assume that the semi-finished products inventory is managed according to a base-stock policy. Under this policy, each demand arrival triggers the immediate release of raw materials to the MTS stage and the immediate release of orders to the MTO stage as soon as semi-finished products become available at the intermediate buffer (see e.g. [3, 9, 10, 11, 12]).

This research work gives a contribution to fill the research gap in the area, using discrete event simulation to model and analyse the performance of a two-stage manufacturing system when operated under the above-referred materials flow control mechanisms. In particular the following research question is addressed: How controlled release of orders to both stages of the production system impacts system performance?

The remainder of the paper is organized as follows. In Section 2, we present the simulation study carried out, including the simulation model, the experimental set-up and the performance measures considered. In Section 3, we discuss the results of the simulation study, and finally, in Section 4 of the paper, we summarize key results and managerial implications.

2   Simulation Study

Simulation will next be used to model building and experimentation towards answering the above research question. A discrete event simulation model was developed using Arena® software.

2.1   Manufacturing System

In this study, we consider a hypothetical two-stage manufacturing system with an intermediate buffer of semi-finished products (see Figure 1). Stage one consists of workstations 1, 2 and 3, and manufactures standard components from raw materials. Stage two consists of workstations 4, 5 and 6, and manufactures end products to order from the components made at stage one, i.e., according to the customer specifications. Production flows at the system are unidirectional with each production order having exactly the same routing.

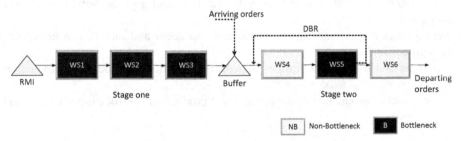

Fig. 1. Two-stage manufacturing system

Whenever a customer order arrives at the production system, a standard component from the intermediate buffer is allocated to the order. We assume that each customer order requires just one unit of the standard components. However, when a customer order arrives and finds the intermediate buffer empty, the order is backordered. Backorders are filled after the standard components are made available at the intermediate buffer following processing at stage one. The first stage is capable of manufacturing two different types of standard components or semi-finished products that are then customised in the second stage into, virtually, an infinite number of end products.

As customer orders arrive to the production system, their operation times are identified and due dates established. It is assumed that all orders are accepted and enough raw materials inventory is always available in the beginning of the first stage. Orders inter-arrival times follow an exponential distribution, due dates are market driven and set by adding a uniformly distributed time allowance to the time of order arrival. In this study, the allowance varies between 25 and 45 time units. This leads to approximately 12% of orders being tardy when immediate release of orders to the second stage is used, for a fill rate level of 80%. This has been verified through preliminary simulation tests. This fill rate level means that 80% of arriving customer orders are filled from the semi-finished products inventory and then made immediately available for release into the second stage.

In the simulation model, operations' processing times follow an exponential distribution, with a mean of one time unit. The arrival rate combined with the routings and processing times ensures that utilisation is 90% at all workstations, except at work stations four and six. These have 20% of protective capacity. Protective capacity is defined as a given amount of extra capacity at non-constraints above the system constraint's capacity, used to protect against statistical fluctuations [13]. Workstations with protective capacity are non-bottleneck. This means that on stage one the bottleneck will shift across workstations 1 to 3, since utilisation is equal across workstations, while on stage two workstation five (WS5) is the bottleneck for most of the time. Additionally, following assumptions are adopted:

- Workstations operate asynchronously, so production orders can be loaded whenever material or inventory is available and the required production authorisations have been received. These take the form of available production control cards when required by the production control mechanism.
- Workstations capacity remains constant over time and no breakdowns have been modelled.
- Set-up times are assumed to be sequence-independent and included in the operation processing times.
- Distances and transportation times between workstations and between production stages are assumed to be negligible.
- Information of production control events and production control cards are transmitted instantly.

The simulation model presented here was kept simple in order to ensure easy and correct interpretation of the effect of combining MTO and MTS and getting results that may contribute for the understanding of the behaviour of more complex production systems.

2.2 Materials Flow Control

Materials Flow Control addresses two main functions: order release and priority dispatching. Order release determines the time and the orders to be released into each production stage. Release decisions are usually based on the orders' urgency and on their influence on the current shop floor situation [14]. Priority dispatching determines which orders in queue should be selected next for processing once a workstation becomes idle.

In the manufacturing system considered, an arriving customer order will consume a standard component from the intermediate buffer of semi-finished products and immediately flows into a pre-shop pool, waiting its release to the second stage of processing for customisation. This means that orders are not immediately released to the shop as they seize the semi-finished products that they need. Rather, they must wait for capacity availability at the second stage. The use of a pre-shop pool is expected to reduce the level of work-in-process (WIP) and allow better control over the flow of production orders through the shop. Orders in the pool are sequenced according to their urgency, i.e., due date, and released under the drum-buffer-rope control mechanism (DBR), see Figure 1.

There are three major components of DBR: the drum; the buffer; and the rope. The drum represents the bottleneck workstation (WS5 in our manufacturing system), which defines the overall pace of the system, the buffer is a time mechanism that protects the bottleneck against starvation and the rope drives the release of orders to the shop. For this purpose, production authorisation cards are used, which are attached to production orders at the beginning of stage two and detached from the order after processing at the bottleneck workstation. Cards are not part number specific and can be acquired by any order waiting release in the pre-shop pool. Detached cards are sent back to the first workstation of the second stage, where they can be attached to new production orders entering the system. In our study we consider that one order requires just one production authorisation card from each pair of workstations in the routing of the order.

When a customer order arrives at the production system or when a semi-finished product is consumed from the intermediate buffer, depending on the mechanism applied (Base-stock or CONWIP, see section 2.3), a MTS order is also released to the first stage for the replenishment of the standard component that will be (or was) consumed from the semi-finished product buffer.

The role of priority dispatching is a very modest one when order release control is applied, because the choice among jobs is limited due to short queues [15]. Thus in this study shop floor dispatching at both stages is based on *first-come-first-served* (FCFS) priority dispatching rule that supports the natural flow of the orders through the shop, stabilizing operation throughput times.

2.3   Experimental Design and Performance Measures

The experimental factors and simulated levels of the study are summarised in Table 1. Thirty simulation cases are tested (2 production control strategies; 5 card counts; and 3 levels of the fill rate), and each test case runs 100 replicates. The time horizon for a simulation case is 200 000 time units and only data of the last 190 000 time units are collected, i.e., a warm-up period of 10 000 time units is considered.

Table 1. Experimental factors and levels

Experimental factor	Levels		
Materials Flow Control Strategies	B-DBR		C-DBR
Card counts	10, 12, 15, 18 and infinity		
Fill rate	80%	90%	99%

Two materials flow control strategies are applied to release orders to the shop, namely, B-DBR and C-DBR. The former combines Base-stock with DBR (B-DBR) to release orders to first and second stages, respectively. The latter combines CONWIP with DBR (C-DBR) for the same purpose.

Under Base-stock control, demand information is instantaneously transmitted to all workstations of the first stage when a customer order arrives to the manufacturing system. The idea is that all workstations know about each customer order as it arrives to the system and start immediately to manufacture a replacement item. For that, Base-stock maintains a certain amount of inventory in the input buffer on each workstation. This amount of inventory is called base stock level. Thus the particularity of this mechanism is their immediate reactivity to demand. In our study all base stock levels are zero, except for the semi-finished products. This complies with previous studies e.g. [16].

Under CONWIP control, each time a semi-finished product is seized by a customer order, the release of a new job (i.e., MTS order) to the first stage is authorized. CONWIP uses cards from a single card type to control the total amount of work-in-process (WIP) permitted in the first processing stage. Cards are attached to the order at the beginning of the first stage and detached from the order (i.e., semi-finished product) when it is seized by an arriving customer order.

The mechanism applied to release orders to the second stage of processing, DBR, was tested at 5 card counts, including infinity. Card counts are sets of cards to operate the manufacturing system. When infinity is assumed, this means that the number of cards in the set imposes no restriction on the number of jobs, and thus on the workload, that can be released to the shop.

The order fill rate, defined as the percentage of orders that is immediately filled from the semi-finished products buffer when a customer order arrives, was tested at three levels: low (80%), medium (90%) and high (99%). Note that the fill rate is expected to approach 100% as the semi-finished products inventory increases and tends to infinity. The inventory replenishment mechanisms used aim at determining the base-stock level or the number of CONWIP cards, depending on to the mechanism applied at first stage, to achieve the desired fill rate, i.e., 80%, 90% or 99%. This was determined through exhaustive searching using pre-test simulation runs.

We use three types of criteria to evaluate the system's performance: (1) the ability to deliver orders on time, (2) the ability to provide short delivery times, and (3) the ability to keep the inventory levels low. To measure performance with regard to the first, the percentage of tardy orders (P_{tardy}) and the standard deviation of lateness ($SD_{lateness}$) are recorded. To measure performance with regard to the second, the shop throughput time (TT) and the total (or system) throughput time (TTT) are used. The shop throughput time refers to the time that elapses between order release to the second stage and order completion. The total throughput time is the shop throughput time plus the pool delay and plus the time that orders wait for semi-finished products availability. To measure performance with regard to the third, work-in-process (WIP) at stage one and the average inventory of semi-finished products (SFPI) at the intermediate buffer are used.

3   Simulation Results and Discussion

This section discusses the results of the simulation study described in the previous section. Comparisons between materials flow control strategies are based on the Student paired t-test with $\alpha=0.05$.

The overall results are summarised in Table 2. In what concerns the C-DBR strategy only the results of an infinity number of cards are shown as it was observed that there are no statistical performance differences between the two materials flow control strategies, i.e. C-DBR and B-DBR, for TT, TTT, SDlateness and Ptardy.

Figure 2 plots the percentage of tardy orders against the shop throughput time for different combinations of the experimental factors under the B-DBR strategy. By comparing plotted curves we can determine performance differences for different values of card counts. A marker on a curve is the result of simulating DBR at a specific card count. Five card counts have been simulated, including infinity. Infinity means unrestricted release of orders to the second stage of shop and refers to the rightmost mark on each curve.

From Figure 2 it can be observed that increasing the fill rate from 80% to 99%, leads to a lower percentage of tardy orders. A higher fill rate means a higher probability of orders being filled from the intermediate buffer of semi-finished products, and therefore, the time that orders wait for semi-finished products availability tends to be lower. This makes the total throughput time lower and percentages of tardy orders also lower (see Table 2). Note that a lower percentage of tardy orders may result from a lower average lateness (as a results of lower total throughput times), but also from a lower variance of the lateness. In this case it results from both, as can be observed from Table 2. However, the lower percentage of tardy orders is obtained at the cost of having a higher inventory of semi-finished products between production stages and a higher WIP at the MTS stage, as Table 2 shows.

Increasing the fill rate from 80% to 99% allows a reduction on the total throughput time in more than 13% and on the percentage of tardy orders in more than 38%, under unrestrictive release, depending on the materials flow control strategy. However, this requires increasing the average inventory of semi-finished products in more than 231%, and WIP at stage one in more than 87%, depending on the materials flow control strategy. Most of the reduction on the percentage of tardy orders is achieved when the fill rate increases from 80% to 90%. This requires a moderate increase in WIP and in the stock level of semi-finished products, sees Table 2.

Table 2. Performance Results

Control strategy	DBR card counts	Fill rate	WIP	SFPI	TT	TTT	SD$_{lateness}$	P$_{tardy}$
C-DBR	infinity	80%	41.00	15.91	15.24	18.48	15.24	12.17
		90%	51.00	24.78	15.48	16.81	13.41	8.95
		99%	80.00	52.69	15.75	15.87	12.29	7.23
B-DBR	infinity	80%	42.69	15.38	15.36	18.34	14.87	11.94
	18				13.58	18.40	14.71	11.70
	15				12.86	18.54	14.87	11.69
	12				11.88	18.89	14.95	12.21
	10				11.01	19.53	15.42	13.53
B-DBR	infinity	90%	51.23	23.93	15.51	16.88	13.36	9.13
	18				13.60	16.93	13.33	8.68
	15				12.88	17.11	13.45	8.74
	12				11.90	17.42	13.54	9.28
	10				11.07	18.24	14.07	10.78
B-DBR	infinity	99%	80.12	52.85	15.79	15.92	12.40	7.34
	18				13.71	16.02	12.29	6.84
	15				12.94	16.14	12.34	6.87
	12				11.91	16.47	12.48	7.42
	10				11.09	17.40	13.13	9.01

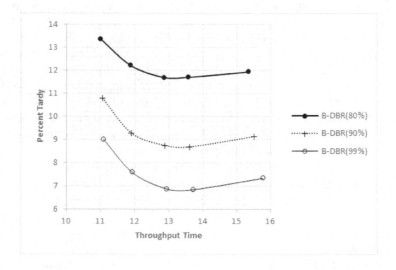

Fig. 2. Performance results for the percentage of tardy orders under the B-DBR strategy

Figure 2 also shows that when card counts are reduced, i.e. moving from right to left along the curve, the percentage of tardy orders decrease. Thus we may conclude that controlled release of orders allows improving performance. However, card counts cannot be set excessively low in order to avoid deteriorating performance. We also may observe in Table 2 that C-DBR performs slightly better than B-DBR in what concerns WIP at stage one, but only when the fill rate is low. This may be attributed to the CONWIP part of this control strategy, which only releases an MTS order to the first stage when a semi-finished product is consumed by a customer order, therefore avoiding increasing WIP. On the contrary, Base-stock releases MTS orders as soon as customer orders arrive to the manufacturing system.

4   Conclusions and Managerial Implications

This study investigates the impact of two materials flow control strategies in the hybrid MTS-MTO manufacturing. The study also analyses how the percentage of tardy orders is affected by the semi-finished products inventory between the MTS and the MTO stages of manufacturing required to achieve a given fill rate. Results led us to conclude that: (1) controlled release of orders to both stages contributes to reduce the percentage of tardy orders; (2) CONWIP may result in a lower work-in-process at stage one, but only when a low fill rate is allowed; (3) A trade-off exists between the percentage of tardy orders and the semi-finished products inventory required to achieve a given fill rate. However, most of the reduction on the percentage of tardy orders is achieved for a moderate increase in the stock level of semi-finished products.

Our future research work will extend the study to other materials flow control strategies and shop configurations in context of this hybrid production environment.

Acknowledgements. This study had the financial support of FCT-Fundação para a Ciência e Tecnologia of Portugal under the project PEst2015-2020: UID/CEC/00319/2013.

References

1. Nyhuis, P., Wiendahl, H.-P.: Fundamentals of Production Logistics: Theory, Tools and Aplications. Springer-Verlag, Heidelberg (2009)
2. Åhlström, P., Westbrook, R.: Implications of Mass Customisation for Operations Management. International Journal of Operations and Production Management **19**(3), 262–274 (1999)
3. Kaminskya, P., Kayab, O.: Inventory positioning, scheduling and lead-time quotation in supply chains. International Journal of Production Economics **114**(1), 276–293 (2008)
4. Kimball, G.: General principles of inventory control. Journal of Manufacturing and Operations Management **1**(1), 119–130 (1988)
5. Lee, Y.J., Zipkin, P.: Tandem queues with planned inventories. Operations Research **40**(5), 936–947 (1992)

6. Spearman, M.L., Woodruff, D.L., Hopp, W.J.: CONWIP: a pull alternative to kanban. The International Journal of Production Research **28**(5), 879–894 (1990)
7. Goldratt, E.M., Fox, R.E.: The Race. North River Press, New York (1986)
8. Fry, T.D., Karwan, K., Steele, D.: Implementing drum-buffer-rope to control manufacturing lead time. The International Journal of Logistics Management **2**(1), 12–18 (1991)
9. Aviv, Y., Federgruen, A.: Capacitated multi-item inventory systems with random and seasonally fluctuating demands: implications for postponement strategies. Management science **47**(4), 512–531 (2001)
10. Gupta, D., Benjaafar, S.: Make-to-order, make-to-stock, or delay product differentiation? A common framework for modeling and analysis. IIE Transactions **36**, 529–546 (2004)
11. Almehdawe, E., Elizabeth Jewke, E.: Performance analysis and optimization of hybrid manufacturing systems under a batch ordering policy. International Journal of Production Economics **144**(1), 200–208 (2013)
12. Fernandes, N.O., Silva, C., Carmo-Silva, S.: Order release in a hybrid MTO-MTS two-stage production system. In: Pre-prints of the 18th International Working Seminar on Production Economics, Innsbruck, Austria, February 24–28, 2014
13. Cox III, J.F., Blackstone Jr., J.H. (eds.): APICS Dictionary Alexandria. APICS, VA (2002)
14. Henrich, P., Land, M., Gaalman, G.J.C.: Exploring applicability of the workload control concept. International Journal of Production Economics **90**(2), 187–198 (2004)
15. Land, M.J., Gaalman, G.: The performance of workload control concepts in job shops: Improving the release method. International Journal of Production Economics **56–57**(1), 347–364 (1998)
16. Bonvik, A.M., Couch, C.E., Gershwin, S.B.: A comparison of production-line control mechanisms. International Journal of Production Research **25**(3), 789–804 (1997)

A New Modelling Approach of Evaluating Preventive and Reactive Strategies for Mitigating Supply Chain Risks

Abroon Qazi[1(✉)], John Quigley[1], Alex Dickson[1], and Barbara Gaudenzi[2]

[1] Strathclyde Business School, University of Strathclyde, Glasgow, UK
{abroon.qazi,j.quigley,alex.dickson}@strath.ac.uk
[2] Faculty of Business Economics, University of Verona, Verona, Italy
barbara.gaudenzi@univr.it

Abstract. Supply chains are becoming more complex and vulnerable due to globalization and interdependency between different risks. Existing studies have focused on identifying different preventive and reactive strategies for mitigating supply chain risks and advocating the need for adopting specific strategy under a particular situation. However, current research has not addressed the issue of evaluating an optimal mix of preventive and reactive strategies taking into account their relative costs and benefits within the supply network setting of interconnected firms and organizations. We propose a new modelling approach of evaluating different combinations of such strategies using Bayesian belief networks. This technique helps in determining an optimal solution on the basis of maximum improvement in the network expected loss. We have demonstrated our approach through a simulation study and discussed practical and managerial implications.

Keywords: Supply chain risks · Preventive and reactive strategies · Bayesian belief networks · Network expected loss · Simulation study

1 Introduction

Supply chains have become complex because of the globalization and outsourcing in manufacturing industries. Supply chain risk is characterized by both the probability of an event and its severity given that an event occurs. Supply chain risk management (SCRM) is an active area of research that deals with the overall management of risk events ranging across the entire spectrum of the supply chain including external risk factors. "SCRM aims to identify the potential sources of supply chain risk and implement appropriate actions to avoid or contain supply chain vulnerability" [1]. Vulnerability is defined as an exposure to serious disturbances from risks within the supply chain as well as risks external to the supply chain [2]. Supply chain risk is an event that may cause disruption to the flow of activities within the supply chain. Recently, there has been a shift in the interest of researchers towards exploring impact of disruption on global supply chains. Global sourcing and lean operations are the main drivers of supply chain disruptions [3].

© Springer International Publishing Switzerland 2015
F. Corman et al. (Eds.): ICCL 2015, LNCS 9335, pp. 569–585, 2015.
DOI: 10.1007/978-3-319-24264-4_39

Bayesian belief network (BBN) is a an acyclic directed graphical model comprising nodes representing uncertain variables and arcs indicating causal relationships between variables whereas the strength of dependency is represented by the conditional probability values. BBNs have started gaining the interest of researchers in modelling supply chain risks [4]. BBNs offer a unique feature of modelling risks combining both the statistical data and subjective judgment in case of non-availability of data [5]. Researchers have used the BBNs to model specific domains of supply chain risks and validated these models through case studies.

1.1   Research Problem and Contribution

It is extremely important to consider the interdependency between risks in modelling supply chain risks. However, capturing the probabilistic interaction between risks and resulting losses is not sufficient for managing risks as risk management process necessitates selecting cost-effective strategies. Selection of optimal mix of risk mitigation strategies has never been explored within the realm of interconnected risks across different segments of a supply network. This paper bridges the research gap and presents a new modelling approach of evaluating mix of preventive and reactive strategies taking into account the supply network configuration, interdependency between risks and associated costs and benefits of different combinations of risk mitigation strategies. The technique will help researchers develop robust models of managing supply chain risks and benefit practitioners in understanding interaction between risks and selecting optimal mix of risk mitigation strategies.

1.2   Outline

We present brief overview of the research conducted in SCRM in Section 2. New modelling approach of evaluating risk mitigation strategies is described in Section 3. Application of the proposed method is demonstrated through a simulation study in Section 4. Furthermore, results are also discussed in detail followed by the explication of managerial implications. Finally, conclusion and future research agenda are presented in Section 5.

2   Literature Review

2.1   Supply Chain Risk Management

Risk management is an established field in some areas of organizational life like finance but it is still a developing theme within the realm of Supply chain management [6]. Despite the ongoing debate on the objective and subjective nature of risk, there is a consensus among researchers on treating the risk management as a process comprising three stages of risk identification, risk estimation and risk evaluation [7]. "SCRM is the management of supply chain risks through coordination or collaboration amongst the supply chain partners so as to ensure profitability and continuity" [8].

Simulation has been extensively used by researchers in modeling supply chain risks. It provides a systematic approach for understanding the interactive impact of factors for different scenarios. Simulation techniques used in the realm of supply chain risk management include agent-based modeling, Monte Carlo simulation, discrete event simulation, system dynamics modeling and Petri-Net simulation [9]. Researchers have also used mixed methods in their research. Analytical hierarchy process has been considered as an effective technique for modelling and managing supply chain risks [10].

The major limitation of existing models is their lack of capturing the holistic nature of supply chain risks. Many techniques are not able to account for risk propagation [11]. Furthermore, existing methods and models have not taken into consideration the network configuration of a supply chain. The limited focus of these models in solving specific problems results in evaluating locally optimal solutions. BBNs present a useful technique of capturing interaction between risk events and performance measures [4]. Another advantage of using BBNs for modelling supply chain risks is the ability of back propagation that helps in determining the probability of an event that may not be observed directly. There are certain problems associated with the use of BBNs. Firstly, with the increase in number of nodes representing supply chain risks, a considerable amount of data is required in populating the network with (conditional) probability values and it might not be feasible to elicit huge data from the experts. Secondly, there are computational challenges associated with the increase in number of nodes.

2.2   Bayesian Belief Network Based Models

Lockamy and McCormack [12] developed a model for benchmarking supplier risks incorporating risk events related to supplier network, internal operations and external factors. They used surveys and interviews for collection of data from both the internal and external company sources and applied the model on a group of 15 automotive casting suppliers for a major automotive company in US. Dogan and Aydin [13] developed a supplier selection model combining Total Cost of Ownership and BBN methods and applied the model in automotive industry to help Tier-1 suppliers select their own suppliers. They found the method to be suitable in dealing with incomplete or uncertain information of buyers about the suppliers.

Badurdeen et al. [4] developed supply chain risk taxonomy and a risk network map capturing interdependencies between risks and applied the model on the Boeing company and its Tier 1 Suppliers. Their model presents an effective tool to capture the interaction of risk factors and helps in identifying key suppliers. Risk propagation across multiple tiers is not explored in their study. Furthermore, modelling of resulting losses and mitigation strategies with associated costs is not considered and therefore, risk management process is not explored through BBNs comprehensively.

Garvey et al. [11] presented a Bayesian network approach of modelling risk propagation in a supply network. Their proposed model takes into consideration the interdependencies between risks and the structure of a supply network. They introduced different risk measures on the basis of this model and conducted a simulation study in order to demonstrate the use of risk measures in a supply network setting. However, evaluation of their proposed risk measures is not feasible in case of a complex network structure. Furthermore, they did not focus on the risk evaluation stage of risk management process.

2.3   Limitations and Research Gap

Most of the existing studies in SCRM have focused on specific domains in supply chain without considering the holistic view. Qualitative techniques are not able to capture the interaction of risks exclusively whereas many quantification methods treat risks as independent [4], [13]. Limited studies have considered modelling interdependency between risks and resulting losses. However, it is not sufficient to model the probabilistic interaction between risks and resulting losses. Risk evaluation is an equally important stage of the risk management process that necessitates evaluating the costs and benefits associated with different combinations of risk mitigation strategies. Risk evaluation has gained limited attention of the researchers in SCRM and no study has focused on integrating the probabilistic interaction between risks, resulting losses and impact of mitigation strategies. It is, therefore, important to investigate an effective approach of not only assessing risks but also evaluating different mitigation strategies within a framework of interconnected risks and mitigation strategies.

3   New Modelling Approach

Based on the efficacy of BBNs in capturing interdependencies between risks, we consider BBN based modeling of a supply network as an effective approach. Such a modeling technique can help managers visualize supply chain risks and take effective mitigation strategies [5], [9]. BBNs have been already explored in the literature of SCRM, however, our proposed BBN based modelling approach is unique in terms of introducing new risk measures that capture the impact of loss propagation across the entire network and demonstrating the efficacy of BBNs in evaluating risk mitigation strategies.

3.1   Framework

We follow the butterfly view of supply chain risks ranging from the causes to actual risk events to consequences [14]. Furthermore, we classify risks as process, upstream, downstream and external risks. Process risks relate to the risks directly associated with the main focal firm and comprise inventory, operational, quality and management risks. Downstream and upstream risks arise from the interaction between the focal firm and its customers and suppliers respectively. External risks are driven by external events like weather, earthquakes, political and market forces [15]. Supply chain risks can be considered as an interconnected web of events spanning across the entire network as shown in Fig. 1.

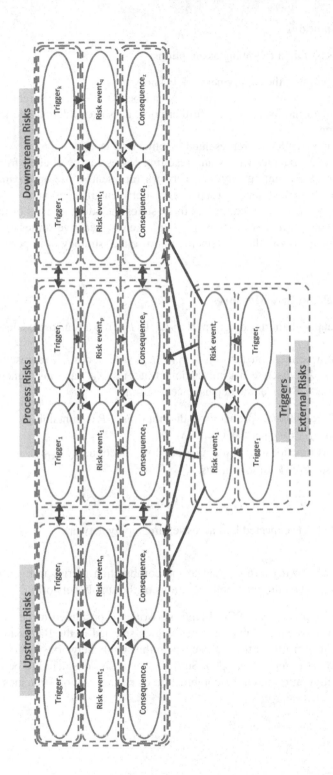

Fig. 1. Framework capturing interdependency between triggers, risk events and consequences

3.2   Assumptions

Our model is based on following assumptions:

1. Entire structure of the supply network is known
2. Risk triggers, events and consequences can be assigned to different locations and links between the locations and furthermore, all stakeholders agree to share such information
3. All random variables are represented by binary states
4. Conditional probability values and resulting losses can be elicited from the stakeholders and the resulting Bayesian network represents close approximation to the actual perceived risks and interdependency between different risks
5. Each mitigation strategy comprises three states including options of taking no action, adopting preventive strategy and implementing reactive strategy
6. Costs associated with the implementation of either strategy at important nodes are known

3.3   Model and Risk Measures

A discrete supply chain risk diagram $N = (X, G, P, L)$ is a four-tuple consisting of

- a directed acyclic graph (DAG), $G = (V, E)$, with nodes, V, representing discrete risk events, X_R, discrete risk mitigation strategies, X_S, and loss functions, L, and directed links, E, encoding dependence relations
- a set of conditional probability distributions, P, containing a distribution, $P(X_R|X_{pa(R)})$, for each risk event, X_R
- a set of loss functions, L, containing one loss function, $l(X_{pa(V)})$, for each node v in the subset $V_l \in V$ of loss nodes.

$$EL(X) = \prod_{X_v \in X_R} P(X_v|X_{pa(v)}) \sum_{w \in V_L} l(X_{pa(w)}) \tag{1}$$

where $EL(X)$ is the expected loss across entire supply network

Definitions. Following terms relate to the combination of risk mitigation strategies corresponding to two different configurations of the supply network:

- *Standard Configuration (SC).* Supply network is considered to be in its standard configuration when risk mitigation strategies selected in the Bayesian network reflect real-time profile of these strategies in the supply network.
- *Contingency Configuration (CC).* Supply network is considered to be in its contingency configuration when the combination of risk mitigation strategies satisfies the objective function.

Risk Measures. We introduce two risk measures in order to evaluate the relative contribution of each risk factor towards the loss propagation across entire network.

- *Loss Propagation Containment Measure (LPCM).* Loss propagation containment measure is the ratio between relative improvement in the network expected loss corresponding to complete mitigation of the risk factor and network expected loss for the standard configuration.

$$LPCM_{X_{R_i}} = \frac{EL(X) - EL(X|X_{R_i}=false)}{EL(X)_{SC}} \tag{2}$$

$$Avg. LPCM\ (\overline{LPCM}) = 1/n \sum_1^n LPCM_{X_{R_i}} \tag{3}$$

- *Loss Propagation Spread Measure (LPSM).* Loss propagation spread measure is the ratio between range of network expected loss corresponding to the two extreme states of the risk factor and network expected loss for the standard configuration.

$$LPSM_{X_{R_i}} = \frac{EL(X|X_{R_i}=true) - EL(X|X_{R_i}=false)}{EL(X)_{SC}} \tag{4}$$

$$Avg. LPSM\ (\overline{LPSM}) = 1/n \sum_1^n LPSM_{X_{R_i}} \tag{5}$$

3.4   Modelling Process

Following steps must be followed in developing the Bayesian network based model of a given supply network and evaluating the optimal combination of mitigation strategies:

1. Define the boundaries of supply network and identify stakeholders
2. Following the supply network process flow, classify risks as triggers, risk events and consequences on the basis of input received from each stakeholder
3. Refine the qualitative structure of the resulting network involving all stakeholders
4. Elicit (conditional) probability values, loss values resulting from risks and costs associated with implementing different mitigation strategies and populate the Bayesian network with all values
5. Define the objective function
6. Run the model and export array of values corresponding to different combinations of strategies to Microsoft Excel
7. Repeat the previous step for instantiation of each risk factor to the extreme states
8. Analyze the results and select optimal combination of strategies satisfying the objective function
9. Validate the model output involving stakeholders

4   Simulation Study

We demonstrate our proposed method through a simple supply network [11] as shown in Fig. 2. The model was developed in GeNIe software. The supply network comprises a raw material source, two manufacturers, a warehouse and retailer. Risks are represented by oval shaped nodes whereas resulting losses and control strategies are represented by diamond and rectangular shaped nodes respectively. Each risk factor is represented by a unique number appearing at top of the node. Though each domain of the supply network may comprise a number of triggers, risk events and consequences, we consider limited risks for the sake of simplicity. Furthermore, we consider the significance of losses and mitigation strategies at the interface of different domains. However, it is equally important to consider internal risks and related mitigation strategies in managing supply chain risks.

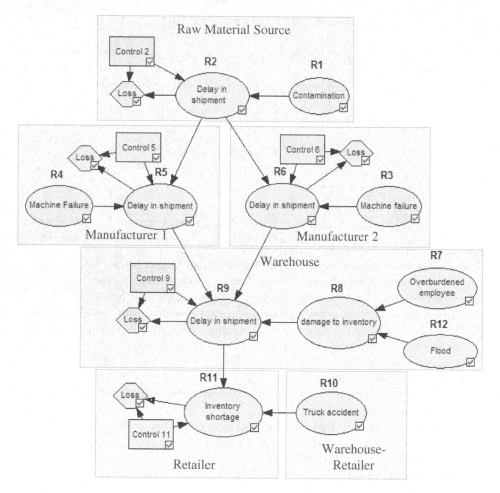

Fig. 2. Bayesian network based model of a supply network (adopted from Garvey et al. [11])

Each control node comprises three states; no mitigation strategy, preventive strategy and reactive strategy. (Conditional) probability values of risks (given no mitigation strategy) for the network are shown in Table 1. Loss values and costs associated with each strategy are shown in Table 2. We also assume that under standard configuration, 'no mitigation strategy' is selected for all the control nodes. Conditional probability values of risks (given preventive or reactive strategy) are given as follows:

$$P(risk = True(T)|strategy = Preventive) = 0.0001 \qquad (6)$$

$$P(risk = False(F)|strategy = Preventive) = 0.9999 \qquad (7)$$

$$P(risk = T|strategy = Reactive) = P(risk = T|strategy = No) \qquad (8)$$

$$P(risk = F|strategy = Reactive) = P(risk = F|strategy = No) \qquad (9)$$

Table 1. (Conditional) probability values ($P(risk = F|parents) = 1 - P(risk = T|parents)$

Parents				P(risk|parents)					
R1	R2	R3	R4	R1 T	R2 T	R3 T	R4 T	R5 T	R6 T
				0.4					
T					0.8				
F					0.3				
						0.2			
							0.3		
		T	T					0.7	
		T	F					0.4	
		F	T					0.6	
		F	F					0.1	
	T	T							0.9
	T	F							0.6
	F	T							0.5
	F	F							0.2

Parents							P(risk|parents)					
R5	R6	R7	R8	R9	R10	R12	R7 T	R8 T	R9 T	R10 T	R11 T	R12 T
							0.4					
		T				T		0.8				
		T				F		0.3				
		F				T		0.6				
		F				F		0.2				
T	T	T							0.9			
T	T	F							0.5			
T	F	T							0.6			
T	F	F							0.3			
F	T	T							0.4			
F	T	F							0.3			
F	F	T							0.3			
F	F	F							0.2			
										0.4		
			T	T							0.9	
			T	F							0.7	
			F	T							0.6	
			F	F							0.2	
												0.2

Table 2. Loss values and costs for different mitigation strategies

Risk	Loss (no mitigation strategy)	Loss (preventive strategy) [Cost]	Loss (reactive strategy) [Cost]
R2	500	500 [300]	250 [100]
R5	100	100 [70]	50 [30]
R6	220	220 [130]	110 [70]
R9	940	940 [600]	470 [300]
R11	30	30 [25]	15 [10]

4.1   Problem Statement

Given different options of preventive and reactive strategies and associated costs available at different nodes of the supply network, what is the optimal combination of these strategies yielding maximum improvement in the network expected loss taking into consideration the associated mitigation cost?

Objective Function. In this study, we aim to maximize the improvement in network expected loss keeping in view the costs associated with different mitigation strategies.

$$\underset{\gamma_{x_s} \in \gamma_{X_S}}{max} \quad EL(X_{\gamma_{X_{SC}}}) - EL(X_{\gamma_{x_s}}) - C_{\gamma_{x_s}} \tag{10}$$

where $\gamma_{X_{SC}}$ is the combination of different states of n mitigation strategies under standard configuration

γ_{X_S} is a set of all possible orderings of different states of n mitigation strategies $(x_{s_1} \times x_{s_2} \times ... \times x_{s_n})$

$C_{\gamma_{x_s}}$ is the cost of implementing γ_{x_s} combination of mitigation strategies

4.2   Results and Discussion

Once the Bayesian network was updated, array of network expected loss values was exported to Microsoft Excel. Because of availability of three options at each of the five control nodes, there were 243 different combinations of control strategies. Under standard configuration with no mitigation strategy selected at any control node, the network expected loss was 747.52 units. Risk measures of all risk factors are shown in Table 3. Risk spectrum representing the graphical dimension of risk measures is shown in Fig. 3. R9 is the most important risk factor having maximum values of LPCM and LPSM. As risk factors appearing at the interface of different supply network domains were considered important in our model, and therefore assigned loss values and control strategies, high values of LPCM and LPSM could be observed for all these risk factors. If other risk factors were also assigned loss values, the resulting risk measures would be higher in magnitude. Furthermore, external risk triggers affecting multiple organizations within the network would also result in achieving high values of the risk measures. Without considering the cost factor, it seems viable to implement a control strategy for mitigating R9, however, it might not be feasible after capturing dynamics of all significant factors.

Table 3. Risk measures of risk factors under standard configuration

Risk	Standard Configuration			
	Expected Loss (True)	Expected Loss (False)	LPCM	LPSM
R1	963.72	603.39	0.1928	0.4820
R2	1107.85	387.19	0.4820	0.9641
R3	834.42	725.80	0.0291	0.1453
R4	834.21	710.37	0.0497	0.1657
R5	1053.26	567.96	0.2402	0.6492
R6	1068.74	473.88	0.3661	0.7958
R7	760.79	738.68	0.0118	0.0296
R8	871.34	687.09	0.0808	0.2465
R9	1431.92	352.66	0.5282	1.4438
R10	753.40	743.60	0.0052	0.0131
R11	964.46	518.39	0.3065	0.5967
R12	812.38	731.31	0.0217	0.1085
	$EL(X)$	747.52		

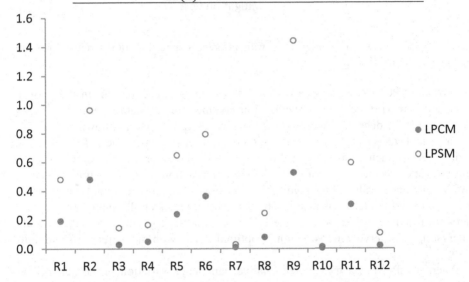

Fig. 3. Risk spectrum of the supply network under standard configuration

Network expected loss is an important parameter that reflects the risk level of the supply network under given conditions. Variation of network expected loss with all combinations of control strategies is shown in Fig. 4. Generally, network expected loss decreases with the increase in mitigation cost. However, corresponding to different cost regimes, it might not be viable to implement costly strategies because of the interdependent nature of these strategies with risks across the network. For each cost value, the optimal combination of strategies is represented by a solid circle whereas hollow circles represent inefficient solutions. This model helps in identifying inefficient solutions as well.

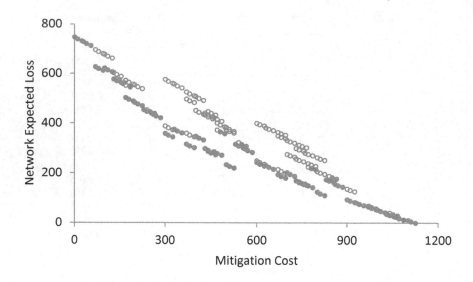

Fig. 4. Variation of network expected loss with different combinations of risk mitigation strategies and associated cost

Average LPCM is a measure of relative percentage improvement in the network expected loss with the overall average improvement in the state of each risk factor. Average LPCM decreases with the increase in mitigation cost as shown in Fig. 5. It means that because of the implementation of control strategies, the risk condition of individual risk factors improves and therefore, the relative margin of improvement for the network expected loss is reduced. Each combination of control strategies representing minimum value of average LPCM corresponding to specific mitigation cost is shown in solid circle. Implementing preventive strategies at all control nodes of the network results in achieving average LPCM of 0 at the cost of 1125 units. It is also interesting to observe wide variation of optimal points with the increase in mitigation cost.

Average LPSM is a measure of relative percentage variation in the network expected loss with the overall average variation in the state of each risk factor. In general, average LPSM also decreases with the increase in mitigation cost as shown in Fig. 6. In case of implementing reactive strategies, LPSM decreases as the resulting loss is reduced, however, choice of a preventive strategy reduces the probability of risk event without affecting the value of resulting loss and therefore, LPSM is not reduced. It can be observed that average LPSM starts increasing after a certain value of mitigation cost (approx. 640 units) because of incorporating preventive strategies in the portfolio of mitigation strategies. Each combination of control strategies representing minimum value of average LPSM corresponding to specific mitigation cost is shown in solid circle. Similar to the case of average LPCM, it is also interesting to observe wide variation of optimal points with the increase in mitigation cost.

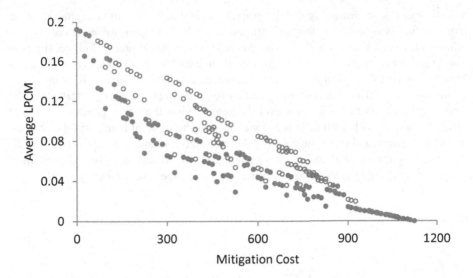

Fig. 5. Variation of average LPCM with different combinations of control strategies and associated cost

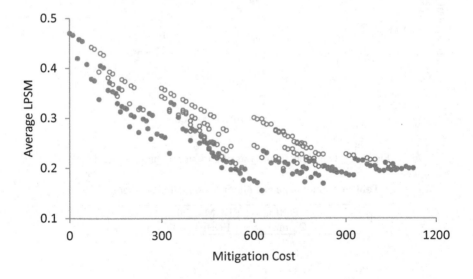

Fig. 6. Variation of average LPSM with different combinations of control strategies and associated cost

As our objective function necessitated selection of an optimal combination of strategies resulting in the maximum value of relative improvement of network expected loss taking into account the associated cost of mitigation strategies, it is important to consider the variation of this function with different combinations of control strategies as shown in Fig. 7. The graph reveals that the maximum value of objective function is achieved at the mitigation cost of 300 units. However, there are two other inefficient solutions and without the help of this modelling technique, the relative impact of each specific combination of strategies might not be appreciated. Combinations of optimal and inefficient strategies are presented in Table 4. It is interesting to find that one of the inefficient solutions requires implementing a strategy at the most important risk factor R9, however, keeping in view the interdependency between different factors, such a solution is not viable.   Furthermore, it is important to consider that a decision maker might not treat the expected loss and mitigation cost equally in evaluating the optimal choice of strategies. Expected loss may be assigned more weightage keeping in view the reputational risks and other non-monetary factors.

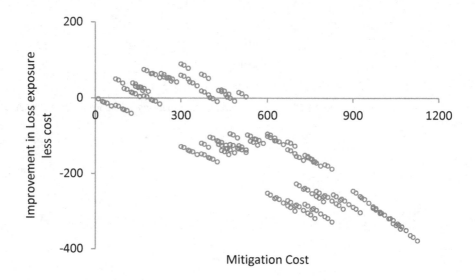

Fig. 7. Cost and benefit analysis of various mitigation strategies

Table 4. Combinations of optimal and inefficient strategies

Risk	Portfolio of Risk Mitigation Strategies		
	Optimal	Inefficient 1	Inefficient 2
R2	Reactive	No	Preventive
R5	Preventive	No	No
R6	Preventive	No	No
R9	No	Reactive	No
R11	No	No	No
$EL(X)$	357.62	575.56	387.26
Total Cost		300	

Risk measures of all risk factors under contingency configuration are shown in Table 5 and risk spectrum representing the graphical dimension of risk measures is shown in Fig. 8. As preventive strategies were implemented at R5 and R6, their

LPCM values are 0. LPCM and LPSM values for R3 and R4 are all 0 because their impact is blocked by their descendant nodes. Although no mitigation strategy is implemented at R9, its LPCM and LPSM values have decreased because of the impact of strategies implemented at R5 and R6. R9 still remains a critical risk factor, however, keeping in view the relative costs of implementing strategies, it is not viable to protect this node.

Table 5. Risk measures of risk factors under contingency configuration

Risk	Contingency Configuration			
	Expected Loss (True)	Expected Loss (False)	LPCM	LPSM
R1	432.62	307.62	0.0669	0.1672
R2	482.62	232.62	0.1672	0.3344
R3	357.62	357.62	0.0000	0.0000
R4	357.62	357.62	0.0000	0.0000
R5	615.36	357.60	0.0000	0.3448
R6	672.86	357.59	0.0000	0.4218
R7	364.48	353.05	0.0061	0.0153
R8	421.65	326.37	0.0418	0.1275
R9	1088.45	135.83	0.2967	1.2744
R10	363.98	353.38	0.0057	0.0142
R11	527.93	213.83	0.1924	0.4202
R12	391.16	349.24	0.0112	0.0561
	$EL(X)$	357.62		

Evaluation of risk mitigation strategies through our proposed approach results in an optimal mix of preventive and reactive strategies. As our approach incorporates interdependency between supply network elements, risks and mitigation strategies and follows rigorous technique of BBNs, the resulting solution can be considered as viable. However, it is assumed that all the stakeholders would be willing to share their private information and furthermore, elicited values would truly reflect the real-time risk scenario. Besides the limitations associated with modelling huge supply networks, these assumptions are deemed as challenges to our proposed approach.

4.3   Managerial Implications

The proposed modelling approach can help supply chain managers visualize interdependency between supply chain risks across the supply network. Stakeholders can identify important triggers and risk events and evaluate the impact of different risk mitigation strategies on the entire web of interconnected risks. Furthermore, if stakeholders consider only their domain of the supply network, they might implement strategies yielding sub-optimal solutions and therefore, it is extremely important to involve all stakeholders in this modelling process for achieving the global optimal solution. Causal mapping (qualitative modelling of BBNs) is beneficial to the managers in identifying important risks and understanding the dynamics between these risks. It is also important to realize that crucial decision of selecting an optimal mix of preventive and reactive strategies can only be made after following the proposed rigorous approach of modelling interdependency between risks and mitigation strategies.

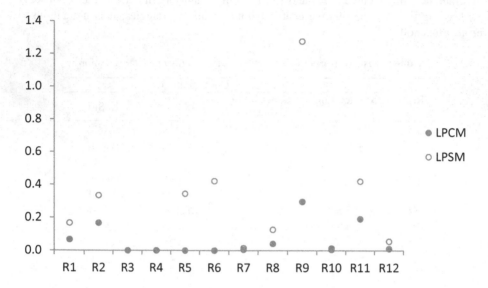

Fig. 8. Risk spectrum of the supply network under contingency configuration

5   Conclusion and Future Research

Generally, available models in the field of Supply chain risk management address specific problems, whereas, few models capturing interdependency between risks do not cover all stages of risk management process. We have bridged this important research gap and proposed a new approach of modelling interdependency between risks and evaluating different control strategies (preventive and reactive). Optimal combination of strategies can only be selected after adopting a rigorous modelling approach of capturing supply network configuration, probabilistic interdependency between risks, resulting losses and costs associated with different risk mitigation strategies. Our proposed risk measures are easy to compute and reflect the contribution of risk factors towards the network expected loss. We have also demonstrated use of our proposed method through a simple simulation study.

Our model is based on a number of assumptions. Firstly, the method may be feasible for a limited network and in case of a large network, elicitation of (conditional) probability values may be cumbersome. However, this problem can be tackled with introducing some assumptions in the model itself like Noisy-OR function. Secondly, we assume that stakeholders would be willing to share true information of the risks and loss values, however, it might not be in the best interest of stakeholders to share private information and therefore, they would need to be incentivized for developing the model and sharing real data.

We have also assumed binary states for all the risk factors. However, future research may focus on representing risks by continuous variables. Furthermore, a control strategy may also be represented by a continuum of control levels and associated costs. Our proposed method can help researchers develop robust models for managing supply chain risks. Supply chain managers can visualize the interaction between different risks and appreciate the importance of key risk factors. In future, the proposed method may be applied in modelling real supply networks in order to evaluate its efficacy.

References

1. Jüttner, U., Peck, H., Christopher, M.: Supply chain risk management: outlining an agenda for future research. International Journal of Logistics Research and Applications **6**(4), 197–210 (2003)
2. Christopher, M., Peck, H.: Building the Resilient Supply Chain. International Journal of Logistics Management **15**(2), 1–14 (2004)
3. Son, J.Y., Orchard, R.K.: Effectiveness of policies for mitigating supply disruptions. International Journal of Physical Distribution and Logistics Management **43**(8), 684–706 (2013)
4. Badurdeen, F., Shuaib, M., Wijekoon, K., Brown, A., et al.: Quantitative modeling and analysis of supply chain risks using Bayesian theory. Journal of Manufacturing Technology Management **25**(5), 631–654 (2014)
5. Qazi, A., Quigley, J., Dickson, A.: A novel framework for quantification of supply chain risks. In: 4th Student Conference on Operational Research. University of Nottingham, UK (2014)
6. Khan, O., Burnes, B.: Risk and supply chain management: creating a research agenda. International Journal of Logistics Management **18**(2), 197–216 (2007)
7. White, D.: Application of systems thinking to risk management: a review of the literature. Management Decision **33**(10), 35–45 (1995)
8. Tang, C.S.: Perspectives in supply chain risk management. International Journal of Production Economics **103**(2), 451–488 (2006)
9. Qazi, A., Quigley, J., Dickson, A.: Supply chain risk management: systematic literature review and a conceptual framework for capturing interdependencies between risks. In: 5th International Conference on Industrial Engineering and Operations Management, Dubai, UAE (2015)
10. Gaudenzi, B., Borghesi, A.: Managing risks in the supply chain using the AHP method. International Journal of Logistics Management **17**(1), 114–136 (2006)
11. Garvey, M.D., Carnovale, S., Yeniyurt, S.: An analytical framework for supply network risk propagation: A Bayesian network approach. European Journal of Operational Research **243**(2), 618–627 (2015)
12. Lockamy, A., McCormack, K.: Analysing risks in supply networks to facilitate outsourcing decisions. International Journal of Production Research **48**(2), 593–611 (2009)
13. Dogan, I., Aydin, N.: Combining Bayesian Networks and Total Cost of Ownership method for supplier selection analysis. Computers and Industrial Engineering **61**(4), 1072–1085 (2011)
14. Sodhi, M.S., Tang, C.S.: Managing supply chain risk, International Series in Operations Research and Mangement Science, vol. 172. Springer, New York (2012)
15. Wagner, S.M., Bode, C.: An empirical investigation into supply chain vulnerability. Journal of Purchasing and Supply Management **12**(6), 301–312 (2006)

Site Selection of the New Mexico City Airport from the Perspective of Maximizing the Sum of Expected Air Pax Demand

Rafael Bernardo Carmona-Benítez[1(✉)], Octavio Fernandez[1], and Esther Segura[2]

[1] School of Business and Economics, Universidad Anáhuac México Norte, Av. Universidad Anahuac no. 46, Col. Lomas Anáhuac 52786, Huixquilucan, State of Mexico, Mexico
{rafael.carmona,tavosfz}@anahuac.mx
[2] Institute of Engineering, Universidad Nacional Autónoma de México (UNAM), Torre de Ingenieria Piso 2 Ala Norte 04510, Coyoacan, Mexico City, Mexico
ESeguraP@iigen.unam.mx

Abstract. The Mexican government studies the possibility of building a new international airport (NAICM) in ZFLT or Tizayuca. The aim of this paper is to determine which the best location site of the NAICM is (ZFLT or Tizayuca) considering the maximization of the sum of expected air pax demand as main factor. To solve such problem, we propose: a mathematical formulation with the objective of maximizing the sum of expected air pax demand and a methodology to estimate air pax demand at each demand point based on an index to measure wealth. Results indicate that Tizayuca is the place where the NAICM should be located for a catchment area smaller than 500km or 4 hours travel time, and ZFLT is the place where the NAICM should be constructed for a catchment area longer than 500km or 4 hours travel time.

Keywords: Airport site selection · Facility location model · Maximum coverage location model · Pax demand estimation · Decay function

1 Introduction

The lack of capacity to meet demand requirements at major airports in the world, is a serious problem facing aviation worldwide [1]. Air passenger (pax) demand is not fully satisfied. This results in airport congestion and delay operations. The capacity of the current Mexico City airport (AICM) was increased by building terminal 2. However, it did not solve the problem. Therefore, the Mexican government has studied the possibility of building a new international airport for Mexico City (NAICM) in two places: Zona Federal del Lago de Texcoco (ZFLT) and Tizayuca, 15.3 km and 59.5 km far from AICM respectively [2]. The Mexican government choose these sites for their technical and aeronautical advantages, project cost-benefit, minimum environmental impact, and economic benefits that result indirectly from the project [2]. Since both sites are suitable to locate the new airport, the maximization of the total expected pax demand is perhaps the decision that the Mexican government should take before

© Springer International Publishing Switzerland 2015
F. Corman et al. (Eds.): ICCL 2015, LNCS 9335, pp. 586–601, 2015.
DOI: 10.1007/978-3-319-24264-4_40

investing in such infrastructure. Therefore, this paper aims to: first, propose a mathematical formulation for solving the problem of airport site selection decision with the objective of maximizing the sum of expected pax demand, second propose an approach to estimate pax demand at each demand point based on the development of a wealth index (*WI*), and fourth, answer, which of the two proposed sites is the best option for the construction of the NAICM from the perspective of maximizing the sum of expected pax demand.

This paper proposes to estimate pax demand at each demand point by considering the economic factors that compose the Marginalization index (*MI*) per demand point [3], the total population per demand point, and distances from each demand point to each possible airport location site.

Location problems show up from the need to place facilities such as distribution centers (DCs), manufacturing plants, landfills, fire and police stations, ambulance, airports, etc. [4] classified location problems as: continuous models, network models, and discrete models. Continuous models determine Cartesian coordinates for a number of facilities with the objective of minimizing the sum of distances between facilities and demand points [5]. In network models, the demand occurs only at the facilities of a network and facilities can only be located within the network. In discrete models, the demand usually arise at demand points and facilities can only be located in a finite set of candidate sites. In this case study, discrete models are suitable to locate the NAICM because the geographical location of the NAICM is only possible at two candidate sites (ZFLT or Tizayuca).

In literature, four fundamental types of discrete facility location models can be used to select the potential of an airport site: the p-median problem (PMP), the uncapacitated facility-location problem (UFLP), the p-centre problem, and location covering problems. All these models take into account quantitative criteria. The PMP involves location of *p* number of facilities on a network in such a way that the total weighted distance of serving all demand is minimized [6]. The UFLP is to minimize costs of serving and satisfying all demand from an undetermined number of facilities [7]. The p-centre problem minimizes the distance needed to supply all demand points with *p* facilities [8]. Finally, location covering problems can be used to minimize the number of sites needed to cover all demand points (set covering location problem) or to maximize the total number of demand points covered with *p* facilities (maximum covering location problem).

Maximizing the sum of expected pax demands means covering as many demand points as possible to meet demand. Therefore, from the analysis of the facility location problems (FLPs) literature, and because the aim of this paper is to design a mathematical formulation that maximize covered demand, the maximum coverage location model (MCLM) is chosen as the most suitable covering problem to locate the NAICM, in ZFLT or Tizayuca, from a perspective of maximizing the sum of expected pax demand. The application and adaptation of the MCLM to answer such question is the first contribution of this paper.

An approach to estimate demand at airports, coming from demand points, is proposed, and is the second contribution of this paper. This approach is based on a decay function whose variables are *WI*, population (*Pop*), and distances (*d*) from demand points to each possible site for airport location, and is the third contribution of this paper. In this paper, *WI* is proposed as an opposite index to the *MI*. As a consequence, *WI* measures household economic status, economic growth, and human well-being per demand point, and is the fourth contribution of this paper. Therefore, the proposed pax demand estimation approach considers the more developed demand points have better economy and purchasing power. This is consistent with the economic theory and is called *wealth effect* [20].

The paper is organized as follows: Section 2 describes a brief review on previous works for airport site selection using optimization. In Section 3, the mathematical formulation for problem of airport site selection decision is developed. In Section 4, an approach to estimate demand at airport site locations coming from each demand point is proposed. In Section 5, experimental data from 2010 is presented for the NAICM case study. In Section 6, the approach to estimate demand at airport site locations coming from each demand point and the mathematical formulation for airport site selection are used to locate the NAICM. The model is solved by the state-of-the-art commercial software CPLEX. Results are shown. Finally, conclusion and references are included.

2 Mathematical Programming Models for Airport Site Selection

Studies that addressed the problem of airport site selection are presented by [9], [10], [11], [12], [13], [14], [15], [16], and [17].

[9] Study the airport site selection problem of the new airport in Mexico City. However, contrary to our paper, [9] do not consider wealth index per demand point as decision factors. [10] Study the airport site selection problem of an airport in The Netherlands. [11] Study the airport site selection problem of a new airport in Sydney. [12] Study the airport site selection problem considering capacity and demand constraints. [13] Study the airport site selection problem considering government regulations, demography and status of the local economy. [14] Study the airport site selection problem considering demographic, social and political factors. [15] Study the airport site selection problem based on social, political, and environmental factors. [16] Study the airport site selection problem by translating the opinions of managers/experts into quantitative data. Finally, [17] Study the airport site selection problem by translating the opinions of specialists to quantitative data.

For all above airport site selection problem studies, the lack of considering the maximization of the expected pax demand as main aim for airport site selection is detected.

3 Mathematical Formulation for Airport Site Selection

In this paper, the MCLM is applied to select the location of airports within a set of potential sites for airport location. Therefore, the MCLM locates *p* number of airports to maximize the number of covered pax demand (p is a parameter in the model). The model distinguishes between big and small demands and allow some demand points to be uncovered what can happen when the number of airports needed to cover all demand points exceeds p. This depends on minimal travelling distance (d) or travelling time (t) between each site for airport location (L) and each demand point (M).

Let A be a set of airport location sites ($1, 2, ..., A$) and V be a set of demand points ($1, 2,..., V$). Y_i's are decision variables; they indicate if M_i is covered by L_j. a_{ij}'s are parameters that indicate L_j covering ratio or *catchment area*. In other words, a_{ij} indicates if d_{ij} between L_j and M_i is larger or shorter than the distance covered (Dc). Dc is a parameter in the model that can be changed by a parameter that expresses the time coverage (Tc). In both cases, they express the L_j covering ratio or *catchment area* where M_i's inside this ratio are covered by L_j (a_{ij}'s = 1), and M_i's outside this ratio are not covered by L_j (a_{ij}'s = 0). Finally, X_j's are decision variables; they locate p number of airports at the best possible L_j's to maximize the number of covered pax demand.

Dc or Tc are determined by the airport *catchment area* which is the area and *Pop* attended by the airport.

$$a_{ij} = \begin{cases} 1 \text{ if } d_{ij} \text{ between } M_i \text{ and } L_j \text{ is smaller or equal to } Dc \\ 0 \text{ otherwise} \end{cases} \quad \forall i \in V, \forall j \in A$$

$$Y_i = \begin{cases} 1 \text{ if } M_i \text{ is covered} \\ 0 \text{ otherwise} \end{cases} \quad \forall i \in V$$

$$X_j = \begin{cases} 1 \text{ if airport is located at airport location site } L_j \\ 0 \text{ otherwise} \end{cases} \quad \forall j \in A$$

The MCLM mathematical formulation for a given integer value of $p > 0$ is the following:

$$\text{Max } Z = \sum_{i=1}^{V} D_i Y_i \tag{1}$$

Subject to:

$$\sum_{j=1}^{A} \left(a_{ij} X_j \right) \geq Y_i \quad \forall i \in V, \forall j \in A \tag{2}$$

$$\sum_{j=1}^{A} \left(X_j \right) \leq p \quad \forall j \in A \tag{3}$$

$$Y_i \in [0,1] \quad \forall i \in V \tag{4}$$

$$X_j \in [0,1] \qquad \forall j \in A \tag{5}$$

The objective function maximizes the total number of covered pax demand (Equation 1).Where D_i is the pax demand at each M_i. Equation (2) states that demand D_i at M_i cannot be covered unless one of the potential sites for airport location L_j that covers M_i is selected to build an airport. M_i's that can be covered by L_j are located in a shorter distance than Dc ($a_{ij} = 1$) or shorter time than Tc. Constraints (Equation 3) indicates that no more than p airports are located. Finally, constraints (4) and (5) are the integrality constraints on the decision variables.

4   Pax Demand Estimation

In this section, we propose an approach to estimate pax demand at L_j's, coming from each M_i's. In this approach WI and the Decay function are calculated for each M_i under certain assumptions.

4.1   Marginalization Index

The MI is calculated using the statistical method of principal component analysis (PCA). This technique uses an orthogonal transformation to convert a set of variables that are possibly correlated into a set of values of linearly uncorrelated variables called principal components. The method is used for data analysis, factor analysis, and to design predictive models. [18] explains in detail the PCA methodology applied to calculate the MI for the states, districts, and municipalities in Mexico every five years.

The MI is a reliable indicator of socioeconomic status of a country at location level. This index is a measure to differentiate states, municipalities and/or districts in any country according to the economic shortcomings faced by the Pop. In Mexico, the MI socioeconomic indicators are [18]:

- Percentage of the Pop aged 15 years or more illiterate.
- Percentage of the Pop aged 15 years or more without complete primary school.
- Percentage of the Pop living in households without drain or toilet.
- Percentage of the Pop living in households without electricity.
- Percentage of the Pop living in households without piped water.
- Percentage of households with some level of overcrowding.
- Percentage of the Pop living in households with dirt floors.
- Percentage of the Pop living in towns with less than 5,000 inhabitants.
- Percentage of the Pop employed with income up to 2 minimum wages.

The MI is calculated in a range of qualification [0, 100] where zero represents no presence of deficits that measures the socioeconomic indicators, and 100 when the entire Pop in a location of analysis suffers deprivation of such socioeconomic indicators. In other words, locations that have a high socioeconomic status have a near zero MI.

Scale effects and transformed variables are eliminated for the calculation of *MI*, so that variables that have great variance are not predominant in determining the *MI* due to standardization of socioeconomic indicators values by using the mean and standard deviation [19]. That is why the *MI* measures socioeconomic disparities between states/municipalities/districts of a country, and what makes *MI* a reliable and accepted index to measure marginalization [19].

MI is a household characteristic that allows for the identification of unequal access for poor people to the economic markets in comparison with the wealthy. It is an important index, especially in countries without reliable data on income expenditures which are the normal indicators of household economic status. Therefore, the *MI* allows identifying how much household economic status is at each demand point.

4.2 Wealth Index

In this paper, the *WI* is calculated as the complement to 100 of the *MI*. For the *WI*, zero represents the presence of deficits that measures each of the socioeconomic indicators that calculate the *MI* and 100 when all the people living in a location of analysis do not suffer deprivation of such socioeconomic indicators. Therefore, the *WI* represents the purchasing power of states/municipalities/districts of a country. The purchasing power of a location of analysis is high as its *WI* gets close to 100. This is consistent with the economic theory and is called *wealth effect*. This effect relates the evolution of wealth with the expansion of private consumption. The sense of larger (smaller) household wealth supposedly leads to increase (reduce) consumption levels affecting positively (negatively) the aggregate demand function [20].

4.3 Decay Function for Pax Demand Estimation

Pax demands at L_j coming from M_i is estimated as follows:

$$W_{ij} = \frac{Pop_i WI_i}{d_{ij}} \qquad \forall i \in V, \forall j \in A \qquad (6)$$

Where:

W_{ij} =	L_j attractiveness of passenger demand at M_i per km	[person/km]
Pop_i =	M_i population	[person]
WI_i =	M_i wealth index	[-]
d_{ij} =	distance from M_i to L_j	[km]

Equation 6 calculates a factor W_{ij} which indicates how attractive L_j is to M_i's. Equation 6 considers that the farther is M_i from L_j the less attractive is L_j to M_i and demand grows as *Pop* grows what proves this equation to be consistent with literature [21]. Now, the argument is that L_j's vary in attractiveness to M_i's. Therefore, in this paper, we set Equation 7 to be the probability (P_{ij}) that a M_i demands air pax services at L_j where W_{ij} is the attractiveness of I_j which depends on Pop_i, WI_i, and distance between L_j and M_i.

$$P_{ij} = \frac{W_{ij}}{\sum\limits_{i=1}^{V} W_{ij}} \qquad \forall i \in V, \forall j \in A \qquad (7)$$

Pax demand (h_{ij}) at L_j coming from M_i is estimated by Equation 8 which multiplies P_{ij} by the total number of passengers (H_i) that are currently transported through the airports in the region of L_j.

$$h_{ij} = H_i P_{ij} \qquad \forall i \in V, \forall j \in A \qquad (8)$$

Where:

h_{ij}	=	pax demand at L_j coming from M_i	[persons]
H_i	=	total number of passengers that are currently transported through the airports that are in the region of L_j.	[persons]

5   NAICM Case Study Experimental Data

In this case study, data is obtained for the Federal District (Mexico City) and the 31 States of Mexico. In the case of Mexico City, data are obtained for its 16 districts, and in the case of the State of Mexico data are obtained for 8 regions which include its 125 municipalities. Therefore, 55 M_i's are considered in this case study. Mexico City and the State of Mexico together form the Metropolitan Area of the Valley of Mexico (ZMVM) with more than 20% of the total country Pop. The ZMVM has the largest number of businesses, commercial activities and Pop throughout the country. Hence, this breakdown is necessary because the districts and municipalities that are part of the ZMVM have more impact than other municipalities in the rest of the country for the construction of NAICM. Pop and MI indicators data at state, municipal, and district levels [18] are constructed based on information provided by the Population and Housing Census 2010 "Censo nacional de población y vivienda 2010" [22].

The road distances (d_{ij}) from the 55 M_i's to two L_j's (Tizayuca and ZFLT) are calculated using the software Google Maps [23] Table 1 shows the data base used in this case study. Demand point M3 is the richest district or municipality in Mexico followed by M11; M35 is the poorest state in Mexico followed by M29; M19 is the demand point with most Pop followed by M43; M12 and M10 are the districts or municipalities with less Pop in the sample; M15 is the nearest demand point to AICM; M2 is the nearest demand point to Tizayuca; M10 is the nearest demand point to ZFLT; M26 is the farthest state from AICM, Tizayuca and ZFLT.

Finally, the total number of passengers (H_j) that are currently transported through the AICM, which is the nearest airport to ZFLT and Tizayuca, is 24,130,535 pax [24].

Table 1. Data base used in this case study

Demand Point (M)	Code	AICM (d_{ij})	Tizayuca (d_{ij})	ZFLT (d_{ij})	MI	WI	Pop
Alvaro Obregon	M1	20.7	71.4	42.9	6.26	93.74	727034
Azcapotzalco	M2	16.9	62.6	42.1	5.18	94.82	414711
Benito Juarez	M3	13.3	64.3	37.1	1.21	98.79	385439
Coyoacan	M4	19.6	70	40.8	3.86	96.14	620416
Cuajimalpa de Morelos	M5	26.6	89.7	48.8	6.98	93.02	186391
Cuauhtemoc	M6	11.9	58.1	32.2	4.60	95.40	531831
Gustavo A. Madero	M7	11.2	50.1	29.6	7.15	92.85	1185772
Iztacalco	M8	6.2	66.3	27.8	5.86	94.14	384326
Iztapalapa	M9	11	67.6	29.9	8.89	91.11	1815786
La Magdalena Contreras	M10	26.6	76.4	20.6	7.86	92.14	239086
Miguel Hidalgo	M11	18.5	70.1	40.7	3.56	96.44	372889
Milpa Alta	M12	39.1	113	75.3	15.07	84.93	130582
Tlahuac	M13	17	73.2	35.6	9.10	90.90	360265
Tlalpan	M14	30	80.1	52.2	7.40	92.60	650567
Venustiano Carranza	M15	2.7	62.7	23.8	6.11	93.89	430978
Xochimilco	M16	23.5	80.3	45.5	9.10	90.90	415007
Toluca de Lerdo	M17	71.5	130	93.7	12.38	87.62	2003879
Zumpango de Ocampo	M18	56.2	13.1	59.2	9.35	90.65	4550642
Texcoco de Mora	M19	24.6	55.6	23	10.67	89.33	6572778
Tejupilco de Hidalgo	M20	21.3	72.8	40	32.31	67.69	197331
Atlacomulco de Fabela	M21	25.4	68.2	48.3	28.65	71.35	1197326
Coatepec Harinas	M22	143	202	166	26.22	73.78	392559
Valle de Bravo	M23	147	206	169	26.17	73.84	119709
Jilotepec de Molina Enríquez	M24	102	98.1	105	24.60	75.40	141638
Aguascalientes	M25	512	489	513	15.24	84.76	1184996
Baja California	M26	2845	2772	2781	10.35	89.65	3155070
Baja California Sur	M27	1676	1669	1679	20.14	79.86	637026
Campeche	M28	1143	1168	1164	43.93	56.07	822441
Chiapas	M29	828	854	850	84.14	15.86	4796580
Chihuahua	M30	1438	1417	1441	23.59	76.41	3406465
Coahuila	M31	1054	1033	1067	10.35	89.65	2748391
Colima	M32	670	663	673	18.06	81.94	650555
Durango	M33	952	931	955	35.80	64.20	1632934
Guanajuato	M34	329	308	332	35.97	64.03	5486372
Guerrero	M35	323	376	344	88.72	11.28	2665018
Hidalgo	M36	95	38.3	94.9	48.79	51.21	3388768
Jalisco	M37	552	545	555	17.08	82.92	7350682
Michoacán	M38	377	371	380	45.90	54.10	4351037
Morelos	M39	140	193	155	28.87	71.13	1777227
Nayarit	M40	793	786	796	37.28	62.72	1084979
Nuevo León	M41	914	893	917	5.16	94.84	4653458
Oaxaca	M42	456	481	477	80.48	19.52	3801962
Puebla	M43	124	150	146	49.88	50.12	5779829
Querétaro	M44	219	213	222	29.04	70.96	1827937
Quintana Roo	M45	1419	1444	1440	25.76	74.24	1325578
San Luis Potosí	M46	421	400	424	46.72	53.28	2585518
Sinaloa	M47	1296	1289	1299	29.13	70.87	2767761
Sonora	M48	2000	1993	2003	19.67	80.33	2662480
Tabasco	M49	797	822	818	44.76	55.24	2238603
Tamaulipas	M50	753	700	756	19.28	80.72	3268554
Tlaxcala	M51	112	129	123	31.48	68.52	1169936
Veracruz	M52	526	551	547	57.63	42.37	7643194
Yucatán	M53	1379	1404	1400	43.70	56.30	1955577
Zacatecas	M54	607	586	610	36.89	63.11	1490668

Table 2. AICM, Tizayuca and ZFLT catchemtn areas

| | AICM | Tizayuca | ZFLT | AICM | Tizayuca | ZFLT | | AICM | Tizayuca | ZFLT | AICM | Tizayuca | ZFLT |
	Tc = 4 and s = 80			Tc = 4 and s = 100				Tc = 6 and s = 80			Tc = 6 and s = 100		
M1	1	1	1	1	1	1	M1	1	1	1	1	1	1
M2	1	1	1	1	1	1	M2	1	1	1	1	1	1
M3	1	1	1	1	1	1	M3	1	1	1	1	1	1
M4	1	1	1	1	1	1	M4	1	1	1	1	1	1
M5	1	1	1	1	1	1	M5	1	1	1	1	1	1
M6	1	1	1	1	1	1	M6	1	1	1	1	1	1
M7	1	1	1	1	1	1	M7	1	1	1	1	1	1
M8	1	1	1	1	1	1	M8	1	1	1	1	1	1
M9	1	1	1	1	1	1	M9	1	1	1	1	1	1
M10	1	1	1	1	1	1	M10	1	1	1	1	1	1
M11	1	1	1	1	1	1	M11	1	1	1	1	1	1
M12	1	1	1	1	1	1	M12	1	1	1	1	1	1
M13	1	1	1	1	1	1	M13	1	1	1	1	1	1
M14	1	1	1	1	1	1	M14	1	1	1	1	1	1
M15	1	1	1	1	1	1	M15	1	1	1	1	1	1
M16	1	1	1	1	1	1	M16	1	1	1	1	1	1
M17	1	1	1	1	1	1	M17	1	1	1	1	1	1
M18	1	1	1	1	1	1	M18	1	1	1	1	1	1
M19	1	1	1	1	1	1	M19	1	1	1	1	1	1
M20	1	1	1	1	1	1	M20	1	1	1	1	1	1
M21	1	1	1	1	1	1	M21	1	1	1	1	1	1
M22	1	1	1	1	1	1	M22	1	1	1	1	1	1
M23	1	1	1	1	1	1	M23	1	1	1	1	1	1
M24	1	1	1	1	1	1	M24	1	1	1	1	1	1
M25	0	0	0	0	0	0	M25	0	0	0	1	1	1
M26	0	0	0	0	0	0	M26	0	0	0	0	0	0
M27	0	0	0	0	0	0	M27	0	0	0	0	0	0
M28	0	0	0	0	0	0	M28	0	0	0	0	0	0
M29	0	0	0	0	0	0	M29	0	0	0	0	0	0
M30	0	0	0	0	0	0	M30	0	0	0	0	0	0
M31	0	0	0	0	0	0	M31	0	0	0	0	0	0
M32	0	0	0	0	0	0	M32	0	0	0	0	0	0
M33	0	0	0	0	0	0	M33	0	0	0	0	0	0
M34	0	1	0	1	1	1	M34	1	1	1	1	1	1
M35	0	0	0	1	1	1	M35	1	1	1	1	1	1
M36	1	1	1	1	1	1	M36	1	1	1	1	1	1
M37	0	0	0	0	0	0	M37	0	0	0	1	1	1
M38	0	0	0	1	1	1	M38	1	1	1	1	1	1
M39	1	1	1	1	1	1	M39	1	1	1	1	1	1
M40	0	0	0	0	0	0	M40	0	0	0	0	0	0
M41	0	0	0	0	0	0	M41	0	0	0	0	0	0
M42	0	0	0	0	0	0	M42	1	0	1	1	1	1
M43	1	1	1	1	1	1	M43	1	1	1	1	1	1
M44	1	1	1	1	1	1	M44	1	1	1	1	1	1
M45	0	0	0	0	0	0	M45	0	0	0	0	0	0
M46	0	0	0	0	1	0	M46	1	1	1	1	1	1
M47	0	0	0	0	0	0	M47	0	0	0	0	0	0
M48	0	0	0	0	0	0	M48	0	0	0	0	0	0
M49	0	0	0	0	0	0	M49	0	0	0	0	0	0
M50	0	0	0	0	0	0	M50	0	0	0	0	0	0
M51	1	1	1	1	1	1	M51	1	1	1	1	1	1
M52	0	0	0	0	0	0	M52	0	0	0	1	1	1
M53	0	0	0	0	0	0	M53	0	0	0	0	0	0
M54	0	0	0	0	0	0	M54	0	0	0	0	1	0

Table 3. AICM, Tizayuca and ZFLT catchemtn areas

	AICM	Tizayuca	ZFLT	AICM	Tizayuca	ZFLT		AICM	Tizayuca	ZFLT	AICM	Tizayuca	ZFLT
	Tc = 8 and s = 80			Tc = 8 and s = 100				Tc = 10 and s = 80			Tc = 10 and s = 100		
M1	1	1	1	1	1	1	M1	1	1	1	1	1	1
M2	1	1	1	1	1	1	M2	1	1	1	1	1	1
M3	1	1	1	1	1	1	M3	1	1	1	1	1	1
M4	1	1	1	1	1	1	M4	1	1	1	1	1	1
M5	1	1	1	1	1	1	M5	1	1	1	1	1	1
M6	1	1	1	1	1	1	M6	1	1	1	1	1	1
M7	1	1	1	1	1	1	M7	1	1	1	1	1	1
M8	1	1	1	1	1	1	M8	1	1	1	1	1	1
M9	1	1	1	1	1	1	M9	1	1	1	1	1	1
M10	1	1	1	1	1	1	M10	1	1	1	1	1	1
M11	1	1	1	1	1	1	M11	1	1	1	1	1	1
M12	1	1	1	1	1	1	M12	1	1	1	1	1	1
M13	1	1	1	1	1	1	M13	1	1	1	1	1	1
M14	1	1	1	1	1	1	M14	1	1	1	1	1	1
M15	1	1	1	1	1	1	M15	1	1	1	1	1	1
M16	1	1	1	1	1	1	M16	1	1	1	1	1	1
M17	1	1	1	1	1	1	M17	1	1	1	1	1	1
M18	1	1	1	1	1	1	M18	1	1	1	1	1	1
M19	1	1	1	1	1	1	M19	1	1	1	1	1	1
M20	1	1	1	1	1	1	M20	1	1	1	1	1	1
M21	1	1	1	1	1	1	M21	1	1	1	1	1	1
M22	1	1	1	1	1	1	M22	1	1	1	1	1	1
M23	1	1	1	1	1	1	M23	1	1	1	1	1	1
M24	1	1	1	1	1	1	M24	1	1	1	1	1	1
M25	1	1	1	1	1	1	M25	1	1	1	1	1	1
M26	0	0	0	0	0	0	M26	1	1	1	0	0	0
M27	0	0	0	0	0	0	M27	1	1	1	0	0	0
M28	0	0	0	0	0	0	M28	1	1	1	0	0	0
M29	0	0	0	0	0	0	M29	1	1	1	1	1	1
M30	0	0	0	0	0	0	M30	1	1	1	0	0	0
M31	0	0	0	0	0	0	M31	1	1	1	0	0	0
M32	0	0	0	1	1	1	M32	1	1	1	1	1	1
M33	0	0	0	0	0	0	M33	1	1	1	1	1	1
M34	1	1	1	1	1	1	M34	1	1	1	1	1	1
M35	1	1	1	1	1	1	M35	1	1	1	1	1	1
M36	1	1	1	1	1	1	M36	1	1	1	1	1	1
M37	1	1	1	1	1	1	M37	1	1	1	1	1	1
M38	1	1	1	1	1	1	M38	1	1	1	1	1	1
M39	1	1	1	1	1	1	M39	1	1	1	1	1	1
M40	0	0	0	1	1	1	M40	1	1	1	1	1	1
M41	0	0	0	0	0	0	M41	1	1	1	1	1	1
M42	1	1	1	1	1	1	M42	1	1	1	1	1	1
M43	1	1	1	1	1	1	M43	1	1	1	1	1	1
M44	1	1	1	1	1	1	M44	1	1	1	1	1	1
M45	0	0	0	0	0	0	M45	1	1	1	0	0	0
M46	1	1	1	1	1	1	M46	1	1	1	1	1	1
M47	0	0	0	0	0	0	M47	1	1	1	0	0	0
M48	0	0	0	0	0	0	M48	1	1	1	0	0	0
M49	0	0	0	1	0	0	M49	1	1	1	1	1	1
M50	0	0	0	1	1	1	M50	1	1	1	1	1	1
M51	1	1	1	1	1	1	M51	1	1	1	1	1	1
M52	1	1	1	1	1	1	M52	1	1	1	1	1	1
M53	0	0	0	0	0	0	M53	1	1	1	0	0	0
M54	1	1	1	1	1	1	M54	1	1	1	1	1	1

5.1   Possible Location Sites Catchment Areas

a_{ij}'s are parameters that form a matrix that indicates L_j covering ratio or *catchment area*. a_{ij} is equal 1 if t_{ij} from M_i to L_j by road vehicle is shorter than Tc, a_{ij} is equal 0 otherwise. t_{ij} is calculated using the average velocity formula (Equation 9).

$$t_{ij} = d_{ij} / s \qquad \forall i \in V, \forall j \in A \tag{9}$$

Where:

s =   vehicle average speed   [km/hr]

The traffic regulations issued by the Ministry of Communications and Transportation indicates that speed ranges for highways are from 80 km/hr to 100 km/hr in Mexico [25].

The Ministry of Social Development sets that the catchment area of the NAICM must be larger than a radius of 500 km or a travel time longer than 4 hours [26].

Therefore, in this paper, twenty four matrixes are calculated to indicate the *catchment area* of the AICM, the ZFLT and Tizayuca for two average speeds (s), 80 km/hr and 100 km/hr, and for four different t_{ij}'s: 4, 6, 8, and 10 hrs (Table 2 and Table 3).

6   NAICM Site Selection from the Perspective of Maximizing the Sum of Expected Pax Demand

6.1   Pax Demand Estimation at Possible Location Sites

Table 4 shows the results of the pax demand estimation at the possible location sites for the NAICM. Equation 6 calculates W_{ij}, Equation 7 calculates P_{ij}, and Equation 8 calculates h_{ij} using the case study data base (Table 1).

Table 4 results indicate that AICM attractiveness of pax demand is highest at M19, M9 and M15. Tizayuca and ZFLT attractiveness of pax demand is highest at M18, M19 and M9. AICM, Tizayuca and ZFLT attractiveness of pax demand is the lowest at M27, M28, and M23.

Table 4 results point out that M19, M9 and M25 are the demand points with the highest probability to demand air pax services at AICM. M18, M19 and M36 are the demand points with the highest probability to demand air pax services at Tizayuca. M19, M18 and M9 are the demand points with the highest probability to demand air pax services at ZFLT. These results are because these M_i's are close to AICM, Tizayuca and ZFLT and their *Pop* are big. M27, M26, M29, and M45 are the demand points with the lowest probability to demand air pax services at AICM, Tizayuca, and ZFLT. These demand points are the states farthest from AICM, Tizayuca, and ZFLT.

Table 4 results identify that the current location of the AICM benefits the *Pop* and the economy of in first place Mexico City, in second place the State of Mexico, and in third place the State of Puebla. The pax demand estimation approach calculates 14,010,440 pax demand coming from Mexico City, 7,531,489 pax demand coming from the State of Mexico, and 462,781 pax demand coming from Puebla. Contrary,

6,013 pax demand coming from the State of Baja California Sur which is the state that demands less air pax services from the AICM.

Table 4. Pax demand estimation approach results

Code	AICM Wij	Tizayuca Wij	ZFLT Wij	AICM Pij	Tizayuca Pij	ZFLT Pij	AICM hi	Tizayuca hi	ZFLT hi
M1	3,292,410.35	954,522.33	1,588,645.55	0.00%	1.31%	2.16%	652,180.52	316,419.34	521,674.14
M2	2,326,749.56	628,148.04	934,015.86	1.91%	0.86%	1.27%	460,896.60	208,227.91	306,709.02
M3	2,862,942.36	592,179.37	1,026,337.83	2.35%	0.81%	1.40%	567,108.91	196,304.48	337,025.40
M4	3,043,235.44	852,105.92	1,461,946.44	2.50%	1.17%	1.99%	602,822.45	282,468.82	480,069.11
M5	651,828.95	193,295.99	355,300.20	0.54%	0.27%	0.48%	129,118.21	64,076.65	116,672.30
M6	4,263,675.72	873,282.98	1,575,706.24	3.50%	1.20%	2.14%	844,574.64	289,488.91	517,425.18
M7	9,830,579.24	2,197,654.44	3,719,678.63	8.07%	3.02%	5.06%	1,947,300.50	728,511.38	1,221,455.70
M8	5,835,246.45	545,679.16	1,301,385.90	4.79%	0.75%	1.77%	1,155,880.86	180,889.89	427,344.77
M9	15,039,990.37	2,447,335.71	5,533,106.82	12.35%	3.36%	7.53%	2,979,212.12	811,279.46	1,816,943.21
M10	828,199.30	288,352.11	1,069,422.39	0.68%	0.40%	1.46%	164,054.72	95,587.27	351,173.37
M11	1,943,920.75	513,017.60	883,600.34	1.60%	0.70%	1.20%	385,063.56	170,062.75	290,153.74
M12	283,646.81	98,146.82	147,285.40	0.23%	0.13%	0.20%	56,186.47	32,535.18	48,365.09
M13	1,926,442.92	447,397.94	919,930.61	1.58%	0.61%	1.25%	381,601.45	148,310.17	302,083.75
M14	2,008,105.16	752,099.31	1,154,083.42	1.65%	1.03%	1.57%	397,777.60	249,317.13	378,974.08
M15	14,986,860.90	645,367.22	1,700,190.10	12.30%	0.89%	2.31%	2,968,687.91	213,935.98	558,302.77
M16	1,605,229.42	469,774.49	829,074.53	1.32%	0.65%	1.13%	317,973.54	155,727.88	272,248.74
M17	2,455,690.66	1,350,629.86	1,873,872.81	2.02%	1.86%	2.55%	486,438.04	447,727.00	615,336.12
M18	7,339,975.02	31,489,053.13	6,968,016.82	6.03%	43.26%	9.48%	1,453,946.58	10,438,462.52	2,288,134.19
M19	23,868,001.28	10,560,302.73	25,528,383.98	19.59%	14.51%	34.74%	4,727,917.84	3,500,687.17	8,382,925.82
M20	627,067.89	183,469.04	333,913.65	0.51%	0.25%	0.45%	124,213.39	60,819.06	109,649.45
M21	3,363,213.31	1,252,575.05	1,768,646.34	2.76%	1.72%	2.41%	666,205.60	415,222.32	580,782.20
M22	202,527.50	143,373.43	174,466.46	0.17%	0.20%	0.24%	40,117.87	47,527.57	57,290.72
M23	60,127.31	42,906.38	52,300.08	0.05%	0.06%	0.07%	11,910.38	14,223.25	17,174.13
M24	104,696.87	108,859.13	101,705.53	0.09%	0.15%	0.14%	20,738.99	36,086.25	33,397.72
M25	196,174.32	205,401.33	195,791.91	0.16%	0.28%	0.27%	38,859.39	68,089.51	64,293.50
M26	99,425.34	102,043.68	101,713.44	0.08%	0.14%	0.14%	19,694.77	33,826.97	33,400.32
M27	30,354.35	30,481.66	30,300.11	0.02%	0.04%	0.04%	6,012.77	10,104.52	9,949.85
M28	40,344.36	39,480.82	39,616.50	0.03%	0.05%	0.05%	7,991.65	13,087.69	13,009.13
M29	91,878.73	89,081.49	89,500.69	0.08%	0.12%	0.12%	18,199.89	29,530.06	29,389.94
M30	181,017.69	183,700.38	180,640.83	0.15%	0.25%	0.25%	35,857.08	60,895.75	59,318.24
M31	233,772.14	238,524.52	230,923.93	0.19%	0.33%	0.31%	46,307.00	79,069.68	75,830.03
M32	79,559.80	80,399.80	79,205.15	0.07%	0.11%	0.11%	15,759.69	26,652.13	26,009.12
M33	110,123.69	112,607.69	109,777.75	0.09%	0.15%	0.15%	21,813.97	37,328.88	36,048.45
M34	1,067,684.46	1,140,481.12	1,058,036.71	0.88%	1.57%	1.44%	211,493.39	378,063.75	347,434.57
M35	93,040.67	79,925.89	87,360.86	0.08%	0.11%	0.12%	18,430.06	26,495.03	28,687.27
M36	1,826,595.95	4,530,721.02	1,828,520.71	1.50%	6.22%	2.49%	361,823.16	1,501,911.20	600,443.55
M37	1,104,188.23	1,118,370.46	1,098,219.64	0.91%	1.54%	1.49%	218,724.27	370,734.18	360,629.71
M38	624,380.09	634,477.88	619,450.78	0.51%	0.87%	0.84%	123,680.98	210,326.22	203,413.19
M39	902,953.43	654,992.12	815,570.84	0.74%	0.90%	1.11%	178,862.47	217,126.59	267,814.44
M40	85,816.05	86,580.32	85,492.63	0.07%	0.12%	0.12%	16,998.96	28,700.94	28,073.78
M41	482,868.77	494,224.02	481,289.04	0.40%	0.68%	0.65%	95,649.56	163,832.77	158,044.10
M42	162,741.40	154,282.91	155,576.69	0.13%	0.21%	0.21%	32,236.80	51,144.01	51,087.75
M43	2,336,265.58	1,931,312.88	1,984,225.56	1.92%	2.65%	2.70%	462,781.59	640,220.49	651,573.39
M44	592,248.99	608,932.06	584,245.63	0.49%	0.84%	0.80%	117,316.26	201,857.91	191,852.64
M45	69,349.59	68,148.94	68,338.24	0.06%	0.09%	0.09%	13,737.19	22,591.03	22,440.68
M46	327,226.18	344,405.56	324,910.90	0.27%	0.47%	0.44%	64,818.94	114,168.71	106,693.16
M47	151,361.06	152,183.04	151,011.50	0.12%	0.21%	0.21%	29,982.51	50,447.91	49,588.65
M48	106,945.03	107,320.65	106,784.85	0.09%	0.15%	0.15%	21,184.32	35,576.26	35,065.66
M49	155,158.82	150,439.88	151,175.53	0.13%	0.21%	0.21%	30,734.80	49,870.06	49,642.52
M50	350,375.09	376,903.49	348,984.72	0.29%	0.52%	0.47%	69,404.41	124,941.61	114,598.44
M51	715,748.18	621,424.78	651,738.18	0.59%	0.85%	0.89%	141,779.72	205,999.18	214,015.62
M52	615,677.25	587,742.71	592,040.65	0.51%	0.81%	0.81%	121,957.07	194,833.75	194,412.34
M53	79,853.82	78,412.28	78,030.31	0.07%	0.11%	0.11%	15,813.96	25,993.27	25,822.33
M54	154,981.20	160,535.14	154,219.00	0.13%	0.22%	0.21%	30,699.61	53,216.59	50,641.92

Table 4 results reveal that location site Tizayuca benefits the *Pop* and the economy of in first place the State of Mexico, in second place Mexico City, and in third place State of Hidalgo. The pax demand estimation approach calculates 14,960,755 pax demand coming from the State of Mexico, 4,143,143 pax demand coming from Mexico City, and 1,501,911 pax demand coming from Hidalgo. Contrary, 10,105 pax demand coming from the State of Baja California Sur which is the state that demands less air pax services from Tizayuca.

Table 4 results identify that location site ZFLT benefits the *Pop* and the economy of in first place the State of Mexico, in second place Mexico City, and in third place State of Puebla. The pax demand estimation approach calculates 12,084,690 pax demand coming from the State of Mexico, 7,946,620 pax demand coming from Mexico City, and 651,573 pax demand coming from Puebla. Contrary, 9,950 pax demand coming from the State of Baja California Sur which is the state that demands less air pax services from ZFLT.

Table 4 results probe that the pax estimation approach behaves as an exponential decay function. Therefore, results are consistent with literature since the farther is M_i from L_j the less attractive is L_j to M_i and demand grows as *Pop* grows [21].

6.2   MCLM Application for the NAICM Case Study

Although the MCLM can consider more than two potential sites for the location of the NAICM, in this case study the MCLM only selects between ZFLT or Tizayuca because these are the sites chosen by the government of Mexico to build the NAICM due to their technical and aeronautical advantages, project cost-benefit, minimum environmental impact, and economic benefits that result indirectly from the project.

The state of the art commercial software CPLEX is used to solve the MCLM. The software CPLEX decides the optimum location site based on a mathematical programming language OPL.

Table 5 shows the results for the 8 scenarios analyzed: *Tc* equal to 4, 6, 8 and 10 hrs, and *s* equal to 80 and 100 km/hr.

Table 5. MCLM results for the NAICM site selection problem, eight scenarios

Tc	4 hrs		6 hrs		8 hrs		10 hrs	
s	80 km/hr	100 km/hr	80 km/hr	100 km/hr	80 km/hr	100 km/hr	80 km/hr	100 km/hr
Lj	Tizayuca	Tizayuca	ZFLT	Tizayuca	ZFLT	ZFLT	ZFLT	ZFLT
Cover demand in millions	22.25	22.60	22.69	23.34	23.36	23.53	23.53	23.81
% cover demand	92.20%	93.66%	94.05%	96.72%	96.82%	97.52%	97.52%	98.66%

Table 5 shows the optimum location site for the NAICM under 8 different scenarios from a standpoint of maximizing the sum of expected pax demand. First case,

$Tc = 4$ hrs and $s = 80$ km/hr, the optimum location site is **Tizayuca** with coverage equal to 22.25 million pax (92.20%) from the total number of pax currently transported through the AICM, 24.13 million pax. Second case, $Tc = 4$ hrs and $s = 100$ km/hr, the optimum location site is **Tizayuca** with coverage equal to 22.60 million pax (93.66%) from the total number of pax currently transported through the AICM. Third case, $Tc = 6$ hrs and $s = 80$ km/hr, the optimum location site is **ZFLT** with coverage equal to 22.69 million pax (94.05%) from the total number of pax currently transported through the AICM. Fourth case, $Tc = 6$ hrs and $s = 100$ km/hr, the optimum location site is **Tizayuca** with coverage equal to 23.34 million pax (96.72%) from the total number of pax currently transported through the AICM. Fifth case, $Tc = 8$ hrs and $s = 80$ km/hr, the optimum location site is **ZFLT** with coverage equal to 23.36 million pax (96.82%) from the total number of pax currently transported through the AICM. Sixth case, $Tc = 8$ hrs and $s = 100$ km/hr, the optimum location site is **ZFLT** with coverage equal to 23.53 million pax (97.52%) from the total number of pax currently transported through the AICM. Seventh case, $Tc = 10$ hrs and $s = 80$ km/hr, the optimum location site is **ZFLT** with coverage equal to 23.53 million pax (97.52%) from the total number of pax currently transported through the AICM. Finally, eighth case, $Tc = 10$ hrs and $s = 100$ km/hr, the optimum location site is **ZFLT** with coverage equal to 23.81 million pax (98.66%) from the total number of pax currently transported through the AICM.

The Ministry of Social Development sets that the *catchment area* of the NAICM must be larger than a radius of 500 km or a Tc longer than 4 hours [26]. Therefore, ZFLT is the optimum site to construct the NAICM from the perspective of maximizing the sum of expected passenger demands because this site covers slightly more demand than Tizayuca for the majority of scenarios with Tc longer than 4 hours.

7   Conclusions

The first and main contribution of this paper is the application and adaptation of the MCLM to answer: Which is the best site to locate the NAICM, ZFLT or Tizayuca, from a perspective of maximizing the sum of expected passenger demands? The results indicate that Tizayuca is the optimum site for *catchment areas* shorter than 4 hrs, and ZFLT is the optimum site for *catchment areas* longer than 4 hours. However, the Ministry of Social Development sets that the *catchment area* of the NAICM must be larger than a radios of 500km or a travel time longer than 4 hours. Therefore, ZFLT is the place where the NAICM should be constructed from the perspective of maximizing the sum of expected passenger demands. In such decision, the ZMVM is the area that would get must of the economic benefits. Specifically, the State of Mexico is the state that would get must of the economic benefits follow by Mexico City and the State of Puebla. The States of Baja California Sur, Campeche, Baja California Norte, Yucatan y Quintana Roo would get less economic benefits.

Answering this paper main question involves estimating pax demand at each demand point. Therefore, the second contribution of this paper is an approach to estimate pax demand at each possible airport location site coming from each demand point. This approach is based on a decay function, third contribution of this paper, whose variables are WI, Pop, and d from M_i´s to each possible L_j´s. WI is proposed as an opposite index to the MI. As a consequence, WI measures standard of living and purchasing power per M_i and is the fourth contribution of this paper. The economic factors that form the MI allow the estimation of pax demand for each M_i assuming the *wealth effect*, which relates the evolution of wealth with the expansion of private consumption. Hence, the estimation approach considers that M_i´s with high MI do not demand as much pax services as M_i´s with low MI do.

The optimal solution is obtained using the CPLEX software, however it is important to mention that for the case study with only two potential sites for airport location, the MCLP can be optimally solved multiplying a_{ij} values by M_i´s demands.

It is important to mention that the application and adaptation of the MCLM, feed it with the outputs resulting from the proposed approach to estimate pax demand, can be applied to select between a number p of airport sites (not only two sites), from the perspective of maximizing the sum of expected passengers demand, in any place.

As future works, first applied the proposed MCLP and pax demand estimation approach to select the NAICM optimum site between more than two possible sites for airport location, second applied the proposed MCLP and pax demand estimation approach to select optimum sites for airport location in other countries; third, applied the proposed MCLP and pax demand estimation approach to locate hub airports in Mexico and other countries; fourth, use the proposed MCLP and pax demand estimation approach to compare the coverage of the NAICM against a multi-hub system; fifth, compare the pax demand estimation approach against real data, unfortunately obtaining these data is very expensive; and sixth, develop forecasting methods to estimate pax demand per M_i and the evolution of WI for the long-term, the goal would be to verify if ZFLT remains as the optimum site for the location of the NAICM in the future.

References

1. Herrera, A.: Alternativas de Solución para Problemas de Capacidad Aeroportuaria. SCT, Mexico City (2006)
2. Domínguez, J.C.: Ventanas de oportunidad y coaliciones de política pública: el caso del proyecto para un nuevo aeropuerto en la Ciudad de México desde una perspectiva histórica. Instituto Mora, Mexico City (2011). ISSN: 0186-0348
3. Bartolo, D., Ruíz, A.: Índice de Marginación por Entidad Federativa y Municipio 2010. Consejo Nacional de Población, Mexico City (2011). http://www.conapo.gob.mx
4. Daskin, M.S.: Network and Discrete Location. Models, Algorithms, and Applications. John Wiley & Sons Inc., New York (1995)
5. Weiszfeld, E.: Sur le point pour lequel la somme des distances den points donnes est minimum. Tohoku Mathematical Journal **43**, 355–386 (1937)
6. Hakimi, S.: Optimum Location of switching centers in a communication network and some related graphs theoretic problems. Operation Research **13**, 462–475 (1965)
7. Erlenkotter, D.: A dual-based procedure for uncapacitated facility location. Operatiion Research **26**, 992–1009 (1978)

8. Drezner, Z.: The p-Centre Problem-Heuristic and Optimal Algorithms. The Journal of the Operational Research Society **35**(8), 741–748 (1984)
9. Neufville, R., Keeney, R.L.: Use of decision analysis in airport development for Mexico City. Analysis of Public Systems. MIT Press, Cambridge (1972)
10. Paelinck, J.: Qualitative multicriteria analysis: an application to airport location. Environment and Planning A **9**, 883–895 (1977)
11. Neufville, R.: Successful siting of airports: Sydney example. ASCE Journal of Transportation Engineering **116** (1990)
12. Saatcioglu, O.: Mathematical programming models for airport site selection. Transportation Research Part B - Methodological **16**(6), 435–447 (1982)
13. Min, H., Melachrinoudis, E., Wu, X.: Dynamic expansion and location of an airport: A multiple objective approach. Transportation Research Part A - Policy and Practice **31**(5), 403–417 (1997)
14. Aldrich, D.: Location, location, location: selecting sites for controversial facilities. Singapore Economic Review **53**(1), 145–172 (2008)
15. Partidário, M.R., Coutinho, M.: The Lisbon new international airport: The story of a decision-making process and the role of Strategic Environmental Assessment. Environmental Impact Assessment Review **31**, 360–367 (2011)
16. Dağ, S., Önder, E.: Decision-making for facility location using vikor method. Journal of International Scientific Publication: Economy and Business **7**(1), 308–330 (2013)
17. Zhao, A., Sun, P.: Scheme Comparison of New Airport Site Selection Based on Lattice Order Decision Making Method in the Integrated Transportation System. International Journal of Online Engineering (iJOE) **9**, 90–94 (2013)
18. CONAPO: Metología de estimación del índice de marginación (2010). http://www.conapo.gob.mx
19. De la Vega, S., Romo, R., González, A.: Índice de Marginación por Entidad Federativa y Municipio 2010. Consejo Nacional de Población (2014). http://www.1.gob.mx
20. Menezes, V.: El efecto riqueza en la crisis global actual: el caso de los países de la Eurozona. XIII Reunión de Economía Mundial, pp. 1–22. Central Bank of Brazil, Brazil (2011)
21. Drezner, T., Drezner, Z.: The gravity p-median model. European Journal of Operational Research **179**, 1239–1251 (2007)
22. INEGI: Censo de Población y Vivienda 2010 (2010). http://www.inegi.org.mx/est/contenidos/proyectos/ccpv/cpv2010 (accesed on 1 April 2015)
23. GoogleMaps.com. https://maps.google.com.mx (accesed on 1 April 2015)
24. AICM. Estadísticas del AICM. http://www.aicm.com.mx/categoria/estadisticas/ (accesed on 1 April 2015)
25. Mendoza, A., Abarca, E., Mayoral, E., y Quintero, F.: Recomendaciones de Actualización de Algunos Elementos del Proyecto Geométrico en Carreteras. IMT. Queretaro, Mexico **03**(007), 1–64 (2004)
26. CONAPO. Implicaciones Territoriales de las Alternativas de Localización del Nuevo Aeropuerto Internacional del Valle de México. Dirección General de Desarrollo Urbano. Documentos Técnicos. CONAPO, Mexico City, pp. 1–86 (2001)

Rescheduling Railway Traffic Taking into Account Minimization of Passengers' Discomfort

Francesco Corman[1]([✉]), Dario Pacciarelli[2], Andrea D'Ariano[2], and Marcella Samà[2]

[1] Section of Transport Engineering and Logistics, Delft University of Technology and Center for Industrial Management, Katholieke Universiteit Leuven, Leuven, Belgium
f.corman@tudelft.nl
[2] Dipartimento di Ingegneria, Università degli Studi Roma Tre, Rome, Italy

Abstract. Optimization models for railway traffic rescheduling in the last decade tend to develop along two main streams. One the one hand, train scheduling models strives to incorporate any relevant detail of the railway infrastructure having an impact on the feasibility and quality of the solutions from the viewpoint of operations managers. On the other hand, delay management models focus on the impact of rescheduling decisions on the quality of service perceived by the passengers. Models in the first stream are mainly microscopic, while models in the second stream are mainly macroscopic. This paper aims at merging these two streams of research by developing microscopic passenger-centric models, solution algorithms and lower bounds. Fast iterative algorithms are proposed, based on a decomposition of the problem and on the exact resolution of the sub-problems. A new lower bound is proposed, consisting of the resolution of a set of min-cost flow problems with activation constraints. Computational experiments, based on a real-world Dutch railway network, show that good quality solutions and lower bounds can be found within a limited computation time.

Keywords: Train scheduling · Delay management · Passenger routing · MILP · Min-cost flow

1 Introduction

In the last years, many railway companies, at least in Europe, are experiencing increasing difficulties to face the ever increasing transport demand while ensuring good quality of service (QoS) to the passengers, also due to the limited space and funds to build new infrastructure in bottleneck areas. These facts stimulated the interest of practitioners and theoreticians for new effective approaches to railway traffic rescheduling aiming at the reduction of delays of trains and passengers. As a matter of fact, the literature on this subject experienced a significant growth in the last years, see, e.g., Cacchiani et al. (2014).

This paper aims to provide a synthesis of two main lines of research that have been in the academic focus recently, namely operation-centric approaches (minimizing

© Springer International Publishing Switzerland 2015
F. Corman et al. (Eds.): ICCL 2015, LNCS 9335, pp. 602–616, 2015.
DOI: 10.1007/978-3-319-24264-4_41

delays of trains and considering precise movements of train vehicles) and passenger-centric approaches (which minimize travel time of passengers, and consider larger scale networks by which less train traffic is modelled very roughly).

The former is typically termed *Train Scheduling* (TS) problem, and its complexity stems from the limited overtaking capacity of railway lines and from the constraints of the safety system, caused by the signal status and speed restrictions. The competition of trains for the available capacity can be modelled only when a sufficient level of detail is considered. One of the most effective approaches to tackle such complexity is based on the blocking time theory (see, e.g., Hansen and Pachl 2014) and on the alternative graph formulation of the blocking job shop scheduling model with no-swap constraints (Mascis and Pacciarelli 2002). Advanced scheduling approaches based on the alternative graph model are able to quickly solve real-life instances in which train arrival times, orders and routes, are considered variable (see e.g. D'Ariano et al. 2007, Mannino and Mascis 2009, Corman et al. 2011). Other approaches based on Mixed Integer Linear Programs (MILPs) are reported, e.g., in Törnquist Krasemann (2011), Meng and Zhou (2014), Pellegrini et al. (2014). The goal of all these approaches is to find a *train schedule*, i.e., a departure/passing time for each train et each relevant point of the railway network, compatible with the real time position of each train and such that a suitable function of the train delays is minimized. Such goal can be achieved by all these approaches in practical size networks and within a computation time compatible with real-time operations. One weakness of all these models is the limited view of passenger needs and expectations, which are taken into account only indirectly, e.g., by penalizing train delays.

The alternative stream of research directly faces the optimization of the QoS perceived by the passengers, and is based on the concept of customer-oriented dispatching introduced in Schöbel (2001). The *delay management* (DM) problem is to decide whether to keep or not transfer connections during operations, a decision that directly affect passenger QoS. Dollevoet et al. (2012) enlarge the scope of DM to include the possibility of rerouting passengers in order to reduce their travel time. The approaches in this stream of research are currently based on macroscopic models, i.e. they consider only arrival and departure at stations, neglecting the actual capacity of platforms, interlocking areas and block sections. As a result, the promised passenger delay is only a lower bound of the one achievable in practice, furthermore the proposed solution might turn to be infeasible when implemented in practice. To overcome these drawbacks, more recent works have tried to include some capacity constraints in the models, though in approximated form along lines (Schachtebeck and Schöbel 2010) and at stations (Dollevoet et al. 2014A). Though the trend in the literature on DM is for the inclusion of an increasing level of detail in the models, a microscopic DM model with passenger routings is still missing.

Very recently, research has started addressing the interaction of passenger flows with train scheduling. Sato et al. (2013) address the problem of minimizing passenger inconvenience on simple railway lines, taking into account disruptions that might require adjustment of vehicle schedules. The passenger inconvenience is divided into three components, i.e., the time spent onboard the trains, the waiting time at platforms and the number of transfers. Passenger flows are routed along path of minimum inconvenience, and then considered fixed while the timetable is adjusted to a minor extent. Capacity at stations is approximated by means of headway times along the line. A combination of the delay management approach with the microscopic models based on the alternative graph concept is proposed by Dollevoet et al. (2014B), in which passengers delays are optimized by iteratively solving a microscopic train scheduling problem (without knowledge of passenger flows) and a macroscopic delay management problem (without explicit modelling of limited infrastructure capacity). Passengers are always assigned to a shortest path between their origin and destination. The procedure delivers in few iterations good feasible solutions.

This paper aims at merging these two lines of research by developing microscopic passenger-centric models, i.e., *microscopic delay management* (MDM) models, addressing several issues that have not been fully considered by previous research. We integrate microscopic railway traffic rescheduling and passenger point of view into a single MILP model. We consider the minimization of the time spent by the passengers in the system as objective function. Passenger flows are modelled based on Origin-Destination description, with possibility of transfer connections and rerouting. A lower bound and fast heuristic algorithms are proposed. Computational experiments on a real-world Dutch network allow us to evaluate the overall approach. Comparison with the optimal or the best solution known demonstrates the potential of the proposed approaches.

The paper is organized as follows. Section 2 introduces the problem and notations. Section 3 reports on lower bounds and algorithms to compute upper bounds. Section 4 reports on the computational experiments on a rail Dutch network. Section 5 concludes the paper.

2   Problem Definition

We address the problem of computing in real time a schedule for all trains and a routing for each passenger so that passengers have the least possible discomfort. We relate discomfort to the time spent in various conditions (Wardman 2004).

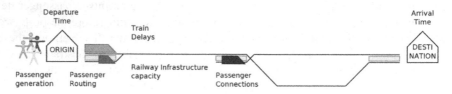

Fig. 1. Pictorial representation of the elements of the MDM problem

Figure 1 gives a graphical summary of all aspects of the model.

Train scheduling decisions are necessary whenever *train delays* occur, making infeasible the plan of arrivals/departures described by the timetable. Such decisions must take into account the limited *capacity* of the *railway infrastructure*, which limits the possibility of rescheduling train movements. This capacity depends on railway safety regulations, which make use of the signalling system to limit the speed of each train depending on the position of other trains in the network. Formally, the railway network is partitioned in block sections, separated by signals; when a block section is occupied by a train, no other train can enter it. Relevant characteristics include the *running time* necessary to traverse a block section and the *dwell time* at the platform of a scheduled stop. Moreover, additional constraints prescribe that a train cannot depart from a station before its scheduled departure time and its departure from a station can be constrained to be sufficiently larger than the arrival of another (feeder) train so that the passengers can move from the latter to the former.

A train is late when its arrival time at a station is larger than its scheduled arrival time. Delays are caused either by external disturbances or by the propagation of delays from one train to another along the infrastructure. Primary delays are due to external disturbances that can be recovered only to a certain extent by exploiting running time supplements of the timetable. Secondary delays are determined by rescheduling decisions in response to primary delays, and are the result of a delay propagation of some conflicts. A *conflict* occurs whenever two trains require the same block section at the same time. The conflict is typically solved by specifying a passing order for the trains at the block section. Determining the train order and the entrance time of each train in each block section is the main subject of the TS problem. We assume train traffic can be controlled towards specific states, maximizing some performance measure. More detailed descriptions of the TS definition and formulation can be found, e.g., in D'Ariano et al. (2007) and Corman et al. (2014B) and (Mascis and Pacciarelli 2002). In this paper we deal with *timetable perturbations*, i.e., with primary delays that can be managed without the need for train cancellations or rerouting. We neglect disruptions, failures, accidents resulting in large part of the traffic not running according to the plans, and requiring changes to the plan of vehicles and crew. We base our model on the train rescheduling model of D'Ariano et al. (2007).

The passenger routing problem (or passenger assignment problem) studies the distribution of passengers onto the railway network. Passengers start from an origin station at a given arrival time and want to reach a destination station as soon as possible. We consider a time discrete model for passenger arrivals at each station. Hence, we assume to know the number of passengers willing to reach the same destination $d \in D$ from the same origin $o \in O$, starting their journey at the same time w, for a discrete set of arrival times W. The discrete model is justified by the observation that all the passengers with the same destination arriving at a station between two consecutive train departures will move together in the network as a group, as each train is assumed to have infinite capacity and each passenger aims at reaching his/her destination in the minimum time. We refer to a group of passengers going from o to d and arriving in o at time w as a triple odw, hereinafter denoted as *demand*, and let ODW be the set of all demands odw. Note that, once the train schedule is fixed, each demand odw moves in the network independently from the other triples, i.e., the choice of a particular routing for a given odw does not influence the routing of any other odw. Moreover, we assume that all passengers in a demand odw will follow the same OD path (we assume this path as unique, possibly breaking ties arbitrarily).

We call *passenger routing* the definition of a route for each demand from the associated origin to the associated destination stations, possibly including transfers between pairs of connected trains at intermediate stations. We assume that passengers are rational and informed, and that each demand aims at reaching the destination within the shortest time from the arrival at the origin station. To this aim, transfers between trains are used by passengers whenever convenient, i.e., each demand follows the fastest route to destination given the train schedule. Hence, the passenger routing aspect of the MDM problem is similar to a multi-commodity flow problem on a graph $(N, F \cup S)$, in which a commodity is associated to each odw triple. The only difference is that passengers may change train only at scheduled stops if a connection exists, i.e., only if the connected train departs from the station sufficiently later that the arrival of the passengers. To take into account this difference, we introduce a set of *connection* arcs C, each associated to a pair (i, j) of operations, where i is the operation associated to the arrival of the feeder train at the station and j is the operation associated to the departure of the connected train from the station. Each arc has a weight c_{ij} equal to the minimum time for transferring passengers from the feeder train to the second one. Each arc in $(i, j) \in C$ is active only if $h_j \geq h_i + c_{ij}$. Thus, the passenger routing aspect of the MDM problem can be modelled as a multi-commodity flow problem where passengers may flow only through the arcs of F and through the active arcs of C.

3   The MDM Mathematical Model

We now introduce a detailed MILP model for the MDM problem combining train rescheduling and passenger routing decisions. This mathematical model represent an exact and comprehensive approach to describe quantitatively the problem.

We introduce a disjunctive graph $G^P = (N \cup N^{ODW}, F \cup F^{ODW} \cup C, A)$ where N, F and A are the sets of nodes, fixed arcs and alternative pairs of the Alternative Graph model (see Mascis and Pacciarelli 2002 for the basic terminology and definition) describing the train circulation and the constraint due to the signalling system. Instead, N^{ODW}, F^{ODW} and C are the sets of nodes, fixed arcs and connection arcs necessary to take into account passenger routing. The set N^{ODW} contains two nodes for each demand $odw \in ODW$, namely a source node $start^{odw}$ with supply equal to 1 and a sink node end^{odw} with demand equal to 1. These nodes take into account the origin and destination of the flow associated to odw. Fixed arcs in F^{ODW} link arriving/departing passengers of an odw to the first/last train they may take on their journey. Let δ_{start}^{odw} be the set of nodes associated to train departures from the origin station of odw and δ_{end}^{odw} be the set of arrivals at the destination station of odw, F^{ODW} is the union set of arcs $(start^{odw}, j)$ with $j \in \delta_{start}^{odw}$ plus the arcs (i, end^{odw}) with $i \in \delta_{end}^{odw}$. C is the set of connection arcs. There is an arc $(i, j) \in C$ for each pair of nodes i, associated to a train arrival, and j, associated to a train departure, at/from the same station, for all stations. The connection is active if $h_j \geq h_i + c_{ij}$, i.e., if a passenger can transfer from the feeder to the connected train.

In order to translate G^P into a MILP model, we use two kinds of binary variables: x_{ijkl} associated to the choice of an alternative arc in the pair $((j, k), (l, i)) \in A$, representing a decision on train orders, and q_{ij}^{odw} associated to the use of connection

$(i, j) \in C$ by the passengers on odw, representing the assignment of passengers to arcs in $F \cup F^{odw}$. Besides the binary variables, the model makes use of real variables h_i, equal to the starting time of each operation in $N \setminus \{0\}$, where 0 is a dummy operation representing the starting time of the scheduling horizon, and T_{odw}, equal to the arrival time at destination of the passengers in odw. We quickly summarize all the notation used.

Parameters

- $F = \{(i, j), \dots\}$ are fixed directed arcs representing running, departure, arrival, dwell, origin, destination of each train;
- $C = \{(i, j), \dots\}$ are connection arcs between train arrivals and departures;
- $A = \{((j, k), (l, i)), \dots\}$ are pairs of alternative arcs representing train orders;
- p_{ij} is the weight on fixed arcs;
- s_{ki} is the weight on alternative arcs;
- c_{ij} is the weight on connection arcs;
- ODW are demands, i.e., groups of passengers moving from o to d starting at time w;
- $start^{odw}$ is the origin node for passengers in $odw \in ODW$;
- end^{odw} is the destination node for passengers in $odw \in ODW$;
- δ_{start}^{odw} are nodes, associated to the departure of trains from the origin station of odw;
- δ_{end}^{odw} are nodes, associated to the arrival of trains at the destination station of odw;
- δ_i^{out} are arcs in $F \cup F^{ODW} \cup C$ outgoing node i that can be used by passengers;
- δ_i^{in} are arcs in $F \cup F^{ODW} \cup C$ ingoing node i that can be used by passengers;
- F^{ODW} are arcs $(start^{odw}, j)$ with $j \in \delta_{start}^{odw}$ plus arcs (i, end^{odw}) with $i \in \delta_{end}^{odw}$;
- π_{odw} is the arrival time at origin station $o \in O$ of demand odw;
- n_{odw} is the number of passengers for demand odw.

Variables

- h_i is the starting time of operation $i \in N \setminus \{0\}$;
- x_{ijkl} is 1 if arc (l, i) is selected from $((j, k)(l, i)) \in A$, i.e., if $h_i \geq h_l$, 0 otherwise;
- q_{ij}^{odw} is 1 if arc $(i, j) \in F \cup F^{ODW} \cup C$ belongs to the path of odw, 0 otherwise;
- T_{odw} arrival time at end^{odw} of passengers in odw.

The MDM formulation is as follows:

$$\min \sum_{odw \in ODW} n_{odw} (T_{odw} - \pi_{odw})$$

$$h_j \geq h_i + p_{ij} \qquad\qquad\qquad \forall (i,j) \in F \qquad\qquad (A1)$$

$$h_i \geq h_l + s_{li} - M(1 - x_{ijkl}) \qquad \forall ((j,k),(l,i)) \in A \qquad (A2)$$

$$h_k \geq h_j + s_{jk} - M x_{ijkl} \qquad\quad \forall ((j,k),(l,i) \in A \qquad (A3)$$

$$\sum_{j \in \delta^{odw}_{start}} q^{odw}_{start,j} = 1 \qquad\qquad\quad \forall\, odw \in ODW \qquad (A4)$$

$$\sum_{i \in \delta^{odw}_{end}} q^{odw}_{i,end} = 1 \qquad\qquad\quad \forall\, odw \in ODW \qquad (A5)$$

$$\sum_{(i,j) \in \delta^{out}_i} q^{odw}_{ij} = \sum_{(i,j) \in \delta^{in}_i} q^{odw}_{ij} \qquad \forall\, i \in N\backslash\{0\}, \forall\, odw \in ODW \quad (A6)$$

$$h_j \geq \pi_{odw} + M\big(q^{odw}_{start,j} - 1\big) \qquad \forall\, j \in \delta^{odw}_{start}, \forall\, odw \in ODW \quad (A7)$$

$$h_j \geq h_i + c_{ij} - M(1 - q^{odw}_{ij}) \qquad \forall (i,j) \in C, \forall\, odw \in ODW \quad (A8)$$

$$T_{odw} \geq h_i - M\big(1 - q^{odw}_{i,end}\big) \qquad \forall\, i \in \delta^{odw}_{end}, \forall\, odw \in ODW \quad (A9)$$

The objective function is the minimization of the total time spent in the system by all passengers. Constraints (A1) relate to fixed arcs, e.g., to running, dwell, and departing operations. Constraints (A2)-(A3) model the choice of an arc from each pair of alternative arcs in set A, i.e., choose the orders of trains over each infrastructure element with limited capacity. Constraints (A4)-(A6) define a min-cost flow problem to assign a path from o to d to the passengers in each triple odw, as departure, arrival, and flow balance respectively. Constraints (A7)-(A9) model the interaction between train and passenger arrival/departure times. (A7) constrains a train carrying passengers in odw to depart from o after the arrival time of passengers, (A8) describes passengers transfer from a train to another and ensure that a suitable transfer time has elapsed; (A9) computes passengers arrival time at destination.

4   Lower and Upper Bounds

The formulation introduced in the previous section can be solved by commercial solvers. Anyway, it is computationally hard to find solutions or to assess the quality of a solution found; this section proposes to this aim a lower bound, and a set of heuristic procedures based on decomposing the MILP problem.

4.1   Lower Bound

We propose a lower bound which neglects the interactions between different OD pairs. Each OD pair is evaluated independently from the others by exploiting all the routing alternatives available to reach a destination $d \in D$ from an origin $o \in O$ in the given time horizon. Therefore, in what follows, all the demands odw considered in the lower bound computation share the origin and destination and differ only for the arrival time w. We name *train combination* a sequence of trains and passenger transfers, that allows to reach the destination d starting from the origin o. Each combination j has a minimum departure time τ_j, equal to the earliest departure time of the train leaving o, and can be delayed by any amount of time if useful to reduce the travel time of the passengers travelling from o to d. For each combination, the running time r_j is also given, that we assume to be constant even if the train departure is delayed, since each train disregards the presence of other trains in the network. Note that, for each train leaving o, only the combination reaching d with minimum travel time is relevant to compute a lower bound. Therefore, the number of combinations to be considered is equal to the number of trains departing from o in the given time horizon.

The lower bound is obtained by solving the problem of assigning all the demands odw associated to the same origin o and destination d to the available train combinations connecting o and d. In what follows, we order the demands associated to the pair od for increasing arrival time, and use the index i to denote the i-th demand associated to the pair od. Therefore, π_i and n_i denote the arrival time and the number of passengers of the i-th demand. Clearly, the departure time of the train combination j is the maximum between τ_j and the arrival time π_i of the latest demand assigned to j. The travel time of the i-th demand assigned to combination j is then equal to r_j plus the difference between the departure time of j and π_i. As a consequence of the above discussion, in the optimal solution of this relaxation it is sufficient to consider only a limited set of departure times for each combination, namely τ_j and all the values $\pi_i \geq \tau_j$. We formulate the relaxed problem for a given pair od as an uncapacitated min-cost flow problem with additional constraints on the digraph $(N_1 \cup N_2, A_1 \cup A_2)$.

Nodes in N_1 are associated to the demands $i=1,\ldots,W$ and nodes in N_2 are associated to the train combinations $j=1,\ldots,J$. We assume the demands/combinations are numbered for increasing arrival/departure times, i.e., $i > h$ implies $\pi_i \geq \pi_h$ and $j > k$ iimplies $\tau_j \geq \tau_k$. There are two sets of direct arcs: *waiting* arcs in A_1 between pairs of consecutive nodes in N_1 and *travelling* arcs in A_2 between a node in N_1 and a node in N_2. More precisely, there is a waiting arc $(i,i+1)$ between the i-th demand with the next one, for $i=1,\ldots,W-1$, having weight $\gamma_{i,i+1} = \pi_{i+1} - \pi_i$. For each pair $(i$-th demand, combination $j)$ such that $\pi_i \leq \tau_j < \pi_{i+1}$ there is an arc $(i,j) \in A_1$ having weight $\gamma_{ij} = \tau_j - \pi_i + r_j$. For each pair (i, j) such that $\pi_i > \tau_j$ there is an arc $(i,j) \in A_2$ having weight $\gamma_{ij} = r_j$. Each node $i \in N_1$ is a source node with supply n_i, while each node $j \in N_2$ is a sink node accepting any non-negative flow.

We formulate the problem as follow:

$$min \sum_{(i,j) \in A_1 \cup A_2} \gamma_{ij} u_{ij}.$$

$u_{i,i+1} - u_{i-1,i} + \sum_{(i,j) \in A_2} u_{ij} = n_i$	$\forall\, i \in N_1$	(B1)
$u_{ij} \leq M v_{ij}$	$\forall (i.j) \in A_2$	(B2)
$\sum_{i:(i,j) \in A_2} v_{ij} = 1$	$\forall\, j \in N_2$	(B3)
$u_{ij} \geq 0$	$\forall (i,j) \in A_1 \cup A_2$	(B4)
$v_{ij} \in \{0,1\}$	$\forall (i,j) \in A_2$	(B5)

were constraints (B1) represent the flow conservation in each node, (B2) the activation of each arc $(i, j) \in A_2$ with $M = \sum_{i \in N_1} n_i$ and (B3) the choice of one arc $(i, j) \in A_2$ ingoing each node $j \in N_2$. Also, this formulation includes two sets of variables: the (real) flow variables u_{ij}, and the (binary) activation variables v_{ij} , (, which are required to express the constraint that for each train combination exactly one departure time must be chosen, i.e., only one arc ingoing each $j \in N_2$ must be activated. The objective function is the minimization of the flow cost.

4.2   Heuristic H1

The first heuristic H1 we consider is inspired by the last phase (reducing passenger inconvenience) reported in the work by Sato, Tamura, and Tomii (2013). We solve the train scheduling problem by simply fixing variables x according to the sequence prescribed by the timetable. In fact, the timetable prescribes a total order of the train departure times from each station (if necessary by breaking ties arbitrarily). Given this order we simply select x_{ijkl} equal to 1 whenever the departure time of the train associated to operations i and j precedes the departure of the train associated to operations k and l. This precedence holds for all the resources shared by the two trains until the first point where the two paths diverge, i.e., until an overtake can be performed.

4.3   Heuristic H2

Heuristic H2 is a speed-up of H1. Starting from the sequence prescribed by the timetable, the train scheduling problem is first solved by fixing both variables x and h in the MDM problem (A1)-(A11). Note that, when a value $\bar{h}_i$ is given to each $i \in N$, the routing options for the passengers are strongly reduced. In fact, the connections that can be used are limited to those $(i, j) \in C$ such that $\bar{h}_j \geq \bar{h}_i + c_{ij}$, that we call *active* connections. We let C_{active} be the set of active connections. Also the set of trains eligible for the passengers in *odw* is restricted to those trains departing from o at time larger or equal to π_{odw}. We call $\beta_{start}^{odw} \subseteq \delta_{start}^{odw}$ the set of nodes associated to the departure of a train from the origin station of *odw* after π_{odw}, i.e., $j \in \beta_{start}^{odw}$ if and only if $(start^{odw}, j) \in F^{ODW}$. The advantage of H2 is the strongly reduced computation time with respect to H1, since train departure times are simply computed by shifting all traffic ahead to account for the train delays. The disadvantage is that train departure times are fixed without taking passengers into account. Therefore, passengers have less routing options, and this fact may deteriorate the performance of H2.

4.4   Heuristic H3

Heuristic H3 is an iterative heuristic which aims at improving the performance of H2. It solves alternatively a train scheduling problem and a passenger routing problem until no improvement is possible. Starting from the solution of H2, a new instance of the train scheduling problem is solved by taking into account the number of passengers assigned to each train, in order to reduce passenger travel time. In order to introduce the problem, let us define a set $E \subseteq N$ of operations associated to the train arrivals at some scheduled stops, and let a_e be the scheduled arrival time of $e \in E$. Let also f_e be the number of passengers disembarking the train according to the passenger routing solution, either because they have reached their final destination or because of a transfer. With this notation, the quantity $z_e = max\{0, h_e - a_e\}$ is the delay of the associated train at the associated station that is experienced by the f_e passengers disembarking the train. The new instance of the train scheduling problem aims at rescheduling trains for the purpose of reducing this delay for all passengers, i.e., the objective function is the minimization of $\sum_{e \in E} f_e z_e$.

Figure 2 summarizes the behaviour of H3. Given a train scheduling solution, the DM problem computes a passenger routing, and the procedure iteratively continues until one of the two problems finds the same solution obtained in the previous iteration.

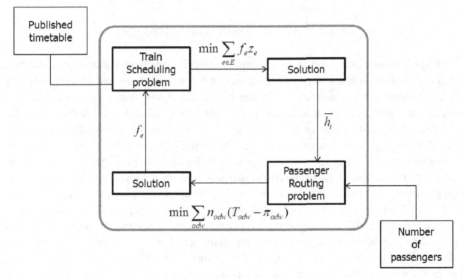

Fig. 2. Flowchart of H3

5   Experimental Assessment

5.1   Description of the Instances

The instances studied in this paper are based on the Dutch railway network between Utrecht and Den Bosch, a line long about 40 km that comprises about two hundreds block sections. There are three major stations, Utrecht (Ut), Geldermalsen (Gdm), and Den Bosch (Ht). In all the instances we consider all trains stop at those three stations. Furthermore, there are 8 minor stations, as detailed in Figure 3. Only local trains stop at all those minor stations. We consider trains running in both directions along the line, with the two traffic directions basically independent from each other. Trains can overtake each other at the outbound interlocking area in Utrecht, at the 4-tracks area around Houten, at Geldermalsen, and at the outbound interlocking area of Den Bosch.

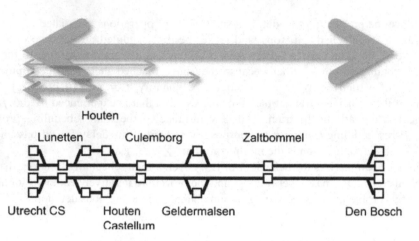

Fig. 3. The railway infrastructure and OD pairs

The actual timetable used in operations in 2010 is considered, that is periodic with a period of 30 minutes. For passenger trains, we consider three sets of instances, one with the same train frequency as in the actual timetable, and other two sets with lighter timetables, having a reduced number of trains. Namely, the actual timetable schedules 4 intercity trains and 2 local trains per hour per direction between Utrecht and Den Bosch, and 2 local trains per hour per direction between Utrecht and Geldermalsen. This is the default timetable with 16 trains/hour. Lighter timetables are generated by removing two intercity trains per hour per direction (12 trains / hour) and removing the two local trains between Utrecht and Geldermalsen (8 trains / hour).

Due to the unavailability of detailed real data about passenger flows, we resort to realistic synthetic OD data based on the average flow of passengers at the considered stations as published by the infrastructure manager. This is translated to an average rate of passenger generation per OD, per time unit. Out of the theoretically 56 possible combinations of origin and destination stations, we consider the 8 OD pairs with the largest amount of passenger flow, as reported in Figure 3.

We restrict the time horizon of traffic control to different lengths, namely time horizons of 30, 45 and 60 minutes. A time horizon of 45 minutes with the timetable scheduling 16 trains per hour corresponds to an instance with 12 trains, on average, and considering 8 OD pairs corresponds to having 39 demands *odw,* on average.

Entrance delays, for all trains in the network, are defined based on a three-parameter Weibull distribution. We consider for every combination of the other parameters 10 instances with normal traffic conditions, generated with the same Weibull distribution used in Corman et al. (2011) and 10 instances with more perturbed traffic conditions, generated by using a Weibull distribution with the same scale and shift parameters of the first 10 instances and a doubled shape parameter. All results are the average over this combination of 10 + 10 instances.

The experiments are executed on a PC with a processor Intel i5 CPU at 3.20 GHz, 8 GB memory. The commercial solver CPLEX 12.4 is used to solve the MILP.

5.2   Experiments Up to 1 Hour Time Horizon

We next report on the experiments for the instances with 8 OD pairs and a time horizon varying from 30 to 60. The instances result in about 2100 till 100000 binary variables, from the simplest case (8trh, 30 min) to the most complicated case (16trh, 60 min), for the MDM model. Tables 1 and 2 report on the average values of the objective function and on the computation time of all approaches. We show the average travel time of each passenger instead of the total travel time of all passengers, to make the comparison easier when instances with different number of passengers are considered. Each line reports the average result over 20 instances with the same train frequency and time horizon. The following results are reported in the tables: the best upper bound known, and the best lower bound known; the value found by H1, H2, H3 within 3 minutes of computation. The last columns report the values found by MDM within 3 minutes and 4 hours of computation, and the lower bound computed. When H1 or MDM was not able to find a feasible solution for some instances, within the time limit of computation, we consider under H1 the solution found by H2, that is always computed within a few seconds.

Table 1. Value of the average passenger travel time [sec] obtained by the various approaches.

trains /hour	time hor	Best UB	Best LB	H1 3 min	H2 3 min	H3 3 min	MDM 3 min	MDM 4 h	Lower Bound
8trh	30 m	1729.4	1729.4	**1729.4**	1730.3	1730.7	**1729.4**	1729.4	1687.9
8trh	45 m	1734.4	1734.4	1736.0	1755.2	1738.1	**1734.4**	1734.4	1660.3
8trh	60 m	1654.9	1655.4	1662.3	1755.1	1747.1	1712.7	**1654.9**	1540.7
12trh	30 m	*1544.6*	1544.8	1557.3	1570.8	1558.1	1545.3	**1544.8**	1463.1
12trh	45 m	*1883.3*	1887.2	1901.4	1975.8	1969.4	1911.1	**1885.8**	1720.6
12trh	60 m	1844.1	1779.9	1855.4	1855.4	**1844.1**	1950.8	1872.1	1621.0
16trh	30 m	1684.0	1684.8	1713.1	1736.0	1711.1	1690.1	**1684.8**	1585.6
16trh	45 m	*1734.4*	1718.2	1756.0	1768.9	1741.5	1953.4	**1741.4**	1620.6
16trh	60 m	1706.4	1575.3	1740.9	1740.9	**1706.4**	1740.9	1740.9	1566.7
Average		*1724.0*	*1701.1*	*1739.1*	*1765.4*	*1749.6*	*1774.2*	*1732.1*	*1607*

For each group of instances, the approach achieving the best average result is highlighted in bold; in a few cases (highlighted in bold italic) the best upper bound for the different instances in the same group is found by different approaches. As expected, the rank of the best results sees the exact MDM model as best, and then the heuristics H1, and H3. MDM is able to solve to optimality the easier instances, but the most complex ones are solved at best by H3; MDM is unable to outperform H3 even after 4 hours of computation. The lower bound proposed is very good for the largest instances, with less than 45 seconds of computation on average, and a quality deterioration of less than 0.6% with respect to the best known lower bound. On average, the optimality gap is below 6%.

Table 2. Computation time [sec] for the approaches considered

Trains/ hour	time hor	H1 3 min	H2 3 min	H3 3 min	MDM 3 min	MDM 4h	LB
8trh	30 min	0.2	0.2	0.4	0.3	0.1	3.4
8trh	45 min	0.7	0.3	0.8	1.4	0.8	5.4
8trh	60 min	176.3	0.7	2.1	180.0	3858.0	14.0
12trh	30 min	115.5	0.5	1.3	173.5	2264.0	10.0
12trh	45 min	180.0	1.5	4.4	180.0	3129.6	15.0
12trh	60 min	180.0	2.2	5.7	180.0	12273.0	27.8
16trh	30 min	180.0	0.7	2.2	180.0	2323.4	14.1
16trh	45 min	180.0	1.4	4.2	180.0	10434.8	20.7
16trh	60 min	180.0	3.5	9.9	180.0	14150.2	44.6
Average		*132.5*	*1.2*	*3.5*	*139.5*	*5381*	*17.2*

Table 2 details the average computation time of the different approaches. When no feasible solution is found, the timetable solution is used, and the total time limit of computation is reported. H2 and H3 are the fastest heuristics, being able to deliver, on average, a solution within 10 seconds even for the largest instances. For the iterative approach H3, the average number of iterations is 1.9, (min 1.2 , max 2.1 iterations). The amount of iterations for all instances never exceeds 3. H3 is the best heuristic, providing good solutions and short computation time.

5.3   Experiments with 2 Hour Time Horizon

This subsection presents our computational experience with significantly larger instances compared to the previous subsection, with two hours of time horizon and with a timetable of 16 trains/hour, i.e., the actual train frequency observed in real-life. Similarly to the previous subsection, 20 instances are generated with the distributions of Section 8.1. Each instance has more than 12000 passengers grouped in 119 demands. The resulting MDM models have more than 400 thousands variables, and CPLEX is unable to solve them in 8 hours; the same applies for H1.We thus report on the performance of H2 and H3 only, in Table 3. H3 converges after 2.5 iterations on average (5 iterations at max). The optimality gap is 11% for H3 and 13.7% for H2.

Table 3. Average performance on the 20 two-hour traffic instances.

	H2	H3	Lower bound
Average Passenger Travel Time (sec)	1810.7	1767.1	1591.9
Computation time (sec)	18.9	68.7	11.1

6   Conclusions and Future Research

This paper integrates train scheduling and delay management visions into an MDM model to control railway traffic in real-time with the objective of minimizing passenger travel time. Research on TS and DM in the recent years has been very active, even if this paper represents the first attempt to fully incorporate the passengers' point of view into a microscopic railway traffic rescheduling model.

The MDM problem is modelled as a MILP that can be solved to optimality by commercial solvers for small-size instances. A new lower bound provides good values within a short computation time also for the largest instances. Three heuristic procedures are developed, based on decomposing the problem into a train scheduling problem and a passenger routing problem. Two of the three heuristics are able to find near-optimal solutions also for large cases, for which the MDM approach fails to compute a feasible solution. The time to compute lower and upper bounds is quite limited, and compatible with real-time applications. Overall, computational experiments on a real-life network with a large set of OD pairs show that H3 is promising to increase railway customer satisfaction in response to real-time perturbations.

A more detailed analysis of the problem for a full-scale paper should investigate in depth the quality of the heuristics and the optimality gap for different configurations of passenger demand, network, train traffic and computation time. To this aim, more accurate lower bounds can be provided, based on other relaxations of the problem; or algorithmic speed up based on problem characteristics. Moreover, a study of longer time horizons and extended set of origin destination for passengers traveling in the network can help showing the value of the proposed heuristics for a realistic case.

There are moreover many directions open for future research. More efficient approaches are needed to control large networks in real time, with a large set of OD pairs, both in terms of lower and upper bounds. The lower bound proposed in this paper might be used within a heuristic or exact approach for computing good solutions within a short computation time. The MDM model could be enriched to take into account the finite capacity of each train and/or more sophisticated measures of the passenger discomfort. A further line of research concerns with the design of more sophisticated models for the passengers' behaviour: how are passengers going to react when a change to their preferred path is suggested? Are they going to stick to their (offline) decision or are they going to follow the real-time suggestion for alternative modes of connectivity? Approaches based on discrete choice theory might help to model these questions.

References

1. Cacchiani, V., Huisman, D., Kidd, M., Kroon, L., Toth, P., Veelenturf, L., Wagenaar, J.: An overview of recovery models and algorithms for real-time railway rescheduling. Transportation Research B **63**, 15–37 (2014)
2. Corman, F., D'Ariano, A., Pacciarelli, D., Pranzo, M.: Dispatching and coordination in multi-area railway traffic management. Computers and Operations Research **44**(1), 146–160 (2014)

3. Corman, F., D'Ariano, A., Hansen, I.A., Pacciarelli, D.: Optimal Multi-Class Rescheduling Of Railway Traffic. Journal of Rail Transport Planning and Management **1**(1), 14–24 (2011)
4. D'Ariano, A., Pacciarelli, D., Pranzo, M.: A Branch And Bound Algorithm For Scheduling Trains In A Railway Network. European Journal Of Operational Research **183**(2), 643–657 (2007)
5. Dollevoet, T., Huisman, D., Schmidt, M., Schöbel, A.: Delay Management With Rerouting Of Passengers. Transportation Science **46**(1), 74–89 (2012)
6. Dollevoet, T., Huisman, D., Kroon, L., Schmidt, M., Schöbel, A.: Delay Management including Capacities of Stations. Transportation Science (2014A, in press)
7. Dollevoet, T., Corman, F., D'Ariano, A., Huisman D.: An iterative optimization framework for delay management and train scheduling. Journal of Flexible Services and Manufacturing (2014B, in press). doi:10.1007/s10696-013-9187-2
8. Hansen, I.A., Pachl, J.: Railway timetabling and operations: analysis, modelling, optimization, simulation, performance evaluation. Eurailpress, Hamburg (2014)
9. Mannino, C., Mascis, A.: Optimal Real-Time Traffic Control In Metro Stations. Operations Research **57**(4), 1026–1039 (2009)
10. Mascis, A., Pacciarelli, D.: Job Shop Scheduling With Blocking And No-Wait Constraints. European Journal Of Operational Research **143**(3), 498–517 (2002)
11. Meng, L., Zhou, X.: Simultaneous train rerouting and rescheduling on an N-track network: A model reformulation with network-based cumulative flow variables. Transportation Research B **67**, 208–234 (2014)
12. Pellegrini, P., Marlière, G., Rodriguez, J.: Optimal train routing and scheduling for managing traffic perturbations in complex junctions. Transportation Research Part B: Methodological **59**, 58–80 (2014)
13. Sato, K., Tamura, K., Tomii, N.: A MIP-based timetable rescheduling formulation and algorithm minimizing further inconvenience to passengers. Journal of Rail Transport Planning Management **3**(3), 38–53 (2013)
14. Schachtebeck, M., Schoebel, A.: To Wait or Not to Wait—And Who Goes First? Delay Management with Priority Decisions. Transportation Science **44**(3), 307–321 (2010)
15. Schöbel, A.: A model for the delay management problem based on mixed-integer programming. In: Proceedings of the 1st Workshop on Algorithmic Methods and Models for Optimization of Railways, Crete, Greece. Electronic Notes in Theoretical Computer Science, vol. 50(1), pp. 1–10 (2001)
16. Törnquist Krasemann, J.: Design Of An Effective Algorithm For Fast Response To The Re-Scheduling Of Railway Traffic During Disturbances. Transportation Research C **20**, 62–78 (2011)
17. Wardman, M.: Public transport values of time. Transport Policy **11**, 363–377 (2004)

Design of an Efficient Algorithm to Determine a Near-Optimal Location of Parking Areas for Dangerous Goods in the European Road Transport Network

María D. Caro, Eugenio M. Fedriani, and Ángel F. Tenorio[✉]

Department of Economics, Quantitative Methods and Economic History,
Pablo de Olavide University, Ctra. Utrera Km 1, 41013 Seville, Spain
{mdcarvel,efedmar,aftenorio}@upo.es

Abstract. This paper deals with the problem of locating the minimal number of parking areas being necessary for dangerous goods in the European Road Transport Network. To obtain a near-optimal solution for this problem, we introduce the design of a new graph-based algorithm to locate parking areas in such a way that drivers can obey the regulations related to driving and resting times. This restriction is imposed to the problem as follows: each point in the European Road Transport Network has to be at a distance lower than 200 km from a parking area in the Network.

Keywords: Efficient algorithm · Near-optimal solution · Dangerous goods · Parking areas · European Road Transport Network

1 Introduction

In the European Union, drivers of vehicles transporting dangerous goods must satisfy several legal restrictions and stipulations about parking. Their conditions can be summarized as follows: these vehicles must remain separated from other road users and they must be permanently supervised by security personnel [15]. In addition, lorry drivers must strictly obey other regulations about stops according to parameters of resting and driving times. Indeed, these goods must be delivered through the European Road Transport Network.

Unfortunately, the infrastructure of parking areas adapted for vehicles transporting dangerous goods is not sufficient to allow drivers to observe the regulations. Moreover, there are no studies about how many locations must be considered to assure the correct and safe stops for this kind of transportation; in fact, best locations for this type of parking areas have not been determined yet to build as few as possible. Only some attempts have been performed in particular countries (e.g. Berbeglia et al. [2]) but nobody has considered the global problem for the whole European Union and its European Road Transport Network [5] to date.

© Springer International Publishing Switzerland 2015
F. Corman et al. (Eds.): ICCL 2015, LNCS 9335, pp. 617–626, 2015.
DOI: 10.1007/978-3-319-24264-4_42

According to the current European legislation [4], drivers of heavy vehicles transporting goods must keep rest stops along the route. More specifically, they must take breaks of at least 45 minutes (decomposable into one of 15 minutes followed by another of 30 minutes) after passing four and a half hours from the last break, using appropriate places that assures the regulations of the European Union and each country member with respect to security for the load and the population.

The goal of this paper is to provide an efficient graph-based algorithm to obtain a near-optimal solution of the problem of locating additional parking areas adapted for transportation of dangerous goods throughout the European Road Transport Network. This is carried out by providing a set of locations (being minimal in number or as near as possible to this amount) where new adapted parking areas must be built to assure the correct compliance of regulations about parking. In short, we are designing a minimal-cost connected network with maximal distance of 400 km between nodes (and, more concretely, of 200 km between a point in the network and a node of a particular type) by addition of new nodes to a given (weighted) network.

Let us note that the already-existing literature includes many paper about location [1,7,12], parking areas [13,14] and dangerous goods [16,8,3] but, to the authors' knowledge, the location of parking areas for dangerous goods has not been studied looking for the number of these areas being necessary to cover all the European Road Transport Network in such a way that lorry drivers can comply the legal restrictions about resting and driving times. Our proposal is not limited to decide how many additional parking areas are needed and where they should be built, but we are also modeling the problem using graph theory in order to obtain the above-mentioned algorithm to obtain efficient near-optimal solutions for the problem considered in this paper.

2 Modeling the Problem

We have modeled the problem by using a graph-theory approach. The reader can consult [9] for a general overview on graphs. Our model consists in defining an undirected weighted graph G, placing nodes in the following points of the Transport Network:

1. existing parking areas (first-type nodes);

2. loading-and-unloading areas (second-type nodes);

3. road intersections (second-type nodes).

We distinguish between nodes (for example, with a graph coloration) in order to indicate which of them correspond to locations of parking areas (fist-type nodes). Besides, in the model, edges represent the road section between two nodes, considering its distance (in km) as a weight. Since the network only consists of highways and other double-way roads, we can omit the edge orientation.

This is just a preliminary approach to the problem, since the above-mentioned regulations refer to time instead of length. However, the algorithm can be easily adapted to consider time, with only changing the input data set and the unit of measure.

In addition, this model allows us to add progressively new nodes when imposing additional restrictions to make the model more complex (e.g. regulations on tunnels –and their schedule to use them– would involve more nodes in the graph).

Since our problem consists in minimizing the number of additional parking which should be built being adapted for dangerous goods, this must be translated into the following graph problem: design a minimal-cost connected network by addition of new first-type nodes to the original network in such a way that every point (not necessarily a node) in the final network has a maximal distance of 200 km from some first-type node. Let us note two considerations: First, the meaning of 'minimal-cost' in this case is referring to the number of additional nodes (representing parking areas) which have to be added to the original network to provide sufficient coverage to the complete network. Secondly, the final network only differs from the original network in the additional nodes being inserted and in the new edges resulting from the subdivision of the already-existing edges when adding the additional nodes.

All the information needed to generate our graph G comes from two databases: TRANS-TOOLS (source about the European Road Transport Network [10]) and TRANSPark (including all the parking areas in the European Union [11]). To define the nodes representing parking areas and how to add others, we have considered two regulations: Core network corridors on TEN-T [5] and Regulation EC 1315/2013 (European Commission [6]) and the European Agreement concerning the International Carriage of Dangerous Goods by Road (United Nations [15]).

To manage the huge amount of data to obtain the location of parking areas to be built, we need to automate all the computations by means of algorithms implemented and/or run in the appropriate software. For information processing and overlapping, we are using ArcGIS 10.0; whereas data processing to obtain a near-optimal solution will be carried out with an efficient algorithm designed to be implemented with Mathematica 9. The latter is the goal of the following step, returning a (near-)minimal location set of new parking areas for dangerous goods starting from those already available.

When we are indicating that we want to give an efficient algorithm, we are referring to the fact that the algorithm works correctly and the computations are carried out with as little time as possible and the solution provided by the algorithm as output satisfies the properties required when designing the problem.

3   Designing the Algorithm

As we have commented above, we want to design an algorithm which allows us to obtain a near-optimal solution for the problem of minimizing the number of new parking areas to be built being adapted for dangerous goods. To do so, we have assumed that the distance between two consecutive parking areas consists of 400 kilometers (which is the distance estimated after traveling four hours and a half). This assumption provides a solution for the following problem: each point of the European Road Transport Network is at a distance lower than 200 km from a parking area adapted for transportation of dangerous goods. In this sense, we have designed the following algorithm to solve this problem:

Algorithm:

Input: Map of the European Road Transport Network with the locations of already existing parking areas, loading-and-unloading areas, and road intersections.

Step 1: Translate locations into nodes (first-type for parking areas and second-type otherwise) and translate each section of road between two locations as an edge whose weight equals its length, in kilometers.

Step 2: Insert additional first-type nodes to represent one parking area in each harbor (or loading-and-unloading area with relevance in transportation of dangerous goods).

Step 3: Insert a second-type node for each endpoint of an edge.

Step 4: Determine the points on the edges (i.e. roads) within a distance of 200 km from the already-existing first-type nodes (including harbors, previously considered); and delete all those points from the graph.

Step 5: Insert a second-type node for each endpoint of an edge.

Step 6: Compute the connected components of the graph (from this step on, the algorithm runs in parallel over each connected component).

Step 7: For each connected component, determine those nodes with maximal eccentricity (i.e. maximal distance from the graph center).

Step 8: Detect if the connected component contains any cycle.

Step 9.1: If there are no cycles in the component, select one of the most eccentric nodes (from Step 7) and fix a new fist-type node 200 km away from this eccentric node (in the only way to the graph center).

Step 9.2: If there are cycles in the component, select the furthest point from the center in the graph (not necessarily a node), and fix a new second-type node at this point. Next, fix a new fist-type node 200 km away from this eccentric node (in one of the shortest ways to the graph center).

Step 10: Go back to Step 4.

Output: List with all the first-type nodes representing locations of new parking areas.

In order to illustrate how our algorithm works, we explain the above-mentioned steps when applying them to a graph modeling a road network. More specifically, we can consider the road network shown in Figure 1, where there are two harbors and one parking area adapted for dangerous goods. Let us note that the value assigned to each road corresponds to its distance (in km).

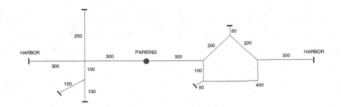

Fig. 1. Example of road network to apply our algorithm.

Next, we model the road network as a (weighted) graph applying Steps 1 to 3 of our algorithm. By using Step 1, the location for the parking area is represented as a first-type node and is marked as a round node. On the contrary, the locations for intersection roads are represented by second-type nodes, which have been marked as triangular nodes. From here on, the road sections between nodes are modeled as weighted edges between nodes and the distance (in km) of each road section is saved as the weight of its associated edge. See Figure 2.

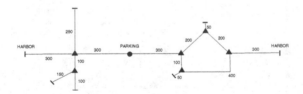

Fig. 2. Road network after applying Step 1.

When applying Step 2, we must insert first-type (i.e. round) nodes in each location assigned to harbors. Analogously, we must insert second-type (i.e. triangular) nodes to the road ends in Figure 2. After applying this step, we have obtained the graph-based model for the road network under study, which is illustrated in Figure 3.

To apply Step 5, we need to consider the three fist-type nodes (those representing the harbors and the parking area). Starting from each of them, we have computed a distance of 200 (km) from each of them on the edges. In Figure 4, we have marked with squares the points (not necessarily nodes) indicating such

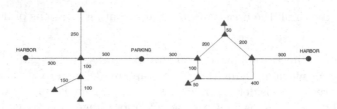

Fig. 3. Graph modeling road network after applying Steps 2 and 3.

distances in the graph. Next, we have deleted all the points on the graph between each first-type node and the squares coming from this. The resulting graph is shown in Figure 5, where Step 5 has been applied by inserting second-type nodes in the endpoints (those marked as squares).

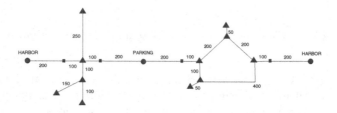

Fig. 4. Marking points at distance of 200 from some first-type node.

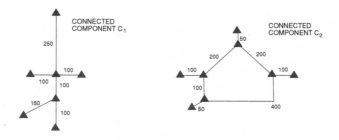

Fig. 5. Graph (with 2 connected components) resulting from applying Steps 4 and 5.

As can be observed in Figure 5, the new graph consists of two connected components (Step 6) in each of which we must run the next steps of our algorithm. To apply Step 7, we need to find the graph center for each connected component. Let us recall that the center of a connected graph G is the set of all the nodes v of G such that the greatest distance $d(v, w)$ to other nodes w of G is minimal; i.e. those nodes being solution of the optimization problem

$$\min_{v} \max_{w \neq v} d(v, w),$$

where the definition of distance $d(v, w)$ between two nodes v and w of G is given by the minimal weight for paths between v and w. For the connected component C_1 in our example, the distance is determined by the only path between two nodes because C_1 is a tree. However, when considering the connected component C_2, there may exist more than one path between two nodes and we must choose that of minimal weight to determine the distance between such nodes. Figure 6 shows the center of C_1 and of C_2.

Since Step 7 requires the nodes having maximal distance from the center for each connected component, we only need to check the distance from the center to the rest of nodes in its connected component. In the connected component C_1, the maximal distance from the center is 250, which correspond to two nodes. Analogously, in the connected component C_2, this maximal distance is 350 and there exists a unique node at this distance. In Figure 6, we have marked the above-mentioned nodes of maximal distance from the center of their corresponding connected component.

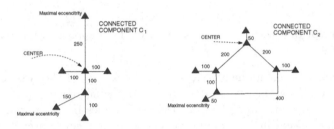

Fig. 6. Centers and most eccentric nodes (Step 7).

Next, our algorithm works in a different way for each connected component in our example. This is due to the test carried out in Step 8. Whereas the connected component C_1 is a tree and does not contain cycles, there exists a cycle in the connected component C_2. Hence, we must apply Step 9.1 to C_1 and Step 9.2 to C_2. Consequently, for C_1, we choose one of the most eccentric nodes in Figure 6 and then we must insert a new first-type node (i.e. a new parking area) at a distance of 200 (km) from that eccentric node (see Figure 7). Due to the existence of cycles in C_2, we must find the furthest point from the center in C_2. Taking into account which is the most eccentric node of C_2, it is trivial to check that the furthest points are on the edge of weight 400 and they are at a distance of 400 from the center. We have inserted a second-type node on one of these points in Figure 7 and then we have inserted a new first-type node at a distance of 200 from it using the shortest path to the center.

Now we must apply Step 10 which involves going back to Step 4 and deleting all the points at a distance less than 200 from the first-type nodes which have been previously computed. The result of this deletion, applying Steps 4 and 5 again, is shown in Figure 8, consisting of two connected components (one from C_1 and another from C_2).

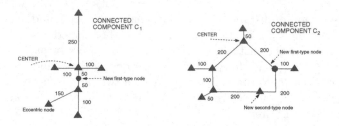

Fig. 7. Applying Step 9 to obtain two new first-type nodes.

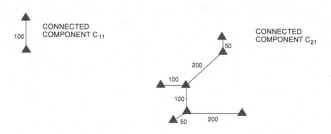

Fig. 8. Connected components resulting from applying Step 10.

In the connected component C_{11}, we can choose any of the two nodes as one of first-type, deleting the other. Regarding the connected component C_{21}, we must compute its center and the most eccentric nodes in order to insert a new first-type node taking into account that C_{21} does not contain cycles. Figure 9 shows the computations carried out by our algorithm at this stage.

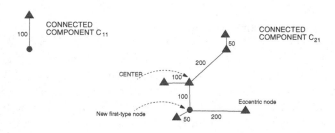

Fig. 9. Running again Steps 4 to 9.

Once this is done, we must go back to Step 4 and perform the last iteration with the unique connected component resulting from the deletion of the first-type nodes obtained in the previous iteration. See Figure 10 to observe the component (which is a tree) and the new nodes to be inserted.

In summary, our algorithm has obtained a set of five locations to build new parking areas adapted for dangerous goods in order to cover the whole road network used in our example. The near-optimal solution given by our algorithm corresponds to that shown in Figure 11.

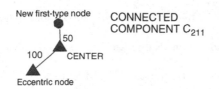

Fig. 10. The last iteration.

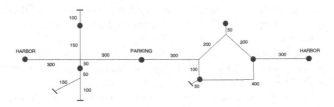

Fig. 11. A near-optimal solution for our example of road network.

4   Conclusion

The previous algorithm provides a general solution for the design of parking areas for dangerous goods over the whole European Union. However, some aspects of the real problem have been simplified. We have assumed that a lorry can always reach the next parking area (400 kilometers ahead) independently from the road conditions or any other circumstances. Even more, we force the drivers to make long stops instead of shorter ones (according to the Regulation EC 561/2006), to be able to drive 400 kilometers without stopping. Obviously,although our algorithm provides a valid solution, our model would be more realistic (and consequently more complicated and with a higher complexity in its solution) if we consider time instead of distance, and different conditions of traffic and resting times.

Acknowledgments. The authors would like to thank the ERDF of European Union for financial support via project "Localización de áreas de estacionamiento para mercancías peligrosas en Andalucía y la Red Transeuropea" of the "Programa Operativo FEDER de Andalucía 2007-2013". We also thank to Public Works Agency and Regional Ministry of Public Works and Housing of the Regional Government of Andalusia.

References

1. Brandeau, M.L., Chiu, S.S.: An Overview of Representative Problems in Location Research. Management Science **35**, 645–674 (1989)
2. Berbeglia, G., Cordeau, J., Laporte, G.: Dynamic pickup and delivery problems. European J. Oper. Res. **202**, 8–15 (2010)
3. Caro-Vela, M.D., Paralera, C., Contreras, I.: A DEA-inspired approach to selecting parking areas for dangerous-goods trucks. Eur. J. Transp. Infrast. Res. **13**, 184–195 (2013)

4. European Commission: Regulation EC 561/2006 about driving time and rest periods (2006)
5. European Commission: Trans-European Transport Network: TEN-T Core Network Corridors (2013)
6. European Commission: Regulation EC 1315/2013 on Union guidelines for the developtment of the trans-European transport network (2013)
7. Farahani, R.Z., SteadieSeifi, M., Asgari, N.: Multiple criteria facility location problems: A survey. Applied Mathematical Modelling **34**, 1689–1709 (2010)
8. Gusik, V., Klumpp, M., Westphal, C.: International comparison of dangerous goods transport and training schemes. Ild Schriftenreihe Logistikforschung, No. 23. Leibniz Information Centre for Economics (2012)
9. Harary, F.: Graph Theory. Addison-Wesley, Massachusetts (1969)
10. Institute for Prospective Technological Studies and DG Tren: TRANSTOOLS v2.5. Joint Research Centre of European Comission (2010)
11. International Road Transport Union and International Transport Forum: TRANSPark database (2013)
12. Prodhon, C., Prins, C.: A survey of recent research on location-routing problems. European J. Oper. Res. **238**, 1–17 (2014)
13. Robert, M., Drago, P.: Applicability of information technologies in parking area capacity optimization. Interdisc. Manag. Res. **6**, 143–151 (2010)
14. Rodier, C.J., Shaheen, S.: Commercial Vehicle Parking in California: Exploratory Evaluation of the Problem and Possible Technology-Based Solutions. Institute of Transportation Studies, Working Paper Series UCD-ITS-RR-07-36. University of California, Davis (2007)
15. UNECE: European agreement concerning the international carriage of dangerous goods by road (ADR). ECE/TRANS/225 vol. I and II, United Nations Economic Commission for Europe (2012) (applicable as from 1 January 2013)
16. Verma, M., Verter, V.: A lead-time based approach for planning railtruk intermodal transportation of dangerous goods. European J. Oper. Res. **202**, 696–706 (2010)

Capacity Analysis of Freight Transport with Application to the Danish and Southern Swedish Railway

L. Blander Reinhardt[✉], S. Nordholm, and D. Pisinger

Technical University of Denmark, Lyngby, Denmark
lbre@dtu.dk
http://www.dtu.dk

Abstract. A model for capacity analysis of freight transport with a time aspect is presented and applied. The model involves the analysis of the impacts of investments in possible new connections. In this capacity analysis we combine the knowledge of origin and destination of the demand with business knowledge of desired departure and arrival times. The model for the analysis is an integer multi-commodity flow model. From the output of this model congested track segments are found together with the time of week the congestion occurs. To illustrate the application of the model a capacity analysis of the railways in Denmark and Southern Sweden based on forecasts of the transportation flow in 2030 is presented.

1 Introduction

Electrified trains are a green form of transportation when using hydro and wind energy sources. Using trains for containerized freight is an environmentally friendly alternative to trucks and vessels. Therefore to reduce pollution and CO_2 emission taxes and fees are placed to move goods from other transport forms such as truck and ship to the railway. When introducing such policies it is important to ensure that the railway can in fact accommodate the swift in transport modes. In this paper we present an analysis of the capacity of the network under different policy assumptions. When analyzing the capacity of a railway segment with respect to estimated future demands the origins and destinations outside the segment are often not considered. In this paper we include the knowledge of origin and destination of the demand with general business knowledge of desired departure and arriving times of the demand. For this type of capacity analysis we have applied techniques developed for track allocation.

The aim of this project is to develop a model for analyzing the capacity of the links of the network over the duration of a week when provided with amount, origin and destination for forecasted future demands in different scenarios. When evaluating the network without considering time and cost the capacity of the

The project was partly funded by the EU-project EWTC-II.

F. Corman et al. (Eds.): ICCL 2015, LNCS 9335, pp. 627–647, 2015.
DOI: 10.1007/978-3-319-24264-4_43

network may appear as sufficient although a more detailed analysis will show that some time periods are saturated. For instance if there is no need for trains between 2:00 and 5:00 then the capacity available at that time cannot be used to satisfy the demand at other time windows. This is a major concern when it comes to passenger trains; however, with freight trains the time of the transportation is less important. Even though freight trains do not have as extensive time restrictions as passenger trains, there are time constraints which apply to the freight trains. The constraints can be working hours for loading and unloading at the departure and the arrival terminal, the cost of operating a train and the working hours of the operators. Moreover a somewhat even weekly distribution of the arrivals from a specific location is generally desired.

As previously mentioned a desired time window is considered for the departure and the arrival of the train. A general forecast based on market knowledge is used to set a departure time window and an arrival time window. These time windows are soft with an associated penalty for breaking them. However, a hard time window encapsulates these soft time windows. The hard time window does not allow for delays exceeding a given threshold. It is required that the train travel through the network without waiting at intermediate stations because of capacity issues, moreover the trains between a given origin and destination must have a somewhat even distribution during the week. Using these requirements it is possible to evaluate the utilization of the network at different times.

In the problem studied the cost of the train journey is only relevant when prioritizing the paths, to minimize delays when selecting departure times and in cases where trains must be canceled. Therefore only direct costs are included and socio-economic costs covered in [18] are not considered. It is assumed that it is always more profitable to route a train than to cancel it. This means that only capacity limitations can result in canceled trains, however, the canceled trains will by the model be selected so that the most expensive train on the capacity exceeded link is canceled. Thus trains will only be canceled due to lack of capacity in the acceptable time period.

The paper is organized as follows. In the following section a short literature review is presented and afterwards in Section 3 the time expanded network is described and a mathematical model using this representation is presented in Section 4 and 5. In Section 6 we discuss the forecast transportation demands and how these demands are converted to train schedules with specific time demands. Section 7 describes the train network of the case Denmark and Southern Sweden and future expansions of the network are discussed. Finally, Section 8 presents the optimal results for routing the trains through the network based on various scenarios. The paper is concluded in Section 9 with a short summary of the found results.

2   Literature Review

Exact methods using combinatorics has not been applied to the problem even though it has been extensively applied to the similar track allocation problem.

The modeling of rail transportation can be regarded as a network where the nodes are stations and the links are lines of track. An early survey by Assad [5] from 1980 on rail transport modeling includes aspects concerning yard queueing and simulation of passenger transports. However, these aspects are not relevant here. A more recent extensive review published in 1998 by Cordeau et al. [10] shows that since 1980 the research in the area of train transportation increased significantly and several details and aspects of the routing and scheduling problem of rail transport were considered.

Caprara et al. [9] investigated the configuration of trains and their routes on a railway corridor. This was done in connection with the European Union REORIENT project (2004-2007) where a railway corridor connecting southern and northern Europe through eastern Europe is analyzed. In [9] the capacity in the form of the number of trains is predetermined on the route and the assignment of demand to trains is optimized with respect to the demand travel time and travel cost. When demand is routed on a capacitated network a form of capacity analysis is performed. Given a demand Caprara et al. considers how to compose the trains and how to route them on a provided network so that overall cost is minimized. In the problem presented in this paper the composition of trains is not considered as the problem is not viewed from the operators perspective and therefore the composition of trains is not part of the study presented here. However the minimum cost of the routes is still considered so that the owner is able to offer attractive routes to the operators.

Burdett and Kozan [8] develop a model for very detailed capacity analysis where the speed of the individual trains and possible headway is determined. This method is relevant for capacity analysis of a current network and for a very near future situation. However when making changes to the network one often plan more than 10 years ahead, and in these situations the speed and mix of trains and head times are uncertain.

In this project the goal is to find routes for the generated trains so that the forecasted demand is satisfied with respect to an arrival and a departure time window and capacity while minimizing cost. The cost includes a fixed track charge, an infrastructure tax per kilometer and a delay cost. This is similar to the method used by Borndörfer et al. [7] and Schlechte et al. [15] for macroscopic case of the track allocation problem. However here we do not consider different train types as we were not provided information on trains and their type from the forecast. The problem in the project is a simplification of the problem described by Zhu et al. [21]. In the mentioned paper blocking and service selection is combined using a heuristic method. Here we only consider a service selection and solve it using an exact method. In [3] Andersen and Christiansen design new European north south rail freight services through Poland using an exact method. The problem solved in [3] considers the routing of rolling material in more detail than covered in the model presented here and is solved for very small instances containing at most 20 services. Andersen et al. [4] study the design of rail services in an intermodal network with the aim of reducing transhipment times. Jarrah et al. [12] consider a large-scale less-than truckload service network design. In this problem the objective is to determine a planned origin - destination paths for all anticipated freight while minimizing overall transportation and other ancillary costs. The problem can be formulated as a capacitated multi-commodity fixed-charge network design problem (CMND). Lium et al. [13] study a service network design problem taking into account demand stochasticity. They show that solutions based on an uncertain demand can differ significantly from solutions based on a deterministic demand. Although we do not explicitly study the design of a railway network, the results in [13] indicate that stochasticity should be taken into account when modeling network flow. However, we do not at present have information about the stochastic distribution of demands and travel times. For a thorough review of tactical planning problems in the literature related to long-distance freight distribution we refer the reader to the review by Wieberneit [20].

The problem solved in this paper is based on a variant of the integer multi-commodity flow problem. The integer multi-commodity flow problem is known to be NP-hard on a directed graph, as shown by Even [11].

Capacity analysis is usually performed using more detailed information about the network and equipment such as signal systems, train speeds and so forth. However when looking at forecasts more than 10 years in the future under different policies these details are no longer available and cannot be forecasted to the detail used in the cited articles.

Therefore a reduced version of the track allocation path based model produced by Borndörfer et al. [7] and Schlechte et al. [15] is used. Due to the amount of detail considered by Borndörfer and Schlechte hours are used for solving the problems. However in real-life applications hours of calculation time is often considered undesirable as long running times requires a very thorough preparation of input data and therefore a capacity analysis may take several months to perform which is too long in the political decision process and thus possibilities of useful expansions to the current network maybe lost. We here present a very simple capacity analysis which can help find and solve capacity problems for future demand levels. The development of the problem and model has been done in close cooperation with the Danish traffic authority and has been applied to a real-life case. This model can be used for comparison between different extensions to a network with the goal of ensuring good service under a future demand level.

3   Time-Expanded Network

The capacity of a track segment is measured in trains per hour, thus we have chosen to represent the network as a time-expanded network with a node per terminal or connection point representing each hour. Since we are looking at a time period of one week there will for each station be $24 \cdot 7 = 168$ vertices in the time-expanded graph. A connection in the original network between two nodes i and j will in the time-expanded network be represented by an edge for each time-expanded node of station i to the corresponding time-expanded node of station j representing a direct connection. The corresponding time-expanded node of station j is the first node which is larger than or equal to the time of the time-expanded node at i plus the travel time needed to reach j. It should be noted that due to the fact that it is not desirable to allow the trains to wait at intermediate stations on their journey, only timewise direct connections are represented in the time-expanded network. Therefore a time-expanded node i_t has the same number of incoming edges and outgoing edges as the station i in the original network.

4 Modeling the Problem

In this section we will describe the model applied to the problem. In the model each demand corresponds to a train between a specific origin and destination and with a specified time window. This capacity model has been developed in cooperation with the traffic authorities [17] and the model is therefore in accordance with actual practices of a traffic authority. The goal is to maximize the number of trains scheduled and to minimize the total delay. For a demand let O and D be the origin and destination respectively.

Constraints to be Considered

- A train must be routed continuously through the links.
- The arrival and departure may create a penalty if a time window is violated
- Capacity on the links must not be exceeded
- For each train going from O to D there must be a train going from D to O. This is to ensure the return of the rolling stock.

An edge based model is presented in Section 5.1. In the edge based model the number of variables corresponds to the number of combinations of trains and edges. However since the number of edges in the time-expanded graph corresponds to 168 time-expanded links for each link in the original graph, the number of variables can amount to several millions for even small networks with a heavy load of freight trains. This many variables can be a problem for even state-of-the-art solvers. Moreover this model may construct routes which are unacceptable for the operators. Such routes could be routes which travel for parts in the opposite direction of the destination to ensure arrival at links when capacity is available.

To be able to solve the test illustration in Section 8 we also develop a path based model, which is presented in Section 5.2. In the path based model each origin destination pair has a set of possible paths. The acceptable paths for the trains through the network are provided by the operators and the time-dependent paths are generated in the program. Using this method we ensure that only acceptable paths are generated; however, we also limit our selves to the operator's knowledge of paths. The number of time-dependent paths corresponds to the number of variables in the IP problem. As explained in Section 8, the running time is mostly spent setting up the model while only a few seconds were

used on solving the model. Therefore, the model is likely to scale well for even
larger problems than the real-life scenario presented. When capacity analysis is
done the rail network which is subject to the capacity analysis is often a subset of
a larger network. To accommodate this we define terminals or stations as entry
points to the evaluated network. This means that a routed train has both an O,
D pair and entry exit point pair. The point where a train enters the considered
subset is denoted by S and the point where the train exits the subset by E. Note
that before a train is routed there may be several possible points at which the
train can enter or exit the subset. To avoid creating impossible conditions for
the network connecting to the subnetwork we suggest defining a demand by its
origin, destination and entry, exit point to the capacity analyzed subnetwork.

5   Integer Programming Model

The problem of routing a number of trains on capacitated links is an integer
multi-commodity flow problem. The integer multi-commodity flow problem is
known to be NP-hard on a directed graph, as shown by Even [11]. Therefore several decomposition methods have been developed for the integer multi-
commodity flow problem (see [6] and [2]). Although Barnhart et al. [6] show
Cplex 3.0 to be inferior to their branch-cut-and-price algorithm, Alvelos and
Carvalho [2] showed that in 2003 Cplex 7.5 was already competitive with several Branch-and-price algorithms for small instances. One of the main problems
with both the polynomially solvable splitable multi-commodity flow problem and
the unsplitable multi-commodity flow problem is the number of variables in the
formulation as shall be discussed later.

For the model we define the following sets:

N The set of nodes
E The set of connections in the time-expanded graph
O The set of demands where each demand is calculated for each O-D pair. Each $k \in$ **O**
    represent a single train.
Sr^k The time-expanded set of the origin terminal of demand $k \in$ **O**. Thus containing
    the feasible time-expanded origin nodes.
Sk^k The time-expanded set of the destination terminal of demand $k \in$ **O**. Thus con-
    taining the feasible time-expanded destination nodes.
O_{od} The set of trains with the same origin station o and destination station d.

In the model we use the following parameters

q_{ij} The capacity per hour on a link $e \in$ **E**.
a_p^k The start time for the soft time window for departure of demand k
b_d^k The end time for the soft time window for arrival of demand k
pd^+ Penalty for departure before a_p^k
pa^+ Penalty for arrival after b_d^k
c_{ij}^k The cost of demand $k \in$ **O** traveling on connection ij where the penalty for late
    arrival is also introduced for each demand on the connections from the departing
    station and to the arrival station.
P^k Penalty for not routing demand $k \in$ **O**

5.1 Edge Model

Using the definition described in Section 5 the edge variable model can be formulated by using the variable $x^k_{i_t j_{t'}}$, which is 1 if demand k is transported on a direct connection between i_t and $j_{t'}$ and 0 otherwise. Here t is the time at station i and t' is the time at j. The variable h^k is 1 if demand k is routed and 0 other wise. Let t_{ij} be the travel time on connection i, j and t_i be the time of node i in the time-expanded graph.

$$\text{Min: } \sum_{k \in O} \left(P^k h^k + \sum_{i_t \in N} \sum_{j_{t'} \in N} c^k_{i_t j_{t'}} x^k_{i_t j_{t'}} \right) \tag{1}$$

s.t.

$$\sum_{j \in N} x^k_{ji} = \sum_{j \in N} x^k_{ij} \qquad \forall k \in O, \forall i \in N \setminus \{Sr^k \cup Sk^k\} \tag{2}$$

$$\sum_{j \in N} \sum_{i \in Sr^k} x^k_{ij} - \sum_{j \in N} \sum_{i \in Sk^k} x^k_{ji} = 0 \qquad \forall k \in O \tag{3}$$

$$\sum_{j \in N} \sum_{i \in Sk^k} x^k_{ij} \leq 1 \qquad \forall k \in O \tag{4}$$

$$\sum_{j \in N} \sum_{i \in Sr^k} x^k_{ji} \leq 1 \qquad \forall k \in O \tag{5}$$

$$\sum_{j \in N} \sum_{i \in Sk^k} t_i x^k_{ji} \leq 24 + b^k_d \qquad \forall k \in O \tag{6}$$

$$\sum_{k \in O} x^k_{ij} \leq q_{ij} \qquad \forall i, j \in N \tag{7}$$

$$\sum_{j \in N} \sum_{i \in Sr^k} x^k_{ij} + h^k \geq 1 \qquad \forall k \in O \tag{8}$$

$$\sum_{k \in O_{od}} h^k - \sum_{k \in O_{do}} h^k = 0 \qquad \forall O_{od} \in O \tag{9}$$

$$x^k_{ij} \in \{0, 1\} \qquad \forall i, j \in N, \forall k \in O \tag{10}$$

$$h^k \in \{0, 1\} \qquad \forall k \in O \tag{11}$$

Constraints (2) ensure that a train k entering a node will also leave the node unless the node is the origin or destination of the train. Constraints (3) ensure that a train k which departs also arrives. Constraints (4) and (5) ensure that a train journey leaves its start location and enters its end location at most once. Constraints (6) will prevent trains from arriving more than 24 hours late at the end location. The capacity constraints (7) ensure that the hourly capacity of the track is not exceeded. Constraints (8) introduce a penalty if a train is not scheduled. Finally, constraints (9) ensure that if a train k between o and d is unscheduled then a train in the opposite direction is also unscheduled. This is to ensure that all trains return. It should be noted that there are no variables x^k_{ij} where i and j are time expanded vertices of the same station. This model has $O(|K||E|)$ variables. In the case where $|E|$ contains several thousand edges due to the time-expanded graph a small increase in the number of commodities will increase the number of variables significantly. In the three real-life test instances tested in Section 8 there are between 900 and 2500 trains to be routed in both directions. Therefore there are more than 1 million variables in the instances. Clearly some of these variables can be removed using the time window restriction however the number of variables removed will only be a small portion of the entire set. Preliminary tests with variables removed using the time window restriction resulted in instances not solvable within several hours. Therefore a different approach for solving the problem was investigated. As mentioned earlier this edge based model may construct routes which are undesirable for the train operators.

5.2   Path Model

To solve the problem of many variables and to ensure that the routes constructed are acceptable for the operators, we have chosen to decompose the model. In the decomposition each train has a set of possible paths to choose from. The acceptable paths for the trains through the network is provided by the operators and for these paths time-dependent paths are enumerated in the subproblem. The goal is to maximize the number of trains scheduled and to minimize the total delay.

Master Problem: The master problem is the problem which selects a set of paths which will not exceed the capacity on the links in the time-expanded graph and which minimizes the cost for the cancelation penalty, the travel cost and the delay cost.

To select the paths we use the variable λ_{Pt}^k which indicates if path Pt is selected for demand k. The parameter α_{ij}^{Pt} is 1 if the connection between time-expanded nodes i and j in the time-expanded graph is part of the path Pt. The variable h^k is 1 if demand k is routed and 0 otherwise.

$$\textbf{Min:} \sum_{k \in \mathbf{O}} \left(P^k h^k + \sum_{Pt \in P(k)} \lambda_{Pt}^k c_{Pt}^k \right) \tag{12}$$

s.t.

$$\sum_{Pt \in P(k)} \sum_{k \in \mathbf{O}} \alpha_{ij}^{Pt} \lambda_{Pt}^k \leq q_{ij} \qquad \forall i, j \in \mathbf{N}, \forall k \in \mathbf{O} \tag{13}$$

$$\sum_{Pt \in P(k)} \lambda_{Pt}^k + h^k \geq 1 \qquad \forall k \in \mathbf{O} \tag{14}$$

$$\sum_{k \in O_{od}} h^k - \sum_{k \in O_{do}} h^k = 0 \qquad \forall O_{od} \in \mathbf{O} \tag{15}$$

$$\lambda_{Pt}^k \in \{0, 1\} \qquad \forall k \in \mathbf{O} \tag{16}$$

$$h^k \in \{0, 1\} \qquad \forall k \in \mathbf{O} \tag{17}$$

In the objective function (12) the cost c_{Pt}^k is the cost of the path Pt with respect to demand k. This also corresponds to the sum $\sum_{i,j \in \mathbf{N}} c_{ij}^k \alpha_{ij}^{Pt}$ for a path

$Pt \in P(k)$. The objective function (12) will clearly minimize the delay penalty on the departure through the cost c_{Pt}^k. By making the penalty P_k for not scheduling a train large enough we can ensure that trains are only unscheduled if no other option is possible. Note that this ensures that the number of unscheduled trains is minimized. Using the presented objective, trains which are more costly will be chosen as the ones to be unscheduled. This could be trains that travel far and therefore have a larger travel cost and/or have a large delay penalty. In this **Master problem** we have capacity constraints (13) to ensure that the capacity on the links is not exceeded. Constraints (14) correspond to the constraints (8) where it is ensured that if no path is used for a commodity then a penalty for not scheduling the train is paid. Finally the constraints (15) ensure that when a train is unscheduled, a train in the opposite direction is also unscheduled. This is to balance the rolling stock.

Enumeration of Paths: For each S-E pair a set of paths is defined in advance by a user with knowledge of which transportation paths are acceptable. This can in later versions be changed so that the acceptability of a path is calculated from the increase in cost using some threshold value. For each of the given paths, the program generates a path for each valid time period of start and end. In our case we look at hourly departures and a path will be created for each of those time intervals as long as they are valid according to the hard time window of the demand. The cost of the path is calculated with respect to the desired time window of the demand. As shown in Section 8 this results in fewer variables and a fast running time for solving the model.

6   The Freight Demands for the Danish and Southern Swedish Network Application

The model is used for analyzing the capacity of the Danish and Southern Swedish network. The data used for this analysis is from a flow analysis based on transportation forecasts [1] provided by Tetraplan [16]. These forecasts were generated using the program Trans-Tools [14].

The forecasts contain the freight in tons per year between 47 different zones in Europe. There is a forecast for the following three scenarios:

2010 Scenario. The amount of demand transported on rail in 2010.

2030 Base Scenario. The amount of demand estimated to be transported on rail in 2030 under the assumption that the policies are the same as those of 2010.

2030 Green Scenario. The amount of demand estimated to be transported on rail under the assumption of higher fees on CO_2 emission.

The demand estimates for the different scenarios was provided in an origin destination (O-D) matrix as well as maps showing the cargo flow transported through the Danish and Southern Swedish region. For each zone a terminal is

Fig. 1. The zones in Europe used for the O-D matrix.

selected and all cargo with origin or destination in a given zone, starts and ends at the selected terminal for that zone. Figure 1 shows a map of the zones in Europe.

From this we were able to extract the start and end terminals (S-E pair) in the Danish and Southern Swedish region for the flow through the region and also the amount of freight from each O-D pair going through the analyzed region. It should be noted that transport between an O-D pair may not go through the analyzed region. Moreover for an O-D pair some percentage of the cargo may be transported through the analyzed region while the rest may not, or the cargo may be split so that some enters the region at one point and some at another even though the origin and destination is the same.

The O-D matrix provided by Tetraplan [16] represents the volume in terms of tons. For each O-D S-E pair the number of trains needed to transport the forecast amount of cargo was calculated. It is assumed that the trains operate on a weekly schedule since the capacity of the tracks is scheduled with a weekly cycle. We have been informed by the Danish traffic authority [17] that a single weekly departure of a full train can transport between 22000 and 37000 tons freight per year. If less than 15000 tons is to be transported on an O-D S-E pair, then it would be better to relocate the cargo to other modes of transport or distribute it on existing trains instead of allocating a train for the small amount of freight. The 22000-37000 tons freight per year for a weekly departure presumes 52 week schedule per year however it does allow for one or two cancelations due to public holidays.

The weekly number of train departures ϕ between O-D entering and leaving the Danish and Southern Swedish region at the terminals S-E is thus calculated as follows:

$$\phi = \left\lfloor \frac{\sigma}{22000} \right\rfloor + \left(\left\lfloor \frac{\sigma - 22000 \lfloor \frac{\sigma}{22000} \rfloor}{15000} \right\rfloor \right) \tag{18}$$

Where σ is the amount of freight from O to D which enters and leaves the analyzed network for at the point SE. Here the amount which can be transported on a train per year with one weekly departure is 22000 tons.

Clearly, we do not know which days and times trains are to be scheduled in 2030 therefore we have used a distribution pattern which estimates how the weekly departures in practice are distributed. It is assumed for business purposes that a single train departure for an O-D S-E pair will depart on a Wednesday and so on as it is assumed that O-D S-E trains should be spread evenly as to minimize the time goods is stored at origin or destination. The trains are distributed somewhat evenly during the week according to the distribution pattern shown in Table 1 obtained from the Danish traffic authority [17]. The pattern will continue as shown for a higher number of weekly departures. Note that freight trains are not scheduled for departure during the weekends. Trains may travel during the weekends but are not scheduled for departure as the terminals are often partly shutdown for operations during the weekends. Usually the freight

Table 1. Distribution of train departures during a week. For instance if 3 trains are needed per week, then one train is scheduled for Monday, Wednesday and Friday.

Number of needed trains	Monday	Tuesday	Wednesday	Thursday	Friday	Saturday	Sunday
1			1				
2		1		1			
3	1		1		1		
4		1	1	1	1		
5	1	1	1	1	1		
6	1	1	2	1	1		
7	1	2	1	2	1		
8	2	1	2	1	2		
9	1	2	2	2	2		
10	2	2	2	2	2		
⋮	⋮	⋮	⋮	⋮	⋮	⋮	⋮

is loaded on the train during the afternoon and therefore the operators desire a departure for the train in the evening between 8 pm and 2 am. Moreover, since the freight is unloaded at the destinations during the morning hours it is desired that the train arrives between 10 pm and 6 am. For the departure it would be a problem if the train was scheduled to depart at 2 pm as it may not be possible to load the freight before departure. The same is the case for an arrival after 6 am as it may not be possible to unload the goods so they can arrive at the customers in due time. Therefore a penalty is associated with departing early and with arriving late. However, it is not possible to arrive more than 24 hours past the end time of the arrival time window nor to depart more than 24 hours before the start time of the departure as this would generate an unacceptable distribution of departures for the operators. This may result in the cancelation of trains even though there is available capacity on the links. A table with distance and time from the terminals of the zones in Figure 1 to the entrypoints of the modeled network shown in Figure 2 and 3 was provided by the Danish traffic authority [17]. Note that all freight to and from a specific zone will in our model start and end at the terminal. Therefore one must be careful when interpreting the results.

If an O-D pair has more than one departure on a day the second departure is scheduled for departure between 10 am and 4 pm and arrival between noon and 10 pm and a third departure would be scheduled with a desired departure between 6 am and noon and arrival between 8 am and 2 pm. For the 4th or more departure on a day for the same O-D S-E pair the departure time window is the entire day and the arrival time window is the entire day of estimated arrival.

Since rolling material return to their origin, the number of trains from O to D is to be the same as the number of trains from D to O. This means that the trains and cars may travel empty in one direction. Note that this does not mean that the number of trains in one direction on a specific link is the same as the number of trains in the other direction on that link. As seen later there are links where the numbers may vary. Moreover, for a single day the number of trains on a link may be very different in the two directions.

7   The Train Network of Denmark and Southern Sweden

On the rail network of Denmark and Southern Sweden, two different networks are studied: One representing the rails in 2010 and one representing the rails in 2030. These two networks are shown in Figure 2 and 3. The network in Figure 2 represents the network as it is today. The network in Figure 3 incorporates all projected expansions of the rail network. The new links are shown in red in Figure 3. The projected expansion of capacity (extra tracks) on existing links are not shown in Figure 3 but will be discussed later. The cargo starts and ends at the nodes defined as Terminals. The freight train may have an origin and destination outside the network and will in that case enter or leave the network at a terminal, also called an entrypoint.

The fixed link between **Helsingør** and **Helsingborg** was discussed when modeling the network. However to establishing this link one would also include need to establish a new connection from **Helsingør** to **Ringsted**. This link, if implemented, is not realistic to be completed by 2030. Hence, we have included a connection between **Helsingborg** and **Ringsted** in some of the tests of the 2030 network so that this alternative can be considered. The link is represented by an edge between Helsingborg and Ringsted.

The links have associated travel times and costs. The travel times has been made available by the Danish traffic authority [17]. The cost of traversing a link

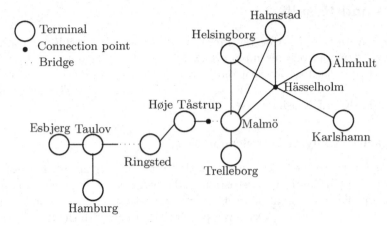

Fig. 2. Considered network year 2010

contains several expenses. In this model only very elementary costs are included as the cost function is used for the selection of path and departure time. The costs included in the model are estimates provided by the Danish traffic authority [17]. The costs are a capacity and bridge cost which is a fixed cost imposed on some links. Moreover estimates of infrastructure, locomotive and carriage charges are included in the cost of the links. All other costs are ignored as these are less important for the model since alternative transportation modes such as trucks and vessels are not considered.

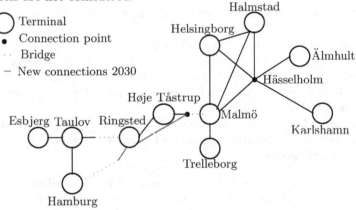

Fig. 3. Considered network year 2030

The costs estimates are given as parameters to the solver, and can easily be changed. For each link the capacity is given in the form of the number of freight trains that can pass per hour in each direction. These capacities are described in Section 8.

8   Tests and Results

In this section we will describe the input provided and the results of running the path based model on this input. It should be noted that the test results of the model are based on forecast data provided by Tetraplan [16] and hence are subject to the same uncertainty as the underlying data. The model was implemented in CPLEX using C++.

8.1   Capacity Analysis Test Scenarios

From Tetraplan three scenarios were provided representing an estimate of the past situation in 2010 and two forecasts for 2030 with a baseline scenario and a green scenario. For each scenario an O-D matrix with the tons of cargo transported between the O-D pairs was developed by Tetraplan with the use of Trans-Tools [14]. This matrix is the basis for our analysis. For each scenario, maps showing flow through a few selected arcs was delivered. Together with the Danish traffic authority [17] the specific flow through the network was estimated by combining the knowledge provided by the maps and the information in the O-D matrix. This resulted in an O-D S-E table from which a set of trains is created by converting the tonnage to trains, as described in Section 6. On the three data sets, one for each scenario, the capacity of the network is analyzed using the different capacity settings described later in this section.

2010: From the transportation given in tons in this scenario, 926 trains were created.

2030 Baseline: From the transportation given in tons in this scenario, 2246 trains were created.

2030 Green: From the transportation given in tons in this scenario, 2354 trains were created under the assumption of higher fees on CO_2 emission.

2030 Baseline SK: Is the 2030 Baseline where all freight with origin **Sundsvall** and destination **Karlshamn** is removed possibly assuming a direct link **Älmhult Karlshamn**.

2030 Green SK: Is the 2030 Green where all freight with origin **Sundsvall** and destination **Karlshamn** is removed possibly assuming a direct link **Älmhult Karlshamn**.

The last two data sets were developed to account for the possibility of transport between **Sundsvall** and **Karlshamn** using a track not represented in the model of the network or a origin or destination in **Blekinge** other than **Karlshamn** with a better connection.

The connections each have an associated capacity. The capacities are given per hour which allows the edges to be distributed in the time-expanded graph with one hour intervals. The capacities provided by the Danish and Swedish traffic authorities [17], [19] are shown in Figure 4. These capacities are also denoted **cap1**.

The model was used on the scenarios using the capacities from Figure 4. The capacities shown in Figure 4 are developed together with the Danish and Swedish

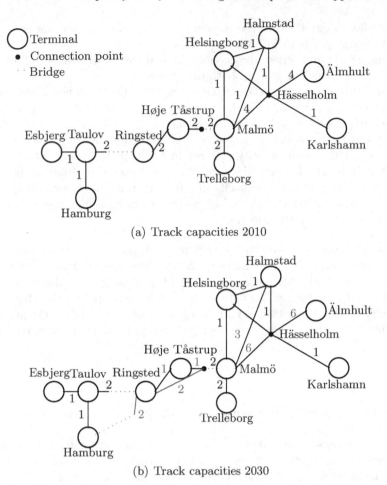

(a) Track capacities 2010

(b) Track capacities 2030

Fig. 4. The capacity as freight trains per hour on the individual track segments in 2010 and 2030

traffic authorities. From analyzing the results of these capacities, variations on the capacities were generated. These variations on capacities are based on political suggestions and public discussions of possible extensions to the network in the parts where a bottleneck could be relieved. The variations constructed so that they may help suggest to both traffic authorities and politicians where an investment would be beneficial. The variations are described using **cap1** (Figure 4 (a) and (b) for respectively 2010 and 2030) as the basis.

cap1: The capacities presented in Figure 4.
cap2: Similar to **cap1** where the capacity of Vigerslev Malmö link is set to 3 freight trains per hour in both directions
cap3: Similar to **cap1** where the capacity of Karlshamn Hässleholm link is set to 2 freight trains per hour in both directions

cap4: Similar to **cap1** where the capacity of Vigerslev Malmö link is set to 4 freight trains per hour in both directions

cap5: Similar to **cap1** where the capacity of Karlshamn Hässleholm link is set to 3 freight trains per hour in both directions

cap6: Similar to **cap1** where the capacity of Karlshamn Hässleholm link is set to 2 freight trains per hour in both directions and the capacity of the Vigerslev Malmö edge is set to 3 in both directions

HH: Similar to **cap1** where the capacity of Helsingborg Ringsted link over Helsingør is included with capacity of 2 freight trains per hour in both directions

HH2: Similar to **cap1** where the capacity of Helsingborg Ringsted link over Helsingør is included with capacity of 2 freight trains per hour in both directions and the connection **Hässleholm Helsingborg** is increased to 2 freight trains per hour in both directions.

For the 2010 scenario only the **cap1** is applied. All capacity sets are applied to the Baseline and Green scenario of 2030. Especially the capacity on the **Øresunds** connection has been discussed at meetings with different traffic authorities and therefore it is a natural area to investigate in this setting. The rail capacity on the connection to **Karlshamn** is interesting due to the projected increase in transport from the East possibly through the **Kleipeda Karlshamn** sea link.

8.2   Results

The model was applied to the three scenarios applying the different capacity sets described in Section 8.1.

For the scenarios tested 70 000 to 500 000 variables are generated using the model presented in Section 5.2, which is well within the limits of the standard solvers. The different scenarios are solved by the CPLEX solver in 5-15 minutes and the majority of the time is spent setting up the model. The CPLEX solver uses less than a minute on solving the resulting model.

The number of trains which was accepted on the network applying the individual capacity sets is reported in Table 2. In Table 3 the number of delayed trains and the number of minutes of delays are shown. Tables 4 and 5 show the total number of trains traversing a given link in each direction during a week for the generated schedule on respectively the 2010, Baseline 2030 and Green 2030 scenarios.

In Table 2 the number of routed trains are reported. The results **cap4** and **cap5** are the same as the results of respectively **cap2** and **cap3** and therefore to make the overview more simple they are not reported in the table. From the results in Table 2 we can see that a capacity increase on the **Karlshamn Hässelholm** connection increases the capacity of the network (see **cap3** (and **cap5**)). However, the model used may not correctly reflect the capacity to **Karlshamn** as we believe that the cargo from **Sundsvall** may take an alternative route to **Karlshamn** not included in the network. The developed model show that in 2030 the freight to and from **Hamburg** will use the **Femern** connection.

Table 2. The number of routed trains using the different capacity sets.

scenario	Number of trains	Trains routed in the considered network and capacity scenario					
		cap1	cap2	cap3	cap6	HH	HH2
2010	926	926	-	-	-	-	-
2030 Baseline	2246	1808	2078	1962	2244	2078	2078
2030 Baseline SK	1814	1530	1812	1530	1812	1812	1812
2030 Green	2354	1806	2042	2064	2322	2042	2042
2030 Green SK	1922	1632	1920	1632	1920	1920	1920

Table 3. The number of delayed trains and the total minutes of delays in the schedule.

scenario		Trains routed in the considered network and capacity scenarios					
		cap1	cap2	cap3	cap6	HH	HH2
2010	Number of trains delayed	242	-	-	-	-	-
	Total minutes of delay at origin	71394	-	-	-	-	-
	Total minutes of delay at destination	83382	-	-	-	-	-
2030 Baseline	Number of trains delayed	584	903	503	997	899	885
	Total minutes of delay at origin	21750	112271	18509	104037	96617	96803
	Total minutes of delay at destination	159244	261986	140583	325119	291344	289695
2030 Green	Number of trains delayed	707	922	758	1142	897	887
	Total minutes of delay at origin	18884	84275	28200	85542	60829	61015
	Total minutes of delay at destination	178478	223979	267387	385441	265074	263610
2030 Baseline SK	Number of trains delayed	409	703	413	705	678	676
	Total minutes of delay at origin	13272	99730	13752	99430	84263	83615
	Total minutes of delay at destination	130545	250933	130065	251233	262390	261646
2030 Green SK	Number of trains delayed	445	740	454	736	671	666
	Total minutes of delay at origin	10059	94804	9328	94733	61470	61236
	Total minutes delay of at destination	133053	255171	132771	254175	212036	210807

This can be seen in Tables 4 and 5. From Table 2 it is indicated that increasing the capacity on the **Øresunds** bridge from 2 to 3 trains per hour will provide capacity for many of the unscheduled trains (see **cap2**). However, when increasing this capacity to 4 trains per hour (**cap4**) no difference is recorded in the number of scheduled trains. This is probably due to the capacity on the links the trains can use to continue from **Vigerslev** sum to 3 trains per hour where the link to **Højo Tåstrup** has capacity of 1 train per hour and the link to **Ringsted** from **Vigerslev** has capacity of 2 trains per hour. When increasing both the capacity of the **Øresunds** bridge from 2 to 3 trains per hour and the **Karlshamn Hässelholm** connection from 1 to 2 trains per hour all trains are scheduled with our model (except for one train between Sundsvall and Athens). For the usage of the link between **Malmö** and **Vigerslev** availability spots are present in the Excel sheets[1] described earlier for **cap2** and **cap6**, whereas for **cap1** there is no unused capacity on the link using the model. In Table 2 it can also be seen that a connection between **Helsingborg** and **Ringsted** via **Helsingør** will give the same benefits as the extra capacity on the **Øresunds** bridge (**cap2**). However, Table 3 shows that the delays may possibly be less using the **Helsingborg Ringsted** connection.

In Table 3, the number of delayed trains and the total number of minutes of delay are reported. It can be seen from the results on the 2030 Baseline

Table 4. Number of trains per link per week for each capacity set reported for the Green 2030 scenario and the Green 2030 scenario with Sundsval-Karlshamn demand removed assuming direct link between Älmhult and Karlshamn.

Connections	2030									
	Green					Green SK				
	cap1	cap2	cap3	cap6	HH	cap1	cap2	cap3	cap6	HH
Malmø->Halmstad	103	167	107	167	63	97	167	97	167	65
Malmø<-Halmstad	103	167	106	167	65	97	167	97	167	68
Malmø->Helsingborg	2	2	2	2	1	2	2	2	2	1
Malmø<-Helsingborg	2	2	2	2	1	2	2	2	2	0
Malmø->Trelleborg	157	157	157	157	157	157	157	157	157	157
Malmø<-Trelleborg	157	157	157	157	157	157	157	157	157	157
Malmø->Vigerslev	336	454	336	467	335	336	480	336	480	335
Malmø<-Vigerslev	336	454	336	467	330	336	480	336	480	331
Malmø->Hasselholm	581	635	584	655	616	594	668	594	668	622
Malmø<-Hasselholm	581	635	585	655	619	594	668	594	668	624
Karlshamn->Hasselholm	156	156	296	296	156	95	95	95	95	95
Karlshamn<-Hasselholm	156	156	296	296	156	95	95	95	95	95
Halmstad->Helsingborg	5	5	5	5	108	5	5	5	5	105
Halmstad<-Helsingborg	5	5	5	5	109	5	5	5	5	107
Halmstad->Hasselholm	3	4	19	19	3	18	19	18	19	18
Halmstad<-Hasselholm	3	4	18	19	4	18	19	18	19	19
Høje Taastrup->Vigerslev	139	134	16	141	83	31	151	31	151	101
Høje Taastrup<-Vigerslev	133	129	18	134	115	33	148	33	148	117
Høje Taastrup->Ringsted	135	131	9	123	117	14	129	14	129	98
Høje Taastrup<-Ringsted	141	136	7	130	85	12	132	12	132	82
Taulov->Esbjerg	0	0	0	0	0	0	0	0	0	0
Taulov<-Esbjerg	0	0	0	0	0	0	0	0	0	0
Taulov->Ringsted	6	136	7	130	127	12	132	12	132	131
Taulov<-Ringsted	8	128	5	123	123	10	129	10	129	128
Taulov->Padborg	8	128	5	123	123	5	124	5	124	123
Taulov<-Padborg	6	136	7	130	127	7	127	7	127	126
Helsingborg->Hasselholm	31	31	31	31	50	31	31	31	31	77
Helsingborg<-Hasselholm	31	31	31	31	46	31	31	31	31	74
Almhult->Hasselholm	749	802	841	907	802	620	693	620	693	693
Almhult<-Hasselholm	749	802	841	907	802	620	693	620	693	693
Hamburg->Padborg	6	136	7	130	127	7	127	7	127	126
Hamburg<-Padborg	8	128	5	123	123	5	124	5	124	123
Hamburg->Putgarten	332	320	320	326	329	305	329	305	329	330
Hamburg<-Putgarten	330	328	322	333	333	307	332	307	332	333
Vigerslev->Ringsted	203	325	318	333	220	303	332	303	332	218
Vigerslev<-Ringsted	197	320	320	326	247	305	329	305	329	230
Ringsted->Putgarten	330	328	322	333	333	307	332	307	332	333
Ringsted<-Putgarten	332	320	320	326	329	305	329	305	329	330
Helsingborg->Ringsted					119					145
Helsingborg<-Ringsted					124					149

scenario that a decrease in the number of delayed trains does not always result in a decrease in the total minutes of delays. Note that unscheduled trains are disregarded in these numbers. When compared to the number of unscheduled trains reported in Table 2 fewer cancelations do not always result in fewer delays. This is only natural as scheduling more trains may result in more total delay minutes since more trains can be delayed. An example of this can be seen for **cap2** and **cap6** where **cap2** has more cancelations than **cap6** in Table 2, however in Table 3 **cap6** has more delayed trains than **cap2** for both Green and Baseline scenario. When the capacity is large enough the delay should also be reduced as can be seen in Table 3 for **HH** and **HH2**.

Table 5. Number of trains per link per week for each capacity set reported for scenario 2010, Baseline 2030 and Baseline 2030 with Sundsval-Karlshamn demand removed assuming direct link between Älmhult and Karlshamn.

| Connections | 2010 | | 2030 | | | | | | | | | |
| | | SK | Baseline | | | | | Baseline SK | | | | |
	cap1	cap1	cap1	cap2	cap3	cap6	HH	cap1	cap2	cap3	cap6	HH
Malmø->Halmstad	70	70	98	170	117	170	59	97	170	97	170	59
Malmø<-Halmstad	70	70	98	170	117	171	58	97	170	97	170	58
Malmø->Helsingborg	0	0	2	2	2	2	1	2	2	2	2	1
Malmø<-Helsingborg	0	0	2	2	2	2	0	2	2	2	2	0
Malmø->Trelleborg	88	88	165	165	165	165	165	165	165	165	165	165
Malmø<-Trelleborg	88	88	165	165	165	165	165	165	165	165	165	165
Malmø->Vigerslev	150	150	336	471	336	477	336	336	477	336	477	336
Malmø<-Vigerslev	150	150	336	471	336	477	334	336	477	336	477	334
Malmø->Hasselholm	295	295	590	653	571	659	628	591	659	591	659	628
Malmø<-Hasselholm	295	295	590	653	571	658	632	591	659	591	659	632
Karlshamn->Hasselholm	71	10	147	147	230	230	147	14	14	14	14	14
Karlshamn<-Hasselholm	71	10	147	147	230	230	147	14	14	14	14	14
Halmstad->Helsingborg	2	2	5	5	5	5	118	5	5	5	5	118
Halmstad<-Helsingborg	2	2	5	5	5	5	116	5	5	5	5	116
Halmstad->Hasselholm	2	2	2	3	3	3	2	3	4	3	4	3
Halmstad<-Hasselholm	2	2	2	3	3	4	3	3	4	3	4	4
Høje Taastrup->Vigerslev	150	150	129	144	9	145	94	9	147	9	147	91
Høje Taastrup<-Vigerslev	150	150	129	143	11	144	124	11	145	11	145	125
Høje Taastrup->Ringsted	150	150	133	147	14	147	128	14	148	14	148	128
Høje Taastrup<-Ringsted	150	150	133	148	12	148	98	12	150	12	150	94
Taulov->Esbjerg	0	0	0	0	0	0	0	0	0	0	0	0
Taulov<-Esbjerg	0	0	0	0	0	0	0	0	0	0	0	0
Taulov->Ringsted	150	150	6	148	12	148	140	12	150	12	150	145
Taulov<-Ringsted	150	150	8	144	10	147	139	10	147	10	147	144
Taulov->Padborg	147	147	8	144	5	142	139	5	142	5	142	139
Taulov<-Padborg	147	147	6	148	7	143	140	7	145	7	145	140
Helsingborg->Hasselholm	19	19	31	31	31	31	56	31	31	31	31	62
Helsingborg<-Hasselholm	19	19	31	31	31	31	51	31	31	31	31	57
Almhult->Hasselholm	367	306	758	820	809	896	820	613	680	613	680	680
Almhult<-Hasselholm	367	306	758	820	809	896	820	613	680	613	680	680
Hamburg->Padborg	147	147	6	148	7	143	140	7	145	7	145	140
Hamburg<-Padborg	147	147	8	144	5	142	139	5	142	5	142	139
Hamburg->Putgarten			334	327	327	332	335	327	330	327	330	335
Hamburg<-Putgarten			332	331	329	333	336	329	333	329	333	336
Vigerslev->Ringsted			207	328	325	333	212	325	332	325	332	211
Vigerslev<-Ringsted			207	327	327	332	240	327	330	327	330	243
Ringsted->Putgarten			332	331	329	333	336	329	333	329	333	336
Ringsted<-Putgarten			334	327	327	332	335	327	330	327	330	335
Helsingborg->Ringsted							135					141
Helsingborg<-Ringsted							137					143

For each test case the program used 10-15 minutes to find the optimal solution. This shows that the program can easily be applied to larger networks. This time was mostly spent setting up the model while only a few seconds were used on solving the model.

9   Conclusion

The track allocation model from [15] has been adapted to analyze the capacity of the rail network. We show that this model can be used in combination with business knowledge about desired arrival and departure times to give more detailed knowledge of the capacity problems. The presented method makes it possible to perform capacity analysis with different possibilities of extensions to the network. With the knowledge of the train operators and railway planner this model should be able to aid in the decision process of railway expansions and planning. This will hopefully help ensure that the investments for costly railway expansions are placed in areas where they contribute the most.

Assuming that the forecast for the freight transport through the Danish and Southern Swedish region holds and that the other assumptions such as the weekly distribution of trains Table 1 and departure and arrival times are representative, the tests identified the bottle necks and show that increasing the capacity between **Malmø** and **Vigerslev** from 2 to 3 trains per hour will make it possible to transport all the freight in the forecast by train. However, even by increasing the capacity between **Malmø** and **Vigerslev** to 3 trains per hour there are still many delays in the network and the usage is for some links close to 100% over the entire week. This could indicate that the estimate for the amount of freight to be transported by rail is much higher than expected. An alternative to increasing the capacity on the link between **Malmø** and **Vigerslev (Øresund)** is to build a new link between **Helsingborg** and **Ringsted** with capacity for 2 trains per hour. Moreover alternatives such as a **Helsingborg Ringsted** was tested. The model can not only be used to evaluated if a given network will be able to satisfy an increased demand or changes in demand but the model can also easily evaluate the effect of alternative new links on the network.

Another issue is the freight between **Northern Sweden** represented by **Sundsval** and **Blekinge** represented in the model by **Karlshamn**. The developed model of the network can not provide an analysis of this issue since we do not know the specific origin and destinations of the freight. Therefore we cannot conclude if and where a link is needed and a more detailed study for that area is needed.

Comparing the results for the two scenarios **Baseline 2030** and **Green 2030** one surprisingly sees that even though the **Green 2030** scenario has more freight transported by train the challenges can be overcome by the infrastructure investments required for the **Baseline 2030**.

The model can as shown be used to evaluate the effect of various future investments in the railway infrastructure. Here two different scenarios with different political and environmental assumptions are shown and several different infrastructure projects are evaluated in terms of their effect on the flow and congestion.

Acknowledgments. The authors wish to thank Mikkel Krogsgaard Niss, Eva Lindborg and Jens Brix for valuable discussions and input to the project. We also wish to thank the EU project the East West Transport Corridor (EWTC-II) for supporting the project.

References

1. T.E.W. 6B. http://www.ewtc2.eu/ewtc/reports-and-results.aspx
2. Alvelos, F., de Carvalho, J.M.V.V.: Comparing branch-and-price algorithms for the unsplittable multicommodity flow problem. In: Proceedings of the International Network Optimization Conference, pp. 7–12 (2003)
3. Christiansen, M., Andersen, J.: Designing new european rail freight services. Journal of the Operational Research Society **60**(3), 348–360 (2009)
4. Crainic, T.G., Christiansen, M., Andersen, J.: Service network design with management and coordination of multiple fleets. European Journal of Operational Research **193**(2), 377–389 (2009)
5. Assad, A.A.: Models for rail transportation. Transportation Research Part A **14A**, 205–220 (1980)
6. Barnhart, C., Hane, C., Vance, P.: Using branch-and-price-and-cut to solve origin-destination integer multicommodity flow problems. Operations Research **48**(2), 318–326 (2000)
7. Borndörfer, R., Schlechte, T., Swarat, E.: Railway track allocation - simulation, aggregation, and optimization. In: Ni, Y.-Q., Ye, X.-W. (eds.) Proceedings of the 1st IWHIR, Vol. 2. LNEE, vol. 148, pp. 53–70. Springer, Heidelberg (2012)
8. Burdett, R.L., Kozan, E.: Techniques for absolute capacity determination in railways. Transportation Research Part B **40**, 616–632 (2006)
9. Caprara, A., Malaguti, E., Toth, P.: A freight service design problem for a railway corridor. Transportation Science **45**, 147–162 (2011)
10. Cordeau, J.-F., Toth, P., Vigo, D.: A survey of optimization models for train routing and scheduling. Transportation Science **32**, 380–404 (1998)
11. Even, S., Itai, A., Shamir, A.: On the complexity of timetable and multicommodity flow problems. SIAM Journal on Computing **5**, 691–703 (1976)
12. Jarrah, A.I., Johnson, E., Neubert, L.C.: Large-scale, less-than-truckload service network design. Operations Research **57**(3), 609–625 (2009)
13. Lium, A.G., Crainic, T.G., Wallace, S.W.: A study of demand stochasticity in service network design. Transportation Science **43**(2), 144–157 (2009)
14. Rich, J., Hansen, C.O., Vuk, G., Nielsen, O.A., Korzenewych, A., Bröcker, J.: Traffic flow: Scenario, traffic forecast and analysis of traffic on the ten-t, taking into consideration the external dimension of the union. Technical report, TRANS-TOOLS version 2; Model and Data Improvements (2009)
15. Borndörfer, R., Erol, B., Graffagnino, T., Schlechte, T., Swarat, E.: Aggregation methods for railway networks. In: Pacciarelli, R., Rodriguez, L., Wendler, H. (eds.) Proceedings of 4th International Seminar on Railway Operations Modelling and Analysis (IAROR), vol. 4 (2011)
16. Tetraplan. http://www.tetraplan.dk
17. Trafikstyrelsen. The danish traffic authority. http://www.trafikstyrelsen.dk
18. Trafikverket. Network statement 2012 part 1 (edition 10-12-2010)
19. Trafikverket. The swedish traffic authority. http://www.trafikverket.se
20. Wieberneit, N.: Service network design for freight transportation: A review. OR Spectrum **30**(1), 77–112 (2008)
21. Zhu, E., Crainic, T.G., Gendreau, M.: Integrated service network design for rail freight transportation. Technical report, CIRRELT (2009)

Order Management in the Offshore Oil and Gas Industry

Henrik Andersson[1], Eirik F. Cuesta[1], Kjetil Fagerholt[1,2(✉)],
Nora T. Gausel[1], and Martine R. Hagen[1]

[1] Department of Industrial Economics and Technology Management, Norwegian University of
Science and Technology, Trondheim, Norway
kjetil.fagerholt@iot.ntnu.no
[2] The Norwegian Marine Technology Research Institute (MARINTEK), Trondheim, Norway

Abstract. The supply order management problem (SOMP) is an important planning problem in the offshore oil and gas industry. The SOMP consists of determining, for a given departure for an offshore supply vessel following a fixed route, which orders to and from offshore oil and gas installations to serve and which orders to postpone. We propose a mixed-integer programming (MIP) model for this purpose. By setting up the model in a number of ways and running simulations using the model, we compare the performance of various planning strategies. As a case study, we use data from Petrobras, which is the main state-owned oil company in Brazil. It is shown that reductions in the amount of critical order delays can be achieved with careful planning using the proposed MIP model.

Keywords: Offshore oil and gas industry · Supply vessels · Order management

1   Introduction

The oil and gas industry is essential for the world, as it supplies the majority of the energy needed. It is also an industry associated with very large monetary values, with costly operations and regulations, and highly advanced technology, especially for the part of the industry that takes place offshore. The upstream sector includes exploration and production of hydrocarbons, while downstream consists of refining, distribution and retailing. In this paper, we limit ourselves to consider the upstream segment of the offshore oil and gas industry. Figure 1 shows an overview of the offshore oil and gas supply chain.

The oil and gas producing offshore installations need regular supplies of various commodities from land. It is common practice that the installations place orders for the different commodities required and that specialized offshore supply vessels (OSVs) are used to bring these orders from onshore supply depots to the offshore installations. These OSVs operate on weekly routes and schedules that are fixed in advance to make visits to the offshore installations predictable. The operator of the installations is also responsible for the operation of the OSVs. For a given route, an OSV departs from the onshore supply depot, visits a number of offshore installations

© Springer International Publishing Switzerland 2015
F. Corman et al. (Eds.): ICCL 2015, LNCS 9335, pp. 648–657, 2015.
DOI: 10.1007/978-3-319-24264-4_44

in a given sequence before returning to the depot. Since the weekly routes are fixed, it also means that a given offshore installation is serviced by an OSV a given number of times throughout the week, depending on their requirements.

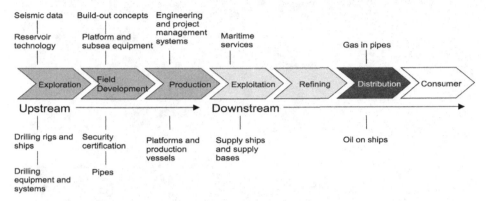

Fig. 1. The offshore oil and gas supply chain

Since the OSVs operate on fixed routes and schedules, it is given which offshore installations that will be visited and serviced on a given departure/voyage. Therefore, the routing of the OSVs is not considered in this paper. However, due to capacity limitations on the OSVs, there are often orders to or from offshore installations on the voyage that sometimes must be left behind and serviced on a later departure/voyage.

In contrast to what we do in this paper, most papers related offshore supply logistics consider routing a key feature of the problems studied. This is the case in Aas ct al. (2007), where a base model for an OSV routing problem is presented. A single vehicle pickup and delivery problem that models the operations of an OSV is studied in Gribkovskaia et al. (2008). Other variations of OSV routing problems that also include fleet composition decisions can be found in Shyshou et al. (2012) and Halvorsen-Weare et al. (2012). A general presentation of the practices and issues found in offshore supply logistics is found and discussed in Aas et al. (2009).

This paper considers the supply order management problem (SOMP), which simply consists of determining, for a given OSV departure, which orders to serve and which orders to postpone. Our contribution is to propose a mixed-integer programming (MIP) model for this problem, as well as to test a number of alternative planning strategies (using this model) through simulation. As a case study, we use data from Petrobras, which is the main state-owned oil company in Brazil operating along the Brazilian coastline. We use data from their operation for the offshore installations in the Campos Basin, which are supplied from the onshore supply depot in Macaé, see Figure 2.

Section 2 gives a detailed description of the SOMP, while the proposed MIP model is presented in Section 3. A computational study, showing that reductions in the amount of critical order delays can be achieved from careful planning using the proposed MIP model, is presented in Section 4. Section 5 provides concluding remarks.

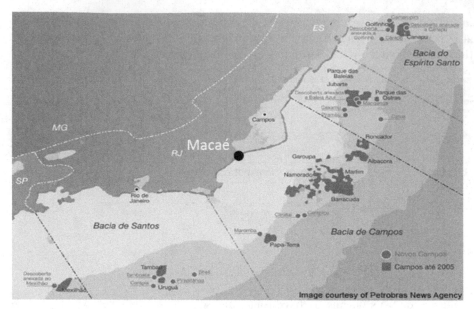

Fig. 2. Basins southeast of Brazil

2   The Supply Order Management Problem

Offshore installations place orders more or less continually. When an offshore installation places an order, this order is received and placed in an order pool at the logistics central at the onshore supply depot where the OSVs are prepared for departure. In
the case study described in this paper, this depot corresponds to the port of Macaé,
servicing the offshore installations on the Campos Basin, see Figure 2.

An order is either a request for delivery of a given amount of a specific commodity
from the port to the offshore installation or a pickup order for commodities that must
to be brought back to the port. The logistics central at the port must make decisions
about which orders to ship out on the next scheduled departures. Petrobras operate
with fixed routes and departure schedules for the OSVs. For a given voyage/departure
an OSV leaves the port and visits a number of offshore installations in a given sequence before returning to the port. In the following we use the terms departure and
voyage interchangeably to describe a given voyage scheduled to depart at a given
time of the week.

Figure 3 shows an example of two OSV voyages. The first voyage services offshore installations 1, 2, 5, 6, and 4 in sequence, while the second voyage services
installations 3, 9, 8, and 7. Most installation must be serviced more than once per
week. The given schedule for the Campos Basin includes 13 voyages per week, two
per day except for Sundays. Several of these voyages may include a visit to a given
offshore installation. The visits to a given installation are typically evenly distributed
throughout the week.

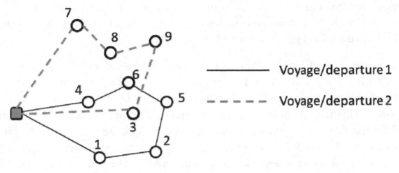

Fig. 3. Example of OSV voyages/departures

A fleet of OSVs is scheduled to perform the voyages, although a given OSV may perform more than one voyage per week depending on the duration of the voyages. An OSV voyage typically takes two or three days. Since the OSVs have limited capacity, it is often not possible to service all orders on the next voyage visiting the given offshore installations.

The supply order management problem (SOMP) can simply be stated as follows: Given a set of orders and a fixed weekly OSV schedule, determine which orders to service on the next departure and which to postpone for later departures visiting the same installations.

Since the routes are fixed, only the set of orders for the installations that will be visited on the next voyage must be considered. The chosen orders are removed from the order pool, while the other orders remain in the pool together with the orders for the offshore installations that are not visited on the next voyage. It should be noted that there can be more than one order in the order pool for a given installation, and only a subset of these might be chosen.

The decision about which orders to service on a given departure can be seen in a rolling horizon framework, see for example Sethi and Sorger (1991) where the order pool represents the currently available orders and decisions are made at decision points prior to each departure. New orders are revealed while the time rolls from one decision point to the next. Hence, the SOMP is solved as a sequence of small problems, i.e. one for each departure.

3   Mathematical Model

Before presenting the notation and the mathematical model, we state some important assumptions:

— The model is formulated for one departure at a time (it will later be tested how different planning strategies influence the performance using simulation and the rolling horizon framework described in Section 2).

— Orders cannot be split, i.e. a given order can only be serviced by one OSV on one departure. However, it is allowed to only choose a subset of the orders to service among the orders for a given offshore installation.

Let P be the set of offshore installations to be visited on the departure. If we consider voyage/departure 1 from the example in Figure 3, $P = \{1,2,4,5,6\}$ since these are the offshore installations visited on this departure. We let O_p be the set of orders for installation p. This may include both delivery and pickup orders. K is the capacity of the OSV for the departure (given in square meters of deck area, which is the binding constraint), while Q_i is the size of order i (also given in square meters). Q_i is positive for delivery orders and negative for pickup orders. There are no time windows associated with orders. However, it is assumed that, if possible, one wants to service each order on the next voyage/departure visiting the given installation after the order has been placed. We define C_i as the cost of not serving order i on the next departure. This cost is not a real cost, but a fictitious model cost which can be calibrated to provide solutions that are desirable to the planner. For example, a high-priority (emergency) order will typically have a higher cost than other orders. It can also be natural to let large-sized orders have higher costs than small-sized orders. Furthermore, following the rolling horizon framework described in Section 2, if an order already has been postponed, it is natural to increase this cost to make it more likely that it will be serviced on the next departure. Since orders do not have time windows and the scheduled plans include much slack between departures for a given OSV and the availability of OSVs is good, we do not need to consider the timing aspect of each OSV route.

Let u_i be a binary variable that takes the value 1 if order i is served on the departure and 0 otherwise. Furthermore, let l_p be the load onboard the OSV when leaving offshore installation p or the port if $p = 0$ (given in square meters).

The function $p(k)$ ensures that we are moving between installations in the sequence given by the route, and returns the installation visited as number k in the route.

Now, the SOMP can be formulated as follows:

$$\min \sum_{p \in P} \sum_{i \in O_p} C_i \cdot (1 - u_i) \tag{1}$$

subject to

$$l_0 - \sum_{p \in P} \sum_{i \in O_p | (Q_i > 0)} Q_i u_i = 0 \tag{2}$$

$$l_{p(k)} - l_{p(k-1)} + \sum_{i \in O_{p(k)}} Q_i u_i = 0, \quad k = 1, \dots, |P| \tag{3}$$

$$u_i \in \{0,1\}, \quad p \in P, i \in O_p \tag{4}$$

$$0 \le l_p \le K, \quad p \in P \cup \{0\} \tag{5}$$

The objective function (1) minimizes the costs of unserved orders, while constraint (2) initializes the load onboard the OSV to be equal to the sum of the order sizes for the served delivery orders. The summation is over the orders whose demand is greater than zero, since the pickup orders are not part of the initial load when leaving the port. Constraints (3) ensure that the load onboard the OSV is updated for each offshore installation visited. The load when leaving an installation is thus equal to the load when entering the installation minus the net demand at the platform. The net demand is the sum of all orders served at the respective installation, both deliveries and pickups, and can in some cases be a negative number. Constraints (4) and (5) are merely defining the variables, where u_i is the binary variable stating whether an order is served or not, and l_p is the non-negative load when leaving offshore installation p or the port, which cannot be greater than the capacity K.

4   Computational Study

To test alternative planning strategies we do a simulation over a one-year period in a manner which has several similarities with the studies described by Fagerholt et al. (2009) and Richetta and Larson (1997). Over a one-year period there are 676 departures (13 per week), where orders are randomly generated from distributions to mimic the ordering process. Historic data is used to calibrate the distributions to provide a realistic ordering behavior from the 53 offshore installations that are included in the data set. On average, each installation has two delivery orders and two pickup orders per week. The order sizes are generated randomly from uniform distributions with upper limit of 90 m^2 and lower limit of 10 m^2. On average 21 000 m^2 and 7 000 m^2 are transported monthly on the fronthaul and backhaul respectively. This corresponds to historical data from Petrobras. .

Table 1. Key figures for the case study

Total number of generated orders (per year)	10 980
Total order demand (square meters)	338 580
Total delivery demand (in square meters)	250 926
Total pickup demand (in square meters)	87 654
Vessel capacity (square meters)	600
Number of departures per year	676
Number of platforms	53

Table 1 provides some key figures for the simulated data used in our computational study. Note that even though OSVs come with different capacities, we have used a standard capacity of 600 m^2 for all departures in our case study.

When performing this simulation, we follow the rolling horizon framework described in Section 2. This means that for each of the 676 departures, we solve the model described in Section 3 before moving to the next departure. In between each model run, we maintain the order pool by adding new orders that have been generated and removing the orders that were chosen to be served on the previous departure. The model presented in Section 3 has been implemented and solved with the commercial optimization software Xpress-IVE 1.24.00 64-bit with modeling language Xpress Model version 3.4.2.All departures solve to optimality within one second of run time.

Section 4.1 presents the results from the case study where a number of planning strategies are evaluated and compared. A planning strategy is in this context simply alternative ways to set the order delay costs, C_i, based on the priorities defined by the strategy. Since Petrobras in practice experience an extensive degree of no-shows, i.e. orders that have been chosen but for some reason do not become available for loading on the given departure, we also consider this case in Section 4.2. Here we also test alternative overbooking strategies to reduce the negative effects from no-shows on the utilization of the OSVs.

4.1   Computational Results Without No-Shows

In the following we compare the results from simulating over one year with four different planning strategies:

1. First in – first out (FIFO)
   In this strategy we set the order delay costs such that orders for a given offshore installation always are served in the order the orders are placed. This means that an order will never be chosen for a given departure if there exists another order for the same installation that have been placed before and is still not served. The order delay cost function is $C_i(t) = 5 + 1000t^2$, where t is the number of departures visiting the relevant offshore installation counted from the time order i is generated. If order i is served on the first possible departure, $C_i(0) = 5$, if it is delayed and served on the second possible departure, $C_i(1) = 1005$, if it is served on the third possible departure, $C_i(2) = 1000005$, and so on.

2. Same delay costs for all orders (SAME)
   All orders have the same delay cost given by the function $C_i(t) = 5 + 5t$.

3. Size- and delivery-based priority (SIZE)
   Large-sized orders are given priority over smaller orders. Furthermore, since it is often considered more important to perform deliveries than pickup from the offshore installations, delivery orders are given priority over pickup orders. The order delay cost function is $C_i(t) = \begin{cases} 5 + 5t - 0.2Q_i & Q_i < 0 \\ 5 + 5t + 0.4Q_i & Q_i \geq 0 \end{cases}$.

4. Priority-based delay costs (PRIO)
   In reality, some of the orders are so-called high-priority orders. In this strategy, we assume that 10 % of the orders are such high priority orders (randomly chosen), which are given priority over other orders. The order delay cost function is $C_i(t) = \begin{cases} 5 + 5t & i \notin O^P \\ 5 + 1000t & i \in O^P \end{cases}$, where O^P is the set of high priority orders.

Table 2 presents the main results from the one-year simulations with the four different planning strategies. The row with "# 1 period delays" shows the number of orders that are delayed until the next departure to the relevant offshore installations, while the row with "# 2 period delays" shows the number of orders that must wait until the third departure before being served, and so on. The row with the total demand delay shows the total number of square meters of orders that have been postponed at least one departure, while the row with total priority delay shows the number of prioritized orders that have been postponed at least one departure.

Table 2. Computational results from the one-year simulation for the different planning strategies (without no-shows)

	FIFO	SAME	SIZE	PRIO
# 1 period delays	511	436	536	374
# 2 period delays	65	87	48	108
# 3 period delays	0	19	0	26
# 4 period delays	0	0	0	2
Total demand delay (sq. meters)	33 276	36 756	32 434	36 440
Total priority delay (# orders)	67	77	66	0

The results presented in Table 2 shows that the four different strategies provide rather different solutions. If for example large-sized orders are given priority over smaller orders (strategy 3, SIZE), we see that the total demand that is delayed is decreased compared with the other strategies. We also note that if some orders are given priority due to their importance, using strategy 4 (PRIO) makes sure that none of these orders is delayed even though the total demand delayed is higher than for the SIZE and FIFO strategies.

It is impossible to state which planning strategy is best as this depends on the planner's preferences. However, testing alternative strategies through a simulation, as shown here, may help the planner in choosing one that performs well according to his/her preferences.

4.2   Computational Results with No-Shows and Overbooking

In practice Petrobras experience approximately 25 % no-shows, i.e. 25 % of the delivery orders chosen for a given departure are not available when the OSV is loaded for its departure. This is due to a very congested port in Macaé and low reliability from some of the suppliers. This has several major negative effects on the system, such as low utilization of the OSVs resulting in a need for a higher number of expensive OSVs. To remedy this problem overbooking can be introduced, i.e. more goods than the OSV's capacity are booked for a departure. However, using overbooking might lead to orders that cannot be served on the given departure when the amount of no-shows is less than normal. These orders must either be served on a later departure or so-called high cost express deliveries can be used, i.e. chartering in an additional vessel to handle these orders. Since the offshore installations expect these orders to arrive on time, we assume in the following that express deliveries are used.

Table 3 shows the results from testing three overbooking policies, i.e. no over-booking, 10 % overbooking and 20 % overbooking. These tests have been performed using the FIFO planning strategy. Table 3 also repeats the results from using the FIFO strategy without no-shows in the column denoted Orig. in order to compare and analyze the effects of no-shows.

Table 3. Computational results from the one-year simulation for the different overbooking policies (with no-shows). The FIFO planning strategy is used in all tests.

	Orig.	0 %	10 %	20 %
# 1 period delays	511	538	488	461
# 2 period delays	65	218	203	196
# 3 period delays	0	0	0	0
# 4 period delays	0	0	0	0
Total demand delay (sq. meters)	33 276	48 334	43 729	41 276
Express deliveries	0	0	36	42

If we compare the results without no-shows (Orig.) with the results with no-shows, it is easy to see the major negative impact that no-shows have on the system's performance. We see that the total demand delay increases from 33 276 to 48 334 because of the no-shows (in the case where we do not use any overbooking policy). The number of delayed orders increases correspondingly. We can also see from Table 3 that overbooking is effective when it comes to reducing the delayed orders. However, it comes with a cost for express deliveries.

This type of analyses using simulation can also be used to evaluate the effects of reductions in the amount of no-shows. We tested a scenario with only 15 % no-shows using the 10 % overbooking policy. In this case the number of 1 and 2 period delays was reduced from 488 to 470 and 203 to 150, respectively, while the number of express deliveries was reduced by one.

5   Concluding Remarks

We have considered the supply order management problem, which consists of determining, for a given voyage for an offshore supply vessel (OSV) following a fixed route, which orders to and from offshore oil and gas installations to serve and which orders to leave behind (postpone delivery). We proposed a mixed-integer programming (MIP) model for this purpose, which was used in a rolling horizon simulation to compare a number of alternative planning strategies. As a case study, we used data from Petrobras, which is the main state-owned oil company in Brazil operating along the Brazilian coastline. It was shown that reductions in the amount of critical order delays can be achieved from careful planning using the proposed MIP model.

Since it is common to experience no-shows (i.e. orders chosen for the next departure do not become available for some reason), we also tested different overbooking policies. It was shown that overbooking can improve the utilization of the fleet of OSVs. It was also shown how a simulation study can be used to evaluate the effects of reducing the amount of no-shows.

A simulation study, as shown in this paper, can also be used to test the effect from alternative weekly routes and schedules on the amount of delayed orders. We emphasize that even though the analyses in this paper were performed with data from Petrobras, the same methodology can also be used on other similar problems.

Acknowledgement. We are grateful to Even A. Holte at MARINTEK for providing information about the supply order management problem and to Petrobras for providing data. Thanks are due to the reviewers for their valuable comments.

References

Aas, B., Gribkovskaia, I., Halskau, Ø., Shlopak, A.: Routing of supply vessels to petroleum installations. International Journal of Physical Distribution & Logistics Management **37**(2), 164–179 (2007)

Aas, B., Halskau, Ø., Wallace, S.W.: The role of supply vessels in offshore logistics. Maritime Economics & Logistics **11**(3), 302–325 (2009)

Fagerholt, K., Christiansen, M., Hvattum, L., Johnsen, T., Vabø, T.: A decision support methodology for strategic planning in maritime transportation. Omega **38**(6), 465–474 (2009)

Gribkovskaia, I., Laporte, G., Shlopak, A.: A tabu search heuristic for a routing problem arising in servicing of offshore oil and gas platforms. Journal of the Operational Research Society **59**(11), 1449–1459 (2008)

Halvorsen-Weare, E.E., Fagerholt, K., Nonås, L.M., Asbjørnslett, B.E.: Optimal fleet composition and periodic routing of offshore supply vessels. European Journal of Operational Research **223**(2), 508–517 (2012)

Richetta, O., Larson, R.C.: Modeling the increased complexity of New York City's refuse marine transport system. Transportation Science **31**(3), 273–293 (1997)

Sethi, S., Sorger, G.: A theory of rolling horizon decision making. Annals of Operation Research **29**(1), 387–415 (1991)

Shyshou, A., Gribkovskaia, I., Laporte, G., Fagerholt, K.: A large neighborhood search heuristic for a periodic supply planning problem arising in offshore oil and gas operations. INFOR **50**(4), 195–204 (2012)

A Review of Real Time Railway Traffic Management During Disturbances

Wenhua Qu[✉], Francesco Corman, and Gabriel Lodewijks

Department of Maritime and Transport Technology,
Delft University of Technology, Delft, The Netherlands
{W.Qu,F.Corman,G.Lodewijks}@tudelft.nl

Abstract. This paper gives an over view of real time traffic management of the railway network in case of disturbances. After briefly introducing the problem of disturbance management and basic mathematical formulations, this paper overviews the existing literatures according to the typologies of traffic and levels of detail in the infrastructure models used for railway traffic network representation. A precise placement is made based on the effect of management decisions towards the various stakeholders. The application of these models in real life railway system is discussed based on the special constraints considered, the size of the railway network and the calculation time. Most railway disturbance management models are tested in an experiment setting at present, and if applied in practice they can be helpful to dispatchers to provide a higher quality service for all stakeholders involved.

Keywords: Railway network · Real time traffic management · Disturbance management · Train types

1 Introduction

Railway network operates according to a pre-planned timetable, which specifies the route choice of the trains through the infrastructures and regulates the precise time slot of the trains' departure or arrival. Intercity trains or express trains stop mainly at big stations, regional trains or regular trains stop almost at every station. In the stage of timetable designing, in order to provide convenient to passengers, and coupling of express trains and regular trains are well considered at stations where passengers' transfers take place, not only at "hub" stations. The occurrence of delay and its propagation can be reduced by making delay-resistant timetables or improve the robustness of a railway system, see Liebchen and Stiller (2006), Liebchen et al. (2007), and Dewilde (2014).

However, there are always some unavoidable disturbances causing deviation from the original timetable, which calls for more effective real time trains management. The real time traffic management in case of disturbance (RTTM-disturbance) should make a decision whether to maintain or drop the pre-planned connections in the timetable. Besides, the management needs to deal with possible conflicts resulting from

© Springer International Publishing Switzerland 2015
F. Corman et al. (Eds.): ICCL 2015, LNCS 9335, pp. 658–672, 2015.
DOI: 10.1007/978-3-319-24264-4_45

delayed trains require access to infrastructures pre-assigned to another train at the same time. It takes the current train time-space position and the traffic regulations as input, gives out a series of corresponding adjustments to the train schedule before execution, and aims at bringing the traffic status back to the normal timetable as soon as possible and limiting the economic loss caused.

Except for very few applications, in practice RTTM-disturbance is usually performed by dispatchers. Due to the complexity of the problem, dispatchers utilize some simplifying rules to implement their decisions and resolve conflicts accordingly. From the view of system effectiveness and efficiency, their decisions should be supported with appropriate tools because their immediate decisions may cause considerable train delay propagation in future interferences. Many scholars have studied the RTTM-disturbance problem in many ways and from various perspectives over the years, to assist the decision makers to make more effective decisions, avoiding a suboptimal through put out. The application of those approaches in practices constitutes a scientifically challenging and promising perspective.

The existing researches use different approaches to address models and algorithms for RTTM-delay. A recent state-of-the-art paper about recovery models and algorithm for real-time railway rescheduling is Cacchiani et al. (2014). This review differs from the existing review articles in the following ways.

1. We concentrate on the RTTM in case of disturbance, and waive the questions concerning the RTTM-disruption. Delays can be categorised into disturbances and disruptions, however there is not a sharp distinction between disturbances and disruptions in term of time length. According to Cacchiani et al. (2014), disturbances are relative small perturbation to the railway system that can be handled by modifying the timetable, but without modifying the duties of rolling stock and crew. Disruptions are relatively large incidents, requiring both the timetable and the duties for rolling stock and crew to be modified. Railway operating companies are mostly faced with disturbances, instead of disruptions. For more information on railway disruption management, please refer to Jespersen-Groth et al. (2007).

2. The literatures on RTTM-disturbance are reviewed from the perspective of the classes of traffic, i.e., distinguishing between passenger trains, freight trains, approaches considering unspecified traffic, or explicitly both at the same time, as shown in Figure 1. Here the unspecified traffic means the train types are not emphasized and distinguished in the models. Passenger and freight trains should be distinguished because they differ a lot in served clients, body structures, organization of train operations, etc. Since they might share the same corridor, there is interplay in terms of infrastructures and time. It is worthwhile studying how to integrate different types of train traffic, with respect to the diversities.

3. We discuss the dispatch decisions from the point view of different stakeholders. Early studies mainly aim at bringing down the overall train delays yet ignore the service quality perceived by passengers. In the last decades, scholars start to focusing on the passengers' interest, addressing the management and keeping of passenger connections, discomfort caused by congestion, value of time, etc. In addition, some RTTM models try to get a balance between the train delays and passenger delays.

2   Background Information

The RTTM-disturbance strategy can be retiming, rerouting, reordering, and cancelling the connections, explained in Sec. 2.1. And Sec. 2.2 introduces the commonly used mathematical formulations.

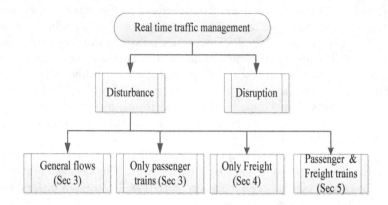

Fig. 1. Basic categories of the RTTM according to the train types

2.1   Operation Strategy

In case of disturbance, the traffic deviate from the original timetable and the timetable need to be up-dated to a new one, the so-called disposition timetable. The problem of finding a disposition timetable is also called re-scheduling, which may consist retiming, rerouting, reordering or cancelling the passenger connections.

- **Retiming:** Decision makers may adjust the time slots of one train entering or leaving one block section, arriving or departing from the stations.
- **Rerouting:** Decision makers may assign a new route from a set of feasible routes (inside one station or between stations) to a train, instead of executing the train's pre-planned route.
- **Reordering:** Decision makers may change the order of a pair of consecutive trains' access to the infrastructure.
- **Cancelling connections:** If the pre-planned passenger connection is dropped, there is no adjustment to the movement of the feeder trains. The decision of maintaining or dropping a connection (or wait-no-wait decisions) is called pure delay management.

2.2   Mathematical Formulation

The RTTM-disturbance model can be divided into *microscopic* model and *macroscopic* models, according to the different levels of detail in the infrastructure models used for railway traffic network representation. Macroscopic models consider the railway network at a relative high level, and have a more aggregated representation of some resources, i.e., stations are represented by nodes of a graph and tracks by arcs. Besides, signals are not considered. Most macroscopic models use *Event-Activity* mathematics to formulate the railway network.

While in microscopic models, the above aspects are considered in detail, and they include a lot more detail (e.g. a station is composed of a complex set-up of pieces of tracks separated by switches and signals). Most microscopic models use *Alternative Graph* mathematics to formulate the railway network.

3   RTTM-Disturbance of General/Passenger Trains

Sec 3 discusses the RTTM-disturbance literatures of general or passenger trains, first microscopic and then macroscopic models. The basic structure is listed in Table 1 and Table 2. Some papers in this section do deal with the freight trains, however, they do not distinguish passenger trains (high speed or normal ones) and freight trains in the model. All trains are taken as the same in terms of value of time or travel time reliability. These models do not discuss the differences of passenger and freight transportation, such as the carrying vehicles, clients' perception and evaluation to the transportation service. The consequential differences, such set of priority in access to the infrastructures, are not discussed. Therefore, we classify them as models on general train flows.

3.1   Microscopic RTTM-Disturbance Model of General/Passenger Trains

Much of the literatures at a microscopic level are based in the Alternative Graph model introduced in Section 2.2.

The delay management is a series of adjustment decisions, which can affect both the trains and passengers. If all connecting trains wait for the delayed feeder trains to provide passengers with smooth transfers, which however increases the overall train delays. On the other hand, if all connecting trains depart punctually to make an early arrival, passengers missed their connections and total passenger waiting time will be enormous. According to the stakeholders involved in the wait or no wait decisions, the existing literatures are sorted according to the objective functions: trains orientation (i.e., aim at minimizing the total train delays), passenger orientation (i.e., aim at minimizing total passenger delays) or a trade-off between the two criteria.

Train Orientation. D'Ariano et al. (2007) studies the train RTTM-disturbance on a regional railway network, by giving new conflict-free timetable of feasible arrival and departure times. It is modelled with an alternative graph formulation, by which the authors explicitly include the no-store constraints. A branch & bound (B&B) algorithm is adopted to speed up the computation time. The lower bound is achieve from Jackson pre-emptive schedule in Jackson (1955), and the upper bound as the best value obtained by three heuristics: "First Come First Served" dispatching rule, "First

Leave First Served" dispatching rule and greedy algorithm AMCC described in Mascis and Pacciarelli (2002). The objective function is to minimize the deviation between the disposition timetable and the original timetable. Computational experiments based on the Schiphol area, a bottleneck of the Dutch railway, show that the truncated version of the algorithm provides proven optimal or near optimal solution within short time limits (120 seconds).

Table 1. Basic category of the microscopic RTTM-disturbance models according to train types

Objective functions	Special constraints	Related Literature	Test network	Calculation time
Train orientation	train retiming	D'Ariano et al. (2007)	Schiphol, 2h (20km)	<120 s
	train retiming & rerouting	D'Ariano et al. (2008a)	Utrecht Den Bosch	<30s
		D'Ariano et al. (2008b)	Schiphol	<30s
		Corman et al. (2010)	Utrecht Den Bosch (1h)	<1 s
	track choices, extra-stops	Gély et al. (2006)	Line between Tours and Bordeaux (8h)	-
	junctions areas	Rodriguez (2007)	Pierrefitte-Gonesse junction	<180 s
	congested bottlenecks	Caimi et al. (2012)	Berne area (10 scenarios)	< 1 min
	speed control	Albrecht et al. (2011)	Utrecht to 's-Hertogenbosch	-
Passenger orientation		Wegele and Schnieder(2005)	Deutsche Bahn AG (24 h)	-
	passenger rerouting	Corman et al. (2015)	Utrecht and Den Bosch (2 h)	About 1m
A trade-off		Corman et al. (2012)	Utrecht Central (1 h)	<30s

In D'Ariano et al. (2007), trains are not allowed to change routes from the original timetable, while in practical, better solutions can be achieved by rerouting. D'Ariano et al (2008, 2008a) integrate trains' rerouting and extend it into a real time traffic management system ROMA (Railway traffic Optimization by Means of Alternative graphs). Still improvements are possible in term of computation time, especially when dealing with large-scale network.

D'Ariano et al. (2008b) put out "flexible timetable" in comparison with "rigid timetable", by relaxing some timetabling constraints in the ROMA model. The authors construct a flexible timetable by replacing the scheduled arrival and departure times with maximum arrival and minimum departure times. Experimental results are performed on the congested area around Schiphol Amsterdam Airport with randomly generated disturbances. The results show that flexible timetables are promising. The best solution is always found within 30 s of computation time.

RTTM differs from the timetabling significantly in the required time, since that RTTM needs to bring the traffic status back to the normal timetable as soon as possible. On the basis of ROMA, Corman et al. (2010) develop a Tabu Search (TS) scheme to address the train conflict detection and resolution (CDR) problem. Tabu Search improves the calculation speed of the local research method by using memory structures called Tabu list which describe the visited solutions. The new TS algorithm can enhance significantly the performance of ROMA.

Gély et al. (2006) present a quite detailed mathematical model to describe the RTTM-disturbance problem. The model presents continuous variables (arrival or departure times of trains from each visited each node at a given order), track choices, and extra-stops. The objective is to minimize the total accumulated delay of trains. They use evolutionary algorithms and hybrid techniques to solve the problem. Test based to real-life instances of railway lines between Tours and Bordeaux of the French railway company between 15:00 and 23:00 shows the feasibility and the effectiveness of decision support systems.

High traffic density and heterogeneous traffic networks make the railway operations more sensitive to delays. There have been increasing studies on congestion related RTTM.

Small disruptions are amplified through the junction area. Rodriguez (2007) points out that a disturbance which is at origin only a few seconds long can quickly lead to a delay of over 5 min. Thus, the researcher presents a constraint-programming model for rerouting and rescheduling of trains at a junction area. The model has been applied to a set of problem instances. Preliminary test results based on a real case study of traffic on the Pierrefitte-Gonesse node, North of Paris show that the model yields a significant improvement in performance within an acceptable computation time.

A special concern can be the congested bottleneck areas, where delays easily propagate from one train to another. Caimi et al. (2012) propose a dispatching assistant system in the form of a model predictive control framework for railway traffic management in bottleneck areas, aimed at maximizing customer satisfaction. In particular, they propose a closed-loop discrete-time control system, which suggests rescheduling trains according to solutions of a binary linear optimization model. The system is tested in collaboration with the Swiss Federal Railways, and successfully applied for an operational day at the central railway station area. The computation time is less than 1 minute.

Albrecht et al. (2011) introduce the concept of target points and target windows to distinguish and specify the management operations in stations dealing with different traffic intensity. Target points correspond to arrival and departure times for the purpose of maintaining passenger connections. When there is no need to consider connections (often in minor stations), target windows can be considered. Target windows impose an upper limit within which the planned time can be exceeded by a delay. The authors propose a two-level optimization approach: optimization of speed between consecutive target points, and optimization of running times between target windows, if target windows exist between the target points. Case study on parts of the Dutch and German railway networks shows that the method is able to improve timetable adherence, to save energy, and to improve throughput in the system-related bottlenecks.

Passenger Orientation. Most early papers aim to minimize the train delays or the number of cancelled trains. However, a growing number of papers begin to consider minimizing the negative effects of disturbances for passengers.

Wegele and Schnieder (2005) use genetic algorithm to achieve objective function of minimizing customers' annoyance, e.g., delays, change of platforms and missed connections. The method is tested with a real data from part of the German Railways. The evaluation runtimes in both cases lied at few minutes.

Corman et al. (2015) integrate microscopic railway traffic rescheduling and passenger point of view into a single mixed integer linear programming. The objective function is to minimize the time spent by the passengers in the railway network. They use a fast iterative algorithms based on a decomposition of the problem and on the exact resolution of the sub-problems. Computational experiments based on a real-world Dutch railway network show that good quality solutions and calculation time within a limited computation time.

A Trade-Off. Transfer connections are relevant to the passenger satisfaction but do not affect the feasibility of railway operations, therefore one of the possible dispatching countermeasures to reduce delay propagation is to cancel some of scheduled connections. This operation reduces overall train delays but cause an extra delay to the passenger because of the missed connections. Train operating companies are clearly also interested in keeping as many connections as possible even in the presence of disturbed traffic condition.

As a series of coherent research work, Corman et al. (2012) combine the microscopic formulation with the minimization of passenger dissatisfaction in Ginkel and Schöbel (2007) (introduced in Sec 3.2). The authors consider the needs of different stakeholders (infrastructure company, train operating companies, passengers, etc.), and get a compromise solution between the minimization of train delays and missed connections. Test based on a complex and densely occupied Dutch railway network put out accurately the Pareto front in a limited computation time.

3.2   Macroscopic Model of General/Passenger Trains

In this section, we discuss RTTM-disturbance at a macroscopic level. Also the literatures are sorted from the point view of train orientation or passenger orientation.

Train Orientation. Schöbel (2009) provides a disturbance management model including the track capacity constraints. The author develops a branch-and-bound algorithm and several heuristic approaches to solve the problem. The macroscopic approach allows treating the most important capacity constraints using headway time constraint. The algorithmic approaches have been tested at a real-world data from the region of Harz, Germany with a calculation time within seconds.

Table 2. Basic category of the macroscopic RTTM-disturbance models according to train types

Objective functions	Special constraints	Related papers	Test network	Calculations
Train orientation		Min et al. (2011)	Seoul metropolitan railway network	< 1 min
		Dündar and Şahin (2013)	single track in Turkey (150 km)	not mentioned
	Track capacity	Schöbel (2009)	Deutsche Bahn	within seconds
	Station capacity	Dollevoet (2015)	Zwolle to Utrecht network (1 h)	< 3 min
Passenger orientation		Schöbel (2001)	Rheinland-Pfalz and the Saarland	within seconds
	Passenger rerouting	Dollevoet (2014)	Zwolle to Utrecht network (1 hour)	< 1 min
	Dynamic interacting	Kanai et al. (2011)	Japanese railway (130 km)	< 6 min
A trade-off		Ginkel and Schöbel (2009)	Verkehrsverbund Rhein-Neckar (30 m)	< 1 min

Dollevoet et al (2015) point out the limited capacity of the stations in disturbance management problem. They develop an integer programming (IP) formulation that takes into account the capacity within stations and allow rescheduling the platform track assignment. First, a fixed platform track assignment is used, and then the platform track assignment is improved systematically, using iterative heuristic.

Min et al. (2011) propose a MIP formulation to solve the RTTM-disturbance problem in Seoul Railway, South Korea. They prove that when the railway network gets as large as a metropolitan area network, the computation times can be extensive and fluctuate significantly on the instances. They proposed a heuristic Fix and Regenerate Algorithm that exploits the structure of the problem iteratively. Tests based on the Seoul metropolitan railway network (passenger trains, subway trains, and freight trains) shows that the model provides a new timetable within 1 min.

Dündar and Şahin (2013) study real-time management of railway traffic on a single-track railway line of about 150 km in Turkey. They develop a Genetic Algorithm (GA) to reschedule the trains on this line, and in particular to determine the meets and passes of trains in opposite directions. This model can be used for solving the smaller instances to optimality. However, this model cannot solve the larger instances.

Passenger Orientation. Schöbel (2001) firstly using an IP model the delay (disturbance) management problem, deciding which connections should be maintained and which other connections can be dropped. The objective function is to minimize the total passenger delays at their destination stations.

In a following paper, Dollevoet et al. (2014) point out that, different from the typical assumption in classic DM models, passengers can choose another route instead of taking their original planned route and waiting for one cycle time when delays occur. They adopt an IP formulation to manage the passenger re-routing and delay management at the same time. Computational experiments based on real-world data from part of Netherlands Railways show that significant improvements can be obtained by integrating the re-routing of passengers.

Kanai et al. (2011) attach high importance of passenger dynamic interaction and level of service to the RTTM-disturbance problem. A dynamic interaction means a phenomenon such that if a train is delayed for some time, more passengers than usual get on at the next station and the dwell time becomes longer than usual and the train is delayed further. In Japan, railway companies have to densely operate express trains and regular trains and transport a massive of passengers. The authors develop a delay management algorithm combining simulation and optimization. They adopt Tabu search algorithm to finding good strategies for the management of train connections. The model is tested on data of the Japanese railway network with promising results, with an average computation time of about 6 min.

A Trade-Off. Ginkel and Schöbel (2007) present a bi-criteria model for the DM problem, aiming at a trade-off between the delay of the vehicles and the number of passengers who miss their connections. They present an IP formulation and a graph-theoretic approach based on discrete time/cost project network. The test based on south-west Germany show the applicability of the approach.

Table 1 and Table 2 show that when the main focus of RTTM is the feasibility of railway operations, the related papers take into account the constraints on the limited capacity of the railway network disregarding the passenger inconvenience. On the other hand, when the focus is on the minimization of passenger inconvenience, the network capacity is not taken into account.

4   Disturbance Management of Freight Trains

At moment, there are only limited literatures studding the freight delay management. However, there is an environmental and European political vision for an increased use of the railway, especially for long-distance freight transportation. Thus, it is increasingly promising to investigate the freight transport management.

4.1   Differences between Passenger Transport and Freight Transport

Different Speed. passenger trains usually run at a higher speed than freight trains, thus have speed limited by construction. Passenger trains and freight trains are marshalling separately. In timetable designing, freight trains are inserted among the fixed schedule of passenger trains.

Different Value of Time, and Travel Time Reliability. In case of disturbance, the loss caused can be different according to value of time. For detailed information, please refer to the report by Jong et al. (2007). Based on the value of time, researchers can get a set of priority order for different train flows, as discussed in Sec 5.

Different Number of Stops Alongside the Trips. Normally freight transport provides a point-to-point service to clients. However, there can be frequent stops along the lines. Clients are concerned with the total delivery time, instead of the stops or changing between different lines.

Different Operations. Passengers can accomplish the boarding/alighting themselves, on the platform. But for freight transport, the cargo handlings take place at the yards. Off-peak and night-time deliveries are widely considered in Freight transportation to avoid some of the traffic network congestion at peak hours.

4.2   Disturbance Management of Freight Trains

The railway freight transportation can be affected by the regional factors, such as the transportation demand, operations, policies, etc. The European railway freight transportation tends to have a schedule, while the US or Canadian Railways would more often wait to dispatch a train, scheduling only happens when sufficiently many cars have been accumulated.

Kraay and Harker (1995) present a MIP model for the optimization of RTTM-disturbance over the entire freight network based on the American railway networks. The model aims to provide a link between strategic schedules (which might be decided every month) and line dispatching or computer assistant dispatching models (which need the scheduled arrival and departure times of each train at the ends of each lane at very frequent intervals). The model considers the current position of each train and the relative importance of the train. The model generates the time that each train should be at each major point in its itinerary. The model is tested on a portion of a major North American railroad to ascertain its efficiency and efficacy. These results were significantly better than the initial standard heuristic at that time in many of the problem instances.

Kuo et al. (2010) point out that the demand of freight transportation in North America is not fixed. Instead, it is a function of the frequency of service. The researchers develop a train slot selection model for scheduling railway services. The freight scheduling methodology equilibrates between the performance of the freight transport system (given schedules, delays and user costs under different levels of demand) and the demand (given level of service provided). The objective function is to minimize both operating costs incurred by carriers and delays incurred by shippers, while ensure that the schedules and levels of demand are mutually consistent. They propose a column generation-based methodology for train slot selection to meet the frequency requirements. Its utility is illustrated through the development of weekly train and ferry timetables for the international freight services.

Oetting et al. (2015) put forward an evaluation approach to assess the effect of DM measures on transportation service quality based on European freight transportation. The so called monetarization analysis of delays is a customer-based cost-benefit-analysis for operations addressing changes infrastructure, operations and vehicle characteristics. Based on expert interview and a survey with 55 companies, the study gives an approach to integrate the effects of delays in a monetarized way, i.e., resulting cost arising from the effects of delays on production and logistics. It concludes in a non-linear time-and-process dependent valuation function for delays with assigned costs caused by delays to the customer.

5   Disturbance Management of Passenger and Freight Trains

Different from Section 3, literature in this section clearly distinguishes passenger and freight transportation in the model.

When passenger and freight trains use the same corridor, it creates a quite heterogeneous traffic flow. In case of delays, both passengers and freight transportations are affected. Passengers experience it as late arrival, broken connections, insufficient seating capacity, cancelled trains, etc. Also freight trains suffer from delays mainly in the form of rerouted trains and late arrivals. Also they compete for the same part of the train system at the same time. Decisions have to be made about which train can go first, and thus there arise the problem of priority orders among different traffic types.

Törnquist and Persson (2007) propose a MIP model which takes into account both passenger and freight trains. The model in a geographically large and fine-grained railway network with highly interacting traffic, consider reordering and rerouting of trains. This model can formulate a highly complex setting such as a railway network composed of segments with a large number of tracks which can be unidirectional (only permitting one-way traffic) and bidirectional. There are two goals, to minimize the total traffic delays, and to minimize the cost function based on the train delays. The cost function allocates different delay cost per minute, different tolerance time windows and different fixed penalty cost and to different passenger and freight trains. The model is tested on the southern part of the Swedish railway network. Since the model contains a lot detail and deal with large-scale network, the computational time can be long. Still this model does not give more analysis of the interaction between passenger and freight trains when they can have some conflict with the occupation of the infrastructure resources.

A prompt decision is quite important in RTTM. Törnquist (2012) improves Törnquist and Persson (2007) using a heuristic greedy approach. In general the heuristic provides solutions that are good enough very fast, but the author holds that it could be further improved.

Acuna-Agost et al. (2011) also extend the model presented in Törnquist and Persson (2007). In particular, they use hard and soft fixing of integer variables with local-branching-type cuts. Tests based on instances of French railways show a best compromise can be obtained with the Iterative MIP based local search procedure. Good solutions (average gap<1%) can be got within 5 min.

All the above literatures are macroscopic models. The models distinguish passenger trains and freight trains using delay cost. However, in real practices, dispatchers can always meet such difficulties, some high-speed passenger trains should recover to the origin timetable as soon as possible. At this moment, slow freight trains are not in the scope of the emergency, and their recovery can be postponed to "some other time". Corman et al. (2011) propose an innovative microscopic model to cope with the passenger and freight train rescheduling, using a set of priority. At each step, the procedure focuses on the current priority class, preserving solution quality from the higher priority classes and neglecting the lower priority classes in the optimization of train orders and times. The iterative process is implemented from the highest one to the lowest one until a new network disposition timetable is finished. They use the alternative graph to formulate and a sophisticated B&B algorithm to solve the multi-class rescheduling problem. The test result based on Utrecht Central shows an interesting gap between single-class and multi-class rescheduling problems in terms of delay minimization.

Similar studies can be referring to Godwin et al. (2007). They describe a situation in Indian Railway system that freight trains are routed and scheduled in a railway network where passenger trains must adhere to a strict schedule. The freight train movements can be inserted at any time or as demands arise, and should not disrupt passenger trains. They adopt a binary (0-1) MIP and a hierarchical permutation heuristic. The computational experiences for solving various problems are based on real data.

6   Conclusions and Future Research

This paper gives an overview of the state-of-the-art in models and algorithms for real time traffic management in case of disturbance in railway network. In particular, we describe various approaches in terms of the train types, stakeholders, and constraints. We draw the following conclusions:

1. Due to regional differences and other reasons, most research focus on passenger traffic management. Some American and Japanese researchers study railway freight transportation management. The European ongoing deregulation has created multiple competing actors such as different train operating companies for passenger and freight traffic, competing on the same tracks. Thereby infrastructure managers are to be neutral and cope with multiple conflicting requests and demands. The majority of previous research approaches does not account explicitly for this new situation. Furthermore, the complexity of the problem of having mixed traffic is often mentioned but less investigated. This is a clear direction of future research, about simultaneous management of railway traffic of different classes, including the diversity and interplay between passenger and freight trains.

2. There are two main tendencies of real time disturbance management models for railway traffic. Microscopic models consider all elements of the railway infrastructure for computing safe movements, thus are able to check feasibility and quality of the solutions from the viewpoint of operations managers. On the other hand, macroscopic models transfer the focus from minimizing train delays to improving the quality of service perceived by the passengers, i.e., less waiting time, more convenient transfers.

3. There are several challenges left open for research when dealing with optimization in the level of service, such as management of congestion on board or at stations, passenger behaviours, etc. Passengers' behaviour means their reactions when disturbance occur and lead to a change to their pre-planned path. Will they stick to their

original plans or follow the real-time suggestion for alternative modes of connectivity? The analysis of recorded passenger flows might provide insights on how passenger flows react to unexpected events as investigated, for example, by van der Hurk et al. (2013).

4. Improvement in calculation time can be important, to give a quick response in the real time management. There is a trend to integrate more detail (such as track capacity, station capacity, passenger behaviour, interactions, etc.) in the model, thus the RTTM becomes increasingly complex. The development of algorithms for RTTM is currently still mainly an academic field, where the research is still far ahead of what has been implemented in practice. Some approaches are implemented in practice, despite being far from the academic results.

5. Although most of the presented models show promising results in the described experiments, most researches mainly focus on instances representing relatively small railway networks (see Table 1 and Table 2). It will be quite a challenge to get the calculation results for large-scale network in short time when bring these methods into real operations.

Nevertheless, there are signals that practice has discovered the added value that can be provided by real-time management methods, based on the successes that have been achieved by the application of optimization methods in the railway planning stage, see Caprara et al(2002). Despite the large amount of research that has been accomplished in the last decades, the regular application of the research results in practice will still need quite some time.

References

1. Acuna-Agost, R., Michelon, P., Feillet, D., Gueye, S.: A MIP-based local search method for the railway rescheduling problem. Networks **57**(1), 69–86 (2011)
2. Albrecht, T., Binder, A., Gassel, C.: An overview on real-time speed control in rail-bound public transportation systems. In: Proceedings of the 2nd International Transportation Conference-Leuven, Belgium (2011)
3. Błażewicz, J., Domschke, W., Pesch, E.: The job shop scheduling problem: Conventional and new solution techniques. Eur. J. Oper. Res. **93**(1), 1–33 (1996)
4. Cacchiani, V., Huisman, D., Kidd, M., Kroon, L., Toth, P., Veelenturf, L., Wagenaar, J.: An Overview of Recovery Models and Algorithms for Real-time Railway Rescheduling. Transportation Res. Part B **63**, 15–37 (2014)
5. Caimi, G., Fuchsberger, M., Laumanns, M., Lüthi, M.: A model predictive control approach for discrete-time rescheduling in complex central railway station areas. Compt. & Operations Res. **39**, 2578–2593 (2012)
6. Caprara, A., Fischetti, M., Toth, P.: Modeling and solving the train timetabling problem. Oper. Res. **50**(5), 851–861 (2002)
7. Corman, F.: Bi-objective conflict detection and resolution in railway traffic management. Transportation Res. Part C **20**, 79–94 (2012)
8. Corman, F., D'Ariano, A., Hansen, I.A., Pacciarelli, D.: Optimal multi-class rescheduling of railway traffic. J. Rail Transport Planning & Management **1**, 14–24 (2011)
9. Corman, F., D'Ariano, A., Pacciarelli, D., Pranzo, M.: A Tabu search algorithm for rerouting trains during rail operations. Transportation Res. Part B **44**(1), 175–192 (2009)

10. Corman, F., D'Ariano, A., Pacciarelli, D., Samá, M.: Railway Traffic Reschedule in with Minimization of Passengers' Discomfort. Proceedings of the MT, ITS (2015)
11. D'Ariano, A.: Improving real-time train dispatching: models, algorithms, and applications. TRAIL Thesis Series, T2008/6, The Netherlands (2008)
12. D'Ariano, A., Corman, F., Pacciarelli, D., Pranzo, M.: Reordering and local rerouting strategies to manage train traffic in real time. Transportation Science 42(4), 405–419 (2008)
13. D'Ariano, A., Pacciarelli, D., Pranzo, M.: A branch and bound algorithm for scheduling trains in a railway network. European J. Operational Res. 183(2), 643–657 (2007)
14. D'Ariano, A., Pacciarelli, D., Pranzo, M.: Assessment of flexible timetables in real-time traffic management of a railway bottleneck. Transportation Res. Part C 16(2), 232–245 (2008)
15. Dewilde, T.: Improving the robustness of a railway system in large and complex station areas. Doctoral thesis (2014)
16. Dollevoet, T., Huisman, D., Kroon, L., Schmidt, M., Schöbel, A.: Delay Management including Capacities of Stations. Transportation Science 49(2), 185–203 (2015)
17. Dollevoet, T., Huisman, D., Schmidt, M., Schöbel, A.: Delay management with rerouting of passengers. Transportation Science 46(1), 74–89 (2012)
18. Dündar, S., Şahin, I.: Train re-scheduling with genetic algorithms and artificial neural networks for single-track railways. Transportation Res. Part C: Emerging Technologies 27, 1–15 (2013)
19. Gély, L., Dessagne, G., Lerin, C.: Modelling train re-scheduling with optimization and operational research techniques: results and applications at SNCF. In: Proceedings of WCRR, Montréal (2006)
20. Ginkel, A., Schöbel, A.: To wait or not to wait? The criteria delay management problem in public transportation. Transportation Science 41(4), 527–538 (2007)
21. Godwin, T., Gopalan, R., Narendran, T.T.: A heuristic for routing and scheduling freight trains in a passenger rail network. International J. Logistics Systems and Management 3(1), 101–133 (2007)
22. Jespersen-Groth, J., Potthoff, D., Clausen, J., Huisman, D., Kroon, L.G., Maroti, G., Nielsen, M.N.: Disruption Management in Passenger Railway Transportation, Informatics and Mathematical Modelling, Technical University of Denmark, Kgs. Lyngby, Denmark (2007)
23. Jong, G., Tseng, Y., Kouwenhoven, M., Verhoef, E., Bates, J.: The Value of Travel Time and Travel Time Reliability. Prepared for The Netherlands Ministry of Transport, Public Works and Water Management (2007)
24. Kanai, S., Shiina, K., Harada, S., Tomii, N.: An optimal delay management algorithm from passengers' viewpoints considering the whole railway network. J. Rail Transport Planning & Management 1, 25–37 (2011)
25. Kraay, D.R., Harke, P.T.: Real-time scheduling of freight railroads. US Transportation Res. Part B 29(3), 213–229 (1995)
26. Kuo, A., Elise, M.H., Mahmassani, H.S.: Freight train scheduling with elastic demand. Transportation Res. Part E 46, 1057–1070 (2010)
27. Liebchen, C., Schachtebeck, M., Schöbel, A., Stiller, S., Prigge. A.: Computing delay-resistant railway timetables. Technical report, ARRIVAL Report TR-0071, Georg-August Universität, Göttingen, Germany (2007)
28. Liebchen, C., Stiller, S.: Delay resistant timetabling. Technical Report 2006/24, Technische Universität Berlin, CASPT 2006 (2006)

29. Mascis, A., Pacciarelli, D.: Job shop scheduling with blocking and no-wait constraints. European Journal of Operational Res. **143**(3), 498–517 (2002)
30. Oetting, A., Keck, A.-K.: Monetarization of delay valuation for freight. In: 6th International Conference on Railway Operations Modelling and Analysis - RailTokyo2015 (2015)
31. Rodriguez, J.: A constraint programming model for real-time train scheduling at junctions. Transportation Res. Part B **41**, 231–245 (2007)
32. Schöbel, A.: A model for the delay management based on mixed integer programming. Electronic Notes Thoret. Comput. Sci. **50**(1), 1–10 (2001)
33. Schöbel, A.: Integer programming approaches for solving the delay management problem. In: Geraets, F., Kroon, L.G., Schoebel, A., Wagner, D., Zaroliagis, C.D. (eds.) Railway Optimization 2004. LNCS, vol. 4359, pp. 145–170. Springer, Heidelberg (2007)
34. Schöbel, A.: Capacity constraints in delay management. Public Transport **1**(2), 135–154 (2009)
35. Törnquist, J.: Design of an effective algorithm for fast response to the rescheduling of railway traffic during disturbances. Transportation Res. Part C **20**, 62–78 (2012)
36. Törnquist, J., Persson, J.A.: N-tracked railway traffic re-scheduling during disturbances. Transportation Res. Part B **41**(3), 342–362 (2007)
37. Van der Hurk, E., Kroon, L.G., Maroti, G., Bouman, P., Vervest, P.H.M.: Network reduction and dynamic forecasting of passenger flows for disruption management. In: Proceedings of Rail Copenhagen Conference, Denmark (2013)
38. Wegele, S., Schnieder, E.: Dispatching of train operations using genetic algorithms. In: Hansen, I.A., Dekking, F.M., Goverde, R.M.P., Heidergott, B., Meester, L.E. (eds.) Proceedings of Rail Delft Conference, The Netherlands (2005)

Model Predictive Control for Maintenance Operations Planning of Railway Infrastructures

Zhou Su$^{(\boxtimes)}$, Alfredo Núñez, Ali Jamshidi, Simone Baldi, Zili Li,
Rolf Dollevoet, and Bart De Schutter

Delft Center for Systems and Control & Section of Railway Engineering,
Delft University of Technology, 2628 CD Delft, The Netherlands
{Z.Su-1,A.A.NunezVicencio,A.Jamshidi,S.Baldi,Z.Li,
R.P.B.J.Dollevoet,B.DeSchutter}@tudelft.nl

Abstract. This paper develops a new decision making method for optimal planning of railway maintenance operations using hybrid Model Predictive Control (MPC). A linear dynamic model is used to describe the evolution of the health condition of a segment of the railway track. The hybrid characteristics arise from the three possible control actions: performing no maintenance, performing corrective maintenance, or doing a replacement. A detailed procedure for transforming the linear system with switched input, and recasting the transformed problem into a standard mixed integer quadratic programming problem is presented. The merits of the proposed MPC approach for designing railway track maintenance plans are demonstrated using a case study with numerical simulations. The results highlight the potential of MPC to improve condition-based maintenance procedures for railway infrastructure.

Keywords: Health condition monitoring and maintenance · Model Predictive Control (MPC) · Track maintenance · Railway engineering

1 Introduction

A railway track infrastructure system is composed of a set of different assets. All of those assets are distributed and interconnected over the railway network, continuously working together to keep the railway service reliable, safe, and fast. Each asset has a different need for maintenance, at different times and according to its degradation process, which is influenced by geographic position, tonnage of the track, health condition of the rolling stock, among many other factors. Thus, to sustainably manage railway assets, a step forward from the current policy of "find and repair" towards a more integrated methodology containing condition-based monitoring and predictive maintenance is required to improve the entire whole system performance. In the Netherlands, over forty percent of the maintenance costs is related to track maintenance [1]. Due to this fact, a condition-based maintenance decision support system can facilitate the infrastructure manager to decide where and which type of maintenance should be

© Springer International Publishing Switzerland 2015
F. Corman et al. (Eds.): ICCL 2015, LNCS 9335, pp. 673–688, 2015.
DOI: 10.1007/978-3-319-24264-4_46

performed. Moreover, if a prediction capability is incorporated in the decision making, we can expect maintenance actions that will anticipate problems and will take corrective measures before a failure become costly or unsafe for the users. This study proposes a model based predictive maintenance strategy using condition-based monitoring. We in particular show how this strategy can be applied to maintenance planning for ballast degradation and for treating squats.

The role of ballast is to provide support to the tracks with hard stones aiming to distribute loads over the sleepers while the train is passing. It also allows rain and snow to drain, thermal expansion, and weight variance; and it inhibits the growth of weed and vegetation. In the deterioration process of ballast, some stones may be displaced due to the vibrations and some others will get a white rounded shape losing their properties (see Figure 1a). When the ballast is in a bad condition, it will be reflected in the rail geometry. In order to keep the performance level at a satisfactory condition, tamping (packing the track ballast under the railway track) and ballast replacement are the principal maintenance actions to consider. In the literature, different studies have been proposed on how to predict changes in the track geometry condition. In some studies the ballast deterioration is modeled deterministically based on the average growth of track irregularities [2–4]. Other studies have linked stochastic degradation process with the effects of possible maintenance and renewal options [5,6].

Squats are a type of Rolling Contact Fatigues (RCFs) that initiate on the rail surface and evolve into a network of cracks beneath the surface of the track that when not treated on time can evolve into rail breakage. Treating RCFs to avoid a reduced life cycle of the track is very expensive. Early stage squats can be efficiently treated with grinding, while the only solution for late stage squats is track replacement (See Figure 1b). There are different methods to detect squats, like non-automatic inspection using human inspectors, photo/video records, and non-destructive testing such as ultrasonic and eddy current test [7,8]. For automatic detection of squats in an early stage, axle box acceleration (ABA) systems can be efficiently employed [9]. Predictive and robust models for squats evolution have been proposed in [10]. In [11], it is suggested to consider clusters of squats to facilitate grinding maintenance operations; however, the maintenance actions were obtained under static scenarios. In this paper, the main contribution is to propose a suitable model that incorporates the dynamics in the decision process of railway track maintenance operations, together with a rolling horizon methodology that can deal with discrete integer control actions.

The major benefit of applying Model Predictive Control (MPC) to maintenance operations planning is that the resulting strategy is flexible. By updating the degradation model using health condition monitoring methodologies regularly, the maintenance plans can be adapted dynamically. Especially when severe problems are predicted within the prediction horizon, MPC will suggest more frequent or more effective maintenance operations, resulting in a more efficient plan. This is a big step from current practice in railway maintenance, where cyclic preventive maintenance prevails, which, as a myopic strategy, is unable to predict the evolution of the degradation process, and treats severe problems

(a) Loose ballast indicated by the presence of white dust

(b) Severe squats (type C)

Fig. 1. Two different defects in railway infrastructures

only when they occur. Another merit of the proposed predictive methodology is that the objective function explicitly captures the trade-off between maintenance costs and the health condition of the track. This is crucial for railway infrastructure managers, who require transparent tools that facilitate the decision making process. Moreover, other factors concerning the management of railway infrastructures, like closure time due to maintenance, can also be conveniently added to the MPC optimization problem. In addition, limits on the admissible degradation level can be included effortlessly as constraints in MPC, which is especially useful for the maintenance of safety-critical components.

This paper is organized as follows: first a brief introduction to MPC is presented in Section 2; then Key Performance Indicators (KPIs) and maintenance options for railway infrastructures are explained in Section 3; the proposed MPC approach is explained in detail in Section 4 and illustrated by the case study in Section 5; finally a short summary and remarks on future work is provided in Section 6.

2 Model Predictive Control (MPC)

Model Predictive Control (MPC) is an advanced design methodology for control systems, which has gained wide popularity in the process industry since the last decade. MPC was pioneered simultaneously by Richalet et al. [12,13] and Cutler and Ramaker [14] in the late 1970s. The main reasons for the success of MPC in the process industry are:

- Easy handling of multi-input-multi-output (MIMO) processes, non-minimum phases processes, processes with large time delay, and unstable processes;
- Easy tuning of parameters (in principle only three parameters need to be tuned);
- Natural embedding of constraints in a systematic way;
- Easy handling of structural changes by regularly updating the process model.

Five elements are essential for MPC:

1. A process model
2. A cost criterion
3. Constraints
4. Optimization algorithms
5. Receding horizon principle.

For maintenance operations planning in railway network, the process model can be the degradation model or the performance indicator of an asset, the cost criterion can be a trade-off between track condition and maintenance cost, and the constraints can be an upper bound on the maximum degradation level and budget. Depending on the process model, which might contain continuous and discrete variables, the cost criterion, and the imposed constraints, the computation of a sequence of future control actions at each sample step will result in different optimization problems, which must be solved by some mathematical programming algorithm. For railway maintenance, since the degradation of the track condition is a continuous process and maintenance operations are intrinsically discrete, the planning of maintenance operations should in general result in a mixed integer programming problem. This optimization problem must be solved at each sample step, providing a sequence of optimal discrete control actions. The length of the sequence is called prediction horizon when using a receding horizon approach. Instead of using the whole sequence of predicted control actions, only the first entry is applied, and a new sequence is computed at the next sample step with updated information, e.g. new measurements of the track condition.

Despite its success in the process industry, the applications of MPC in railway maintenance operations are scarce, although the application of mathematical models and optimization is not uncommon in maintenance [15,16]. The process model associated with most operations planning problems usually contains both continuous and discrete dynamics. In [17] an MPC scheme is applied to plan risk mitigation actions together with other control variables, using a mixed integer quadratic formulation. For complex decision making problems, a hierarchical or distributed approach is often applied to render the problem tractable. See [18] for an application of hierarchical distributed MPC to risk management of a network of irrigation canals, and [19] for applications of hybrid MPC to interventions in behavioral health and inventory management in supply chains. As a model-based decision making approach, MPC can be viewed as an extension of condition-based maintenance, as it does not only take into consideration the current track condition, but also predicts the track condition, using updated track measurements, as well as knowledge on the process, e.g. degradation models.

3   Railway Maintenance

A brief introduction on railway maintenance is presented, explaining how the track condition is measured in practice, as well as typical operations on track maintenance.

3.1   Key Performance Indicators (KPIs) for Maintenance Planning

To ensure the proper functioning of railway tracks, both temporal and spatial characteristics need to be considered in the maintenance decisions. For this purpose, Key Performance Indicators (KPIs) are developed to capture the dynamics of track deterioration and the evolution of defects. These KPIs usually consider a broad set of measurements from different sources and define the health condition of the track as a single number. When normalized, 0 would mean a healthy track, while 1 a track with very bad condition. This health number changes over time, and when reaching some threshold corrective maintenance is performed.

In the case of ballast, the track bed positioning and alignment changes in terms of speed and number of passing trains have to be considered in the design of KPI. The following measurements are usually considered [20,21]: (1) cyclic top, which is a measure of resonant frequencies, (2) rail spacing compared to the standard gauge, (3) a measure of cant variation over 3 m and 5 m, (4) lateral geometry (alignment) - rail alignment, averaged over the left and right rail, expressed as short and long wave standard deviations.

In [10] some KPIs are proposed for maintenance operations related to squats using axle box acceleration measurements. The number of squats of type A (light squats in early stage), number of squats of type B or C (severe squats), number of potential risk points, and density of squats are the KPIs proposed. Field observations also revealed that different squats have different rates of growth, thus three different evolution scenarios were proposed: slow growth, average growth, and fast growth. Due to the big number of KPIs, temporal dependence and scenarios, one global KPI using a fuzzy inference system was proposed to facilitate maintenance decisions. This global KPI for squats represents the health condition of a cluster of defects and it is represented by a score between zero (representing a healthy state of the track) and two (indicating an unhealthy condition of the track).

3.2   Maintenance Options

This paper evaluates three possible maintenance options: (1) to do nothing, (2) corrective maintenance: tamping for ballast or grinding for squats, (3) replacement: full ballast replacement or track replacement. Next, a short description of the maintenance actions is given.

In the case of tamping, the track geometry is adjusted when the track alignment is outside the accepted tolerances. Tamping machines are able to pack the ballast under the sleepers in order to correct the alignment of the rails using measurements of the track geometry, estimating the needed adjustments, lifting/inserting the track and at the same time vibrating tamping arms [22]. Tamping can improve the track condition. However, in the worst case, vibrating arms into the ballast could lead some break-up of the stones which can accelerate the ballast degradation. When the ballast has reached the end of its useful life, then ballast renewal must be carried out.

In the case of grinding, the Dutch railways use a cyclic grinding strategy that is not based on the condition of the track. This mean that sections that are healthy are ground, and also sections that need replacement are ground in spite of its inefficiency. Squats in early stage can be removed by grinding, because they have not developed the network of crack beneath yet. Therefore, early detection of RCF rail defects is cost-effective when a grinding campaign is scheduled appropriately in time. Furthermore, grinding is not efficient for cracks deeper than 5-7 mm. Grinding severe squats can delay rail replacement but may accelerate the squat evolution, because the cracks are not yet removed.

When the conditions of either ballast or track has worsened, and tamping or grinding is ineffective, then replacement will be the only option. With predictive models that incorporate the degradation process of the ballast or the track, it is possible to estimate the life cycle of the track and to inform the infrastructure manager about the tentative time for replacing. This is crucial information because replacement campaigns are extremely costly and the track needs to be unavailable for a long period. In the case of ballast replacement, keeping a similar total volume of stones before and after the replacement is essential. Long segments with deteriorated ballast will require a higher packing level of the damaged ballast [23]. In the case of rails, they are typically replaced according to predefined estimated life cycle, tonnage, wear limit, fatigue, and weather conditions. Determining the optimal rail replacement interval is a critical issue for rail industry, due to its high cost and consequences over the entire performance of the infrastructure.

Figure 2 shows a generic KPI and the typical effect of corrective maintenance or replacement. While a corrective maintenance (grinding or tamping) will improve the performance, a general drop of the performance is usually observed. In the case of replacement, while more expensive than corrective maintenance, it usually leads into a healthy status for a longer period of time. In the next section, a hybrid MPC methodology is proposed to capture the principal dynamics of railway maintenance operation.

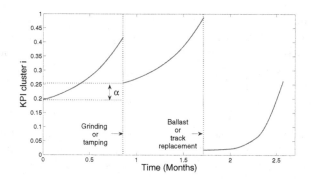

Fig. 2. Generic KPI evolution over time.

4 MPC for Maintenance Operation Planning

A maintenance model describing the degradation dynamic of the track condition is presented, with three maintenance operations as inputs. This linear model with discrete inputs is then transformed into a standard Mixed Logic Dynamic (MLD) system, and an MPC scheme is designed for this MLD system.

4.1 Maintenance Model Description

We consider the following discrete-time state space model for the degradation dynamic (unhealthy condition) of a certain asset (e.g. track with squats, or ballast) in a segment of track:

$$
\begin{aligned}
x_1(k+1) &= a_1 x_1(k) + f_1(x(k),\, u(k)) \\
x_2(k+1) &= x_2(k) + f_2(x(k),\, u(k))
\end{aligned}
\tag{1}
$$

with constraint
$$
m \le x_i(k) \le M \quad \forall i \in \{1, 2\}
\tag{2}
$$

The state vector is $x(k) = \begin{bmatrix} x_1(k) & x_2(k) \end{bmatrix}^{\mathrm{T}}$. In particular, x_1 represents the level of degradation of a part of the track regarding a certain type of fault, e.g. the average length of the squats in a cluster. The parameter a_1 is the degradation rate of the track, which is assumed to be larger than 1 so that the track condition deteriorates exponentially as observed in late stage of degradation. The state x_2 records the level of degradation upon the last corrective maintenance operation. This is necessary because corrective operation will be unlikely to bring the track back to a condition healthier than the previous corrective operation. The states are bounded in the interval $[m,\, M]$ by the constraint (2), with m and M representing the lowest and highest admissible degradation level, respectively.

The input $u(k) \in \{1, 2, 3\}$ is a discrete input representing the three major maintenance operations: do nothing, corrective maintenance, and replacement, respectively. The interpretation of the input u is given in Table 1.

Table 1. Interpretation of maintenance operations and the corresponding value of input

Input value	Maintenance operation	Effect on the track condition
1	do nothing	no effect
2	corrective maintenance	bring the track condition to a healthier level, but usually not as healthy as the condition upon the last corrective maintenance
3	replacement	bring the track condition to a state with no degradation

The effects of the maintenance operations are captured by the discontinuous functions f_1 and f_2, which take the following representation:

$$f_1(x(k),\, u(k)) = \begin{cases} 0 & \text{if } u(k) = 1 \\ -a_1 x_1(k) + x_2(k) & \text{if } u(k) = 2 \\ -a_1 x_1(k) + m & \text{if } u(k) = 3 \end{cases} \quad (3)$$

and

$$f_2(x(k),\, u(k)) = \begin{cases} 0 & \text{if } u(k) = 1 \\ \alpha & \text{if } u(k) = 2 \\ -x_2(k) + m & \text{if } u(k) = 3 \end{cases} \quad (4)$$

with α, which usually takes a small positive value, indicating the offset of the effect of one corrective maintenance from the last corrective maintenance, i.e. a corrective maintenance can only bring the condition to a level which is α worse than that just after the previous corrective maintenance operation.

4.2   Transformation into an Mixed Logic Dynamic (MLD) Systems

The system (1) can be viewed as a hybrid system with linear plant model (degradation process) and switching control. The difficulty of designing a controller for such systems lies in the different conditions triggered by different values of the control input (equations (3)–(4)). By associating the three conditions triggered by the three control actions with two binary variables $\delta_1(k)$ and $\delta_2(k)$, the system (1) can be transformed into a Mixed Logic Dynamic (MLD) system. The translation from the control input $u(k)$ to the binary variables $\delta_1(k)$ and $\delta_2(k)$ is shown in Table 2.

Table 2. Translation from control input to binary variables

$u(k)$	$\delta_1(k)$	$\delta_2(k)$
1	0	0
2	0	1
3	1	0

We eliminate the fourth option ($\delta_1 = \delta_2 = 1$) by adding the constraint:

$$\delta_1(k) + \delta_2(k) \leq 1 \quad (5)$$

After translating the control input $u(k)$ into binary variables $\delta_1(k)$ and $\delta_2(k)$, system (1) can be rewritten as

$$\begin{aligned} x_1(k+1) &= a_1 x_1(k) + \delta_2(k)(-a_1 x_1(k) + x_2(k)) + \delta_1(k)(-a_1 x_1(k) + m) \\ &= a_1 x_1(k) - a_1 \delta_1(k) x_1(k) - a_1 \delta_2(k) x_1(k) + \delta_2(k) x_2(k) + \delta_1(k) m \\ x_2(k+1) &= x_2(k) + \alpha \delta_2(k) + \delta_1(k)(-x_2(k) + m) \\ &= x_2(k) - \delta_1(k) x_2(k) + m \delta_1(k) + \alpha \delta_2(k) \end{aligned} \quad (6)$$

The system (6) is non-linear in the state $x(k)$ and in the two binary variables $\delta_1(k)$ and $\delta_2(k)$. The non-linear system can be transformed into the following linear system:

$$\begin{bmatrix} x_1(k+1) \\ x_2(k+1) \end{bmatrix} = \begin{bmatrix} a_1 & 0 \\ 0 & 1 \end{bmatrix} \begin{bmatrix} x_1(k) \\ x_2(k) \end{bmatrix} + \begin{bmatrix} m & 0 \\ m & \alpha \end{bmatrix} \begin{bmatrix} \delta_1(k) \\ \delta_2(k) \end{bmatrix} + \begin{bmatrix} -a_1 & -a_1 & 1 & 0 \\ 0 & 0 & 0 & -1 \end{bmatrix} \begin{bmatrix} z_1(k) \\ z_2(k) \\ z_3(k) \\ z_4(k) \end{bmatrix} \tag{7}$$

by introducing four auxiliary variables

$$z_1(k) = \delta_1(k)x_1(k) \qquad\qquad z_2(k) = \delta_2(k)x_1(k)$$
$$z_3(k) = \delta_2(k)x_2(k) \qquad\qquad z_4(k) = \delta_1(k)x_2(k)$$

The equation for each auxiliary variable

$$z_p(k) = \delta_i(k)x_j(k) \quad p \in \{1, 2, 3, 4\}, \ i, j \in \{1, 2\}$$

is equivalent to the following four inequality constraints [24,25]:

$$\begin{cases} z_p(k) \le M\delta_i(k) \\ z_p(k) \ge m\delta_i(k) \\ z_p(k) \le x_j(k) - m(1 - \delta_i(k)) \\ z_p(k) \ge x_j(k) - M(1 - \delta_i(k)) \end{cases} \tag{8}$$

which results in sixteen inequality constraints in total.

Finally, the mixed logical dynamic (MLD) system [24] described by the linear dynamics (7) and linear constraints (2), (5), (8) can be formulated in the following compact form [1]:

$$x(k+1) = Ax(k) + B_1\delta(k) + B_2z(k) \tag{9}$$
$$E_1x(k) + E_2\delta(k) + E_3z(k) \le g \tag{10}$$

with $\delta(k) = \begin{bmatrix} \delta_1(k) & \delta_2(k) \end{bmatrix}^{\mathrm{T}}$ and $z(k) = \begin{bmatrix} z_1(k) & z_2(k) & z_3(k) & z_4(k) \end{bmatrix}^{\mathrm{T}}$

4.3   The MLD-MPC Problem and its Solution via MIQP

Consider the MLD system (9)–(10). Denote by $\hat{x}(k+j|k)$ the estimated state at sample step k with information available at sample step $k+j$. Likewise, define $\hat{z}(k+j|k)$ as the estimate of the auxiliary variable at sample step $k+j$. Let N_{p} be the prediction horizon[2], and define

$$\tilde{x}(k) = \begin{bmatrix} \hat{x}^{\mathrm{T}}(k+1|k) & \dots & \hat{x}^{\mathrm{T}}(k+N_{\mathrm{p}}|k) \end{bmatrix}^{\mathrm{T}}$$

---

[1] Since the introduced binary variable δ is a full replacement of the original discrete control input u, which no longer appears in the resulting MLD system, we treat δ as control input for the MLD-MPC problem.

[2] Here we set the control horizon equal to the prediction horizon.

as the estimates of the future state at sample step k. The estimates of input and auxiliary variables ($\tilde{\delta}(k)$ and $\tilde{z}(k)$) can be defined in a similar way. Grouping the input and auxiliary variables together we further define

$$\tilde{V}(k) = \left[\tilde{\delta}^{\mathrm{T}}(k)\ \tilde{z}^{\mathrm{T}}(k)\right]^{\mathrm{T}}$$

After successive substitution of (9), the state prediction equation can then be written in the following compact form

$$\tilde{x}(k) = M_1\tilde{V}(k) + M_2 x(k) \tag{11}$$

The goal of maintenance operations planning is to minimize degradation with the lowest possible maintenance cost, which can be formulated by the following objective function

$$J(k) = J_{\mathrm{Perf}}(k) + \lambda J_{\mathrm{Cost}}(k) \tag{12}$$

with $J_{\mathrm{Perf}}(k)$ and $J_{\mathrm{Cost}}(k)$ representing the performance and the cost of maintenance operations, respectively, while the weighting parameter $\lambda > 0$ captures the trade-off of the two conflicting objectives.

More specifically, if a weighted 2-norm is considered for performance, i.e. $J_{\mathrm{Perf}}(k) = \|\tilde{x}(k)\|_P^2$, with P positive definite weighting matrix, a mixed integer quadratic programming (MIQP) problem will be obtained. Alternatively, a 1-norm or an $\infty-$norm can also be applied, with $J_{\mathrm{Perf}}(k) = \|P\tilde{x}(k)\|_1$ or $J_{\mathrm{Perf}}(k) = \|P\tilde{x}(k)\|_\infty$, and P a matrix with non-negative entries. If a 1-norm or an $\infty-$norm is applied, the optimization problem can be recast as a mixed integer linear programming (MILP) problem, which is generally easier to solve than an MIQP problem.

The cost of maintenance operations $J_{\mathrm{Cost}}(k)$ has the following linear representation:

$$J_{\mathrm{Cost}}(k) = R\tilde{\delta}(k) = Q\tilde{V}(k)$$

with R a matrix with non-negative entries assigning weights to different maintenance operations, i.e. the cost of corrective maintenance and replacement. Since no weights are assigned to the auxiliary variables, we have $Q = \begin{bmatrix} R\ 0 \end{bmatrix}$.

For illustration purposes, we consider now a weighted 2-norm for J_{Perf}. Given the weighting matrices P and Q, the objective function can be rewritten as:

$$J(k) = \tilde{x}(k)^{\mathrm{T}} P\tilde{x}(k) + \lambda Q\tilde{V}(k) \tag{13}$$

$$= (M_1\tilde{V}(k) + M_2 x(k))^{\mathrm{T}} P(M_1\tilde{V}(k) + M_2 x(k)) + \lambda Q\tilde{V}(k) \tag{14}$$

$$= \tilde{V}^{\mathrm{T}}(k) S_1 \tilde{V}(k) + \left(S_2 + x^{\mathrm{T}}(k) S_3\right) \tilde{V}(k) + S_4 \tag{15}$$

Note that S_4 is a constant and can be removed from the objective function without changing the solution of the optimization problem. Finally we can formulate the MLD-MPC problem as a standard MIQP problem with decision variable $\tilde{V}(k)$:

$$\min_{\tilde{V}(k)} \tilde{V}^{\mathrm{T}}(k) S_1 \tilde{V}(k) + (S_2 + x^{\mathrm{T}}(k) S_3) \tilde{V}(k) \tag{16}$$

$$\text{s.t. } F_1 \tilde{V}(k) \leq F_2 + F_3 x(k) \tag{17}$$

MIQP problems are identified as NP-hard [26], indicating that in practice the solution time might grow exponentially with the problem size. Among the major algorithms for solving MIQP and MILP problems, branch-and-bound methods [27] are generally regarded as the most efficient ones.

5 Case Study

Now we consider a simple case study to illustrate the proposed approach. An MPC controller for the MLD system (9)–(10) with quadratic objective function (16) is implemented in Matlab, and the MIQP optimization problem at each sample step is solved using the Gurobi Optimizer 5.6.3, which can solve MIQP and MILP problems. The parameters for the degradation dynamics, as well as the performance criteria (in particular, the parameters for the objective function) are given in the appendix. We present the simulation results with three different prediction horizons ($N_{\mathrm{p}} = 5, 10, 15$), and three different weights ($\lambda = 0.1, 1, 10$).

A simple cyclic preventive maintenance approach with the same objective function is also implemented and optimized in Matlab for a comparison. The two decision variables for the cyclic approach are the period for corrective maintenance (T_{c}) and the period for replacement (T_r). The latter is usually fixed as a multiple of the former, i.e. $T_r = n T_{\mathrm{c}}$, thus we determine the multiple n instead of T_r. The planning horizon is the whole simulation time, and an iteration of all possible combinations of T_{c} and n is applied to generate the best possible cyclic maintenance plan for a given cost criterion.

The simulation results from the MPC approach are given in Figure 3–5 and the results from the cyclic approach are given in Figure 6. The flexibility of MPC

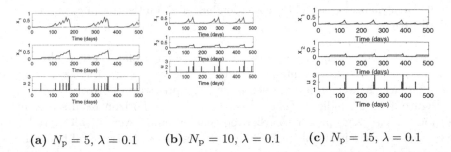

    (a) $N_{\mathrm{p}} = 5, \lambda = 0.1$ **(b)** $N_{\mathrm{p}} = 10, \lambda = 0.1$ **(c)** $N_{\mathrm{p}} = 15, \lambda = 0.1$

Fig. 3. Predicted state x and control input u for different prediction horizons and a small λ

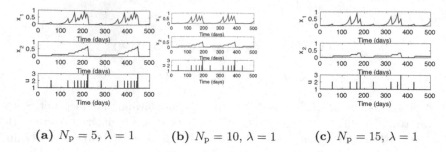

(a) $N_p = 5,\ \lambda = 1$ (b) $N_p = 10,\ \lambda = 1$ (c) $N_p = 15,\ \lambda = 1$

Fig. 4. Predicted state x and control input u for different prediction horizons and a medium λ

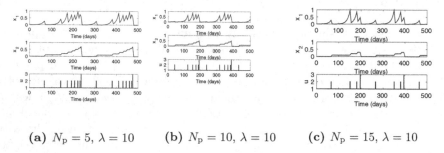

(a) $N_p = 5,\ \lambda = 10$ (b) $N_p = 10,\ \lambda = 10$ (c) $N_p = 15,\ \lambda = 10$

Fig. 5. Predicted state x and control input u for different prediction horizons and a big λ

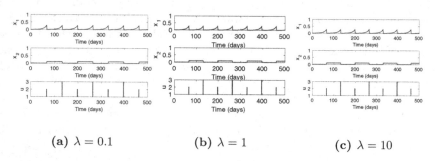

(a) $\lambda = 0.1$ (b) $\lambda = 1$ (c) $\lambda = 10$

Fig. 6. Maintenance plans and the corresponding effect on the track degradation level with different λ

is clearly demonstrated by the resulting maintenance plans, which all suggest more frequent corrective maintenance as the track condition deteriorates, despite the differences in weighting parameters and the prediction horizon.

Figure 3–5 also indicate that a longer prediction horizon results in a more cautious maintenance plan, i.e. earlier replacement and lower overall degradation level. The weight λ in the objective function represents the trade-off between the track condition and the maintenance cost. This is also shown in Figure 3–5, where it can be noticed that for a larger λ, the first replacement is suggested at a later time step, for a given N_p. On the contrary, the cyclic approach suggests the same

Table 3. Evaluation of closed-loop objective function for MPC (J_{MPC}) and cyclic approach (J_{CYC}). For a given λ, the lowest objective function value is marked in bold.

λ	J_{MPC}			J_{CYC}
	$N_p = 5$	$N_p = 10$	$N_p = 15$	
0.1	31.85	22.08	**11.88**	12.65
1	125.63	107.80	**90.23**	97.25
10	797.53	726.80	**702.25**	943.25

optimal maintenance plan for the three different λ (corrective maintenance every 65 days and replacement every 130 days).

The values of the closed-loop objective function for both approaches are given in Table 3. It can be seen that with a long enough prediction horizon, the maintenance plan generated by MPC always out performs the plan generated by the cyclic approach.

6 Conclusions

In this contribution a hybrid Model Predictive Control (MPC) approach with discrete input has been developed to support decision making in railway maintenance. We have provided a detailed procedure to illustrate how to transform the model-based optimization problem into a standard mixed integer quadratic programming problem. Numerical simulations have been performed for a case study with different parameter settings, and the results indeed demonstrate the potential of MPC as an optimization-based approach to aid decision making in maintenance of railway infrastructures.

Future work includes developing a more extensive process model with parameters obtained from track measurements, and extending the current approach from maintenance operations planning for a single segment of track to joint decision making for multiple segments.

Acknowledgments. Research sponsored by the NWO/ProRail project "Multi-party risk management and key performance indicator design at the whole system level (PYRAMIDS)", project 438-12-300, which is partly financed by the Netherlands Organisation for Scientific Research (NWO).

Appendix

The values and interpretation of the parameters for the degradation dynamics (1) are given in Table 4. The initial condition is $x(0) = [m\,m]^T$, and the sampling time is 5 days.

Table 4. Parmaters for degradation dynamics

Parameter	Value	Interpretation
a_1	1.09	degradation rate
α	0.1	offset for corrective maintenance
m	0.001	minimum degradation level
M	1	maximum allowed degradation level

The matrix P is a square matrix consisting of diagonal replications of the diagonal matrices $P_{Sub} = \text{diag}(1, 0)$:

$$P = \text{diag}\left(\underbrace{P_{Sub}, \ldots, P_{Sub}}_{N_p \text{ times}}\right)$$

The matrix Q is a block-row matrix containing N_p horizontal replications of the diagonal matrix $Q_{Sub} = \text{diag}(r, 1, 0, 0, 0, 0)$:

$$Q = \left(\underbrace{Q_{Sub}, \ldots, Q_{Sub}}_{N_p \text{ times}}\right)$$

where the parameter r is the ratio of the cost of one replacement over the cost of one corrective maintenance. For the case study we assume replacement is 30 times more costly than corrective maintenance, thus $r = 30$.

References

1. Zoeteman, A.: Yardstick for condition based and differential planning of track and turnout renewal: a major step towards full decision support. In: Proceedings of the 7th World Congress on Railway Research (WCRR), Montreal, Canada (1993)
2. Chrismer, S., Selig, E.: Computer model for ballast maintenance planning. In: Proceedings of 5th International Heavy Haul Railway Conference, Beijing, China, pp. 223–227 (1993)
3. Sato, Y.: Optimum track structure considering deterioration in ballasted track. In: Proceedings of the 6th International Heavy Haul Conference, Cape Town, South Africa, pp. 576–590 (1997)
4. Sadeghi, J., Askarinejad, H.: Development of improved railway track degradation models. Structure and Infrastructure Engineering **6**, 675–688 (2010)
5. Shafahi, Y., Hakhamaneshi, R.: Application of a maintenance management model for Iranian railways based on the Markov chain and probabilistic dynamic programming. International Journal of Science and Technology. Transaction A: Civil Engineering **16**, 87–97 (2009)
6. Podofillini, L., Zio, E., Vatn, J.: Risk-informed optimisation of railway tracks inspection and maintenance procedures. Reliability Engineering & System Safety **91**, 20–35 (2006)

7. Magel, E., Tajaddini, A., Trosino, M., Kalousek, J.: Traction, forces, wheel climb and damage in high-speed railway operations. Wear **265**, 1446–1451 (2008)
8. Peng, D., Jones, R.: Modelling of the lock-in thermography process through finite element method for estimating the rail squat defects. Engineering Failure Analysis **28**, 275–288 (2013)
9. Molodova, M., Li, Z., Núñez, A., Dollevoet, R.: Automatic detection of squats in railway infrastructure. IEEE Transactions on Intelligent Transportation Systems **15**, 1980–1990 (2014)
10. Jamshidi, A., Núñez, A., Li, Z., Dollevoet, R.: Maintenance decision indicators for treating squats in railway infrastructures. In: Proceedings of the 94th Annual Meeting of the Transportation Research Board, Washington D.C., USA (2015)
11. Jamshidi, A., Núñez, A., Li, Z., Dollevoet, R.: Maintenance decision indicators for treating squats in railway infrastructures. In: Proceedings of the Joint Rail Conference 2015 (JRC2015), San Jose, CA, USA (2015)
12. Richalet, J., Rault, A., Testud, J.: Algorithmic control of industrial processes. In: Proceedings of the 4th IFAC Symposium on Identification and System Parameter Estimation, Tbilisi, URSS, pp. 1119–1167 (1976)
13. Richalet, J., Rault, A., Testud, J., Papon, J.: Model predictive heuristic control: Applications to industrial processes. Automatica **14**, 413–428 (1978)
14. Cutler, C., Ramaker, B.: Dynamic matrix control - a computer control algorithm. In: Proceedings of the Joint Automatic Control Conference, vol. 1., p. WP5–B (1980)
15. Scarf, P.: On the application of mathematical models in maintenance. European Journal of Operational Research **99**, 493–506 (1997)
16. Dekker, R.: Applications of maintenance optimization models: A review and analysis. Reliability Engineering & System Safety **51**, 229–240 (1996)
17. Zafra-Cabeza, A., Ridao, M., Camacho, E.: A mixed integer quadratic programming formulation of risk management for reverse osmosis plants. Desalination **268**, 46–54 (2011)
18. Zafra-Cabeza, A., Maestre, J., Ridao, M., Camacho, E., Sánchez, L.: A hierarchical distributed model predictive control approach to irrigation canals: A risk mitigation perspective. Journal of Process Control **21**, 787–799 (2011)
19. Nandola, N., Rivera, D.: An improved formulation of hybrid model predictive control with application to production-inventory systems. IEEE Transactions on Control Systems Technology **21**, 121–135 (2013)
20. Parida, A., Stenström, C.: Performance measurement for managing railway infrastructure. International Journal of Railway Technology **2**, 1–14 (2013)
21. Stenström, C., Parida, A., Galar, D., Kumar, U.: Link and effect model for performance improvement of railway infrastructure. Proceedings of the Institution of Mechanical Engineers, Part F: Journal of Rail and Rapid Transit (2013) (0954409713492956)
22. Prescott, D., Andrews, J.: Modelling maintenance in railway infrastructure management. In: Proceedings of the 2013 Annual Reliability and Maintainability Symposium (RAMS), pp. 1–6 (2013)
23. Lam, H., Wong, M., Yang, Y.: A feasibility study on railway ballast damage detection utilizing measured vibration of in situ concrete sleeper. Engineering Structures **45**, 284–298 (2012)
24. Bemporad, A., Morari, M.: Control of systems integrating logic, dynamics, and constraints. Automatica **35**, 407–427 (1999)

25. Williams, H.: Model Building in Mathematical Programming. Wiley (1993)
26. Schrijver, A.: Theory of Linear and Integer Programming. John Wiley & Sons (1993)
27. Fletcher, R., Leyffer, S.: Numerical experience with lower bounds for MIQP branch-and-bound. SIAM Journal on Optimization **8**, 604–616 (1998)

An Original Simulation Model to Improve the Order Picking Performance: Case Study of an Automated Warehouse

Francisco Faria[✉] and Vasco Reis

Instituto Superior Técnico, Universidade de Lisboa, Lisbon, Portugal
{francisco.faria,vascoreis}@tecnico.ulisboa.pt

Abstract. Order picking is a labour-intensive operation and so it represents significant expenditures, with any underperformance leading to high operational costs for the entire supply chain. Hence, this manuscript reports a research aimed to enhance the order picking process at an automated warehouse. The research included an assessment and restructuring of the storage assignment in the picking area and the picking process, namely the routing method.

A simulation model was developed to assess the performance of the order picking, taking in account multiple scenarios, in a total of sixteen scenarios (including three storage assignment policy and five routing methods plus a base case), varying in storage assignment policy and routing method.

The results evidence that gains above 30% could be achieved in certain scenarios (e.g.: class-based storage assignment policy with s-shape routing).

Keywords: Storage assignment · Routing methods · Discrete events simulation · Order picking · Warehousing · Logistics

1 Introduction

Order picking is the most labour-intensive operation in warehouses with manual systems, and a very capital-intensive operation in warehouses with automated systems, with any underperformance leading to unsatisfactory service and high operational cost for the whole supply chain. Studies estimate the picking costs to be above 50% of the total warehouse operating expense (see van den Berg & Zijm, 1999; Ruben & Jacobs, 1999; Broulias et al., 2005; Eisenstein, 2008; De Koster et al, 2007; Rushton et al., 2006). Therefore, in the current competitive paradigm driven by cost reductions, warehousing professionals consider order picking as the highest priority area for productivity improvements (Goetschalckx & Ashayeri, 1989; De Koster et al., 2007).

Henceforth, the all-embracing objective of the work presented in this manuscript was to assess and restructure the storage assignment in the picking area and the order picking process (namely the routing method) in order to enhance the order picking performance of an automated warehouse, so-called Carregado 2 Logistic Operations Centre (C2). This warehouse is run by a major Portuguese logistics company – Grupo

© Springer International Publishing Switzerland 2015
F. Corman et al. (Eds.): ICCL 2015, LNCS 9335, pp. 689–703, 2015.
DOI: 10.1007/978-3-319-24264-4_47

Luis Simões (LS). To accomplish this objective a methodology was developed to assess the performance of the order picking in C2, taking in account various scenarios, respectively before and after the implementation of various storage assignment policies and routing methods. To this end a simulation model, based on discrete-event simulation (DES), was created, using picking time as measure of performance. A set of alternative storage assignment policies and routing methods was tested.

The remainder of the manuscript is organized as follows. Section 2 is a brief literature review focusing on order picking systems optimization. Section 3 presents the Carregado 2 Logistic Operations Centre – the case study. In Section 4 the simulation model is described, while in Section 5 it is applied to the case study. Lastly, the final conclusions of this work are offered on section 6.

The research reported in this manuscript was developed within the scope of a Master Dissertation[1] carried out at the University of Lisbon, Portugal.

2   Literature Review on Order Picking Systems Optimization

The most common objective of order picking systems is to maximise the service level while respecting resource constraints. The uttermost important relation between the order picking and service level is that the faster the picking occurs, the better (De Koster et al., 2007). Travel represents 50% of order-picker's time in a typical picker-to-parts warehouse (Tompkins et al., 2003). It is, therefore, the first and most promising candidate for enhancement.

Following De Koster et al., (2007), to optimize travel time (or travel distance) in low level, manual-pick order picking processes one can focus on ideal (internal) layout design, storage assignment methods, routing methods, order accumulation, order batching and zoning (Fig. 1).

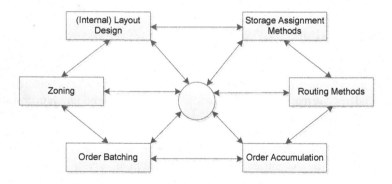

Fig. 1. Optimization of low level, manual-pick order-picking processes.

---

[1]   The interested reader is referred to:
https://fenix.tecnico.ulisboa.pt/homepage/ist165183/thesis

The optimization of these six policies has the advantage of remaining within the tactical and operational levels, which is critical for a built warehouse where strategic decisions are already taken and are difficult and expensive to change.

Please note that, while these six optimization objectives are strongly interdependent, including all decisions in one model is complex. Consequently, researchers restrict their studies to one or few decision areas at a time (De Koster et al., 2007).

The internal layout design concerns the determination of the number of blocks, and the number, length and width of aisles in each block of a picking area. The objective is to find the best warehouse layout with respect to a certain objective function, taking in consideration a set of constraints and requirements. Again, the most common objective is the minimisation of travel distance.

The order picking area can be divided into zones, i.e. zoning. To each zone a picker is assigned, picking the part of the order that is in his assigned zone. Possible advantages of zoning include the fact that each picker is confined to a smaller area, reducing traffic congestion and allowing the familiarisation with the item locations within the zone. The central disadvantage of zoning is that if orders are split, then consolidation before shipment to the customer is required (De Koster et al., 2007).

Order batching is the method of grouping a set of orders into a number of sub-sets, each of which can then be retrieved by a single picking tour. According to Choe and Sharp (1991), there are basically two criteria for batching: the proximity of pick locations and time windows.

When batching and/or zoning are applied some additional effort is usually needed to congregate the items per customer order. These processes are frequently called accumulation/sorting (A/S) (De Koster et al., 2007). The performance of an A/S system depends not only on the equipment capacity (i.e. sorter capacity and conveyor speed) but also on operating policies like shipping lane assignment.

2.1   Routing Methods

The objective of routing policies is to sequence the items on the pick list so that a good route through the warehouse is ensured. So, by definition, the problem of routing order pickers in a warehouse classifies as a Steiner Travelling Salesman Problem (De Koster et al., 2007). The difficulty with the (Steiner) Travelling Salesman Problem is that it is in general not solvable in polynomial time (De Koster et al., 2007).

In practice, and because of the disadvantages of optimal routing, the problematic of routing order pickers in a warehouse is mostly resolved using heuristics (De Koster et al., 2007).

Hall (1993), Petersen (1997) and Roodbergen (2001) distinguish several heuristic methods for routing order pickers, with examples of a number of routing methods for a single-block warehouse being presented in Table 1.

Petersen (1997) carried out a number of numerical experiments to compare six routing methods: the S-shape, return, largest gap, mid-point, composite and optimal in a situation with random storage. He concludes that a best heuristic solution is on average 5% over the optimal solution.

Table 1. Routing Methods for a single-block warehouse.

S-shape (or traversal) heuristic	
Description	Routing order pickers by using the S-shape method means that any aisle containing at least one pick is traversed entirely. Aisles without picks are not entered. From the last visited aisle, the order picker returns to the depot. For single-block random storage warehouses S-shape provides routes that, on average, are between 7% and 33% longer than the optimum solutions (see De Koster and Van der Poort (1998) and De Koster et al. (1998)).
Advantages	One of the simplest heuristics for routing order pickers.
Drawbacks	Outperformed by more complex heuristics.
Return method	
Description	An order picker enters and leaves each aisle from the same end. Only aisles with picks are visited.
Advantages	Another simple heuristic for routing order pickers.
Drawbacks	Outperformed by more complex heuristics.
Midpoint method	
Description	The midpoint method essentially divides the warehouse into two areas. Picks in the front half are accessed from the front cross aisle and picks in the back half are accessed from the back cross aisle. The order picker traverses to the back half by either the last or the first aisle to be visited.
Advantages	According to Hall (1993), this method performs better than the S-shape method when the number of picks per aisle is small (i.e. one pick per aisle on average).
Drawbacks	More intricate practical implementation that S-shape or return heuristics.
Largest gap method	
Description	The largest gap strategy is similar to the midpoint strategy except that an order picker enters an aisle as far as the largest gap within an aisle, instead of the midpoint. If the largest gap is between two adjacent picks, the order picker performs a return route from both ends of the aisle. The largest gap within an aisle is therefore the portion of the aisle that the order picker does not traverse.
Advantages	The largest gap method always outperforms the midpoint method and the S-shape when the pick density is less than about 4 picks per aisles (see Hall, 1993).
Drawbacks	From an implementation point of view, the midpoint method is simpler.
Combined (or composite) heuristic	
Description	Aisles with picks are either entirely traversed or entered and left at the same end. However, for each visited aisle, the choice is made by using dynamic programming (see Roodbergen and De Koster, 2001).
Advantages	Outperforms the other heuristics in many instances. Roodbergen and De Koster (2001) compared six routing methods in 80 warehouse instances and reported that the combined+ heuristic gives the best results in 74 of the 80 instances they analysed.
Drawbacks	Being dynamic, doesn't allow the human order picker to familiarize with the routing heuristics.

2.2   Storage Assignment

Products need to be distributed into storage locations before they can be picked to complete customer orders. To assign products to storage locations a set of rules, designated storage assignment policy, can be applied (De Koster et al., 2007). Table 2 summarizes the storage assignment polices, along with their main advantages and drawbacks. The information in this table was summarized from the work of De Koster et al., (2007).

Various possibilities exist for positioning the A-, B- and C-areas in class based low-level picker-to-part systems. The optimum storage strategy depends on the routing policies (and on warehouse size and number of SKUs per pick route). In the warehousing literature, there is no set rule to define class partition (number of classes, percentage of items per class, and percentage of the total pick volume per class) for low-level picker-to-part systems, though many studies on the subject exist (De Koster et al., 2007).

Table 2. Storage assignment policies.

Random storage	
Description	Assigned location is selected randomly from all eligible empty locations with equal probability.
Advantages	High space utilisation (or low space requirement).
Drawbacks	Increased travel distance.
Closest open location storage	
Description	The first empty location that is encountered is used to store the products.
Advantages	Similar performance to the random storage policy (if products are
Drawbacks	moved by full pallets only).
Dedicated storage	
Description	Each location is dedicated to a product.
Advantages	Order pickers become familiar with product locations.
Drawbacks	Space utilisation is lowest among all storage policies.
Full turnover storage	
Description	Locations are assigned to products according to their turnover. Products with the highest sales rates are located at the easiest accessible locations.
Advantages	Decreased travel distance (outperforms class-based storage).
Drawbacks	Each change in demand rates and product assortment requires a new ordering of products. Requires a more "information intensive" approach than random storage.
Class based storage	
Description	Products are grouped into classes in such a way that the fastest moving class contains only about 20% of the products stored but contributes to about 80% of the turnover. Each class is then assigned to a dedicated area of the warehouse. Storage within an area is random.
Advantages	Fast-moving products can be stored close to the depot and simultaneously the flexibility and low storage space requirements of random storage are applicable.
Drawbacks	Full-turnover storage outperforms class-based storage in regards to the travel distance. Class-based storage requires more rack space than randomised storage.

3   The Case Study: Carregado 2 Logistic Operations Centre

The Carregado 2 logistics operation centre (C2) project was the response to the necessity of LS, as a market leader, to search for solutions that increase the competitive edge and further differentiate the company from other competitors. The initial goal of this project was to implement a multi-client and multi-product warehouse in which the operations where the human resources do not add value would be automated. It was also needed to maintain the flexibility of a conventional warehouse and integrate the automatic operations with the remaining manual operations. The end result was a state of the art 20,000 square metres warehouse. With its clever design, C2 has the capacity for 55432 stored pallets and 3700 picking positions. Currently, it receives forty to fifty trucks and dispatches seventy to seventy-five trucks each day (Fernandes, 2010).

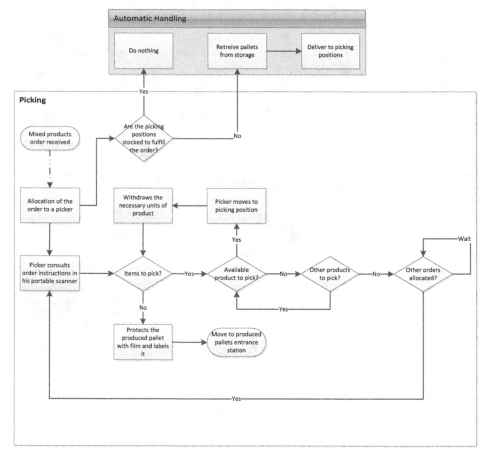

Fig. 2. Flowchart of the picking event

In Carregado 2 it is possible to identify six separated processes: reception, dispatch, automatic handling, co-packing, picking, reverse logistics. Besides these six processes there is also a support process, inventory.

The picking is a very important process in C2. Being a vital service to the LS clients, the C2 was specifically designed to support picking. The outcome was a picking area that consists in corridors in the ground floor, below the storage shelves, and is served by the CPAs that operate between the corridors.

The picking event (Fig. 2) is triggered by the influx of orders containing pallets with mixed products. This pallets need to be produced by a picker. Once the picking pallets are produced they are stored in the warehouse, in a buffer zone. Their dispatch is then processed normally.

4   Methodology: Discrete Event Modelling

Simulation is an extensively used technique for warehouse performance evaluation in the academic world as well as in practice. The simulation model[2] was primary based on Discrete Event Simulation (DES), since process-centric modelling is used widely in logistics and warehousing in particular (AnyLogic, 2014).

4.1   Model Structure

The network based discrete event model developed for this work can be described theoretically as including three layers: infrastructure, process and population.

The infrastructure is the network that guides the picker movements, containing all the available picking positions and produced pallets entrance stations. In the scope of the case study it was decided to simulate a full week of orders (week 45, 2014) from one client, which occupies a third of the warehouse (aisle 21 to 30, from 30 aisles) and it is served by up to eleven pickers. Warehouse schematics were drawn to serve as network, the backbone of the model space-awareness.

As for the process, the model working logic is conceptually represented in Fig. 3. The key events are:

1. A source object introduces orders, controlled by an arrival schedule mimicking the real arrivals.
2. Pickers are selected and allocated to an order and the simulation of their movement begins with a delay object (acceleration).
3. A decision object ponders the occurrence of an incident and the corresponding downtime, for added realism.
4. A movement object moves the picker to its picking position, movement that is controlled by the aforementioned network associated to the model. This network represents the warehouse.

---

[2] Other details and information about the simulation model are available in the document mentioned in Footnote 1.

5. After moving, a delay object accounts for the deceleration of the picker. The existence of separate delays representing acceleration and deceleration permits the definition of the pickers in the network with their cruising speed, while still ensuring that simulation of movement is realistic.
6. After decelerating, picking takes place and, if the order list continues, the model becomes iterative, proceeding to the acceleration object.
7. If every product of the order list is picked a decision object evaluates which produced pallets entrance station is closer, taking into account the last picking location.
8. After movement to the appropriate pallet entrance, the picker is released and the order exists the model via a sink object.

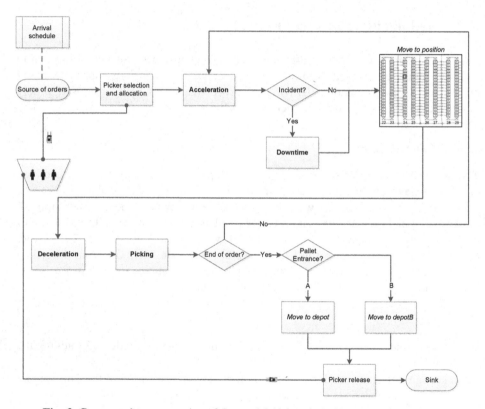

Fig. 3. Conceptual representation of the model (delays in bold, movements in italic)

When programming the model (to achieve the concept represented in Fig. 3), the authors chose a structure with two main blocks: order entry and exit and picking. In both blocks extensive Java programing was applied along with the typical DES objects to fulfil the model needs.

Order entry and exit simulates the arrival of orders and their allocation to a picker as well as the liberation of the picker and exit of the order after fulfilment. The source object mimics the arrival of orders on week 45, 2014. As for the picking block, it consists of eleven blocks one for each of the pickers that can be allocated to this client. By the authors' observation in loco, it was decided that two of those pickers would be faster than average and one would be slower.

All picking blocks have the same structure, varying only the proprieties of some events. Respecting the framework (Fig. 3), the picking block has an iterative nature to guarantee that an order keeps getting picked until it is completed, accurately simulates the pickers movements and is embedded with the possibility of incidents. Please note that, in order to obtain the values for the events, pickers were observed and timed in action, always consulting with representatives of LS about the values acquired for validation. The duration of events is represented by a triangular distribution.

Lastly, the model population consists of "Orders", the entity of the model, and "Pickers", the resource. The performance measure (time) is registered in seconds.

4.2   Verification and Validation of the Model

If a model is to be accepted and used in general, verification and validation is an essential phase of the model development process. Referring back to Reis (2010) for definitions: verification refers to the steps, processes or techniques the modeller deploys to ensure the model behaves according to every initial specification and assumption, while validation refers to the steps, processes or techniques the modeller (and any other interested party) deploys to ensure the model adequately represents and reproduces the behaviours of the real world phenomenon.

In this work, the process of verification of the model embraced several steps and tests that were performed repeatedly throughout the development of the model. Besides verification, the model was subject to validation. The validation technique adopted in this dissertation was based in the work of Reis (2010). The validation also included interviews and the comparison of outcomes between the model and real world results within the case study.

5   Case Study Application

As further elaborated in section 2, improvements in low level, manual-pick order-picking processes is achieved commonly by focusing on six policies (please refer to Fig. 1) that normally stay within the sphere of tactical and operational levels, which is critical for a built warehouse where strategic decisions are already taken and are difficult and expensive to change. However there are specifics in C2, resultant primarily from the fact that C2 is a fully functioning automated warehouse. Because of the restrictions the case study presented, namely the lack of flexibility in the floor plan, lack of available space and difficulties to install different equipment, the authors chose the storage assignment and routing as the dimensions to improve. Within the case study, these dimensions were the only that would allow the implementation of conclusions in reality with a short cost and time frame.

In this section the different scenarios chosen by the authors for simulation will be presented, as well as results and conclusions. As explained, there are two dimensions for these scenarios: storage assignment policy (SAP) and routing method. The scenarios fluctuate between three storage assignment policies: current, turnover, and ABC1. As for routing methods, five were selected for this work: return (scenario 1), random (scenario 2), "LSPickers" (scenario 3), s-shape (scenario 4), and midpoint (scenario 5). These five routing methods are combined with every storage assignment policy. For comparison, a routing method identified as "original" (scenario 0) is also applied in the current storage assignment. Table 3 summarizes the scenarios, within the C2 case study.

Table 3. Case study scenarios.

Scenarios	Current SAP (A)	Turnover SAP (B)	ABC1 SAP (C)
Return Routing (1)	A1	B1	C1
Random Routing (2)	A2	B2	C2
"LSPickers" Routing (3)	A3	B3	C3
S-shape Routing (4)	A4	B4	C4
Midpoint Routing (5)	A5	B5	C5
"Original" Routing (0)	A0	-	-

5.1   Characterization of Scenarios

As the name indicates, the current policy (scenario A) mimics the actual positions of each product in week 45, 2014. The positions of this policy respect a class-based storage policy already implemented by LS in C2. Supported by literature, a turnover (scenario B) and a class-based (scenario C) storage assignments are also evaluated.

Scenario B is the full turnover policy, a policy where products are distributed over the storage area according to their turnover. The products with the highest turnover are located closer to the entrance stations, whereas slow moving products are at the back of the warehouse. In this work the authors used the actual turnover (or pick volume) as measure, obtained from the orders supplied by LS. By corresponding the turnovers with the positions distance vector the storage assignment was obtained. This full turnover policy, by definition, outperforms class-based storage. However it requires a new ordering of products every time the demand rates change.

Scenario C is a class-based storage policy. It consists of three classes (A, B and C) each with a dedicated area of the warehouse. The use of three classes is common as further divisions, while providing additional gains in some cases, increase the space requirements. For the same reasoning of the full turnover policy, the class with the highest turnover products (A area) is closer to the produced pallets entrance stations and slow moving products (class C) are at the back of the warehouse. Since there is no firm rule to define a class partition, the authors selected an 80/19/1 turnover split specifically for this scenario. This split was achieved by analysis of the cumulative turnover curve, whilst minding the frequently applied Pareto principle (or the 80-20 rule). So, to A class was assigned 20% of the products, responsible for 80% of the turnover, precisely as predicted by the Pareto principle, and B class was designated to approximately the next 40% of the products (39% to be exact), responsible, along with A class products, for 99% of the turnover. The remaining 40% of the products, which account only to 1% of the turnover, were allocated to class C. Within each class the product distribution was random, using for that purpose Visual Basic (VBA) programing. Please note that by assuming that automated supply of the picking positions works flawlessly, scenarios B and C only assign one position to every product, which not always happens in scenario A.

In regards to the literature routings, return and s-shape were selected for their simplicity while midpoint was selected because, though it is more intricate to implement, it performs better than the s-shape method when the number of picks per aisle is small (Hall, 1993).

As for the other routings, random routing, where the routing is completely random, was selected to serve as a comparison point. "LSPickers" was a routing created to somehow simulate the comportment of the real life pickers in C2. Finally, regarding the "original" routing (scenario 0), it represents the actual travels made by the pickers, obtained from the order list provided by LS.

These scenarios were entered in the model using a bi-dimensional array, consisting of order lists and the positions within each list. To create inputs for the model the authors used extensive VBA programing within Excel, using as basis the order list provided by LS (Fig. 4). By analysing on the case study picking log, the current SAP positions and original routing were subtracted. Then VBA assisted in the creation of a key for the routings and the selection of positions for the SAPs. Ultimately the model input was arranged.

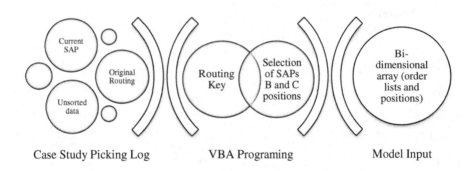

Fig. 4. Creation of model inputs

5.2   Results

Lets now address the results of the experiment runs. Every scenario was run 250 times with different seeds and the picking times of all simulations were statistically treated to withdraw meaningful results. The descriptive statics obtained made it clear that the model results were consistent.

One important aspect to take in consideration about the value of the results is that the picking times resulting from the model represent a picking operation completely unhindered and where the pickers operate always with no drops in productivity. Please note that while not always corresponding to reality, this high productivity of the picking model does not disrupt the authors' conclusions as every scenario ran in the same optimum picking ambience.

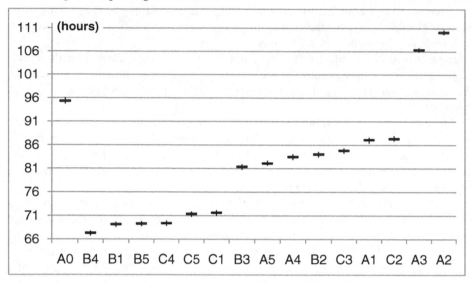

Fig. 5. Ordered box-and-whisker diagram (in hours) of the picking time under the different scenarios

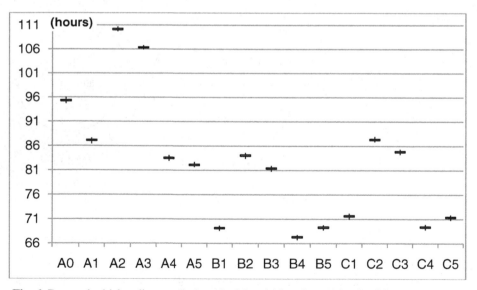

Fig. 6. Box-and-whisker diagram (in hours) of the picking time under the different scenarios.

The results are presented in box-and-whisker diagrams (Fig. 5 and Fig. 6). These diagrams include minimum, first quartile, third quartile and maximum values for each scenario, all in hours for simpler reading and understanding.

Through the analysis of Fig. 5, scenario A (current SAP) is the worst, and both scenarios B (turnover) and C (ABC1) present a similar and worthy performance. Also, routings 1, 4 and 5 (return, s-shape and midpoint) achieve the best results.

In absolute terms, scenario B4 (combining s-shape routing and turnover SAP) represents the fastest picking times, with a significant performance gap vis-à-vis the current situation represented by A0. Scenarios B1, B5 and C4 follow closely, with high performances.

The main conclusions to be drawn from these results, grounded on the attained results (see Fig. 6), are that in relation with the storage assignment methods:

- The turnover SAP presents the best results, as expected by definition;
- The ABC1 SAP presents results closer to the turnover SAP in every routing, while being easier to implement and requiring less time to administer;
- The proximity of turnover and ABC1 performance renders the turnover SAP, with its added complications, less attractive;
- As for the current SAP, it is grossly outperformed by the other two in every routing method, although there are extenuatory circumstances that could help explain the lack of performance like the product demand taken into consideration corresponding to 90 days and the fact that scenarios B and C only assigned one position to every product which not always happens in scenario A.

As for the routing methods:

- Three groups of routing methods exist;
- One, consisting of random and LSPickers, is by far the worst performing, thus assuring that a random behaviour is categorically hurtful to the productivity;
- A second group, comprising only the original routing, serves as proof that the on-the-fly routing decisions of the pickers equal a substantial loss of time over a week;
- The third and final group consists of the best performing methods, return, s-shape and midpoint, all widely studied and applied. These three methods are the better performing methods, particularly s-shape and midpoint;
- Under better performing turnover and ABC1 SAPs the performance gap between the random routings and the literature routings decreases.

As main results:

- It is clear that scenario A (current SAP), is seriously underperforming and that scenarios B (turnover) and C (ABC1) present a comparable and admirable performance. Additionally routing 1, 4 and 5 (return, s-shape and midpoint respectively) present the best results;
- In absolute terms, scenario B4 (combining s-shape routing and turnover SAP) represents the quickest picking time, with a significant performance gap to the current situation represented by A0. Scenarios B1, B5 and C4 follow with similar performance.

6   Conclusions

This work's utmost motivation was the importance and costs of logistics. Today's world would simply not function without logistics, being it the support of our everyday activities. Warehousing is an integral part of every logistics system that plays a vital role in providing a desired level of customer service at the lowest possible total cost. And within warehouses and distribution centres, picking has come under increased scrutiny. Order picking is the most labour-intensive operation in warehouses with manual systems, and a very capital-intensive operation in warehouses with automated systems, with any underperformance in leading to unsatisfactory service and high operational cost for the whole supply chain. Therefore, order picking is considered as the highest priority area for productivity improvements (Goetschalckx & Ashayeri, 1989; De Koster et al., 2007).

Henceforth, the all-embracing objective of the present work is to assess and restructure the storage assignment in the picking area and the order picking process (explicitly the routing method) of a warehouse, Carregado 2 Logistic Operations Centre. Order picking is a labour-intensive operation, especially in an automated distribution centre like C2, and so it represents significant costs.

To accomplish this objective a methodology was developed to assess the performance of the order picking in C2, taking in account various scenarios, respectively before and after the implementation of various storage assignment policies and routing methods. To this end a simulation model, based on discrete-event simulation, was created. To provide evidence for supporting or refuting the hypothesis of each scenario, validating theories and, ultimately, the conclusions of this dissertation, the model collected the dimension time. This allowed assessing the performance, using picking time as measure, of the order picking in C2 under various scenarios. By analysing the results the current paradigm of the order picking was evaluated, as were possible modifications in storage assignment policies and routing methods.

In total sixteen scenarios were evaluated. These bi-dimensional scenarios consist, in one dimension, of three storage assignment policies; current SAP (scenarios A), a full-turnover SAP (scenario B) and a class based SAP named ABC1 (scenario C). As for the other dimension, routing method, five methods were combined with every SAP; return (scenarios 1), random (scenarios 2), LSPickers (scenarios 3), s-shape (scenarios 4) and midpoint (scenarios 5). Also, the current SAP was also combined with the routing that was actually applied by LS pickers (named "original" and represented by a 0). This scenario (A0) was necessary to evaluate the current performance of picking and to serve as benchmark for comparisons.

For C2, the results suggest that a class-based storage policy equal or similar too ABC1 is applied and that s-shape routing is enforced (scenario C4). This suggestion is backed by the top tier performance of this scenario, the previously mentioned advantages of class-based storage over a full-turnover policy and by the fact that s-shape routing is already implemented in the warehouse management system. These alterations, combined with perfect picking supply, would amount to serious performance improvements of more than 30%.

In general, the authors would like to point out that inadequate routing only enhances the SAP shortcomings and, in what the authors think is the single most important conclusion of this dissertation, that a culture of method should always prevail over cunning actions, as the perceived short-term gains that pickers seek with their in-the-moment decisions do not compensate the losses in productivity caused by the deviation from proven methods over a longer period of time.

References

AnyLogic: Discrete Event - AnyLogic Simulation Software (2014). Retrieved December 15, 2014 from AnyLogic Simulation Software: http://www.anylogic.com/discrete-event-simulation

Berg, Jv, Zijm, W.: Models for warehouse management: Classification and examples. International Journal Production Economics **59**, 519–528 (1999)

Broulias, G., Marcoulaki, E., Chondrocoukis, G., Laios, L.: Warehouse management for improved order picking performance: an application case study from the wood industry. In: Papadopoulos, C. (ed.) Proceedings of the 5th International Conference on Analysis of Manufacturing Systems – Production Management, pp. 17–23. Zakynthos (2005)

Choe, K., Sharp, G.: Small parts order picking: design and operation (1991)

De Koster, R., Van der Poort, E.: Routing orderpickers in a warehouse: A comparison between optimal and heuristic solutions. IIE Transactions **30**, 469–480 (1998)

De Koster, R., Le-Duc, T., Roodbergen, K.J.: Design and control of warehouse order picking: A literature review. European Journal of Operatonal Research **182**, 481–501 (2007)

De Koster, R., Van der Poort, E., Roodbergen, K.: When to apply optimal or heuristic routing to orderpickers. In: Fleischmann, B., van Nunen, J., Speranza, M., Stahly, P. (eds.) Advances in Distribution Logistics, pp. 375–401. Springer, Berlin (1998)

Eisenstein, D.D.: Analysis and Optimal Design of Discrete Order Picking Technologies Along a Line. Naval Research Logistics (2008)

Fernandes, A.: Projecto Carregado 2 "Centro Logístico do Futuro". Grupo Luís Simões, Lisboa (2010)

Goetschalckx, M., Ashayeri, J.: Classification and design of order picking. Logistics Information Management **2**(2), 99–106 (1989)

Hall, R.: Distance approximation for routing manual pickers in a warehouse. IIE Transactions **25**, 77–87 (1993)

Petersen, C.: An evaluation of order picking routing policies. International Journal of Operations & Production Management **17**(11), 1098–1111 (1997)

Reis, V.: Development of Cargo Business in Combination Airlines: Strategy and Instrument. Ph.d. Thesis. Universidade Técnica de Lisboa, Lisbon (2010)

Roodbergen, K.: Layout and routing methods for warehouses. Ph.D. Thesis. RSM Erasmus University, Netherlands (2001)

Roodbergen, K., De Koster, R.: Routing methods for warehouses with multiple cross aisles. International Journal of Production Research **39**(9), 1865–1883 (2001)

Ruben, R., Jacobs, F.: Batch construction heuristics and storage assignment strategics for walk/ride and picking systems. Management Science **45**(4), 575–596 (1999)

Rushton, A., Croucher, P., Baker, P.: The Handbook of Logistics and Distribution Management, 3rd edn. Kogan Page, Great Britain (2006)

Tompkins, J.A., White, J.A., Bozer, Y.A., Tanchoco, J.: Facilities Planning. John Wiley & Sons, New Jersey (2003)

Designing Bus Transit Services for Routine Crowd Situations at Large Event Venues

Jiali Du[✉], Shih-Fen Cheng, and Hoong Chuin Lau

School of Information Systems, Singapore Management University,
Singapore, Singapore
{jiali.du.2012,sfcheng,hclau}@smu.edu.sg

Abstract. We are concerned with the routine crowd management problem after a major event at a known venue. Without properly design complementary transport services, such sudden crowd build-ups will overwhelm the existing infrastructure. In this paper, we introduce a novel flow-rate based model to model the dynamic movement of passengers over the transportation flow network. Based on this basic model, an integer linear programming model is proposed to solve the bus transit problem permanently. We validate our model against a real scenario in Singapore, where a newly constructed mega-stadium hosts various large events regularly. The results show that the proposed approach effectively enables routine crowd, and achieves almost 24.1% travel time reduction with an addition of 40 buses serving 18.7% of the passengers.

Keywords: Crowd management · Bus transit service · Vehicle routing problem

1 Introduction

In architectural and urban design community, there is a growing trend to design and build increasingly larger facilities that integrate diverse functions [18]. Examples of such facilities include stadiums, convention centers and airports. Operating such facilities with high volumes of human traffic is very challenging and needs to be carefully planned. Issues related to the operation of such facilities include, but not limited to, wayfinding inside the facility, routine crowd management, and emergency egress. In particular, to serve the transportation needs of crowds moving into and out of such facilities, an important consideration is to integrate mass transit to the facilities.

In this paper we focus on designing a bus transit service to complement mass transit during the routine (i.e. non-emergency) situation after an event in order to minimize total journey time of crowds. While such crowd dynamic is predictable in both volume and timing (the planner should know exactly how many people will be leaving the facility, and at what time), and all utilities can be assumed to be in perfect working condition (which contrasts the case of emergency egress, where the timing is uncertain, and some utilities could be faulty), the planning problem is still challenging. The major challenge in the

© Springer International Publishing Switzerland 2015
F. Corman et al. (Eds.): ICCL 2015, LNCS 9335, pp. 704–718, 2015.
DOI: 10.1007/978-3-319-24264-4_48

routine crowd management problem is to avoid bottlenecks and crowd buildups, which is hard to avoid since mass transit is designed to satisfy regular transport demands and not demand surges. A popular solution adopted by many planners is to complement mass transit with bus transit services, yet despite the long history of using such services, optimizing its delivery has not received much attention; in the end, results in the fixed-route and ad-hoc policies.

In the area of disruption management, however, there are rich literatures on how to optimally utilize bus transit services to make up for the lost link or capacity due to disruptions (for instance, in [5], [7], a two-step framework for bus transit service planning is proposed). Despite the similarity between disruption response and routine crowd management, they are fundamentally different, in the following aspects. For disruption response, the priority is on restoring as much connectivity as possible, and as a result, the modeling effort has been mostly on maximizing the amount of flow that can pass through the point of disconnection. For routine crowd management problem, on the other hand, the focus is on experience management, which aims at minimizing total journey time including both travel and waiting time. To accurately account for the journey time, we have to modify the classical flow network so that both travel and waiting times can be quantified and thus minimized.

The objective of this paper is to formulate and study the design of bus transit services for routine crowd situations at event venues. In doing so, we make the following three major contributions:

1. We formulate routine crowd scenario as a normalized flow network in which the total journey time can be easily calculated.
2. We model the introduction of bus transit services as an increase to the link capacities in the above normalized flow network, and we create an integer programming model to derive the *optimal design* of the bus transit service that would minimize the total journey time for all flows to reach destinations.
3. We demonstrate the practical usage of our model by solving instances inspired by a real-world scenario. The key parameters of this scenario are derived from a real-world public transport dataset in Singapore.

2   Literature Review

Operating the large-scale venue is very challenging due to the massive crowd after the public events. Accelerating the crowd diffusion process is explored in many aspects. On one hand, researchers seek for the optimal design of the egress in the facilities[18],[1]. On the other hand, it is crucial to provide effective strategies to handle the crowds at these venues by complementing the existing public transportation network. In the literatures, majority of existing works related to such topics focus on emergency evacuation planning [17],[14]. Stella et al. in [17] talks about the way to speed up the egress under emergency. By adopting proper strategies, they demonstrated the optimality with two benchmark performances. Victor et al. in [14] introduces a variant of the vehicle routing problem and models the evacuee arrival behavior in a realistic manner. By applying capacity-constrained buses, the problem aims at providing efficient services to minimize the waiting time at locations for all of the evacuees. However, in [2], Vinayak et al. addressed that there are fundamental differences exist in the evacuation traffic dynamics and routine non-emergency operations. The variations are described in the features including free flow speeds and maximum flow rates. But the planning problem during non-emergency period receives much less attention. A network optimization-based approach is proposed in [3] to support the efficient movement of pedestrians. In [8], Lassacher et al. addressed some applicable methodologies to deal with the routine crowd after an event, including traffic signal retiming, and real-time traffic monitoring. In [11], the authors divided the routine crowd problem into three sub-stages: leaving the venue, walking from the venue exit to the bus station and being dispersed by means of transportation at the bus station. In our work, we put our focus on the third stage where we provide bus transit services to help disperse the massive people flow at venues after large events.

In public transportation field, there are various works discussing about the vehicle route planning problem with regard to three major topics: network design, line planning and timetabling. Unlike the these works, whose focus were on the strategic planning under daily traffic situations and improving the service quality during a long term period, our work put the emphasis on complementing the existing mass transit system during the large events through establishing the temporary bus links. Reasonable bus planning strategy in context of the daily situations might not be applicable under the large event scenarios as the passengers demand change dramatically during special hours. Moreover, daily bus service that is suitable for the long term period is unnecessary with respect to the special cases, since the impact results from the event only last for a few hours. Therefore, we seek strategic planning for the transportation services under special situations.

One of the special cases is the metro infrastructure disruption management problem. Contingency plans were investigated in case of disruption, which can be found in [4] and [12]. A survey did by Pender et al. on the various practices to manage the disruption in [13] , which indicated that bus transit service is the most common way to minimize the negative impact of the disruption.

In [7], Konstantinos et al. proposed a methodological framework for planning the bus services. There were two key steps: bus routes planning on the network and shuttle bus assignment over the selected routes. The optimal bus routes were generated by using a shortest path algorithm and improved by a heuristic approach. Following this framework, Jin et al. in [5] formulated the problem by applying a different approach for generating candidate bus routes compared to [7]. Though the the two-step framework makes the problem tractable to some extent, separation of the two processes, namely candidate routes selection and resources assignment, may cause some inconsistencies. Whereas we optimize the planning problem in an integrated manner, which covers both processes in one optimization model and guarantees optimality for the two simultaneously.

3 Normalized Flow Model for Routine Crowd at Facilities with Ultra High Demand

3.1 Background

Defined formally, our problem can be represented by a graph incorporating existing public transport service lines, where stations are denoted as nodes and connectivities denoted as directed links. An example can be seen in Figure 1a, where there are three lines, each represented by a different line style. Stations along all lines are represented as hollow nodes in Figure 1a, the node with ultra-high demand is shaded as node s. Note that node s is not necessarily connected to existing stations, and visitors at node s might need to find their ways to the closest station. This might be feasible during normal circumstances, yet when the demand is beyond planned capacity, this sudden inflow of demands might overwhelm the service provided at the nearby stations.

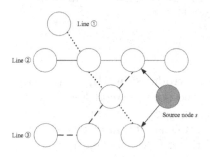

(a) An example of public transportation network with a node emitting ultra high demands.

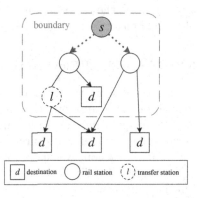

(b) An example of individual's trip over the transportation networks

Fig. 1. Problem description

3.2 Overview

The problem is defined on a graph $\hat{G} = (\hat{N}, \hat{E})$, where the set $\hat{N}$ represents all stations, and the set $\hat{E}$ represents directed links connecting stations. Every link is defined with a link-specific flow capacity, which will be defined next. In this context, the bus transit service between two stations is essentially a way to *add capacity* to the graph: if the selected two stations are not already connected, a link with corresponding flow capacity will be created; if the selected two stations are already connected, its flow capacity will be increased accordingly. The planning horizon is discretized into T time units with equal intervals, where T

is large enough for all travelers to reach their destinations even without any transit service. The planned bus transit service can be dynamic, which means that it can change over time. The total number of buses that can be deployed is bounded by B.

Let $s \in \hat{N}$ be the source node where surge demands originate. To focus only on the part of graph where the transit service can reach within *reasonable amount of time*, we define $N \subseteq \hat{N}$ to be the set containing only nodes that can be reached from node s within X minutes (X is empirically set to be large enough to contain all nodes we will ever consider). Similarly, we define $E \subseteq \hat{E}$ to contain all edges between nodes in N. The reduced graph $G = (N, E)$ will be our focus for the rest of the paper. To accurately estimate total journey time, for a passenger who travels to a destination node d not in N, a transfer node $l \in N$ that's closest to node d will be chosen as the transfer node, and the remaining travel time will be accounted for from l to d. In other words, the total journey time should contain two components: (1) from node s to transfer node l, and (2) from transfer node l to destination d. For travelers whose destination nodes are already in N, the transfer time will be set to 0. Figure 1b illustrates an example of individual's trip over the transportation networks.

3.3   Normalized Flow Network Model

In classical flow network models (such as the one introduced in [7]), the primary focus is on flows, and journey time cannot be derived from the model directly. To enable the quantification of journey time from flow networks, we introduce *time periods* to the model. To ensure that the model is still tractable after we introduce the time dimension, we make following assumptions. (a). The time period has equal length; (b). Train arrives with equal frequencies; (c). Travel time on each link is equivalent to the train frequency. With these assumptions, we can then simply recover journey time by summing up flows waiting at all nodes across all time periods. However, having uniform time periods implies that the travel time between any pair of nodes has to be set to the same (single time period) as well. To enable such normalization, for each edge we will calculate the *normalized flow rate* to replace capacity, which intuitively refers to the amount of flow that can pass through the edge within a single time period. (To understand how this works, assume that it takes 5 minutes for a train with the capacity of 100 to travel from a to b, the normalized flow rate for edge (a, b) is then 20 per minute.)

Formally speaking, we define $n_{u,t}^{l,d}$ to be the amount of flow waiting at node u in time t, with destination node being d and transfer node being l. Similarly, we define $x_{u,v,t}^{l,d}$ to be the flow going through the edge (u, v) in time t, with destination node being d and transfer node being l. The normalized capacity of the edge (u, v) in time t is defined as $c_{u,v,t}$. In other words, for time period t, at most $c_{u,v,t}$ units of flow can pass from u to v. The normalization procedure will be described in detail in Section 3.4.

3.4   Deriving Normalized Flow Capacity

As highlighted earlier, total journey time is composed of two major components: the time required to move from s to the transfer node l, which is denoted as $\delta_{s,l}$, and the time required to move from l to the final destination d, which is denoted as $\phi_{l,d}$. If $d \in N$, $\phi_{l,d}$ will be set to 0, otherwise it will be pre-computed. $\delta_{s,l}$, on the other hand, will be computed from the normalized flow network as follows:

$$\delta_{s,l} = \sum_{t,u,d,l,u \neq l} n_{u,t}^{l,d}. \tag{1}$$

The journey time can be computed as above since flow waiting at any nodes other than the transfer node will require one time period to move forward. Next we will explain how we can compute the normalized capacity.

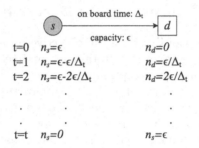

Fig. 2. An example to illustrate the normalization procedure.

Figure 2 shows an example with two nodes explaining the rationality of the normalization procedure, where ϵ is the capacity between the start point s and destination d and Δ_t is the travel time from s to d before normalization.

The purpose of the normalization procedure is to normalize the capacity of the link to be the amount of flow that can pass through in one time unit. The normalized capacity is therefore ϵ/Δ_t. After normalization, at the time step $t = 1$, the total journey time, which consists of wait time and travel time, for the first ϵ/Δ_t unit of flow who successfully pass through the link is $(1 + 0) \times \epsilon/\Delta_t = \epsilon/\Delta_t$. Similarly, the total journey time for the second ϵ/Δ_t unit of flow is $(1 + 1) \times \epsilon/t = 2\epsilon/t$. Generally, the total journey time for the $i^{th}\epsilon/\Delta_t$ unit of flow is $(i - 1 + 1) \times \epsilon/t = i\epsilon/\Delta_t$. Thus the total journey time for all ϵ units of flow is $\sum_{i=1}^{t} i\epsilon/t = (1 + t)\epsilon/2$, which indicates the journey time over the link is $(1+\Delta_t)/2$. To correct the bias, we can adding a constant $\Delta_t - (1+\Delta_t)/2 = (\Delta_t - 1)/2$ to the final average journey time via normalization. As in an optimization model, adding constant to the objective function does not change the solution, therefore, we maintain the calculation of $\delta_{s,l}$ as formula 1.

Total travel time out of the boundary can be measured according to the number of passengers at transfer node l at the last time step $n_{l,T}^{l,d}$ and the estimated shortest travel time from l to d: $\phi_{l,d}$. Therefore, the total journey time that we seek to minimize will be:

$$\sum_{s,l} \delta_{s,l} + \sum_{l,d} n_{l,T}^{l,d} \cdot \phi_{l,d}. \tag{2}$$

Finally, the bus transit service in our context can be thought of as either creating a new edge with capacity $\alpha_{u,v}$ or increasing the existing capacity $c_{u,v,t}$ by $\alpha_{u,v}$. $\alpha_{u,v}$ is the normalized capacity that corresponds to a particular bus service connecting u and v. The transit can be time dependent, yet every assigned bus need to complete its current service before being re-assigned to serve another route. Our goal is to come up with a bus transit service that would minimize the above total journey time.

4   The Integer Linear Programming (ILP) Model for Dynamic Bus Transit Service During Routine Crowd

As highlighted in the previous section, the objective of introducing bus transit service in our paper focuses on reducing total journey time, not making up for the lost capacity (as in the cases of disruption management). The major innovations we introduce in our mathematical model are: 1) normalization of link capacity to reflect uniform time period length, and 2) the separation of node delay and link delay. With these two modeling innovations, we can now formally introduce the integer linear programming model for optimizing dynamic bus transit service during the routine crowd. In our model, the objective is to minimize the total journey time experienced by all travelers.

$$\min \sum_{s,l} \delta_{s,l} + \sum_{l,d} n_{l,T}^{l,d} \cdot \phi_{l,d}.$$

Let $q_{s,t}^d$ be the demand size that comes out of node s with destination d in time t. With such dynamic demand, (3) is to ensure the flow conservation for demand node s, which states that the flow at s in time t is constrained by the flow in time $(t-1)$ plus the difference between new demands and outgoing flow. Flow conservation for other nodes is described by (4). The next two constraints, (5) and (6), state that outgoing flow of a node u should not exceed the flow at node u as well as the capacity of the edge taken.

$$\sum_l n_{s,t}^{l,d} = \sum_l n_{s,t-1}^{l,d} + q_{s,t}^d - \sum_{l,u} x_{s,u,t-1}^{l,d} \quad \forall s,t,d, \tag{3}$$

$$n_{u,t+1}^{l,d} = n_{u,t}^{l,d} + \sum_w x_{w,u,t}^{l,d} - \sum_v x_{u,v,t}^{l,d} \quad \forall u,l,d,t, \tag{4}$$

$$\sum_v x_{u,v,t}^{l,d} \le n_{u,t}^{l,d} \quad \forall u,l,d,t, \tag{5}$$

$$\sum_v x_{u,v,t}^{l,d} \le c_{u,v,t} \quad \forall u,l,d,t. \tag{6}$$

The decision variable $a_{s,u,r}^{k,t}$ is set to 1 if bus k is assigned to link (s,u) in time t. This decision will add additional capacity of $\alpha_{s,u}$ units to edge (s,u), and is expressed in constraint (7).

$$c_{s,u,t} = c_{s,u,0} + \sum_{k,r} a_{s,u,r}^{k,t} \cdot \alpha_{s,u}, \quad \forall s,u,t. \tag{7}$$

In our formulation, each bus k is allowed to make one intermediate stop before reaching its destination. In other words, a bus route should contain leg 1 and leg 2, and is denoted as index r. The dependency between two legs of the same bus route is specified in constraint (8).

$$a_{s,u,1}^{k,t} \leq b_{s,u,1}^{k,t-1} + \sum_{w} a_{w,s,0}^{k,t-1} \quad \forall s,u,k,t. \tag{8}$$

Although our model allows the same bus to be assigned to different routes over time, it cannot be re-assigned unless it has completed the current assignment. This temporal relationship is ensured by both (9) and (10). $b_{s,u,r}^{k,t}$ is a derived decision variable that is set to 1 when bus k starts its current trip, and its value would increase monotonically by 1 at a time, until it ends its current service. After the service terminates, the value of $b_{s,u,r}^{k,t}$ will be reset to 0, and bus k can be utilized in other service route, as noted by (11).

$$b_{s,u,r}^{k,t} \leq \tau_{s,u} \cdot a_{s,u,r}^{k,t} \quad \forall s,u,k,t,r, \tag{9}$$

$$b_{s,u,r}^{k,t} = \begin{cases} 0 & \text{if } b_{s,u,r}^{k,t-1} + a_{s,u,r}^{k,t} = \tau_{s,u}; \\ b_{s,u,r}^{k,t-1} + a_{s,u,r}^{k,t} & \text{otherwise;} \end{cases} \quad \forall s,u,k,t,r, \tag{10}$$

$$\sum_{w} a_{u,w,0}^{k,t} = 1 \text{ if } a_{s,u,0}^{k,t-1} + b_{s,u,0}^{k,t-1} = 1 \quad \forall s,u,k,t. \tag{11}$$

Both (10) and (11) are nonlinear and have to be linearized. To linearize (10), we introduce two additional variables $y_{s,u,r}^{k,t}$ and $\lambda_{s,u,r}^{k,t}$. Let L and U be the lower and upper bounds of $b_{s,u,r}^{k,t}$, which equal 0 and $\tau_{s,u} - 1$ respectively. The nonlinear constraint (10) can be re-written as:

$$\begin{cases} b_{s,u,r}^{k,t-1} + a_{s,u,r}^{k,t} \geq L \cdot y_{s,u,r}^{k,t} + \tau_{s,u} \lambda_{s,u,r}^{k,t} \\ b_{s,u,r}^{k,t-1} + a_{s,u,r}^{k,t} \leq \tau_{s,u} \lambda_{s,u,r}^{k,t} + U y_{s,u,r}^{k,t} \\ y_{s,u,r}^{k,t} + \lambda_{s,u,r}^{k,t} = 1 \\ U(1 - \lambda_{s,u,r}^{k,t}) \geq b_{s,u,r}^{k,t} \\ (1 - U)\lambda_{s,u,r}^{k,t} \leq b_{s,u,r}^{k,t} - (b_{s,u,r}^{k,t-1} + a_{s,u,r}^{k,t}) \\ U(1 - y_{s,u,r}^{k,t}) \geq b_{s,u,r}^{k,t} - (b_{s,u,r}^{k,t-1} + a_{s,u,r}^{k,t}) \\ y_{s,u,r}^{k,t}, \lambda_{s,u,r}^{k,t} \in \{0,1\} \end{cases} \tag{12}$$

(11) can be linearized similarly, and in the interest of space, we will skip it. Budget constraint (14) is to reflect the limited number of buses that are available. The amount of demand with destination d is represented by β_d and (13) is to

make sure that in the last time period, all travelers must reach their respective final destinations (either their true destinations, or the transfer nodes leading to their real destinations that are outside of the boundary). Finally, the domains of decision variables are listed as the last two constraints.

$$\sum_l n_{l,T}^{l,d} = \beta_d \quad \forall d, \tag{13}$$

$$\sum_{k,s,u,r} a_{s,u,r}^{k,t} \leq B \quad \forall t, \tag{14}$$

$$a_{s,u,r}^{k,t} \in \{0,1\} \quad \forall s,u,k,t,r, \tag{15}$$

$$b_{s,u,r}^{k,t} \in \{0, \tau_{s,u} - 1\} \quad \forall s,u,k,t,r. \tag{16}$$

5   Experiment

The effectiveness of our model is demonstrated by a real-world inspired scenario in Singapore, where a newly constructed multi-purpose national stadium is designed to host large events. In this section, we first estimate passengers' travel demands based on a real-world public transport dataset. We then perform computational experiments to measure the effectiveness of our ILP model. We solve the ILP model using CPLEX 12.5.

5.1   Dataset Description

The public transport dataset we obtained from our industry partners is called EZlink[1] dataset, which contains each passenger's boarding and alighting information (the boarding/alighting stations and times). It contains over one million card users' tap records from 1 *Nov 2011* to 31 *Jan 2012*. We use only records from work days for consistency.

Inferring Destinations. For each card holder h, we maintain a list of candidate destinations and append the station s' to the list if: (1) s' is the first station that h registered as boarding in the morning (before 12 : 00) of a day; or (2) s' is the last station that h has registered as alighting during a day after 16 : 00. The intuition behind this filtering process is based on the assumption that majority of public transport users would depart from homes in the morning, and leave their workplaces in the afternoon. By aggregating records collected over three months, we can obtain the frequency of visited stations from the list.

Figure 3 plots an example of the candidate list extracted from 4 card holders. Card holders maintain a set candidate destination stations. It is observed that most of the card holders (1,2,3) in the figure have one dominant station s' whose frequency is much higher than the rest. This pattern is common when we process the dataset. We consider a station s' to be the home location for card holder h if its appearance frequency is over 80%.

---

[1] http://www.transitlink.com.sg/PSdetail.aspx?ty=catart&Id=1

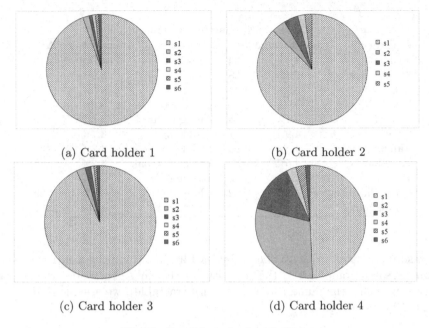

(a) Card holder 1   (b) Card holder 2

(c) Card holder 3   (d) Card holder 4

Fig. 3. Candidate destination list

If no dominant station can be detected in the list, we will try to cluster stations based on their distance. If the combined frequency of all stations belonging to the same cluster is high enough, we will consider the home station to be within the cluster. For example, card holder 4 in Figure 3d maintains a list of 6 stations. Although no dominant station can be found, we can identify the cluster of $(s1, s2, s3)$ as they are less than 800 meters from each other. And the combined frequency for these 3 stations is 90.3%, well above the threshold. In this case, we conclude that all of them are close enough to card holder 4's real home and thus we use station $s1$ as the representative home station. If dominant home station cannot be found for a card hold after the above two checks, we will remove this card from consideration.

In total, we have extracted $|\mathcal{D}| = 22$ important destinations. The distribution of each station s and the travel times from the national stadium s_0 to $s \in \mathcal{D}$ are shown in table 1. We treat the set of card users that we identified as representative of the whole city.

Inferring Edge Capacity. We obtain the aggregate number of passengers on rail way link (u, v) at time t from the EZLink dataset. The actual flow rate $c_{u,v,t}$ on each link is extracted according to train frequencies. The edge capacity $c_{u,v,t}$ in the model is represented by the additional flow rate, which is defined as the spare space available for passengers and can be inferred from the designed flow rate and actual flow rate .

$$c_{u,v,t} = dc_{u,v} - ac_{u,v,t}. \tag{17}$$

Table 1. Destination distributions.

station s	percentage	$\Delta t_{s_0,s}$	station s	percentage	$\Delta t_{s_0,s}$
Yishun	7.6%	34	Aljunied	4.0%	10
Sembawang	7.4%	38	Simei	3.9%	21
Admiralty	6.9%	41	Hougang	3.8%	20
Yew Tee	6.0%	44	Boon Lay	3.8%	40
Ang Mo Kio	5.4%	24	Tiong Bahru	3.8%	16
Khatib	4.9%	32	Sengkang	3.7%	24
Tampines	4.5%	23	Bukit Batok	3.7%	36
Lakeside	4.5%	37	Bukit Gombak	3.7%	38
Pioneer	4.3%	42	Woodlands	3.6%	44
Choa Chu Kang	4.0%	42	Clementi	3.4%	29
Serangoon	4.0%	16	Toa Payoh	3.3%	22

We assume that the capacity of each bus is 140. In our experiment, the capacity of bus is small compared to the capacity on the links. To reduce the solution space (and make the numerical experiments tractable), we assume that we will assign 4 buses at a time.

5.2   The Scenario

Let the stadium be the demand originator (s_0) with up to 30,000 people. Time horizon is assumed to be $T = 12$ and is enough for all passengers to reach their respective destinations. Each time period refers to 6 minutes. In total, there are 19 nodes (stations) and 38 links within the boundary.

5.3   Effectiveness

We first discuss the effectiveness of our approach by comparing our ILP model to a rule-of-thumb assignment policy. After consulting industry experts on this problem from a sports complex, they recommend a rule-of-thumb assignment policy to create a recurrent bus service line running between the sports facility and a major nearby station (called Cityhall station). Finally, we also assume that the egress for all 30,000 visitors would occur at the same time. Travel time reduction for both ILP model and rule-of-thumb approach is shown in Figure 4a. Travel time decreases along the y-axis for both approaches as the number of available buses increases along the x-axis. When the number of buses is set to be 0, it shows the very baseline indicating the situation of assigning no bus. On one hand, in terms of the average waiting time reduction, our ILP model improve the total journey by 15.7 minutes, i.e., a 24.1% reduction, compared to the no bus situation. On the other hand, with a fixed budget, the journey time reduction of our ILP model is larger than the rule-of-thumb method, which indicates that the ILP model is more effective in planning the bus transit services. For example, with 40 buses, the ILP model saves almost 4 minutes (8% reduction) for each passenger compared to the rule-of-thumb assignment. This result

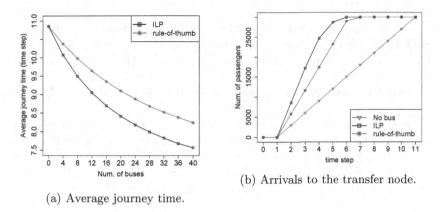

(a) Average journey time.

(b) Arrivals to the transfer node.

Fig. 4. Effectiveness.

is not surprising as the rule-of-thumb assignment only considers the approximate demand and does not change its strategy over time as need.

Figure 4b depicts the number of passengers that arrives at their target transfer nodes over time horizon under 3 different situations. Arriving at the transfer node is the first step of the whole trip. When there is no bus services incorporated, passengers gradually approach to the target transfer node with a much slower pace. Before $t = 7$, when all things being equal, the naive rule-of-thumb approach serves a increase of around 20% passengers when the planning horizon is going up. This is a stark contrast to our ILP model, in which almost 82% of passengers were sent to the transfer node in time $t = 4$.

One phenomenon observed from Figure 4b is that the ILP approach is not only effective in sending people to the final destinations but also efficient in sending passengers to the transfer node. However, the rate of sending passengers towards the transfer node after $t = 4$ decreases significantly. On the other hand, such rate for the rule-of-thumb approach keeps the same even after $t = 4$. This is because the rule-of-thumb strategy requests all of the buses serving on the edge from s_0 to the preselected station, Cityhall, hence passengers quickly diffuse to the transfer node. When $t = 6$, most of the passengers are sent to the transfer node and serving on the route $(s_0, \text{Cityhall})$ does not help any more. Rest of passengers who did not reach the transfer node would have to rely on regular train services and this accounts for the slower movement pace during this $t = 6$ and $t = 7$.

In our problem, besides the trip within the boundary, another significant factor that affect the total journey time is the trip from transfer nodes to destinations. In addition to the fact that the ILP model can disperse the crowd to the transfer nodes quickly, it also assign passengers to the optimal nodes l for making transfers. While for the rule-of-thumb approach, it fails to assign passengers to the optimal transfers which lead to the situation that people may take longer time to their final destinations.

5.4   Effect of Stop

In this section, we discuss the effect of having alighting stops in our bus transit service. For simplicity, we assume that buses can only start their services from the demand node s_0 and operate in 2 different ways: 1) creating a *direct* link connecting two stations, and 2) creating a route with one alighting stop. We assume that all 30,000 passengers exit the source node simultaneously at time $t = 0$.

We show the map illustrating the optimal bus routes taken by the above two services in Figure 5. In Figure 5a, buses start from the national stadium (label A with red circle) to a set of stations with label B. In figure 5b, buses start from the national stadium and have one alighting stop labeled as B and then at the same station, start their service towards the end of the service stop.

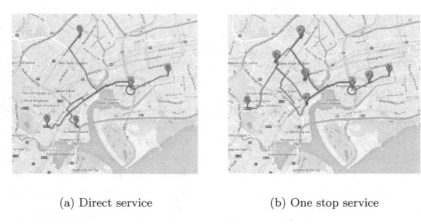

(a) Direct service   (b) One stop service

Fig. 5. Bus routes

Figure 6 plots the average journey time experienced by passengers when the number of employed buses varies along the x-axis. Intuitively, we observe that for both services, the average journey time reduces as the number of bus increases. Another observation from Figure 6 is that direct bus service is more effective compared to setting an alighting stop under our scenario.

In our ILP model, buses serve for two major roles: (1) facilitate the movement of crowds out of congested area near the demand node s_0 (which reduce the travel time within the boundary); (2) adjust passengers' trip and accommodate them to the proper transfer node l at lower-density area, which reduce the travel time beyond the boundary. Easing the congestion near the demand node is the key factor that affect passengers' total journey time. Adjusting the transfer node further improve passengers' travel experience. As the number of buses is too small to handle the demand (48 buses provides services for over 2% passengers), plenty of passengers are clogged near station s_0.

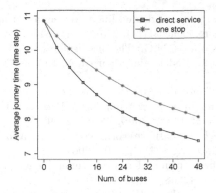

Fig. 6. Direct service vs one stop service

6   Conclusion

In this work, we presented a novel normalized flow network approach to model the routine crowd of a large-scale facility. With such movement model, we propose an ILP-based approach to generate the optimal bus transit services. The results from a real-world scenario show that our ILP formulation obtains 24.1% journey time reduction with only 40 buses providing services for 18.7% of the passengers. Even compared to the rule-of-thumb strategy, where authorities set a bus route based on experience, it is able to save 8% of the journey time for each passenger. Furthermore, we learn that setting an alighting node along the bus route is not a good choice when the number of available buses is not enough. The future research is to seek more efficient approaches to handle problem instances on a larger scale. In addition, we also look at extending the existing model to provide online planning strategies.

Acknowledgments. This research is supported by the Singapore National Research Foundation under its International Research Centre @ Singapore Funding Initiative and administered by the IDM Programme Office, Media Development Authority (MDA).

References

1. Chertkoff, J.M., Kushigian, R.H.: Don't panic: The psychology of emergency egress and ingress. Praeger Publishers (1999)
2. Dixit, V., Wolshon, B.: Evacuation traffic dynamics. Transportation research part C: Emerging Technologies **49**, 114–125 (2014)
3. Feng, L., Miller-Hooks, E.: A network optimization-based approach for crowd management in large public gatherings. Transportation Research Part C: Emerging Technologies **42**, 182–199 (2014)
4. Janarthanan, N., Schneider, J.B.: Computer-aided design as applied to transit system emergency contingency planning. Computers, Environment and Urban Systems **9**(1), 33–52 (1984)
5. Jin, J.G., Teo, K.M., Odoni, A.R.: Optimizing bus bridging services in response to disruptions of urban transit rail networks. Transportation Science (2015)

6. Kaspi, M., Raviv, T.: Service-oriented line planning and timetabling for passenger trains. Transportation Science **47**(3), 295–311 (2013)
7. Kepaptsoglou, K., Karlaftis, M.G.: The bus bridging problem in metro operations: conceptual framework, models and algorithms. Public Transport **1**(4), 275–297 (2009)
8. Lassacher, S., Veneziano, D., Albert, S., Ye, Z.: Traffic management of special events in small communities. Transportation Research Record: Journal of the Transportation Research Board **2099**, 85–93 (2009)
9. Lee, Y.J., Vuchic, V.R.: Transit network design with variable demand. Journal of Transportation Engineering **131**(1), 1–10 (2005)
10. Liebchen, C.: The first optimized railway timetable in practice. Transportation Science **42**(4), 420–435 (2008)
11. Liu, Q., Lu, H., Yang, H., Zhang, W.: Study on the evacuation of people flow in the venue of olympic games. Journal of the Eastern Asia Society for Transportation Studies **6**, 4365–4380 (2005)
12. Meyer, M.D., Belobaba, P.: Contingency planning for response to urban transportation system disruptions. Journal of the American Planning Association **48**(4), 454–465 (1982)
13. Pender, B., Currie, G., Delbosc, A., Shiwakoti, N.: Disruption recovery in passenger railways. Transportation Research Record: Journal of the Transportation Research Board **2353**(1), 22–32 (2013)
14. Pereira, V.C., Bish, D.R.: Scheduling and routing for a bus-based evacuation with a constant evacuee arrival rate. Transportation Science (2014)
15. Schöbel, A.: Line planning in public transportation: models and methods. OR Spectrum **34**(3), 491–510 (2012)
16. Schöbel, A., Scholl, S.: Line planning with minimal traveling time. In: ATMOS 2005–5th Workshop on Algorithmic Methods and Models for Optimization of Railways. Internationales Begegnungs-und Forschungszentrum für Informatik (IBFI), Schloss Dagstuhl (2006)
17. So, S.K., Daganzo, C.F.: Managing evacuation routes. Transportation Research part B: Methodological **44**(4), 514–520 (2010)
18. Tubbs, J., Meacham, B.: Egress design solutions: A guide to evacuation and crowd management planning. John Wiley & Sons (2007)
19. Zhao, F., Ubaka, I.: Transit network optimization-minimizing transfers and optimizing route directness. Journal of Public Transportation **7**(1), 63–82 (2004)

Application of Discrete-Event Simulation to Capacity Planning at a Commercial Airport

L. Douglas Smith[1(✉)], Liang Xu[1], Ziyi Wang[1], Deng Pan[1],
Laura Hellmann[2], and Jan F. Ehmke[2]

[1] University of Missouri-St. Louis, One University Blvd., St. Louis, MO 63121, USA
ldsmith@umsl.edu
[2] Freie Universität Berlin, Garystraße 21 14195, Berlin, Germany

Abstract. We describe the construction, calibration and application of a discrete-event simulation model to estimate the potential effects of changes in airport infrastructure, operating procedures, and traffic intensity upon system performance. Logistic and regression models provide time-varying parameters for probability distributions used for physical processes. Detailed event logs of simulated aircraft activity and corresponding logs of actual aircraft operations allow us to validate the model and analyze the effects of normal disruptions and extraordinary events. With multivariate statistical analysis, we assess the influence of design capacity, airline scheduling practices and uncontrollable events on flight delays. We also estimate the effects of selectively removing airport assets from service for major maintenance.

1 Introduction

In recent years, major U.S. airlines have altered their route structures and schedules to concentrate their flight activity at a few mega-hubs. Consolidation of this sort and additional flights of express freight carriers strain some airports while others find themselves with unplanned excess capacity. Airport planners thus seek ways of better utilizing existing assets in some environments, intelligently expanding them in others, and selectively removing assets from service to reduce operating costs where precipitous drops in traffic have occurred.

Highly sophisticated simulation models have been used for decades to aid in the design of airports and simulate air traffic with remarkable realism [1,2,3,4,5,6,7,8,9, 10,11,24]. These detailed engineering models are excellent for studying system behavior in microscopic detail but they carry enormous overhead for studies that are more strategic in nature. Traditional operational research models, in contrast, have been used for optimizing aspects of airport activity such as timing pushbacks, sequencing arrivals or departures, performing regular gate services, or performing special services such as de-icing aircraft [14,15,19,20,25,29]. The OR models, however, tend to ignore stochastic aspects of system behavior or necessary interactions with other parts of the system [6,17,23,26]. In developing our models, we strive to capture the essential interactions of key system components, represent the system with sufficient

F. Corman et al. (Eds.): ICCL 2015, LNCS 9335, pp. 719–733, 2015.
DOI: 10.1007/978-3-319-24264-4_49

granularity, and facilitate the efficient conduct of experiments with multiple replications of a wide range of planning scenarios and operating rules. The integrative conceptual framework is the representation and control of the system as a network of staged queues [12,21,22].

2   Staged Queues as the Integrating Framework

We model the three domains (airline operations, airport facilities and ATC) by moving simulated aircraft through a network of staged queues – some physical, others conceptual. Aircraft arrivals are generated according to daily schedules of individual airlines but with random deviations appropriate for the scenario being simulated. The scenario is defined by local weather conditions, weather in airspace sectors through which arrivals and departures take place, and conditions at major hub airports which may cause bunching of arrivals and traffic holds for departures. For Lambert St. Louis, arriving aircraft are placed in conceptual queues at the final approach fix (FAF) for an active runway (Figure 1). Movements of aircraft are simulated from the FAF until the designated flight's activity at the airport is completed (with termination at the gate, or, if continuing to another destination, after turnaround and departure). At Frankfurt, the flight data contain the time at which flights enter the terminal environment "10 minutes out" for vectoring to the final approach. For Frankfurt, therefore, we impute a FAF for the runway with an appropriate offset of time to reach the imputed FAF.

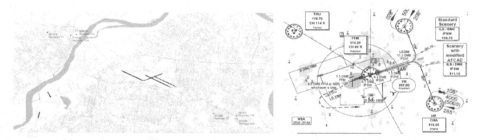

Fig. 1. Final Approach Fixes for Arrivals at Lambert St. Louis and Frankfurt, Germany

Simulation entities for flights that terminate at the airport are removed from the simulation after reaching the gate and the gate is made available for originating flights that are generated by the model according to schedule (with random perturbation if desired) or for a new arrival.

Figure 2 illustrates the physical layout of runways, taxiways and ramp areas with key intersections that aircraft traverse from the points of touchdown to the gates and from the gates to the points of liftoff. We identify points on the airport surface where aircraft may be staged as they progress from runways to gates and vice versa. Routes between staging points across ramps and along taxiways are mapped and aircraft are directed to the next staging point depending on which runways are in use for landings and takeoffs and which staging points between their current position and airport destination (gate or runway) can accommodate them. Aircraft may be held at a staging point until the next segment of its route is available to traffic in the desired direction. They cannot enter a segment of a taxiway, for example, earlier than when it would be vacated by aircraft currently traversing it in the opposite direction. Some staging points may have sufficient maneuvering space to allow re-sequencing of queued aircraft for the next segment of their taxi routes; others may require the aircraft to be processed in order of their arrivals. Unlike SIMMOD and other highly realistic simulators for real-time simulation of ground operations, we do not indicate the specific physical locations of each aircraft waiting at staging points; nor do we regulate the speed of aircraft to maintain realistic physical separation while they are in motion.

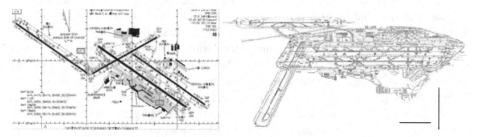

Fig. 2. Airport Layouts at Lambert St. Louis and Frankfurt, Germany

To accommodate airlines' independent behavior in managing their own resources on the ground and dispatching their flights, we designate separate staging areas on the ramp for each airline's arrivals and departures. Arriving aircraft are staged in queues in one area of the ramp pending the availability of a gate (and clear path to it). Departing aircraft (which may be held on the ground by ATC for weather or traffic control) are staged at another area if they must clear a gate to accommodate arriving aircraft. Figure 3 shows the gate staging areas and taxiing routes to the gates for four major airlines with gates at Terminal 1 and another with gates at Terminal 2 at St. Louis Lambert Airport. Areas on the airfield may be designated for spillover when physical capacity is reached at the primary ramp locations for staging the airlines' arrivals and departures.

Other areas on the airfield may be designated as staging points for departing aircraft when there is a backlog for takeoffs, traffic holds due to weather conditions in departure sectors, or holds due to weather or congestion at hub destinations. In addition to queues that are associated with physical positions on the airport property, aircraft are placed in conceptual queues to control the sequences of operations. Aircraft whose routes involve sectors of airspace temporarily restricted by severe weather, for example, may be held in a common queue and released in sequences determined by the simulated scheduling regime in effect.

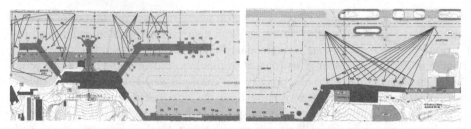

Fig. 3. Staging Points on Ramps for Arrivals and Departures of Individual Airlines

3   Data Required for Model Calibration and Validation

Calibration and validation of the model require integration of gate data maintained by individual airlines and flight data that are maintained by ATC systems for aircraft that operate under instrument flight rules (IFR). The analytical process is illustrated in Figure 4. From airline data we acquire information about aircraft type, origin and destination for the flight leg, and the scheduled and actual times of arrival or departure (pushback) at the gate. From ATC data, we obtain the time when an arriving flight reached the FAF and when it landed (touched down) on the runway. For departing flights, ATC data indicate the takeoff (liftoff) time. Merging these data, we are able to determine the itineraries of flights that arrive at the airport with continuing legs and generate the files used to activate arrivals and originating flights in the simulation model. Routings along taxiways and staging of aircraft to coordinate traffic on the airport surface occur at the discretion of ATC ground controllers who are located in the airport control tower alongside controllers of traffic in the local airspace. Direct observation and interviews with ATC controllers are required to understand the combinations of runways, taxiways and staging points used for arrivals and departures under different wind and weather conditions. Separation standards (used to space arrivals at the FAF and provide appropriate time intervals between successive takeoffs from the same runway) are derived from operating policy manuals. Airports at the point of origin for inbound flights and airports at the destination of outbound flights are grouped according to ATC sectors. This enables deviations from schedule to contain systematic elements related to wind and weather – which affect arrival itineraries and runways in use.

Aviation is particularly prone to the effects of severe weather and airport operations can be affected by conditions or events outside the immediate vicinity. Historical data of weather reports at the airport, at connected hubs and at airports in adjacent ATC sectors through which flights occur allow us to determine the conditions under which the operations took place and to design simulation scenarios accordingly.

4   Modeling Tools

For the discrete-event simulation, we use ARENA 14.7 on a Windows platform. Heuristic scheduling and sequencing procedures are able to be written in C++ or Visual

Basic and called by "event" blocks when the modeling logic requires them. The simulation is run in replicating mode (suppressing animation) to allow statistical tests of the effects of factors or strategies covered in the experimental scenarios. Adverse weather conditions in airspace sectors and at hub airports that affect traffic movements into and out of the local airspace are simulated by blocking aircraft from entering designated sectors (using either user-defined schedules or exponential probability distributions for successive events and their duration) and placing affected aircraft in queues for orderly release when the traffic restrictions expire.

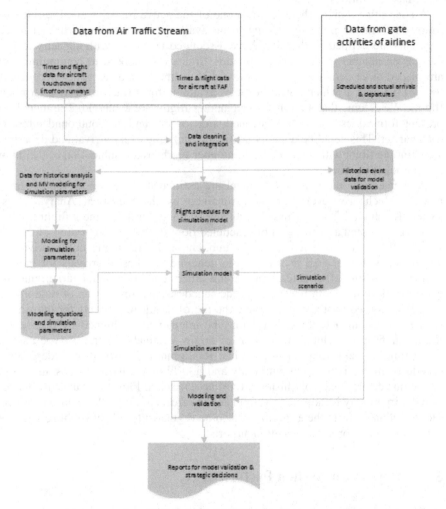

Fig. 4. Analytical Process

Arrivals for scheduled service in each simulation replication are generated with random variation imposed on their scheduled arrival times and stacked at the FAF. The file of arrivals is read by Arena, which creates a simulation entity (aircraft) that progresses through the system depending on its scheduled activity and availability of required resources (taxiways, ramps, staging points, gates, personnel and equipment) as simulated events occur. Arrivals and departures for other (general aviation) aircraft are generated randomly through the day (using exponential distributions at the highest hourly rate and thinned randomly to create hourly intensity determined by historical patterns of flight activity or exogenous planning assumptions). Airport locations (gates) for arrivals and departures of general-aviation aircraft are assigned randomly (as each flight is generated) in conformity with levels of activity at the respective fixed-base operations.

A subroutine assigns the aircraft to one of the active runways and the route to be followed from the point of landing to an available gate for the airline. Taxi-route segments are defined so that they have associated resources with capacity to hold a designated number of aircraft. Originating flights (as opposed to continuing flights) are placed at an available gate for the airline at the later of its scheduled departure time or the time at which a gate becomes available for it (i.e., freed by a terminating flight). We assume that aircraft for originating flights are available. The model, in its present form, does not force a reconciliation of inbound and outbound aircraft for each carrier. This could be done by artificially defining every arrival and departure as a continuing flight with a unique flight number (perhaps a combination of the inbound and outbound number).

Parameters for the simulation model are estimated using logistic and regression models which are developed and maintained by the Statistical Analysis System (SAS). Likelihood (and length of) of an arrival delay for an airline's flight might, for example, be stated as a function of scheduled hour of day, total duration of the flight, whether the flight originated at a major hub, and an interaction term for arrival sector and runways in use. SAS is also used to generate the files of arrivals for individual airlines (with some flights terminating and others continuing after turnaround at the gate) in conformity with historical airline schedules and imposition of random variation. SAS is used similarly to generate the file of originating flights for the simulated scenario. Scheduled flight activity may be intensified or thinned by inserting new flights (indicating airline, flight number, origin, destination, aircraft type and scheduled time) or removing existing flights. Randomness in arrivals and departures of scheduled flights is imposed with daily and hourly time-varying means and standard deviations determined from historical airline gate data. Flows inbound from a sector or hub airport may be adjusted to simulate the effects of unusual conditions or events. Flows outbound from the airport may also be regulated to reflect flight restrictions in departure sectors or into destination airports.

5   Metrics for System Performance

Airport activity varies throughout the day, with a tendency for flights to concentrate in popular times. Table 1 contains statistics for departures that occurred over 364 consecutive days at Lambert St. Louis Airport. Note how delays propagate through the schedules as the day progresses. Some delays (such as weather) are highly correlated among carriers depending on schedules and routes flown (in our case, represented by airspace sectors and major connecting hubs). Others (such as equipment failure) are random. A comprehensive simulation model for airport operations must produce information in a form that allows one to investigate the dynamic performance of the system.

At minimum, performance statistics of airport activity would include:
– Number of arrivals and departures for each hour of the day
– Distributions of delays (differences between actual and scheduled times for arrivals at the gate and departures (pushbacks) from the gate)
– Percentage of delays that constitute a significantly late arrival or departure (e.g., delays in excess of 20 minutes)
– Distributions of time required to taxi from touchdown on the runway to the designated arrival gate
– Distributions of time from pushback at the gate to liftoff
– Frequencies with which different runways are used for landings and departures
– Frequency, duration and timing of ramp and gate holds for weather events
– Frequency, duration and timing of ramp and gate holds for traffic congestion at destination hubs

Table 1. Departure Delays over 364 Days at Lambert St. Louis Airport

Scheduled Flights and Delays		Airline					
		American	Delta	United	US Air	Southwest	Overall
Flights	Hour of Day						
	6AM to 8AM	2,284	1,557	1,179	1,430	3,168	9,618
	8AM to 10AM	2,165	1,005	1,166	1,031	5,144	10,511
	10AM to 12PM	2,387	742	913	325	4,100	8,467
	12PM to 2PM	2,608	458	928	673	4,080	8,747
	2PM to 4PM	2,272	787	893	666	3,663	8,281
	4PM to 6PM	2,629	1,045	1,641	1,024	3,722	10,061
	6PM to 8PM	2,030	699	1,560	317	4,684	9,290
	8PM to 10PM	1,046	24	38	134	3,626	4,868
	After 10PM	10	21	.	.	16	47
	Overall	17,431	6,338	8,318	5,600	32,203	69,890
Av. Delay	Hour of Day						
	6AM to 8AM	3.6	7.2	6.7	6.6	1.2	4.2
	8AM to 10AM	4.2	8.9	10.7	10.4	3.4	5.6
	10AM to 12PM	6.0	11.2	11.2	15.9	4.8	6.8
	12PM to 2PM	6.5	10.3	20.8	15.0	6.9	9.1
	2PM to 4PM	5.9	9.9	21.2	8.2	11.2	10.5
	4PM to 6PM	11.0	16.1	27.3	11.6	13.5	15.2
	6PM to 8PM	10.7	12.0	29.0	12.4	17.6	17.4
	8PM to 10PM	1.3	35.7	10.8	4.5	23.1	17.9
	After 10PM	14.4	20.6	.	.	12.5	16.5
	Overall	6.6	10.7	19.2	10.2	10.1	10.4

For reporting of simulation results, we create detailed logs of simulated activity (written to flat files) and perform the analysis with SAS. Table 2 illustrates information that is saved for individual aircraft. Separating the simulation and analysis in this fashion, we can use data from multiple replications to investigate thoroughly how system performance varies through time. We can also assess the differential effects that physical or operational changes have on individual airlines or types of aircraft and estimate the extent to which variation is attributable to systematic versus random effects. With similar recording of information as planes leave or arrive at key queuing points, we can retrospectively deduce the state of the system at any point in simulated time (e.g., gates in use, queues at various stages for arriving and departing flights, simulated aircraft in motion on the ground, aircraft holding on a ramp or taxiway, and aircraft in the simulated airspace).

Strategies for dealing with weather interruptions are employed by both airline operations and ATC. Our modeling framework readily allows an exploration of alternative actions from individual airlines, on one hand, and from ATC ground control on the other hand, if flights to some destinations need to be held. Ground controllers may hold an aircraft at the gate or direct it to a staging position elsewhere on the field if its departure would be delayed by weather or traffic on its planned route. Since delays are calculated as deviations from scheduled pushback rather than liftoff, the staged queuing strategy to cope with traffic holds has a significant impact on actual and reported performance for an airline. Moving an aircraft to free a gate may make it possible for an airline to accommodate incoming traffic without interruption and enable an "on-time" departure, but it may also create congestion elsewhere on the ground that interferes with other departures.

Table 2. Excerpt from the Simulation Event Log for Aircraft Movements

Obs	Replic. No.	Event time	Event	Airline	Flight Number	Lambert Gate	City	Continuing	Next City	Next Departure Time
450	1	1523	2: Arrival	WN	2544	E8	MCI	Yes	RSW	1545
451	1	1525	5: Liftoff	DL	2158	A2	ATL	Yes	ATL	1515
452	1	1525	4: Pushback	UA	5276	A9	CLE	Yes	CLE	1517
453	1	1527	2: Arrival	WN	1657	E16	BWI	Yes	HOU	1545
454	1	1528	3: Originate	UA	3820	A9	EWR	No	000	0000
455	1	1528	4: Pushback	UA	3820	A9	EWR	No	000	0000

Simulation of such actions can occur by using dynamic priorities for individual aircraft in the staged queues. To investigate how the effects of different operating conditions and practices would be revealed in practice, multiple replications are required with stochastic times for activities and random generation of interfering events (equipment failure, weather) in accordance with their historical frequencies and durations. We illustrate below the measures of system performance produced in 100 replications of a scenario to test the potential effects of gate holds and ramp holds imposed in St. Louis for flights destined to Chicago airports because of severe weather. Affected were flights to ORD (served by American and United Airlines) and to MDW (served by Southwest Airlines). As ramp and taxiway capacities allowed, flights to other destinations were permitted. Random delays were imposed at departure gates using lognormal distributions with means and standard deviations determined from historical data considering time of day and whether the flight is continuing or originating. Other activity times (for taxiing, etc.) were generated using lognormal distributions with a 20% coefficient of variation. Arrivals were assumed to accrue at the FAF according to schedule (with no random variation). To perform 100 replications of a day's schedule with simple scheduling rules (FCFS except for aircraft subject to gate and ramp holds) and pre-designated taxiing routes for active runways, less than two minutes of CPU time were required on a workstation with an Intel® Core™2DuoCPU E8400 processor @ 3.0GHZ and 3.5GB of RAM.

Table 3 shows the simulated performance for a simulated extreme weather event that results in gate holds and ramp holds for flights destined to ORD and MDW in the morning. Table 4 reflects the results of the same weather scenario without gate holds but imposition of holds on a ramp when the ramp capacity for flights staged for departure was reduced. In the latter case, aircraft were pushed back when ready for departure but they were held at the staged queuing area on the ramp until the holds on flights to Chicago were lifted. The result is fewer flights registering pushback delays (i.e., better "on-time performance") but longer resulting waits on taxiways and ramps (with higher fuel burn and emissions). Also, with reduced space for staging flights near the departure end of the runway, flights released from the gate cause interference with departures of airlines not destined to Chicago and the latter suffer delays that did not occur when the Chicago-bound flights were held at the gate. Without the reductions in ramp capacity, the flights not destined to Chicago did not suffer delays. These results were generated using preliminary parameters estimated from the 364-day history and would not reflect actual experience over a year of flight activity. They simply verified that the modeled performance behaved as expected when the experimental changes to dispatching practices were imposed.

Table 3. Stochastic Simulation with 100 Replications of Severe Weather Scenario at Major Destination Hub and Affected Aircraft Held at Gate and Ramp

		Delay (minutes)		Flights with Pushback Delay		Ramp and Taxi time
		Flights	Av. Delay	Number	P(>20 min.)	Av. Minutes
airline	event					
American	2: Arrival	3,000	7.1	0	0.000	7.1
	4: Departure	3,596	17.1	551	0.153	8.1
Delta	2: Arrival	1,800	7.0	0	0.000	7.0
	4: Departure	1,900	5.8	104	0.055	7.7
United	2: Arrival	2,500	7.4	22	0.009	7.4
	4: Departure	3,297	27.4	888	0.269	8.4
US Air	2: Arrival	1,500	7.0	0	0.000	7.0
	4: Departure	1,600	6.7	105	0.066	7.6
Southwest	2: Arrival	7,900	7.5	0	0.000	7.5
	4: Departure	7,899	6.9	859	0.109	8.2
Overall		34,994	10.5	3E3	0.072	7.7

Table 4. Results of Stochastic Simulation with 100 Replications for Severe Weather Event with Ramp Hold, Restricted Ramp Capacity, and No Gate Hold

airline	event	Delay (minutes)		Flights with Pushback Delay		Ramp and Taxi time
		Flights	Av. Delay	Number	P(>20 min.)	Av. Minutes
American	2: Arrival	3,000	7.1	0	0.000	7.1
	4: Departure	3,599	9.4	389	0.108	20.7
Delta	2: Arrival	1,800	7.1	0	0.000	7.1
	4: Departure	1,900	5.7	96	0.051	13.3
United	2: Arrival	2,500	7.0	0	0.000	7.0
	4: Departure	3,297	14.7	584	0.177	24.0
US Air	2: Arrival	1,500	7.0	0	0.000	7.0
	4: Departure	1,600	5.9	79	0.049	10.6
Southwest	2: Arrival	7,900	7.5	0	0.000	7.5
	4: Departure	7,894	8.8	766	0.097	13.0
Overall		34,990	8.4	2E3	0.055	12.0

6   Generalization, Validation and Application

We performed extensive multivariate statistical analysis on detailed activity data for Lambert and Frankfurt airports to get a sense of the factors that need to be considered in calibrating, validating and applying the model to local conditions. From detailed data for individual flight operations in St. Louis and in Frankfurt for an entire year, we examined the likelihood and length of delays at both airports and found, as expected, that delays tend to be greatest when traffic is most intense (depending on time of day and day of week), in times of inclement weather (depending on month of year), for carriers with flights from major hub airports, when direction of landing (into the wind) tends to involve longer approach paths or taxiing times for major carriers, or when flights involve busy airspace sectors. In Table 5 we present results of fitting logistic regression models for the likelihood of delays in departures at individual gate groups (used by specific airlines) with data from Frankfurt and St. Louis. Each of the aforementioned factors is highly statistically significant at both airports; yet there are individual differences in the magnitude of their impact. The effects of changing design parameters and operating practice at the airport can differentially affect individual airlines. They are affected by scheduling practices of the airlines, the physical resources they employ and the concentration of activity where they are located.

In constructing the simulation model, we accommodate normal operating variation by adjusting for systematic effects with regression and logistics models (using combinations of indicator variables and partitioning of data with separate calibration for factors where there is significant interaction and sufficient data), impose randomness to reflect the residual variance from such models, and impose further variation by creating disruptive scenarios. Some factors are interdependent (e.g., fleet mix, scheduled activity and connecting cities for an airline) – hence the difference in individual variables used for the models illustrated in Table 5. It is a challenge to screen out exceptional cases when fitting the multivariate models, to create parameters for elemental operations (such as

preparing a plane for departure or taxiing on a taxiway segment) that result in appropriate behavior cumulatively, and to validate model's behavior under realistic scenarios
(and overall) using higher-level statistics available from operating data.   An iterative
analytical process is required – which involves continuous looping through the stages
represented in Figure 4. Constructing regression models from the simulated data and
comparing their structure with those derived from historical data (for the base set of
operating assumptions) helps to ensure that relevant factors are considered and that their
influence is consistent with theory and operational history.

Table 5. Factors Affecting the Likelihood of Delays for flights from a Gate Group in Frankfurt
(left) and in St. Louis (right)

Parameter	DF	Schätzwert	Standard-fehler	Waldsches Chi-Quadrat	Pr > ChiSq	Parameter	DF	Schätzwert	Standard fehler	Waldsches Chi-Quadrat	Pr > ChiSq
Intercept	1	0.1539	0.3530	8.4424	0.0037	Intercept	1	−2.59	0.0675	1480.3474	<.0001
hourbef6	1	−0.5819	0.0769	57.2675	<.0001	hourbef6	1	−1.0051	0.4241	5.6167	0.0178
hour6to8	1	−0.3812	0.0496	59.0683	<.0001	hourof6to8	1	−1.0934	0.1225	79.2590	<.0001
hour8to10	1	−0.3974	0.0441	81.5722	<.0001	hour10to12	1	0.3371	0.0748	20.3374	<.0001
hour10to12	1	−0.1997	0.0442	20.4488	<.0001	hour12to14	1	0.8410	0.0668	158.5462	<.0001
hour16to18	1	0.3932	0.3418	88.2823	<.0001	hour14to16	1	1.3742	0.0651	445.5213	<.0001
hour18to20	1	−0.2153	0.0431	25.0046	<.0001	hour16to18	1	1.5742	0.0657	573.6536	<.0001
houraf22	1	−0.9344	0.1522	37.7022	<.0001	hour18to20	1	1.8975	0.0616	949.3157	<.0001
may	1	−0.1383	0.0481	8.2804	0.0040	hour20to22	1	2.3613	0.0647	1331.2957	<.0001
july	1	−0.1235	0.0476	6.7405	0.0094	houraft22	1	2.2328	0.7162	9.7180	0.0018
august	1	−0.2084	0.0483	18.6217	<.0001	january	1	0.2196	0.0625	11.6000	0.0006
september	1	0.1576	0.0471	11.2001	0.0008	march	1	0.4815	0.0587	67.1080	<.0001
october	1	0.1638	0.0465	4.5762	0.0257	april	1	0.3558	0.0646	30.3237	<.0001
november	1	−0.3171	0.0496	40.9015	<.0001	may	1	0.7345	0.0628	135.4061	<.0001
rwy07C	1	−0.1491	0.1045	21.9196	<.0001	june	1	0.7807	0.0641	148.5153	<.0001
rwy25L	1	−0.2696	0.0542	52.0043	<.0001	july	1	0.6143	0.0649	88.5107	<.0001
rwy25C	1	−0.9432	0.0634	150.6153	<.0001	august	1	0.7671	0.0656	136.7958	<.0001
rwy25R	1	0.1324	0.0522	16.5391	<.0001	december	1	0.5861	0.0579	102.3110	<.0001
NW	1	0.1568	0.0576	17.4344	<.0001	rwy127	1	−0.1837	0.0583	13.3299	0.0003
SW	1	0.2821	0.0527	51.4297	<.0001	rwy29	1	0.2785	0.0912	9.3373	0.0022
classM	1	−0.2618	0.0421	38.6954	<.0001	rwy30L	1	0.1909	0.0517	13.5531	0.0002
classL	1	−0.6304	0.0766	67.7005	<.0001						

To show the correspondence between historical delays and those generated by the
model for the most frequent operating practice, we present statistics for 364 days of
actual airport activity in Table 6 and statistics for 100 days of simulated activity in
Table 7.   This simulation scenario is a base case involving the use of RWY 30R for
arrivals and RWY 30L for departures and an assumed level of general aviation activity similar to recent months.   The statistic "average delay" in Table 6 includes negative values (early arrivals and departures).   The "truncated delays" are computed by
treating an early arrival or departure as having a delay = 0.

Table 6. Actual Delays Computed from 364 Days of Gate Activity

linecode	Recorded Arrivals	Av. Arrival Delay (min.)	Av. Arrival Delay (min.) Truncated	Prop. Arrival Delays >15 min.	Recorded Departures	Av. Departure Delay (min.)	Av. Departure Delay (min.) Truncated	Prop. Departure Delays >15 min.
AA	9,699	7.93	13.96	0.21	9,694	10.64	10.69	0.15
CP	3,421	0.44	1.72	0.02	7,737	1.12	1.38	0.02
DL	7,708	1.85	9.92	0.14	6,338	7.18	10.65	0.13
UA	8,920	17.73	22.86	0.29	8,318	15.54	19.15	0.25
US	5,579	8.34	14.26	0.18	5,600	6.82	10.24	0.14
WN	32,011	5.56	9.85	0.15	32,203	10.03	10.14	0.17

For this base case, we placed scheduled airline flights at the final approach fix (FAF)
with random deviations based on a regression fitted with historical data. Deviations

from schedule for gate arrivals are shifted back to the FAF using average approach and taxi times for the runway in use. We defined 0-1 indicator variables for each hour of the day and used the resulting regression models to generate flight delays for each carrier. For example, the equation for arrival delays of one carrier took the form:

$$\text{expminutesdelay} = 8.0 - 15.6 * \text{hour7} -7.8 * \text{hour8} -5.8 * \text{hour9} -5.7 * \text{hour11}$$
$$+ 8.1 * \quad \text{hour16} +10.0 * \text{hour17} + 14.6 * \text{hour18} +3.6 * \text{hour19}$$
$$+ 13.4 * \quad \text{hour20} +3.5 * \text{hour21} +11.8 * \text{hour22}$$
$$+ 2.2 * \text{nesector} -4.4 * \text{swsector}.$$

The residual standard error for that regression model was 36.0. The deviation from schedule for that airline's individual flights was set at max{-20,int(expminutesdelay+ 36.0 * (standard normal deviate))}. In contrast, for general aviation, we generate arrivals and flight originations used exponential inter-arrival times at the highest hour-ly rate for the day and "thin" them to create the expected time-of day variation.

Departure delays in the simulated activity for scheduled flights were the result of a two-step process involving pairs of logistic and regression models that were fitted separately for continuing flights and originating flights of individual carriers. For the former, we used a logistic regression model such as the following to determine the probability of a delay for an airline's flight:

$$\text{probpbdelay} = 1/(1+\exp(0.54 + 1.48 * \text{hour6} + 1.18 * \text{hour7} + 1.11 * \text{hour8}$$
$$+ 1.04 * \text{hour9} + 0.89 * \text{hour10} + 0.58 * \text{hour11} + 0.34 * \text{hour15}$$
$$+ 0.37 \text{hour18} + 0.83 * \text{hour20} -0.28 * \text{nesector} --0.49* \text{swsector}$$
$$+ 0.84 * \text{sesector})).$$

We then used regression equations calibrated with cases that experienced delays to estimate the lengths of delays, given they occur.

Table 7. Delays Computed from 100 Days of Simulated Activity

airline	event	Delays (av. min. delay)		Flights with Delay > 15 min.		Ramp and Taxi time
		Flights	Av. Delay	Number over 15 min.	P(>15 min.)	Av. Minutes
American	2: Arrival	2,598	1.4	727	0.280	6.2
	4: Departure	2,600	5.9	279	0.107	13.1
Cape Air	2: Arrival	2,500	-6.4	49	0.020	6.5
	4: Departure	2,499	3.7	219	0.088	8.4
Delta	2: Arrival	1,876	-5.7	302	0.161	6.1
	4: Departure	1,600	4.7	121	0.076	14.9
GA	2: Arrival	0	.	0	0.000	7.2
	4: Departure	0	.	0	0.000	5.0
United	2: Arrival	3,280	8.3	1,260	0.384	6.1
	4: Departure	3,300	5.9	375	0.114	15.2
US Air	2: Arrival	1,400	0.6	367	0.262	6.0
	4: Departure	1,400	2.8	77	0.055	13.6
Southwest	2: Arrival	9,495	0.5	2,229	0.235	7.4
	4: Departure	9,500	10.0	1,258	0.132	12.1
Overall		42,048	3.8	7,263	0.134	8.9

7   Achieving Proper Analytical Balance in Future Research

Our simulation prototype was created to facilitate the analysis of airport ground operations with due consideration of the major intersecting spheres of activity and responsibility. It captures essential characteristics of the system in each operational sphere and links them with staged queues at the interfaces. Optimizing heuristics may be embedded in portions of the Arena simulation model and the effects of their solutions may be tested with consideration of stochastic system behavior. Solutions from deterministic optimizing models may also be driven through the model to see their effects on other aspects of the operation and to examine whether promised gains from their use are achievable in a stochastic environment.

The prototype was originally constructed to represent traffic in the dominant operating environment at St. Louis Lambert Airport (using runways 30L and 30R for departures and arrivals) and behavior was validated using complementary flight data for just a few weather scenarios. The model has since been extended and calibrated for opposite traffic flows (using runways 12L and 12R); occasional traffic on runway 6-24 when strong crosswinds require such use; and use of runway 11-29 for occasional westerly departures from Terminal 1 and occasional easterly arrivals to Terminal 1. With a full year of complementary flight data (giving times at the FAF and indications of runways used for arrivals and departures), we will be able to refine the statistical models for arrival delays to take landing direction (and needs for circling to the FAF) into account. Lambert Airport is to be simulated with the current configuration of taxiways and with new taxiway designs conforming to current FAA standards. In the process, crude estimates of taxi-time distributions will be refined with additional measures from direct observation. Models for fuel burn considering taxi time and idle times under power will be appended to the report generators to assess economic and environmental effects of alternative airport configurations and operating practices. Further refinements estimating stop-and-go behavior on runways and taxiways to give better estimates of fuel burned and resulting emissions are also possible.

Despite the common factors that affect system performance at different airports, the impact of improved decision-making processes in airside operations is highly dependent on the specific problem domain and on the conditions under which the system operates. Traffic levels have dropped since Lambert Airport was a major hub to TWA and American Airlines; so the impact of innovative scheduling methods there will have to be assessed by concentrating on scenarios involving artificially inflating traffic to the higher historical levels, or situations where the system is under stress from factors such as severe weather. For investigation of strategies to improve performance of systems with traffic closer to design limits, we are applying the model to flight operations at Frankfurt Airport, Germany. Conceptually the problem is the same and the layouts of the airfields are quite similar. Selection of taxi routes from points of landing to staging points for arrival at gates and from gates to staging points for departure may be more complex (and dynamic) in the Frankfurt environment, with more opportunities for intersecting traffic.

8   Discussion and Conclusion

As we seek balance between the highly detailed engineering simulations of airspace and airports with microscopic detail, on one hand, and operations research models designed for strategic optimization of parts of the system, on the other hand, we strive to incorporate necessary details of the operating environment and avoid the "flaw of averages" when studying airside operations of commercial airports. We also try to keep the investigation of strategic alternatives computationally tractable. We believe that our analytical framework involving networks of staged queues and discrete-event simulation with embedded heuristics offer a good balance.

We finally recognize that airline personnel and ATC respond to situational opportunities in a more flexible manner than our model (and others) allow. Ultimately, the effects of operating with different physical constraints, operating rules and supporting resources are determined by the motivation and creativity of actors in the real system. With further applications and refinement of our models in North American and European settings, however, we hope to identify opportunities for better utilizing existing assets and efficiently deploying new assets for air transportation.

References

1. Atkin, J.A.D., Burke, E.K., Greenwood, J.S., Reeson, D.: An examination of take-off scheduling constraints at London Heathrow airport. Public Transport 1(1), 169–187 (2009)
2. Atkin, J.A.D., Burke, E.K., Ravizza, S.: The airport ground movement problem: past and current research and future directions. In: 4th International Conference on Research in Air Transportation, Budapest, June 01–04, 2010, pp. 131–138 (2010)
3. Bazargan, M., Fleming, K., Subramanian, P.: A simulation study to investigate runway capacity using TAAM. In: Proceedings of the 2002 Winter Simulation Conference, pp. 1235–1242 (2002)
4. Bertino, J., Boyajian, E.: 21st Century Fast-time Airport and Airspace Modeling Analysis with Simmod. Managing the Skies 2011, 21–23 (2011)
5. Brentnall, A.R., Cheng, R.C.H.: Some Effects of Aircraft Arrival Sequence Algorithms. The Journal of the Operational Research Society 60(7), 962–972 (2009)
6. Bubalo, B., Daduna, J.R.: Airport capacity and demand calculations by simulation – the case of Berlin-Brandenburg International Airport. Netnomics 12, 161–181 (2011)
7. Capozzi, B., Brinton, M., Churchill, A., Atkins, S.: The metroplex simulation environment. In: 2013 IEEE/AIAA 32nd Digital Avionics Systems Conference (DASC), p. 1E5-1) (2013)
8. Federal Aviation Administration. SIMMOD Reference Manual AOR-200, Office of Operations Research, Federal Aviation Adminstration, Washington, D.C. (FAA, 1989). http://www.tc.faa.gov/acb300/how_simmod_works.pdf
9. Fishburn, P.T., Golkar, J., Taafe, K.: Simulation of transportation systems. In: Proceedings of the 1995 Winter Simulation Conference, pp. 51–54 (1995)
10. Gilbo, E.P.: Airport capacity – representation, estimation, optimization. IEEE Transactions on Control Systems Technology 1, 144–154 (1993)
11. Gotteland, J.B., Durand, N., Alliot, J.M., Page, E.: Aircraft ground traffic optimization. In: 4th USA/Europe Air Traffic Management Seminar, pp. 04–07 (2001)

12. Gue, K.R., Kang, K.: Staging queues in material handling and transportation systems. In: Peters, B.A., Smith, J.S., Medeiros, D.J., Rohrer, M.W. (eds) Proceedings of the 2001 Winter Simulation Conference, pp. 1104–1108 (2001)
13. Herrero, J.G., Berlanga, A., Molina, J.M., Casar, J.R.: Methods for operations planning in airport decision support systems. Applied Intelligence **22**(3), 183–206 (2005)
14. Horstmeier, T., de Haan, F.: Influence of groundhandling on turn round time of new large aircraft. Aircraft Engineering and Aerospace Technology **73**(3), 266–270 (2001)
15. Khadilkar, H., Balakrishnan, H.: Network congestion control of airport surface operations. Journal of Guidance, Control and Dynamics, 19 (2013)
16. Norin, A., Granberg, T.A., Varbrand, P., Yuan, D.: Integrating optimization and simulation to gain more efficient airport logistics. In: Eighth USA/Europe Air Traffic Management Research and Development Seminar (2009)
17. Odoni, A.R., Bowman, J., Delahaye, D., Deyst, J.J., Feron, E., Hansman, R.J., Khan, K., Kuchar, J.K., Pujet, N., Simpson, R.W.: Existing and required modeling capabilities for evaluating ATM systems and concepts, International Center for Air Transportation, Massachusetts Institute of Technology (1997)
18. Offerman, H.: Simulation to Support the Airport Stakeholder Decision-Making Process. Air and Space Europe **3**(1/2), 60–67 (2001)
19. Ravizza, S., Chen, J., Atkin, J.A.D., Burke, E.K., Stewart, P.: The trade-off between taxi time and fuel consumption in airport ground movement. Public Transport **4**(1–2), 25–40 (2013)
20. Sherali, H.D., Hobeika, A.G., Trani, A.A., Kim, B.J.: An integrated simulation and dynamic programming approach for determining optimal runway exit locations. Management Science **38**(7), 1049–1049 (1992)
21. Smith, L.D., Nauss, R.M., Mattfeld, D.C., Li, J., Ehmke, J.F.: Scheduling Operations at System Choke Points with Sequence-dependent Delays and Processing Times. Transportation Research Part E **47**(5), 669–691 (2011)
22. Smith, L., Ehmke, J.F., Mattfeld, D.C., Waning, R., Hellmann, L.: Strategic decision support for airside operations at commercial airports. In: González-Ramírez, R.G., Schulte, F., Voß, S., Ceroni Díaz, J.A. (eds.) ICCL 2014. LNCS, vol. 8760, pp. 132–150. Springer, Heidelberg (2014)
23. Snowdon, J.L., MacNair, E., Montevecchi, M., Callery, C.A., El-Taji, S., Miller, S.: IBM journey management library: An arena system for airport simulations. The Journal of the Operational Research Society **51**(4), 449–456 (2000)
24. Wei, G., Siyuan, J.: Simulation study on closely spaced parallel runway analysis using SIMMOD Plus. In: 2010 International Conference on Intelliget Computation Technology and Automation, pp. 344–347. IEEE (2010)
25. Yan, S., Shieh, C., Chen, M.: A simulation framework for evaluating airport gate assignments. Transportation Research Part A **36**, 885–898 (2002)
26. Zografos, K.G., Madas, M.A.: Development and demonstration for an integrated decision support system for airport performance analysis. Transportation Research Part C **14**, 1–17 (2006)

Discrete Speed in Vertical Flight Planning

Zhi Yuan[1]([✉]), Liana Amaya Moreno[1], Armin Fügenschuh[1], Anton Kaier[2],
and Swen Schlobach[2]

[1] Professorship of Applied Mathematics, Department of Mechanical Engineering,
Helmut Schmidt University, Hamburg, Germany
{yuanz,lamayamo,fuegenschuh}@hsu-hh.de
[2] Lufthansa Systems AG, Kelsterbach, Germany
{anton.kaier,swen.schlobach}@lhsystems.com

Abstract. Vertical flight planning concerns assigning optimal cruise altitude and speed to each trajectory-composing segment, such that the fuel consumption is minimized, and the arrival time constraints are satisfied. The previous work that assigns continuous speed to each segment leads to prohibitively long computation time. In this work, we propose a mixed integer linear programming model that assigns discrete speed. In particular, an all-but-one speed discretization scheme is found to scale well with problem size with only negligible objective deviation from using continuous speed. Extensive experiments with real-world instances have shown the practical effectiveness and feasibility of the proposed speed discretization approach.

Keywords: Flight planning · Mixed integer programming · Variable discretization · Piecewise linear interpolation

1 Introduction

Air transport is an important component of many international logistics networks, including transportation of goods and people. Planning a fuel-efficient trajectory for each flight is a practically important and computationally hard optimization problem. Such a flight trajectory is in general four-dimensional (4D), which consists of horizontally a 2D route on the earth surface, vertically, a number of discrete admissible altitude levels, and a time dimension controlled by aircraft speed such that the flight can arrive within a certain strict time window. Due to the computational difficulty of such a 4D optimization problem, in practice, it is usually approached in two separate phases [2]: a horizontal optimization phase that searches for a trajectory on the earth surface consisting of a set of segments, to which an optimal altitude and speed is assigned to in the subsequent vertical optimization phase.

In this work, we focus on the vertical flight planning problem. The vertical profile of a flight includes five stages: take-off, climb, cruise, descend, and landing. Here we focus on the cruise stage, since it consumes the most fuel and time during a flight, while the other stages are relatively short and usually have fixed procedures due to safety considerations, which leaves little flexibility for fuel

F. Corman et al. (Eds.): ICCL 2015, LNCS 9335, pp. 734–749, 2015.
DOI: 10.1007/978-3-319-24264-4_50

optimization. Computing an optimal altitude profile in the absence of wind can also provide estimated altitude for the 2D horizontal trajectory optimization [12]. Such a steady-atmosphere optimal altitude profile increases approximately linearly as fuel burns, however, it becomes irregular if altitude-dependent wind is considered [9]. A recent research by Lovegren and Hansman [10] confirmed a potential fuel saving of up to 3.5% by reassigning only altitude and speed to fixed flight trajectories, based on a study of 257 real flight operations in US. However, no time constraint is taken into account in their computation as in real-world airline operations. In such case, there exists a backward dynamic programming approach to compute fuel-optimal vertical profile [17].

A practical challenge in airline operations is to handle time constraints, especially delays, due to disruptions such as undesirable weather conditions, unexpected maintenance requirements, or waiting for passengers transferring from other already delayed flights. Such delays are typically recovered by increasing cruise speed, such that the next connection for passengers as well as for the aircraft and the crew can be reached [1]. Varying cruise speed may also be useful, e.g., to enter a time-dependent restricted airspace before it is closed (or after it is open), or when an aircraft is reassigned to a flight that used to be served by a faster (or slower) aircraft. The industrial standard suggests using a cost index procedure to vary cruise speed. This requires inputing a value that reflects the importance between time-related cost and fuel-related cost. The use of cost index was criticized due to the difficulty to quantify the time-related cost in the presence of delay, thus a dynamic cost index approach has been proposed to this end [6]. However, such approach still cannot handle explicitly hard time constraints, such as the about-to-close airspace. Aktürk et al. [1] formulate the time constraint explicitly into their MIP model in the context of aircraft rescheduling. Their model uses only constant speed. Yuan et al. [17,18] explicitly include the time constraint and the use of variable speed in the vertical flight planning.

In [17,18], the vertical flight planning problem with variable continuous speed is identified as a mixed-integer second-order cone programming (MISOCP) problem. The second-order cone constraints consist in calculating the flight time, and the integer variables consist in the 2D piecewise linear interpolation of the fuel consumption function, as well as the selection of discrete admissible altitude levels. The MISOCP model is reformulated as a mixed-integer linear programming model by applying linear approximation techniques [4,8] and various piecewise linear approximation techniques. Despite the performance boost by using the linear approximation of the MISOCP model, the long computation time still prevents it from being a practically feasible approach.

In this present work, we study an alternative model for the vertical flight planning problem with discrete speed, i.e., only a set of speed levels can be selected for each segment. The use of speed discretization replaces the quadratic cone constraints by linear constraints, and it also reduces the 2D piecewise linear fuel function to 1D, at the expense of introducing more binary variables. We experimentally investigate the computation scalability of the discrete speed model, and carefully analyze the discretization error that leads to differences in the objective value. In particular, to balance the computational scalability and the discretization error, an all-but-one discretization, which discretizes speed on all but one segments, appears to be the most practically viable approach.

2   Vertical Flight Planning: The Problem Description

In the vertical flight planning problem (VFP), we are given a set of segments that compose the flight trajectory. The wind information for each segment is given in both the track direction (flight direction) and cross-track direction. The task is to assign an altitude and a speed to each segment, such that the flight consumes the least fuel while the arrival time constraints are satisfied. The altitude and the speed on each segment are invariant, and they can only be changed at the beginning of each segment, due to safety requirements. The cruise stage under consideration in this work starts after the initial climb has brought the aircraft above the crossover altitude of around 29 000 feet. Depending on the flight direction (eastwards or westwards), a set of discrete admissible flight altitudes are allowed. We consider IFR RVSM flight levels [13], where two adjacent flight levels usually differ by 1 000 feet, and the eastwards and westwards flights are allowed to fly in alternate flight levels.

The aircraft manufacturers provide the aircraft performance data as unit distance fuel consumption, which depends on three factors: aircraft speed, altitude, and weight. Each aircraft's unit distance fuel consumption data is measured at discrete levels of each of the three factors. For a given value that does not lie on these measured levels, it needs to be linearly interpolated by adjacent grid points. An illustrative example is given in Fig. 1. As can be observed, in general, the heavier the weight, the more fuel is consumed; besides, the higher the altitude, the less fuel is burnt. If no time constraint is considered, a fuel-optimal vertical profile can be determined by a backward dynamic programming approach [17] by enumerating all speed and altitude levels from the last segment to the first segment. However, if the arrival time constraint is enforced, such as to avoid delays and missing connections, assigning speed and altitude is not an easy task. Our previous works [17,18] modeled the vertical flight planning problem as a mixed-integer nonlinear programming (MINLP) model. We further observed, if the arrival time window enforces speeding up the aircraft from its unconstrained fuel-optimal vertical profile, such as to avoid delays, then the MINLP model can be formulated as a mixed-integer second order cone programming (MISOCP) model. In this work, we compared our proposed discrete speed model to the continuous speed model in MISOCP, and adopted the instances in [17,18] for speeding up the aircraft. But the discrete speed model can be potentially also applied to cases when the aircraft needs slowing down.

3   Vertical Flight Planning with Continuous Speed

To the best of our knowledge, the first mathematical programming model for the vertical flight planning problem was proposed in [18], which studies the use

Fig. 1. Unit distance fuel consumption with respect to aircraft weight (in kg), altitude (in feet), and speed (in Mach number).

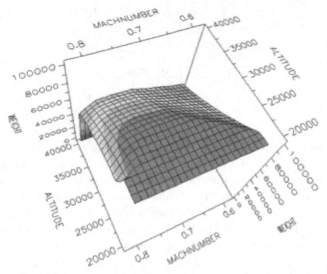

of variable speed during a flight in the absence of wind. This model is further extended in [17] to include wind. Both models assign continuous speed to each segment, and can be identified as mixed integer second-order cone programming (MISCOP), if the aircraft needs to be speeded up. These two models are briefly presented in this section.

3.1   Vertical Flight Planning without Wind (VFP-C)

In [18], a mathematical model for vertical flight planning without wind (VFP-C) is presented as follows. The unit distance fuel consumption F of an aircraft is given as measured data at discrete levels of the three dependent factors: speed V, altitude H, and weight W, as illustrated in Figure 1. If no wind is considered, given speed and weight, the optimal altitude can be precomputed by checking all possible altitudes, thus it is not necessary to include its computation in the optimization model. Other input parameters include a set of n segments $S :=$ $\{1, \ldots, n\}$ with length L_i for all $i \in S$; the minimum and maximum trip duration $\underline{T}$ and $\overline{T}$; and the dry aircraft weight W^{dry}, i.e. the weight of a loaded aircraft without trip fuel (reserve fuel for safety is included in the dry weight). The variables include the time vector t_i for $i \in S \cup \{0\}$, where t_{i-1} and t_i denote the start and end time of segment i; the travel time Δt_i spent on a segment $i \in S$; the weight vector w_i for $i \in S \cup \{0\}$ and w_i^{mid} for $i \in S$ where w_{i-1}, w_i^{mid}, and w_i denote the start, middle, and end weight at a segment i; the speed v_i on a segment $i \in S$; and the fuel f_i consumed on a segment $i \in S$. A general mathematical model for VFP-C can be stated as follows:

$$\min \quad w_0 - w_n \tag{1}$$

$$\text{s.t.} \quad t_0 = 0, \quad \underline{T} \le t_n \le \overline{T} \tag{2}$$

$$\forall i \in S: \quad \Delta t_i = t_i - t_{i-1} \tag{3}$$

$$\forall i \in S: \quad L_i = v_i \cdot \Delta t_i \tag{4}$$

$$w_n = W^{dry} \tag{5}$$

$$\forall i \in S: \quad w_{i-1} = w_i + f_i \tag{6}$$

$$\forall i \in S: \quad w_{i-1} + w_i = 2 \cdot w_i^{mid} \tag{7}$$

$$\forall i \in S: \quad f_i = L_i \cdot \widehat{F}(v_i, w_i^{mid}). \tag{8}$$

The objective function (1) minimizes the total fuel consumption measured by the difference of aircraft weight before and after the flight; (2) ensures the flight duration within a given interval; time consistency is preserved by (3); the basic equation of motion (4) is enforced on each segment; (5) initializes the weight vector by assuming all trip fuel is burnt during the flight; weight consistency is ensured in (6), and the middle weight of each segment calculated in (7) will be used in the calculation of fuel consumption of each segment in (8), where $\widehat{F}(v, w)$ is a piecewise linear function interpolating F for all the continuous values of v and w within the given grid of $V \times W$. $\widehat{F}$ can be formulated as a MILP submodel using Dantzig's convex combination method [7,16], a.k.a. lambda method. Our previous work [18] presents a variant of the 2D lambda method tailored for this problem. The quadratic constraint (4) can also be formulated as second-order cone constraint, if the time constraint (2) requires the aircraft to speed up from its unconstrained fuel-optimal travel time. A variable transformation technique to formulate it into a standard second-order cone constraint is presented in [18]. The resulting MISOCP can be solved by applying the linear approximation formulation for the second-order cone constraints that was proposed by Ben-Tal and Nemirovski [4] and refined by Glineur [8] (see [18] for more details).

3.2   Vertical Flight Planning with Wind (VFPW-C)

In practice, wind plays an important roll in planning a fuel-optimal flight trajectory. In vertical flight planning, the wind also depends on the flight altitude. Since the segments S are given, the track wind component $U_{i,h}^t$, i.e., the wind in the flight direction, as well as the cross-track wind component $U_{i,h}^c$, i.e., the wind perpendicular to the flight direction, can be precomputed for each segment i at each altitude h. The mathematical model without wind presented in Section 3.1 is extended in [17] to include wind influence. Firstly, a further binary variable $\mu_{i,h}$ is introduced to indicate whether a segment i is flown on altitude h. Then

$$\forall i \in S: \quad \sum_{h \in H} \mu_{i,h} = 1 \tag{9}$$

guarantees only one altitude is assigned to each segment. With the help of variable μ, the wind can be assigned to each segment by

$$\forall i \in S: \quad u_i^t = \sum_{h \in H} \mu_{i,h} \cdot U_{i,h}^t, \tag{10}$$

$$\forall i \in S: \quad u_i^c = \sum_{h \in H} \mu_{i,h} \cdot U_{i,h}^c. \tag{11}$$

The equation of motion (4) is reformulated based on the wind triangle (Figure 2):

Fig. 2. Wind triangle. v^{ground} denotes the ground speed; v^{air} denotes the aircraft speed; v^t and u^t denote the aircraft speed and wind speed in the track direction, respectively; u^c denotes the cross-track wind speed.

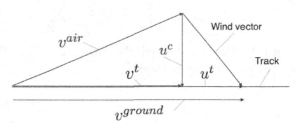

$$\forall i \in S: \quad L_i = v_i^{ground} \cdot \Delta t_i \tag{12}$$

$$\forall i \in S: \quad v_i^{ground} = v_i^t + u_i^t \tag{13}$$

$$\forall i \in S: \quad (v_i^{air})^2 = (v_i^t)^2 + (u_i^c)^2. \tag{14}$$

The two quadratic constraints (12) and (14) can be transformed into second-order cone if speeding up the aircraft is enforced, and thus can be reformulated by linear approximation [17]. Furthermore, the fuel consumption per segment in (8) should be reformulated using the air speed and air distance as

$$\forall i \in S: \quad f_i = \sum_{h \in H} \mu_{i,h} \cdot \widehat{F}_{i,h}^L(v_i^{air}, w_i^{mid}), \tag{15}$$

where $F_{i,h}^L(v, w)$ denotes the fuel consumed by flying a segment i on an altitude h, which can be computed in the preprocessing phase by

$$\forall (v, w) \in V \times W: \quad F_{i,h}^L(v, w) = F(v, w) \cdot L_i \cdot \frac{v}{\sqrt{v^2 - (U_{i,h}^c)^2} + U_{i,h}^t}$$

based on the wind triangle. $\widehat{F}_{i,h}^L(v, w)$ is the 2D piecewise linear interpolation of the data $F_{i,h}^L(v, w)$ for all continuous values of (v, w) in the grid of $V \times W$, and thus can be solved by the 2D piecewise linear function techniques. In particular, the lambda method is found to outperform the delta method for this model [17].

4   Speed Discretization in Vertical Flight Planning

The continuous speed models introduced in Section 3 can be classified as mixed-integer second-order cone programming models. The drawback of such models is their unpractically long computation time. In this section, another modeling alternative by discretizing the aircraft speed is presented.

4.1   Discrete Speed in VFP without Wind (VFP-D)

We first focus on the vertical flight planning model without wind. Given a discrete set of aircraft speed V, we can further introduce binary variables $\mu_{i,v}$, which indicates whether a discrete speed level v is used when flying on segment i. Then only one speed level can be assigned to each segment by

$$\forall i \in S: \qquad \sum_{v \in V} \mu_{i,v} = 1. \qquad (16)$$

With the discretized speed, the travel time $\Delta T_{i,v}$ for segment i with speed v can be calculated in preprocessing,

$$\forall i \in S, v \in V: \qquad \Delta T_{i,v} = \frac{L_i}{v},$$

such that the quadratic constraint (4) can be linearized as:

$$\forall i \in S: \qquad \Delta t = \sum_{v \in V} \mu_{i,v} \cdot \Delta T_{i,v}. \qquad (17)$$

Besides, the 2D matrix $F(v,w)$ can be reduced to $F_v(w)$ of 1D by precomputing:

$$\forall v \in V: \qquad F_v(w) = F(v,w),$$

such that the fuel consumption (8) can be reformulated as

$$\forall i \in S: \qquad f_i = L_i \cdot \sum_{v \in V} \mu_{i,v} \cdot \widehat{F}_v(w_i^{mid}). \qquad (18)$$

Therefore, the speed discretization is the "stone that kills two birds": it linearizes the quadratic travel time constraint and reduces the 2D piecewise linear fuel function to 1D.

4.2   Discrete Speed in VFP with Wind (VFPW-D)

Similarly as in the VFP-D model in Section 4.1, speed discretization can help to simplify the travel time equation as well as the fuel interpolation in the VFPW-C model. Firstly, the binary variables $\mu_{i,h}$ in the VFPW-C model are extended to $\mu_{i,h,v}$ by one more dimension $v \in V$. Then (9) is replaced by

$$\forall i \in S: \qquad \sum_{h \in H, v \in V} \mu_{i,h,v} = 1 \qquad (19)$$

to ensure only one altitude and one speed level is assigned to each segment. Then the travel time $\Delta T_{i,h,v}$ for a segment i traveled on altitude h with speed v can be precomputed based on the wind triangle:

$$\forall i \in S, h \in H, v \in V: \qquad \Delta T_{i,h,v} = \frac{L_i}{\sqrt{v^2 - (U_{i,h}^c)^2 + U_{i,h}^t}}.$$

Then the travel time computation given by (12, 13, 14) can be simply replaced by linear constraint

$$\forall i \in S: \quad \Delta t = \sum_{h \in H, v \in V} \mu_{i,h,v} \cdot \Delta T_{i,h,v}. \tag{20}$$

And replacing 2D matrix $F_{i,h}^L(v, w)$ by 1D vector $F_{i,h,v}^L(w)$ as

$$\forall v \in V: \quad F_{i,h,v}^L(w) = F_{i,h}^L(v, w),$$

reduces the 2D piecewise linear function (15) by one dimension:

$$\forall i \in S: \quad f_i = \sum_{h \in H, v \in V} \mu_{i,h,v} \cdot \widehat{F}_{i,h,v}^L(w_i^{mid}), \tag{21}$$

4.3   Univariate Piecewise Linear Interpolation

Here we review three different techniques to model the univariate piecewise linear function such as $\widehat{F}_v$ and $\widehat{F}_{i,h,v}^L$ into mixed integer linear programming. Despite being mathematically equivalent (in the sense that they all describe the same set of feasible solutions), their performances in terms of computation time are problem dependent. Given an index set $K_0 := \{0, 1, \ldots, m\}$, and the values for the parameters $W_0 := \{w_0, w_1, \ldots, w_m\}$ are specified as $F(w_k)$ for $k \in K_0$. We further denote $K := K_0 \setminus \{0\}$ for the index set of intervals. A piecewise linear function $\widehat{F} : [w_0, w_m] \to \mathbb{R}$ interpolating F can be modeled as follows.

The Convex Combination (Lambda) Method. A variant of the *convex combination* or *lambda method* [7] can be formulated as follows. To interpolate F we introduce binary decision variables $\tau_k \in \{0, 1\}$ for each $k \in K$, and continuous decision variables $\lambda_k^l, \lambda_k^r \in [0, 1]$ for each $k \in K$.

$$\sum_{k \in K} \tau_k = 1 \tag{22a}$$

$$\forall k \in K: \quad \lambda_k^l + \lambda_k^r = \tau_k \tag{22b}$$

$$w = \sum_{k \in K} (w_{k-1} \cdot \lambda_k^l + w_k \cdot \lambda_k^r) \tag{22c}$$

$$\widehat{F}(w) = \sum_{k \in K} (F(w_{k-1}) \cdot \lambda_k^l + F(w_k) \cdot \lambda_k^r) \tag{22d}$$

Note that our variant uses twice as many lambda variables compared to the original version of Dantzig [7], but in our numerical experiments it turned out that problem instances can be solved significantly faster.

The Special Ordered Set of Type 2 (SOS2) Method. Instead of introducing decision variables for the selection of a particular interval (the τ_k above), we mark the lambda variables as belonging to a special ordered set of type 2 (SOS2). That is, from an ordered set (or list) of variables $(\lambda_0, \lambda_1, \ldots, \lambda_m)$ it is required, that at most two of them are positive, and these two have to be adjacent with respect to the ordering. This information is implicitly treated by the solver in the solution process when branching on such special ordered set. SOS2 branching was introduced by Beale and Tomlin [3]. We introduce continuous decision variables $0 \leq \lambda_k \leq 1$ for each $k \in K_0$, and the following constraints:

$$\text{SOS2}(\lambda_0, \lambda_1, \ldots, \lambda_m) \tag{23a}$$

$$w = \sum_{k \in K} (w_{k-1} \cdot \lambda_{k-1} + w_k \cdot \lambda_k) \tag{23b}$$

$$\widehat{F}(w) = \sum_{k \in K} (F(w_{k-1}) \cdot \lambda_{k-1} + F(w_k) \cdot \lambda_k) \tag{23c}$$

The Incremental (Delta) Method. The *incremental (delta) method* is the oldest of the three, introduced by Markowitz and Manne [11]. It uses binary decision variable $\tau_k \in \{0,1\}$ for $k \in K$ and continuous decision variables $\delta_k \in [0,1]$ for $k \in K$, and the following constraints:

$$\forall k \in K : \quad \tau_k \geq \delta_k \tag{24a}$$

$$\forall k \in K \setminus \{n\} : \quad \delta_k \geq \tau_{k+1} \tag{24b}$$

$$w = w_0 + \sum_{k \in K} (w_k - w_{k-1}) \cdot \delta_k \tag{24c}$$

$$\widehat{F}(w) = F(w_0) + \sum_{k \in K} (F(w_k) - F(w_{k-1})) \cdot \delta_k \tag{24d}$$

4.4   All-but-one Speed Discretization

Variable discretization often leads to a discretization error and thus a loss of optimality in the objective value. In particular, when an aircraft needs speeding up, the shorter the flight time, the more fuel is consumed. Thus it is usually fuel-optimal to arrive at the exact arrival time upper bound. But this is usually not possible with discretized speed as it is with continuous speed. Therefore, it may result in an unnecessary speedup on some segments, and the speed on some segments may need to be adjusted from its optimal setting in order to arrive as close to the prescribed time boundary as possible. This problem can be solved by leaving one segment with continuous speed while discretizing the speed for all other segments. More specifically, we pick the last segment to use continuous speed by the method described in Section 3, and the discrete speed is used on the rest of the segments and solved as described in this section.

5   Experimental Results

5.1   Experimental Setup

Two of the most common aircraft types, Airbus 320 (A320) and Boeing 737 (B737), are used for the empirical studies in this work. The aircraft performance data and the upper air data are provided by Lufthansa Systems AG. Two vertical flight planning problems are considered, the one without wind (VFP), and the other with wind (VFPW). For VFP, the instances considered in [18] for continuous speed are adopted here, including two speedup factors (flying 2.5% and 5% faster than unconstrained optimal). Five instances sizes are considered for A320, ranging from 15, 20, 25, 30, and 35 segments, each of which is 100 nautical miles (NM) long,[1] which results in flight ranges from 1500 NM to 3500 NM; four B737 instance sizes are considered: 8, 12, 15, 18, i.e., flight ranges from 800 NM to 1800 NM, totalling 18 instances. For VFPW, we adopted the instances considered in [17], with two different wind fields (one for westwards, and one for its eastwards return trip), three speedup factors: 2%, 4%, and 6%, and three different instance sizes: 10, 20, and 40 segments of 75 NM each for A320, and 10, 15, 20 segments of 75 NM each for B737, totaling 36 instances. Instances of both problems use full speed levels and weight levels as in the aircraft performance data, including 12 weight levels and 7 speed levels for B737, and 15 weight levels and 12 speed levels for A320. The speed discretization takes the same speed levels as in the continuous speed, i.e., a discretization step of 0.01 Mach number. All experiments ran on a computing node with a 12-core Intel Xeon X5675 CPU at 3.07 GHz and 48 GB RAM. Three MIP solvers are considered: SCIP 3.1, Cplex 12.6, and Gurobi 6.0.0. Each solver run uses 12 threads, and an instance is considered optimally solved, when the MIP gap is within 0.01%, which corresponds to a maximum fuel error of 1 kg for B737, and maximum 2 kg for A320.

5.2   Solver Comparison in Continuous Speed

The MISOCP model for continuous speed is extensively studied in [17]. The use of the linear approximation for the second-order cone constraints plus the lambda method for the 2D piecewise linear fuel interpolation are found to be the best performing MIP model. In this work, we compare three MIP solvers on our best continuous speed model, including SCIP, Cplex and Gurobi. The runtime development plot for this comparison is shown in Figure 3, with the VFP-C on the left and VFPW-C on the right. On the horizontal axis, the solver performance is displayed in terms of computation time in seconds. For VFP-C, Cplex is faster than SCIP by an average factor of 7, while Gurobi is faster than SCIP by an average factor of 30. For VFPW-C, the average speedup factor of Cplex over SCIP is 5, while Gurobi is in average 15 times faster than SCIP. The best performing solver Gurobi also scales best as the instance size grows. Its speedup is more significant for large instances than for small instances. The largest real-world instances can be solved with Gurobi within 100 seconds when no wind is considered, and require around 1 hour when wind is included.

---

[1] Note that we currently considered segments of maximum 100 NM, based on our previous accuracy studies on using middle-weight segment fuel estimation [18]. In fact, longer segments can also be used to reduce the number of segments, if the segment fuel consumption is precomputed without using middle weight, e.g., using a numerical integral approach of the unit distance fuel consumption function [5].

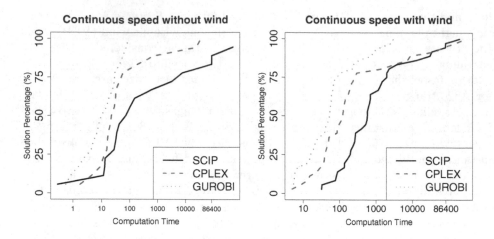

Fig. 3. The comparison of three MIP solvers: SCIP, Cplex, and Gurobi, in the best continuous speed models without wind (VFP-C, left) and with wind (VFPW-C, right).

5.3   Comparison of Piecewise Linear Methods in Speed Discretization

The use of speed discretization replaces the second-order cone constraints with linear constraints, and it also reduces the 2D piecewise linear function for fuel computation to 1D. The three 1D piecewise linear interpolation techniques, namely, lambda, delta, and SOS methods, are empirically studied in this section with the two commercial MIP solvers Cplex and Gurobi. The comparison can be visualized in the plots in Figure 4, where the model without wind VFP-D is shown on the left, and the right plots with wind VFPW-D. The maximum cutoff time is set to 4 hours (14400 seconds), and their gap between the upper and lower bound after cutoff is also compared. For both models, Gurobi outperforms Cplex in almost all cases. For VFP-D, the delta method solved by Gurobi appears to be the best performing one, and solves all instances within 2 seconds. While the SOS method scales the worst for VFP-D, it appears to be the fastest solver for 90% of the VFPW-D instances as shown on the right of Figure 4. However, it scales poorly for the largest instances, and leaves the largest gap (close to 0.1%) after 4 hours. The best approach for VFP-D, the delta method by Gurobi (Del-G), appears to be the most robust and scalable approach also for VFPW-D, and solves the largest instances to optimality in around one minute.

5.4   Comparison of Discrete Speed and Continuous Speed

The best approach for discrete speed studied in Section 5.3, namely Del-G, is compared with the best approach for continuous speed (see Section 5.2), in terms of computational performance as well as discretization error. As shown in Figure 5, the use of discrete speed substantially speeds up the continuous speed

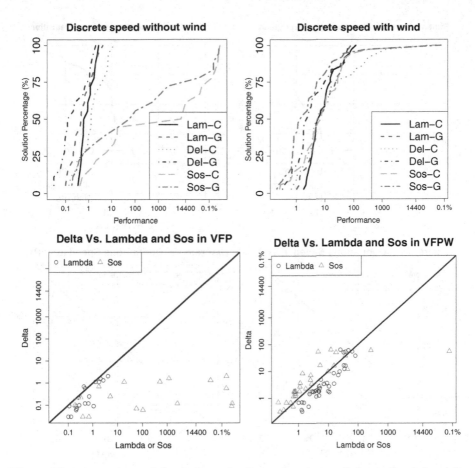

Fig. 4. The comparison of three piecewise linear function techniques (lambda, delta, SOS) solved by two commercial MIP solvers (Cplex and Gurobi) on the vertical flight planning models without wind (left) and with wind (right). The scatter plots show comparison of the delta with lambda and SOS methods with Gurobi.

across all instances. The average speedup factor is 44 for VFP without wind, and 15 for VFP with wind. Note that the scalability of the discrete speed model is especially noticeable for the largest instances. For instances that take more than 30 seconds by VFP-C, the average speedup of using discrete speed is of factor 80; while for instances that take over 30 minutes by VFPW-C, using discrete speed is in average over 50 times faster. The computation time of the largest instance is shortened from one hour to one minute by applying discrete speed.

However, the drawback of using fully discretized speed is its discretization error. The objective deviation from using continuous speed is shown in the columns of VFP-D and VFPW-D in Fig. 6. The use of discrete speed results in an increase in the objective value of over 0.1% in VFP without wind, and even over 0.5% for VFPW, which translates to a possible fuel increase of 50 kg for aircraft B737 or 100 kg for A320.

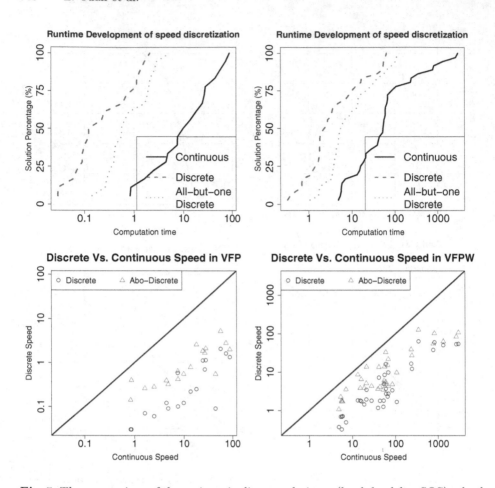

Fig. 5. The comparison of three piecewise linear techniques (lambda, delta, SOS) solved by two commercial MIP solvers (Cplex and Gurobi) on the vertical flight planning models without wind (left) and with wind (right).

The all-but-one (abo) speed discretization proposed in Section 4.4 can be used to reduce the discretization error. The speed discretization leaving one segment with continuous speed significantly lowers the discretization error as shown in Figure 6 in columns VFP-A and VFPW-A. As visualized in the box plot, around 75% of the instances in both models without or with wind have an objective deviation of less than 0.01%, which is the solver termination MIP gap, and it translates to maximum 1 kg fuel consumption for B737 and 2 kg for A320. Besides, the maximum objective deviation is reduced to 0.02% from 0.5%. With such practically negligible discretization error, the abo-discretization is still in average 13 times faster than using continuous speed in VFP without wind, and 6 times faster when wind is considered. Furthermore, the abo approach scales especially well for large instances, as shown in Figure 5, since only one segment is

Fig. 6. The percentage discretization error in terms of objective increase over using continuous speed. VFP-D and VFP-A denote the fully discrete and all-but-one-discrete (abo-discrete) approach for VFP without wind, while VFPW-D and VFPW-A denote the fully discrete and abo-discrete approach for VFPW.

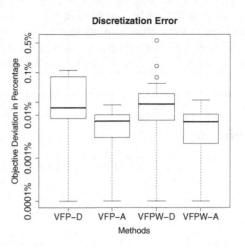

assigned with continuous speed. For the largest instances that require more than 30 seconds by VFP-C as well as largest instances that need over 30 minutes by VFPW-C, abo is in average around 30 times faster than continuous speed. The largest instance without wind is solved within 2 seconds, and the largest instance with wind can be solved within 2 minutes. Considering both the computational scalability and discretization error, the Abo-discretization appears to be the most practically viable approach for vertical flight planning.

6   Conclusions and Future Works

In this work, we address the vertical flight planning problem, which concerns assigning optimal altitude and speed to each composing segment of a flight trajectory. The previous work has employed a mixed integer second-order cone programming (MISOCP) model to assign continuous speed to segments. However, such model usually takes hours to solve instances of realistic sizes. In this work, we studied an alternative MIP model by assigning discretized speed. The speed discretization leads to significant speedup, since it not only transforms the quadratic constraints for travel time determination into linear constraints, but also reduce the 2D piecewise linear fuel interpolation into 1D. Computational experiments with various real-world instances have confirmed the effectiveness of the proposed discrete speed model, which can deliver optimal solution within minutes. To cope with the discretization error, an all-but-one (abo) discretization scheme that discretizes speed for all but one segments is proposed. The abo approach is confirmed to scale well to especially large instances, and deliver solution that are under 0.02% discretization error within 2 minutes, thus proves to be a practically viable approach.

Our experiments so far have focused on the instances with time constraint that speeds up the aircraft from its unconstrained fuel-optimal vertical profile, in order to compare with the MISOCP formulation for continuous speed. In the future, it will also be interesting to compute the optimal vertical profile with time constraints that require slowing down the aircraft. Advanced techniques for modeling piecewise linear function such as spatial branching [14] and a logarithmic model [15] may be applied to further speed up our discrete speed model.

Acknowledgments. This work is supported by BMBF Verbundprojekt E-Motion.

References

1. Aktürk, M.S., Atamtürk, A., Gürel, S.: Aircraft rescheduling with cruise speed control. Operations Research **62**(4), 829–845 (2014)
2. Altus, S.: Flight planning - the forgotten field in airline operations. presented at AGIFORS Airline Operations (2007). http://www.agifors.org/studygrp/opsctl/2007/
3. Beale, E.L.M., Tomlin, J.A.: Global Optimization Using Special Ordered Sets. Mathematical Programming **10**, 52–69 (1976)
4. Ben-Tal, A., Nemirovski, A.: On Polyhedral Approximations of the Second-Order Cone. Mathematics of Operations Research **26**(2), 193–205 (2001)
5. Blanco, M., Hoang, N.D.: Personal communication on segment fuel estimation in Erlangen, Germany, April 21, 2015
6. Cook, A., Tanner, G., Williams, V., Meise, G.: Dynamic cost indexing-managing airline delay costs. Journal of Air Transport Management **15**(1), 26–35 (2009)
7. Dantzig, G.B.: On the significance of solving linear programming problems with some integer variables. Econometrica **28**(1), 30–44 (1960)
8. Glineur, F.: Computational Experiments with a Linear Approximation of Second-Order Cone Optimization. Tech. rep., Image Technical Report 0001, Faculté Polytechnique de Mons, Belgium (2000)
9. Liden, S.: Optimum cruise profiles in the presence of winds. In: Proceedings of IEEE/AIAA 11th Digital Avionics Systems Conference, pp. 254–261. IEEE (1992)
10. Lovegren, J.A., Hansman, R.J.: Estimation of potential aircraft fuel burn reduction in cruise via speed and altitude optimization strategies. Tech. rep., ICAT-2011-03, MIT International Center for Air Transportation (2011)
11. Markowitz, H.M., Manne, A.S.: On the solution of discrete programming problems. Econometrica **25**(1), 84–110 (1957)
12. Ng, H.K., Sridhar, B., Grabbe, S.: Optimizing aircraft trajectories with multiple cruise altitudes in the presence of winds. Journal of Aerospace Information Systems **11**(1), 35–47 (2014)
13. IVAO: IFR cruise altitude or flight level. http://ivao.aero/training/documentation/books/SPP_ADC_IFR_Cruise_Altitude.pdf
14. Tawarmalani, M., Sahinidis, N.V.: A polyhedral branch-and-cut approach to global optimization. Mathematical Programming **103**(2, Ser. B), 225–249 (2005)
15. Vielma, J.P., Nemhauser, G.L.: Modeling disjunctive constraints with a logarithmic number of binary variables and constraints. In: Lodi, A., Panconesi, A., Rinaldi, G. (eds.) IPCO 2008. LNCS, vol. 5035, pp. 199–213. Springer, Heidelberg (2008)
16. Wilson, D.: Polyhedral Methods for Piecewise-Linear Functions. Ph.D. thesis, University of Kentucky (1998)

17. Yuan, Z., Amaya Moreno, L., Maolaaisha, A., Fügenschuh, A., Kaier, A., Schlobach, S.: Mixed integer second-order cone programming for the horizontal and vertical free-flight planning problem. Tech. rep., AMOS#21, Applied Mathematical Optimization Series, Helmut Schmidt University, Hamburg, Germany (2015)
18. Yuan, Z., Fügenschuh, A., Kaier, A., Schlobach, S.: Variable speed in vertical flight planning. In: Operations Research Proceedings. 6 pages. Springer (2014, to appear)

Author Index

Printed in the United States
By Bookmasters